HANDBOOK OF

Organizational Learning and Knowledge

GOTTLIEB DAIMLER- UND KARL BENZ-STIFTUNG

The editors gratefully acknowledge the support of the Gottlieb Daimler and Karl Benz Foundation in preparing this handbook.

HANDBOOK OF
Organizational Learning and Knowledge

Edited by

Meinolf Dierkes, Ariane Berthoin Antal,
John Child, and Ikujiro Nonaka

OXFORD
UNIVERSITY PRESS

OXFORD

UNIVERSITY PRESS

Great Clarendon Street, Oxford OX2 6DP

Oxford University Press is a department of the University of Oxford.
It furthers the University's objective of excellence in research, scholarship,
and education by publishing worldwide in

Oxford New York

Athens Auckland Bangkok Bogotá Buenos Aires Cape Town
Chennai Dar es Salaam Delhi Florence Hong Kong Istanbul Karachi
Kolkata Kuala Lumpur Madrid Melbourne Mexico City Mumbai Nairobi
Paris São Paulo Shanghai Singapore Taipei Tokyo Toronto Warsaw

with associated companies in Berlin Ibadan

Oxford is a registered trade mark of Oxford University Press
in the UK and in certain other countries

Published in the United States
by Oxford University Press Inc., New York

British Library Cataloguing in Publication Data

Data available

Library of Congress Cataloging in Publication Data
Handbook of organizational learning and knowledge/
edited by Meinolf Dierkes . . . [et al.].
p. cm.
Includes bibliographical references and index.
1. Organizational learning—Handbooks, manuals, etc. 2. Knowledge
management—Handbooks, manuals, etc. I. Dierkes, Meinolf.
Hd58.82 .H36 2001   658.4'038—dc21   2001021816

ISBN 0–19–829583–9

10 9 8 7 6 5 4 3 2

Typeset by Kolam Information Services Pvt. Ltd. Pondicherry, India
Printed in Great Britain
on acid-free paper by
T. J. International Ltd., Padstow, Cornwall

PREFACE

The *Handbook of Organizational Learning and Knowledge* is the focal product of the *Ladenburger Kolleg* on 'Organizational Learning in Various Environmental Conditions'. Between October 1994 and Fall 2000 more than thirty academics, managers, and consultants from ten countries worked together in the framework of the *Kolleg* to clarify the state of the art in the field and to extend the boundaries of knowledge. Professor Meinolf Dierkes undertook the tremendous task of coordinating the work of the group and of editing this handbook in cooperation with Professors Ariane Berthoin Antal, John Child, and Ikujiro Nonaka.

Ladenburger Kollegs are interdisciplinary research groups sponsored by the Gottlieb Daimler and Karl Benz Foundation. A *Kolleg* is established by the Foundation to work for a period of three to five years on a specific topic, and the results are then published and made available to a wide readership. The Foundation thereby fulfills its goals of supporting science and research that focuses on the interrelationship between humans, the environment, and technology. This overarching theme raises complex issues that can be dealt with only through interdisciplinary and problem-oriented research and analysis.

The Foundation identifies the topics for *Kollegs* through a process of discourse involving scientists from different disciplines and other experts from industry, associations, and public administration. The forum for this discussion is the *Ladenburger Diskurs*. The topic of organizational learning was the subject of three such *Diskurs* meetings beginning in 1993, in which the research program for the new *Kolleg* was prepared, leading to its inauguration in 1994.

The Gottlieb Daimler and Karl Benz Foundation decided to invest in the study of organizational learning for several reasons. Rapid technological change and a wealth of information and communication media have transformed businesses all around the world. Organizations of almost every kind, including those in the public sector, have undergone fundamental transformations in their structures, management, and goals. Furthermore, public interest in the performance of organizations, especially private companies, has increased in nearly all societies. Industrial accidents, for example, can generate such intense public criticism that the continued existence of a company is endangered. These phenomena represent challenges to organizations, and their effective management requires the generation of new knowledge.

The Foundation therefore considers organizational learning to be a central topic in the context of worldwide processes of transformation. Earlier *Ladenburger Kollegs* have treated related topics, such as the *Kolleg* on 'Security in Communication Technology', and the *Kolleg* on 'Understanding and Shaping Globalization'. The *Ladenburger Kolleg* on 'Organizational Learning in Various Environmental Conditions' completes the analysis of new global trends in the framework of the Foundation's program.

This handbook represents an unusually comprehensive approach to the field of organizational learning and knowledge. The authors worked in the *Kolleg* over a five-year period, and they succeeded in bringing together experiences and research findings from numerous disciplines and different sociopolitical, cultural, and economic environments. They conducted innovative research projects and drew on the collective wisdom of senior executives from a wide range of organizations: major business corporations, unions, United Nations agencies, and the armed forces. The handbook is also the final capstone of the multifaceted work of the *Kolleg*'s many publications, not the least of which is the *Annotated Bibliography of Organizational Learning*, which is edited by Meinolf Dierkes and several other members of the *Kolleg*.

On behalf of the Gottlieb Daimler and Karl Benz Foundation, we would like to take this opportunity to thank the editors, Professors Dierkes, Berthoin Antal, Child, and Nonaka, as well as the authors of the handbook for their tremendous effort and the members of the *Kolleg* for their contributions. We specifically would like to acknowledge the central role of the leader of the Kolleg, Professor Meinolf Dierkes, for having put together such an outstanding group. Lastly, we thank Oxford University Press for publishing this handbook.

Prof. Gisbert zu Putlitz (chairman)

Dr. Diethard Schade

Board of Management of the
Gottlieb Daimler and Karl Benz Foundation

Ladenburg
October 2000

ACKNOWLEDGMENTS

The preparation of a volume of such broad scope as this one is a process that involves many people. The editors are particularly grateful to Professor Gisbert Freiherr zu Putlitz, Dr. Horst Nienstedt, Dr. Jörg Klein, Thomas Schmitt, and Petra Jung at the Gottlieb Daimler and Karl Benz Foundation for their generous support and practical assistance throughout the project's life span. The members of the international network funded by the Foundation engaged in many lively debates that led to this handbook. The collegiality that grew out of these discussions is something we editors will value and build on for many years to come. Without a doubt, the very special atmosphere of the Foundation's villa (which was originally the home of the Benz family) in the picturesque medieval town of Ladenburg, where many of our meetings were so generously hosted by the Foundation, played a significant role in stimulating the collegial atmosphere.

The role of coordinator for this network, first held by Katrin Hähner-Ketteler from 1994 to 1995, followed by Lai Si Tsui-Auch from 1996 to 1998, and then by Anne Vonderstein from 1998 to 2000 was central to the success of the undertaking. The handbook has profited especially from Anne Vonderstein's professional dedication. Her attention to detail was combined with the skills in international diplomacy that are required for eliciting top quality manuscripts from authors around the world. The editors also thank Casey Teele for helping prepare the introductory notes to many of the sections of the handbook, thereby providing a useful navigational tool for readers.

All the contributors to the handbook, and above all we, the editors, are deeply indebted to the technical editing experience that David Antal brought to their chapters. His keen eye for logic and his sense of style increased the clarity of argumentation and improved the scholarship in every chapter. In addition, several contributions benefited from his skillful translation of the German original texts. His team, Ginger Diekman and Ginna Edwards, attended to the multitude of details involved in polishing the academic product. Without the unflagging and meticulous attention of Barbara Schlüter, the corrected manuscripts would never have reached the publisher in legible form. At Oxford University Press, David Musson showed admirable patience during the long gestation period required for this handbook, and his team (Sarah Dobson, Lynn Childress) provided valuable help in finalizing the manuscript.

CONTENTS

List of Figures   xiv

List of Tables   xvi

Notes on Contributors   xviii

Abbreviations   xxiv

Introduction: Finding Paths through the Handbook   1
Ariane Berthoin Antal, Meinolf Dierkes, John Child, and Ikujiro Nonaka

PART I INSIGHTS FROM MAJOR SOCIAL SCIENCE DISCIPLINES

INTRODUCTION   11

1 **Psychological Perspectives of Organizational Learning**   14
Günter W. Maier, Christiane Prange, and Lutz von Rosenstiel

2 **The Sociological Foundations of Organizational Learning**   35
Silvia Gherardi and Davide Nicolini

3 **The Treatment of Organizational Learning in Management Science**   61
Peter Pawlowsky

4 **A Review and Assessment of Organizational Learning in Economic Theories**   89
Christopher S. Boerner, Jeffrey T. Macher, and David J. Teece

5 **Anthropology and Organizational Learning**   118
Barbara Czarniawska

6 **The Underestimated Contributions of Political Science to Organizational Learning**   137
Joseph LaPalombara

7 **Thinking Historically about Organizational Learning**   162
Jeffrey R. Fear

PART II EXTERNAL TRIGGERS FOR LEARNING

INTRODUCTION   195

8 Change in Socioeconomic Values as a Trigger of
   Organizational Learning   198
   Lutz von Rosenstiel and Stefan Koch

9 Social Movements and Interest Groups as Triggers
   for Organizational Learning   221
   Jürgen Kädtler

10 Triggers of Organizational Learning during the
   Transformation Process in Central European
   Countries   242
   Hans Merkens, Mike Geppert, and David Antal

11 Organizational Learning as Guided Responses to
   Market Signals   264
   John M. Stopford

12 Technological Visions, Technological Development,
   and Organizational Learning   282
   Meinolf Dierkes, Lutz Marz, and Casey Teele

PART III FACTORS AND CONDITIONS SHAPING ORGANIZATIONAL LEARNING

INTRODUCTION   305

13 The Social Constitution of Organizations and its
   Implications for Organizational Learning   308
   John Child and Sally J. Heavens

14 How Organizations Learn from Success and Failure   327
   William H. Starbuck and Bo Hedberg

15 The Role of Time in Organizational Learning   351
   Christiana Weber and Ariane Berthoin Antal

16 Effects of Emotion on the Process of Organizational
   Learning   369
   Klaus R. Scherer and Véronique Tran

PART IV AGENTS OF ORGANIZATIONAL LEARNING

INTRODUCTION   395

17 The Individual as Agent of Organizational Learning   398
Victor J. Friedman

18 Leadership and Organizational Learning   415
Philip Sadler

19 The Role of Boards in Facilitating or Limiting
Learning in Organizations   428
Risto Tainio, Kari Lilja, and Timo J. Santalainen

20 Labor Unions as Learning Organizations and
Learning Facilitators   446
Andreas Drinkuth, Claudius H. Riegler, and Rolf Wolff

21 Consultants as Agents of Organizational Learning:
The Importance of Marginality   462
Ariane Berthoin Antal and Camilla Krebsbach-Gnath

PART V PROCESSES OF ORGANIZATIONAL LEARNING AND KNOWLEDGE CREATION

INTRODUCTION   487

22 A Theory of Organizational Knowledge Creation:
Understanding the Dynamic Process of Creating
Knowledge   491
Ikujiro Nonaka, Ryoko Toyama, and Philippe Byosière

23 Media Choice and Organizational Learning   518
Bettina Büchel and Steffen Raub

24 Organizing, Learning, and Strategizing:
From Construction to Discovery   535
Bo Hedberg and Rolf Wolff

25 Power and Politics in Organizations: Public and
Private Sector Comparisons   557
Joseph LaPalombara

26 **Identity, Conflict, and Organizational Learning** 582
Jay Rothman and Victor J. Friedman

27 **Rules and Organizational Learning:**
The Behavioral Theory Approach 598
Alfred Kieser, Nikolaus Beck, and Risto Tainio

PART VI INTERORGANIZATIONAL
LEARNING AND KNOWLEDGE IN A
GLOBAL CONTEXT

INTRODUCTION 627

28 **Learning in Multinationals** 631
Klaus Macharzina, Michael-Jörg Oesterle, and Dietmar Brodel

29 **Learning through Strategic Alliances** 657
John Child

30 **Organizational Learning in International Joint**
Ventures: The Case of Hungary 681
Marjorie A. Lyles

31 **Organizational Learning in Supplier Networks** 699
Christel Lane

32 **Learning in Global and Local Networks: Experience of**
Chinese Firms in Hong Kong, Singapore, and Taiwan 716
Lai Si Tsui-Auch

33 **Learning in Imaginary Organizations** 733
Bo Hedberg and Mikael Holmqvist

PART VII DEVELOPING LEARNING
PRACTICES

INTRODUCTION 755

34 **Creating Conditions for Organizational Learning** 757
Victor J. Friedman, Raanan Lipshitz, and Wim Overmeer

35 **Practices and Tools of Organizational Learning** 775
Peter Pawlowsky, Jan Forslin, and Rüdiger Reinhardt

36 **Intellectual Capital and Knowledge Management: Perspectives on Measuring Knowledge** 794

Rüdiger Reinhardt, Manfred Bornemann, Peter Pawlowsky, and Ursula Schneider

PART VIII PUTTING LEARNING INTO PRACTICE

INTRODUCTION 823

37 **Integrated Information Technology Systems for Knowledge Creation** 827

Ikujiro Nonaka, Patrick Reinmöller, and Ryoko Toyama

38 **Scenarios and Their Contribution to Organizational Learning: From Practice to Theory** 849

Graham S. Galer and Kees van der Heijden

39 **Barriers to Organizational Learning** 865

Ariane Berthoin Antal, Uwe Lenhardt, and Rolf Rosenbrock

40 **Applying Theory to Organizational Transformation** 886

Camilla Krebsbach-Gnath

41 **Multimodal Organizational Learning: From Misbehavior to Good Laboratory Practice in the Pharmaceutical Industry** 902

Christoph de Haën, Lai Si Tsui-Auch, and Marcus Alexis

PART IX CONCLUSION

42 **Organizational Learning and Knowledge: Reflections on the Dynamics of the Field and Challenges for the Future** 921

Ariane Berthoin Antal, Meinolf Dierkes, John Child, and Ikujiro Nonaka

Name Index 941
Subject Index 958

LIST OF FIGURES

3.1 A simplified process model of organizational learning 79
3.2 A conceptual framework for the management of organizational learning 79
8.1 Process model of organizational learning as a result of changing values 198
8.2 Determinants of behavior 200
8.3 Child-rearing objectives of parents in the Federal Republic of Germany, 1951–1995 201
8.4 Actual and desired goals of organizations as seen by incumbent and future managers 211
11.1 Elements of organizational learning as guided responses to market signals 265
12.1 Interaction of visions and forms of learning in three environments 289
13.1 Three channels of communication and relationship necessary for effective organizational learning 314
14.1 Behavioral learning 331
14.2 Cognitive learning 334
19.1 Widening performance gap as decline deepens 431
19.2 The changing role of a board at the various stages of a performance path 436
19.3 The types of boards 437
21.1 Type and level of consultant activity *vis-à-vis* the client 468
21.2 Typology of clients 469
22.1 Three layers of the knowledge-creation process, including *ba* (platforms for knowledge creation) and SECI (socialization–externalization–combination–internalization processes) 493
22.2 The four modes of knowledge conversion and the evolving spiral movement 498
22.3 *Ba*, the shared space for interaction 500
22.4 Four categories of knowledge assets 502
22.5 Leading the knowledge-creation process with *ba* (platforms for knowledge creation) and SECI (socialization–externalization–combination–internalization processes) 507
22.6 The hypertext organization 512
23.1 Media richness and media scope 523
24.1 Single-loop and double-loop learning 538
24.2 Evolutionary growth of competencies and customer bases 550
24.3 The sense-making cycle 551
24.4 Myth cycles as sense-makers and bases for action in organizations 552
27.1 The cycle of organizational learning and its interruptions 610

28.1 Double-feedback model of knowledge generation and
knowledge exploitation in multinational corporations 633

29.1 A framework for comparing strategic alliances with other forms
of interorganizational cooperation 658

30.1 Capabilities affecting high knowledge acquisition in international
joint ventures (IJVs) in transitional economies 685

33.1 The structure of an imaginary organization (IO) 737

33.2 Four models of learning in imaginary organizations 738

33.3 Skandia Assurance and Financial Services (AFS): A mediator
between two global markets 744

33.4 Arenas for knowledge creation in imaginary organizations 746

33.5 Trust-building loops in imaginary organizations 748

34.1 Conditions for organizational learning 761

35.1 Toolbox: Categorization of organizational learning tools 776

36.1 Conceptual framework for integrating general management,
the management of intellectual capital, and knowledge
management 814

37.1 The necessity of managing the knowledge-creation spiral—
socialization, externalization, combination, and internalization
(SECI)—through information technology (IT) and platforms
of knowledge work (*ba*) 831

37.2 Four levels of utilizing customer or supplier knowledge 833

37.3 Action–reflection-triggering systems for knowledge creation 834

37.4 Conversion-support tools, action–reflection-triggering systems,
and platforms of knowledge-work (*ba*) at Seven-Eleven Japan 841

37.5 Conversion-support tools, action–reflection-triggering systems,
and platforms of knowledge work (*ba*) at Wal-Mart 843

38.1 Kolb's (1991) learning model 856

39.1 Learning cycle and interruptions 866

40.1 The process of learning 889

LIST OF TABLES

2.1 Narratives of organizational learning according to five sociological traditions   46

3.1 Organizational knowledge concepts   70

3.2 Examples of different types of organizational learning   77

4.1 Modifications made in orthodoxy in order to accommodate learning   92

4.2 Categories of learning in the innovation literature   104

8.1 Development of types of values in West Germany, 1987/1988–1997   203

8.2 Perceptual organs of an organization at the interface with change in a society's socioeconomic values   205

8.3 Value-oriented personnel policy: Example of operationalizing an area of values   213

9.1 A profile of political and moral conflict between social movements and three companies   233

9.2 The course of organizational crises   235

10.1 Similarities and differences in the approach to transformation in central Europe   244

10.2 Types of organizational learning during the transformation in central Europe   249

10.3 Top ten foreign investments in the Czech Republic, Hungary, and Poland, 1990–2002   253

10.4 An anatomy of triggers of organizational learning in the transformation process of selected eastern European companies   258

16.1 Major classes of emotion and their effects on organizational learning   388

20.1 Union and management learning in ICA   452

20.2 From single-loop learning to boundary-transcending   455

22.1 Tacit and explicit knowledge   494

22.2 The factors constituting the knowledge-conversion process in companies   496

22.3 Comparison of three management models of knowledge creation   506

23.1 Media and their features   522

23.2 Match between learning processes, learning context, and media choice   530

24.1 From 'strategic fit' to 'strategic intent'   541

24.2 Organizing, strategizing, and organizational learning— A historical simplification   543

24.3 Four learning situations   545

24.4 A conceptual model of organizational learning   548

26.1 The frames of conflict and organizational learning   585

33.1 Comparison between three types of organizational framework   748

35.1 Classification categories for organizational learning tools   777

35.2 Overview and categorization of learning tools   791
36.1 Examples of the process perspective on intellectual capital   797
36.2 Intellectual capital: Examples of dimensions, categories, and
       measures based on the Skandia Navigator   800
36.3 Investor valuation of nonfinancial performance improvement   808
36.4 Characteristics of knowledge assets and tangible assets   813
37.1 Resemblance and identity: Information technology at Seven-Eleven
       Japan and Wal-Mart   836
38.1 Principal characteristics of the world of business and the world of
       management   859
38.2 The purposes of scenarios   863
42.1 The development of organizational learning as a field of inquiry   926

NOTES ON CONTRIBUTORS

Marcus Alexis

Professor, J. L. Kellogg Graduate School of Management, Northwestern University, Evanston, Illinois

David R. Antal

Editor and translator, specialized fields: psychology, sociology, political sciences, and history, Berlin

Nikolaus Beck

Research Fellow at the Chair of Business Administration and Organizational Behavior and Sonderforschungsbereich 504, University of Mannheim

Ariane Berthoin Antal

Program leader for Organizational Learning, Research Unit on Organization and Technology at the Wissenschaftszentrum Berlin für Sozialforschung (WZB) (Social Science Research Center, Berlin); Visiting Professor at Henley Management College, and lecturer at the Technical University of Berlin and the Leipzig Graduate School of Business

Christopher S. Boerner

Doctoral Candidate in Business and Public Policy at the Walter A. Haas School of Business and the University of California, Berkeley

Manfred Bornemann

Assistant Professor, Department of International Management, Karl Franzens University, Graz, Austria

Dietmar Brodel

Chancellor and Managing Director, Stuttgart Institute of Management and Technology, Professor of Organizational Behavior

Bettina Büchel

Professor of Strategy and Organization, International Institute for Management Development (IMD), Lausanne

Philippe Byosière

Associate Professor at the Japan Advanced Institute of Science and Technology (JAIST), Graduate School of Knowledge Science, Japan

John Child

Professor of Commerce, University of Birmingham, U.K., Visiting Professor, University of Hong Kong. Founding Director, Centre for International Business and Management, University of Cambridge and Chinese Management Centre, University of Hong Kong

Barbara Czarniawska

Skandia Professor of Management at the Gothenburg Research Institute, School of Economics and Commercial Law, Göteborg University, Sweden; Titular Professor at the European Institute for Advanced Studies in Management

Christoph de Haën

Group Scientific Advisor, Chairman of the Scientific Committee, Bracco Imaging S.p.A., Milan, Italy

Meinolf Dierkes

Director, Research Unit on Organization and Technology at the Wissenschaftszentrum Berlin für Sozialforschung (Social Science Research Center, Berlin); Professor for the Sociology of Science and Technology, Technical University of Berlin; recurrent visiting Professor at University of California, Berkeley, and Research Professor at the Shanghai Academy of Social Sciences

Andreas Drinkuth

Labor advisor for technology and innovation with the German Metalworkers' Union (IG Metall), Frankfurt am Main

Jeffrey R. Fear

Assistant Professor for History at the School of Arts and Sciences, University of Pennsylvania, Philadelphia

Jan Forslin

Professor for Industrial Economy and Organisation at the KTH, Sweden

Victor J. Friedman

Senior Lecturer, Ruppin Institute, Israel

Graham S. Galer

Independent consultant associated with the Global Business Network, Emeryville, California, former Head of Planning Support in Group Planning, Shell International Petroleum Company, Ltd., London, U.K.

Mike Geppert

Assistant Professor, European Business Management School, University of Wales, U.K.

Silvia Gherardi

Professor at the Department of Sociology and Social Research, Research Unit on Organizational Cognition and Learning, Università di Trento, Italy

Sally J. Heavens

Research Associate at the Judge Institute of Management Studies, University of Cambridge, U.K.

Bo Hedberg

Professor of Management at the School of Business, Stockholm University

Kees van der Heijden

Professor of Strategic Management, University of Strathclyde, Glasgow, Scotland, and a director of Global Business Network, Emeryville, California

Mikael Holmqvist

Assistant Professor at the School of Business, Stockholm University

Jürgen Kädtler

Sociological Research Institute, Georg-August University, Göttingen, Germany

Alfred Kieser

Chair of Business Administration and Organizational Behavior and Priority Research Area (*sh*) 504, University of Mannheim

Stefan Koch

Assistant Professor for Industrial and Organizational Psychology, German University of Administrative Sciences, Speyer

Camilla Krebsbach-Gnath

Partner of K-G & D Management Consultancy, Kronberg, Germany

Christel Lane

Reader in Economic Sociology at the University of Cambridge, Faculty of Social and Political Sciences, and a Fellow of St. John's College

Joseph LaPalombara

Arnold Wolfers Professor of Political Science and Management, Yale School of Management, Yale University, New Haven, Connecticut

Uwe Lenhardt

Fellow, Research Group on Public Health Policy, Wissenschaftszentrum Berlin für Sozialforschung (WZB) (Social Science Research Center, Berlin); Lecturer, Institute of Public Health, Technical University of Berlin

Kari Lilja

Professor of Organization and Management at the Helsinki School of Economics and Business Administration

Raanan Lipshitz

Senior Lecturer, Department of Psychology, Haifa University, Israel

Marjorie A. Lyles

Professor of International Strategic Management, Kimball Faculty Fellow, Kelley School of Business, Indiana University

Klaus Macharzina

President of the University of Hohenheim, Chair of Management, Organization and Human Resources Management, Director of the Center for Research in Export and Technology Management, University of Hohenheim, Stuttgart

Jeffrey T. Macher

Assistant Professor, Robert E. McDonough School of Business, Georgetown University

Günter W. Maier

Assistant Professor of Industrial and Organizational Psychology, Department of Psychology, University of Munich

Lutz Marz

Research Fellow, Research Unit on Organization and Technology, Wissenschaftszentrum Berlin für Sozialforschung (WZB) (Social Science Research Center, Berlin)

Hans Merkens

Professor of Educational Sciences, Research Unit for Empirical Studies, Free University of Berlin

Davide Nicolini

Senior Social Scientist, The Tavistock Institute, London, and Senior Researcher, Research Unit on Organizational Cognition and Learning, University of Trento, Italy

Ikujiro Nonaka

Professor at the Graduate School of International Corporate Strategy, Hitotsubashi, Tokyo; University Xerox Distinguished Professor in Knowledge, HAAS School of Business, University of California, Berkeley; Visiting Dean and Professor, Center for Knowledge and Innovation Research, Helsinki School of Economics and Business Administration

Michael-Jörg Oesterle

Professor of International Management, University of Bremen

Wim Overmeer

Professor of Intelligence in Action, The Duxx Graduate School of Business Leadership, Monterrey, Mexico

Peter Pawlowsky

Professor for Personnel Management and Leadership Studies and Director at the Research Institute for Labor Economics, Chemnitz University of Technology, Germany

Christiane Prange

Head of Corporate Development, in a Multimedia Agency, Berlin

Steffen Raub

Adjunct Professor of Management, HEC-University of Geneva, and visiting Professor, HEC-University of Lausanne, Switzerland

Rüdiger Reinhardt

Assistant Professor, Institute for Personnel Management and Leadership Studies, Chemnitz University of Technology, Germany

Patrick Reinmöller

Assistant Professor, Japan Advanced Institute of Science and Technology (JAIST), Graduate School of Knowledge Science, Japan

Claudius H. Riegler

Economic historian, Ystad, Sweden

Rolf Rosenbrock

Senior Fellow, Wissenschaftszentrum Berlin für Sozialforschung (WZB) (Social Science Research Center, Berlin), Professor of Public Health Policy, Technical University of Berlin

Lutz von Rosenstiel

Professor of Industrial and Organizational Psychology, Department of Psychology, University of Munich

Jay Rothman

President of the ARIA Group, Director of the Action-Evaluation Research Institute, and Scholar-in-Residence at Antioch University McGregor School, Yellow Springs, Ohio

Philip Sadler

Independent Consultant. Former CEO of Ashridge Management College

Timo J. Santalainen

President of Stratnet, Geneva, and Adjunct Professor of Strategy and International Management, Helsinki School of Economics and Business Administration

Klaus R. Scherer

Professor of Psychology, University of Geneva

Ursula Schneider

Professor, Department of International Management, Karl Franzens University, Graz, Austria

William H. Starbuck

ITT Professor of Creative Management, Stern School of Business, New York University

John M. Stopford

Professor of International Business, London Business School and Harry Reynolds Visiting Chair Professor, the Wharton School, University of Pennsylvania

Risto Tainio

Professor of Organization and Management, Helsinki School of Economics and Business Administration

David J. Teece

Mitsubishi Bank Professor and Director of the Institute of Management, Innovation, and Organization at the Walter A. Haas School of Business at the University of California, Berkeley

Casey Teele

Research Assistant, Research Unit on Organization and Technology, Wissenschaftszentrum Berlin für Sozialforschung (WZB) (Social Science Research Center, Berlin)

Ryoko Toyama

Assistant Professor at the Japan Advanced Institute of Science and Technology (JAIST), Graduate School of Knowledge Science, Japan

Véronique Tran

Ph.D. Candidate, Geneva Emotion Research Group, Department of Psychology, University of Geneva

Lai Si Tsui-Auch

Assistant Professor, Nanyang Business School, Division of Strategy, Management and Organization, Nanyang Technological University, Singapore

Christiana Weber

Senior Associate, Research Unit on Organization and Technology, Wissenschaftszentrum Berlin für Sozialforschung (WZB) (Social Science Research Center, Berlin); former Investment Manager, Gruner & Jahr Multimedia Ventures GmbH, Hamburg

Rolf Wolff

Professor of Sustainability Management at Chalmers University of Technology and Dean of the School of Economics and Law, Gothenburg University, Göteborg, Sweden

ABBREVIATIONS

APSR	*American Political Science Review*
ART	action–reflection-triggering
ASTD	American Society for Training and Development
BPR	business process reengineering
CFO	Chief Financial Officer
CKO	Chief Knowledge Officer
CLO	Chief Learning Officer
CSCW	computer-supported cooperative work
CSTools	conversion-support tools
EVA	economic value-added
FAQ	Frequently Asked Questions
FDA	Food and Drug Administration (United States)
FDI	foreign direct investment
GAAP	generally accepted accounting procedures
GLP	good laboratory practices
GUI	graphical user interfaces
HC	human capital
HRA	human resource accounting
HRM	human resource management
HTML	Hypertext Markup Language
IC	intellectual capital
IDF	Israel Defense Force
IJV	international joint venture
I-model	innovation model
IO	*International Organization*
IP	intellectual potential
ISDN	Integrated Services Digital Network
IT	information technology
JIT	just-in-time
LAN	Local Area Network
MNC	multinational corporation
MVA	market value-added
NASA	National Aeronautics and Space Administration (United States)
OC	organizational capital
OECD	Organization for Economic Cooperation and Development
OLM	organizational learning mechanisms
PCS	personal communications systems
POS	point of sale
Project	Project Scientific Activity Predictor from Patterns with Heuristic Origins
SAPPHO	

QMI	quick market intelligence
RegNeg	regulation negotiation
ROI	return on investment
SC	social capital
SECI	socialization–externalization–combination–internalization
SMS	Strategic Management Society
SOE	state-owned enterprise
SOP	standard operating procedure
S–R	stimulus–response
SRB	solid rocket booster
TQM	total quality management
U-model	Uppsala internationalization process model
UTE	Elementary Technical Unit
VAIP	value-added intellectual potential
VSAT	very small aperture satellites

Introduction

Finding Paths through the Handbook

Ariane Berthoin Antal, Meinolf Dierkes,
John Child, and Ikujiro Nonaka

The Origins and Intentions of this Handbook

This handbook is arguably a product of two types of approaches to the field of organizational learning—one focusing on how existing knowledge is shared, used, and stored; the other, on how new knowledge is created. It is designed to bring together the current streams of thinking on organizational learning that are dispersed in different disciplines and subdisciplines and to extend the boundaries of work in this area. The idea of publishing such a volume emerged from discussions among members of the 'Kolleg on Organizational Learning in Various Environmental Conditions'. The Gottlieb Daimler and Karl Benz Foundation in Germany funded this special international network of scholars and practitioners under the leadership of Meinolf Dierkes in order to explore organizational learning through regular discussions and joint research over several years.

The members of this network on organizational learning came from sixteen countries and met biannually for two or three days from 1994 through 1998 (see http://duplox.wz-berlin.de/oldb/). Considering the diversity among the members and the multifaceted nature of organizational learning, it is not surprising that the meetings were often characterized by controversial discussions about how to make sense of the state of the field and how to develop it further. Members reported on their ongoing research projects and sought advice from colleagues in the range of disciplines represented in the network and from practitioners based in companies, unions, universities, consultancies, and other organizations.

These discussions revealed the need for various kinds of guides to the field. As a subject of inquiry, organizational learning continues to attract newcomers from a variety of backgrounds. They are seeking help in finding their way through the burgeoning literature on the topic. Two types of orienting publications resulted from this recognition. The first was the *Annotated Bibliography of Organizational Learning and Knowledge Creation*, 2nd edn. (Dierkes *et al.* 2001), which was prepared by a group of network members who reviewed the publications in their disciplines and selected the ones they felt were the most significant for the topic of organizational learning. It was published as a book with a CD-ROM that allows users to search the database. The first edition is also available on the Internet (http://duplox.wz-berlin.de/oldb/bibliography.html).

The second type of orienting publication is the present work, the *Handbook of Organizational Learning and Knowledge*. In deciding to prepare it, the members of the network set themselves the challenge of providing a comprehensive review of the field. The goal was to produce a volume that would enable readers to appreciate the richness and liveliness of discussions and practices of organizational learning and knowledge creation. They wanted to provide an overview of key contributions from different theoretical perspectives and to explore a variety of facets of organizational learning. Most of the authors were recruited from the network; some were sought through the members' own networks to write additional chapters needed to cover the field.

The very act of preparing such a handbook entailed the creation of new knowledge because the contributors wrote original chapters, building on their areas of expertise in order to push into new territory. The process was an intensely social one, for many chapters were written by multiple authors, and early drafts of chapters were discussed among colleagues in small groups that met at the Foundation's villa, in the offices of network members in various countries, and through E-mail conferences. The conversations that started in the network meetings continued as we editors reviewed each draft of each chapter at length and shared our suggestions with authors through E-mail, by telephone, and in personal meetings around the world. As the preparation of the handbook advanced, the discussions moved from a primarily face-to-face process to a dyadic electronic mode, which was effective at focusing issues and securing rapid agreement on them. Nevertheless, face-to-face meetings were still required for two purposes: to brainstorm on chapters needing new ideas and to secure personal commitment, which can otherwise gradually drain away. In short, such an intellectual undertaking of global proportions requires many means of communication, not the least important one being long dinners with good food and wine that enable the members of a network to deepen their exploration and understanding of each other's ways of thinking.

The term 'handbook' risks conveying the impression that a field has arrived at a state of order, possibly even its zenith, and that it deserves monumental documentation. However, the spirit in which this handbook was conceived was one of continuous exploration. The dynamic development of organizational learning as a field of inquiry implies that it would be contradictory to try to provide a conclusive map at this time. It is not closure that is being sought. In order to provide directions for future work, we are instead looking for orientation to what already exists and what is emerging. The discussions in the network meetings showed that the field is alive with varied and, at times, competing views stemming from different disciplinary and cultural backgrounds. The authors of this handbook were therefore encouraged to give voice to multiple perspectives. There is still a great deal of territory to be charted, and diversity of approach enhances the process of discovery. The dynamic nature of the field is reflected in the fact that this project, which started under the heading of organizational learning, expanded to encompass emerging work on knowledge as well because the boundaries of the field remain permeable and continue to move. Further evidence of the ongoing nature of the learning that has been triggered by work on this handbook is that members have embarked on new projects, courses, and publications on the subject, often in new partnerships that grew from conversations within the network.

Paths through the Handbook

There are different ways to proceed through a publication as comprehensive as this one. A reader may want to work from front to back, focus on one or two sections, or select specific chapters in various sections. The handbook is organized into eight major parts, each with an introduction identifying key themes and issues treated in its chapters. Part I provides a review of the contributions by various disciplines, laying the groundwork for the rest of the book. Parts II, III, IV, and V are explorations of organizational learning from a variety of angles: the triggers for organizational learning, the factors shaping such learning, the agents involved in that shaping process, and the processes of organizational learning, respectively. Part VI focuses on interorganizational learning in several different constellations that are becoming increasingly important in the global economy. In Parts VII and VIII, the authors examine organizational learning in practice. Specific approaches to stimulating and implementing organizational learning are presented, and a variety of case studies illustrate how the theoretical concepts and practical tools can be applied. Part IX closes the handbook with the editors' reflections on the development of organizational learning and knowledge and with their ideas for future work by scholars and practitioners interested in advancing the field further.

Part I: Gaining Insights from Major Social Science Disciplines

Numerous disciplines have shaped thinking about organizational learning over the past decades. The founding fathers most frequently cited are Argyris and Schön (1978), Cyert and March (1963), and March and Olsen (1975). All of them are closely associated with studies on management but bring varied perspectives to their analyses, for they come from such different areas as psychology, sociology, economics, and political science. Part I therefore defines the disciplinary scope of the handbook by detailing the relation between organizational learning and seven fields of scholarly inquiry.

The topic of learning is generally thought of as having its closest links with psychology. Although many of the scholars and practitioners who have become interested in the field do not have a grounding in psychology, they draw on concepts borrowed from that discipline. Part I therefore commences with a chapter that lays foundations for the subsequent discussions, analyses, proposals, and perspectives pertaining to the ways in which behavioral and cognitive psychologists have treated learning processes and to their suggestions for applying their ideas to organizations. The dominance of management studies in literature on organizational learning to date stems from the search for concepts that can help the private sector deal with rapid changes in markets and technologies and can assist it in using new information technology

capabilities to support such processes. The legacy of this disciplinary background has been a strong focus on senior managers as drivers of learning and on an orientation to achieving their goals for the organization without exploring the political dimensions of the process.

The exercise of stock-taking was extended to cover other disciplines that have already influenced the field of inquiry or could contribute to it: sociology, anthropology, economics, political science, and history. Sociology has a rich and varied tradition of critical observation of organizations, and leading sociologists such as Durkheim, Weber, and Giddens have had a major impact on scholars in other disciplines. A close look at the implications of different sociological theories for the study of organizational learning promises to enable scholars to generate questions more incisive than those posed thus far. The curiosity of the members of the network led them to wonder whether research in anthropology could throw fresh light on organizational learning. It is no coincidence that growth of interest in organizational learning followed the wave of research on organizational culture, which itself had been significantly influenced by concepts borrowed from anthropology. The topic of learning is not new to economics, but because cross-fertilization between economics and the social sciences remains limited, no real dialogue has been established yet. Thus, the idea of including a chapter on how economists have thought about learning and how their ideas could be applied to organizational learning is an experiment in interdisciplinary communication.

Possibly the most surprising disciplinary explorations in this volume are found in the chapters from political science and history. The fact that political scientists have not been highly visible participants in the field of organizational learning over the last few decades should not be taken as an indicator of their past or future potential contributions to this area. In retrospect, political scientists such as Mary Parker Follett said a great deal that is relevant to organizational learning, albeit with different terminology. The work by political scientists on public organizations has received too little attention from scholars of organizational learning, who have focused on the private sector in recent years. Concepts from political science may well become increasingly useful as the political dimension of learning processes comes to the fore.

The connection between organizational learning and historians' approaches may at first glance appear tenuous because managers and scholars of management are constantly looking for new concepts, even to the point of generating or falling prey to rapidly changing fads. However, since knowledge accumulates and is thus embedded in the past, people tend to look to history as a source of lessons for the future. Furthermore, there are increasingly frequent calls for longitudinal studies as the limitations of conclusions based on simultaneous 'snapshots' become evident. Researchers in organizational learning can avoid making naive errors by understanding the kinds of questions historians pose. The commonalities between current trends in sociology and in history suggest that scholars from these two disciplines may be able to cooperate far more than they have thus far in their efforts to understand organizations undergoing change.

Part II: Understanding External Triggers for Organizational Learning

In most models of organizational learning, it is posited that changes in the external environment trigger the need for learning.[1] In light of the turbulence experienced by organizations today, Part II responds to the need for a close look at how different sources of change can affect learning. Socioeconomic values are shifting significantly in many countries, making it crucial for organizations to acquire and maintain an acute ability to perceive and make sense of the new expectations of their multiple external and internal stakeholders. Social movements form around selected issues and put various forms of pressure on organizations to learn how to deal with these issues. It would be a mistake to conceive of changes in the environment as something organizations respond to passively, for developments in technologies and in the market can be shaped by organizations in which learning is actively managed. The complex nature of the interaction between external triggers and internal learning processes becomes particularly evident under conditions of extreme change, such as the transformation processes in former eastern European countries.

Part III: Recognizing Factors and Conditions that Shape Organizational Learning

Although organizational learning takes place, by definition, within an organizational context, that context has not always been adequately taken into account. Learning and knowledge creation are triggered, shaped, and constrained by the social constitution of the organizations within which these processes take place. In other words, the structuring of roles, interests, and power between different organizational elements, such as departments or hierarchical levels, generates various paradoxes and tensions that bring into play a set of dynamics that have an impact on learning processes. These dynamics are associated with people's sense of social identity and can release strong emotions, the effects of which may also foster or hinder learning, depending on the kind of emotion and the specific context involved. Consequently, organizations often fail to learn from their previous relevant successes and failures. Experience that is uncomfortable may be screened out or sanitized, and lack of time may prevent relevant experience from being adequately recorded or disseminated. In practice, the time required for effective organizational learning is often underestimated, a miscalculation that can create exaggerated expectations that jeopardize the learning process.

---

[1] This is not to say that organizational learning is triggered only externally. It can also be triggered internally, a point made throughout this handbook.

Part IV: Identifying Agents of Organizational Learning

Theories of organizational learning are predicated on the assumption that the agents of organizational learning are the members of the organization, not the organization itself. To date, however, little attention has been devoted to exploring how different types of people in organizations contribute to organizational learning and knowledge creation, and even less attention has been dedicated to how people outside the organization can influence its learning. This handbook therefore contains several chapters about how individuals at various levels of the organization can define their roles as agents of organizational learning and how they can influence the overall climate for learning in an organization. This section also includes explorations of the impact of agents who are not full-time members of the organization: board members, unions representatives, and consultants. In keeping with the recognition that organizational learning is a social rather than a purely individual process, the chapters highlight how the interaction between the various agents can stimulate or block organizational learning.

Part V: Delving into Processes of Organizational Learning

Processes of organizational learning and knowledge creation can be conceived of in a number of different ways. Part V not only reflects the models that dominate the field but also challenges them to adapt to evolving conceptualizations of 'organization'. Research in the traditional paradigm treats learning as a stepwise process, focusing on how knowledge is acquired, distributed, and stored in memory. Research conducted in the recently developed knowledge-creation paradigm explores how an organization can not only process information but also generate new knowledge. The process in this paradigm is captured by a spiral image. This part of the handbook presents work done in both paradigms, illustrating that they can be

seen as competing or complementary points of view. The purpose of these chapters is also to highlight specific dimensions of organizational learning processes. Because organizational memory is a key facet of organizational learning, a chapter is dedicated to processes in which acquired or created knowledge is stored and embedded as rules and procedures in organizations. Power and conflict are possibly the most understudied dimensions of organizational learning processes, a deficit we seek to begin correcting by dedicating two chapters to these topics in Part V and by touching on them in chapters of other parts.

Part VI: Exploring Interorganizational Learning in a Global Context

Research on organizational learning and knowledge has traditionally focused on the private sector, and even there, almost exclusively on learning within individual companies. The authors in this part of the handbook advance understanding of the field by looking at processes of learning and knowledge creation between organizations. Various kinds of constellations are considered: units within multinational companies, strategic alliances and joint ventures between companies, customer–supplier networks, regional networks, and imaginary organizations. The growing importance of these organizational constellations is largely attributable to the global expansion of transactions. This expansion requires forms of collaboration that increasingly open up organizations so that information and learning can be shared between them. The insights in these chapters challenge some of the concepts of organizational learning that have been generated solely on the basis of existing knowledge about individual learning or learning within closed units.

Parts VII and VIII: Putting Organizational Learning into Practice

The development of the field of organizational learning and knowledge has been shaped significantly by the attention it has attracted from scholars and practitioners alike. These two communities, with their highly dissimilar goals and methods, do not always make good partners in learning. However, the tension has often been creative because managers and consultants have posed many questions and have exerted pressure on academics to generate communicable results. Scholars have profited from the access that curious practitioners have afforded field research. Within the network the presence of practitioners contributed significantly to focusing and deepening the discussions. Their emphasis on outcomes and implementation and their insistence that theories be grounded in specific contexts have been valuable for the development of the field. Furthermore, many of the academics in the network could draw on their own practical experience as managers or consultants.

The handbook's chapters on learning practices and case studies were thus written with the needs of practitioners in mind. The chapters about learning practices (Part VII) present approaches and tools with which reflective practitioners in all kinds of organizations may want to experiment. The case studies (Part VIII), which deal with organizations in Japan, the United States, and Europe, draw together and illustrate in practical terms the theoretical insights generated throughout the handbook. Common to all these chapters is the recognition that the use of practices in different settings, like the process of effectively translating ideas from one language and culture into another, always requires a creative learning process of its own.

Part IX: Conclusion

We editors, too, have engaged in the network and in the creation of this handbook as learners. Through the intense collaboration with the diverse authors and through our own ongoing research over the past few years, we have gained new insights into the dynamics of the field. Among the most striking developments we see are (a) the emergence of a shared language that draws on concepts from multiple disciplines, (b) a move away from an assumption of universality based on Anglo-Saxon cultures and toward a global scope and increased cultural differentiation, (c) penetrating inquiry that goes beyond intraorganizational learning processes to include interorganizational learning, and (d) a shift from a focus on top management to a recognition of manifold sources of knowledge and power that are needed for organizational learning. We offer our perspectives as an orientation to the current state of the art, and we convey our sense of where the stimulating challenges lie.

We recommend that readers seek paths through the field of organizational learning and knowledge in the same spirit as they would explore a lively Middle Eastern bazaar or Chinese market. The bazaar offers a comprehensive range of goods and has its own kind of order, one very different from the tidy, distinct departments of a modern supermarket. It would be misleading and sterile to treat the various aspects of organizational learning as though they could best be understood in terms of neatly defined packages. The bazaar is alive with multiple voices competing for attention, not the soothing canned music of the supermarket. As our colleague Victor Friedman pointed out to us, this handbook is the product of a healthy intellectual process in which the network members plied their wares, haggled over ideas, and made all kinds of interesting exchanges and partnerships. They set up stalls, moved them around, combined them, split them up, and placed them next to each other not according to some overarching, logical plan but in a rather organic and fluid fashion. It is symptomatic of this fluidity that the handbook's table of contents changed many times as fresh drafts of chapters suggested different connections between ideas and hence alternative ways of ordering the chapters and sections. The outcome of this creative process is not a place for quick shopping nor is it a chaotic jumble. There are sections and rows in a bazaar, but they are characterized by great intricacy, complexity, color, and richness rather than by linearity. We hope that the interested reader may even dare to get lost at times but then discover new passages and make exotic finds that will stimulate further learning and creativity.

References

Argyris, C. and Schön, D. A. (1978). *Organizational Learning: A Theory of Action Perspective*. Reading, Mass.: Addison-Wesley.

Cyert, R. M. and March, J. G. (1963). *A Behavioral Theory of the Firm*. Englewood Cliffs, NJ: Prentice Hall.

Dierkes, M., Alexis, M., Berthoin Antal, A., Hedberg, B. L. T., Pawlowsky, P., Stopford, J. M., and Vanderstein, A. (2001). *The Annotated Bibliography of Organizational Learning and Knowledge Creation*, 2nd ed., Berlin: edition sigma. First edition available: http://duplox.wz-berlin.de/oldb/bibliography.html

March, J. G. and Olsen, J. P. (1975). 'The Uncertainty of the Past: Organizational Learning under Ambiguity'. *European Journal of Political Research*, 3: 147–71.

PART I

INSIGHTS FROM MAJOR SOCIAL SCIENCE DISCIPLINES

Introduction

Because scholars of organizational learning and knowledge have come from different backgrounds and have borrowed ideas from many areas of scientific inquiry, this field has been shaped by a wide range of thinking. The chapters in Part I lay the groundwork for the handbook by tracing how key disciplines have influenced the theories and concepts currently used to understand processes and features of organizational learning. The authors also explore ways to increase the degree to which these disciplines are tapped as sources for this field of study.

Not surprisingly, the most comprehensive and direct contributions to organizational learning are to be found in management science. As Pawlowsky points out, the centrality that the relationship between the organization and its environment has in theory-building on change has placed learning processes onto the research agenda. His chapter provides a framework for making sense of the multiplicity of theoretical approaches, models, and concepts that have been generated by scholars over the past decades. A useful classification differentiates between five directions of research: organizational decision-making and adaptation, systems theory, cognitive and knowledge perspective, organizational culture, and action learning. This overview makes it possible to specify four dimensions of organizational learning and knowledge creation that a comprehensive theory needs to address: system levels of learning, learning modes, learning types, and phases of organizational learning. (The practical implications of these classifications are subsequently developed by Pawlowksy, Forslin, and Reinhardt in Part VII).

The contributions from sociology are almost as manifold as those in management science, and therefore also require a comprehensive review of the field. Gherardi and Nicolini discuss five sociological traditions and the implications that each has for organizational learning, thereby illustrating the wide range of possible ontological and epistemological choices available to scholars. For example, they explore how the rational–utilitarian tradition enables organizational learning to be conceptualized as a problem-driven search, as the activation of an exchange network, and as an ecology of learning. The discourses that grow out of the Durkheimian tradition, the microinteractionist perspective, and theories of power take quite different routes, as does the discourse that stems from the younger stream of postmodernist thinking.

The place occupied by the subject of organizational learning in the other four disciplines reviewed in Part I is quite different. A common message running through the chapters on psychology, economics, political science, and anthropology is that although organizational learning is relevant for these disciplines, it has received very little attention in the mainstream. Such 'disciplinary obscurity', as LaPalombara so aptly puts it when describing the treatment of organizational learning in political science, has various reasons. For example, in psychology the focus on individuals, and in history on nations or great men, has made organizations and their internal workings invisible or uninteresting as units of analysis in these two disciplines. In the chapter on economics, Boerner, Macher, and Teece show that, although the capacity to learn is arguably crucial for competitiveness, the topic receives little attention because it challenges perceived wisdom in mainstream economics. Anthropology's traditional focus on cultures has essentially excluded organizations as objects of study, and the discipline's interest in continuity has relegated innovation and change to the shadows. Nevertheless, in all of these disciplines, subfields have treated issues related to organizational learning. For example, economists who have studied innovation, as well as their colleagues who have worked on developing the theory of the firm, have identified tacit knowledge as a source of competitive advantage because it is very difficult to imitate. Political scientists specialized in international relations have long been interested in how ideas from one system are learned in another, and the recent work in historical institutionalism promises to provide new insights into what governmental organizations have learned in the course of developing and implementing public policies. Czarniawska points out that studies of modernization by anthropologists highlight the complex and paradox-ridden role of elites in either preventing or fostering learning. She also stresses that a central insight to be drawn from anthropological studies is that the greater part of organizational learning happens through the circulation of stories, a factor that tends to be overlooked in management thinking that emphasizes tables, lists, and other taxonomies.

Having read and reread these chapters several times while compiling this handbook, we are struck by how much more can be mined in the disciplines than has been used by researchers of organizational learning. Considering the amount of work that has been done on power by sociologists and political scientists in particular, it is striking how little attention has been paid to this issue in research on organizational learning and knowledge creation. By drawing on the theories and concepts that have been developed already, some of the contributors to this volume were able to make great strides in covering this insufficiently charted territory (see Rothman and Friedman, Ch. 26 in this volume). Similar benefits are obtainable by drawing on the historian's skill at meticulously reconstructing the sequences of decisions, contexts, and reasons justifying a course of action. If these skills could help unveil the mistakes, failures, alternative paths, and setbacks that organizations encountered in their learning processes, then they could avoid the deceptive impression that streamlined and purposive learning processes are generally expected to culminate in success (see Starbuck and Hedberg, Ch. 14 in this volume, for a step in this direction).

All the chapters in this part raise questions and challenges that are worth keeping in mind while reading the subsequent contributions to the handbook. Maier, Prange, and Rosenstiel's review of contributions by psychologists serves to warn readers not to equate successful learning with improved performance, not only because improvements can come from sources other than learning but also because an organization is as likely as an individual is to learn dysfunctional behaviors. When Czarniawska asks 'how do ideas travel?' and questions the appropriateness of the metaphor of diffusion, she touches on an issue that is addressed in many other chapters. Equally stimulating is her question about the relationship between learning and organization: 'Does learning determine what organizing will look like, or does the present mode of organization determine what learning will look like?' (This line of inquiry is explored at some length particularly by the authors in Part III.) Fear, in his review of historical thinking, concludes by speculating about how theories of organizational learning help legitimate new global corporate practices, identity, and memory of a corporation's own history. Such questions cannot be answered conclusively at the moment, but the reader who approaches the ideas in this handbook with the spirit of critical reflexivity called for by many of the contributors is likely to enjoy the learning process greatly.

1 Psychological Perspectives of Organizational Learning

Günter W. Maier, Christiane Prange, and Lutz von Rosenstiel

In recent years the term 'organizational learning' has appeared increasingly in scientific and nonscientific publications alike. It stems from an analogy, namely, the idea that a goal-oriented social structure, such as an organization, is able to learn like an organism. This interest in organizational learning is fueled by social and economic challenges confronting many organizations: the globalization of markets and ever keener worldwide competition, the shortening of development cycles for individual products, demographic shifts in the world's industrialized countries, and reduction in the half-life of knowledge, among others (e.g. Prange 1999). To meet these challenges now and in the future, organizations must have a broad spectrum of competence, including the ability to foster their acquisition of knowledge (Starbuck 1992; Tenkasi and Boland 1996). 'Organizational learning' is a concept that has been proposed to describe this knowledge acquisition by organizations (Garratt 1987; Garvin 1993; Probst and Büchel 1994).

Interest in organizational learning has all but exploded in management literature. Whereas academic journals carried only about 50 articles on the subject in the 1980s, 184 additional publications treating it had appeared by the mid-1990s (Crossan and Guatto 1996). In psychology, particularly industrial and organizational psychology, the concept of organizational learning has attracted far less attention. Organizational learning is found as a keyword for the years 1980

to 1998 in only two volumes of the *Annual Review of Psychology* (1995 and 1997). Similarly, a computer search of the literature in journals especially relevant to industrial and organizational psychology (i.e. *Academy of Management Journal, Academy of Management Review, Journal of Applied Psychology, Organizational Behavior and Human Decision Processes, Personnel Psychology*) yielded only two articles with the keyword 'organizational learning' in the period from 1988 through 1998. Nevertheless, research on individual learning processes among animals and humans has a long tradition in psychology. Psychology as a scientific discipline is scarcely more than a century old, but phenomena of learning and memory have been a scholarly focus in that field from the very outset. In 1885, for example, Ebbinghaus published a book about experimental studies on human memory. Other early and very influential investigations into this topic and associated ones were subsequently conducted by such pioneers as I. Pavlov (1849–1936), E. L. Thorndike (1874–1949), C. Hull (1884–1952), E. C. Tolman (1896–1959), and B. F. Skinner (1904–1990).

Management literature contains basically two views on the relation between organizational learning and the learning processes studied in psychology. First, organizational learning is used as an analogy of individual learning (e.g. Walsh and Ungson 1991). From this perspective knowledge about processes of individual learning can be used to understand

The work on this chapter was made possible by a grant received by Lutz von Rosenstiel from the Gottlieb Daimler- and Karl Benz-Foundation. We thank Meinolf Dierkes, the reviewers, and Petra Bles for comments on earlier versions of the manuscript, and David Antal for the translation of our manuscript.

the initially unfamiliar hypothetical construct of organizational learning. Second, individual learning is a basis for organizational learning (e.g. Argyris and Schön 1978; Cangelosi and Dill 1965; Duncan and Weiss 1979; Hedberg 1981; March and Olsen 1975). According to this view, increases in organizational knowledge—an indicator of organizational learning—are based on the growth by knowledge acquisition of the individuals in an organization.

Close examination of the learning processes studied in psychology can enrich both views. If the analogy between individual learning and organizational learning is accepted, learning processes hitherto investigated in psychology can give clues about which factors could be salient in organizational learning as well. If individual learning is regarded as a basis of organizational learning, learning processes studied in psychology may indicate ways to promote organizational learning. Moreover, familiarity with the years of research on social cognition as investigated in social and applied psychology is central to organizational learning because processes in a social aggregate's acquisition and use of knowledge can be studied within a manageable context.

The goal in this chapter is, first, to define the psychological concept of learning and to introduce learning theories and research paradigms in order to demonstrate the various forms of individual learning. The investigation is then broadened to include group learning processes. The chapter concludes with a discussion of what the findings on individual and group learning mean for organizational learning.

Individual Learning: A Definition and Its Implications for Definitions of Organizational Learning

All organisms are capable of learning at different levels. The survival of each species demands that the members of the species adapt to their particular environment. This behavioral adaptation can emerge in two ways, through evolution of the species as a whole and through adaptation by individual members. In the first case, features that have proven especially useful for survival are passed down from generation to generation within the species. In the second case, the organism learns and then adopts new behavior that optimizes its survival. Of these two types of behavioral changes, evolutionary adaptation has the advantage that each individual is endowed with capabilities or skills for successful survival. Adaptation through learning is inherently risky because the individual does not know for certain how to react to the environment during the learning process and therefore might be killed before acquiring the necessary skills for survival.

If learning is such a precarious way of adapting to the environment, why are not *all* skills and capabilities inherited? The reason is that evolutionary adaptation is not flexible enough to permit adequate response to a constantly changing environment. Human beings are no exception. The members of each generation must, for instance, deal with their self-induced technological revolutions, such as automotive innovations and the development of new technologies in other domains of life. They can do so only if they have the capacity to adapt flexibly to a changing environment.

Although the aspects of learning that are accentuated in definitions of learning concepts differ from one psychological approach to the next (e.g. behaviorism and cognitivism), learning in general can be defined as a 'process by which relatively permanent changes occur in behavioral potential as a result of experience' (Anderson 1995: 4). Because learning is described as a *process*, it is bound to take more time than a single event. A short learning process can have a negative effect on the learner's performance if previously well-learned and successful procedures and strategies must be 'unlearned' before new and more useful practices can be employed (Friedrich and Mandl 1992). For example, a person who must first unlearn the two-finger technique of typing in order to use the more efficient ten-finger technique will initially type more slowly with all ten fingers and initially make more typing errors in the learning process than was the case with the two-finger technique. Moreover, it is often *necessary* for the learner to make mistakes during the learning process, for only through these errors can the person understand associations and principles (Frese and Brodbeck 1989; Strike and Posner 1985). The errors can also lead to inferior levels of performance. Knowledge about the process, or the how, of learning facilitates corrections that stimulate or accelerate learning.

Not every kind of behavioral change can be regarded as learning. As the concept of 'permanent change' suggests, all forms of temporary change are excluded. Behavioral change induced by fatigue, for example, is not seen as learning, for the old pattern of behavior merely reasserts itself after the individual has rested.

The term 'behavioral potential' in the definition of learning encompasses two aspects. First, the results of the learning process should be observable in the individual's behavior. Second, the term 'potential' calls attention to the fact that not every learning process inevitably culminates in overt behavior. The pilot of a passenger plane, for instance, uses a flight simulator to learn the correct behavior for making emergency landings, but given the low probability of an aviation accident, this learned behavior is unlikely to be exhibited in real life.

Lastly, learning is defined as the result of experience, for learning has to be differentiated from maturation processes and from performance limitations due to situational constraints. Maturation processes are defined primarily as genetically determined growth of the nervous system (e.g. Hall 1989). Situational constraints include the absence of the resources (e.g. information) that are needed for taking action. In all such cases behavioral changes that may occur are not the result of learning processes, for they are not influenced by experience, be it personal or vicarious.

This definition of individual learning contains no reference to performance, for learning does not necessarily lead to improvement in performance (Domjan and Burkhard 1982; Hall 1989). There are three main reasons why learning should not be equated with improved performance. First, results of learning processes are not the only determinants of individual behavior and performance (Campbell 1990). An individual's behavior is influenced by a variety of factors (Rosenstiel 2000): the individual's abilities (e.g. skills), personal volition (e.g. motives), social approbation (e.g. group norms), and the possibilities arising from given circumstances (e.g. situational constraints). Even the execution of such simple manual tasks as mounting a single electronic component on a printed circuit board is affected by all these factors. Just because better skills have been acquired through learning does not necessarily mean that they translate into improved performance. The other determinants of action (e.g. group norms) may block the use of the behavior. If one is to assume that the outcome of learning processes is the cause of improved performance, one has to be able to discount the other determinants of behavior and performance as alternative explanations. Second, it is possible to learn any kind of behavior, not just those that can help improve performance. Absenteeism (e.g. Johns 1997) and antisocial behavior (e.g. Robinson and O'Leary-Kelly 1998) such as causing damage to an organization's property or deliberately delivering substandard work are examples of 'undesired', ultimately performance-limiting behaviors. It follows, therefore, that learning processes can even result in a deterioration of performance.

In some common definitions of *organizational* learning (for an overview, see Prange 1999), learning is equated with intentional learning whose purpose is to achieve an improvement in performance or efficiency. An example of this linkage is the representation and study of learning curves in which the production efficiency of organizations increases with their production experience (e.g. Argote 1993). Another example consists in definitions according to which there have to be demonstrable improvements in performance before one can speak of organizational learning (e.g. Argyris and Schön 1978; Fiol and Lyles 1985). In many cases researchers assume the increase in production efficiency to be a direct indicator of learning and do not consider that the increase could result from other factors, too, such as the mix of products (McGrath and O'Conner 1996). It would therefore certainly be helpful to define organizational learning irrespective of changes in performance. Divorcing the two dimensions would make it possible to investigate all processes and content of organizational learning and to avoid rashly excluding key aspects, such as the question of whether learning is based on the wrong models or why something that has been successfully learned is not manifested as improved performance.

Each part of the definition of individual learning can be operationalized for empirical study. Operationalization allows one to judge whether a study was focused on phenomena of learning or perhaps on some other set of processes instead. As in other areas of study, attempts have been made in the field of organizational learning to introduce operational definitions. Referring to organisms and organizations alike, Huber (1991) wrote that 'an entity learns if, through its processing of information, the range of its potential behaviors is changed' (p. 89). In order to arrive at a definition of organizational learning, it is first necessary to clarify theoretically which alternative constructs also have to be considered for explaining individual parts of the definition. An organization's behavior can be affected, for example, by both successful learning and favorable economic conditions (e.g. lack of competition or chance access to desired resources; see Reber 1992). Hence, either the corresponding parts in the definition of learning have to be operationalized in such a way that they cannot be explained by alternative constructs, or the alternative constructs have to be operationalized also. In empirical studies one can thereby rule out the possibility that changes in an organization's behavior are attributable to, say, favorable economic conditions and can state definitively that the changes are due to learning effects instead.

Basic Concepts and Theories of Individual Learning

In the literature on organizational learning, one finds three basic concepts—learning, memory, and knowledge—that were originally used for individual processes (e.g. Huber 1991). Together, these three concepts deal with the acquisition and recall of new information formally acquired by the individual. The difference between learning and memory processes can be explained in terms of the three-part sequence constituted by the acquisition, encoding, and recall of information. Generally, the concept of learning focuses on processes that occur during the acquisition of new behavior, whereas the concepts of memory, or information-processing, focus on the storage and recall of information (Crowder 1976). Unlike the concepts of learning and memory, the concept of knowledge generally has to do with the content of the information and its appropriate and spontaneous use.

Behavioral Learning Theories

The most prominent behavioral theories of learning are those of classical conditioning and instrumental learning (for an overview, see Schwartz 1989). According to these theories, new behaviors are acquired through the formation of associations between stimuli and reactions or between reactions and consequences. These theories have been extensively tested in experiments, particularly with animals. Although many of the experiments have involved learning at only a very simple level, the underlying mechanisms of learning can be used to understand human behavior acquisition, which is more complex than that of animals.

Classical Conditioning

Through successive pairing of an unconditioned stimulus and a conditioned stimulus, the unconditioned stimulus (which had initially been neutral) elicits a conditioned response. This principle of learning was

accidentally discovered by Pavlov. While studying the digestive system of dogs, he observed
that the animals salivated in anticipation of
being fed when they heard the footsteps of
their keeper. Pavlov then conducted a series of
experiments in which he formulated the basis
of classical conditioning: An important unconditioned stimulus (food) that elicits an innate
reflex (salivation) is presented at the same time
as a neutral conditioned stimulus (such as
the steps of the animal keeper), and after a few
pairings of the unconditioned and conditioned
stimuli, a conditioned response (salivation) is
elicited by the unconditioned stimulus alone;
that is, the subject associates a neutral stimulus
and a response. The learning of emotional
responses is a well-investigated example of processes of classical conditioning (Oehman, Dimberg, and Estevers 1989; Scherer and Tran, Ch. 16
in this volume). The mechanism by which such
responses come to be associated with particular
stimuli is often exploited in advertisements
(Rosenstiel and Neumann 1991). Commercial
products are paired with stimuli that elicit positive emotional responses (e.g. babies or leisure
time).

In organizations it is frequently the case that
employees have a pronounced fear of their
supervisors (Rosenstiel 2000). It is often a generalized fear associated not only with the supervisor personally but also with stimuli in the
environment of that person. Under certain circumstances the very sight of the superior's
office or the voice of his or her secretary can
elicit fear in the employee who has learned that
the two stimuli usually coincide.

Instrumental conditioning

When a certain behavior and a consequence are
successively paired, one can reduce or increase
the frequency of that behavior. In contrast to
classical conditioning, in which stimuli are
paired, instrumental conditioning has to do
with the formation of an association between
a certain response and its consequences. This
learning theory was formulated by Thorndike
at about the same time that Pavlov was working
on his theory of classical conditioning and was

restated by Skinner (Schwartz 1989; Domjan
and Burkhard 1982). The assumption that trial-
and-error learning and the law of effect underlie the central learning sequence is drawn from
Thorndike. He observed that an organism will
make several different attempts (trial-and-
error) to solve a problem. If a particular behavior of this organism is positively reinforced (by
pleasant stimuli such as food or praise) several
times in succession, the likelihood increases
that this type of behavior will recur in a future
situation (the law of effect).

Analysis of problematic behavior in organizations is often facilitated by a check for
unknown reinforcers of the behavior, for it
may have been learned through instrumental
conditioning. For example, if an employee
habitually presents spontaneous ideas without
thinking them through, the reason might be
that the supervisor has been reinforcing that
employee with social attention. If a more
reflective production of ideas is desired, the
supervisor's behavior must change completely.
He or she should bestow attention only if
the employee shows the desired behavior. The
supervisor should be consistent, otherwise the
undesired behavior will become increasingly
manifest. Praise, appreciation, or wage increases are only a few of the positive consequences that are used as reinforcers intended
to shape employee behavior (for an overview,
see Weiss 1990). Luthans and Kreitner's (1985)
model for modifying organizational behavior,
which has been successfully used to improve
the task performance of employees (Stajkovic
and Luthans 1997), is based especially on instrumental conditioning.

Social Learning

In the learning principles presented above, the
individual always showed the target behavior
and either learned the pairing with the formerly unconditioned stimulus or experienced
the consequences of his or her behavior. Generally, no new behaviors are learned through
the mechanisms described in behavioral learning theories. Those mechanisms only increase

the probability of eliciting specific behaviors. By contrast, social learning and modeling are based on the principle of individual learning through observation (Bandura 1969, 1977). If individuals see a model rewarded for its behavior, they will probably imitate that behavior. Accordingly, the behavioral repertoire of individuals is thought to be changed not by their own experience but by their observation of the model's behavior and experience. Modeling appears to be especially suitable for complex behavioral learning, such as driving a car. Bandura (1977) compiled a list of characteristics that facilitate social learning:

- The desired behavioral pattern is seen to be rewarded.
- The model is regarded as positive (e.g. a generally respected employee or supervisor).
- The model is similar to the observer (e.g. same gender, same major field of study).
- The observer's close attention to the model is rewarded.
- The model's behavior is very different from other possible models.
- The model's behavior lies within the behavioral capacity of the observer.

There are many models to learn from in an organization. One's own work group may have a successful colleague whose example can be learned from. Supervisors are often used as role models. Organizational myths often present individuals who can be regarded as models of how one climbs the ladder in the organization. Models also enable a person to learn what the organization marks as desirable or undesirable behavior. A brilliant employee who severely criticizes a decision made by the board of directors and is consequently fired is depicted as a model warning against always expressing one's opinions openly.

These three classical learning theories—classical conditioning, instrumental conditioning, and social learning—illustrate that individuals can learn behavior patterns in different ways: by pairing conditioned and unconditioned stimuli, by pairing behavior with specific consequences, or by observing models. No conscious learning is necessary for any of these processes. Often, the different learning principles complement each other, forming new behavior patterns in real-life situations (Domjan and Burkhard 1982).

Memory and the Information-processing Approach

The information-processing approach has to do with how external information is encoded, stored in, and retrieved from memory (e.g. Anderson 1990, 1995; Eysenck 1993; Howes 1990). Encoding encompasses processes of perception and interpretation that are necessary for transforming external stimuli into cognitive representations of those stimuli. The analysis of external stimuli occurs through bottom-up and top-down processes of perception. Information-processing controlled solely through stimulus input is known as the bottom-up process. However, purely stimulus-driven processes are not the only ones affecting the interpretation and analysis of new information; existing knowledge is always part of the process as well. The ways in which previous experience and existing knowledge affect perception are known as top-down processes. Existing knowledge is stored as schemata and scripts (Anderson 1990). Schemata are cognitive frameworks representing the structure of objects or concepts. The schema 'house', for example, comprises the knowledge that a house is a kind of building, that the discrete parts of a house are 'rooms', that it is built of wood or stone, that it serves as a dwelling, that it consists of right angles, and so forth. Scripts are a special kind of schemata. They refer to events, such as a visit to a restaurant, attendance at a theater performance, the acquisition of a new customer, or the presentation of project results to managers (Schank and Abelson 1977).

Schemata and scripts help a person process information because they make it unnecessary to analyze all aspects of received information (e.g. Gioia 1986). Recognizing salient features of familiar schemata or scripts suffices to enable the receiver to activate them and interpret incoming information. Usually, these cognitive frameworks function without the receiver being aware of it. However, the identification of information is aided at the cost of precision. The analysis of new information ceases if that information can be classified into familiar schemata. Such association frequently leads to erroneous or incomplete absorption of information.

In the social context, that is, in a person's interaction with others, a special form of schemata comes into play, stereotypes. Stereotypes are beliefs that members of a particular group (e.g. men, women, employees, or leaders) all have the same characteristics (e.g. Aronson, Wilson, and Akert 1994). Stereotypes, too, are often used without the users being aware of it. If people perceive features of group affiliation in another person, then a few general group traits will be implicitly ascribed to the perceived person. For instance, college students characterize typical leaders in different contexts (e.g. military, educational, or business) with such attributes as *intelligent*, *decisive*, *informed*, or *determined* (Lord and Maher 1993).

The extent to which these stereotypes play a role in the process of perception seems to be governed by two conflicting factors, the need to be accurate and situational constraints that preclude accuracy (Fiske 1993*a*, *b*; Fiske and Morling 1996). The need to be accurate, and hence perception that goes beyond stereotypes, is affected mainly by people's need for control. In an asymmetrical social context—a context in which a person (e.g. a supervisor) has control over the outcome of actions taken by other persons (e.g. by employees)—the people concerned have different interests in the precision of their perception. The powerful person in such a situation tends to be contented with stereotypical perceptions of those who are less powerful, seeing them as a group. The powerful person thereby reduces the effort he or she invests in processing information. By contrast, the less powerful people perceive the powerful person as an individual to a greater extent than that person sees them as individuals. The less powerful participants in this situation tend to dispense with stereotypical categories of perception. They are motivated to adopt this more complicated mode of information-processing because they expect it to increase the precision of their perception of the powerful person and, hence, to improve their ability to predict that person's responses. In this way they hope to increase their control over the outcome of their own actions.

Storage refers to the manner in which encoded cognitive representations are depicted in the memory. Knowledge about language and the world is called semantic knowledge (e.g. Anderson 1990; Eysenck 1993). It is stored as terms arranged into networks according to their semantic affinity. The characteristics of each term are categorized under it (e.g. Adam Smith is a Scottish moral philosopher). The greater the similarity between the elements of knowledge expressed, the closer the relation between them. This semantic organization of memory has implications for the use of memory, that is, for the storage of new information or the recall of existing content. The closer the relation between two terms, the faster one term can be recalled if the other is already active. Studies on the differences between novices and experts in such domains of knowledge as chess games, physics, and computer programming show that experts not only have greater knowledge but that the organization of their knowledge is a key factor in their high level of achievement (e.g. Ericsson 1996; Glaser and Chi 1988). Their knowledge tends to be organized according to natural laws relevant in specific domains of content, and it is contexualized, linked with the circumstances in which it usually has to be recalled (Bransford, Brown, and Cocking 1999).

Lastly, retrieval refers to the processes of recalling cognitive representations stored in memory. Retrieving information from memory is an active process governed partly by schemata. It is an active process because the storage of information is economical; only the relevant aspects are stored. Additional characteristics of terms are then reconstructed for retrieval, depending on the existing schemata and networks of terms. As a result, an event is recalled in a form that does not correspond exactly to what originally happened.

Knowledge—Substance and Application

Whereas behavioral learning theories focus on the process of acquiring new information, the information-processing approach focuses on the storage and retrieval of information. Investigation of knowledge structures, however, shifts the emphasis to the substance of knowledge.

In cognitive psychology a distinction is frequently made between declarative and procedural knowledge (e.g. Anderson 1976; Squire 1987). Declarative knowledge is 'knowing what'. It consists of facts like dates, the routine sequence of opening a bank account, or the details of an employee's area of responsibility in an organization. Individuals are aware of this sort of knowledge, and they are able to report these facts.

Procedural knowledge is 'knowing how'. It is typified by action-based knowledge and encompasses the execution of such skills as driving a car, writing an article, and using word-processing software on a computer. Often, people are not fully aware of this sort of knowledge. Frequently, both forms of knowledge supplement each other. Bank employees, for example, are required to know precisely each step in opening a bank account, but the use of the software needed in order to perform the task is a highly automatic action on which they are unable to report. Procedural knowledge is acquired in three stages: cognitive, associative, and autonomous (Anderson 1995). In the cognitive stage, the individual deals mostly with problem-solving. A person who learns a word-processing system is confronted, say, with typing errors that have to be corrected. The acquired knowledge in this stage is still expressed as declarative knowledge. Therefore, one often finds 'how to do' lists during this stage. In the associative stage the declarative knowledge of the learning material is carried over into action (procedural knowledge). The action becomes much smoother and far freer of error than it was in the preceding stage because the coordination of the different steps demands less attention. Finally, in the autonomous stage the skill becomes even more automatic. As a consequence, individuals often cannot verbally describe how they perform the action. Experienced typists are typically unable to say from memory where a letter is found on the keyboard, although they are able to type flawlessly without looking at the keyboard.

Inductive Learning

The learning theories discussed above have usually been studied in simple contexts where the behavior to be learned is unambiguous. These theories explain how behavior is learned through the reinforcement of certain actions. It is assumed that the responses of the environment are largely consistent. In the everyday world of work, however, people are often confronted by completely unstructured situations in which they draw causal inferences and conclusions from information, in many cases without feedback. In the absence of feedback, people apply their causal inferences and conclusions as general rules (e.g. Holland, Hoyoak, Nisbett, and Thagard 1989; Stevenson, Busemeyer, and Naylor 1990).

In unstructured settings, new cognitive structures or rules are not learned through reasoning alone. This learning of complex structures and rules in certain domains is called inductive learning (Anderson 1995). A key question about inductive learning is how people draw causal inferences from existing experience and thereby learn generalized rules. Causal inferences occur in many areas of organizational action. A certain sound leads a maintenance technician to infer that there is a certain malfunction in a machine, for that technician has often heard the sound in connection with that malfunction. Certain symptoms lead a physician to diagnose the cause of a disorder, certain statements by an applicant lead the interviewing manager to infer the applicant's suitability, and turbulence on Asian markets leads a broker to expect a decline in the prices of certain U.S. stocks.

Einhorn and Hogarth (1986) described four key components by means of which people arrive at causal judgments, which are the basis for the rules or structures learned in that process. First, inferences are made in a certain context or field. The context is crucial because it provides the basis on which a person can judge whether an event is normal. Explanations are then sought only for abnormal events (Weiner 1985). The context in which a certain event occurs affects judgment about different variables as conditions or possible causes. Upon hearing of a small company's bankruptcy, for example, one might assume ineptitude on the part of the general manager. Keeping in mind the broader context—the fact that all the other suppliers of a conglomerate have also declared bankruptcy—one might look for other explanations.

Second, certain cues-to-causality increase the likelihood that one event will be assumed to be the cause of another event (Einhorn and Hogarth 1986). Customary cues are temporal order, contiguity, and similarity. If one event precedes another, then the assumption will very probably be that the earlier one caused the later one. Temporal or spatial proximity (contiguity) of two events likewise suggests a causal linkage, as does a similarity of two events.

Third, according to this model, people combine the context of events and the cues-to-causality in order to ascertain the likelihood of a causal linkage between various events in a certain context. Fourth, alternative explanations for why one event could be the cause of another event are weighed in the process of ascertaining the likelihood of a causal linkage.

The learning of new rules and terms through inferences is often paralleled by an utter lack of awareness that new terms and rules have to be learned. One particularly serious obstacle to the recognition of a need to learn is known as the 'illusion of validity' (Einhorn and Hogarth 1978; Tversky and Kahneman 1974). It is an unjustified confidence that there is a causal link between incoming information and the prediction of events. The illusion of validity stems from systematic cognitive biases (for examples beyond those discussed in the following passage, see Feldman 1986).

One factor contributing to the illusion of validity is a person's tendency to register the frequency of events more than their probability. An explanation for this tendency is that probability is more difficult to register, for it requires attention to be directed to the nonoccurrence of events. For instance, it might be that personnel decisions have usually favored male candidates because many male candidates have eventually worked out well. A cognitive bias builds when only the absolute frequency of positive outcomes is contemplated rather than the number of eventually successful employees as a percentage of all candidates hired.

A second factor that increases the illusion of validity is the impossibility of gathering information about alternative assumptions if action is based on a hypothesis. If a certain kind of compensation is introduced in a company, then it is no longer possible to find out if alternative kinds of compensation would be successful.

A third factor in the illusion of validity is disregard of base-rate information (Tversky and Kahneman 1982). For example, executives are hired in an organization on the basis of an invalid instrument, such as a nonstandardized interview, but these individuals are from a population with a high success rate (base-rate) of 72 per cent. Because the only information involved is about the persons who were eventually hired, and because individuals tend to ignore base-rate information, the future job success of the candidates for executive positions seems to be correctly predicted through the interviews.

A fourth factor that might increase the illusion of validity is known as the self-fulfilling prophecy (e.g. Darly and Fazio 1980), that is, a behavior manifested in individuals or groups because it was expected. A study by Eden (1990) demonstrated the role this effect had in the training of soldiers. In the experimental group platoon leaders were told that their soldiers would have above-average potential, although their actual potential was the same as that of the soldiers in the control group. The platoon leaders of the control group received no information about the potential of their soldiers. After 10 weeks of training, the soldiers of the experimental group scored higher on objective written and practical tests than did the soldiers of the control group. The example shows that the application of incorrect rules or convictions creates facts that appear to confirm those rules or convictions. This apparent confirmation fosters the illusion of validity and prevents recognition that existing information should be analyzed in order to learn better rules and concepts from the causal inferences drawn from it.

Motivation as a Moderator of Individual Learning

In most cases, behavior underlies learning and learning processes, so learning, too, is determined by a number of factors. Behaviorally oriented approaches have usually involved experiments with animals, whose behavior reflects their desire to allay their hunger, quench their thirst, or satisfy other basic needs. The learning behavior of school children takes place in specific learning activities, such as the constant recitation of facts to be learned by heart, the restructuring of class notes, or the solving of problems given as homework. The execution of these behaviors is an essential part of intentional learning. Both the frequency of these behaviors and the fundamental willingness to engage in them depend on the motivation of the learner. This variable of learning success has been studied primarily in educational psychology (see Gage and Berliner 1992; Slavin 1994).

As a phenomenon, motivation is a state in which an individual directs his or her activities to a desired goal (Geen 1995). In terms of an individual's behavior, motivation refers to the initiation, intensity, and persistence of an action. A person with high achievement motives, for example, is apt to behave competitively in a neutral social situation and exhibits such behavior frequently and persistently in this situation. Motivation originates in an interplay between a person's characteristics (e.g. the achievement motive or power motive) and a situation's characteristics that stimulate

certain motives (Heckhausen 1991). Motivation can have a bearing on when, how, what, and with which degree of success a person learns in the educational (Schunk 1991) and occupational (Noe and Ford 1992) context. The goal-setting theory and the self-efficacy theory are widely used to explain learning motivation (for an overview, see Pintrich and Schunk 1996).

The main tenet of the goal-setting theory is that difficult and specific goals lead to high achievement, as opposed to do-your-best conditions or unspecific goals, which lead to low achievement (Locke and Latham 1990). Although this theory was developed primarily in order to explain task performance in work settings, it has also contributed a great deal to the understanding of learning motivation (Pintrich and Schunk 1996). The setting of high, specific goals increases learning success because it directs the learner's attention to content that is relevant to the goals and relates learner's effort to attain the high goal level (Locke and Latham 1990).

The existence of goals is a basic part of Bandura's self-efficacy theory (1986, 1997) as well. Self-efficacy is defined as 'people's judgments of their capabilities to organize and execute courses of action required to attain designated types of performances' (Bandura 1986: 391). A person's perceived self-efficacy determines the goal level, the person's commitment to the goal, the selection of strategies with which to attain the goal, and the degree of effort made in pursuit of it (Bandura 1997: 136). A person's assessment of self-efficacy and the effect it has on the person's learning behavior and learning success may have nothing to do with his or her actual abilities (e.g. Bouffard-Bouchard 1990; Bouffard-Bouchard, Parent, and Larivée 1991; Schunk 1989).

Individual Learning: Implications for Organizational Learning

What implications do the concepts and theories of individual learning have for organizational learning?

1. *Learning is not always intentional.* As with social learning, the behavioral approaches to learning demonstrate that unintentional learning processes take place in many cases. Individuals tend to favor previously successful behavior, especially when a change in conditions calls for different behavior. Basically, organizations respond in the same way (see also Starbuck and Hedberg, Ch. 14 in this volume, who show that simple behavioral learning principles can be applied both to individual organizations and populations of organizations).

2. *Individuals learn from models.* Individuals tend to adopt behaviors of people whom they experience as being similar to themselves. These behaviors are those that individuals observe directly, think themselves capable of emulating, and judge to have positive effects on others. The implications for organizations are that successful and unsuccessful behavior should be openly communicated and observable within the organizations and that successful and unsuccessful behaviors of similar organizations should be analyzed and regarded as benchmarks. In the U.S. metal industry, those companies whose R&D employees judiciously exchanged information bit-by-bit with their counterparts at competing firms have been more successful than those companies who did not engage in such communication (Schrader 1990). In Europe, Daimler-Benz and BMW once supported a rival company, Audi, in its development of an eight-cylinder engine in order to serve the overriding mutual goal of enhancing the image of German-made eight-cylinder engines on the world market. Similarly, it is conceivable that common interest in defending automotive transport against rail and air competitors on the market is leading many car manufacturers to inform each other about advances and setbacks in their efforts to increase the efficiency, environmental compatibility, and safety of motor vehicles.

3. *Previous knowledge is always important and sometimes hazardous.* Existing structures of knowledge are a key aspect of learning processes. These structures play an important role in the interpretation of new information. The better the quality of the knowledge structures, the greater the capacity to acquire new knowledge and the better that knowledge can be retrieved in the appropriate situation. At the organizational level, too, this previously available knowledge is a key determinant of the 'absorptive capacity' of an organization, that is, its ability to transpose new knowledge into products ready for the market (Cohen and Levinthal 1990). In the long term, however, great expertise in a domain of knowledge can also hamper information in-take, learning, and performance. These drawbacks can be manifested as paralysis in dealing with unexpected events, whether at the level of the individual (Sternberg 1996) or the organization (Walsh and Ungson 1991).

4. *Learning results from making causal inferences.* In many situations people in organizations must infer rules from ambiguous information. The inferred rules are, in turn, applied to new situations and one's own actions. In other words, these rules have been learned. The process by which they are learned, however, is highly vulnerable to error. Researchers have identified a number of factors that lead individuals to infer rules incorrectly or to fail to check whether they are correct. People acting on the basis of faulty rules then make wrong decisions and take inappropriate action. In these cases learning can therefore mean that something will continue to be done improperly despite systematic attempts at problem-solving and despite subsequent efforts at rule creation.

The danger in wrongly applying rules, or of applying the wrong rules, is that one cannot recheck what has been learned. Under these circumstances, learning is not a positive outcome. Only the systematic search for and use of feedback can help repeatedly check rules once they have been acquired (see Starbuck and Hedberg, Ch. 14 in this volume). In the area of organizational learning, Sitkin (1992) advocated that management decision-making be approached in a more daring, experimental fashion than has been the case thus far. An experimental approach of the kind he proposed would permit management to make strategic and intelligent errors that help identify and then correct faulty rules.

5. *Learning is motivated behavior.* The cognitive processes that constitute learning are only part of learning behavior as a whole. With intentional learning in particular, people must also be motivated to begin learning activities and pursue them successfully. For intensely motivated learning, high, specific learning goals and self-efficacy are essential. Little research has been devoted to the significance that motivational variables have in organizational learning. One reason for this lack of attention may be that the definitions of organizational learning are often nonuniform, very narrow, or all but impossible to operationalize.

From Individual to Group Learning: The Sociocognitive Approach

Organizations are social structures formed by individuals and groups (Rosenstiel 2000). As defined by Guzzo and Shea (1992), a group is 'a social system that has the following properties: It is perceived to be an entity by its members and by nonmembers familiar with it; its members have a degree of interdependence; and a differentiation of roles and duties takes place in the group' (p. 272). The meaning that groups have for organizations is steadily increasing because the work that used to be done by individuals is often done by groups today (Guzzo and Shea 1992; Moreland 1999). Even strategic decisions of large and complex organizations are being shaped more and more by top management teams (e.g. Murray 1989; Wiersema and Bantel 1992). Moreover, individual managers usually do not have all the needed information; instead, it lies spread among various persons or groups (see Hollenbeck *et al.* 1995). The significance that work groups therefore have in organizations means that

knowledge acquisition by individuals is an indispensable, but usually insufficient, component of organizational learning. For that reason the special features of group learning are examined in this section.

New approaches in research on social cognition indicate that cognitive processes of encoding, storage, retrieval, and the use of information can be observed and analyzed at both the group and the individual levels (Larson and Christensen 1993; Hinsz, Tindale, and Vollrath 1997). For example, overall information-processing by groups working on decision-making tasks is often qualitatively compared to cognitive performance by individuals on the same tasks. Such study is useful in efforts to find out whether and under what conditions information available to a group's individual members can be used by the group as a whole to make a correct decision (Brodbeck and Greitemeyer 2000).

At the group level, encoding has to do with the identification and interpretation of relevant information. The perception of the members that their group is a unit is expressed in group culture, which has been defined in many different ways (e.g. Shrivastava and Schneider 1984; van Maanen and Barley 1984). Common to all the definitions is the notion that group culture contains, among other things, a set of thoughts shared among the group members (Levine and Moreland 1991). These shared thoughts encompass knowledge about the group (e.g. group norms), about group members (e.g. skills of the prototypical group member), and about the work of the group (e.g. work goals). They can facilitate or obstruct recognition of relevant information or problems (Moreland and Levine 1992). In the early phases of cognitive processing of information, groups as a whole have to identify information as thematically relevant for their tasks in order to integrate it in the useable knowledge structure of the group. If harmony and cohesion is highly regarded in a group's culture, then the group tends to eschew open discussions because they may open the way for problems that might entail conflicts among the group's members. By contrast, groups that are committed by group norms to constant innovation and improvement in performance may instead tend to encourage their members to address differing positions and information. This practice may improve the group's understanding of its tasks and augment the benefit that the members derive from the information distributed to them (Larson and Christensen 1993).

The capacity of groups to store knowledge seems to be superior to that of individuals (Clark and Stephenson 1989; Hartwick, Sheppard, and Davis 1982). Wegner (1987) described this superiority as transactive memory in a group. This transactive memory consists in the collective storage of the group's knowledge across various members and in all members' awareness of what knowledge is stored with whom. Among the members there is usually a specialization in certain domains of knowledge, and that specialization is known to the members to varying degrees (Levine and Moreland 1991). Each of the specialists in the group becomes responsible for storing the information relevant to a domain, with each member actively passing on information to the pertinent specialist. The knowledge stored in this decentralized manner is then useful to the group as a whole if each member knows who is responsible for storing what kind of information. Liang, Moreland, and Argote (1995) confirmed that the formation of a transactive memory system in groups whose members went through training together accounts for their superior performance in comparison to that of groups whose members went through the same training individually. The findings from studies by Henry (Henry 1993, 1995a, b; Henry, Strickland, Yorges, and Ladd 1996) and Littlepage (Littlepage, Robinson, and Reddington 1997; Littlepage, Schmidt, Whisler, and Frost 1995; Littlepage and Silbiger 1992) demonstrate that the better groups are at recognizing the expertise of their members, the better they are able to make decisions.

The superiority of group memory over the memory of individuals is also often explained by the advantages of group retrieval of information. Groups can tap the recall ability of their individual members. When compiling and collating the information, the members are able to correct each other (Hinsz 1990). An additional explanation for the superiority of group recall is that group members bringing together this information give each other cues that facilitate its retrieval (e.g. Martell and Borg 1993).

The variously documented superiority of the capacity of groups to store and retrieve information is not always reflected as an improved use of information. Group work has repeatedly been shown to be susceptible to what is referred to as process loss (e.g. Diehl and Stroebe 1987; Stasser 1992; Steiner 1972), the phenomenon that a group's performance is frequently less than optimal because its members have to be coordinated. Process loss explains why the achievement of groups is lower than the summed achievement of a comparable number of individuals performing the same tasks. Referring especially to the gathering and use of information, Stasser (1992) pointed out that information possessed by all members as a group is more likely to be talked about in a group discussion than information possessed only by a single member. This phenomenon of the biased sampling of information becomes especially obstructive in group decisions if the distribution of information among members produces a 'hidden profile' (Stasser 1988). In hidden-profile situations, parts of the information that a group has vary somewhat from member to member. A group can arrive at the best decision only if all the information is taken into account equally by all the members. Many studies have shown that groups are not optimally able to retrieve from their members all the information necessary for making the best group decision (e.g. Larson, Foster-Fishman, and Keys 1994; Stasser and Titus 1985; Stasser, Taylor, and Hanna 1989). Such phenomena also surface in real work groups that have to make daily diagnostic decisions by pooling information (Larson, Christensen, Abbott, and Franz 1996). In group discussion of this sort, managers often inherit the role of counteracting the tendency of the group by repeatedly bringing in unshared information (Larson et al. 1996).

Group Learning: Implications for Organizational Learning

Research on social cognition deals with the collection, storage, and retrieval of information in a social aggregate, the group. This work thereby complements the learning processes hitherto examined only in relation to individuals. Findings of research on social cognition are important to organizational learning because the use of knowledge in organizations is a social phenomenon in many cases. Employees specialize in certain domains of knowledge, so it is crucial that this unequally distributed information be taken into account jointly as organizational decisions are made. Researchers of social cognition are beginning to study the conditions under which, for example, groups succeed at using unequally distributed information knowledge in such a balanced way that the best decision can be made by a group. What implications does sociocognitive research have for organizational learning?

1. *Social aggregates possess more knowledge than individuals do*. Studies on the memory processes of groups have demonstrated that groups have greater storage capacity than individuals do. This superiority is due to two factors: (a) the specialization of individual group members in certain domains of knowledge, and (b) all members' knowledge of this specialization. Whereas specialization is fairly manageable in a small group, particularly because all members have direct contact with each other, the situation is different in organizations, for the specialists are entire departments or small departmental units, not just individuals. If organizations, too, are to tap the potential knowledge existing within them, the spheres of responsibility must be known and there must be confidence in the reliability of the specializations.

2. *Groups cannot use all information equally.* Although the storage capacity of groups is potentially greater than that of individuals, groups in decision-making situations are often evidently unable to draw on this knowledge as much as they need to. The risk is that inform-

ation known only to some of the members will not enter into group decision-making.

3. *There are differences between small groups and organizations.* Studies based on the sociocognitive approach have been conducted primarily as small-group experiments. However, some factors operating in real work groups within organizations have thus far been excluded from such controlled settings and have therefore had to be left unconsidered in this research (Anand, Manz, and Glick 1998).

A frequent premise in studies based on the sociocognitive approach is that information is stored solely in the memories of a group's members. However, information storage in organizations is not confined to the members of a group alone; knowledge can be recorded in and retrieved from other media as well, such as printed material and formalized routines. Moreover, organizations, unlike the experimental small groups of scientific studies, are open systems. Information in organizations can therefore also be retrieved through modern information media outside the organizations (McGrath and O'Connor 1996).

The degree to which knowledge in organizations is stored mainly in its individual members is indicated by research on the effects that turnover has at least on indirect measures (e.g. performance) of learning processes and information-processing. Argote, Beckman, and Epple (1990), for example, reported that the productivity of the company they studied was unaffected by turnover among its production workers. They supposed that the jobs performed by the production workers were so standardized and that the company had such a highly formalized production configuration that the turnover of production employees had no influence on the company's production knowledge. In a group experiment, Argote, Insko, Yovetich, and Romero (1995) showed that turnover in fact reduced the group performance. This effect was much stronger in the groups that performed simple tasks than it was in groups that had complex tasks. In a simulation study, Carley (1992) showed that the knowledge elements of teams was affected by the turnover of group members rather than by hierarchical structures. In teams, knowledge is distributed among the members, so team decisions depend heavily on the current members. In hierarchical structures, one person's knowledge can be compensated for because the gathering of knowledge involves a variety of analysts.

These studies point out a few special features of learning processes and information processes—features that continue to warrant attention when the sociocognitive approach is applied to the study of organizational learning. In order to ascertain the significance of the knowledge possessed by individual members of an organization or group, one must consider the type of task, the degree to which task performance is standardized or formalized. It is also important, particularly with regard to learning processes in entire organizations, to specify the level of hierarchy at which losses due to the turnover of individuals are likely.

Contributions of and Gaps in the Psychological Study of Organizational Learning

So far we have discussed the psychological construct of 'learning' as it is applied to and studied at the level of individuals and groups. Can this construct also be useful at other levels, such as organizations? Can organizations be attributed characteristics or abilities ascribed only to individuals? How can one circumvent the problem of anthropomorphizing social units?

Walsh and Ungson (1991) argued that 'organizational memory' is an analogy. The use of analogy is justifiable because it helps explain something abstract or difficult to understand by showing its similarity to something concrete or easy to understand. The description of a construct, such as 'learning', can begin abstractly (Morgeson and Hofmann 1999), but applying a construct to an individual, a group, an organization, or some other level requires one to define the outcomes that the construct is intended to explain. The important thing is

that the construct's constitutive processes can be different at each level. That is, basic processes of an individual's learning occur within the nervous systems; basic processes of organizational learning occur between individuals taking action in specific structures, in organizations (e.g. Larson and Christensen 1993). If organizational learning must always be assumed to require learning processes at a lower level of analysis—namely, individuals—then it is always necessary to specify how effects of learning as a construct at the level of the individual influence processes of learning as a construct at the level of organizations (House, Rousseau, and Thomas-Hunt 1995).

The psychological approaches to the study of learning by individuals and groups do not necessarily imply that learning leads to increased success. Successful learning and improved performance have to be considered separately. Learning more efficient behavior or concepts can be one reason that performance improves, but there are also many other factors that affect the performance of an individual. If performance does not improve, it does not automatically mean that no learning has taken place. Learning can occur unintentionally, as demonstrated by the behavioral approaches and by social learning. These unintentional forms of learning may explain why undesired or dysfunctional behaviors (e.g. anxiety responses) are sometimes learned along with 'best practice'. Past knowledge guides the interpretation of new information, a cognitive function that facilitates the uptake of information but reduces the precision of its processing.

Groups are superior to individuals in the total amount of stored information. In groups, however, process losses can occur in the use of information. Often, not all potentially available information can be retrieved from group members and therefore cannot fully contribute to the choice of the right decision.

Psychological theories leave many special aspects of organizational learning unconsidered. Important differences between organizational learning and the factors studied through psychological approaches are that the knowledge in organizations can be stored in a great variety of ways, including diagrams created by employees themselves, work flows, office layouts, and standard operating procedures. Alternatively, it can encompass less visible matters such as identity, culture, and vision (e.g. Levitt and March 1988; Walsh and Ungson 1991). The significance that these different possibilities have for storage is largely unstudied in psychological research.

Another important difference is that knowledge in organizations can be unequally distributed not only within a group but across many units as well. So that this knowledge can become part of organizational decisions as well, it must be gathered by decision-makers or decision-making groups; it must become communicable, shared knowledge (Duncan and Weiss 1979; Nonaka 1994).

People are often unable to say much about important aspects of their knowledge, for that knowledge is tacit (Sternberg 1999). These aspects are important because high performers differ in their tacit knowledge from moderate-to-low performers. The use and transfer of individual tacit knowledge into communicable, explicit, organizational knowledge is often problematic, as shown in the studies of work psychology (Frese and Zapf 1994; Hacker 1986, 1992). For example, Hacker (1992) reported that machines operated by highly productive workers ran idle less than did the machines operated by less productive persons but that the high performers were largely unable to explain how they knew when their machines needed new spools. To enable all the production workers to share this relevant knowledge, it is essential to pinpoint the signals (e.g. specific sounds or a particular sequence of actions) that prompt the high performers to feed the machine on time. Explanatory tacit knowledge can be attained by interviews (Hacker and Jilge 1993; Spencer and Spencer 1993) or by team-based interventions such as the formation of self-organizing teams (Nonaka 1994) or systematic variation in group composition (Mohrman, Cohen, and Mohrman 1995). When this knowledge becomes explicit and communicable, it can be conveyed in training programs or built into systems of production that will raise the level of productivity and quality.

This chapter has focused on psychological theories about the learning, information-processing, and knowledge of individuals and groups. We have pointed out that learning by individuals can lead to improved performance but that dysfunctional behaviors or concepts are also learned in many cases. It has also been shown that both information-processing and learning through causal inferences is prone to error in individuals. The study of learning processes in groups broadens the scope to social processes that have a major impact on the acquisition and use of information. Social cognition research appears to be significant for organizational learning because organizations are intent on gathering knowledge distributed across individuals, groups, or both. There has been little investigation into aspects especially relevant to organizational learning, such as the different ways of storing knowledge or the conditions under which individual or group knowledge become shared knowledge in an organization.

References

Anand, V., Manz, C. C., and Glick, W. H. (1998). 'An Organizational Memory Approach to Information Management'. *Academy of Management Review*, 23: 796–809.

Anderson, J. R. (1976). *Language, Memory, and Thought*. Hillsdale, NJ: Erlbaum.

——(1990). *Cognitive Psychology and Its Applications* (3rd edn). New York: Freeman.

——(1995). *Learning and Memory: An Integrated Approach*. New York: John Wiley and Sons.

Argote, L. (1993). 'Group and Organizational Learning Curves: Individual, System and Environmental Components'. *British Journal of Social Psychology*, 32: 31–51.

Argote, L., Beckman, S. L., and Epple, D. (1990). 'The Persistence and Transfer of Learning in Industrial Settings'. *Management Science*, 36: 140–54.

——Insko, C. A., Yovetich, N., and Romero, A. A. (1995). 'Group Learning Curves: The Effects of Turnover and Task Complexity on Group Performance'. *Journal of Applied Social Psychology*, 25: 512–29.

Argyris, C. and Schön, D. A. (1978). *Organizational Learning: A Theory of Action Perspective*. Reading, Mass.: Addison-Wesley.

Aronson, E., Wilson, T. D., and Akert, R. M. (1994). *Social Psychology: The Heart and the Mind*. New York: Harper Collins.

Bandura, A. (1969). *Principles of Behavior Modification*. New York: Holt, Rinehart and Winston.

——(1977). *Social Learning Theory*. Englewood Cliffs, NJ: Prentice Hall.

——(1986). *Social Foundations of Thought and Action: A Social Cognitive Theory*. Englewood Cliffs, NJ: Prentice Hall.

——(1997). *Self-efficacy: The Exercise of Control*. New York: Freeman.

Bouffard-Bouchard, T. (1990). 'Influence of Self-efficacy on Performance in a Cognitive Task'. *Journal of Social Psychology*, 130: 353–63.

——Parent, S., and Larivée, S. (1991). 'Influence of Self-efficacy on Self-regulation and Performance among Junior and Senior High-school Age Students'. *International Journal of Behavioral Development*, 14: 153–64.

Bransford, J. D., Brown, A. L., and Cocking, R. R. (1999). *How People Learn: Brain, Mind, Experience, and School*. Washington, DC: National Academy Press.

Brodbeck, F. C. and Greitemeyer, T. (2000). 'A Dynamic Model of Group Performance: Considering the Group Members' Capacity to Learn'. *Group Processes and Intergroup Relations*, 3: 159–82.

Campbell, J. P. (1990). 'Modeling the Performance Prediction Problem in Industrial and Organizational Psychology', in M. D. Dunnette and L. M. Hough (eds.), *Handbook of Industrial and Organizational Psychology* (Vol. 1) (2nd edn). Palo Alto, Calif.: Consulting Psychologists Press, 687–732.

Cangelosi, V. and Dill, W. R. (1965). 'Organizational Learning: Observations toward a Theory'. *Administrative Science Quarterly*, 10: 175–203.

Carley, K. (1992). 'Organizational Learning and Personnel Turnover'. *Organization Science*, 3: 20–46.

Clark, N. K. and Stephenson, G. M. (1989). 'Group Remembering', in P. B. Paulus (ed.), *Psychology of Group Influence*. Hillsdale, NJ: Lawrence Erlbaum, 357–91.

Cohen, W. M. and Levinthal, D. A. (1990). 'Absorptive Capacity: A New Perspective on Learning and Innovation'. *Administrative Science Quarterly*, 35: 128–52.

Crossan, M. and Guatto, T. (1996). 'Organizational Learning Research Profile'. *Journal of Organizational Change Management*, 9/1: 107–12.

Crowder, R. G. (1976). *Principles of Learning and Memory*. Hillsdale, NJ: Erlbaum.

Darly, J. M. and Fazio, R. H. (1980). 'Expectancy Confirmation Process Arising in the Social Interaction Sequence'. *American Psychologist*, 35: 867–81.

Diehl, M. and Stroebe, W. (1987). 'Productivity Loss in Brainstorming Groups: Toward the Solution of a Riddle'. *Journal of Personality and Social Psychology*, 53: 497–509.

Domjan, M. and Burkhard, B. (1982). *The Principles of Learning and Behavior* (2nd edn). Pacific Grove, Calif.: Brooks/Cole.

Duncan, R. and Weiss, A. (1979). 'Organizational Learning: Implications for Organizational Design', in B. M. Staw (ed.), *Research in Organizational Behavior: An Annual Series of Analytical Essays and Critical Reviews* (Vol. 1). Greenwich, Conn.: JAI Press, 75–123.

Ebbinghaus, H. (1885). *Über das Gedächtnis*. Leipzig: Altenberger.

Eden, D. (1990). 'Pygmalion without Interpersonal Contrast Effects: Whole Group Gain from Raising Manager Expectations'. *Journal of Applied Psychology*, 75: 394–8.

Einhorn, H. J. and Hogarth, R. M. (1978). 'Confidence in Judgement: Persistence of the Illusion of Validity'. *Psychological Review*, 85: 395–416.

——(1986). 'Judging Probable Cause'. *Psychological Bulletin*, 99: 3–19.

Ericsson, K. A. (1996). 'The Acquisition of Expert Performance: An Introduction to Some of the Issues', in K. A. Ericsson (ed.), *The Road to Excellence*. Mahwah, NJ: Erlbaum, 1–50.

Eysenck, M. W. (1993). *Principles of Cognitive Psychology*. Hillsdale, NJ: Erlbaum.

Feldman, J. (1986). 'On the Difficulty of Learning from Experience', in H. P. Sims and D. A. Gioia (eds.), *The Thinking Organization: Dynamics of Organizational Social Cognition*. San Francisco: Jossey Bass, 263–92.

Fiol, C. M. and Lyles, M. A. (1985). 'Organizational Learning'. *Academy of Management Review*, 10: 803–13.

Fiske, S. T. (1993a). 'Controlling Other People: The Impact of Power on Stereotyping'. *American Psychologist*, 48: 621–8.

—— (1993b). 'Social Cognition and Social Perception'. *Annual Review of Psychology*, 44: 155–94.

—— and Morling, B. (1996). 'Stereotyping as a Function of Personal Control Motives and Capacity Constraints: The Odd Couple of Power and Anxiety', in H. Higgins and E. Tory (eds.), *Handbook of Motivation and Cognition: The Interpersonal Context* (Vol. 3). New York: Guilford, 323–46.

Frese, M. and Brodbeck, F. C. (1989). *Computer in Büro und Verwaltung: Psychologisches Wissen für die Praxis*. Berlin: Springer.

—— and Zapf, D. (1994). 'Action as the Core of Work Psychology: A German Approach', in H. C. Triandis, M. D. Dunnette, and I. M. Hough (eds.), *Handbook of Industrial and Organizational Psychology* (Vol. 4) (2nd edn). Palo Alto, Calif.: Consulting Psychologists Press, 271–340.

Friedrich, H. F. and Mandl, H. (1992). 'Lern- und Denkstrategien—ein Problemaufriß', in H. Mandl and H. F. Friedrich (eds.), *Lern- und Denkstrategien: Analyse und Intervention*. Göttingen: Hogrefe, 3–54.

Gage, N. L. and Berliner, D. C. (1992). *Educational Psychology*. Boston: Houghton Mifflin.

Garratt, B. (1987). *The Learning Organization*. Aldershot: Gower.

Garvin, D. A. (1993). 'Building a Learning Organization'. *Harvard Business Review*, 71/4: 78–91.

Geen, R. G. (1995). *Human Motivation: A Social Psychological Approach*. Pacific Grove, Calif.: Brooks/Cole.

Gioia, D. A. (1986). 'Symbols, Scripts, and Sensemaking: Creating Meaning in the Organizational Experience', in H. P. Sims and D. A. Gioia (eds.), *The Thinking Organization: Dynamics of Organizational Social Cognition*. San Francisco: Jossey-Bass, 49–74.

Glaser, R. and Chi, M. T. H. (1988). 'Overview', in M. T. H. Chi, R. Glaser, and M. J. Farr (eds.), *The Nature of Expertise*. Hillsdale, NJ: Erlbaum, xv-xxviii.

Guzzo, R. A. and Shea, G. P. (1992). 'Group Performance and Intergroup Relations in Organizations', in M. D. Dunnette and L. M. Hough (eds.), *Handbook of Industrial and Organizational Psychology* (Vol. 3) (2nd edn). Palo Alto, Calif.: Consulting Psychologists Press, 269–313.

Hacker, W. (1986). *Arbeitspsychologie*. Bern: Huber.

—— (1992). *Expertenkönnen: Erkennen und Vermitteln*. Göttingen: Verlag für angewandte Psychologie.

—— and Jilge, S. (1993). 'Vergleich verschiedener Methoden zur Ermittlung von Handlungswissen'. *Zeitschrift für Arbeits- und Organisationspsychologie*, 37: 64–72.

Hall, J. F. (1989). *Learning and Memory* (2nd edn). Boston: Allyn and Bacon.

Hartwick, J., Sheppard, B. H., and Davis, J. H. (1982). 'Group Remembering: Research and Implications', in R. A. Guzzo (ed.), *Improving Group Decision Making in Organizations*. New York: Academic Press, 41–72.

Heckhausen, H. (1991). *Motivation and Action*. New York: Springer.

Hedberg, B. L. T. (1981). 'How Organizations Learn and Unlearn', in P. C. Nystrom and W. H. Starbuck (eds.), *Handbook of Organizational Design*: Vol. 1. *Adapting Organizations to Their Environments*. Oxford: Oxford University Press, 3–27.

Henry, R. A. (1993). 'Group Judgment Accuracy: Reliability and Validity of Postdiscussion Confidence Judgments'. *Organizational Behavior and Human Decision Processes*, 56: 11–27.

—— (1995a). 'Improving Group Judgment Accuracy: Information Sharing and Determining the Best Member'. *Organizational Behavior and Human Decision Processes*, 62: 190–7.

—— (1995b). 'Using Relative Confidence Judgements to Evaluate Group Effectiveness'. *Basic and Applied Social Psychology*, 16: 333–50.

Henry, R. A., Strickland, O. J., Yorges, S. L., and Ladd, D. (1996). 'Helping Groups Determine Their Most Accurate Member: The Role of Feedback'. *Journal of Applied Social Psychology*, 26: 1153–70.

Hinsz, V. B. (1990). 'Cognitive and Consensus Processes in Group Recognition Memory Performance'. *Journal of Personality and Social Psychology*, 59: 705–18.

——Tindale, R. S., and Vollrath, D. A. (1997). 'The Emerging Conceptualization of Groups as Information Processors'. *Psychological Bulletin*, 121: 43–64.

Holland, J. H., Holyoak, K. J., Nisbett, R. E., and Thagard, P. R. (1989). *Induction: Processes of Inference, Learning, and Discovery*. Cambridge, Mass.: MIT Press.

Hollenbeck, J. R., Ilgen, D. R., Sego, D. J., Hedlund, J., Major, D. A., and Phillips, J. (1995). 'Multilevel Theory of Team Decision Making: Decision Performance in Teams Incorporating Distributed Expertise'. *Journal of Applied Psychology*, 80: 292–316.

House, R., Rousseau, D. M., and Thomas-Hunt, M. (1995). 'The Meso Paradigm: A Framework for the Integration of Micro and Macro Organizational Behavior', in L. L. Cummings and B. M. Staw (eds.), *Research in Organizational Behavior: An Annual Series of Analytical Essays and Critical Reviews* (Vol. 17). Greenwich, Conn.: JAI Press, 71–114.

Howes, M. B. (1990). *The Psychology of Human Cognition*. New York: Pergamon.

Huber, G. P. (1991). 'Organizational Learning: The Contributing Processes and the Literatures'. *Organization Science*, 2: 88–115.

Johns, G. (1997). 'Contemporary Research on Absence from Work: Correlates, Causes, and Consequences', in C. L. Cooper and I. T. Robertson (eds.), *International Review of Industrial and Organizational Psychology*. London: Wiley, 115–74.

Larson, J. R., Jr., and Christensen, C. (1993). 'Groups as Problem-solving Units: Toward a New Meaning of Social Cognition'. *British Journal of Social Psychology*, 32: 5–30.

——————Abbott, A. S., and Franz, T. M. (1996). 'Diagnosing Groups: Charting the Flow of Information in Medical Decision-making Teams'. *Journal of Personality and Social Psychology*, 71: 315–30.

——————Foster-Fishman, P. G., and Keys, C. B. (1994). 'The Discussion of Shared and Unshared Information in Decision Making Groups'. *Journal of Personality and Social Psychology*, 67: 446–64.

Levine, J. M. and Moreland, R. L. (1991). 'Culture and Socialization in Work Groups', in L. B. Resnick, J. M. Levine, and S. D. Teasley (eds.), *Perspectives on Socially Shared Cognition*. Washington, DC: American Psychological Association, 257–79.

Levitt, B. and March, J. G. (1988). 'Organizational Learning'. *Annual Review of Sociology*, 14: 319–40.

Liang, D. W., Moreland, R. L., and Argote, L. (1995). 'Group versus Individual Training and Group Performance: The Mediating Role of Transactive Memory'. *Personality and Social Psychology Bulletin*, 21: 384–93.

Littlepage, G. E., Robinson, W., and Reddington, K. (1997). 'Effects of Task Experience and Group Experience on Group Performance, Member Ability, and Recognition of Expertise'. *Organizational Behavior and Human Decision Processes*, 69: 133–47.

——Schmidt, G. W., Whisler, E. W., and Frost, A. G. (1995). 'An Input–Process–Output Analysis of Influence and Performance in Problem-solving Groups'. *Journal of Personality and Social Psychology*, 69: 877–89.

——and Silbiger, H. (1992). 'Recognition of Expertise in Decision-making Groups: Effects of Group Size and Participation Patterns'. *Small Group Research*, 23: 344–55.

Locke, E. A. and Latham, G. P. (1990). *A Theory of Goal Setting and Task Performance*. Englewood Cliffs, NJ: Prentice Hall.

Lord, R. G. and Maher, K. J. (1993). *Leadership and Information Processing*. London: Routledge.

Luthans, F. and Kreitner, R. (1985). *Organizational Behavior Modification and Beyond*. Glenview, Ill.: Scott, Foresman.

March, J. G. and Olsen, J. P. (1975). 'The Uncertainty of the Past: Organizational Learning under Ambiguity'. *European Journal of Political Research*, 3: 147–71.

Martell, R. F. and Borg, M. R. (1993). 'A Comparison of the Behavioral Rating Accuracy of Groups and Individuals'. *Journal of Applied Psychology*, 78: 43–50.

McGrath, J. E. and O'Connor, K. M. (1996). 'Temporal Issues in Work Groups', in M. A. West (ed.), *Handbook of Group Psychology*. Chichester: Wiley, 25–52.

Mohrman, S. A., Cohen, S. G., and Mohrman, A. M., Jr. (1995). *Designing Team-based Organizations: New Forms of Knowledge Work*. San Francisco: Jossey Bass.

Moreland, R. L. (1999). 'Transactive Memory: Learning Who Knows What in Work Groups and Organizations', in L. Thompson, D. Messick, and J. Levine (eds.), *Shared Cognition in Organizations: The Management of Knowledge*. Hillsdale, NJ: Erlbaum, 3–31.

—— and Levine, J. M. (1992). 'Problem Identification by Groups', in S. Worchel, W. Wood, and J. A. Simpson (eds.), *Group Processes and Productivity*. Newbury Park, Calif.: Sage, 17–47.

Morgeson, F. P. and Hofmann, D. A. (1999). 'The Structure and Function of Collective Constructs: Implications for Multilevel Research and Theory Development'. *Academy of Management Review*, 24: 249–65.

Murray, A. (1989). 'Top Management Group Heterogeneity and Firm Performance'. *Strategic Management Journal*, 10: 125–41.

Noe, R. A. and Ford, J. K. (1992). 'Emerging Issues and New Directions for Training Research'. *Research in Personnel and Human Resources Management*, 10: 345–84.

Nonaka, I. (1994). 'A Dynamic Theory of Organizational Knowledge Creation'. *Organization Science*, 5: 14–37.

Oehman, A., Dimberg, U., and Estevers, F. (1989). 'Preattentive Activation of Aversive Emotions', in T. Archer and L.-G. Nilsson (eds.), *Aversion, Avoidance, and Anxiety: Perspectives on Aversively Motivated Behavior*. Hillsdale, NJ: Erlbaum, 169–93.

Pintrich, P. R. and Schunk, D. H. (1996). *Motivation in Education*. Englewood Cliffs, NJ: Prentice Hall.

Prange, C. (1999). 'Organizational Learning—Desperately Seeking Theory?', in M. Easterby-Smith, J. Burgoyne, and L. Araujo (eds.), *Organizational Learning and the Learning Organization*. Newbury Park, Calif.: Sage, 1–21.

Probst, G. and Büchel, B. (1994). *Organisationales Lernen*. Wiesbaden: Gabler.

Reber, G. (1992). 'Lernen, organisationales', in E. Frese (ed.), *Handwörterbuch der Organisation*. Stuttgart: Poeschel, 1240–55.

Robinson, S. L. and O'Leary-Kelly, A. M. (1998). 'Monkey See, Monkey Do: The Influence of Work Groups on the Antisocial Behavior of Employees'. *Academy of Management Journal*, 41: 658–72.

Rosenstiel, L. von (2000). *Grundlagen der Organisationspsychologie*. Stuttgart: Schäffer-Poeschel.

—— and Neumann, P. (1991). *Einführung in die Markt- und Werbepsychologie* (2nd edn). Darmstadt: Wissenschaftliche Buchgemeinschaft.

Schank, R. C. and Abelson, R. (1977). *Scripts, Plans, Goals, and Understanding: An Inquiry into Human Knowledge Structures*. Hillsdale, NJ: Erlbaum.

Schrader, S. (1990). *Zwischenbetrieblicher Informationstransfer*. Berlin: Duncker and Humblot.

Schunk, D. H. (1989). 'Self-efficacy and Cognitive Skill Learning', in C. Ames and R. Ames (eds.), *Research on Motivation in Education*, 57: 149–74.

—— (1991). 'Self-efficacy and Academic Motivation'. *Educational Psychologist*, 26: 207–31.

Schwartz, B. (1989). *Psychology of Learning and Behavior* (3rd edn). New York: W. W. Norton.

Shrivastava, P. and Schneider, S. (1984). 'Organizational Frames of Reference'. *Human Relations*, 10: 795–809.

Sitkin, S. B. (1992). 'Learning through Failure: The Strategy of Small Losses', in B. M. Staw and L. L. Cummings (eds.), *Research in Organizational Behavior: An Annual Series of Analytical Essays and Critical Reviews* (Vol. 14). Greenwich, Conn.: JAI Press, 231–66.

Slavin, R. E. (1994). *Educational Psychology*. Boston: Allyn and Bacon.

Spencer, L. M. and Spencer, S. M. (1993). *Competence at Work: Models for Superior Performance*. New York: Wiley.

Squire, L. R. (1987). *Memory and Brain*. New York: Oxford University Press.

Stajkovic, A. D. and Luthans, F. (1997). 'A Meta-analysis of the Effects of Organizational Behavior Modification on Task Performance, 1975–95'. *Academy of Management Journal*, 40: 1122–49.

Starbuck, W. H. (1992). 'Learning by Knowledge-intensive Firms'. *Journal of Management Studies*, 29: 713–40.

Stasser, G. (1988). 'Computer Simulation as a Research Tool: The DISCUSS Model of Group Decision Making'. *Journal of Experimental Social Psychology*, 24: 393–422.

——(1992). 'Pooling of Unshared Information During Group Discussion', in S. Worchel, W. Wood, and J. A. Simpson (eds.), *Group Process and Productivity*. Newbury Park, Calif.: Sage, 48–67.

——Taylor, L. A., and Hanna, C. (1989). 'Information Sampling in Structured and Unstructured Discussions of Three- and Six-person Groups'. *Journal of Personality and Social Psychology*, 57: 67–78.

——and Titus, W. (1985). 'Pooling of Unshared Information in Group Decision Making: Biased Information Sampling During Group Discussion'. *Journal of Personality and Social Psychology*, 48: 1467–78.

Steiner, I. D. (1972). *Group Process and Productivity*. New York: Academic Press.

Sternberg, R. J. (1996). 'Costs of Experience', in K. A. Ericsson (ed.), *The Road to Excellence*. Mahwah, NJ: Erlbaum, 347–54.

——(1999). 'What Do We Know about Tacit Knowledge? Making the Tacit Become Explicit', in R. J. Sternberg and J. A. Horvath (eds.), *Tacit Knowledge in Professional Practice: Researcher and Practitioner Perspective*. Mahwah, NJ: Erlbaum, 231–6.

Stevenson, M. K., Busemeyer, J. R., and Naylor, J. C. (1990). 'Judgment and Decision-making Theory', in M. D. Dunnette and J. M. Hough (eds.), *Handbook of Industrial and Organizational Psychology* (Vol. 1) (2nd edn). Palo Alto, Calif.: Consulting Psychologists Press, 283–374.

Strike, K. A. and Posner, G. J. (1985). 'A Conceptual Change View of Learning and Understanding', in L. H. T. West and A. L. Ping (eds.), *Cognitive Structure and Conceptual Change*. Orlando, Fla.: Academic Press, 211–31.

Tenkasi, R. V. and Boland, R. J. (1996). 'Exploring Knowledge Diversity in Knowledge-intensive Firms: A New Role for Information Systems'. *Journal of Organizational Change Management*, 9/1: 79–91.

Tversky, A. and Kahneman, D. (1974). 'Judgment under Uncertainty: Heuristics and Biases'. *Science*, 185: 1124–31.

————(1982). 'Evidential Impact of Base Rates', in D. Kahneman, P. Slovic, and A. Tversky (eds.), *Judgment under Uncertainty: Heuristics and Biases*. Cambridge: Cambridge University Press, 153–60.

Van Maanen, J. and Barley, S. R. (1984). 'Occupational Communities: Culture and Control in Organizations', in B. M. Staw and L. L. Cummings (eds.), *Research in Organizational Behavior: An Annual Series of Analytical Essays and Critical Reviews* (Vol. 6). Greenwich, Conn.: JAI Press, 287–366.

Walsh, J. P. and Ungson, G. R. (1991). 'Organizational Memory'. *Academy of Management Review*, 16: 57–91.

Wegner, D. M. (1987). 'Transactive Memory: A Contemporary Analysis of the Group Mind', in B. Mullen and G. R. Goethals (eds.), *Theories of Group Behavior*. New York: Springer, 185–208.

Weiner, B. (1985). ' "Spontaneous" Causal Thinking'. *Psychological Bulletin*, 97: 74–84.

Weiss, H. M. (1990). 'Learning Theory and Industrial and Organizational Psychology', in M. D. Dunnette and L. M. Hough (eds.), *Handbook of Industrial and Organizational Psychology* (Vol. 1) (2nd edn). Palo Alto, Calif.: Consulting Psychologists Press, 171–221.

Wiersema, M. F. and Bantel, K. A. (1992). 'Top Management Team Demography and Corporate Strategic Change'. *Academy of Management Journal*, 35: 91–121.

2 The Sociological Foundations of Organizational Learning

Silvia Gherardi and Davide Nicolini

The purpose of this chapter is to illustrate the specific contribution that general sociology and the sociology of organizations can make to the study of organizational learning. The first part provides an overview of the possible ontological and epistemological choices available to scholars who undertake one of the various possible readings of organizational learning from a sociological standpoint. In the second part of the chapter, our epistemological choice is to see organizational learning as a root metaphor. It is on that basis that we attempt to determine what contribution a social constructionist approach has made to the study of organizational learning through the concepts of participation and reflexivity.

The concept of participation highlights the fact that learning does not take place solely or principally in the minds of individuals but rather stems from the participation of individuals in social activities. Working and organizing are social practices engaged in through a set of activities situated in specific contexts of interaction. Organizational learning is learning-in-organizing, because working, learning, and organizing are not distinct activities within a practice. The concept of participation, therefore, gives access to the study of organizational learning that takes place in action and through action.

The concept of reflexivity is tied closely to participation in that reflexivity occurs when the flow of experience is interrupted and the subject reflects on knowledge. Reflexivity refers to ways of seeing that act back on and reflect existing ways of seeing; reflexivity gives rise to the institutionalization of knowledge. The principal feature of reflexivity is that reflection produces the setting that contains its object as well as its expected and unexpected outcomes. In other words, reflexivity ensures that the social production of that area of studies known as 'organizational learning' will produce the very phenomenon that it studies.

Five Sociological Traditions

Just as is it difficult to mark the boundaries around any discipline in any historical period —the watchword being 'blurring disciplinary boundaries' (Linstead 1994: 3)—it is equally difficult to describe differentiation within them. Numerous authors have attempted the task, and we certainly have no intention of proposing a new classification. Aware of the fictitious and arbitrary nature of any endeavor to recount the history of a discipline, we refer instead to the scheme proposed by Collins (1994) and supplemented by other contributions in order to discuss the fact that the insights into organizational learning yielded by sociology vary greatly depending on the sociological approach chosen. Collins identified four sociological traditions: the tradition of conflict,

This chapter is the result of an entirely collaborative effort by the two authors: if, however, for academic reasons individual responsibility must be assigned, Silvia Gherardi wrote the second, third, and fourth sections; Davide Nicolini wrote the first section, the introduction, and the conclusions. The authors thank Adrian Belton for editing an earlier version of the text.

which he traced back to Marx, Engels, and Weber; the rational-utilitarian tradition begun by Homans, Blau, Cook, and Simon; the Durkheimian tradition, in which functionalism takes the name of its outstanding theoretician; and the microinteractionist tradition of such authors as Peirce, Mead, Husserl, Schutz, and Garfinkel.

We flank these four traditions with an approach that, given its youth, cannot properly be called a tradition but that has nevertheless been a stimulating reflection on knowledge: postmodernism.

The Tradition of Conflict

This tradition represents a line of thought that directs attention to the structure of dominant and subordinate interest groups, to social conflict, and to power systems. Its principal thesis is that society is based on conflict and that, in the absence of open conflict, a process of domination prevails. In this tradition the social order is perceived as the outcome of a struggle between groups and individuals seeking to ensure that their own interests predominate over those of others. Also, organizations are not innocuous instruments in the hands of their creators, and political interpretation of organizational life can be found in Michels (1911), Selznick (1949), Gouldner (1954), Dalton (1959), Etzioni (1961), and Crozier (1963). For Marxism and the Frankfurt school, the economy is what determines politics, law, and human culture; the materialistic dynamic is what produces the inevitable contradictions and transformations identified by Hegel (1807). Conflict is expressed and masked by ideology. Every social class tends to view the world in a particular way, and its ideas mirror its economic interests and the social circumstances that define those interests. As ideology, ideas are exalted by people and are used to cloak interests in respectable guise.

Weber's (1922/78) thought has exerted its influence on the sociology of organization through the model of bureaucracy and its functionalist misinterpretation (Clegg 1995). But the sociological tradition of conflict has continued to exacerbate the contradiction between substantial rationality (the capacity of humans to understand that certain means lead to certain ends) and formal rationality (obedience to norms and written rules), a type of behavior first highlighted by Mannheim (1935), then developed by critical theory, and today theorized by Beck (1992) in the concept 'risk society', a society that escapes human control because formal rationality has supplanted substantial rationality.

The theme of control is mirrored by the theme of power, both within organizations and among them. Not only has modernization produced a society of organizations (Perrow 1991; Presthus 1978), but forms of control have gradually changed from external control (direct or mediated by technology) to normative control, which is internalized and based on the control of decisional and cultural assumptions. In postindustrial societies, power-based social divisions have become more ramified, and, with the increasing use of knowledge for productive purposes, the linkage between knowledge and power has given rise to social conflicts that are more articulated and complex than the property-based class conflicts that characterized the onset of industrialization (Clegg 1990; Rothman and Friedman, Ch. 26 in this volume).

The use of knowledge on a vast scale has produced a new class of technicoscientific experts, and neologisms such as 'knowledge-firm' (Starbuck 1992) and 'knowledge-workers' (Zuboff 1988) have appeared in scientific as well as everyday language. The term 'organizational learning' also belongs to this rhetoric, whose system of persuasion is grounded in knowledge (Alvesson 1993).

Drawing on both the interpretative tools of sociology and the tradition of conflict, one can interpret the theme of organizational learning in three ways.

1. *Organizational learning as the ideology of particular power groups.* The ideas subsumed under the heading 'organizational learning' are extolled. As a consequence, the label 'learn-

ing organization' has been coined to celebrate an organizational identity and draw a social distinction between those organizations conforming to a bureaucratic model and those in which a 'new' managerial philosophy is propounded (Easterby-Smith, Snell, and Gherardi 1998). This philosophy may become first a methodology, then a technique, as the prescriptiveness of its contents increases, and as its capacity to discipline members of an organization grows (Gherardi 1999). Management is one of the social actors interested in developing a managerial theory of organizational learning that will give it legitimacy, but it is not the only power group that can use this ideology to mask its interests. Traditional occupational groups of experts and new occupational groups that may emerge as experts on organizational learning will also develop various versions of the ideology in order to legitimate covert power struggles against other communities of experts that possess their own knowledge resources and compete against them (Snell and Chack 1998).

2. *Organizational learning as a policy of mobilizing power.* In both organizations and society, knowledge is a resource for social stratification insofar as it gives rise to positions of relative power that, by virtue of their intrinsic instability, must be defended and possibly reinforced. To create knowledge is to produce a value resource that can be exchanged. Transmitting knowledge involves transferring a value; utilizing knowledge entails exploiting a resource that is offered for exchange on a political (and economic) market. Historically, the professions arose out of the monopolization and institutionalization of sources that had the legitimacy to produce and transmit knowledge. Within organizations, that which individuals or groups learn gives them power over those who 'do not know' or who 'know less efficiently', and it is a source of potential conflict (Coopey 1995). The circulation of knowledge within organizations, its exploitation for productive purposes, and its codification as useful, good, correct, or prescribed take place within the micropolitics of quotidian power relationships (Gherardi, Nicolini, and Odella 1998b). In other

words, power and conflict render the circulation of knowledge nontransparent and conceal the social conditions of its production.

3. *Organizational learning as an attempt to manage the tension between substantial and formal rationality.* Learning conditioned by substantial rationality is learning acquired through experience, with logical connections being established between the means, the ends, and the consequences of action, and behavior being modified on the basis of these inferences. Put differently, substantial rationality is the learning that people acquire in their work, but this learning cannot automatically be transferred to the rules and regulations that govern organizational behavior. Consequently, obedience to formal rationality gives rise to unintended effects that fail to take account of learning from experience. The literature on how and why organizations do not learn (Hedberg 1981) highlights this loss of meaning caused by the social mechanisms that reproduce instrumental rationality. Rationalization is the enemy of rationality, *hence* of organizational learning, a term that can be regarded as an oxymoron (Merkens, Geppert, and Antal, Ch. 10 in this volume; Weick and Westley 1996). In fact, learning and organizing can be defined as antithetical processes. The former focuses on a disorganization and increase of variety; the latter, on a forgetting and reduction of variety.

The Rational–Utilitarian Tradition

Utilitarianism has distant origins in British social philosophy, and later became a discipline in the field of economics. Collins (1994: 85) argued that the utilitarian tradition is not sociological in a strict sense, though it has numerous points of contact with sociology. In the 1950s a broader intellectual movement known as 'rational choice (or action) theory' arose, taking the name of 'public choice' theory in political science and 'exchange theory' in sociology.

Rational utilitarianism in sociology has a great deal in common with conflict theory in the sense that society, from both points of view, is considered to be a set of groups and individuals who pursue interests and calculate advantages. Unlike conflict theory, however, rational utilitarianism is not focused on political conflict, social stratification, or inequality. Instead, rational utilitarians seek to explain society in terms of people's rational motivations and the manner in which they rationally perform exchanges so that everything functions in the best possible way.

In sociology, utilitarians have provoked a controversy known as the micro/macro problem (Collins 1994). They conceive of society as being held together by the actions of individuals at the microlevel, and they reject the idea of society as a macrostructure existing above and beyond individuals. For example, they dispute the notion that culture is determined by the actions of people. Utilitarians instead seek to understand what motivates individuals to act beyond their own self-interest. Accounting for selfless behavior by individuals is one of the paradoxes that has enriched rational utilitarianism, and it well illustrates the method used in this tradition of thought: On the assumption that individuals are rational and intent on maximizing their interests, utilitarians analyze the limits of rationality, as in the phenomenon of free riding (Olson 1965), or the prisoner's dilemma (Luce and Raiffa 1957).

A pioneer of utilitarianism in sociology was George Homans (1950, 1961). Disagreeing with Parsons's (1951) functionalism, Homans claimed that not only is the social system a myth, but so, too, are the standards according to which individuals act (the role system), which are inculcated in them by the socialization process. Homans argued that the more individuals interact as equals and on the basis of reciprocity, the more they come to accept, assimilate, and conform to a common standard. As individuals interact, cohesive groups form and develop a shared culture and a normative system, both at the workplace and in the neighborhood. According to Homans, the reason for this emergence of a shared culture and a normative system is the reward intrinsic to the interaction, social approval, for the group will remain united as long as its members exchange these rewards. Other authors, such as Blau (1964), have studied the patterns of exchange and the exchange networks in which individuals negotiate approval among themselves (Cook *et al.* 1983).

The tradition in which Homans, Blau, and Cook *et al.* stand includes the premise that power derives from the unequal exchange of resources and that each of the parties to an exchange adjusts its manner of negotiating according to the resources at its disposal. This conception of exchange has been highly influential in the sociology of organizations, where the rational-choice paradigm is recognized as one of the classical theories expounding on the paradoxes of rationality in organizational decision theory (March 1988; Simon 1957).

This strand of studies has provided one of the most coherent accounts of organizational learning as adaptation (Levitt and March 1988). The recognition of a performance gap stimulates actors within an organization to search for knowledge about alternative courses of action that might reduce the gap between current and desired performance. Searches may be based on existing knowledge and existing views of the world or on the creation of new knowledge through formal investigations, environmental scanning, individual experiential learning, or armchair theorizing.

The contributions of the rational–utilitarian tradition to organizational learning can be summarized in three conceptualizations.

1. *Organizational learning serves as a problem-driven search* when the organization's performance does not meet aspiration levels. This kind of organizational learning is the conscious learning that takes place within an adaptive learning system in which a great deal of behavior takes place through standard operating procedures. The study by Cyert and March (1963) was the landmark of this neorationalist approach, although the most strictly sociological contribution was made by research into incomplete learning cycles (March and Olsen 1976; see also Berthoin Antal, Lenhardt, and Rosenbrock, Ch. 39 in this volume). Cyert and March (1963) pointed out where the paradoxes

of rationality arise, and they highlighted the impact of ambiguity on interpretation processes as well as the emotional and cultural factors that mould adaptation to experience (Kieser, Beck, and Tainio, Ch. 27; Pawlowsky, Forslin, and Reinhardt, Ch. 35 in this volume).

2. *Organizational learning serves as the activation of an exchange network* that takes the form of a market for knowledge and skills. Knowledge is input into the production process, and firms acquire it externally in the form of people in possession of it, patents, and the technologies that embody and produce it. The more that knowledge is explicit, codified, and universal, the more it acquires the transferable nature of a commodity. Conversely, the more that knowledge is implicit, tacit, and situated, the more it becomes an asset of the people and groups that possess it and the more it is embodied in skills and specific practices. The 'invisible assets' of an organization (specific skills and tacit expertise) are based on idiosyncratic forms of knowledge (Baumard 1996; Nonaka and Takeuchi 1995; Spender 1996a). Workplace control has historically changed hands in the presence of a different market: Knowledge work-groups are characterized by high levels of autonomy and self-management, trust relations with customers, and uncertain and ambiguous tasks (Butera, Donati, and Cesaria 1998). Control becomes concentrated in the product rather than in the process of work.

3. *Organizational learning as an ecology of learning* located within distributed, multiactor routines rather than within individual minds (Arujo 1998). Organizations learn by taking inferences from past experience and encoding them into the routines, rules, procedures, conventions, strategies, and technologies that guide behavior (Levitt and March 1988). This approach revives Bateson's (1972) work on the logical levels of learning, but it is also concerned with the specific rationality of corporate actors and the societal consequences of the power that those actors acquire by monopolizing knowledge, institutionalizing forms of systemic myopia, or imitating maladaptive learning (Levinthal and March 1993). Nelson

(1991) and Tsoukas (1992) viewed firms as hierarchies of routines and argued that most of the knowledge possessed by firms is tacit and resides not in the heads of individuals but in teams of individuals with shared experiences and with only a partial view of what constitutes a particular routine.

The Durkheimian Tradition

Durkheim's work remains the central tradition of sociological thought, and both sociology and social anthropology have developed within it. Durkheim's followers used the term 'ethnology' for empirical descriptions of tribal societies and the term 'sociology' to denote the theoretical analysis of society. They believed that tribal societies were simpler than modern society and that tribal societies most clearly evinced the 'elementary forms' of social life, by which was meant, as Collins (1994) put it, the sentiments, emotions, morality, the sacred, and the religious that together constitute the essence of every society as expressed in its symbolism.

Although Durkheim (1912) forcefully argued for the influence of 'nonrational' elements in the shaping of society, he is important to the history of sociology as the founder of sociological method and of sociology as the science of the social order. Paradigmatic of Durkheim's work is his study of suicide (1897), in which the circumstances in which a phenomenon occurs were compared with circumstances in which it does not. Accordingly, suicide—or, as in this handbook, learning—can be treated as a variable. The researcher examines the rates of incidence of the variable 'suicide' (or learning) as well as its variations in the presence of certain factors (e.g. age, religion, civil status, and climate), and sets it in relation to the social structure. On the basis of empirical indicators, therefore, alternative explanations can be systematically tested and theoretical generalizations or 'laws of the social' formulated. In fact most structuralist studies of organizational learning follow the Durkheimian model, with organizations conceived of as social contexts for learning.

In the Durkheimian tradition society is conceived of as operating 'from outside', so to speak. Society works externally, on narrow social groups and society as a whole, exerting pressure, constraining social action, and shaping sentiments and collective ideas. As regards suicide, for example, members of groups with high social density are less likely to kill themselves. Social density is not physical density; it is, rather, moral density, that is, the extent to which organic solidarity is present in a community with a 'shared life', a life in which individuals take part in rituals and ceremonies that focus the emotions of the individual onto the group. Individuals belong to a broad society that constrains and moulds them. But they can also withdraw and meet together to practice those rituals of everyday life that produce social density. Society has a nonrational grounding in ritual, and utilitarian considerations alone cannot hold it together. The Durkheimian tradition therefore incorporates two currents, one focused on the macroaspects of society, the other on the microaspects. The former current developed through an emphasis on the theory of the social division of labor and scientific method, resulting in the functionalism of Merton (1957) and Parsons (1951). The second current concentrating on the microaspects of society has maintained its links with social anthropology and the analysis of ritual through the work of Durkheim's nephew, Mauss (1968), and then through the work of Goffman (1967, 1971) and Bernstein (1971–1975). Analogously, organizational learning can be either analyzed as a dependent variable, so that one looks for the (macrostructural) conditions that favor or impede it, or conceptualized as a socialization process to specific cultural codes.

In brief, in the first current of the Durkheimian tradition *organizational learning is defined as a dependent variable*. Other variables (strategy, structure, or culture) define the conditions that facilitate or hinder organizational learning (Duncan and Weiss 1979; Tomassini 1993; Warglien 1990). Learning is conceived of as one of the functions of the organizational system, which engenders change on some occasions and conservation on others. The theory of cybernetics is drawn upon both in its simple feedback version, in which a change of state occurs when environmental conditions alter, and in its double-loop version (Argyris and Schön 1974, 1978; Fiol and Lyles 1985), in which parameters change by virtue of self-organization or learning. At bottom, the functions attributed to organizational learning explain its dynamics and its position in the organization. The manifest function of organizational learning is to achieve the results that individuals consciously strive for, including adjustment to changed operational or informational circumstances and the ability to develop fresh approaches to situations, to experiment, or to innovate (Starbuck 1983). The latent function of organizational learning is generated by the social system itself, one example being the protection of the advantages gained through the operation of mechanisms requiring modification. Organizational learning can be both explorative and exploitative (March 1996).

The second current, represented by such scholars as Bernstein (1971–1975), Douglas (1970), and Collins (1979), has furnished insights that formulate a structural theory of occupational or professional cultures and subcultures. Durkheim's legacy to the analysis of organizational cultures is immense, as Ouchi and Wilkins (1985) stressed when they examined the contribution made by sociology to the analysis of organizational cultures.

This sociological tradition, therefore, conceptualizes organizational learning as socialization to specific cultural codes. Socialization, in fact, sensitizes subjects to the different orders of society because it acts selectively on their life-chances, creating a sense of a given social order's inevitability and restricting the amount of change that is permitted. The contexts of socialization identified by Bernstein (1971–1975) can be transferred from child to adult socialization and from an extended social context to a restricted one, such as an organization. Accordingly, in different contexts of socialization, specific contents of organizational learning are activated when individuals join specific occupational communities within a particular organization. These contexts of socialization are—

- the regulatory context formed by the authority relationships that sensitize individuals to the rules of the moral order and their underlying structures. The social reproduction of the hierarchy and the moral order that regulates relationships among occupational groups with differing endowments of knowledge and power are actuated in this context.
- the educational context, in which individuals are instructed on the objective nature of objects and people, and in which they learn various skills. This context pertains to the reproduction of expertise.
- the imaginative or innovative context, in which individuals are encouraged to experience the world on its own terms. This context is internal to occupational communities in which self-images and individual and collective identities are produced through experimentation and negotiation.
- the interpersonal context, in which people learn to know their own affective states and those of others. This context pertains to socialization in the appropriate social relationships that grant membership in a community. In this case, the organization is a social structure external to the contexts of socialization, which it structures into one form rather than another by promoting, or impeding learning processes.

The Microinteractionist Tradition

The microinteractionist tradition owes a twofold debt to philosophy: First, to Peirce's pragmatism (1931–1935), and second, to Schutz's phenomenology. Peirce coined the term 'semiotics' (the science of signs) and developed the theory that individuals cannot perceive things or think about the world without the mediation of signs. Consequently, meaning always exists in a three-way relationship between the sign, the object, and the internal referent (the thought). Peirce thus introduced a social element into theories on the mind of the individual because, as he explained, thought is always realized in a community, and what the community considers to be 'true' and 'objective' is only what is based on habitus (the historical product of previous individual and collective practices). People, Peirce maintained, are nothing but the sum of their thoughts, the historical accumulation of their social experiences.

The social theory of the mind was refined by Cooley (1964), who maintained that thought consists of an imaginary conversation with the self and that society is the mind of all individuals. Thus, society is a relationship among ideas, and the ways in which individuals imagine each other are the 'concrete facts' examined by sociology. Much more influential in the sociology of thought than Cooley, however, was Mead (1934), who posited that society is grounded on reflectivity, or the ability of the self to reflect upon itself. The self is a point of view. Every individual possesses a plurality of selves, and thought is a form of conversation conducted by individuals with themselves.

Mead's social theory of the mind exerted a profound influence on Blumer (1969) and the symbolic interactionist approach, which had also assimilated insights from Dewey (1922) and his critique of the doctrine of 'rational man'. Alfred Schutz's social phenomenology influenced Garfinkel (1967), Goffman (1967), and the ethnomethodological movement. Both in symbolic interactionism and ethnomethodology society is conceived of not as a structure but as a process. People do not assume ready-made roles but rather create and re-create them according to the given situation. Social institutions exist only insofar as individuals come into contact with each other and jointly construct actions.

Social action comes about because individuals project various social 'me's' onto future situations; they then assume the role of the Other, predict the consequences, and model their actions accordingly. This process of continuous negotiation yields 'definitions of the situation' and the social construction of reality (Berger and Luckman 1966).

The concept of 'definition of the situation' was developed by Thomas and celebrated in his aphorism, 'If one defines a situation as real, then it is real in its consequences' (Thomas 1928: 512). Reality is fluid and susceptible to rapid changes, and if the way in which individuals define a certain situation changes, then so, too, does the type of behavior that it induces. Social life has a peculiar tendency to become whatever people think it is.

A microinteractionist approach is the cradle of the concept of *organizational learning as the transmission of knowledge within occupational communities*. The theory starts from the hypothesis that occupations (or professions) are forms of interaction negotiated by subjects engaged in work practices. Doctors, janitors, lawyers, social workers, and so on produce not only 'work' but also social relations, identities, and self-images. As they work, members of an occupational community are intent on hiding the 'dirty' aspects of their work and the 'dodges' known only to initiates. They do so in order to manipulate their public image and to increase their bargaining power *vis-à-vis* members of other occupational communities or the public in general. Studies of the noncanonical practices in professions (or occupations) shed a great deal of light on the purportedly 'transparent' transmission of knowledge (Boland and Tenkasi 1995; Brown and Duguid 1991; Suchman 1987). This line of inquiry, in fact, is indebted to the ethnomethodological approach (see Czarniawska, Ch. 5 in this volume). The term 'ethnomethodology' (Flynn 1991) indicates that this approach is an examination of social reality through observation (ethnography) and that researchers who use it seek to uncover the methods that individuals employ in order to give meaning to experience (methodology). Learning therefore has to do with participating, with becoming a member of a community, because social relations are important for the transmission of knowledge, the mastering of a situated curriculum (Gherardi, Nicolini, and Odella 1998*a*), and the relational development of identity (Blackler 1995; Wenger 1998). Consequently, learning is always situated in the sphere of social interaction.

The social dimension of learning suggests the existence of a 'group mind' that takes the form of cognitive interdependence centered on memory processes. People working together give life to a single transactive memory system, complete with differentiated responsibility for remembering their experiences. The behaviors of people in organizations, like to the neuron connections in the brain, may be spontaneously and tacitly activated and then interconnect so that they coordinate an intelligent action. Social learning is thus a network of collective behaviors based on distributed knowledge (Tsoukas 1996).

The microinteractionist account of learning as social and cultural process has also developed through studies on communities of practice (Brown and Duguid 1991; Lave and Wenger 1991; Orr 1993; Stopford, Ch. 11 in this volume; Stucky 1995; Zucchermaglio 1995). Lave and Wenger (1991) are taken to be the representatives of the so-called situated learning theory. They define a community of practice as 'a set of relations among persons, activity, and world, over time and in relation with other tangential and overlapping communities of practice. A community of practice is an intrinsic condition for the existence of knowledge, not least because it provides the interpretative support necessary for making sense of its heritage' (p. 98). Working, learning, and innovating are not distinct activities; they are, rather, closely bound up with each other in a local practice and in the culture of that practice.

A similar concept, that of the occupational community, has been developed in studies of organizational cultures (Barley 1991; Gherardi 1990; Kunda 1986; Strati 1986; van Maanen and Barley 1984). It focuses on the growth of local cultures, the socialization of their members, and the 'organization' that results from negotiation within communities and between the communities external and internal to a given organization. Both concepts share the Weberian idea of the dynamic between *Gemeinschaft* and *Gesellschaft*, which is inherent in the concept of community, but they differ in the emphasis that they place on either practice or occupation.

The distinctive features of the microinteractionist tradition are its constructionist epistemology (the idea that society is constituted in and by the interpretative practices of its members) and its stress on the role of language as the medium of such social construction. Speech acts are units of language and action; they are part of practice. They are not descriptions but, rather, types of action like any other action in a given practice. Language is not only the expression of social relations; it is also the medium for their creation (Czarniawska-Joerges 1991). The previous point implicitly highlights the impact of the 'linguistic turn' (Alvesson and Deetz 1996: 205) in organization studies. The turning point came with the notion that language does not describe or represent reality (language is not tied to meaning or perception); rather, it constructs the 'objects' and 'subjects' of reality.

The contribution of this sociological tradition is the study of *organizational learning as a label that both produces a socially constructed reality and is produced by that reality*. The label 'organizational learning' gives identity to a scientific community whose social practices are grounded in such pursuits as writing and talking about organizational learning, organizing conferences, and founding new journals (Nicolini and Meznar 1995; Spender 1996b). Indeed, a wholly sociological phenomenon is the social process by which a term, organizational learning, is coined for managerial practices; a new subjectivity is socially created; firms that define themselves as 'learning organizations' appear; and social researchers proliferate and, equipped with survey tools, set off in quest of 'learning organizations', determined to measure the properties of this new 'object' in the physical world (Gherardi 1999). Words, labels, metaphors, and platitudes produce the reality that people experience as 'out there'.

The characteristic features of constructionism are contingency, negotiation, breakdown, discontinuity, heterogeneity, and fragmentation. Accordingly, in a social constructionist approach organizational learning is seen as situated; knowledge is seen to stem from negotiations, breakdowns, and discontinuities; and knowing is seen as heterogeneous and frag-

mented. The process of learning can therefore be better understood when it is located in the domains of knowledge, language, and interpretation rather than in action and its outcomes. These features are at odds with the traditional psychological models of learning (based on stimulus–response theory), which are acritically transferred to the study of organizational learning (Maier, Prange, and Rosenstiel, Ch. 1 in this volume; Weick 1991). Within the microinteractionist tradition an antithesis to modernist thought has thus begun to appear. In the next section we examine the insights that such postmodernist thought can offer.

The Postmodern Tradition?

It is only with a certain amount of irony that one can talk of a postmodern tradition in sociology, given that systematic criticism of modernist thought dates back only to the late 1980s. Although postmodernism originated in aesthetics and philosophy (Lyotard 1984; Vattimo 1985), sociologists soon declared themselves for or against this silent cultural revolution (Clegg 1990; Giddens 1990). Preeminent in the postmodern approach to organizations is the influence of French poststructuralism, deconstructionism (Derrida 1971), and Foucault's theory of discourses (1980) as contingent systems of thought that inform both linguistic and material practices through specific technologies of power producing specific forms of subjectivity.

The central theme of the debate on the postmodern, or on postmodernisms, is the critique of that modernism which is characterized by grand narratives, the concepts of totality and development, and essentialism. Although postmodernism is generally defined by default in the literature, the topics on the postmodern agenda can be summarized as

the constructed nature of people and reality, emphasizing language as a system of distinctions which are central to the construction process, arguing against grand narratives and large-scale theoretical systems, such as Marxism, or functionalism, emphasizing the power–knowledge connection and the role of claims of expertise in systems of domination, emphasizing the fluid and hyperreal nature of the contemporary world and the role of mass-media and information technologies, and stressing narrative/fiction/rhetoric as central to the research process. (Alvesson and Deetz 1996: 192)

The role of research in postmodern thought is not that of 'discovering the truth' but of challenging the conventional wisdom, routines, static meanings, and axioms of 'normal' science, thereby exposing knowledge to non-dogmatic forms of thought (Astley 1985; Gergen 1992).

In discussing how the topic of organizational learning is addressed in the postmodern tradition, we consider here those issues on the postmodern agenda that are relevant to learning: the relationship between knowledge and power, the central importance of language and discourse, and fragmented identity.

The relationship between knowledge and power is crucial, both because it challenges the existence of any universalistic foundation to knowledge and because learning is intimately bound up with the production of knowledge. Every attempt to label something as 'knowledge' is made by a specific social community belonging to a network of power relations, and not by a world consisting purely of ideas. Hence, no knowledge is universal or supreme; instead, all knowledge is produced within social, historical, and linguistic relations grounded in specific forms of conflict and the division of labor. Power is implicit in the language that draws distinctions, hierarchizes terms, permits modes of reasoning and discursive practices that, in turn, organize the social institutions and produce one type of subject rather than another. Therefore, in the sense of the 'narrative turn' (Bruner 1990: 1), stories told and retold in organizations become important because memory is retained not so much in propositions as in stories. Stories are vehicles of organizational memory, and the development of stories constitutes organizational learning (Sims 1999).

The obvious implication for the study of organizational learning is that the concept and its adoption should be situated within the network of knowledge/power relations that produces it. Take, for example, managerial knowledge. It shapes the identity of a group of people; creates a bond of solidarity, shared interests, and a profession; establishes criteria for selection, remuneration, membership, and exclusion; and allocates power and resources with which to discipline the behavior of members and nonmembers. Townley (1993) discussed Foucault's (1977) concept of discipline, applying it to human resource management in order to show that this form of expert knowledge is used to exert control over another social group.

As Foucault (1977) argued, a discipline can be conceived of as a specific technology of power: 'Disciplinary power is exercised through its invisibility; at the same time it imposes on those it subjects a compulsory visibility. In discipline, it is the subjects who have to be seen. It is the fact of being constantly seen that maintains the disciplined individual in his subjection' (p. 187). Foucault (1988) defined four major technologies of self-understanding that enter into the power game of truth:

1) technologies of production, which permit us to produce, transform, or manipulate things; 2) technologies of sign systems, which permit us to use signs, meanings symbols, or signification; 3) technologies of power, which determine the conduct of individuals and submit them to certain ends or domination, an objectivizing of the subject; and 4) technologies of the self, which permit individuals to effect by their own means or with the help of others a certain number of operations on their own bodies and souls, thoughts, conduct, and the way of being, as to transform themselves in order to attain a certain state of happiness, purity, wisdom, perfection, or immortality. (p. 18)

A Foucauldian reading of the managerial use of the concept of organizational learning is therefore the interpretation of the use of this concept as a technology of power used to discipline organizational members.

Although postmodern analysis in organization studies is only in its beginnings, it has provided significant insights, as in accounting, where terms are meaningless if isolated from the specific accounting practices that sustain them (Hopwood 1987; Munro and Mouritsen

1996; Power and Laughlin 1992). Other interesting proposals relate to knowledge-firms and the production of specific technologies of power that are used to control knowledge-workers (Deetz 1996). Although there is no direct linkage between those who produce the social object 'knowledge-firm' by studying it and those who investigate organizational learning and the 'learning organization', the two communities of scholars closely resemble each other in the social effects of their practices, effects that deconstructionism can reveal.

In the postmodern approach the task of the researcher is to deconstruct (Cooper 1989; Linstead 1993) the so-called objects that are taken to be objective and self-evident in organizational life. Organizational discourses do not use language as the mirror of reality or of mental states. Instead, language is figurative, metaphorical, and fraught with contradictions, opacities, and incoherencies (Cooper and Burrell 1988). It is not universal but local; it is precarious and fragmented (Linstead and Grafton-Small 1990). Consequently, postmodernism takes social constructionism one step further: Language constitutes identity, that is, the subject's position within a discursive practice. Rather than being focused on persons with a unitary identity (the locus of will and self-determination), postmodernism is a consideration of the narratives of identity. Identity as a human property and the foundation of subjectivity is one of the great narratives of modernism. Its critique by postmodernism has generated the concept of 'identities' constructed by means of unstable and multiple discourses (Czarniawska-Joerges 1995).

Whereas modernism views knowledge as a collection of real entities located in people's minds, with learning as the process of internalizing them and context as the container of decontextualized knowledge, postmodernism asserts that the boundary between culture and the world has dissolved. The problem of decontextual and contextual knowledge is bound up with the arguments between modernism and postmodernism and with traditional cognitive learning theory on the one hand and emergent situated learning theory on the other (Fox 1997). Decontextualized knowledge is valued because it is taken to represent the hidden unity of the world. In cognitive theory the context is conceived of as the container of decontextualized knowledge, and the interpretation process is ultimately impersonal, detached, and ahistorical. But if it is assumed that science, too, is a cultural phenomenon and that interpretation itself is a textually mediated process, then one has to agree with Fox (1997), who stated that 'modernism, like science, hides or represses the socially skilled craft work which goes into producing the "real" with textual materials and accounts' (p. 741).

Postmodernism is consistent with situated learning theory's valorization of emergent social contexts. Theory therefore becomes a contextualized practice in which communities of practitioners work to construct a 'scientific theory' or a body of knowledge out of textual materials.

Within the postmodern tradition one may say that *organizational learning is viewed as a discursive practice*. Every discourse on organizational learning unfolds within a network of knowledge/power relations that shapes the subjectivity of those who participate as speakers and those who are excluded and that sustains concrete practices based on specific technologies of power (Boje 1994). A subject position incorporates both a conceptual repertoire and a location for persons within the structure of the rights pertaining to those who use this repertoire. A position is created in and through conversations as speakers and listeners construct themselves as persons: It creates a location in which social relations and actions are mediated by symbolic forms and modes of being. Through practices of mutual accountability, speaking subjects not only make the world more intelligible but also choose a discursive position for themselves and for others.

Because organizational learning is thus located within the discursive practices of a scientific community, the researcher's concern is to examine how this social object is formed and to render this object of knowledge unstable, incomplete, and always open to fresh interpretations.

The Metaphorical Nature of the Concept 'Organizational Learning'

Accepting a postmodern stance, we find that the sociological contribution to the field of organizational learning is socially constructed by eleven discursive positionings (or in Reed's [1996: 34] terminology, analytical narratives) that stem from five sociological traditions. Researchers in this field can choose different ontological and epistemological positions and thereby give different accounts of their object of knowledge. Each account presupposes a narrative capacity, an ability to narrate their experience and that of others when making sense of the world. Therefore, we resume our analysis of the sociological contribution to the study of organizational learning by examining several narratives (see Table 2.1) that stem from as many theoretical discourses and merge into one conversation.

The conversation metaphor has been used (Clegg and Hardy 1996b) to map the debate in organization theory as 'nothing less, nothing more, nothing other than its practices of representation' (p. 676). In conversations between researcher and researched, both parties may learn, and the aim of such conversations is to open up multiple narratives with multiple meanings, resist conventional narratives, and avoid marginalizing narratives that do not conform to accepted wisdom. These conversations are socially organized (in professions, academic disciplines, and specialized journals), and they organize a social process. No conversation is more valid than any other, but all conversations offer opportunities for understanding and action within different discursive practices, whether theoretical, practical, professional, or daily.

One discursive practice predominant in the conversation about organization theory is the narrative of organizational learning as learning by an organization that, according to a more or less cybernetic model, produces change, real or potential, after a shift in the relationship between thought, organizational action, and environmental response (Tsang 1997). From

Table 2.1. Narratives of organizational learning according to five sociological traditions

Sociological traditions	Narratives of organizational learning
The tradition of conflict	• Organizational learning as the ideology of particular power groups • Organizational learning as a policy of mobilizing resources of power and conflict • Organizational learning as an attempt to manage the tension between substantial and formal rationality
The rational–utilitarian tradition	• Organizational learning as a problem-driven search • Organizational learning as the activation of an exchange network • Organizational learning as an ecology of learning
The Durkheimian tradition	• Organizational learning as a dependent variable • Organizational learning as socialization to specific cultural codes
The microinteractionist tradition	• Organizational learning as the transmission of knowledge within occupational communities • Organizational learning as a label producing and produced by a socially constructed reality
The postmodern 'tradition'	• Organizational learning as a discursive practice

functionalism, which, according to Burrell and Morgan (1979), is the dominant paradigm in the sociology of the organization, organization scholars have inherited a realistic postulate (and a positivistic methodology) that concerns both learning and the organization: Learning is a 'real' event that takes place in those 'real' places that are called organizations (and one can measure learning). Both organizations and learning are considered to be empirical objects, and the organization came to be anthropomorphized as the subject of learning, or, in order to avoid this dilemma, came to be the container of individual and collective learning.

By contrast, we argue that this 'reality' results from discursive practices based on the metaphorical use of a term, organizational learning, which yields a particular account of organizations. Organizational learning is a metaphor that encompasses two concepts, learning and organization, and enables the exploration of an organization as though it were a subject that learns, processes information, reflects on experiences, and possesses a stock of knowledge, skills, and expertise. This metaphor opens the way for critical examination of the relationship between organization and knowledge, between organization and the social and cognitive processing of knowledge, and between organizational action and organizational thought; it activates a 'conversation' that recognizes some aspects of the organization and not others (Gherardi 1994, 1996).

Metaphors can be a medium of important elements of culture that 'persuade us to see, understand, and imagine situations in partial ways' (Morgan 1997: 348). Moreover, 'metaphor encourages us to think and act in new ways. It extends horizons of insight and creates new possibilities' (Morgan 1997: 351). The assumption that the concept organizational learning is a metaphor implicitly allows one to start a conversation about knowledge, knowing, and learning in organizational processes.

The epistemological premises that allow this transition from a realistic to a metaphorical conception reside in the semantic shift from the term 'organization' to the term 'organiz-ing'. Organizing refers 'to the embeddedness of organizing within distinct local practices of language, of culture, of ethnicity, of gender' (Clegg and Hardy 1996a: 4). Accordingly, we, too, propose a semantic change. Instead of 'organizational learning', we explore the concept of 'learning-in-organizing'. This expression denotes a representational system, a way of organizing a theoretical discourse on organizing and organizations that eschews the concept of organization as a unified (and reified) entity. The term, therefore, refers to a social process inherent in the social construction of society and signifies no recognition of boundaries between one organization and another or between an organization and its environment. In the following sections we argue that sociology has contributed two concepts to learning-in-organizing: participation and reflexivity.

Learning-in-organizing and Participation in a Practice

Sociologists approach learning not as something that takes place in the mind but as something produced and reproduced in the social relations of individuals when they participate in society. 'Learning is unhampered participation in a meaningful situation', wrote Illich (1971: 65). Consequently, the various forms assumed by individuals engaged in goal-oriented activities are important for understanding how people become members of a community of practice and how they come to master the specific knowledge embedded in the various activities. Learning and knowing may therefore be understood 'as competent participation in a practice' (Wenger 1998: 137). The study of situated learning reveals the intended uses of knowledge in situations (Brown, Collins, and Duguid 1989).

The concept of learning through participation in a practice requires exploration of practice as a concept because it is laden with diverse traditions of thought: phenomenological, Marxist, and linguistic. These three traditions have been described (Ehn 1988) in terms of practice-as-work (the transformation of a given work process), practice-as-morality (the politics and power of the different groups or social classes involved in a given work process), and practice-as-language (professional language and interaction within a given work process). We briefly recall them in this context in order to illustrate how practice-based theorizing reshapes the concept of knowledge and helps dissolve the artificial separation of levels of learning based on the learning subject (the individual, group, organization, and networks).

Heidegger (1962) and the phenomenological school used the term *Dasein* to denote this 'being-in-the-world', whereby subject and object are indistinguishable. Both subject and object are part of a situation and exist in a social and historical setting. An illuminating example of the relationship between subject, object, environment, and knowledge is found in Winograd and Flores (1986), who used hammering as a paradigmatic instance of prereflexive learning, of comprehension that takes place in situations of involvement in a practice when subject and object are not separated. Consider a carpenter hammering a nail into a piece of wood. In terms of the carpenter's practical activity, the hammer does not exist as an object with given properties. It is as much a part of his world as the arm with which he wields it. The hammer belongs to the environment and can be unthinkingly used by the carpenter. The carpenter does not need to 'think a hammer' in order to drive in a nail. His capacity to act depends on his familiarity with the act of hammering. His use of the practical item 'hammer' constitutes its significance to him in the setting 'hammering' and 'carpentry'. When the carpenter's hammering is unimpeded, the hammer with its properties does not exist as an entity. Only when some breakdown or situation of nonusability occurs will the carpenter's activity of hammering become problematic. The hammer exists as an entity when it no longer works or is missing. That is to say, when it becomes unusable. In the usable environment, the understanding of situations is a prereflexive activity. Reflexive, investigative, theoretical knowledge requires that something that was previously usable now becomes unusable. The world of objects thus becomes 'simply present' (*vorhanden*), no longer understood. This breakdown occurs only when the carpenter has already understood the hammer in practice.

The concept of tacit knowledge is very close to the phenomenological tradition. This affinity is what Polanyi (1962: 105–6) meant when he said that we know much more than we know we know. He asked whether an analytical description of how to keep one's balance on a bicycle suffices as instruction to someone wanting to learn how to ride a bicycle? His answer: 'Rules of art can be useful, but they do not determine the practice of an art; they are maxims, which can serve as a guide to an art only if they can be integrated into the practical knowledge of the art. They cannot replace this knowledge' (p. 50).

In order to convey what he meant by 'tacit knowledge' in the practice of skills, Polanyi (1962) distinguished between two types of awareness: focal and subsidiary:

When we use a hammer to drive in a nail, we attend to both nail and hammer, *but in a different way*. We *watch* the effect of our strokes on the nail and try to wield the hammer so as to hit the nail most effectively. When we bring down the hammer we do not feel that its handle has struck our palm but that its head has struck the nail. (p. 55; emphasis in the original)

The focal awareness is on driving in the nail, the subsidiary awareness is on what is felt on the palm of the hand. The phenomenological thinker pays close attention to these feelings not because they are the object of one's attention but because they are the instruments of that attention. The conclusion is that, in general, people do not have focal awareness of the instruments over which they have achieved mastery. The implication for studying a practice is not how to make explicit what is tacit knowledge but how to deal with what von Hippel (1994) called 'sticky information': all that is unsayable and kept within the usable environment and the docile instruments in it.

To participate in a practice is to learn the logic of that practice (what Bourdieu [1990] called *sens pratique* as opposed to the logic of discourse). *Sens pratique* is prereflexive, unlike the logic of discourse, which functions by making the work of thought explicit in a linear series of signs that the mind perceives as simultaneous instead. The logic of practice is necessary for the order and continuity of an organization because practical knowledge is kept within the habitus, which produces historical 'anchors' and ensures the correctness of practices and their constancy over time more reliably than formal and explicit rules do (Bourdieu 1990).

In the phenomenological tradition, therefore, the concept of practice shows how comprehension in situations where one is 'thrown headlong into use' (Heidegger 1962: 57) is prereflexive and does not draw distinctions between subject, object, thing, or environment. The concept of practice also shows how reflexive understanding arises at moments of breakdown. It signifies that organizations as systems of practices exist in the world of tacit knowledge that is simply usable and that becomes the object of reflection when a breakdown occurs.

The phenomenological concept of practice is, however, less well known than the Marxist use of the term, which assigns to it an emancipating force. Practice is a notion central to Marxist epistemology, where it contrasts with the Cartesian notion of detached reflection and separation of mind and body and is at odds with rationalism, positivism, and scientism. Practice is an epistemological principle, and activity theory (Engestrom 1987) draws on the work of Vygotsky (1962, 1978), Luria (1976), and Leontyev (1981) from the Russian school of social psychology in order to show how the analysis of human activity must begin with the study of material actions and contexts of action. Human activity systems are distinguished from animal activity by the presence of (a) manufactured objects and concepts that mediate the interaction between individuals and concepts; (b) traditions, rituals, and rules that mediate the interaction between individuals and the community; and (c) the division of labor that mediates the interaction between the community and the actions of its members. In redefining the study of work, psychologists, sociologists, and cognitive scientists are increasingly turning to an interdisciplinary approach to work as mindful practice (Engestrom and Middleton 1996). Analyzing work as culturally mediated practice requires a consideration of both the 'mindfulness' of human action (remembering, reasoning, seeing, learning, and inventing) and the social relations and artifacts in which cognition and communication are embedded.

In other words, the activity in which knowledge is developed and applied is not separable from or ancillary to learning, and conceptual knowledge shares significant features with tools. As Brown, Collins, and Duguid (1989) explained: 'they [tools] can only be fully understood through use, and using them entails both changing the user's view of the world and adopting the belief system of the culture in which they are used' (p. 33). This analogy between knowledge and tools stresses the materiality of knowledge and is also expressed by Law's (1994) concept of relational materialism: 'ordering has to do both with humans *and* non-humans' (p. 24; emphasis in the original).

Practice is a system of activities in which knowing is not separate from doing and situations might be said to coproduce knowledge through activity (Blackler 1993; Hutchins 1993; Resnik 1993; Rogoff and Lave 1984; Zuccermaglio 1996). If the old vocabulary of technology as 'designed', 'implemented', and 'impact producing' is abandoned in favor of seeing technological systems as malleable artifacts, that is, cultural objects leading to new routines despite their initial purpose and design, then an innovative arena for negotiating the materiality of knowledge opens up. Take, for example, computer-based information systems, which, despite the characteristics usually attributed to information technologies (standardization, routinization of tasks, and centralization), are open and dynamic artifacts (Ciborra and Lanzara 1990). Computer-based information systems are embodiments not just of data flows and work routines but also of organizational cultures and archetypes: 'Computers are able to interact with *both* the structural and institutional arrangements associated with a given division of labor *and* the assumptions, frames, and mental images people have while enacting and practicing routinely that division of labor' (Ciborra and Lanzara 1990: 149; emphasis in the original). Technology, argued Latour (1991), is society made durable.

Finally, language is a distinctive feature of human activity systems, an observation that brings us to Wittgenstein's notion of practice as a linguistic game. Language is a social, not a private, fact: Linguistic terms arise within a social practice of constructing meaning. Participation in a practice entails taking part in a professional language game and mastering and being able to use its rules. To have grasped a concept means that one has learned to obey the rules within a given practice. Those who participate in the practice of a linguistic game must share in the 'life form' that makes that practice possible: Intersubjective consensus is more a matter of shared environment and language than a lack of opinions (Wittgenstein 1953).

Sharing in a life form is the prerequisite for understanding and transmitting so-called procedural knowledge, the type of knowledge acquired through the practical understanding of an operation. For example, carpenters participate in a professional language game, and they are able to 'articulate' the procedures that they follow in making a chair. But this 'know-what' kind of knowledge that can be acquired in this way is different from the practical understanding, the real operation, of making a chair. The practical knowledge of how to make a chair and how to describe this process is qualitatively different from knowing how to use a carpenter's plane or knowing when its blade needs changing.

Some knowledge is transmitted through the senses and stored in sensory maps (Gagliardi 1990) by virtue of one's familiarity with previous situations and the refinement of one's sensitivity. This type is the connoisseur's knowledge (Turner 1988) and is possessed by individuals, professional communities, and industries. The manufacture of flutes is an example (Cook and Yanow 1993). Knowing how to describe the sound of a flute is part of the practice of knowing how to identify a flute from other flutes and how to manufacture it. Practical understanding (Strati 1986) is often inarticulate, aesthetic, and tacit. In cases where this description of practical understanding applies to flute-makers, its pertinence does not stem from an inability to talk about the range of sounds but to the flute-makers' capacity to talk about participating in that language game and to the fact that this knowledge requires the presence of the person(s) possessing it. Whereas 'objective' knowledge is accessible through tangible artifacts (e.g. books, films), subjective knowledge is possessed by those who participate in a practice. It is impossible to learn how to recognize the sound of a flute from other instruments solely through books. It can only be learned by interacting with other people who are skilled in the activity.

In other words, learning-in-organizing is not only a way to acquire knowledge in practice but also a way to change or perpetuate such knowledge and to produce and reproduce society. A practice can be the hammering of a carpenter or more complex practices such as organ transplantation, bridge-building, or the execution of a safety plan. If learning is understood as participation in such practices, the artificial separation of learning into levels (e.g. individual, collective, organizational, interorganizational, institutional) dissolves because a practice may cross all levels and link all relevant knowing and knowledge. The empirical starting point for practice as a framework is the 'logic of action' formulated and pursued by social actors, and to accept this view of practice is to reject the concept of organization as a unified entity (Reed 1992: 115). The notion of practice includes both the mental and the material, the verbal and the nonverbal, the textual and the nontextual, and the human and nonhuman as the instruments surrounding everyone in everyday organizational life, as the 'missing masses' (Latour 1992) that are meant whenever social actions are described.

Amid the diverse schools of thought about organizational learning, the specific contribution that practice-based theory has made to the analysis of the knowledge intrinsic in practice can be summarized as follows:

1. Learning is acquired through participation in communities of practice (Brown and Duguid 1991; Lave and Wenger 1991; Wenger 1998).

2. Organizing can be seen as an activity system that reveals the tentative nature of knowledge and action (Blackler 1993, 1995; Blackler, Crump, and McDonald 1998). Incoherencies, inconsistencies, paradoxes, and tensions are integral to activity systems.

3. Knowledge and action are located in ecologies of sociomaterial relations (Fujimura 1995; Star 1995).

4. Knowing is enacted (Weick 1979), situated (Billett 1994; Suchman 1987), resilient but provisional (Unger 1987), and public and rhetorical (Vattimo 1985).

5. Practice involves the establishment of alignments across human and nonhuman elements (Latour 1986; Law 1994) at particular positionings at a particular time within a network of relations (Suchman 1998).

An emphasis on practice focuses the research on organizational learning on the 'doing' and the materiality of social relations, detaching it from idealist tradition and cognitive approaches.

Learning-in-organizing and Reflexivity

Learning-in-organizing can be defined as the enactment of a practice-based knowledge and its unfolding over time. Whereas in the previous section we stated that practice is both the production of the world and the result of this process, in this section we illustrate how reflexivity is the link between knowing *in* practice and knowing *a* practice. Learning a practice means participating competently in the knowledge embedded in that practice (i.e. knowing

in practice); knowing a practice entails disembedding knowledge through an act of reflexive logic. Reflexivity betrays the logic of practice because it inserts distance, reflection, and separation of subject and object where there had been no distinction between the subject and the world because both were totally present and caught up by the 'matter at hand'. The previous example of the carpenter hammering a nail is an illustration of his 'being in the world' while absorbed by carpentry. And it is also an illustration of what is meant by prereflexivity in the phenomenological tradition.

Situated practices are both prereflexive (i.e. they depend on unstated assumptions and shared knowledge for the mutual comprehensibility of the participants) and reflexively constitutive of the situated members' contexts from which they arise. Reflexivity results from the separation of or breakdown between subject and object and, for ethnomethodologists, from the need for accountability, by which is meant making the world comprehensible to oneself and to the other members of a collectivity: 'Reflexivity refers to the dynamic self-organizational tendency of social interaction to provide for its own constitution through practices of accountability and scenic display' (Flynn 1991: 28).

Reflexivity, therefore, is a characteristic of all order-producing social activities. Moreover, 'the essential reflexivity of accounts' (Garfinkel 1967: 67) is used to create a sense of orderliness for action, but it reflexively creates that selfsame context. The term 'organizational learning' not only acquires meaning from the context in which it appears but also reflexively creates that context.

Reflexivity, individual and systemic, is therefore the process whereby the carpenter in the previous section translates his or her practical knowledge of hammering and carpentry into explicit knowledge that can, for example, be transmitted to an apprentice; codified as standard operating routines, books, models, or instruments; and used as a knowledge base for innovation.

The concept of reflexivity therefore comprises three elements: (a) self-monitoring as its cognitive element, which produces knowledge; (b) accountability as its social element, which creates a discursive order; and (c) institutionalization as its normative element, which produces and reproduces the social institutions. The term 'institutional reflexivity' (Giddens 1976: 6, 1990: 12) refers to the fact that the institutional work of society reproduces the social order that has produced its institutions. It does so by means of a twofold hermeneutics, that is, the constant reinterpretation of previous interpretations.

Learning-in-organizing can only occur in relation to reflexivity, for reflexivity enables both cybernetic self-monitoring, the institutionalization of knowledge, and hence change as the result of a learning process. Both positions are continuations of the Enlightenment tradition of modernity (Bauman 1992), and in German sociology they are taken up, albeit with different emphases, by Luhmann (1984), Habermas (1975), and Beck (1992): Social change is a learning process.

This conceptualization of reflexivity in mainly cognitive terms differs from the notion of aesthetic reflexivity (Lash 1993, 1994; Strati 1999), according to which reflexivity does not occur solely by virtue of cognitive categories (self-monitoring) but involves hermeneutic categories as well. That is to say, it is a process of self-interpretation and aesthetic judgment that involves the imagination and intuition specifically.

Reflexivity as a phenomenon typically tied to modernity has given rise to an interesting sociological debate (Beck, Giddens, and Lash 1994) that has engendered something akin to a 'third way' between modernism and postmodernism: 'reflexive modernization'. Whether modernity is over and done with or whether it has entered a new phase, proponents of reflexive modernization have asserted that 'the more societies are modernized, the more agents acquire the ability to reflect on the social conditions of their existence and to change them in that way' (Beck 1994: 174). Of course, what is meant by reflexivity, and what the subjects, the medium, and the consequences of reflexive modernization are, change from one author to

the next. Be that as it may, the social construction of organizational learning by organizational scholars also contributes to the process of reflexive modernization and exemplifies institutional reflexivity.

In Giddens's terms (1994), institutional reflexivity means the dis-embedding and re-embedding of industrial society's ways of life by new ones under the general conditions of the welfare state in a developed society based on industrial labor. The subjects of reflexive modernization are organizations, institutions, and individuals, and the medium is knowledge in its various forms: scientific knowledge, expert knowledge, everyday knowledge. Reflexive modernization is a theory of the ever-growing powers of social actors (agency) to shape structure (Lash 1994). The reflexive modernity of the organizational learning approach lies in its progressive liberation of the practice and theory of organizing from the 'cage' of order-producing structure and contingency. The purpose of that liberation is to create more space for the organizational agency and its activity of self-monitoring or self-interpreting uncertainty and ambiguity.

We therefore conclude that the concept of reflexivity can make a twofold contribution to the social foundation of learning. First, reflexivity is a methodological guide for analyzing how practical knowledge is communicated to and institutionalized at all levels of society. This knowledge is communicated and institutionalized through—

- the community of practice based upon it;
- the organizational subsystem where this community interacts with other communities;
- the organization as a corporate actor that possesses the power to legitimate some forms of expert knowledge and discredit others;
- the interorganizational network created by a system of practices and within which they circulate, by imitation, diffusion, or translation;
- varyingly institutionalized forms of knowledge reproduced by knowledge-brokering

organizations, such as training agencies, consortia for certification, and organizational consultants; and

- the institutional environment that creates the conditions for the reproduction (or change) of knowledge institutionalized into rules and regulations or granted to universities, national research institutes, and similar institutions authorized to manage knowledge.

In this sense, institutional reflexivity constitutes the grounds for a rather different view of learning than the one that underpins most of the views of organizational learning shown in Table 2.1. As Star (1995) argued, an alternative view of cognition emphasizes the situated and shared character of learning, the uncertain and fluid boundaries of knowledge in formal organizations, and the social and material practices that make up learning, knowledge, and skills.

Second, the concept of reflexivity enables a community of practice (the organizational learning scholars) to exert reflexive control over both the knowledge that it produces and the social effects that arise from this production in all their ambiguity. Learning, in fact, is a term that is often part of a final vocabulary, an axiomatic value. The positive connotations associated with the word induces the a priori assumption of what needs to be empirically demonstrated. Learning, as the founding myth of the scientific community of scholars, obscures the social construction of organizational practices that, inasmuch as they are called 'learning', produce learning (Nicolini and Meznar 1995) in the form of discourses that normalize and discipline the thought of individuals. The exploitative ethos of many discourses on organizational learning is part of the theoretical construction of the field as a discourse of disciplining when such discourse is preselected as a managerial technique biased specifically toward systematic and purposeful learning, improvement, and particular norms (Gherardi 1999). These biases and others—toward individual action, environmental adaptation, or planned learning, for example (Huys-

man 1999)—constitute a specific structuring of power/knowledge that sustains and perpetuates them as a discourse of power even though other discursive positions are possible.

Conclusions

The specific disciplinary contribution of sociology to the study of organizational learning lies in its depiction of learning as a social process involving social relations (shaped by social institutions) and learning itself (a 'cultural object' created by artful practices of cultural work). However, sociology is not a body of incremental knowledge. Consequently, various sociological traditions have produced many sociological discourses on learning (see Table 2.1), which can be discerned in the specialist and multidisciplinary field of organizational studies.

We have used an analytical approach that ideally draws on a constructionist ontology. Accordingly, we have argued that the notion of organizational learning is like an open conversation and that we can contribute to this conversation through two sociological concepts: participation and reflexivity.

The concept of participation directs the attention of the scholar of organizational learning to the fact that learning is not an activity distinct from other activities, organizational or otherwise, but rather a part of becoming a member of an organization and that it is intrinsic to the practices that sustain an organization. The logic of practice does not draw a distinction between subject and object; instead, it involves 'knowing how to be competent' in a usable environment. This concept therefore invites the study of prereflexive knowledge, tacit knowledge, aesthetic understanding, knowledge in action—in short, of what we have called learning-in-organizing. By contrast, the concept of reflexivity relates to a particular moment of separation between the knowing subject and the object of its knowledge: the moment that produces the conditions of the context. Reflexivity directs organizational analysis to the processes of knowledge institutionalization. It invites investigation of the organizational network engaged in the social process of extracting the-oretical knowledge from practical knowledge and then transforming it into the normative knowledge that produces the operating conditions of practical knowledge.

References

Alvesson, M. (1993). 'Organization as Rhetoric: Knowledge-intensive Firms and the Struggle with Ambiguity'. *Journal of Management Studies*, 30: 997–1016.

——and Deetz, S. (1996). 'Critical Theory and Postmodernism Approaches to Organizational Studies', in S. R. Clegg, C. Hardy, and W. R. Nord (eds.), *Handbook of Organization Studies*. London: Sage, 191–217.

Argyris, C. and Schön, D. A. (1974). *Theory in Practice: Increasing Professional Effectiveness*. San Francisco: Jossey-Bass.

——— (1978). *Organizational Learning: A Theory of Action Perspective*. Reading, Mass.: Addison-Wesley.

Arujo, L. (1998). 'Knowing and Learning as Networking'. *Management Learning*, 29: 317–36.

Astley, G. (1985). 'Administrative Science as Socially Constructed Truth'. *Administrative Science Quarterly*, 30: 497–513.

Barley, S. (1991). 'Semiotics and the Study of Occupational and Organizational Cultures', in P. J. Frost, L. F. Moore, M. R. Louis, C. C. Lundberg, and J. Martin (eds.), *Reframing Organizational Culture*. Newbury Park, Calif.: Sage, 39–54.

Bateson, G. (1972). *Steps to an Ecology of Mind: A Revolutionary Approach to Man's Understanding of Himself*. New York: Ballantine Books.

Bauman, Z. (1992). *Intimations of Postmodernity*. London: Routledge.

Baumard, P. (1996). 'Organizations in the Fog: An Investigation into the Dynamics of Knowledge', in B. Moingeon and A. Edmondson (eds.), *Organizational Learning and Competitive Advantage*. London: Sage, 74–91.

Beck, U. (1992). *The Risk Society: Towards a New Modernity* (M. Ritter, trans.). London: Sage. (Original work published 1986)

—— (1994). 'Self-dissolution and Self-endangerment of Industrial Society: What Does This Mean?' in U. Beck, A. Giddens, and S. Lash (eds.), *Reflexive Modernization*. Cambridge: Polity Press, 174–83.

—— Giddens, A., and Lash, S. (1994). *Reflexive Modernization*. Cambridge: Polity Press.

Berger, P. L. and Luckmann, T. (1966). *The Social Construction of Reality: A Treatise in the Sociology of Knowledge*. Garden City, NY: Doubleday.

Bernstein, B. (1971–1975). *Class, Codes, and Control* (Vols. 1–3). London: Routledge and Kegan Paul.

Billett, S. (1994). 'Situated Learning: A Workplace Experience'. *Australian Journal of Adult and Community Education*, 34/2: 112–30.

Blackler, F. (1993). 'Knowledge and the Theory of Organizations: Organizations as Activity Systems and the Reframing of Management'. *Journal of Management Studies*, 30: 863–84.

—— (1995). 'Knowledge, Knowledge Work and Organizations: An Overview and Interpretation'. *Organization Studies*, 16: 1021–46.

—— Crump, N., and McDonald, S. (1998). 'Managing Experts and Competing through Collaboration: An Activity Theoretical Analysis'. *Organization*, 6: 5–31.

Blau, P. M. (1964). *Exchange and Power in Social Life*. New York: Wiley.

Blumer, H. (1969). *Symbolic Interactionism*. Englewood Cliffs, NJ: Prentice Hall.

Boje, D. M. (1994). 'Organizational Storytelling—The Struggles of Premodern, Modern and Post-modern Organizational Learning Discourses'. *Management Learning*, 25: 433–61.

Boland, R. and Tenkasi, R. (1995). 'Perspective Making and Perspective Taking in Communities of Knowing'. *Organization Science*, 6: 350–72.

Bourdieu, P. (1990). *The Logic of Practice*. Stanford, Calif.: Stanford University Press.

Brown, J. S., Collins, A., and Duguid, P. (1989). 'Situated Cognition and the Culture of Learning'. *Educational Researcher*, 18/1: 32–42.

—— and Duguid, P. (1991). 'Organizational Learning and Communities-of-Practice: Toward a Unified View of Working, Learning, and Innovation'. *Organization Science*, 2: 40–57.

Bruner, J. (1990). *Acts of Meaning*. Cambridge, Mass.: Harvard University Press.

Burrell, G. and Morgan, G. (1979). *Sociological Paradigms and Organizational Analysis*. Aldershot: Gower.

Butera, F., Donati, E., and Cesaria, R. (1998). *I lavoratori della conoscenza* (Knowledge Workers). Milan: Angeli.

Ciborra, C. U. and Lanzara, G. F. (1990). 'Designing Dynamic Artifacts: Computer Systems as Formative Contexts', in P. Gagliardi (ed.), *Symbols and Artifacts: Views of the Corporate Landscape*. Berlin: de Gruyter, 147–65.

Clegg, S. R. (1990). *Modern Organization: Organization Studies in the Postmodern World*. London: Sage.

——(1995). 'Of Values and Occasional Irony: Max Weber in the Context of the Sociology of Organizations', in S. B. Bacharach, P. Gagliardi, and B. Mundell (eds.), *Studies of Organizations in the European Tradition*. Greenwich, Conn.: JAI Press, 1–46.

—— and Hardy, C. (1996a). 'Organizations, Organization and Organizing', in S. R. Clegg, C. Hardy, and W. R. Nord (eds.), *Handbook of Organization Studies*. London: Sage, 1–28.

—— —— (1996b). 'Representations', in S. R. Clegg, C. Hardy, and W. R. Nord (eds.), *Handbook of Organization Studies*. London: Sage, 676–708.

Collins, R. (1979). *The Credential Society: A Historical Sociology of Education and Stratification*. New York: Academic Press.

——(1994). *Four Sociological Traditions*. Oxford: Oxford University Press.

Cook, K. S., Emerson, R. M., Gillmore, M., and Yamagishi, I. (1983). 'The Distribution of Power in Exchange Networks'. *American Journal of Sociology*, 89: 275–305.

Cook, S. D. N. and Yanow, D. (1993). 'Culture and Organizational Learning'. *Journal of Management Inquiry*, 2: 373–90.

Cooley, C. H. (1964). *Human Nature and the Social Order*. New York: Shocken.

Cooper, R. (1989). 'Modernism, Postmodernism and Organizational Analysis 3: The Contribution of Jacques Derrida'. *Organization Studies*, 10: 479–502.

—— and Burrell, G. (1988). 'Modernism, Postmodernism and Organizational Analysis: An Introduction'. *Organization Studies*, 9: 91–112.

Coopey, J. (1995). 'The Learning Organization: Power, Politics and Ideology'. *Management Learning*, 26: 193–214.

Crozier, M. (1963). *Le Phénomène bureaucratique*. Paris: de Seuil.

Cyert, R. M. and March, J. G. (1963). *A Behavioral Theory of the Firm*. Englewood Cliffs, NJ: Prentice Hall.

Czarniawska-Joerges, B. (1991). 'Culture Is the Medium of Life', in P. J. Frost, L. F. Moore, M. R. Louis, C. C. Lundberg, and J. Martin (eds.), *Reframing Organizational Culture*. Newbury Park, Calif.: Sage, 285–97.

——(1995). 'Autobiographical Acts and Organizational Identities', in S. Linstead, B. Grafton-Small, and P. Jefcutt (eds.), *Understanding Managements*. London: Sage, 157–71.

Dalton, M. (1959). *Men Who Manage: Fusions of Feeling and Theory in Administration*. New York: Wiley.

Deetz, S. (1996). 'Discursive Formations, Strategized Subordination, and Self-surveillance: An Empirical Case', in A. McKinlay and K. Starkey (eds.), *Managing Foucault: A Reader*. London: Sage, 157–71.

Derrida, J. (1971). *L'Écriture et la différence*. Paris: de Seuil.

Dewey, J. (1922). *Human Nature and Conduct*. New York: Holt.

Douglas, M. (1970). *Natural Symbols*. London: Routledge & Kegan Paul.

Duncan, R. and Weiss, A. (1979). 'Organizational Learning: Implications for Organizational Design', in B. M. Staw (ed.), *Research in Organizational Behavior: An Annual Series of Analytical*

Essays and Critical Reviews (Vol. 1). Greenwich, Conn.: JAI Press, 75–123.

Durkheim, E. (1897). *Le Suicide: Étude de sociologie.* Paris: Presses universitaires de France.

——(1912). *Les Formes élémentaires de la vie religieuse: Le Système totemique en Australie.* Paris: Alcan.

Easterby-Smith, M., Snell, R., and Gherardi, S. (1998). 'Organizational Learning and Learning Organization: Diverging Communities of Practice?' *Management Learning*, 29: 259–72.

Ehn, P. (1988). *Work-oriented Design of Computer Artifacts.* Stockholm: Arbetlivscentrum.

Engestrom, Y. (1987). *Learning by Expanding: An Activity Theoretical Approach to Developmental Research.* Helsinki: Orienta Konsultit.

——and Middleton, D. (1996). *Cognition and Communication at Work.* Cambridge: Cambridge University Press.

Etzioni, A. (1961). *A Comparative Analysis of Complex Organizations.* New York: Free Press of Glencoe.

Fiol, C. M. and Lyles, M. A. (1985). 'Organizational Learning'. *Academy of Management Review*, 10: 803–13.

Flynn, P. (1991). *The Ethnomethodological Movement.* New York: Mouton de Gruyter.

Foucault, M. (1977). *Discipline and Punish: The Birth of the Prison* (A. Sheridan, trans.). New York: Pantheon. (Original work published 1975)

——(1980). *Power/Knowledge: Selected Interviews and Other Writings 1972–1977* (C. Gordon, trans.). New York: Pantheon.

——(1988). 'Technologies of the Self', in L. Martin, H. Gutman, and P. Hutton (eds.), *Technologies of the Self: A Seminar with Michel Foucault.* Amherst: University of Massachusetts Press, 16–49.

Fox, S. (1997). 'Situated Learning Theory versus Traditional Cognitive Learning Theory: Why Management Education Should Not Ignore Management Learning'. *Systems Practice*, 10: 727–47.

Fujimura, J. (1995). 'Ecologies of Action: Recombining Genes, Molecularizing Cancer, and Transforming Biology', in S. L. Star (ed.), *Ecologies of Knowledge.* Albany: State University of New York Press, 302–46.

Gagliardi, P. (1990). 'Artifacts as Pathways and Remains of Organizational Life', in P. Gagliardi (ed.), *Symbols and Artifacts: Views of the Corporate Landscape.* Berlin: de Gruyter, 3–37.

Garfinkel, H. (1967). *Studies in Ethnomethodology.* Englewood Cliffs, NJ: Prentice Hall.

Gergen, K. (1992). 'Organization Theory in the Postmodern Era', in M. Reed and M. Hughes (eds.), *Rethinking Organizations.* London: Sage, 207–26.

Gherardi, S. (1990). *Le microdecisioni nelle organizzazioni* (Microdecisions in Organizations). Bologna: Il Mulino.

——(1994). 'Imparare a decidere' (Learning for Decision-making), in D. Demetrio, D. Fabbri, and S. Gherardi (eds.), *Apprendere nelle organizzazioni.* Rome: Nuova Italia Scientifica, 161–208.

——(1996). 'Organizational Learning', in M. Warner (ed.), *International Encyclopedia of Business and Management.* London: Routledge, 3934–42.

——(1999). 'Learning as Problem-driven or Learning in the Face of Mystery?' *Organization Studies*, 20: 101–24.

——Nicolini, D., and Odella, F. (1998a). 'Toward a Social Understanding of How People Learn in Organizations: The Notion of Situated Curriculum'. *Management Learning*, 29: 273–98.

—— —— ——(1998b). 'What Do You Mean by Safety? Conflicting Perspectives on Accident Causation and Safety Management Inside a Construction Firm'. *Journal of Contingencies and Crisis Management*, 7/4: 202–13.

Giddens, A. (1976). *New Rules of Sociological Method.* London: Hutchinson.

——(1990). *The Consequences of Modernity.* Cambridge: Polity Press.

——(1994). 'Living in a Post-traditional Society', in U. Beck, A. Giddens, and S. Lash (eds.), *Reflexive Modernization.* Cambridge: Polity Press, 68–109.

Goffman, E. (1967). *Interaction Ritual.* Garden City, NY: Doubleday.

——(1971). *Relations in Public.* New York: Harper & Row.

Gouldner, A. W. (1954). *Patterns of Industrial Bureaucracy: A Study of Modern Factory Administration.* Glencoe, Ill.: Free Press.

Habermas, J. (1975). *Legitimation Crisis* (T. McCarthy, trans.). Boston: Beacon. (Original work published 1973)

Hedberg, B. L. T. (1981). 'How Organizations Learn and Unlearn', in P. C. Nystrom and W. H. Starbuck (eds.), *Handbook of Organizational Design*: Vol. 1. *Adapting Organizations to Their Environments*. Oxford: Oxford University Press, 3–27.

Hegel, G. W. F. (1807). *Die Phänomenologie des Geistes*. Bamberg: Goebhardt.

Heidegger, M. (1962). *Being and Time* (J. Macquire, trans.). New York: Harper & Row. (Original work published 1927)

Homans, G. C. (1950). *The Human Group*. New York: Harcourt Brace.

—— (1961). *Social Behavior: Its Elementary Forms*. New York: Harcourt Brace.

Hopwood, A. (1987). 'The Archeology of Accounting Systems'. *Accounting, Organizations and Society*, 12: 207–34.

Hutchins, E. (1993). 'Learning to Navigate', in S. Chaiklin and J. Lave (eds.), *Understanding Practice: Perspectives on Activity and Context*. Cambridge: Cambridge University Press, 35–63.

Huysman, M. (1999). 'Balancing Biases: A Critical Review of the Literature on Organizational Learning', in M. Easterby-Smith, L. Araujo, and J. Burgoyne (eds.), *Organizational Learning and the Learning Organization: Developments in Theory and Practice*. London: Sage, 59–74.

Illich, I. (1971). *Deschooling Society*. London: Calder and Boyars.

Kunda, G. (1986). *Engineering Culture: Control and Commitment in a High-tech Organization*. Philadelphia: Temple University Press.

Lash, S. (1993). 'Reflexive Modernization: The Aesthetic Dimension'. *Theory, Culture and Society*, 10: 1–23.

—— (1994). 'Reflexivity and Its Doubles: Structure, Aesthetics, Community', in U. Beck, A. Giddens, and S. Lash (eds.), *Reflexive Modernization*. Cambridge: Polity Press, 110–73.

Latour, B. (1986). 'The Powers of Association', in J. Law (ed.), *Power, Action and Belief: A New Sociology of Knowledge?* London: Routledge & Kegan Paul, 264–80.

—— (1991). 'Technology Is Society Made Durable', in J. Law (ed.), *A Sociology of Monsters*: *Essays on Power, Technology and Domination*. London: Routledge, 103–31.

—— (1992). 'Where Are the Missing Masses? The Sociology of a Few Mundane Artifacts', in W. E. Bijker and J. Law (eds.), *Shaping Technology/Building Society: Studies in Sociotechnical Change*. Cambridge, Mass.: MIT Press, 225–58.

Lave, J. and Wenger, E. (1991). *Situated Learning: Legitimate Peripheral Participation*. Cambridge: Cambridge University Press.

Law, J. (1994). *Organizing Modernity*. Oxford: Blackwell.

Leontyev, A. N. (1981). *Problems of the Development of the Mind*. Moscow: Progress. (Original work published 1959)

Levinthal, D. A. and March, J. G. (1993). 'The Myopia of Learning'. *Strategic Management Journal*, 14 (Winter special issue): 95–112.

Levitt, B. and March, J. G. (1988). 'Organizational Learning'. *Annual Review of Sociology*, 14: 319–40.

Linstead, S. (1993). 'Deconstruction in the Study of Organizations', in J. Hassard and M. Parker (eds.), *Postmodernism and Organizations*. London: Sage, 49–70.

—— (1994). 'The Responsibilities of Betrayal: Deconstruction and Ethnographic Praxis'. *Blurring Genres*, 6: 1–27.

—— and Grafton-Small, R. (1990). 'Theory as Artifact: Artifact as Theory', in P. Gagliardi (ed.), *Symbols as Artifacts: Views of the Corporate Landscape*. Berlin: de Gruyter, 387–420.

Luce, R. and Raiffa, H. (1957). *Games and Decisions*. New York: Wiley.

Luhmann, N. (1984). *Soziale Systeme: Grundriß einer allgemeinen Theorie*. Frankfurt am Main: Suhrkamp.

Luria, A. R. (1976). *Cognitive Development: Its Cultural and Social Foundations*. Cambridge, Mass.: Harvard University Press.

Lyotard, J. (1984). *The Postmodern Condition*. Manchester: Manchester University Press.

Mannheim, K. (1935). *Mensch und Gesellschaft im Zeitalter des Umbaus*. Leiden: Sijthoff's Vitgeversmaatschappij.

March, J. G. (1988). *Decisions and Organizations*. Oxford: Basil Blackwell.

——(1996). 'Exploration and Exploitation in Organizational Learning', in M. D. Cohen and L. S. Sproull (eds.), *Organizational Learning*. Thousand Oaks, Calif.: Sage, 101–23.

—— and Olsen, J. P. (1976). 'Organizational Choice Under Ambiguity', in J. G. March and J. P. Olsen, *Ambiguity and Choice in Organizations*. Bergen: Universitetsforlaget, 10–23.

Mauss, M. (1968). *Œuvres*. Paris: Édition de Minuit.

Mead, G. H. (1934). *Mind, Self, and Society: From the Standpoint of a Social Behaviorist*. Chicago: University of Chicago Press.

Merton, R. K. (1957). *Social Theory and Social Structure*. New York: Free Press.

Michels, R. (1911). *Zur Soziologie des Parteiwesens in der modernen Demokratie: Untersuchungen über die oligarchischen Tendenzen des Gruppenlebens*. Leipzig: Werner Klinkhardt.

Morgan, G. (1997). *Images of Organization* (2nd edn). Beverly Hills, Calif.: Sage.

Munro, R. and Mouritsen, J. (1996). *Accountability: Power, Ethos and the Technologies of Managing*. London: Thomson Business Press.

Nelson, R. R. (1991). 'Why Do Firms Differ, and How Does It Matter?' *Strategic Management Journal*, 12 (Winter special issue): 61–74.

Nicolini, D. and Meznar, M. B. (1995). 'The Social Construction of Organizational Learning'. *Human Relations*, 48: 727–46.

Nonaka, I. and Takeuchi, H. (1995). *The Knowledge-creating Company: How Japanese Companies Create the Dynamics of Innovation*. New York: Oxford University Press.

Olson, M. (1965). *The Logic of Collective Action*. Cambridge, Mass.: Harvard University Press.

Orr, J. (1993). 'Sharing Knowledge, Celebrating Identity: War Stories and Community Memory among Service Technicians', in D. S. Middleton and D. Edwards (eds.), *Collective Remembering: Memory in Society*. Beverly Hills, Calif.: Sage, 169–89.

Ouchi, W. and Wilkins, A. (1985). 'Organizational Culture'. *Annual Review of Sociology*, 11: 457–83.

Parsons, T. (1951). *Toward a General Theory of Action*. Cambridge, Mass.: Harvard University Press.

Peirce, C. (1931–1935). *Collected Papers*. Cambridge, Mass.: Harvard University Press.

Perrow, C. (1991). 'A Society of Organizations'. *Theory and Society*, 20: 725–62.

Polanyi, M. (1962). *Personal Knowledge*. London: Routledge & Kegan Paul. (Original work published 1958)

Power, M. and Laughlin, R. (1992). 'Critical Theory and Accounting', in M. Alvesson and H. Willmott (eds.), *Critical Management Studies*. London: Sage, 113–35.

Presthus, R. (1978). *The Organizational Society*. New York: St. Martin's Press.

Reed, M. (1992). *The Sociology of Organizations*. Hemel Hempstead: Harvester.

——(1996). 'Organizational Theorizing: A Historically Contested Terrain', in S. R. Clegg, C. Hardy, and W. R. Nord (eds.), *Handbook of Organization Studies*. London: Sage, 31–56.

Resnick, L. B. (1993). 'Shared Cognition: Thinking as a Social Practice', in L. Resnick, J. Levine, and S. D. Teasley (eds.), *Perspectives on Socially Shared Cognition*. Washington, DC: American Psychological Association, 57–73.

Rogoff, B. and Lave, J. (eds.) (1984). *Everyday Cognition: Its Development in Social Context*. Cambridge, Mass.: Harvard University Press.

Schutz, A. (1971). *Collected Papers*. The Hague: Nijhoff.

Selznick, P. (1949). *TVA and the Grass Roots: A Study in the Sociology of Formal Organization*. Berkeley: University of California Press.

Simon, H. A. (1957). *Administrative Behavior: A Study of Decision-making Processes in Administrative Organization* (2nd edn). New York: Free Press.

Sims, D. (1999). 'Learning as the Development of Stories', in M. Easterby-Smith, L. Araujo, and J. Burgoyne (eds.), *Organizational Learning and the Learning Organization: Developments in Theory and Practice*. London: Sage, 44–58.

Snell, R. and Chak, A. M. (1998). 'The Learning Organization: Learning and Empowerment for Whom?' *Management Learning*, 29: 337–64.

Spender, J. C. (1996a). 'Competitive Advantage from Tacit Knowledge? Unpacking the Concept and Its Strategic Implications', in B. Moingeon and A. Edmondson (eds.), *Organizational Learning and Competitive Advantage*. London: Sage, 56–73.

—— (1996b). 'Organizational Knowledge, Learning, and Memory: Three Concepts in Search of a Theory'. *Journal of Organizational Change Management*, 9/1: 63–78.

Star, S. L. (1995). *Ecologies of Knowledge*. Albany: State University of New York Press.

Starbuck, W. H. (1983). 'Organizations as Action Generators'. *American Sociological Review*, 48: 91–102.

—— (1992). 'Learning by Knowledge-intensive Firms'. *Journal of Management Studies*, 29: 713–40.

Strati, A. (1986). 'Lavoro e Simbolismo Organizzativo' (Work and Organizational Symbolism). *Studi Organizzativi*, 17/2–3: 65–85.

—— (1999). *Organization and Aesthetics*. London: Sage.

Stucky, S. (1995). 'Technology in Support of Organizational Learning', in C. Zucchermaglio, S. Bagnara, and S. Stucky (eds.), *Organizational Learning and Technological Change*. New York: Springer, 4–15.

Suchman, L. (1987). *Plans and Situated Action*. Cambridge: Cambridge University Press.

—— (1998). *Organizing Alignment: A Case of Bridge-building*. Paper presented at The Academy of Management Annual Meeting, San Diego, Calif., Symposium on 'Situated Learning, Local Knowledge, and Action: Social Approaches to the Study of Knowing in Organizations', 10–12 August.

Thomas, W. (1928). *The Child in America*. New York: Knopf.

Tomassini, M. (1993). *Alla ricerca dell'organizzazione che apprende* (In Search of the Learning Organization). Rome: Edizioni Lavoro.

Townley, B. (1993). 'Foucault, Power/Knowledge, and Its Relevance for Human Resource Management'. *Academy of Management Review*, 18: 518–45.

Tsang, E. W. K. (1997). 'Organizational Learning and the Learning Organization: A Dichotomy between Descriptive and Prescriptive Research'. *Human Relations*, 50: 73–89.

Tsoukas, H. (1992). 'Ways of Seeing—Topographic and Network Representations in Organization Theory'. *Systems Practice*, 5: 441–56.

—— (1996). 'The Firm as a Distributed Knowledge System: A Constructionist Approach'. *Strategic Management Journal*, 17 (Winter special issue): 11–25.

Turner, B. (1988). 'Connoisseurship in the Study of Organizational Cultures', in A. Bryman (ed.), *Doing Research in Organization*. London: Routledge & Kegal Paul, 108–22.

Unger, R. (1987). *False Necessity*. Cambridge: Cambridge University Press.

van Maanen, J. and Barley, S. R. (1984). 'Occupational Communities: Culture and Control in Organizations', in B. M. Staw and L. L. Cummings (eds.), *Research in Organizational Behavior: An Annual Series of Analytical Essays and Critical Reviews* (Vol. 6). Greenwich, Conn.: JAI Press, 287–366.

Vattimo, G. (1985). *Fine della modernità* (The End of Modernity). Milan: Garzanti.

von Hippel, E. (1994). ' "Sticky Information" and the Locus of Problem Solving: Implications for Innovation'. *Management Science*, 40: 429–39.

Vygotsky, L. S. (1962). *Thought and Language*. New York: Wiley.

—— (1978). *Mind in Society*. London: Harvard.

Warglien, M. (1990). *Innovazione e impresa evolutiva: Processi di scoperta e apprendimento in un sistema di routines* (Innovation and the Evolutionary Firm: Discovery and Learning in a Routine System). Venice: Cedam.

Weber, M. (1978). *Economy and Society: An Outline of Interpretive Sociology* (2 vols., E. Fischoff, H. Gerth, A. M. Henderson, F. Kolegar, C. W. Mills, T. Parsons, M. Rheinstein, G. Roth, E. Shils, and C. Wittich, trans.). G. Roth and C. Wittich (eds.). Berkeley: University of California Press. (Original work published 1922)

Weick, K. E. (1979). *The Social Psychology of Organizing* (2nd edn). Reading, Mass.: Addison-Wesley.

—— (1991). 'The Nontraditional Quality of Organizational Learning'. *Organization Science*, 2: 116–24.

—— and Westley, F. (1996). 'Organizational Learning: Affirming An Oxymoron', in S. R. Clegg, C. Hardy, and W. R. Nord (eds.), *Handbook of Organization Studies*. London: Sage, 440–58.

Wenger, E. (1998). *Communities of Practice: Learning, Meaning and Identity*. Cambridge: Cambridge University Press.

Winograd, T. and Flores, F. (1986). *Understanding Computers and Cognition: A New Foundation for Design*. Norwood, NJ: Ablex.

Wittgenstein, L. (1953). *Philosophical Investigations* (G. E. M. Anscombe, trans.). Oxford: Blackwell.

Zuboff, S. (1988). *In the Age of the Smart Machine: The Future of Work and Power*. New York: Basic Books.

Zucchermaglio, C. (1995). 'Organization and Cognitive Design of (Technological) Learning Environment', in C. Zucchermaglio, S. Bagnara, and S. Stucky (eds.), *Organizational Learning and Technological Change*. New York: Springer, 61–74.

——(1996). *Vygotskij in Azienda* (Vygotskij in the Workplace). Rome: La Nuova Italia Scientifica.

3 The Treatment of Organizational Learning in Management Science

Peter Pawlowsky

A theme commonly found in the literature on management is the need for concepts of organizational change that are suitable for an increasingly turbulent and complex business environment. However, the interpretative framework for these concepts encompasses a number of scenarios, including ones for a post-industrial society, a service economy, and a knowledge society. All these scenarios capture aspects of radical change that is occurring in economic and social conditions: a declining importance of physical assets and a growing importance of intangible assets. Management is confronted not only with new combinations and patterns of old variables but also with fundamental shifts in the logic of business itself and in the assets with which business deals.

Since early industrialization, management concepts and tools have been focused primarily on the transformation of physical resources through work systems based on the division of labor. Indeed, value-added by economic activities continues to be measured as the difference between raw materials and the output of the production process. What management has yet to learn is the transformation of informational and knowledge resources in *integrated* work systems. Innovation, growth, and productivity gains do not result from separating tasks in the workflow of a knowledge-intensive operation but rather from integrating and combining knowledge in order to develop new ideas and jointly develop solutions through problem-solving processes. Aside from the increases in speed and decreases in failure that

are due to learning curves, little is known about the role of knowledge and learning as a promoter of change and added value.

Thus, one of the major challenges for management is to understand the role of knowledge and learning for organizational change and business success. Quinn (1992), for example, argued that the organization of enterprises and effective corporate strategies increasingly depends more on the development and deployment of intellectual resources than on the management of physical assets: 'As a company focuses ever more on its own internal knowledge and service skills and those of its suppliers, it increasingly finds that managing shifts *away from* the overseeing and deployment of fiscal and physical assets and *toward* the management of human skills, knowledge bases, and intellect both within the company and in its suppliers' (p. 72). Similarly, Boisot (1995) concluded that 'we have an economic theory that can help us to understand and manage the production and exchange of tangible goods but [that] is unable to help us understand and manage intangibles like knowledge' (p. 4).

Even traditional accounting principles are being questioned and altered in order to capture the true value-generating resources (Kaplan and Norton 1996; Sveiby 1997). Drawing on studies of performance measurement, Kaplan and Norton (1996) argued that financial indicators of business success are no longer sufficient, that companies in the information society have to invest in their intellectual capital and have to assess new indicators beyond conventional financial results in order to succeed (see also Reinhardt, Bornemann, Pawlowsky, and Schneider, Ch. 36 in this volume). According to Sveiby (1997), knowledge-intensive organizations in particular have to free themselves from the mental straitjackets of the industrial age by employing strategies that focus on intangible rather than tangible assets if they want to succeed.

Which solutions can management science offer to organizational decision-makers in order to cope with these challenges of the information society? To answer this question, it may be helpful to begin by reviewing the development of theoretical insights into organizational change learning and inquiring into the practical relevance that such learning has for management.

Theoretical Perspectives on Organizational Change

The topic of organizational change is not new to management science. Ever since it became apparent that there is no one best way to manage an organization in all circumstances, there has been the question of which solution fits which circumstances best. Hence, the relation between an organization and its environment is a central issue of theoretical perspectives on organizational change. The differences between the approaches lie mainly in the assumptions of what constitutes correct solutions to the management of this relationship. Several authors have grouped the theoretical approaches according to different schools or lines of thinking. Astley and van de Ven (1983) distinguished deterministic from voluntaristic orientations. Pfeffer (1982) differentiated three perspectives: (a) purposive, intentional, goal-directed, and rational perspectives; (b) externally constrained and controlled models; and (c) emergent, almost random perspectives. Scott (1992) used two basic dimensions for his systematization of organizational theory, distinguishing not only between closed systems models and open system models but

also between different levels of analysis (e.g. social psychological, structural, and ecological).

Looking more closely at these theoretical approaches, one sees that early deterministic approaches are rooted in economic thinking based on the assumption that a firm exists in a state of equilibrium. From that point of view, organizational behavior takes shape only in direct response to market prices and demands. There is only one best way to manage a business that is strictly determined by markets (Debreu 1954; Jensen 1983; Schreyögg 1996; Schumann 1976; Zimmerman 1961): keep the organization in balance with these market forces. In evolutionary approaches, such as population ecology, one does not define rules but rather interprets the survival of organizations in terms of environmental selection (Hannan and Freeman 1989; McKelvey and Aldrich 1983; Nelson and Winter 1982). This selection is determined by evolutionary processes. Organizations are conceived of as self-reproducing, closed systems that develop variance in practice. The 'best practices' are those that enable organizational survival. Organizations cannot escape this selection process. The process of organizational change proceeds along the phases of variation—selection and retention, with management being considered the initiator of the variation and retention necessary in order to keep the system alive.

Contingency approaches, too, are basically deterministic if one considers various aspects of environmental influences on organizations, aspects such as the nature of the environment or technological factors. They give management a standard by which to adapt internal structures and processes. In the adaptation perspective the management of change requires the identification of environmental characteristics and the design of organizational architecture and procedures according to changing external influences (Burns and Stalker 1961; Lawrence and Lorsch 1967; Thompson 1967; Woodward 1965). In order to adapt organizations to changing contingencies, management has to focus primarily on technological complexity and develop a best fit.

Child (1972) argued that contingency approaches have a mechanistic flavor and that there are strategic choices for management. The strategic-choice view and strategic-contingency approach open room for strategic choice, for there is no one best way. However, they also open several ways of managing change successfully. This range of possibilities implies that environmental forces are not seen only as the sole determining factor of organizational structures and behavior but also as a dependent variable that can be influenced by organizational strategies under certain circumstances. In order to develop strategic advantages, management has to analyze contingencies and design strategies on the basis of the organization's strengths and weaknesses (e.g. Porter 1985).

Beyond these basic theoretical perspectives of adaptation, evolution, selection, contingency, and strategic-choice view, organizational change is also conceptualized in connection with models of organizational change and maturation. In this regard, an analogy is drawn between organizational change and biological concepts, with the firm's development being seen as a continuum of maturation stages extending from the founding phase to the firm's death. Because these shifts are associated primarily with severe problems or even symptoms of crisis in organizations, management's task is primarily to support the transition from one phase to the next (Greiner 1972; Lievegoed 1974; Mintzberg 1979; Quinn and Cameron 1983).

Numerous models of intended organizational change do not explicitly relate to organizational theory. Based on early research on resistance to change (Lewin 1947) and on the development of survey-feedback methods (Likert 1961; Mann 1961), concepts of planned organizational development include many practices of organizational development and methods of systemic intervention such as survey feedback, T-groups, grid development, and team-development and paradox intervention (e.g. Blake and Mouton 1969, 1985; French and Bell 1973; Selvini Palazzoli et al. 1988; Schein 1969).

Lastly, organizational change is dealt with in a growing number of organizational learning concepts in which organizations are neither victims of natural selection nor solely dependent variables of determining environmental forces. Rather, organizations are conceived of as active learning institutions that can develop according to goals and intentions of their founders and members and that also learn to move beyond these original goals. Similarly, as the basic differentiation between individual stimulus–response learning (operant conditioning and classic conditioning) and intentional cognitive learning, the organizational learning approach allows one to regard learning not merely as adaptation to contingencies but also as learning through insight, understanding, and interpretation.

In summary, the different approaches to organizational learning are rooted in a wide variety of theoretical foundations. Thus far, there is no theoretical platform that can serve as a common basis for further development of the concept.

Perspectives on Organizational Learning in Management Literature

Since Cyert and March (1963) first spoke of 'organizational learning' and especially since Argyris and Schön's *Organizational Learning: A Theory of Action Perspective* (1978), the concept has been used in different ways in different disciplinary traditions. The amount of literature that has appeared on the subject in the past two decades is overwhelming. The scope and the heterogeneity of the contributions obviously make it necessary to describe the concept of organizational learning from different perspectives. What are the relevant perspectives on organizational learning? What are the core assumptions that can be traced in the literature in order to derive a conceptual framework for the management of organizational learning?

Most scholars confronted with the literature on organizational learning have major problems in organizing, systematizing, and grouping the array of contributions. Not much has changed since Fiol and Lyles (1985) argued that a

systematic assessment of the strategic management literature suggests an interesting dilemma: Although there exists widespread acceptance of the notion of organizational learning and its importance to strategic performance, no theory or model of organizational learning is widely accepted. Major research . . . along with more modest efforts provide the basis for initial attempts to define, to develop, and to differentiate organizational learning and its components. Each has approached the subject from different perspectives, leading to more divergence. (p. 803)

Indeed, the divergence of perspectives has increased, and so far no single analytical or conceptual model serves as a framework for research by scholars of organizational learning. It is difficult to judge whether new contributions should be valued as increases in knowledge about organizational learning or whether they just add to the growing diversity that characterizes the joint process of constructing complex reality in the mental models of organization researchers.

Maybe the answer to this question reflects two paradigms of research, one focused on adding knowledge through analysis and empirical inquiry and, it is to be hoped, on gradually eliminating false assumptions, and another that adds interpretations and thereby continues the aspiration for a joint construction of meaning over time. Whatever the result may be, the current growth of literature on organizational learning coincides with a sense of ambiguity, lack of consensus (Barnett 1998), and even growing confusion (Edmondson and Moingeon 1998; Tsang 1997; Wahren 1996; Wiegand 1996). Attempts at integrative theorizing are the exception.

Shrivastava (1983) was the first researcher to differentiate four distinct and contrasting perspectives on organizational learning systematically. Referring to the decision-making approach by Cyert and March (1963), he labeled one line of thinking 'adaptive learning' (p. 10) (Cangelosi and Dill 1965; March and Olsen

1976). Citing Argyris and Schön (1978), he described a second perspective on organizational learning as 'assumption sharing' (p. 9). Both concepts are rooted in sociological theories of knowledge (e.g. Berger and Luckmann 1966). A third perspective on organizational learning was referred to by Shrivastava as 'development of the knowledge base' (p. 10), with the emphasis being on the development of knowledge about action–outcome relationships relevant to organizational activities as elaborated in Duncan and Weiss (1979). The fourth perspective labeled by Shrivastava was what he called 'institutionalized experience effects' (p. 10). It covers the approaches to institutionalized experiences on learning curves (Abernathy and Wayne 1974).

Wiegand (1996) referred to seven theoretical perspectives on organizational learning, all based on the historical development of the contributions as well as on their conceptual distinctions. First, the pioneer approach by James March is presented in relation to different stages of development in his works (Cyert and March 1963; Levitt and March 1988; March and Olson 1975). The second line of thinking is linked to Chris Argyris, who focused primarily on the individual as the acting agent of the organization. In this theoretical perspective, too, a number of phases are distinguishable. Argyris started with the question of 'integrating the individual and the organization' (1964). In a second phase of thought on organizational learning, Argyris and Schön (1978) explored the promotion of organizational learning through interventions. It was at that time that they presented the main body of their work on theories-in-action.[1] A third phase of work on

[1] 'Organizational learning occurs when individuals within an organization experience a problematic situation and inquire into it on the organization's behalf. They experience a surprising mismatch between expected and actual results of action and respond to that mismatch through a process of thought and further action that leads them to modify their images of organization or their understanding of organizational phenomena and to restructure their activities so as to bring outcomes and expectations into line, thereby changing organizational theory-in-use. In order to become organizational, the learning that results from organizational inquiry must become embedded in the images of organization held in its members' minds and/or

organizational learning is associated with the facilitation of organizational learning through the circumvention of organizational defenses (Argyris 1990) and through a promotion of higher-order learning and Model II theory-in-use (Argyris and Schön 1996).

Drawing on these two basic theoretical foundations by March and Argyris, Wiegand described a third perspective on organizational learning: knowledge-based approaches. Among the concepts it incorporates are those by Duncan and Weiss (1979), Huber (1991), Imai, Nonaka, and Takeuchi (1985), Pautzke (1989), Pawlowsky (1992, 1994), and Walsh and Ungson (1991). Although most approaches to organizational learning somehow relate to knowledge as the starting and end point of learning, the contributions clustered in this third perspective focus on different types of knowledge and organizational processes connected with knowledge creation and diffusion. The fourth of the seven perspectives identified by Wiegand (1996) is what he called 'eclectic approaches' (p. 154), referring to Senge (1990b) and Hedberg (1981), both of whom bring a variety of theoretical elements into their respective approaches. Whereas Senge's approach originated in a research project initiated by the Massachusetts Institute of Technology and large U.S. corporations in order to develop systems thinking as a way of fostering organizational learning, Hedberg (1981) conceptualized organizations as cognitive systems that are developed by individual perceptions and interpretations.

A fifth perspective described by Wiegand (1996) consists of integrative approaches to organizational learning. Common to these approaches is the reference to a wide spectrum of organizational learning literature characterized by theoretical integration. This body of work subsumes Bomke, Kreuter, and Stegmüller (1993); Dodgson (1993); Fiol and Lyles (1985); and Shrivastava (1983). A sixth group of publications deals with systemic thinking and systems theory (Klimecki, Probst, and Eberl 1991; Reinhardt 1993; Schreyögg and Noss 1995). Lastly,

in the epistemological artifacts (the maps, memories, and programs) embedded in the organizational environment' (Argyris and Schön 1996: 16).

Wiegand (1996) pointed to an 'individualistic-normative' (p. 154) perspective consisting of approaches in the tradition of organizational development (e.g. Garratt 1990; Pedler, Burgoyne, and Boydell 1991).

Edmondson and Moingeon (1998) presented a framework with which to organize the diverse scholarly contributions into 'meaningful categories' (p. 6). They distinguished between four approaches:

1. Residues: Organizations as residues of past learning. The theme is that lessons of the past are embodied in current routines (e.g. Cyert and March 1963; Nelson and Winter 1982).

2. Communities: Organizations as collections of individuals who can learn and develop. This research is mainly descriptive (e.g. Brown and Duguid 1991; Pedler, Burgoyne, and Boysell 1991; Stata 1989).

3. Participation: Organizational improvement through intelligent activity of individuals. Authors of this work view organizational learning as an outgrowth of policies that engage individuals in contributing to the organization (e.g. Hayes, Wheelwright, and Clark 1988).

4. Accountability: organizational improvement through development of individuals' mental models. According to this approach, effectiveness depends on properties of individual cognition (e.g. Argyris and Schön 1974; Brown and Duguid 1991; Senge 1990b).

These distinctions between organizational learning approaches may be of help in understanding the basic assumptions of organizational learning, but only to the extent that they use the same analytical dimensions in defining theoretical clusters. With the exception of Shrivastava's (1983) typology, the perspectives presented above either consist of different analytical dimensions, such as the chronological development of a theory (e.g. pioneer approaches), or have the author as the main anchor of a perspective. Furthermore, there are different content dimensions, such as integration or eclecticism, as criteria for distinguishing between the approaches. In order to demarcate theoretical perspectives on organizational learning, it might prove useful to apply a consistent analytical approach. One could, namely, organize the key contributions to organizational learning according to theoretical traditions. A review of the literature to date suggests five clusters of theories: (a) the perspective of organizational decision-making and adaptation, (b) the systems-theory perspective, (c) the cognitive perspective, and the knowledge perspective, (d) the cultural perspective, and (e) the action-learning perspective. By examining each in turn, one can extract core assumptions for the management of organizational learning.

Obviously, the different perspectives are not mutually exclusive, for most approaches have a number of different views and theoretical bases. Over time, authors such as March and Argyris have changed their ideas about organizational learning and have added new aspects. The line between the frameworks, such as that between the adaptive learning approach and the cognitive and epistemological approaches, are blurred. Nevertheless, most approaches seem to be centered on clearly distinguishable theoretical assumptions that make it possible to define genuine qualitative clusters.

The Perspective of Organizational Decision-making and Adaptation

The early work of Cyert and March (1963) revolved around a stimulus–response (S–R) behavioral approach to learning and was based on a contemporary conceptualization of decision-making processes in organizations. Looking at March and Simon (1958), one sees that their understanding of the learning process and their postulates about human organism were rooted in Tolman's (1932) goal-directed behaviorism. Although the human organism is considered a complex information-processing system, human memory is seen to include 'all sorts of partial and modified records of past experiences and programs for responding to environmental stimuli' (March and Simon 1958: 10). The internal states are divided into evoked and unevoked parts. External stimuli are triggers to evoke certain parts of the memory.

When one of these elements is evoked by a stimulus, it may also bring into the evoked set a number of other elements with which it has become associated through the learning process. Thus if a particular goal has been achieved on previous occasions by execution of a particular course of action, then evocation of that goal will be likely to evoke that course of action again. (p. 10)

In March and Simon's understanding of organizational learning, this mechanistic stimulus–response (S–R) conception of the learning process is transferred to organizational learning, whereas the individual concept of memory is exchanged by standard operating procedures at the organizational level. Cyert and March (1963) were the first scholars to conceive of organizational learning as a concept located at the organizational level:

Organizations learn: to assume that organizations go through the same processes of learning as do individual human beings seems unnecessarily naive, but organizations exhibit (as do other social institutions) adaptive behavior over time. Just as adaptations at the individual level depend upon phenomena of the human physiology, organizational adaptation uses individual members of the organization as instruments. However, we believe it is possible to deal with adaptation at the aggregate level of the organization, in the same sense and for the same reasons that it is possible to deal with the concept of organizational decision making. (p. 123)

In Cyert and March's (1963) understanding, organizational learning is triggered by external shocks. An uncontrollable external source of disturbance or shock to the system makes adaptation necessary (p. 99). The organization has a number of internal decision-making variables and decision-making rules. Each combination of external shocks and decision variables in the system changes the state of the system. Organizations learn by memorizing disturbances and reaction combinations according to decision variables. Standard operating procedures are referred to as the memory of the organization. By learning new combinations of external disturbances and internal decision-making rules, the organization increases its adaptability to differing environmental states. Any decision rule that leads to a nonpreferred state at one point is less likely to be used in the future. Just as the probability of a specific individual behavior decreases with the expectation of negative outcomes in behavioral learning theory, 'organizations exhibit . . . adaptive behavior over time' (p. 123). 'We argue . . . that a business organization is an adaptive institution. In short, the firm learns from its experience' (p. 100). This concept of organizational learning is based on a perception of adaptive learning that can result in uncertainty avoidance, problemistic search (search that is motivated by a problem and is directed toward finding a solution to that problem), and organizational learning (adaptation of goals, adaptation in attention rules, and adaptation in search rules) (p. 126). The outcome of organizational learning is an adaptation or change of organizational rules and standard operating procedures. Organizational learning does not depend on an increase of knowledge of its members. Rather, it is seen as organizational memorization of S–R combinations. Learning, therefore, is regarded as reactive adaptation in line with S–R learning principles; there is no cognitive or knowledge-related learning.

Unlike Cyert and March (1963), March and Olson (1976) associated organizational learning primarily with 'organizational intelligence' (p. 55) and cognitive processes. To them, organizational learning was clearly conceptualized as experiential learning based on 'cognitions and preferences', 'models of the world', ideas, beliefs, and attitudes that members of the organization hold (March and Olson 1976: 338). Individual capabilities of correctly interpreting environmental ambiguity, which rely on cognitive processes and their limitations, are of central importance to organizational learning in March and Olson's model. In comparison to the mechanistic S–R learning model by Cyert and March (1963), March and Olson (1976) extended the concept of organizational learning to include social psychological factors and cognitive structures as important elements. The incomplete learning cycle takes into account not only the individual psychological 'pre-

existing structure of related values and cognitions' (1976: 60) but also social psychological aspects such as role constraints.

Levitt and March (1988) developed the concept of organizational learning still further. In their approach 'organizations are seen as learning by encoding inferences from history into routines that guide behavior. The generic term "routines" includes the forms, rules, procedures, conventions, strategies, and technology around which organizations are constructed and through which they operate' (p. 320). Levitt and March explicitly added: 'It also includes the structure of beliefs, frameworks, paradigms, codes, cultures, and knowledge that buttress, elaborate, and contradict the formal routines' (p. 320). These routines are considered independent of the individual actors, and they are capable of surviving considerable turnover in organizational actors. These routines are more than standard operating procedures (Cyert and March 1963); they open the way to conceptualizing collective bases of organizational knowledge that are the result of learning from direct experience; learning from interpretations such as stories, paradigms, frames of reference, and culture; and learning from the experience of others.

It is clear that March's understanding of organizational learning has changed considerably from the early mechanistic concept of standard operating procedures. It moved to the intermediate notion of a learning cycle that includes subjective interpretations of reality and gives the individual in organizations an important function in shaping the organizational learning process and, subsequently, to Levitt and March's (1988) concept of routines, which went one step further by including a broad range of organizational knowledge bases that are seen as a result of different individual learning histories.

The Systems-theory Perspective[2]

By defining organizations as systems of 'consciously coordinated activities or forces of two

[2] Systems theoretical- and epistemological approaches can be distinguished by the notion of first-versus

or more persons', Barnard (1956: 75) was presumably the first to root management thinking in a systems perspective. The systems approach has a long tradition and has ramified considerably. Bertalanffy (1951) developed the principles of a general systems theory as a means of linking different disciplines. It is the basis for a number of approaches that conceptualize organizations as open systems that are confronted with environmental pressure to which they somehow must adapt.

With respect to organizational learning, at least three distinctive approaches have developed. First, the traditional approaches to a system-based management perspective and to system–environment relations can be identified. Kast and Rosenzweig (1970), among others, rested their organization and management approach on a systems view. They used the systems perspective as an analogy rather than in a strictly theoretical way. With the development of an early systems perspective, organizational environments were perceived as exerting pressure on organizations, pressures that management had to deal with. For example, Ashby's (1956) 'law of requisite variety' implies that 'only variety can destroy variety' (p. 207). Organizations that have to cope with environmental complexity have to generate structures that can deal with complexity. Thus, a complex environment needs a complex 'inside' of organizational structures. This perception of organizations as open systems in the context of a general-systems view was further developed by other scholars. Katz and Kahn (1978), for example, stated that 'The organization lives only by being open to inputs, but selectively, its continuing existence requires both the property of openness and

selectivity' (p. 31; see also Emery 1969; Emery and Trist 1965).

Second, there are concepts based on the assumptions of self-organization processes.[3] These concepts take self-referentiality into account as basic processes to deal with in organizations (e.g. Beer 1972, 1979; von Foerster 1985; Malik 1987, 1992; Probst 1987; Reinhardt 1993; Steinmann and Schreyögg 1993; Ulrich 1984; Willke 1987a, b, 1998). Organizational learning is conceived of as problem-solving potential of social systems that are derived from institutional learning (Klimecki, Probst, and Eberl 1991). According to the authors adopting this perspective, institutions have to build organizational slack in order for self-referential processes to take place and thereby raise the organization's level of development. Management is advised to allow autonomous developments in systems and to design structural preconditions in organizations that promote such self-referential processes.

Third, there is the systems-dynamics approach, which originates in population analysis. It was developed by Forrester (1961) and others. The concept plays an important role in both Senge's (1990a, b) approach to organizational learning and in the St. Gallen school's view on organizational development (Gomez 1981; Klimecki, Probst, and Eberl 1991; Morecroft 1988; Senge, Kleiner, Roberts, Ross, and Smith 1994; Ulrich and Probst 1984, 1990; Vester 1991). The assumption underlying the systems-dynamics approach is that once one has reduced the complexity of a network system by analyzing the features of all relevant factors and their dynamic relations over time, this knowledge can be used to understand the functioning of complex systems networks and to intervene accordingly. All outputs of systems are seen as input to other systems, so learning means understanding the complex relations of social systems and their dynamics. In this

second-order cybernetics: First-order cybernetics is based on the assumption that systems do exist as an ontological reality and therefore can be identified and improved by tools on the basis of prescriptions. Second-order cybernetics, or autopoietic systems theory, refers to the idea that systems are mental constructions (von Foerster 1985; see also Luhmann 1984; Maturana and Varela 1987). Hence, changing systems first must take into account the role of the observer explicitly, a prerequisite that means, for example, that different stakeholders have, or must have, different goals because of their observer positions and interpretation modes.

[3] In order to avoid misunderstandings, one must distinguish between self-organizational and autopoietic, or epistemological, approaches: Self-organization is an element of autopoiesis but not vice versa. Autopoiesis implies self-creation *and* self-maintaining on the basis of self-organizing processes. The notion 'self-organization' lacks the aspect of self-maintaining (e.g. Heijl 1982).

approach, looking at one system level, say, the organization, also implies defining the elements of this system at a lower level—groups or individuals—and describing the larger system into which the system of interest is integrated. This methodological procedure is based on both an analysis and synthesis: One is to look at the elements of a system (analysis), aggregate to the next system level through synthesis, and describe the learning relations accordingly.[4] Basically the systems-dynamics perspective is derived from a cybernetic concept of single-loop learning, for the model builds on feedback loops and the idea of stabilizing systemic structures by balancing loops. Because Senge's (1990b) propositions about systems archetypes (p. 378) are based on assumptions resulting from reflection about higher-order rules, they can perhaps be interpreted in terms of Bateson's (1972/1992) Type II or Type III learning. Senge (1990b: 57) saw systems thinking as the essential fifth discipline[5] for organizational learning. As reiterated in Senge and Sterman (1992), 'organizational learning processes are most effective when they help managers develop a more systemic and dynamic perspective' (p. 354).

The Cognitive Perspective and the Knowledge Perspective

The cognitive perspective on organizational learning is based on the early works about decision-making processes in organizations, but it has developed far beyond the concepts of bounded rationality in terms of its ability to integrate the value and belief perspective. In this view of organizational learning, cognitive systems are the basic concepts applied at the individual and collective levels. There is only a

gradual transition between Levitt and March's (1988) 'routines' (p. 320) and cognitive conceptions of organizational learning. Basically the cognitive perspective centers on the assumption 'that all deliberate action had a cognitive basis, that it reflected norms, strategies, and assumptions or models of the world which had claims to general validity. . . . Human action and human learning could be placed in the larger context of knowing' (Argyris and Schön 1978: 10). Essential to the cognitive notion is the conscious character of learning. Members of organizations are not merely a storage bin of past rational experiences but interpreters of reality according to the specificities of their cognitive system.

The cognitive and knowledge perspectives of organizational learning also include a variety of clusters, each of which emphasizes different aspects. First, there are two cognitive approaches that have received a considerable amount of interest: (a) structural approaches also called 'representationism' (von Krogh and Roos 1996), which focus on information-processing abilities, depending on the structural characteristics of the cognitive system (Axelrod 1976; Bartlett 1964; Dörner, Kreuzig, Reither, and Stäudel 1983; Dörner 1989; Huber 1991; Rumelhart 1984; Scholl, Hoffmann, and Gierschner 1993; Schroder, Driver, and Streufert 1975; Streufert and Streufert 1978; Streufert and Swezey 1986), and (b) corporate epistemology (von Krogh, Roos, and Slocum 1996: 157), in which the interpretation process and the cognitive construction of reality is regarded as the central issue of importance in learning (Daft and Weick 1984; Reinhardt 1993; Sims and Gioia 1986; Smircich 1983; Smircich and Stubbart 1985; von Krogh and Roos 1996; Weick and Bougon 1986). I now examine these two approaches in more detail.

The assumption that both learning and decision-making depend on the structure of the knowledge system is not new to psychological thought. Much of cognitive psychological research has shown that the capacity of human information-processing depends on the characteristics of individual cognitive structures (the individual knowledge system) or stages of

---

[4] The idea that a lower system level also constitutes an element of a higher system level indicates the necessity of differentiating between first- and second-order cybernetics. The 'element relation' makes sense only within an ontological interpretation of systems (first-order cybernetics).

[5] The other four disciplines, according to Senge (1990b), are (a) personal mastery, (b) management of mental models, (c) development of shared visions, and (d) team learning.

moral development. Research on the dynamics of organizational social cognition also suggests the applicability of the cognitive construct idea to the organizational and group levels (e.g. Streufert and Swezey 1986). 'Organizational mind' and 'collective cause' maps are two approaches to organizational knowledge systems (see Table 3.1). In this perspective, organizational learning can be considered a modification in the organizational knowledge system that enables organizations to improve their understanding and evaluation of the internal and external environments. As Fiol and Lyles (1985) argued: 'Learning enables organizations to build an organizational understanding and interpretation of their environment. . . . [I]t results in associations, cognitive systems, and memories that are developed and shared by members of the organization' (p. 804). Thus, knowledge systems are both antecedents and results of organizational learning processes. If this duality really exists, then characteristics of organizational knowledge systems can be thought of as determinants of the organizational learning process, and one can observe the results of learning processes by looking at the characteristics of knowledge systems. In the literature on organizational learning, a number

Table 3.1. Organizational knowledge concepts

Author	Concept
Boulding (1956)	Image
Wilensky (1967)	Organizational intelligence
Argyris and Schön (1978)	Organizational theories-in-action
Tushman and Nadler (1978)	Information-processing system
Duncan and Weiss (1979)	Knowledge about the relationship between specific actions and outcomes
Starbuck (1982)	Logically integrated clusters of belief
Daft and Weick (1984)	Organizational interpretation systems
Hall (1984)	Organization's cause map
Shrivastava and Schneider (1984)	Organizational frames of reference
Salancik and Porac (1986)	Distilled ideologies
Sims and Gioia (1986)	Organizational schemata
Weick and Bougon (1986)	Collective 'cause maps'
Sandelands and Stablein (1987)	Organization mind
Lundberg (1989)	Operational cause map
Pautzke (1989)	Organizational knowledge base
Senge (1990b)	Shared mental models
Klimecki, Probst, and Eberl (1991)	Joint construction of reality
Lyles and Schwenk (1992)	Organizational knowledge structures and shared belief structures
Baitsch (1993)	Local theory
Nonaka and Takeuchi (1995)	Organizational knowledge-base layer

Source: See List of References for the authors cited.

of concepts of organizational knowledge systems can be identified.

There is a considerable amount of work on human information-processing and complexity theory to build on. This line of research is associated with Bieri (1968); Schroder, Driver, and Streufert (1975); and Scott (1969) and has been developed considerably in the complexity theory by Streufert and Streufert (1978). In keeping with Lewin's, Heider's, and Scott's thinking, the assumptions of complexity theory are basically that cognitive structures can be analyzed according to content and structure. The Streuferts and others have concentrated only on the structural aspects, that is, with the notion that complexity is concerned with how people think, not what they think. Structures of individual knowledge systems are defined in terms of dimensions of differentiation (dimensionality in the cognitive semantic space) and integration (the flexible relationships among various dimensions with regard to specific stimulation). Practically, individual differences have a significant impact on managers' cognitive styles (which relate to the structure of their knowledge systems) and hence on executive performance (Streufert, Pogash, and Piasecki 1988). This research seems to offer interesting ways of accessing individual knowledge systems, which are measurable and which have prognostic validity for business success. Moreover, research has effectively utilized simulation procedures—Strategic Management Simulation (SMS)—with decision-making processes in groups (Streufert, Pogash, and Piasecki 1988). The concept may be used to assess teams of decision-makers who must, for example, cope with complex, uncertain, and fluid task environments. This theoretical perspective affords at least partial access to the quality of a knowledge system at the group level and allows one to evaluate efficient learning in teams. Organizational learning in this context implies distinguishing between structural characteristics of collective knowledge systems, in other words, groups learn to evaluate and discuss in a more differentiated and integrated way than in the past if they have a number of ways of interpreting and reflecting on topics or of observing

processes from different angles. By the same token, a more differentiated and integrated collective knowledge system is necessary before a team can acquire a differentiated perception and experience effective learning.

With regard to corporate epistemology, the emphasis is on the question of how organizations develop knowledge. Essentially, these approaches do not define knowledge as an 'objective' mental reflection of reality but rather as a coexisting and conflicting interpretation of reality that is based on the history of each participating member of a joint knowledge system. Weick (1969) coined the phrase 'enacted environment' (p. 64), meaning that 'the human *creates* the environment to which the system then adapts. The human actor does not *re*act to an environment, he *en*acts it' (Weick 1969: 64). Subjective construction of meaning is developed on the basis of symbols and language (von Krogh, Roos, and Slocum 1996: 157). Organizational reality thus is constructed by interaction between members of the organization who are developing a joint interpretation. Drawing on Maturana and Varela (1987), von Krogh, Roos, and Slocum (1996), like Reinhardt (1993), built a bridge between the cognitive-rooted approach and autopoiesis theory. To Maturana and Varela, knowledge is a result of the self-productive (autopoietic) process and is embodied in the individual (pp. 163–4). This 'private' knowledge can be conveyed to organizational knowledge through interactions: 'Knowledge of the organization is shared knowledge among organizational members' (von Krogh, Roos, and Slocum 1996: 166; see also Weick 1969: 33, 'double interact'). Therefore, the epistemological perspective suggests cooperative experimentation and interactive methods, especially language games as means of promoting knowledge development and hence organizational learning (Vicari, von Krogh, Roos, and Mahnke 1996; von Krogh, Roos, and Yip 1996).

The second major theoretical cluster in the cognitive and knowledge perspective consists of approaches to organizational learning that center around (a) core competencies and (b) knowledge creation and development processes. Certainly, the previously mentioned aspects play a role in this cluster, too, but the main focus is on other aspects. The basic assumption of the core-competence approach is that an organization's competitive advantage depends on the knowledge and skills it possesses in a distinct area. Core capabilities in organizations are seen as the 'wellsprings' of organizational learning processes (Leonard-Barton 1995). This line of thinking is influenced by the traditional approach to the diffusion of innovations (Rogers 1983), for the central question is about the identification, development, and diffusion of core competencies in organizations (e.g. Grundy 1994; Hamel and Prahalad 1994; Jelinek 1979; Jelinek and Schoonhoven 1990; Leonard-Barton 1995; Lullies, Bollinger, and Weltz 1993; Prahalad and Hamel 1990; Wikström and Normann 1994). The main emphasis is on discovering both the core rigidities and the core capabilities that are considered 'interlocked *systems* of knowledge bases and flows' (Leonard-Barton 1995: xiv). In order to promote organizational learning, different activities such as integrated problem-solving across different cognitive and functional barriers, implementation of new methodologies, experimentation, and importation of know-how are suggested (Leonard-Barton 1995: xv).

The second line of thinking, the knowledge-development and creation approaches, are closely related to epistemological concepts of organizational learning and build on Polanyi's understanding of explicit and implicit knowledge in organizations (Polanyi 1966). Explicit knowledge is understood to be insights that can be articulated and transferred by language. Implicit, or tacit, knowledge is based on individual experience and cannot be transferred and articulated by language. Knowledge development is described as an interactive process between these two types of knowledge at different levels of the organization. The crucial question of knowledge creation lies in mobilizing the tacit knowledge in organizations and transferring it to the organizational and group levels so that collective system levels can learn (see the SECI-Model presented in Nonaka, Toyama, and Byosière, Ch. 22 in this volume). In other

words, individual knowledge and experience, which often are implicit, have to be articulated and experienced by other members of the organization. Using a phase model, one can derive a number of tools and methods that facilitate the necessary transfer of knowledge and promote the creation of knowledge. From this perspective one can also discuss and analyze intercultural differences in typical knowledge management styles and emphasize the distinction between the Japanese approach to knowledge, which stresses the awareness of tacit knowledge in organizations (Nonaka 1988, 1991; Nonaka and Konno 1998; Nonaka and Takeuchi 1995; Pautzke 1989), and Western management styles that rely mainly on explicit knowledge.

The Cultural Perspective

The cultural perspective has its roots in an interpretative approach to human behavior and builds on the notion that members of organizations create a set of intersubjective meanings (construction of reality) that can be assessed by artifacts such as symbols, metaphors, ceremonies, and myths and that are tied together by values, beliefs, and emotions. The scholars who have focused on the culture concept view organizational learning as a change in defensive routines within organizations, as the development of an organizational learning culture, or as both (e.g. Argyris 1990; Cook and Yanow 1993; Dierkes 1988, 1992; Frost, Moore, Louis, Lundberg, and Martin 1991; Hawkins 1991; Klimecki, Probst, and Eberl 1991; Mitroff and Kilmann 1976; Sackmann 1991; Schein 1984, 1991). 'At the simplest conceptual level . . . we can say that culture is the shared common learning output' (Schein 1991: 247). Cook and Yanow (1993) described the distinctive way in which organizational learning is viewed in the culture approach: 'Our intention . . . is to outline a "cultural perspective" on organizational learning. . . . We see this perspective as a complement to, not a substitute for, the cognitive perspective' (p. 374). They argued that the cognitive perspective focuses only on the individual level, whereas the cultural perspective can capture learning at a collective level. Organizational learning is therefore seen as a process 'when a group acquires the know-how which enables it to carry out its collective activities' (p. 379). This perspective is closely linked to the epistemological approaches, as Cook and Yanow make clear by defining culture as the 'set of values, beliefs, and feelings, together with the artifacts of their expression and transmission (such as myths, symbols, metaphors, rituals) that are created, inherited, shared, and transmitted within one group of people and that, in part, distinguish that group from others' (p. 379). Culture and joint construction of reality are basically the common core.

Several contributions have built on the cultural dimension, helping bridge the gap between individual and collective concepts of learning. Sackmann's (1991) concept of 'cultural knowledge in organizations', for example, is based on the assumption 'that culture can be conceptualized as the collective construction of social reality' (p. 33). Sackmann (pp. 34–9) distinguished between four classes of cultural knowledge, which additionally are divided up into several categories. Class 1 is dictionary knowledge, which describes organizational reality (e.g. the strategy of a firm) that members of a given cultural setting consider relevant with that setting. The descriptive dictionary knowledge can be elicited by 'what?' questions. Class 2 cultural knowledge is directory knowledge and represents commonly held theories of action, which contain causal-analytical attributions. The directory knowledge can be elicited by 'how?' questions. Class 3 is recipe knowledge, which consists of normative prescriptions or causal-normative attributions. Recipe knowledge can be elicited by 'what-should-be?' questions. Class 4 cultural knowledge is axiomatic knowledge—causes, assumptions, and beliefs. Axiomatic knowledge can be elicited by 'why-are-things-done-the-way-they-are?' questions.

This approach makes it possible to link cultural changes to the process of organizational learning: Dictionary knowledge is closely related to functional domains, the implications being that changing dictionary knowledge occurs, say, through changes in incentive and reward systems. Making changes in directory knowledge can be interpreted as an organization-wide learning process, which is driven in part by the change of organizational control mechanisms. A change in recipe knowledge can be triggered by the degree of autonomy that exists within the organization and by selection procedures. A change in axiomatic knowledge is closely related to the learning of top management teams (e.g. by the sharing of beliefs within those groups).

Argyris (1990) impressively explained that organizational defense mechanisms against learning processes reside at a cultural and emotional level of the organization. He distinguished between two types of cultures in organizations: Model I Theory-in-Use and Model II Theory-in-Use. 'Model I Theory-in-use instructs individuals to seek to be in unilateral control, to win, and not to upset people' (p. 13). 'Model I theory-in-use is designed to produce defensive consequences and therefore requires defensive reasoning' (p. 23). 'Model II is the new theory-in-use. The governing values of Model II Theory-in-use are valid information, informed choice, and responsibility to monitor how well the choice is implemented' (p. 104). The predominant values in the context of Model I (to have control, to win and not to lose, to avoid negative feelings), lead to defensive routines in organizations: 'For example, whenever human beings are faced with any issue that contains significant embarrassment or threat, they act in ways that bypass, as best they can, the embarrassment or threat. In order for the bypass to work, it must be covered up. The basic strategy involves bypass and cover-up' (Argyris 1990: 25). Organizational learning as cultural change thus also implies affective and emotional aspects of common culture (see Scherer and Tran, Ch. 16 in this volume). Therefore, knowledge systems in organizations cannot be seen only as joint constructions of reality; they are also general constructions of meaning with affective connotations. If one regards this cultural perspective as the affective component of collective knowledge systems, a broad variety of approaches that are closely linked to the cognitive perspective outlined above opens up under the generic term 'management of meaning' (cf. Gioia 1986a, b; Gray, Bougon, and Donnellon 1985; Pondy, Frost, and Morgan 1983; Schein 1991; Smircich 1983; Smircich and Stubbart 1985).

The Action-learning Perspective

The action-learning perspective derives its assumptions from several traditions. Essential to action learning is the idea that learning occurs through acting. The basic notion is that the understanding of content is enhanced through a reflection process that follows action. Pure cognitive learning may be memorized, but it does not allow for understanding. Reflection on one's own experiences is necessary for action-relevant learning. The action-learning approach is quite heterogeneous, consisting of theoretical and conceptual models such as Kolb's (1976, 1984) learning circle as well as the practical action-behavior orientation that can be found in Revans (1980), who applied action learning to different learning situations since the 1950s, and in the approach of Pedler et al. (1991) approach to organizational learning practices. In these approaches behaviorally oriented intervention was conceptualized as the starting point for learning processes in a theoretical framework of experiential learning (Argyris and Schön 1978; Dewey 1910; Forslin and Thulestedt 1993; Inglis 1994; Kolb 1976, 1984; Pedler 1997; Revans 1982).

According to Revans (1982), learning occurs from experience, the basic idea being that a person has an experience and then thinks and reflects on this experience by relating it to former experiences. As Inglis (1994) explained, 'We continue to think about the experience, but now we are making generalizations and fitting the results into our personal view of reality. And finally we test our conclusions by using a modified approach the next time a similar set of circumstances arises' (p. 14). Similarly, the necessity of organizational adaptation to changing environments is regarded as the trigger to learning. Following Revans (1982), one can express the learning process as $L = P + Q$ (where L

stands for learning; P for programmed knowledge; and Q for the ability to pose questions) (Inglis 1994: 8). Inglis (1994) extended the formula to $L = P + Q + I$, where I is implementation. 'Action learning requires action to be taken, not merely recommended' (p. 9).

Practically speaking, action learning, with its roots in the British sociotechnical tradition, is a popular approach in leadership and management development programs. Its main advantage is learning based on experience and the simultaneous processes of learning and congruent change in the client system. It also offers a flexible and meaningful learning situation for the individual and provides support in problem-solving. Action learning is also viable, however, for collective, experiential learning. In terms of higher-order (double-loop) learning, an action-learning set (a group of participants who work on forming shared knowledge) is a powerful instrument. Experiences are shared, analysis is enhanced, and new concepts are gradually developed and understood in order to meet the needs of the group. The learning and problem-solving process is supported by the introduction of relevant external knowledge, and typically the process is managed by a facilitator. Learning sets can consist of members from the same organization or from separate cooperating organizations (e.g. in a network). The participation in a learning set is an experience that highlights the learning aspects of problem-solving, and the set develops an attitude toward what could be seen as a case of deutero-learning. That is, the set learns to learn.[6] Pedler (1997) suggested that action learning be given a constructionist interpretation that 'frees us from the limitations of individual action and learning' (p. 261). In the constructionist's eyes action learning helps to develop 'a shared process of meaning-making, helping to create frameworks of understanding within which to act' (p. 261). This conceptual extension allows the integration of an epistemological perspective, enabling one to see that organizational meaning and the action taken

---

[6] Thanks to Jan Forslin for his discussion and contribution on this perspective.

by organizational members are closely connected at the organizational level.

Management of Organizational Learning: A Conceptual Framework and Practical Suggestions

What implications do these perspectives have for the management of organizational learning? The assessment offered in literature on management science clearly reveals, first, distinct perspectives on organizational learning that differ with respect to certain basic assumptions, such as the assumption that organizations act rationally, that an organization and its environment are either objective reality or a subjective construction of reality, and that organizations emphasize certain aspects of organizational learning such as the cognitive, the cultural, or the action perspective. Second, besides these differences that result from distinctive theoretical traditions, these approaches to action learning have similarities, that reappear, albeit sometimes with other labels. In one way or another, all approaches to organizational learning refer to the problem of how to transfer learning from the individual level to a group or organizational level. Most approaches also distinguish between, say, simple adaptive learning and higher-order reflective learning. Third, the differences between cognitive, cultural, and action approaches are diminishing, for authors from all theoretical sides seem to be calling for an integration of cognitive, cultural, and action-related aspects into their approaches to organizational learning. In other words, basic building blocks for an integrative model of organizational learning are beginning to emerge. These development can not only help researchers define hypotheses that are open to empirical research and thus refine the understanding of organizational learning, they can also help managers and consultants identify relevant organizational factors that influ-

ence learning. A close look at the analytical edifice that is taking shape suggests that there are four integrative dimensions of organizational learning: (a) different system levels of learning (from individual to network); (b) different learning modes, such as cognitive, cultural, and action learning; (c) different learning types (single-loop, double-loop, deutero), and (d) different phases of a collective learning process (see also the discussion of boundary-transcending learning and new-ball-game learning by Drinkuth, Riegler, and Wolff, Ch. 20 in this volume).

System Levels

Organizational learning must be distinguished from individual learning. In most concepts of learning, learning is therefore defined for levels above that of the individual. The group, or team, level is of special interest as a gateway to organizational learning. Systems perspectives and knowledge-creation approaches in particular have pointed to the essential function of groups in this regard. As Senge (1990b) put it, 'Team learning is vital because teams, not individuals, are the fundamental learning unit in modern organizations. This is where "the rubber meets the road," unless teams can learn, the organization cannot learn' (p. 10). As Nonaka and Takeuchi (1995: 198) pointed out, however, awareness of the group's importance in organizational learning varies. Among Japanese managers the focus on groups is a traditional part of the Japanese culture, whereas Western managers usually deal with individuals.

Groups are not only the link between the individual and the organization but also the crucial intervening social system in which 'sharing' (Jelinek and Litterer 1994), learning, and organizational behavior take place. Groups are where the individual's view of the world is shared, mediated, and influenced. The early research on group dynamics (e.g. Bales 1950; Bion 1968; Cartwright and Zander 1968; Katzenbach and Smith 1993; Lewin 1947; Likert and Likert 1976; Weick 1969) provides much knowledge that can be revitalized for questions of organizational learning. Elaborating how research on groups can be transferred to problems of organizational learning, Wiegand (1996) has argued that groups play a central role in the emotional support of individual learning and that phases of group development can be reinterpreted as learning phases that promote learning and open new opportunities for interventions (see also the discussion about the learning networks tool in Pawlowsky, Forslin, and Reinhardt, Ch. 35 in this volume).

The next level, often conceptualized, is intraorganizational learning, where the main question is how the organization can learn as an entity. Rarely are there any attempts to define precisely what collective learning means at this level. And beyond the individual, the group, and the intraorganizational levels, the network or *inter*organizational level of learning has been the subject of much attention (Sydow 1992), particularly the issue of how external knowledge systems can be used to support learning. Basically, any conceptual framework for organizational learning theory should therefore incorporate at least four analytical levels of learning systems: individual learning, group or interpersonal learning, organizational or intraorganizational learning, and network, or interorganizational learning.

Learning Modes

As noted above, most current approaches to organizational learning are based on one or more of three orientations: the cognitive, the cultural, and the action-learning perspectives. They correspond to three existential stances on the human condition: knowing, feeling, and acting. 'Throughout the classical tradition, from Plato and Aristotle on, theorists repeatedly proposed the same three components of attitude under their latinized names of cognitive, affective, and conative' (McGuire 1968: 155). Rather than excluding one of these perspectives on organizational learning, and rather than harmonizing the differences between them, I assume that all three components—knowledge, feelings, and action—must be considered complementary if organ-izational learning is to be promoted. Management of learning makes it necessary to understand learning not only as a matter of cognitive learning but also of values, emotions, and behavior. Research in the field of social psychology indicates that the relation between these three components is likely to be an important aspect of attitude change. People in organizations not only have to understand or create new realities, they have to feel that it is right to adopt new hypotheses or views and that they are able to act accordingly. Neither the 'sharing' of tacit knowledge in groups nor the 'suspension' of assumptions[7] that is necessary for true dialogue has a chance if people are afraid to lose in such a process. Management of learning thus makes it necessary to establish, create, and nurture a culture of mutual trust (e.g. Bleicher 1995; Cohen 1998: 36; Luhmann 1989; Seifert and Pawlowsky 1998; Zand 1977).

Learning Types

The third dimension of organizational learning frequently found in the literature is based on Bateson's (1972/1992) three learning levels—Learning I ('proto-learning', p. 371), Learning II ('deutero-learning', p. 378), and Learning III ('Changes in the deutero process of learning', p. 389)—and Argyris and Schön's (1978) distinction between single-loop, double-loop, and deutero-learning. As shown in Table 3.2, other authors have developed similar learning typologies, which basically rest on the assumption that there are differences between learning as a conditioned response (in keeping with behavioristic learning theory) and learning as a result of reflection, insight, and maturation.

The common division of organizational learning into three prototypes of learning can be thought of as Type I, the correction of deviations ('idiosyncratic adaptation', Pawlowsky 1994). This type of learning consists in the

---

[7] 'To "suspend" one's assumptions means to hold them, as it were, "hanging in front of you," constantly accessible to questioning and observation. . . . This cannot be done if we are defending our opinions. Nor, can it be done if we are unaware of our assumptions' (Senge 1990b: 243).

Table 3.2. Examples of different types of organizational learning

Authors	Learning types		
	Type 1	Type 2	Type 3
Bateson (1972/1992)	Learning 0 and Learning I	Learning II	Learning III
Starbuck and Hedberg (1977)	First-order learning	Second-order learning	
Argyris and Schön (1978)	Single-loop learning	Double-loop learning	Deutero-learning
Hedberg (1981)	Adjustment learning	Turnover learning	Turnaround learning
Shrivastava (1983)	Adaptive learning	Assumption sharing	Development of knowledge base
Fiol and Lyles (1985)	Lower level learning	Higher level learning	
Morgan (1986)	Self-organization		Holographic learning
Lundberg (1989)	Learning as organizational change	Learning as organizational development	Learning as organizational transformation
Senge (1990b)	Adaptive learning		Generative learning
Garratt (1990)	Operational learning cycle	The policy learning cycle	The integrated learning cycle

Source: See List of References for the authors cited.

detection of performance gaps and their elimination in line with the standard operating procedures that have been defined. Type II organizational learning implies an adjustment to the environment. This learning prototype is based on the assumption that organizations have theories-in-use, interpretation systems, and frames of reference that guide and determine organizational behavior. If the organization's environmental feedback challenges the organization's assumptions, and if these assumptions are differentiated, redefined, or altered completely in order to fit the environmental demand, then one can say that learning of Type II has occurred. Type III is referred to as problem-solving learning ('learning to learn'). This kind of organizational learning requires collective reflection on governing rules and assumptions. Garratt (1990) described the necessary state as a 'helicopter view' (p. 127) and Senge (1990b) spoke of 'metanoia' (p. 13). Type III learning is a construction of higher-order

rules based on experiences and insight. According to Bateson (1972/1992), Learning III involves attainment of knowledge about the development and the meaning of habits (Learning II) and is only rarely possible for individuals because it occurs only in religious and spiritual experiences or in psychotherapy.

Managers should keep in mind that learning types differ and that a given learning type may be more appropriate under some circumstances than under others. Learning may well necessitate only simple adjustment in order for norms and standard operating procedures to be defined, but it may also require a profound reflection process if severe consequences are possible.

Phases of a Collective Learning Process

In most descriptions of organizational learning, a distinction is made between different phases of the process. Cyert and March (1963) differentiated between 'information taken into the firm'; 'the distribution of information inside the organization'; 'the condensing of input information'; and the output of information 'through orders to suppliers, deliveries to consumers, advertising, petitions for patents, and in many other ways' (1963: 107). Hedberg (1981) broke the organizational learning process down into four phases: perception of environmental stimuli, selection of stimuli, interpretation of stimuli, and reaction. Kolb's model (1976, 1984: 30), too, is made up of four phases: 'concrete experience', 'reflective observation', 'abstract conceptualization', and 'active experimentation'. Huber (1991) regarded the organizational learning process as consisting of knowledge acquisition, distribution, interpretation, and memorization. Similar process phases are also described by Lundberg (1989) and Nonaka (1992).

Basically, the process phases of learning are described in terms of four steps, which are not necessarily sequential:

(1) the identification of information that seems relevant to learning, to the creation (generation) of new knowledge, or both (e.g. Lundberg's 'puzzles' [1989: 65]; Nonaka's 'socialization' [1994: 14]);

(2) the exchange and diffusion of knowledge, either from the individual to the collective level or at the collective level itself (e.g. Duncan and Weiss's 'exchange' [1979: 79] and Huber's 'distribution' [1991: 89]);

(3) the integration of knowledge into existing knowledge systems at a collective level, an individual level, or both, or into procedural rules of the organization, whereby either integration or modification of the adopting system can take place[8] (Boulding's 'addition' [1956: 97]);

(4) the transformation of the new knowledge into action and the application of the knowledge to organizational routines so that it has effect on organizational behavior (e.g. a development of new leadership styles or of new products and services).

[8] A third way of coping with 'new' knowledge is to ignore it. Ignoring knowledge, however, implies an absence of learning, an option not discussed in this chapter.

These process dimensions of organizational learning can be visualized as shown in Figure 3.1.

In summary, four dimensions play a conceptual role in the literature on organizational learning. These dimensions can be regarded as basic cornerstones of an integrative conceptual framework for organizational learning theory and as the basic architecture for knowledge management designed to promote organizational learning (see Fig. 3.2).

The management of organizational learning thus revolves around several key issues. One of them is that different system levels and their interconnectiveness must be taken into account through a process of learning to deal with complexity and interdependent variables at different system levels. Individuals, with their learning capabilities and possible emotional defenses derived from anxiety and fear of uncertainty in unstable settings; teams as social systems that function according to specific laws of group dynamics; and knowledge networks of relations between the members of the core organization and external suppliers, customers, knowledge workers, all interact with each other in the organization and their relationship must be managed.

Second, the management of learning modes is necessary if management is to understand that learning is a matter not only of cognitive, programmed learning but also of emotions and behavior (see also Scherer and Tran, Ch. 16 in this volume). People have to understand new knowledge and feel that it is right to adopt new assumptions and routines. That is, knowing, feeling, and acting have to be balanced. A learning culture therefore depends not only on an organization's learning infrastructure and investment in human resource development but also on the trust that members have in one another and in management trust, for example, that they will not become the victims of their own innovations.

The third central issue in managing organizational learning is to take into account different learning types. What type of problem-solving process makes sense in which problem situation? The correction of simple deviations in

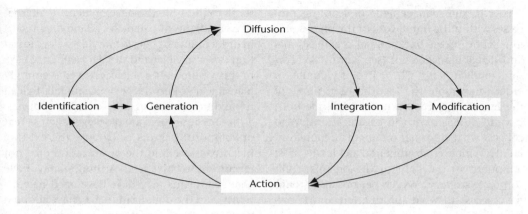

Fig. 3.1. A simplified process model of organizational learning

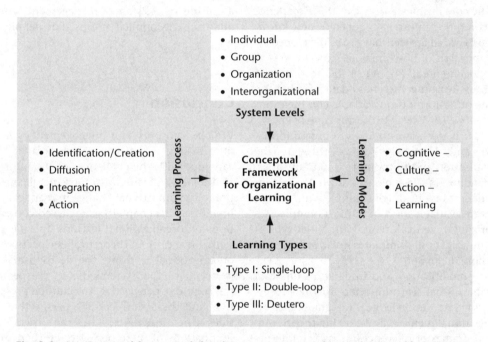

Fig. 3.2. A conceptual framework for the management of organizational learning

the outcomes of actions (single-loop learning, such as adjustments to given standards) should be delegated as far down in the organizational hierarchy as possible. By contrast, action-outcome deviations that can have crucial ef-fectzs on the organization[9] call for reflective

learning processes in which assumptions and views of organizational members are questioned.

Gore, which has defined different categories of decisions. Decisions that are 'under the water line' of the organizational vessel and that therefore can have crucial consequences for the organization have to be handled with special caution. In this instance the 'learning' procedure is linked to a collective security net.

[9] An example of a standard operating procedure for ensuring different learning types is found in the company

Fourth, the management of learning processes within the framework of the phases outlined above is the backbone of organizational knowledge management (see Pawlowsky, Forslin, and Reinhardt, Ch. 35 in this volume). In order to promote the identification phase of the learning process, a number of questions have to be dealt with in organizations. Who collects what information about the environment? Which environmental fields are most important in the light of the organization's corporate strategy? Which persons and groups have access to what information and knowledge?

Similarly, the phase of creation needs specific attention. What knowledge (experience) exists in the core business? How can this experience be combined in order to generate new knowledge? Further answers have to be developed for the question of how previous experience is to be documented. Should it be recorded in memos, learning histories, data warehouses, some other form, or in variable combinations thereof? With respect to the diffusion of knowledge, it is necessary to analyze how information and knowledge flows through the organization and to promote important links, depending on the types of knowledge and information involved. For example which channels are available for communication processes (horizontal, vertical, temporal)? What type of communication dominates (instruction, discussion, dialogue)?

The modification and integration phase of organizational learning refers to the process by which new knowledge is integrated into organizational memory and existing theories-in-use or frames of references. It is therefore necessary to question existing theories-in-use, reflect on the assumptions that are guiding people's everyday behavior in the organizations and modify these assumptions on the basis of new insights.

With respect to important issues such as the core business strategy, it may be useful to check and question these assumptions frequently, at least if the outcomes of organizational learning deviate significantly from expected developments. In some business areas it may make sense to promote the development of alternative paradigms or paradoxes (Handy 1995, 1997) in order to invent new futures for the organization (see also Galer and van der Heijden, Ch. 38 in this volume). In some cases even seemingly plausible new knowledge or insight fails to lead to modifications in assumptions and routines, either because there are blockages such as fear of committing errors or because the existing incentive system in the organization may not reward innovativeness. Attitudes may have changed, teams may have developed new insights, and the organization may have adopted new standard operating procedures, but people do not behave accordingly. If such inertia stems from organizational defenses and a culture of resistance, management should question the implicit norms that people act on.

Conclusion

Which solutions can management science offer managers and consultants so that they can cope with the challenges of the information society? Starting with the general conception of organizational change in management literature, this chapter has reviewed contributions on organizational learning and has presented five distinct theoretical perspectives on organizational learning: the decision-making perspective, the systems-theory perspective, the cognitive perspective, the cultural perspective, and the action-learning perspective. Besides the differences in the theoretical foundations of these perspectives, there are a number of conceptual similarities that reappear in most other perspectives as well and that make up the core architecture of a conceptual model of organizational learning. By projecting the different theoretical assumptions onto this conceptual framework, one can outline the relevant dimensions of managing organizational learning. The manager of organizational learning thus should focus on system levels, learning modes, learning types, and learning phases by thinking about learning in terms of systems; by considering different learning modes, such as cognitive, cultural, and action learning; by selecting appropriate learning types that are useful under different learning circumstances; and by taking into account different obstacles to the organization's learning process.

Within the discipline management science, recognition of the new territory represented by the information and knowledge society is clearly emerging. The contributions to this field also show that there are many assumptions about ways to move in this new environment. But these guidelines are based more on a rudimentary theoretical framework than on empirical evidence, of which there is little to inspire confidence in the direction being taken

and in the decisions being made. Do these new rules contribute significantly to organizational success? In addition to refining the conceptions of organizational knowledge systems and knowledge processes in organizations, researchers need to study the relevance of learning processes and knowledge for economic success. There is a great variety of assumptions about the determining factors of organizational learning but almost no knowledge about the effects or consequences those factors have for organizations. The dependent variables of the models on organizational learning clearly need more attention if the business and scientific communities are to understand the accepted economic necessity and value of learning and knowing.

References

Abernathy, W. J. and Wayne, K. (1974). 'Limits of the Learning Curve'. *Harvard Business Review*, 52/5: 56–72.

Argyris, C. (1964). *Integrating the Individual and the Organization*. New York: Wiley.

——(1990). *Overcoming Organizational Defenses: Facilitating Organizational Learning*. Boston: Allyn and Bacon.

——and Schön, D. A. (1974). *Theory in Practice: Increasing Professional Effectiveness*. San Francisco: Jossey-Bass.

————(1978). *Organizational Learning: A Theory of Action Perspective*. Reading, Mass.: Addison-Wesley.

————(1996). *Organizational Learning*: Vol. 2. *Theory, Method, and Practice*. Reading, Mass.: Addison-Wesley.

Ashby, W. R. (1956). *An Introduction to Cybernetics*. London: Chapman & Hall.

Astley, W. G. and Van de Ven, A. H. (1983). 'Central Perspectives and Debates in Organization Theory'. *Administrative Science Quarterly*, 28: 245–73.

Axelrod, R. (1976). *Structure of Decision: The Cognitive Maps of Political Elites*. Princeton: Princeton University Press.

Baitsch, C. (1993). *Was bewegt Organisationen?* Frankfurt am Main: Campus.

Bales, R. F. (1950). *Interaction Process Analysis: A Method for the Study of Small Groups*. Chicago: University of Chicago Press.

Barnard, C. I. (1956). *The Functions of the Executive*. Cambridge, Mass.: Harvard University Press.

Barnett, C. K. (1998). Book Review 'Organizational Learning'. *Administrative Science Quarterly*, 43: 208–12.

Bartlett, F. C. (1964). *Remembering: A Study in Experimental and Social Psychology*. Cambridge: Cambridge University Press.

Bateson, G. (1992). *Ökologie des Geistes: Anthropologische, psychologische, biologische und epistemologische Perspektiven* (6th edn) (H. G. Holl, trans.). Frankfurt am Main: Suhrkamp. (Original work published 1972)

Beer, S. (1972). *Brain of the Firm*. London: Penguin.

——(1979). *The Heart of Enterprise*. London: Penguin.

Berger, P. L. and Luckmann, T. (1966). *The Social Construction of Reality: A Treatise in the Sociology of Knowledge*. New York: Doubleday.

Bertalanffy, L. v. (1951). 'General Systems Theory: A New Approach to the Unity of Science'. *Human Biology*, 23: 302–61.

Bieri, J. (1968). 'Cognitive Complexity and Judgment of Inconsistent Information', in R. P. Abelson, E. Aronson, W. J. McGuire, T. M. Newcombe, M. J. Rosenberg, and P. H. Tannenbaum (eds.), *Theories of Cognitive Consistency*. Chicago: Rand McNally, 633–40.

Bion, W. R. (1968). *Experiences in Groups*. London: Tavistock.

Blake, R. R. and Mouton, J. S. (1969). *Building a Dynamic Corporation through Grid Organisation Development*. Reading, Mass.: Addison-Wesley.

———— (1985). *The Managerial Grid III*. Houston: Gulf.

Bleicher, K. (1995). 'Confidence as a Success Critical Factor in Change Management'. *Zeitschrift Führung und Organisation*, 64: 390–5.

Boisot, M. H. (1995). *Information Space: A Framework for Learning in Organizations, Institutions and Culture*. London: Routledge.

Bomke, P., Kreuter, A., and Stegmüller, R. (1993). *Diskussion einer Konzeption des organisatorischen Lernens: Wurzeln, Alternativen und Erkenntnisinteresse*. Unpublished manuscript, University of Mannheim, Germany.

Boulding, K. E. (1956). *The Image: Knowledge in Life and Society*. Ann Arbor: University of Michigan Press.

Brown, J. S. and Duguid, P. (1991). 'Organizational Learning and Communities-of-Practice: Toward a Unified View of Working, Learning, and Innovation'. *Organization Science*, 2: 40–57.

Burns, T. and Stalker, G. M. (1961). *The Management of Innovation*. London: Tavistock.

Cangelosi, V. and Dill, W. R. (1965). 'Organizational Learning: Observations toward a Theory'. *Administrative Science Quarterly*, 10: 175–203.

Cartwright, D. and Zander, A. (eds.) (1968). *Group Dynamics: Research and Theory*. New York: Harper & Row.

Child, J. (1972). 'Organizational Structure, Environment, and Performance: The Role of Strategic Choice'. *Sociology*, 5: 1–22.

Cohen, D. (1998). 'Toward a Knowledge Context: Report on the First Annual U.C. Berkeley Forum on Knowledge and the Firm'. *California Management Review*, 40/3 (Special issue on Knowledge and the Firm): 22–39.

Cook, S. D. N. and Yanow, D. (1993). 'Culture and Organizational Learning'. *Journal of Management Inquiry*, 2: 373–90.

Cyert, R. M. and March, J. G. (1963). *A Behavioral Theory of the Firm*. Englewood Cliffs, NJ: Prentice Hall.

Daft, R. L. and Weick, K. E. (1984). 'Toward a Model of Organizations as Interpretation Systems'. *Academy of Management Review*, 9: 284–95.

Debreu, G. (1954). 'Existence of an Equilibrium for a Competitive Economy'. *Econometrica*, 22: 265–90.

Dewey, J. (1910). *How We Think*. Boston: D. C. Heath.

Dierkes, M. (1988). 'Unternehmenskultur und Unternehmensführung—Konzeptionelle Ansätze und gesicherte Erkenntnisse'. *Zeitschrift für Betriebswirtschaft*, 58: 554–75.

—— (1992). 'Leitbild, Lernen und Unternehmensentwicklung: Wie können Unternehmen sich vorausschauend veränderten Umfeldbedingungen stellen?', in C. Krebsbach-Gnath (ed.), *Den Wandel in Unternehmen steuern*. Frankfurt am Main: Frankfurter Allgemeine Zeitung Verlag, Bereich Wirtschaft, 19–36.

Dodgson, M. (1993). 'Organizational Learning: A Review of Some Literatures'. *Organization Studies*, 14: 375–94.

Dörner, D. (1989). *Die Logik des Miplingens: Strategisches Denken in komplexen Situationen*. Reinbek bei Hamburg: Rowohlt.

—— Kreuzig, H. W., Reither, F., and Stäudel, T. (1983). *Lohhausen: Vom Umgang mit Unbestimmtheit und Komplexität*. Berlin: Huber.

Duncan, R. and Weiss, A. (1979). 'Organizational Learning: Implications for Organizational Design', in B. M. Staw (ed.), *Research in Organizational Behavior: An Annual Series of Analytical Essays and Critical Reviews* (Vol. 1). Greenwich, Conn.: JAI Press, 75–123.

Edmondson, A. and Moingeon, B. (1998). 'From Organizational Learning to the Learning Organization'. *Management Learning*, 29: 5–20.

Emery, F. E. (1969). *Systems Thinking*. Harmondsworth: Penguin.

—— and Trist, E. L. (1965). 'The Causal Texture of Organizational Environments'. *Human Relations*, 18: 21–32.

Fiol, C. M. and Lyles, M. A. (1985). 'Organizational Learning'. *Academy of Management Review*, 10: 803–13.

Forrester, J. W. (1961). *Industrial Dynamics*. Cambridge, Mass.: MIT Press.

Forslin, J. and Thulestedt, B. M. (1993). *Lärande Organisation: Att utveckla kompetens tillsammans* (The Learning Organization: Joint Development of Competences). Stockholm: Publica.

French, W. L. and Bell., C. H., Jr. (1973). *Organization Development: Behavioral Science Interventions for Organization Improvement*. Englewood Cliffs, NJ: Prentice Hall.

Frost, P. J., Moore, L. F., Louis, M. R., Lundberg, C. C., and Martin, J. (eds.) (1991). *Reframing Organizational Culture*. Newbury Park, Calif.: Sage.

Garratt, B. (1990). *Creating a Learning Organisation: A Guide to Leadership, Learning and Development*. Cambridge: Director Books.

Gioia, D. A. (1986*a*). 'Conclusion: The State of the Art in Organizational Social Cognition: A Personal View', in H. P. Sims, Jr. and D. A. Gioia (eds.), *The Thinking Organization: Dynamics of Organizational Social Cognition*. San Francisco: Jossey-Bass, 336–56.

—— (1986*b*). 'Symbols, Scripts, and Sensemaking: Creating Meaning in the Organizational Experience', in H. P. Sims, Jr. and D. A. Gioia (eds.), *The Thinking Organization: Dynamics of Organizational Social Cognition*. San Francisco: Jossey-Bass, 49–74.

Gomez, P. (1981). *Modelle und Methoden des systemorientierten Managements*. Bern: Haupt.

Gray, B., Bougon, M. G., and Donnellon, A. (1985). 'Organizations as Constructions and Destructions of Meaning'. *Journal of Management*, 11: 83–98.

Greiner, L. E. (1972). 'Evolution and Revolution as Organizations Grow'. *Harvard Business Review*, 7/8: 37–46.

Grundy, T. (1994). *Strategic Learning in Action: How to Accelerate and Sustain Business Change*. London: McGraw-Hill.

Hall, R. I. (1984). 'The Natural Logic of Management Policy Making: Its Implications for the Survival of an Organization'. *Management Science*, 3/8: 905–27.

Hamel, G. and Prahalad, C. K. (1994). *Competing for the Future: Unleashing the Power of the Workforce*. Boston: Harvard Business School Press.

Handy, C. (1995). *The Age of Unreason*. Boston: Harvard Business School Press.

—— (1997). 'Finding Sense in Uncertainty', in R. Gibson (ed.), *Rethinking the Future*. London: Brealey, 16–33.

Hannan, M. T. and Freeman, J. (1989). *Organizational Ecology*. Cambridge, Mass.: Harvard University Press.

Hawkins, P. (1991). 'The Spiritual Dimension of the Learning Organization'. *Management Education and Development*, 22: 172–87.

Hayes, R. H., Wheelwright, S. C., and Clark, K. B. (1988). *Dynamic Manufacturing: Creating the Learning Organization*. New York: Free Press.

Hedberg, B. L. T. (1981). 'How Organizations Learn and Unlearn', in P. C. Nystrom and W. H. Starbuck (eds.), *Handbook of Organizational Design*: Vol. 1. *Adapting Organizations to Their Environments*. Oxford: Oxford University Press, 3–27.

Heijl, P. M. (1982). *Sozialwissenschaft als Theorie selbstreferentieller Systeme*. Frankfurt am Main: Campus.

Huber, G. P. (1991). 'Organizational Learning: The Contributing Processes and the Literatures'. *Organization Science*, 2: 88–115.

Imai, K., Nonaka, I., and Takeuchi, H. (1985). 'Managing the New Product Development Process: How Japanese Companies Learn and Unlearn', in K. B. Clark, R. H. Hayes, and C. Lorenz (eds.),

The Uneasy Alliance: Managing the Productivity–Technology Dilemma. Boston: Harvard Business School Press, 337–81.

Inglis, S. (1994). *Making the Most of Action Learning*. Aldershot: Gower.

Jelinek, M. (1979). *Institutionalizing Innovation: A Study of Organizational Learning Systems*. New York: Praeger.

——and Litterer, J. A. (1994). 'Toward a Cognitive Theory of Organizations', in C. Stubbart, J. R. Meindel, and J. F. Porac (eds.), *Advances in Managerial Cognition and Organizational Information Processing* (Vol. 5). Greenwich, Conn.: JAI Press, 3–41.

——and Schoonhoven, C. B. (1990). *The Innovation Marathon: Lessons from High Technology Firms*. Oxford: Basil Blackwell.

Jensen, M. C. (1983). 'Organization Theory and Methodology'. *The Accounting Review*, 58: 319–39.

Kaplan, R. S. and Norton, D. P. (1996). *The Balanced Scorecard: Translating Strategy into Action*. Boston: Harvard Business School Press.

Kast, F. E. and Rosenzweig, J. E. (1970). *Organization and Management: A Systems and Contingency Approach*. New York: McGraw-Hill.

Katz, D. and Kahn, R. L. (1978). *The Social Psychology of Organizations* (2nd edn). New York: Wiley. (Original work published 1966)

Katzenbach, J. R. and Smith, D. K. (1993). *The Wisdom of Teams*. Boston: Harvard Business School Press.

Klimecki, R., Probst, G., and Eberl, P. (1991). 'Systementwicklung als Managementproblem', in W. H. Staehle and J. Sydow (eds.), *Managementforschung* (Vol. 1). Berlin: de Gruyter, 103–62.

Kolb, D. A. (1976). 'Management and the Learning Process'. *California Management Review*, 18/3: 21–31.

——(1984). *Experiential Learning: Experience as the Source of Learning and Development*. Englewood Cliffs, NJ: Prentice Hall.

Lawrence, P. R. and Lorsch, J. W. (1967). *Organization and Environment: Managing Differentiation and Integration*. Cambridge, Mass.: Harvard University, Graduate School of Business Administration.

Leonard-Barton, D. (1995). *Wellsprings of Knowledge: Building and Sustaining the Sources of Innovation*. Boston: Harvard Business School Press.

Levitt, B. and March, J. G. (1988). 'Organizational Learning'. *Annual Review of Sociology*, 14: 319–40.

Lewin, K. (1947). 'Frontiers in Group Dynamics: II. Channel of Group Life; Social Planning and Action Research'. *Human Relations*, 1: 143–53.

Lievegoed, B. C. (1974). *Organisationen im Wandel*. Bern: Haupt.

Likert, R. (1961). *New Patterns of Management*. New York: McGraw-Hill.

——and Likert, J. G. (1976). *New Ways of Managing Conflict*. New York: McGraw-Hill.

Luhmann, N. (1984). *Soziale Systeme: Grundriß einer allgemeinen Theorie*. Frankfurt am Main: Suhrkamp.

——(1989). *Legitimation durch Verfahren*. Frankfurt am Main: Suhrkamp.

Lullies, V., Bollinger, H., and Weltz, F. (1993). *Wissenslogistik: Über den betrieblichen Umgang mit Wissen bei Entwicklungsvorhaben*. Frankfurt am Main: Campus.

Lundberg, C. C. (1989). 'On Organizational Learning: Implications and Opportunities for Expanding Organizational Development'. *Research in Organizational Change and Development*, 3: 61–82.

Lyles, M. A. and Schwenk, C. R. (1992). 'Top Management, Strategy, and Organizational Knowledge Structures'. *Journal of Management Studies*, 29: 155–74.

Malik, F. (1987). 'Selbstorganisation im Management', in K. W. Kratky and F. Wallner (eds.), *Grundprinzipien der Selbst-Organisation*. Darmstadt: Wissenschaftliche Buchgesellschaft, 96–102.

——(1992). *Strategie des Managements komplexer Systeme: Ein Beitrag zur Management-Kybernetik evolutionärer Systeme*. Bern: Haupt.

Mann, F. C. (1961). 'Studying and Creating Change', in W. G. Bennis, K. D. Benne, and R. Chin (eds.), *Planning of Change*. New York: Holt, Rinehart and Winston, 605–15.

March, J. G. and Olsen, J. P. (1975). 'The Uncertainty of the Past: Organizational Learning under Ambiguity'. *European Journal of Political Research*, 3: 147–71.

—— —— (1976). *Ambiguity and Choice in Organizations* (2nd edn). Bergen: Universitetsforlaget.

—— and Simon, H. A. (1958). *Organizations*. New York: Wiley.

Maturana, H. and Varela, F. J. (1987). *Der Baum der Erkenntnis*. Bern: Scherz.

McGuire, W. J. (1968). 'The Nature of Attitudes and Attitude Change', in G. Lindzey and E. Aronson (eds.), *The Handbook of Social Psychology* (Vol. 3). Cambridge, Mass.: Addison-Wesley, 136–314.

McKelvey, B. and Aldrich, H. E. (1983). 'Populations, Natural Selection, and Applied Organizational Science'. *Administrative Science Quarterly*, 28: 101–28.

Mintzberg, H. (1979). *The Structuring of Organizations: A Synthesis of the Research*. Englewood Cliffs, NJ: Prentice Hall.

Mitroff, I. I. and Kilmann, R. H. (1976). 'On Organizational Stories: An Approach to the Design and Analysis of Organizations through Myths and Stories', in R. H. Kilmann, L. R. Pondy, and D. P. Slevin (eds.), *The Management of Organization Design*: Vol. 1. *Strategies and Implementation*. New York: North Holland, 189–207.

Morecroft, J. D. W. (1988). 'System Dynamics and Micro-words for Policymakers'. *European Journal of Operational Research*, 35: 301–20.

Morgan, G. (1986). *Images of Organization*. Newbury Park, Calif.: Sage.

Nelson, R. R. and Winter, S. G. (1982). *An Evolutionary Theory of Economic Change*. Cambridge, Mass.: Belknap Press.

Nonaka, I. (1988). 'Creating Organizational Order out of Chaos: Self-renewal in Japanese Firms'. *California Management Review*, 30/3: 57–73.

—— (1991). 'Managing the Firm as an Information Creation Process', in J. R. Meindl, R. L. Cardy, and S. M. Puffer (eds.), *Advances in Information Processing in Organizations: A Research Annual* (Vol. 4). Greenwich, Conn.: JAI Press, 239–75.

—— (1992). 'Wie japanische Konzerne Wissen erzeugen'. *Harvard Manager*, 2: 95–103.

—— (1994). 'A Dynamic Theory of Organizational Knowledge Creation'. *Organization Science*, 5: 14–37.

—— and Konno, N. (1998). 'The Concept of "Ba": Building a Foundation for Knowledge Creation'. *California Management Review*, 40/3: 40–54.

—— and Takeuchi, H. (1995). *The Knowledge-creating Company: How Japanese Companies Create the Dynamics of Innovation*. New York: Oxford University Press.

Pautzke, G. (1989). *Die Evolution der organisatorischen Wissensbasis: Bausteine zu einer Theorie des organisatorischen Lernens*. Herrsching: B. Kirsch.

Pawlowsky, P. (1992). 'Betriebliche Qualifikationsstrategien und organisationales Lernen', in W. H. Staehle and P. Conrad (eds.), *Managementforschung* (Vol. 2). Berlin: de Gruyter, 177–237.

—— (1994). *Wissensmanagement in der lernenden Organisation*. Unpublished postdoctoral dissertation, University of Paderborn, Germany.

Pedler, M. (1997). 'Interpreting Action Learning', in J. Burgoyne and M. Reynolds (eds.), *Management Learning: Integrating Perspectives in Theory and Practice*. London: Sage, 248–64.

—— Burgoyne, J., and Boydell, T. (1991). *The Learning Company: A Strategy for Sustainable Development*. London: McGraw-Hill.

Pfeffer, J. (1982). *Organizations and Organization Theory*. Boston: Pittman.

Polanyi, M. (1966). *The Tacit Dimension*. London: Routledge & Kegan Paul.

Pondy, L. R., Frost, P. J., and Morgan, G. (eds.) (1983). *Organizational Symbolism*. Greenwich, Conn.: JAI Press.

Porter, M. E. (1985). *Competitive Advantage*. New York: Free Press.

Prahalad, C. K. and Hamel, G. (1990). 'The Core Competence of the Corporation'. *Harvard Business Review*, 68/3: 71–91.

Probst, G. (1987). 'Selbstorganisation und Entwicklung'. *Die Unternehmung*, 41: 242–55.

Quinn, J. B. (1992). *Intelligent Enterprise: A Knowledge and Service Based Paradigm for Industry*. New York: Free Press.

Quinn, R. E. and Cameron, K. S. (1983). 'Organizational Life Cycles and Shifting Criteria of Effectiveness: Some Preliminary Evidence'. *Management Science*, 29: 33–51.

Reinhardt, R. (1993). *Das Modell organisationaler Lernfähigkeit und die Gestaltung lernfähiger Organisationen*. Frankfurt am Main: Lang.

Revans, R. W. (1980). *Action Learning: New Techniques for Management*. London: Blond and Briggs.

—— (1982). 'The Enterprise as a Learning System', in R. W. Revans (ed.), *The Origins and Growth of Action Learning*. Goch: Bratt Institut für Neues Lernen, 280–6.

Rogers, E. M. (1983). *Diffusion of Innovations* (3rd edn). New York: Free Press.

Rumelhart, D. E. (1984). 'Schemata and the Cognitive System', in R. S. Wyer and T. K. Srull (eds.), *Handbook of Social Cognition* (Vol. 1). Hillsdale, NJ: Lawrence Erlbaum, 161–88.

Sackmann, S. A. (1991). *Cultural Knowledge in Organizations: Exploring the Collective Mind*. Newbury Park, Calif.: Sage.

Salancik, G. R. and Porac, J. F. (1986). 'Distilled Ideologies: Values Derived from Causal Reasoning in Complex Environments', in H. P. Sims and D. A. Gioia (eds.), *The Thinking Organization: Dynamics of Organizational Social Cognition*. San Francisco: Jossey-Bass, 75–101.

Sandelands, L. E. and Stablein, R. E. (1987). 'The Concept of Organization Mind', in S. B. Bacharach (ed.), *Research in the Sociology of Organizations* (Vol. 5). Greenwich, Conn.: JAI Press, 135–62.

Schein, E. H. (1969). *Process Consultation: Its Role in Organization Development*. Reading, Mass.: Addison-Wesley.

—— (1984). 'Coming to a New Awareness of Organizational Culture'. *Sloan Management Review*, 25/2: 3–16.

—— (1991). 'What Is Culture?', in P. J. Frost, L. F. Moore, M. R. Louis, C. C. Lundberg, and J. Martin (eds.), *Reframing Organizational Culture*. Newbury Park, Calif.: Sage, 243–53.

Scholl, W., Hoffmann, L., and Gierschner, H. C. (1993). *Innovation und Information: Wie in Unternehmen neues Wissen produziert wird*. Unpublished manuscript. Institut für Arbeits-, Sozial- und Organisationspsychologie, Humboldt University of Berlin.

Schreyögg, G. (1996). *Organisation*. Wiesbaden: Gabler.

—— and Noss, C. (1995). 'Organisatorischer Wandel: Von der Organisationsentwicklung zur lernenden Organisation'. *Betriebswirtschaft*, 55: 169–85.

Schroder, H. M., Driver, M. J., and Streufert, S. (1975). *Menschliche Informationsverarbeitung*. Weinheim: Beltz.

Schumann, J. (1976). *Grundzüge der mikroökonomischen Theorie*. Berlin: Springer.

Scott, W. A. (1969). 'Structure of Natural Cognitions'. *Journal of Personality and Social Psychology*, 12: 261–78.

Scott, W. R. (1992). *Organizations: Rational, Natural, and Open Systems*. Englewood Cliffs, NJ: Prentice Hall.

Seifert, M. and Pawlowsky, P. (1998). 'Innerbetriebliches Vertrauen als Verbreitungsgrenze atypischer Beschäftigungsformen'. *Mitteilung aus der Arbeitsmarkt- und Berufsforschung*, 3: 599–611.

Selvini Palazzoli, M., Anolli, L., Di Blasio, P., Giossi, L., Pisano, J., Ricci, C., Sacchi, M., and Ugazio, V. (1988). *Hinter den Kulissen der Organisation* (3rd edn). Stuttgart: Klett-Cotta.

Senge, P. M. (1990a). 'The Leader's New Work: Building Learning Organizations'. *Sloan Management Review*, 32/1: 7–23.

—— (1990b). *The Fifth Discipline: The Art and Practice of the Learning Organization*. New York: Bantam Doubleday.

—— Roberts, C., Ross, R. B., Smith, B. J., and Kleiner, A. (1994). *The Fifth Discipline Fieldbook: Strategies and Tools for Building a Learning Organization*. New York: Currency Doubleday.

—— and Sterman, J. D. (1992). 'Systems Thinking and Organizational Learning: Acting Locally and Thinking Globally in the Organization of the Future', in T. A. Kochan and M. Useem (eds.), *Transforming Organizations*. New York: Oxford University Press, 353–71.

Shrivastava, P. (1983). 'A Typology of Organizational Learning Systems'. *Journal of Management Studies*, 20: 7–28.

Shrivastava, P. and Schneider, S. (1984). 'Organizational Frames of Reference'. *Human Relations*, 37: 795–809.

Sims, H. P., Jr. and Gioia, D. A. (eds.) (1986). *The Thinking Organization: Dynamics of Organizational Social Cognition*. San Francisco: Jossey-Bass.

Smircich, L. (1983). 'Organizations as Shared Meanings', in L. R. Pondy, P. J. Frost, and G. Morgan (eds.), *Organizational Symbolism*. Greenwich, Conn.: JAI Press, 253–312.

—— and Stubbart, C. (1985). 'Strategic Management in an Enacted World'. *Academy of Management Review*, 10: 724–36.

Starbuck, W. H. (1982). 'Congealing Oil: Inventing Ideologies to Justify Acting Ideologies Out'. *Journal of Management Studies*, 19: 3–27.

—— and Hedberg, B. L. T. (1977). 'Saving an Organization from a Stagnating Environment', in H. B. Thorelli (ed.), *Strategy + Structure = Performance*. Bloomington: Indiana University Press, 249–58.

Stata, R. (1989). 'Organizational Learning: The Key to Management Innovation'. *Sloan Management Review*, 30/3: 63–74.

Steinmann, H. and Schreyögg, G. (1993). *Management—Grundlagen der Unternehmensführung: Konzepte, Funktionen, Fallstudien*. Wiesbaden: Gabler.

Streufert, S., Pogash, R., and Piasecki, M. (1988). 'Simulation-based Assessment of Managerial Competence: Reliability and Validity'. *Personnel Psychology*, 41: 537–57.

—— and Streufert, S. C. (1978). *Behavior in the Complex Environment*. New York: Wiley.

—— and Swezey, R. W. (1986). *Complexity, Managers, and Organizations*. Orlando, Fla.: Academic Press.

Sveiby, K. E. (1997). *The New Organizational Wealth: Managing and Measuring Knowledge-based Assets*. San Francisco: Berret-Koehler.

Sydow, J. (1992). *Strategische Netzwerke*. Wiesbaden: Gabler.

Thompson, J. D. (1967). *Organizations in Action*. New York: McGraw-Hill.

Tolman, E. C. (1932). *Purposive Behavior in Animal and Men*. New York: Appleton Century.

Tsang, E. W. K. (1997). 'Organizational Learning and the Learning Organization: A Dichotomy between Descriptive and Prescriptive Research'. *Human Relations*, 50: 73–89.

Tushman, M. L. and Nadler, D. A. (1978). 'Information Processing as an Integrating Concept in Organizational Design'. *Academy of Management Review*, 3/7: 613–24.

Ulrich, H. (1984). *Management*. Bern: Haupt.

—— and Probst, G. J. B. (eds.) (1984). *Self-organization and Management of Social Systems*. Heidelberg: Decker.

—— —— (1990). *Anleitung zum ganzheitlichen Denken und Handeln: Ein Brevier für Führungskräfte*. Bern: Haupt.

Ulrich, P. (1984). 'Systemsteuerung and Kulturentwicklung'. *Die Unternehmung*, 38: 303–25.

Vester, F. (1991). *Neuland des Denkens: Vom technokratischen zum kybernetischen Zeitalter* (7th edn). Stuttgart: Deutsche Verlags Anstalt.

Vicari, S., von Krogh, G., Roos, J., and Mahnke, V. (1996). 'Knowledge Creation through Cooperative Experimentation', in G. von Krogh and J. Roos (eds.), *Managing Knowledge: Perspectives on Cooperation and Competition*. London: Sage, 184–202.

von Foerster, H. (1985). *Sicht und Einsicht*. Braunschweig: Vieweg.

von Krogh, G. and Roos, J. (eds.) (1996). *Managing Knowledge: Perspectives on Cooperation and Competition*. London: Sage.

—— —— and Slocum, K. (1996). 'An Essay on Corporate Epistemology', in G. von Krogh and J. Roos (eds.), *Managing Knowledge: Perspectives on Cooperation and Competition*. London: Sage, 157–83.

—— —— and Yip, G. (1996). 'A Note on the Epistemology of Globalizing Firms', in G. von Krogh and J. Roos (eds.), *Managing Knowledge: Perspectives on Cooperation and Competition*. London: Sage, 203–17.

Wahren, H. K. (1996). *Das lernende Unternehmen—Theorie und Praxis des lernenden Unternehmens*. Berlin: de Gruyter.

Walsh, J. P. and Ungson, G. R. (1991). 'Organizational Memory'. *Academy of Management Review*, 16: 57–91.

Weick, K. E. (1969). *The Social Psychology of Organizing*. Menlo Park, Calif.: Addison-Wesley.

—— and Bougon, M. G. (1986). 'Organizations as Cognitive Maps: Charting Ways to Success and Failure', in H. P. Sims, Jr. and D. A. Gioia (eds.), *The Thinking Organization: Dynamics of Organizational Social Cognition*. San Francisco: Jossey-Bass, 102–35.

Wiegand, M. (1996). *Prozesse organisationalen Lernens*. Wiesbaden: Gabler.

Wikström, S. and Normann, R. (1994). *Knowledge and Value: A New Perspective on Corporate Transformation*. London: Routledge.

Wilensky, H. L. (1967). *Organizational Intelligence: Knowledge and Policy in Government and Industry*. New York: Basic Books.

Willke, H. (1987a). 'Strategien der Intervention in autonome Systeme', in D. Bäcker (ed.), *Theorie als Passion*. Frankfurt am Main: Suhrkamp, 333–61.

——(1987b). *Systemtheorie*. Stuttgart: Fischer.

——(1998). *Systemisches Wissensmanagement*. Stuttgart: Lucius und Lucius.

Woodward, J. (1965). *Industrial Organization: Theory and Practice*. New York: Oxford University Press.

Zand, D. E. (1977). 'Vertrauen and Problemlösungsverhalten von Managern', in H. E. Lück (ed.), *Vertrauen, Verantwortung: Ergebnisse der Erforschung prosozialen Verhaltens*. Stuttgart: Klett, 61–74.

Zimmerman, L. J. (1961). *Geschichte der theoretischen Volkswirtschaftslehre*. Cologne: Bund.

4 A Review and Assessment of Organizational Learning in Economic Theories

Christopher S. Boerner, Jeffrey T. Macher, and David J. Teece

One principal goal of economics is to help understand innovation and change. It is therefore surprising to many observers that mainstream economics has largely failed to develop a coherent approach to one of the primary means by which individuals innovate and change: learning. For the purposes of this chapter, learning is defined as the acquisition and use of existing knowledge and/or the creation of new knowledge with the purpose of improving economic performance. Strictly speaking, only individuals possess the ability to create knowledge. However, organizations provide a context within which individual learning takes place (Marshall 1965).

In particular, organizations have the capacity to support and channel individual knowledge creation in specific directions. Thus, organizational learning can be thought of as the capability of a firm to facilitate knowledge creation or acquisition, disseminate it throughout the organization, and embody it in products, services, and systems (Nonaka and Takeuchi 1995). So defined, organizational learning is a central concern of economics. Such learning enables firms to modify and develop new technologies, structures, and operating practices in the face of changing economic and business conditions. It enables the creation of intangible assets that are the basis of enduring competitive advantage (Burgelman 1990; Senge 1990; Teece 1998).

Despite the centrality of learning in fundamental economic issues, its treatment in the orthodox economics literature is sparse, and frequently a caricature. In spite of a substantial and growing body of economics literature that characterizes various aspects of learning, mainstream economics continues to ignore learning, not because it is unimportant but because embracing it tends to undermine perceived wisdom. It is admittedly difficult to define and differentiate a mainstream economics approach to learning. Indeed, organizational learning is given scant attention in standard graduate economics textbooks. With the exception of a brief discussion of learning curve models, neither the *New Palgrave Dictionary of Economics* (Eatwell, Milgate, and Newman 1987) nor the *Fortune Encyclopedia of Economics* (Henderson 1993) dealt with an economic perspective of learning. Indeed, the *International Encyclopedia of Business and Management* (Warner 1996) failed even to mention the subject (Albach and Jin 1998). Progress is nevertheless being made, for scholars in two subfields of economics have endeavored to grapple head-on with learning: the economics of innovation, and the theory of the firm.

In some sense, this slighting of organizational learning in economics is not surprising. As other chapters in this volume illustrate, inadequate theoretical appreciation of organizational learning is not unique to economics. The management science, history, and anthropology chapters, for example, highlight the difficulty that scholars in other disciplines have had in developing a coherent theoretical framework.

The neglect of learning in economics stems in part from the fact that economics is built upon a set of highly stylized assumptions about the behavior and decision-making processes of economic agents. In the environment based on these assumptions, agents are perfectly rational and able to respond optimally and instantaneously to changing conditions. The stylized nature of such an environment is summarized by Nelson and Winter (1982): 'Never is such a theoretical actor confused about a situation or distracted by petty concerns; never is he trapped in a systematically erroneous view of the problem; never is a plain old mistake made' (p. 8). Information asymmetries may exist in such models, but they come and go according to the model-builder's whim. Learning is generally not recognized; if it is, it is simply turned on and off in the model, with no attention being given to the mechanism itself. Within such theoretical confines, economists have been handicapped in developing useful models of organizational learning. The effort to develop an economic approach to organizational learning in the orthodox literature, therefore, has had to focus on moving away from this highly stylized setting.

In the next section of this chapter we explore a number of approaches that economists have employed to modify traditional assumptions and study issues related to learning. Although by no means exhaustive, the seven approaches examined are among the most prominent models of learning found in the orthodox literature. These approaches have also heavily influenced much of the subsequent work on learning found in other fields within economics. In the third and forth sections of the chapter we explore the treatment of organizational learning in two relatively influential fields in economics: the economics of innovation and the theory of the firm. These two streams of literature provide important new insights into individual learning processes and how individual learning is transformed into organizational learning. They also extend orthodoxy by examining not only how firms acquire and utilize existing knowledge but also how they create new knowledge. This extension is essential in progressing toward a more comprehensive and more dynamic framework for

understanding organizational learning than exists today.

Orthodox Models of Learning

In the overview of his graduate economics textbook, Kreps (1990) stated that microeconomic theory concerned 'the behavior of individual economic actors and the aggregation of their actions in different institutional frameworks' (p. 3). In this one sentence Kreps introduced four important economic concepts: actors, their behavior, the institutional framework, and equilibrium analysis. In most traditional microeconomic models there are two types of actors: consumers and firms. The behavior of these actors is portrayed as the selection from a specified set of options that maximizes some objective function. Consumers, for example, are typically assumed to maximize utility to the extent that budget constraints allow. Firms, on the other hand, maximize profits given production constraints. The maximizing choices that firms and consumers make are dependent upon the opportunities available in a given institutional setting. The institutional framework in economics describes the options that each actor faces and the outcomes that ensue from each action, given the behavior of all the other players. In most orthodox models, the institutional setting is an impersonal marketplace governed by prices. Finally, the actions that firms and consumers select, and the results that ensue, are predicted using various forms of equilibrium analysis. Generally speaking, equilibrium is a feedback system that aggregates individual actions into an overall outcome that, in turn, determines the constraints that individuals face and the outcomes they receive (Kreps 1990). Equilibrium in most economic models is a situation in which each individual agent is assumed to be doing as well as possible, given the actions taken by others and the institutional environment.

As the above description suggests, the assumptions that are typically associated with the core concepts in microeconomics depict a highly simplified world in which learning is generally absent. Economic actors have stable, well-defined preferences, rationally maximize utility, profits, or some other entity against those preferences, and operate in a completely transparent market in which prices reveal all relevant information. Behavioral adjustments are instantaneous, and changes in market conditions are known by all. Although these simplifying assumptions help derive important insights, they do not allow for meaningful analysis of learning. Indeed, economic agents in traditional neoclassical models have neither a need nor an incentive to learn.

In an effort to incorporate learning into traditional neoclassical models, economists since the early 1950s have attempted to modify the stylized setting depicted above. Much of the research on learning found in the mainstream literature can be seen as an effort to relax traditional assumptions about the behavior of economic actors, the institutional setting in which these actors operate, or the equilibrium conditions that are used to model outcomes. Though not exhaustive, Table 4.1 illustrates the primary modifications to basic assumptions that have been made so that learning dynamics can be recognized. These changes are now discussed in some detail.

Behavioral Modifications

Bounded Rationality

In traditional economic models it is assumed that decision-makers are rational. An agent is economically rational if decisions are based on (a) a known set of conceivable alternatives with corresponding outcomes, (b) an established rule or set of relations that produces a preference ordering of the alternatives, and (c) a maximization criterion (Alexis and Wilson 1967). Simon (1955) was one of the first economists to stress that the real world is such that these assumptions are not abstractions but gross distortions. Specifically, Simon formalized the idea that human cognitive limitations significantly affect the ability of economic agents to optimize. Rather than the hyperrationality as-

cribed to agents in traditional models, Simon (1957b) suggested the concept of bounded rationality, noting that 'the capacity of the human mind for formulating and solving complex problems is very small compared with the size of the problems whose solution is required for objectively rational behavior in the real world' (p. 198). Simon suggested that the 'key to the simplification of the choice process . . . is the replacement of the goal of *maximizing* with the goal of *satisficing*, of finding a course of action that is good enough. . . . [T]his substitution is an essential step in the application of the principle of bounded rationality' (Simon 1957b: 204–5).

Thus, for Simon, the complexity of real-life decision-making problems means that firms are simply unable to maximize over the entire set of conceivable options. Rather, firms employ simple decision-making rules and procedures to guide their actions. Due to the cognitive limits of individuals within firms, the decision-making rules that firms employ cannot be characterized as optimal in the sense that they reflect the results of global calculations (Nelson and Winter 1982). Rather, firms pick outcomes that are satisfactory, given certain targets and objectives. Simon (1955) suggested that this approach is analogous to the behavior of individuals selling a house. When selling a house, individuals typically have some reservation price and are willing to accept any offer that meets this price. (Unlike the concept of reservation prices in standard economic models, which are set where the expected gains from searching equal the costs, Simon's concept simply reflects a price with which people are satisfied.) This idea is similar to Alchian's (1950) assertion that firms are more likely to search for positive profits than for some universal optimum.

Simon's model of rationality has a number of useful properties with respect to organizational learning. First, the computational skills ascribed to managers are far less stringent than those ascribed to them in traditional models. Rather than computing the global optimum, managers must simply be able to compare outcomes to some predefined goal. Second,

Table 4.1. Modifications made in orthodoxy in order to accommodate learning

	Behavioral assumptions	Institutional environment	Equilibrium concept
Orthodoxy	• Hyperrationality • Certainty	• Frictionless adjustment	• Instantaneous adjustment
Modifications to orthodoxy	• Bounded rationality • Uncertainty	• Social learning • Path dependency	• Game-theoretic approaches • Bayesian updating • Learning-by-doing and learning curve models

economic agents need not be able to create a complete preference ordering of all conceivable alternatives. Instead, it is sufficient for managers to create partial orderings of relevant alternatives. Finally, because agents are assumed to be '*intendedly* rational, but *limitedly* so' (Simon 1957a: xxiv; Simon's emphasis), they are free to update their preferences as additional information is revealed. Similarly, managers may acquire a better understanding of relationships between actions and outcomes the more exposure they have to a given set of decision-making problems.

These properties explicitly open the door for learning to enter economic analysis. Because agents are no longer assumed to have full cognizance of all the possible actions they may take and of the associated consequences, it is conceivable that learning takes place through trial and error or through the discovery of new or additional information. Models incorporating bounded rationality, many of which have implications for organizational learning, have been employed extensively in orthodox economics since Simon's early work (Conlisk 1996; Ellison and Fudenberg 1993; Heiner 1983; Winter 1971; for additional discussion of learning models based on bounded rationality, see Kreps 1990 and Conlisk 1996). Conlisk (1996), for example, applied bounded rationality to innovation. He noted that models employing complete rationality predict that many technological innovations should have occurred far earlier than they actually did. Bounded ration-

ality, according to Conlisk, is a major determinant of technological change. In Ellison and Fudenberg's (1993) model of learning by boundedly rational agents, decision-making is improved when agents incorporate into their decision-making processes the popularity of different actions. The authors modeled two learning situations, one in which the same technology is optimal for all players and one in which the optimal technologies differ. In both cases, players used rules of thumb that ignore historical information but may incorporate the popularity of the technology. Ellison and Fudenberg (1993) found that in some cases these simple heuristics can lead to efficient decisions in the long run.

Although learning models based on bounded rationality have been frequently employed in economics, two factors have hindered the development of a cumulative research tradition. First, bounded rationality models are far more complex mathematically than are models employing complete rationality (Alexis 1999). Second, although the concept of satisficing is appealing and has been employed extensively in other disciplines (e.g. psychology), it is one to which economists have had difficulty relating (Williamson 1996). Indeed, until recently the field of economics had few models in which satisficing is explicitly applied (Aumann 1985). These critiques notwithstanding, the concept of bounded rationality has been useful in exploring how economic agents learn in the face of cognitive limitations.

Uncertainty

A related way in which mainstream economists have modified traditional neoclassical assumptions in order to model organizational learning has been to explicitly include uncertainty. In economic theory it is frequently assumed that firms possess all the relevant information necessary to maximize profits. Alchian (1950), however, noted that firms operate in an uncertain world and typically lack the data and, in many cases, the skills to perform maximizing calculations. Whereas traditional models portray success as a function of firms' abilities to predict in these situations, Alchian argued that two types of learning may be operative. First, firms may engage in imitation. In particular, firms may choose, for lack of information or computational skills, to imitate other firms that appear to be doing well. Interestingly, this imitation may actually lead to unintended innovation. In attempting to copy the configuration or behavior of other successful players, firms may make mistakes and, as a result, end up with configurations that are even more successful (for an additional discussion of imitation learning, see Czarniawska, Ch. 5 in this volume). Second, Alchian suggested that trial-and-error learning may also be an important determinant of a firm's success in the face of uncertainty. He qualified this statement, however, noting that in order for trial-and-error learning to be effective it must be possible for economic agents to make inferences about the results of past trials. Alchian suggested that this possibly may not exist if the environment is changing rapidly. This discussion of imitation and trial and error suggests that learning may be partially influenced by chance. That is, economic actors may appear to be learning when in fact they are discovering decision-making rules that happen to be useful in a given situation.

Consumer learning in the context of uncertainty is also a central theme in Akerlof's (1970) examination of the market for 'lemons'. In this paper, Akerlof modeled how uncertainty about product quality can lead to market inefficiencies and, in the extreme case, to the elimination of markets altogether. Although the context for his paper was the market for used cars, he actually addressed the general problem of adverse selection. Adverse selection occurs when one party to a transaction has an informational advantage over another party. This lack of information leads to a condition in which only agents with unfavorable characteristics are willing to transact. In the case of used cars, adverse selection results in only the lowest quality cars (i.e. what Americans call 'lemons') being placed on the market.

The important point from the perspective of organizational learning is that, in the face of adverse selection, some type of learning or adaptation mechanism must be introduced if markets are to function properly. Four possible mechanisms for learning in this context are signaling, repeated interaction, advertising, and product branding. Each of these approaches allows the parties to a transaction to learn about the relevant quality characteristics of the products being exchanged.

Lastly, Stigler (1961) developed a model of uncertainty in which learning is a prominent feature of market transactions. In all markets, prices change. In response, buyers engage in a costly search for sellers offering the best deals. Likewise, sellers engage in a search for buyers. Searching in this context is costly for a number reasons. First, buyers may incur the costs of physically searching multiple stores for the best prices. Second, buyers may find it costly to determine what constitutes the best deal in a given context. Finally, buyers and sellers may incur costs associated with communicating with one another. Because of these costs, economic agents do not search indefinitely but rather until the additional cost of searching just equals the additional expected benefit associated with the search.

These models of uncertainty have two important implications for learning. First, they reinforce the previously made point that, in the face of cognitive limitations and uncertainty, economic agents may economize on learning by using simple heuristics and imitation. Rather than striving for complete information, economic agents select an optimal amount of learning such that costs and benefits are equated. Second, given cognitive limitations and positive search costs, various mechanisms arise to assist agents in learning relevant information. In the case of buyers searching for sellers offering the best deals, for instance, Stigler (1961) observed that advertising and specialized traders assist in reducing search costs.

Institutional Modifications

Social Learning

In the preceding discussion we noted that economic agents frequently use simple heuristics when faced with complex decision-making problems in order to compensate for cognitive limitations. One implication of this research is that agents acquire cues about appropriate behavior in a given instance by observing their institutional environment. A number of economists have therefore explored organizational learning by modifying the institutional framework within which economic agents operate so as to allow for learning. Recall that the institutional framework in economics describes the options faced by actors as well as the outcomes that ensue from each action, given the behavior of other players. In most real-world settings the behavior of other players has a direct impact on how a given economic agent perceives the environment in which he or she operates. Put simply, agents learn from one another. For instance, economic actors frequently accept certain ideas or approaches to solving problems simply because others do. Ellison and Fudenberg (1993) defined this form of learning as 'social learning'. Everyday examples of social learning abound: Individuals often decide where to shop, which restaurants to frequent, and even where to send their children to school according to the behavior and actions of others.

The concept of social learning has been studied extensively in economics, and recent explicit treatments include Bala and Goyal (1998), Banerjee (1992), Blonski (1999), Neeman and Orosel (1999), and Scharfstein and Stein (1990). Social learning is also an implicit feature in many other economic models. Keynes (1936), for example, though not referring to social learning directly, suggested that similar processes are operative in the behavior of investors in asset markets. Indeed, to the extent that social learning underpins the use of learning heuristics such as imitation, it is implicit in many of the models examined in this chapter and elsewhere in economics.

In an economic model of social learning developed by Banerjee (1992), economic agents rationally respond to the decisions of others because these decisions may reflect privately held information. One result of this model is herd behavior—everyone does what everyone else is doing even when their own private information suggests that they should do something different. As an example, consider the decision of a firm to enter a given market. In addition to the private information that each firm has about the long-term profitability of this market, the decision of other firms to enter may provide a signal of the market's value. If other firms enter that market, a potential entrant may become convinced that the market is in fact highly profitable. After a sufficient number of firms have entered the market, all potential entrants do the same regardless of their own private information (Albach and Jin 1998). Bikhchandani, Hirschleifer, and Welch (1998) referred to this learning process as an 'informational cascade' (p. 154), where it is optimal for an observer of preceding individuals to follow their behavior without regard to his or her own information. In the context of organizational learning, informational cascades may have dangerous consequences for firms. If a few investors have received wrong signals, all investors may end up worse off.

A major contribution of this literature has been the explicit recognition that the institutional environment in which economic actors operate not only provides a context for learning but also may facilitate learning. By observing the behavior of others, economic agents gain insight about the outcomes associated with certain actions and, thus, learn what action is best in a given situation. Although this interaction may or may not produce efficient outcomes, it is certainly important in understanding economic learning activities.

Path Dependency

The phenomenon of social learning suggests that the behavior of a given economic agent may depend upon learning that takes place among all agents. In a similar way, economists have recognized that learning processes may also depend upon the past behavior of economic agents (Arthur 1989, 1990; David 1986, 1990). That is, knowledge acquisition and creation may be path dependent. Arthur (1989), for example, developed a simple model that illustrates the evolutionary and path-dependent nature of technological improvement. The model consists of a large number of agents who have been divided equally into two groups, Type R and Type S. Each agent chooses between two types of technology, A and B. Type R agents are assumed to prefer technology A; Type S agents, technology B. The payoff to each agent from picking a given technology is equal to a payoff that is specific to that agent plus a returns parameter multiplied by the number of people using a given technology. This setup allowed Arthur to explore how the returns to technology (i.e. the change in the benefits of a technology given a change in its amount of use) influence the type of technology that is adopted. Three scenarios are considered in the model: increasing, constant, and decreasing returns. Arthur found that one can accurately predict the proportion of agents using each technology in the constant and decreasing returns cases but that there is no predictability in the case of increasing returns. Because there are increasing returns, the benefits from increased use of a given technology will eventually outweigh any individual preferences for other technologies. Thus, with increasing returns, it is likely that all agents will eventually prefer a single technology. Because timing is important, the technology that is ultimately chosen in the model is strongly influenced by the type of agent that moves first.

Arthur's model suggests that the development of technology may be subject to self-reinforcing cycles that, once initiated, may channel future development into a particular path. In this framework, even small, random events may have substantial downstream effects. Interestingly, the path of development that is followed need not be socially optimal *ex post*. David's (1990) account of the QWERTY typewriter keyboard provides a classic illustration of this phenomenon. In spite of what is presumed to be a superior *ex post* alternative, the QWERTY keyboard design became 'locked in'.[1] Other examples of technological lock-in are provided in Arthur (1990) and David (1990). The fundamental insight of this research is that initial conditions and chance events can dictate how economic agents acquire new knowledge. Put another way, 'history matters' in organizational learning (for a more extensive discussion of the impact of history on organizational learning and change, see Fear, Ch. 7 in this volume).

Equilibrium Modifications

Game Theory

A third approach used in economics to examine organizational learning is to change the equilibrium concept that is used to model outcomes in traditional models. An equilibrium concept can be thought of as a feedback system that aggregates individual actions into an overall outcome (Kreps 1990). Traditionally, this feedback system is assumed to be instantaneous, with players performing as well as they possibly can, given the behavior of others. The growing literature in economic game theory modifies this feedback concept to explicitly examine the ways in which players interact and learn about the benefits of certain actions from past performance and to gain an understanding of their opponents' strategies. Game theory has become one of the most popular means by which economists approach individual and organizational learning.

[1] Oliver Williamson (1996) provided an interesting critique of this literature, suggesting that many of the 'inefficiencies' highlighted in discussions of path dependency are irremediable. That is, no feasible alternative can be articulated and implemented.

An underlying theme in most of the game-theoretic literature is that history and the structure of the game enable players to learn about their environment and about the beliefs and strategies of their opponents, affording the players increased payoffs due to superior knowledge of the game (Alexis 1999). Although the game-theoretic literature on learning is extensive, two general approaches can be distinguished (Knight 1996; Milgrom and Roberts 1991). The first set of game-theoretic models deals with games that are played repeatedly and emphasizes specific rules according to which players form expectations about their opponents' current moves as a function of previous plays. The basic assumption is that a player's actions in period $t + 1$ can be perfectly predicted by actions in period t. This approach, frequently referred to as best-reply dynamics, has been used extensively in economics to study learning (Bernheim 1984; Moulin 1986) and is the basis for Cournot's (1960) analysis of duopoly. A variant of this approach, known as 'fictitious-play' logic, bases expectations of current play on the entire set of past plays of the game (Brown 1951; Milgrom and Roberts 1991). Players pick their strategies so as to maximize their returns, given the prediction that the probability distribution of opponents' play in round t will be the same as the empirical frequency distribution in the $t-1$ previous rounds. (Fictitious-play games are a game-theoretic variant of Bayesian learning, which is examined in the next section.)

A second set of learning models in game theory examines information about the payoffs in a game rather than about the past behavior of players. In models employing this approach (Aumann 1987; Bernheim 1984), actors use their knowledge of existing payoffs and their understanding of the rationality and information possessed by others to derive expectations about the behavior of their opponents (Knight 1996).

These two approaches to learning in game theory provide insights into how economic agents learn from the past or through an understanding of the structure of their environment and the behavior of others. Although they have

been used extensively in the literature, they are of limited utility. In many cases, for example, 'past-play' approaches place too much emphasis on recent events, ignoring important information from previous periods. Fictitious-play models, on the other hand, may overemphasize the distant past by weighting the first play equally with the last play, thereby ignoring the possibility that learning takes place in the interim (Milgrom and Roberts 1991). Finally, approaches that stress payoffs may ignore potentially useful information that one can gain by analyzing the relationship between payoffs and the types of players who seek those payoffs (Knight 1996). In an effort to overcome these limitations, Milgrom and Roberts (1991) developed a 'sophisticated' learning model that combines the knowledge that players have about the past with whatever information they have about their competitors' rationality, alternatives, and payoffs. Although relatively recent in its development, this approach reflects recognition that economic agents employ a variety of learning strategies and, as a result, may yield new insights into how individuals and organizations learn in different environments.

Bayesian Learning

In economics, as in most applied social sciences, deductive reasoning is used to solve problems. That is, economists typically derive hypotheses from practical experiences and test them against empirical observations (Albach and Jin 1998). As Popper (1959) noted, however, these tests can never definitively prove that a statement about the real world is true. The best that can be hoped for is that repeated tests will continue to decrease uncertainty and, in turn, increase confidence in the validity of a particular hypothesis. This updating process, known as Bayesian learning, is among the most widely utilized approaches to learning in economics. In traditional neoclassical models it is typically assumed that Bayesian updating is perfect and instantaneous. However, recent research combining psychology and economics is replete with reasons why perfect Bayesian updating may be implausible or simply too costly (Conlisk 1996; Rabin 1998; Tversky and Kahneman 1974, 1983). In these cases, more realistic and less costly forms of learning become important.

To understand Bayesian learning and its problems, it is useful to consider an example. Suppose an individual wants to know whether the demand for a given product next year will exceed demand this year. One approach is to survey customers and use the responses as a signal of next year's market demand. No matter how carefully survey techniques are implemented, one can never infer the true market demand from the results of the survey. However, it is possible to use the information gleaned from the survey to update prior beliefs about demand. Hence, a positive signal from the survey results would lead one to make an upward adjustment of expectations about demand. In other words, the new probability of increased demand exceeds the prior probability (Albach and Jin 1998). If one continues to receive positive signals through repeated surveying, the confidence that next year's demand will be higher than this year's will converge toward one. In the extreme, if an agent is able to observe the environment for a sufficiently long time, the agent will eventually acquire truth, at least in a probabilistic sense.

In traditional orthodox models it is frequently assumed that economic agents can observe and correctly interpret past signals over a sufficiently long period and thereby achieve probabilistic truth. However, Rabin (1998) and Kahneman and Tversky (1982) suggested that a variety of factors limit the ability of agents to engage in perfect updating. Economic agents, for example, tend to cling to previously held beliefs in spite of new signals, a phenomenon known as belief perseverance. Similarly, agents tend to look for signals that conform to strongly held prior beliefs (i.e. confirmatory biases). Finally, overconfidence in one's own judgment may inhibit perfect Bayesian updating. Once the reliability of signals or the ability of agents to correctly interpret received signals is questioned, it is no longer true that Bayesian learning will lead to probabilistic truth. In these cases, economic agents may employ quicker

and less costly forms of learning. March and Simon (1993), for instance, suggested that imitation may be a more effective form of learning in these contexts. Likewise, firms may employ simple heuristics to solve problems (Grether 1980) or utilize predefined procedures or solutions (Cohen, March, and Olsen 1972). Unlike traditional Bayesian approaches, these other forms of learning take into account that the feedback mechanisms used by economic agents in decision-making are imperfect and subject to biases.

Learning-by-doing and Learning Curve Models

In traditional neoclassical models it is typically assumed that feedback mechanisms work instantaneously. A substantial and growing body of research in economics, however, shows that the experience gained by individuals and organizations actually improves performance over time. There are two main variants of these so-called learning-by-doing models. The first branch focuses on learning by individuals. Economists have typically assumed that increases in individual productivity and skills result either from learning-by-doing on the job or from investments made in training. In the first case, productivity gains in human capital result from being able to increase the quality or speed of job performance as a result of previous exposure to a given set of tasks (Arrow 1962; Rosen 1972). Perhaps the most noted example of this form of learning is in Adam Smith's (1776/1976) example of a pin factory, in which repeated exposure to individual tasks in the pin-making process enabled workers to increase production substantially.

An alternative approach to individual learning is associated with Becker's (1964) training model of human capital accumulation. In this model, experience improves individual skills and productivity through a portion of experience that is invested in training. Unlike the pure learning-by-doing approach, in which individuals learn through current productive activities, the investment in training model is based on the assumption that workers dedicate a portion of their workday to training and thereby trade off current production for increases in future productive performance. For instance, when a firm sends an individual to a training program to learn how to use a new machine, the firm is giving up a portion of that worker's current productive capacity for expected increases in future capacity. (For a useful effort to combine this training focus with the learning-by-doing approach to human capital, see Killingsworth 1982, who developed a model in which human capital accumulation occurs through both training and learning-by-doing.) In both Becker's human capital model and models of individual learning-by-doing, organizations are assumed to reap the benefits of productivity gains resulting from individual learning. However, the mechanisms by which individual learning is transformed into organizational learning are rarely clearly specified.

The second major approach focuses on learning in organizations. Learning-by-doing in firms may take place through individuals gaining knowledge through experience, improved capital usage, firm knowledge gained through experience with a given technology, capital design improvement, and improved coordination (Arrow 1962). Thus, an important distinction between this approach and the individual learning models described above is that firm learning can increase productivity in multiple factors, whereas individual learning is focused solely on human capital. Gruber (1992) provided a classic example of learning-by-doing at the organizational level in his examination of semiconductor firms. Gruber found that the process of semiconductor chip manufacturing is so sensitive to production processes that many of the chips produced in early stages are unusable. Yields in later stages increase considerably, primarily because of gained experience. As firms become increasingly proficient at specific tasks, they are said to move along their 'learning curve', which depicts the relationship between a firm's cumulative experience and productivity. Hatch and Mowery (1998) also examined semiconductor manufacturing and the relationship between process innovation

and learning-by-doing. Yield improvements are shown empirically to be the product of deliberate activities by the semiconductor manufacturer, rather than the incidental by-product of production volume. Interestingly, some of the knowledge gained through learning-by-doing during new process development is specific to the production environment where the process is developed and is effectively lost when the new process is transferred to the manufacturing environment. Likewise, Teece (1977) found that strong learning exists in the process of technology transfer. The first effort to transfer manufacturing technology abroad is typically fraught with hazards and cost overruns, whereas subsequent efforts occasion much lower costs. Typically, economists assume that as cumulative output increases the production costs per unit decrease because of experience efficiencies. Average costs will decrease with increases in production until the firm eventually reaches a point when no additional gains to learning can be realized.

Learning curve models have been explored in many firms in both the manufacturing and service sectors. Some of the first applications were in aircraft production (Alchian 1963; Asher 1956; Wright 1936). Wright (1936), for example, noticed that labor, material, and overhead requirements declined with increased aircraft production, and he estimated that production input requirements decreased by 20 per cent for every doubling of cumulative past production. Similarly, Alchian's (1963) examination of twenty-two different types of World War II military aircraft revealed that learning rates varied significantly across plane types. Learning curve effects have also been found in a variety of industries, including shipping (Rapping 1965), power plants (Joskow and Rose 1985; Zimmerman 1982), machine tools (Hirsch 1952, 1956), and electronics (Adler and Clark 1987; for other applications of learning curve models, see Argote and Epple 1990 and Dutton and Thomas 1984).

One recent application of learning curve models is Benkard's (1999) analysis of commercial aircraft production. Utilizing a unique data set covering the entire production of the

Lockheed L-1011 Tri-Star, Benkard found support for the traditional learning curve hypothesis about declining average costs of production. Interestingly, Benkard also found considerable support for organizational forgetting, or the hypothesis that the firm's production experience depreciates over time, as well as for incomplete spillovers of production expertise from one generation of aircraft production to another. Specifically, labor costs per plane decreased as expected during the first portion of the L-1011's production, but then took a striking upturn during later production periods. Benkard suggested that this rise could be explained by the depreciation in Lockheed's human capital due to turnover, relatively low aircraft production rates, and the introduction of a new 500-series aircraft, which had a fundamentally different design than previous models. Benkard argued that the skills needed to produce previous models were not entirely relevant to the production of the 500-series aircraft and that the firm consequently experienced both a setback in learning and increased production costs for the whole program. These results add another level of complexity to traditional learning models and have important implications for many areas of industrial organization. Notably, this research suggests that learning may be a stochastic process. That is, during task completion, learning takes place in some instances but not in others. This characteristic of learning suggests a need to better understand what properties of the firm and of production are most important in determining when learning and forgetting occur (for additional discussion of the implications that learning curve models have for industrial organization, see Cabral and Riordan 1994).

Summary

As the above subsections illustrate, a substantial and growing body of literature in mainstream economics explores various aspects of individual and organizational learning. By modifying traditional neoclassical assumptions, mainstream economists have made at least three major contributions to the understanding of organizational learning. First, by relaxing traditional behavioral assumptions, economists have somewhat clarified the picture of how cognitive limitations and environmental uncertainty affect how economic agents update their prior beliefs. Second, utilizing various game-theoretic and non-game-theoretic techniques, economists have considerably sharpened their awareness of how strategic interaction and history affect learning processes. Lastly, over the past half-century economists have explored the productivity effects of one important form of learning, learning-by-doing.

These contributions notwithstanding, the orthodox literature's treatment of learning is far from adequate. First, the portrayal of learning is still highly stylized. For the most part, learning is presented as a relatively simple, automatic, and low-cost process. In the case of learning-by-doing, for example, organizational learning is essentially a free good: a joint output of productive activity. Second, mainstream economists frequently ignore the various sources of organizational learning and ways in which internal firm processes and capabilities interact and affect learning. Finally, and perhaps most important, many of the portrayals of learning in the mainstream economics literature are fundamentally static, detailing how firms acquire and utilize existing knowledge. Much of the strategic value of learning, however, comes not from utilizing existing knowledge but from creating *new* knowledge.

Learning and Innovation

Although critical aspects of learning have been largely neglected in mainstream economics, the process by which organizations create knowledge is of central importance in a large and growing stream of research examining the economics of innovation. Broadly speaking, innovation concerns the processes by which firms acquire and put into practice new product and process technologies (Nelson and

Rosenberg 1993). Since the early work of Schumpeter (1942) and Hayek (1945), economists interested in innovation have attempted to define the nature and character of these processes. A central theme of the innovation literature is that the means by which firms develop new product and process technologies are not random; rather, technological innovation is structured and orderly and typically occurs within fairly well-defined frameworks (Dosi 1982; Dosi and Orsenigo 1988; Pavitt 1987; Zuscovitch 1986). In an effort to improve understanding of these identifiable and well-defined structures, innovation scholars have placed considerable emphasis on organizational learning processes (Metcalfe 1995). The insights provided by these scholars build upon and, in important ways, extend the treatment of learning found in the mainstream literature.

An important insight coming out of the innovation literature pertains to the complex nature of technology. Developing a new product or process is a highly uncertain venture, entailing the interaction of a host of frequently complex technological and market factors (Kline and Rosenberg 1986). Successful development involves bringing together knowledge from a variety of sources and effectively meeting performance criteria that differ along multiple dimensions (Patel and Pavitt 1998). Complexity means that knowledge, which can be easily codified, is rarely a sufficient guide to practice. As Patel and Pavitt (1998) noted, 'theoretical laws and models, often developed "under laboratory conditions," or assuming "other things being equal," are unable to predict the operating performance of complex technological artifacts' (p. 11). Rather, firms frequently rely on knowledge that is difficult, if not impossible, to articulate and codify (Polanyi 1967; Winter 1987). This tacit knowledge is acquired through experience and on-the-job training in multiple learning activities, including design, production engineering, testing, and development. Frequently, this knowledge is embodied in an organization's system of coordinating and managing tasks, that is in its organizational routines (Nelson and Winter 1982).

The tacit component of technological knowledge makes its transfer between organizations difficult. As a result, a portion of an organization's technological knowledge is often highly specific to that firm or research entity. This fact explains why imitation costs (the costs of copying an existing process or product design) are frequently on par with the costs of innovation (the costs of developing a new product or process design). Mansfield, Schwarz, and Wagner (1981), for example, showed that imitation costs are on average as much as 70 per cent of innovation costs. As with innovation, success in imitation requires the ability to control many variables with complex interactions (Patel and Pavitt 1998). These interactions can rarely be reduced to simple, codifiable algorithms, so trial and error and operating experience are required. The specificity of technological knowledge also explains why the diffusion of new technology frequently depends on the mobility of engineers and scientists (Teece 1977). Because tacit knowledge is often embodied in human capital, transferring that knowledge may depend critically on the movement of experienced personnel.

The explicit recognition of the complexity of technology has enabled scholars to derive a number of insights about organizational learning and, ultimately, the nature of technological innovation. At least three main implications for organizational learning can be distinguished in this literature (Malerba 1992; Metcalfe 1995). First, various types of learning processes can be identified, each of which is associated with different activities that take place within the firm. Second, learning involves the interaction of internal and external sources of knowledge. Third, learning is cumulative and supports localized and primarily incremental innovation. Each of these insights is explored in the remainder of this section.

Types of Learning Processes

Among the most important contributions of the innovation literature to the study of organizational learning has been the explicit recognition that learning within firms occurs in many different varieties. Technological innovation has usefully been described as consisting of several different categories of learning, each of which is relevant in varying degrees during the different activities associated with the innovation process (Rosenberg 1982). Four categories of learning processes within the firm are frequently highlighted in this literature. As noted above, much of the attention given to organizational learning in economics has focused on learning-by-doing, a category of learning that is most closely associated with manufacturing activities (Malerba 1992; Rosenberg 1982). During this stage, learning primarily involves the acquisition of increasing skills in production in order to reduce input factor costs per unit of output. However, the traditional view of learning-by-doing is but one category of learning that affects only one part of a spectrum of activities related to technological innovation.

A second category of learning, scientific learning, is most frequently associated with basic research but is also operative in other stages of the innovation process. Scientific learning entails acquiring knowledge about the fundamental laws of science and nature. As the stock of scientific knowledge increases, the cost of undertaking science-based invention decreases (Rosenberg 1974). Nelson and Winter (1982) argued that the importance of science in the learning process is that it narrows the set of research options and directs attention to approaches that appear to hold the most promise of success. Evenson and Kislev (1976) enriched this view, suggesting that another role of science in the learning process is that it may enlarge the pool of approaches to solving a particular technological problem. As the number of candidate approaches increases, the likelihood of success and the expected payoff increase, albeit at the cost of broadening the search (Cohen 1998). Cohen and Klepper (1992) offered a related argument according to which a strong base of scientific knowledge, rather than simply increasing the number of approaches to achieving a given objective, actually increases the number of technological

objectives that a firm may pursue. In each of these views, scientific learning plays an essential role in the processes of technological change. It provides not only many of the tools that are useful in the search for new products and processes but also a powerful heuristic that guides this search process (Cohen 1998).

A third form of learning identified in the innovation literature is learning-by-searching. Whereas basic research is most closely, though not exclusively, associated with research activities, learning-by-searching entails searching out and discovering the optimal design of a new product or process (Rosenberg 1982). This form of learning is most closely associated with development activities and has a strong commercial dimension. For example, firms may engage in a search to discover the specific product characteristics that are desired in the marketplace and then seek to incorporate them into their designs. Firms may also attempt to innovate by scanning the technology sets of rival firms (Metcalfe 1995). A number of authors have examined the various search routines that firms employ in the context of innovation (Dosi 1988a; Nelson and Winter 1982; Winter 1986). All these scholars found that firms are unlikely to survey the entire stock of knowledge before making their technological choices. Because technological knowledge is often highly tacit and specific to a given firm, innovation decisions are frequently made with reference to a firm's current technological capability. Thus, firms will seek to improve and diversify their technology by searching in those zones that best exploit and enhance their existing technological base (Dosi 1988a). The use of relatively narrow search routines is one explanation of why technological innovation tends to be cumulative.

As Rosenberg (1982) noted, the three forms of learning identified thus far relate to generating knowledge that is either incorporated into the designs of new products and processes or used to improve the production process associated with new products. A final type of learning frequently discussed by innovation scholars occurs only after new products are used. Learning-by-using is the process by which the performance and maintenance characteristics of a new product are determined through feedback from consumers who have extensive experience with the product (Rosenberg 1982). This form of learning is particularly important in determining the optimal characteristics of new, highly complex technologies. Rosenberg (1982) stated:

For in an economy with complex new technologies, there are essential aspects of learning that are a function not of the experience involved in producing the product but of its utilization by the final user. . . . For a range of products involving complex, interdependent components or materials, . . . the outcome of the interaction of these parts cannot be precisely predicted. In this sense, we are dealing with performance characteristics that scientific knowledge or techniques cannot predict very accurately. The performance of these products, therefore, is highly uncertain. (p. 122)

Learning-by-using generates two different types of knowledge that assist in alleviating this uncertainty. First, the feedback from users deepens understanding of the relationship between a product's design and its performance. This information can subsequently be used to make necessary product design modifications. For instance, user feedback about the failure under stress of jet engine turbine blades in the Boeing 747 during the late 1960s led to aircraft design modifications (Rosenberg 1982). Second, learning-by-using may result in product-related knowledge that leads to new performance or operating practices. In this case, the information revealed by utilization never actually becomes embodied in the product's design. Rather, learning-by-using leads to new practices that lengthen the product's life or reduce its operating costs. In the airline industry, for example, early operating experience generated data about how various flight conditions affect airplane fuel consumption and overall performance. Although such information might not get incorporated into aircraft designs, it would likely be used to modify training and operating procedures (Rosenberg 1982).

This discussion of the various categories of learning suggests that what is typically referred to as research and development (R&D) is a mul-

tifaceted learning process. In conducting R&D, firms employ different types of learning methods. Although each of these types of learning is closely associated with a particular set of innovative activities their utility is by no means limited to these activities. Rather, firms employ these various approaches to learning during multiple stages of innovation. For example, scientific learning is not confined to basic research activities, but rather takes place at all points along the chain of innovation (Kline and Rosenberg 1986). Kline and Rosenberg (1986) noted that complex feedback loops between innovative activities frequently allow knowledge acquired during one stage of innovation to be incorporated into other activities. Moreover, distinctions within these four categories of learning can be sharpened. For instance, innovation scholars point out that a firm's specific types of scientific learning differ across the various stages of innovation. During initial analytic design activities, for example, pure, long-range scientific learning is frequently important, whereas during development activities the emphasis is on applied learning (Kline and Rosenberg 1986). Thus, in explicitly recognizing that organizations employ various categories of learning, innovation scholars not only have created a useful taxonomy but also have facilitated the examination of many subtle aspects of organizational learning.

Sources of Knowledge

In addition to the recognition that firms employ many different types of learning processes, a second important insight of the innovation literature is that learning is linked to different sources of knowledge that may be either internal or external to the firm (Malerba 1992). As noted above, a portion of a firm's existing knowledge base is highly tacit and, thus, idiosyncratic to a given organization or research unit. Other knowledge, however, can be articulated and even codified in journals, manuals, and precise algorithms (Dosi 1982). This knowledge can be easily transferred between organizations and may actually exist in the public domain. Even knowledge that is privately held or that is highly tacit frequently spills over organizational boundaries through, for instance, the movement of experienced personnel. These spillovers of technological knowledge, experience, and skills are essentially externalities that flow between adjacent users and producers of innovation (Geroski 1998). As a result of these externalities, interdependencies and synergies between sectors, firms, and even business units or production stages within a given firm are created (Dosi 1988a). The level of learning achieved in a given organization depends not only on its own research efforts but also on the entire pool of knowledge that is available to it and on its ability to take advantage of these spillovers (Griliches 1998). Understanding the dynamics of internal and external spillovers, therefore, is critical to developing a comprehensive view of organizational learning.

The importance of knowledge spillovers to learning at various organizational levels has been examined extensively in the innovation literature. Westney and Sakakibara (1986), Mansfield (1988), Odagiri and Goto (1993), and Rosenberg and Steinmueller (1988) noted the importance of spillovers at the national level. Odagiri and Goto, for example, observed that the ability of firms to absorb Western economic and technological knowledge rapidly has been critical to Japanese industrial growth since the mid-nineteenth century. Similarly, industry-level spillovers have been documented in a number of sectors, notably the aluminum and computer industries (Bresnahan 1986; Brock 1975; Peck 1962). At the organizational level, learning from spillovers may take the form of drawing on knowledge generated by various external sources, such as rival firms, universities, and government research organizations (Griliches 1991). Arora and Gambardella (1990), Jaffe (1989), and Mansfield (1991) each noted that firm-level innovation is strongly influenced by spillovers of knowledge from university research (for economic models of these externalities, see Griliches 1979 and Romer 1990). Alternatively, March and Simon (1958: 34–47) observed that organizations may learn

by imitating and borrowing from their rivals. Rosenberg and Steinmueller (1988), for instance, argued that the economic success of Japanese firms is due in part to their ability to imitate the successful practices of U.S. firms. Research on the sources of innovation supports the observation that imitation is an important means of technological diffusion and change (Cohen and Levinthal 1990). Finally, knowledge spillovers are important at the intraorganizational level. Considerable research suggests that a firm's innovative performance is strongly influenced by knowledge generated outside the firm's formal R&D unit (Mansfield 1968; Patel and Pavitt 1998).

Taken together, the research discussed thus far in this section suggests that an organization's innovative performance is strongly influenced by a variety of internal and external sources of knowledge. Table 4.2 highlights the various sources of learning. The specific factors that affect the ability of organizations to assimilate and absorb knowledge from these internal and external sources are examined by Cohen and Levinthal (1990). These authors argued that the ability of an organization to recognize the value of new information, assimilate it, and apply it to commercial ends (i.e. a firm's absorptive capacity) is a function of the firm's level of prior related knowledge. Drawing on cognitive research that indicates that learning is cumulative, Cohen and Levinthal suggested that organizations are better able to absorb external knowledge when it is closely related to the organization's existing stock of knowledge than when it is not. Thus, firms that invest in R&D are not only generating new knowledge but also enhancing their ability to learn in the future. This twofold effect suggests that an organization's innovative performance is partially path-dependent, for failure to invest adequately in an area of technological expertise may foreclose the future development of capabilities in that area (Cohen and Levinthal 1990).

Similarly, an organization's current learning processes may limit its ability to recognize and respond to external changes. Henderson and Clark (1990), for example, argued that, in an

Table 4.2. Categories of learning in the innovation literature

Type of learning	Locus	Innovative focus
Learning-by-doing	Internal to the firm	Production activities
Learning-by-searching	Primarily internal to the firm	Commercial focus mainly R&D-related
Scientific learning	Internal and external to the firm	Absorption of new scientific and technological knowledge
Learning-by-using	Internal to the firm	Use of products and inputs
Spillover learning	External to the firm	Absorbing external knowledge and imitating the practices of rivals

Note: For a discussion of these basic learning types, see Malerba 1992.

environment in which a given technology's design is stable, an organization will tend to focus its learning efforts on a specific product architecture. That is, engineers within the organization will concentrate on learning about the product's components and the way these components relate to one another. Eventually, this knowledge becomes embedded in the practices and procedures of the organization, a useful property as long as the product's fundamental design is stable. When this product's architecture changes, however, two problems arise. First, established organizations may be slow to respond to these technological changes. Because the organization's active learning is focused on the old technological architecture, the organization may fail to recognize the importance of technological changes immediately. Second, once an organization has recognized the nature of an architectural innovation, it may be unable to respond effectively. Because knowledge of the old product architecture is embedded in the organization, responding to the new innovation entails fundamentally switching from one mode of learning to another. This switch is complicated by the fact that the organization must build new architectural knowledge in a context in which some of its old architectural knowledge may be relevant. Thus, a firm's existing learning processes may fundamentally handicap it in the face of certain types of technological changes. This same theme is also featured in work by Anderson and Tushman (1990) and Christensen and Rosenbloom (1995).

Incremental and Cumulative Learning

The discussion of the previous two subsections suggests that organizational learning is often an incremental and cumulative process. Dosi (1982, 1988a) made this point explicitly, arguing that technological innovation frequently evolves in certain path-dependent ways, contoured and channeled by what can be thought of as technological paradigms. A technological paradigm contextually defines a firm's opportunities for innovation and the basic procedures that are available to exploit these opportunities. The crucial point is that paradigms are fundamentally shaped by an organization's prior technological performance. As noted above, both the search routines that a firm employs in developing new products and processes and the ability of that firm to absorb external knowledge are largely determined by the organization's current stock of technology. In such a circumstance, organizational learning tends to be incremental (Dosi 1988a; Malerba 1992). The technological problems and opportunities that an organization perceives frequently relate to its current activities. Thus, a considerable portion of a firm's innovative activities consists of modifications and improvements to existing products and processes. In many instances, incremental innovations result not from any deliberate research activities but rather from improvements discovered during a product's manufacturing process or through a feedback from users (Dosi 1988*a*). Because firms differ in their stock of knowledge and in the learning processes they employ, the trajectories of incremental technological change also differ (Malerba 1992). Therefore, one would expect that new product and process developments for a particular organization lie in the technological neighborhood of previous successes (Nelson and Winter 1982; Teece 1996; for an additional discussion of the importance of technological paradigms in learning processes, see Dierkes, Marz, and Teele, Ch. 12 in this volume).

This last point also suggests that technology development, particularly within a given paradigm, proceeds *cumulatively* along the path defined by that paradigm. According to Dosi (1988*a*), '[w]hat the firm can hope to do technologically in the future is heavily constrained by what it has been capable of doing in the past. Once the cumulative and firm specific nature of technology is recognized, its development over time ceases to be random, but is constrained to zones closely related technologically to existing activities' (p. 225). To the extent that innovative learning is local and specific to a given technology paradigm but is shared by other firms operating on that technology, one is likely to see the sort of industry lock-in and path dependence discussed in David (1975, 1985) and Arthur (1989, 1990). Alternatively, to the extent that learning is local and cumulative at the level of individual organizations, firm-specific lock-in and path dependence are likely to be operative. In this case, an organization's technical capabilities are likely to be 'close in' to previous technological accomplishments (Teece 1996: 195). For instance, specific technological skills in one field (e.g. pharmaceuticals) may be applicable to closely related fields (e.g. pesticides) but are not likely to be useful in distant areas (e.g. airplanes) (Teece 1988).

Summary

In some sense, all technological innovation entails organizational learning. Thus, any attempt to summarize the contribution of the innovation literature to organizational learning in a few pages is bound to be inadequate. Nevertheless, in this section we identified three main contributions of this kind. The first two insights—that there exist different categories of learning involving internal and external sources of knowledge—are summarized in Table 4.2. This table, along with the above discussion, suggests that learning is not the free good it is portrayed as being in much of the economics literature but rather that learning is a costly and multifaceted process (Malerba 1992). Moreover, this discussion dispels the notion that learning takes place in a vacuum. Instead, various internal and external sources are instrumental in the accumulation of a firm's stock of knowledge. It is this existing pool of knowledge capital and the specific learning processes employed by a firm that generate unique trajectories of incremental and cumulative technological innovation, the third major insight of this literature. Taken together, these three insights present a more realistic and comprehensive picture of organizational learning processes. In the next section we examine how contributions from the innovation literature are influencing emerging work on the economic theory of the firm.

Organizational Learning and the Theory of the Firm

Much of the work reported in the innovation literature suggests that, to the extent that learning is localized in individual firms, one is likely to observe that firms with specific technological competencies follow unique trajectories of innovation. Any useful treatment of economic learning, therefore, must address a key question: How do firms organize so as to develop and exploit their specialized competencies for knowledge creation in the best way? For this purpose, we turn to emerging economic theories of the firm. The literature in economics exploring the theory of the firm and the economics of organization emerged during the late 1930s but did not receive focused theoretical and empirical attention until the late 1970s. One main thrust of this literature is that the principal objective of economic organization is to adapt to changing circumstances (Barnard 1938; Hayek 1945; Williamson 1996). Given the importance of adaptation in learning processes (Huber 1991; Levitt and March 1988), much of this literature can therefore be seen as fundamentally addressing how organizations learn. (Various literature reviews of organizational learning note that the terms 'adaptation' and 'learning' are frequently used interchangeably; see Nonaka and Takeuchi 1995: 54.) Indeed, work coming out of this branch of economics has been central in developing a coherent and dynamic approach to organizational learning.

Antecedents

Learning and learning processes have long been central components in the understanding of the economics of organization. The early Austrian economist Frederich von Hayek (1945) was among the first to draw attention to the role of the market form of organization in facilitating learning among economic agents. According to Hayek, the process of a market reaching its equilibrium is fundamentally a learning process. In reaching this conclusion, Hayek made a distinction between two types of economic knowledge: knowledge of general rules and principles (i.e. scientific knowledge) and knowledge of particular circumstances of time and location. Whereas the former type of knowledge is mainly of interest to theorists, it is the latter type that is most relevant in determining economic outcomes. The main problem of economic organization in Hayek's view, is coordinating the use of this dispersed, context-specific knowledge in the face of changing circumstances that continually redefine the relative importance of the knowledge

possessed by any given individual. According to Hayek,

The peculiar character of the problem of a rational economic order is determined precisely by the fact that the knowledge of the circumstances of which we must make use never exists in concentrated or integrated form but solely as dispersed bits of incomplete and frequently contradictory knowledge which all the separate individuals possess. The economic problem of society is thus not merely a problem of how to allocate 'given' resources[,] . . . it is a problem of the utilization of knowledge not given to anyone in its totality. (pp. 519–20)

It is the price mechanism, Hayek (1945) argued, that provides the solution to this core economic problem. Although its workings may not be fully understood by market participants, the price system serves as a communication network that allows agents to share relevant economic information. It is through this fundamentally spontaneous process that economic learning occurs.

Whereas Hayek (1945) concentrated on the role of the market in facilitating economic learning, Ronald Coase (1937) emphasized the limits of market learning. Coase was the first to observe that what is unique about firms and markets is that they are alternative means for organizing the same transactions. Whether economic activity is organized in one mode or another in a given instance hinges largely on the costs of managing the transaction inside the firm as compared with the costs of mediating it through the market. For Coase, the central transaction cost associated with the market mode of organization is that of learning what the relevant prices are. These costs of learning are largely eliminated when transactions are internalized inside the firm. Thus, from Coase's perspective, firms arise in part because of difficulties of learning in markets. Unlike Hayek (1945), who extolled the virtues of markets in this respect, Coase (1964) recognized that all forms of organization (including markets) are flawed and that the central problem of organizations is determining which arrangements work best in practice. Researchers interested in learning and innovation, therefore, are encouraged to examine which organizational arrangement is most conducive to knowledge creation and exploitation in a given instance.

Transaction-cost Economics

Though first suggested by Coase (1937), this comparative institutional approach has been most fully developed in the work of Oliver Williamson (1975, 1985, 1996) and scholars working in transaction-cost economics (e.g. Joskow 1987; Klein, Crawford, and Alchian 1978; Masten 1996; Masten, Meehan, and Snyder 1991; Williamson 1985, 1996; for more thorough review of the empirical work in transaction-cost economics, see Shelanski and Klein 1995). Consistent with Coase, transaction-cost economists maintain that economizing on transaction costs is mainly responsible for the choice of one form of organization over another. The theory's main prediction is that transactions, which differ in their attributes, are aligned with governance structures, which differ in their costs and competencies, in a discriminating and mainly transaction-cost-economizing fashion (Williamson 1996). The primary ways in which transactions differ, it is argued, are frequency, uncertainty, and the degree to which the assets involved can be redeployed for alternative uses or to alternative users without loss of productive value (i.e. asset specificity). Though all three characteristics are important, many of the strongest refutable implications are associated with asset specificity (Williamson 1985). Where assets are largely nonredeployable, contracting parties become locked into the transaction. This condition of bilateral dependency creates the potential that one or both parties will behave in ways that do not maximize joint profits when contractual conditions change in ways not fully accounted for in the original agreement. As a consequence, economic agents will be inclined to devise governance structures that better align the parties' incentives and limit the scope of *ex post* opportunistic behavior (Williamson 1996). As asset specificity and other contractual hazards increase, added (i.e. more hierarchical) modes of governance will be required to safeguard the transaction.

Although transaction-cost economics has been remiss in addressing organizational learning directly (Williamson 1999), its insights have been used extensively to improve understanding of how innovative activities should be organized. Teece (1988) and Dosi (1988b), for instance, observed that market transactions involving innovative activities generally exhibit the following characteristics: (a) incomplete specifications of contracts due to uncertainty about the outcomes of innovative activities, (b) high monitoring costs, (c) a lack of adequate protection for proprietary knowledge (i.e. appropriability problems), (d) weak incentives to least-cost performance, and (e) bilateral dependencies among research suppliers. Given these inherent hazards, the authors suggested that innovative activities are rather likely to occur in more formal organizations (e.g. R&D laboratories in vertically integrated firms, government and university labs) than in markets involving individual innovators. Performing R&D activities in formal organizations has a number of potential benefits. Williamson (1985), for example, noted that, in integrated firms, the flow of information between R&D laboratories and the people in the firm who implement new technologies is superior to that in markets. Kogut and Zander (1996) similarly suggested that firms facilitate the sharing and transfer of knowledge. In addition, there may be important appropriability benefits to hierarchical modes of governance. Dosi (1988b), for instance, observed that formal organizations limit cross-organization information leaks. Liebeskind (1996) likewise suggested that firms have particular institutional capabilities that enable them to protect knowledge from expropriation better than markets do. Teece (1996) pointed out that if the innovation at issue is a process technology, the vertically integrated firm may be able to use the technology in-house and take profits not by selling the technology but by selling the products that embody or use the process. Because contracting in these cases is entirely internal, specialized assets are better protected than in markets and recontracting hazards are attenuated.

The above discussion does not imply that innovative activities *never* occur outside a formal integrated setting. Indeed, one often observes market and hybrid transfers of innovations through, for example, licensing and joint ventures (Dosi 1988b; Teece 1989, 1992; Teece, Pisano, and Shuen 1997). However, these alternative modes are not all-or-nothing substitutes for in-house research. In fact, the work of Cohen and Levinthal (1990) cited in the third section of this chapter suggests that firms must possess considerable capabilities in order to absorb many of the innovations that are obtained through market mechanisms. Thus, this literature suggests that industrial research will *primarily* occur in integrated research organizations. This prediction is largely substantiated by studies documenting the growth of R&D activities in American industry over the last century (Mowery 1980; Rosenberg 1985; Teece and Armour 1977).

Resource-based and Evolutionary Theories of the Firm

In addition and, in many respects, complementary to the transaction-cost economics perspective discussed above, a growing number of theories of learning and knowledge creation in firms emphasize organization-level factors. Penrose (1959) was a pioneer in these approaches, arguing that the firm is fundamentally a repository of knowledge and that learning is central to the firm's growth. According to Penrose, the firm is 'both an administrative organization and a collection of productive resources, both human and material' (p. 31). The services rendered by these resources are the primary inputs into a firm's production processes and are firm-specific in the sense that they are a function of the knowledge and experience that the firm has acquired over time. When services that are currently going unused are applied to new lines of business, these services also function as a growth engine for the firm. In Penrose's view, a firm possesses idle resources primarily because of learning that enables the organization to utilize its re-

sources better and more efficiently than it has previously. By implication, then even firms that maintain a constant level of capital may nevertheless be able to grow as services are freed up for new uses as a result of organizational learning. Thus, Penrose's analysis suggests that a firm's resources and learning processes have an important impact on strategic performance and growth.

This basic idea underpins much of the research by scholars working on the resource-based theory of the firm (Dierickx and Cool 1989; Prahalad and Hamel 1990; Stalk, Evans, and Shulman 1992). In the resource-based approach it is argued that unique and difficult-to-imitate resources are the primary source of sustainable competitive advantage for firms. These resources enable firms to have markedly lower costs or offer high-quality products and performance than their competitors. Because of the inability of firms to quickly develop new competencies internally or to acquire often highly tacit skills and knowledge externally, resource endowments can differentiate performance and provide for competitive advantage. At least in the short run, therefore, firms with superior competencies will tend to be more profitable than their competitors. Although much of this literature focuses on the importance of existing firm-specific resources and does not directly address learning in organizations, this perspective does invite consideration of managerial strategies for developing *new* resources. In fact, because controlling difficult-to-imitate resources is a crucial source of economic profits, the management of knowledge and learning are critical strategic issues (Shuen 1994; Wernerfelt 1984). These issues are examined below.

The importance of knowledge and learning in firms was also addressed extensively in Nelson and Winter's work on the evolutionary nature of the firm (Nelson and Winter 1982; Winter 1988). Consistent with Penrose (1959) and Hayek (1945), Nelson and Winter (1982) suggested that business firms are essentially repositories for a range of highly specific productive knowledge. This knowledge, these authors argued, can be thought of as residing in an organization's standard operating procedures, or routines. Much like the genes of biological evolutionary theory, routines are patterns of interactions that represent successful solutions to particular problems. These patterns of interaction are fundamentally social in nature and are thus most often resident at the group level, though certain subroutines may be operative in individual behavior. An important aspect is that organizational routines shape how firms comprehend and address both familiar and unfamiliar situations. Organizational routines are therefore central to organizational learning. Although the character of routines varies within and across organizations, one unifying feature is that the knowledge embodied in them is typically highly tacit (Nelson and Winter 1982; Winter 1988). This characteristic implies that routines can rarely be fully codified or articulated. As a result, the routines themselves and the ability of managers to call upon them as needed are crucial aspects of an organization's learning capabilities.

Teece, Rumelt, Dosi, and Winter (1994) distinguished two main types of routines. Static routines are those that enable firms to replicate previously performed functions. Although these routines are constantly being updated and thus are not truly static, they nevertheless reflect responses to relatively familiar situations. The learning curve economies discussed in the second section of this chapter frequently reflect the presence of static routines. In contrast, dynamic routines are directed at new learning and the development of novel products and processes. The search routines that firms employ in innovative activities, for example, typically rely on dynamic routines. These routines assist firms in deciding where, how, and how long to search for innovations (Teece et al. 1994).

The above discussion suggests that routines have at least two important qualities with respect to learning. First, by storing previously successful responses to familiar and repetitious problems, routines enable organizations to improve the performance of everyday tasks. Second, by patterning useful approaches to innovation, routines facilitate experimenta-tion and the identification of new production opportunities. In short, routines embody the common codes of communication and coordination that are essential to all aspects of organizational learning. Moreover, because the knowledge embodied in routines is typically highly tacit, copying routines from one context to another is often difficult. In this respect, routines contribute to a firm's distinctive learning capabilities and are largely responsible for the regular and predictable behavioral patterns that differentiate firms from one another (Winter 1988; for an additional discussion of routines, see Kieser, Beck, and Tainio, Ch. 27 in this volume).

Dynamic Capabilities and the Knowledge-creating Organization

Nelson and Winter's work on dynamic routines began to explore the internal processes by which firms learn and develop new, strategically relevant competencies. Research examining the dynamic nature of firm capabilities has further developed these issues. First fully elaborated in the work of Teece and Pisano (1994), the dynamic capabilities approach traces its intellectual origins to early work by Joseph Schumpeter (1951), who argued that the emergence of new products and processes results from new combinations of knowledge. In a similar vein, it is argued in the dynamic capabilities approach that competitive success arises from the continuous development and reconfiguration of firm-specific assets (Teece and Pisano 1994; Teece, Pisano, and Shuen 1997). Whereas Penrose and resource-based scholars recognize the competitive importance of firm-specific capabilities, researchers of the dynamic capabilities approach attempt to outline specifically how organizations develop and renew internal competencies. Thus, the latter approach is concerned with a subset of a firm's overall capabilities, namely, those that allow firms to create new knowledge and to disseminate it throughout the organization. Stated differently, proponents of the dynamic capabilities approach attempt to isolate those internal factors that facilitate organizational learning.

Teece and Pisano (1994) highlighted the importance of three main factors: the firm's managerial and organizational processes, its strategic position, and the paths that are available to the firm. Managerial and organizational processes refer essentially to how things get done in firms (Teece and Pisano 1994). Central in this regard is how well management organizes, coordinates, and integrates various internal firm processes. A number of empirical studies, for example, suggest that the organization and coherence of production processes can lead to important differences in competencies across firms (Clark and Fujimoto 1991; Garvin 1988). Likewise, a firm's learning routines are a critical dimension of its managerial and organizational processes. The strategic position of a firm pertains to its current endowment of technology and intellectual property as well as its customer base and upstream relations with suppliers (Teece and Pisano 1994). Particularly important in this respect are difficult-to-replicate assets and those complementary assets that are required to produce and deliver new products and services (Teece 1986). Finally, the paths that are available to a firm are the strategic alternatives that it faces. As noted in the work of Dosi (1988a), Arthur (1989), and David (1985, 1986), the path a firm can take is largely constrained by its current position. Path dependencies and established technological trajectories shape the productive and technological opportunities faced by firms and the attractiveness of these opportunities.

Economists who focus on dynamic capabilities suggest that these three factors shape the ability of an organization to learn, adapt, change, and renew itself over time. Central to the dynamic capabilities approach is the idea that, in the face of a changing business environment, competitive success depends on the ability of firms to reconfigure internal and external organizational skills and resources appropriately. This sentiment is echoed in Kogut and Zander (1992), who argued that organizational learning is a function of a firm's 'combinative capabilities' to generate new

applications from existing knowledge. Underlying Kogut and Zander's claim is the idea that a firm's capabilities cannot be separated from how it is currently organized. The main advantage of learning through recombinations is that it enables firms to take advantage of existing relational structures. Other similar approaches to firm-learning can be found in Dierickx and Cool (1989), Prahalad and Hamel (1990), and Stalk, Evans, and Shulman (1992). The chief contribution of these dynamic views is that they explore not only how firms acquire and utilize existing knowledge but also how they generate and benefit from new knowledge.

This image of a knowledge-creating organization—as opposed to simply a knowledge-using organization—is further refined and extended in recent work by Nonaka (1991, 1994) and Nonaka and Takeuchi (1995). Because other chapters in this volume examine this work directly, it is redundant to summarize it here. However, research by Nonaka complements the work examined in this chapter in that he has attempted to provide a comprehensive and dynamic theory of firm-learning. Particularly useful in this regard is Nonaka and Takeuchi's (1995) discussion of the specific organizational factors that facilitate the 'knowledge spiral' (p. 70) through which learning occurs. These insights help clarify how it is that individual learning is transformed into group knowledge and, ultimately, into new *organizational* knowledge. Nonaka and Takeuchi noted that this knowledge, once embodied at the organizational level, can then be made available to affiliated organizations, such as subsidiaries, customers, suppliers, or even competitors. The specific mechanisms by which these interorganizational transfers of knowledge occur have become the subject of considerable interest among economists. Recent work by Mowery, Oxley, and Silverman (1996, 1998), for example, suggested that interorganizational collaboration provides a means by which firm-specific knowledge can be exchanged between organizations. Likewise, Hamel (1991) and Kogut (1988) observed the use of joint ventures as a means of transferring knowledge between firms (see also Merkens, Geppert, and Antal, Ch. 10 in this volume).

Interorganizational learning in a global perspective is also explored in Part VI of this volume.

Summary

In this section we have reviewed the contributions that various economic theories of the firm have made to organizational learning. Building on much of the economics and innovation research reviewed in the previous sections, this literature has been instrumental in the progress toward a comprehensive and dynamic understanding of organizational learning processes. In particular, three contributions are evident. First, the economic theory of the firm developed in the early work of Hayek and Coase and extended by Williamson stressed the central role of economic organization in facilitating adaptation and articulated the fundamental distinctions between various modes of organization. These authors' insights highlighted the limitations and possibilities for learning associated with different forms of economic organization. Second, subsequent work by resource-based scholars and those working on the evolutionary theory of the firm have emphasized the crucial dimensions along which individual firms vary in their ability to acquire and exploit knowledge. The importance of organizational routines and firm-specific assets and capabilities have generally been cited as driving this heterogeneity. Lastly, in their recent work on the dynamic aspects of firm strategy scholars have begun to recognize the organizational processes and mechanisms that firms employ not only to acquire and utilize existing knowledge but also to create new knowledge. The distinction between a knowledge-using company and a knowledge-creating company has been articulated. This final contribution has been central in the development of a dynamic theory of organizational learning.

Conclusion

In this chapter we have explored the contribution of economics to the study of organizational learning. We hope it is apparent that learning is by no means a novel concept in economics. Few, if any, modern economists would question the paramount importance of learning and learning processes to a firm's competitive performance. Moreover, many of the field's most noted forefathers, including Schumpeter, Coase, Hayek, and Marshall, made important early contributions to the study of learning. However, as we noted above, the ability of economists to develop a comprehensive, realistic, and dynamic theory of organizational learning has been substantially limited by the highly stylized assumptions that ground much research in mainstream economics. Indeed, many of the contributions to learning that have been made in economics result from modifications to a number of these restrictive assumptions. The contributions of the mainstream literature notwithstanding, we note that many of the most valuable insights into organizational learning come from two main branches within economics. Researchers studying the economics of innovation have highlighted the various types of learning that organizations employ and have noted that organizations take advantage of various internal and external sources of learning. This literature also points to the incremental and cumulative nature of learning and innovation. Economists working on the theory of the firm have utilized these insights into the nature and sources of learning in order to explore how internal firm processes affect the ability of economic organizations to develop and exploit new and existing forms of knowledge. What emerge from economics, therefore, though not a complete portrait of organizational learning, are useful vignettes of various critical aspects of learning processes. Considerable work remains to be done in piecing these snapshots together in order to provide a comprehensive and unified theory of how organizations learn.

References

Adler, P. and Clark, K. (1987). *Behind the Learning Curve: A Sketch of the Learning Process.* Boston: Harvard Business School, Harvard University.

Akerlof, G. A. (1970). 'The Market for "Lemons": Quality Uncertainty and the Market Mechanism'. *Quarterly Journal of Economics,* 84: 488–500.

Albach, H. and Jin, J. (1998). 'Learning in the Market', in H. Albach, M. Dierkes, A. Berthoin Antal, and K. Vaillant (eds.), *Organisationslernen—institutionelle und kulturelle Dimensionen. WZB Jahrbuch 1998.* Berlin: edition sigma, 355–72.

Alchian, A. (1950). 'Uncertainty, Evolution, and Economic Theory.' *Journal of Political Economy,* 58: 211–21.

—— (1963). 'Reliability of Progress Curves in Airframe Production'. *Econometrica,* 31: 679–93.

Alexis, M. (1999). 'The Treatment of Organizational Learning in Economics', in M. Dierkes, M. Alexis, A. Berthoin Antal, B. L. T. Hedberg, P. Pawlowsky, J. Stopford, and L. S. Tsui-Auch (eds.), *The Annotated Bibliography of Organizational Learning.* Berlin: edition sigma, 143–292.

—— and Wilson, C. (1967). *Organizational Decision Making.* Englewood Cliffs, NJ: Prentice Hall.

Anderson, P. and Tushman, M. L. (1990). 'Technological Discontinuities and Dominant Designs: A Cyclical Model of Technological Change'. *Administrative Science Quarterly,* 35: 604–33.

Argote, L. and Epple, D. (1990). 'Learning Curves in Manufacturing'. *Science,* 247: 920–4.

Arora, A. and Gambardella, A. (1990). 'Complementarity and External Linkages: The Strategies of the Large Firms in Biotechnology'. *Journal of Industrial Economics,* 38: 361–80.

Arrow, K. J. (1962). 'The Economic Implications of Learning by Doing'. *Review of Economic Studies,* 29: 155–73.

Arthur, W. B. (1989). 'Competing Technologies, Increasing Returns, and Lock-in by Historical Events'. *Economic Journal,* 99/394: 116–31.

—— (1990). 'Positive Feedbacks in the Economy'. *Scientific American,* 262/2: 92–9.

Asher, H. (1956). *Cost–quantity Relationships in the Airframe Industry.* Santa Monica, Calif.: Rand.

Aumann, R. (1985). 'What Is Game Theory Trying to Accomplish?' in K. J. Arrow (ed.), *Frontiers of Economics.* Oxford: Basil Blackwell, 28–78.

—— (1987). 'Correlated Equilibrium as an Expression of Bayesian Rationality'. *Econometrica,* 55: 1–18.

Bala, V. and Goyal, S. (1998). 'Learning from Neighbours'. *Review of Economic Studies,* 65: 595–621.

Banerjee, A. V. (1992). 'A Simple Model of Herd Behavior'. *Quarterly Journal of Economics,* 107: 797–817.

Barnard, C. I. (1938). *The Functions of the Executive.* Cambridge, Mass.: Harvard University Press.

Becker, G. S. (1964). *Human Capital: A Theoretical and Empirical Analysis, with Special Reference to Education.* New York: Columbia University Press.

Benkard, L. C. (1999). *Learning and Forgetting: The Dynamics of Aircraft Production.* Palo Alto, Calif.: Graduate School of Business, Stanford University.

Bernheim, B. D. (1984). 'Rationalizable Strategic Behavior'. *Econometrica,* 52: 1007–28.

Bikhchandani, S., Hirschleifer, D., and Welch, I. (1998). 'Learning from the Behavior of Others: Conformity, Fads, and Informational Cascades'. *Journal of Economic Perspectives,* 12/3: 151–70.

Blonski, M. (1999). 'Social Learning with Case-based Decisions'. *Journal of Economic Behavior and Organization,* 38: 59–77.

Bresnahan, T. (1986). 'Measuring the Spillovers from Technical Advance: Mainframe Computers in Financial Services'. *American Economic Review,* 76: 742–55.

Brock, G. W. (1975). *The U.S. Computer Industry.* Cambridge, Mass.: Ballinger.

Brown, G. W. (1951). 'Iterative Solution of Games by Fictitious Play', in T. C. Koopmans (ed.), *Activity Analysis of Production and Allocation: Proceedings of a Conference.* New York: Wiley, 374–80.

Burgelman, R. A. (1990). 'Strategy-making and Organizational Ecology: A Conceptual Framework', in J. V. Singh (ed.), *Organizational Evolution: New Directions.* Newbury Park, Calif.: Sage, 164–81.

Cabral, L. M. B. and Riordan, M. H. (1994). 'The Learning Curve, Market Dominance, and Predatory Pricing'. *Econometrica*, 62: 1115–40.

Christensen, C. M. and Rosenbloom, R. S. (1995). 'Explaining the Attacker's Advantage: Technological Paradigms, Organizational Dynamics, and the Value Network'. *Research Policy*, 24: 233–57.

Clark, K. B. and Fujimoto, T. (1991). *Product Development Performance: Strategy, Organization, and Management in the World Auto Industry*. Boston: Harvard Business School Press.

Coase, R. H. (1937). 'The Nature of the Firm'. *Econometrica*, 4: 386–405.

——(1964). 'The Regulated Industries: Discussion'. *American Economic Review*, 54: 194–7.

Cohen, M. D., March, J. G., and Olsen, J. P. (1972). 'A Garbage Can Model of Organizational Choice'. *Administrative Science Quarterly*, 17: 1–25.

Cohen, W. M. (1998). 'Empirical Studies of Innovative Activity', in P. Stoneman (ed.), *Handbook of the Economics of Innovation and Technological Change*. Oxford: Blackwell, 182–264.

——and Klepper, S. (1992). 'The Tradeoff between Firm Size and Diversity in the Pursuit of Technological Progress'. *Small Business Economics*, 4: 1–14.

——and Levinthal, D. A. (1990). 'Absorptive Capacity: A New Perspective on Learning and Innovation'. *Administrative Science Quarterly*, 35: 128–52.

Conlisk, J. (1996). 'Why Bounded Rationality'. *Journal of Economic Literature*, 34: 669–700.

Cournot, A. (1960). *Researches into the Mathematical Principles of the Theory of Wealth*. London: Hafner.

David, P. A. (1975). *Technical Choice, Innovation and Economic Growth*. London: Cambridge University Press.

——(1985). 'Clio and the Economics of QWERTY'. *American Economic Review*, 75: 332–7.

——(1986). 'Technology Diffusion, Public Policy, and Industrial Competitiveness', in R. Landau and N. Rosenberg (eds.), *The Positive Sum Strategy: Harnessing Technology for Economic Growth*. Washington, DC: National Academy Press, 373–91.

——(1990). 'The Dynamo and the Computer: An Historical Perspective on the Modern Productivity Paradox'. *American Economic Review*, 80: 355–61.

Dierickx, I. and Cool, K. (1989). 'Asset Stock Accumulation and Sustainability of Competitive Advantage'. *Management Science*, 35: 1504–14.

Dosi, G. (1982). 'Technological Paradigms and Technological Trajectories: A Suggested Interpretation of the Determinants and Directives of Technological Change'. *Research Policy*, 11: 147–62.

——(1988a). 'The Nature of the Innovative Process', in G. Dosi, C. Freeman, R. Nelson, G. Silverberg, and L. Soete (eds.), *Technical Change and Economic Theory*. New York: Pinter, 221–38.

——(1988b). 'Sources, Procedures, and Microeconomic Effects of Innovation'. *Journal of Economic Literature*, 26: 1120–71.

——and Orsenigo, L. (1988). 'Coordination and Transformation: An Overview of Structures, Behaviors, and Change in Evolutionary Environments', in G. Dosi, C. Freeman, R. Nelson, G. Silverberg, and L. Soete (eds.), *Technical Change and Economic Theory*. New York: Pinter, 13–37.

Dutton, J. and Thomas, J. (1984). 'Treating Progress Functions as a Managerial Opportunity'. *Academy of Management Review*, 36: 235–47.

Eatwell, J., Milgate, M., and Newman, P. (eds.) (1987). *The New Palgrave Dictionary of Economics*. London: Norton.

Ellison, G. and Fudenberg, D. (1993). 'Rules of Thumb for Social Learning'. *Journal of Political Economy*, 101: 612–43.

Evenson, R. E. and Kislev, Y. (1976). 'A Stochastic Model of Applied Research'. *Journal of Political Economy*, 84: 265–81.

Garvin, D. A. (1988). *Managing Quality*. New York: Free Press.

Geroski, P. (1998). 'Markets for Technology: Knowledge, Innovation and Appropriability', in P. Stoneman (ed.), *Handbook of the Economics of Innovation and Technological Change*. Oxford: Blackwell, 90–131.

Grether, D. M. (1980). 'Bayes' Rule as a Descriptive Model: The Representativeness Heuristic'. *Quarterly Journal of Economics*, 95: 537–57.

Griliches, Z. (1979). 'An Exploration of a Production Function Approach to the Estimation of the Returns to R&D'. *Bell Journal of Economics*, 10: 92–116.

—— (1991). *The Search for R&D Spillovers*. Cambridge, Mass.: National Bureau of Economic Research.

—— (1998). 'R&D and Productivity: Econometric Results and Measurement Issues', in P. Stoneman (ed.), *Handbook of the Economics of Innovation and Technological Change*. Oxford: Blackwell, 52–89.

Gruber, H. (1992). 'The Learning Curve in the Production of Semiconductor Memory Chips'. *Applied Economics*, 24: 885–94.

Hamel, G. (1991). 'Competition for Competence and Inter-partner Learning within International Strategic Alliances'. *Strategic Management Journal*, 12 (Summer special issue): 83–103.

Hatch, N. W. and Mowery, D.C. (1998). 'Process Innovation and Learning by Doing in Semiconductor Manufacturing'. *Management Science*, 44: 1461–77.

Hayek, F. A. v. (1945). 'The Use of Knowledge in Society'. *American Economic Review*, 35: 519–30.

Heiner, R. A. (1983). 'The Origin of Predictable Behavior'. *American Economic Review*, 73: 560–95.

Henderson, D. (ed.) (1993). *The Fortune Encyclopedia of Economics*. New York: Warner.

Henderson, R. M. and Clark, K. (1990). 'Architectural Innovation: The Reconfiguration of Existing Product Technologies and the Failure of Established Firms'. *Administrative Science Quarterly*, 35: 9–30.

Hirsch, W. Z. (1952). 'Manufacturing Progress Functions'. *Review of Economics and Statistics*, 34: 143–55.

—— (1956). 'Firm Progress Ratios'. *Econometrica*, 24: 136–43.

Huber, G. P. (1991). 'Organizational Learning: The Contributing Processes and the Literatures'. *Organization Science*, 2: 88–115.

Jaffe, A. (1989). 'Characterizing the "Technological Position" of Firms, with Application to Quantifying Technological Opportunity and Research Spillovers'. *Research Policy*, 18: 87–97.

Joskow, P. L. (1987). 'Contract Duration and Relation Specific Investments: Empirical Evidence from Coal Markets'. *American Economic Review*, 17: 168–85.

—— and Rose, N. L. (1985). 'The Effects of Technological Change, Experience, and Environmental Regulation on the Construction Cost of Coal-burning Generating Units'. *Rand Journal of Economics*, 16: 1–27.

Kahneman, D. and Tversky, A. (1982). 'On the Study of Statistical Intuitions'. *Cognition*, 11: 123–41.

Keynes, J. M. (1936). *The General Theory of Employment, Interest and Money*. London: Macmillan.

Killingsworth, M. R. (1982). ' "Learning by Doing" and "Investment in Training": A Synthesis of Two Rival Models of the Life Cycle'. *Review of Economic Studies*, 49: 263–71.

Klein, B., Crawford, R. G., and Alchian, A. A. (1978). 'Vertical Integration, Appropriable Rents, and the Competitive Contracting Process'. *Journal of Law and Economics*, 21: 297–326.

Kline, S. J. and Rosenberg, N. (1986). 'An Overview of Innovation', in R. Landau and N. Rosenberg (eds.), *The Positive Sum Strategy: Harnessing Technology for Economic Growth*. Washington, DC: National Academy Press, 275–305.

Knight, J. (1996). *Institutions and Social Conflict*. Cambridge: Cambridge University Press.

Kogut, B. (1988). 'Joint Ventures: Theoretical and Empirical Perspectives'. *Strategic Management Journal*, 9: 319–32.

—— and Zander, U. (1992). 'Knowledge of the Firm, Combinative Capabilities, and the Replication of Technology'. *Organization Science*, 3: 383–97.

—— —— (1996). 'What Firms Do? Coordination, Identity, and Learning'. *Organization Science*, 7: 502–18.

Kreps, D. M. (1990). *A Course in Microeconomic Theory*. Princeton: Princeton University Press.

Levitt, B. and March, J. G. (1988). 'Organizational Learning'. *Annual Review of Sociology*, 14: 319–40.

Liebeskind, J. P. (1996). 'Knowledge, Strategy, and the Theory of the Firm'. *Strategic Management Journal*, 17: 93–107.

Malerba, F. (1992). 'Learning by Firms and Incremental Change'. *Economic Journal*, 102: 845–59.

Mansfield, E. (1968). *Industrial Research and Technological Innovation*. New York: W. W. Norton.

—— (1988). 'The Speed and Cost of Industrial Innovation in Japan and the United States'. *Management Science*, 34: 1157–68.

—— (1991). 'Academic Research and Industrial Innovation'. *Research Policy*, 20: 1–12.

—— Schwarz, M., and Wagner, S. (1981). 'Imitation Costs and Patents: An Empirical Study'. *Economic Journal*, 91: 907–18.

March, J. G. and Simon, H. A. (1958). *Organizations*. New York: John Wiley.

—— —— (1993). *Organizations* (2nd edn). Cambridge, Mass.: Blackwell.

Marshall, A. (1965). *Principles of Economics*. London: Macmillan.

Masten, S. E. (ed.) (1996). *Case Studies in Contracting and Organization*. New York: Oxford University Press.

—— Meehan, J., and Snyder, E. (1991). 'The Costs of Organization'. *Journal of Law, Economics, and Organization*, 7: 1–22.

Metcalfe, S. (1995). 'The Economic Foundations of Technology Policy: Equilibrium and Evolutionary Perspectives', in P. Stoneman (ed.), *Handbook of the Economics of Innovation and Technological Change*. Oxford: Blackwell, 409–512.

Milgrom, P. and Roberts, J. (1991). 'Adaptive and Sophisticated Learning in Normal Form Games'. *Games and Economic Behavior* 3: 82–100.

Moulin, H. (1986). *Game Theory for the Social Sciences*. New York: New York University Press.

Mowery, D. C. (1980). *The Organization of Industrial Research in Great Britain, 1900–1950*. *Economics*. Palo Alto, Calif.: Stanford University, 351–74.

—— Oxley, J. E., and Silverman, B. S. (1996). 'Strategic Alliances and Interfirm Knowledge Transfer'. *Strategic Management Journal*, 17 (Winter special issue): 77–91.

—— —— —— (1998). 'Technological Overlap and Interfirm Cooperation: Implications for the Resource Based View of the Firm'. *Research Policy*, 27: 507–23.

Neeman, Z. and Orosel, G. O. (1999). 'Herding and the Winner's Curse in Markets with Sequential Bids'. *Journal of Economic Theory*, 85: 91–121.

Nelson, R. R. and Rosenberg, N. (1993). 'Technological Innovation and National Systems', in R. R. Nelson (ed.), *National Innovation Systems: A Comparative Analysis*. New York: Oxford University Press, 3–21.

—— and Winter, S. G. (1982). *An Evolutionary Theory of Economic Change*. Cambridge, Mass.: Belknap Press.

Nonaka, I. (1991). 'The Knowledge-creating Company'. *Harvard Business Review*, 69/6: 96–104.

—— (1994). 'A Dynamic Theory of Organizational Knowledge Creation'. *Organization Science*, 5: 14–37.

—— and Takeuchi, H. (1995). *The Knowledge-creating Company: How Japanese Companies Create the Dynamics of Innovation*. New York: Oxford University Press.

Odagiri, H. and Goto, A. (1993). 'The Japanese System of Innovation: Past, Present, and Future', in R. R. Nelson (ed.), *National Innovation Systems: A Comparative Analysis*. New York: Oxford University Press, 76–114.

Patel, P. and Pavitt, K. (1998). 'Patterns of Technological Activity: Their Measurement and Interpretation', in P. Stoneman (ed.), *Handbook of the Economics of Innovation and Technical Change*. Oxford: Basil Blackwell, 14–51.

Pavitt, K. (1987). 'The Objectives of Technology Policy'. *Science and Public Policy*, 14: 182–8.

Peck, M. J. (1962). 'Inventions in the Postwar American Aluminum Industry', in R. R. Nelson (ed.), *The Rate and Direction of Inventive Activity*. Princeton: Princeton University Press, 279–98.

Penrose, E. T. (1959). *The Theory of the Growth of the Firm*. Oxford: Basil Blackwell.

Polanyi, M. (1967). *The Tacit Dimension*. Garden City, NY: Doubleday.

Popper, K. (1959). *The Logic of Scientific Discovery*. London: Hutchinson.

Prahalad, C. K. and Hamel, G. (1990). 'The Core Competence of the Corporation'. *Harvard Business Review*, 68/3: 79–91.

Rabin, M. (1998). 'Psychology and Economics'. *Journal of Economic Literature*, 36: 11–46.

Rapping, L. (1965). 'Learning and World War II Production Functions'. *Review of Economics and Statistics*, 47: 81–6.

Romer, P. M. (1990). 'Endogenous Technological Change'. *Journal of Political Economy*, 98: 71–102.

Rosen, S. (1972). 'Learning by Experience as Joint Production'. *Quarterly Journal of Economics*, 86: 366–82.

Rosenberg, N. (1974). 'Science, Innovation, and Economic Growth'. *Economic Journal*, 84: 90–108.

—— (1982). *Inside the Black Box*. Cambridge: Cambridge University Press.

—— (1985). 'The Commercial Exploitation of Science by American Industry', in K. B. Clark, R. H. Hayes, and C. Lorenz (eds.), *The Uneasy Alliance: Managing the Productivity–Technology Dilemma*. Cambridge, Mass.: Harvard Business School Press, 19–51.

—— and Steinmueller, W. E. (1988). 'Why Are Americans Such Poor Imitators'. *American Economic Review*, 78: 229–34.

Scharfstein, D. and Stein, J. (1990). 'Herd Behavior and Investment'. *American Economic Review*, 80: 465–79.

Schumpeter, J. A. (1942). *Capitalism, Socialism and Democracy*. London: Allen and Unwin.

—— (1951). *The Theory of Economic Development*. Cambridge, Mass.: Harvard University Press.

Senge, P. M. (1990). *The Fifth Discipline: The Art and Practice of the Learning Organization*. New York: Doubleday.

Shelanski, H. A. and Klein, P. G. (1995). 'Empirical Research in Transaction Cost Economics'. *Journal of Law, Economics, and Organization*, 11: 335–61.

Shuen, A. (1994). *Technology Sourcing and Learning Strategies in the Semiconductor Industry*. Doctoral dissertation, Walter A. Haas School of Business, University of California at Berkeley.

Simon, H. A. (1955). 'A Behavioral Model of Rational Choice'. *Quarterly Journal of Economics*, 69: 99–118.

—— (1957a). *Administrative Behavior: A Study of Decision-making Processes in Administrative Organization*. New York: Macmillan.

—— (1957b). *Models of Man: Social and Rational; Mathematical Essays on Rational Human Behavior in a Social Setting*. New York: Wiley.

Smith, A. (1976). *The Wealth of Nations*. Chicago: University of Chicago Press. (Original work published 1776)

Stalk, G., Evans, P., and Shulman, L. E. (1992). 'Competing on Capabilities: The New Rules of Corporate Strategy'. *Harvard Business Review*, 70/2: 57–69.

Stigler, G. J. (1961). 'The Economics of Information'. *Journal of Political Economy*, 69: 213–25.

Teece, D. J. (1977). 'Technology Transfer by Multinational Firms: The Resource Cost of Transferring Technological Know-how'. *Economic Journal*, 87: 242–61.

—— (1986). 'Profiting from Technological Innovation: Implications for Integration, Collaboration, Licensing and Public Policy'. *Research Policy*, 15: 285–305.

—— (1988). 'Technological Change and the Nature of the Firm', in G. Dosi, C. Freeman, R. R. Nelson, G. Silverberg, and L. Soete (eds.), *Technical Change and Economic Theory*. New York: Pinter, 256–81.

—— (1989). 'Inter-organizational Requirements of the Innovation Process'. *Managerial and Decision Economics*, 10 (Spring special issue): 35–42.

—— (1992). 'Competition, Cooperation, and Innovation: Organizational Arrangements for Regimes of Rapid Technological Progress'. *Journal of Economic Behavior and Organization*, 18: 1–25.

—— (1996). 'Firm Organization, Industrial Structure, and Technological Innovation'. *Journal of Economic Behavior and Organization*, 31: 193–224.

—— (1998). 'Capturing Value from Knowledge Assets: The New Economy, Markets for Know-how, and Intangible Assets'. *California Management Review*, 40/3: 55–79.

—— and Armour, H. O. (1977). 'Innovation and Divestiture in the U.S. Oil Industry', in D. J. Teece (ed.), *R&D in Energy Implications of Petroleum Industry Coorganization*. Palo Alto, Calif.: Institute for Energy Studies, Stanford University, 7–93.

—— and Pisano, G. (1994). 'The Dynamic Capabilities of Firms: An Introduction'. *Industrial and Corporate Change*, 3: 537–56.

—— —— and Shuen, A. (1997). 'Dynamic Capabilities and Strategic Management'. *Strategic Management Journal*, 18: 509–33.

—— Rumelt, R., Dosi, G., and Winter, S. (1994). 'Understanding Corporate Coherence: Theory and Evidence'. *Journal of Economic Behavior and Organization*, 23: 1–30.

Tversky, A. and Kahneman, D. (1974). 'Judgment under Uncertainty: Heuristics and Biases'. *Science*, 185: 1124–31.

—— —— (1983). 'Extensional versus Intuitive Reasoning: The Conjunction Fallacy in Probabilistic Judgment'. *Psychological Review*, 90: 293–315.

Warner, M. (ed.) (1996). *International Encyclopedia of Business and Management*. New York: Routledge.

Wernerfelt, B. (1984). 'A Resource-based View of the Firm'. *Strategic Management Journal*, 5: 171–80.

Westney, D. E. and Sakakibara, K. (1986). 'The Role of Japan-based R&D in Global Technology Strategy', in M. Hurowitch (ed.), *Technology in the Modern Corporation*. London: Pergamon, 217–32.

Williamson, O. E. (1975). *Markets and Hierarchies: Analysis and Antitrust Implications*. New York: Free Press.

—— (1985). *The Economic Institutions of Capitalism: Firms, Markets, Relational Contracting*. New York: Free Press.

—— (1996). *The Mechanisms of Governance*. New York: Oxford University Press.

—— (1999). *Strategy Research: Governance and Competence Perspectives*. Berkeley: Business and Public Policy.

Winter, S. G. (1971). 'Satisficing, Selection, and the Innovation Remnant'. *Quarterly Journal of Economics*, 85: 237–61.

—— (1986). 'Schumpeterian Competition in Alternative Technological Regimes', in R. Day and G. Elliasson (eds.), *The Dynamics of Market Economies*. Amsterdam: North Holland, 199–232.

—— (1987). 'Knowledge and Competence as Strategic Assets', in D. J. Teece (ed.), *The Competitive Challenge: Strategies for Industrial Innovation and Renewal*. Cambridge, Mass.: Ballinger, 159–84.

—— (1988). 'On Coase, Competence, and the Corporation'. *Journal of Law, Economics, and Organization*, 4: 163–80.

Wright, T. P. (1936). 'Factors Affecting the Cost of Airplanes'. *Journal of the Aeronautical Sciences*, 3: 122–8.

Zimmerman, M. B. (1982). 'Learning Effects and the Commercialization of New Energy Technologies: The Case of Nuclear Power'. *Bell Journal of Economics*, 13: 297–310.

Zuscovitch, E. (1986). 'The Economic Dynamics of Technologies Development'. *Research Policy*, 15: 175–86.

5   Anthropology and Organizational Learning

Barbara Czarniawska

The concept of organizational learning does not often appear in anthropological literature. The only instance I have found of the term's use in that field is in Hutchins (1995), where it is borrowed from organization theory. There are several reasons for this paucity, and it might be instructive to take a look at some of them.

One of the main reasons concerns the definition of 'organization' in both anthropology and organization theory. In the social sciences, the word 'organization' was traditionally understood not as a social unit but as a state, an attribute or an activity, and the relevant adjective was 'organized', not 'organizational'. This usage was first replaced in the 1960s by a notion of organizations as open systems separated by 'boundaries' from their 'environments' (Waldo 1961). In anthropology the analogy with open systems was reserved for 'cultures', a plural, that also begun to appear in the literature of the field at approximately the same time (Mead 1959).

However, there are ways of closing this interpretive gap. One is rapprochement achieved by the 'organizational culture' approach in the 1980s but announced earlier in such works as Jaques (1951), Gouldner (1954), and Dalton (1959). Following the anthropologists' example by using 'cultures' rather than 'organizations' to depict their objects of study, students of organizations gain legitimate entry into anthropological literature. Authors of this literature, although not using the same term, often speak about something that could be called 'organ-

izational learning', or learning in the context of social rather than economic organization. Indeed, many contemporary transnationals, seen as collectives of people, are far bigger than many of the traditional cultures that have been studied (on anthropology of complex organizations, see Czarniawska-Joerges 1992). Furthermore, anthropologists themselves provided arguments for treating the two concepts synonymously: 'Cultures are organizations for doing something, for perpetuating human life and themselves' (Sahlins and Service 1960: 24).

Another way of building a bridge between anthropological and organization theory is to conceive of organizations as processes rather than as structures. The call for such an approach existed in organization theory even before Weick's pledge in 1979. In anthropology it was formulated by Wolf (1994) who was worried by the anthropological lack of attention to organization and saw processual redefinition as the remedy:

Organization is key, because it sets up relationships among people through allocation and control of resources and rewards. It draws on tactical power to monopolize or share out liens and claims, to channel action into certain pathways while interdicting the flow of action into others. Some things become possible and likely; others are rendered unlikely. At the same time, organization is always at risk. Since power balances always shift and change, its work is never done; it operates against entropy. (p. 223)

This chapter was made possible by the unparalleled generosity of Kajsa Ekholm and Jonathan Friedman of the Anthropology Department, Lund University, neither of whom, however, bears any responsibility for its contents. As an excursion into a neighboring discipline, this text bears the inevitable signs of such intellectual tourism: simplification and generalization. It is also biased toward Anglo-Saxon anthropology.

Another set of reasons for the apparent neglect of the issue of organizational learning in anthropological literature is connected more with the worldviews dominant in anthropology than with the specific terminology used. Generally speaking, the approach used in traditional studies of 'pre-modern' cultures was static (Firth 1951). It was assumed that these cultures reproduced themselves with minor deviations and that they could only be 'transformed' by structural, exogenous forces, which did not leave much room for learning. At first, such changes were not considered to be an appropriate topic of study for the anthropologist, who was supposed to be concerned with the 'untouched primitive' (Mair 1957). This methodological purity was increasingly called into question by historical realities. As early as the nineteenth century two schools were emerging. Transformation could be seen either as evolution, which culminated in modern Western societies (with non-Western societies being relegated to the status of some kind of cultural fossil) or as a process initiated by an invention and spread by a process of diffusion, to be incorporated in a process of acculturation. Neither of these two views explicitly related to learning, but because they both affected understandings of this phenomenon, they are addressed at greater length below.

The static picture of the cultures studied does not have to be explained solely in terms of anthropologists' world view. To a great extent it was produced, somewhat as a byproduct, by the methods employed. As Redfield (1953) pointed out, anthropologists did not look for change, their task was 'to record what is usual and institutional, not what is unusual and creatively novel' (p. 14). This tendency was reinforced by a preference for writing in the 'ethnographic present', a style whose practitioners, often unintentionally, produced what Firth (1951) called 'literary embalming' (pp. 80–1).

Also, the concept of 'learning' contains at least the tacit assumption that a diachronic study is involved, however short its time span may be. Although anthropologists spent long periods in the field, they used to treat learning

as one moment in time. They often returned after a certain interval, but, as Firth (1959: 22) noted about his Tikopia study (1929, repeated in 1952), the approach was *dual-synchronic* rather than diachronic. In 1929, for example, the Tikopia did not use money, but they started to do so in 1952. What had happened in between? How would the learning continue? A traditional anthropologist had to resort to speculation on such matters. The much criticized 'in-and-out' method of the organizational scholar—short, but repetitive, visits to the field rather than one prolonged stay—has, after all, some advantages (for critique, see Van Maanen 1988, 1995 and Traweek 1992; for defense, Czarniawska 1998).

The lack of attention paid to organizational, social, and even individual learning has more specific historical reasons that vary from one school of thought to another. Social (structuralist) anthropologists emphasized macrosystemic variables, whereby learning was considered 'too micro' to be taken into account, no doubt as part of the fight that representatives of this branch of anthropology waged against the kind of cultural approach that professed culture as personality writ large. Similarly, interpretive anthropologists, trying to weaken their ties with this kind of cultural approach, took a more institutionalist line, in which learning is regarded as unnecessary psychologizing. 'Accretion of innovation' is a term more fitting of this vocabulary than 'organizational learning' is (Fox 1991: 109).

Learning as a concept appears mainly in cognitive or psychological anthropology (Suarez-Orozco, Spindler, and Spindler 1994) and is applied to individuals, not to groups. Psychological anthropologists are most likely to quote Bateson (1972), who among nonanthropologists is considered to have made anthropology's main contribution to learning theory. In recent decades, however, the anthropologists seem to have sold Bateson to psychology and sociology[1]

---

[1] I should probably say that they seem to have sold shares in Bateson. Bateson's genius expressed itself in a unique combination of radical behaviorism and radical humanism, the heritage of Descartes and of Gianbattista Vico, as Rappaport (1994) put it. Whereas until recently Bateson was

in exchange for such influences as Weber and Freud. This development also seems to be connected with the ambiguous treatment of psychological anthropology by anthropologists in the rest of the discipline. The form that the shift took varied (see Spindler 1978; Suarez-Orozco, Spindler, and Spindler 1994), but the main criticism—the scantiness of the attention paid to societal phenomena, especially power—remained stable over time.

Below I try to sketch a history of topics that have generated many contemporary approaches (which continue to use the above or similar concepts) and many studies that have produced insights of potential importance to the understanding of organizational learning.

Early Approaches to Social (Culture) Change[2]

One of the most important early attempts by anthropologists to conceptualize social change was evolutionism, which can be traced back to the nineteenth century and the works of Edward Burnett Tylor, a contemporary and associate of Darwin, Galton, and Spencer (Stocking 1995). The notion of evolution had 'savage tribes' at one end of a continuum whose other end was occupied by the European nations. Generally conceived of as a hierarchy, this view was based on the assumption of progress and of the unquestionable superiority of European civilization. The best known name associated with evolutionism is James George Frazer, who exerted a profound influence over many generations of anthropologists, although many, like Rivers and Malinowski, later retracted their early evolutionary ideas.

Evolutionism was attacked most spectacularly by Franz Boas for its adherents' ethno-

centric assumption of a 'superior civilization' and for their juggling with the evidence that was meant to corroborate it. Other criticisms followed: Evolutionism was speculative ('armchair theory'), and it ran counter to the main task of anthropology, namely, to record living cultures. Boas (1904/1974) proposed replacing it by 'historicalism' the theory that cultural elements are transferred through contact.[3] Its main concepts included 'invention', 'diffusion', and 'acculturation' (the third term being coined in 1880 but not properly defined or widely used until the 1920s; see Keesing 1953).

In time historicism itself came to be criticized for its atomism and lack of scientific rigor. Remedies against this state of affairs were sought, and one such attempt led to a concerted effort to study acculturation, which was defined by Redfield, Linton, and Herskovits (1936) as follows:

Acculturation comprehends those phenomena which result when groups of individuals having different cultures come into continuous first-hand contact, with subsequent changes in the original cultural patterns of either or both groups. Under this definition acculturation is to be distinguished from *culture-change*, of which it is but one aspect, and *assimilation*, which is at times a phase of acculturation. It is also to be differentiated from *diffusion*, which while occurring in all instances of acculturation . . . frequently takes place without the occurrence of the types of contact between peoples . . . [and] constitutes only one aspect of the process of acculturation. (p. 149)

This definition, which readily lends itself to the context of organizational learning (e.g. to a discussion of mergers and acquisitions), is typical of the period during which functionalism and structuralism were successfully replacing previous schools of thought. Malinowski began with a static functionalist approach but changed it later for a more dynamic one. Alas, his work on the dynamics of culture change was never completed. Radcliffe-Brown (1952) came closer to evolutionism in the organistic

thus 'borrowed from' selectively, the postmodernists have reclaimed him precisely for the collage-like, paradoxical quality of his work.

[2] In accordance with contemporary conventions, I use 'social' and 'cultural' synonymously, ignoring the historical feud over what ought to be the subject of anthropology — 'society' or 'culture'.

[3] In some other versions, historicalism became known as 'diffusionism'. The German version of diffusionism was also known as *kulturkreis* theory; the British version was dubbed (by its critics) pan-Egyptianism. Both were closer to evolutionism than the U.S. school of diffusionism.

undertone of his structuralism and his perception of society as an adaptive system. He used the Durkheimian concepts of 'eunomia' and 'dysnomia' (in place of *anomie*) and brought British social anthropology to a wider audience after his transfer to the University of Chicago.

During the 1930s the dynamic approach among U.S. anthropologists moved from historicalism to psychoanalytically oriented cultural anthropology (represented by Boas's students: Edward Sapir, Ruth Benedict, Margaret Mead, Clyde Kluckhohn, Alfred Kroeber, and Robert Lowie). It was also in the 1930s that learning emerged as an explicit concern of anthropology in the 'Yale learning theory', developed in collaboration between cultural anthropologists and experimental psychologists led by John Dollard (Keesing 1953: 34–5). Psychological anthropology subsequently developed in both psychoanalytic and behaviorist directions, but the first of these trends enjoyed more visibility and legitimacy than the second until the late 1970s, when a wave of radical critique swept through all the social sciences. It is only recently that another version of psychological anthropology, cultural cognition theory, seems to be regaining legitimacy (Dougherty 1985; Holland and Quinn 1987; Bloch 1994; Hutchins 1995). This school, however, is close to the European alternative to psychological anthropology, that is, the anthropology of knowledge that stems from the works of Durkheim and Mauss. Cultural anthropology is most strongly represented at present in interpretive or symbolic anthropology (Geertz 1973, 1995a).

In the 1940s the topic of change acquired respectability in anthropology, first becoming established under the label of 'cultural dynamics' and then diversifying in many directions, including the new variants of evolutionism (see, for instance, Sahlins and Service 1960), sometimes renamed the 'transformation of cultures' (Wolf 1964, 1994; Rappaport 1994). The new evolutionists kept some elements of the evolutionist vocabulary, where the closest equivalent to 'organizational learning' would probably be 'adaptive advance', albeit defined in terms of results rather than processes. As evolution theory went through radical reinterpretations in biology at the hands of such biologists as Stephen J. Gould and Richard Lewontin, so, too, did evolutionist anthropology, where, for example, the notion of maladaptation was introduced (Edgerton 1992).

In recent years, the topic of culture transformation has received a great deal of attention (see, for example, Sahlins 1995), and the concept of *cultural translation* has been much in use. This development was inspired and aided by the so-called linguistic turn initiated in social sciences in the 1970s, when the students of language and of society united forces in their attempt to understand culture. Steiner (1975/1992) stated, significantly, that 'a culture advances spiralwise via translations of its own canonic past' (p. 459). As I show later, the concept of translation can also be useful in the understanding of organizational learning.

Although the further development of topics associated with social (culture) change ramified, traces of the two original approaches can always be found. Change is induced either by contact with another culture (diffusion and acculturation) or by a kind of internal dynamics of needs (evolution and adaptation). The possibility that both may happen is least explored, a fact that seems to indicate that both perspectives are 'labels for various points of view which we adopt in our studies' (Bateson 1935: 178). Because the difference between the approaches is not highly pronounced in later works, I structure the following account according to topics rather than schools of thought.

Organizational Learning as Organizational Teaching: The Modernizers

One phenomenon described in many anthropological reports is a group, sometimes consciously created and maintained and sometimes just noted sociologically, that learns in order to teach the rest of the population (a tribe, a nation, a community). Such phenomena are often associated with modernization programs.

An instructive example is Geertz (1963), who told of economic change in two Indonesian towns, Modjokuto and Tabanan. Geertz pointed out that, unlike the fathers of the industrial revolution in Europe, the innovators in the two towns were neither engineers nor inventors. The skills they acquired and developed were organizational and administrative, namely mobilizing existing social and economic resources, disciplining the untrained labor force, managing production, and marketing. What is more, the peak of such skills lay not in introducing novelties but in joining the old with the new, smoothly and effortlessly. 'It is in their ability to operate at once in the traditional world of established custom and in the modern world of systematic economic rationality which is their resource' (1963: 152).

This capacity to cope with paradoxes comes up again and again as an attribute of successful elites. An additional point of interest is that such elites may be successful at either preventing change or fostering it. In either case, the literate elite plays a crucial role in the practices and actions of a local community, inducing 'organizational learning'. An analogy with management consultants comes to mind (see Berthoin Antal and Krebsbach-Gnath, Ch. 21 in this volume).

Taking up the issue of the learning of Islamic tradition in western Sudan, Wilks (1968) described the fate of the Dyula communities scattered throughout Sudan. According to his account, they tended to acquire the characteristics of their immediate neighborhood. He explained that this process was being intentionally counteracted by the Dyula's educated elite, which provided for the renewal and revitalization of the Muslim content of the Dyula culture and for a bridging of the gap between the general precepts of Islam and local practices. Wilks pointed out that these men of learning became teachers or officials of central importance to the community. Similar phenomena have been described in the context of Buddhism, where Buddhist monks have played the same role (Bechert 1972; Tambiah 1972).

The contrasting case is described in A. Cohen's (1981) famous study of the Creole elite in Sierra Leone. He showed how the Creole group educated themselves (at British universities) for the role of a political elite, a role they long maintained and with great success, first bridging the gap between the British and the locals and then the growing gap between the Mendes and the Temnes, the two other peoples of Sierra Leone. The education of the Creole elite also served to organize them into a group that was able to bring about the first change of government by democratic elections in sub-Saharan Africa. Their own learning helped them organize themselves successfully, a result that then allowed them to help the whole community reorganize itself.

Although it was not so intended, Cohen's ultimate understanding of the process of elite formation could well offer a way of conceptualizing organizational learning, namely, as 'a collective endeavor embodying the cumulative efforts, rational and non-rational, creative and routine, of all the men and women in the group. It is a construction which is continuously questioned, continuously modified, continuously created' (1981: 230).

The contrasting aims (those of preventing or promoting change) are also worth attending to. It is said that they reflect a crucial difference between the desired role of education in nonmodern and modern societies. As Mead (1943) said in the vocabulary of her times:

Primitive education was a process by which continuity was maintained between parents and children. . . . Modern education includes a heavy emphasis upon the function of education to create discontinuities—to turn the child of the peasant into a clerk, of the farmer into a lawyer, of the Italian immigrant into an American, of the illiterate into the literate. (p. 637)

Modern education, continued Mead, is grounded in the belief 'that it was possible by education to build a new world—a world that no man had yet dreamed' (p. 639).

Apter (1967), who studied the modernization of political systems in Ghana and Uganda, took up the same theme, contrasting traditionalism and modernism in a novel way:

Traditionalism, as distinct from tradition, we can define as validations of current behavior stemming from immemorial prescriptive norms. It is not that traditionalist systems do not change, but rather that innovation . . . has to be mediated within the social system and charged to antecedent values. Modernism, in contrast, presupposes a much remoter relationship between antecedent values and new goals. (p. 349)

The application of this classification to contemporary organizations leads to the surprising reflection that most organizational learning in fact happens under the auspices not of modernism but of traditionalism. This insight is also to be found in work by students of organization who have used historical and anthropological perspectives (see, for example, Pettigrew 1985; Smith, Child, and Rowlinson 1991). The prescriptive norms are not perhaps 'immemorial' but are usually old enough and taken-for-granted enough to act as a mediating link. And, at least in Apter's eyes, traditionalism is undoubtedly positive, for it 'puts novelty on trial rather than the people that novelty is supposed to serve' (Apter 1967: 348). Does it make modernism an impossible proposition? Are no dramatic transformations and complete ruptures possible? Obviously they are, but the two different instances of change throw a more complex light on the issue of the relationship between microchanges and macrochanges, between learning and change, and between change and transformation.

Thus, although the aims of the educated elites of Modjokuto and Tabanan, of the Dyula, and of the Creoles of Sierra Leone differed and appeared to aim at producing either continuity or rupture, their *modus operandi* was very similar. This common *modus operandi* is worth looking at because what the anthropologists observed was a personification of a hermeneutic principle: A group of people take upon themselves to bridge the old and new, the known and unknown, the part and the whole. This bridging is perceived by many anthropologists as a *sine qua non* of modernization. As

Berque (1972) succinctly put it, 'either modernism will be based upon the traditional, or it will remain colonial in form, which means it will not exist at all' (p. 244).

Recent trends have radicalized the concerns of the earlier modernizers. Until the 1980s the modernizers worried that modernization was not proceeding swiftly enough, whereas the critics of modernization worried that it was proceeding too rapidly. They all worried unnecessarily, claimed Sahlins (1994). In the meantime, the 'natives' managed to invent both their own tradition, as Europeans did in the nineteenth century, and their own modernity. These two phenomena, the invention of tradition and the indigenization of modernity, now call for study, said Sahlins. It does not seem too far-fetched to transfer these concerns to organization studies. For example, according to Alexandersson and Trossmark's (1997) study of an attempted spiritual renewal in Denmark Radio, the main step consisted of inventing a coherent past against which such change could take place.

Organizational Learning and Institutional Change: An Ambiguous Relationship

I have already mentioned the reported cases of organizational learning aimed at preventing modernization. In the previous section I interpreted these cases as meaning 'learning prevents change', but this statement can be reinterpreted by asking, 'change at what level?' No doubt the cases of organizational learning aimed at preventing modernization provoked a fair amount of organizational change. Among teachers of Islam and Buddhism such learning revitalized tradition that may have been moribund or even extinct. In fact, one could claim that most organizational learning aims to protect and revitalize the existing institutional order rather than change it, as is the case with modernization projects or revolutions.

For instance, Firth's two field studies of Tikopia, which he conducted in 1929 and 1952, led him to conclude that 'the basic social structure of the Tikopia had remained intact over a generation' (Firth 1959: 50). His detailed report contained a description of an interesting event that could be of great importance to an understanding of organizational learning. Describing the Tikopia reactions to the famine in 1952, he wrote: 'Conceding a great deal to the force of circumstances, they nevertheless managed to keep the greater part of the structure of their institution unimpaired; they made many organizational but few structural adaptations' (1959: 105).[4] This passage throws further light on the complex and perhaps paradoxical connection between organizational learning and institutional change. It is generally assumed that the relationship between the two should be positive: Learning fosters change, change fosters learning. Although this assumption may be true at the organizational level, it could be incorrect at the institutional level. Firth (1951, 1959) pointed out that learning and consequent organizational change might preserve the institutional order that runs into turbulence. Similarly Acker (1994) showed how the major reorganization of a Swedish bank, which required a substantial amount of organizational learning, reproduced exactly the old gender relationships in the new organizational form. Herskovits's (1973) dictum, that 'form changes more readily than meaning' seems particularly appropriate here. He called this phenomenon 'cultural reinterpretation' (p. 180).

A. Cohen (1974) considered it in a different context, that of political change. Symbolic or cultural changes tend to lag behind even the most radical political changes, and the 'cultural revolution' seems to have destroyed many people and a large number of the cultural artifacts rather than the symbolic system of meaning. No wonder, for according to Cohen: 'One of the major characteristics of symbolic formations is their multiplicity of meaning' (p. 36). Symbols are ambiguous and open to inter-pretation, a characteristic that makes them different from signs. Many anthropological studies, including Cohen's own (1974, 1981) show how the traditional symbols of a society become the hallmarks of its modernization.

In a similarly paradoxical vein, some anthropological studies show how an attempt at change, initiated from outside, may lead to intense organizational learning because of unintended consequences. Nandy (1972: 132), in his reading of the changing political culture in India, observed that, in reaction to a newly established colonial system, the native leadership first tried to show that system's disruptive impact in native terms. But important elements in the same political elite felt that this response was not enough, that it was necessary both to organize in order to redefine the nature of the challenge and to design adaptive strategies that were congruent with the self-respect of the community. Nandy (p. 132) felt no doubts when answering the question I formulated in the previous section: What causes the change of an institutional order? It happens, he said, as a result of changes in the society's definition of the human condition, and although a planned change might unintentionally trigger those changes, it cannot control them.[5]

What does produce institutional changes, then? One might still expect it to be organizational learning and the consequent organizational change, but mainly as a result of 'unintended consequences'. It is difficult to deduce any shape or timing for institutional change from studies of organizational learning. In Firth's (1959) terms, 'organizational change may lead to structural change' (p. 341), but to capture this progression, genuinely diachronic studies are needed. Firth offered a set of useful concepts that allow one to grasp those dynamics of social change that, in his opinion, could be initiated either inside or outside a given community. In a constructivist vein, he postulated that although individuals do not change society by acts of will or by single

---

[4] Firth consistently contraposed 'structure' and 'organization' in his work. I translate the two concepts as 'institutional order' and 'organizing practice', respectively.

[5] One could claim, as Yalman (1972) did, that cultural revolutions manage to control a massive change of institutional thought structure, but history has meanwhile shown that cultural revolutions are reversible.

deeds, it is the change in individual action patterns that, reinforced by interaction, will change other people's action patterns by means of the same interaction (Firth 1951: 85). Firth suggested two micromechanisms that could be interesting in the context of organizational learning: *social convection*, that is, the reactions, including negative ones, of community members to change in the action patterns of some members of the community; and *social conduction*, or the unintended consequences of change, which require further change and adjustment (p. 86). These mechanisms are triggered by planned change but operate beyond its control.

Although the works reviewed above focused on encounters between cultures, or 'organizations' as one might call them in the present context, it has been pointed out that cultures, especially in contemporary global culture, influence one another in such a mediated way that it is difficult to claim that an actual contact ever took place.

How Do Ideas Travel?

The mechanism of diffusion is a classic anthropological answer to the quest of how ideas travel. Originally, diffusion was envisaged quite literally, in the sense that cultural artifacts 'spilled over' from cultures that were full of them to others that were without them. Soon, however, it began to be treated more or less metaphorically. In the definition of acculturation quoted above, Redfield, Linton, and Herskovits (1936) pointed out that '*diffusion* . . . frequently takes place without the occurrence of the types of contact between people' (p. 149). In the version that became popular in management theory via marketing (Rogers 1962; Levitt and March 1988), the emphasis was still on artifacts (consumer products or technologies), but the spreading of innovation led more and more to the spreading of ideas, even ideologies. This process is no doubt a central concern in the whole issue of organizational learning.

But is diffusion an appropriate metaphor? It seems certain that even ideas do travel as things, incorporated in books, overheads, documents, designs, or models (Czarniawska and Joerges 1996); it is the method of locomotion that remains in doubt. Attempts to change a physical metaphor into a biological one (e.g. 'infection', 'catching'), probably inspired by the ideas of the bacteriologist and philosopher of science Ludwig Fleck (who was popularized in anthropology by Mary Douglas), do not solve the problem. Analogies to nature may make the process itself more acceptable (Douglas 1986) but will not increase one's understanding of it. In what sense can one 'catch' an idea, or how can an innovation 'diffuse'?

Diffusion suggests a physical process subject to the laws of physics, so explanations of phenomena using this term provoke a further train of physical metaphors, such as 'saturation' or 'resistance'. All these terms are in fact widely used in organizational practice. They are good examples of how scientific metaphors can conquer the field, but when they are gathered in from the field again for analytical purposes, they can become misleading. It is true that people speak about ideas as if they were objects moving in time and space by virtue of some *inherent* properties. Like other field metaphors, diffusion has an economic value, rendering the less known in terms of the more familiar, the immaterial in terms of the material. But adopting the metaphor for analytical purposes leads to an impasse. It may be plausible to say that ideas move from 'more satiated' to 'less satiated' environments, but saying so also means suggesting that the law of inertia applies to ideas as it does to physical objects.

This interpretation is hardly convincing in the light of what is known of such phenomena as braindrain, for which a reverse interpretation is more apt. Ideas travel from less satiated to more satiated environments, so another physical metaphor is necessary, that of 'critical mass'. Rather than bring in new physical metaphors to defend those already in use, one can look again to anthropology for a different kind of metaphor. Latour, who formulated a program of symmetrical anthropology (1993), also made a suggestion concerning diffusion:

[T]he model of diffusion may be contrasted with another, that of the model of translation. According to the latter, the spread in time and space of anything—claims, orders, artifacts, goods—is in the hands of people; each of these people may act in many different ways, letting the token drop, or modifying it, or deflecting it, or betraying it, or adding to it, or appropriating it. (1986: 267)

The translation model answers the question about the energy needed if ideas or objects are to move around. It is people, whether regarded as users or as creators, who energize an idea every time they translate it for their own or somebody else's use. Watching ideas travel, '[w]e observe a process of translation—not one of reception, rejection, resistance or acceptance' (Latour 1992: 116).

It is important to stress, though, that the meaning of 'translation' in such a context goes beyond its linguistic interpretation. It means 'displacement, drift, invention, mediation, creation of a new link that did not exist before and modifies in part the two agents' (Latour 1993: 6), the two agents being those who translated and that which is translated. The idea of translation and the program of symmetrical anthropology (treating 'premodern' societies at the same level as the 'modern' ones) helped contemporary anthropology break out of the impasse in which it had landed as a result of political refigurations. Instead of lamenting either the loss of 'native culture' or the misuse of modern imports, the symmetrical anthropologist can now document the emerging postmodern cultures, in which the elements of 'native' and 'Western' cultures are creatively translated into local inventions (Sahlins 1994).

This richness of meaning, evoking associations with both movement and transformation, embracing both linguistic and material objects, makes translation a key concept for understanding organizational change (Czarniawska and Sevón 1996). It comprises what exists and what is created; it comprises the relation between humans and ideas, ideas and objects, and humans and objects. There is no doubt that it could be usefully introduced into the topic of organizational learning, as I have already attempted to do (Czarniawska 1997).

Enculturation

In the previous sections the anthropologists' interest in phenomena akin to organizational learning in situations of social (culture) change has been explored. Another type of context in which similar phenomena are likely to appear entails the opposite situation, namely, enculturation, whereby a community's ways of living are inculcated in its new members.

Enculturation undoubtedly constitutes social learning, for it is society (community, group) that teaches the newly acquired members. The process is usually studied in the case of children, but immigrants have recently also been the focus of such research, although in their case it is rather a question of acculturation. To a large extent enculturation proceeds through the inculcation of notions of right and wrong, through punishment for undesirable actions and reinforcement of desirable ones (Campbell 1973: xix–xx). Another element—a more subtle one, as Campbell pointed out—consists in excluding alternatives, in enhancing the 'taken-for-granted' attitudes. This exclusion is possible because 'most of our knowledge of the world is vicarious, acquired through the observations and reports of others' (p. xix).

P. S. Cohen (1969) surveyed studies of the role of myths in society and pointed out that although the central role of myths is to offer explanations of the origins or transformations of things, by doing so they actually block off competing explanations; by legitimizing certain social institutions and practices, they delegitimate others; by maintaining and expressing solidarity, they create the notion of deviancy. Cohen's analysis is directly transferable to the realities of contemporary organizations, and it reveals the typical paradox of organizational learning: that the acquisition of new techniques, ideologies, viewpoints, and so on blocks off learning, and learning about, the alternative techniques, ideologies, and viewpoints. And enculturation is not just any learning; it is the initial learning that is expected to have a major formative influence on children and other organizational newcomers.[6]

The significant insight to emerge from enculturation studies, as compared to socialization studies, concerns the crucial role of rites and ceremonies (see, for example, Cohen 1974, 1981). In terms of learning one could speak here of a total experience, of learning *of*, rather than learning *about*. The wave of organizational culture studies revealed that those supposedly premodern ways of teaching and learning have a legitimate and prominent place in modern organizations (Rosen 1988). Organizational rituals and ceremonies aim at creating the same kind of total experience, which can advance enculturation much more efficiently than any transfer of abstract knowledge. As the great theoretician of ritual, Turner (1982), put it, '[t]hey confer on the actors, by nonverbal as well as verbal means, the experiential understanding' (p. 78).

The topic of nonverbal learning has been reverberating in anthropology at least since Kluckhohn and Kelly's (1945) famous article on 'culture', which, presented as a conversation between specialists in different professions, contained the following passage:

THE PSYCHOLOGIST: I suppose that branch of psychology which is most intimately related to 'culture' is what we today call 'learning theory'. Wouldn't you agree that the transmission of culture can be understood only in so far as learning and teaching are understood?

FIRST ANTHROPOLOGIST: Yes, inasmuch as all human beings of whatever 'races' seem to have about the same nervous system and biological equipment generally, we would anticipate that the basic processes of learning are very similar if not identical among all groups. We therefore look to the psychologist to inform us about the laws of learning. On the other hand, we can show that *what* is learned, from whom learning takes place, and when the learning of certain skills usually occurs, varies according to culture. Also I should like

[6] Enculturation in organizations is most often studied under its sociological name, socialization.

to point out that there is one danger in speaking of culture as being 'taught.' 'Teaching' is not limited, as in the popular sense, to conscious instruction. Individuals learn—'absorb' more nearly suggests, in nontechnical language, the process—much of their culture through imitation of both 'matched-dependent' and 'copying' types. (p. 80)

Imitation, matching, and copying are well-known concepts in organizational learning, and only recently has their taken-for-granted understanding been questioned (Sevón 1996). An interesting possibility for anthropologists and organization scholars alike opens with the following example by literary theorists who drew on the Aristotelian concept of *mimesis*:

An imitation is a copy that in one way or another advertises the fact that it is a copy. 'Mimesis' as used, for example, by Aristotle, on the other hand, still carries the force of its origin in dance or mime. Mimesis is an inward act of reproduction whereby the thing imitated is internalized by the imitator and so learned. In mimesis the thing imitated is then turned into an action and thereby externalized, brought out in the open for the imitator or for those who watch the imitation. In mimesis the imitated becomes exposed to knowledge. (Miller 1993: 155)

Although mimetic isomorphism is mentioned in organization theory (DiMaggio and Powell 1983), the focus is not on investigating how this process occurs. Prolonged fieldwork, another loan from anthropology, might throw more light on such peculiar organizational enculturation.

In contemporary anthropology linguistic and nonlinguistic enculturation constitute the main interest of cognitive anthropology, originating in the works of Goodenough (see, for example, Goodenough 1981). If folk thought models (Quinn and Holland 1987) are compared with connectionist models of brain operations, for instance, it soon appears that, far from being 'natural knowledge', the former are in fact culturally acquired (Bloch 1994; Strauss and Quinn 1994). Thus, in terms of an understanding of organizations, cultural cognition theory has more to offer than its competitor, cognitive psychology, whose representatives are far more prone to accept cultural thought models as universal truth about learning. There are some notable exceptions, such as Churchland (1979), who said: 'In large measure we *learn*, from others, to perceive the world as everybody else perceives it. But if this is so, then we might have learned, and may yet learn, to conceive/perceive the world in ways other than those supplied by our present culture' (p. 7). Cultural cognition theorists try to go a step further and offer an 'insight into those conditions under which cultural models are endowed with directive force and hence with ideological potential' (Quinn and Holland 1987: 13). This advance is possible, according to Bloch (1994), because of a technique that is essential in anthropology, participant observation. Unlike other cognitive scientists, the anthropologist is present when nonlinguistic learning takes place, a circumstance that necessarily extends the anthropological understanding of learning.

The traditional division between the 'individual' and the 'social' in cultural cognition theory is nevertheless maintained, sometimes vociferously (Strauss and Quinn 1994). Afraid as they are of the 'collectivization of the individual mind', cognitive anthropologists tend to forget the other side of the coin: If culture and cognition are in 'people's heads', what then constitutes 'the public' or 'the social' and what is so threatening? Does society vanish when everybody is at home? This quandary is common to cognitive anthropology and to many organizational learning studies, but it is absent from cognitive anthropology's older cousin, the anthropology of knowledge.

The Anthropology of Knowledge

Comparative studies of literate and nonliterate societies (Goody 1968, 1977, 1986) do not contain any specific reference to organizational learning, and yet they offer profound insight into the social character of learning. Goody was concerned with differences between oral and literate cultures and the ways of learning that

are accessible to both. In *The Domestication of the Savage Mind*, he analyzed three forms of text that the existence of script makes possible: tables, lists, and recipes. Because the first two present items of information in a disjointed, abstracted way, they differ from the narrative, a typical knowledge carrier in oral cultures. When memorizing a list or a table, a person must resort to mnemonic devices in order to make up for the lack of connections. This necessity does not mean that lists or tables are in any sense defective narratives—they serve a different purpose. A narrative imitates social life, re-presenting the complexity of its connections. Taxonomies of all kinds are helpful in the analysis of social life because they separate it into discrete entities. The recipe, for instance, is based on the assumption of a chronological connection and thus seems to resemble a narrative, but in fact recipes lack the propelling force of a cause or an intention, the plot of the narrative. Clouds lead to rain, and greed leads to crime; the sifting of flour does not lead to the breaking of eggs. The recipe fulfills the learning function of the narrative in that it provides the learner with a vicarious experience, but in a way that is closer to that of tables or lists. One could say that recipes are lists, but they are lists of actions, not of objects.

Tables, lists, and recipes are undoubtedly the modern props of organizational learning. But if one agrees with Latour (1993) that we have never become completely modern, then it can be interesting to take a look at nonmodern ways of learning that are still present in contemporary organizations. It appears, for instance, that the extent to which the modern props of learning, and the technologies of writing that support them, are used in organizations varies. My own studies of city management revealed, for example, that in Stockholm's city hall many important deals are made on the phone, whereas in Warsaw every agreement has to be confirmed in writing. Stockholm, however, was flooded with leaflets, brochures, and memos, whereas in Warsaw there was very little such material and important information was conveyed face-to-face only (Czarniawska 1997). Both practices have their advantages and disadvantages, but it seems obvious that the method of circulating information must affect learning.

Another insight to emerge from anthropological studies is that contemporary organizations, in their eager desire to be as modern as possible, tend to ignore the role of narrative in learning, at least in their programmatic attempts to influence organizational learning. Tables and lists (many 'models' and taxonomies are simply lists) are given priority as teaching aids. Although they can fulfill certain functions that narratives cannot, the reverse applies even more. Almost certainly, the greater part of organizational learning happens through the circulation of stories.

Yet another similarity, and difference, concerns collective memory. With something of an evolutionist undertone, Goody and Watt (1968) wrote that

[t]he social function of memory—and forgetting— can thus be seen as the final stage of what may be called the homeostatic organization of the cultural tradition in non-literate society. The language is developed in intimate association with the experience of the community, and it is learned by the individual in face-to-face contact with the other members. What continues to be of social relevance is stored in the memory while the rest is usually forgotten. (pp. 30–1)

The picture sketched above does not have to be seen as something exotic, something never to be met in literate societies. In the first place, as Goody and Watt themselves pointed out, non-literate societies have various mnemonic techniques at their disposal. Second, the above picture can be applied to any interpretive community in which written texts play a role secondary to that of face-to-face contacts, facilitated by the modern media. One could say of any contemporary company that 'what continues to be of social relevance is stored in the memory while the rest is usually forgotten'. One would only need to specify that 'forgetting' means filing away, storing in an archive. Goody and Watt (1968) pointed out that even in a literate culture the oral tradition remains the primary mode of cultural orientation, a rather fortunate circumstance in light of the unlim-

ited variety and fragmentation of the written sources available.

The notion of collective memory brings up another classic topic in the anthropology of knowledge: categorization and classification (Durkheim and Mauss 1903/1963; Levi-Strauss 1966; Leach 1970; Ellen and Reason 1979; Ardener 1989). It has in fact been postulated that classification is the principal form for the organization of consciousness in contemporary Western cultures (Reason 1979: 223). Marxist anthropologists postulated that the mode of production determines the mode of categorization. Reason (1979) reinterpreted the work of Thomas and Znaniecki, showing that Polish peasants perceived America in terms known to them from their own agricultural past, failing to grasp the economic complexities of the host country. Here again there is an interesting insight for students of organizational learning. Does learning determine what organizing will look like, or does the present mode of organization determine what learning will look like? This undoubtedly mutual influence has not yet been sufficiently explored in organization studies. As often happens, though, cross-cultural encounters give rise to reflection. Holden and Cooper (1994), reflecting on their experience in teaching Russian managers in the construction industry, noted that the course participants did not consider its contents relevant to their situation. Their classification system did not contain any categories to match what is regarded as Western management knowledge, although they had come to Manchester for the explicit purpose of acquiring it.

As the realization grows of the crucial role that language and speech acts have in organizing, students of organizations will learn to appreciate Reason's claim that classification and, even more, categorization should be regarded as a historical, situated discursive practice (1979: 243). Researchers busy studying *how* learning occurs often forget to ask where the content of learning comes from.

Among the authors who brought the Durkheimian-Maussian concern about primitive classifications close to organization studies are Mary Douglas and Karin Knorr Cetina. Douglas

(1986) paved the way for the return of institutionalist thinking into organization studies by pointing out two critical elements in Weber's thought, which is crucial to organization theory: the firm assumption of the steady evolution of human consciousness and, consequently, of an irreparable breach between 'primitive' and 'modern' societies. Knowledge of the former, in Weber's opinion, gave no advantage for understanding the latter. Durkheim, as Weber's contemporary, was guilty of the same bias but, luckily, failed to pursue it consistently. He introduced two forms of solidarity, or grounds for collective action: classificatory (primitive societies) and economic (modern societies). Although he mourned the loss of primitive solidarity in modern societies, he, together with Marcel Mauss, put much effort into understanding the classificatory work performed by institutions.

Now, when the supposed breach between primitive and modern societies has been definitively called in question, the work of Durkheim and Mauss can be brought to bear on contemporary societies. Although the existence of collective action may be due mainly to economic motives, collective action acquires direction from shared classifications. And although the work of classifying and negotiating classifications continues all the time and in all kinds of interaction, it is made possible and facilitated by shared classifications of greater stability: institutions. 'Institutions systematically direct individual memory and channel our perceptions into forms compatible with the relations they authorize. They fix processes that are essentially dynamic, they hide their influence, and they rouse our emotions to a standardized pitch on standardized issues' (Douglas 1986: 92). 'The high triumph of institutional thinking is to make the institutions completely invisible' (p. 98).

This dictum can be unfailingly applied in the context of organizational learning studies that, following cybernetic and biological models, focus on how to teach/learn more, more quickly, and more efficiently. Yet one is forcefully reminded of Kluckhohn and Kelly (1945), who said that although they looked to psychologists to learn the how of learning, the anthropologists could provide the answer to what. What is learned, both in the sense of what (at a given time and place) is considered worth learning and what appears to be learned, resides in the realm of institutions.

The program suggested by Knorr Cetina, herself an ethnographer and student of organizations, thus seems highly relevant. There is no reason to despair, said Knorr Cetina (1994), referring to the postmodernist discovery that facts are produced (a 'fact' known to anyone who has ever bothered to check the etymology of the word). Modern institutions run on fictions, as all institutions always have, and the task of the scholar is to study how these fictions are constructed and sustained. Knorr Cetina listed three main kinds of such fiction: symbolic ('primitive') classifications, social simulations, and systems of knowing (p. 8). All three are of direct relevance to organizational learning: The process itself is an exercise in reclassification, it often uses simulation, and it is situated in and dependent upon a relevant system of knowing.[7]

What Can Knowledge of the Other Contribute to the Understanding of Organizational Learning?

In previous sections I have noted the use of concepts close to the notion of organizational learning and related theory-building within the frame of general social theory. Remaining at this level, however, means abandoning anthropology's specificity (except in the participant–observation method), treating it as no more than a social science that uses exotic field

[7] I hasten to add that such a program is still perceived as radical within anthropology, where, as in other social sciences, the term *fiction* remains anathema (see, for instance, I. L. Jarvie's (1990) violent rebuke to Strathern (1990) for her redefinition of anthropology as 'persuasive fiction'). Organization theory, however, perhaps because of its basically cross-disciplinary character, has become known for being first in incorporating notions considered too radical for other social sciences.

examples. But the main contribution of anthropology lies in its unique opportunities for throwing light from outside one's culture onto one's own cultural concepts. I spoke above of the way concepts associated with organizational learning might be able to improve the understanding of alien cultures. Now it is time to ask how a knowledge of other cultures can enrich the concept of organizational learning.

One obviously relevant issue concerns the definition of person, or self. Whereas the idea of organizational learning takes for granted the modern institution of individuality, the accompanying definition of the person as an individual, 'a bounded, unique, more or less integrated motivational and cognitive universe, a dynamic career of awareness, emotion, judgment, and action organized into a distinctive whole and set contrastively both against other such wholes and against its social and natural background, is . . . a rather peculiar idea within the context of the world's cultures' (Geertz 1976: 225). For example, the Samoan language does not include any terms to denote personality or self (Shore 1982). '[I]nstead of our Socratic "know thyself," Samoans say "take care of the relationship"' (Marcus and Fischer 1986: 65).

The definition of person, or self, is a matter of greater value than merely a point for cultural relativism: 'they think so, and we think otherwise'. In a growing wave of reflection on the conditions of modernity, the idea of 'self' and of 'individuals' is perhaps the most frequent subject of critical contemplation. It no longer seems impossible that one of the crucial institutions of contemporary times, individual identity, is going to be transformed before people's very eyes. The units of a life are relations, not persons, claimed Kenneth Gergen (1994), and such a redefinition of 'person' cannot leave the concept of learning untouched.

In the same vein, Rosaldo (1989) spoke of relational knowledge in telling the story of his learning of Ilongot knowledge and culture. Equipped with a eurocentric assumption of universality, he believed that his learning mirrored the process of enculturation that Ilongot children experience—until he learned enough to notice that his 'teachers' treated him not as a child but as a grown up man who did not know their customs and that they taught him accordingly ('relationally'). In the end, said Rosaldo, this intercultural experience might have taught him more about his own identity than about the Ilongots he was purportedly studying. Rosaldo seemingly projected on the Ilongots an attitude typical for immigration authorities in Western countries, who proclaim their goal to be acculturation even as they enact an enculturation, treating immigrants as children. The difference between the two processes, acculturation and enculturation, may be of interest in the context of organizational learning, not least for moral reasons.

The increasing reflection upon the institution of individual identity has had a remarkable effect on anthropology itself. After anthropologists had gained deepened insight into their own professional identity, they came to recognize that the modernization of developing countries does not mean that they 'learn how to be us' but that they 'learn how to be themselves'—learning as identity-construction. The most venturesome works in the trend of ethnographies are profoundly concerned with the shaping and transformation of identities 'of one's subjects, of their social systems, of the nation-states with which they are associated, of the ethnographer and the ethnographic project itself' (Marcus 1992: 312).

The subject of identity formation and transformation has always been present, however marginally, in the study of organizational learning, as a question of imitation. Bringing this issue into the focus of interest throws light on a variety of fascinating phenomena that previously remained in the shadows. For example, what identity models or blueprints are offered to those willing to learn (Löfgren 1993; Sevón 1996)?

The most pertinent of such blueprints is the concept of homo oeconomicus, as the identity model (usually male) supposedly grounded in 'human nature' and thus offered to those who have as yet to realize its full potential. As pointed out by Herskovits (1973), among many others, it is surprising how few brows were raised by the permanent presence of such a model in analyses of the 'developing countries'. Leach (1972) compared homo oeconomicus with a Buddhist whose 'ambitions are strictly personal and escapist; the most he is prepared to hope for is a future existence which is rather less unpleasant than this one' (p. 50). To what extent the notion of organizational learning is tied to homo oeconomicus is an open question that is worth examining in depth. A sound lesson learned from anthropology is that it is both worthwhile and necessary to take the crucial notions that one uses and examine them for the ideological ties they entail.

Organizational Learning—A Projected Category?

While I was working on this chapter, the most hotly discussed issue in anthropology concerned the death of Captain Cook at the hands of Hawaiians in 1779 and the duel between Sahlins (1995) and Obeysekere (1995) over its correct interpretation. Sahlins claimed that a series of random circumstances had led the Hawaiians to take Cook for a god and worship him accordingly until he had left the island. But when a mast broke on his ship and he had had to return, they had killed him, an act that restored the holy order, which had not foreseen such an occurrence. Obeysekere read this interpretation as an example of a typical Western imperialistic vision that imputed to the Hawaiians a naive veneration for Westerners. He countered with his own reading of the Hawaiians as pragmatic and rational.

In anthropology the argument about projecting Western categories of interpretation onto non-Western cultures dates back long before the era of political correctness. It was, in fact, a cornerstone of the critique of evolutionism. Before using the above example of the Buddhist, Leach (1972) said:

Those who believe that there is a law of Nature which declares that all underdeveloped countries will 'progress' to the stage of industrialization tend to assume that all those who are so progressing must necessarily welcome the prospect with open arms. In other words, they assume that the basic Christian dogma of the coming millennium when all mankind shall live in peace and happiness in the New Jerusalem is shared by all the world. But this is not the case. (p. 50)

It could be claimed that Leach, while mounting a convincing critique of the supposed 'natural supremacy' of Western values, was nevertheless still using alien categories ('personal', 'escapist') in his comments on Buddhism. Similarly, Geertz (1995b), in his insightful and well-balanced commentary on the Sahlins–Obeysekere quarrel, pointed out the peculiarity of Obeysekere's own stance. Obeysekere is not Hawaiian but Sri Lankan, and he was 'defending' Hawaiians from what could be called, with a dose of irony, a universal local standpoint. Also, in Hawaiians' 'defense', Obeysekere uses another set of Western categories (pragmatism, rationalism, individualist psychology).

It seems to me that the fact that all interpreters use certain interpretive categories-at-hand is not the same as assuming the existence of universal categories. It is especially not the same as assuming that universal categories are identical with Western categories. Although Hawaiians do not use the concept of organizational learning in interpreting the famous deeds of Kamehameha II, who apparently abolished the traditional order single-handedly (by eating with women in public and committing many similar sins), there is no reason why a Western scholar should not do so. Recontextualizing past events by means of new and unexpected vocabularies has always been the main grounds of creativity. If a scholar's vocabulary clashes with a local one, then an interesting dialogue may develop, perhaps enriching both vocabularies.

In other words, so long as the concept of organizational learning is found to be useful and meaningful, it can be fruitfully applied to many studies of alien cultures, which up to now have been interpreted in different terms. It could also enrich the understanding of organizational learning in organization theory itself. The present chapter is intended to mark a first step, not an end, to such an endeavor.

References

Acker, J. (1994). 'The Gender Regime of Swedish Banks'. *Scandinavian Journal of Management*, 10/ 2: 117–30.

Alexandersson, O. and Trossmark, P. (1997). *Konstruktion av fàrnyelse i organisationer* (The Construction of Renewal in Organizations). Lund: Lund University Press.

Apter, D. E. (1967). 'The Role of Traditionalism in the Political Modernization of Ghana and Uganda', in P. Bohannan and F. Plog (eds.), *Beyond the Frontier: Social Process and Cultural Change*. New York: Natural History Press, 347–74.

Ardener, E. (1989). *The Voice of Prophecy*. Oxford: Blackwell.

Bateson, G. (1935). 'Culture Contact and Schismogenesis'. *Man*, 35: 178–83.

——(1972). *Steps to an Ecology of Mind: A Revolutionary Approach to Man's Understanding of Himself*. San Francisco: Chandler Press.

Bechert, H. (1972). 'Sangha, State, Society, "Nation": Persistence of Traditions in Post-traditional Buddhist Societies', in S. N. Eisenstadt (ed.), *Post-traditional Societies*. New York: Norton, 85–95.

Berque, J. (1972). 'Tradition and Innovation in the Maghrib', in S. N. Eisenstadt (ed.), *Post-traditional Societies*. New York: Norton, 239–50.

Bloch, M. (1994). 'Language, Anthropology, and Cognitive Science', in R. Borofsky (ed.), *Assessing Cultural Anthropology*. New York: McGraw-Hill, 276–82.

Boas, F. (1974). 'The History of Anthropology', in G. W. Stocking. Jr. (ed.), *A Franz Boas Reader*. Chicago: University of Chicago Press, 23–41. (Original work published 1904)

Bohannan, P. and Plog, F. (eds.) (1967). *Beyond the Frontier: Social Process and Cultural Change*. New York: Natural History Press.

Campbell, D. T. (1973). 'Herskovits, Cultural Relativism, and Metascience'. Introduction to M. J. Herskovits, *Cultural Relativism*. New York: Random House, v–xxiii.

Churchland, P. M. (1979). *Scientific Realism and the Plasticity of Mind*. Cambridge: Cambridge University Press.

Cohen, A. (1974). *Two-dimensional Man*. London: Routledge & Kegan Paul.

——(1981). *The Politics of Elite Culture: Explorations in the Dramaturgy of Power in a Modern African Society*. Berkeley: University of California Press.

Cohen, P. S. (1969). 'Theories of Myth'. *Man*, 4: 337–53.

Czarniawska, B. (1997). 'Learning Organizing in a Changing Institutional Order: Examples from City Management in Warsaw'. *Management Learning*, 28: 475–95.

——(1998). *A Narrative Approach to Organization Studies*. Thousand Oaks, Calif.: Sage.

——and Joerges, B. (1996). 'Travels of Ideas', in B. Czarniawska and G. Sevón (eds.), *Translating Organizational Change*. Berlin: de Gruyter, 13–48.

——and Sevón, G. (1996). 'Introduction', in B. Czarniawska and G. Sevón (eds.), *Translating Organizational Change*. Berlin: de Gruyter, 1–12.

Czarniawska-Joerges, B. (1992). *Exploring Complex Organizations: A Cultural Perspective*. Thousand Oaks, Calif.: Sage.

Dalton, M. (1959). *Men Who Manage: Fusions of Feeling and Theory in Administration*. New York: Wiley.

DiMaggio, P. J. and Powell, W. W. (1983). 'The Iron Cage Revisited: Institutional Isomorphism and Collective Rationality in Organizational Fields'. *American Sociological Review*, 48: 147–60.

Dougherty, J. W. D. (ed.) (1985). *Directions in Cognitive Anthropology*. Chicago: University of Chicago Press.

Douglas, M. (1986). *How Institutions Think*. Syracuse, NY: Syracuse University Press.

Durkheim, E. and Mauss, M. (1963). *Primitive Classifications*. London: Cohen and West. (Original work published 1903)

Edgerton, R. B. (1992). *Sick Societies: Challenging the Myth of Primitive Harmony*. New York: Free Press.

Ellen, R. F. and Reason, D. (eds.) (1979). *Classifications in Their Social Context*. London: Academic Press.

Firth, R. (1951). *Elements of Social Organization*. London: Watts.

——(1959). *Social Change in Tikopia*. London: George Allen and Unwin.

Fox, R. G. (1991). 'For a Nearly New Culture History', in R. G. Fox (ed.), *Recapturing Anthropology: Working in the Present*. Santa Fe, N. Mex.: School of American Research Press, 93–113.

Geertz, C. (1963). *Peddlers and Princes: Social Development and Economic Change in Two Indonesian Towns*. Chicago: University of Chicago Press.

——(1973). *The Interpretation of Cultures: Selected Essays*. New York: Basic Books.

——(1976). 'From the "Native's" Point of View: On the Nature of Anthropological Understanding', in K. H. Basso and H. A. Selby (eds.), *Meaning in Anthropology*. Albuquerque, N. Mex.: University of New Mexico Press, 221–37.

——(1995a). *After the Fact: Two Countries, Four Decades, One Anthropologist*. Cambridge, Mass.: Harvard University Press.

——(1995b). 'Culture Wars'. *New York Review of Books*, 30 November: 4–6.

Gergen, K. (1994). *Realities and Relationships*. Cambridge, Mass.: Harvard University Press.

Goodenough, W. H. (1981). *Culture, Language, and Society* (2nd edn). Menlo Park, Calif.: Benjamin-Cummings.

Goody, J. (ed.) (1968). *Literacy in Traditional Societies*. Cambridge: Cambridge University Press.

——(1977). *The Domestication of the Savage Mind*. Cambridge: Cambridge University Press.

——(1986). *The Logic of Writing and the Organization of Society*. Cambridge: Cambridge University Press.

——and Watt, I. (1968). 'The Consequences of Literacy', in J. Goody (ed.), *Literacy in Traditional Societies*. Cambridge: Cambridge University Press, 27–68.

Gouldner, A. W. (1954). *Patterns of Industrial Bureaucracy: A Study of Modern Factory Administration*. Glencoe, Ill.: Free Press.

Herskovits, M. J. (1973). *Cultural Relativism*. New York: Random House.

Holden, N. J. and Cooper, C. (1994). 'Russian Managers as Learners: Implications for Theories of Management Learning'. *Management Learning*, 25: 503–22.

Holland, D. and Quinn, N. (eds.) (1987). *Cultural Models in Language and Thought*. Cambridge: Cambridge University Press.

Hutchins, E. (1995). *Cognition in the Wild*. Cambridge, Mass.: MIT Press.

Jaques, E. (1951). *The Changing Culture of the Factory*. London: Tavistock.

Jarvie, I. C. (1990). 'Comments', in M. Manganaro (ed.), *Modernist Anthropology: From Fieldwork to Text*. Princeton: Princeton University Press, 122–5.

Keesing, F. M. (1953). *Culture Change*. Stanford, Calif.: Stanford University Press.

Kluckhohn, C. and Kelly, W. H. (1945). 'The Concept of Culture', in R. Linton (ed.), *The Science of Man in the World Crisis*. New York: Columbia University Press, 78–106.

Knorr Cetina, K. (1994). 'Primitive Classification and Postmodernity'. *Theory, Culture, and Society*, 11: 1–22.

Latour, B. (1986). 'The Powers of Association', in J. Law (ed.), *Power, Action and Belief: A New Sociology of Knowledge?* London: Routledge and Kegan Paul, 261–77.

——(1991). 'Technology Is Society Made Durable', in J. Law (ed.), *A Sociology of Monsters: Essays on Power, Technology and Domination*. London: Routledge, 103–31.

——(1993). *We Have Never Been Modern*. Cambridge, Mass.: Harvard University Press.

Leach, E. (1970). *Levi-Strauss*. London: Fontana.

——(1972). 'Buddhism in Post-colonial Burma', in S. N. Eisenstadt (ed.), *Post-traditional Societies*. New York: Norton, 29–54.

Levi-Strauss, C. (1966). *The Savage Mind*. London: Weidenfeld and Nicolson.

Levitt, B. and March, J. G. (1988). 'Organizational Learning'. *Annual Review of Sociology*, 14: 319–40.

Löfgren, O. (1993). 'Materializing the Nation in Sweden and America'. *Ethnos*, 3–4: 161–96.

Mair, L. (1957). 'Malinowski and the Study of Social Change', in R. Firth (ed.), *Man and Culture: An Evaluation of the Work of Bronislaw Malinowski*. London: Routledge and Kegan Paul, 229–44.

Malinowski, B. (1929). *The Sexual Life of Savages in North-western Melanesia*. New York: Holcyon House.

Marcus, G. (1992). 'Past, Present and Emergent Identities: Requirements for Ethnographies of Late Twentieth-century Modernity Worldwide', in S. Lash and J. Friedman (eds.), *Modernity and Identity*. Oxford: Blackwell, 309–30.

—— and Fischer, M. M. J. (1986). *Anthropology as Cultural Critique*. Chicago: University of Chicago Press.

Mead, M. (1943). 'Our Education Emphases in Primitive Perspective'. *American Journal of Sociology*, 48: 633–9.

—— (1959). 'Preface', in R. Benedict, *Patterns of Culture*. New York: Mentor Books, v–viii.

Miller, J. H. (1993). 'Is Literary Theory a Science?', in G. Levine (ed.), *Realism and Representation*. Madison: University of Wisconsin Press, 155–68.

Nandy, A. (1972). 'The Making and Unmaking of Political Cultures in India', in S. N. Eisenstadt (ed.), *Post-traditional Societies*. New York: Norton, 115–37.

Obeysekere, G. (1995). *The Apotheosis of Captain Cook: European Mythmaking in the Pacific*. Princeton: Princeton University Press.

Pettigrew, A. M. (1985). *The Awakening Giant: Continuity and Change in Imperial Chemical Industries*. Oxford: Blackwell.

Quinn, N. and Holland, D. (1987). 'Culture and Cognition', in D. Holland and N. Quinn (eds.), *Cultural Models in Language and Thought*. Cambridge: Cambridge University Press, 3–40.

Radcliffe-Brown, A. R. (1952). *Structure and Function in Primitive Society*. Glencoe, Ill.: Free Press.

Rappaport, R. A. (1994). 'Humanity is Evolution and Anthropology is Future', in R. Borofsky (ed.), *Assessing Cultural Anthropology*. New York: McGraw-Hill, 153–66.

Reason, D. (1979). 'Classifications, Time and the Organization of Production', in R. F. Ellen and D. Reason (eds.), *Classifications in Their Social Context*. London: Academic Press, 221–47.

Redfield, R. (1953). *The Primitive World and Its Transformations*. Ithaca, NY: Cornell University Press.

—— Linton, R., and Herskovits, M. J. (1936). 'Memorandum for the Study of Acculturation'. *American Anthropologist*, 38: 149–52.

Rogers, E. M. (1962). *Diffusion of Innovations*. New York: Free Press.

Rosaldo, R. (1989). *Culture and Truth*. Boston: Beacon Press.

Rosen, M. (1988). 'You Asked for It: Christmas at the Bosses' Expense'. *Journal of Management Studies*, 25: 463–80.

Sahlins, M. (1994). 'Goodbye to *Tristes Tropes*: Ethnography in the Context of Modern World History', in R. Borofsky (ed.), *Assessing Cultural Anthropology*. New York: McGraw-Hill, 377–94.

—— (1995). 'How "Natives" Think, about Captain Cook, for Example'. Chicago: University of Chicago Press.

—— and Service, E. R. (eds.) (1960). *Evolution and Culture*. Ann Arbor: University of Michigan Press.

Sevón, G. (1996). 'Organizational Imitation in Identity Transformation', in B. Czarniawska and G. Sevón (eds.), *Translating Organizational Change*. Berlin: de Gruyter, 49–66.

Shore, B. (1982). *Sala'ilua: A Samoan Mystery*. New York: Columbia University Press.

Smith, C., Child, J., and Rowlinson, M. (1991). *Reshaping Work*. Cambridge: Cambridge University Press.

Spindler, G. (1978). *The Making of Psychological Anthropology*. Berkeley: University of California Press.

Steiner, G. (1992). *After Babel: Aspects of Language and Translation*. Oxford: Oxford University Press. (Original work published 1975)

Stocking, G. W., Jr. (1995). *After Tylor: British Social Anthropology 1888–1951*. Madison: University of Wisconsin Press.

Strathern, M. (1990). 'Out of Context: The Persuasive Fictions of Anthropology', in M. Manganaro (ed.), *Modernist Anthropology: From Fieldwork to Text*. Princeton: Princeton University Press, 80–122.

Strauss, C. and Quinn, N. (1994). 'A Cognitive/Cultural Anthropology', in R. Borofsky (ed.), *Assessing Cultural Anthropology*. New York: McGraw-Hill, 284–97.

Suarez-Orozco, M. M., Spindler, G., and Spindler, L. (eds.) (1994). *The Making of Psychological Anthropology II*. Orlando, Fla.: Harcourt Brace.

Tambiah, S. J. (1972). 'The Persistence and Transformation of Tradition in Southeast Asia, with Special Reference to Thailand', in S. N. Eisenstadt (ed.), *Post-traditional Societies*. New York: Norton, 55–84.

Traweek, S. (1992). 'Border Crossings: Narrative Strategies in Science Studies and among Physicists in Tsukuba Science City, Japan', in A. Pickering (ed.), *Science as Practice and Culture*. Chicago: University of Chicago Press, 429–66.

Turner, V. (1982). *From Ritual to Theatre*. New York: Performing Arts Journal Publications.

Van Maanen, J. (1988). *Tales of the Field*. Chicago: University of Chicago Press.

——(1995). 'An End to Innocence: The Ethnography of Ethnography', in J. Van Maanen (ed.), *Representation in Ethnography*. Thousand Oaks, Calif.: Sage, 1–35.

Waldo, D. (1961). 'Organization Theory: An Elephantine Problem'. *Public Administration Review*, 21: 210–25.

Weick, K. E. (1979). *The Social Psychology of Organizing* (2nd edn). Reading, Mass.: Addison-Wesley.

Wilks, I. (1968). 'The Transmission of Islamic Learning in the Western Sudan', in J. Goody (ed.), *Literacy in Traditional Societies*. Cambridge: Cambridge University Press, 161–97.

Wolf, E. R. (1964). *Anthropology*. Englewood Cliffs, NJ: Prentice Hall.

——(1994). 'Facing Power: Old Insights, New Questions', in R. Borofsky (ed.), *Assessing Cultural Anthropology*. New York: McGraw-Hill, 219–27.

Yalman, N. (1972). 'Some Observations on Secularism in Islam: The Cultural Revolution in Turkey', in S. N. Eisenstadt (ed.), *Post-traditional Societies*. New York: Norton, 139–68.

6   The Underestimated Contributions of Political Science to Organizational Learning

Joseph LaPalombara

Introduction: Disciplinary Obscurity of Organizational Learning

Organizational theory and, therefore, organizational learning, an important dimension of the former, have rarely attracted the attention of political scientists. Etheredge (1981) noted this situation two decades ago, but he added that 'Government learning is a new interdisciplinary field of social science inquiry' (p. 73). This judgment was premature for political science, even though in those same years the discipline moved sharply in the direction of trying to provide improved explanations for what encouraged or impeded 'effective' government. A good deal of the attention focused on the executive branch, which was Etheredge's primary focus as well (1981: 76–82).

Etheredge (1981: 86–8) also noted that, unlike organizations in the private sector, government institutions almost always have a powerful and central normative dimension. This aspect of public-sector organizations is of critical import (see also LaPalombara, Ch. 25 in this volume).

The time is certainly ripe for a reevaluation of organizational learning in the public/political sector. The formal institutions of government and the ever-increasing number of organizations that are directly involved in the political processes of most countries interact in ways that make it imperative to have a deepened understanding of all of these structures. This many-faceted organizational articulation is called 'political pluralism'. It has now come to characterize even once-repressive political systems as they try to democratize. The salience to politics of so many organizations brings about a complex organizational mosaic that consists of organizations representing both civil society and the state. The impact of organizations on daily life and, indeed, on the fortunes of individuals and of nations impel one to ask whether these organizations learn and to what effect.

Some Explanations of Neglect

To deepen the understanding of the salience to politics of organizations *as organizations*, political scientists need to overcome the misapprehension that 'organization theorists have been talking to themselves' (Hall and Quinn 1981: 18). Even a cursory look at some of the classic works in organizational learning (e.g. Argyris and Schön 1978, 1996) makes plain the intellectual advantages that would derive from an analysis of public/political-sector organizations in terms of, for example, their capacity to experience single-loop and double-loop learning. In the public/political sphere, it is quite difficult for organizations to modify the means they utilize in goal achievement, especially when (as is typically the case) the organizations involved are responsible for the implementation of public policies. And when double-loop learning prescribes a modification or abandonment of the goals or policies themselves, this step is next to impossible.

The point to stress here is that an improved cross-disciplinary integration of political science into the fields of organizational theory and organizational learning requires increased intellectual openness on both sides of the disciplinary divide. An intellectual interchange of this type would almost certainly bring about conceptual and theoretical modifications. They would not only reduce intellectual isolation and parochialism but would almost certainly also enrich organizational theory and organizational learning.

Etheridge (1981) made an eloquent plea for such disciplinary cross-fertilization, but it has not yet materialized. One reason is that scholars who specialize in the study of organizations and organizational learning lack consensus even as a working hypothesis, on a precise denotation of the concept 'organizational learning'. Hence, those outside the organizational learning subfield are typically at a loss as to how the learning aspects of organizations might be systematically and empirically measured. Even more daunting is the challenge to show what might be the effects on organizations—internally or in what they do—were they to improve their capacity to learn (Rist 1994: 189–93).

Problems of this kind have led some political scientists (Palumbo 1975: 319) to conclude, somewhat unfairly, that organizational learning amounts to nothing more than research activity in search of an identity. Palumbo argued in addition that, because organizations of interest to political scientists differ systematically from those in the private sector, extant theories about organizational learning are, at best, of limited relevance to their discipline (pp. 320–6). This judgment remains dominant among political scientists, even though, as suggested below, there is some evidence that it is withering away.

The history of political science's origins is another factor that underlies this discipline's neglect of organizational theory and organizational learning. Like American sociology, political science in the United States, at its origins, was deeply influenced by European intellectuals and scholarship. In sociology, the European precursors include world-renowned names such as Weber, Simmel, Durkheim, and Pareto. These scholars stressed the importance of well-crafted theories and their empirical validation. They also showed the value of looking at different aspects of social organizations. These aspects included their origins and purpose, their place in the broad social scheme of things, their internal workings, their interactions with other segments of society, and, of course, their propensity and capacity to learn and, on this basis, to modify their behavior and, indeed, their goals. Thus, it is no accident that the first theoretically rich, in-depth empirical study in the United States of a major governmental institution came from a sociologist (Selznick 1949).

Like sociologists and scholars in other fields, a number of early American political scientists went to Europe, particularly to Germany, in order to pursue postgraduate study. They gravitated, however, toward leading legal philosophers, such as von Gierke, Jellinek, Bluntschlii, and von Jhering. American political science's early elite came to believe that the organizational contours, internal processes, and operational norms of political institutions would conform, one-to-one, with what was laid down in the constitutions, laws, executive orders, administrative regulations, and other official expressions of the polities in which they were located. Deviations from such conformance were actually treated by those in the discipline as political pathologies.

This overly simplified conception of organizations (and indeed of politics!) saddled political science with a highly legalistic and formalistic approach to institutions and organizations, an approach that, with a few exceptions, persisted until after World War II. This situation encouraged neither the innovative building of theory about organizations nor empirical investigations into how the institutions in the public/political sector actually operate in practice. The question of whether organizations learn simply never surfaced.

Some Exceptions

There were some exceptions to this hyperformalism about organizations and the consequent failure to develop and test empirical theories about them. In the subfield of public administration (where attention to organizations as such appears to be the essence of the enterprise), the name Mary Parker Follett looms large. Follett, in the early years of the twentieth century, viewed public-administrative organizations as organic, dynamically active and reactive systems that influenced and, equally important, were influenced by the environments in which they were located (Follett 1942). Long before the corporate community discovered the tendency of senior executives to imbue the firm with a particular culture, Follett was providing brilliant insights into this phenomenon. The pity is that her work had a much greater impact on the disciplines of social psychology and management theory than it did on political science, where she long remained an obscure figure or was paid only lip service (Graham 1995; Heap and Ross 1992). The same can be said of Chester Barnard's (1938) seminal book on executive leadership, which was not paid any attention at all in political science until several decades after it appeared.

Follett showed that even in organizations characterized by extreme hierarchy, including those that were seemingly governed or regulated by very precise laws and executive orders, variables such as norms, values, personality, and culture profoundly affected the organizations' actual behavior. She pioneered the exploration of the impact on organizations of, for example, individualism, norms such as egalitarianism, the nature of interaction between levels of leadership, the capacity of individuals within an organization to modify their interactions on the basis of what is learned, and the different styles of organizational leadership.

Follett's work is of value even today, for it provides a broad perspective on, and shrewd insights into, the weight that contextual variables, including politics, have in shaping organizations. Some of these conditions greatly inhibit the ability of some public/political-sector organizations to engage in and profit from learning experiences. The simple truth is that, when politics is at the center of an organization's *raison d'être*, it is typical that one group of leaders will try to undo what may have gone before, no matter how efficacious these earlier expressions of organizational life, shaped by their predecessors, may have been.

In effect, 'creative destruction' (Schumpeter 1950)—the impulse, on the basis of what is learned, to replace existing organizational structures with better ones—is as rare in the public/political sector as it may actually be alien to it. In this context, organizational change, if it occurs at all, is more likely to be motivated by ideology, political partisanship, or both than by anything so rational as that implied in the idea that ends and means should be efficiently associated with each other. Thus, a universal challenge to leaders and managers in the public/political sphere is to find the means to overcome political obstacles that impede learning. Equally challenging, when learning does occur, is to put this knowledge to good use, including its use, when necessary, as a justification for organizational change. To be successful in this sense demands an unusual combination of managerial skills.

An even earlier organizationally focused work is that by the Swiss writer Robert Michels (1915/1962), whom political scientists claim as one of their own. Writing a bit earlier than Follett, Michels provided an unprecedented empirical study of the internal workings of the German Social Democratic Party (SPD). In it he formulated his famous Iron Law of Oligarchy. The brilliance of this study lies not so much in the banal discovery that, even in an organization ideologically committed to maximizing democratic participation, actual rule is carried out by a small elite. Rather, it lies in the sophisticated explication of the dynamic relationships between leaders, militants, and ordinary rank-and-file members within the SPD. By implication, Michels's striking findings apply to other organizations as well. The work is a pioneering examination of the sociopsychological aspects, as well as the necessary and sufficient conditions, of effective leadership within complex organizations.

Michels (1915/1962) was also remarkably prescient in his understanding of the vital importance of control and exploitation of an organization's channels of communication, as a means used by the organization's leaders in order to perpetuate their privileged places in them. Homeostasis, the condition whereby the survival of the organization comes to replace the purposes for which it was created in the first place, is the probable outcome of such leadership behavior. Michels treated this condition and the processes that bring it about with the acuity and the irony they deserve.

Earlier than either Follett or Michels, the political scientist Moisie Ostrogorski, writing in France late in the nineteenth century, was the first to look at many political parties *as* organizations and to explore their internal workings (Ostrogorski 1889/1926, 1964). He was particularly fascinated by the United States, which, because of the early extension of suffrage there, was the first country to experience mass-based parties. In Ostrogorski's work, too, one finds pioneering insights into the relationship between the form of an organization and its capacities to achieve its goals. Ostrogorski stressed the need for parties to make tactical and strategic adaptations to external factors and to changes in their environments. How well this type of adaptation occurs depends on the organization's learning capacity, which, as he showed, is, in turn, related to the party's structural configuration.

Several decades later, a few distinguished political scientists made a quantum leap in their understanding of organizations. Among the most prominent were Herbert Simon and James March. Simon's attempt, with two colleagues, to place the study of public-administrative organizations on more solid conceptual and empirical footing (Simon, Smithburg, and Thompson 1950) had relatively little impact.

Written as a textbook, the volume, had it been widely adopted, would radically have changed the formulations applied by political scientists to public-administrative bodies.

These authors showed every sign of having read and digested the works of writers like Follett and Barnard as well as organizationally focused works in sister disciplines. They stressed that the form of an organization, the type of persons recruited to lead it, the organization's degree of complexity, and the nature of its interactions with others in its immediate and broader spheres deeply affects its operations. The fact that such considerations then shape organizational behavior itself implied, as Etheridge (1981) noted, that public-administrative organizations can and do learn (p. 76).

Simon's study a few years later (Simon 1957), which delineated the contours of decision-making processes in complex organizations, certainly influenced what was later to be called the 'behavioral revolution' in political science. But even as this important shift in conceptual, theoretical, and methodological orientation evolved in the 1960s and 1970s, not many political scientists thought to treat organizations as the unit of analysis. Almost never does one encounter research that treats as independent variables the internal structural characteristics of organizations, or aspects of organizations' environments, that might affect their behavior.

As a consequence, the seminal work by March and Simon (1958), which underscored this need, had immensely more influence in several of the social sciences other than the one (political science) in which both of these innovative scholars were trained. Little wonder, then, that both of these political scientists abandoned that discipline and went on to do their creative work elsewhere: Simon primarily in economic and organizational theory (Simon 1982, 1991), March in the field of management studies (March 1991; March and Olsen 1976).

Peter Blau (1955, 1956) is another of the handful of political scientists who have brought sharp insight into the internal processes of public-administrative organizations. He is also the author of the *International Encyclopedia of the Social Sciences* article on 'Theories of Organizations' (Blau 1968). It is indicative of political science's aloofness from the fields of organizational theory and organizational learning that, of the nineteen authors he cited, only five, including Simon, March, and Blau, himself, are trained political scientists.

Organizational Learning and Political Science Subfields

As defined in the United States, the subfields of political science are generally said to include: American Government and Politics, Comparative Politics, Political Parties and Pressure Groups, Political Philosophy or Normative Theory, Public Administration, Policy Studies, Public Law, Political Economy or Public Choice, and International Relations and Organization. The number and variety of organizations encompassed by this list are enormous. Knowing more about them has certainly been one of the central impulses of the discipline's practitioners, but the questions of whether such organizations engage in learning and, if so, how and with what effects have rarely been at the center of their scientific concerns.

There are, of course, exceptions to this statement. Moreover, in all of the subfields, one can find many works that actually do reveal the structural characteristics and dynamics that encourage or impede organizational learning. It could not be otherwise, given that political scientists have from the beginning been concerned with questions such as choice of public policies, why some policies turn out to be more successful than others, and why some policies are more rather than less easy to administer— or, more rather than less acceptable to those organizations and persons who themselves are the objects of the policies. A glimpse of this disciplinary landscape is now in order.

Public Law

The easiest place to begin is with one of the oldest of the discipline's subfields, the one that deals with constitutions and basic laws as the foundations for the polity itself. Governmental organizations not only are created by such public laws; they and those who manage them are deeply constrained by them as well. For persons who operate in the public sphere, and especially for those among them who hold bureaucratic or public-administrative positions, learning is an imperative. That is, at the very least, these persons must learn what the laws that govern their agencies, and their authority within them, will or will not allow. Indeed, they must also learn what it is that the laws require. These public servants operate under the Sword of Damocles, that impels them to pay careful attention to acts of malfeasance and nonfeasance (Spiro 1969: 86–7). The more delicate or controversial the policy realm in which these governmental agencies are located, the greater will be the attention paid to what the law will or will not permit.

Lawgivers and institution-builders are highly conscious of the salience of law, not just as it is written but also how it will be administered. Public-sector organizations are often designed with exactly such considerations in mind. Once the laws are enacted, and agencies created or empowered to administer them, the organizations involved are imbued with an aura of permanency. Those who are thereafter inclined to make changes in the organizations—in response, for example, to unexpected or unwanted developments—are well advised to proceed with great care. One way or another, questions will arise about whether the would-be changes are in conformance with existing laws. If they are not, little change can actually take place without, for example, modification of the laws or official regulations involved. In limited cases, existing laws must be abolished before changes can proceed (Dean 1981; Gortner, Mahler, and Nicholson 1987: 60–9).

In addition, as Moe (1989: 85–7) pointed out, the legal straitjacket imposed on public organizations may in itself work in ways that prevent any kind of useful learning from taking place. Thus, even in cases where there may be a strong commitment to effecting change, even with what Levin and Sanger (1994) called the 'entrepreneurial executive' (p. 171) who may be bent on change, his or her freedom to act will be 'constrained . . . by rules, regulations and clearance points' (p. 171) that tie the hands and impede learning-based change.

The obvious weight of public law on institutions, even though widely recognized in the discipline of political science, has not led many of the specialists in this field to explore the effects of formal rules on an organization's learning. The legacy of formalism described earlier in this chapter is a key reason for this inattention. Any view holding that a public-sector organization worthy of the name should conform to written law and that deviations from such constraints amount to a form of pathology is not likely to generate much interest in phenomena of organizational learning and adaptation. The presumption, more often begged than demonstrated, is that law by itself describes not only what an organization is but also what it will be permitted to become.

Legislative Organizations

Research on the U.S. Congress, without doubt the legislative body most studied by political scientists in the United States, is another striking example of the scant attention paid to organizational theory and organizational learning. For example, Bailey's (1950) postwar study of the passage of the U.S. Federal Employment Act of 1946 brims over with insights into the nature of Congress, particularly of its interactions with organizations that were deeply enmeshed in the legislative process itself. Bailey offered a dazzling description of these interactions. Anyone who wishes to see up close just how variegated and complex legislative bodies can be, and what kinds of internal and external factors lie in the way of rational choice or efficacious decision-making within them, still does well to read this book.

This study contains all manner of information about what was learned as the legislative battle unfolded, who did the learning, and how this knowledge was used in pursuit of highly partisan goals. Among its merits is the empirical justification it provides for the caveats articulated by Cyert and March (1963: 100–25) about what lies in the way of rational organizational learning. When the organization is constituted of many subgroups, whose goals are different and whose information-seeking and utilization strategies are highly biased, it is, to say the least, unproductive to impute rational impulses to such bodies. To be sure, learning is an integral part of this process, for both the individuals involved and for the organization as a whole. Why they learn, how they learn, and what they do with what is learned are exactly the interesting questions that should never be begged.

Legislatures, like many other organizations in the public sphere, are by definition arenas designed both to accommodate conflict over ends and means and to assure that conflict itself will remain within reasonable bounds. Far from being pathological, this type of conflict typically contributes to the stability of the larger system of which the organization is a part (Lindblom 1971: ch. 8). Over time, monumental encounters and conflicts take place of the kind that accompany major pieces of legislation, such as the one studied by Bailey. Such encounters test the capacity of legislative organizations to learn from past experiences in the performance of this delicate stabilizing role. But these aspects of Congress or of the organized groups that intervened in the legislative process were not systematically treated by Bailey. Consequently, the book's rich theoretical implications for organizational learning were simply overlooked.

Fenno (1973) published distinguished research on structural and institutional aspects of Congressional committees. As with Bailey's pathbreaking study, Fenno's work reflects an intellectual journey of a kind taken by few others. On the other hand, many studies center on actual attempts to reform one or the other branch of Congress. This focus implies an interest in showing why the changes were proposed and adopted in the first place and what their subsequent effects were. Clearly, such reforms would rarely be introduced were it not for some learning that took place about what the organization does that is found to be unacceptable or that, in any case, might be improved. Such learning occurs either diachronically, when an organization assesses its own past, or synchronically, when it looks across space to see how things are done elsewhere. Similar learning is involved even when reforms are imposed from outside the organization, a relatively frequent phenomenon in the public/political sphere (see the chapters on external triggers to organizational learning in Part II of this volume).

An excellent study of this kind is by Smith and Deering (1984). It was motivated by the reforms of Congress, most of them highly controversial, that were instituted in the early 1970s. This study (ch. 9) was particularly helpful in showing again how fragmented and decentralized the learning capacity of some complex organizations is, and it established this point more systematically than Bailey (1950) did. Smith and Deering (1984) also pointed up some of the unintended consequences of organizational reforms, many of which produce perverse results, unwanted by the reformers themselves or, indeed, by their opponents. Studies of this kind underscore that in the political sphere organizational learning and change take place principally on a trial-and-error basis.

Examples of structural aspects of national legislative organizations that are designed to bring about more or less democratic representation and more or less efficiency in both the passage of laws and the legislative oversight of laws' administration are also found in the subfield of comparative politics (Blondel 1973, 1982). There is also information from European and other national settings on how the behavior of legislative bodies is affected by their organizational configurations, the basic rules that govern their internal procedures, their formal and informal relationship to the executive branch and to outside interest groups, the modalities through which their members are chosen, and many other structural factors (Loewenberg and Patterson 1979; Loewenberg, Patterson, and Jewell 1985; Mayhew 1974).

Literature of this kind rarely poses research questions in organizational learning terms. Much of it can nevertheless be read with profit, because organizational learning is an intimate aspect of all such institutional processes. The introduction in recent decades of specialized committees in many different national legislatures would not have proceeded as it has were it not for the example set by the U.S. Congress. Similarly, the spread of the institution of the 'ombudsman', as a means of improving the legislature's oversight of the executive and public-administrative sector is a direct result of what has been learned about this institution in the Scandinavian countries. Similar examples of learning abound—of deliberate or accidental cross-national learning and acculturation that then emanate in organizational and institutional change in the public and governmental spheres.

Political Parties

Political parties and the courts, the former arguably the most important organizations in any representative democratic system, also have rarely been studied as organizations and as entities that engage in learning from their environment and experiences. V. O. Key is a striking exception, particularly because he delineated (Key 1942) the organizational interactions between parties and interest groups and, even more significant from the standpoint of organizational theory and organizational learning, showed the impact of local culture and norms on political party organizations (Key 1949). Key's acute insights into the U.S. political system and process produced overwhelming evidence that the political parties that emerged and operated within the fourteen states that make up the secessionist American Southern states not only shared very specific cultural characteristics. These organizations also exchanged useful information—about internal party organization as well as laws—that would help them maintain one-party domination of their respective states. This communication was organizational learning *par excellence*, and its nefarious electoral and related political effects in the 'Solid South' endured for over a century.

The first important book after Ostrogorski's work to treat systematically the internal organizational aspects of political parties in a variety of national settings was that by Maurice Duverger (1954), a French political scientist. He provided insightful, even if not always empirically based, observations on the internal dynamics of these organizations. Duverger correctly noted that it would make a considerable difference whether a political party emerged from within existing governmental institutions, dominated by a given socioeconomic elite, or whether it was created instead on the outside, so to speak, by those who would challenge this same elite. Among other things, the capacity of these organizations to make timely and effective adaptations to changes in the broader political and electoral environments (i.e. to learn) would be deeply affected by such characteristics. An enduring value of this work lies in its differentiation between mass parties according to why and with what effects one or another organizational form comes into existence.

More than thirty years later, Angelo Panebianco (1988), an Italian political scientist, produced the first volume worthy of being included in the tradition of Michels and Ostrogorski. Panebianco's study overflows with powerful, empirically supported arguments about, for example, the relationship between degrees and kinds of centralization and what a party will be capable of doing. He laid out a variety of constraints on party organizations, which, among other things, tell how these organizations will read and learn about their environment and what kinds of adaptations they are likely to make to what is learned. It turns out, in this regard, that the party's place and moment of origin, its early structural configuration, the milieu in which it operates, and the kinds of leaders and members it develops during its early years will long dominate the party's behavior. This organizational DNA, so to speak, will tend to freeze a political party organization into certain structural and behav-

ioral modes. Whether and to what extent it is then able to learn, and, on this basis, to modify its institutional and behavioral modes is to some extent preordained.

Panebianco's book (1988) is a deliberate application to political parties of the sociology of complex organizations. He offered a typology of these organizations (ch. 4) that accounts for varying patterns of internal conflict, relationships between leaders and rank-and-file members, and the probability that a given party will achieve deep institutionalization. One interesting form of organizational learning he highlights is the tendency of party leaders to change the size of the organization in the interest of prolonging their control of it. The most dramatic empirical examples of this phenomenon are changes in the size and sometimes in the organization of revolutionary political parties over time.

Above all, Panebianco showed (ch. 14) that some political parties manage to change, and indeed sometimes are radically transformed, precisely because they learn how to make adaptations that assure their continuity and survival. Over time, parties once driven by ideology and tightly related to given segments of society are replaced by what Panebianco (1988) called the 'electoral professional' party (p. 273). The so-called Third Way of today, which has brought radical transformations in so many of Europe's once social democratic parties, is a prime example of this type of transformation. Predicted by Kirscheimer (1966) so many years ago, the emergence of these 'catch-all parties' represents quintessential evidence of organizational learning (pp. 177–200).

As in other subfields of political science, the work on political parties and party systems rarely treats these organizations as such and therefore rarely introduces questions about organizational learning. The one striking exception is the subfield of international relations, where, particularly in recent years, the issue whether and how organizations learn has clearly gained a great deal in saliency. I return to this point below, but first a few general observations about this subfield in the study of politics are in order.

International Relations

As in many other spheres, in the relationships among nations, conflict is the other side of collaboration. And, again as elsewhere, competition among states can and often does get out of hand. Unlike the case with other organizations, however, those who are responsible for managing the external affairs of states are exceptionally impelled to learn from their mistakes. The ability to read the environment accurately, to make timely and valid adaptations to it, and to change these adaptations as circumstances may require is not only a potential comparative advantage where states are concerned; it may also be, literally speaking, a matter of life and death—of survival itself—for its citizens as well as the nation.

From the very beginning, the literature in this subfield, has been rich in materials that are highly suggestive of factors that may facilitate or lie in the way of useful learning on the part of the state and its prime institutions. Historians and others warn that the dismal recurrence of violent conflicts, including the most deadly of wars in the twentieth century, is evidence that the learning capacities of the nation-state, and of the organizations that make it up, are remarkably limited. If history is doomed to repeat itself, this cliché implies either that learning does not occur or, if it does, that such knowledge is rarely a guide for state action (see Fear, Ch. 7 in this volume).

In contrast to this picture is another according to which, for centuries, even those nations otherwise in conflict with each other have found the ways and means (i.e. they have learned) to reach mutually beneficial modes of collaboration. In addition, there are the advocates of *realpolitik*, many of whom remind their listeners that the hard-headed pursuit of national self-interest would scarcely be possible were it not for the fact that at least some state leaders and organizations do know how to read the environment well and do learn well from the past. Illustrations of this approach to international politics are found in the writings of political scientists Hans Morgenthau (1948), Arnold Wolfers (1962), and many others. Even

in this sphere, however, it is only in very recent years that analysts have turned a bit of their attention to the self-conscious study of the organizations of the state involved in these processes.

A striking exception is Ernst Haas, a pioneering political scientist who almost single-handedly established the so-called functional approach to the empirical study of relations between nations. In his now classic work on the European Communities, Haas (1968) took the view that the inexorable integration of the nations that make up the European Economic Community (EEC) would proceed, gradually and step by step. The process would be driven by persons assigned either to the new institutions of the EEC or to national organizations that would have to deal with the former. Interactions among such persons would lead them, he argued, to develop common values and cognitive systems and therefore common interests. Over time, they would improve understanding of the benefits of collaboration and therefore shape organizations to achieve this end.

In Haas's formulation, this entire process takes place on the basis of organizational learning. More precisely, the specialists and leaders of the organizations involved in specialized activities learn first. They then pass along this learning to others who interact with the EEC's institutions. In Haas's words, 'the answer to maximizing the learning process lies in extending the range of participation in practical problem-solving' (1968: 13). It is this oil-slick effect, this gradual extension born of organizational learning, that will eventually bring about a successful supranational political entity.

The functionalist school has been criticized on many grounds, not the least salient of which is that it places so much emphasis on the role of specialists in policy-making and implementation that it fails to take adequate account of the fact that all processes of the kind represented by the European Community are deeply infused with politics (Webb 1983: 10–12). In other words, whenever the policy issues that these international organizations confront are no longer narrowly technical but of the kind that attracts relatively broad public attention, the issues become politicized (Scheinman 1971: 210–19). When this change happens, when matters on the policy agenda develop a high and sharp political profile, the organizations involved open up considerably to the behaviorally constraining factors mentioned above (see also LaPalombara, Ch. 25 in this volume). In effect, what those who manage these organizations come to learn, sometimes painfully, is that the member nations of the EEC (and now also the European Union) may not permit them to act at all on certain matters, even when these matters are, at least in theory, within their jurisdiction. The give-and-take struggles that then ensue are much more political than they are technical or rational (Allen 1977: 108–10).

Be that as it may, Haas and others who have been associated with this scholar are exceptional in political science because they identify learning as perhaps the central phenomenon that brings about organizational change. Haas (1968) believed that the way to induce change is to maximize the amount of learning open to the experts in organizations (p. 12). Collaboration among experts is the primary channel for the spatial diffusion of knowledge (p. 14). Indeed, through such learning processes 'power-centered governmental pursuits evolve into welfare-oriented action' (pp. 47–8). So powerful are these pressures, in his view, that they bring about double-loop learning, in the form of a redefinition of an organization's interests, and the organizational instruments through which these interests are pursued (p. 48). 'Men', Haas concluded on a highly positive note, 'are not condemned merely to act out a systemic tragedy because through learning they are able to change the system itself' (p. 81).

Haas and others (Haas, Williams, and Babai 1977) constructed case studies to provide empirical validation for such assertions. They sought to show that learning proceeds essentially from new knowledge, that the search for it is a necessary condition for organizational learning, and that the use of past experience as a basis for action will impede this type of learning (pp. 117–18). Indeed, Haas, Williams, and Babai argued that when learning takes place within a dynamic of this type, there is often a narrowing of the antagonistic gap that separates the makers of political policy from those who are called on to administer it (1977: 184). Far from asserting that this dynamic process brings about increased rationality, they simply noted that the incremental accumulation of new knowledge will reduce antagonism and increase cognitive convergence among actors (pp. 326–30). The cases cited by these authors in support of this conclusion are similar to those mentioned by William Wallace (1983) in his concluding reflections on another set of case studies of different segments of the European Community's institutions.

Some Quantitative Indicators

Works of the kind cited above have had little influence on the intellectual pursuits of political scientists, and progress in this direction has been slower than one might expect. A rough measure of the current state of affairs in political science is provided by a tally I conducted of articles in two leading political science journals, *American Political Science Review* (*APSR*) and *International Organization*, for the period from 1989 through 1998. The purpose was to discern whether authors of the articles that treated any public/political organization were testing theories or propositions about organizational theory or organizational learning.

In the *APSR*, about half of the 448 articles and research notes published during the designated period dealt with political organizations, broadly defined. This count included all items that treated one or more organizations, even if they were not the main focus of the research. In this journal, it is extremely rare to find any item that inquires into how an organization learns—how, for example, it may change its operational code or its goals—on the basis of what it may learn about itself, about its relationship to its clients, or about its broader environment. Some of the articles do address the issue of organizational reform, but such changes are typically described as occurring not because of internal reflection but, rather, because of politically motivated intervention from outside the organization itself.

In the *APSR*, about 20 per cent (48) of the items that did deal with organizations involve the use of formal modeling and rational choice theories and methods. Of these items, twenty-three focused on the U.S. Congress, and the rest dealt with were scattered among executive or judicial bodies in the United States or abroad, political parties or pressure groups, local authorities, or international organizations. Twenty-six of the forty-eight items were said to involve empirical testing of hypotheses about organizations, but in fact they did not. That is, the articles were only spuriously empirical. They typically displayed one or more of the shortcomings of this type of work signaled by Green and Shapiro (1994). Equally spurious in this literature were explicit observations that individual actors who are members of organizations modify their behavior (e.g. in strategic bargaining) on the basis of what each of them 'learns' in the legislative or other 'game' being played.

The other articles did little more than lay out in chronological order what a legislative body or administrative agency or executive office or political party did from time to time. Only in a virtual handful of the items did authors recognize and/or treat systematically (as opposed to describing, even if with sharp insights) matters such as organizational complexity, hierarchy, internal conflict and conflict resolution, dynamic interactive processes, leadership or organizational change. One searches in vain for research propositions about the internal organizational aspects of courts, bureaucratic agencies, executive offices, political parties, interests groups, and so on. Warwick's (1975) comment that political scientists tend to treat organizations in nontheoretical, nonanalytical fashion is an apt description of most of the works surveyed.

The tally of articles in *International Organization* supports this conclusion. From 1989 through 1998, this journal published 182 articles, twenty-three of which might be said to reflect research on organizations. The articles are heavily skewed toward describing interactions (often bilateral) between governmental organizations and international organizations, or both. Little attention is paid to leadership, conflict, conflict resolution, and other phenomena that are *internal* to the organizations, or that derive from one or more aspects of the organization's characteristics.

A number of these articles are also of the rational choice or formal modeling variety. Using such models, the authors purported to illuminate the games that nations play. A central characteristic of these models is that the players (in this case nations or negotiators who are surrogates for them) *learn* as the interactions proceed. However, these articles, too, display the same aloofness from systematic empirical proof found in the *APSR*. Among other things, the articles in both journals contain the repeated mistake of equating the organization with its leaders (see Fear, Ch. 7 in this volume, for a discussion of a similar phenomenon in writings by historians). This extreme reification fails to draw conceptual distinctions between the organization as such and those who are its leaders or members.

Signs of Change?

The so-called new institutionalism in political science, of which the rational choice group is a vibrant part, may nevertheless bring additional rigorous empirical attention not just to the rules (formal or implied) that govern the games of politics but also to the formal organizations themselves, to which the rules apply and within and through which the games are played. The more promising work on this score comes from the group identified with the approach known as historical institutionalism. Political scientists such as Skowronek (1982), Hattam (1993), Skocpol (1995), and Weir (1992) have provided us with new insights into the evolution of public policies in past decades. There is now improved information about what was learned by governmental organizations and by other organizations with which they interacted and about how that learning brought certain public policies or their modifications into existence.

This research is closely related to earlier work in Europe (Mayntz and Scharpf 1975) and represents a potentially major impulse for political scientists to focus deliberate attention on organizational learning. There is also a distinctive interdisciplinary quality to it, which brings well-developed concepts and empirical work in sociology more self-consciously than has been the case thus far into research directed at public-sector organizations of interest to political scientists (Powell and DiMaggio 1991). Historical institutionalism is also tied in with early work by the American political scientist Heclo (1974, 1978), who helped political scientists to understand how bureaucrats and their organizations learn from each other, even across national boundaries. Such learning both arises from and actually creates and reinforces networks among specialized managers of public-sector organizations. From this type of learning, as Heclo documented, there emerge new organizational approaches to the examination, promotion, adoption, and administration of public policies.

This new institutionalism should bring more political scientists to look carefully at some of the well-established conceptual schemes of organizational theory, such as those that address the behavioral study of the firm, and the growing literature in the field of organizational learning. With such cross-fertilization in mind, I wish to turn to aspects of political science research that relate to organizational learning. On the one hand, it is manifest that governmental and political organizations do indeed learn and, on this basis, modify, reorient, and restructure what they do. In some instances learning will also bring about changes in the goals and/or the structural aspects of the organizations themselves.

It is essential not to lose sight of the significant ways in which public/political-sector organizations differ from those in the private sector, on which most of the work in organizational learning has been concentrated. Perhaps the mutual integration of knowledge across disciplines will strengthen the field of organizational learning and increase the self-conscious and active participation of political scientists in the further development of knowledge about organizational learning.

That integration, I believe, will be considerably assisted by a broadened knowledge of what political science does in fact have to offer to those interested in organizational learning, as well as by the fact that, as shown below, there are indeed several subfields of the discipline, in addition to international relations, in which organizations are, for many reasons, at the very center of scholarly attention.

Learning in Political Organizations

Organizations studied by political scientists are not limited to the formal institutions of government. These institutions include executive offices, public-administrative agencies, legislatures and their committees, judicial bodies, the military, quasi-judicial and quasi-legislative regulatory agencies—in effect, all institutions established by law or by constitutions, or simply by custom, that are involved in the processes of government. Equally of interest in the subfield of international organization, relations, and diplomacy is the political capstone organization, namely, the nation-state.

But the list is not exhausted with such organizations. Political scientists also have a keen interest in all modes of organization in civil society that become involved, sometimes very intricately, in the governmental process. Politics is an umbrella term for all such organizations (as well as for individuals and social movements) involved in the formation, implementation, and adjudication of public policies.

The most prominent of these public, but nongovernmental, organizations are political parties. Almost as important, however, are those organized interest groups that in all societies, but especially in pluralist democracies, play a key role in the process of government. Among the most obvious examples of such groups are organized labor and organized business. In addition, there are large numbers of groups that represent the media, geographic areas, the professions, religious and fraternal associations, age groups, social movements, and other categories or dimensions of civil society (see Kädtler, Ch. 9 in this volume).

Given the variety of organizations, formal and informal, public and private, that are intrinsically involved in the process of government, there is much in the literature of political science that is intricately connected to organizational learning. A few illustrations from this literature follow.

Policy Studies

It is in this subfield that public/political organizations are often treated as purposeful and examined in terms of what facilitates or impedes their effectiveness (La Porte 1975; Pressman and Wildavsky 1984). Although political scientists are not the only social scientists writing in this field, they number among its most prominent exponents.

The 'fountainhead' of policy studies was Harold D. Lasswell, a distinguished political scientist who wrote with sometimes breathtaking creativity in almost all of the discipline's subfields. Lasswell addressed the ways in which personality shapes political leadership as well as the organizations within and through which leadership is exercised (Lasswell 1930). His study of political power (Lasswell and Kaplan 1950) remains a landmark effort to bring clarity and logical rigor to this most elusive of concepts. His treatise on what politics is all about (Lasswell 1936) may have jarred the legalists and idealists of that era, but it remains as basic to our understanding of politics as any other major work in the field.

While so many political scientists were still treating political and administrative organizations as if they were exact, concrete expressions of their legal and formal descriptions, Lasswell (1956) broke new ground. One of his major concerns was to show how to improve research into and the understanding of decision-making in these complex organizations. There is little doubt that his work influenced Herbert Simon (with whom he studied at the University of Chicago) as well as James March, who was one of his graduate students at Yale University. He was also a major factor in leading Karl Deutsch (1963) to write his seminal book on the communication and other internal aspects of governmental organizations. The Deutsch study, among other things, clearly showed how the internal structure of an organization and the types of persons named to occupy certain roles within it will facilitate or impede organizational learning.

Lasswell deplored that so few of his political science colleagues paid sophisticated attention to such matters. Many of his early efforts were directed toward improving the theories and methodologies that might be used in policy analysis (Lerner and Lasswell 1951). He himself provided some empirical evidence on the ways in which structure, personality, and interpersonal relations come to impinge on the internal workings of organizations (Rubenstein and Lasswell 1966). He also shocked many of his colleagues by insisting that, in all organizations, people are driven by power-seeking impulses and that some of these people tend to aggregate to themselves all manner of privileges and other scarce resources (Lasswell 1997).

Beyond his unexcelled ability to theorize about politics, Lasswell was a quintessential empiricist. Whether he was writing about world politics and relations between nations, the formation of public opinion and its impact on the political process, or the psychodynamics of political corruption (Rogow and Lasswell 1963), his focus was sharply centered on the organizations involved in the political process and how these organizations and their leaders and members are influenced in what they do by a wide range of social, sociopsychological, personality-related, and cultural variables.

Other Yale-related political scientists who were deeply influenced by Lasswell's policy science approach include Brewer (1971, 1983), Pressman (Pressman and Wildavsky 1984), and Wildavsky (1964, 1974, 1979). The latter remains a towering figure who has fashioned and tested many propositions about factors that lie in the way of efficacious policy choice and implementation. Much of his work showed how indviduals and organizations located far from the decisional center (Wildavsky 1974) or at different hierarchical levels can frustrate or derail goal attainment by organizations.

Wildavsky enriched the literature by illustrating how important it is for organizations to learn about power and how it is exercised. This issue is missing in an oversight in the literature of organizational theory and organizational learning, a gap that may well be in the process of being filled in (Fairholm 1990a: 149; see also Gherardi and Nicolini, Ch. 2; and LaPalombara, Ch. 25 in this volume). Wildavsky (1979) also believed that an organization should be 'self-evaluating' (p. 213). Indeed, he contended that the ways in which an organization goes about seeking knowledge 'uniquely defines its character' (p. 234). Thus, the organization should carefully monitor its own methods for goal achievement, change them when they do not work well and, if necessary, consider modifying the policies themselves. Wildavsky argued that evaluative activities had to be continuous and that internal and external obstacles to this process had to be overcome in order to achieve this sophisticated level of single- and double-loop learning (pp. 214–15; 225). Like Wilensky (1967: 319–34), Wildavsky believed that this type of learning was a precondition for organizational goal attainment and other earmarks of effectiveness.

Wildavsky (1979: 218) and others (Smith and Deering 1984: 252–71) did not believe that learning of this kind is fostered by decentralized decision-making and policy administration. Similarly, given the kinds of political considerations that weigh so heavily in the public sector, the danger remains high that organizational leaders will grow overcautious. This response is reflected in their timidity to make even those changes, suggested by organizational learning, that might be widely accepted. In effect, the fear of upsetting the existing power equilibrium is in itself an impediment to efficacious organizational learning (Wildavsky 1979: 229).

Public/political-sector organizational efforts to scan and learn from the environment are also fraught with other uncertainties and impediments. Bias in information-gathering, present everywhere, is likely to be an immensely noxious problem in the public/political sphere because of the salience there of ideology, conflicting interests, powerful conflict over normative issues, radically different political agendas, and the kind of vulnerability to outside forces that are endemic to these bodies. For similar reasons, the risk of information overload (Cyert and March 1963: 95–101) is also greater in the public/political sector than in other sectors. Despite these problems, Wildavsky believed, along with others (Argyris and Schön 1978: ch. 6), that the intelligent adaptation of an organization to its environment remains an essential condition for optimal performance, regardless of the sector in which the organization is found.

Very much in the Wildavsky tradition is the work of the German scholars Renate Mayntz and Fritz Scharpf. Scharpf also studied at Yale during the Lasswell era, and his outstanding research has deepened the Lasswell quest to understand organizations. Mayntz and Scharpf (1975) clarified a major point on the varying weight likely to be exercised by bureaucratic agencies in the choice (and not just the implementation) of public policies. For example, this influence is likely to vary with the sector of policy involved as well as with the complexity of the policies themselves. A high degree of technical complexity tends to inhibit great attention to a policy by the media and the public, thus allowing the bureaucrats greater freedom and influence. As I noted above about high-profile issues, the more attention proposed policies engender, especially from the press and public opinion but also from competing interest groups, the more limited and circumspect will be the influence exerted by bureaucratic bodies (see also Kädtler, Ch. 9 in this volume).

Scharpf (Scharpf and Hanf 1978) edited papers from an important symposium that showed how, in the political sphere, levels of complexity and conflict over turf, and indeed over values, can reach such levels that organizational goal attainment becomes impossible, no matter how much learning actually occurs. More recently, in an effort to improve the perspective on abstract rational-choice models of organizations, Scharpf (1997) further illuminated the kinds of power- and-influence patterns that emerge in governmental organizations. Not only is the sphere of politics separated from the private sector, the organizations found in politics involve a complex, dizzying network of relationships and interactions that call for carefully tailored conceptual schemes as well as analytical tools that take such matters into account.

Interest Groups and Public Bodies

Those who would influence public policies must organize for this purpose. Exactly how this organization should proceed is conditioned, in the first place, by how the government and its agencies are themselves organizationally structured (LaPalombara 1963). That is, the way in which the branches and agencies of government are organized tends to influence, in turn, the organizational contours of interest groups. This case holds especially for those groups that are the object of governmental regulations. In effect, the group's effort to optimize its influence over policy leads it to shape its organizational form, as well as its personnel, so that it mirrors the governmental agencies. This form of aping is present everywhere. It represents organizational learning of a highly rational and instrumental nature.

Organized pressure groups and lobbying emerged as a major phenomenon first in the United States. The separation and division of power among branches of government at the national and state levels made it highly efficient in the United States for pressure groups to intervene directly in the legislative process as well as elsewhere in the realm of government and administration. The fact that earlier political scientists considered such interventions pathological distortions of what constitutions prescribed served only to guarantee that these scholars garnered, at best, only a partial or, at worst, a highly distorted understanding of the governmental process itself. For as long as there have been organized interest groups, the quest

to learn where and how to optimize leverage over public policies has been at the very center of their learning agenda.

In parliamentary systems, such as those in Europe, where prime ministers exercise great powers over their cabinets, where cabinets dictate legislative policy, and where political parties exercise noteworthy discipline over the legislative behavior of their members, organizational intervention typical of American interest groups is much less efficacious. Hence, other means of access to critical points of policy-making and policy implementation must be found, which requires that groups must organize themselves somewhat differently if they wish to be effective. And they do, as reflected, for example, in the large number of European legislators who are recruited directly from leading interest group categories and organizations. The point is that, if the organized group is to be successful, it must learn how to tailor its own structure, including those who are recruited to represent it, to the particular configuration found on the governmental side.

Thus, as European parties continue to decline, in the sense of exercising discipline over their own deputies, and as individual candidates intensify their use of the mass media in direct appeals for support from voters, interest groups make adaptations to these changes. This process of adaptation has already happened, for the work of legislatures has become increasingly technical and specialized and has therefore become dominated by specialized committees and outside experts. In short, as political systems and governmental institutions come more and more to resemble each other, so, too, will the interest group organizations. The dynamic at work in this process is not unlike that described by Haas (1968) and discussed earlier in this chapter.

Over the years, changes occur in all pluralist democratic systems. Ministries proliferate or are combined or reduced. Powers may shift from one branch or level of government to another. The structure of power and influence may be subtly or radically changed because of electoral outcomes, war, economic depression, or myriad other factors. Organized groups bent on intervening in the governmental process must either learn about such changes and their implications, adapt to them, or risk the loss of effectiveness. The things that governments do, and the organizational arrangements through which these undertakings proceed, will impel attentive groups in the private sectors to learn and to change their own organization and behavior accordingly (Meyer 1979).

Trade unions have been particularly sensitive to the need for this type of transformation. Gone are the days when the only major weapon used by these organizations was the strike. They have radically changed the array of persons who work within their midst and who represent them in complex negotiations with the other social partners—organizations representing business. Twentieth-century learning on the part of these organizations has brought them into the policy-making process in strikingly different ways from the past (Golden 1988; Golden and Pontusson 1992).

Such adaptation has also been true of the corporate community. To begin with, as the other social partner, it joins the trade unions in carrying on with governmental bodies a wide range of negotiations. It, too, must learn to make the organizational changes that permit its representative associations to interact effectively with the other partners. The more technical the problems to be resolved and the more specialized the areas of public policy addressed, the more likely will be the similarity between those from both the private and public sectors involved in these interactions.

Peak associations that represent specific industrial sectors or industry as a whole are not the only organizations that have adapted to these environmental changes. Individual, large-scale multinational corporations have done so as well. One indicator of this shift is the creation of corporate units responsible for 'external affairs', which come either to supplement or to replace earlier units dealing with 'public relations'. This step alone brings about substantial modification of the kind of dialogue and exchange of information that takes place between the governmental and corporate communities.

Another such indicator is the increased amount of time that senior corporate officers and managers devote to contacts and relationships with governmental bodies. Indeed, such relationships have now been widely institutionalized. In recent decades, individual firms and units representing industrial and commercial associations have cropped up in Washington DC, London, Paris, and essentially all of the national (and often regional) capitals of the industrial democracies. As increasing proportions of gross domestic product continue to pass through governmental institutions, corporations (at least the more alert ones) take judicious note of this flow and develop a variety of organizational responses to such conditions. It would be irrational to do otherwise, given that in so many countries national and local governments are not only the biggest 'businesses' around but also, for private-sector business firms, the biggest customers.

The process of organizational adaptation can be nicely traced in a place like Brussels, where the key institutions of the European Union (EU) are based. Over the decades, trade union and employers associations, as well as individual industries, have opened permanent offices there. The considerable and still-growing regulatory powers of the EU make this step not just convenient; this type of direct presence may well be a necessary condition for continuing viability in the marketplace. Failure to engage in and exploit this sort of learning would sooner or later create for the firm difficulties that might otherwise be finessed. When interest groups change in this way, they conform very closely to the dynamic imperatives of organizational learning noted by Ernst Haas (1968) and other writers of the so-called functionalist school.

Similar learning and adaptive processes are at work in the public-administrative sector. For one thing, administrative agencies are often highly dependent on organized groups for technical information as well as for feedback on how well or poorly policies are being implemented. It is well known in political science that high levels of interdependence grow out of such situations. As Downs (1967) showed, in situations (such as public policy implementation) where there is no market that provides information, the agencies involved must seek to maximize the number of sources from which information relevant to their mission can be gleaned. Where interest groups that typically provide this type of information and feedback do not exist, the government itself, and particularly its administrative branches, will go to great pains to bring them into existence. The post–World-War-II histories of the New Nations etch this phenomenon in bold relief, for their governmental and administrative organizations were, so to speak, starting from scratch (Kothari 1970). And what is true for field administrative behavior within nations is true as well in the international sphere. Programs of the United Nations, for example, are influenced, for better and for worse, by what organizations called upon to implement its policies manage to learn about what actually happens in the field (Sharp 1961).

It is also the case that policy-making organizations, such as legislatures, can learn how to exercise effective control over what the bureaucrats do. The ombudsman, mentioned earlier, is one way to acquire this control. But, as Wood and Waterman (1994: ch. 4) demonstrated, there are other methods as well. The legislators, as 'principals', can use their powers over budgetary allocations, their ability to influence the kind and number of agency personnel, and other instruments to keep their bureaucratic 'agents' in line.

It is clear that bureaucratic structures respond to such stimuli, so it may be said that a good deal of organizational learning is at work on both sides of this equation. True though this conclusion may be, the principal–agent relationship that this type of reasoning implies should not lead back to a previous misconception in political science—the idea that the making of public policy can be empirically (as opposed to conceptually) separated from its implementation because both process and policy content may be technical (Gulick and Urwick 1937). Fallacious thinking of this kind,

as Wildavsky (1964) and others have shown, perpetuated the hyperformalism in political science mentioned early in this chapter. Such errors persist because, once some of the concepts associated with the scientific-management movement insinuated themselves into the political science literature, it has remained difficult to remove them (Nood and Rourke 1975).

Nonetheless, organizational learning aspects of this relationship are undeniable. As Etheridge (1981) noted, public administrative agencies typically must resolve a 'design problem' (p. 83). That is, they are under pressure to devise a framework and *modus operandi* that raise the probability that policy-makers will get the right information about the environment—on time and in the quantity and quality needed. Without them, policies will almost always be at high risk of being wrong or otherwise failing. However, of the nineteen theories surveyed by Etheridge on how the problem is attacked, he rightly warned that much of this knowledge 'has been derived from the private profit-making sector' (p. 123). This fact alone may guarantee a bad fit of such theories with public/political-sector organizational life (see LaPalombara, Ch. 25 in this volume).

As corporations become more global, more complex and differentiated in their internal structures, and more subject to pressures that derive from the different cultures in which they are located, they will also begin to experience the same kinds of challenges to effectiveness that have long bedeviled national governments. For this reason, among many others, it may pay large dividends if increased attention is paid to organizations in the public/political sector, particularly to what lies in the way of what they can learn, how such obstacles may be overcome, and how they can then beneficially utilize what is learned.

Organizational Learning and Adaptation

Such learning has certainly been manifest in political parties. Over time they have been structured, and then have changed organizationally, in terms of their central purposes, the nature and quality of their leadership, and their *modus operandi* (Panebianco 1988). As Duverger (1954) noted, they could behave like exclusive clubs only so long as the electorate was limited and illiteracy endured. In these circumstances, the choice of candidates and indeed of public policies remained the purview of a tightly organized elite. When such environmental factors changed, however, parties either changed as well, or they risked going out of existence, as, indeed, some of them did.

Universal suffrage, for example, impelled political parties to remake their organizations. Benjamin Disraeli, in the 1860s recognized the implications of a broadened suffrage base. Thus, while the Liberals were in office in England, he spent more than a decade restructuring the British Conservative Party. For the first time, the party was organized at the local level, with carefully structured relationships of communication, authority, and control between the local units and the organization's central offices. Gladstone's Liberal Party followed this example with reorganization of its own. Both organizations showed admirable capacity to put what was learned to good use. Additional examples of good, bad, indifferent, or disastrous readings and adaptations might readily be cited.

No better manual on how to tailor organizations in order to optimize the achievement of their primary purpose(s) is available than Lenin's (1929) famous publication 'What Is to Be Done?' This work represents a splendid example of organizational engineering, based on what the author had learned about the organization of other mass parties of the political left. Although it may sound banal today, Lenin's insistence that a party that wants to make revolution cannot be organized as were the social democratic parties of his time was then considered a shockingly new idea. The spread of Communist systems in the twentieth century, however ill-starred this movement appears in retrospect, was closely tied to emulation and repetitions of the Leninist organizational formula (Selznick 1952).

The introduction of the direct primary election in the United States is another example of organizational learning and change that were impelled by existential circumstances. The direct primary replaced older, much more tightly controlled (by party leaders) methods of nominating candidates for public office. The shift of this important function to mass influence compelled party leaders to develop new skills of negotiation and persuasion, compromise, and coalition-building. Indeed, new units were added to the party organizations, in order to accommodate the fact that decision-making could no longer proceed on the basis of strong hierarchical relationships. And new laws were needed (e.g. the closed primary) to keep out members of opposing parties who might vote in primary elections in order to nominate the party's weakest candidates.

Similarly, today's political parties are having to adapt to the growing importance of television and the Internet in electoral politics. Democracies may not yet be at the point where citizens vote from their personal computers. But it is apparent that, all over the world, political parties continue to explore the types of changes that this new existential aspect of political life will require. Thus, certain organizational units once relied upon by the parties to keep members clustered within each party's subculture have simply atrophied and disappeared. The definition of party membership has changed. New structures that give voice to subgroups within the party have come into existence.

As with centralized trade unions, parties, too, have learned that tight control from the center is highly problematic (see Drinkuth, Riegler, and Wolff, Ch. 20 in this volume). Such control was difficult even for Communist parties that, in their heyday, practiced 'democratic centralism' (Hellman 1988: 155–66; 196–9). The more geographically widespread the organization, the greater freedom its members will have to access information on their own. The more varied the local conditions in which the party's units are located, the more difficult it will be for the party to establish and make stick a single culture, a single overall strategy, or an undifferentiated operational code, of the kind, for example, discussed by Selznick (1952). Even when a party's auxiliary organizational units, such as trade unions, are enmeshed in a party's larger web of power and authority, it is highly problematical that a single party line can be made to stick everywhere and in the same way (Golden 1988).

A limiting case that illustrates this point, including the failure of central organizational leaders to utilize single- or double-loop learning, is offered by Hough (1969). In the center–periphery relationships analyzed by Hough, a Soviet Communist Party, fashioned by Stalin, sent its most trusted managers into different parts of the Soviet Union to assure that the industrial policies established at the center were in fact carried out. The results of this strategy were that these trusted managers, one way or another, were themselves integrated into the regional or local systems. Indeed, they were psychologically coopted by the local organizations and their elite leaders. These Communist agents of the center, far from doing what the center expected, came instead to share the local (as opposed to the central) norms. Thus, far from helping to solve the problem of conformance to goal achievement dictated by the center, they themselves became part of the problem and not its solution.

One of the morals of this case is that some organizations may be so blindly and rigidly driven by ideology or by absolute-value types of rationality that they are unable either to read the environment accurately or to adapt to aspects of the environment, which they would rather deny. In both the public/political and private spheres, the dustbins of history provide ample evidence about the consequences of this organizational incapacity.

Nations as Organizations

The history of relations among nations provides a plethora of examples of good and bad organizational learning, good and bad adaptations to environmental conditions that fluctuate, sometimes abruptly and with violence.

Nations in particular are well advised to steer clear of rigid, absolute-value approaches to their relationships with others. Good political management of these organizations requires that leaders and officials learn when it is both possible and expedient to collaborate rather than to fight. Nations whose managers learn to recognize such occasions better than their counterparts, have a clear competitive advantage over others.

As in the policy sciences, topics such as scanning and assessing environments, learning from such activity, and making necessary organizational changes on this basis have received much attention in the international relations subfield. Past theories of *realpolitik* and of balance-of-power politics have been refurbished, for example, by adding highly sophisticated measures of one's own capabilities in the international sphere against those of one's enemies and allies. Proficiency in such exercises is expected to improve a nation's bargaining capability and promote the stability and longevity of international agreements (Lockart 1979).

Growing attention also is paid to the range of factors that affect, again for good or for bad, leaders who are compelled to make decisions under conditions of extreme stress. It is now widely recognized that states do indeed learn and that, moreover, they will be conditioned, in the production and utilization of this knowledge, by the way in which they are organized (Levy 1994: 297–9). In this sphere of research, additional important conceptual and empirical distinctions are drawn between the types of learning that apply to the individual within an organization or to the organization itself, as a collectivity (Goldstein and Keohane 1993).

There is also consensus that the perceptive capacities of those who lead and manage international organizations must be carefully assessed and, where possible, improved. As in the private sector, lack of such capacities is one of several near-universal leadership shortcomings that can adversely affect organizations, and for this reason alone it requires more scholarly attention (Fairholm 1990b). Negotiations and relationships between nations are often adversely affected by misperceptions that plague their representatives at all levels of authority. Political scientists are now able to delineate, with great sophistication, structural aspects of organizations that are directly associated with such weaknesses (Breslauer 1991; Jervis 1976). There has also been pioneering theoretical work in political science on the ways and means that leaders of organizations involved in international politics overcome tendencies toward conflict and move instead in the direction of greater and more fruitful collaboration. Axelrod's (1984) work in particular has drawn favorable attention from organizational theorists in several of the social sciences.

Many of the leading works in this subfield suggest that the cross-fertilization with organizational theory and organizational learning is already in high gear. Practitioners implicitly agree with Rothman and Friedman (Ch. 26 in this volume) that failure to include well-developed knowledge about conflict and its resolution in conceptual schemes will hobble otherwise valuable attempts to achieve single- and double-loop learning.

A critically important dimension of conflict management is skill in negotiation. In the literature on international relations, considerable attention has been paid to the negotiating styles of nations, the implication being that, in each of many problematic areas, this variable will go a long way to explain and, indeed, predict success or failure (Iklè 1968). Knowledge about style and other aspects of negotiations, particularly when the negotiations involve more than one national culture, also has direct implications for the modern corporate community. The use of groups in decision-making, the flattening of corporate hierarchies, and the emphasis on communication and participation imply, or should imply, that policies reflect negotiated agreements and not something dictated from high (Wilson 1995). If relationships are fundamentally interactive rather than hierarchical, if they take place on a relatively level playing field, and if consensus is to be reached, primarily through the use of negotiating skills (Nicotera 1995: 260–3), then much that would be useful to organizational learning can be

gleaned from the international relations literature. Indeed, international relations is an area where previous ideas about span of control and its incident problems in organizations can be profitably revised in the light of what organizational theory and organizational learning now can teach about the plusses and minuses of flat organization in the corporate sphere.

Levy (1994: 287–91) nicely illustrated the marked growth of organizational theory and organizational learning in the international relations field. He judiciously warned against any leap to the conclusion that the mere fact of a change in foreign or international policies implies learning (p. 290). Nevertheless, the literature he reviewed underscored how a number of scholars have actually used learning models in their explications of the behavior of nation-states and the organizations that represent them. In addition, he provided several examples of organizational reforms in a variety of nations, all of them designed to improve the quality of information produced and analyzed as well as to raise the quality of an organization's memory (1994: 286–9).

Levy (1994) was well aware of several problems that have emerged in the field of organizational learning. Not the least important of them is that of showing cause and effect between what an organization learns and what it does (p. 289). Focusing on organizations in the foreign policy sphere, he provided an interesting summary of characteristics that impinge on any effort to clarify this type of cause and effect (pp. 300–10). He noted that people in organizations learn different things; that they struggle to have their interpretations prevail over those of others; that the outcomes of such struggles have little or nothing to do with whose perceptions or cognitive systems are the most accurate; that the struggle is indeed often ideological or normative; and that the organization's behavior is usually the product of this internal dynamic, no matter what else may be going on in the outside environment. Presumably, many of these characteristics would also apply to private-sector organizations, although it would be of considerable interest to explore exactly what the limits of these similarities are.

Scanning and Evaluations

My final observation brings the focus back to politics. Political science retains as one of its central concerns the nature, possession, and exercise of power. This concern tends both to overshadow and to transcend almost everything else that occurs in the public/political sphere. This fact about the discipline is a critically important consideration that warrants extensive treatment (see LaPalombara, Ch. 25 in this volume). Power comes to represent the fulcrum around which scanning and evaluations or attempts on the part of organizations to learn are placed in motion. As Wildavsky (1979) once observed, 'Evaluative man does seek knowledge, but he also seeks power... One is useless without the other' (p. 231). He went on to point out that, if scanning and evaluations are to be translated into discernible (presumably ameliorative) changes, some way must be found to 'institutionalize these efforts' (p. 234).

Where a minimum of this type of institutionalization has occurred, shifts in power equilibria represent not only threats but also opportunities. In the public sector, organizations with higher than minimal learning capacity can capture moments of disequilibria and turn them into improved capacities in goal achievement. This aspect of bureaucratic politics in the public/political sphere has been insightfully documented for the U.S. Department of State (Allison 1971) and for other governmental branches and agencies (Hall 1993).

Allison's (1971) research indicated another wrinkle in the ways in which public/political-sector organizations learn: The leaders of these organizations pay a lot of attention to history, and this type of learning actually becomes the basis for subsequent decisions. The reference groups for presidents and prime ministers, secretaries of state and other cabinet members, and even senior-level bureaucrats will tend to be those who in the past have held similar positions or sat at the very desks present persons now occupy. These persons also will make historical information and learning the basis for accepting or rejecting alternative policies, lines of action, or both (Neustadt and May 1986). The fact that many public-sector organizations endure over very long periods makes this approach to learning and its uses more natural, perhaps, than is true of the private sector. But even private-sector reference groups for senior executives often include the so-called captains of industry who, like great political leaders, easily take on legendary proportions (see Sadler, Ch. 18 in this volume).

These observations may be simply another way of saying, in conclusion, that, like organizations in the private sector, those that are public/political in nature engage in scanning and evaluations in order to use 'information in ways that enhance effectiveness and clearly contribute to successful governance' (Rist 1994: 190). Writing about the international relations field, Levy (1994: 297) believed that organizations are much better at using information effectively than individuals are. And Rose (1993) extended this judgment to governmental organizations in general.

I agree on both counts and I add one further consideration: The organizations most studied by political scientists are in many important ways quite different from those found in the private sector. As long as this basic truth goes unrecognized or, even worse, is denied, the kind of intellectual cross-fertilization that is desired will come to nothing. This outcome would be a pity, for the structural characteristics of organizations, well-treated in the literature of organizational theory and organizational learning, definitely impinge on the quality of learning in the public/political sector as well (Deutsch 1963; Hedberg 1981: 5–15).

It may be true, as Huber (1991) argued, that much of the activity associated with organizational learning can be generalized to all organizations, in whatever sphere they may be located. Learning, however it may occur, is a response to underlying impulses to make discoveries that are instrumental for organizations as well as for their leaders. The instrumental side of life, however, inevitably raises questions about power and much more in public/political sector organizations (see LaPalombara, Ch. 25 in this volume).

References

Allen, D. (1977). 'Policing or Policy-making: Competition Policy in the European Communities', in H. Wallace and W. Wallace (eds.), *Policy-making in the European Community*. New York: Wiley, 91–112.

Allison, G. (1971). *Essence of Decision: Explaining the Cuban Missile Crisis*. Boston: Little Brown.

Argyris, C. and Schön, D. A. (1978). *Organizational Learning: A Theory of Action Perspective*. Reading, Mass.: Addison-Wesley.

——— (1996). *Organizational Learning*: Vol. 2. *Theory, Method, and Practice*. Reading, Mass.: Addison-Wesley.

Axelrod, R. (1984). *The Evolution of Cooperation*. New York: Basic Books.

Bailey, S. J. (1950). *Congress Makes a Law: The Story behind the Unemployment Act of 1946*. New York: Columbia University Press.

Barnard, C. I. (1938). *The Functions of the Executive*. Cambridge, Mass.: Harvard University Press.

Blau, P. (1955). *Dynamics of Bureaucracy*. Chicago: University of Chicago Press.

—— (1956). *Bureaucracy in Modern Society*. New York: Random House.

—— (1968). 'Theories of Organizations', in D. L. Sills (ed.), *International Encyclopedia of the Social Sciences* (Vol. XI). New York: Macmillan, 297–305.

Blondel, J. (1973). *Comparative Legislatures*. Englewood Cliffs, NJ: Prentice Hall.

—— (1982). *The Organization of Government: A Comparative Analysis of Governmental Structures*. Beverly Hills, Calif.: Sage.

Breslauer, G. W. (1991). 'What Have We Learned about Learning', in G. W. Breslauer and P. E. Tetlock (eds.), *Learning in U.S. and Soviet Foreign Policy*. Boulder, Colo.: Westview, 825–56.

Brewer, G. (1971). *The Policy Sciences Emerge: To Nurture and Structure a Discipline*. Santa Barbara, Calif.: Rand Corporation.

—— (1983). *The Foundations of Policy Analysis*. Homewood, Ill.: Dorsey.

Cyert, R. M. and March, J. G. (1963). *A Behavioral Theory of the Firm*. Englewood Cliffs, NJ: Prentice Hall.

Dean, A. L. (1981). 'General Propositions of Organization Design', in P. Szanton (ed.), *Federal Reorganization: What Have We Learned?* Chatham, NJ: Chatham House, 131–54.

Deutsch, K. (1963). *The Nerves of Government*. Glencoe, Ill: Free Press.

Downs, A. (1967). *Inside Bureaucracy*. Boston: Little, Brown.

Duverger, M. (1954). *Political Parties: Their Organization and Activities in the Modern State*. New York: Wiley and Sons.

Etheredge, L. S. (1981). 'Government Learning: An Overview', in L. S. Long (ed.), *The Handbook of Political Behavior* (Vol. 2). New York: Plenum, 73–161.

Fairholm, G. W. (1990a). 'Organization and Management Theory', in M. L. Whicker and T. W. Areson (eds.), *Public Sector Management*. New York: Praeger, 129–52.

—— (1990b). 'Leadership', in M. L. Whicker and T. W. Areson (eds.), *Public Sector Management*. New York: Praeger, 153–79.

Fenno, R. (1973). *Congressmen in Committees*. Boston: Little, Brown.

Follett, M. P. (1942). *Dynamic Administration: The Collected Papers of Mary Parker Follett* (H. C. Metcalf and L. Urwick, eds.). New York: Harper & Brothers.

Golden, M. (1988). *Labor Divided: Austerity and Working Class Politics in Contemporary Italy*. Ithaca, NY: Cornell University Press.

—— and Pontusson, J. (eds.) (1992). *Bargaining for Change: Union Politics in North America and Europe*. Ithaca, NY: Cornell University Press.

Goldstein, J. and Keohane, R. O. (eds.) (1993). *Ideas and Foreign Policy: Beliefs, Institutions, and Political Change*. Ithaca, NY: Cornell University Press.

Gortner, H. F., Mahler, J., and Nicholson, J. B. (1987). *Organization Theory: A Public Perspective*. Chicago: Dorsey.

Graham, P. (ed.) (1995). *Mary Parker Follett: Prophet of Management*. Boston: Harvard Business School Press.

Green, D. F. and Shapiro, I. (1994). *The Pathologies of Rational Choice Theory.* New Haven: Yale University Press.

Gulick, L. and Urwick, L. (eds.) (1937). *Papers on the Science of Administration.* New York: Institute of Public Administration, Columbia University.

Haas, E. (1968). *Beyond the Nation-state: Functionalism and International Organization.* Stanford, Calif.: Stanford University Press.

—— Williams, M. P., and Babai, D. (1977). *Scientists and the World Order: The Use of Technical Knowledge in International Organizations.* Berkeley: University of California Press.

Hall, P. (1993). 'Policy Paradigms, Social Learning, and the State'. *Comparative Politics,* 25: 275–96.

Hall, R. A. and Quinn, R. E. (eds.) (1981). *Organizational Theory and Public Policy.* Berkeley: Sage.

Hattam, V. C. (1993). *Labor Unions and State Power.* Princeton: Princeton University Press.

Heap, S. H. and Ross, A. (eds.) (1992). *Understanding the Enterprise Culture: Theories in the Work of Mary Douglas.* Edinburgh: Edinburgh University Press.

Heclo, H. (1974). *Modern Social Politics in Britain and Sweden.* New Haven: Yale University Press.

—— (1978). 'Issue Networks and the Executive Establishment', in A. King (ed.), *The New American Political System.* Washington, DC: American Enterprise Institute, 87–124.

Hedberg, B. L. T. (1981). 'How Organizations Learn and Unlearn', in P. C. Nystrom and W. H. Starbuck (eds.), *Handbook of Organizational Design:* Vol. 1. *Adapting Organizations to Their Environments.* Oxford: Oxford University Press, 3–27.

Hellman, S. (1988). *Italian Communism in Transition: The Rise and Fall of the Historic Compromise in Turin, 1975–1980.* New York: Oxford University Press.

Hough, J. B. (1969). *The Soviet Prefects: The Local Party Organization in Decision Making.* Cambridge, Mass.: Harvard University Press.

Huber, G. (1991). 'Organizational Learning: The Contributing Processes and the Literatures'. *Organization Science,* 2: 88–115.

Iklè, F. (1968). 'Negotiating Skill: East and West', in L. B. Muller (ed.), *Dynamics of World Politics.* Englewood Cliffs, NJ: Prentice Hall, 20–43.

Jervis, R. (1976). *Perception and Misperception in International Politics.* Princeton: Princeton University Press.

Key, V. O. (1942). *Politics, Parties, and Pressure Groups.* New York: Crowell.

—— (1949). *Southern Politics in State and Nation.* New York: Knopf.

Kirscheimer, O. (1966). 'The Transformation of European Party Systems', in J. LaPalombara and M. Weiner (eds.), *Political Parties and Political Development.* Princeton: Princeton University Press, 177–200.

Kothari, R. (1970). *Politics in India.* Boston: Little, Brown.

LaPalombara, J. (1963). *Interest Groups in Italian Politics.* Princeton: Princeton University Press.

La Porte, T. (1975). *Organized Social Complexity: Challenge to Politics and Policy.* Princeton: Princeton University.

Lasswell, H. D. (1930). *Psychopathology and Politics.* New York: Viking.

—— (1936). *Politics: Who Gets What, When, How.* London: McGraw-Hill.

—— (1956). *Decision Process: Seven Categories of Functional Analysis.* College Park: University of Maryland Press.

—— (1997). *Essays on the Garrison State* (J. Stanley, ed.). New Brunswick, NJ: Transaction Books.

—— and Kaplan, A. (1950). *Power and Society: A Framework for Political Inquiry.* New Haven: Yale University Press.

Lenin, V. I. (1929). *What Is to Be Done? Burning Questions of Our Movement* (J. Fineberg and G. Hanna, trans.). New York: International Publishers. (Original work published 1929)

Lerner, D. and Lasswell, H. D. (1951). *The Policy Sciences: Recent Developments in Scope and Method.* Stanford, Calif.: Stanford University Press.

Levin, M. A. and Sanger, M. B. (1994). *Making Government Work: How Entrepreneurial Executives Turn Bright Ideas into Real Results.* San Francisco Calif.: Jossey-Bass.

Levy, J. S. (1994). 'Learning and Foreign Policy: Sweeping a Conceptual Minefield'. *International Organization,* 48: 279–312.

Lindblom, C. E. (1971). *The Policy-making Process*. Englewood Cliffs, NJ: Prentice Hall.

Lockart, C. (1979). *Bargaining in International Conflicts*. New York: Columbia University Press.

Loewenberg, G. L. and Patterson, S. C. (eds.) (1979). *Comparing Legislatures*. Boston: Little, Brown.

—————— and Jewell, M. E. (eds.) (1985). *Handbook of Legislative Research*. Cambridge, Mass.: Harvard University Press.

March, J. G. (1991). 'Exploration and Exploitation in Organizational Learning'. *Organization Science*, 2: 71–87.

—— and Olsen, J. P. (1976). *Ambiguity and Choice in Organizations* (2nd edn). Bergen: Universitetforlaget.

—— and Simon, H. A. (1958). *Organizations*. New York: Wiley.

Mayhew, D. (1974). *Congress: The Electoral Connection*. New Haven: Yale University Press.

Mayntz, R. and Scharpf, F. (1975). *Policy-making in the German Federal Bureaucracy*. New York: Elsevier.

Meyer, M. W. (1979). *Change in Public Bureaucracies*. London: Cambridge University Press.

Michels, R. (1962). *Political Parties*. New York: Free Press. (Original work published 1915)

Moe, T. (1989). 'The Politics of Bureaucratic Structure', in J. Chubb and P. Paterson (eds.), *Can the Government Learn?* Washington, DC: Brookings Institution, 85–7.

Morgenthau, H. J. (1948). *Politics among Nations*. New York: Alfred Knopf.

Neustadt, R. and May, E. R. (1986). *Thinking in Time: The Uses of History for Decision-makers*. New York: Free Press.

Nicotera, A. M. (1995). 'Integrating the Chapters: Where Does This Collection Leave Us?', in A. M. Nicotera (ed.), *Conflict and Organizations*. New York: State of New York Press, 259–73.

Nood, M. L. and Rourke, F. E. (1975). 'Bureaucracies', in F. I. Greenstein and N. W. Polsby (eds.), *Handbook of Political Science* (Vol. 5). Reading, Mass.: Addison-Wesley, 429–573.

Ostrogorski, M. (1926). *Democracy and the Party System in the United States* (F. Clarke, trans.). New York: Macmillan. (Original work published 1889)

—— (1964). *Democracy and the Organization of Political Parties* (F. Clarke, trans., S. M. Lipset, ed.). Chicago: Quadrangle Books.

Palumbo, D. J. (1975). 'Organization Theory and Political Science', in F. I. Greenstein and N. W. Polsby (eds.), *Handbook of Political Science* (Vol. 2). Reading, Mass.: Addison-Wesley, 319–89.

Panebianco, A. (1988). *Political Parties: Organization and Power*. Cambridge: Cambridge University Press.

Powell, W. W. and DiMaggio, P. J. (eds.) (1991). *The New Institutionalism in Organizational Analysis*. Chicago: University of Chicago Press.

Pressman, J. and Wildavsky, A. (1984). *Implementation* (3rd edn). Berkeley: University of California Press.

Rist, R. C. (1994). 'The Preconditions of Learning: Lessons from the Public Sector', in F. L. Leeuw, R. C. Rist, and R. C. Sonnichsen (eds.), *Can Governments Learn? Comparative Perspectives on Evaluation and Organizational Learning*. New Brunswick, NJ: Transaction Books, 189–205.

Rogow, A. and Lasswell, H. D. (1963). *Power, Corruption, and Rectitude*. Englewood Cliffs, NJ: Prentice Hall.

Rose, R. (1993). *Lesson Drawing in Public Policy*. Chatham, NJ: Chatham House.

Rubenstein, R. and Lasswell, H. D. (1966). *The Sharing of Power in a Psychiatric Hospital*. New Haven: Yale University Press.

Scharpf, F. (1997). *Games Real Actors Play: Actor Centered Institutionalism in Policy Research*. Boulder, Colo.: Westview.

—— and Hanf, K. (eds.) (1978). *Interorganizational Policy Making: Limits to Coordination and Central Control*. Beverly Hills, Calif.: Sage.

Scheinman, L. (1971). 'Economic Regulation and International Administration', in R. Jordon (ed.), *International Administration*. New York: Oxford University Press, 187–227.

Schumpeter, J. A. (1950). *Capitalism, Socialism, and Democracy*. New York: Harper Brothers. (Original work published 1942)

Selznick, P. (1949). *TVA and the Grass Roots: A Study of the Sociology of Formal Organization*. Berkeley: University of California Press.

—— (1952). *The Organizational Weapon: A Study of Bolshevik Strategy and Tactics*. New York: McGraw-Hill.

Sharp, W. (1961). *Field Administration in the United Nations System: The Conduct of Economic and Social Programs*. New York: Praeger.

Simon, H. A. (1957). *Administrative Behavior: A Study of Decision-making Processes in Administrative Organizations* (2nd edn). New York: Macmillan.

—— (1982). *Models of Bounded Rationality*. Cambridge, Mass.: MIT Press.

—— (1991). 'Bounded Rationality and Organizational Learning'. *Organization Science*, 2: 125–34.

—— Smithburg, D. W., and Thompson, V. (1950). *Public Administration*. New York: Knopf.

Skocpol, T. T. (1995). *Social Policy in the United States: Future Possibilities in Historical Perspective*. Princeton: Princeton University Press.

Skowronek, S. (1982). *Building a New American State: The Expansion of National Administrative Capacity*. Cambridge: Cambridge University Press.

Smith, S. S. and Deering, C. J. (1984). *Committees in Congress*. Washington, DC: CQ Press.

Spiro, H. J. (1969). *Responsibility in Government: Theory and Practice*. New York: Van Nostrand Reinhold.

Wallace, W. (1983). 'Less than a Federation, More than a Region', in H. Wallace, W. Wallace, and C. Webb (eds.), *Policy-making in the European Community* (2nd edn). New York: Wiley, 403–36.

Warwick, D. P. (1975). *A Theory of Public Bureaucracy*. Cambridge, Mass.: Harvard University Press.

Webb, C. (1983). 'Theoretical Perspective and Problems', in H. Wallace, W. Wallace, and C. Webb (eds.), *Policy-making in the European Community* (2nd edn). New York: Wiley, 1–41.

Weiner, M. (1957). *Party Politics in India: The Development of a Multi-party System*. Princeton: Princeton University Press.

Weir, M. (1992). *Politics and Jobs: The Boundaries of Employment Policy in the United States*. Princeton: Princeton University Press.

Wildavsky, A. B. (1964). *The Politics of the Budgetary Process*. Boston: Little, Brown.

—— (1974). *Implementation: How Great Expectations in Washington Are Dashed in Oakland*. Berkeley: University of California Press.

—— (1979). *Speaking Truth to Power: The Art and Craft of Policy Analysis*. Boston: Little, Brown.

Wilensky, H. L. (1967). *Organizational Intelligence: Knowledge and Policy in Government and Industry*. New York: Basic Books.

Wilson, S. R. (1995). 'Cultural Communication Processes in International Business Negotiations', in A. M. Nicotera (ed.), *Conflict and Organizations*. New York: State of New York Press, 201–32.

Wolfers, A. (1962). *Discord and Collaboration: Essays in International Politics*. Baltimore: Johns Hopkins University Press.

Wood, B. D. and Waterman, R. W. (1994). *Bureaucratic Dynamics: The Role of Bureaucracy in a Democracy*. Boulder, Colo.: Westview.

7 Thinking Historically about Organizational Learning

Jeffrey R. Fear

The literature on organizational learning and evolutionary theories of the enterprise often evoke the phrase 'path dependency', a social science translation of the insight that 'history matters'. History matters because learning—be it social, organizational, or personal—is a difficult process, requiring one to evaluate the past, and perhaps reconsider it, to alter the present and confront the future. Schiller (1784/1970) viewed history unfolding as 'a long chain of events [that] extends from the present moment back down to the beginning of the human race, which mesh into one another as cause and effect' (p. 370). If one agrees with Schiller, then persons, organizations, or nations can never entirely escape the past. In order to forge a new link in the historical chain, they must still acknowledge the past 'chain of events', even if they reject it by taking a stand against previous ways of thinking and acting. By definition, then, learning implies having some sense, some knowledge, of one's accumulated experience so that one can initiate change.

Organizational learning, moreover, is somewhat more complicated because the metaphor of individual learning is inadequate for organizational learning, which must be understood as a complex intersubjective process. Any definition of organizational learning needs to address issues of change, transformation, processes, routines, practices, perception, intersubjectivity, knowledge creation, memory, and past experience (Nonaka and Takeuchi 1995: 44–6). Such issues open a Pandora's Box of questions for historians. How exactly did past experience shape the present organization and its routines? How does an organization create knowledge about its past and present circumstances? Why did it alter its routines or policies based on this new knowledge at a given point in time? Remembering past experience, however, means that an organization must have a sense of its own history, which can prove highly problematic. Important decisions, documents, turning points, motivations, and even people vanish, lost in the fogs of time. Police experiences with eyewitnesses at crime scenes attest to the fleeting reliability of memory and perception, not to mention complicated questions of organizational or collective memory. In addition, people, organizations, and nations fashion their own histories, constructing and passing down life trajectories as narratives, stories, or myths. Although all people, organizations, or nations operate with some visceral understanding and memory of their shared past, this understanding is not necessarily accurate or transparent, let alone critically evaluated. The very telling of any history (oral, informal, and written), moreover, creates knowledge about the past, but not necessarily relevant or correct knowledge. How do organizations create a vision of their histories? If organizational memory legitimizes a process of learning or unlearning, then what exactly is being remembered and learned, and for what ends? What are the organizational implications of such a history or memory? Immensely complicated questions about memory, knowledge, legitimacy, and power inside organizations are at stake.

In theory, historians have much to offer a theory of organizational learning, for the craft of history specializes in showing the choices people made to change their lives and how the past has shaped potential futures and the present. In the first section of this essay, I explore how path dependent models of organizational change have implicitly used history in ways that obscure more than they reveal, and I examine why historians have not engaged with a theory of organizational learning more actively than they have so far. The second section concentrates on how traditional, 'modernist' directions in the historical profession can positively contribute to a theory of organizational learning. These modernist directions emphasize the accurate reconstruction of the sequence of the process of organizational change and learning—who, how, what, when, where, and why— and the use of original, primary sources to 'tell it like it really was' (*wie es eigentlich gewesen*) (Ranke 1824/1874: vii). The third section focuses on recent 'postmodern' or cultural history approaches, greatly influential in the profession since the 1980s. Whereas in modernist conceptions, histories objectively reflect and reconstruct the past with relative accuracy (or 'bias'), in postmodernist approaches the very telling of stories, narratives, accounts, or histories actively *create* and *construct* knowledge and vision of the collective past. In the postmodernist view, histories become a more or less convincing representation of the past and thus have an agenda for present purposes. This question about the possibilities of objectivity and truthfulness in historical writing has, in fact, split the academic historical profession as practiced in the United States ('New Historical Society Formed', 1998). (For excellent overviews on the state of the discipline, see Appleby, Hunt, and Jacob 1994; Evans 1997; Fay, Pomper, and Vann 1998; Hunt 1989; Novick 1988; Wehler 1998.)

Part I: Thinking Historically

Is the Past a Source of Inertia or an Inheritance?

An implicit view about the impact of the past drives some social science theories about

organizational change. Path dependency is actually past dependency. But whereas some organizational theorists assume that the past is a link in the chain that needs to be broken, others see the past as a living heritage. Both views, however, cannot be upheld without careful historical research. Historians begin their research where these theories end.

In a classic article, Stinchcombe (1965) argued that vested interests, forces of traditionalism, or an ideological position deemed legitimate provided the main sources of inertia in an organization. He wrote that this social constellation potently 'imprints' the organization, particularly at its inception. These founding conditions, he added, fundamentally constrain the organization's ability to adapt to new situations or competitive forces. Population ecology theorists, such as Hannan and Freeman, also view the past as source of lethargy and conservatism. To them, new technologies and changes in markets (e.g. new entries and growth in competitive populations) disrupt this cozy stability by 'generating turmoil' and by challenging the learning capacities of individuals and organizations in the population pool (Freeman 1990: 53–5, 74–5; Hannan and Freeman 1989). Like Stinchcombe, they do not, however, adequately dissect and explore the sources of inertia. They assume the past is inert (or has reached some form of equilibrium) until exogenous forces such as new competition, technologies, or a shift in the relative importance of existing resources (market prices) impels change, overcoming a sluggish past. Both Stinchcombe and Freeman tend to view the past as a constraint that organizations need to overcome.

A historian immediately asks if it is true that a vested interest, a traditional force, a shift in resources, or a legitimized ideological position immobilized an organization. Historians find all of these sources of inertia, so defined, maddeningly abstract. They represent hypotheses at the beginning, not the end, of a historical inquiry. Each of Stinchcombe's listed causes imply very different types of historical explanation: one is power-political, one economic, and one cultural. Each cause of inertia suggests a different history and an entirely different set of methodologies for analyzing an organization. Stinchcombe also falls into the trap the great French historian Marc Bloch warned against: the search for origins—as though the founding or origin constituted the most important point of time in an organization's life, as though 'ancestry' acted as an explanation (Bloch 1953: 29–35). Are there not other critical inflection points in the evolution of an organization? For instance, Mitsui and Yasuda began as 'political merchants' in the Tokugawa era, licensed to handle tax revenues and exchange money. Other than their names, how are these massive *keiretsu* really the *same* companies today as at their founding? Finally, for a historian, these theorists locate sources of organizational change in a very narrow range of potential causes. In most neoclassical explanations, technologies and market competition drive change by disrupting equilibrium. History lurches from equilibrium to equilibrium.

In contrast to the above authors, Nelson and Winter created an evolutionary model for economic organizations, one that depicts a process of cumulative, historical change (Nelson and Winter 1982; Winter 1990). For Nelson and Winter, the large-scale modern business corporation is the crucial driver of innovation by virtue of its productive competence, its ability to know how to make and do things. Underlying an organization's competence and its process of innovation are its routines, a sort of genetic code or organizational memory. In empirical work on national innovation systems, Nelson (1993) argued that technological innovation does not originate as an exogenous force but rather is ingrained in a country's historical legacy, more specifically, its science-oriented institutions and business organizations. In contrast to Hannan and Freeman, he asserted that institutions, organizations, and history itself help generate technological, market, and organizational innovation. Not surprisingly, Winter (1990) used a positive metaphor for past successes and institutionalized routines, viewing them not as sources of 'inertia', but as an 'inheritance'.

In general, this evolutionary approach is much more amenable to most historians because it measures the developmental process of an organization over a sequential period of time. But a historian has to go beyond Nelson and Winter to identify who, how, when, where, and why change took place. Are organizations, particularly large-scale ones, the main source of change in the present economy? (Considerable historical debate surrounds just this question, see Chandler and Hikino 1997; Dosi 1997; Piore and Sabel 1984; Sabel and Zeitlin 1997.) What defines a routine, and how did it work in practice? What causes a routine to be born or die? What role do active individuals play in organizational life? The metaphor of biological evolution makes the evolutionary system larger than individuals. Yet, to what extent is history, including organizational history, driven by great individuals (be it a Roosevelt, a Rockefeller, or a Renault) or groups of people (sans-culottes, workers, slaves, suffragettes, peasants, or engineers and accountants) who make and shape their own destinies? This question of human agency is a classic problem within the historical discipline. Finally, evolutionary theories assume incremental change over time. Yet, are there not ruptures and discontinuities in the history of societies and organizations: wars, revolutions, depressions, bankruptcies, or unexpected deaths of entrepreneurs? Nelson and Winter (1982: 9–11) were aware of these problems, but their model did not include them.

If organizational learning is dependent on past experience, then the question about the past as inertia versus inheritance needs to be addressed. Neither view can necessarily be upheld without careful historical, empirical analysis.

The Trouble with Learning Lessons from History

It is precisely at this point that historians can contribute most effectively to a theory of organizational learning. However, the classic, nonhistorian vision of history as the field in which people learn 'lessons' from the past, where history provides a moral guidebook or serves as a compass for distinguishing 'good' from 'bad' behavior and heroes from the fools, actually proves counterproductive to a theory of organizational learning.

It is not hard to think of ways in which people have created or altered organizations after learning from history. The military, the first large-scale organization in history, offers a rich source of past learning. The lessons of Vietnam obsessively dominate present American military thinking. The lack of clear political objectives for military intervention in Vietnam and the public shock of viewing row upon row of body bags on the evening news forced new strategies. By the time of the Gulf War, the American military controlled media access to the front, even forming press departments to manage media exposure, and established clear objectives for engagement and withdrawal. Important world institutions such as the International Monetary Fund (IMF) and the World Bank were derived from lessons learned after failure to win the peace after World War I and failure to secure international cooperation in the interwar economy (Feinstein, Temin, and Toniolo 1997). Meiji Japan offers an outstanding national learning example of the modern age. Japanese reformers initiated one of the great ventures of 'creative conservatism', completely transforming Japanese society—right down to its hairstyles—in order to preserve it (see Gluck 1985; Westney 1987). Moreover, learning lessons from history can just as often lead to failure. The French Maginot Line, built after World War I to hold off the Germans in a future war, is one of the major symbols of how to learn the wrong lesson from history. There is a good deal of truth to the classic refrain that militaries fight the previous war.

This use of history, though intuitive, is often naive. What makes a particular lesson appropriate and relevant to present conditions? From the vast repertoire of events and people in history, why are certain lessons selected and not others? One problem with lessons is that they are based on the presumption that history repeats itself in a recognizable way. It is not always clear whether the examples or situations are really that similar. For instance, the lessons drawn from the genocide of Jews led to policy confusion about whether to intervene in Bosnia (Linenthal 1995: 260–72). Learning from history in this manner proved more complicated than at first glance. If circumstances are new, modern, and unprecedented, how can people learn from history, for it is dated, obsolete, and past? Henry Ford put this problem famously and bluntly: 'History is more or less bunk' (Interview in the *Chicago Tribune*, 25 May 1916, quoted in Nevins and Hill 1957: 138).

As stated, the examples show that learning took place, but they shed little light on the learning process, the creative process of thinking, selecting, adopting, and innovating involved with learning from history. As with the French Maginot line, contemporaries 'learned' from the previous war, but drew the wrong conclusions. In the case of Japanese borrowing, Westney (1987) clearly showed that the Japanese chose Western models for a host of reasons, including prestige, a 'contagion' effect, and sheer random access to people and knowledge from some countries (and not others). A measure of contingency, not rational-choice, was involved. At most, the learning-lessons-from-history approach identifies places to begin, not end, research. Ascertaining an outcome is often less important for a theory of organizational learning than showing the actual process leading to an outcome. Close micro-oriented historical analyses of organizational change would be useful.

Often the use of such lessons says less about history or learning itself than about contemporaries legitimating a present course of action by making recourse to the past (see the final section on learning, knowledge, and legitimacy). Organizational theorists should be wary about using history as a means of trawling for lessons or examples. They can be misleading as well as insightful. Ironically, it was the father of modern history, Leopold von Ranke, who tried to disabuse readers and future historians of using history in this way: 'To history has been attributed the office to judge the past and to instruct the present to make its future useful. At such high functions this present work does not aim—it merely wants to show how things really were' (Ranke 1824/1874: vii). Showing 'how things really were' has been one of the most consistent objectives and claims of historians over the last two centuries.

What Is History?

If the discipline of history can potentially offer rich material and approaches to a theory of organizational learning, why then have historians—in general—not addressed the question more adeptly than they have? First, there are mundane, but decisive, practical problems of archival access, particularly for the study of business corporations. Most importantly, however, historians' main concerns classically lie outside organizations. Business or organizational history, for instance, remains a relatively small subdiscipline within the profession as a whole. Even when historians study a particular organization, they tend to use it as an archaeological site of inquiry and archival research, not as the analytical theme of the research. Mainstream historiographic methods pass over the issue of organizational change and learning. Historians tend to shift their sights to the goal of understanding people, not organizations. At most, they study the behavior of people in organizations, but not the organization *per se*. This quasi-automatic shift to understanding people rather than organizational life immediately diverts detailed examination of how organizations shape human behavior and life. Ultimately, historians are interested in what it means to be human. What it means to be organizational beings is not quite the same question.

As with anthropologists, when historians speak of social organization they speak of generalized structures, institutions, or shared meanings that bind collectivities of people together. Historians, however, do not merely understand people in a disembodied or innocent fashion. States, nations, great people (usually men), societies, communities, culture, the modernization process, or class, and, more recently in postmodern accounts, race, gender, and ethnicity (identity formation) figure large in the oeuvre of historians. Both Ranke and Marx, for instance, took the study of 'people' as their starting point. Ranke, however, viewed these people organized into states as opposed to other states, giving primacy to balance-of-power politics and foreign policy. Ranke offered a history of diplomacy and statecraft, the classic locus of traditional historians' work. Marx's 'people', however, were organized into classes and were implicitly international. Control over the means of production became the central issue. These conceptual points of departure shaped their analytical gaze so that they passed over organizations, those smaller creatures of modern life, to larger game.

Studies of organizational life rarely rose off the ground in traditional history, for historians focused on big events, historical turning points, the great philosopher, the religious figure, the king or queen, the great military leader who alters the trajectory of History writ large. Under this view, Carlyle (1841/1993) wrote: 'The History of the World is but the Biography of great men' (pp. 3, 13, 26). Moreover, in traditional historical narratives, top political leaders *represent* their countries. Nowhere can this practice be seen more dramatically than in the famous photograph of Roosevelt, Churchill, and Stalin at Yalta. They personified their countries. Great military leaders personified their armies. Likewise, great business entrepreneurs, such as Carnegie, Rockefeller, Krupp, Renault, and Toyoda personify their firms, effacing the organization of the firm itself (for a critique, see Lauschke and Welskopp 1994: 7–14). This version of writing history can be called a history of the commanding heights. Organizations and organizational learning remain overshadowed by the bright lights of big 'events' and important people.

Throughout the nineteenth century, historians' narratives increasingly became identified with the nation-state. National histories slowly replaced histories of kingdoms. Historians' narratives about the nation-state also tended to conflate state and society (Albrow 1997: 41–4). Only recently, with the theoretical studies of nationalism itself and the recent move to world history in the last few years, has this 'natural' national approach to organizing and writing history come under fire.

The late nineteenth and early twentieth centuries, the high point of modernism, bequeathed to historians the major intellectual directions of post-1945 mainstream history until the mid-1980s: Marxism, the Annales school, and modernization theory. Respectively, the three most important thinkers, as much historians as sociologists, were Karl Marx, Emile Durkheim, and Max Weber. These early decades also saw the creation and professionalization of now standard university disciplines (history, anthropology, economics, psychology, and sociology). Despite their very different approaches, scholars in all three streams turned their attention to broad social structures and social change, away from the commanding heights of political events to issues of class and society. By the 1960s and 1970s, however, these foci had become mainstream or dominant historiographical approaches (Appleby, Hunt, and Jacob 1994: 78–90; Novick 1988: 438–45). Carr, in his standard work, *What is History?* (1961), advocated social history as an alternative to traditional political history, and the book appeared precisely at the time when left-leaning historians in particular turned to social history.

Marx turned traditional History, writ large, on its head and looked for underlying laws of historical motion in the material world of industry and economy. By uncovering hidden laws of social change, the oppressed could theoretically harness a science of society for their own revolutionary ends. This approach relegated the study of organizations to a study of their political connections and their material bases, not their internal life—although intellectual, ideological struggles within socialist movements played a large role in scholarship.

Both inspired and horrified by the alienating effects of modern life, Durkheim focused on the wide-ranging shift from community to society and on long-term social processes, or 'laws of the social' (see also Gherardi and Nicolini, Ch. 2 in this volume). His approach found their fullest expression in the work of the French Annales School. Not surprisingly, many Annales-school historians took community studies and examined how long-term demographic and economic processes of material life affected these communities. Coalescing as a distinct direction in the 1940s and 1950s, the Annales school of thought increasingly focused on the quantification of long-term 'social facts' such as population trends, fertility and mortality patterns, and trade. Annales' historians often combined a type of fact fetishism with a close scrutiny of community structures and ritual. Much like Marx, they viewed causation in history from the ground up. Much like ocean currents, geography and climate influenced population trends over the *longue durée*. The real story lay in the 'deep structures' and rhythms of human life.

The Annales approach tended to focus on how communities created bonds of meaning rather than how societies created new types of bonds, rituals, and meanings. Not surprisingly, the Annales school focused primarily on medieval and early modern history up until the transition to modernity. This approach also relegated a closer study of organizational life to the epiphenomen of human experience, curiously, at the same time when states and business corporations built huge, new organizational apparatuses to administer society and markets (Ross 1995: 165–96). By implication, most modern society's organizations and bureaucracies lacked meaning, loyalty, and affect. An organization bound together by impersonal, anonymous rules, functional specialization by office, not to mention its rituals or internal life, did not warrant the same close attention. These are just some reasons why the word 'community' radiates an almost visceral sense of warmth; the word 'organization' remains cool, if not downright frozen.

The final influential figure, Max Weber, most explicitly fitted a theory of historical, social change to a theory of organizations, that is, the bureaucratization and rationalization of society. Unlike Marx, Weber emphasized the role of ideas, religion, and the semiautonomous nature of the state and political leaders. Unlike Durkheim, Weber focused more on how new, formally rational institutions bound greater numbers of people together rather than on how bonds of community dissolved. Interpreted particularly through Talcott Parsons' structural-functional approach, Weber's influence underlies most post-1945 American and German economic, business, and social history, which emphasized national development, society-wide social changes, and modernization. (Classic examples of this approach include Dahrendorf 1967; Moore 1966; Wehler 1973/1985, 1987.)

Jürgen Kocka's (1969) seminal book on Siemens exemplified how social historians can look specifically at the growth of corporate organization, but the real theme of the book lay elsewhere. Kocka focused most intently on the new class of corporate white-collar employees dominated, as he argued, by a specifically German, state bureaucratic, 'preindustrial' mentality. He questioned whether corporate organization fits Weber's theory of bureaucracy, but he did not move beyond it. Kocka concentrated more on social or class stratification and organizational structure than on organizational process or learning. Weber himself developed a theory of organization to elucidate the increasing rationalization and modernization of society, not to study organizational life *per se*. As asserted by one of the best business histories about the chemical company IG Farben during the Third Reich: 'the organizing framework for good and evil in the modern age is not capitalism or socialism, but industrialization and its corollaries of bureaucratism and professionalism' (Hayes 1987: xix). Hayes's work on IG Farben is another good example of how historians tended to use corporate organizations as an archaeological site for the analysis of something else. Hayes investigated the company's relationship to the Nazi regime, explicitly forgoing a discussion of its internal operations, managerial styles, or its organizational processes. Like most historians and sociologists, Weber, too, chased after larger game—describing structural change and explaining how societies become modern—rather than how individual organizations work and learn. In this respect, examining or-

ganizational change and learning would be aiming too low and would be too micro-oriented; the topic would be at most a jigsaw piece in the larger puzzle.

Ironically, Weber's conception of bureaucracy tended to remove organizational life and learning from the practice of history. (It did not have this effect on sociologists and organizational theorists, however.) In Weber's theory of organization, bureaucracy is an instrument, a tool, or a technology of power (*Herrschaft*). Crucially, bureaucracy is not defined as a field of social processes or rich, intersubjective human behavior, but as a set of functions. Bureaucratization meant the growth of formally rational rules and procedures, a set of offices, files, paperwork, a hierarchy, and a career path. In short, it was defined in terms of structural characteristics. Bureaucracies also have a power-political dimension in that they institutionalize a given value orientation, usually through a charismatic, visionary figure. But the apparatus itself was viewed as an internally consistent organic whole that ensured regularity and enforcement. In a strict sense, bureaucracies do not learn but execute. Historians passed over them.

Unlike many of his students, Weber had a profoundly ambivalent, if not downright pessimistic, attitude toward bureaucracy and the imminent direction of modernity. Weber's famous *Protestant Ethic* (1904–5/1958) ended chillingly with a warning about the dangers of society's increasing rationalization and bureaucratization, which would lead into an 'iron cage' (p. 181). Weber chimed in that modern men were in danger of becoming 'specialists without spirit, sensualists without heart' (p. 182), interested in narrow career paths instead of the great questions of the day, comfortable in their little cubicles. This basic attitude fundamentally influenced many studies of organizational men (Mills 1951; Whyte 1956). As with Durkheim, there is almost a degenerative, consumptive quality emanating from such studies about their modern subjects.

This vague discomfort with organizations and organizational life does not stimulate historians in the same way as, say, the study of oppressed groups who hold out an alternative path and promise for the future. Much like anthropologists, who went to distant lands allegedly untouched by modernity to recover a more innocent time, historians tried to save these forgotten groups 'from the enormous condescension of posterity' (Thompson 1966: 12). The examination and history of the managerial class of the twentieth century is much less thorough in its density than that of the working class.

Business history, the natural subdiscipline where historians might place organizational learning under the microscope, has its own particular afflictions. For decades, the main sources of information about businesses came through commissioned, usually anniversary histories by the companies themselves, especially in Germany. They were of extremely mixed quality, generally discrediting the field in the eyes of the profession. Many of these anniversary histories are better utilized as exemplars about how the company wanted to represent itself to the outside world, as a type of cultural history or public relations, than as a source of information about organizational learning inside the business firm.

The dean of American business history, Alfred D. Chandler, nearly single-handedly helped transform this highly uneven collection of individual business histories into a comparative, social-science-oriented subdiscipline of history with a coherent set of clear hypotheses, questions, and proofs—an impressive achievement in its own right. Chandler's work on corporations and management paralleled the increasing use of social-science methods by other historians, who tended to focus on labor and broad social change. (Note as well that Chandler was employed by a business school, not by a history department.) His formidable theoretical reach has positively influenced the writing of business history on at least three continents (Coleman 1992; Jaeger 1992; Morikawa 1992). Over the course of his own career, however, Chandler became increasingly 'structural', focusing less on internal organizational change processes than on organizational and industrial structures (Chandler 1962, 1977, 1990).

Partly, this trajectory occurred naturally as he broadened his basic model to other countries (Chandler, Amatori, and Hikino 1997), but it also derived from theoretical tendencies in his own work.

Through Talcott Parsons, Max Weber's theories exerted a powerful influence on Chandler (McCraw 1988: 18–21, 301–6). Weber tended to presume a clear separation of fact and value, means and ends, often leading to the accusation that he is decisionistic (Habermas 1984). Applied to organizations, the bureaucracy, as Weber saw it, executes the will in a rationalized manner and regularizes the value orientation permeating the organization from the top down. This ends–means distinction played into the top-down tendencies of most business histories, which already focused on the great entrepreneur, a 'great-man' version of writing history. Historians neglected the bottom-up influence that the organization has on those at the top. Until quite recently, internal organizational life in business history tended to be subsumed under a narrative of senior management.

Chandler derived his basic categorization of business enterprises—actually Weberian ideal-types—from the person at the top of the firm, whether that person was a family member, an entrepreneur, or a manager. This categorization was not based on the organization or processes of the firm itself. Chandler did outline two ideal-types of organization, unitary functional and multidivisional *structures*, but, being cut out from an American cloth, these typologies have distinct limitations when they travel abroad to Germany or Japan. More important, for a theory of organizational learning, Chandler's emphasis on structure—not processes—cannot adequately deal with organizational change (for a more extensive critique of these categories, see Fear 1997: 555–61; Fruin 1998: 128–31). This weakness is reflected in Chandler's famous formulation, 'structure follows strategy', which tends to make organization a structure, not a process or a culture.

In his more recent work, Chandler has increasingly emphasized the importance of organizational capabilities and continuous learning to explain the competitive strengths and weaknesses of firms (Chandler 1992; Chandler and Hikino 1997: 34–7). Although Chandler now acknowledges that organizational learning is central to his discussion—problem solving through trial and error, feedback, and evaluation—it remains largely defined structurally in terms of his 'three-pronged investment' in manufacturing, marketing, and management. Paradoxically, the more Chandler has spread his scope to encompass more businesses and more countries, the more structure-oriented he has actually become, yet to an inversely proportional degree, his theory stresses process: organizational evolution, capabilities, and learning. *Strategy and Structure* (Chandler 1962) actually showed organizational process and learning more than *Scale and Scope* (Chandler 1990) did. His emphasis on internal organizational form tends to miss the 'intersubjective dimension of structure', that is, 'managers' shared ideas and beliefs and the way these shape decision-making' (Tiratsoo 1997: 78; also Fruin 1998: 130–1). Although Chandler 'places the problem of coordination squarely at the center of business history . . . [and] focused attention on large firms' dependence on managerial coordination, he actually had surprisingly little to say about how this coordination was achieved throughout the organization' (Lamoreaux and Raff 1995: 3–4). In order to bring organizational learning processes to light, one needs to reconstruct micropolitical decision-making processes and the history of organizational routines *inside* individual business firms.

The internal organizational life of business corporations is still largely *terra incognita*. Even among business historians, the history of internal decision-making processes and organizational routines below senior management is only just beginning, led in many respects by studies of Japanese enterprise. Two recent historical studies from Germany and Japan (Hilger 1996; Morikawa 1992) explicitly make organization a variable, but they tend to be descriptive rather than analytical. Reasons compelling organizational change, the way in which executives actually managed their companies, and

the internal decision-making *process* within these structures, all of which might disclose organizational learning, remain vague, if not opaque. In a comparative synthesis of European big business, Cassis (1997) pointed out that very little is known about the internal organization of most European business before 1945. Very little is known about how businesses actually made their decisions and strategic choices. Very little is known about the depth or size of middle management, let alone the actual work of managers within businesses. Research on such questions is 'still in its infancy' (pp. 157–67). It is a testament to how little is known about structure, not to mention internal organizational processes and learning, that the most vaunted organizational form of the twentieth century, the multidivisional structure, appeared in Japan and Germany before it did in its ostensible 'home', in the United States. Without a lot of sophisticated theorizing, a whole wealth of material about organization can be brought to light if one is willing to refer back to primary documents inside the business firm.

Finally, a more mundane, but extremely important, consideration keeps historians from addressing organizational learning directly, especially within business enterprises. Following the Rankean imperative, historians work above all with archival records. Because company records tend to be private, such questions remain 'enshrined in secrecy'—especially for the period after 1945. Historically speaking, business organizations, large-scale ones in particular, are of relatively recent vintage. Although extensive managerial hierarchies began to grow in the late nineteenth century, large-scale business organizations became the norm only in the mid-part of the twentieth century. Access to archives (where extant) therefore remains a problem for a good portion of large enterprises' histories. Furthermore, legal questions of privacy or protection of company information might cover a good portion of a company's history. And where archives are open, oftentimes crucial decisions and the process of organizational learning cannot be fully reconstructed from the available documentation. In order to write on organizational learning effectively, a historian needs access to a broad range of materials and people inside the organization, not just at the senior management level where written protocols may exist. Much middle-level management material may be lost. Interviews with participants may help a historian, but working from memory has its own pitfalls. All of these methodological and practical problems have largely quieted historians on the issue of organizational learning.

Part II: Telling It Like It Really Was

How, then, can historians contribute positively to a theory of organizational learning? The traditional approach to history, founded on historians' 'noble dream' of objectivity and 'telling it like it really was', has many virtues (Novick 1988: 2–6). Historians still tend to approach their subject matter in chronological, sequential fashion with an emphasis on longitudinal process. Reconstructing sequential process with the use of primary, archival sources—the Rankean imperative—is particularly useful for overcoming the snapshot, or 'in-and-out', before-and-after, method utilized so often by organizational theorists. In the anthropology chapter of this volume (Ch. 5), Czarniawska indicated the need for more diachronic studies of learning, the process of learning being more important than *what* was learned.

Historians need to focus on the 'micropolitical' decision-making process within business organizations to disclose organizational learning processes. The meticulous reconstruction of sequences of decisions, context, and reasons justifying change provides one strategy for showing how organizations learned. Moreover, historians' traditional narrative craft can nicely convey the mistakes, failures, options, alternative paths, and setbacks that an organization corrected and institutionalized into new procedures or routines, which affected later decisions. Such narrative analysis can give a

critical perspective on how management coped with crisis and change (Lauschke and Welskopp 1994: 10–3). With the following examples, I want to show how recent, ground level, archival work in business history has begun to illuminate these internal organizational processes.

This learning process can be conveyed through the early development of the Japanese cotton textile industry. A close, sequential narrative reveals a series of interlocking personnel, financial, technological, manufacturing, and marketing decisions that transformed the organization and operations of firms in the industry for more than two decades before they could compete successfully. The government did provide credit, opened state-operated mills, and subsidized private operations, but despite this support, only one of these companies achieved real success, that of Itó Denschichi. Itó, however, had already spent years dissembling and 'mutilating' an American hand-operated spinning machine to learn its secrets—a tactile learning-by-doing experience. Still, he had great difficulties and died heavily in debt. Not until years later did his son turn to another 'model' of operation pioneered by the privately owned Osaka Spinning Mill. Again, after years of frustration and perseverance, including a major fire, did Mie Cotton Textiles eventually prove successful. Even then, these pioneering companies used mule-spinning with the advice of British manufacturers, but Japanese industry increasingly moved to ring-spinning, employed young female workers, shifted to higher quality raw cotton, and changed their target markets to low-income consumers. On this basis, Japanese cotton-spinning firms eventually challenged British preeminence in Asian markets around the time of World War I.

The growing success and scale of cotton textile firms posed a new organizational dilemma around 1900. Who should run the companies and what role should trained engineers play in the firm? The historian Nakagawa stressed that the experience abroad and thought patterns shaped by training in technical and academic disciplines quickly led to internal organizational conflict within Japanese business. As with the steel and ship-building industries, merchant financiers vied with trained engineers for leadership within firms. This struggle was not just a question of personal authority or competence but also of corporate strategy, for engineers tended to stress expensive technical standards and long-term growth rather than short-term financial dividends. New standards of professionalism also created conflict over the methods and authority of corporate control. In addition, classic problems associated with the separation of ownership from control worked themselves out slowly over the next decades (Francks 1992: 44–6, 180–5; Nakagawa 1989: 1–6, 14–27; Tsurumi 1990: 34–46; Yamamura 1997: 310–14).

Because 'effective learning was the basis of survival', Japan offers a rich source of examples where historians have utilized the concept of learning-by-doing and organizational learning most explicitly (Fruin 1994: 40–9, 73–5). Because the Meiji government, acting 'as an organization-creating organization' (Westney 1987: 30), helped channel one of the most systematic learning experiences in history, historians questioned the significance of state industrial policy. In pursuing this broader question, historians uncovered a wealth of material about inner-organizational learning. The example of the Japanese cotton textile industry also indicates that only fine-grained historical research could disclose this difficult learning process, whose success came after considerable persistence and failure. With much of available business history, the organizational theorist still needs to read closely between the lines and supplement the basic story with close archival research. (For further examples from Japan, see Westney 1987; on Japanese silk-reeling, see McCallion 1989; for a similar argument pertaining to South Korea and, by implication, other late-industrializing countries, see Amsden 1989: 329.) In another case from Germany, two historians have gone back to the archives to study decision-making among German universal banks and industrial firms to test if banks, 'finance capital', had significant leverage over the strategies of German firms before the 1930s. They found a story very different from that normally assumed about German banking power. In many cases, German firms had significant leverage over banks (Wellhöner 1989; Wixforth 1995). Without a close narrative, telling how it really was, this learning process by entrepreneurs and organizations would remain hidden.

Analysts who remain on the surface and do not dive into the history of the organization itself, might miss crucial aspects of organizational learning. Let me take two opposing examples, Toyota and Thyssen, that illustrate the effectiveness of a close reading. In the first case, the shift from Toyoda to Toyota, from a textile machinery manufacturer to a carmaker, appears first as a major organizational discontinuity. In the second example, that of Thyssen, the shift from one steel-making site to another appears to be an organizational continuity. Without a close historical perspective, key aspects of these transitions would be lost.

Although the building of automatic looms has apparently little to do with the building of automobiles, a number of continuities in organizational values and routines bind the history of the Toyota Motor Works to the Toyoda Automatic Loom Works through three generations. Above all, Toyota's famous methods of 'lean production' rested on organizational legacies taken from textiles and loom-manufacturing. Sakichi Toyoda, the founder, encouraged his son, Kiichiro, to continue his tinkering with automobiles, just as he, the father, had with looms, and he allotted funds and factory floor space to his son to develop automobiles, long before the Toyoda Automatic Looms Company established the Toyota Motor Company in 1937. As obsessive about waste as his father was about looms, Kiichiro made 'just in time' one of his founding organizational principles. This phrase referred not only to punctuality but also to the production of precise quantities of parts as needed to reduce parts inventories. Machinery should be flexible enough to perform different tasks and should be located to improve product flows. After World War II, Taiichi Ohno, a manufacturing expert from Toyoda Spinning & Weaving, revived Kiichiro's ideas.

Ohno took the principle of the Toyoda auto-matic loom, which was a self-working device (*jidoka*) that stopped if it ran out of thread and applied it to the assembly line. His machines operated as automatically as possible. Also in-spired by the example of American supermar-kets, which replaced goods only if they moved off the shelf, Ohno revived Kiichiro's just-in-time principle by introducing a *kanban*, a sign-board, announcing the precise quantity of a specific part needed by the next station on the line. This change helped reduce stockpiling and inventories through improved communi-cation. Eventually, Ohno's system extended to first-tier suppliers, then to all of the company's subcontractors after the 1970s. Eiji Toyoda, Kii-chiro's cousin and Toyota managing director, aggressively backed Ohno over the resistance of unions and subcontractors (Bernstein 1997). Thus the corporate values (cost-saving through small inventories, self-working processes, ob-sessive work, perseverance) and routines of lean production passed down almost as an 'in-heritance' from father to son to cousin, from Toyoda to Toyota.

Without denying the dramatic differences between textile machinery and automobile production, one can say that the legacy of the Toyoda past conferred a positive set of values, principles, and experiences for the future of Toyota. The continuity lay not in the product but in the implicit organizational values and routines of Toyoda. Moreover, like the Japanese experience with cotton textiles, Toyota's learn-ing and implementation process was neither easy nor automatic; it took years of single-minded work before Toyoda or Toyota achieved success. Knowledge of past routines and values (Ohno) bridged an apparent discontinuity in company life, a discontinuity between textiles and automobiles and between products of the first and second industrial revolution. Theorists who argue in terms of path dependency tend to assume that businesses or economic history are inescapably locked into certain patterns or in-stitutions (witness the myriad arguments about British economic and business decline) but the past can also have polyvalent applications for the future. The theoretical issue about the na-ture of past-dependency is the same one that underlies the difference between Stinchcombe (the past as inertia) and Nelson and Winter (the past as inheritance).

Whereas Toyota illustrates a striking level of continuity in an apparent discontinuity, the example of Thyssen, a German steel-maker, shows a striking level of discontinuity where, on the surface, considerable continuities lie. Thyssen needed to increase scale in his steel plant. He had already worked successfully for nearly two decades at the Thyssen & Co. rolling mills, which had a small Siemens-Martin steel plant on site. So he decided to set up his own integrated steelworks with a larger scale. At the end of 1891, the Gewerkschaft Deutscher Kaiser (GDK), the predecessor of today's Thyssen AG, cast its first steel ingot. But the new steelworks continued to lose money. Thyssen turned to outside consultants to figure out why. They advised him that the type of steel was inap-propriate to the market and that the plant was a disorganized 'hovel'. Thyssen and his man-agers had essentially transferred their twenty-year successful production model at Thyssen & Co. to the GDK, but it was inappropriate for new markets, although production processes seemed similar. First annoyed at his con-sultants' critiques, Thyssen eventually hired one of them to redesign the steelworks. Even-tually, Thyssen's GDK became one of the lar-gest, most profitable producers of crude steel in Germany.

In this example, Thyssen recognized in time that market conditions were changing rapidly and took preventative measures. The new firm had the right machines but used the wrong methods and was outfitted for the wrong mar-kets. Thyssen had to turn to outside advisors in order to break away from his previous, success-ful experience (Fear 1997). Without a careful look inside the trajectory of the business firm, the Thyssen story would, on the surface, seem more continuous than it actually was, and the Toyoda/Toyota story would appear more dis-continuous.

What is the effect of this shift in perspective? Historians wrestle constantly with this prob-lem of continuity or discontinuity because it goes to the heart of questions about causation, periodization, and identity. Company histories of Toyota emphasize the spiritual continuity between Toyoda textiles and Toyota automobiles. But Thyssen AG's official history begins with the GDK in 1891, its legal predecessor, not with Thyssen & Co., which was founded in 1871. Indeed, the move to the GDK did mark a break with previous operating ideas. These notions of continuity or discontinuity, however, help shape the corporate identity of these two companies just as national histories create a national heritage (for a similar debate about the modernization of Japan, see Gluck 1985; Smith 1988; Howell 1995). Histories themselves play a crucial role in shaping corporate and national identity.

By dissecting the sequence and sources of internal organizational decision-making, historians can contribute to a theory of organizational learning. Nonaka and Takeuchi (1995) have shown the importance of a 'middle-up-down management process for knowledge creation' (pp. 124–59) in Japanese companies. Even in classic top-down hierarchies, the initiative for change does not necessarily come from the top. In my own work on management practices inside Thyssen, led by one of Germany's most famously autocratic entrepreneurs, August Thyssen, I have found a high degree of managerial autonomy and decentralized decision-making within his operations. Initiatives for organizational and strategic change did not necessarily come from the entrepreneur or senior management but frequently from young engineers and managers deep inside the business organization. Thyssen's organization forged final strategies, often after intensely competitive negotiations among managers, in a bottom-up process of managing tradeoffs and learning rather than a top-down process (Fear 1993; Galambos 1993). The typical approach in business histories—to use the top executive as a kind of shorthand for the entire company— creates the illusion of top-down decision-making. Other shorthands, such as 'Daimler-Benz decided . . .', elides the decision-making, the people, the process of organizational learning about decisions regarding strategy and investment, and the ways in which the firm realized its objectives.

A reconstructive historical approach can isolate the where, when, how, and why initiatives for organizational change arise more precisely than such shorthand can. Debates, disagreements, and contending viewpoints inside the business organization are more important for a theory of organizational learning than an ultimate outcome is, for they can disclose the process of learning, unlearning, or not learning. Strategies or reasons not taken into consideration may be more important for a theory of organizational learning than is the course eventually taken. Internal disagreements over strategy illuminate organizational behavior and various understandings about the situation of the firm, just as conflicts in national politics expose the character of society and its contradictions. Historians excel in this sort of portrayal in political histories but less so in business history (for an exception, see Carlson 1995).

Required is a careful, accurate reconstruction through archival research of the firm's objective situation, the key players, their perceptions of this situation, their reasoning in favor of one path or another, and contemporary statements from participants explaining why they considered the chosen path to be the correct one. With the passage of time, the disagreements and setbacks in the organizational learning process tend to fade in people's minds, especially if the firm succeeds. Such dimming of memory is one reason why historians since Ranke pay close attention to contemporary archival sources in order to provide an accurate reconstruction of events through *Quellenkritik*, or critical review of primary documents, a procedure that maximizes precision. Returning to the archives often reveals forgotten reasons, embarrassing lapses in judgment, and ugly truths.

Close historical research can also identify why companies failed to learn to use new institutional forms or technologies or processes. For instance, when the German government anchored works councils in the constitution of German firms by law during and after

World War I, industrialists vehemently objected, citing them as an incursion into their entrepreneurial turf. Antagonism between labor and management remained quite high in the 1920s. Yet one historian, Werner Plumpe, delved into the archives at Bayer in Leverkusen and found a high degree of cooperation between the works councils and management within the firm even during the heady, revolutionary days of early Weimar. In 1931, the director of the Social Policy Department of IG Farben in Leverkusen (Bayer) found managers who enthusiastically endorsed the forum. At Siemens, management thought that the works council improved communication channels within the firm. Not surprisingly, acceptance of factory councils varied dramatically depending on the industry, firm, and individual director. In general, the more management or labor construed the factory council in political, ideological, and symbolic terms, the less effectively and less pragmatically it acted at the firm level. The effectiveness (or lack thereof) of works councils derived less from the institution's actual role within the firm than the symbolic legitimacy attributed to it by participants. By accepting or even merely tolerating the new forum, a firm's management could learn to make the works council function for the firm rather than against it (Bellon 1990: 152–203; Plumpe 1992, 1994).

Finally, for a theory of knowledge creation, one needs to see how the firm organizes and disseminates knowledge through a history of organizational information systems. If, as Nelson and Winter (1982) argued, organizational routines are crucial for shaping decision-making and creating institutional memory, then a great many more histories are needed about the communicative process and procedures inside firms. These internal routines, too, have a history. I have already pointed out the importance of the kanban for Toyota's organizational operations, but a good deal of work still needs to be accomplished on reconstructing the history of these internal routines, procedures, and organizational dynamics. Yates (1989), for instance, pioneered the study of genres of communication within American enterprises. Most modern business decision-making rests on statistical information, but until the creation of the physical apparatus that is now taken for granted—typewriters, copiers, letterpress printing, filing systems, punchcards, and computers, all of which create, manage, and store organizational memory—such information was not easily accessible or disseminated. In short, organizational knowledge depended on certain types of information that first had to be assembled before they could replace more informal, personal ways of managing a business. But replacing cumbersome and centralized letterpress printing, vertical filing, and card files also altered paths of authority and communication within the firm. Likewise, the present impact that network computer systems have on corporate communication channels cannot be underestimated for organizational processes. Yates, however, did not simply offer a history of technologies. Each of these practices engendered new genres of business communication such as the memo with their own manner of evaluation and interpretation in much the same way that genres of literatures alter reading habits.

In the related field of management accounting, Johnson and Kaplan (1991) questioned the relevance of traditional management accounting. They argued that the type of information created by management, which affects its perception and decision-making, is increasingly inadequate in today's business world. In making their case, they provided a history of the assumptions and practices of U.S. managerial accounting, which bias managerial decision-making in particular ways. Communicative procedures and types of information affect the recognition and transmission of knowledge throughout the organization. Obviously, they, too, are shaped by the organizational structure and informal networks within an organization, but these procedures and types of information construct the manner in which people conceive and shape historical memory about the organization.

Theories of organizational learning would be greatly aided by histories of organizational routines, communication processes, genres of business information, or administrative procedures, all of which create organizational memory and coherence. Such studies require thematic, historical approaches. As March, Sproull, and Tamuz (1996) once stated: 'historical events are observed, and inferences about historical processes are formed, but the paucity of historical events conspires against effective learning' (p. 1). Viewing history as an interlocking chain of discrete 'events' or 'great people' is a primary reason why less work than desired has been accomplished in matters of crucial interest to organizational learning. As important as key turning points, figures, or legends are for understanding the culture of the company, it is precisely the hidden processes and routines that help form the collective identity and unconscious structures of company organizations. Internal decision-making of corporate organizations needs to be placed in a coherent, historical, and comparative context. Only when one gets inside the business firm will organizational evolution and learning come to light with all of its failures, setbacks, confusions, and debates—those bumps in the road—that the organization *learned* to overcome, integrate, institutionalize, circumvent, or simply forget.

However, researchers need methods more sophisticated than simply a return to the archives and 'telling it like it really was' in order to conceptualize a theory of organizational learning in historical perspective. A documentary reconstruction of sequence cannot answer the question of how the facts become evidence and how evidence is transformed into a meaningful story. The following example illustrates how one version of Hohner's company history—and not another—shaped its strategic choices and vision. In a strange way, the use and abuse of business history itself contributed to the future of the famous German harmonica company, Hohner.

By the 1960s, Hohner had ossified into a reflection of its own past. In the eyes of its aging director, who became increasingly interested in his social and communal legacy, the firm was a purveyor of stable tradition, focusing on harmonica production and a stable marketing

strategy. Other managing directors, however, tried to emphasize an alternative version of the firm's history. They viewed the history of Hohner as a series of experiments, breaks, and flexible innovations in production and marketing over the last century. For these directors, this dynamic vision of the firm's history opened the firm to new directions and possibilities. The leading director, however, overrode them, and the official version of the firm's history overshadowed their interpretation, thus eliminating strategic options from the table (Berghoff 1997: especially 584).

The Hohner example illustrates how recourse to historical 'truths' says less about the past than about contemporaries who try to legitimize a course of action in the present. Present agendas shape how people interpret the past and what they find meaningful in the past. As many historians noted long before the 'postmodern' turn in history, a dialectical relationship between past and present exists. Because there is no immediate access to the past, except through documents, stories, and memory, recovering past experience is trickier than one immediately supposes. Going back to the archives in order to 'tell it like it really was' is naive. Recent approaches to history offer needed theoretical guides and are more sensitive than earlier approaches have been to how historical narratives construct knowledge (and the creation of knowledge) about past experience. They are also better capable of handling broad thematic issues about learning, such as the role and creation of identity, culture, knowledge, interpretation, and legitimacy within organizations.

Part III: History 'Turns'

Since the 1980s, historians have turned increasingly to the study of how language, culture, and meaning shape human action, thinking, and identity. These approaches are popularly known as the 'linguistic turn' or 'cultural studies'. The postmodern turn tends to shift the question from an emphasis on uncovering hidden causes to locating shifts in meaning, from the question 'what is history' to 'how has history been told'. The difference lies less in the level of theory employed (economic history or social science history are highly theoretical) than in the claims of reaching some objective truth.

Dissatisfaction with social and economic models for explaining human action grew first out of the attempt to understand class and class formation. In a seminal work entitled *The Making of the English Working Class*, Thompson (1966) examined the way people experienced material circumstances in cultural terms, although 'productive relations' ultimately determined class. The historians of the French Annales school supported a strong stream of research focusing on the history of *mentalités*. By the 1980s, they increasingly viewed cultural practices and language as determinant of, if not primary to, economic relations. Historians studied the language of class to see how it shaped the claims and identity of ordinary laborers (Sewell 1980). In Germany, new approaches to *Alltagsgeschichte*, or the historical anthropology of everyday life, made some headway (see the debate between Kocka 1984 and Peukert 1984; see also Lüdtke 1995). Many U.S. and German historians turned to the anthropologist Clifford Geertz, who used 'thick description' and an explicit theory of culture to explain how ordinary people give meaning to their experiences (see, for example, Geetz 1973, 1983; Darnton 1985). In tune with the times, organizational theorists, too, paralleled this shift in the historical profession with their focus on symbolic politics and corporate culture (Schein 1992). U.S. and French historians, in particular, stirred into this brew Michel Foucault's influential approach to discourse and power—that is, how language and meanings order objects to create truth and knowledge that guide society's institutions—and one had a full-fledged break from structural social science approaches and Marxism (O'Brien 1989).

Most postmodern approaches to historical writing emphasize interpretation, that is, the malleable, if not entirely fictional, quality of writing about the past. Some historians drew heavily on linguistic theory stemming more or less from Ferdinand de Saussure: theoreticians such as Roland Barthes, Jacques Derrida, Dominick La Capra, and Hayden White, all of whom took their deconstructive skills to works of history. (For an introduction, see Eagleton 1983; Fay, Pomper, and Vann 1998; LaCapra and Kaplan 1987; White 1978.) These intellectual figures have forced historians to think more reflexively and self-consciously about the nature of historical knowledge and narrative.

These intellectuals highlighted the unbridgeable difference between the word and the world, the signifier and the signified, the text and the reality, historical narratives and the past. At best, historians could re-present an elusive past. There is simply no way to squeeze a four-dimensional (space-time) past with a cast of hundreds of millions onto black-and-white pages, no matter how thick the tome. Roland Barthes scathingly described histories as 'an inscription of the past pretending to be a likeness of it, a parade of signifiers masquerading as a collection of facts' (quoted in Evans 1997: 94). Narrative objectivity was a 'referential illusion', 'a product of ideology, or rather of imagination', that created a 'reality effect' by 'sheltering behind the apparent omnipotence of the referent' and a 'tissue of quotations' allegedly signifying what really happened (Barthes 1970: 149, 153–4; see also Barthes 1967: 19–40; Barthes 1977: 114–24, 142–48). For postmodernists, the question became how historians created truth-effects through their writing. Historians did not find facts in the archives but 'founded' facts by rhetoric in the act of writing. Moreover, the 'facts', the documents themselves, were already scattered shards of some other mirror, warped by contemporaries' ideological aims and past discourses. No one could 'tell it like it was'. Telling stories actually manufactured the past rather than reflected it innocently as a mirror. In the funhouse of mirrors past, historians became storytellers who created narrative coherence where none existed. History was a profoundly literary act, constructing (not reconstructing) the past with more or less explicit ideological agendas. Historians could never escape the game of creating knowledge for present purposes.

Postmodern approaches undermined the classic, 'modernist' position of historians as omniscient, impartial narrators with their claims to scientific objectivity and value neutrality, a position stemming from Enlightenment ideals. Instead, postmodern approaches offer stories about contested outcomes, forgotten alternatives, competing versions of history and identity, and history as the constant rewriting of cultural codes and ruptures of paradigms. These approaches created a new type of interpretive historicism, calling into question the idea of progress or historians' ability to approach truth and objectivity in their writing. This issue is especially contentious in the history of science (Appleby, Hunt, and Jacob 1994: 160–97; Kuhn 1962). Ultimately, these criticisms forced historians to be more attentive to narrative forms, underlying ideologies, or assumptions that created the 'facts' that the historian then used as evidence.

Postmodern, constructivist approaches involve deep philosophic and professional issues that cannot be delved into in this chapter. For instance, postmodern theorists such as Foucault—maddeningly—tend to skirt the issue of 'why' in history. They are fearful of listing 'causes' but are highly sensitive to how language meanings guide historical action. A cause might be a cause by any other name. (For sympathetic and hostile critiques, see Appleby, Hunt, and Jacob 1994: 198–237; Evans 1997; Fay, Pomper, and Vann 1998; Jenkins 1995; Wehler 1998.) One need not accept all of their claims to understand that the major issue at stake here is the accessibility of the past and the construction of knowledge itself.

This radical critique provides crucial insights for organizational learning. If organizational learning is based on knowledge-creation, learning, and communication, then historical forms of information, meaning, and signification need more explicit examination. Both the linguistic and cultural turns emphasize how information, knowledge, and the telling of stories help create national, organizational, and personal identities and help manufacture a common past that shapes present outlooks and future decisions. With these insights, for instance, historians have deconstructed national histories as narratives of power and legitimacy.

The transformation of a social science-oriented, positivistic approach to history into one that rests on the analysis of meaning, culture, and discourse is best illustrated by the shift from women's history to gender history (Scott 1988). As many historians turned to the study of ordinary people, there was little 'objective' evidence or 'real' sociological reason why women should disappear from the archives and much of history unless *categories of thought and meaning* systematically excluded or devalued women's contributions. Historians needed to analyze the history of those categories of thought (in this case, sexual difference) that could not be explained by recourse to empirical reality itself, for such categories obviously helped constitute social reality itself. Facts found in documents, the foundation of the historical method, began to be viewed as broken fragments of a larger discourse as opposed to transparent evidence. Meanings, metaphors, and language itself give rise to distinctive historical constellations of meaning in which people organize facts, conceptualize the world, and create knowledge. Meanings, metaphors, and language thereby transform human thought and guide action. Such linguistic or meaning constellations were prior to facts and knowledge. Such constellations of values also deeply influence broad social institutions and cultural practices: sexuality, family, respectability, clothing, the economic division of labor, state policies, medicine, politics, or even diplomacy (see Costigliola 1997; Hull 1996). One could say that the categories and meanings associated with sexual difference relegated women to the home, largely eliminating them from public life and history.

Analogous to the exclusion of women from history, the constellation of meanings associated with markets, entrepreneurs, management, labor, skill, or business have distinctive histories that shape organizational behavior or individual action, possibly eliminating alternatives or people from decision-making power. In the following passages I give a few examples illustrating how recent approaches in history can provide insights into three areas: organizational cultures, ways in which organizations create knowledge about themselves, and the use of this knowledge to legitimize change in organizational regimes. Knowledge creation and organizational learning are crucially linked to issues of strategy and power.

Shaping Organizational Culture

Schein (1993) defined organizational culture as the 'accumulation of past learning' (p. 87). But how does one know about this 'accumulation'? How does one know about the past? If one follows recent ideas about the nature of the past, then stories themselves invent organizational culture. Human memory about the past is intimately linked to what people tell themselves. I have shown how a particular understanding of the firm's history affected Hohner's strategic choices. As historians have often found in the history of nations, the meanings and implications surrounding particular legends shift subtly over time, or new versions of such legends are reimagined, erasing an old understanding of national history. For instance, U.S. political culture regularly returns to the Founding Fathers to reformulate its continuity with certain founding principles. Yet, as Wills (1992) argued, the mythology of the United States being founded on the basis of 'all men are created equal' begins with the Civil War not the Revolutionary War. The Declaration of Independence was and is one of the founding documents and legends of the United States, but its *meaning* for U.S. history changed profoundly after the Civil War. Historians have usually found that the meanings associated with key legends, stories, icons, or principles are surprisingly mutable and more historically contingent than one is likely to believe at first glance. A person taking a historical approach to organizational stories and knowledge must have to explore the alternative meanings and,

possibly, tensions deriving from these legends or founding principles over time.

Organizational cultures also create patterns of behavior that allow the organization to perceive and respond to its environment. Recent work in history, however, has shown that perception is highly transient and affected by present political and cultural issues. For instance, German attitudes toward America have changed greatly over the last century. Before World War I, Germans generally saw America as an exotic and dynamic, but slightly barbarous and uncivilized, land (the spitting of chewing tobacco!) populated by cowboys and Indians. This vision of America is attributed almost exclusively to the imagination of the German writer, Karl May, who had never visited America, or to Buffalo Bill's traveling show. By the 1920s, Germans had altered their vision of America, which became reimagined as a land of smokestacks, assembly lines, Model Ts, efficient kitchens, and dangerously independent 'new women'. By the 1950s and 1960s, however, America had became a land of mass, if somewhat crass, consumption, with Hollywood, Coca-Cola, and GIs threatening to swamp European culture (Kuisel 1993; Nolan 1994; Pells 1997). At issue, then, is less what America was really like than how attitudes and perceptions, rightly or wrongly, affect responses and behavior. The responses said more about the state of Germany than they did about the state of America.

Metaphors indicate a particular way of conceptualizing knowledge and a way of seeing (or not seeing). Nonaka and Takeuchi (1995: 59), for instance, used the metaphor, 'amplifier', to describe an organization's impact on learning (see also Morgan 1986). But amplifiers not only make sound louder, they can also squelch or drown out other sounds, metaphorically speaking, other options or people (on metaphor and organizational learning, see Gherardi and Nicolini, Ch. 2 in this volume). In recent work historians have increased their attention to language and metaphor as guides to deeper value systems shaping human behavior, institutions, and social and cultural practices. Language and metaphor help create the limits or boundaries of collective identity by including and excluding. Gender studies can be used as a metaphorical approach to show how constructed categories and meanings influence social perception and practices, possibly amplifying or squelching alternative perspectives, options, or talent.

Downs (1995) showed how assumptions about women's 'nature' helped reorder shopfloor organizational practices before and during World War I. French and British metalworking industries did not employ women, for assumptions about what constituted men's work kept women largely outside the industry. Women's arrival during the war reshuffled the job classifications and organization of female and male work on the shopfloor (pp. 79–118). Looking at the German textile industry, Canning (1996) demonstrated that women and men had remarkably similar work patterns and turnover rates in spite of gender segregation on the shopfloor. Male employers and workers assumed (falsely) that women did not develop a work identity, although they were as 'attached' to their jobs at least as much as men were in a social historical, empirical sense. But women continued to be defined by their identity as mothers. By contrast, men were defined primarily by their work and job skills, not by their identity as fathers—a possibility by today's standards. In addition, working-class organizations demanded a 'family-wage', which implicitly put working-class women back in the home (Canning 1996). The creation of a feminized clerk, or secretary, can be explained only by reference to the vocabulary of gender (Kwolek-Folland 1994). The assumption that financial issues are 'hard' and human resource issues are 'soft' is a common refrain with real-life ramifications for men and women of the corporation. Smith (1998) has shown the deeply gendered manner in which the practice of history has worked and how people have understood history. Women *have* written numerous histories, but they were considered 'amateurs' or tended to focus on different historical subjects considered 'lower', 'superficial', or trivial. Real history was weighty, solid, professional, and focused on important matters such as

state politics or diplomacy. Such meaningful categorization was prior to writing history itself, prior to empirical 'facts', and determined how people regarded events, evidence, or people as important, significant, or relevant.

In each of these cases, gender (meanings associated with biological difference) shaped perceptions, responses, choices, and organizational work practices; it helped define 'what is history' and helped demarcate the limits of the possible. Organizational learning specialists could turn their attention to the historical uses of language categories and demonstrate their subsequent impact on organizational practice and behavior. (Gender is merely one type of meaningful category of analysis.) Shifts in language, metaphor, and meaning create points of focus and attention, but they can also create blind spots for organizational life. Historians have increasingly turned to such cultural studies because their authors explore the underlying constellation of values constructing contemporaries' actions and offer useful approaches for confronting crosscultural issues in the age of globalization. Informed by a historical perspective, organizational theorists can better place the qualitative perception and responses of an organization over time by paying close attention to the long-term change in meanings and language attributed to elements of the environment. A historical analysis of language, meaning, and discourse helps determine how 'facts' became significant and created knowledge.

Creating Significant Knowledge

Knowledge creation always involves questions of significance or relevance that guide how people select, interpret, and communicate information. French historian-philosopher Michel Foucault addressed most directly how people 'order things' and create significant knowledge. Foucault's influence on the historical profession has been both immense and controversial precisely because of the links he made between knowledge, culture, and power. Foucault inverted the traditional narrative about the emancipation of the individual since the Enlightenment. Instead, he showed how individuals have become 'disciplined' *subjects*, increasingly subjected to new powers of modern life such as the welfare state, prisons, new forms of surveillance, and new disciplines of knowledge and professions. In this respect Foucault is a direct successor to Max Weber's or Friedrich Nietzsche's critique of modernity. (Classic texts are Foucault 1965, 1970, 1978; straightforward introductions are Bouchard 1980; Rabinow 1984; O'Brien 1989: 32–44.)

How does the ordering of information—discourse—generate knowledge as a technology of power? Without delving into a detailed exploration of Foucault's thought (see also Gherardi and Nicolini, Ch. 2 in this volume), a few examples illustrate some fruitful intersections applied to business organizations. Arguably, the accounting and information system is the single most important representation of a business firm. It is an 'account', a story about the firm, and it embodies the firm's organizational memory. Over the last century professional societies established increasingly sophisticated accounting conventions and practices that shaped the way company organizations 'see' themselves objectively and truthfully. But what types of information provided by the accounts are most relevant to decision-making? How are accounts and statistics constructed? In one manner, the national state helped set accounting conventions according to historical political contingencies and national cultural values (Gallhofer and Haslam 1991: 491–500), which might not be most appropriate. Johnson and Kaplan (1991) offered an excellent example of how a historical perspective can facilitate critical examination of hidden assumptions underlying seemingly objective cost criteria. They argued that the accounting standards advocated by the profession and utilized by individual businesses have generated the wrong sort of information, misrepresented costs in a systematic way, and created the wrong knowledge about the operations of the firm. In a work on labor history, Biernacki (1995) showed how cultural meanings constituted the practice and disciplining of labor in textile firms, fabri-

cating the understanding of labor commodification in different ways in Britain and Germany. Biernacki showed how British managers tended to understand labor as the amount of 'materialized labor' or product that workers manufactured, whereas German managers understood labor as the 'timed appropriation of workers' labor power and disposition over workers' labor activity' (p. 12). This distinction underlay and shaped work practices, forms of remuneration, standards for piece-rates, disciplinary procedures, the type of accounting statistics kept, and the types of supervision within factories. Both these works utilize historical methods and perspectives to deconstruct statistical, information, and professional practices.

Like a language code, the accounting and information system helps inform action, transform decision-making, and create organizational reality (Hopwood and Miller 1994; Jones 1995: 118–43). These representations of company and labor performance become institutionalized in the standard operating routines and the culture of the firm itself. A historian using a 'postmodernist' approach emphasizes how the *discourse* about management or the accounting profession constructs meaningful organizational knowledge in particular ways.

Knowledge, Legitimacy, and Power

Foucault's broader point about the nexus between power and knowledge, or 'technologies of power', is crucial for understanding how new knowledge and new stories legitimate change in organizational 'regimes'. All regimes, or those in power, wield a particular symbolic rhetoric or resort to specific institutional practices or rituals that legitimate their rule. If knowledge, professional practices, and discourses confer authority, then those who tell the stories, write the reports, or collect critical information are crucial figures in creating the basis for claims to legitimacy within organizations. In political theory, legitimacy refers to a symbolic or rhetorical justification that links, explains, and dignifies a claim or right to rule. Such references carry authority because they tap into the core values of a given culture, society, or, as in the context of this volume, an organization (see Kubik 1994: 7–15). Accounting practices, for instance, fundamentally gain their authority through the profession's claims to accuracy, transparency, objectivity, and rationality. Legitimacy, then, is a type of rhetorical ground for making claims to truth, which justify choices, actions, a type of rule, or a specific ruler.

How might the historical studies of regime change and symbolic legitimacy contribute to organizational learning? One of the most vibrant areas of historical research today is the analysis of the nation-state and nationalism. Historical approaches to the use of knowledge, symbolic authority, and power within nations should prove effective in illuminating the sources of legitimacy within business organizations, their institutional practices, and the right of certain managers (and not others) to form corporate strategy. The study of nationalism is particularly revealing of how contesting claims to legitimacy and power have been made over time. New strategies, new symbols, new rhetoric, new tactics, new practices, new histories formed to justify authority and the right to use power in nation-states.

A dramatic case in point can be seen with the French Revolution. The French Revolution fundamentally challenged the divine right of kings to rule, the previous and then persuasive basis of political legitimacy. Taking a Foucaultian approach to symbolic action, Hunt (1984: 52–86) showed that in order to replace the king as a symbol of legitimacy, literally chopping his head off in the guillotine, revolutionaries had to invent a new rhetorical king to replace the old one. They turned to an abstract 'people', who were fashioned into a new type of man, with new symbols (Liberty or Marianne), new national colors, new festivals, even new clothes. Europeans slowly replaced symbols of kings with new symbols such as flags or national holidays and institutional practices such as elections, parliaments, or majority rule that demonstrated that the regime in charge represented the will of the people. Defining who exactly the people were, however,

remained a bone of legal and rhetorical contention throughout the nineteenth century in Europe. Different groups in society also contested one vision of the people against another. But the rhetorical recourse to the people, to the nation, increasingly helped give governments authority for holding onto power.

Since the French Revolution, national histories have been founded on the study of the people. Historians—national storytellers—created new knowledge about the past and reviewed history to find undisclosed national heritages. Historians enthusiastically jumped into the preservation and restoration of past artifacts, folklore, monuments, and documents as relics of national identity and customs. Historians imbued the people's past as a cultural heritage, immemorial, venerable, and thus worthy of loyalty—often whether they were true or not. Nation-states are relatively recent historical phenomena, yet they often claim to have an ancient past. For instance, the 'immemorial' pomp and ceremony of British royalty and George VI's 1937 coronation could really be traced all the way back to 1901. The famous Scottish Highland kilt did not hark back to medieval pre-English times, but to an eighteenth-century English Quaker industrialist, who wanted a better set of clothes for his factory workers. The question that still needs to be researched more effectively is why these 'invented traditions' proved so surprisingly convincing and legitimate (Hobsbawm and Ranger 1983; Lowenthal 1985: 332–7, 389–95). Thus, the very writing of these new national histories and the creation of new knowledge and symbols helped found a people as an 'imagined community' (Anderson 1983). Historical narratives help 'invent' nations, not the other way around (Appleby, Hunt, and Jacob 1994: 91–116). The same narrative of history invented a tradition to legitimate the rulers of new nations who worked for the national will. The stories about the nation gave people a sense of their own history and identity within a national framework. These traditions and stories proved immensely powerful ways of engendering powerful emotional bonds to an 'imagined community', a loyalty that corporate organizations can rarely match in affective loyalty. These emotional bonds can also animate protest movements. For instance, Kubik (1994) examined how the Polish Solidarity protest movement managed to appropriate symbolic legitimacy away from the Communist regime. This national narrative, a particular genre and institutional practice, has become one of the most fundamental organizing principles for history departments around the world. Historians are only just beginning to unravel the strands of the nation, nationalism, state, territory, citizenship, immigration, and legitimacy (Cesarani and Fulbrook 1996). It is not surprising, then, in this age of globalization that for some people nation-states have become less convincing frameworks for analysis.

To illuminate organizational learning, a historian would deconstruct the way legitimacy was rhetorically and symbolically created within the organization *over time*, not just in a particular snapshot of time. To examine this process of change, organizational learning theorists could analyze crucial turning points in time when previous forms of legitimate reasoning made way for new ones. This approach would also provide a historical perspective on present forms of legitimacy and organizational practices. What constellation of values did contemporaries evoke to ground new strategies or policies? When did a particular form of rhetorical justification or use of a particular type of knowledge practice become important for organizational decision-making? For instance, key rhetorical devices or measures of competitiveness, which imply particular, but different, organizational practices, include production efficiency, labor productivity, market share, revenues, the maintenance of shareholder value, or price–earnings ratios, or return-on-investment ratios. All these devices and measures imply a way of maintaining the business organization's competitiveness and profitability, but the target values each imply different organizational practices. They divert the bulk of managerial attention to certain types of operations, possibly to the detriment of others. Each measure or target ratio also signifies that managers value different types of relevant

information about the firm's activities. Management would design the firm's reporting system in different manners to reflect these priorities and would know about the firm through this information system. Taking a Foucaultian approach, moreover, an analyst could treat the provided accounting and statistical information as a set of symbols used in professional and organizational discourses that discipline behavior and construct how managers view their range of choices and their own organization, thus linking knowledge, legitimacy, and power.

Another historian, who has analyzed modes of writing history, Hayden White, has emphasized how *genres* of written communication map information in particular ways so as to create meaning and relevant knowledge. White has taken historians who write in the narrative mode to task for not being aware of the way the narrative genre itself mobilizes a particular developmental story, prefiguring how information becomes encoded and communicated and how knowledge becomes relevant, guiding the practice of writing history. These are various forms of 'emplotment', that is, the 'encodation of the facts contained in the chronicle as components of specific kinds of plot structures' (White 1998: 17). For White the narrative form is just one kind of plot, just one way of encoding knowledge, of constructing how one creates a meaningful past and how one sees one's own history. Because of these critiques, historians today have become much more sensitive than previous historians used to be to the ways in which genres or emplotment actually constitute knowledge and make sense of reality. The *form* of communication helps create significance and the 'story'. For White, the form becomes content (White 1978, 1998; for a critique, see Carroll 1998).

Likewise, organizational learning specialists could turn their attention to the genres of communication coursing through an organization. They could look closely at the 'stories' organizations tell themselves about their own history and present practices. Organizational theorists have already emphasized the importance of 'legends' as guiding principles or stories for

organizational life. But a historian would critically analyze these stories to see whether they
were historically true (what Ranke originally
emphasized) or when and why they became
persuasive representations of the organization's past (see the Hohner example, above).
These legends, stories, reports, accounts, statistical information, target values, memoranda—
genres of communicated information—change
over time. To create new knowledge, new sorts
of information and new genres of communication are needed. In any case, they all imply a
way of seeing, of making aspects of the organization visible or invisible. They have a history
and can be deconstructed or demythologized.
Again, one need not turn into a radical decon-
structionist or view the organization as a pure
'text' to appreciate the way in which the communicative process, knowledge, and learning
within organizations is shaped by legends, particular stories or genres, certain types of statistical information, or professional practices.
Organizational learning itself is a new way of
reconceptualizing the business enterprise.

Finally, according to many postmodern theories, all histories have an underlying agenda
with a 'present-day purpose and inspiration,
which may be moral or political or ideological'
(Evans 1997: 195). This assertion is not entirely
false. Traditional history with its emphasis on
diplomacy, state politics, or national narratives
was deeply implicated in the state and nation-
building project. In a telling way, all three
dominant directions in twentieth-century historiography became deeply imbricated in the
Cold War battle of ideologies: In the United
States and The Federal Republic of Germany,
modernization theory became dominant; in
communist countries, Marxism got locked
into its worst, most rigid form, Marxist-Lenin-
ism. In western Europe, one found a more pragmatic and influential Marxist analysis of
society, a type of social democratic Marxism.
Postmodern theorists, such as Jenkins (1995),
however, oversimplify, for historians do not
just embody the dominant ideologies of their
time. A good many historians have critical
views about dominant ideologies. Nevertheless, the theory and writing of history, which

creates knowledge about the past, always has its
more or less explicit politics. New stories do
create new knowledge, which can justify and
legitimate not only one course of action over
another but also some groups of people who
have a stake in such knowledge over others.
Knowledge-creation itself is always tied to
questions of power and legitimate authority.

Conclusion

Many of these postmodern ideas already have
analogs in organizational theory because historians, anthropologists, political scientists,
and sociologists often draw from a common
pool of influential intellectuals. As pointed
out in the preceding section, however, there
are specific ways in which a historical approach
can help a theory of organizational learning.

First, historians tend to concentrate on the
peculiarities and uniqueness of special cases—
one of the reasons why members of other disciplines become frustrated by historians who
point out exceptions, degrees of nuance, or
complexity not taken into consideration by
broader approaches. But that complexity is
the great virtue of histories, for they emphasize
the contingent, fluid, messy historical reality.
The exceptions to the rule may generate new
ways of thinking about the general theory. Historians' virtue is the fine-grained analysis. Just
because a historian may offer one case, such as a
biography or a study of a specific organization,
does not mean that it cannot shed light on
more general matters. Historians also tend to
revel in bringing new, archival material to light,
which could only help other disciplines for
other purposes. A close, accurate narrative
story that emphasizes sequence and process
within the organization can enable a theory of
organizational learning to multiply examples,
which can then be synthesized into more simplified models of organizational learning.

Second, histories can offer a sense of this
messy process of organizational learning, overcoming snapshot, before-and-after, input–
output approaches. Outcome may be less

important than a description and analysis of the process of learning itself. Historians can detect when problems become perceived, how the organization reacts to changes in its environment, what triggers an attempt to change, and how the organization did (or did not) overcome this challenge.

Third, histories can disclose past or present alternatives unpursued by organizations. These historical alternatives need to be rescued from the enormous condescension of the present. Even heretics or witches are a stock in trade for the historian. They, too, shed light on the boundaries of society or, by analogy, the limits of an organization. Sometimes, such as with Martin Luther, they point the way to the future. Usually, any important strategic move in business always generates an opposition, whose rationales are not necessarily unreasonable at the time. They may provide insight into alternative paths for an organization. In this context, it might even be useful for active business people to go back to the original reasons and decisions for entering a market or developing a new product to see if the original assumptions still hold.

Fourth, historians usually spend a good deal of time reconstructing past events, revitalizing past contexts, and rediscovering past meanings and assumptions that helped guide people's behavior and actions in their time. These contemporary meanings and language helped construct thinking and decisions at a previous point in time. Such historical illumination could shed light on present organizational assumptions and historicize the organization's use of language, metaphors, symbols, and present culture.

Thus, a historical approach or sensibility can provide a perspective, a base of vicarious experience, or a basis for contrast. If one develops a sense of how categories and meanings shift over time, this perspective might create a distancing from present practices, initiating reflexivity and learning (see Gherardi and Nicolini, Ch. 2 in this volume). It might open possibilities, rather than foreclose them. This distancing might be more valuable than learning 'lessons' from history, which might appear

more conclusive but might actually hinder this process of reflection. Moreover, this perspective might initiate a *proactive* reflexive learning process without waiting for a breakdown or crisis to trigger organizational change. Analyzing an organization's history also opens the organization up to a constant reinterpretation of previous behavior and actions. Do they still make sense under new conditions? This historical perspective can also provide a deep spring of skepticism about new ideas or claims. For instance, recent years have seen an amazing resurgence of the virtues and values of entrepreneurship and leadership over mere management (Hinterhuber and Popp 1992; Zaleznik 1992). Yet this literature also reinvents an older literature that has been forgotten (Hartmann 1959; Schumpeter 1942).

Finally, a historical perspective can provide a vantage point for reflecting on organizational learning itself. Why does this theory arise now? Why is organizational learning a concept for *its* time? According to the business historian Mark Fruin (1994):

Modern corporations represent a stage of development where organizational learning became paramount, that is when internalized and institutionalized routines, methods, and processes superseded idiosyncratic, expedient, and frankly entrepreneurial measures. Newer organizational forms were only weakly connected with past institutions, although there was a considerable degree of interaction and even borrowing between them. To disregard that interaction is to deny the importance of organizational learning. (p. 74)

Fruin equated organizational learning with the rise of managerial hierarchies, but why, then, does the concept or theory, not the reality, of organizational learning appear just now in the late 1980s and 1990s? Organizational learning is a means of reimagining the history and nature of corporate organization.

Part of the answer grows out of the ultimate inability of the classic paradigms to explain modern life. The major directions of modernist historiography emanating from the great social theorists of the nineteenth century are less wrong or irrelevant than have run their course. If society is completely bureaucratized, rationalized, commodified, and urbanized, then at this historical juncture new tools and new concepts are needed with which to distinguish behavior in societies that have reached this point. It is not surprising that new discussions about postmodernism, gender, race, ethnicity (identity politics) have arisen at this time, discussions that emphasize the construction of difference rather than some macro-homogenizing convergence process. Likewise, the presumption underlying organizational learning is that a good portion of learning now takes place within 'bureaucracies'.

If new methods, new knowledge, and new histories arise out of present concerns, how does organizational learning relate to the present context? In *The Borderless World*, Kenichi Ohmae (1990) emphasized how the internal life of the organization is critical to reaching a new stage of globalism, at which the organization can draw on talent from around the world as its corporate identity increasingly transcends mother-country identity. This assertion may be debatable in reality, but Hannerz (1996) argued that, in Ohmae's vision, corporate identity

becomes an alternative, a transnational source of solidarity and collective identity . . . while the na-

tion at the same time becomes defined as little more than an environment, a local market. . . . In the shared life and personal ties of the corporation, it is implied, cultural resonance can again be found. The corporation may even have a history, a mythology of the past, and celebrate it. More certainly, it will offer some vision for the future. (p. 86)

Indeed, in 1996, the Atlanta-based Coca-Cola company announced that it would eliminate the organizational distinction between domestic and international operations. One of the premier symbols of Americana went 'one world' (Collins 1996). As huge corporations grow beyond the bounds of their national contexts, the procedures, routines, objectives, mission, and culture of transnational firms need new ways of binding people together and legitimating their actions across the globe. Is it surprising that corporations are starting to conceive of themselves as effective learning organizations with their own coherent, autonomous identity, according to their own organizational practices? In national school systems, learning is always associated with a socialization process. How do the new theories of organizational learning help legitimate new global corporate practices, identity, and memory of a corporation's own history?

References

Albrow, M. (1997). *The Global Age: State and Society beyond Modernity*. Stanford, Calif.: Stanford University Press.

Amsden, A. H. (1989). *Asia's Next Giant: South Korea and Late Industrialization*. New York: Oxford University Press.

Anderson, B. (1983). *Imagined Communities: Reflections on the Origin and Spread of Nationalism*. London: Verso.

Appleby, J., Hunt, L., and Jacob, M. (1994). *Telling the Truth about History*. New York: W. W. Norton.

Barthes, R. (1967). *Writing Degree Zero* (A. Lavers and C. Smith, trans., with a preface by S. Sontag). New York: Hill and Wang.

——(1970). 'Historical Discourse', in M. Lane (ed.), *Structuralism: A Reader*. London: Jonathan Cape, 145–55.

——(1977). *Image, Music, Text* (S. Heath, trans.). New York: Hill and Wang.

Bellon, B. P. (1990). *Mercedes in Peace and War: German Automobile Workers, 1903–1945*. New York: Columbia University Press.

Berghoff, H. (1997). *Zwischen Kleinstadt und Weltmarkt: Hohner und die Harmonika 1857–1961: Unternehmensgeschichte als Gesellschaftsgeschichte*. Paderborn: Ferdinand Schöningh.

Bernstein, J. R. (1997). 'Toyoda Automatic Looms and Toyota Automobiles', in T. K. McCraw (ed.), *Creating Modern Capitalism: How Entrepreneurs, Companies, and Countries Triumphed in Three Industrial Revolutions*. Cambridge, Mass.: Harvard University Press, 398–438.

Biernacki, R. (1995). *The Fabrication of Labor: Germany and Britain 1640–1914*. Berkeley: University of California Press.

Bloch, M. (1953). *The Historian's Craft: Reflections on the Nature and Uses of History and the Techniques and Methods of the Men Who Write It*. New York: Vintage Books.

Bouchard, D. F. (ed.) (1980). *Language, Countermemory, Practice: Selected Essays and Interview by Michel Foucault*. Ithaca, NY: Cornell University Press.

Canning, K. (1996). *Languages of Labor and Gender: Female Factory Work in Germany 1850–1914*. Ithaca, NY: Cornell University Press.

Carlson, W. B. (1995). 'The Coordination of Business Organization and Technological Innovation within the Firm: A Case Study of the Thomson-Houston Electric Company in the 1880s', in N. R. Lamoreaux and D. M. G. Raff (eds.), *Coordination and Information: Historical Perspectives on the Organization of Enterprise*. Chicago: University of Chicago Press, 55–94.

Carlyle, T. (1993). *On Heroes, Hero-worship and the Heroic in History: Six Lectures*. Berkeley: University of California Press. (Original work published 1841)

Carr, E. H. (1961). *What Is History?* New York: Vintage Books.

Carroll, N. (1998). 'Interpretation, History, and Narrative', in B. Fay, P. Pomper, and R. T. Vann (eds.), *History and Theory: Contemporary Readings*. Oxford: Blackwell, 34–56.

Cassis, Y. (1997). *Big Business: The European Experience in the Twentieth Century*. Oxford: Oxford University Press.

Cesarani, D. and Fulbrook, M. (eds.) (1996). *Citizenship, Nationality and Migration in Europe*. London: Routledge.

Chandler, A. D., Jr. (1962). *Strategy and Structure: Chapters in the History of the American Industrial Enterprise*. Cambridge, Mass.: MIT Press.

——(1977). *The Visible Hand: The Managerial Revolution in American Business*. Cambridge, Mass.: Belknap Press.

——(1990). *Scale and Scope: The Dynamics of Industrial Capitalism*. Cambridge, Mass.: Belknap Press.

——(1992). 'Organizational Capabilities and the Economic History of the Industrial Enterprise'. *Journal of Economic Perspectives*, 6/3: 79–100.

——Amatori, F., and Hikino, T. (eds.) (1997). *Big Business and the Wealth of Nations*. Cambridge: Cambridge University Press.

—— and Hikino, T. (1997). 'The Large Industrial Enterprise and the Dynamics of Modern Economic Growth', in A. D. Chandler, Jr., F. Amatori, and T. Hikino (eds.), *Big Business and the Wealth of Nations*. Cambridge: Cambridge University Press, 24–57.

Coleman, D. C. (1992). 'The Uses and Abuses of Business History', in D. C. Coleman (ed.), *Myth, History and the Industrial Revolution*. London: Hambledon Press, 203–19.

Collins, G. (1996). 'Coke Drops "Domestic" and Goes One World'. *New York Times*, 13 January: A17, A19.

Costigliola, F. (1997). 'The Nuclear Family: Tropes of Gender and Pathology in the Western Alliance'. *Diplomatic History*, 21: 163–83.

Dahrendorf, R. (1967). *Society and Democracy in Germany*. New York: W. W. Norton.

Darnton, R. (1985). *The Great Cat Massacre and Other Episodes in French Cultural History*. New York: Vintage Books.

Dosi, G. (1997). 'Organizational Competences, Firm Size, and the Wealth of Nations: Some Comments from a Comparative Perspective', in A. D. Chandler, Jr., F. Amatori, and T. Hikino (eds.), *Big Business and the Wealth of Nations*. Cambridge: Cambridge University Press, 465–79.

Downs, L. L. (1995). *Manufacturing Inequality: Gender Division in the French and British Metalworking Industries 1914–1939*. Ithaca, NY: Cornell University Press.

Eagleton, T. (1983). *Literary Theory: An Introduction*. Minneapolis: University of Minnesota Press.

Evans, R. J. (1997). *In Defence of History*. London: Granta Books.

Fay, B., Pomper, P., and Vann, R. T. (eds.) (1998). *History and Theory: Contemporary Readings.* Oxford: Blackwell.

Fear, J. R. (1993). *Thyssen & Co. Mülheim (Ruhr): The Institutionalization of the Corporation.* Doctoral dissertation, Stanford University, Calif.

—— (1997). 'Constructing Big Business: The Cultural Concept of the Firm', in A. D. Chandler, Jr., F. Amatori, and T. Hikino (eds.), *Big Business and the Wealth of Nations.* Cambridge: Cambridge University Press, 546–74.

Feinstein, C. H., Temin, P., and Toniolo, G. (1997). *The European Economy between the Wars.* Oxford: Oxford University Press.

Foucault, M. (1965). *Madness and Civilization: A History of Insanity in the Age of Reason* (R. Howard, trans.). New York: Random House. (Original work published 1961)

—— (1970). *The Order of Things: An Archaeology of the Human Sciences.* New York: Random House. (Original work published 1966)

—— (1978). *History of Sexuality*: Vol. 1. *An Introduction* (R. Hurley, trans.). New York: Random House. (Original work published 1976)

Francks, P. (1992). *Japanese Economic Development: Theory and Practice.* London: Routledge.

Freeman, J. (1990). 'Ecological Analysis of Semiconductor Firm Mortality', in J. V. Singh (ed.), *Organizational Evolution: New Directions.* Newbury Park, Calif.: Sage, 53–77.

Fruin, W. M. (1994). *The Japanese Enterprise System: Competitive Strategies and Cooperative Structures.* Oxford: Clarendon Press.

—— (1998). 'To Compare or Not to Compare: Two Books that Look at Capitalist Systems across Centuries, Countries and Industries'. *Business History Review,* 72: 123–36.

Galambos, L. (1993). 'The Innovative Organization: Viewed from the Shoulders of Schumpeter, Chandler, Lazonick, *et al.*'. *Business and Economic History,* 22: 79–91.

Gallhofer, S. and Haslam, J. (1991). 'The Aura of Accounting in the Context of a Crisis: Germany and the First World War'. *Accounting, Organizations and Society,* 16: 487–520.

Geertz, C. (1973). *The Interpretation of Cultures: Selected Essays.* New York: Basic Books.

—— (1983). *Local Knowledge: Further Essays in Interpretative Anthropology.* New York: Basic Books.

Gluck, C. (1985). *Japan's Modern Myths: Ideology in the Late Meiji Period.* Princeton: Princeton University Press.

Habermas, J. (1984). *The Theory of Communicative Action* (2 vols., T. McCarthy, trans.). Boston: Beacon Press. (Original work published 1981)

Hannan, M. T. and Freeman, J. (1989). *Organizational Ecology.* Cambridge, Mass.: Harvard University Press.

Hannerz, U. (1996). *Transnational Connections: Culture, People, Places.* London: Routledge.

Hartmann, H. (1959). *Authority and Organization in German Management.* Princeton: Princeton University Press.

Hayes, P. (1987). *Industry and Ideology: IG Farben in the Nazi Era.* Cambridge: Cambridge University Press.

Hilger, S. (1996). *Sozialpolitik und Organisation: Formen betrieblicher Sozialpolitik in der rheinisch-westfälischen Eisen- und Stahlindustrie seit der Mitte des 19. Jahrhunderts bis 1933.* Stuttgart: Franz Steiner.

Hinterhuber, H. H. and Popp, W. (1992). 'Are You a Strategist or Just a Manager?' *Harvard Business Review,* 70/1: 105–13.

Hobsbawm, E. and Ranger, T. (eds.) (1983). *The Invention of Tradition.* Cambridge: Cambridge University Press.

Hopwood, A. G. and Miller, P. (eds.) (1994). *Accounting as Social and Institutional Practice.* Cambridge: Cambridge University Press.

Howell, D. L. (1995). *Capitalism from within: Economy, Society, and the State in a Japanese Fishery.* Berkeley: University of California Press.

Hull, I. V. (1996). *Sexuality, State, and Civil Society in Germany 1700–1815.* Ithaca, NY: Cornell University Press.

Hunt, L. (1984). *Politics, Culture, and Class in the French Revolution.* Berkeley: University of California Press.

——(ed.) (1989). *The New Cultural History*. Berkeley: University of California Press.

Jaeger, H. (1992). 'Unternehmensgeschichte in Deutschland seit 1945: Schwerpunkte—Tendenzen—Ergebnisse'. *Geschichte und Gesellschaft*, 18: 107–32.

Jenkins, K. (1995). *On 'What Is History?' From Carr and Elton to Rorty and White*. London: Routledge.

Johnson, H. T. and Kaplan, R. S. (1991). *Relevance Lost: The Rise and Fall of Management Accounting*. Boston: Harvard Business School Press.

Jones, T. C. (1995). *Accounting and the Enterprise: A Social Analysis*. London: Routledge.

Kocka, J. (1969). *Unternehmensverwaltung und Angestelltenschaft am Beispiel Siemens 1847–1914: Zum Verhältnis von Kapitalismus und Bürokratie in der deutschen Industrialisierung*. Stuttgart: Ernst Klett.

——(1984). 'Historisch-anthropologische Fragestellungen—ein Defizit der historischen Sozialwissenschaft?', in H. Süssmuth (ed.), *Historische Anthropologie: Der Mensch in der Geschichte*. Göttingen: Vandenhoeck & Ruprecht, 73–83.

Kubik, J. (1994). *The Power of Symbols against the Symbols of Power: The Rise of Solidarity and the Fall of State Socialism in Poland*. University Park: Pennsylvania State University Press.

Kuhn, T. S. (1962). *The Structure of Scientific Revolutions*. Chicago: University of Chicago Press.

Kuisel, R. (1993). *Seducing the French: The Dilemma of Americanization*. Berkeley: University of California Press.

Kwolek-Folland, A. (1994). *Engendering Business: Men and Women in the Corporate Office 1870–1930*. Baltimore: Johns Hopkins University Press.

LaCapra, D. and Kaplan, S. L. (eds.) (1987). *Modern European Intellectual History: Reappraisals and New Perspectives*. Ithaca, NY: Cornell University Press.

Lamoreaux, N. R. and Raff, D. M. G. (1995). 'Introduction: History and Theory in Search of One Another', in N. R. Lamoreaux and D. M. G. Raff (eds.), *Coordination and Information: Historical Perspectives on the Organization of Enterprise*. Chicago: University of Chicago Press, 1–9.

Lauschke, K. and Welskopp, T. (eds.) (1994). 'Einführung: Mikropolitik im Unternehmen: Chancen und Voraussetzungen beziehungsanalytischer Ansätze in der Industrie- und Arbeitergeschichte', in K. Lauschke and T. Welskopp (eds.), *Mikropolitik im Unternehmen: Arbeitsbeziehungen und Machtstrukturen in industriellen Großbetrieben des 20. Jahrhunderts*. Essen: Klartext, 7–15.

Linenthal, E. T. (1995). *Preserving Memory: The Struggle to Create America's Holocaust Museum*. New York: Penguin Books.

Lowenthal, D. (1985). *The Past Is a Foreign Country*. Cambridge: Cambridge University Press.

Lüdtke, A. (ed.) (1995). *The History of Everyday Life: Reconstructing Historical Experiences and Ways of Life*. Princeton: Princeton University Press.

March, J. G., Sproull, L. S., and Tamuz, M. (1996). 'Learning from Samples of One or Fewer', in M. D. Cohen and L. S. Sproull (eds.), *Organizational Learning*. Thousand Oaks, Calif.: Sage, 1–19.

McCallion, S. W. (1989). 'Trial and Error: The Model Filature at Tomioka', in W. D. Wray (ed.), *Managing Industrial Enterprise: Cases from Japan's Prewar Experience*. Cambridge, Mass.: Harvard University, Council on East Asian Studies, 89–118.

McCraw, T. K. (1988). *The Essential Alfred Chandler: Essays toward a Historical Theory of Big Business*. Boston: Harvard Business School Press.

Mills, C. W. (1951). *White Collar: The American Middle Class*. New York: Oxford University Press.

Moore, B. (1966). *Social Origins of Dictatorship and Democracy: Lord and Peasant in the Making of the Modern World*. New York: Beacon Press.

Morgan, G. (1986). *Images of Organization*. London: Sage.

Morikawa, H. (1992). *Zaibatsu: The Rise and Fall of Family Enterprise Groups in Japan*. Tokyo: University of Tokyo Press.

Nakagawa, K. (1989). 'The "Learning Industrial Revolution" and Business Management', in T. Yui and K. Nakagawa (eds.), *Japanese Management in Historical Perspective*. Tokyo: Tokyo University Press, 1–27.

Nelson, R. R. (ed.) (1993). *National Innovation Systems: A Comparative Analysis*. New York: Oxford University Press.

——and Winter, S. G. (1982). *An Evolutionary Theory of Economic Change*. Cambridge, Mass.: Belknap Press.

Nevins, A. and Hill, F. E. (1957). *Ford: Expansion and Challenge 1915–1933* (Vol. 2). New York: Charles Scribner's Sons.

New Historical Society Formed (1998). *Perspectives: American Historical Association Newsletter*, 36, 6 September: 3–6.

Nolan, M. (1994). *Visions of Modernity: American Business and the Modernization of Germany*. Oxford: Oxford University Press.

Nonaka, I. and Takeuchi, H. (1995). *The Knowledge-creating Company: How Japanese Companies Create the Dynamics of Innovation*. New York: Oxford University Press.

Novick, P. (1988). *That Noble Dream: The 'Objectivity Question' and the American Historical Profession*. Cambridge: Cambridge University Press.

O'Brien, P. (1989). 'Michel Foucault's History of Culture', in L. Hunt (ed.), *The New Cultural History*. Berkeley: University of California Press, 25–46.

Ohmae, K. (1990). *The Borderless World*. New York: Harper Business.

Pells, R. (1997). *Not Like Us: How Europeans Have Loved, Hated, and Transformed American Culture since World War II*. New York: Basic Books.

Peukert, D. (1984). 'Neuere Alltagsgeschichte und Historische Anthropologie', in H. Süssmuth (ed.), *Historische Anthropologie: Der Mensch in der Geschichte*. Göttingen: Vandenhoeck & Ruprecht, 57–72.

Piore, M. J. and Sabel, C. F. (1984). *The Second Industrial Divide: Possibilities for Prosperity*. New York: Basic Books.

Plumpe, W. (1992). 'Die Betriebsräte in der Weimarer Republik: Eine Skizze zu ihrer Verbreitung, Zusammensetzung und Akzeptanz', in W. Plumpe and C. Kleinschmidt (eds.), *Unternehmen zwischen Markt und Macht: Aspekte deutscher Unternehmens- und Industriegeschichte im 20. Jahrhundert*. Essen: Klartext, 42–60.

——(1994). 'Mikropolitik im Unternehmen: Die Reaktion der Farbenfabriken vorm. Bayer & Co. in Leverkusen auf die Novemberrevolution 1918/19', in K. Lauschke und T. Welskopp (eds.), *Mikropolitik im Unternehmen: Arbeitsbeziehungen und Machtstrukturen in industriellen Großbetrieben des 20. Jahrhunderts*. Essen: Klartext, 123–60.

Rabinow, P. (ed.) (1984). *Foucault Reader*. New York: Pantheon Books.

Ranke, L. (1874). *Sämmtliche Werke*: Vols. 33–4. *Geschichte der romanischen und germanischen Völker von 1494 bis 1514*. Leipzig: Duncker und Humblot. (Original work published 1824)

Ross, K. (1995). *Fast Cars, Clean Bodies: Decolonization and the Reordering of French Culture*. Cambridge, Mass.: MIT Press.

Sabel, C. F. and Zeitlin, J. (eds.) (1997). *World of Possibilities: Flexibility and Mass Production in Western Industrialization*. Cambridge: Cambridge University Press.

Schein, E. H. (1992). *Organizational Culture and Leadership* (2nd edn). San Francisco: Jossey-Bass.

——(1993). 'How Can Organizations Learn Faster? The Challenge of Entering the Green Room'. *Sloan Management Review*, 34/2: 85–92.

Schiller, F. (1970). 'Was heisst und zu welchem Ende studiert man Universalgeschichte? Eine akademische Antrittsrede', in K.-H. Hahn (ed.), *Schillers Werke. Nationalausgabe*: Vol. 17. *Historische Schriften, Teil I*. Weimar: Heumann Böhlaus Nachfolger, 359–76. (Original work published 1784)

Schumpeter, J. A. (1942). *Capitalism, Socialism and Democracy*. New York: Harper & Row.

Scott, J. W. (1988). *Gender and the Politics of History*. New York: Columbia University Press.

Sewell, W. H. (1980). *Work and Revolution in France: The Language of Labor from the Old Regime to 1848*. Cambridge: Cambridge University Press.

Smith, B. (1998). *The Gender of History: Men, Women, and Historical Practice*. Cambridge, Mass.: Harvard University Press.

Smith, T. (1988). *Native Sources of Japanese Industrialization 1750–1920*. Berkeley: University of California Press.

Stinchcombe, A. L. (1965). 'Social Structure and Organizations', in J. G. March (ed.), *Handbook of Organizations*. Chicago: Rand McNally, 142–93.

Thompson, E. P. (1966). *The Making of the English Working Class*. New York: Vintage Books. (Original work published 1963)

Tiratsoo, N. (1997). 'British Management 1945–64: Reformers and the Struggle to Improve Standards', in E. Abé and T. Gourvish (eds.), *Japanese Success? British Failure? Comparisons in Business Performance since 1945*. Oxford: Oxford University Press, 77–97.

Tsurumi, E. P. (1990). *Factory Girls: Women in the Thread Mills of Meiji Japan*. Princeton: Princeton University Press.

Weber, M. (1958). *The Protestant Ethic and the Spirit of Capitalism* (T. Parson, trans. [1930], with an introduction by A. Giddens). New York: Charles Scribner's Sons. (Original work published 1904–5)

Wehler, H.-U. (1985). *The German Empire 1871–1918* (K. Traynor, trans.). New York: Berg Publishers. (Original work published 1973)

——(1987). *Deutsche Gesellschaftsgeschichte* (2 vols.). Munich: C. H. Beck.

——(1998). *Die Herausforderung der Kulturgeschichte*. Munich: C. H. Beck.

Wellhöner, V. (1989). *Großbanken und Großindustrie im Kaiserreich*. Göttingen: Vandenhoeck & Ruprecht.

Westney, D. E. (1987). *Innovation and Imitation: The Transfer of Western Organizational Patterns to Japan*. Cambridge, Mass.: Harvard University Press.

White, H. (1978). *Tropics of Discourse: Essays in Cultural Criticism*. Baltimore: Johns Hopkins University Press.

——(1998). 'The Historical Text as Literary Artifact', in B. Fay, P. Pomper, and R. T. Vann (eds.), *History and Theory: Contemporary Readings*. Oxford: Blackwell, 15–33.

Whyte, W. (1956). *The Organization Man*. New York: Simon and Schuster.

Wills, G. (1992). *Lincoln at Gettysburg: The Worlds that Remade America*. New York: Simon and Schuster.

Winter, S. G. (1990). 'Survival, Selection, and Inheritance in Evolutionary Theories of Organization', in J. V. Singh (ed.), *Organizational Evolution: New Directions*. London: Sage, 53–77.

Wixforth, H. (1995). *Banken und Schwerindustrie in der Weimarer Republik*. Cologne: Böhlau.

Yamamura, K. (1997). 'Entrepreneurship, Ownership, and Management in Japan', in K. Yamamura (ed.), *The Economic Emergence of Modern Japan*. Cambridge: Cambridge University Press, 294–352.

Yates, J. (1989). *Control through Communication: The Rise of System in American Management*. Baltimore: Johns Hopkins University Press.

Zaleznik, A. (1992). 'Managers and Leaders: Are They Different?' *Harvard Business Review*, 70/2: 126–35.

PART II

EXTERNAL TRIGGERS FOR LEARNING

Introduction

As explored in Part I, organizational learning is grounded in a wide range of social science disciplines. Just as the theoretical foundations are diverse, so are the factors that stimulate learning. The chapters in this part are all manifestations of a common theme: that fundamental changes in society are linked to a shift in socioeconomic values. Each of the authors in this part explore how value changes are mediated through social and environmental movements, political transformations, markets, and technological visions to influence organizational learning. These changes or discontinuities in existing patterns in the environment can be perceived as either opportunities or threats and can thereby stimulate different responses within organizations.

The first contribution, by von Rosenstiel and Koch, sets the tone for the section by discussing how socioeconomic values trigger organizational learning. Drawing on a wide range of surveys conducted over time, the authors analyze how the emergence of new value systems stimulates changes in the perceptions, views, and behaviors of organizations. They conclude that the traditional values associated with industrialization have merged with the new 'postindustrial' values, which mirror the 'post-modern' and 'neocapitalistic views' of the world. Values such as personal responsibility and self-development have emerged and placed new pressures and demands on organizations. The spread of postmodern values has been accompanied by an even greater trend toward value pluralization. The authors suggest that organizations seeking to enhance their ability to address these changes must concentrate on their ability to perceive change and integrate learning into their organization. That focus calls for organizations to place the willingness to learn very high among their core values.

Social movements and interest groups also mediate value change in modern societies. The chapter by Kädtler deals with the relation between social movements, organizational crisis, and organizational learning. He describes the emergence of three different movements, highlighting the strategies, the issues, and the general ability of social movements to cause organizational crisis. The argument that emerges from his examples is that social movements, because they are located outside the institutionalized values and procedures of the organization, often create tensions between the internal and external environment. To reconcile these differences, organizations must establish new priorities and cognitive frameworks to insure the social legitimacy of individual and collective actions.

Kädtler concludes that organizations thereby learn and develop new competencies.

The chapter by Merkens, Geppert, and Antal examines organizational learning in the changing economic contexts and cultures that have resulted from the dramatic sociopolitical and economic transformations in central and eastern Europe. Their analysis focuses on the stimuli that have triggered these transformation processes and the learning that has developed as a result of profound changes in the environment. They provide examples of the variety of organizations that face the challenge of internalizing new structures, processes, and behaviors in order to operate successfully under new and unfamiliar conditions. Learning by imitation has been the most frequent initial response and often the preferred strategy. However, as the examples indicate, imitation learning seldom results in success. The eventual failure of this strategy, in combination with other factors such as human resources, the available knowledge base, and time, significantly influences learning. The authors further suggest that the probability of successful processes of learning and reorganizing increases if a company first undergoes a period of disorganizing, which offers the organization the opportunity to understand the inner dynamics of synthesizing past experiences with current demands.

The pace of change in markets and the multiple developments occurring simultaneously in many industries around the world expose organizations to an overwhelming number of signals, all representing potential triggers for learning. The speed and depth of change in markets manifest themselves in reconfigured industry boundaries, the emergence of new competitors, and the erosion of traditional client bases. Information overload and organizational inertia are two key barriers to be overcome if organizations are to learn from markets. Stopford points out that it is impossible to respond to all the many changes that present themselves, so it is crucial for organizations to be able to distinguish between those market signals that require attention and those that can be ignored. He proposes an analytical framework based on the concept of strategy as guided evolution, whereby the organization's leadership plays a key role in shaping the destiny of the enterprise. Stopford stresses that management, when it selects the environment signals that the organization should respond to and learn from, it fulfills a critical sense-making function for the organization. To illustrate dimensions of his framework, he draws on a rich variety of examples ranging from Apple, Xerox, and Royal Dutch/Shell to the Scottish knitwear industry.

The contribution by Dierkes, Marz, and Teele focuses on the role of overarching and organizational visions of technology and on the introduction of new system-related technologies as triggers to organizational learning. The chapter links the three classical forms of learning—single-loop learning, double-loop learning, and deutero-learning—to changes in over-all technological visions and related technological developments. Using three case studies, the authors conclude that, as technological developments become more complex, organizations are confronted with the need to change their underlying organizational visions to increase their emphasis on learning. They argue that new and more advanced learning strategies are needed so that changes in overarching technological visions and in the potential of their technologies can be responded to and incorporated into current organizational visions. The authors highlight, in particular, the increasing importance of deutero-learning within organizations. This learning strategy, they suggest, will be a key to ensuring the survival and growth of an organization in the face of increasing globalization and technological competition.

Each author in this section stresses that an organization's response to external triggers to learning is based on the ability of an organization to recognize and make sense of the complex interrelations between the organization and its environment. As Stopford points out, organizations are not inert, and members, particularly senior and middle managers, can take an active role in perceiving and adapting to external changes, thereby triggering learning. Learning is most effective when leaders take a proactive stance and meld the existing culture and processes of the organization into those of the new environment, thereby creating a sense of stability in the midst of the rapid and profound changes in the environment. However, all the authors in the handbook illustrate that the existing culture and social construct of an organization often predetermines its response to change. Organizational visions are part of this construct and can thus be an important factor contributing to or hindering an organization's ability to learn. The task of organizational leaders is thus to create an internal environment conducive to learning. One should also remember, as Kädtler and many other authors point out, that organizations have the choice not to change, even despite heavy external pressures. The decision not to change may also be associated with high learning and great awareness.

8   Change in Socioeconomic Values as a Trigger of Organizational Learning

Lutz von Rosenstiel and Stefan Koch

Organizational learning is a vital process by which organizations adapt to change in their social, political, or economic setting. Organizational learning triggered by a shift in socioeconomic values constitutes a special case of such change. Learning can be considered at two levels: as direct behavioral adaptation and as the development of general strategies of learning and adaptation (Argyris and Schön 1978). This chapter is focused on a particular process of organizational learning, one characterized by value change, a phenomenon that requires adaptation. Because processes of learning and adaptation to the environment also result in a change in the organization as a system (Gherardi and Nicolini, Ch. 2 in this volume), we take a look at specific implications that value change has for an organization's strategies of adaptation and its culture. However, our description of the special process is not to be interpreted as a normative concept for a learning organization (Easterby-Smith 1997).

Integral elements of this process are the change in a society's socioeconomic values, the interface between society and the organization, and the processes of change and learning within the organization. These three main elements can be arranged as shown in Figure 8.1.

For several decades many industrialized societies have been witnessing a shift in the socioeconomic values of the population in general. This value change involves the interfaces between the organization and its environment, through which the manifestations of value change enter the organization or can be perceived by it if the proper 'perceptual organs' are activated. By perceptual organs we mean the functions or areas of the organization that have an identifiable interface with the environment. Ultimately, some of the change processes

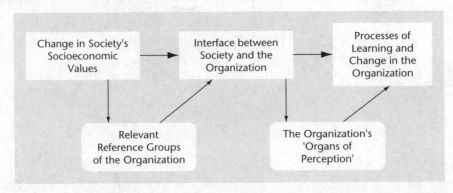

Fig. 8.1. Process model of organizational learning as a result of changing values

triggered in the organization are responses to the phenomena of value change that have become manifest at the interfaces. These processes can be interpreted as adaptation or organizational learning.

The chapter is organized around the distinction between these three main elements. The first section deals with values and value change. In the second section ways in which organizations can be receptive to value change are examined. The final section presents areas in which learning processes can take place in the organization.

Socioeconomic Values and Change in Them

One can generally assume that different cultures and societies are characterized by mutable socioeconomic values that underlie the actions of people and of their political and economic institutions (Gensicke 1999; Inglehart 1997; Klages 1984, 1999; Klages, Hippler, and Herbert, 1992; Klages and Kmieciak 1984; Noelle-Neumann 1978; Rosenstiel, Djarrahzadeh, Einsiedler, and Streich 1993). A society's values are therefore both a guide for action and a visible expression of that society's culture. But what is meant by 'values', what is value change, and what is their relevance to the behavior of individuals and organizations?

Toward a Definition of Values and Their Behavioral Relevance

Building on earlier approaches (Allport, Vernon, and Lindzey 1960; Kluckhohn 1951; Lewin 1951; Spranger 1924), Rokeach (1973) established values as a main concept of social science. We follow his approach in defining values as concepts or convictions that pertain to desirable behavior or objectives (Feather 1990, 1996; Schwartz 1996; Schwartz and Bilsky 1990; Trommsdorff 1996). In a further step, values can be interpreted as conscious, cognitive representations of universal human needs

(Schwartz and Bilsky 1990). As a general concept, values are not linked to specific situations and events but rather are crystallized in attitudes toward certain objects. Such crystallization occurs, for example, when a person devoted to the abstract value of freedom has to decide between pursuing a secure career as a civil servant and becoming an entrepreneur. In discretionary situations, values determine the selection and assessment of alternatives for action. They may be thought of as 'internal guiding factors of human behavior' (Klages 1984, our translation). Values not only guide individuals but also characterize societies. Values held in society as a whole are adopted and internalized more or less by individual people within it. Values as a social construct are therefore to be distinguished from the value orientations of individuals. Value orientations emerge through social interaction. It can be assumed that two mechanisms are involved in the individual acquisition of socioeconomic values (Mandler 1993). First, people can adopt values from their social context. Second, experiences that a person gains in the social context coalesce into a stable schema by which to look at the world. Schematized experiences thereby constitute a structural source of values indicating what is and is not compatible with the 'correct' social world (Mandler 1993).

To focus on values that really are behaviorally relevant, researchers can consider either very specific value orientations or entire clusters of values. The relation between values and behavior is presumed to be close if values are considered in domain-specific rather than general terms (Seligman and Katz 1996). In an alternative approach, values are grouped into aggregates according to thematic structure (Schwartz 1996; Schwartz and Bilsky 1990). It is assumed that action taken in a situation is determined not by individual values but by considerations of and balances between several values. If thematically related values are aggregated into types and if these types are then grouped into contrary sets, the types enable one to predict behavior more consistently than would be possible on the basis of the individual values (Schwartz 1996).

In summary, the correlations between values and behavior are weak (Kristiansen and Hotte 1996). Human behavior is affected by many factors, of which values is only one (see Figure 8.2). Volition and social norms are directly a function of values represented by a person or that person's social context. Ability and situational enablement influence action in that they are in general judged by a person subjectively before he or she decides to act. Someone favorably disposed to the value of community involvement could be prevented from showing this behavior by lack of personal confidence about being able to engage in a social activity or by failure to find an institutional setting in which to do so.

Value Change

Value change is usually taken to mean the change of average value orientations within a society over time. In research, such changes are expressed in survey results. A graphic example is the development of educational objectives in the Federal Republic of Germany from 1951 through 1995 (see Figure 8.3). The value of independence has clearly risen since the 1960s, whereas the value of obedience has declined.

The Study of Value Change: Its Relevance to Organizations

Our definition of values emphasized that values are behaviorally relevant, albeit indirectly and to a limited degree. For that reason the value orientations of groups of people who are relevant in some way to an organization will influence their behavior toward the organization. An organization's relevant reference groups consist of members or employees, customers and suppliers, and, at a more abstract level, institutions such as churches, unions, parties, consumer or environmental associations, local communities, and states (Dierkes, Hähner, and Berthoin Antal 1997). The performance of an organization's employees may differ significantly, depending on whether they are committed to such values as discipline and obedience or to personal responsibility. Similarly, the purchasing behavior of a car buyer may depend heavily on whether he or she embraces environmental protection or hedonism as a value. In groups of employees and customers, too, an aggregate shift in values will

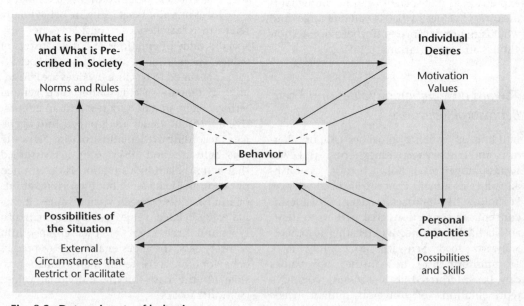

Fig. 8.2. Determinants of behavior

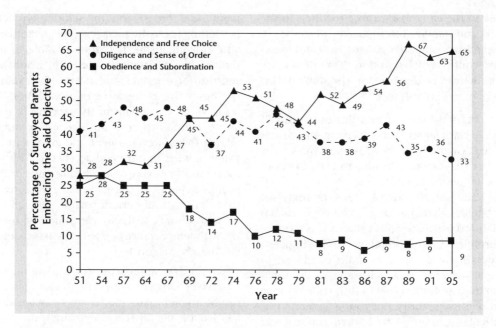

Fig. 8.3. Child-rearing objectives of parents in the Federal Republic of Germany, 1951–1995

Based on Klages 1999: 1–20.

follow in the wake of a macrosocial change in values, resulting in the possibility of systematic rather than just isolated appearance of the effects described above. The examples show two major ports of entry for value change in organizations: the demands of the market and the needs of the members.

The Study of Value Change

Values are an abstraction; they cannot be observed directly. They have to be inferred from indicators. Such indicators can be (a) observable human behavior, (b) human artifacts, or (c) verbal statements by persons about their value orientations. A society's religiosity, for instance, can be manifested in the frequency of church attendance (behavior), the construction of churches (artifacts), or the percentage of people who, when asked, say that they believe in God (verbal statements). Research on value change is generally confined to the third kind of indicator—data from surveys. In surveys, respondents are requested either to rank statements about values in some way (Rokeach 1973; Ingelhart 1990) or to rate their degree of agree-

ment with those statements (see Klages 1984). These surveys always provide statements about aggregates of persons, that is, a cross-section of society or particular subgroups. These subgroups are differentiated according to simultaneously gathered sociodemographic information, such as age, education, or social status. In order to study value change, researchers repeat the surveys at intervals of several years, but not with the same respondents. Known as trend studies, these surveys each involve a representative sample of the population. In this context, then, value change always refers to a change of value orientation in a society's population in general, not to changes among individuals (Trommsdorff 1996). There has been little research on the latter changes; past research has indicated that they only occur relatively infrequently and under extreme circumstances (Mandler 1993).

Value Change in Industrialized Cultures

The phenomenon of value change was originally observed in the countries of western Europe and North America. This value change arose in the early 1960s, came to a halt in the 1970s, and stabilized in the 1980s (Klages 1984). Research on value change has a long and somewhat controversial tradition. Three basic approaches can be discerned in the study of this phenomenon (Barth 1998).

1. Loss of values. The meaning of traditional middle-class values of achievement and virtues rooted essentially in the Protestant work ethic is said to have eroded, leading to a lack of values (Noelle-Neumann 1978).

2. Value substitution. As stated by Inglehart (1977, 1990), there has been a change from materialist to postmaterialist values, or, as recently reformulated, from modern to postmodern values (Inglehart 1997). In studies conducted in several Western democracies, researchers began with the assumption that in times of economic and political security the young generation is particularly oriented to higher, nonmaterial values in the sense meant by Maslow (1954). It was shown that postmaterialist values as conceived by Inglehart (1977, 1990, 1997)—such as beautification of the environment or increased grass-roots participation in decision-making—were spreading especially among younger generations at the expense of materialist values (such as economic growth, economic security, and law and order), which were gradually being replaced in society at large (Inglehart 1977, 1990, 1997). However, this approach is subject to the limitation that value change, for methodological reasons, can only be ascertained unidimensionally—in terms of materialism versus postmaterialism. Serious methodological objections (Klages 1992; Witte 1996) have challenged the usefulness of results indicating a change to postmaterialist values.

3. Bidimensional value space. Values research confined to the Federal Republic of Germany has provided nuanced insights (Gensicke 1999; Klages 1984; Klages, Hippler, and Herbert 1992) because a two-dimensional value space has been studied. The objective of this approach consists in ascertaining a population's entire spectrum of values. Two dimensions, or groups, of values are differentiated: (a) duty and acceptance (e.g. discipline, obedience, achieve-ment, and order) and (b) self-development (including idealistic social critique, hedonism, and individualism). It is thus possible to describe a loss of values (in both dimensions), a substitution of values, and a synthesis of values (crosses between the two groups of values). In terms of postmaterialism, this approach, too, led to identification of an increase in values related to self-development and a decrease in values related to duty and acceptance (Klages 1984). Another expression of value shifts in the Federal Republic of Germany since the 1950s is the fact that the importance of independence as an educational goal has continuously risen, while the importance of obedience has steadily declined (see Figure 8.3).

There are two approaches for explaining the observed change in values (Barth 1998). First, it can be argued that a higher level of education has led people to turn increasingly to post-materialist values of self-development. As the level of education rises, these values grow in the population. The second line of argumentation is that increasing affluence awakens other, nonmaterial needs in people (Inglehart 1977). This 'elevator effect' (Beck 1986; Schnierer 1996), according to which society at large has raised its level of prosperity, serves to explain increasing individualism in society. Both explanations can be interpreted to mean that members of the young generation in particular serve as the vehicle of value change, profit from a high level of education, and acquire their value orientations under affluent conditions. With older, materially minded generations dying off at the same time, this up and coming generation is bringing about a shift in the demographic average.

Findings from the 1990s

Recent results of research in Germany, for example, give a complex and varied picture of current value change. In the 1990s the classic polarity between groups with conventional, traditional values and groups with values of individualism and self-development was bridged by the emergence of populations incorporating both camps (Gensicke 1999;

Herbert 1993). In addition, there crystallized a third important group of values consisting in a combination of hedonism and materialism that has united heretofore seemingly irreconcilable elements of the two original groups. The population group with these values—people known as hedomaterialists—has grown considerably since the 1980s, especially because it is much more prominent among the younger generations than the older ones (Gensicke 1998; see Table 8.1). Another strong group, accounting for more than one-third of the population, is called the realists. They are committed equally to all three sets of values and likewise transcend the old polarity.

This development is striking, first, for the fact that material values are regaining acceptance. It seems to reflect the rise of the Yuppies and the turn toward luxury that began in the 1980s (Dierkes, Hätiner, and Berthoin Antal 1997). Moreover, the change and pluralization of value structures has sparked growth in the diversity of population groups with dissimilar patterns of value orientations. The clearest example of the change in the context of values is that hedonistic and meritocratic values have meanwhile come to coexist in some population groups. That is, both enjoyment and discipline are highly regarded (Meulemann 1996). Additionally, change in socioeconomic values seems to reflect an increased need for personal autonomy and the linkage between initiative and meaningful, intrinsically motivating activities, not least in working life (Klages 1999). These facts are consistent with forecasts about development in the world of work (Opaschowski 1997). The general trend is expressed by the occurrence a key basic value that can be related to future social challenges: personal responsibility (Gensicke 1998; Klages 1999). Personal responsibility combines the individualistic element of self-determination with the individual's responsibility for his or her own actions in the social context. Current society reserves a special place for personal responsibility as a value providing the foundation of self-determined initiative and civic commitment (Klages 1999).

Value change outside industrialized cultures

Other phenomena analogous to value change have been studied worldwide, with The World Value Survey, for instance, now covering forty-three societies (Inglehart 1997). The results show

Table 8.1. Development of types of values in West Germany, 1987/1988–1997 (in percentages)

	Conventionalists	Resigned	Realists	Hedomaterialists	Idealists
All respondents					
1987/88	25	14	30	14	17
1990	20	14	32	15	19
1993	17	15	33	18	17
1997	18	16	36	14	16
18–30-year-olds					
1987/88	14	13	30	18	25
1990	9	13	29	23	26
1993	10	10	34	31	15
1997	7	15	38	22	18

Source: Based on Gensicke 1998.

a substitution of postmaterialist for materialist values not only in the eight western European states studied but also in the United States, Japan, eastern Europe, and many other countries. Only two countries, India and Nigeria, have shown no shift toward postmaterialist values among the young generations. These changes occur at very different levels of postmaterialist value orientations, with affluent states (especially in western Europe and North America) achieving the highest levels. By contrast, the higher the rate of economic growth in a country, the greater the value shift, with South Korea being the leading example (Inglehart 1997). The dimension of materialism is also bound up with orientations relating to politics, religion, and sexual norms, areas of life in which a global shift toward liberal, postmodern values is taking place (Inglehart 1997).

However, methodological doubts have been raised about comparative study of values and value change across different cultures. If values are regarded as culture specific, then situational analysis is required in order to arrive at useful, comparative results (Schwartz and Bilsky 1990; Trommsdorff 1996). For example, one may find equally high levels of consensus on an abstract value such as justice in two cultures. Assessed in a specific situation, however, justice could in one culture be taken to mean distributional justice (to each an equal share) as opposed to input justice (to each according to his or her performance; Trommsdorff 1996). Comparing values and value change on the basis of specific situations yields far more cautious statements about value shift in other cultures. Other difficulties lurk as well. For example, individualist values play a larger role in Europe than in Asia, but in certain situations people in Asia are oriented to both very different kinds of values (Ralston, Egri, Steward, Terpstra, and Yu 1999; Trommsdorf 1996). Lastly, the assessment of values is influenced by the very language in which they are formulated (Ralston, Cunniff, and Gustafson 1995).

Value Change and Political Upheaval

Recent findings reveal a number of things about value change associated with radical sociopolitical change, such as the collapse of the socialist system in the former German Democratic Republic (GDR) and other eastern European countries. In the wake of modernization after World War II, the GDR underwent a value change similar to that experienced in other industrialized states (Gensicke 1995a, b; 1996). The population responded to the surge of hedonistic and materialist values in the late 1980s by turning away from the socialist system (Gensicke 1995b). This aspect of the value change preceding the collapse of the East German state was observable among young members of society by at least 1975 (Friedrich 1990; Gensicke 1992). In short, the political developments were heralded by a value change in the young generation. No major shifts in values have occurred since German unification (Gensicke 1996, 1999). Instead, the value structures in the eastern and western parts of the country have largely merged.

A second nation whose twentieth-century history has been marked by great sociopolitical upheaval is China, which continues to undergo change associated with modernization and the process of opening up to the Western, capitalist economic system (Ralston et al. 1999; Ralston, Gustafson, Terpstra, and Holt 1995). China's experience is similar to that of former GDR in that this change is accompanied by significant differences between the value orientations of successive generations (Ralston et al. 1999). The youngest generation of Chinese managers, for example, is clearly more given to individualist values than older generations are. Conversely, commitment to collectivist and traditional Chinese values is declining generation by generation.

Interfaces between the Organization and Macrosocial Change in Values

In the preceding section the phenomenon of value change was described, and the reference groups through which this phenomenon passes into the organization were identified.

There lie the interfaces between the organization and society at large, or between the system and its environment (see Figure 8.1). These interfaces have to be permeable in order for the phenomenon to be perceived and further processed within the organization, where it can trigger processes of adaptation. The system must not be a closed one. Hence the question about the organization's mechanisms and structures behind the interfaces—or, metaphorically, the organization's organs of perception at the interface with value change—that pass on information and thereby trigger learning processes (Berthoin Antal, Dierkes, and Hähner 1997; see Table 8.2). Information about the socioeconomic environment can come from an organization's internal sources (employees) or from external sources such as customers, suppliers, publications, or institutions. More important, however, is whether information is internally accessible. Information from customers as a source can be internally accessible through orders, complaints, and similar channels. Other external sources such as mass media, as reflected by the organization's employees, are also available to some extent. All these sources can be used unsystematically (say, on the initiative of individuals) or systematically (through the creation of special functions).

Initiatives of Individuals

Anecdotes about individuals who recognize changes in society in a timely fashion and respond accordingly usually refer to the type of person embodied by the far-sighted entrepreneur or board member (Neuberger and Kompa

1987; Sadler, Ch. 18 in this volume). Such figures have become rare in modern management culture, particularly because managers adopt a rather short-term perspective in the name of self-optimization rather than consider the long-term development of the company (Freimuth 1997; Rosenstiel and Kaschube 1999). Systems theory—according to which the individual has less influence than the inertia of the organization as a system, which maintains the status quo (Neuberger 1995)—has further demystified the legend that charismatic leaders have major impacts on organizations. Organizational learning is shaped to an important degree by an appropriate culture of leadership, not only by singular leaders (Sadler, Ch. 18 in this volume). If the task of perceiving changes in the environment is left to the initiative of individuals within the organization, it is in general likely to be undertaken only unsystematically and rather randomly.

In any case, fresh ideas and perspectives different from mainstream thinking can also be brought in by people occupying less prominent positions than charismatic leaders do. Such people can act as engines of change (Freimuth 1997), of whom three types are distinguishable. 'Intrapreneurs' are dogged and daring in their use of discretionary latitude within organizations in order to achieve their visionary ideas of innovation against manifold economic and political resistance (Pinchot 1985). 'Brain workers' have the intellectual ability to think in interdisciplinary, integrative, and future-oriented ways. They are able to argue successfully for the decisions that have to be made in the complex issues involved. With their visions and insights, both intrapreneurs and

Table 8.2. Perceptual organs of an organization at the interface with change in a society's socioeconomic values

	Internally available sources	External sources
Unsystematic perception	Initiatives of individuals	Cooperation with external partners
Systematic perception	Knowledge management	Institutionalization of perceptional functions

brain workers are predisposed to reflect value changes in society. In this context, however, the most interesting group is the 'gatekeepers' (Berthoin Antal 1992; Freimuth 1997). They have strong contacts to the organization's environment, particularly to key developments and discussions, and have internal communicational competencies not only for being a source of initiative for change but also for making such initiatives 'digestible' for the organization.

The individuals described thus far are often complemented by others filling the roles of mentors or godfathers, who support the non-mainstream thinker (Witte 1973), protecting him or her from internal resistance (Freimuth 1997). According to Dierkes and Raske (1994), one can distinguish between two organizational learning forms and constellations of people to fulfill the function of organs of perception in each firm. In the first learning form, top managers and their closest associates are responsible for initiating change. In the second learning form, learning from outside the mainstream occurs through the complementary roles of high-ranking sponsors and champions who are located lower in the organization (Berthoin Antal 1992; Berthoin Antal, Dierkes, and Hähner 1997). The likelihood that personal initiative will be taken to disseminate new ideas and values increases when the organization offers a supportive environment and fosters people who think differently. Boundary-spanning functions of organizations, such as departments for human resource development, also play an important role because they have decisive influence over whether people outside the mainstream will be recruited into the company.

Example 1. An example illustrates how personnel selection can enable or limit the entry of nonmainstream thinkers into the company. In the 1980s a young physicist with excellent qualifications, the garb of a guru's disciple, and close ties to Germany's environmental party applied for a job at Volkswagen (VW AG). The personnel officers did not know what to make of him. Finally, he was sent to the management board member responsible for quality, which plainly recommended that the applicant be hired because highly qualified, 'unusual' types of people were welcome and because the company had to learn what was being thought and done outside.

Cooperation with External People and Institutions

In addition to hiring nonmainstream types of people, companies can also learn through frequent cooperation with external people whose potential knowledge and experience diverges from that of the average members of the organization. Such people are hence able to bring to the organization external competence pertaining to phenomena of value change. The principle behind this approach of cooperating with external people is that they are outsiders but nevertheless know and understand at least the basic characteristics of the organization (Berthoin Antal, Dierkes, and Hähner 1997). The most important persons and institutions that come to mind in this context are universities, research institutes, federations of economic associations, and business consulting companies. In example 3 (see p. 212), we describe a company's cooperation with scientists in the marketing area. Probably the most frequent case is that organizations contract business consulting services. On the whole, one can assume that these corporate contacts with external institutions improve the company's perception of such relevant topics as value change (Dierkes, Hähner, and Berthoin Antal 1997). Another, more systematic form of cooperation is to build up external networks with other organizations and institutions (Berthoin Antal 1992).

Knowledge Management

In the context of this chapter, an interesting topic is the systematic development and use of the organization's available internal knowledge (Davenport and Prusak 1998; Nonaka and Takeuchi 1995; Nonaka, Reinmöller, and

Toyama, Ch. 37 in this volume) about societal values that diverge from the operative values within the organization and of knowledge from which these values can at least be inferred. In principle, company employees have knowledge about relevant values in society because they themselves are citizens of it. However, it is solely through selection processes that the value orientations of the employees are likely to diverge from those of the population at large. Especially in successful companies that are able to recruit their young managers from elites, the problem sometimes arises that the management has little feeling for the broad reality in society.

Consequently, implicit knowledge about valid socioeconomic values is represented less by management than by ordinary employees. The functions of boundary-spanning between the organization and the environment are automatically performed also by groups of employees who have direct contact with the customers, as in the areas of sales and service (Berthoin Antal 1992; Meyer and Ertl 1998). In many major companies there are employees in customer service whose daily experience exposes them far more than the board to the faults that the average customer finds with the company's products. Because these employees are frequently not asked, however, the board may make decisions that fail to respond to the needs and value orientations of the customers. The task of managing knowledge consists in gathering and structuring this knowledge and making it available as a basis for decisions in the company. Communication between employees and management takes place, for example, through internal marketing (Meyer and Ertl 1998).

Instruments designed to facilitate the development of new knowledge and recognition of new developments can be an additional component of knowledge management (Koch and Mandl 1999; Pawlowsky, Forslin, and Reinhardt, Ch. 35 in this volume). These instruments include workshops with young, innovative groups of employees who are trying to grasp and anticipate contemporary developments of values in society. A particularly

systematic instrument is the scenario technique (Galer and van der Heijden, Ch. 38 in this volume; Preissler, Roehl, and Seemann 1997). Experts from different corporate areas come together in workshops to design model worlds of the future and play through the impacts that possible developments may have on the company (Preissler, Roehl, and Seemann 1997). Lastly, early warning systems for detecting signs of impending changes can be developed on the basis of models used in economics (Bach and Homp 1998). The objective of all the instruments mentioned above is to provide the knowledge necessary for strategic decision-making by corporate management.

Institutionalization of Perceptual Functions

An increasing number of companies are establishing offices for scanning political and social developments and positioning the company in its environment. These offices represent as it were the institutionalized ability of organizations to perceive changes in their political and social environments. In the earlier section on the initiatives of individuals, we described the function of the gatekeeper, who has good contacts to the company's environment and communicates its demands inside the company (Freimuth 1997). This informal function of boundary-spanning personnel may be defined as an explicit responsibility (Berthoin Antal 1992). Establishment of an office for public affairs (Post, Murray, Dickie, and Mahon 1983; Wood 1991) as an institutionalized interface with society has been on the rise in Europe since the 1980s, following the experience of companies in the United States. The two most important activities in this area are issues management and stakeholder management, that is, the response to political and social matters and to interest groups relevant to the activity of the organization (Greening and Gray 1994; Wood 1991). As a result, functions that often used to be performed partly by generalists in the corporate management are transferred to specialists. Increasingly, political and social competence is being acquired from outside the company. For example, at least two German companies now have executive policy departments headed by former senior politicians. The high priority accorded these functions in the company is a further condition for perceiving and responding to social demands such as value change (Dierkes, Hähner, and Berthoin Antal 1997).

Example 2. The purpose of this example is to outline the activity of a public-affairs department that reports directly to the policy officer on the board of BMW. The department is described as having the task of communicating policy and shaping the company's corporate social responsibility. The activity consists in working with a variety of external information sources: reviewing press and other media, specialized congresses, and legislation and cultivating contacts with political parties, parliament, national economic institutes, the World Bank, Greenpeace, and other institutions. The department commissions its own trend studies. The department also has access to governmental networks and other special contacts. By presenting company positions in forums that tend to be critical of business (schools, universities, and church conventions), the public affairs department actively seeks critical feedback in order to adjust its positions to social currents.

Ascertained in this manner, the relevance of political and social issues is communicated to the company along a variety of channels. Every two months the department brings out a bulletin that spells out the positions of the company (and the works council) on current topics—a publication that circulates widely within the organization. Lastly, the department writes speeches and prepares documents for the board and is consulted on relevant subjects during the decision-making process. The success of the work by the public affairs department is reflected in new company initiatives and activities pertaining to environmental issues, management culture, and sales-areas in which value orientations are especially pronounced.

Company-specific Impacts on the Faculty of Perception

Several factors of the perception of value change differ from one organization to the next. One factor is the variable degree to which companies feel the external impacts of changes in values. For example, a manufacturer of environmentally damaging products can be particularly affected by changes in the environmental values of its customers. On the other hand, companies can differ in the internal effectiveness and preferred uses of certain interfaces for perceiving change and their receptiveness to it. One corporate area in which these differences are felt is issues management. Differences in this area can be due to the size of the organization, with large companies addressing this topic more actively than small and medium-sized companies (Berthoin Antal 1992; Greening and Gray 1994); to the management's commitment to the particular issue; and to external pressure.

Apart from the question of which interfaces are entailed, Dierkes, Hähner, and Berthoin Antal (1997) and Berthoin Antal, Dierkes, and Hähner (1994, 1997) studied how a major German chemical company responded over several decades to socioculturally related value changes in its environment. They documented that corporate culture had an influence on whether the company took up topical sociocultural issues of its environment and integrated them into its own culture. The company accommodated social changes if they overlapped thematically with several traditional elements of its corporate culture. If no such overlap existed, or if corresponding elements of the corporate culture were still weak, the company did not perceive the social changes. As long as the corporate social policy toward the employees continued to promote traditional family structures, the company only dimly perceived the change in the value attached to equal opportunity for men and women. It was important, too, that the substance and language, line of reasoning, or perspective of public discourse about issues of the day had to fit the organization's perceptual schema (Dierkes, Hähner, and

Berthoin Antal 1997). For example, the chemical company had always conscientiously provided for the social welfare of its employees but nonetheless ignored the issue of drug abuse as long as it was publicly discussed as a phenomenon of adolescent fringe groups. So defined, the subject had no obvious relevance for the firm and its point of view. When drug abuse was redefined in public discussion as an illness, however, the company responded rather quickly, in keeping with its generally high sensitivity in the field of health policy.

Processes of Change and Learning within the Organization as a Result of Changes in Values

Change in the socioeconomic values held in a given social context can result in an actual or impending discrepancy between the action of an organization and the demands of its environment. The actions of organizations are oriented to theories that have developed over time and that serve as a source for certain expectations of what it takes to run a successful business. Constant comparison between these expectations and daily experience makes the discrepancies apparent. In particular, they are likely to surface in comparisons between a theory-in-use and an espoused theory (Argyris and Schön 1978). For example, an organization's espoused theory could be that customer loyalty is won by means of good value for the money. In reality, however, many dissatisfied customers are held onto by means of discounts. Experience shows that customers who go elsewhere are dissatisfied with the quality, say, because they are more interested in quality than in quantity. Awareness of such discrepancies is brought into the organization first by individuals, and it then spreads by means of changes in cognitive concepts within the company, especially its management (Argyris and Schön 1978; Dixon 1994). Through a process of organizational learning, the theory-in-use—and hence the range of organizational

behavior that is possible—changes with the acquired knowledge (Huber 1991).

Socioeconomic values may be discrepant at two levels. First, there is the possibility that the values cherished within the organization diverge from those outside it. Second, the organization's concept of values held by reference groups, which is at the center of the organization's behavior and strategy, may not coincide with the values to which these groups are actually oriented. In that case, knowledge about the values relevant to society is lacking. Analogously, two approaches to organizational learning are possible, and they start at different levels. Organizational learning is oriented either to the organization's cherished values and changes in them or to the necessary knowledge about society's values, its acquisition, and its application (Sinkula, Baker, and Noordewier 1997). Accordingly, the first of the four following sections is about corporate culture, which provides both the mooring for the values of the organization and the necessary context for all processes of organizational learning. The subsequent three sections each deal with the reference groups whose value orientations are brought into the organization by virtue of membership, commercial relations, and social responsibility or interests: employees, customers, and social groups.

Corporate Culture

Corporate culture is a concept incorporating a number of facets, among them the level of conscious values shared by the vast majority of the organization's members (Schein 1985, 1990). Socioeconomic values are not identical with the spectrum of values that makes up corporate culture and that also includes norms and ideologies (Kaschube 1993), but they do constitute part of it. Because corporate cultures are rooted in a consensus on values, they are directly affected by value change. That consensus is reduced or threatened by divergence between the values passed down within the organization and the values that have changed in the society surrounding it but that are partly represented by the members of the organization. If the corporate culture is interpreted as an intersection between the values of corporate management and those of the employees, changing values are almost bound to trigger a process of change in the culture. The changes proceed very slowly because the members of an organization are rarely aware of the culture's implicit assumptions and values, and, therefore, they do not perceive any need for change at the organizational level. Changes in values within an organization are scarcely detectable over the course of a few years (Kabanoff and Holt 1996), so there are rarely abrupt changes in the organization's policies or action (Berthoin Antal, Dierkes, and Hähner 1997). Given this lack of sensitivity, the action of companies is frequently based not on their perception but on pressure from customers or employees to adapt the company's values to reality outside the organization (Dierkes, Hähner, and Berthoin Antal 1997).

Corporate cultures, or internal values, can be changed intentionally in order to consolidate or rejuvenate an organization's internal consensus on values. From this functionalist perspective, organizational culture serves the coordination of objectives and the integration and motivation of employees. The conscious development of a company's values and norms in keeping with changes in society as a whole (Barth 1998) appears to be useful because classical value change seems to foster the normative as opposed to the utilitarian organization. The latter type are classical business organizations and rest on the continuance commitment (Meyer and Allen 1997) of their members, who are tied to the organization by means of reward or remuneration (Etzioni 1975). By contrast, normative organizations, as embodied, for example, by religious communities and political parties, have 'morally' involved members, who are bound together by shared values. Most findings on value change indicate that many people have high regard for activities that they can define themselves and that they feel to be purposeful. This fact stems from the increasing significance of postmaterialist values (Inglehart 1997) or values centered on self-development

(Klages 1999). Such desires can be realized in an organization that respects the values of the members, forges a consensus with them, and normatively binds them to the organization by giving them responsibility for achieving its objectives. Instrumentally rational, merit-based organizations are increasingly finding themselves faced with the demand to make the purpose, conditions, and consequences of achievement transparent (Fürstenberg 1995).

However, is the normative organization suited to dealing with value change? Barth (1998) argued that the findings in the 1990s show a stronger trend toward a pluralization of values than toward a general spread of postmaterialism or self-development values (Gensicke 1998). This research suggests that employees bring very individual needs to the organization and prefer a flexible, continuance commitment, a desire that cannot be met by an offer of shared values (Barth 1998). Similar considerations underlie differential job design, by which alternative work structures are intended to optimize the development of different personalities (Ulich 1998). Intentional attempts at change encounter further difficulties because new cultural elements that are to be established in a company have very different chances of taking hold (Dierkes, Hähner, and Berthoin Antal 1997). Resistance to these innovations builds if existing elements of the corporate culture are ignored or contradicted. The same fate is likely, however, with elements of culture that fail to gain sufficient support from the employees. In one major German company, for instance, it was difficult to build consensus on the necessity for globalization because the employees attached great importance to working for a 'German' company (Dierkes, Hähner, and Berthoin Antal 1997).

Personnel Policy

Values transmitted over a long period in an organization and accepted as foundations of its corporate culture become embedded in artifacts and rituals. In organizations, such reified values (Rosenstiel 1984) are reflected as working arrangements, divisions of labor, production processes, and modes of control. Punctuality, hard work, modesty, and other values related to one's sense of duty and acceptance still characterize these structures and processes (Klages 1984). They now seem alien especially to freshly hired young people, whose orientations have shifted predominantly to personal responsibility and self-development as a result of changes in values (Klages 1999). Rosenstiel and Stengel (1987) showed that many people perceive a discrepancy between the goals they hold dear and the actual goals of business organizations (see Figure 8.4). Among students who were about to enter the world of work as well as among managers, there was sometimes considerable discrepancy between the ratings that they gave the goals they thought the organization should have and ratings that they gave the organization's actual goals. This discrepancy can adversely affect both the affective commitment of the organization's members (i.e. their degree of identification with and involvement in the organization) and their normative commitment (the degree of their obligation and loyalty to the organization) (Meyer and Allen 1997). Lack of commitment, in turn, reduces employee motivation and effort.

The area of personnel policy in particular has had a long tradition of coping with effects of value change. Full employment and labor shortages in the 1960s and 1970s led, especially in northern Europe, to efforts to make jobs attractive for the people who held them (Antoni 1996). Programs promoting industrial democracy (Emery and Thorsrud 1982) and the quality of work life (Rosenstiel and Weinkamm 1980) were developed in order to move away from monotonous and alienating activities performed in authoritarian structures and toward a form of work that was both meaningful to the individual and capable of permitting him or her a measure of self-development. The key component of these attempts was the introduction of semiautonomous work groups, whose participants were allowed to make their own decisions on many matters of their work. This

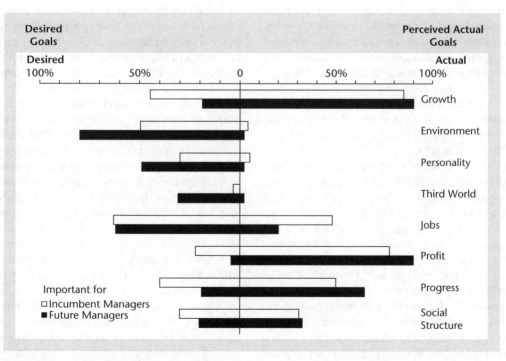

Fig. 8.4. Actual and desired goals of organizations as seen by incumbent and future managers

form of work accommodated value orientations that had in fact emerged from changes
in values at that time (Klages 1984). Although
semiautonomous group work was initially rejected for political reasons (Granel 1980), group
work and some of the demands made at that
time became established in the personnel policies of many companies (Antoni 1996).

Against this background, it seems to make
sense for organizations to use what is known
about value change in order to respond to its
impacts with appropriate personnel policies.
One attempt to deal with value change through
suitable learning processes within the company is value-oriented personnel policy at
BMW, the Bavarian automotive company
(Bihl 1993, 1995; Rosenstiel 1989). The objective
is to bring the company and its employees to a
consensus on values (see example 3, below). A
similar route is offered by what is known as
identification policy (Wunderer and Mittmann
1995). Its premise is that the effectiveness of
extrinsic, or material, incentives is limited because they do not satisfy the employees' need for
identification now that values have changed.
Suitable ways of promoting employees' identification with the company are suggested.
Designing meaningful jobs, managing relations in work groups and the corporate management, and providing a corporate culture
that means something to the individual are
important elements that are expected to influence the employee motivation (Wunderer and
Mittmann 1995).

Example 3. In the early 1980s the task of personnel policy at BMW was seen to lie in raising
employee motivation and commitment. This
task led to the concept of matching the values
that workers held in everyday life and the
values they held in the world of work. The
matching was to be accomplished by bringing
BMW's values into line with those of the population. Cooperating with external experts, the
personnel department developed relevant
areas of values. In workshops with managers,
each area was rated for the degree to which it
was represented in society, in the company, and
in personnel work. All items were referenced to
the present and the future. The results showed
that the current situation in the company and
current personnel work were associated mostly
with traditional values in society and were very
remote from society's new values. Desirable
personnel policy was often associated with the
new values.

The opportunity offered by BMW's study was
also used to experiment with the concept of
value-oriented personnel policy in the newly
constructed BMW factory. For most of the
value areas, the company decided and implemented objectives, strategies, and operation-
alizations as shown in Table 8.3 for the area
pertaining to independence and individuality.
Although the multitude of variables involved
prevent an exact calculation of the economic
effects incurred by value-oriented personnel
policies, this concept has been judged a success
at BMW (Bihl 1995). This assessment is borne
out by the benchmarks for product quality,
absenteeism, and fluctuation at the new plant.

Marketing

Increased competition and customer expectations have led to the frequently cited change
in the seller's and buyer's market in many areas
of the economy. Intense focus on customer
needs has increased the importance of market
orientation, a development reinforced by a
shift to the tertiary (service) sector of the economy (Meyer 1998; Nerdinger 1994). Service,
especially personal service, requires direct communication with customers and responses to
their expectations, wishes, and value orientations. In general, a market orientation means
development of the ability to anticipate customer needs and to improve the service one
provides to the customer. The main task of
marketing is to initiate information-processing
and base it on appropriate norms through
which a learning process can be shaped across
the entire organization (Slater and Narver 1995).
Information relevant to the market is gathered,
distributed throughout the organization, and
interpreted uniformly (Huber 1991; Sinkula
1994). External sources of this information are
market research, consultants, organizations cooperating with one's own company, and take-

Table 8.3. Value-oriented personnel policy: Example of operationalizing an area of values

Society/employees basic values	Goals	Personnel policy strategies/concepts	Instruments/measures
Independence and individuality	• Creation of personal room for maneuver and options	• Increased flexibility of additional benefits • Increased flexibility of work hours	• Cafeteria system • Part-time • Distinction between work hours/business hours • Flexitime • Flexible scheduling to bridge work between holidays • Early retirement • Alternative shift schedules
	• Fostering of independence	• Support for taking personal or joint responsibility	• Management style • Principles of delegation (assigning tasks, authority, and responsibility) • Project management, teamwork
		• System for agreeing on goals	• Employee participation in agreeing on goals
		• The right of employees to participate in decisions that affect them	• Learning workshops, quality circles • Measures for organizational development • Inclusion of employees in work-design groups

overs (Sinkula 1994). Internal sources are knowledge rooted in the company's founding, past experience, and innovations and ideas that originated in the organization.

Whereas value orientations are relatively stable, changing primarily over generations, the classical instrument of market research often has to do with the rapidly changeable opinions and attitudes only loosely associated with value orientations. If the issue being investigated is not explicitly defined in terms of research on values (see example 4, below), market research is unlikely to contribute directly to the anticipation of value change. For that purpose, it would be more helpful to analyze *existing* sources of data on this topic (desk research)

for points relevant to the organization (Meyer and Ertl 1998). For instance, increasing hedonistic values make it likely that so-called experience consumption will grow and that consumption to meet needs will decrease (Opaschowski 1997). Accordingly, the success of many companies may depend on their ability to offer consumers products that are fun to consume and not just products that they can use. Another example is the observation that a young generation of Chinese managers is relatively receptive to Western values such as individualism (Ralston *et al.* 1999). This group of persons could therefore develop into an interesting sales market for companies operating in an international context.

There are findings that document the positive effects that intensive information-processing in the marketing area has on organizational behavior on the market and that focus on implemented innovations, rapid adaptation, and relatively high awareness of customer needs and desires (Hult and Ferrell 1997; Hurley and Hult 1998; Menon, Bharadwaj, Adidam, and Edison 1999; Narver and Slater 1990; Sinkula, Baker, and Noordewier 1997). These behaviors can be interpreted as indicators of learning processes. After learning processes have been rapidly translated into competitive advantage on the market (Hurley and Hult 1998), the choice of rather quantitative indicators seems justified. Qualitative insight into market-oriented organizational learning permits the description in example 4, below. As a higher-order learning process (Argyris and Schön 1978), the recognition that product and marketing policy must anticipate value change is anchored in organizational structures and processes. In addition, basic considerations and procedures of the project were implemented for extended periods, certain procedures were institutionalized, and long-term planning of product policy was established (Grabner 1993). A company's learning ability in the marketing area depends directly on the values rooted in the corporate culture, specifically, on the value of the willingness to learn (Hurley and Hult 1998; Sinkula, Baker, and Noordewier 1997; Slater and Narver 1995). In the marketing area of organizations, with its ongoing search for new ideas and knowledge that will win customers, it can be assumed that the willingness to learn from value change is relatively high. After all, topics having especially favorable chances of being perceived by a company and of becoming part of its corporate culture are those closely associated with economic success, as is the case with questions of marketing and sales (Dierkes, Hähner, and Berthoin Antal 1997).

A variety of factors can be critical for the success of market-oriented learning processes. An excessively narrow and one-sided emphasis on short-term changes of the market is at odds with anticipation of such profound develop-

ments as value change and can be avoided by expanding the company's concept of the market (Slater and Narver 1995). A broader approach, one in which internal and interaction marketing is considered as well as traditional sales marketing, includes the processing of information supplied by employees and various stakeholders (Meyer and Ertl 1998). Organizational learning based on information-processing depends whether the right kind of information is available and whether the complexity of the environment can really be reduced (Sinkula 1994). In this case, information overload in particular could become a threat. Large companies with bureaucratic structures tend to rely on readily available information, whereas younger and smaller companies develop active search strategies (Daft and Weick 1984), patterns that can be substantiated by the behavior of managers in both types of companies (Sinkula 1994). At best, organizational learning buffers the organization from the environment by making it possible to anticipate changes and thus avoid environmental shocks, to reduce complexity, and to develop strategies of adaptation (Slater and Narver 1995).

Example 4. This example is intended to show which paths companies can take in order for their marketing to anticipate a value change. It is also an example of how companies can systematically seek out external contacts in order to enhance their ability to perceive social developments. The 'Quality Enhancement—Long-term Quality Planning' group at VW AG initiated a cooperative project with organizational psychologists. The task was to expand the concept of quality, which was understood primarily in technical terms, to include aspects of the quality experienced by the customer. Because product development takes so long in the automotive industry, another purpose of the project was to find out what the customer's automotive needs may be in twenty years. Both aspects are largely a function of customers' value orientations and their future development.

Nondirective interviews about aspects that had to do with cars, competing means of transport, and the basic context of traffic were conducted with about fifty prominent persons and experts who represented broad areas of the society and whose professions involved issues concerning the future of society and technology. Their statements were condensed and translated by the project team into demands upon future passenger cars (Volkswagen AG Qualitätsförderung 1986). This research led at that time to relatively compact cars with large, variable interiors (vans) and two-seater city cars. The suggestions were presented to VW's large product commission but were not adopted completely. Both concepts are represented on the market now, though VW was not the first manufacturer to introduce them.

Corporate Social Performance

Society has economic, legal, and ethical expectations of business organizations. Such expectations also express or are manifested in socioeconomic values (Greening and Gray 1994). Business responds to these expectations by assuming corporate social responsibility. It is expressed in the principles of the organization, its responsiveness to social demands, and its specific policies (Wood 1991). The social responsibility of a company exists at three levels (Berthoin Antal 1992; Wood 1991). First, the organization is obligated to act in the interests of its stakeholders, especially its employees, customers, and investors, to whom it owes its survival. Second, the company has a public responsibility for problems resulting from its activity, or even just relating to it. Examples are environmental impacts, transport problems, unemployment, and health damages that occur in the sphere in which the company operates. Lastly, the members of the organization must behave individually in a manner that meets standards of social responsibility.

By living up to its social responsibility and thereby adapting to the values that society and society's institutions stand for, the company tries to avoid imposition of government regulations or sanctions by other institutions (Wood 1991). An example of such regulations is the mandating of catalyzers for passenger cars, a measure introduced over the objections of the automotive industry, which refused to accept social responsibility for the noxious emissions from motorized traffic. A second example shows the damage a company can inflict upon itself if it fails to take at least credible steps to assume its social responsibility. In 1995, Greenpeace successfully waged a boycott against Shell after the oil company announced its intention to dispose of the oil-storage platform known as the *Brent Spar* by sinking it in the North Sea. The purpose behind a policy of assuming social responsibility is to initiate voluntary and anticipatory learning processes within the organization so that it will not ultimately be forced to adapt to its environment. Given the complex interrelations an organization has with its socioeconomic environment, the importance of its ability to control its own strategies is growing (Fürstenberg 1995). By reducing uncertainty and dependence on external groups, organizations try to preserve their autonomy and freedom of action (Greening and Gray 1994).

Conclusion

Generalizing from the findings discussed in this chapter, one can say that the value change occurring in nearly all countries in the wake of their modernization or industrialization is accompanied by a parallel development of organizations. In the socioeconomic area regard for conventions and authority has declined, and the value of individualism and self-development has risen. The next step has been an increasing differentiation and pluralization of people's value orientations. It is no longer possible to talk of 'the' generally accepted values. The basic tenor of developments within organizations is their increased openness toward the environment, an attitude expressed by such concepts as corporate social performance and an orientation to customers, markets, employees, and learning.

These areas are the places in which to look for organizational learning that is triggered by value change. Organizations have discovered and emancipated their relevant reference groups and are trying to open themselves to a broadened range of values and interests that they perceive in their environment. When interacting with the outside world, organizations are relying less on conventional and statutory structures than on the dynamic balance between needs and interests (McLean Parks and Kidder 1994; Rousseau 1997), adapting, for example, by means of flexible working hours and cooperation with other organizations. A visible sign of this development is the fact that the learning organization has been established as a normative vision, as 'an organization skilled at creating, acquiring, and transferring knowledge, and at modifying its behavior to reflect new knowledge and insights' (Garvin 1993: 80). The success of such organizations is attributed to their ability to continue change in a pluralistic environment and to pursue a degree of organizational self-development. The gap between the Taylorist concept of the disciplined and perfectly functioning organization and the idea of a learning organization clearly reflects the change in values of society as a whole.

References

Allport, G. W., Vernon, P. E., and Lindzey, G. (1960). *A Study of Values*. Boston: Houghton Mifflin.

Antoni, C. (1996). *Teilautonome Arbeitsgruppen: Ein Königsweg zu mehr Produktivität und einer menschengerechteren Arbeit?* Weinheim: Psychologie Verlags Union.

Argyris, C. and Schön, D. A. (1978). *Organizational Learning: A Theory of Action Perspective*. Reading, Mass.: Addison-Wesley.

Bach, N. and Homp, C. (1998). 'Objekte und Instrumente des Wissensmanagements'. *Zeitschrift Führung + Organisation*, 67/3: 139–46.

Barth, M. (1998). *Unternehmen im Wertewandel*. Konstanz: Hartung-Gorre.

Beck, U. (1986). *Risikogesellschaft: Auf dem Weg in eine andere Moderne*. Frankfurt am Main: Suhrkamp.

Berthoin Antal, A. (1992). *Corporate Social Performance: Rediscovering Actors in Their Organizational Contexts*. New York: Campus.

——Dierkes, M., and Hähner, K. (1994). 'Business in Society: Perceptions and Principles in Organizational Learning'. *Journal of General Management*, 20/2: 55–77.

————(1997). 'Business Perception of Contextual Change: Sources and Impediments to Organizational Learning'. *Business and Society*, 36: 387–407.

Bihl, G. (1993). 'Unternehmen und Wertewandel: Wie lauten die Antworten für die Personalführung?' in L. von Rosenstiel, M. Djarrahzadeh, H. E. Einsiedler, and R. K. Streich (eds.), *Wertewandel: Herausforderungen für die Unternehmenspolitik in den 90er Jahren* (2nd edn). Stuttgart: Schäffer-Poeschel, 83–94.

——(1995). *Wertorientierte Personalarbeit: Strategie und Umsetzung in einem neuen Automobilwerk*. Munich: Beck.

Daft, R. L. and Weick, K. E. (1984). 'Toward a Model of Organizations as Interpretation Systems'. *Academy of Management Review*, 9: 284–95.

Davenport, T. H. and Prusak, L. (1998). *Working Knowledge: How Organizations Manage What They Know*. Boston: Harvard Business School Press.

Dierkes, M., Hähner, K., and Berthoin Antal, A. (1997). *Das Unternehmen und sein Umfeld: Wahrnehmungsprozesse und Unternehmenskultur am Beispiel eines Chemiekonzerns*. Frankfurt am Main: Campus.

——and Raske, M. (1994). 'Wie Unternehmen lernen—Erfahrungen und Einsichten von Managern'. *Manager Magazine*, 24/7:142–54.

Dixon, N. (1994). *The Organizational Learning Cycle: How We Can Learn Collectively*. Maidenhead: McGraw-Hill.

Easterby-Smith, M. (1997). 'Disciplines of Organizational Learning: Contributions and Critiques'. *Human Relations*, 50: 1085–113.

Emery, F. E. and Thorsrud, E. (1982). *Industrielle Demokratie: Bericht über das norwegische Programm der industriellen Demokratie*. Bern: Huber.

Etzioni, A. (1975). *A Comparative Analysis of Complex Organizations*. New York: Free Press.

Feather, N. T. (1990). 'Bridging the Gap between Values and Action: Recent Applications of the Expectancy-value Model', in E. T. Higgins and R. M. Sorrentino (eds.), *Handbook of Motivation and Cognition: Foundations of Social Behavior* (Vol. 2). New York: Guilford, 151–92.

—— (1996). 'Values, Deservingness, and Attitudes toward High Achievers: Research on Tall Poppies', in C. Seligman, J. M. Olson, and M. P. Zanna (eds.), *The Psychology of Values: The Ontario Symposium* (Vol. 8). Mahwah, NJ: Erlbaum, 216–51.

Freimuth, J. (1997). 'Querdenker und Querschnittsqualifikationen. "Ich denke, also spinn' ich!" ', in J. Freimuth, J. Haritz, and B.-U. Kiefer (eds.), *Auf dem Wege zum Wissensmanagement*. Göttingen: Verlag für angewandte Psychologie, 191–203.

Friedrich, W. (1990). 'Mentalitätswandelungen in der Jugend der DDR'. *Aus Politik und Zeitgeschichte: Beilage zur Zeitung Das Parlament*, 40/16–17: 25–37.

Fürstenberg, F. (1995). 'Die Zukunft der Leistungsorganisation', in V. Kreyher and C. Böhret (eds.), *Gesellschaft im Übergang: Problemaufrisse und Antizipationen*. Baden-Baden: Nomos, 213–19.

Garvin, D. A. (1993). 'Building a Learning Organization'. *Harvard Business Review*, 71/4: 78–91.

Gensicke, T. (1992). 'Mentalitätswandel und Revolution: Wie sich die DDR-Bürger von ihrem System abwandten'. *Deutschland Archiv*, 25: 1266–82.

—— (1995a). 'Pragmatisch und optimistisch: Über die Bewältigung des Umbruchs in den neuen Bundesländern', in H. Bertram (ed.), *Ostdeutschland im Wandel: Lebensverhältnisse—politische Einstellungen*. Opladen: Leske + Budrich, 127–54.

—— (1995b). 'Modernisierung, Wertewandel und Mentalitätsentwicklung in der DDR', in H. Bertram, S. Hradil, and G. Kleinhenz (eds.), *Sozialer und demographischer Wandel in den neuen Bundesländern*. Berlin: Akademie Verlag, 101–40.

—— (1996). 'Ostdeutschland 1989–1995 im Wandel: Objektive und subjektive Umbrüche'. *Journal für Sozialforschung*, 36/1: 41–72.

—— (1998). 'Sind die Deutschen reformscheu? Potentiale der Eigenverantwortung in Deutschland'. *Aus Politik und Zeitgeschichte: Beilage zur Zeitung Das Parlament*, 48/18: 19–30.

—— (1999). 'Deutschland am Ausgang der 90er Jahre: Lebensgefühl und Werte', in H. Klages and T. Gensicke (eds.), *Wertewandel und bürgerschaftliches Engagement an der Schwelle zum 21. Jahrhundert* (Speyerer Research Report 193). Speyer: Forschungsinstitut für öffentliche Verwaltung, 21–52.

Grabner, L. (1993). 'Unternehmen und Wertewandel: Die Auswirkungen auf die Produktanforderungen', in L. von Rosenstiel, M. Djarrahzadeh, H. E. Einsiedler, and R. K. Streich (eds.), *Wertewandel: Herausforderung an die Unternehmenspolitik in den 90er Jahren* (2nd edn). Stuttgart: Schäffer-Poeschel, 95–114.

Granel, M. (1980). 'Zusammengefaßter Abschlußbericht der Volkswagenwerk AG zum Forschungsvorhaben Vergleich von Arbeitsstrukturen in der Aggregatefertigung', in Bundesminister für Forschung und Technologie (ed.), *Gruppenarbeit in der Motorenmontage*. Frankfurt am Main: Campus, 13–54.

Greening, D. W. and Gray, B. (1994). 'Testing a Model of Organizational Response to Social and Political Issues'. *Academy of Management Journal*, 37: 467–98.

Herbert, W. (1993). *Wandel und Konstanz von Wertstrukturen*. Frankfurt am Main: Campus.

Huber, G. P. (1991). 'Organizational Learning: The Contributing Processes and the Literatures'. *Organization Science*, 2: 88–115.

Hult, G. T. M. and Ferrell, O. C. (1997). 'A Global Learning Organization Structure and Market Information Processing'. *Journal of Business Research*, 40: 155–66.

Hurley, R. F. and Hult, G. T. M. (1998). 'Innovation, Market Orientation, and Organizational Learning: An Integration and Empirical Examination'. *Journal of Marketing*, 62/7: 42–54.

Inglehart, R. (1977). *The Silent Revolution: Changing Values and Political Style among Western Publics*. New York: Princeton.

—— (1990). *Cultural Shift in Advanced Industrial Society*. Princeton: Princeton University Press.

Inglehart, R. (1997). *Modernization and Postmodernization: Cultural, Economic, and Political Change in 43 Societies*. Princeton: Princeton University Press.

Kabanoff, B. and Holt, J. (1996). 'Changes in Espoused Values of Australian Organizations, 1986–1990'. *Journal of Organizational Behavior*, 17: 201–19.

Kaschube, J. (1993). 'Betrachtungen der Unternehmens- und Organisationskulturforschung aus (organisations-)psychologischer Sicht', in M. Dierkes, L. von Rosenstiel, and U. Steger (eds.), *Unternehmenskultur in Theorie und Praxis: Konzepte aus Ökonomie, Psychologie und Ethnologie*. Frankfurt am Main: Campus, 90–146.

Klages, H. (1984). *Wertorientierungen im Wandel: Rückblick, Gegenwartsanalyse, Prognosen*. Frankfurt am Main: Campus.

——(1992). 'Werte und Einstellungen', in E. H. Witte (ed.), *Einstellung und Verhalten* (Vol. 32). Braunschweig: Braunschweiger Studien, 93–112.

——(1999). 'Zerfällt das Volk? Von den Schwierigkeiten der modernen Gesellschaft mit Gemeinschaft und Demokratie', in H. Klages and T. Gensicke (eds.), *Wertewandel und bürgerschaftliches Engagement an der Schwelle zum 21. Jahrhundert* (Speyerer Research Report 193). Speyer: Forschungsinstitut für öffentliche Verwaltung, 1–20.

——Hippler, H. J., and Herbert, W. (1992). *Werte und Wandel*. Frankfurt am Main: Campus.

——and Kmieciak, P. (eds.) (1984). *Wertewandel und gesellschaftlicher Wandel* (3rd edn). Frankfurt am Main: Campus.

Kluckhohn, C. (1951). 'Values and Value Orientation in the Theory of Action: An Exploration in Definition and Classification', in T. Parsons and E. Shils (eds.), *Toward a General Theory of Action*. Cambridge, Mass.: Harvard University Press, 388–433.

Koch, S. and Mandl, H. (1999). *Wissensmanagement—Anwendungsfelder und Instrumente für die Praxis*. Research Report No. 103. Munich: Ludwig-Maximilians-Universität, Lehrstuhl für Empirische Pädagogik und Pädagogische Psychologie.

Kristiansen, C. M. and Hotte, A. M. (1996). 'Morality and the Self: Implications for the When and How of Value–Attitude–Behavior Relations', in C. Seligman, J. M. Olson, and M. P. Zanna (eds.), *The Psychology of Values: The Ontario Symposium* (Vol. 8). Mahwah, NJ: Erlbaum, 77–105.

Lewin, K. (1951). *Field Theory in Social Science: Selected Theoretical Papers* (D. Cartwright, ed.). New York: Harper & Row.

Mandler, G. (1993). 'Approaches to a Psychology of Values', in M. Hechter, L. Nadel, and R. E. Michod (eds.), *The Origin of Values*. New York: de Gruyter, 229–58.

Maslow, A. H. (1954). *Motivation and Personality*. New York: Harper.

McLean Parks, J. and Kidder, D. L. (1994). ' "Till Death Us Do Part." Changing Work Relationships in the 1990s'. *Trends in Organizational Behavior*, 1: 111–36.

Menon, A., Bharadwaj, S. G., Adidam, P. T., and Edison, S. W. (1999). 'Antecedents and Consequences of Marketing Strategy Making: A Model and a Test'. *Journal of Marketing*, 63/4: 18–40.

Meulemann, H. (1996). 'Wertewandel in modernen Gesellschaften: Erwartungen und Entwicklungen am Beispiel der Bundesrepublik Deutschland vor 1990', in E. Jannsen, U. Möhwald, and H. D. Ölschleger (eds.), *Gesellschaften im Umbruch? Aspekte des Wertewandels in Deutschland, Japan und Osteuropa*. Munich: Judicium, 41–63.

Meyer, A. (1998). *Handbuch Dienstleistungs-Marketing* (2 vols.). Stuttgart, Germany: Schäffer-Poeschel.

——and Ertl, R. (1998). 'Marktforschung von Dienstleistungs-Anbietern', in A. Meyer (ed.), *Handbuch Dienstleistungs-Marketing* (Vol. 1). Stuttgart: Schäffer-Poeschel, 204–46.

Meyer, J. and Allen, N. (1997). *Commitment in the Workplace: Theory, Research, and Application*. Thousand Oaks, Calif.: Sage.

Narver, J. C. and Slater, S. F. (1990). 'The Effect of a Market Orientation on Business Profitability'. *Journal of Marketing*, 54/10: 20–35.

Nerdinger, F. W. (1994). *Zur Psychologie der Dienstleistung: Theoretische und empirische Studien*. Stuttgart: Schäffer-Poeschel.

Neuberger, O. (1995). *Mikropolitik: Der alltägliche Aufbau und Einsatz von Macht in Organisationen*. Stuttgart: Enke.

——and Kompa, A. (1987). *Wir, die Firma*. Weinheim: Beltz.

Noelle-Neumann, E. (1978). *Werden wir alle Proletarier? Wertewandel in unserer Gesellschaft*. Zürich: Edition Interfrom.

Nonaka, I. and Takeuchi, H. (1995). *The Knowledge-creating Company: How Japanese Companies Create the Dynamics of Innovation*. New York: Oxford University Press.

Opaschowski, H. W. (1997). *Deutschland 2010: Wie wir morgen leben—Voraussagen der Wissenschaft zur Zukunft unserer Gesellschaft*. Hamburg: British-American Tobacco.

Pinchot, G., III (1985). *Intrapreneuring: Why You Don't Have to Leave the Corporation to Become an Entrepreneur*. New York: Harper & Row.

Post, J. E., Murray, E. A., Dickie, R. B., and Mahon, J. F. (1983). 'Managing Public Affairs: The Public Affairs Function'. *California Management Review*, 26/1: 135–50.

Preissler, H., Roehl, H., and Seemann, P. (1997). 'Haken, Helm und Seil: Erfahrungen mit Instrumenten des Wissensmanagements'. *Organisationsentwicklung*, 16/2: 4–16.

Ralston, D. A., Cunniff, M. K., and Gustafson, D. A. (1995). 'Cultural Accommodation: The Effect of Language on the Responses of Bilingual Hong Kong Chinese Managers'. *Journal of Cross-Cultural Psychology*, 26: 714–27.

——Egri, C. P., Steward, S., Terpstra, R. H., and Yu, K. (1999). 'Doing Business in the 21st Century with the New Generation of Chinese Managers: A Study of Generational Shifts in Work Values in China'. *Journal of International Business Studies*, 30: 415–27.

——Gustafson, D. A., Terpstra, R. H., and Holt, D. A. (1995). 'Pre–post Tienanmen Square: Changing Values of Chinese Managers'. *Asia Pacific Journal of Management*, 12: 1–20.

Rokeach, M. (1973). *The Nature of Human Values*. New York: Free Press.

Rosenstiel, L. v. (1984). 'Wandel der Werte—Zielkonflikte bei Führungskräften?', in R. Blum and M. Steiner (eds.), *Aktuelle Probleme der Marktwirtschaft in gesamt- und einzelwirtschaftlicher Sicht*. Berlin: Duncker und Humblot, 203–34.

——(1989). 'Kann eine wertorientierte Personalpolitik eine Antwort auf den Wertewandel in der Gesellschaft sein?', in R. Marr (ed.), *Mitarbeiterorientierte Unternehmenskultur: Herausforderung für das Personalmanagement der 90er Jahre*. Berlin: Schmidt, 21–32.

——Djarrahzadeh, M., Einsiedler, H. E., and Streich, R. K. (eds.) (1993). *Wertewandel: Herausforderung für die Unternehmenspolitik in den 90er Jahren* (2nd edn). Stuttgart: Schäffer-Poeschel.

——and Kaschube, J. (1999). *Attribution von Erfolg im Management: Eine Studie an Top-Managern*. Unpublished manuscript. Munich: Ludwig-Maximilians-Universität.

——and Stengel, M. (1987). 'Manager von morgen: Alternativ oder Grün?' *Psychologie heute*, 14/11: 50–5.

——and Weinkamm, M. (eds.) (1980). *Humanisierung der Arbeitswelt—Vergessene Verpflichtung?* Stuttgart: Poeschel.

Rousseau, D. M. (1997). 'Organizational Behavior in the New Organizational Era'. *Annual Review of Psychology*, 48: 515–46.

Schein, E. H. (1985). *Organizational Culture and Leadership: A Dynamic View*. San Francisco: Jossey-Bass.

——(1990). 'Organizational Culture'. *American Psychologist*, 45: 109–19.

Schnierer, T. (1996). 'Von der kompetitiven Gesellschaft zur Erlebnisgesellschaft? Der "Fahrstuhl-Effekt", die subjektive Relevanz der sozialen Ungleichheiten und die Ventilfunktion des Wertewandels'. *Zeitschrift für Soziologie*, 25/1: 71–82.

Schwartz, S. (1996). 'Value Priorities and Behavior: Applying a Theory of Integrated Value Systems', in C. Seligman, J. M. Olson, and M. P. Zanna (eds.), *The Psychology of Values: The Ontario Symposium* (Vol. 8). Mahwah, NJ: Erlbaum, 1–24.

Schwartz, S. H. and Bilsky, W. (1990). 'Toward a Theory of Universal Content and Structure of Values: Extensions and Cross-cultural Replications'. *Journal of Personality and Social Psychology*, 58: 878–91.

Seligman, C. and Katz, A. N. (1996). 'The Dynamics of Value Systems', in C. Seligman, J. M. Olson, and M. P. Zanna (eds.), *The Psychology of Values: The Ontario Symposium* (Vol. 8). Mahwah, NJ: Erlbaum, 53–75.

Sinkula, J. M. (1994). 'Market Information Processing and Organizational Learning'. *Journal of Marketing*, 58: 35–45.

Sinkula, J. M., Baker, W. E., and Noordewier, T. (1997). 'A Framework for Market-based Organizational Learning: Linking Values, Knowledge, and Behavior'. *Journal of the Academy of Marketing Science*, 25: 305–18.

Slater, S. F. and Narver, J. C. (1995). 'Market Orientation and the Learning Organization'. *Journal of Marketing*, 59/3: 63–74.

Spranger, E. (1924). *Lebensformen*. Halle: Niemeyer.

Trommsdorff, G. (1996). 'Werte und Wertewandel im kulturellen Kontext aus psychologischer Sicht', in E. Jannsen, U. Möhwald, and H. D. Ölschleger (eds.), *Gesellschaften im Umbruch? Aspekte des Wertewandels in Deutschland, Japan und Osteuropa*. Munich: Judicium, 13–40.

Ulich, E. (1998). *Arbeitspsychologie* (4th edn). Zürich: VDF/Schäffer-Poeschel.

Volkswagen AG Qualitätsförderung—Langfristplanung Qualität & Arbeitsgruppe Wirtschaftspsychologie (1986). *Anforderungen an die Qualität zukünftiger Personenkraftwagen: Zentrale Aussagen Thesen, Interpretationen und mögliche Empfehlungen*. Wolfsburg: Volkswagen AG.

Witte, E. H. (1973). *Organisation für Innovationsentscheidungen: Das Promotorenmodell*. Göttingen: Schwartz.

——— (1996). 'Wertewandel in der Bundesrepublik Deutschland (West) zwischen 1973–1992: Alternative Interpretationen zum Inglehart-Index'. *Kölner Zeitschrift für Soziologie und Sozialpsychologie*, 48: 534–41.

Wood, D. J. (1991). 'Corporate Social Performance Revisited'. *Academy of Management Review*, 16: 691–718.

Wunderer, R. and Mittmann, J. (1995). *Identifikationspolitik: Einbindung des Mitarbeiters in den unternehmerischen Wertschöpfungsprozeß*. Stuttgart: Schäffer-Poeschel.

9 Social Movements and Interest Groups as Triggers for Organizational Learning

Jürgen Kädtler

Deutsch (1963) once defined power as 'the ability to afford not to learn' (p. 111), adding that making use of this ability might be a risky option: 'When carried to its extremes, such narrow power becomes blind, and the person or organization becomes insensitive to the present, and is driven, like a bullet or torpedo, wholly by the past' (Deutsch 1963: 111). This chapter deals with situations in which this power is questioned by collective actors from outside.

Organizational learning that is triggered by social movements or interest groups is a form of involuntary learning. It takes place because the organization is confronted with problems it has not chosen to deal with and, in order to cope, must develop competences it would not have developed without being forced to.

Social movements and interest groups become important in organizational learning when they are able to cause organizational crisis. By condensing and focusing social problems and interests, they can create the critical mass that compels organizations—and other social actors—to give a response, be it rejection, avoidance, acceptance, active treatment, or some combination of all these possibilities. Which of these options are taken by the organization, and whether the organization acquires the capacity to manage the crisis and deal with the concern of social movements or interest groups, is determined by organizational learning. This refers to the tension between an analytical and a normative perspective on

organizational learning, discussed systematically by Gherardi (1999) and Berthoin Antal (1998: 39–43). Both hard-headed resistance to and active treatment of the concerns of sound movements can result in organizational learning. In either case new organizational competencies have to be acquired if critical issues are to be addressed successfully.

It follows then, that organizations have to be analyzed as a category of systems of collective action (see Friedberg 1993). These systems are distinguished from others by their significantly higher level of formalization, structure, and finalization. Their consistency and capacity to act as organizations consists in a complex of relatively stable balances of powers and influence and in a stock of conventions that makes it possible to decide questions of adequacy and legitimacy in a generally accepted manner (see Boltanski and Thévenot 1991; Orléan 1994). The organization's knowledge and cognitive framework is part of this complex system of collective action and cannot be isolated from other parts. The development, modification, and restructuring of organizational knowledge and cognitive frameworks is therefore part of organizational learning in a more general sense: the process of finding, developing, modifying, or restructuring this system of balances and conventions. (For the dialectic of the social constitution of organizations and organizational learning, see Child and Heavens, Ch. 13 in this volume.)

In this chapter, I concentrate on the organizational learning of enterprises. I view enterprises as the 'archetype of organization in the context of complex collective learning' (Favereau 1994: 128, translation by the author). This focus, however, is not based on generalizing microeconomic explanations. On the contrary, I assume that collective learning processes can be analyzed best in situations where demands are highest. Such situations are found in enterprises that have to deal not only with the complexity of their respective internal or external organizational environments but also with the challenge of connecting the two kinds of environment in a productive way. The following analysis of company cases is therefore not confined to a more or less important special case, it encompasses organizational learning in general. This purpose requires a concept of enterprises as socially constituted collective systems of action that excludes their reduction to mere economic considerations (for the contrary position, see Williamson 1985; for a critique of Williamson, see Gomez 1996).

I begin by explaining the underlying concept of social movements, interest groups, and organizational crisis. I then analyze real crises in enterprises and examine subsequently organizational changes. In the final section, I explain possible conclusions about the way organizations deal with unwanted learning constellations that may nevertheless be essential for processes of innovation.

Social Movements, Interest Groups, Organizational Crisis, and Organizational Learning

The relation between social movements, interest groups, organizational crises, and organizational learning, as outlined above, rests on a particular interpretation of these terms. But what do they mean? Having been borrowed from theoretical and pragmatic contexts going well beyond this brief introduction, these terms call for explanation before the argument proceeds.

Social Movements and Interest Groups: A Pragmatic Operationalization

In academia it is anything but clear what is meant by the expression 'social movements'. It is even less clear in everyday communication. There are theoretical approaches in which the aim of a fundamental change in society constitutes an indispensable defining quality (Touraine 1981, 1985). At the other extreme, everyday use of the term has inflated it. Political sectarians, for instance, speak of social movements in order to make themselves appear more important. An example in Germany is the 'Movement of the seventh of June' which in fact was a small group of terrorists. Exponents of specific economic interests or management concepts use the word to communicate a sense of dynamics and broad commitment, as in 'human relations movement' and 'total-quality movement'.

In between is the mainstream of current academic debate, with its broad range of micro- and mesotheoretical approaches that are applied in attempts to analyze and classify situational, institutional, and organizational conditions under which social movements can emerge and develop. The perspectives offered by these approaches are mainly complementary but in some ways also totally antithetical (Klandermans and Tarrow 1988; Kriesberg and Spencer 1991; Lyman 1995; McAdam, McCarthy, and Zald 1996; Rucht 1991; Zald and McCarthy 1979, 1987). My approach to clarifying what is meant by the terms 'social movements' and 'interest groups' is a bit arbitrary, for it is contingent on the plausibility of the idea that all the different ways of using the term 'social movement' at least implicitly share a semantic core with which they are compatible. I talk of a movement or a social movement to the degree that political or social aims are the subject of collective action that is based on a minimum degree of public acceptance and that is thus able to mobilize people. Through that mobilization, the movement can tap areas of action that are, at least to some extent, located outside the institutionalized paths and procedures of decis-ion-making (see Kitschelt 1991; Tarrow 1991; Zald 1991).

This definition is admittedly vague, span-ning political systems of action (see Rucht 1994: 79) that range from 'grand old' social movements such as the labor movement to 'new' environmental or women's movements and single-issue movements such as the peace movement. The definition even applies to in-terest groups if they manage to achieve a mini-mum amount of public attention, approval, and support outside official channels. It is far more inclusive than, say, Touraine's definition (1985), which restricts the term 'social move-ment' to cases in which the aim of collective action is to bring about fundamental changes in the structures of societies.

The inclusion of interest groups, however, should not blur basic differences. Social move-ments are public activities; interest groups are more private ones. Social movements strive to integrate their general aspirations into the sys-tem of values and norms that constitute legitim-acy in a society. Interest groups seek concrete advantages for the specific and clearly defined interests of their members. But the difference between social movements and interest groups can become fluid or even obsolete, as when interest groups are able to mobilize public sup-port for their partial and specific aims, or when they even make those aims part of more general social aspirations. The rise of shareholder activ-ism and its influence on corporate control illus-trate this point well (Davis and Thompson 1994). Under these conditions, the difference between interest groups and social movements can indeed be disregarded in the logic of organizational learning.

Organizational Crisis and Organizational Learning

Social movements or interest groups with a capacity to mobilize public support can im-mediately trigger organizational learning, a possibility that rests on their ability to induce organizational crisis. The important thing is the ability to do so, not the actual outbreak of crisis. Anticipation, too, imbues social move-ments and interest groups with a sense of real-ity that is relevant for organizational learning. This concept of organizational crisis is very sim-ilar to that of industrial crisis as introduced by Shrivastava, Mitroff, Miller, and Miglani (1988), whose treatment of the term, however, relates to manifest crises.

Shrivastava et al. (1988) see industrial crises as 'organizationally-based disasters which cause extensive damage and social disruption, in-volve multiple stakeholders, and unfold through complex technological, organiza-tional and social processes' (p. 285). Such crises represent 'the dark side of the Faustian bargain that modern society has struck with technol-ogy, a bargain whose down side risks are not fully known to us' (Shrivastava 1988: 283). Indus-trial crises represent 'a significant opportunity for learning' (p. 284) because they instantly show this still unknown side of the use of tech-nology and because the responsible party comes under pressure to reduce the concomi-tant risks as much as possible by developing new competencies for dealing with technology and its risks.

Shrivastava (1988) stated that industrial crises 'are caused by organizational and interorgan-izational failures' (p. 283). In other words, it is insufficient and shortsighted to interpret crises merely in terms of 'human error' or 'technolo-gical failure' as causes of disaster. The way in which technologies are used depends on how collective and cooperative work relations are organized in a given context. Adverse effects of this use must therefore be seen as con-sequences of insufficient organizational hand-ling of the concomitant processes and their risks.

The idea of examining organizational learn-ing through the lens of industrial crisis calls to mind spectacular, local, environmental cata-strophes—'sudden destructive events' (Shri-vastava et al. 1988: p. 288)—caused either by accidents with immediate, far-reaching impacts (as in the 1984 disaster at the Union Carbide pesticide plant in Bhopal, India, and the severe 1976 chlorine accident at the Hoffmann–La Roche plant in Seveso, Italy, or by a long-term cumulation of effects that dramatically come to public attention (as with Minamata disease in Japan during the 1950s and the discovery of chromosomal damage due to toxic chemical wastes in Love Canal, Pennsylvania). Basically, however, this approach covers more ground than other kinds of analysis do. It includes cases in which damages are indirect and far apart and in which the concentration of damage leading to crisis is achieved by compiling and presenting individual effects of industrial activities in a way that commands public attention. The approach can be applied, for example, to analysis of organizational learning triggered by damages associated with aggressive marketing in countries of the Third World (Nestlé), by the health hazards posed by asbestos, and by the risk of cancer caused by smoking.

Nonetheless, the severity of an incident does not guarantee that it can be used to bring about organizational learning. Shrivastava *et al.* (1988) pointed out that even in spectacular catastrophes such as those mentioned above enterprises and public organizations alike tend to limit themselves to the recovery of immediate damages and do not necessarily draw any further organizational consequences. In these instances, too, long-term political and social pressure is necessary in order to prompt organizational learning and not merely coping routines and defensive reactions.

To the degree that immediate impressions of disasters lose their topicality, special actors—interest groups of directly affected persons or social movements—are needed to keep the topic on the public agenda. These actors are of utmost importance from the start, particularly in cases where the underlying facts and incidents have acquired the quality that will enable them to trigger organizational crises at the mere act of drawing connections or interpreting and articulating interests.

Organizations and Social Movements: The Rearrangement of the Organization's Internal and External Environments

From the perspective adopted in this chapter, organizational learning is triggered by the latent or manifest collision of existing organizations and social movements.[1] This space explicitly includes organizations, such as labor unions, which have their roots in social movements and which, as social-movement organizations, may even participate in the dynamics of social movements. As consolidated organizations, they are subject to the same mechanisms, regardless of their aims and external effects, a point demonstrated by the examples below.[2]

Social movements may lead to latent or manifest organizational crisis and may thereby engender organizational learning by establishing new priorities for determining the social legitimacy of individual or collective actions. New values and aspirations gain importance; others are pushed to the background or lose their importance completely. For organizations, these changes mean new chances or opportunities for action as well as new pressures and constraints. Whether the new opportunities are regarded as such and how organizations deal with new pressures and constraints depends on the extent to which the objectives of organizations and the foundations of collective action in organizations are affected. For example, producers of trekking equipment may have suffered less from the social influence of the eco-

---

[1] By concentrating on this point of view, I exclude collective learning *within* social movements, which, in the context of these vaguer and more fluid kinds of collective action, is the basis of new organizations.

[2] Under the pressure of 'their' respective social movements, these organizations can be both objects and triggers of organizational learning at the same time. Especially in those situations, for instance, German labor unions were important triggers for organizational learning in enterprises, employers' associations, and government organizations. In this context, the unions were subject to massive, uncontrolled influence of their rank and file and were thus forced into organizational learning themselves. See Schumann, Gerlach, Geschlüssl, and Milhofer (1971) and Kädtler (1986: 249–65).

logical movement than the chlorine chemical industry has.

The situation is not usually as clear as this example might suggest. What looks like a great chance at first sight or what subsequently proves to have been a crucial opportunity for organizational learning might represent a high-risk matter as initially seen inside the organization. In most cases the issue is not the improvement of what are seen as inadequate organizational practices and business strategies. The point is to question a behavior that appears to work sufficiently for the organization. That behavior may, for instance, relate to the organization's portfolio. It is clear, for instance, that the tobacco industry's scope for responding to antismoking campaigns is extremely narrow, whereas the chemical industry, whose knowledge is necessary for the establishment of new environmental norms, has a greater number of far-reaching options. But theoretical possibilities for a new line of thinking must have a foothold, or at least the opportunity to gain a foothold, within the organization before they can be realized. The more an organization questions all the core beliefs, conventions, balances of power and influence, and well established claims that stand for the integration of collective action within it, the riskier those theoretical possibilities become. The chapters in the following section of this handbook, particularly those on social constitution and on identity and conflict, deal with these internal dynamics of organizational learning.

Because such questioning is based upon a fragile balancing of myriad independent interests in large organizations and companies, there is a widespread tendency to respond cautiously to the challenges of social movements so as to avoid interfering with the established modalities of collective action.

Social Movements, Organizational Crisis, and Organizational Learning in Reality: Three Case Studies

Real processes of organizational learning based on a single, clear, and consistently executed option in the course of confrontation with the demands of social movements are the rare exception rather than the rule. Normally, one finds changes in different options or sees chronological changes of strategies. This seeming lack of continuity is due to the fact that the results of learning processes are not predetermined for either organizations or individuals. In this context, carrying through on just one option can be seen as an expression of power in the sense of the ability to afford not to learn.

The three case studies presented below are about situations in which this kind of power did not exist. The companies involved saw themselves in organizational crises that inevitably required organizational learning. In each case, the organizational crises and the learning processes they triggered occurred only because interest groups took up certain themes and because social movements, functioning as sounding boards, amplified the importance of the message.

The three cases were chosen because they represent distinct variations in the mode, intensity, and duration of organizational learning within a common pattern of events. Like Dyllick (1989), I distinguish between three phases: a period of latency, during which enterprises are confronted with demands but can still avoid dealing with them, a period of escalation, during which enterprises are forced to react by the pressure of social movements; and a period of de-escalation, when enterprises learn to manage the conflict by using new organizational competencies.

In the course of this development, enterprises repeatedly switch between different strategic options. I distinguish between three strategic options: resistance, symbolic policy, and active engagement, which express different degrees of problem acceptance. These options, whose rationale is examined later in this chapter, have had a distinct influence on the course and the result of organizational learning in each of the three cases.

Each case study summarizes central facts and the basic course of events in a given company. The studies particularly focus on the influence exerted by conflict, situational conditions, and the strategic actions of enterprise or movement representatives at crucial stages of the development described. Furthermore, the cases highlight gains in competence that were observable in the enterprises as a result of these developments. An analytical summary follows the entire set.

Nestlé and the Conflict over Infant Formula

The boycott that hit Nestlé between 1978 and 1984, particularly in the United States, is probably the literature's best described and analyzed confrontation between an enterprise and a social movement (see Dyllick 1989; Johnson 1986; Sethi 1994). The most important facets and milestones of the case are as follows:

- The object of the quarrel was not the product, infant formula, but Nestlé's aggressive marketing in developing countries. It was argued that the marketing reduced breastfeeding and the attendant protection afforded by the human immune system. It was also asserted that infants were endangered because many of the countries targeted by Nestlé's marketing lacked the hygienic and sanitary conditions necessary for the product's safe use.
- The markets in the developing countries were seen as future growth markets as markets in industrial countries became more and more saturated.
- To some extent, Nestlé became the target of the boycott for contingent reasons, which Kitschelt (1986), writing in a different context, summed up with the term 'political opportunity structure': the company was (and still is) the market leader for infant formula in

the developing countries, and the critics had no opportunities to exert influence internally, say, through proposals by shareholders. Most important, however, was the behavior of the enterprise itself.

- Nestlé repeatedly refused to accept criticism, for the product was of proven quality and there was no conclusive evidence of a causal relation between instant-formula marketing, a decline in breastfeeding, and infant mortality. For a long time, Nestlé maintained a 'basic attitude of general confrontation' (Dyllick 1989: 313) toward critics, merely adjusting its strategy from 'offensive image cultivation' (p. 312) to that of 'minimal visibility' (p. 312) before listing external experts to deal with criticism. Blatant mistakes during that period, such as defamation charges brought against the editors of *Nestlé kills Babies* (Arbeitsgruppe Dritte Welt Bern 1974) in Basel and the narrow-minded, opinionated testimony of Nestlé's representative at a hearing of the Kennedy subcommittee in 1978 (U.S. Senate 1978), strongly contributed to the anti-Nestlé movement by making the company look socially irresponsible to the public. The shift from latency to escalation was largely caused by the company itself.
- Internally, Nestlé was oriented to technical and scientific criteria of product quality and production efficiency; externally, to market success. The company had neither the experience nor the organizational capacity for a political and moral justification of its economic conduct. There was high turnover in the relevant departments (Dyllick 1989: 303), and the task of dealing with the boycott was passed to a number of public relations companies in succession for a long time (Sethi 1994: 218–19). In addition, a complex matrix structure that granted individual affiliates a great deal of autonomy stood in the way of a coherent strategy for the group as a whole.

To de-escalate the boycott and eventually end it, it was important for the group to change its strategy. It therefore shifted from intransigently resisting all reproaches and demands of the boycott movement to actively communicating and agreeing with those critics who were concerned with the ethical and humanitarian problems of child nutrition in developing countries. Rather than asserting Nestlé's position, the group now tried to work with its critics to find mutually satisfactory solutions. This new tack was based on central management's insight that the problem, because of its impact on the group as a whole, had to be handled as a strategic task. Moreover, changes in Nestlé's top management meant that the strategy could be changed without loss of face for those in charge.

This strategic change was expressed and supported through two new institutions, the Nestlé Coordination Center for Nutrition (NCCN) and, initiated by this body, the Nestlé Infant Formula Audit Commission (NIFAC). The NCCN was a unit that operated outside from the normal chain of command, possessed immediate access to top management, and had extensive responsibilities. Staff was recruited externally and, besides professional expertise, had specific experience in dealing with companies' socially or politically driven crisis of acceptance. The strategic approach consisted of talking with the well-meaning supporters of the boycott, whose motivation was humanitarian or religious and of convincing them to participate in finding solutions together with the company. NIFAC was an additional independent body for the verification of reproaches against Nestlé. Senator Edward Muskie, whose reputation was beyond any doubt, presided over the commission, which was authorized to conduct its own investigations and issue public statements.

Arrived at in this way, the resolution of the boycott problem was mainly due to Nestlé's acceptance of collaboration with social groups and the inclusion of their demands pertaining to company strategy. The technical and economic orientation within the enterprise and the market was supplemented by justification of the company's economic action and by communication with external groups and consideration of their demands. This change implied a fundamental break with Nestlé's traditions and corporate culture, a departure that was controversial within the company. However, top management's support of the shift helped overcome internal resistance. The most crucial question regarding organizational learning is to assess whether this exceptional learning constellation had lasting consequences for the organization. If the most important aspect of ending the boycott was that the company publicly presented itself 'as part of the solution rather than the problem' (Sethi 1994: 222), then the key question in terms of organizational learning is to what extent the company's contribution to the problem is understood internally.

The evidence cited by Sethi (1994: 319–54) and IGBM (1997) shows that Nestlé has little understanding of its contribution to the problem that brought about the boycott. In particular, the way Nestlé retrospectively interpreted the conflict gives no indication that relevant causes of the crisis within the organization had been identified (see Dobbing 1988). In the company's view, the boycott *was* the crisis, which therefore came from outside. Accordingly, the NCCA had been seen as a task force formed in order to end the boycott. After the goal was achieved, the task force lost influence and was eventually abolished. NIFAC survived until 1990, when it was replaced by an ombudsman at the level of the business association Infant Food Manufacturers (IFM). This institution was given very little authority, and there was no indication that Nestlé had supported a stronger one like NIFAC. By streamlining and by emphasizing a line orientation of corporate organization, Nestlé has enhanced its ability to respond to problems with a coherent strategy. The wave of U.S. public resentment that hit Nestlé at the end of the 1980s, when the company tried to introduce infant-formula products on the U.S. market (Sethi 1994: 341–9), shows two things: First, Nestlé had by that time never been penetrated by the NCCA's idea that the ability to deal with conditions for political and moral acceptance of products—and with the corresponding groups and their demands—should be viewed as a core competence of the company. Second, Nestlé's flexibility and efficiency in dealing with this kind of problem have meanwhile increased considerably. The economic performance of the organization since the end of the first boycott clearly indicates that it has sufficiently learned to achieve political and moral acceptance of its products without significantly changing.

Asbestos

The asbestos campaign and the development of the Eternit group under its influence is well documented (see Albracht and Schwerdtfeger 1991; Dyllick 1989; Selikoff and Lee 1978). In this case, the object of the campaign was the product itself. It had been known since the early twentieth century that asbestos could cause severe health damages. Acknowledgment of asbestosis, lung cancer, and mesothelioma as occupational diseases came first in Britain in 1931, and respective industrial safety regulations were passed.

For a long time the spectacular increase of asbestos use was not affected. In Germany, for instance, where the diseases were registered in 1937, 1942, and 1977 (former West Germany), asbestos consumption rose from 10,000 to almost 180,000 tons per year between 1950 and the mid-1970s, remaining at the higher level until the end of the 1970s. This rise was due not only to the usefulness of asbestos but also to the fact that the threshold for having a particular disease acknowledged as occupational was very high. For decades, there were recognized asbestos-related diseases, but few certified asbestos patients.

The origin and rise of the Eternit group was inseparably connected with the triumphant advance of asbestos, the ultrastability, or 'eternity', of which had given the enterprise its name. Every criticism directed at the use of asbestos aimed at the very mainstay of the company. At first, the enterprise uncompromisingly relied on a strategy of resistance, rejecting all criticism of its product. For instance, when practitioners of industrial medicine started to attack the use of asbestos early in the 1970s, the companies using asbestos founded an independent academic council of

the asbestos industry. This council, which was headed by the leading representatives of common practice, had the declared objective of cutting the so-called asbestos doctors down to size (Albracht and Schwerdtfeger 1991: 406). This approach proved to be successful. Even the publication of new U.S. epidemiological results (IG Metall 1976), which revolutionized the academic debate of the asbestos issue, prompted no immediate change in the attitude of authorities and enterprises.

A public campaign launched by unions and political parties eventually brought the Swedish industrial safety authority—against its original intention—to ban the use of asbestos in building construction as early as 1976. Eternit's Swedish subsidiary had to file for bankruptcy two years later. Speaking of the way in which the ban was pushed through, the designated heir of the company described the experience as his 'Swedish shock' (Dyllick 1989: 346).

In Germany, the asbestos industry, along with Eternit, came under pressure from 1979 on. Until then, industrial safety had received little public attention and had not been perceived as a political issue. Union-related industrial safety experts used the broad public recognition of the then recently developed environmental movement to put industrial safety—seen as industrial environment politics—on the agenda of the overall environmental movement. Exploiting the environmental movement's ability to mobilize public opinion and resources, these experts had found an efficient new source of power with which to assert their positions on industrial safety. The asbestos campaign constituted the prototype of this strategy.

The occasion was afforded by a rather unspectacular learning process in a small company. By persistent effort, a member of the works council had succeeded in having authorities acknowledge that eight deaths caused by asbestos had been work related. Additionally, he proved 50 cases of asbestos-related illnesses in a firm with an average of only 50 to 60 employees. The works council and the employer informed the public and in 1979 achieved a ban on the use of gunned asbestos, moving asbestos to the center of public interest. Mass media took up the cause, authorities issued asbestos bans for public buildings, and West Germany's Federal Environment Agency prepared a report that would have led to a *de facto* ban on all uses of asbestos had it not been momentarily stayed through intervention by Eternit's works council (see Kädtler and Hertle 1997).

The strategy of the enterprises was a blend of resistance, symbolic policy, and active engagement. The intention was to prevent an immediate ban on the use of asbestos and, in the long term, to develop new technologies that were certain to allow the continued use of asbestos without endangering customers. In 1979 a specialized research institute called the 'Asbestos Institute for Industrial Safety and Environmental Protection' was founded by the industry (Dyllick 1989: 380). Through expertise and reports, the organization attempted to influence the industrial safety debate to the benefit of the asbestos industry. The battle for public opinion, however, was no longer winnable by these means. The estimated figure of 10,000 asbestos-related deaths a year sparked a broad public response, and the Federal Minister of the Interior called for an asbestos ban, albeit not an immediate one. The conflict had definitely reached the escalation phase.

The asbestos cement firms thereupon pulled the emergency brakes as it were. In 1982 and 1984 they voluntarily agreed with the federal government to abandon the use of asbestos in building construction step-by-step while developing measures and techniques to promote safe use of the material. In an additional act of voluntary self-control, Eternit appointed the most distinguished environmental politician of the federal government as a member of the company's supervisory board. As a quid pro quo, they expected political trust during the negotiated time span and the approval to use asbestos in underground engineering in the future.

This agreement remained in place even in the light of a new asbestos crisis that broke out when a large number of kindergardens, schools, gymnasiums, and other public buildings had to be closed because the air in them had been found to contain excessively high levels of asbestos. At that point, however, authorities declared that all use of asbestos products had to end upon expiration of the voluntary agreement with the federal government. Since the early 1990s, Eternit has been successful in the old markets with a new product portfolio free of asbestos, and has been advertising its merits in abandoning asbestos.

This trailblazer role is also exemplified by an antiasbestos campaign that has existed in France since 1974 (Senat français 1997), when extremely high asbestos values were measured in the air of new university buildings in Paris-Jussieu. This campaign had led to a ban on gunned asbestos in mid-1977, one and a half years earlier than in West Germany. For fifteen years thereafter, however, little action against the use of asbestos had been taken. At last, in 1992, union representatives were able to publicly substantiate the cases of several employees suffering from asbestos-related diseases, and the mass media became interested. By 1996, the public pressure generated by the campaign was so great that on 3 July the French parliament banned the use of asbestos as of the end of the year. Then, in the traditional presidential address delivered on France's national holiday, 14 July, Jacques Chirac announced the immediate evacuation of the universities of Jussieu (40,000 students). The nation had its asbestos scandal, and, looking at neighboring countries, the media asked why it had taken that long.

In addition to the industrial-safety authorities, the behavior of the two main manufacturers of asbestos products became the center of attention: St. Gobain and the French subsidiary of Eternit. In the early 1980s, a standing committee on asbestos had been founded and maintained by the asbestos industry as a forum for objective discussion by all people involved. Moreover, there had been some steps toward product conversion in French Eternit plants, too. But while exporting asbestos-free products to neighboring countries, they had continued to use asbestos-laden products domestically. An inquiry report (Senat français 1997) that was accepted unanimously by the French senate came to a devastating judgment of those activities. The companies, so it stated, had selected the information that had gone to the committee, had put economic aims above public health, and had pursued the goal of delaying product conversion as long as possible. Moreover, the inspection of an Eternit plant early in 1996 had shown serious shortcomings in industrial safety.

Eternit can claim the right to call itself a 'pioneer of the exit from asbestos' (Albracht and Schwerdtfeger 1991: 409) because the company managed product conversion, developed new products, and acquired the necessary know-how, partly in cooperation with other companies. Nevertheless, its actors, from management to works council, appeared to be driven by external forces. They defended the status quo as long as possible, giving in only when a definite asbestos ban was threatening. As shown by a comparison of the French and the German responses to the hazards of asbestos even the speed of innovation was a direct function of the activities of national antiasbestos movements and their ability to mobilize public support.

Royal Dutch/Shell Group—Brent Spar

In the spring of 1995, a public debate developed about a plan to sink a former oil-drilling platform, the 'Brent Spar', in the North Sea became a highly volatile organizational crisis for the Royal Dutch Shell Group (for a detailed description and thorough analysis of this case, see Scherler 1996). The dispute centered on an issue of industrial waste disposal that transcended this individual case, for there were (and still are) many oil platforms in the North Sea, and Europe, unlike the United States, was new to the problem of disposing of them.

Shell UK, the British subsidiary in charge, had decided on dumping the platform at sea because experts had described this solution as the most ecological, economical, and occupationally safe course of action. A year-old Greenpeace study that had come out against disposal at sea had not been considered.

The Brent Spar platform gave Greenpeace an opportunity to put the disposal of oil-drilling

facilities on to the public political agenda. Using vivid, symbolic, and emotional appeals, the organization made people politically aware of North Sea pollution, which was largely invisible and anonymous. Greenpeace created the image of small people trying (and being politically compelled) to act in an ecologically sound manner and accepting inconveniences and costs although large enterprises were simply dumping their waste into the sea.

The campaign was immediately directed at the 4th North Sea Conference, which took place in Esbjerg, Denmark in June 1995. According to Scherler (1996: 252), the objective was to pass a general ban on the dumping of offshore equipment. (A similar agreement was eventually passed in Lisbon in July 1998.) Greenpeace succeeded. Several daring occupations by Greenpeace activists, combined with scenes of rude eviction, were given spectacular coverage by the mass media.

As in the previous two cases reviewed in this chapter, the enterprise involved in the Brent Spar issue—represented by its British subsidiary—stubbornly followed the strategy of resistance. Pointing out that their disposal concept had been approved by the British energy minister, company officials refused to engage in any political debate about the Brent Spar platform. The violent execution of a British court's eviction order against Greenpeace activists only spotlighted the campaign and won it broad public recognition. In this regard—and others—similarities between the cases of Royal Dutch/Shell Group, Eternit, and Nestlé cannot be denied. The fact that Shell started to transport the drilling platform to the dumping location only 24 hours after the vast majority of delegates at the North Sea Conference had voted for a ban on dumping certainly did not curry support from politicians, who were under public pressure in their own countries to support the decision. Given the politically and emotionally charged situation and the stalemate among the experts involved, the company's stubborn legalism could only be perceived by the public at large as arrogant callousness.

Another analogy to the Nestlé case in particular is that the Shell subsidiaries were attacked as a group but were unable to act as one. Dealing with the Brent Spar oil-drilling platform was the sole responsibility of Shell UK, but it meant trouble for the group as a whole, especially for Shell Germany, whose own symbolic policy became a liability. Shell Germany had consciously related to the broad influence of the environmental movement in Germany and presented itself as a company particularly responsive to environmental matters, but the Brent Spar controversy made the subsidiary appear hypocritical and untrustworthy in the eyes of an indignant public. In Germany, the ensuing boycott of Shell gas stations had much approval and active support from the public, politicians of all parties, and groups of enterprises, the subsidiary's turnover contracted drastically, and gas station managers suffered severe economic damage.

At first, Shell did not feel the pressure where the controversial policy was carried out but rather where it caused the strongest outrage. This discrepancy caused growing tensions between Shell UK and Shell Germany, a rift that became apparent even to the public, forcing company headquarters to intervene. On 20 June 1995, just before the Brent Spar had reached the planned location for dumping, Shell rescinded its decision to sink the platform at sea, and the oil platform was towed to a Norwegian harbor. After advertised bidding, an order for onshore disposal of the Brent Spar was issued in 1996. The future disposal of off-shore equipment and the labor intensity of on-shore disposal gave new perspectives to economically weak coastal areas, hopes that were then discussed in a positive way by Shell. In a lecture, the CEO at that time demanded that the company take a fundamental, critical look at itself on the basis of reflections that were triggered by the organizational crisis it had experienced and by a subsequent campaign against the company's policies towards the Ogoni people in Nigeria.[3] He focused on the question of why the organization had not been able to respond adequately to changes in the social environment.

One major reason . . . was a type of technological arrogance which is rather common in companies with a strong technical base. Most of us in Royal Dutch/Shell come from a scientific, technological background. That type of education, along with our corporate culture, teach[es] us that we must identify a problem, isolate it and then fix it. That sort of approach works well with a physical problem—but it is not so useful when we are faced with, say, a human right issue. For most engineering problems there is a correct answer. For most social and political dilemmas there is a range of possible answers—almost all compromises. (Herkströter 1996)

Commenting on the environmental movement and other aspiration groups, the CEO stated:

Of course, we dealt with environmentalist groups, consumer groups and so on, but we tended to let the public affairs department deal with them. They were important—but they were not as important as government, industry organizations and so on. In essence, we were somewhat slow in understanding that these groups were tending to acquire authority. Meanwhile those institutions we were used to dealing with, were tending to lose authority. We underestimated the extent of these changes—we failed to engage in a serious dialogue with the new groups. (Herkströter 1996)

This analysis had several practical impacts. For instance, Shell has withdrawn from the Global Climate Coalition (GCC), a group of U.S. enterprises that strictly rejects the assumption of a greenhouse effect and that therefore fight all measures intended to protect the atmosphere. Though Shell's management still has reservations about the greenhouse thesis, it has embraced a 'nonregret policy', meaning that the company accepts the necessity of preventive measures because no one can exclude the possibility of severe consequences if it is true. In October 1997 a further positive change in business strategies was signaled through the establishment of a new line of business, 'renewable energies', in which, for example, the

---

[3] The planned dumping of an oil platform in the North Sea was given much more public attention and exerted much more pressure on the company than did the severe damage to the living conditions of a people and the execution of their speakers in Africa. This fact points to the problem of opportunity structures for social movements. It is obvious that the murder of Ken Saro-Wiwa became a publicity problem for Shell, at least in Europe, only because the company had lost credibility during the Brent Spar affair anyway.

world's largest manufacturing plant for solar collector panels is being built in Gelsenkirchen, Germany. It is also remarkable that a main figure of the environmental movement in Germany was appointed as a member of the executive board of Shell Germany. Lastly, Shell's restructuring into divisions, which gives more power to headquarters, can be seen as a response to the weakness the company had displayed during the political and moral conflicts that had played out when it was widely decentralized.

The company and its different lines of business (and their interests) still have unresolved tensions with the environmental movement. However, these relations are no longer seen as an external disturbance but—whether Shell likes it or not—as integrated aspects of the company's strategy. In this case, the development of new competencies is clearly not aimed at improving the protection of internal corporate structures from the external environment but rather, in the sense of active engagement, at partially opening them to new problems and aspirations that create pressure for internal processes of change.

Summing Up

Table 9.1 gives a partial overview of the three cases examined in this chapter. It refers to the profile, strategic focus, and resources for the mobilization of particular social movements and to the companies they have affected.

Social Movements and Organizational Learning: The Effectiveness of 'learning that cannot be willed'[4]

The results of the preceding case analyses are systematically discussed below, and conclu-

[4] See Elster's (1983) discussion of 'willing that cannot be willed' (pp. 44–52), that is, 'states that are essentially by-products'.

sions are drawn for conditions, opportunities, and limitations of organizational learning that are triggered by social movements.

Foundations of Social Mobilization: Collective Norms or Individual Altruism

The pressure that enterprises feel exposed to and the range and intensity of learning processes triggered by that pressure differ greatly according to the kind of social movement and the corporate weak spot involved. Collective norms and individual altruism can be seen as two poles of a continuum along which constellations of social movements form (for a systematic discussion of social norms and altruism as different individual motivations for collective action, with altruism defined as nonselfish individual rationality, see Elster 1989: 43–9). The environmental and occupational safety conflicts described in the preceding case are typical for constellations of social movements that revolve around collective norms. The risks and interests of the population that is to be mobilized are the focus of attention. To the degree the population has internalized the corresponding aims and attitudes and perhaps even sees them as socially and morally binding behavioral norms, social movement organizations (SMOs) can achieve broad, highly dynamic mobilizing effects by making examples of vivid cases. This process, the social embodiment of norms represented by a movement, is the most important result of the latency period in the cases analyzed above. By the same token, the vulnerability of the enterprises involved was that they failed to see or correctly estimate this process or the commitment that went along with it.

Once sparked in society, the energy of a social movement can be sustained by appropriate news and events, especially because mutual feedback and reinforcement of public awareness and media interest build. Where movements successfully focus on a clearly defined goal and are able to convert social mobilization into political pressure on state institutions,

Table 9.1. A profile of political and moral conflict between social movements and three companies

Company	Social movement	Strategic focus	Target	Strategy of social movements
Nestlé	Third-World groups Appeal to moral engagement	Marketing strategy (indirect effects of product application under Third-World conditions)	Company's image Consumer acceptance	Media campaign Consumer boycott
Eternit	Union activists Evocation of environmental risk	Core-product (industrial diseases and general health risks caused by core product)	Government intervention	Media campaign
Royal Dutch/ Shell Group	Social Movement Organization (Greenpeace)	Industrial waste disposal (single case of limited importance but high symbolic potential)	Company's image Government regulation	Highly professional campaign (focus on media strategy; physical confrontation; consumer boycott)

the pressure on enterprises increases further because state regulations or bans ensuing from a single case automatically apply to most such cases in the future (lock-in effects). Under these conditions, SMOs can pursue a strategy of short campaigns and decisive battles.

The second constellation of social movements—typically driven by individual altruism, as exemplified by the struggle over aggressive marketing of infant formula in countries of the Third World, is characterized by conditions for mobilization that are far more indirect than those of the first pole. The target group has to be made interested in the topic first. The focus is not the group's own interest but its willingness to become committed to the interest of others for moral reasons. Mobilization does not happen by itself; it must be initiated by heterogeneous coalitions. A common denominator must be found for stated aims and for the interests of potential supporters, and it must extend to as much of the movement's concern as possible. And the aim itself, that of drawing the line between morally acceptable and morally unacceptable business practices, is normally a difficult process of definition, interpretation, and bargaining. Under these conditions, it is difficult to drive companies into an organizational crisis unless they actively contribute to it. Most of all, however, the ripple effect, which bred a self-sustaining dynamic of organizational crisis in the Eternit and Shell cases, takes much more time to achieve the desired change in corporate behavior than collective norms do. Indeed, time works against the social movement.

For example, the long conflict over the activities of Royal Dutch Shell in Nigeria was profoundly similar to the clash over Nestlé's marketing of infant formula. However, the Nigerian controversy became a real problem for Royal Dutch Shell only in the wake of the Brent Spar crisis, even though the environmental and human rights issues in Nigeria were much more severe.

Defensive and Offensive Forms of Organizational Learning

At the risk of being schematic, I suggest that there are three typical ways in which organizations deal with actual or impending crises caused by social movements. New strategies and competencies that have to be developed represent different ways and reaches of organizational learning. With respect to the three cases treated in this chapter, Table 9.2 provides an overview of the courses of the various conflicts, their phases, the activities pursued by the selected enterprises, and the main results of organizational learning. (The terms 'resistance', 'symbolic policy', and 'active engagement' lead to the considerations presented in the concluding section.)

1. The first type of response that organizations give the claims of social movements is resistance. It can take the form of a rationally planned and executed strategy of the organizations' or the companies' management. Lobbying and public and internal opinion-making campaigns are examples of such resistance. It can also be—and at least in the asbestos case at times really was—a more or less spontaneous or natural collective reaction, particularly if the members of an organization feel collectively pilloried or consider the claims of social movements to be an attack on the shared *raison d'être*.

2. The second type of organizational response to the claims of social movements can be characterized as symbolic politics. In the cases presented in this chapter, this type was manifested through the creation of 'independent' scientific institutes and through efforts to give the company an environmentalist image. Generally, all types of organizations and companies create specific functions for handling environmental or women's issues. Companies in high-risk industries establish telephone hot lines for the public and organize public visits. Labor unions opt for the ecological restructuring of industrial society. For these changes to occur, it is crucial for managers of organizations to recognize that the new norms and claims being pressed by social movements cannot be overtly ignored if the organization is to protect its image.

3. The third type of response is active engagement. The problems highlighted by the social movements are seen as shortcomings of the organization itself, as a chance for further development, or as both. Practices or production lines are dispensed with or replaced, and new activities or business lines are developed. Competencies that used to be marginal become central, and operative functions become central management tasks. The organization is restructured in this sense, and balances of power and influence and the conventional bases of internal coherence are newly adjusted and defined. Organizational learning in this context is manifested as a revision of organizational objectives, knowledge, and cognitive frameworks.

To the extent that these variations have to do with or depend on growing organizational competence, the first two can be described as a defensive form of organizational learning; the final variation as an offensive form. At the same time, the three case analyses presented in this chapter clearly show that organizational learning processes are often characterized by connections between and intermediate stages of these variations of organizational learning and development.

Unambiguously resisting social movements, for example, can, and in reality often does, correlate with rather sophisticated diagnosis and internal efforts to find other solutions. What was initially resistance can afterwards be seen as a strategy of minimizing risks and, therefore, as an opportunity for active engagement, which is more far-reaching than the first two types of organizational learning. The asbestos case (Eternit) is an outstanding example of this learning constellation. The path taken by Eternit West Germany—the transformation of a new industry through voluntary agreements with state authorities—was subsequently described as a 'model innovation' by the company's CEO. This view is tenable only if one takes into account the social

Table 9.2. The course of organizational crises

Company	Latency period	Escalation	De-escalation	Results of organizational learning
Nestlé	*Resistance*: Problem denial Denial of company's responsibility	*Resistance*: One-way communication Law suit against critics *Symbolic Policy*: Council for industrial self-control *Responsibility*: Subordinate units	*Active engagement*: Engagement in dialogue with critics *Implementation of new responsibilities*: • Highly empowered task force inside the company • Independent control from outside	Strategic upgrading and partial centralization of public policy capacities (i.e. sophisticated competence for resistance)
			Duration: 11 years	
Eternit	*Resistance*: Problem denial Pressure on critics	One-way communication Law suit against critics		Product innovation
	Symbolic policy: Creating 'independent' scientific institutes			
		Active engagement: Development of new application engineering	Development of new products	
		Duration: 3 years (France: 23 years)		
Royal Dutch Shell Group	(Symbolic policy: Creation of an environmental company image in Germany)	*Resistance*: One-way communication Law suit against critics	Canceling the company's position by strategic top-management decision leads to active engagement	Social acceptance as central criterion for business strategy Partial recentralization Prominent environmentalist as top-manager 'No regret policy' Renewable energies as expanding new business
	(Resistance: Global Climate Coalition in the United States)	*Responsibility*: National subsidiary Public policy department		
		Duration: 8 weeks		

Note. Underlining indicates the four types of organizational learning. Parentheses indicate that these strategies for achieving environmental aspirations become relevant for the conflict and the learning process in the escalation and de-escalation phase but that they cannot be seen as a latency phase of this special conflict with its specific focus.

pressure that made the company move in that direction.

Although symbolic politics might at first glance be nothing more than a special form of defense, it sets new points of reference that internal actors can use in order to improve the foundations of their positions. Furthermore, the holders of 'symbolic' functions can benefit from external and internal pressures to build and expand real influence on the organization and its development. In this way, an instrument of defense can become a means of organizational learning. The environmentalist image cultivated by Shell Germany was at first mainly a marketing strategy chosen because alternative options had already been adopted by competitors but the dynamics of the Brent Spar conflict made the image a critical commitment.

Mutations in the opposite direction also occur. What starts as vast organizational reconfiguration may end as symbolic politics because internal resistance has prevailed, because external pressure has disappeared, or both. Nestlé's appointment of an industry-wide ombudsman in place of highly empowered internal and external departments illustrates this regression from active single-issue engagement to a primarily defensive way of dealing with the aspirations of social movements. This retreat does not completely end active engagement but does reduce it to the organizational or strategic aspects that are crucial for increasing the sophistication of an organization's defense against challenges by social movements.

Lastly, changing the matter of conflict and the point of reference for assessment can also change the light in which a given behavior is regarded. For example, trying to reduce the consumption of fertilizer, energy, and raw materials by breeding genetically engineered plants that are resistant to diseases and pests can be interpreted as a proactive response to an old issue or, in the eyes of the movement against novel food, simply as resistance. In other words, organizational learning that represents active engagement with a former matter of conflict can produce new conflicts. To describe how organizations deal with those

conflicts, Berry and Rondinelli (1998) drew a line that ascends from the development of unprepared to reactive and then to proactive corporate environmental management. To me, the curve looks rather like a spiral, so I have preferred to use the more neutral term 'active engagement' when almost identical circumstances are involved.

Common Aspects and Elements of Organizational Learning Triggered by Social Movements

The fact that conflict patterns and coping strategies can, and empirically do, vary in many ways does not mean that they are completely contingent. There are many similarities as well as differences between the three cases presented in this chapter. The first similarity is the fact that a dispute never becomes a crisis solely because of social movements. Companies have a very active part in its escalation. Once a situation seems to go out of control, it is crucial to question resistance strategies, not intensify them. But companies commonly take legal action against their critics or call for government force. Both responses only abet the opponents in their efforts to mobilize opinion and resources in their own support. If defensive learning (refined resistance) helps at an early stage, then major organizational innovations are essential if a conflict is escalating into a crisis.

The companies in all three cases suffered from an underlying kind of technical or legal 'autism' (in the sense of ignoring or failing to perceive important aspects of reality). Technical excellence, superior product and quality standards, and legality were seen as sufficient, indeed as the only, acceptable standards of corporate activity and responsibility, particularly because this philosophy had proven to be economically successful. The demands of social movements were therefore seen not only as immediate economic threats but as generally ill-informed, irrelevant, and illegitimate challenges to the companies' core beliefs. This attitude resulted in a strict antidialogue policy toward social groups and their demands.

In all the cases, giving up this attitude was a central condition of de-escalating and ending the crisis. Each company at least temporarily ceased applying exclusively technical or unambiguous legal standards to its behavior and accepted the need to adopt socially negotiated standards. In all cases, this change was induced by central actors among the owners, the members of top management, or both. In one case, a personnel change preceded the development; in another, the replacement of top managers followed it. (For a systematic treatment of the role of leaders, see Sadler, Ch. 18 in this volume.)

This temporary transition from one-sided application of one's own 'right' product and behavioral standards by all legal means to the negotiation of socially accepted standards is related to a wholesale redefinition and upgrading of company functions that have to do with political and social representation: Interaction with the public is elevated from a marginal operative activity to a strategic function. In the cases presented in this chapter, the situation improved at least for the duration of the crisis when public relations or public policy departments had the task to 'sell' internally fixed positions to the public and to authorities. At that point the perception of and cooperative response to public criticism became part of the strategic core business. In the long run, these changes laid the foundation for mechanisms of permanent organizational learning.

To the extent that the corporate function of working in public and with the public is newly defined and upgraded, a general inherent organizational contradiction emerges. The various responsibilities have to be integrated into increasingly decentralized business processes, yet they also have to be managed in a coherent and unified manner in order to serve as strategic company functions. The solutions to the crises analyzed in this chapter illustrate this contradiction more than they point to a conclusion. Nestlé created temporary *ad hoc* organizations that had no effect beyond management of the crisis facing the company. Eternit and the Shell

Group solved the problem simply through top-management decisions. The perspective for an evolutionary solution has more of a personal than a structural dimension. It requires top management to assume strategic responsibility and to adopt a strategic staff policy (see Berthoin Antal, Dierkes, and Hähner 1994). Organizational decentralization of responsibility is thus partially thwarted by personal networking.

A final common feature of the three cases analyzed in this chapter is the institutionalization of credibility. Besides voluntary commitment to transparency—such as environmental reports, audits, and external control—the personnel aspects of interaction with the public played an important role. Appointing experts or mutually trusted persons as managers or members of control bodies of companies helped establish credibility in external relations, brought additional competence into the companies, and improved the long-term perspectives for learning from tensions with social movements.

Organizational Learning and Force— Limits, Perspectives, and Contradictions

The variety of forms and relations that were subsumed by the common features of the chapter's three case analyses and the corresponding range of scopes, intensities, and long-term effects of organizational learning, are an outcome of different constellations of conflicts and interests and of the course the conflicts took. This final section focuses on that link, especially on similarities and differences between the learning processes that result from conflicts within the companies (see also Rothman and Friedman, Ch. 26 in this volume). In other words, forced compromises can be—but do not have to be—related to a reduced perspective for organizational learning.

The case of Nestlé's infant formula illustrates one constellation of conflicts and interests. The boycott movement centered on the conditions under which an undisputably high-quality product was used. Mobilization consisted in transferring high moral and ethical values of actors who were not personally affected but nonetheless willing to put their own practical everyday interests last. The aim involved a difficult task of interpretation: to draw the line between acceptable and unacceptable side effects. The extreme duration of the conflict reflected the intractability of the problem (on the importance of time as an independent factor, see Weber and Berthoin Antal, Ch. 15 in this volume). The rules imposed by the social movement were regarded by Nestlé as limitations on the capacity to maneuver on the market. Accepting these limitations gains a company no immediate advantage. On the contrary, acceptance might mean ceding advantage to competitors who do not abide by the rules, for incriminated use of a product, unlike problems with product quality or raw materials, can be solved only by social changes that are beyond the influence of any one company. Such problems cannot be solved by product innovation. Because the accepted restrictions are an expression of an unfavorable balance of power, the main option of the company is to change this balance in its own favor and to use the improved situation to delay the restrictions. This logic, too, promotes defensive organizational learning. The organization develops competence in order to deal with the demands of social movements better without giving in to them.

The other two cases in this chapter seem to illustrate a second constellation of conflicts and interests. Both companies saw themselves confronted with social movements that added immediate interests, problems, and commonly shared political priorities of their target groups and that were able to mobilize those groups by efficient media work. In view of the political pressure that was brought to bear by these social movements, one company had to accept a compromise within a few years and then had to accept a disadvantageous revision of this compromise. The other company suffered defeat within but a few weeks, albeit only a partial one. In both cases there followed extensive processes of organizational learning, which was manifested as a revision of organizational objectives, knowledge, and cognitive frame-

works, though in one of the two companies, it mainly had to do with lock-in effects. Investment in a new core competence, in alternative products, created new business interests that stood in the way of revising the original compromise, a complication that worsened the longer the negotiations lasted.

The second company's defeat, which appeared to have limited impact on the matter concerned, nevertheless proved to be paradigmatic and had strategic consequences. It triggered a fundamental revision of reality perception and decision patterns within the organization's traditional corporate culture. The range of such learning impetus, however, depends on whether the conflicts caused by these changes can be dealt with through a new frame of reference and different rules.

Social movements can provide an impetus for organizational learning because even the most highly developed technological civilization depends on the good faith of the majority of its members. If scientific experts lose this support, or if it is neutralized by well-documented contradictions, then the decision about the desirability of a particular solution falls back to society. Nothing seems to support the idea that under the condition of uncertainty worse solutions are found through societal consensus than by particular scientific expertise. The message beyond specific conflicts and individual cases is that companies cannot rely on external agents or regulation systems to make them address ethical issues and risks of business activities and must not allow themselves to withdraw from such discussion. Organizations that view—and actively try to achieve—social acceptance as an important aspect of their strategy are less likely than others to run the danger of being embroiled in conflicts brought about by the erosion of that acceptance.

Learning processes triggered by social movements have their greatest reach and duration where they lead to lock-in effects. Such effects can include binding and effectively controlled conditions and bans that enterprises must abide by. The assertion of minority rights by the U.S. civil rights movement, the extension of these rights by decisions on individual legal cases, and the development of affirmative action and diversity programs by companies are other impressive examples of organizational learning ensured by legal lock-ins—and of the problems that can derive from such learning (Tomasson, Crosby, and Herzberger 1996). But even more constructive in the context of organizational learning is that lock-in effects can also be generated by organizational innovations that alter the core competence, and hence the objectives, of a company. These alternatives are not mutually exclusive, and the threat or imposition of state regulation often triggers innovation activities by enterprises.

The conditions for organizational learning as a process of developing and optimizing existing strengths are best when enterprises address demands of social movements voluntarily and early. These demands are normally a common denominator of vague multiple objectives that have to be interpreted and stated clearly in order for practical policy to be shaped. The earlier companies become engaged in these processes, that is, the earlier they regard a sincere response to these problems as an aspect of their own core competence and develop commensurate abilities, the earlier they will be able to influence their environmental conditions and find solutions that ideally reconcile internal and external organizational environments.

The more they sacrifice this opportunity, the more focused the aims of social movements will become and the greater the confrontation with them will be for companies. The longer companies wait to deal with such demands, the more organizational learning becomes reactive adaptation to external forces instead of independent innovations that combine internal potential and external scope for action. Insufficient use of internal potential may lead to solutions that are far from perfect from a social perspective, too.

The consequence is clearly paradoxical. Many innovation processes that could grow out of a company's own potential and that probably would have better results without external pressure than with it, often commence only because of pressure from social movements. These circumstances are likely to persist. Social movements, the mobilization of social interests, will probably continue to trigger organizational learning processes whose results, if there are any, are arguably inferior to what could have been achieved in the absence of those processes. Ultimately, this paradox probably cannot be resolved, but it can be strategically moderated if the problems and demands articulated by social movements are acknowledged early and dealt with actively.

References

Albracht, G. and Schwerdtfeger, O. A. (eds.) (1991). *Herausforderung Asbest*. Wiesbaden: Universum Verlagsanstalt.

Arbeitsgruppe Dritte Welt Bern (ADWB) (eds.) (1974). *Nestlé tötet Babys*. Bern: ADWB.

Berry, M. A. and Rondinelli, D. A. (1998). 'Proactive Corporate Environmental Management: A New Industrial Revolution'. *Academy of Management Executive*, 12/2: 38–50.

Berthoin Antal, A. (1998). 'Die Dynamik der Theoriebildungsprozesse zum Organisationslernen', in H. Albach, M. Dierkes, A. Berthoin Antal, and K. Vaillant (eds.), *Organisationslernen—institutionelle und kulturelle Dimensionen. WZB Jahrbuch 1998*. Berlin: edition sigma, 31–52.

——Dierkes, M., and Hähner, K. (1994). 'Business in Society: Perceptions and Principles in Organizational Learning'. *Journal of General Management*, 20/2: 55–77.

Boltanski, L. and Thévenot, L. (1991). *De la justification*. Paris: Gallimard.

Davis, G. F. and Thompson, T. A. (1994). 'A Social Movement Perspective on Corporate Control'. *Administrative Science Quarterly*, 39: 141–73.

Deutsch, K. W. (1963). *The Nerves of Government*. London: Collier-Macmillan.

Dobbing, J. (ed.) (1988). *Infant Feeding: Anatomy of a Controversy 1973–1984*. Berlin: Springer.

Dyllick, T. (1989). *Management der Umweltbeziehungen*. Wiesbaden: Gabler.

Elster, J. (1983). *Sour Grapes: Studies in the Subversion of Rationality.* Cambridge, Mass.: Cambridge University Press.

—— (1989). *The Cement of Society: A Study of Social Order.* Cambridge, Mass.: Cambridge University Press.

Favereau, O. (1994). 'Règles, organisation et apprentissage collectif: Un paradigme non standard pour trois théories hétérodoxes', in A. Orléan (ed.), *Analyse économique des conventions.* Paris: Presses Universitaires de France, 113–38.

Friedberg, E. (1993). *Le Pouvoir et la règle.* Paris: Éditions du Seuil.

Gherardi, S. (1999). 'Learning as Problem-driven or Learning in the Face of Mystery?'. *Organization Studies*, 20: 101–24.

Gomez, P.-Y. (1996). *Le Gouvernement de l'entreprise.* Paris: Inter Editions/Masson.

Herkströter, C. (1996). *Dealing with Contradictory Expectations: The Dilemmas Facing Multinationals.* Available: http://195.12.29.164/shellspeech/article.cfm?id=170

IG Metall (ed.) (1976). *IGM-Arbeitssicherheits-Information*, No. 8. Frankfurt am Main: IG Metall.

Interagency Group on Breastfeeding Monitoring (IGBM) (1997). *Cracking the Code.* London: Unicef.

Johnson, D. A. (1986). 'Confronting Corporate Power: Strategies and Phases of the Nestlé Boycott', in J. E. Post (ed.), *Research in Corporate Social Performance and Policy: An Annual Compilation of Research* (Vol. 8). Greenwich, Conn: JAI Press, 323–44.

Kädtler, J. (1986). *Gewerkschaften und Arbeitslosigkeit.* Göttingen: Sovec.

—— and Hertle, H. H. (1997). *Sozialpartnerschaft und Industriepolitik.* Opladen: Westdeutscher Verlag.

Kitschelt, H. P. (1986). 'Political Opportunity Structures and Political Protest: Anti-Nuclear Movements in Four Democracies'. *British Journal of Political Sciences*, 16: 57–85.

—— (1991). 'Resource Mobilization Theory: A Critique', in D. Rucht (ed.), *Research on Social Movements.* Frankfurt am Main: Campus, 323–47.

Klandermans, B. and Tarrow, S. (1988). 'Mobilization into Social Movements: Synthesizing European and American Approaches'. *International Social Movement Research*, 1: 1–38.

Kriesberg, L. and Spencer, M. (eds.) (1991). *Research in Social Movements: Conflicts and Change* (Vol. 13). Greenwich, Conn.: JAI Press.

Lyman, S. F. (ed.) (1995). *Social Movements: Critiques, Concepts, Case-Studies.* Houndmills: Macmillan.

McAdam, D., McCarthy, J. H., and Zald, M. N. (eds.) (1996). *Comparative Perspectives on Social Movements.* Cambridge, Mass.: Harvard University Press.

Orléan, A. (ed.) (1994). *Analyse économique des conventions.* Paris: Presses universitaires de France.

Rucht, D. (ed.) (1991). *Research on Social Movements.* Frankfurt am Main: Campus.

—— (1994). *Modernisierung und neue soziale Bewegungen.* Frankfurt am Main: Campus.

Scherler, P. (1996). *Kommunikation mit externen Anspruchsgruppen als Erfolgsfaktor im Krisenmanagement eines Konzerns: Erfahrungen aus dem Fall Brent Spar (Greenpeace vs. Shell).* Basel: Helbing & Lichtenhahn.

Schumann, M., Gerlach, F., Geschlössl, A., and Milhofer, P. (1971). *Am Beispiel der Septemberstreiks.* Frankfurt am Main: Europäische Verlagsanstalt.

Selikoff, I. J. and Lee, D. H. K. (1978). *Asbestos and Disease.* New York: Harper.

Senat français (1997). *L'Amiante dans l'environnement de l'homme: Ses conséquences et son avenir.* Rapport présenté à l'Office parlementaire des choix scientifiques et technologiques le 19 octobre 1997, Paris.

Sethi, S. P. (1994). *Multinational Corporations and the Impact of Public Advocacy on Corporate Strategy: Nestlé and the Infant Formula Controversy.* Boston: Kluwer.

Shrivastava, P. (1988). 'Editorial: Industrial Crisis Management: Learning from Organizational Failures'. *Journal of Management Studies*, 25: 283–4.

—— Mitroff, I. I., Miller, D., and Miglani, A. (1988). 'Understanding Industrial Crises'. *Journal of Management Studies*, 25: 285–303.

Tarrow, S. (1991). 'Kollektives Handeln und politische Gelegenheitsstruktur in Mobilisierungswellen: Theoretische Perspektiven'. *Kölner Zeitschrift für Soziologie und Sozialpsychologie*, 43: 647–70.

'Tobacco and Tolerance—Blowing Smoke—Tobacco Is Not a Social Problem, But the Anti-Smoking Movement Is Quickly Becoming One'. (1997). *The Economist*, 345/8048: 59–61.

Tomasson, R. F., Crosby, F. J., and Herzberger, S. D. (1996). *Affirmative Action*. Washington, DC: American University Press.

Touraine, A. (1981). *The Voice and the Eye: An Analysis of Social Movements*. London: Cambridge University Press.

—— (1985). 'An Introduction into the Study of Social Movements'. *Social Research*, 51: 749–87.

U.S. Senate (1978). *Marketing and Promotion of Infant Formula in the Developing Countries, Hearings before the Subcommittee on Health and Scientific Research of the Committee on Human Resources*, 95th Cong., 2d Session. May 23 (testimony of Dr. Oswald Ballarin).

Williamson, O. E. (1985). *The Economic Institutions of Capitalism: Firms, Markets, Relational Contracting*. New York: Free Press.

Zald, M. N. (1991). 'The Continuing Vitality of Resource Mobilization Theory: A Response to Herbert Kitschelt's Critique', in D. Rucht (ed.), *Research on Social Movements*. Frankfurt am Main: Campus, 348–54.

—— and McCarthy, J. D. (eds.) (1979). *The Dynamics of Social Movements*. Cambridge, Mass.: Winthrop.

—— —— (eds.) (1987). *Social Movements in Organizational Society*. New Brunswick, NJ: Transaction Books.

10 Triggers of Organizational Learning during the Transformation Process in Central European Countries

Hans Merkens, Mike Geppert, and David Antal

Organizational learning during the transformation process experienced in Europe's former socialist countries has taken place under particularly difficult circumstances. The businesses in those regions have had to adjust to an environment that has been changing dramatically since the early 1990s. Their challenge has been to internalize a new type of organizational behavior in order to operate successfully under unfamiliar, market-based conditions. The purpose of this chapter is to explain what triggers the process of developing radically new behavior or of seeking evolutionary behavioral change when an organization's environment is in rapid flux. In the following sections both types of change are regarded as organizational learning.

We identify the main triggers of this process as experienced by selected companies[1] in four central European countries whose transformation from a socialist to a market economy is documented best: the former German Democratic Republic (GDR), the Czech Republic,[2] Poland, and Hungary. For all their differences, these countries are similar in a number of

ways. First, foreign investment in their industries has been greater than that in the industries of other former socialist countries (Child with Czeglédy 1996: 169). Second, all four central European countries boast a well-educated work force and a high level of technical know-how. Third, the former GDR, the Czech Republic, Poland, and Hungary are situated so near western Europe that strong economic relations have been established between them and western European industrial economies since 1990.

The analysis begins with a description of features of the transformation process that has taken place in the four countries and the various companies examined below. Those features are then linked to theories of organizational learning that might appropriately explain our observations. The triggers we identify are then associated with two types of organizational learning: structuralist and constructivist.

The Transformation of the Economic System in Formerly Socialist Countries of Central Europe

In physics, transformation signifies that a well-defined state X_1 is changed into another

---

[1] The term *company* refers in this chapter to the business units operating in a market economy. The term *plant* refers to the production, distribution, and service units of former socialist economies.

[2] We use the adjective *Czechoslavakian* and the noun *Czechoslovakia* to refer to the period before the official separation of the Czech and Slovakian parts of the country on 1 January 1993. The words *Czech* and the *Czech Republic* are used to refer to the period thereafter.

well-defined state X_2. A voltage U_1, for example, is transformed into a voltage U_2. In the social realm, however, neither the starting nor ending point of a transformation process is well defined (Child with Czeglédy 1996: 171; Schomer and Herkenhoff 1994). This ambiguity is demonstrated by the national economies of the four countries in our sample.

Given this diffuseness of transformation in societies, we begin our treatment of the transformation process by pointing out that the former socialist economic systems under consideration did have evident organizational and systemic similarities in addition to the economic and geographical commonalities already noted. First, socialist economies had systems within systems, ranging downwards from the ministries, to the conglomerates, and to the various firms. The need for planning and for regulating these systems within systems required a complex, hierarchical, bureaucratic apparatus at each level (Klein 1996; Kornai 1992). Socialist economies were also characterized by a separation between production and distribution and by the lack of a service sector. For example, each plant had its own large service department with its own craftspersons for carrying out repairs. In that sense, the plants were organized as self-contained entities. Second, throughout the socialist period in all four countries, there was a precapitalist shadow economy on which real goods and products were bartered in the private and public sectors in order to compensate for shortcomings of the socialist economies (Grabher 1995; Srubar 1994).

These pretransformation commonalities notwithstanding, separate courses were sometimes taken when it came to the pursuit of economic affairs. During much of the era after World War II, a strictly socialist economy was practised in Czechoslovakia and the GDR, with the private sector being small. By contrast, elements of a market economy had always existed during the socialist period in Poland (Ulrich 1991: 22) and especially in Hungary (Andorka 1996; Grabher 1995). In Poland agriculture was based largely on private ownership (Duke and Grime 1994: 157). Hungary abandoned centralized economic planning in 1968 (Schomer

and Herkenhoff 1994) and developed a second, market-like, government-sanctioned economy that was a mainstay of the country's service sector (Grabher 1995). Beginning in 1984, state property rights were transferred to joint corporate committees of managers and employees (Heidenreich 1994: 5). Since 1987 it has been permissible to found commercial businesses with shares owned by domestic investors outside the plants and, later, the companies (Móra 1991). Subsequent outsourcing was the first step in reorganizing the highly centralized corporate structure of Hungarian businesses (Heidenreich 1994: 5). In Poland joint ventures with Western companies existed from the mid-1980s on, and centralized economic planning was eliminated in 1989 (Schomer and Herkenhoff 1994: 211–12). In that year the functions of commercial banking were separated from those of the state central bank, and a few private banks were founded (Wenzeler 1995: 47). In the 1980s parts of Poland's industry started creeping down the path of privatization by outsourcing functions hitherto performed within the combines (Heidenreich 1994; Staniszkis 1990, 1991).

Just as the starting point of economic transformation in the Czechoslovakian, former East German, Polish, and Hungarian economies is hard to define, so are the respective endpoints of the transformation. Development in these new market economies has by now diverged widely (Apolte and Cassel 1991; Child with Czeglédy 1996: 168), largely because each country (except the former GDR) had to achieve its transformation mostly with its own national resources (see Dörr and Kessel 1996: 45). Consequently, all four countries have economic systems that resemble a market economy more strongly in some domains than in others (Andorka 1996; Apolte and Cassel 1991), depending primarily upon the manner in which the process of privatization has been conducted (Stark and Bruszt 1998).

- The former GDR, which acceded to the Federal Republic of Germany to form a united nation, now has the strongest market economy of the group under consideration in this chapter. The transformation of corporations was achieved by means of shock therapy (Bryson 1992; Pickel 1992). That is, no social scruples buffered the organizational transformation itself (Wiesenthal 1996: 279). Most of the firms in eastern Germany are now stock companies whose owners are located in western German or other Western industrialized countries (Grabher 1995; Heidenreich 1994; Wiesenthal 1996).

- In the Czech Republic, most firms have been privatized in formal terms but in reality are still controlled by the state (Mladek 1995; Ulrich 1991). Industrial restructuring in particular has progressed little, and few initiatives to restructure have been forthcoming from either managers or corporations (Heidenreich 1994: 9).
- In Hungary the status of most companies is similar to that of companies in the Czech Republic, but the legal arrangements are not as clear (Andorka 1996; Grabher 1995) because, in Hungary, the property rights that had been granted to the joint corporate committees of managers and employees were transferred in 1992 to a state-controlled property agency (Heidenreich 1994: 5). In addition, the linkages between state-owned and private corporations are convoluted. Nonetheless, privatization from the bottom up was successful among small businesses. (For further details about the economic developments in Hungary during the transformation, see Lyles, Ch. 30 in this volume.)
- In Poland, by contrast, the distinction between private and state ownership is clear, with many large corporations remaining state-owned (Bornstein 1997; Srubar 1994; Thieme 1995; Wenzeler 1995; Winiecki 1995). As in Hungary, bottom-up privatization has been important in the process of transformation (Heidenreich 1994: 7). Labor-union resistance to the privatization of state-owned businesses has mounted because union members have feared for their jobs (Srubar 1994: 201).

These similarities and differences in the approach to the transformation in these four central European countries are summarized in Table 10.1.

In addition to recognizing that both the point of departure and the endpoint of transformation may differ from one country to the next, one must also ask whether it is the patterns of organizational learning itself that diverge or whether that learning differs primarily in terms of its speed. And is transformation the sole trigger of organizational learning? Are there other triggers that influence the speed, direction, or results of the learning process?

Table 10.1. Similarities and differences in the approach to transformation in central Europe

Dimension of transformation	East Germany	Czech Republic	Hungary	Poland
Execution of privatization				
Government		X	X	X
Special institutions	X			
Type of privatization				
Voucher		X		X
Mostly state ownership			X	X
Private ownership	X			
Past market experience			X	X

Types of Organizational Learning under the Conditions of Transformation

The enterprises in the Czech Republic, Hungary, the former GDR, and Poland had no concept of organizational learning by which to manage their transformation. They coped with the changes more or less by 'muddling through' (Berthoin Antal, Dierkes, and Marz 1998). Only in retrospect can the term 'organizational learning' be used to describe the process that the companies in these central European countries have been going through. But this view is possible only if one distinguishes between different concepts of organizational learning. Because no commonly agreed-upon definition of organizational learning exists (Berthoin Antal 1998: 32), very different concepts can be drawn upon to describe the processes involved (see also Lyles, Ch. 30 in this volume).

Organizational learning can be described as 'the capacity of an organization to learn how to do what it does, where what it learns is possessed not by individual members of the organization but by the aggregate itself' (Cook and Yanow 1996: 438). This concept focuses on organizations as a whole, not on the particular members of the organization. Moreover, it portrays all organizations as learning organizations and rests on the postulation that they differ only in their needs and capacities for learning (Nevis, DiBella, and Gould 1995). To describe the need for organizations to learn, one could therefore say that the most important challenge in the transformation process of a company's plants in Hungary, Poland, the former GDR, and the Czech Republic has perhaps been that the demands of the central plan had to be replaced by a market-oriented definition of the economic environment.

This insight is not to be taken for granted; it had to be acquired. But where was it to come from? Not from the past. In the beginning of the transformation process, past experience was deemed irrelevant (Rottenburg 1991; Nilsson 1996). New models had to be found in relevant environments (the 'scanning imperative'; see Nevis, DiBella, and Gould 1995: 77), and it was only natural to focus on and try to imitate successful (i.e. Western) corporations (DiMaggio and Powell 1983), for they had not been discredited (Child with Czeglédy 1996: 170). In learning theory the concept of imitation means 'a process by which "matched" or similar acts are evoked in two people and connected to appropriate cues' (Miller and Dollard 1941: 11; see also Hannan and Freeman 1984). At the organizational level during the transformation process in central Europe, the term meant that externally observable features of Western organizations were adopted.

In other words, most central European enterprises initially copied organizational structures of Western companies (Czarniawska-Joerges 1994), a process whose behavioral outcomes can be described as structuralist learning because the change in the subsystems or corporate structure (*Aufbauorganisation*) was intentional. This imitative learning is normal for organizations if they look to a model when they 'map their environments in order to be able to act and react' (Berthoin Antal and Böhling 1998: 216; see also Weick 1987). A specific structural feature used in Hungary more often than in the former GDR, the Czech Republic, and Poland is the holding company (Carlin, Van Reenen, and Wolfe 1995: 443), the legal form into which most of the old combines have been changed. In eastern Germany the combines were broken up, and in many cases their parts were downsized or closed altogether, changes that had to be accomplished selectively for the most part (Cameron 1994: 193). At the same time, however, the resulting divisions or companies had to find new solutions for the new challenges of marketing, sales, and controlling (Berthoin Antal and Merkens 1993; Carlin, Van Reenen, and Wolfe 1995: 433; Mickler, Engelhard, Lungwitz, and Walker 1996; Pocztovski 1995).

The decision to adopt Western organizational structures therefore had multiple ramifications. With the shift away from central planning, the directorates—which had been the direct link between the planning authorities of the combines, those of the respective plants, and the government ministries responsible for industries—were jettisoned early in the process of transformation, for they were simply no longer needed. Directorates for social services were also closed, albeit for a different reason. Reassessing traditional socialist assumptions about social and economic responsibilities and what it took to meet them, emerging companies decided to focus solely on economic priorities and renounced their corporate responsibility for providing social services to workers. This redefinition of responsibility had further ramifications, for the routine procedures (or what Laughlin 1991 called design archetypes) that had once guided the work force in its effort to meet production targets vanished.

The effect of this simultaneous dismantling and building up of organizational structure and of the concomitant changes in work processes can be understood as an oxymoron, a term that Weick and Westley (1996: 440) have applied to organizational learning in the West. To them, organizing and learning are antithetical processes. Organization involves a reduction of variety, whereas learning necessarily entails at least some degree of *dis*organization—an *increase* in variety (see also Haiss 1996). Argyris and Schön (1978) refer to such learning as 'double-loop learning' (p. 21) because companies had to define new alternatives in their environment. More precisely, however, it must be described as 'deutero-learning' (p. 26) or, better, as 'learning II' (response to a change in the set of alternatives that guide choices) or 'learning III' (a response to a change in the number of sets of alternatives that guide choices (Bateson 1972: 292–306)). In the companies struggling to adapt to the changed economic realities of central and eastern Europe, new structures such as marketing and sales and controlling had to be built in order to give the direction that had once been afforded by the plan. Ultimately, the entire economic rationale behind the previous plant's existence and operation had to be changed.

In short, organizational learning has been compelled at two levels during the transform-

ation in the companies examined in this chapter. First, in very human terms, there is the manager trying to ensure his or her sheer survival by anticipating the expectations of other companies operating under market conditions (an allusion to Mead's 1934 concept of the 'generalized other'). Second, superordinate (i.e. external) organizations, such as the *Treuhand* in Germany[3] (see Weber 1996), the twelve investment privatization funds in the Czech Republic, and the National Investment Fund in Poland, have obliged companies to change their structures in prescribed ways. Processes at both levels can be seen as examples of forced learning (Child and Markóczy 1993).

Both levels have consequences for the way employees perform their jobs, for in many cases new structures require their attendant organizational behaviors to be learned. Whereas plants under the previous regime were intended to produce only what the population was 'objectively' said to need (the concept of socialism), companies operating under the new economic conditions of transformation were expected to produce only what they could *sell* (the concept of a market economy). The new behaviors also included the hitherto alien practice of monitoring and reporting the costs, exact inventory, and production level of the company (the concept of controlling). The functioning of the systems can be described with the open-system approach, in which the organization may be seen as answering the challenges of a new environment (Llewellyn 1994). In the newly formed companies in Hungary, Poland, the Czech Republic, and the former GDR, this type of learning has been as difficult as it has been crucial. The companies may have adopted the structures of marketing, sales, and controlling, for example, but when responding to them, the members of the work force have drawn on the only experience they had, namely, that with socialist production organizations. The type of learning that results from such melding of old work habits

---

[3] The government holding company set up in and by the Federal Republic of Germany in the early 1990s to sell off or liquidate the state-owned businesses and property of the former GDR.

and new organizational structures has been labeled *constructivist* (Czarniawska-Joerges 1994; Nilsson 1996; for key assumptions about constructivist learning, see Macharzina, Oesterle, and Brodel, Ch. 28 in this volume). In short, the learning is embedded in work routines (Nonaka 1994: 14). Because constructivist learning is thereby socially embedded yet also accommodating of new structures, it is an integrative concept of learning. It brings about new routines and habits (Clark and Soulsby 1995; Nilsson 1996).

Given the indisputable fact that structural changes have occurred in the former GDR, the Czech Republic, Poland, and Hungary, one may ask whether the organizational learning during that transformation has been structuralist or constructivist (Nilsson 1996). Neither concept of learning alone can explain the divergent experiences that each of the four countries has had since 1990. Arguably, both structuralist and constructivist learning are contained in a model by Laughlin (1991), who distinguished between three levels within organizations: subsystems, design archetypes, and culture. His basic assumption was that making changes (which can be seen as an indicator of organizational learning) is relatively simple at the level of subsystems (structure) but more complicated at the level of design archetypes (e.g. the change from the socialist plan to a controlling function as understood in a market economy). According to Laughlin, making changes in organizations is all but impossible at the level of culture because work habits become obstacles to change. An excellent example of this challenge to change habits is the attempt to move from a centrally to a decentrally run system. In terms of belief systems—another dimension of culture—it is difficult to accept the change from security to risk. Schein (1993) added that anxiety and fear hamper organizational learning. To him, anxiety is based on past experience with unsuccessful organizational behavior.

Drawing on Hofstede (1984), Nasierowski and Mikula (1998) underscored the difficulties of structural learning-by-imitation by pointing out deep cultural differences between Polish and Canadian managers. Those differences amount to a special type of inertia for organizational learning: cultural embeddedness (Espejo, Schumann, Schwaninger, and Bilello 1996). Citing Hannan and Freeman (1984, 1989) and Lounamaa and March (1987), Levinthal (1996) pointed out that at least structural inertia is normally positive for organizational learning. Similarly, Pettigrew (1985) and Child and Smith (1987) argued that organizational learning is more effective if changes are combined with elements of continuity.

Be that as it may, central and eastern European countries *have* undergone cultural changes, some of them profound indeed. As just pointed out, companies have abandoned the assumption that they have responsibility for both the social and economic dimensions and have come to focus almost exclusively on economic criteria. Documented resistance to the loss of the social safety net, such as at Fiat in Poland (Gaciarz and Panków 1996: 145), has been the exception. A second example is that the working class has given up its leading role in companies. The worker representation within the economic decision-making organs of socialist plants was dissolved when market structures were introduced. Formerly sovereign workers overwhelmingly accepted a new role as dependent employees. When it comes to transformation, cultural values are thus evidently just as subject to change as corporate subsystems and design archetypes.

Utter anarchy cannot reign for long, either, however. A certain continuity is bound to exist between past experience and new realities (Greenwood and Hinings 1988; for the U.S. context, see Hitt and Ireland 1987). As explained by Clark and Soulsby (1995), 'the organization's subsystems, structure, and culture will tend to be mutually consistent and supportive, leading to internal resistance to change' (p. 218). In the new companies of the former GDR, the Czech Republic, Poland, and Hungary, this inertia is evident in the constructivist type of learning that has taken place. The rapid adoption of marketing and sales departments did not mean that the workers-turned-salespeople of the companies in our sample suddenly knew how to market their products suitably. Nor did the introduction of costing mean that the employees of former socialist plants had automatically mastered the complexities of break-even-point analysis. The members of the former socialist work force quite often fell back on the thinking and work habits they knew, and the experience of their companies was more successful when they did draw on strengths (Dörr and Kessel 1999; Merkens *et al.* 1994; Merkens *et al.* 1996) than when they did not (Gaciarz and Panków 1996). It takes time to learn new—and appropriate—behavior (on the meaning of time in the process of cultural change in organizations, see Weber and Berthoin Antal, Ch. 15 in this volume).

Under these circumstances, what is learned (and practiced) inevitably differs from pure imitation. In the companies we are considering, cultural traditions and habitualized routines have partially resurfaced to influence the kind of structures and procedures that have emerged from the transformation of the economic environment. In this sense the process of organizational change in the former GDR, Poland, the Czech Republic, and Hungary has been paradoxical. Launched as a reorganization, it has entailed a *dis*organization that has produced a new kind of entity somewhere in-between the socialist plant and the market-oriented company whose imitation had been attempted. The newly formed companies in these four countries have had to find their own *modus operandi*. Various levels of this search are identified in Table 10.2.

In fact, it appears that organizations *must* respond in this way if they are to survive the transformation under discussion in this chapter. Disorganizing (increasing the variety of structures and procedures) parallels the process of organizing (combining previous structures and procedures with new ones). The result is a new mix of these features. Since 1990 the transformation in central Europe has produced organizational forms that differ widely both within Hungary, the Czech Republic, Poland, and the former GDR and across all of them. As shown in the following section, this variety can be explained by different triggers operating in the transformation process.

Empirical Findings: Triggers and Organizational Learning in the Former GDR, the Czech Republic, Poland, and Hungary

Triggers may be defined as the conditions that initiate change. The most general of these conditions for change is a transformation of the economic and societal system in which a company operates. Within this overall framework, one can distinguish between triggers that compel structuralist learning and triggers that can set up constructivist learning. In the following sections the empirical examples of structuralist and constructivist learning focus on three well-documented, comparable dimensions: high investment (the automotive industry and investment goods), suppliers (the automotive industry), and success in domestic markets (the pharmaceutical industry and investment goods).

Triggers of Structuralist Learning

When radical changes occur in a social and economic system, organizations usually adapt their behavior to the new conditions of their environment. Radical change therefore often triggers organizational learning. According to Ulrich (1991: 22–3), the character of the Polish, Czechoslovakian, Hungarian, and former East German economies was revolutionized in at least three ways: the privatization of the markets (through the unfreezing of wages and prices and the introduction of real markets along with the risk of bankruptcy and unemployment), the opening of the markets to foreign competitors (through the elimination of the state monopoly on imports and exports), and the dissolution of socialist monopoly structures. In addition, there are two kinds of change that do not always function as triggers outright but that can serve rather as enabling factors: foreign investment and the introduction and use of new technologies. (In the companies discussed here, however, these two kinds of change do happen to function as triggers.)

Table 10.2. Types of organizational learning during the transformation in central Europe

Dimension of organization	Structuralist		Constructivist	
	Disorganizing	Organizing	Disorganizing	Organizing
Subsystems	Dissolution of socialist organizational units	Opening of departments or functional areas (e.g. marketing and sales)		
Design archetypes	Socialist plan	Controlling	Socialist plan	New decision-making routines
Interpretive schemes			Basic habits: action taken upon order, command, or instruction	Basic habits: action often negotiated before carried out
			Belief systems: security	Belief systems: risk

Trigger 1: Privatization and Opening of Markets

Perhaps the most important trigger in these four central European economies has been the privatization of markets (Mertlik 1996: 94). It has brought about the double risk of both unemployment and bankruptcy. It has altered the relation between the company work force and the corporate management, for under socialism citizens had a right to employment. They could not be fired. With the introduction of Western-style employment practices, this former right became conditional. Each worker had to agree to an employment contract with company management. This process has forged a new relation between the two parties in that some of the economic risk of operation (unemployment) has been shifted from the company as employer to the workers as employees. The result has been a high risk of unemployment in the former GDR, Hungary, and Poland (Myant *et al.* 1996: 104), though it has remained low in the Czech Republic (Dörr and Kessel 1996: 45; on the role of fear and anxiety as obstacles to organizational learning, see Scherer and Tran, Ch. 16 in this volume).

At the same time, the risk of bankruptcy has forced former socialist enterprises to wean themselves from the socialist principle that production units should be self-sufficient, for it proved to be an inefficient way to organize an economy. Since the onset of the transformation in the former socialist economies, the companies therein have had to base their activities on contracted services and resources. This reliance on negotiated contracts is increased further by the need to ensure sales. Customers, in turn, can be won over and kept only if the company can ensure competitive quality and prices. Uncompetitive quality and prices eventually result in bankruptcy, a fate that has been particularly common among enterprises in the former GDR and least common among the state-controlled enterprises in Hungary and Poland.

In Europe's former socialist economies, privatization has been accompanied by the opening of markets to foreign competition. Companies in Poland, Hungary, the Czech Republic, and the former GDR have consequently lost sections of their home market because domestic products and services (e.g. Robotron computers in the former GDR) were inferior to and more expensive than their foreign counterparts. To replace these markets, companies in these former socialist countries have tried to find, create, and dominate niches in foreign markets. Because wages are lower in the former socialist countries than in Western countries, one possibility for pursuing this strategy has been to become a supplier of labor-intensive and low-technology products. Czech companies have been particularly successful in this capacity since the onset of economic transformation. By contrast, the companies of the former GDR have had little hope of competing that way because they have been integrated into Germany's high-wage economy. For Czech companies, however, the long-term effects of pursuing a work-intensive, low-technology strategy are unpromising because the work forces of these organizations have meanwhile learned little about modern manufacturing methods and no longer find their products successful against those of competitors elsewhere in the world.

Trigger 2: Dissolution of the Combines

A further consequence of the privatization and opening of markets in the Polish, Czech, Hungarian, and former East German economies is the collapse of the combines, in which the monopolistic structures of the social economy were rooted. These giant organizations were broken up into independent economic units, or companies, each of which is expected to produce goods or services that it can actually sell (Myant *et al.* 1996). In the Czech Republic the initiative for organizational change came from middle managers and employees in many cases (Carlin, Van Reenen, and Wolfe 1995: 437). In the GDR of 1990, moves toward independence from the combines originated in the directorates of particular plants (Merkens *et al.* 1991), an initiative subsequently pursued by the *Treuhand* (see Weber 1996). The combines, which had afforded their production units protection from competition, vanished (Mertlik 1996: 94). A prime example of the new structures that emerged was the outsourcing of the maintenance, tool-making, and machine-building departments that had existed in the East

German combines and plants before they were dissolved (Geppert and Merkens 1999). These departments became small, independent engineering companies, all of which together offered more capacity than even the unified German economy could absorb. Many of the new companies ultimately went bankrupt.

The dissolution of the combines also posed new challenges to the companies because each company that was formed had to offer products or services for which it saw (or presumed to see) a market. Markets had to be analyzed and segmented, so the companies needed to introduce sales and marketing activities and had to learn to respond to perceived conditions of the market or to define new markets (Myant *et al.* 1996). These activities and responses called for the formation of new departments. Jenoptik, an eastern German company, decided to halt production for half a year on government subsidy in order to have its R&D employees develop new high-tech products and seek markets for them (Merkens *et al.* 1996). The additional task of locating markets for the products fell to these researchers. The attempt failed, whereupon Jenoptik bought smaller companies that had access to specific markets, the idea being to use the smaller companies as conduits for selling Jenoptik's products.

In other words, an initial phase of constructivist trial-and-error learning was followed by a period of surgical intervention in the organizational structure of the companies. It was a period of structural changes during which other, smaller companies (e.g. producers of automotive parts or clean rooms) were acquired in order to increase the market access of the parent company. These acquisitions, in turn, forced the parent company to adjust its products, standards, and prices to its new market realities (Merkens *et al.* 1996). The parent company did so through constructivist learning, in which previous skills were adapted to the new economic situation.

The interdependence of structuralist and constructivist learning is illustrated not only by Jenoptik's futile attempt to assign its researchers the task of sales and marketing but also by a different approach to transformation.

Berlin-Chemie, a pharmaceutical firm of the former GDR, added a new department of marketing and sales to its existing corporate structure. The employees in the new department, however, had been workers in other areas of the company. They had no experience in marketing and sales (Merkens *et al.* 1991; Merkens *et al.* 1992).

The same kind of problem existed in the Czech Republic, Poland, and Hungary, too, where success in overcoming it varied. At one Czech company a reasonably well-qualified middle-management team was molded within six months through a crash program of seminars and subsequent short- and long-term training for employees in all new departments (Myant *et al.* 1996). At Berlin-Chemie, however, such a program was established only for the new department of controlling and finance. The marketing and sales department continued muddling through, and the company's sales steadily declined in its domestic market. Berlin-Chemie did successfully continue along the old path of negotiating contracts with government offices in eastern Europe, and this unchanged behavior did sustain overall sales until late 1993, but the marketing and sales department exhibited little organizational learning until the company was acquired by Menarini, an Italian firm (Merkens *et al.* 1994). The new owner replaced key marketing and sales employees with managers from western Germany who were versed in modern practices of marketing and sales. The company then went on to reconquer much of its traditional domestic market and build an efficient marketing organization in selected eastern European countries (Merkens *et al.* 1994; Merkens *et al.* 1998). The success that Berlin-Chemie enjoyed in the first years of the transformation continued, but it lay on new foundations. As at Jenoptik, the trial-and-error learning in the first phase of the transformation failed at Berlin-Chemie; people engaged in it only as individuals rather than as groups. The surgical intervention in the second phase, however, focused on a broader clientele: key managers who functioned as multipliers by communicating their expertise to their respective departments. Evid-

ently, the likelihood that organizational learning will be initiated successfully is greatly enhanced if members of a department are involved as a unit, not just as individual employees. The organizational structure (the department of marketing and sales) at Berlin-Chemie remained unchanged, and the new, Western managers initiated a process of constructivist learning for the organization as a whole.

These two examples show the profound changes ushered in by organizational behavior that had to be learned as a result of the privatization and opening of eastern European markets. In the transformation process, learning with the aim of developing a new organizational structure and behavior must itself be organized; otherwise, the process of disorganizing as the first step may well not promote learning.

Trigger 3: Privatization of Companies

One trigger influencing especially the speed of organizational learning is the privatization of organizations, more specifically, the *way* in which they are privatized. Some of the approaches are outlined by Stark and Bruszt (1998: 53), who offered four dimensions by which to classify types of privatization: (a) foreign versus domestic ownership, (b) spontaneous privatization versus privatization controlled and directed by state agencies, (c) institutional versus national ownership, and (d) concentrated versus dispersed ownership. Foreign ownership compelled newly founded companies to adopt the corporate structures and expectations of the new owners (Dörr and Kessel 1999; Gaciarz and Panków 1996; Merkens *et al.* 1998). In the former GDR, for example, privatization was, for the most part, controlled and directed by a state agency (the *Treuhand*) and was introduced through dispersed ownership (Geppert and Kachel 1995), an alternative that came to be experienced as shock therapy.

In the other three countries, the range of dimensions for privatizing was broader. The Czech Republic, for instance, availed itself of restitution, municipalization, transformation of cooperatives, and both small- and large-scale privatization (the latter of which included vouchers, public auctions and tenders, direct sales to predetermined buyers, entry on the stock market, free transfers to municipalities, and the establishment of pension funds; see Mladek 1995). In the industrial sector, privatization proceeded primarily in two ways: 'First, the corporatization and subsequent sale of (former) state-owned enterprises to private bodies, and, second, the "voucher method"' (Mertlik 1996: 95), a nontraditional privatization technique that is based upon free distribution of former state-owned-enterprise shares among the general population. In addition, many enterprises remained in state hands (Myant *et al.* 1996: 135), as in Poland, too (Poznanska and Poznański 1996). In all the cases where ownership remained with the state, change in corporate structures, and hence organizational learning, was impeded. Modifying a term ('facilitating factor') used by Nevis, DiBella, and Gould (1995), one may say that vouchers were a *non-facilitating* factor in organizational learning.

In Poland other companies were privatized and then sold to foreign buyers, and some smaller ones were bought out by the employees. These approaches quickly brought such organizations to market-oriented thinking and practice. Some larger companies were partly privatized by means of vouchers or were transformed into joint-stock companies (Thieme 1995; Winiecki 1995).

Trigger 4: Foreign Investment

In all four countries dealt with in this chapter, the automotive industry shows that privatization involving foreign partners attracts high foreign investment (see Table 10.3), which, in turn, often leads to structural changes (Schomer and Herkenhoff 1994). The most instructive case illustrating this trigger of organizational learning (privatization combined with high foreign investment) is Skoda, a Czechoslovakian car manufacturer that was bought by Volkswagen (VW) in a joint venture with the Czechoslovakian government in the early 1990s. The purchasing contract contained,

among other things, the Czechoslovakian government's stipulation that Skoda's entire chain of value creation was to remain intact. This demand, however, eventually collided with VW's production concepts, which allowed for only certain types of, say, chassis and engines throughout the company. Such restrictions have meanwhile come to channel Skoda's activities away from R&D and primarily toward manufacturing (Dörr and Kessel 1997a, 1997b, 1999). Nevertheless, Skoda initiated 'the formation of a further 42 joint ventures at its Czech suppliers. Thanks to the links to Volkswagen and to foreign partners, they have been provided with the necessary financial means, managerial expertise and development capacities to reach the level required for the western European motor industry' (Myant *et al.* 1996: 187). In other words, a process of organizational learning that began at Skoda spread to a large number of suppliers (for a similar case involving Honda and its suppliers in Japan, see Sadler, Ch. 18 in this volume).

An additional important aspect of privatization as a trigger of the organizational learning at Skoda is that the original attempt to transfer methods of production and work processes from Volkswagen to Skoda foundered on the resistance of Skoda's middle management and workers, whose experience with organizing work had been ignored. If cooperation between the two companies was to continue, a third, constructivist path had to be opened: an organization of work that also drew upon what Skoda's Czech work force already knew and had practiced with regard to work processes (Dörr and Kessel 1996: 51).

Effects of foreign investment involved in the privatization of the economy as a trigger of organizational learning are also illustrated by a joint-venture company founded by Suzuki in Hungary (Schomer and Herkenhoff 1994: 232). The new company selected suppliers in Hungary on the basis of technological and financial audits 'covering literally every single aspect of [their] business' (Havas 1995: 40) in order to ascertain their capacity to deliver quality parts dependably. The prospective suppliers had to demonstrate the ability to operate under the

Table 10.3. Top ten foreign investments in the Czech Republic, Hungary, and Poland, 1990–2002[a]

Investor	Local Partner	Share (in %)	Investment (in millions of U.S.$) 1994, 1997	Until 2002
Czech Republic				
Volkswagen Germany	Skoda Automotive Works	79	1,200[b]	2,500[b]
Poland				
Fiat Italy	Fiat FSM[c]	90	1,300[b]	1,800[b]
Hungary				
Volkswagen–Audi Germany	Audi Hungaria Motor (greenfield)	100	360[b]	555[b]
General Motors (USA, Germany)	GM Hungary (greenfield)	67	300[d]	390[b]
Suzuki, C. Itoh, International Finance Corporation (Japan, International)	Magyar Suzuki (joint venture greenfield)	60	250[d]	250[b]

[a] Almost all investment in companies formed from former East German plants was by West German firms, not foreign organizations. For example, plants of the IFA combine were bought by Volkswagen (Mosel) and Daimler Benz (Ludwigsfelde). Opel (Eisenach) opened a new plant but did not take over the work force of the plant in Eisenach. Opel treated the plant as a new founding.

[b] Dörr and Kessel 1999.

[c] Fabryka Samochodow Malolitrazowych (small-car factory).

[d] Kogut 1996.

conditions of total quality management and just-in-time delivery (Havas 1995: 44). The structural and behavioral changes that these demands entailed for Suzuki's suppliers in Hungary can clearly be described as the outcomes of foreign investment as a trigger of organizational learning (for further aspects of organizational learning by suppliers, see Lane, Ch. 31 in this volume).

A second effect of foreign investment as a trigger of organizational learning in Suzuki's case was that most of the company's local suppliers were bought by its worldwide suppliers. For this reason further organizational changes, and hence structuralist learning, became possible and indispensable within these local suppliers. For example, their R&D departments were no longer needed, so they were eliminated by the new foreign owners. This change, however, henceforth confined Suzuki's domestic Hungarian suppliers to a production function (Havas 1995).

In Poland, too, the success of privatized companies has been closely associated with foreign investment. However, the only companies that were privatized and then sold to foreign buyers were those that were economically sound in the first place (Thieme 1995), a practice that was followed throughout Hungary (Galgóczi 1994), the Czech Republic (Myant et al. 1996), and the former GDR. As the case of Suzuki's suppliers shows, 'economically sound' means, at least in part, that a company must have a viable product and the capacity to learn. This

understanding obviously introduces a selection effect that weakens the previously asserted
logical link between privatization and restructuring.

In addition to privatization and foreign investment as direct triggers, there is evidence of
what could even be regarded as indirect triggers. Galgóczi (1994) pointed out that, in economic sectors with a high percentage of
privatized companies, the *non*privatized firms
have demonstrated more organizational learning than have companies in economic sectors
with a lower degree of privatization. Galgóczi's
findings may be interpreted as a further example of linkages between structuralist and
constructivist learning because nonprivatized
companies, too, were forced to initiate processes of organizational learning in order to
survive.

In Poland[4] Fiat forced the three companies it
had bought (two suppliers and one company
that had previously produced Fiat's cars under
license) to restructure along Fiat's lines (Gaciarz
and Panków 1996). Granted, the employees in
Poland did go on strike, and the company was
compelled to 'guarantee a stabilized employment level for a fixed number of years' and to
make major wage concessions (Poznanska and
Poźnanski 1996: 74), but Fiat succeeded in carrying out the desired structural changes (and operations at Fiat in Poland were confined to
production). Evidently, when the foreign
buyer is strong enough and stubborn enough,
then foreign investment can be a trigger for
structuralist learning. If the cultural differences
are too great to bridge easily, as was the case
with Fiat in Poland (Barkema, Shenkar, Vermeulen, and Bell 1997: 431; Czeglédy 1996), and
if relations between the two sides remain
strained, as was also the case (Gaciarz and Panków 1996: 149), then organizational learning
may be reduced to structuralist learning.

All other cases represented in the body and
notes of Table 10.3 also document similar processes by which the companies involved were
reduced to a purely manufacturing function

from the outset. In the central European companies in our sample, it therefore generally appears that a high share of foreign investment
narrows a company's functions (Gaciarz and
Panków 1996; Havas 1995). In this way companies founded in central Europe and acquired
by foreign buyers during the transformation in
central Europe were thrown back on their
previous strengths, the production of goods.
External triggers of structuralist organizational
learning (privatization and foreign investment) are complemented by an internal trigger
of structuralist organizational learning (whatever function the company performs best).

A similar result is discernible with the voucher system in the Czech Republic. Vouchers
brought little money into the companies that
had been transformed (Mertlik 1996; Myant *et
al.* 1996), so these companies *had* to restrict
themselves to low-technology types of production, which, in turn, provided little momentum for reorganizing that area of corporate
activity. For lack of money, no other area in
the companies could be successfully reorganized, either. 'They are typically characterized by
obsolete products and services, bad payment
discipline, low productivity and efficiency, an
excessive number of employees, and a low interest from top management in the implementation of radical change' (Myant *et al.* 1996: 179).
Mertlik (1996: 101) noted another weakness of
these companies as well: a lack of strategic management. Most financially strapped central European companies have remained inflexible and
inefficient (Schmögnerová 1993). For many of
them, organizational learning was concentrated on low-technology activities, a narrowed
scope that compromised their prospects for the
future.

Granted, Czech, Polish, and Hungarian companies that have concentrated on low-tech and
wage-intensive kinds of production have been
rewarded by contracts with Western companies, but they have thereby been locked into
this status. An experimental mind-set has not
been able to develop (Nevis, DiBella, and Gould
1995: 77). This strategy of wage-intensive production is supported by an undervaluation of
the national currency (Myant *et al.* 1996: 116).

---

[4] Fabryka Samochodow Malolitrazowych (small-car factory).

Though the voucher system had the initial advantage of helping keep the unemployment rate low, the unemployment rate has been increasing in the Czech Republic since 1997. In summary, state-owned companies located in Poland, Hungary, or the Czech Republic received no foreign investment, so the characteristics of production have been low-tech or, in some cases, medium-tech products and low value-added (Galgóczi 1994; Havas 1995; Whitley and Czaban 1998).

Trigger 5: The Introduction and Use of New Technologies in a Company

New technologies can spur organizational learning particularly in areas of corporate activity in which the company work force can draw on its skills and knowledge. In manufacturing, for example, new interfaces between production, maintenance, and quality control are created when new technologies are introduced (Malsch 1988). A similar effect is the dynamization of relations between sales and production in and beyond the manufacturing sector (Merkens *et al.* 1994). These triggers function particularly at the level of design archetypes.

The challenge posed by the influx of new technologies is not confined to structural aspects, however. It also elicits constructivist learning: Where there is no disorganizing, there is no subsequent reorganizing. The organizational learning that new technologies spurred in the production area at Skoda illustrates this effect. In that company a level of technology lower than that in the West (though higher than that which existed under socialism) was introduced and was combined with a well-educated work force of native engineers. This synthesis has raised production flexibility to levels exceeding those in the West and has led to a comparable level of quality. Organizational learning in companies of former socialist countries in central Europe thus lies in 'facilitating the ability of indigenous employees to demonstrate their skills in applying themselves to a changing economic environment' (Czeglédy 1996: 331).

Potential Triggers of Constructivist Learning

Whereas triggers of structuralist learning have their source outside companies (at least initially), constructivist learning links external, culturally rooted sources and internal experiences. Three potential triggers of constructivist learning seem to exist.

Top Management's Need for Legitimacy

In the early 1990s organizational learning in the four countries of our investigation was influenced by the need of corporate leadership to establish its legitimacy. In the first phase of transformation, for example, management in former East German and in Czech companies was elected either by the companies' work forces or by the corporate managers themselves (Berthoin Antal and Merkens 1993; Clark and Soulsby 1995). In Poland (Wenzeler 1995) and Hungary (Mellar 1993) large companies remained primarily in state hands, with semi-market conditions prevailing in Hungary. In Poland the labor union Solidarity lent legitimacy to the *government* through the presidency of Lech Walesa, Solidarity's leader. In these various ways corporate leadership in the four formerly socialist economies was, during this phase of the transformation, vested largely in the representatives of the old nomenklatura or in the second-level managers who succeeded them (Mickler *et al.* 1996: 77). Managers were dismissed by employees or the government for political reasons or for the purpose of improving management practices (Carlin, Van Reenen, and Wolfe 1995: 436), but many of the former technical and economic elites survived the transformation process (Pohlmann and Gergs 1996). Accelerating the process of organizational learning by changing managers has thus been a method rarely used in central and eastern European businesses (Wiesenthal 1995: 149). When legitimacy is rooted in the experience and staying power of the old socialist elite, surgical interventions in management echelons are more or less precluded.

Having gained initial legitimacy, postsocialist corporate managers had to prove, both visibly and symbolically, that they could run their companies under the new conditions. This exigency explains the managers' previously mentioned adoption of Western business practices and structures. The managers imitated features that they believed were relevant to their particular situation, a selection process based on what Berthoin Antal, Dierkes, and Marz (1998) have referred to as implicit theories. In the course of such experimentation, top managers learned *individually* from their successes and failures, but those lessons rapidly became triggers of organizational learning for the companies as a whole because corporate subsystems and design archetypes had to be adapted accordingly and new routines had to be developed. Because these essential changes eliminated many intermediate management functions that had existed in the socialist decision-making chain, inertia and resistance developed among middle managers (Carlin, Van Reenen, and Wolfe 1995), who have been the losers of organizational change toward lean management and production programs. For similar reasons, the employees, too, mobilized against labor-shedding programs. It was the process of coping with the new structural and procedural environment that brought these two groups to embark on constructivist learning.

Social embeddedness

As noted in the preceding discussion of constructivist learning, inertia, and cultural roots, change can be at least a partial reversion to earlier practices and attitudes just as it can be a step toward something completely new. In this sense, one trigger of organizational learning, especially learning that results from prolonged, rapid, and radical change (Berthoin Antal, Dierkes, and Marz 1998; Geppert 1996), can be social embeddedness, or tradition (see Child and Heavens, Ch. 13 in this volume). Inertia stemming from social embeddedness promotes the development of behavior that can be combined with both tradition and

new contexts. For this reason various cultural traditions of Hungary, Poland, the Czech Republic, and the former GDR have played a major role in the organizational learning that has occurred in companies located in those countries. In Poland, for example, the ability to put a brake on social change has been the strength of the industrial unions, which have insisted that both the economic and social dimensions of transformation be taken into consideration (Gaciarz and Panków 1996). Hungary, historically an agricultural society, had few industrial traditions on which to base the transformation of its economy. In these two countries, the effort to rescue companies has therefore remained largely within the framework of state ownership rather than privatization. In the Czech Republic and the former GDR, which have much stronger industrial traditions, privatization has figured much more prominently in economic transformation (Heidenreich 1994: 21). The process of disorganization was stronger in the latter two countries because cultural roots supported it.

Culture Clash

The change from a planned economy to a market economy can be seen as a clash between two fundamentally different economic cultures. It was revolutionary rather than evolutionary. The best way of coping with this change was to have managers experienced with the West's industrial, financial, and economic practices (i.e. foreign executives) brought into the top echelons of the decision-making structures in the new companies (Albach 1998: 65; Czeglédy 1996: 329). Skoda and Jenoptik initially followed this strategy by pairing domestic managers with Western managers in a coaching relationship. The idea behind this 'tandem' approach (Dörr and Kessel 1996: 51) was that the advantages of the old corporate culture and insights into it could thereby be combined with Western expertise, including technology, while preserving at least some elements of the new organization's previous corporate identity.

The tandem approach had its weaknesses, however. One reason may be that parent companies are often interested only in imposing their own models of organization on the companies they acquire rather than in making effective use of the knowledge and experience that their expatriates gain during their tenure in the affiliates (Berthoin Antal and Böhling 1998). Linguistic complications were a further weakness of the tandem approach. The technical difficulties that translation from one language into another always entails in international joint ventures were compounded by the contrast between the ideologies involved. For example, the socialist understanding of, say, the word *plan*, differs fundamentally from the meaning of the word in market economics (Berthoin Antal and Merkens 1993). A third problem was the difference between the status of the native managers who were involved and the career outlook of the Western managers they were paired with. Furthermore, the Western managers had not yet developed the managerial maturity that their assigned partners, who were usually older, had spent a lifetime acquiring (Dörr and Kessel 1996: 51). The cross-cultural competencies needed by the Western managers to function in this new environment (e.g. a capacity to communicate respect and the tolerance for ambiguity, as formulated by Richards 1997: 391) seemed to have been scant. Nevertheless, tandems of central European and western European managers may be a way to improve participants' understanding of pronounced cultural differences between partners in international joint ventures (Barkema *et al.* 1997: 431).

The experiment with the tandem approach at Jenoptik and Skoda has meanwhile been phased out. It proved unsuccessful, except in one area. As an illustration of the aforementioned oxymoron, the domestic managers at the two companies survived only in the area of production, where their experience under socialism enabled them to reorganize production activities efficiently after a process of disorganization. Reorganization in all other areas of corporate activity, including marketing and controlling, eventually had to be initiated and

executed by the Western (i.e. external) managers, who had the experience to deal with the new demands. This type of combination thus demonstrates a factor of successful organizational learning (Albach 1998: 66–7).

A Well-educated Work Force

Organizational learning in the Czech Republic, Hungary, the former GDR, and Poland has been influenced by a well-educated work force, specifically, experienced engineers (e.g. those at Jenoptik in the former GDR and at the Suzuki plant in Hungary) and artisans. It is primarily this resource that attracts foreign investment (see trigger 4) and the new technologies that go with it (trigger 5). A well-educated work force becomes an enabling factor mostly in regions where specialists receive low wages and where companies are located close to the buyers of their components, to Western markets, or to both (Havas 1995; Mertlik 1996). This combination of low wages and proximity to markets is successful because the necessary products can be made by companies in which high-tech work processes take place with less automation than is the case with Western manufacturers. Such dynamics can increase the flexibility of the work flow (and can thus constitute a siting advantage). Inevitably, some elements of the Western, high-tech work flow that have been brought to the central European companies considered in this chapter must then be adapted to the new conditions, a disorganization that leads to new types of work organization and hence to organizational learning. In any case, the most successful transitions from socialist economic structures to corporate market structures have been achieved when the experience of a well-educated work force has been tapped. Because the experience of the work forces in former socialist countries was greatest in production activities, it seems logical that Western investment in former socialist production organizations has been forthcoming where the aim has been to replace production systems.

Table 10.4 summarizes the triggers of structuralist and constructivist organizational

Table 10.4. An anatomy of triggers of organizational learning in the transformation process of selected eastern European companies

Triggers of structuralist learning	Triggers of constructivist learning
Privatization and opening of markets	Need for legitimacy
Dissolution of combines	Previous experience with markets and technologies
Privatization of companies	New technologies
Foreign investment	Social embeddedness
New technologies	Culture clash
	Well-educated work force

learning discussed in this section. The reality of their interaction is in most cases not as clear as such an analytical presentation may lead one to believe. In particular, not all these triggers may exist in every organization's context of learning, and those triggers that do exist may not all play a role at the same time. Moreover, the combinations and sequences of such triggers of organizational learning may be quite varied indeed.

Conclusion

The process of organizational learning in the central European companies to which we have drawn attention has a particular pattern. First, the new challenges that the transformation to a market economy posed to former socialist economies—such as the need to build sales and marketing departments within companies and to adopt a cost–benefit mentality—prompted imitation of Western corporate practices. Simultaneously, once-familiar routines of socialist production, such as the formulation and execution of each unit's annual targets, had to be abandoned. To meet these challenges, newly founded companies in Poland, the Czech Republic, Hungary, and the former GDR had to change the design archetypes of their past.

In that process, both the social embeddedness of these companies and that of their em-

ployees were major factors. New routines developed as previous habits and ways of thinking were combined with processes that were presumed to be called for in the new organizational context. From the constructivist point of view, these behaviors tended to oscillate between socialist and Western market practices, resulting in syntheses that differed from one company to the next. Interpreted as an oxymoron, the reorganization of the central European companies discussed above first meant *dis*organization, that is, the increase in the variety of organizational structures available as frameworks of behavior within a company. From this stage, however, new, effective design archetypes emerged as novel ways of organizing corporate processes. In short, organizational learning is usually successful when the organizational behavior that is to be learned can be coupled to the habits and routines of the organization. This link between new processes and old patterns of behavior suggests that organizational learning in societies undergoing transition to a market economy will usually be more successful in the production area than in, say, marketing and sales.

This process of organizational learning was thus triggered by the overall transformation of the economic and societal systems of central and eastern Europe after 1989. Beyond this overriding trigger of organizational learning, we have identified other, subsidiary ones that influence the speed, direction, and results of organizational learning in that transformation. Among these subsidiary triggers are those that compel a company to change its design archetypes and subsystems. These triggers of surface-level, or structuralist, learning are (a) the privatization and opening of markets to foreign competition, (b) the dissolution of combines, (c) the privatization of companies, (d) foreign investment, and (e) the introduction and use of new technologies. Under certain conditions, the latter two triggers can be seen instead as factors facilitating organizational learning. It is evident that triggers for structuralist learning (i.e. intentional changes in the structures of an organization) generally come from outside the organization.

In addition, there are triggers of deep-level, constructivist, learning. They include (f) the need to establish or preserve the legitimacy of a company's top management, (g) previous experience with the market and with technologies, and (h) the presence of an educated work force in a company. Prompted by these different types of triggers, new design archetypes and cultural habits of the work force can emerge. In short, triggers for constructivist learning (i.e. the coupling of new organizational behavior to the habits and routines of the organization) usually come from within the organization.

The combination of the eight triggers identified as having been subsumed in the process of economic and societal transformation in central Europe seems to explain the particular character of organizational learning in the Hungarian, Polish, Czech, and former East German companies referred to in this chapter. Of special interest is the disorganizing that design archetypes first underwent. That is, the companies initially attempted simply to exchange their old archetypes for established Western ones—until it was discovered that previous work patterns and other acquired behaviors did not fit. At that point, the old behaviors had to be jettisoned and the variety of structures needed to cope with the company's new conditions had to increase. This requisite paved the way for the new design archetypes synthesizing past experience with current demands.

It appears that the description of organizational learning as a process of disorganizing followed by reorganizing offers the opportunity to understand the inner dynamics of modern corporate development in a manner that opens new avenues for analysis. It would be fruitful to adopt this point of view when examining these processes in other regions and countries of the world. Particularly useful, for example, would be a similar study of organizational learning in pharmaceutical companies, which operate in an industry where the end consumer (the patient) does not have the discretionary latitude enjoyed by consumers in other sectors.

References

Albach, H. (1998). 'Kreatives Organisationslernen', in H. Albach, M. Dierkes, A. Berthoin Antal, and K. Vaillant (eds.), Organisationslernen—institutionelle und kulturelle Dimensionen. WZB Jahrbuch 1998. Berlin: edition sigma, 55–77.

Andorka, R. (1996). 'Systemtransformation in Ungarn'. Soziologische Revue, 4 (Special issue): 7–15.

Apolte, T. and Cassel, D. (1991). 'Dezentralisierung durch "kapitalistische Marktwirtschaft": Radikaler Systemumbruch', in K.-H. Hartwig and H. J. Thieme (eds.), Transformationsprozesse in sozialistischen Wirtschaftssystemen: Ursachen, Konzepte, Instrumente. Berlin: Springer, 111–51.

Argyris, C. and Schön, D. A. (1978). Organizational Learning: A Theory of Action Perspective. Reading, Mass.: Addison-Wesley.

Barkema, H. G., Shenkar, O., Vermeulen, F., and Bell, J. H. J. (1997). 'Working Abroad, Working with Others: How Firms Learn to Operate International Joint Ventures'. Academy of Management Journal, 40: 426–42.

Bateson, G. (1972). *Steps to an Ecology of Mind: A Revolutionary Approach to Man's Understanding of Himself*. New York: Ballantine Books.

Berthoin Antal, A. (1998). 'Die Dynamik der Theoriebildungsprozesse zum Organisationslernen', in H. Albach, M. Dierkes, A. Berthoin Antal, and K. Vaillant (eds.), *Organisationslernen—institutionelle und kulturelle Dimensionen. WZB Jahrbuch 1998*. Berlin: edition sigma, 31–52.

——and Böhling, K. (1998). 'Expatriation as an Underused Resource for Organizational Learning', in H. Albach, M. Dierkes, A. Berthoin Antal, and K. Vaillant (eds.), *Organisationslernen—institutionelle und kulturelle Dimensionen. WZB Jahrbuch 1998*. Berlin: edition sigma, 215–36.

——Dierkes, M., and Marz, L. (1998). 'Implizite Theorien des Organisationslernens: Ergebnisse empirischer Untersuchungen in China, Deutschland und Israel', in H. Albach, M. Dierkes, A. Berthoin Antal, and K. Vaillant (eds.), *Organisationslernen—institutionelle und kulturelle Dimensionen. WZB Jahrbuch 1998*. Berlin: edtion sigma, 497–522.

——and Merkens, H. (1993). 'Cultures and Fictions in Transition: Challenges Facing Managers and Employees in East German Companies'. *Journal of General Management*, 19/1: 76–86.

Bornstein, M. (1997). 'Non-standard Methods in the Privatization Strategies of the Czech Republic, Hungary and Poland'. *Economics of Transition*, 5: 332–8.

Bryson, P. J. (1992). 'The Economics of Germany's Reunification: A Review of Literature'. *Journal of Comparative Economics*, 16: 163–81.

Cameron, K. S. (1994). 'Strategies for Successful Organizational Downsizing'. *Human Resource Management*, 33: 189–211.

Carlin, W., Van Reenen, J., and Wolfe, T. (1995). 'Enterprise Restructuring in Early Transition: The Case Study Evidence from Central and Eastern Europe'. *Economics of Transition*, 3: 427–58.

Child, J. and Czeglédy, A. P. (1996). 'Managerial Learning in the Transformation of Eastern Europe: Some Key Issues'. *Organization Studies*, 17: 167–79.

——and Markóczy, L. (1993). 'Host-country Managerial Behavior and Learning in Chinese and Hungarian Joint Ventures'. *Journal of Management Studies*, 30: 611–31.

——and Smith, C. (1987). 'The Context and Process of Organizational Transformation—Cadbury Limited in Its Sector'. *Journal of Management Studies*, 24: 565–93.

Clark, E. and Soulsby, A. (1995). 'Transforming Former State Enterprises in the Czech Republic'. *Organization Studies*, 16: 215–42.

Cook, S. D. N. and Yanow, D. (1996). 'Culture and Organizational Learning', in M. D. Cohen and L. S. Sproull (eds.), *Organizational Learning*. Thousand Oaks, Calif.: Sage, 430–59.

Czarniawska-Joerges, B. (1994). 'The Tragicomedy of Errors'. *Industrial and Environmental Crisis Quarterly*, 8/1: 1–26.

Czeglédy, A. P. (1996). 'New Directions for Organizational Learning in Eastern Europe'. *Organization Studies*, 17: 327–41.

DiMaggio, P. J. and Powell, W. W. (1983). 'The Iron Cage Revisited: Institutional Isomorphism and Collective Rationality in Organizational Fields'. *American Sociological Review*, 48: 147–60.

Dörr, G. and Kessel, T. (1996). 'Transformation as a Learning Process: Experiences with Joint Ventures in the Czech Republic and an Example for a New Modern Form of Organizing Production'. *EMERGO*, 3/2: 44–57.

————(1997a). *Eine kreative, aber nicht ganz einfache Kooperation: Erfahrungen aus dem deutsch-tschechischen Joint Venture Unternehmen Skoda-Volkswagen*. WZB Discussion paper FS II 97-601, Wissenschaftszentrum Berlin für Sozialforschung.

————(1997b). *Das Restrukturierungsmodell Skoda-Volkswagen—Ergebnis aus Transfer und Transformation*. WZB Discussion paper FS II 97-603, Wissenschaftszentrum Berlin für Sozialforschung.

————(1999). 'Restrukturierung durch Internationalisierung: Direktinvestitionsprojekte der Automobilindustrie in Ostmitteleuropa', in H.-J. Herr and K. Hübner (eds.), *Der 'lange Marsch' in die Marktwirtschaft: Entwicklungen und Erfahrung in der VR China und Osteuropa*. Berlin: edition sigma, 243–77.

Duke, V. and Grime, K. (1994). 'Privatization in East-Central Europe: Similarities and Contrasts in Its Application', in C. G. A. Bryant and E. Mokrzycki (eds.), *The New Great Transformation? Change and Continuity in East-Central Europe*. London: Routledge, 144–70.

Espejo, R., Schumann, W., Schwaninger, M., and Bilello, U. (1996). *Organizational Transformation and Learning: A Cybernetic Approach to Management*. Chichester: John Wiley & Sons.

Gaciarz, B. and Panków, W. (1996). 'Fiat Auto Polen AG: Konflikte ohne Ende', in R. Deppe and M. Tatur (eds.), *Ökonomische Transformation und gewerkschaftliche Politik: Umbruchprozesse in Polen und Ungarn auf Branchenebene*. Münster: Westfälisches Dampfboot, 136–70.

Galgóczi, B. (1994). 'Der Einfluß der Privatisierung auf die Modernisierung ungarischer Betriebe unter besonderer Beachtung arbeitsmarktpolitischer Aspekte', in A. Bieszcz-Kaiser, R.-E. Lungwitz, and E. Preusche (eds.), *Transformation—Privatisierung—Akteure: Wandel von Eigentum und Arbeit in Mittel- und Osteuropa*. Munich: Hampp, 157–82.

Geppert, M. (1996). 'Paths of Managerial Learning in the East German Context'. *Organization Studies*, 17: 249–68.

——and Kachel, P. (1995). 'Die Treuhandanstalt am Ende—Ein historischer Abriß und kritische Beurteilung aus volkswirtschaftlicher und organisationstheoretischer Perspektive', in R. Schmidt and B. Lutz (eds.), *Chancen und Risiken der industriellen Restrukturierung in Ostdeutschland*. Berlin: Akademieverlag, 69–106.

——and Merkens, H. (1999). 'Learning from One's Own Experience: Continuation and Organizational Change in Two German Firms'. *Human Resource Development International*, 2/1: 25–40.

Grabher, G. (1995). 'The Elegance of Incoherence: Institutional Legacies in the Economic Transformation in East Germany and Hungary', in E. Dittrich, G. Schmidt, and R. Whitley (eds.), *Industrial Transformation in Europe: Process and Contexts*. London: Sage, 33–53.

Greenwood, R. and Hinings, C. R. (1988). 'Organizational Design Types, Tracks and the Dynamics of Strategic Change'. *Organization Studies*, 9: 293–316.

Haiss, R. R. (1996). 'Auswirkungen von Business Reengineering und Organisational Learning auf die Unternehmensstrategie', in H. H. Hinterhuber, A. Al-Ani, and G. Handlbauer (eds.), *Das neue strategische Management*. Wiesbaden: Gabler, 129–57.

Hannan, M. T. and Freeman, J. (1984). 'Structural Inertia and Organizational Change'. *American Sociological Review*, 49: 149–64.

—— —— (1989). *Organizational Ecology*. Cambridge, Mass.: Harvard University Press.

Havas, A. (1995). 'Hungarian Car Parts Industry at a Crossroads: Fordism versus Lean Production'. *EMERGO*, 2/3: 33–55.

Heidenreich, M. (1994). 'Die mitteleuropäische Großindustrie im Transformationsprozeß'. *Zeitschrift für Soziologie*, 23: 3–21.

Hitt, M. A. and Ireland, R. D. (1987). 'Peters and Waterman Revisited: The Unended Quest for Excellence'. *Academy of Management Executive*, 1/2: 91–8.

Hofstede, G. H. (1984). *Culture's Consequences: International Differences in Work-related Values*. Newbury Park, Calif.: Sage.

Klein, W. (1996). 'Der Arbeitsmarkt in den Visegrád-Staaten'. *Osteuropawirtschaft*, 41: 202–23.

Kogut, B. (1996). 'Direct Investment, Experimentation, and Corporate Governance in Transition Economies', in R. Frydman, C. V. Gray, and A. Rapaczynski (eds.), *Corporate Governance in Central Europe and Russia*: Vol. 1. *Banks, Funds, and Foreign Investors*. Budapest: Central European University Press, 293–322.

Kornai, J. (1992). *The Socialist System: The Political Economy of Communism*. Princeton: Princeton University Press.

Laughlin, R. C. (1991). 'Environmental Disturbances and Organizational Transitions and Transformations: Some Alternative Models'. *Organization Studies*, 12: 209–32.

Levinthal, D. A. (1996). 'Organizational Adaption and Environmental Selection: Interrelated Processes of Change', in M. D. Cohen and L. S. Sproull (eds.), *Organizational Learning*. Thousand Oaks, Calif.: Sage, 195–202.

Llewellyn, S. (1994). 'Managing the Boundary: How Accounting Is Implicated in Maintaining the Organization'. *Accounting, Auditing, and Accountability Journal*, 7: 4–23.

Lounamaa, P. H. and March, J. G. (1987). 'Adaptive Coordination of a Learning Team'. *Management Science*, 33: 107–23.

Malsch, T. (1988). 'Konzernstrategien und Arbeitsreform in der Automobilindustrie am Beispiel der Arbeitsintegration', in B. Dankbaar, U. Jürgens, and T. Malsch (eds.), *Die Zukunft der Arbeit in der Automobilindustrie*. Berlin: edition sigma, 62–79.

Mead, G. H. (1934). *Mind, Self, and Society from the Standpoint of a Social Behaviorist*. Chicago: University of Chicago Press.

Mellar, T. (1993). 'Eine ökonomische Bewertung der Privatisierung in Ungarn', in J. Hölscher, A. Jacobson, H. Tomann, and H. Weisfeld (eds.), *Bedingungen ökonomischer Entwicklung in Zentralosteuropa*: Vol. 1. *Aspekte des wirtschaftlichen Umbruchs*. Marburg: Metropolis, 287–305.

Merkens, H., Bergs-Winkels, D., Bieker, C., Dufeu, P., Paoli, S., Rottenburg, R., and Schmidt, F. (1991). *Umdenken auf schwankendem Boden oder 'Die Suche nach einem festen Rahmen'*. Unpublished manuscript, Institut für Allgemeine Pädagogik, Free University of Berlin.

——— Kuper, H., Bronner, U., Ernst, S., Gaedecke, J., Hupka, S., Liedholz-Mattees, C., and Reinders, H. (1998). *Wir können nur produzieren, was wir verkaufen*. Unpublished manuscript, Institut für Allgemeine Pädagogik, Free University of Berlin.

—— Bieker, C., Rottenburg, R., Bergs-Winkels, D., Buss, R., Dürr, W., Hoffmann, A., Möller, M., Paoli, S., and Welz, M. (1992). *Der Ritt über den Müggelsee: Auf dem Weg von einem planwirtschaft-lichen zu einem marktwirtschaftlich-orientierten Unternehmen*. Unpublished manuscript, Institut für Allgemeine Pädagogik, Free University of Berlin.

——— Bergs-Winkels, D., Schmidt, F., Achterberg, B., and Keller, B. (1994). *Wir ergreifen unsere Chance: Berlin Chemie auf dem Weg in seine Zukunft*. Unpublished manuscript, Institut für Allge-meine Pädagogik, Free University of Berlin.

—— Kuper, H., Bergs-Winkels, D., Köstler, K., Kilian, K., Liedholz-Matthees, C., Achterberg, B., and Rheingans, A. (1996). *Nicht die Dinosaurier, sondern die Insekten überleben!* Unpublished manu-script, Institut für Allgemeine Pädagogik, Free University of Berlin.

Mertlik, P. (1996). 'Czech Industry: Organizational Structure, Privatization and Their Consequences for Its Performance'. *EMERGO*, 3/1: 93–104.

Mickler, O., Engelhard, N., Lungwitz, R., and Walker, B. (1996). *Nach der Trabi-Ära: Arbeiten in schlanken Fabriken: Modernisierung der ostdeutschen Autoindustrie*. Berlin: edition sigma.

Miller, N. E. and Dollard, J. (1941). *Social Learning and Imitation*. New Haven: Yale University Press.

Mladek, J. (1995). 'Voucher Privatization in the Czech Republik and Slovakia', in Centre for Cooperation with the Economies in Transition (ed.), *Mass Privatization: An Initial Assessment*. Paris: OECD, 61–85.

Móra, M. (1991). 'The (Pseudo-) Privatization of State-owned Enterprises: Changes in Organiza-tional and Proprietary Forms, 1987–1990'. *Acta Oeconomica*, 43: 37–58.

Myant, M., Fleischer, F., Hornschild, K., Vintrová, R., Zeman, R., and Soucek, Z. (1996). *Successful Transformation? The Creation of Market Economies in Eastern Germany and the Czech Republic*. Cheltenham: Edward Elgar.

Nasierowski, W. and Mikula, B. (1998). 'Culture Dimensions of Polish Managers: Hofstede's In-dices'. *Organization Studies*, 19: 495–509.

Nevis, E. C., DiBella, A. J., and Gould, J. M. (1995). 'Understanding Organizations as Learning Systems'. *Sloan Management Review*, 36/2: 73–85.

Nilsson, K. (1996). 'Practice, Myths, and Theories for Change: The Reconstruction of an East German Organization'. *Organization Studies*, 17: 291–309.

Nonaka, I. (1994). 'A Dynamic Theory of Organizational Knowledge Creation'. *Organization Science*, 5: 14–37.

Pettigrew, A. M. (1985). *The Awakening Giant: Continuity and Change in Imperial Chemical Industries*. Oxford: Blackwell.

Pickel, A. (1992). 'Jump-starting a Market Economy: A Critique of the Radical Strategy for Economic Re-form in Light of the East German Experience'. *Studies in Comparative Communism*, 25: 177–91.

Pocztovski, A. (1995). 'Der Einfluß marktwirtschaftlicher Strukturen auf die Arbeitsorganisation: Forschungsergebnisse Polen', in C. Heidack (ed.), *Arbeitsstrukturen im Umbruch: Festschrift für Professor Dr. Dr. h.c. Friedrich Fürstenberg*. Munich: Hampp, 41–53.

Pohlmann, M. and Gergs, H.-J. (1996). 'Manageriale Eliten im Transformationsprozea', in M. Pohlmann and R. Schmidt (eds.), *Management in der ostdeutschen Industrie*. Opladen: Leske + Budrich, 63–98.

Poznanska, J. K. and Poźnanski, K. Z. (1996). 'Foreign Investment in the East European Automotive Industry: Strategies and Performance'. *EMERGO*, 3/2: 70–82.

Richards, D. (1997). 'Developing Cross-cultural Management Skills: Experiential Learning in an International MBA Programme'. *Management Learning*, 28: 387–407.

Rottenburg, R. (1991). '"Der Sozialismus braucht den ganzen Menschen": Zum Verhältnis zwischen vertraglicher und nichtvertraglicher Beziehungen beim VEB'. *Zeitschrift für Soziologie*, 20: 305–22.

Schein, E. (1993). 'How Can Organizations Learn Faster? The Challenge of Entering the Green Room'. *Sloan Management Review*, 34/2: 85–92.

Schmögnerová, B. (1993). 'Privatisierung in der Übergangphase: Theoretische Überlegungen und einige Lehren aus der Vorgehensweise in der Tschechoslowakei', in J. Hölscher, A. Jacobson, H. Tomann, and H. Weisfeld (eds.), *Bedingungen ökonomischer Entwicklung in Zentralosteuropa*: Vol. 1. *Aspekte des wirtschaftlichen Umbruchs*. Marburg: Metropolis, 233–51.

Schomer, C. and Herkenhoff, R. (1994). 'Technologietransfer nach Osteuropa—Dargestellt am Beispiel der Automobilindustrie für die Reformländer Polen, Ungarn sowie die Tschechische Republik'. *Osteuropawirtschaft*, 39: 211–40.

Srubar, I. (1994). 'Variants of the Transformation Process in Central Europe: A Comparative Assessment'. *Zeitschrift für Soziologie*, 23: 198–221.

Staniszkis, J. (1990). 'Patterns of Change in Eastern Europe'. *East European Politics and Societies*, 4: 77–97.

——(1991). '"Political Capitalism" in Poland'. *East European Politics and Societies*, 5: 127–41.

Stark, D. and Bruszt, L. (1998). *Postsocialist Pathways: Transforming Politics and Property in East-central Europe*. Cambridge: Cambridge University Press.

Thieme, J. (1995). 'The Polish Mass Privatization Programme', in Centre for Cooperation with the Economies in Transition (ed.), *Mass Privatization: An Initial Assessment*. Paris: OECD, 39–46.

Ulrich, R. (1991). *Der Übergang zur Marktwirtschaft in der CSFR, Polen und Ungarn: Ausgangsbedingungen und erste Schritte*. Forschungsgruppe Internationale Beziehungen (FIB) P91–307. Wissenschaftszentrum Berlin für Sozialforschung.

Weber, C. (1996). *Treuhandanstalt—Eine Organisationskultur entsteht im Zeitraffer*. Wiesbaden: Gabler.

Weick, K. E. (1987). 'Perspectives on Action in Organizations', in J. Lorsch (ed.), *Handbook of Organizational Behavior*. Englewood Cliffs, NJ: Prentice Hall, 10–28.

——and Westley, F. (1996). 'Organizational Learning: Affirming an Oxymoron', in S. R. Clegg, C. Hardy, and W. R. Nord (eds.), *Handbook of Organization Studies*. London: Sage, 440–58.

Wenzeler, G. (1995). 'Das polnische Bankensystem', in M. Hein (ed.), *Bankensysteme in Ostmitteleuropa*. Berlin: Spitz, 43–81.

Whitley, R. and Czaban, L. (1998). 'Institutional Transformation and Enterprise Change in an Emergent Capitalist Economy: The Case of Hungary'. *Organization Studies*, 19: 259–80.

Wiesenthal, H. (1995). 'Die Transformation Ostdeutschlands: Ein (nicht ausschließlich) privilegierter Sonderfall der Bewältigung von Transformationsproblemen'. *Leviathan*, 15 (Special issue): 134–59.

——(1996). 'Sozio-ökonomische Transformation und Interessenvertretung', in M. Diewald and K.-U. Mayer (eds.), *Zwischenbilanz der Wiedervereinigung*. Opladen: Leske + Budrich, 279–88.

Winiecki, J. (1995). 'Polish Mass Privatization Programme: The Unloved Child in a Suspect Family', in Centre for Co-operation with the Economies in Transition (ed.), *Mass Privatization: An Initial Assessment*. Paris: OECD, 47–60.

11   Organizational Learning as Guided Responses to Market Signals

John M. Stopford

The recent growth of scholarly interest in the relationship between knowledge flows and strategic management has created a variety of perspectives on how organizations respond to market signals. One perspective is based on the largely implicit assumption that organizations are inert and that organizational learning is not a strongly managed process (see, for example, Hannan and Freeman 1977; Nelson and Winter 1982). In similar vein, scholars such as Lave and Wenger (1991) and Strauss (1978) have explained the flows of knowledge across organizational boundaries in terms of the configuration of 'communities of practice'—relatively small groups of people who together develop shared values and perspectives that give meaning and purpose to their communal work—within any one organization. Organizations are assumed to respond to market signals in ways that are predetermined by their social construction.

From the alternative perspective explored in this chapter, it is assumed that managers play an active role in the process of organizational learning. Though their perspectives and behaviors are conditioned by their place in the community of practice, top managers also have some discretion in selecting which of the many, and often conflicting, market signals for action they should accept and which they should ignore. They are also instrumental in determining how responses to those signals should be managed and built upon consistently over time. This perspective builds on an approach developed by Lovas and Ghoshal (1997), who conceived of strategy as guided evolution. Organizational learning is a central component of the process of guided selectivity in response to external signals.

The theories of organizational learning explored in other chapters of this book provide other perspectives that challenge as well as complement this exploration. The field is still in its infancy and is wrestling with many of the key issues and principles that have preoccupied philosophers and social theorists for many years. The contention in this chapter, however, is that many of the common notions of organizational learning can be linked to parallel work in strategic thinking and management. Together, these perspectives may yet yield a robust framework in which the organization is depicted as providing guidance and consistency to the processes that take the learning in individuals' heads into the domain of learning in the system as a whole. How these requisite processes can be managed adequately over time is a matter for much further research. Yet, as the examples shown in this chapter suggest, the outlines of a framework that goes beyond the purely descriptive and begins to suggest normative implications can already be glimpsed (see Figure 1).

The framework has five interlinked components. First, there is the process used for making sense of the changes and new possibilities created either by new technologies and economics of supply on the one hand and by new patterns of demand on the other. In contemporary markets, the pace of change and, in many industries, the multiple developments occurring

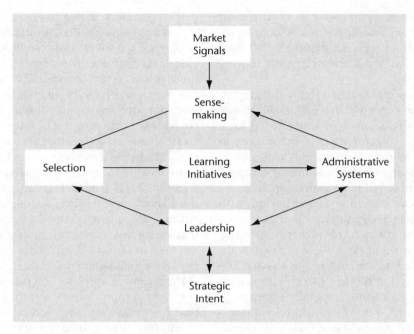

Fig. 11.1. Elements of organizational learning as guided responses to market signals.

Developed from Lovas and Ghoshal 1997: fig. 1.

in many parts of the world simultaneously make it extremely difficult for any organization to know which signals provide intelligence that should spur action and which can safely be ignored. Many individuals will perceive different signals and provide a great variety of knowledge that has to be sifted and evaluated. The question of how to synthesize coherently and consistently individuals' different perspectives and biases is at the heart of the challenge of making the sense-making process work effectively.

The second component, therefore, is the process of selection from among this variety of knowledge of events in the markets and impulses for change. The focus of this component is on experiments and initiatives that provide learning about the possibilities in terms of the effective response the organization is capable of mounting given the existing stock of human and other forms of capital.

The third component is the bundle of administrative systems that determine the routines and incentives within the organization. These

systems provide a form of internal evolutionary environment that complements the external market environment. In some respects, this internal environment with its balance of natural selection mechanisms and traditional features of command and control can be regarded as conditioning the operation of the first two components. These systems intimately involve the work of middle-level managers, whose behaviors have often, and perhaps wrongly on occasion, been regarded as a specific source of inertia.

The fourth component is leadership, discussed in terms of an active role for top management in influencing the processes of organizational learning over time. These processes must be designed to create a positive climate for development and to resist the forces of inertia.

The fifth component is strategic intent: the long-term framework of ambition and definition of purpose. This component is an articulation of top management's preferences for the future evolution of the enterprise. It can act both as a purposeful set of criteria for selecting from among alternative options for investment and as a set of values that help create passion and commitment for moving forward.

The framework shown in Figure 11.1 suggests that multiple perspectives on organizational learning be combined in order to create a sense of the organizational environment in which different types of learning can happen simultaneously. Most definitions of organizational learning point to changes in some aspects of both cognition and behavior. With some behavioral definitions attention is concentrated on the need for a change in actual behavior (Swieringa and Wierdsma 1992) without providing much guidance as to what creates that need in the first place. With others, organizational learning is regarded as creating a potential change (Huber 1991) through 'learning by encoding inferences from history into routines that guide (future) behavior' (Levitt and March 1988: 320; for a critique of the literature on these issues, see Tsang 1997). In this perspective, little consideration is given to the social context that influences both the choice of what potential to develop and the evolutionary environment in which the potential can be turned into action.

The framework explored in this chapter adds theory drawn from evolutionary perspectives and interorganizational ecology to other perspectives on organizational learning. Rather than considering the organization as inert and strategic change as potentially threatening to the organization's survival, one may say that top managers can and do take an active and purposeful role in shaping the destiny of the enterprise. They are regarded as guides and coaches who help instigate changes in the internal environment that permit the firm to adapt to or initiate change in the market environment. In this role, top managers are seen to be constrained by the inertial conservatism of the internal environment and therefore unable to change frequently and at will (see, for example, Child, Ganter, and Kieser 1987), contrary to the assumptions implicit in most economists' models of market behavior.

The framework shown in Figure 11.1 resembles Burgelman's models of strategy-making (1991, 1994) but differs in two crucial respects. First, Burgelman considered that intraorganizational forces operate outside and in addition to the formal mechanisms of management. In common with Lovas and Ghoshal (1997), the contention in this chapter is that these forces and mechanisms act together. Second, the ways in which they interact is shown to be a central component of the organizational learning processes induced by market signals. In addition, the framework introduces sense-making as a critical component of the interactive forces that create and have the capacity to resolve the tensions between signals for change and signals for maintaining the status quo.

The argument in the section below proceeds as follows. A short discussion of the knowledge base that underpins any process of organizational learning is used to set up several questions that are common to each of the components of the model and to establish the theoretical approach. Weick (1976) argued that organizational learning has to be governed by a theory of action, both for the creation of new knowledge and the transfer of old knowledge. In particular, for the purposes of the argument in this chapter, there is a need to define the types and properties of the knowledge under discussion and to regard the firm as an 'integrator' of knowledge (Grant 1996: 109). Each component is then described to introduce the range of issues and some of the arguments in the literature. Along the way examples are used to ground the theory in reality. In a final section I examine the linkages among the components and suggest ways forward in the research agenda that is needed in order to shed more light on interactions among firms and markets that provoke different types of organizational learning with differing degrees of effectiveness.

Knowledge in Organizations

The extensive literature on knowledge and the organization (see, for example, Brown and

Duguid 1998*a*; Hamel and Prahalad 1994; Kogut and Zander 1992, 1996; Leonard-Barton 1995; Nonaka and Takeuchi 1995; Spender 1989) has thrown up many contradictions. Brown and Duguid (1998*b*) went so far as to conclude from the literature that the growing scholarly effort and intellectual rigor has not led to any sense of agreement; indeed, they contended that views on knowledge in an organizational context appear to be diverging. Knowledge comes in different forms and is considered to have various properties, such as:

- Tacitness: Polanyi's (1966) concept of 'tacit', inexpressible knowledge has attracted much scholarly interest. The tacit properties of this type of knowledge make it hard to define and recognize, harder to create in practice, and even harder to detect in research. Yet, many scholars regard tacit knowledge as the foundation of much competitive advantage in turbulent markets.
- Stickiness: Even when knowledge is codified and thus recognizable, many scholars regard it as sufficiently embedded in social structures as to be hard to move. For example, von Hippel (1994) and Szulanski (1996) labeled knowledge as 'sticky'.
- Leakiness: Scientific knowledge, from alchemy onwards, has been regarded as inherently mobile. Liebeskind (1996) considered knowledge to be so 'leaky' (p. 96) that deliberate managerial action is needed to make it immobile and thus capable of being a source of competitive advantage.

Taken one at a time, each of these properties is immediately recognizable. The contradictions, though, suggest that no one type of knowledge can simultaneously be tacit, sticky, and leaky. It seems intuitively obvious that some knowledge can be intangible and sticky, but not sticky and leaky. Yet, there are instances when knowledge seems to combine all three properties at once, as illustrated by the well-known story of Xerox and the development of the personal computer (PC) (Smith and Alexander 1988). A description by John Seely Brown, who was involved at the time, removes the implied contradiction by providing a careful look at how tacitness, stickiness, and leakiness each affects the flow of knowledge across different types of boundary separating communities of practice:

Steve Jobs's famous visit to Xerox PARC, where he saw the elements of what would become the Lisa, the Mackintosh, and later the Windows interface, is usually told as if Apple intercepted an easy catch that Xerox had 'fumbled'—as if corporate blindness within Xerox overlooked what was otherwise universally obvious. In fact, at the time Xerox fumbled, the world [of individuals] capable of catching onto the personal computer was very, very small. The developers within PARC comprised a small, heterodox community within a corporation whose other communities had little understanding of the potential of the personal computer. Few did at the time. But these few made up a vibrant, local world of personal computer enthusiasts, builders, and users. This contrast determined where knowledge would stick and where it was likely to flow. In retrospect, it is not surprising that the line of flow led outside, not across the corporation. To the extent that knowledge did leak out of Xerox, however, it leaked only across this relatively small but congenial social world of similar practices and participants. The understanding that led from Xerox's Alto to Apple's Mac leaked through a world where shared warrants, parallel practice, and the related tacit understanding had prepared the way. As one of the PARC scientists reported of the first discussions with developers from Apple, though these were outsiders, 'it was almost like talking to someone in the [PARC] group.' (Levy 1994: 79) (Brown and Duguid 1998*b*: 16)

New knowledge leaked fairly readily across boundaries where there was shared tacit knowledge. Where there was no such sharing, as between PARC and senior management at headquarters, the same knowledge became sticky. Even within Apple there were diverse communities that might have created boundaries to block the flow, but Apple 'to some extent had a core alignment of communities that lowered the effort needed. . . . It also invested the effort necessary to move this new knowledge against the flow' (Brown and Duguid 1998*b*: 17). In other words, the intuitive understanding of top managers made the necessary investment effort legitimate in Apple. In Xerox, where there was no equivalent senior intuition, proposals for similar investments would most likely have foundered on the rocks of conventional thinking.

Such an example suggests the difficulty of regarding knowledge as something independent of practice; different parts of the story indicate the paradox of simultaneous tacitness, stickiness, and leakiness. The story is also consistent with the sociological literature on organizational learning that emphasizes the extent to which knowledge is embedded within the social practices through which it is produced and deployed (for a thorough and thought-provoking review of the importance of the sociological context for organizational learning, see Gherardi and Nicolini, Ch. 2 in this volume). Though clearly the social construction of the two organizations can explain a good deal of the outcome, managerial discretion and investment determination also played key roles.

The sociological perspective provides valuable insight about ways by which knowledge leaks across the external boundaries of the organization, into and out of what have been called 'knowledge ecologies' (Brown and Duguid 1998b: 17). Similarly, it offers an explanation of the difficulty many firms have with reading signals from the market, with the sense-making processes. If knowledge flows naturally along the path of least resistance, then markets can readily be organized accordingly. In similar vein to Coase (1937), it may be argued that firms exist to push knowledge across discontinuities among social practices, whether inside external boundaries or across them, and so work along the line of greatest difficulty—the source of their competitive advantage. As Brown and Duguid (1998b) put it: 'creating a knowledge continuum against this resistance is hard work and requires organization—indeed it is at the heart of what organizations do' (p. 2).

If firms are to learn from market signals and thereby create new wealth, they have to provide a social and organizational setting that allows knowledge to flow to units within the structure—communities of practice—that can most readily use the knowledge. The first task, however, is to manage the tasks of receiving and selecting signals from the external environment.

Sense-making Processes

It is commonplace to assert that market signals of threat and impending crisis are more potent signals for actions than managers' perceptions of opportunity. Yet, as Baden-Fuller and Stopford (1994) showed in their study of growth in mature markets, there are many examples of firms acting to take advantage of opportunities created by perceived shifts in the market and competitor capabilities. It is equally common to observe leading firms that failed to react to market changes or, like Xerox, to new technical possibilities. One way to examine this set of seeming contradictions is to use the ideas of knowledge in practice and to ask questions about the relationships among data, knowledge, and organizational settings, first to make sense of often contradictory signals and then to select which signals require a response.

Quoting Wallas (1926), Weick (1969) wrote that the main problem was encapsulated in the question 'how can I know what I think until I see what I say?' Weick suggested a recipe of connected sequences of action: enactment → selection → retention. The latter two actions are close to parts of the model discussed below. The enactment phase is a process in which individuals actively create the environments that they face and can deal with. Weick referred to a phase of 'ecological change' (p. 70) in which breaks or change in experience provide the occasion for sense-making, just as was illustrated in the preceding Xerox example. Raw data from the environment are the inputs to the process in which managers 'construct, rearrange, single out, and demolish many "objective" features of their surrounding[s.] . . . People, often alone, actively *put* things out there that they then perceive and negotiate about perceiving. It is that initial implanting of reality that is preserved by the word *enactment*' (pp. 164–5, italics in the original). A collective process complements the individual process.

Enactment can provide misleading percep-tions about changes in the market environ-ment because managers are looking in the wrong places. For example, technology can change industry boundaries by inducing the entry of new competitors that have quite differ-ent resource bundles. Managers who look only at existing customers and competitors can fail to perceive new, crucial sources of market dynamics. Sampler (1998) has introduced the notion of defining 'industry' as a cluster of firms that all possess adequate knowledge of the same market—a perspective that helps identify new entrants early and possibly even helps anticipate their entry. In Sampler's view, competition is increasingly being determined by firms' abilities to develop and leverage com-petence, their relative speeds of learning, and the ways in which knowledge in the digital economy is changing cost structures and com-petitive barriers. This view is close to that of Baden-Fuller and Stopford (1994), who argued that 'David *can* conquer Goliath, sometimes with only modest capital expenditure. For this to be possible, David has to find a way to build an organization capable of handling and further adapting innovative strategies' (p. xii). In other words, competition in many industries is no longer being determined solely or even primarily by the physical resources defined in economists' measures; it is also increasingly a contest among strategies that are based on the human and systemic resources needed to enlarge the available knowledge pool and the capacity to learn and to create new knowledge.

Shifts in industry boundaries exacerbate the well-known problem of information overload. Most organizations can be regarded as informa-tion-rich, but interpretation-poor. Bettis and Prahalad (1995) suggested that organizations use a *dominant logic* to help them filter or funnel information so that it can be turned into intel-ligence. 'Attention is focused only on data deemed relevant by the dominant logic. Other data are largely ignored. "Relevant" data are filtered by the dominant logic and by the ana-lytic procedures managers use to aid strategy development' (p. 7). In other words, the exist-ing frame of reference tends to limit what

people see to what they have either been trained to see or what accords with their prior experience (for similar views, see Daft and Weick 1984; Shrivastava and Schneider 1984). Such biases of perspective influence both the process of sense-making and, as discussed later, the workings of the administrative systems.

For example, the first oil shock caused the major oil corporations to reconsider how they inspected market signals, so as to avoid repeat-ing the great mistake of trying to fit new forces into old frames of reference. Their collective failure to anticipate the fundamental shift in supplier power in the industry spurred some managers in Royal Dutch/Shell to develop the scenario method of planning.[1]

Scenarios deal with both the world of facts and the world of perceptions. The purpose is to develop processes that can transform informa-tion into fresh perspectives (not forecasts) and thereby help managers challenge, change, and reorganize their personal models of reality. In addition, as emphasized by Pierre Wack (1985), one of the architects of the approach, 'scenarios serve two main purposes. The first is protective: anticipating and understanding risk. The sec-ond is entrepreneurial: discovering strategic options of which you were previously unaware (p. 146). He concluded that 'by presenting other ways of seeing the world, decision scenarios allow managers to break out of a one-eyed view. Scenarios give managers something very precious: the ability to perceive reality. In a turbulent business environment, there is more to see than managers normally perceive' (p. 150). De Geus (1988) added that the value of the process does not lie in the plan itself, but in the possibility of changing the mental models of the managers involved. 'Scenario planning . . . remains a craft, with little theoretical back-ground' (Galer and van der Heijden, Ch. 38 in this volume), but that status has not stopped its rapid adoption by many firms around the

---

[1] A few managers within the corporation had under-stood the discontinuity in market structure, but shared understanding of the threat was insufficient to lead to any preemptive action. For a review of the Shell experience and the practical foundations of the scenario method, see Galer and van der Heijden, Ch. 38 in this volume.

world. Growth in practice has, in turn, spurred growing scholarly attention.

However, even in Shell, the process has not yet become sufficiently powerful or pervasive across organizational boundaries to prevent a degree of stasis. Shell is undertaking a program of fundamental transformation designed to increase its rate of innovation and to speed up its responses to market shifts. In other words, a well-honed sense-making mechanism by itself is insufficient to give clear signals for action. That function requires the other components of the proposed framework as well.

Selection

The data received by the organization from sense-making processes are already filtered by the dominant logic at work, so some selection has already been made. But further selection is typically required, for an organization has only a limited ability to handle multiple ideas. Yet there is a need for the sense-making process to reveal multiple ideas and options for the firm. Because many signals for change will prove false, reliance on one alone can be unduly risky. To strike a workable balance between the opposing demands for variety of stimuli and for the consistency determined by dominant logic, Weick (1995) contended that individuals in organizations transform their thoughts and perceptions into collective action by using two processes: action-driven and belief-driven.

Action-driven processes may be thought of as strategic initiatives designed to change part of the firm's position in the market and to create new capabilities. They represent the means by which the firm seeks to justify its continued existence and create value from its relationships with its environment. Sometimes these initiatives are in the form of experiments, sometimes in the form of irrevocable commitments that act to change how the system operates. Such initiatives are often linked to actions that have a proactive impact on the environment. Hedberg, Nystrom, and Starbuck (1976)

labeled this process manipulation, typically manifested in such high-visibility activities as creating protectable market niches, educating clients, forming alliances, advertising, and resolving conflicts.

Belief-driven processes are those in which people connect isolated pieces of data from the environment into larger structures of meaning that can be shared. These processes are conditioned by the intellectual and social capital of the communities of practice scattered across the organization. Intellectual capital refers to the knowledge and capacity for knowing in a social collectivity, such as a firm. This notion is close to the general concept of human capital, which embraces the acquired knowledge, skills, and capabilities that enable people to act in new ways (Coleman 1988). Social capital can be regarded as 'relations among people which have the potential to facilitate productive activity' (Coleman 1990: 304). Intellectual and social capital complement physical and financial capital as resources that create wealth in the market (for a careful review of the issues, see Nahapiet and Ghoshal 1998). Yet, human and social capital have many of the properties of tacitness, stickiness, and leakiness discussed previously. Because the balance among these properties varies across isolated communities of practice, the differences can impede the linking of new initiatives for corporate purposes.

Intellectual and social capital provide distinct resources for the organization. Together they make up much of what has loosely been called 'corporate culture'. They help define 'how things are done around here', for they are intimately linked to the cycle of sense-making ⟶ selection ⟶ retention. They can thus be considered part of the selection process. As argued above with reference to the knowledge base of the organization, the key is to examine how knowledge and beliefs are shared in the relations among individuals, for that analysis will help determine how actions are initiated and enacted.

An example of the link between the sense-making and the selecting processes is provided by detailed data on the Scottish knitwear industry in the mid-1980s. At that time, the

Scottish firms were persistently more profitable than their English rivals and had chosen to develop their product ranges in ways that were regarded as unsustainable in England. The Scots had combined top fashion ranges with mass-market supply, mixing both technologies and brand positions in the markets, whereas the English had two separate groups of producers. English fashion producers had adopted one set of technologies and procedures; mass-market suppliers like Courtaulds had invested for economies of scale and extreme functional specialization based on alternative technologies. English mass-market suppliers blamed their low profitability on cheap imports, though there was little evidence to support the claim of unfair competition (Stopford and Baden-Fuller 1990). Indeed, there was strong evidence that the English views were based on an out-dated model of the industry in which it was easier to blame others than to take aggressive, corrective action. By competing primarily on price, English mass-market suppliers had invested little in managing their channels of distribution and in understanding changing demand patterns.

By contrast, the Scots acted on a quite different set of shared beliefs. Some of these beliefs had to do with how the firms established their distinctive market identities in multiple segments. Other beliefs had to do with how they dealt with related parties in the transactional network of agents, retailers, and consumers (Porac, Thomas, and Baden-Fuller 1989). There were widespread practices of creating new technical resources together with local institutions, and even, in extreme cases, of permitting skilled workers to work on 'loan' to local rivals. Economies of scale would be achieved, in part, by collaboration rather than individual firm-level specialization. Enactment took place as producers and the network around them acted and thought together to limit, label, and influence their environment and to share their experience. Learning in the enactment process went on as like-minded individuals in the network filtered the information. Lengthy discussions were often needed simply to reaffirm the core beliefs that informed action remained

valid or to examine whether fundamental change was needed.

Sense-making for the extended network required a continuous cycle of trials by pursuing initiatives and by filtering and redefining meaning and the related beliefs: an enactment process of managers' shared 'theory' in action. Necessarily, such inquiry and experimental behavior meant that some initiatives failed. Providing an environment that makes at least some types of failure a legitimate and essential part of the process is often a great challenge to the administrative system: different beliefs and measures have to coexist.

Administrative Systems

In this chapter administrative systems are considered to be the means of dividing tasks and organizing work. They are socially embedded configurations of structures, systems, incentives, cultures, and leadership behaviors (see, for example, Granovetter 1985). These systems act together to shape what the firm can do well and what it cannot do. As Meyer (1994) has shown, most people adapt to internal incentives and cues from the organizational environment more often than to stimuli from the external, market environment. Thus, firm behavior is driven by routines, and actions stem more from 'matching procedures to situations than calculating [market] choices' (Levitt and March 1988: 320). Administrative routines are essential as a means of creating efficiency and as a process of retaining the learning from the initiatives selected from the sense-making process. They can, however, become a buffer that insulates the organization from changes in the market environment, or at least acts to delay responses.

Many reasons have been advanced to explain why administrative systems can be such a double-edged sword in influencing and guiding processes of change and of building new capabilities. For example, Bower (1970: 71) considered administrative systems to be the structural context that controls behavior. In effect, the control was based on purely rational calculations of planning that can be highly ineffective, especially in turbulent market conditions. Noda and Bower (1996) observed that 'structural context, once designed and institutionalized as part of a firm's administrative systems and processes, seems to present a strong source of a firm's inertia . . . and continuously exercises strong selecting forces, regardless of possible subsequent changes in top managers' intentions' (p. 186). Similarly, Amburgey and Miner (1992) and Hannan and Freeman (1977) noted that preexisting investments, industry conditions, and managers' cognition based on past experience can reinforce reliance on old routines. Further, Leonard-Barton (1995) extended the arguments of dominant logic by observing that the particular ways in which systems evolve 'bestow status on some skills and functions, and shortchange other skills and knowledge' (p. 47). In other words, the systems can become such a powerful frame of reference for past experience and present norms of behavior that they blind managers to alternatives and thus severely constrain processes of organizational learning and changes in future behavior.

This view of the system as a source of inertia is similar to the view taken by Hedberg (1981) and Nystrom and Starbuck (1984), who considered that organizational learning also requires 'unlearning' and that learning is harder to retrieve after a time lag. It is also consonant with the widely used concept of double-loop learning (Argyris and Schön 1978: 20) in which rational means of adjusting behavior when outcomes fall short of aspirations are exhausted before fundamental questioning of the status quo is attempted. Such a process of confronting deep resistance to questioning and reconstruction of existing perspectives and decision-making rules is widely regarded as so difficult and contentious that managers typically require external facilitation. This view is challenged by the notion of guided evolution, in which it is posited that the administrative system can have an altogether different role.

Seen from the vantage point of organizational knowledge creation, . . . double-loop learning is not a special, difficult task but a daily activity of the organization. Organizations continuously create new knowledge by reconstructing existing perspectives, frameworks, or premises on a day-to-day basis. In other words, double-loop learning is 'built into' the knowledge creating model, thereby circumventing the need to make unrealistic assumptions about the existence of a 'right' answer. (Nonaka, Byosière, Borucki, and Konno 1994: 341)

This argument does not deny the need for unlearning and for versions of double-loop learning. Instead, it suggests that the primary role of the system is to ensure that the variety of signals received from the external environment and the processes of selection are continuously informed by the knowledge and perspectives of individuals and communities of practice within the firm. In this way, the system can play a central role in guiding how the firm learns from and, in turn, affects its market environment.

In many instances, however, the workings of the administrative system are more complex than Nonaka *et al.* (1994) lead one to believe, and the role of top and middle management must be explained more fully than they do. Sull (1996) introduced the concept of 'active inertia' to describe the paradoxical behavior of firms that respond to market changes by making rapid investments in the new developments while delaying necessary disinvestment in outdated facilities and activities. In a careful study of how Firestone reacted to the development of the radial tire and the entry of Michelin to the U.S. market, he showed how a combination of resource allocation processes, commitments, and cognitive biases help explain this phenomenon. In particular, he suggested that

the desire to honor commitments introduces a cognitive bias for investment in the resource allocation process. The general tendency to bias ambiguous data to support options consistent with the decision-maker's previous preferences is well known (Nisbett and Ross 1980). Superiors prefer investment to disinvestment proposals, because the former allow them to honor commitments. The bias enters the decision-making process when superiors evaluate projected return on investment of specific proposals, which rest on inherently uncertain forecasts and require significant judgment. Senior executives and middle managers should, therefore, systematically believe projections . . . more readily than the pessimistic assumptions underlying disinvestment proposals. (Sull 1996: 11)

An additional consideration is the extent to which middle managers truly are the constraint on organizational learning they are so often depicted to be. If top management has systematically developed processes of 'social contracting' (Starr and MacMillan 1990) and established sufficient trust to co-opt middle managers into their thinking, then there can be considerable gains in the decision-making processes and the effectiveness of the implementation (Wooldridge and Floyd 1990). The mobilization of middle managers can also yield valuable new thinking. Baden-Fuller and Stopford (1994) provided the example of one chief executive involved in cutting jobs at a time of business expansion. He said he had 'set a man to the task of finding out what could be done. His evidence was so overwhelming that now everyone agrees that the cuts were necessary and "obvious." . . . Putting people on such projects releases ideas and adds further information and options' (p. 223). Because this chief executive had earlier built a climate of trust, he had been able to set a target, not impose a solution. Indeed, as he added, 'the solution we finally adopted went far beyond what I originally had in mind' (p. 223).

Another example of how processes of cooptation can help accelerate change is provided by Douwe Egberts, a subsidiary of the U.S. firm Sara Lee and a leader in ground coffee and coffee systems in Europe. The company decided to build upon its success by raising its ambitions while it was ahead. The CEO initiated the process in November 1995 by asking the top 20 managers to rethink their ambitions and to develop a new strategy. Five months later, the next 180 managers were told about the new strategy and asked to begin thinking about how they could contribute to making it happen. They were invited to communicate ideas directly to the CEO and to think about how their operating plans and budgets needed adjustment. There was, to be sure, some resistance, but experience showed that they could

quickly get behind the new challenge and work to co-opt others in their own teams. Not only their support but also their active contribution of fresh ideas helped the firm rejuvenate itself (Markides 1998: 37).

How the administrative system can provide a means for consistency in building upon the learning gained at different organizational levels from strategic initiatives is related to the effects of repeated interactions over time between the knowledge 'ecology' and the social system. There are different perspectives on how best firms can organize processes that provide such guidance. One school of thought is that the firm should learn in a series of small steps and build new skills and competencies one at a time, thus preserving focus and limiting the risk in implementing any one strategic initiative (Baden-Fuller and Stopford 1994). Similarly, Sitkin (1992) argued that firms learn most from a 'strategy of small losses'. He did not mean that firms should actively seek out loss-making projects but that they should accept projects amenable to such outcomes: in other words, making failure legitimate. The purpose of such an approach is to foster experimentation, the search for new explanations and meaning, and some tolerance for risk. Progress that is stimulated in part by the spur of possible small losses allows successful firms to steer a fine line between opposing forms of risk. On one side, there is the risk of complacency that can lead to an internal focus on control and risk aversion (Miller 1993). On the other side, there is the risk of large losses, the prospect of which can induce in managers the debilitating effects of denial and rigidity (Staw, Sandelands, and Dutton 1981).

This line of argument is similar in concept to that of Brown and Duguid (1998b), who considered the knowledge base of these evolutionary processes and concluded that 'organizing knowledge is not a process of adding the knowledge of individuals one by one—as if adding bricks to a wall. It is more like mixing colors in a watercolor. To draw on the knowledge resources that lie within them, organizations must look for the practices, the communities, and the collective knowledge that develop together' (p. 7). To help combine the alternative, and perhaps complementary, aspects of the behavior of the administration, one needs to explore the ideas of dominant logic and strategic intent that help guide consistent, and multileveled, choices over time.

Leadership

The elements of the framework presented so far are firmly based on the tradition of the strategy process school and are consistent with Mintzberg's (1980) ideas about emergent strategy and with Quinn's (1980) logical incrementalism. These concepts are rooted in the notion of strategy being shaped by the day-to-day actions and decisions made by many managers and complement the earlier descriptions of knowledge flows among dispersed and different communities of practice. As Mintzberg (1994) noted, much theorizing about strategic management 'involves separating thinking from doing[.] . . . Indeed, strategic planning often spoils strategic thinking' (p. 107). The purpose of the framework, therefore, is to ensure the connections among thinking, learning, and action by grounding it in the evolutionary sequence of enactment $\longrightarrow$ selection $\longrightarrow$ retention. This framework has the elements of a consistent model that can be used to study the behavior and organizational learning processes in a wide variety of social systems (see, for example, March 1994; Nelson and Winter 1982). Burgelman (1994) and Miner (1994) used it as an ecological approach to underpin their frameworks for strategy process research. Levinthal (1994) argued that the approach is robust whether the process is considered to be a 'natural' (emergent) environment for selection and learning or an 'artificial' (rational planning) one.

The role of leadership is a crucial ingredient in the process of guided evolution, actively affecting all phases of the process, directly and indirectly (for a similar perspective on active leadership in organizational learning, see Sadler, Ch. 18 in this volume). This view differs from that taken in most ecological models. These models reflect their origins in models of biological evolution and tend to rest on deterministic explanations of changes over time (Hannan and Freeman 1977). When applied to social systems, they depict top managers as being largely passive in their role, as exercising little choice or leadership.[2] Similarly, Burgelman (1991, 1994) regarded top management as reactive. In his view, strategic initiatives, whether autonomous or induced, create the variety the selective system depends upon. They represent challenges to the status quo, leaving top mangers as judges, a function they carry out by allocating resources. Indeed, many stories of strategic innovation and corporate transformation cast middle managers in the heroic mold, battling with an obdurate central bureaucracy too blind to see what is happening and therefore unable to change the market (see, for example, Markides 1998).

Yet, as shown by the Xerox example, a close look at the knowledge base and associated learning routines indicates the existence of other possible interpretations. Selective and guided responses to environmental changes are possible when the firm has attempted to create an internal environment of selection that mimics the external environment. All initiatives are influenced by the combination of forces determined around the central idea of the strategic intent. Few initiatives are likely when the internal processes are misaligned with the firm's social networks and knowledge ecologies.

In this set of related processes, the active role of top management has been redefined away from resource allocators concerned primarily with maintaining internal efficiency and resolving tensions and toward a more pervasive role in influencing all parts of the enactment $\longrightarrow$ selection $\longrightarrow$ retention cycle (Ghoshal and Bartlett 1997). This view is close to that of Bennis (1993). It is also close to that of Gardner (1995), who casts the great leader in the role of a storyteller, of one able to shape the perspectives and

---

[2] There have been a few attempts to broaden the role accorded to top managers in this perspective (see, for example, Burgelman 1991, on intraorganizational ecology).

values of the people in the organization. The argument is not about the role of the average leader but about the possibilities of exceptional leadership. Gardner (1995), for instance, was concerned about a decline in leadership in major corporations as top managers allow themselves to become ensnared in the routines of maintaining the status quo. An example he used was Roger Smith, the Chairman of General Motors, whom he compared unfavorably with his famous predecessor, Alfred P. Sloan.

The issue of the leadership capabilities of top managers can sometimes be confused with that of the charisma of the individual in question. However, there is compelling evidence from such studies as that by Collins and Porras (1994) that the leadership of 'visionary' firms has frequently been effected by individuals whose primary concerns have been for the values and enduring strength of the organizations, not personal aggrandizement. Such leaders have also given priority to the development of human talent (for similar findings, see Pfeffer 1994). These issues of investing in the creation of new human and social capital assume heightened importance for the learning in multinational corporations, as emphasized by Macharzina, Oesterle, and Brodel, Ch. 28 in this volume. 'Because organizational learning in MNCs can exceed the contributions of single local units, it is useful for MNCs to adopt a broad, cosmopolitan perspective and to develop a non-ethnocentric mind-set' (p. 650). Only an active top management can provide the leadership necessary to overcome the inertia of parochial interests.

Strategic Intent

Strategic intent comprises top managers' choices of long-term goals and their preferences for the future position and capability of the firm (Hamel and Prahalad 1989). These preferences importantly reflect the ambitions of a few key managers and their abilities to share those ambitions with many others. Strategic intent thus establishes a frame of reference for other managers as they make choices and resolve dilemmas. At the same time, however, strategic intent is embodied within the framework of guided evolution, for it is influenced by the processes of organizational learning, the accumulated experience of operations, and the need to react (or choose not to react) to changes in the market environment. Although the need is for 'intent' to provide some form of stability in the decision-making environment, it cannot be cast in stone and remain unaltered; that treatment would be an extreme form of inertia, threatening the survival of the firm.

These competing functions of strategic intent are close to March's (1994) question: What parts of the system are to be optimized in the process of 'engineering' or guiding evolutionary processes in social systems? And how should disparate social systems be connected over time, given the difficulty of predicting the outcome of collaborative efforts? Xerox's development of the PC illustrates the dual nature of the problem. The 'tissues' that connect the parts will be disturbed by decisions to optimize or even to give preferential development attention to one part rather than another. Should the engineers at PARC have been given incentives to collaborate from an early stage with the engineers responsible for high-end office systems? Would such incentives have helped or hindered progress? One might be tempted to conclude that the differences in the behavior of the two 'communities' were so great at the early stages, that neither would have been able to learn from the other without enormous and dysfunctional effort. Yet, over time, Xerox invested in finding ways to manage the migration of the learning in a positive environment. Part of the competitive advantage eventually gained from this investment emerged when the graphical interface capabilities, developed in PARC, were used to provide a key feature of its high-end office systems. Before the event, it was not obvious that the investment could yield such a positive return. As for many other companies, Xerox faced the dilemma that optimizing resources for the immediate future could well conflict with optimization for the long term.

Determining an effective intent requires some clear choices. This process is not an exercise in managing the self-governing systems that have been tightly defined in cybernetics and that are implied in ecology theory. It is an exercise in deliberately stating an ambition for progress and thus challenging the status quo. In this model the nature of the choice is clearly biased toward optimizing long-term performance. This preference has the important benefit of providing a consistent basis for intervening in the evolutionary processes that shape actual behavior and providing a clearly communicated sense of the preferred direction for the strategy-making process.

Clarity of intent can help reduce the costs of creating an undue and unnecessary variety of options for strategic initiatives. The enactment and selection processes can be costly, not just because of the effort involved but also because of the possibilities of persistent errors. One form of error is superstitious learning, that is, the result when a firm draws incorrect inferences from experience and compounds the difficulty by mistakenly applying that learning to prospective experience (Levinthal and March 1993). Another form of error occurs when a firm exploits existing routines that are less appropriate in new environments where the value of prior knowledge rapidly depreciates. These errors are compounded by the difficulties of forgetting, or unlearning (Hedberg 1981) in processes that are unable to create an internal environment of continuous learning from the external environment.

A further role for strategic intent in this model is the determination of what kind of learning is intended from the market. Senge (1990) distinguished between generative and adaptive learning.[3] If the learning is to be generative, it has to be a spur to innovation in the organization, just as Apple could learn from Xerox not to imitate but to create a new generation of machines. Such learning requires a willingness to experiment without a full set of decision-making rules and to invoke the difficulties of the guided process discussed above. If, by contrast, the learning is to be adaptive, or imitative, the task is more focused and more readily managed. There are clear guidelines to be followed. Imitation, nonetheless, can be blocked by the problems of perception that impede the flow of the requisite knowledge. It remains an empirical question whether a system designed to meet the test of imitation can also be good at generative learning. Sull's ideas (1996) on 'active inertia' suggest that doing both well is likely to stretch the connective tissues of the organizational processes to the breaking point, especially when the markets are changing rapidly. For example, Dierkes, Marz, and Teele, Ch. 12 in this volume, argue that Olympia Büromaschinenwerke failed to adapt their typewriter technology to the digital revolution because most of the administrative procedures introduced after 1971 fostered adaptive learning when generative learning was essential. The mistake eventually led to the collapse of the firm in 1994.

All of these considerations make it impossible for an 'intent' to be determined collectively. Deciding what constitutes a compelling and useful vision (i.e. one that can help managers make choices in their daily business) for the future conduct of the firm is essentially a job for top management. The members of that group have the responsibility to make the key choices and then to articulate them in ways that influence all stages of the evolutionary process and thus the conduct of the firm. They also have the responsibility to ensure that their vision does not become a specific block to the needed type of learning, as in Olympia.

This active role of top management in determining strategic intent differs from the assumption of a more reactive, maintenance stance made by others who have concentrated on strategic context, the internal aspects of managing a stream of initiatives (often

---

[3] Senge drew on a rich literature in which equivalent—and more complex—distinctions are made. To Bateson (1972), for example, it was a question of metalearning versus learning-by-experience. To Argyris and Schön (1978), it was metalearning versus double-loop learning, previously discussed in this chapter.

market-inspired ones). For example, Noda and Bower (1996) concluded that the role of top management is limited to being

willing enough to recognize strategically bottom-up initiatives and capitalize on them rather than pass them by. . . . Successful leaders, who know that influence for any manager is based on the success of his interventions, are very cautious in their public position. . . . Deferring the announcement of public commitments until learning reduces the uncertainty in new business development can be a wise choice for top managers who are concerned to preserve and enhance their 'power'. (p. 188)

It is possible that a passive, maintenance role is appropriate for developing new business that relies on imitative learning from the market and that does not change the fundamental beliefs and practices in the existing communities of practice. Care, however, needs to be exercised in considering the flow of initiatives as essentially bottom-up, for the choices made may well have been crucially influenced by the dissemination of perspectives associated with a strategic intent. Top management may, perhaps by default, play an active role in the selection of projects designed for imitation. On the same lines, a reactive stance seems inappropriate for generative learning. Generative learning requires a much more positive and proactive leadership than imitative learning does.

Concluding Remarks

The purpose of this discussion of a framework for examining the possibilities for guided responses to market signals has been to stress the need to link the conventional models of organizational learning with competing models of strategy processes. The perspectives derived from evolutionary and ecology theory are useful as a bridge to explore the extent to which learning in an organization can be actively managed and the extent to which that learning emerges from the social structure of human interaction. The contention in this chapter has been that there are distinct roles for the

management of the learning process and that consistent guidance over time is possible.

The notion of guidance is central to the argument, for the firm's social systems have biases and inertial forces that can corrupt and even suppress signals from the market. Primary attention was paid to the conception and articulation of strategic intent. There remain, however, many puzzles about the concept. To be effective, the objective function for the whole process has to be long term in orientation and constant for a considerable time if it is to act as a consistent conditioning force for short-term behavior. It also has to be flexible to a degree that permits adaptive interpretations of changed market circumstance and of changed capabilities and levels of feasible ambition. When does 'considerable' time become a strait-jacket? When does adaptiveness become ineffective and destabilizing for the workings of a well-aligned internal selection and experimental process? Much work is needed to frame the issues in operational terms so that the effects in practice can be observed. Moreover, little is known about the learning processes that top managers go through in arriving at their determination of strategic intent in the first place. What affects their cognitive biases? How well do their ambitions have to fit with the current capabilities and yet avoid the dangers of complacent Groupthink? When does guidance cease to be leadership and become dictatorship? The extent to which top management can play an active role in changing the status quo, remain sensitive to the social preconditioning of the organization, and still stimulate and accelerate organizational learning throughout the organization remains an empirical question.

Another major challenge is for managers to devise organizational structures and processes that improve the management of the flow of knowledge across the boundaries of 'knowledge ecologies'. The social systems within each of these ecologies tend to develop around shared tasks, values, and enthusiasms, and over time the differences between communities within the same organization are likely to diverge. These social systems have a major impact on what new knowledge is recognized and what data are ignored and thus on the learning processes within the ecology. The very strength of organizational learning within a community may become a source of inertia for the parent organization. Is it possible to increase benefit derived from developing processes of organizational learning that are common across dispersed ecologies without destroying the strength within each of them? Lovas and Ghoshal (1997) have provided detailed longitudinal data on one firm, Oticon in Denmark, which appears to have innovated in all aspects of the model to create an effective answer to this challenge. This success is well known and has been extensively studied by academics and practitioners alike. So far, however, no one seems to have found a way either to codify Oticon's learning in a form that is replicable elsewhere or to provide a workable imitation in practice.

A related challenge concerns learning within networks of firms. In the global market, where the mobility of many of the resources for competitiveness is increasing, there are locations where the key resources appear to be wholly immobile, as in Silicon Valley (for both micro-processors and genetic engineering) and the City of London (for both foreign-exchange dealing and computer graphics). Such 'hotspot' localities are clearly places where there has been much learning both within organizations (as defined by their legal boundaries) and across the local society in the form of specialized infrastructure and dense networks of firms, many of them small. There are strong incentives for firms to collaborate to gain access to and harness the tacit, inexpressible knowledge of others. The aim is to create new, valuable shared resources (Chesbrough and Teece 1996). The phenomenon has been attracting attention (see, for example, Harrison 1992; Saxenian 1996; Stopford 1995), but most attention has concentrated on outcomes, not on causes and processes. Though Powell, Koput, and Smith-Doerr (1996) observed that 'the locus of innovation will be found in networks of learning, rather than in individual firms' (p. 116), it remains unclear precisely how the learning has happened. One possible strand of future work is to regard these networks as a form of market and compare how 'societal learning' resembles or differs from learning within organizations. There is a rich research agenda for the future.

References

Amburgey, T. L. and Miner, A. S. (1992). 'Strategic Momentum: The Effects of Repetitive, Positional and Contextual Momentum on Merger Activity'. *Strategic Management Journal*, 13: 335–48.

Argyris, C. and Schön, D. (1978). *Organizational Learning: A Theory of Action Perspective*. Reading, Mass.: Addison-Wesley.

Baden-Fuller, C. W. F. and Stopford, J. M. (1994). *Rejuvenating the Mature Business*. Boston: Harvard Business School Press.

Bateson, G. (1972). *Steps to an Ecology of Mind: A Revolutionary Approach to Man's Understanding of Himself*. New York: Ballantine Books.

Bennis, W. (1993). *An Invented Life: Reflections on Leadership and Change*. Reading, Mass.: Addison-Wesley.

Bettis, R. A. and Prahalad, C. K. (1995). 'The Dominant Logic: Retrospective and Extension'. *Strategic Management Journal*, 16: 5–14.

Bower, J. L. (1970). *Managing the Resource Allocation Process: A Study of Corporate Planning and Investment*. Boston: Harvard University, Division of Research, Graduate School of Business Administration.

Brown, J. S. and Duguid, P. (1998a). 'Organizing Knowledge'. *California Management Review*, 40/3: 90–111.

———— (1998b). *The Knowledge Continuum: A Practice-based Perspective on Knowledge and the Firm*. Unpublished manuscript.

Burgelman, R. A. (1991). 'Intra-organizational Ecology of Strategy Making and Organizational Adaptation: Theory and Field Research'. *Organization Science*, 2: 239–62.

—— (1994). 'Fading Memories: A Process Theory of Strategic Business Exit in Dynamic Environments'. *Administrative Science Quarterly*, 39: 24–56.

Chesbrough, H. W. and Teece, D. J. (1996). 'When Is Virtual Virtuous?' *Harvard Business Review*, 74/1: 65–73.

Child, J., Ganter, H.-D., and Kieser, A. (1987). 'Technological Innovation and Organizational Conservatism', in J. M. Pennings and A. Buitendam (eds.), *New Technology as Organizational Innovation*. Cambridge, Mass.: Ballinger, 87–115.

Coase, R. H. (1937). 'The Nature of the Firm'. *Economica*, 4, New Series: 386–405.

Coleman, J. S. (1988). 'Social Capital in the Creation of Human Capital'. *American Journal of Sociology*, 94 (Supplement): 95–120.

—— (1990). *Foundations of Social Theory*. Cambridge, Mass.: Harvard University Press.

Collins, J. C. and Porras, J. I. (1994). *Built to Last: Successful Habits of Visionary Companies*. New York: Harper Business.

Daft, R. L. and Weick, K. E. (1984). 'Toward a Model of Organizations as Interpretation Systems'. *Academy of Management Review*, 9: 284–95.

de Geus, A. (1988). 'Planning as Learning'. *Harvard Business Review*, 66/2: 70–4.

Gardner, H. (1995). *Leading Minds: An Anatomy of Leadership*. New York: Basic Books.

Ghoshal, S. and Bartlett, C. A. (1997). *The Individualized Corporation*. New York: Harper Business.

Granovetter, M. (1985). 'Economic Action and Social Structure: The Problem of Embeddedness'. *American Journal of Sociology*, 91: 481–510.

Grant, R. M. (1996). 'Toward a Knowledge-based Theory of the Firm'. *Strategic Management Journal*, 17 (Winter special issue): 109–22.

Hamel, G. and Prahalad, C. K. (1989). 'Strategic Intent'. *Harvard Business Review*, 67/3: 63–76.

———— (1994). *Competing for the Future: Unleashing the Power of the Workforce*. Boston: Harvard Business School Press.

Hannan, M. T. and Freeman, J. (1977). 'The Population Ecology of Organizations'. *American Journal of Sociology*, 82: 929–64.

Harrison, B. (1992). 'Industrial Districts: Old Wine in New Bottles?' *Regional Studies*, 26: 469–83.

Hedberg, B. L. T. (1981). 'How Organizations Learn and Unlearn', in P. C. Nystrom and W. H. Starbuck (eds.), *Handbook of Organizational Design*: Vol. 1. *Adapting Organizations to Their Environments* (Vol. 1). Oxford: Oxford University Press, 3–27.

—— Nystrom, P. C., and Starbuck, W. H. (1976). 'Camping on See-saws: Prescriptions for a Self-designing Organization'. *Administrative Science Quarterly*, 21: 41–65.

Huber, G. P. (1991). 'Organizational Learning: The Contributing Processes and the Literatures'. *Organization Science*, 2: 88–115.

Kogut, B. and Zander, U. (1992). 'Knowledge of the Firm, Combinative Capabilities, and the Replication of Technology'. *Organization Science*, 3: 383–97.

———— (1996). 'What Firms Do? Coordination, Identity, and Learning'. *Organization Science*, 7: 502–18.

Lave, J. and Wenger, E. (1991). *Situated Learning: Legitimate Peripheral Participation*. Cambridge: Cambridge University Press.

Leonard-Barton, D. (1995). *Wellsprings of Knowledge: Building and Sustaining the Sources of Innovation*. Boston: Harvard Business School Press.

Levinthal, D. A. (1994). 'Surviving Schumpeterian Environments: An Evolutionary Perspective', in J. A. C. Baum and J. V. Singh (eds.), *Evolutionary Dynamics of Organizations*. New York: Oxford University Press, 167–78.

—— and March, J. G. (1993). 'The Myopia of Learning'. *Strategic Management Journal*, 14 (Winter special issue): 95–112.

Levitt, B. and March, J. G. (1988). 'Organizational Learning'. *Annual Review of Sociology*, 14: 319–40.

Levy, S. (1994). *Insanely Great: The Life and Time of Macintosh, the Computer that Changed Everything*. New York: Viking.

Liebeskind, J. P. (1996). 'Knowledge, Strategy, and the Theory of the Firm'. *Strategic Management Journal*, 17 (Winter special issue): 93–107.

Lovas, B. and Ghoshal, S. (1997). *Strategy as Guided Evolution*. Working paper, SLRP WP33, London Business School.

March, J. G. (1994). 'The Evolution of Evolution', in J. A. C. Baum and J. V. Singh (eds.), *Evolutionary Dynamics of Organizations*. New York: Oxford University Press, 39–49.

Markides, C. (1998). 'Strategic Innovation in Established Companies'. *Sloan Management Review*, 39/3: 31–42.

Meyer, M. W. (1994). 'Turning Evolution Inside the Organization', in J. A. C. Baum and J. V. Singh (eds.), *Evolutionary Dynamics of Organizations*. New York: Oxford University Press, 109–16.

Miller, D. (1993). 'The Architecture of Simplicity'. *Academy of Management Review*, 18: 116–38.

Miner, A. S. (1994). 'Seeking Adaptive Advantage: Evolutionary Theory and Managerial Action', in J. A. C. Baum and J. V. Singh (eds.), *Evolutionary Dynamics of Organizations*. New York: Oxford University Press, 76–89.

Mintzberg, H. (1980). 'Managerial Work: Analysis from Observation', in H. Leavitt, L. R. Pondy, and D. Boje (eds.), *Readings in Managerial Psychology*. Chicago: University of Chicago Press, 551–9.

—— (1994). 'The Fall and Rise of Strategic Planning'. *Harvard Business Review*, 72/1: 107–14.

Nahapiet, J. and Ghoshal, S. (1998). 'Social Capital, Intellectual Capital, and the Creation of Value in Firms'. *Academy of Management Review*, 23: 242–66.

Nelson, R. R. and Winter, S. G. (1982). *An Evolutionary Theory of Economic Change*. Cambridge, Mass.: Belknap Press.

Nisbett, R. and Ross, L. (1980). *Human Inferences: Strategies and Shortcomings of Social Judgment*. Englewood Cliffs, NJ: Prentice-Hall.

Noda, T. and Bower, J. L. (1996). 'Strategy Making as Iterated Processes of Resource Allocation'. *Strategic Management Journal*, 17 (Summer special issue): 159–92.

Nonaka, I., Byosière, P., Borucki, C. C., and Konno, N. (1994). 'Organizational Knowledge Creation Theory: A First Comprehensive Test'. *International Business Review*, 3: 337–51.

—— and Takeuchi, H. (1995). *The Knowledge-creating Company: How Japanese Companies Create the Dynamics of Innovation*. New York: Oxford University Press.

Nystrom, P. C. and Starbuck, W. H. (1984). 'To Avoid Organizational Crises, Unlearn'. *Organizational Dynamics*, 12/4: 53–65.

Pfeffer, J. (1994). *Competitive Advantage through People: Unleashing the Power of the Workforce*. Boston: Harvard Business School Press.

Polanyi, M. (1966). *The Tacit Dimension*. Garden City, NY: Doubleday.

Porac, J. F., Thomas, H., and Baden-Fuller, C. W. F. (1989). 'Competitive Groups as Cognitive Communities: The Case of Scottish Knitwear Manufacturers'. *Journal of Management Studies*, 26: 397–416.

Powell, W. W., Koput, K. W., and Smith-Doerr, L. (1996). 'Interorganizational Collaboration and the Locus of Innovation: Networks of Learning in Biotechnology'. *Administrative Science Quarterly*, 41: 116–45.

Quinn, J. B. (1980). *Strategies for Change: Logical Incrementalism*. Homewood, Ill: Irwin.

Sampler, J. (1998). 'Redefining Industry Structure'. *Strategic Management Review*, 19 (April special issue): 343–55.

Saxenian, A. (1996). *Regional Advantage: Culture and Competition in Silicon Valley and Route 128*. Cambridge, Mass.: Harvard University Press.

Senge, P. M. (1990). *The Fifth Discipline: The Art and Practice of the Learning Organization*. New York: Doubleday Currency.

Shrivastava, P. and Schneider, S. (1984). 'Organizational Frames of Reference'. *Human Relations*, 37: 795–809.

Sitkin, S. B. (1992). 'Learning through Failure: The Strategy of Small Losses', in B. M. Staw and L. L. Cummings (eds.), *Research in Organizational Behavior* (Vol. 14). Greenwich, Conn.: JAI Press: 231–66.

Smith, D. K. and Alexander, R. C. (1988). *Fumbling the Future: How Xerox Invented, Then Ignored the First Personal Computer*. New York: Morrow.

Spender, J.-C. (1989). *Industry Recipes: An Enquiry into the Nature and Sources of Managerial Judgment*. Oxford: Blackwell.

Starr, J. A. and MacMillan, I. C. (1990). 'Resource Cooptation via Social Contracting: Resource Acquisition Strategies for New Ventures'. *Strategic Management Journal*, 11 (Summer special issue): 79–92.

Staw, B. M., Sandelands, L. E., and Dutton, J. E. (1981). 'Threat-rigidity Effects in Organizational Behavior: A Multilevel Analysis'. *Administrative Science Quarterly*, 26: 501–24.

Stopford, J. M. (1995). 'Competing Globally for Resources'. *Transnational Corporations*, 4/2: 34–57.

—— and Baden-Fuller, C. W. F. (1990). 'Flexible Strategies—The Key to Success in Knitwear'. *Long Range Planning*, 23/6: 56–62.

Strauss, A. (1978). 'A Social World Perspective'. *Studies in Symbolic Interaction*, 1: 119–28.

Sull, D. (1996). *Active Inertia: An Analytical Case Study and Grounded Theory*. Working paper, SLRP WP17, London Business School.

Swieringa, J. and Wierdsma, A. (1992). *Becoming a Learning Organization*. Wokingham: Addison-Wesley.

Szulanski, G. (1996). 'Exploring Internal Stickiness: Impediments to the Transfer of Best Practice within the Firm'. *Strategic Management Journal*, 17 (Winter special issue): 27–43.

Tsang, E. W. K. (1997). 'Organizational Learning and the Learning Organization: A Dichotomy between Descriptive and Prescriptive Research'. *Human Relations*, 50: 73–89.

von Hippel, E. (1994). ' "Sticky Information" and the Locus of Problem-Solving: Implications for Innovation'. *Management Science*, 40: 429–39.

Wack, P. (1985). 'Scenarios: Shooting the Rapids'. *Harvard Business Review*, 63/6: 139–50.

Wallas, G. (1926). *The Art of Thought*. London: Jonathan Cape.

Weick, K. E. (1969). *The Social Psychology of Organizing*. Reading, Mass.: Addison-Wesley.

—— (1976). 'Educational Organizations as Loosely Coupled Systems'. *Administrative Science Quarterly*, 21: 1–19.

—— (1995). *Sensemaking in Organizations*. Thousand Oaks, Calif.: Sage.

Wooldridge, B. and Floyd, S. W. (1990). 'The Strategy Process, Middle Management, and Organizational Performance'. *Strategic Management Journal*, 11: 231–41.

12 Technological Visions, Technological Development, and Organizational Learning

Meinolf Dierkes, Lutz Marz, and Casey Teele

Learning, Visions, and Technology: A Conceptual Framework

Terminological Bases

From sustainable development and lean government to the learning organization and the virtual company, visions as a concept or metaphor have gained a great deal of attention in both the public at large and the business community (Dierkes, Hoffmann, and Marz 1996). In a number of academic disciplines, this growth in general interest has prompted the research community either to begin to explore the concept of visions or to intensify ongoing research, particularly studies related to the relevance, function, and explanatory power that visions have in social processes (Grin and Grunwald 2000).

In management science and, to some extent, business history, the treatment of visions focuses predominately on their role and function within the organization. In this context visions are mostly characterized as being closely linked to charismatic leaders or an organization's founding generation. According to House and Shamir (1992), 'it can be safely concluded that there is a strong convergence of the findings from studies concerned with charismatic leadership and those concerned with transformational and visionary leadership' (p. 84). They suggested that leaders create visions to define the basic goals and strategic intents of their organizations. Since the mid-1990s, authors of management literature have credited visions with a role in the success of organizations in the increasing uncertainty of today's business environment. Scholars have recognized that organizations require not only strong leadership but also a clear vision to coordinate, direct, and guide them to achieve their desired goals. As Grossman and King (1993) stated, 'visionary leadership is not a luxury but a necessity as we compete in the global marketplace with countries that routinely plan in terms of decades' (p. 56).

In both the business community and academic literature, this treatment of visions fails to address three important topics. First, it leaves certain factors in the environment unconsidered, especially broad and overarching visions in society, which influence organizational visions. Second, it seldom cultivates an awareness that visions often exist apart from the presence of charismatic leaders and also outlive the founding generation. Third, it offers no satisfactory explanation of how and why visions shape the life and behavior of an organization.

Our objective is to fill these gaps by theorizing about how visions influence a key dimension of organizational life—the ability or inability of organizations to change perceptions and strategies and to adapt their visions to meet new challenges in the environment. In short, we theorize about the capacity of organizations to learn. In doing so, we concentrate on visions of technology as triggers of learning.

Three case studies are used to illustrate the complex relationship between organizational visions, overarching visions of technology, and subsequent technological developments. The intention is to demonstrate how visions and technological developments can trigger different forms of learning within organizations. We conclude by discussing which factors in this complex interrelationship may stimulate or inhibit learning and thereby either promote or hinder an organization's survival and success.

Organizational Learning

As outlined by Pawlowsky (Ch. 3 in this volume), the conceptual literature on organizational learning largely distinguishes between three types of learning. No unified nomenclature has yet emerged, but most of the authors he analyzes either follow Bateson's (1972) typology—Type I, Type II, and Type III—or can be easily integrated into it. Probably the terms most widely used to characterize the three types of learning are those introduced by Argyris and Schön (1978): single-loop learning, double-loop learning, and deutero-learning.

Bateson's Type I learning, or single-loop learning according to Argyris and Schön, takes place within the existing framework of the organization. It is based on a process of error detection and correction aimed at improving or modifying the strategies and behaviors within the existing structure of the organization in a way that will best enable it to achieve its goals. Although some changes may occur, they do not alter the underlying norms of the organization. The organization continues to pursue its given policies and objectives. Learning in this context thus promotes a certain continuity.

Bateson's Type II learning, to which Argyris and Schön's double-loop learning corresponds, differs from Type I in that the organization recognizes environmental changes that cannot be responded to adequately within the existing context of the organization or its proven strategies and behaviors. The more drastic the change in the organization's environment,

the more profound the changes in the organization need to be in order to ensure its survival, its success, or both. Often, the resulting changes are incompatible with the organization's existing norms and thus engender conflicts, which must be confronted and resolved. Thus, an organization engaging in double-loop learning questions its existing theory of action, reevaluates and modifies its existing priorities, or even sets new priorities. The outcome is new or modified norms, policies, and objectives.

Bateson's Type III learning has its counterpart in Argyris and Schön's deutero-learning. In this category, not only is the behavior of the organization subject to change, but the entire process of learning is questioned as well. Such learning comes from the realization that it is not enough to respond to a particular change in the environment. Deutero-learning requires organizations to learn from previous contexts of learning and to enhance the learning process itself. In other words, the process of 'learning to learn' is integrated by organizations into their strategies and norms.

Although these categories may act as a guide to studying organizational learning, they have several weaknesses when applied to 'real-world' contexts. The main shortcoming is that the three learning types are not always easy to differentiate in practice and that they are highly dependant on the subjective interpretation of a particular event or moment in the life of the organization. One observer may perceive a learning process to be single-loop, whereas another person may convincingly argue that double-loop learning is involved. In many cases, these forms of learning are not even separate or independent processes; often they overlap in both time and scope.

A further weakness in this tripartite classification is that it focuses too narrowly on problem detection and correction as the primary way of learning. Although problems, conflicts, and crises are common stimuli of learning, important learning can also be triggered by opportunities, creative initiatives, and the development or acquisition of new knowledge (Nonaka and Takeuchi 1995; Nonaka, Reinmöller, and Toyama, Ch. 37 in this volume). The categories originally proposed by Bateson (1972) and further defined by Argyris and Schön (1978) are rather limiting in another way as well. They do little to specify how organizational learning is linked to the *external* environment—other than suggesting that the environment often serves as a stimulus and that learning is the response.

Despite these weaknesses, we adopt the learning types. However, we offer an expanded and, we hope, improved concept by including the role that visions play in shaping and influencing forms of learning. This treatment thereby allows for increased flexibility in categorizing types of organizational learning. We also strive to illustrate learning that does not result directly from a process of conflict resolution, and by including overarching visions as a trigger of learning, we show that in many cases learning is not confined by organizational boundaries.

Visions

Thus far, we have used the term 'vision' without specifically defining the concept. In the *Oxford English Dictionary* (Simson and Weiner 1991) it is defined as 'a mental concept of a distinct or vivid kind: an object of mental contemplation especially of an attractive or fantastic character; a highly imaginative scheme or anticipation' and as the 'ability to conceive what might be attempted or achieved'. This definition corresponds with the word's meaning in social theory, where visions have long been understood as a 'particular something that orients society's action and behavior'[1] (Papalekas 1959: 224). Many academics have studied the role that visions play within social systems, particularly their function and relevance within institutions and organizations. Resulting theories have ranged from being rather static to being quite dynamic. In Malinowski's (1944) theory of institutions, according to which institutions adhere to an implicit charter that justifies their existence and survival, the focus was on the stabilizing function of visions. In more dynamic theories institutions are

[1] This chapter's English translations of passages from German sources are our own.

assumed to rest on an *idée directrice* (Gehlen 1956; Hauriou 1925/1965; Willms 1970) that is said to be mutable, partially indeterminate, symbolically portrayable, yet subjectively inachievable. Schelsky (1970), who specifically addressed visions as a concept of their own, developed a theory of institutions that revolved around the phenomenon of social change. He concluded that 'the vision of each institution exists primarily in intersubjective communication and [that] every revival or renewal of . . . the linguistic and symbolic interaction in an institution thereby induces . . . change in the institution' (p. 26).

On a more general level, visions serve as frames for collective action, often representing a mental image of some desired future state of the organization (Bennis and Nanus 1985). Because visions are conveyed as images and metaphors, they are not the same as goals and plans, which are usually more concrete, short-term, and limited in scope. However, this distinction does not imply that visions are too abstract or too broad to be achieved in practical terms. Rogers (1990) noted that 'far-fetched conjectures as well as outlandish sci-fi fancies can be distinguished from *Leitbilds* [visions], mainly in that the latter are considered imaginable and feasible in the foreseeable future' (p. 9).

What visions do contribute within social systems is the unique ability to stimulate orientation, motivation, and coordination. Visions are points of orientation in that they are based on core values and shared perceptions. As Mambrey and Tepper (1992) claimed, 'a vision can be seen as a collective projection, which is ultimately a synchronization of collective assessments and adjustments' (p. 38). The results of these projections open certain horizons of perception, thinking, and decision-making and preclude others. In this regard, visions orient people and organizations and provide guidance, for they offer a particular perspective that people can either accept or reject as they communicate with each other (Dierkes, Canzler, Marz, and Knie 1995; Krupp 1995). The potential of visions to provide orientation becomes especially relevant in periods of change, when familiar criteria for action often lose their validity and people restructure their individual and collective projections of what is desirable and feasible. In this process, visions help individuals, groups, and organizations relocate their basic goals and values and rebuild a shared perception of the environment.

Visions foster motivation because they activate not only the cognitive potential of individuals, groups, and organizations but also their emotional, volitional, and affective potential. Visions do more than just appeal to the logical and rational mind; they touch upon the internalized norms, values, and preconceived notions underlying people's perceptions, thinking, and decisions. People associate visions with certain sympathies or antipathies, attractions or repulsions, and hopes or anxieties. Thus, visions have the power to motivate people to think and act in a particular direction (Krupp 1995; Marz 1993a, b).

Visions facilitate and foster coordination as well, for they are able to mediate between people's different ways of perceiving and thinking (Dierkes and Marz 1991, 1994). They serve as vehicles of communication through which to improve the conceptualization and discussion of abstract processes and future options (Dierkes, Hoffmann, and Marz 1996: 29). Visions also help people understand complex information and link lay and expert ways of perceiving and thinking. Grin and Grunwald (2000) even went so far as to refer to visions as a 'common language' (p. 11) that guides collective action. In this respect visions play a significant role in reducing obstacles to communication and thereby contribute to relatively low-cost and low-loss coordination and cooperation.

Taken individually, the effects of orientation, motivation, and coordination can be quite remarkable. Yet in many cases these three functions are not mutually exclusive. A vision is most persuasive when they work and support each other simultaneously. Visions then have the potential to coordinate the behavior of different individuals, groups, and organizations at different places and sometimes even at different times, becoming powerful tools that can often work on multiple levels.

Visions are situated at the mesolevel of singular contexts within an organization, but they also function at the macrolevel—decontextualized societal evolution, participation, and cohesion (Mambery and Tepper 1992: 49). For our study of the role that technological visions play in organizational learning, it is therefore important to distinguish between two particular types of visions: overarching visions in a society at large or in sectors of a society and visions in individual organizations.

Overarching visions are derived from key elements of the political, social, and economic environment of an entire industry, region, or society. Most of these visions are not restricted to any particular context; they transcend boundaries in order to integrate different contexts. In this sense they function much like a social contract in that they draw upon and bring together the general will of a society or an industry. Often, an individual overarching vision is a fusion of several other visions that come together to represent a wider set of normative considerations. Value congruency, ongoing consent, and moral freedom are, as in social contract theory, essential components of these visions. Overarching visions are related to the culture and values of a shared past just as much as they are projections guiding a shared future (Grin and Grunwald 2000: 176).

Visions often vary in form. They describe macrodevelopments, such as the automotive society or the projected advent of artificial intelligence. Overarching visions can also be relatively specific, as is the case with the paperless office or the fully automated factory. They provide the general framework within which individuals and organizations operate.

By contrast, visions specific to an organization encompass the basic rationale for its existence, including its fields of activity, long-term goals, and strategic intents. In addition, they represent the basic values intended to guide the behavior of individual members and of the organization as a whole, the shared perceptions and images of desired membership, and acceptable or unacceptable patterns of behavior. On the one hand, organizational visions are quite specific. They direct the organization in its efforts to achieve a particular goal and to distinguish itself from others. On the other hand, visions held by organizations are also very general and broad guides and serve as a guide that outlines an organization's strategy and behavior in changing environments and over long periods. Visions form the core ideology of the organization. In short, visions held by an organization describe as clearly as possible its future direction and the characteristics that distinguish it from other organizations.

Some visions have been guiding organizations for decades (Rogers 1990) or even centuries (Collins and Porras 1994), whereas others, often similarly strong and successful, are ephemeral (Weber 1996). Such variability signals that visions must be routinely reevaluated and, if necessary, modified in light of changing contexts in order to ensure the future success and survival of the organization. In most cases new or significantly modified visions are stimulated by crises, which indicate a gap between the organization's strengths or core competence and the demands of the environment in which it operates. However, crisis is not always necessary to promote the development of new visions. Strong new leadership within the organization or a profound, credible reorientation of existing leadership can initiate the creation of a new vision or the revision of a familiar one. One of the main functions of organizational leaders is to explain and, more important, to personify the vision of the organization for other members. Leaders are also responsible for interpreting or reinterpreting the organization's vision in the light of changing environments and determining the level at which reinterpretation is no longer sufficient. It is in this process that visions guide decisions on what elements of the organization are to be preserved and what kind of future it should be steered toward (Collins and Porras 1994: 66).

Generally, if the values, strategies, and behaviors that are derived from a particular vision prove successful, the organization will pursue them until the need for a new drastic change appears. If such a drastic change is necessary, individuals or groups in the organization will undertake efforts to create a new vision. If the new vision is not successful, another vision will have to be developed from the pool of ideas inside and outside of the organization. This process continues as long as there is the will, the time, and the intellectual and financial resources to be invested.

Organizational visions that have been successful for long periods and that are supported by a fairly stable core membership build a strong culture in the organization. Strong organizational cultures derived from strong visions are an additional powerful way to minimize the costs of orientation, coordination, and motivation and are a key source of success for organizations (Dierkes 1988). However, whereas culture describes the actual state of the objectives, values, perceptions, and behavior of the organization as shaped by experience, visions encompass the desirable state.

The Changing Nature of Technology

Technology seems to be among the most powerful of the many forces that are driving change in the environment of organizations. Overarching visions guiding developments in science and technology are therefore important factors shaping the visions of organizations. A wide range of studies on technological trajectories and delphi exercises in nearly all highly industrialized countries strongly indicate that the influence of overarching technological visions and their resulting developments will significantly increase in the forthcoming decades (Fraunhofer-Institut 1998; Fricke 1999). The importance of technology for the development and survival of organizations is steadily growing because of the frequency of its use and because of the ever increasing variety and applications of new technological and scientific developments. Many of these new developments are distinct from their predecessors. They are the result of a profound, but not yet widely discussed, change in the structure of technology, one that is adding a significant new dimension to technological developments and thereby triggering even greater changes in organizations and, indeed, in society as a whole.

The most important change in this context is the shift from artifact-centered technologies to system-centered technologies. Traditionally, technology has been understood as a physical artifact. This view, vociferously articulated by Max Weber (1924), implicitly or explicitly underlies many conceptions of technology in the humanities and social sciences. However, studies on large technical systems (Joerges 1993; La Porte 1991; Mayntz 1993; Mayntz and Hughes 1988; Weingart 1989) have increasingly shown that all conceptions in which technology is reduced solely or primarily to physical artifacts and portrayed as a more or less independent sphere of action do not suffice as a framework for explaining the technological changes that these systems represent. To understand, for example, the digital revolution in information and communications technologies, one cannot equate these technologies only with this or that artifact, for their specific nature no longer consists exclusively in physical matter. They are oriented instead to systems applications. The very complexity and speed of this change from artifact-centered to system-centered technologies brings with it a vast range of consequences that organizations cannot escape. An organization that continues to focus on new technologies only as mere artifacts and ignores their overriding nature as systems will find nothing but paradoxes and unsatisfactory explanations as it tries to manage technologies (Bijker and Law 1992; Jansanoff, Markle, Petersen, and Pinch 1995; Joerges 1994; Latour 1991/1993). By contrast, thinking of new technological developments and visions as systems can pave the way for organizational learning in its various forms.

The Relationship between Visions, Technology, and Learning

Technological visions, new technologies, and organizational visions trigger organizational learning in three ways:

1. New or modified overarching visions open up new technological options for organizations and create opportunities for additional ones to develop. In order to profit from these visions, an organization must first be able to perceive their emergence and understand their potential. That ability helps prompt the organization to test the new overarching vision against the organization's existing vision, strategies, and norms. If the new vision proves to have little or no relevance, the organization may choose not to integrate it into the existing organizational vision. If the vision is considered valuable and the attendant changes minimal, the organization will adapt to the new or modified vision mainly through single-loop learning. This approach leads to modifications in products and modes of production or to other related changes within the framework of the organizational vision.

New or significantly modified overarching visions trigger double-loop learning if they are recognized by an organization but perceived as being so different that they are impossible to profit from within the context of the organization's existing vision. Integration of a new overarching vision into the organization is guided and shaped by the organization's existing vision, which is modified by that very process. This second step of learning also encompasses the creation of new or modified organizational structures and processes, the acquisition of new skills, or both, either through the training of organizational members or through the hiring of people familiar with the technology in question. The more foreign the new technology is to an organization's competencies, the more important double-loop learning becomes and the greater the necessary changes in the organization's vision are.

2. New or improved technological artifacts or systems become available and affect individual organizations (though perhaps not the overarching vision of an entire industry). Presumably, an organization adopts only those technologies that it perceives to be relevant and superior to its existing operations. If the changes are small, they will be integrated into the organization through single-loop learning, that is, within the framework of the existing organizational vision. However, new technologies

that are significantly different from existing ones require double-loop learning that entails changes in the organizational vision. Double-loop learning consequently brings about changes in the organization's structures, processes, and knowledge base.

3. The recent shift from artifact-centered to system-centered technologies and technological visions triggers new forms of organizational learning. The relationship between system-centered technological visions, technological developments, and organizational learning is the most complex and ambiguous of the three presented in this chapter, for often the visions themselves are still in their formative phase. Moreover, new technologies characteristically entail tremendous, unpredictable change because system-centered technologies are only loosely linked to their artifacts, and these artifacts are accessible to nearly every organization prepared to test new visionary ideas. Organizations therefore have little protection from their competitors and must learn how to respond proactively and quickly to these system-centered technological visions and their technologies.

Additional complications arise because often the system elements of new overarching technological visions may not fit an organization's existing vision. To adjust, an organization may first apply single-loop learning in the framework of its existing vision. With minor adjustments it can also integrate new technological visions into its own vision through double-loop learning. In most cases, however, these two options will not be sufficient to deal adequately with the complex changes introduced by system-centered technologies and their visions. Organizations, instead, have to question their single- and double-loop learning patterns and search for new modes of learning. In this environment learning to learn, or deutero-learning, is a necessary element of the organization's vision and culture. This third form of learning, which is always mentioned in classifications but seldom described and analyzed in the reality of organizational life, is often central to survival and success in system-centered fields of technology.

Technological Visions as Triggers of and Obstacles to Organizational Learning: Lessons to be Learned from Case Studies

To illustrate the complex interaction between overarching technological visions and developments, organizational visions, and organizational learning, we have selected three case studies that have a common background: the change in information and communication technologies since the 1960s (see Fig. 12.1). Our focus is on the vision underlying this change, the computerization of the everyday world. In all three cases, scientific breakthroughs led to new or significantly modified technological visions that were either perceived and used by organizations as an opportunity to learn or that were not seen as important enough to stimulate new learning and motivate a change in the original vision of the organization.

The first example is drawn from the word-processing industry. This case shows how an organization, instead of learning and adapting to a new overarching vision, can choose to maintain the status quo, halting additional learning and ultimately causing the organization to become outdated in the face of changing technologies and markets. The second example, from the automotive industry, presents a combination of both stabilizing and innovative reactions to new environmental challenges. Changes within this industry have shaped the visions and behaviors of organizations in a way that has led them to press forward with multiple forms of learning, simultaneously questioning and challenging traditional technologies, yet ultimately preserving them. The final example, the Internet industry, shows the diverse outcomes that can result from two quite different approaches to the same technological challenge. In this industry technological innovation has been, and still is, so fast and revolutionary that organizations pursuing single- and double-loop strategies

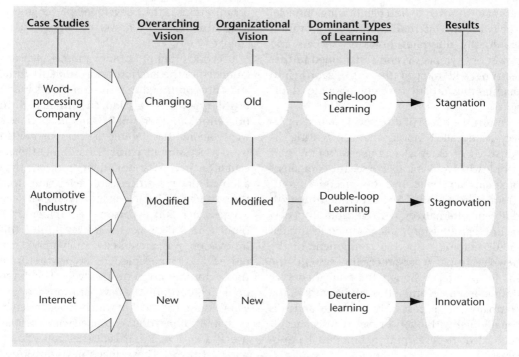

Fig. 12.1. Interaction of visions and forms of learning in three environments

quickly become isolated and then left behind. However, the organizations that proactively undergo deutero-learning become the leaders and shapers of new technology within the industry.

The Vision of the Word-processing Industry: Stagnation of Learning

The first example, the vision of word-processing technologies, is typical of what happens when an organization adheres overwhelmingly to a particular vision. This case is that of AEG Olympia Büromaschinenwerke, a German office-equipment manufacturing company founded in 1903 and dissolved in 1994. In this organization 'the mechanical typewriter [was] the vision in which generations of employees found meaning' (Buhr 1997: 55). Both management and employees at all levels and in all departments were imbued with this vision and had 'unswerving loyalty to the typewriter as a product' (p. 56). From its inception, the typewriter was the core of Olympia's technological vision, and its subsequent success defined and shaped the company's corporate culture. Managers were heard to say 'I wouldn't like to have to see the day when we no longer make typewriters here!' (p. 57). Accordingly, all the learning, work, and activities of thousands of employees revolved around this one product and the aim of perfecting it. It encompassed the projections of what the entire organization held as desirable and feasible, and the employees thrived on this vision.

However, in the mid-1960s signs indicated that the typewriter, the classical form of mechanical writing and the central vision of word-processing technology, would eventually be supplanted by a new technological vision, electronic word-processing systems (Bammé et al. 1983; Hofmann 1997). The company's strong identification with this original vision began to limit the organization's ability to perceive these changes in the environment and ultimately proved to be a debilitating obstacle. The fate of two internal attempts at innovation graphically illustrates how the success and power of Olympia's vision constrained further learning and trapped the organization into maintaining an increasingly obsolete status quo.

In 1971 the board of directors installed a project team called 'nonmechanical writing'. It consisted of external engineers, 'totally new people who would be able to see the company's problems and who had no preconceptions' (Buhr 1997: 58). After first experimenting with different alternatives derived from the new technological vision, this group concentrated on developing a specific component of the new electronic word-processing system, the ink-jet printer. Although the team had very limited resources and although its work in the company was at best only tolerated and was usually met with overt or covert resistance, it succeeded in developing a functional prototype.

Real conflict flared, however, when this new product confronted the traditional, typewriter-centered organizational vision of the company. At the meeting in which the ink-jet printer was presented, it failed to gain the necessary acceptance primarily because it departed too greatly from the organizational vision and the mechanical writing technologies to which the audience was so accustomed. The engineers of the development team tried to reconcile Olympia's employees and management to the new machine by attempting to 'somehow make a typewriter' out of the printer (Buhr 1997: 60). For example, because with typewriters each letter is immediately visible after the corresponding key is struck, they rebuilt the ink-jet printer in such a way that its continuous operation was interrupted after every strike of a key so that the letter could immediately be seen. To accommodate the demand for carbon copies, the engineers used special paper that could be permeated by the ink. However, neither modification was able to change the deeply rooted attachment that management and the employees had to the typewriter-centered vision, and as in most traditionally structured organizations, the development engineers lacked the necessary power to impose such a change.

A second attempt at innovation, which was launched in the late 1970s, was similarly futile and only confirmed that the company's vision of the typewriter was indeed entrenched. In this effort another small team of engineers went about developing a computer-aided word-processing machine. To promote the acceptance necessary for their project, they adopted the typewriter-centered vision from the outset and tried to create 'a hybrid between a typewriter and a personal computer (PC)' (Buhr 1997: 61). Unlike the ink-jet printer, this innovation was presented to Olympia's employees and management as a typewriter from the beginning, not retrospectively. The development group built the new hardware and software around the old, but widely loved, product so that 'the typewriters equipped with a display [were] a kind of PC, except that you [didn't] see it' (p. 61). These machines constituted an attempt to anticipate and tie into the new overarching technological vision of computer-aided office communications. Yet it, too, failed. The PC-disguised-as-a-typewriter was accepted by neither the company nor its customers.

There were no further efforts to adapt Olympia's vision to the new overarching vision in word-processing technology. Despite the technological changes taking place throughout the industry and in the world, the company unwaveringly continued to develop and improve classical typewriters in the firm conviction that they would sell far into the twenty-first century (Buhr 1997: 59). However, as technology progressed, the former leader in word-processing technologies became an outsider to technological change in the industry—and then its victim.

The Vision of the Automotive Industry Challenged: Stagnovation as a Result

The vision of the automotive industry is a second example of the tremendous power and depth that can be associated with techno-logical visions. However, whereas the vision of the typewriter was rooted mainly in a particular organization, the vision of mobility—centered on the automobile as the most desirable form of transport—is rooted in many organizations: automotive firms and their suppliers, police organizations and courts, governments, un-ions, and areas outside the organizational sphere, such as the daily behavior of drivers and their individual and collective projections of what is desirable and feasible (Canzler 1996; Canzler, Knie, and Bertold 1993; Canzler and Marz 1996). This vision, which has been the foundation of the automobile's dominance in all notions of mobility, has structured transport policies throughout the world for decades and must be one of the most widely held, stable, and effective overarching technological visions ever known (Dierkes, Canzler, Marz, and Knie 1995).

The vision of mobility centered on the auto-mobile is currently so powerful that it pervades the learning of almost all organizations in the industry. Thus, the growing crisis of mobility, as indicated by traffic jams, pollution, and the threat to global resources, is treated as though it were merely a variant of other problems that have already been successfully managed. This kind of learning is fixated on retaining the time-tested, technological core of the automo-bile—the 'high-performance, internal combus-tion limousine' (Canzler and Knie 1994: 61)—but upgrading its equipment and accessories to meet society's changing needs. Sensory, op-toelectronic, and information technologies are being used by the automotive industry in the great hope of prolonging the original vision of the automobile. Building upon the traditional technologies of automotive manufacturing and upon technologies hitherto having noth-ing to do with cars, these innovations show that learning has gone beyond the original vi-sion of the industry. The networked and intel-ligent car is the central technology now being propagated in a revised and reshaped vision of the automotive society of the future.

Although people occasionally overestimate the degree to which additional technological

input can enhance the overall efficiency of the automobile-centered transportation system, there is no reason to assume that its potential capacity for solving problems is minor. Specif-ically, a vehicle fully equipped with modern sensory, optoelectronic, and information tech-nologies is expected to bring three kinds of relief from the negative impacts of the automo-tive society (Canzler 1996). First, collective in-formation systems reporting on changes in traffic conditions and parking availability and satellite-aided global-positioning systems (e.g. *autopilot* and *scout*) have been introduced to improve the efficiency with which the existing infrastructure is used. Second, the continued development and integration of information technology is intended to lead to pretravel in-formation systems. Available on-line through personal computers, they are to aid the plan-ning of journeys by expanding the quality and amount of information available to drivers be-fore they depart. An unprecedented level of efficiency in one's planning seems imminent. Third, technological developments have also made it possible to control the volume of traffic by electronic road or congestion pricing. Elec-tronic tolls and restrictions are regarded as a way of introducing market principles into the use of transport infrastructure and of thereby helping minimize undesirable social and envir-onmental side effects.

This process of sustaining the power of an overarching technological vision by modifying it through technological components from other fields of technology can perhaps best be described as stagnating innovation, innovative stagnation, or for short, stagnovation (Canzler and Marz 1996, 1997). This expression commu-nicates that the decade-old vision of the auto-motive society has been neither preserved nor completely reshaped or replaced. Bringing new information technologies into the high-performance limousine creates both virtual and real space for innovations. However, these innovations are ultimately seen as stagnating because they do not transcend the traditional vision of the automobile as a way of satisfying the human demand for mobility, which is likely to grow significantly. Relieving the problems of the automotive system only temporarily will most likely postpone the collapse of the transport infrastructure in metropolitan areas, but it does nothing to eradicate its underlying problems.

The Vision of the Internet Created and Recreated: Learning to Learn

The classical vision of the Internet rests upon a commitment to an open architecture of transmission, a design that distinguishes this network from other communications systems such as the telephone (Dierkes, Hofmann, and Marz 1998). Most of the scientists who originally developed and worked on the Internet's transmission principles were based at universities. It was their projections of what was desirable and feasible that gave the Internet vision its start (Comer 1991; Huitema 1995). The culture of the academic community, where research results can easily be published and discussed and where knowledge is shared and made readily available to others, was mainly responsible for shaping the initial vision and culture of the Internet (Dierkes, Hofmann, and Marz 1998).

The Internet's complex structure and dependence on system-centered technology is in many ways unparalleled, particularly in its vision (Dierkes, Hofmann, and Marz 1998). The founding principle of the vision as stated in *Requests for Comment* (RFC) (Bradner 1996)—that development of Internet standards shall be open—means that anyone with the necessary expertise is invited to contribute (Helmers, Hoffmann, and Hofmann 1997). Design standards, known as Internet drafts, are published, discussed, and then archived in specific series, such as RFC, which are available to all users. Thus, the work on developing Internet standards is a collective effort regulated not through affiliation with a particular organization or committee but instead solely through 'the excellence of the technical work' (Huitema 1995: 24). If a pool of Internet drafts contains two competing designs, and if it is not clear which design is superior, each is developed by a work group until ready for implementation.

The activities of the different groups are transparent and open to objections, critique, and suggestions. The only prerequisite, or running code, for acceptance of a new standard is that it have at least two independent implementations proving that the technical specification in question functions and that it is interoperable with the other technical constituents of the Internet (Alvestand 1997; Bradner 1996). The extent to which a standard then prevails is not subject to the control of specific organizations. The market decides instead. The environment provided by this vision and by the resulting culture of the Internet is highly flexible, cooperative, and decentralized but difficult to manage and regulate.

Not only is the process of developing standards open, but its results are open as well. The Internet's specific transmission principles, called protocols, are not standards in the formal or conventional sense. These protocols are not formally decided upon, introduced, or declared binding in any manner. Instead, they are passed on and offered for discussion, both voluntarily and without cost. In fact, the Internet is as much a collection of communities as it is a collection of technologies, and its success is largely attributable to its record of both satisfying basic public needs and using the community as an effective tool to push the Internet forward (Cerf 1998). Consequently, the speed and transparency of Internet development has been unparalleled.

However, in the early 1990s three parallel processes confronted the Internet's founding groups with a completely new environment. First, government increasingly withdrew its funding as investment from the business community dramatically increased. The centers for the development of standards thereupon shifted away from universities and the academic community to the major users and providers of computer and network technology. As a result, more and more people who were committed to the open development of standards migrated from universities to the business sector (Lehr 1995).

Second, the World Wide Web and its browsers provided new Internet uses whose user-friendliness attracted a mass public able to operate within the system without any training or expertise. This explosion in the number of users not only dramatically increased network traffic (Helmers, Hoffmann, and Hofmann 1996) but also radically changed the methods and content of daily use. Recent figures show that the number of worldwide Internet users doubles every hundred days and that this population is expected to grow from the 70 million registered users in 1997 to 707 million by 2001 (Weingart 1989). Clearly, the classical academic users have lost their preeminence.

Third, this quantitative growth and qualitative shift in the community of users led to the discovery of the Internet as a viable market. Consequently, numerous Internet-specific firms were quickly joined on the net by more and more traditional companies and organizations seeking market exposure and an opportunity to offer their services on-line (Dierkes, Hofmann, and Marz 1998).

The general shift from having a few networks with a modest number of hosts to having many networks has resulted in an entirely new Internet environment, one in which the development of standards has become more crucial than ever. Although the overarching vision remains the same, some groups within the Internet community have begun to challenge the net's traditional methods of standardization. In general, two different approaches to standardization have surfaced: those represented by the International Standards Organization (ISO) and those of the Internet Engineering Task Force (IETF). These organizations have some practices in common: Both of them advance technology through a committee and a process of consensus, and both use some form of parliamentary procedure.

In many other respects, however, particularly in their history, culture, and vision, these communities differ substantially (Piscitello and Chapin 1993: 13). The ISO, for example, tackled the new and fast-paced environment of the Internet industry by applying the traditional vision, strategies, and technologies of their organization's specific competencies. The ISO is a worldwide federation of national standards

bodies from 130 countries (http://www.iso.ch). Its scope is not limited to any particular industry; it is well-established in such diverse fields as information-processing and communications, textiles, packaging, distribution of goods, energy production, and banking and financial services. At the time of Internet development, the ISO and its study group, the International Telegraph and Telephone Consultative Committee (CCITT), had been working closely on the development of public packet-switching standards to coordinate efforts to develop a single international reference model for open-system interconnection (Piscitello and Chapin 1993: 14). Having this experience in standard-setting, the ISO saw the Internet as a related field of technology and tried to use mass support by its member states to set new standards and control basic technological elements in order to gain influence over the Internet (Dierkes, Hofmann, and Marz 1998). Although many dimensions of the basic technology of the Internet were familiar to and shared by the ISO, the body was a closed and traditionally structured standard-setting institution, so its culture and standard-setting procedures were dramatically different from those common to the Internet. The ISO failed to recognize the open, system-centered nature of the Internet and thus did not adapt its vision and procedures to the specific Internet culture. Ultimately, by trying to transfer to the Internet the artifact-based technologies and practices of standardization that had served well for decades in other related fields, the ISO defied the vision of open standardization practiced up to that time (Dierkes, Hofmann, and Marz 1998). As a result, most of the standards developed by the ISO never reached the point where they could be applied to commercial products in the field.

The IETF took a different course. As an independent institution without legal status or formal authority, the IETF had a culture rooted in the original vision of the Internet—the open development of standards—and was championed by work groups composed of engineers and scientists from academic, computer, and telecommunications communities. These work groups were more flexible and fluid than other standard-setting bodies. They were often composed of a diverse, *ad hoc* group of volunteers. They approached the development of Internet standards as a new experience and an opportunity to learn and proactively manage the changing nature of their environment, not just as a mere variant of already familiar tasks. This culture and vision enabled the IETF to become the avant-garde in developing standards openly (Lehr 1995).

Although various companies now employ many of the same people who had been actively involved in the development of the IETF, the vision and practices modeled by this organization have endured. Many companies of the 1990s embrace the overarching vision of the open development of Internet standards and grant their former IETF founders the necessary scope for work in this field (Dierkes, Hofmann, and Marz 1998). These organizations allowed a major share of these employees' available working hours to be dedicated to writing Internet drafts, reading corresponding mailing lists, and discussing current problems. In addition, these companies sent large delegations to IETF meetings, attendance at which had come to range between 1,500 and 2,000 people. Despite their power and influence in the Internet industry, these companies did not try to turn active IETF members into corporate representatives. Any attempt to do so would have been counterproductive because high technical competence and affiliation with the IETF elite was defined in part by the ability to resist such influence-peddling. Esteem and recognition went to those who strictly distinguished the vision of their specific organization from the overarching vision of the Internet as a collective good.

Taking Stock and Looking Ahead

What These Cases Teach about Visions and Learning

In this chapter we have sought not only to illustrate the power of overarching visions and

their related potential for organizational learning but also to demonstrate that visions have limits to their ability to stimulate learning. The three case studies from the word-processing, automotive, and Internet industries show that visions can be either a trigger or a barrier to learning (see Berthoin Antal, Lenhardt, and Rosenbrock, Ch. 39 in this volume, for a detailed discussion of barriers to learning). They also demonstrate why it is necessary to increase attention to the task of developing organizational visions as a mechanism for learning.

The case of Olympia demonstrates how organizational learning can become so constrained by an organization's particular vision and perception of technology that even unmistakable changes in the overarching vision cannot persuade a company to shift to a different type of learning. The learning in this organization was basically confined to single-loop strategies within the framework of the existing vision. The problem was not that the company lacked the capacity to innovate or meet the technological challenges on the market but rather that the typewriter program and its decades of success proved so powerful and deeply embedded in the organization that this legacy blocked management's view to new technologies on the horizons.

Olympia's ability to learn was constrained by boundary rootedness. This boundary reveals the extent to which overarching visions are accepted and anchored in the organization's vision. If a vision is embraced across an organization and even beyond, it takes a long time and unique circumstances for the organization to recognize changes in the overarching vision. Instead, the organization will have a tendency to confine itself to single-loop learning. Coupled with existing leadership and a strong culture, this response may improve existing products and strategies, but the organization will find it nearly impossible to modify its vision and to develop other learning strategies.

This conclusion is supported by a study that Collins and Porras (1994) conducted on the successful habits of visionary companies. They argued that organizational visions must transcend existing products and practices or they can easily become obsolete. If visions are short-sighted or centered on a specific product, they can actually keep learning from going beyond incremental improvements based on single-loop learning: '[B]y confusing core ideology with noncore practices, companies can cling too long to noncore items—things that should be changed in order for the company to adapt and move forward' (p. 81). Over time, the goals, strategies, products, structure, and culture of an organization will most likely need to change in response to the environment. Thus, visions must be flexible, or organizations must be willing to change their vision in order to accommodate the various stages of its life cycle. Although the core ideology of visions must be specific, organizations must separate these core values and goals from their present products and successes. Collins and Porras described visionary companies as those that are able to instill their core ideology into their vision but that are simultaneously prepared to reevaluate and, if necessary, modify other aspects of the existing vision.

The example of the automotive industry portrays many of the same characteristics as that of the word-processing industry: mainly, an industry's or society's dominant, overarching vision and strong visions of new technologies emerging in individual organizations and related fields. However, the potential of these visions and technologies triggered organizational learning throughout the industry. Moreover, organizational learning has extended beyond the original organizational vision and single-loop strategies; double-loop learning was apparent. Organizations modified their specific visions and learned how to improve and modernize by exploiting the given, albeit narrow, scope of action within the overarching vision. Borrowing technologies from other industries by bringing computerization into the vision of the high-performance limousine has opened both virtual and real space for double-loop learning and hence has also modified organizational visions.

The example of the automotive industry illustrates the controlling power of a firmly established overarching technological vision. It has been adopted not only by an entire industry but by society as well to such a degree that the vision has become virtually frozen in time, or at least stagnant. Such stagnation is often the result of barriers to organizational learning processes. Organizations operating within this industry are confronting barriers of control and substance. The barrier of control results from the attempt to take the process of shaping an organization's vision and steer it in a particular direction. In principle, very little, if any, such control is possible. There is one factor, however, that can be powerful enough to influence any vision directly: organizationally perceived change in the overarching vision of the industry. Yet, in order for an organization to respond, it must first perceive this change and then recognize a need to adapt its vision accordingly. Despite current arguments claiming that the automobile is currently pushing the limits of its social desirability, the power and control exerted by the vision that enshrines it has blocked drastic changes or alternative visions from developing.

This inability to look beyond the vision and to the horizon of emerging technologies can stifle the development of new visions and technologies within organizations and thereby hinder learning. Although many organizations within the automotive industry have recognized the need for profound change, the development of new visionary substance has been limited because learning has been confined to single- and double-loop strategies. Organizations within the automotive industry have been able to surmount or at least minimize this barrier of substance by concentrating on marginally modifying their existing vision. The visions, strategies, and culture of this industry continue to focus on the traditional overarching vision of the automobile. But in order to ease the growing problems associated with the automobile, individual organizations have successfully incorporated new technologies from other fields into their own specific visions. Some of this learning has transcended organizational boundaries, and new visions within organizations have triggered incremental changes throughout the entire industry.

Drawing on Collins and Porras (1994), one could say that the automotive industry has been able to preserve its core yet still make progress. However, as the challenges of the automotive society intensify, the human need for mobility will require both the elimination of these barriers and a high level of learning within organizations and the industry as a whole.

The final example, the Internet industry, demonstrates the impact that organizational visions have on single-loop and deutero-learning. The ISO confined its learning to single-loop strategies because it failed to expand its understanding of technologies beyond the traditional, artifact-centered notion of technological development. The ISO's tendency to be political led the organization to embrace multiple solutions to a single problem and to show little concern for developing a real understanding of the underlying technology and its general application (Piscitello and Chapin 1993: 26). The ISO tried to apply to the Internet the same strategies that had brought it previous success in other contexts and different environments. Although a focus on the artifact dimension might have been sufficient to facilitate the construction of global telephone services and standards for other artifact-centered technologies, the rapid changes and developments in system-centered technologies easily overloaded this organization. The ISO's failure to align its vision with the overarching vision in the industry ultimately blocked new visions from triggering the learning necessary to operate within this industry.

The IETF, by contrast, perceived the systems nature of this technology and ensured that its strategic framework coincided with the technological vision and culture of the industry. Parting with the traditional approaches to technological change, the IETF has pressed forward with Internet developments through an innovative kind of decentralized, cooperative, and open coordination rather than adhering to a centralist, hierarchical, and closed organizational model. This more flexible approach promoted permanent learning as an important element of the organizational vision and has thus allowed considerable latitude for adapting the development of standards to the new system-oriented technology that emerged (Piscitello and Chapin 1993: 27).

There are many indications that this form of innovation, the open model for developing technology and standards, emerged from a kind of deutero-learning emancipated from servitude to past programs and experiences. The IETF illustrates how an organization can overcome what can be called the boundary of acceptance. The boundary of acceptance stems from the degree to which the organization's members are involved in the process of creating a new organizational vision. The more they are engaged in the process, the lower the barriers are; the less the members are engaged, the higher the barriers. When a vision is developed without input from organizational members, its power to orient, motivate, and coordinate is usually never brought to bear, so its effect on learning is rather limited.

In the IETF, vision development was unique in that the stakeholders of the technology—the researchers, users, and vendors—were those directly involved in creating and shaping the vision. Membership in the IETF was intentionally left open so that users would be reckoned as part of the actor constellations that help propagate socially desirable innovations (Dierkes, Hofmann, and Marz 1998). Open involvement in shaping an organization's vision can facilitate its acceptance and allow members to learn collectively and make the transition from single- and double-loop learning to deutero-learning. The example of the IETF offers one piece of evidence that developing a successful vision does not require any special form of guidance or control, or even charismatic leadership. If learning is deeply rooted in the organizational vision and, over time, in its culture, the vision will then belong to the entire organization, empowering and stimulating the learning of all its members.

The Conceptual Framework Revised

Review and comparison of the examples presented in this chapter reveal three main relations between technological change, organizational learning, and visions. The first relation has to do with the dimensions of technological change and the way they are perceived. Not all organizations have the organs of perception needed to recognize changes in an overarching vision and sense their potential. Even those organizations that do have such organs or sensors often lack the learning capacity needed to integrate perceived changes into their organizational vision. Furthermore, organizations cannot respond to each and every change and development in their accustomed fields of technology, let alone those in related ones. The opportunities introduced by new technologies are overwhelming, and organizational resources allocated to innovation are often limited. Organizations are therefore forced to decide which options to explore.

In general, organizations welcome new or modified technological visions and new technologies if they can be easily managed within the existing framework of their organizational vision. Even drastic technological changes at the artifact level can still be perceived and responded to with relative ease by organizations, for most of these changes do not disrupt the culture or the operational predictability of the organization's activities. However, the rapid growth of system-centered technological change has challenged this complacency. In the long run, it can be highly problematic for learning processes if organizations recognize or concentrate on only the physical dimension of technological change to the exclusion of the other dimensions. System-centered technological changes require organizations to reconceptualize both their goals and their work activities, or, as Bloomfield and Vurdubakis (1997) referred to it, the 'lifeworld of their professional practices' (p. 647). If an organization does not respond in such a manner, it will often be unable to meet the challenges posed by rapid system-centered technological change, a failure that can ultimately prove fatal.

The second relation between technological change, organizational learning, and visions explored in this chapter is the influence that the different types of learning have on how organizations deal with change in technological visions or developments entailed by new technologies. Organizations are often unprepared for, or do not have the learning capacity to deal with, the many issues raised by changes in technology. The reason is that technological change can erode members' confidence in what they have already learned and the way in which they have learned it. This point applies especially to system-centered technologies, which until recently were still regarded as the essence of science fiction, not everyday reality (Shillingford 2000). Whether and how much an organization is able to adapt to these complex technologies depends greatly upon the type of learning that the organization can resort to. Although single- and double-loop learning can sometimes be sufficient even for significant improvements, time-tested programs and experience will do little, if anything, to help organizations adequately perceive and proactively deal with system-centered technological changes. This deficiency of single- and double-loop learning is especially apparent in industries where major contextual changes are so rapid and revolutionary that they can only be described as discontinuities.

In general, organizational visions and cultures in which learning is valued as an essential and permanent element of practice and procedure is where corporate strategic flexibility and the use of new technology will increase (Hitt, Keats, and DeMarie 1998: 35). Organizations with such visions and cultures are capable of following a pattern of learning that goes beyond single- or double-loop learning. They recognize that technological change has forced the context of organizational learning itself to undergo profound changes, a process that, in turn, calls hitherto successful learning strategies into question and requires development of the capacity to learn and relearn. Although deutero-learning does not guarantee an organization's success, it may well improve the chances that the organization will be able to adapt to fundamental changes in technology.

The third relation explored in this chapter brings the various contexts of technology, learning, and visions together to show the power that visions have in shaping organizational learning in general and each of the learning types in particular. As all three examples illustrate, this power can be extraordinary. In some organizations, visions can be so strongly bound to existing technology that learning is precluded because profound changes of context are either unperceived or are defined as irrelevant and ignored. These types of organizations pursue single-loop learning within the boundaries of existing organizational visions and often stagnate because they are unable to innovate and adapt successfully to new overarching visions. Donald Sull (1999) referred to this condition as 'active inertia' (p. 42), the organization's tendency to follow established patterns of behavior even in response to dramatic environmental shifts. In such cases there is a tendency to force new visions and technologies into existing schemata. Although long-standing visions and success often provide stability by giving organizations a strong, unified sense of strategies and values, they also make the organization and its members reluctant to change. Despite incremental innovation in products and services, these organizations continue to work with old, even outdated processes and structures. Instead of reevaluating strategic frames in light of new overarching visions, they simply accelerate their tried-and-true activities without any real concern for the changing nature of their environment.

The ability to learn requires organizations to scan both their internal and external environments and develop visionary substance and long-range strategies to encompass new goals, values, and behavior patterns. The higher the value that learning has in an organization's existing vision and culture, the more likely it is that the organization will be able to perceive and exploit opportunities for innovation offered by new overarching technological visions, even those quite remote from its current field of activities. The further the organization moves in that direction, the less it will confine itself to preserving and incrementally modernizing traditional concepts.

Each type of learning is based on a different relationship to organizational visions. Visions thoroughly shape forms of learning within an organization. Yet visions, too, are the result of a learning process. They grow from a social field of similar, preexisting, intertwined projections of what is desirable and feasible. Visions are a point of orientation enabling people and organizations to specify and fine tune their individual and collective projections of what is desirable and feasible, a process that stabilizes and reinforces these projections. Visions, therefore, are both a result and a trigger of learning. For this reason a change in an organization's learning process, especially the transition from single- and double-loop learning to deutero-learning, is extremely difficult, if not impossible, without a change in the original organizational vision in which these types of learning are anchored.

Visions are a powerful instrument for guiding organizations. By critically reflecting upon both organizational and overarching visions, organizations have a tool with which to anticipate and prepare for future technological developments. Those visions that rest on the core values of the organization and allow for a degree of openness and flexibility can enhance the responsiveness of organizations and can help them ultimately overcome the problems of active inertia. However, the power of visions to trigger learning depends upon the degree in which learning is integrated into the organizational vision. Organizations that are proactive and able to develop a pool of new potentially visionary ideas and mold them into a viable and widely acceptable vision will have a major advantage in the current state of rapid and unpredictable change. By increasing their ability to meet the growing challenges posed by changes in overarching technological visions and new technologies, organizations can learn to outlive the various changes in technology.

References

Alvestand, H. (1997). 'The Internet Standardisation Process', in B. Trond, F. Hakon, S. Helmers, U. Hoffmann, and J. Hofmann (eds.), *Management and Network Technology: Proceedings from the COST A3 Workshop, Trondheim, Norway, 22–24 November 1995* (Vol. 3). Luxembourg: Office for Official Publications of the European Communities, 59–65.

Argyris, C. and Schön, D. A. (1978). *Organizational Learning: A Theory of Action Perspective*. Reading, Mass.: Addison-Wesley.

Bammé, A., Feuerstein, G., Genth, R., Holling, E., Kahle, R., and Kempin, P. (1983). *Maschinen-Menschen, Mensch-Maschinen: Grundrisse einer sozialen Beziehung*. Reinbek: Rowohlt, 112–14.

Bateson, G. (1972). *Steps to an Ecology of Mind: A Revolutionary Approach to Man's Understanding of Himself*. New York: Ballantine Books.

Bennis, W. and Nanus, B. (1985). *Führungskräfte: Die vier Schlüsselstrategien erfolgreichen Führens*. Frankfurt am Main: Campus.

Bijker, W. and Law, J. (eds.) (1992). *Shaping Technology/Building Society: Studies in Sociotechnical Change*. Cambridge, Mass.: MIT Press, 290–306.

Bloomfield, B. and Verdubakis, T. (1997). 'Visions of Organization and Organizations of Visions: The Representational Practices of Information Systems Development'. *Accounting, Organizations and Society*, 22: 639–68.

Bradner, S. (1996). 'The Internet Standards Process—Revision 3'. *Request for Comments (RFC) 2026*.

Buhr, R. (1997). '"Wenn wir hier mal nicht Schreibmaschinen bauen, das möchte ich gar nicht mehr erleben müssen!"—Betriebliche Innovationsdynamik und Produkleitbilder', in M. Dierkes (ed.), *Technikgenese: Befunde aus einem Forschungsprogramm*. Berlin: edition sigma, 50–61.

Canzler, W. (1996). *Das Zauberlehrlings-Syndrom: Entstehung und Stabilität des Automobil-Leitbildes*. Berlin: edition sigma.

—— and Knie, A. (1994). *Das Ende des Automobils—Fakten und Trends zum Umbau der Autogesellschaft*. Heidelberg: Müller.

—— —— and Bertold, O. (1993). 'Das Leitbild vor seiner Auflösung? Zum Widerspruch von motorischer Aufrüstung und realem Nutzungsverhalten'. *Zeitschrift für Umweltpolitik und Umweltrecht*, 4: 407–29.

—— and Marz, L. (1996). *Festgefahren? Der Automobilpakt im 21. Jahrhundert*. Discussion paper FS II 96–108. Wissenschaftszentrum Berlin für Sozialforschung.

—— —— (1997). 'Stagnovation: Der Automobilpakt und die gedopte Arbeitsgesellschaft'. *Universitas*, 52: 359–71.

Cerf, V. (1998). 'A Brief History of the Internet'. Available: http://www.isoc.org/internet/history/cerf. html

Collins, J. C. and Porras, J. I. (1994). *Built to Last: Successful Habits of Visionary Companies*. New York: Harper Business.

Comer, D. E. (1991). *Interworking with TCP/IP*: Vol. 1. *Principles, Protocols, and Architecture*. Englewood Cliffs, NJ: Prentice Hall.

Dierkes, M. (1988). 'Unternehmenskultur und Unternehmensführung—Konzeptionelle Ansätze und gesicherte Erkenntnisse'. *Zeitschrift für Betriebswirtschaft*, 58: 554–75.

—— Canzler, W., Marz, L., and Knie, A. (1995). 'Politik und Technikgenese'. *Verbund Sozialwissenschaftliche Technikforschung: Mitteilungen*, 15: 7–28.

—— Hoffmann, U., and Marz, L. (1996). *Visions of Technology: Social and Institutional Factors Shaping the Development of New Technologies* (D. Antal, trans.). Frankfurt am Main: Campus. (Original work published 1992)

—— Hofmann, J., and Marz, L. (1998). 'Technological Development and Organisational Change: Differing Patterns of Innovation', in OECD (ed.), *21st Century Technologies: Promises and Perils of a Dynamic Future*. OECD Publications, 97–122.

—— and Marz, L. (1991). 'Technikakzeptanz, Technikfolgen und Technikgenese: Zur Weiterentwicklung konzeptioneller Grundlagen der sozialwissenschaftlichen Technikforschung', in

D. Jaufmann and E. Kistler (eds.), *Einstellungen zum technischen Fortschritt: Technikakzeptanz im nationalen und internationalen Vergleich*. Frankfurt am Main: Campus, 157–87.

Dierkes, M. and Marz, L., (1994). 'Unternehmensverantwortung und leitbildorientierte Technikgestaltung', in W. Zimmerli and V. Brennecke (eds.), *Technikverantwortung in der Unternehmenskultur: Von theoretischen Konzepten zur praktischen Umsetzung*. Stuttgart: Schäffer-Poeschel, 89–114.

Fraunhofer-Institut für Systemtechnik und Innovationsforschung (ed.) (1998). *Studie zur globalen Entwicklung von Wissenschaft und Technik: Zusammenfassung der Ergebnisse*. Delphi—Umfrage im Auftrag des Bundesministeriums für Bildung, Wissenschaft, Forschung und Technologie (BMBF). Karlsruhe: Fraunhofer-Institut für Systemtechnik und Innovationsforschung.

Fricke, W. (ed.) (1999). *1999/2000 Jahrbuch Arbeit und Technik*. Bonn: Dietz.

Gehlen, A. (1956). *Urmensch und Spätkultur: Philosophische Ergebnisse und Aussagen*. Bonn: Athenäum.

Grin, J. and Grunwald, A. (eds.) (2000). *Visions Assessment: Shaping Technology in 21st Century Society*. Berlin: Springer.

Grossman, S. R. and King, M. J. (1993). 'Where Vision Statements Go Wrong'. *Across the Board*, 30/5: 56–7.

Hauriou, M. (1965). *Die Theorie der Institution* (R. Schnur, trans.). Berlin: Duncker and Humblot. (Original work published 1925)

Helmers, S., Hoffmann, U., and Hofmann, J. (1996). '*Netzkultur und Netzwerkorganisation: Das Projekt "Interaktionsraum" Internet'*. Discussion paper FS II 96–103. Wissenschaftszentrum Berlin für Sozialforschung.

—— —— —— (1997). 'Standard Development as Techno-social Ordering: The Case of the Next Generation of the Internet Protocol', in B. Trond, F. Hakon, S. Helmers, U. Hoffmann, and J. Hofmann (eds.), *Management and Network Technology: Proceedings from the COST A3 Workshop, Trondheim, Norway, 22–24 November 1995* (Vol. 3). Luxembourg: Office for Official Publications of the European Communities, 35–57.

Hitt, M., Keats, B., and DeMarie, S. (1998). 'Navigating in the New Competitive Landscape: Building Strategic Flexibility and Competitive Advantage in the 21st Century'. *Academy of Management Executive*, 12/4: 22–41.

Hofmann, J. (1997). 'Über Nutzerbilder in Textverarbeitungsprogrammen: Drei Fallbeispiele', in M. Dierkes (ed.), *Technikgenese: Befunde aus einem Forschungsprogramm*. Berlin: edition sigma, 71–97.

House, R. and Shamir, B. (1993). 'Toward the Integration of Transformational, Charismatic, and Visionary Theories', in M. Chemers and R. Ayman (eds.), *Leadership Theory and Research: Perspectives and Direction*. San Diego: Academic Press, 84–107.

Huitema, C. (1995). *Routing in the Internet*. Englewood Cliffs, NJ: Prentice Hall.

International Organization for Standardization (ISO). Available: http://www.iso.ch

Jasanoff, S., Markle, G. E., Peterson, J. C., and Pinch, T. (eds.) (1995). *Handbook of Science and Technology Studies*. Thousand Oaks, Calif.: Sage.

Joerges, B. (1993). *Große technische Systeme: Zum Problem technischer Größenordnung und Maßstäblichkeit*. Discussion paper FS II 93–507. Wissenschaftszentrum Berlin für Sozialforschung.

—— (1994). *Reden über große Technik*. Discussion paper FS II 94–501. Wissenschaftszentrum Berlin für Sozialforschung.

Krupp, C. (1995). *Klimaänderung und die Folgen: Eine exemplarische Fallstudie über die Möglichkeiten und Grenzen einer interdisziplinären Klimafolgenforschung*. Berlin: edition sigma, 146–58.

La Porte, T. (1991). *Social Responses to Large Technical Systems: Control or Anticipation*. Dordrecht: Kluwer.

Latour, B. (1993). *We Have Never Been Modern* (C. Porter, trans.). Cambridge, Mass.: Harvard University Press. (Original work published 1991)

Lehr, W. (1995). 'Compatibility Standards and Interoperability: Lessons from the Internet', in B. Kahin and J. Abbate (eds.), *Standards Policy for Information Infrastructure*. Cambridge, Mass.: MIT Press, 121–47.

Malinowski, B. (1944). *A Scientific Theory of Culture and Other Essays*. Chapel Hill: University of North Carolina Press.

Mambery, P. and Tepper, A. (1992). *Metaphern und Leitbilder als Instrument: Beispiele und Methoden.* Arbeitspapiere der GMD, No. 651, Gesellschaft für Mathematik und Datenverarbeitung mbH, St. Augustin, Germany.

Marz, L. (1993*a*). *Leitbild und Diskurs: Eine Fallstudie zur diskursiven Technikfolgenabschätzung von Informationstechniken.* Discussion paper FS II 93–106. Wissenschaftszentrum Berlin für Sozialforschung.

—— (1993*b*). *Das Leitbild der posthumanen Vernunft: Zur diskursiven Technikfolgenabschätzung der 'Künstlichen Intelligenz'.* Discussion paper FS II 93–111. Wissenschaftszentrum Berlin für Sozialforschung.

Mayntz, R. (1993). 'Große technische Systeme und ihre gesellschaftstheoretische Bedeutung'. *Kölner Zeitschrift für Soziologie und Sozialpsychologie,* 45: 97–108.

—— and Hughes, T. (eds.) (1988). *The Development of Large Technical Systems.* Frankfurt am Main: Campus.

Nonaka, I. and Takeuchi, H. (1995). *The Knowledge-creating Company: How Japanese Companies Create the Dynamics of Innovation.* New York: Oxford University Press.

Papalekas, J. C. (1959). 'Das Problem der sozialen Leitbilder unter den Bedingungen der entwickelten Industriegesellschaft'. *Jahrbuch für Sozialwissenschaft,* 4/10: 221–37.

Piscitello, D. and Chapin, A. (1993). *Open Systems Networking: TCP/IP and OSI.* Reading, Mass.: Addison-Wesley.

Rogers, R. (1990). *Visions Dancing in Engineer's Heads: AT&T's Quest to Fulfill the Leitbild of a Universal Telephone Service.* Discussion paper FS II 90–102. Wissenschaftszentrum Berlin für Sozialforschung.

Schelsky, H. (1970). 'Zur soziologischen Theorie der Institution', in H. Schelsky (ed.), *Zur Theorie der Institution.* Düsseldorf: Bertelsmann, 9–26.

Shillingford, J. (2000). 'House of the Future Could Bring High-tech Headaches'. *Financial Times,* Section 2, 5 April: XIII.

Simson, A. J. and Weiner, E. S. C. (eds.) (1991). *The Oxford English Dictionary.* Oxford: Clarendon Press.

Sull, D. N. (1999). 'Why Good Companies Go Bad'. *Harvard Business Review,* 77/4: 42–52.

Weber, C. (1996). *Treuhandanstalt—Eine Organisationskultur entsteht im Zeitraffer.* Wiesbaden: Gabler.

Weber, M. (1924). 'Diskussionsrede zu W. Sombarts Vortrag über Technik und Kultur: Erste Soziologentagung Frankfurt 1910', in M. Weber, *Gesammelte Aufsätze zur Soziologie und Sozialpolitik.* Tübingen: Mohr, 1–60.

Weingart, P. (ed.) (1989). *Technik als sozialer Prozeß.* Frankfurt am Main: Campus.

Willms, B. (1970). 'Institutionen und Interesse: Elemente einer reinen Theorie der Politik', in H. Schelsky (ed.), *Zur Theorie der Institution.* Düsseldorf: Bertelsmann Universitätsverlag, 43–57.

PART III

FACTORS AND CONDITIONS SHAPING ORGANIZATIONAL LEARNING

Introduction

The four chapters in this section highlight certain tensions and paradoxes that variously trigger, shape, and constrain organizational learning. Organizations reflect the cultural, political, and intellectual tensions that are inherent in all societies. The dynamics created by the social constitution of the organization, its previous learning experiences, emotional climates, and the dimension of time all have a profound impact on an organization's ability and preparedness to learn. In fact, it is through the exploration of these dynamics that organizational learning may be seen to occur.

The contribution by Child and Heavens provides a theoretical framework for this section. By examining the social construct of organizations, they illustrate the ways in which successful learning organizations harness the dynamics from their environment by reconciling opposing organizational pressures such as continuity and change or control and autonomy. Proceeding on the premise that learning is both promoted and constrained by social boundaries such as action and structure, the authors use the concept of social embeddedness to illustrate that learning capabilities can remain undeveloped because identities are naturally resistant to change. However, if a balance can be found between old and new organizational identities, and if a combination of continuity and change is established, organizations can significantly enhance their competencies and hence the overall learning process. Information brokers, gate keepers, and especially boundary spanning individuals and organizational units can help insure this kind of balance. Thus, the authors suggest that tensions and potential barriers to learning, if strategically managed, can create triggers and motivations for learning.

One of the most profound paradoxes of the learning is that many of the conditions, that initially motivate organizational learning may finally come to constrain it. Several contributors to this section argue that this paradox may be the result of a change in the original context of the rigidities that arise through the routinization of learning, or both. In many cases, it is also an indication that the management of the learning, or both process itself has ceased to be appropriate. Starbuck and Hedberg examine how organizations learn not only from their own previous successes and failures but also from those they observe in other organizations. The two authors analyze the interplay between behavioral and cognitive learning, pointing to the danger of positive feedback, which often signals organizational success yet at the same time fosters the standardization of action programs, ultimately contributing to organizational inertia. Using the U.S. National Aeronautics and Space Administration (NASA) as an example, Starbuck and Hedberg examine this phenomenon within the context of individual companies and within populations of organizations or industries, such as the Swedish construction industry. In both cases they show that the very same learning that initially promotes change and success can also, if not properly managed, limit sense-making frameworks within organizations and hinder further learning.

Temporal factors can also shape the processes of organizational learning. Questions of great concern to many leaders in organizations are whether learning processes can be accelerated or slowed down and whether there is an optimal time period for learning. Weber and Berthoin Antal address these issues in their chapter on the role of time in organizational learning. They argue that time establishes the framework for organizational thinking and action in such a way that it often acts as a behavioral filter. By outlining several dimensions of time in an organization, they illustrate that time frames of organizational learning are often a direct result of the amount and type of information and signals both before and during the learning process. Numerous and often complex processes can set limits on the pace of an organization's learning. Moreover, there are specific points in time in which an organization's initiation of action will have a higher chance of success than at other moments. These 'windows of opportunity' can come at any stage of the organization's development and can thus alter the established time frames. The authors' example of the role that time played in the learning processes of the Treuhandanstalt illustrates this important point.

The last chapter in this part, by Scherer and Tran, examines a key issue that surfaces throughout the handbook—the role that emotions play in the process of organizational learning. Emotions are described as relevance detectors that alert individuals to changes in the environment and thereby help them prepare responses to these events. The authors point out that the emotional climate of an organization is not just a sum of individual emotions but rather a collective phenomenon that can stimulate powerful responses either helping or hindering organizational learning. The authors argue that mechanisms for rewarding or punishing behavior also have a strong effect on learning processes. Similarly, dramatic events play a profound role because they normally provoke extreme emotional responses, which become embedded in the memory of the individual, the organization, or both, and which thus set expectations for future learning processes, especially those that involve double-loop learning. It is the strength of these emotional memories that determines whether any major changes in processes or behaviors will occur. As a result, one finds is difficult to prescribe a particular type of emotion or climate that is most conducive to learning. It is therefore to the advantage of organizations to monitor both individual emotions and the overall emotional climate of the organization. An improved understanding of emotion can greatly enhance learning processes.

The message of this part is that learning is shaped by larger organizational contexts. Although each chapter presents a unique discussion of some of these contexts, the authors all commonly stress that the dynamics created by various organizational contexts are often greatly underestimated and misunderstood. The complex issues that emerge from the social constitution of organizations, the experiences of success and failure, and the role of time and emotion present distinct challenges for learning strategies. The authors do not provide specific recipes for shaping processes in order to ensure successful learning, but they do suggest that successful learning requires an active management process. The type of information made available in organizations, who has access to it, and the points at which it is provided are therefore factors of special significance. Ultimately, that perceptive, flexible, and open organizations have an increased chance of understanding the various dynamics of learning processes, and, therefore, of overcoming the many tensions and paradoxes that can be major obstacles to learning.

13 The Social Constitution of Organizations and its Implications for Organizational Learning

John Child and Sally J. Heavens

Our understanding of organizational learning has been handicapped by the failure to incorporate an adequate conception of organizations. Argyris and Schön (1978) recognized the problem in one of the earliest and most influential publications on the subject, when they posed the question: 'What is an organization that it may learn?' (p. 9). Most discussion since then has focused on one side of this question: how individual learning can be transformed into an organizational property (e.g. Dodgson 1993; Gherardi 1996; Hedberg 1981; Huber 1991; Kim 1993; Levitt and March 1988; Nonaka 1994; Spender 1996; Stata 1989). The other side of this question has received much less attention, namely, how the ways in which organizations are constituted have an impact on the learning that can take place within them.

In focusing on this complementary side of the coin, this chapter introduces a sociological perspective that has largely been absent from previous contributions to organizational learning (see Gherardi and Nicolini, Ch. 2 in this volume). Regarded in this light, organizations can be seen to contain inherent tensions that are of considerable significance for their capacity to learn (Quinn and Cameron 1988). Key characteristics of organizations that give rise to such tensions are (a) their historical embeddedness, which incorporates the benefit of past experience but also can militate against change; (b) their leadership and authority systems, which can both facilitate learning and impose controls that impede it; and (c) their internal and external boundaries, which can provide channels for new information but also create barriers to its assimilation. The chapter explores in turn the implications each of these characteristics and their associated tensions have for organizational learning.

The chapter draws upon research that has been conducted not only on organizational learning *per se* but also on organizational change and innovation. The distinction between these terms therefore requires clarification. The relation between learning and change is controversial, with some authors (e.g. Mintzberg and Westley 1992) arguing that there can be no change without learning. There is nevertheless a distinction between the two. Organizational *change* refers to a transition from one organizational state to another, without that transition necessarily being the result of learning or being beneficial in its consequences. Beneficial change is preferably described as *adaptation*, because it is the type of change that leads to an improved fit between an organization and environmental or other con-

The support of the Daimler-Benz Foundation toward the production of this chapter is gratefully acknowledged. The authors thank Ariane Berthoin Antal, Nicole Biggart, Meinolf Dierkes, Normand Filion, Victor Friedman, Bo Hedberg, Marjorie Lyles, Ikujiro Nonaka, Jay Rothman, Hedwig Rudolf, William Starbuck, and Lai Si Tsui-Auch for their helpful comments on earlier drafts.

tingencies. It therefore involves a degree of learning. *Learning* refers to both the process of acquiring new knowledge and the outcome. The outcome of learning is the acquisition of a new competence: an ability to apply new knowledge to enhance the performance of an existing activity or task or to prepare for new circumstances and thus change in the future (Weick 1991). The distinction between process and outcome indicates that learning provides a potential for change rather than any guarantee of its realization. Indeed, much of the work on organizational change has been concerned with the forces of organizational conservatism and ways of overcoming them (Child, Ganter, and Kieser 1987), and therein lies its considerable practical value for organizational learning.

The chapter also draws from another body of literature, that on *innovation*. Although innovation is often associated with new technologies, the concept applies to all activities. Innovation refers to the introduction of something new. It implies that a learning process has been accomplished; the two concepts are thus intimately connected. Researchers studying innovation have recognized the importance of organizational design and, in particular, the need to reconcile continuity with change, such that the organization is efficiently maintained while innovations are introduced. Other issues in the innovation literature relevant to learning in organizations include the sourcing of new knowledge, its grafting on from outside the organization, and the problems of operating within a differentiated organizational structure while facilitating teamwork to create innovation. For these reasons, senior management is seen to have a critical role in providing a direction for learning (vision), promoting necessary teamwork, and overcoming resistance to change.

Innovation, like learning, is ultimately an organizational property, and common to both is the question of how they might be sustained. In addressing this question, the innovation literature tends to be informed by economic and technological issues. It is instructive to note that, whereas in the learning literature there is a tendency to assume that knowledge generation is a good thing *per se*, within its own literature innovation is often represented in terms of the cost–benefit balance to be drawn between the risk and returns from the investment required. Returns may take a long while to achieve and are not guaranteed (Bolton 1993). This caution can usefully be applied to the evaluation of investments in organizational learning.

The Social Embeddedness of Organizations

Stinchcombe (1965) clearly articulated the relationship between organizations and social systems, pointing up the fact that the former both exist within and are constituted by the latter: 'People found organizations when they find or learn about alternative better ways of doing things that are not easily done within existing social arrangements' (p. 146). He noted that organizations formed at one time typically have a different social structure from those formed at another time, and he asked what kinds of forces internal to the dynamics of passing on an organizational tradition tend to maintain the form in more or less its original shape. This observation highlights the fact that a new organization will have an idiosyncratic social structure and form that will tend to endure through a process of institutionalization. This institutionalization, or social embeddedness, has its own dynamic, even if it is merely one of self-perpetuation.

The concept of social embeddedness was developed by Granovetter (1985), who noted that 'actors do not behave or decide as atoms outside a social context. . . . Their attempts at purposive action are. . . embedded in concrete, ongoing systems of social relations' (p. 482). A similar perspective is apparent in work by Leonard-Barton (1995), who saw managerial systems as a 'core rigidity': 'Because managerial systems grow up in a company to encourage and reward the accretion of particular kinds of knowledge and to bestow status on certain functions, disciplines and roles, other skills and knowledge are shortchanged by those same systems' (p. 47). Johnson (1990) similarly noted that the social systems that underpin an organization may operate to maintain a dominant paradigm, 'a set of core beliefs and assumptions' (p. 185), and so constrain the process of change.

Embedded features, whether knowledge, routines, practices, or culture, may be used by managers to legitimate their authority and so preserve their power base. As noted in the next section, recent studies reveal that managers may be unwilling to share privileged information on what may be seen as their self-prescribed practices, for fear of weakening their position (Ciborra, Patriotta, and Erlicher 1996; Leonard-Barton 1995).

Giddens (1984: 17) took institutions to be those structured practices and properties that have the greatest time-space extension within social totalities. In other words, these are practices that have been embedded within the social fabric in two respects: They have a long past, and they are particularly widespread. For both reasons, institutions are likely to enjoy wide legitimacy. The application of an institutional perspective to organizations is based on the premise that organizations are socially defined and arranged (Powell and DiMaggio 1991; Scott 1987; Zucker 1987). Scott (1995) identified three pillars of institutions, which are the cognitive, normative, and regulative systems that govern organizations through the enforcement, respectively, of interpretative schemes, values and norms, and laws and rules.

In institutional theory, it is recognized that those responsible for organizational practices may learn these practices through a process of seeking to conform to what is accepted wisdom (the cognitive pillar), to what is normatively acceptable to the community or society (the normative pillar), or to what is enforced by regulations or laws (the regulative pillar). The theory implies that significant organizational cultures and practices are not the result of an autonomous learning process, or at least not exclusively so, but rather emanate from what is institutionally embedded in society. As Lu and Lake (1997) wrote: 'This perspective . . .

argues that organizations are not free to pursue their task-related goals for maximizing efficiency. . . . Organizational structures and processes are the product of institutionalization processes (deriving from taken-for-granted rules, norms, culture and social practice), rather than entirely shaped by technical and economic rationality' (p. 77).

The implications of this insight for an appreciation of organizational learning are potentially profound. For they suggest not only that existing organizational practices may be bolstered as conventions that receive social approval but, in addition, that those involved in promoting organizational learning will themselves conceive of what is possible, what is legitimate, and what is lawful in terms that are institutionally defined. In other words, the learning capabilities of organizational members are, at least in part, socially constructed by national, occupational, or other institutions. The effects of institutionalization on organizational learning are often conservative in nature, but they are not necessarily so. Professional associations, for example, provide an important external institutional point of reference for specialist organizational members, especially in the so-called Anglo-Saxon societies (Larson 1979), and their norms may give priority to the improvement of practice through continuous research and learning, albeit within the frameworks of criteria defined by the professional bodies rather than by organizational managers.

It is impossible to address the issue of embeddedness in organizations without considering the role of time in the evolution and reinforcement of routines, myths, and practices (see also Weber and Berthoin Antal, Ch. 15 in this volume). Time can also be seen as a critical factor in the relationship between change and learning processes and the creation of learning capacity within an organization. It takes time to develop this capacity to change, and if the pressures for change are sufficiently severe, then change likely will have to be creatively destructive (Schumpeter 1947/1989), in that organizational unlearning and relearning take place swiftly through the exiting of existing personnel and structures and through the importation of new ones already embodying a new approach and competence.

Thus, where the degree of embeddedness within mature organizations is such that this 'advancing sclerosis . . . is seen to posit [their] transformation as a condition of their survival' (Child and Smith 1987: 568), radical change, with immediacy of effect, may be the only solution. An example is provided by the iconoclastic changes in the U.S. Post Office Department, which was metamorphosed through legislation into the U.S. Postal Service. Biggart (1977) concluded from her study of this process that:

It is not generally recognized that change is an act of destruction as much as of creation. . . . The destructive process must either precede or exist simultaneously with the creative. . . . The organization must systematically destroy former, competing structures before it can successfully implant the new. . . . Among the features a new regime often destroys in the course of conversion are the former formal structure, leadership, ideology, power alliances, decision-making model, and technology. (p. 410)

This transformation excised the old 'service-at-all-costs' ideology, along with many of the officials in whom its practices and values were embedded. 'Such traditional values were held most tightly by the senior employees who had the greatest personal investment in them' (Biggert 1977: 418). Put another way, one can see this transformation as the proscription of one ideology (rooted in service) and the prescription of another (rooted in business): It brought on the destruction of a rigid, inflexible system, prohibitive of learning, and the creation of an organization within which managers had more freedom to innovate than previously, even to make mistakes. Symbolic changes were also made in the name of the organization, its logo, and its vehicle livery, reinforcing the identity of this essentially new organization, the U.S. Postal Service, with its market-driven philosophy.

In another study, of the turnaround at NCR, Leonard-Barton (1995) noted that the phenomenon she termed a 'core rigidity' is comprised of four dimensions—physical systems, skills and knowledge, managerial systems, and values (p. 55). She further distinguished between two kinds of values, generic (or big V) and knowledge-base-specific (little v), where the former are associated with attitudes and beliefs about relations with other people and the latter are associated with attitudes and beliefs about the operationalization of activities (p. 51). Of these four dimensions, values (especially big V) are the most difficult to change. Thus, during the early 1990s, several U.S. corporations forced out their top executives because these corporations perceived that they needed drastic change and that these leaders were too tied to the past to effect such a switch. The incoming chief executive of IBM, for example, was told by the board of directors that 'they needed a manager—a change agent' (p. 44). In situations of crisis, the removal of directors and senior managers who are sustaining a core rigidity is frequently the key that unlocks opportunities for new organizational learning, or at least its emergence from the shadows, and its coming out as a new organization-wide culture and practice (Grinyer, Mayes, and McKiernan 1988; Pettigrew 1985; Sadler, Ch. 18 in this volume).

Entrenched public bureaucracies, such as the U.S. Post Office Department and the U.S. State Department (Warwick 1975), tend to provide the most extreme examples. They clearly demonstrate the power of embeddedness to inhibit and even stultify the learning process within an organization and to impinge on the performance of that organization (Herriott, Levinthal, and March 1985). Knowledge itself can become embedded, as part of the value system of an organization, and as such is also highly resistant to change (Leonard-Barton 1995). This possibility is significant because, of all the features of embeddedness, those which are realized by, and manifested in, the social systems of an organization—ideology, culture, and knowledge-creation processes—are the most difficult to amend and may ultimately necessitate fundamental destruction.

Dramatic examples, such as the U.S. Postal Service present an opposition between institutional continuity and organizational learning.

Other closely researched case studies of major organizational transformations that have taken place over a long period of time indicate that this opposition is not necessarily absolute. Rather, the preservation of some elements of continuity can contribute to the success and permanence of the transformation (Child and Smith 1987; Pettigrew 1985). The apparently paradoxical combination of continuity and change carries forward a basis of legitimacy derived from the preservation of institutionalized practices, and this can enhance the legitimacy of change, and commitment to it, among those who have to live with it. Moreover, from a learning perspective, the combination of continuity with change preserves valuable knowledge, especially tacit knowledge that may not be easily *dis*embedded from those who possess it. Such knowledge often defies codification, sometimes because of resistance by those holding it, and cannot therefore necessarily be reconstituted or replaced in the process of organizational learning. As March (1991: 71) pointed out through his distinction between 'the exploitation of old certainties' and 'the exploration of new possibilities', knowledge gained from past experience can be as essential to organizational learning as that gained from innovative activities.

Leadership and Authority in Organizations

We consider leadership to be an inherent component of organizations, one that defines their direction and shapes control and autonomy within them. It is an important agency for organizational learning, and Sadler (Ch. 18 in this volume) examines the processes involved in the relationship of leadership to learning. Leadership is often required in order to break the mold of embedded thinking and practice, so as to enable learning to take place. Some leadership of the organizational learning process itself is necessary so that it can be directed toward clear goals, coordinated, informed by open channels of communication, and, not

least, provided for with adequate resources. However, leadership in this process implies a degree of top-down direction and control that may not be easily reconciled with the autonomy and open-mindedness commonly regarded as requisites for creative learning. Indeed, the pressures for change and reform emanating from learning within an organization can easily be interpreted as a challenge to the organization's senior leadership. In other words, the inherent tension between leadership and devolved autonomy can also be problematic for organizational learning. The implications for organizational learning of the leadership role and of the tension between control and autonomy are considered in turn below.

Leadership Roles that Promote Learning

Senge (1996: 291) commented that 'leaders are responsible for learning'. Stated baldly, this position is too elitist, but it is nevertheless the case that senior managers are in a privileged position to enhance learning through reshaping the ways in which organizations are socially constituted. Paradoxically, they can themselves become part of that very social constitution and develop a strong vested interest in maintaining it.

The potential contribution of leadership to organizational learning encompasses a number of roles. The most fundamental is that of establishing a culture conducive to organizational learning, if necessary by transforming the embedded legacy of the past from a barrier to an asset. Often, barriers can be broken down through the communication of a vision from the top (Kotter 1995; Strebel 1996). If the barrier proves to be insuperable, however, it may have to be destroyed. Radical moves away from embedded organizational cultural webs, sometimes termed 'frame-breaking' changes or 'transformations', must be led from the top. Tichy (1996) described how John Welch performed this role at General Electric Company. The other side of the coin is that a conservative organizational leader, who clings to an established set of policies and practices, insulating himself or herself against changing realities, can have the power to prevent an organization from learning and adapting (Pfeffer 1993). It is therefore not surprising that radical changes often require the bringing in of new senior managers from outside, as well as the direct involvement of executives in all aspects of the process (Tushman, Newman, and Romanelli 1997).

The need for radical change presents the most dramatic connection between organizational leadership and learning, but the culture that it aims to create must also be sustained on an everyday basis. Sustaining this culture may give rise to tension between the element of control within managerial leadership and the degree of autonomy that is a further condition for effective learning within organizations. Hence, a second leadership role in promoting organizational learning is to support the appropriate culture with a set of accompanying practices that permits the autonomy to encourage the creation of insight and new knowledge, but within a collective effort that is directed toward the present effectiveness and future opportunities of the organization as a whole (Hamel and Prahalad 1994).

A third leadership role specific to organizational learning is to foster the three channels of communication and relationships across internal and external organizational boundaries that are key to the learning process (see below, 'Boundaries within and between Organizations'). The first channel involves the relationship between higher management and other, more specialized groups within an organization. There is a division of function in that higher management will normally be concerned with strategic learning, whereas other groups will work more on systemic and technical learning.[1] Each area of learning needs to

[1] Strategic learning refers to the development of senior managers' mind-sets, especially their criteria of organizational success, their mental maps of their organizations' contexts, and their policies for achieving success within such contexts. Systemic learning refers to the introduction and effective implementation of new organizational arrangements, including systems and procedures. Technical learning refers to the acquisition of new specific techniques. See Child, Ch. 29 in this volume for a fuller discussion of these three levels of organizational learning.

be informed by the others. In particular, the degree of support that higher management gives to learning activities and systems at lower levels of an organization can have a major impact on their progress. The organizationally constituted problems inherent in this 'vertical' relationship are considered shortly.

The other two boundary-spanning responsibilities of organizational leadership are 'horizontal' in nature. One relates to the integration of knowledge contributions from different specialties within an organization, ranging from the management of knowledge databases and systems to the development of effective teamwork across departments and disciplines. The third channel promotes flows of information and knowledge across the boundaries of an organization through communication with and intelligence from other organizations and groups, including customers, suppliers, network partners, competitors, and research institutes. Cross-organizational knowledge flows can occur at any level of an organization, though flows relevant to strategic learning tend to be concentrated at the upper levels and those relevant to organizational and technical learning at levels lower down. These horizontal boundary-crossing channels are considered later. As an *aide-mémoire*, however, the three channels may be summarized graphically as shown in Fig. 13.1.[2]

Control and Autonomy

The question of *what* information is made available, and to *whom* within an organization, involves an element of choice. This choice is a prerogative of top management to the extent that it creates and provides resources for the channels of information. At the same time, fast-changing organizational contexts, characterized by increasing discontinuity and

[2] Communication among parties in other parts of the network to which an organization belongs, such as suppliers with research institutes, can also engender important results for that organization's learning. The relevance of wider organizational networks is considered by Tsui-Auch, Ch. 32, and by Hedberg and Holmqvist, Ch. 33 in this volume.

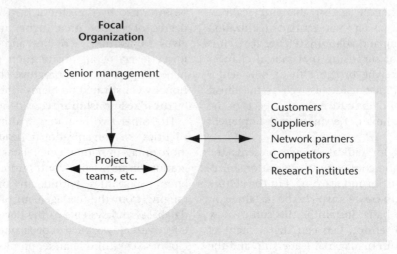

Fig. 13.1. Three channels of communication and relationship necessary for effective organizational learning

turbulence (Ilinitch, D'Aveni, and Lewin 1996), have rendered it even less tenable than previously for top management to hold or even understand all of the information relevant to adapting their organization to these changing conditions. Although it is the role of senior management to make sure that its organization has an appropriate sense of long-term direction, organizational learning also requires a degree of cognitive and behavioral initiative on the part of organizational members who are in close touch with relevant events and developments. The challenge for leadership in facilitating organizational learning therefore lies in maintaining a judicious combination of both control, in the form of guidance and resources, and the autonomy required to motivate knowledge-generators and encourage the free flow of information.[3]

As has been noted, leadership denotes direction. Selznick (1957) commented that 'leadership . . . sets the basic mission of the organization, and . . . creates a social organism capable of fulfilling that mission' (p. 136). Leadership encourages the learning required to realize this fulfillment through the allocation of

resources: money, equipment, personnel, and time. The latter resource is especially significant, for it can be seen to realize a double investment. The time taken up by personnel learning new practices and standing back from a situation in order to assimilate new information is also time that is 'lost' to the organization while learners step out of their usual roles and routines in order to accomplish this learning and assimilation. Drummond (1997) concluded from close investigation that managerial leadership facilitated learning within affiliates of Toshiba Corporation by providing both direction and resources.

There is therefore a need to provide organizational learning with direction sufficient to ensure that it is regarded as significant and thus adequately supported. At the same time, sufficient autonomy for the process must be ensured so that organizational learning is capable of producing new insights. As Turnipseed (1994) commented, 'autonomy in the organization is a positive condition for creativity, but it must be constrained and directed by guidance and control . . . because . . . freedom and order may pull in opposite directions' (p. 188). In this connection, Simons (1995) introduced the concept of interactive control, which is realized through the opening of

---

[3] For a discussion of forms of control that can be combined with autonomy, see Child (1984: 136–71) and Berry, Broadbent, and Otley (1995).

organizational dialogue to encourage learning (p. 83). The management of this control process in tandem with other processes in the areas of beliefs (by communicating core values and missions), boundaries (by specifying and enforcing the rules of the game), and diagnostics (by building and supporting clear targets) attempts to reconcile the simultaneous need for control and creativity within an organization.

An example of how this tension can be resolved to the benefit of learning and innovation is provided by the 3M Corporation (Ghoshal and Bartlett 1995):

Belief in the individual is one of 3M's core values. . . . Generations of top management at 3M have viewed their organization as growing from the bottom—the project team—up. Under a principle the company calls 'grow and divide', successful project teams, consisting of an entrepreneur with an idea and a small team that believes in it, grow into departments. . . . Top management has organized wide, collegial networks that scientists throughout the company can tap into for advice and assistance. . . . It routinely leverages new technologies across two or three divisions and applies them in multiple markets. It is the company's well-oiled competence-building process that has become 3M's real core competence. (pp. 89–94)

These authors further noted that, in companies like 3M, 'top management entrusts the operating units with the challenge of creating the competencies needed to pursue local opportunities. It limits its own role to seeing that those competencies are shared through cross-unit flows of resources, knowledge, and people' (p. 91).

This balance between controlling and creating exemplifies a routinization of creative learning, or innovative, processes at the operational level, coupled with the maintenance, by top management, of an organization's communications network through which these idiosyncratic learning experiences can be made organizationally accessible.

The role of team leader is significant in this regard, with insights from the innovation literature demonstrating how this function can realize necessary links between organizational levels in order to support his or her legitimacy

in generating a collective learning effort. Kidder (1982: 47) graphically described what may be viewed as the *integrative* leadership qualities of Data General's pioneering computer engineer. In another example from the innovation literature, Project SAPPHO (Scientific Activity Predictor from Patterns with Heuristic Origins) was 'conceived as a systematic attempt to identify and evaluate the factors which distinguish innovations which have achieved commercial success from those which have not' (SPRU 1972: 4). The summary findings critically revealed that 'responsible individuals in the successful attempts are usually more senior and have greater authority than their counterparts who fail' and that 'the greater power of the individual innovators in the successful attempts facilitates the concentration of effort on the scale which is needed as well as the integration of R&D and markets (p. 5). Also identified was the importance of effective communications, both internal and external, in innovating firms.

Kidder noted that some of the engineers close to Data General's project leader suspected that if he had no crisis to deal with, occasionally he would create one. Coldwell (1996), in his discussion of catastrophe theory, shed an interesting light on this apparent need for discontinuity in innovation: 'Innovation occurs when there is a sudden and discontinuous change that positively differentiates the changed state from that which preceded it. . . . It seems important to explore the links between innovation, creativity, time, change and competitive advantage' (p. 69).

The example of Data General shows that, although jolts to the status quo may come from innovating units further down the organizational hierarchy, they can also be initiated by top management. The innovation literature is again valuable in pointing up such triggers for learning.[4] For example, Humble and Jones (1989) distinguished between incremental improvement and radical innovation, noting in their discussion of planned obsolescence that, whereas incremental improvement is a

---

[4] See also the chapters in Part IV of this volume on internal triggers for organizational learning and the chapters in Part II on external triggers.

continuing process, 'radical innovation calls for different methods and people. . . . Top management starts with a determination to "obsolete" its products and services, no matter how successful they are' (p. 46). In a similar vein, Nonaka and Takeuchi (1995) commented that 'the willingness to abandon what has long been successful is found in all successful companies' (p. 5), and they noted the 'creative chaos' that 'can be generated intentionally when the organization's leaders try to evoke a "sense of crisis" among organizational members by proposing challenging goals' (p. 79).

Leadership, however, also denotes status, power, and privilege. Hence, those in authority are always liable to seek to defend their positions and, in so doing, may well suppress proposals from below that are at one and the same time opportunities for the organization to learn and challenges to the present establishment. In exercising the right to choose how much power it will delegate downward, the leadership of an organization can determine how many learning opportunities it will make available to subordinates. In making this choice, some managements still agree with the precept of scientific management that in organizations thinking should be separated from doing (Taylor 1911).

This tendency on the part of some managers is clearly illustrated by Fiat S.p.A. In advising the company management on how to achieve their aim of an integrated factory, Ciborra, Patriotta, and Erlicher (1996) recommended the exposure of UTE (Elementary Technical Unit) members (factory workers and supervisors) to the concepts of systems dynamics, which would be a way for them to learn effective strategies to cope with complex breakdowns and bottlenecks. The study also concluded that 'learning new frames and routines, such as the distributed control over flows at the UTE level, which belong to a formative context where the *institutional separation between task direction and execution* is challenged in a deeper way . . . could support the development of the new capabilities' (p. 413, emphasis added).

In delivering an unpublished lecture on this paper (University of Cambridge, 8 December 1995), Ciborra noted that, ultimately, Fiat management elected *not* to make such learning available to the UTE members. Confronted with the challenge of sharing knowledge related to systems dynamics and the mapping of a complex production flow, and thus with sharing control with the workers in order to make the plant operate more efficiently than previously, management 'stepped back from the integrated organization approach'. They were ultimately unwilling to share what they perceived to be their privileged knowledge *as* management. This experience points to the potential that external consultants have in promoting organizational learning but also shows how their recommendations can be rejected because of considerations of maintaining managerial power (see also Berthoin Antal, Lenhardt, and Rosenbrock, Ch. 39 in this volume).

Studies such as Ciborra's highlight the relationship between learning, vertical differentiation, and control. Control can readily be equated with the maintenance of vertical differentiation. This was certainly the perspective of the Fiat management. In reverse, it is also the perspective of shop floor workers who restrict management's access to information on the quality and quantity of production output (Hickson 1961). As a further illustration, Child, Ganter, and Kieser (1987) noted in their discussion of technological innovation within European banks that 'the early introduction of mainframe computers into banks was accompanied by the build-up of well resourced, influential central technical (management services) departments, whose staff tend to see benefit in *the use of new technology to preserve, and indeed strengthen, existing managerial controls*' (p. 96, emphasis added).

Typically, control is manifested in the mechanistic approach to management, through upward reporting via formal, routinized procedures. The main channels through which organizational control is exercised include technology, human resource management, and, in particular, finance. As one vice president of a major American multinational corporation, referring to the company's joint ventures in China, recently explained to the first author: 'you only get to run the operation through the guy who keeps an eye on the money'.

Burns and Stalker (1961) contrasted this hierarchical structure, which is reinforced by 'the location of knowledge of actualities exclusively at the top of the hierarchy, where the final reconciliation of distinct tasks and assessment of relevance is made' (p. 120), with the network structure, which typifies the organic approach to management. In this system, knowledge about the technical or commercial nature of the here-and-now task may be located anywhere in the network, with this location becoming 'the *ad hoc* centre of control authority and communication' (p. 121).

The organic system is more conducive to learning than is the mechanistic system, for it facilitates the crossing of organizational levels and boundaries and the communication of information even to the point of redundancy. Attempts to realize these objectives on a hierarchical basis are not conducive to effective learning, especially in contemporary conditions. Relevant knowledge and expertise is today normally distributed widely among the member groups within organizations. Leaders therefore have to reconcile the need for control and autonomy in a manner that is acceptable to them and that elicits their positive contribution to the learning process.

Having considered how the *vertical* differentiation of organizations can bear upon organizational learning, we can now turn our attention to how their *horizontal* differentiation, in terms of internal and external boundaries, also has an impact on organizational learning. The two aspects of organizational differentiation tend to reinforce each other. An emphasis on hierarchy encourages differentiation between and disassociation of units into separate reporting lines. Horizontal integration by means of teams and the like facilitates autonomy and empowerment and assists in the reduction of vertical differentiation through delayering.

Boundaries within and between Organizations

An important insight that organizational analysis brings to the theory of the firm is that organizations have internal and external boundaries that denote at one and the same time differentiation and integration among the parties to an organizational learning process. Organizational boundaries are social phenomena with significance for their members' identities and actions. Firms, and indeed other organizations, are constituted by much more than the 'set of contracting relationships among individuals' posited by Jensen and Meckling (1976: 310).

Internal Boundaries

Unless they are extremely small, organizations normally develop internal boundaries by distinguishing different specialized groups, departments, or subunits. Each of these specialties will have its own set of competencies and knowledge. However, specialized groups attach their own values to their expertise and express them through their own codes and terminology. As Lawrence and Lorsch (1967) noted, specialization within organizations tends to encourage a 'difference in cognitive and emotional orientation among managers in different functional departments' (p. 11). Specialized personnel may remain attached to their codes and language, seeing in them reflections of their social identity and market value outside a particular organization. In the case of professionalized groups, this identity is bolstered by an external institutional base. It therefore can be difficult to bridge internal boundaries and integrate the contributions of different groups to organizational learning because of contrasts in the technologies they offer, and the goals they attach, to the process.

An organization, nevertheless, must draw upon the specialist competencies and knowledge bases of different intraorganizational groups in order to provide the substantive contributions and insights required for learning. Herriott, Levinthal, and March (1985) referred to an 'ecology of learning' and to the fact that, 'where experience is interdependent, the performance realized by any one actor depends not only on that actor's allocations and competencies, but also on the actions of others' (pp. 298, 300). Hence, effective organizational learning requires a certain level of differentiation and a complementary level of integration, the appropriate balance between them depending on contextual factors such as the complexity, rate of change, and competitive pressures in the organization's environment. Lawrence and Lorsch (1967) concluded from their investigations that high-performing organizations were those that realized this optimum balance.

One of the most incisive analyses of the significance of differentiation and integration for collective learning within organizations remains that offered by Mary Parker Follett. Follett appreciated that conflict is a fact of social and organizational life. Her view was that conflict should be acknowledged and made to work for people, rather than hidden or ignored. In her view, conflict is the legitimate expression of differences of opinion and interest. Without these differences, there would be no progress (Graham 1995: 19–20). This perspective suggests that bringing together people from disparate organizational roles, specialties, and backgrounds should enrich the learning process. The question is how to resolve conflict between people in a constructive way (see also Rothman and Friedman, Ch. 26 in this volume). Follett advocated integration as the most fruitful approach. Integration involves searching for an innovative solution in which all expressed desires and views find a place. Her argument implies that the most fruitful way of dealing with conflict that arises across internal organizational boundaries is to turn it toward collective learning and knowledge creation. If achievable, an innovative solution embodying collective learning stands not only to be enriched by the range of internal organizational specialties: It should also help bridge internal boundaries by offering a mutually attractive solution to the various parties involved.

Others have also made the point that conflict between socially defined groups can play a constructive role. Coser (1964), for example, identified a positive aspect of social conflict when it occurs within an integrative framework: 'In integrated structures, internal contentions may vitalize and strengthen the group's energies' (p. 407). Lawrence and Lorsch (1967) similarly interchanged 'conflict resolution' with 'joint decision-making', their observation being that 'both terms refer to different stages of a single process' (p. 58).

There is, however, no guarantee that integration across internal boundaries can always be realized as a wellspring of collective learning. Coopey (1996) noted that the embeddedness of their norms and practices can present a barrier to learning on the part of specific groups and individuals within an organization. The intergroup conflicts that are liable to arise with differentiation can also constitute an impediment to organizational learning. Child and Loveridge (1990) observed, from their studies of how organizations in European services responded to the availability of new information technologies, that learning can be contested as well as collaborative between the intraorganizational groups involved, such as technical specialists, higher management, personnel specialists, and employee representatives. The introduction of powerful new integrated information technology systems opens up the possibility of radical innovations in the organization of work as well as in the provision of services. It therefore exposes the conflicting interests and perspectives of different occupational groups that might at other times remain relatively subdued.

Scarbrough (1996) concluded similarly, from a study of information systems projects in six financial organizations located in Scotland, that learning proceeds in terms of the possibilities presented by information technology for organizational redesign and that these possibilities are worked through the social construction of different classificatory systems. Scarbrough pointed to the construction of meaning as part of a contested learning process, with the organization being a 'contested terrain across which different classificatory systems slug it out' (p. 200). Each system is fought for by interested parties whose desire is to 'promote classificatory world-views in which their own expertise is central' (p. 200).

The integration of the contributions to learning that organizational subunits have the potential to make involves a process of redefining the frames of meaning within which those contributions are lodged. A prerequisite for this process appears to be a willingness to communicate openly that is based on a minimum level of mutual trust and respect, though open communication in itself is not sufficient to resolve underlying conflicts (see also Nonaka, Toyama, and Byosière, Ch. 22 in this volume). Lawrence and Lorsch (1967) identified managers as the key personnel who effect and mediate the differentiation/integration process and resolve interdepartmental conflict. According to these authors, managers have the responsibility to identify organizational members who possess the appropriate competencies and then to bring them together and help them align the different frames of meaning within which their knowledge is located. There is a political facet to these tasks, however, for where communication between such groupings is mediated rather than open or direct, it becomes vulnerable to reinterpretation, suppression, or reformulation. Significant power can be wielded by those in control of information exchange. Information brokers, or gatekeepers (Pettigrew 1973), therefore play a key role in the facilitation or hindrance of organizational learning. Likewise, those occupying boundary roles between different organizational subunits, such as coordinators and liaison personnel, can also play an important part in securing the integration upon which effective learning depends.

Sometimes external pressures, such as customer complaints, present a need for the organization to learn to improve its integration. This need for integration can act as a catalyst for learning, promoting a gestalt such that the organization becomes more than the sum of its parts. Hedberg (1981) noted that an organization frequently knows less than its members

and that 'problems in communication . . . make it normal for the whole to be less than the sum of the parts' (p. 6). Extrapolating from this observation, one can see the successful organization as one that has brought together its various areas of specialist knowledge to create a synergy, through which organizational learning as process can be realized.

Child (1982) identified another type of integration required to promote learning—that of professional staff into the management structure. He identified higher and lower levels of expertise, the latter being defined as routine and the former (by extrapolation) as nonroutine. Nonroutine expertise is not accessible to 'close definition and procedure' (p. 236) and therefore eludes management control. The characteristics of higher level expertise include 'qualities of expert judgement and mystique which are not readily translated into rationalized, systematized procedures or delegated' (i.e. they are not easily transferred—and some, perhaps, are not transferable at all). A significant point lies in the observation that the 'indeterminate content in professional work will be greater among the upper segments of professional hierarchies where judgement rather than technique is called upon' (p. 236). It is the need to harness the relatively tacit knowledge held by specialists that precipitates attempts at integration both between specialist groups and between specialists and management.

In short, there are two main requirements for securing a contribution by specialist groups to organizational learning. They have to be motivated to offer up their knowledge, and they must be brought together with other participants in the learning process in a way that allows for the constructive conflict of ideas yet also encourages movement toward an actionable conclusion. In the absence of suitable motivational policies in terms of rewards and career prospects, and in the absence of effective mechanisms for bringing together and appropriating the specialist knowledge of experts, such as task forces, the employment of experts is not likely to contribute to organizational knowledge (Mueller and Dyerson 1999).

External Boundaries

Tensions arise from the paradox that an organization's external boundaries must simultaneously be maintained and yet be kept permeable. The boundaries of organizations are enclosures around the legal and contractual realities of ownership and employment. They define the limits of rights and obligations and can also demarcate a common corporate culture and identity. At the same time, these boundaries have to be kept open and information transferred across them so that organizational learning can be stimulated and informed by external developments.

Access to information outside an organization's boundaries and knowledge creation through collaboration with other organizations are becoming increasingly important in many sectors. As Powell, Koput, and Smith-Doerr (1996) noted, 'when the knowledge base of an industry is both complex and expanding, and the sources of expertise are widely dispersed, the locus of innovation will be found in networks of learning, rather than in individual firms' (p. 116).

Learning within and through interorganizational relations is considered at length in Part VI of this volume. The specific point to be noted here is that organizations are in part constituted by their external boundaries. The permeability of those boundaries and the provisions for transferring information across them are consequential for organizational learning. There are, moreover, important parallels between the processes of bridging external and internal organizational boundaries, and the effective transfer of information and knowledge into an organization depends on the effectiveness of both processes.

It is vital for an organization's capacity to innovate and to learn in new ways that it receive relevant new information from its external environment. This information can relate to all levels of organizational activity: strategic, organizational, and technical. Top management, through its external connections, through membership in other companies' boards, trade associations, governmental work-

ing parties, and the like, can be an important conduit for the input of information relevant to strategic learning. At the technical level, which has been the focus for research on innovation, relevant specialists and R&D project teams must maintain effective connections with external sources of technical information, such as universities and research institutes (Ancona and Caldwell 1997).

The inputs to an organization's learning process that flow across its boundaries can vary from ill-structured and scattered items of news to highly codified sets of knowledge. It is generally assumed that the less codified and more tacit the knowledge, the more difficult it will be for the receiving organization to make sense of it, that is, if the organization gains access to that knowledge at all. One of the reasons firms are encouraged to work closely in joint ventures or other forms of collaboration is that working closely together enhances their opportunity to access and make use of the tacit, uncodified knowledge held by and embedded within their partners (Chesbrough and Teece 1996). The alternative is to recruit personnel who hold such knowledge from the other organization(s) and then to graft them onto the 'home' system (Huber 1991).

However, even explicit knowledge is not necessarily imported with ease across an organization's boundaries. Much depends on the receiving organization's 'absorptive capacity' (Cohen and Levinthal 1990), especially the experience to interpret, store, and use the knowledge. Problems can arise because different organizations codify knowledge to suit their own purposes. The imported knowledge may be codified in a form that is specific to a particular purpose or situation that does not apply in the receiving organization. In this case, it is necessary to revert back to the abstract principles that inform the knowledge and to provide the bridge to its reapplication and codification in the new organizational context (Lillrank 1995).

Boundary spanners (Tushman 1977; Tushman and Katz 1980), who work at the interface between their firm and its external environment, play a critical role in the process of transferring information and knowledge into an organization. Boundary-spanning involves three key processes: accessing external knowledge, interpreting and refining it, and directing it to other members of the organization (such as other members of a project team and appropriate senior managers). In this respect, two sets of boundaries must be spanned so that externally sourced information can contribute to internal knowledge enhancement: the external boundaries and the various horizontal and vertical internal boundaries. A commonly occurring problem is that persons who are effective as external boundary spanners, because they belong to the same occupational specialty, share a common social identity (Child and Rodrigues 1996), and use the same language as their external counterparts, may face a significant challenge in spanning the internal boundaries with colleagues who do not share these characteristics.

Both sets of boundaries must be spanned. Tushman (1977), for instance, found in the case of R&D projects that a two-step process was necessary for such projects to be effective means for knowledge creation. The first step was to collect and review outside information. The other step was to communicate this information within the project team. Bearing in mind the findings of Project SAPPHO (SPRU 1972), we add a third necessary step, namely, the communication and interpretation of relevant external information to the project's sponsor in higher management.

Discussion

In this chapter we have sought to locate learning within its organizational setting. In so doing, it has argued for increased attention to social constitution and contextual embeddedness of organizations. The social constitution of organizations encompasses a number of paradoxes. One of them lies in the nature of their structures, which embody both the historical identities and purposes of organizations and the fruits of previous organizational learning. Hence, these structures can be both repositories of experience and knowledge that promote further learning and past-loaded fixtures that stand in the way of such learning. Leadership has the primary role of moving organizations out of their embeddedness, yet, paradoxically, it can also act as a conservative force. Similarly, internal and external boundaries reflect the extant structuring of organizations, with some organizational members seeking to preserve these boundaries and with others seeking to bridge them. The tensions contained in these paradoxes establish dynamic processes that can both stimulate and impede organizational learning, depending partly on how they are managed.

What is being identified in these tensions is the dynamic interplay of action and structure in the organizational learning process. This interplay is captured by Giddens (1984) in his exposition of 'structuration', through which the actions of human agents have a structural realization, though within social systems where existing structures condition those actions. This conditioning is effected in two main ways, which correspond to the realms of cognitive and behavioral learning. In the former case, existing mental frames can impose limitations on the recognition and assimilation of new knowledge—Whittington (1988) referred to this process as action determinism. In the latter case, a structural conditioning of the learning process is manifest in resistance to the application of new insights to existing organizational practice and routine. Giddens's concept therefore recalls not only that learning actors are reconstituting established mental and material structures within organizations but also that their possibilities for conceiving and acting upon new insights are likely to be defined by those structures that are already in being and enjoy legitimacy.

A structuration perspective helps overcome the disjuncture that is present in much current thinking on the subject between reductionism to the individual 'who learns' and reification of the organization 'that learns'. Much discussion of organizational learning has adopted an undersocialized conception of both. As a result, the relations between actors and structures are in danger of being perceived too much in the light of the mechanics of information-processing, to the neglect of the symbolic connotations attached to information in the light of its perceived implications for the position people occupy within the structures of organizations as well as within their wider communities. In other words, the significance of information for organizational learning is not just what it literally says but also where it comes from and how its social implications are interpreted.

Further research is required in order to assist the development of an adequate theory of organizational learning. This chapter and that by LaPalombara (Ch. 25 in this volume) draw attention to the role of power in organizational learning, both as an enabler and a barrier. More attention deserves to be given to power in future research. We have indicated how barriers to organizational learning can be bolstered by embedded interests and mind-sets. The nature and implications of social embeddedness merit further attention. There are, for instance, multiple and complex contours of embeddedness, based on economic, political, ethnic, and ideological boundaries that transcend yet interweave with the organizational boundaries discussed in this chapter. They are all likely to have an impact on the processes through which information is communicated and utilized in the organizational learning process. The extent to which there are social interconnections and shared identities between organizational groups and community groups may also be relevant to the ability of the former to access relevant external information, including the necessary triggers for learning. This issue arises, for example, when multinational companies seeking to enter new territories decide whether they require the assistance of partners who are rooted in the local society in order to learn how to accomplish the entry successfully.

Although this chapter points to a need for increasing the adequacy of theory and research on organizational learning, the themes it contains carry several practical implications as well. Most of them boil down to the conclusion that successful organizational learning requires an active management of the process. In different ways, top management, project coordinators, and specialist experts each have important contributions to make. Senior managers must recognize the significance of organizational learning in order to legitimate the process and encourage it through the provision of suitable resources and incentives. More difficult, senior managers should also be receptive to the possibility that they are standing in the way of organizational learning. Otherwise, as noted earlier, pressures to remove the top management team are liable to build up eventually. The role of project coordinators and leaders is a vital and difficult one, for they must direct their efforts to the challenge of securing integration among different contributors to the learning process. This role involves conflict management and requires a combination of considerable interpersonal skill, an ability to understand disparate corpuses of knowledge, and personal respect within the organization. The potential contribution to organizational learning of specialist holders of both explicit and tacit knowledge is obvious, but their attitude toward and interpretation of organizational learning cannot be taken for granted, especially if they regard its outcome as misguided or even threatening.

Organizational competence is not only a scarce resource but also one that can become politically charged because it resides in different individuals and groups. The garnering of such competence, both to promote new learning within the organization and to mobilize existing sources of knowledge (especially tacit knowledge) effectively, therefore requires active measures to promote a shared sense of purpose and identity among organizational members. In this respect, defining and articulating the purpose of organizational learning is a key to success, just as it is for the promotion and acceptance of organizational change. This requirement again draws attention to the critical role that senior management will normally have to play in the process.

Another practical implication stems from the recognition that both action and structure have an essential part to play in organizational learning and that the two are in dynamic tension with one another. Action is part and parcel of the learning process, whereas structure consolidates and diffuses the benefits of the learning that is achieved. In order to allow scope for both, it may be necessary to plan the organizational learning process as one of 'punctuated equilibrium' (Tushman and Romanelli 1985), that is, one that moves between an emphasis on action and an emphasis on structural consolidation. If this strategy is not realistic because of the pace of external change, then provision must be made for the two to proceed in parallel without one excluding the other. If an organization pursues learning and change to the exclusion of all else, and this pursuit threatens its very social constitution, then the organization is soon likely to suffer the withdrawal of cooperation in that endeavor from the very groups on which the process relies,

for they will have had no opportunity to redefine their roles and identities within the organization in a manner that they can accept. If, on the other hand, too much emphasis is placed on maintaining consensus and 'not rocking the boat', rather little learning (and even less implementation) is likely to take place.

A constructive approach to promoting learning both within and across organizational boundaries requires the creation of communications networks that transcend traditional hierarchical forms. Nevertheless, senior managers are likely to seek to retain some control over these networks because of the political nature of organizational knowledge. Such knowledge can enhance the power of those who control it. What information is made available to whom in an organization remains of special significance, not only for learning but also for management control.

References

Ancona, D. G. and Caldwell, D. F. (1997). 'Making Teamwork Work: Boundary Management in Product Development Teams', in M. L. Tushman and P. Anderson (eds.), *Managing Strategic Innovation and Change*. New York: Oxford University Press, 433–42.

Argyris, C. and Schön, D. A. (1978). *Organizational Learning: A Theory of Action Perspective*. Reading, Mass.: Addison-Wesley.

Berry, A. J., Broadbent, J., and Otley, D. (eds.) (1995). *Management Control: Theories, Issues and Practices*. Basingstoke: Macmillan.

Biggart, N. W. (1977). 'The Creative–Destructive Process of Organization Change: The Case of the Post Office'. *Administrative Science Quarterly*, 22: 410–26.

Bolton, M. K. (1993). 'Organizational Innovation and Substandard Performance: When Is Necessity the Mother of Innovation?' *Organization Science*, 4: 57–75.

Burns, T. and Stalker, G. M. (1961). *The Management of Innovation*. London: Tavistock.

Chesbrough, H. W. and Teece, D. J. (1996). 'When Is Virtual Virtuous?' *Harvard Business Review*, 74/ 1: 65–73.

Child, J. (1982). 'Professionals in the Corporate World: Values, Interests and Control', in D. Dunkerley and G. Salaman (eds.), *The International Yearbook of Organization Studies 1981*. London: Routledge and Kegan Paul, 212–41.

——(1984). *Organization: A Guide to Problems and Practice*. London: Harper & Row.

——Ganter, H.-D., and Kieser, A. (1987). 'Technological Innovation and Organizational Conservatism', in J. M. Pennings and A. Buitendam (eds.), *New Technology as Organizational Innovation*. Cambridge, Mass.: Ballinger, 87–115.

——and Loveridge, R. (1990). *Information Technology in European Services*. Oxford: Blackwell.

——and Rodrigues, S. (1996). 'The Role of Social Identity in the International Transfer of Knowledge through Joint Ventures', in S. R. Clegg and G. Palmer (eds.), *Producing Management Knowledge*. London: Sage, 46–68.

Child, J. and Smith, C. (1987). 'The Context and Process of Organizational Transformation: Cadbury Limited in Its Sector'. *Journal of Management Studies*, 24: 565–93.

Ciborra, C. U., Patriotta, G., and Erlicher, L. (1996). 'Disassembling Frames on the Assembly Line: The Theory and Practice of the New Division of Learning in Advanced Manufacturing', in W. J. Orlikowski, G. Walsham, M. R. Jones, and J. I. DeGross (eds.), *Information Technology and Changes in Organizational Work*. London: Chapman & Hall, 397–418.

Cohen, W. M. and Levinthal, D. A. (1990). 'Absorptive Capacity: A New Perspective on Learning and Innovation'. *Administrative Science Quarterly*, 35: 128–52.

Coldwell, J. B. (1996). 'Quiet Change—Big Bang or Catastrophic Shift: At What Point Does Continuous Improvement Become Innovative?' *Creativity and Innovation Management*, 5: 67–73.

Coopey, J. (1996). 'Crucial Gaps in "the Learning Organization": Power, Politics and Ideology', in K. Starkey (ed.), *How Organizations Learn*. London: International Thomson Business Press, 348–67.

Coser, L. A. (1964). 'The Termination of Conflict', in W. J. Gore and J. W. Dyson (eds.), *The Making of Decisions*. New York: Free Press, 403–10.

Dodgson, M. (1993). 'Organizational Learning: A Review of Some Literatures'. *Organization Studies*, 14: 375–94.

Drummond, A., Jr. (1997). *Enabling Conditions for Organizational Learning: A Study in International Business Ventures*. Unpublished doctoral dissertation, Judge Institute of Management Studies, University of Cambridge, February.

Gherardi, S. (1996). 'Organizational Learning', in M. Warner (ed.), *International Encyclopedia of Business and Management*. London: Routledge, 3934–42.

Ghoshal, S. and Bartlett, C. A. (1995). 'Changing the Role of Top Management: Beyond Structure to Processes'. *Harvard Business Review*, 73/1: 86–96.

Giddens, A. (1984). *The Constitution of Society: Outline of the Theory of Structuration*. Oxford: Polity Press.

Graham, P. (ed.) (1995). *Mary Parker Follett: Prophet of Management*. Boston: Harvard Business School Press.

Granovetter, M. (1985). 'Economic Action and Social Structure: The Problem of Embeddedness'. *American Journal of Sociology*, 91: 481–510.

Grinyer, P. H., Mayes, D. G., and McKiernan, P. (1988). *Sharpbenders: The Secrets of Unleashing Corporate Potential*. Oxford: Blackwell.

Hamel, G. and Prahalad, C. K. (1994). *Competing for the Future: Unleashing the Power of the Workforce*. Boston: Harvard Business School Press.

Hedberg, B. L. T. (1981). 'How Organizations Learn and Unlearn', in P. C. Nystrom and W. H. Starbuck (eds.), *Handbook of Organizational Design*: Vol. 1. *Adapting Organizations to Their Environments*. Oxford: Oxford University Press, 3–27.

Herriott, S. R., Levinthal, D. A., and March, J. G. (1985). 'Learning from Experience in Organizations'. *American Economic Review*, 75: 298–302.

Hickson, D. J. (1961). 'Motives of People who Restrict Their Output'. *Occupational Psychology*, 35: 111–21.

Huber, G. P. (1991). 'Organizational Learning: The Contributing Processes and the Literatures'. *Organization Science*, 2: 88–115.

Humble, J. and Jones, G. (1989). 'Creating a Climate for Innovation'. *Long Range Planning*, 22/4: 46–51.

Ilinitch, A. Y., D'Aveni, R. A., and Lewin, A. Y. (1996). 'New Organizational Forms and Strategies for Managing in Hypercompetitive Environments'. *Organization Science*, 7: 211–20.

Jensen, M. C. and Meckling, W. H. (1976). 'Theory of the Firm: Managerial Behavior, Agency Costs, and Ownership Structure'. *Journal of Financial Economics*, 3: 305–60.

Johnson, G. (1990). 'Managing Strategic Change: The Role of Symbolic Action'. *British Journal of Management*, 1: 183–200.

Kidder, J. T. (1982). *The Soul of a New Machine*. Harmondsworth: Penguin.

Kim, D. H. (1993). 'The Link between Individual and Organizational Learning'. *Sloan Management Review*, 35/1: 37–50.

Kotter, J. P. (1995). 'Leading Change: Why Transformation Efforts Fail'. *Harvard Business Review*, 73/ 2: 59–67.

Larson, M. S. (1979). *The Rise of Professionalism*. Berkeley: University of California Press.

Lawrence, P. R. and Lorsch, J. W. (1967). *Organization and Environment: Managing Differentiation and Integration*. Boston: Harvard Business School Press.

Leonard-Barton, D. (1995). *Wellsprings of Knowledge: Building and Sustaining the Sources of Innovation*. Boston: Harvard Business School Press.

Levitt, B. and March, J. G. (1988). 'Organizational Learning'. *Annual Review of Sociology*, 14: 319–40.

Lillrank, P. (1995). 'The Transfer of Management Innovations from Japan'. *Organization Studies*, 16: 971–89.

Lu, Y. and Lake, D. (1997). 'Managing International Joint Ventures: An Institutional Approach', in P. W. Beamish and J. P. Killing (eds.), *Cooperative Strategies: European Perspectives*. San Francisco: New Lexington Press, 74–99.

March, J. G. (1991). 'Exploration and Exploitation in Organizational Learning'. *Organization Science*, 2: 71–87.

Mintzberg, H. and Westley, F. (1992). 'Cycles of Organizational Change'. *Strategic Management Journal*, 13 (Winter special issue): 39–59.

Mueller, F. and Dyerson, R. (1999). 'Expert Humans or Expert Organizations?' *Organization Studies*, 20: 225–56.

Nonaka, I. (1994). 'A Dynamic Theory of Organizational Knowledge Creation'. *Organization Science*, 5: 14–37.

—— and Takeuchi, H. (1995). *The Knowledge-creating Company: How Japanese Companies Create the Dynamics of Innovation*. New York: Oxford University Press.

Pettigrew, A. M. (1973). *The Politics of Organizational Decision-making*. London: Tavistock.

—— (1985). *The Awakening Giant: Continuity and Change in Imperial Chemical Industries*. Oxford: Blackwell.

Pfeffer, J. (1993). *Managing with Power: Politics and Influence in Organizations*. Boston: Harvard Business School Press.

Powell, W. W. and DiMaggio, P. J. (eds.) (1991). *The New Institutionalism in Organizational Analysis*. Chicago: University of Chicago Press.

—— Koput, K. W., and Smith-Doerr, L. (1996). 'Interorganizational Collaboration and the Locus of Innovation: Networks of Learning in Biotechnology'. *Administrative Science Quarterly*, 41: 116–45.

Quinn, R. E. and Cameron, K. S. (eds.) (1988). *Paradox and Transformation: Towards a Theory of Change in Organization and Management*. Cambridge, Mass.: Ballinger.

Scarbrough, H. (1996). 'Strategic Change in Financial Services: The Social Construction of Strategic IS', in W. J. Orlikowski, G. Walsham, M. R. Jones, and J. I. DeGross (eds.), *Information Technology and Changes in Organizational Work*. London: Chapman & Hall, 197–212.

Schumpeter, J. A. (1989). 'The Creative Response in Economic History', in R. V. Clemence (ed.), *Essays on Entrepreneurs, Innovations, Business Cycles and the Evolution of Capitalism*. New Brunswick, NJ: Transaction Publishers, 221–31. (Original work published 1947)

Scott, W. R. (1987). 'The Adolescence of Institutional Theory'. *Administrative Science Quarterly*, 32: 493–511.

—— (1995). *Institutions and Organizations*. Thousand Oaks, Calif.: Sage.

Selznick, P. (1957). *Leadership in Administration: A Sociological Interpretation*. New York: Harper & Row.

Senge, P. M. (1996). 'The Leader's New Work: Building Learning Organizations', in K. Starkey (ed.), *How Organizations Learn*. London: International Thomson Business Press, 288–315.

Simons, R. (1995). 'Control in an Age of Empowerment'. *Harvard Business Review*, 73/2: 80–8.

Spender, J. C. (1996). 'Organizational Knowledge, Learning, and Memory: Three Concepts in Search of a Theory'. *Journal of Organizational Change Management*, 9/1: 63–78.

SPRU [Science Policy Research Unit, University of Sussex] (1972). *Success and Failure in Industrial Innovation*. London: Centre for the Study of Industrial Innovation.

Stata, R. (1989). 'Organizational Learning—The Key to Management Innovation'. *Sloan Management Review,* 30/3: 63–74.

Stinchcombe, A. L. (1965). 'Social Structure and Organizations', in J. G. March (ed.), *Handbook of Organizations.* Chicago: Rand McNally, 142–93.

Strebel, P. (1996). 'Why Do Employees Resist Change?' *Harvard Business Review,* 74/3: 86–92.

Taylor, F. W. (1911). *The Principles of Scientific Management.* New York: Harper.

Tichy, N. M. (1996). 'GE's Crotonville: A Staging Ground for Corporate Revolution', in K. Starkey (ed.), *How Organizations Learn.* London: International Thomson Business Press, 243–57.

Turnipseed, D. (1994). 'The Relationship between the Social Environment of Organizations and the Climate for Innovation and Creativity'. *Creativity and Innovation Management,* 3: 184–95.

Tushman, M. L. (1977). 'Special Boundary Roles in the Innovation Process'. *Adminstrative Science Quarterly,* 22: 587–605.

—— and Katz, R. (1980). 'External Communication and Project Performance: An Investigation into the Role of Gatekeepers'. *Management Science,* 26: 1071–85.

—— Newman, W. H., and Romanelli, E. (1997). 'Convergence and Upheaval: Managing the Unsteady Pace of Organizational Evolution', in M. L. Tushman and P. Anderson (eds.), *Managing Strategic Innovation and Change.* New York: Oxford University Press, 583–94.

—— and Romanelli, E. (1985). 'Organizational Evolution: A Metamorphosis Model of Convergence and Reorientation', in L. L. Cummings and B. M. Staw (eds.), *Research in Organizational Behavior: An Annual Series of Analytical Essays and Critical Reviews* (Vol. 7). Greenwich, Conn.: JAI Press, 171–222.

Warwick, D. P. (1975). *A Theory of Public Bureaucracy.* Cambridge, Mass.: Harvard University Press.

Weick, K. E. (1991). 'The Nontraditional Quality of Organizational Learning'. *Organization Science,* 2: 116–24.

Whittington, R. (1988). 'Environmental Structure and Theories of Strategic Choice'. *Journal of Management Studies,* 25: 521–36.

Zucker, L. G. (1987). 'Institutional Theories of Organization'. *Annual Review of Sociology,* 13: 443–64.

14   How Organizations Learn from Success and Failure

William H. Starbuck and Bo Hedberg

This chapter analyzes the effects of successes and failures on organizational learning. The analysis contrasts behavioral and cognitive approaches, illustrating these with an example of technological development by an interorganizational coalition and an example of industry-wide development during a business cycle.

Behavioral approaches explain as much behavior as possible without allowing for conscious thought, so learning arises from automatic reactions to performance feedback. Because it is learners' environments that generate this feedback, environments strongly influence what is learned. One advantage of behavioral approaches is that they can explain how effective learning can occur in spite of learners' perceptual errors.

Cognitive approaches describe learners as being able to perceive, analyze, plan, and choose; learning modifies cognitive maps that guide action. Cognitive approaches make effective learning dependent upon realistic perceptions, so these theories have difficulty explaining how learners can improve even though they misunderstand their environments. On the other hand, cognitive approaches can explain how people and organizations suddenly act in dramatically novel ways.

These two approaches coexist because they can explain different phenomena and neither is adequate by itself. Most studies of learning by individual organizations have taken a cognitive approach; most studies of learning by populations of organizations have taken a behavioral approach. However, the distinction between behavior and cognition may be an abstraction that does not exist in the realities of daily life.

Grinyer and Norburn (1975) made a careful study that they had expected to document the beneficial consequences of formal strategic planning. They did find a positive correlation between profitability and the use of formal planning, but the correlation was very weak. Profitable firms were nearly as likely to plan informally as formally, and the same was true of unprofitable firms. This suggests that efforts to forge consensus among managers around rationalizations about effective behavior are unlikely to produce the benefits sought. Furthermore, Grinyer and Norburn found that profitability correlated inconsistently and meaninglessly with the degrees to which senior executives agreed about their firms' objectives or about their personal responsibilities. Since such disagreements indicate that some executives have misperceived, this suggests that perceptual accuracy may not make effective behavior more likely.

These findings illustrate a family of interesting questions: To what degrees do misperceptions prevent organizations from learning effectively? How can organizations learn from feedback if they are making faulty judgments about their performance? How can organizations adapt effectively to outside conditions that they misread? Some theories say that these are central and important issues. Other theories

This chapter has benefited from suggestions by Joel Baum, Philippe Baumard, George Huber, Li Malmström, Danny Miller, and Anne Miner.

say it really does not matter whether people perceive accurately or analyze well because learning is imposed by external forces.

To show that perceptual errors need to be taken seriously, this chapter begins by describing research about managers' perceptions. Then the chapter contrasts two complementary approaches to learning—the behavioral and the cognitive (Glynn, Lant, and Milliken 1994; Leroy and Ramanantsoa 1997). Two examples illustrate these approaches. The first illustrates how evolutionary learning led to the Challenger disaster. The second describes how changing conditions first created a successful growth industry and then devastated it. The chapter concludes with reflections about the integration of behavioral and cognitive approaches.

How Well Do People and Organizations Understand Their Environments?

Research studies have found large errors and biases in people's perceptions both of their organizations' environments and of their organizations. How can organizations improve their behavior if they misunderstand their own capabilities or their environments? Or how should an organization proceed if different people in the organization hold radically different perceptions of their organization and its environments?

Psychological studies of human perception have revealed many biases. Bazerman (1997) lists more than a dozen biases, most of which assert that people do not behave as statisticians recommend. People also update their cognitions more slowly than statistical models recommend, and they see patterns or correlations in random data (Edwards 1968; Singer and Benassi 1981). People search for information in ways that tend to confirm their prior beliefs. Brains involuntarily alter memories to fit new information, and vice versa (Kiesler 1971; Loftus 1979). Brains also invent memories of events that never occurred. Nisbett and Wilson (1977)

concluded that, by and large, people's introspections into their own thoughts are not true insights.

The 'fundamental attribution bias' is a propensity for people to overestimate their own influence on events and to underestimate external or situational influences. For instance, Meindl and Ehrlich (1987) and Meindl, Ehrlich, and Dukerich (1985) argued that both researchers and the general populace attribute too much control and influence to leaders. Based on the behaviors of college students, they inferred that these attributions become more frequent after especially successful performances. Rotter (1966) said that individual people show consistent tendencies either to perceive themselves as causes of events or to see causes arising in their environments.

The 'self-serving bias' denotes a propensity for people to overestimate their own influence on successes and to overestimate external or situational influences on failures (Heider 1958). People also tend to exhibit the opposite biases when interpreting other people's successes and failures. Wagner and Gooding (1997) found that managers who face equivocal information about their own businesses tend to attribute positive outcomes to strengths in their own organizations, while they blame negative outcomes on environmental circumstances. However, when managers are asked to interpret information about businesses managed by others, they attribute positive outcomes to opportunities in the environment and negative outcomes to organizational weakness. Similarly, Huff and Schwenk (1990) observed that Chrysler executives attributed negative company performance mainly to environmental causes while they tied positive performance to forceful managerial actions.

Lawrence and Lorsch (1967) initiated research into the accuracy of managers' perceptions inadvertently. They inferred that firms perform better when their organizational properties match the properties of their market environments. But, Lawrence and Lorsch relied on managers' perceptions, and other researchers wondered how dependable such data might be. Two groups of researchers (Tosi, Aldag, and

Storey 1973; Downey, Hellriegel, and Slocum 1975) asked middle and top managers to describe their firms' markets, and then compared these perceptions with financial reports and industry statistics. The correlations between managers' perceptions and objective measures were all near zero and were negative more often than positive. Thus, on average, managers' perceptions of environmental properties did not correlate with objective measures of those properties.

Obtaining data from middle managers in several companies, Starbuck and Mezias (1999) found considerable variation in perceptual errors. For the most accurately perceived variable, 39 per cent of the managers made errors below 50 per cent, whereas for the least accurately perceived variable, 31 per cent of the managers made errors exceeding 200 per cent. Very large errors were prevalent. Furthermore, contrary to the researchers' expectation, managers with sales experience had no more accurate perceptions of sales-related variables than did managers without such experience. One reason for this, the researchers conjectured, may be that people define their responsibilities and their environments very narrowly. Large organizations divide responsibilities into small compartments, and small organizations focus on small market segments.

Other research suggests that people are ignorant about or misperceive their own organizations. In another study, Mezias and Starbuck are observing managers' perceptions of quality performance by their business units. This company's top management says quality improvement is their top priority. Many personnel have attended training courses, each business unit has a department that focuses on quality improvement, and quality measures are distributed to all managers frequently. Yet, 40 to 80 per cent of the managers report 'I don't know' when asked about current levels of quality performance.

After reviewing many studies in which people described their organizations' structures and cultures, Payne and Pugh (1976: 1168) drew three conclusions: (a) Different employees of the same organization disagree so strongly with each other that it makes no sense to talk about an average perception. 'Perceptual measures of each of the structural and climate variables have varied so much among themselves that mean scores were uninterpretable.' (b) Except for organizational size, employees' perceptions of organizational properties correlate weakly with objective measures of those properties. (c) Differences among employees' perceptions of organizational properties correspond with employees' jobs and hierarchical statuses. For instance, higher-status employees view their organizations more favorably.

Starbuck (1983) gave several reasons why top managers are especially prone to misperceive events and to resist changes (see also Glynn, Lant, and Milliken 1994): They have strong vested interests. They become the targets for blame when current behaviors are judged ineffective. Significant strategic reorientations threaten their dominance. Their high statuses lead them to think they have more expertise than their subordinates. Their expertise tends to be out-of-date. They receive much information through biased channels that conceal or de-emphasize information that might displease them.

Normann (1971) pointed out that people can understand and readily respond to stimuli in domains where they have experience, and that they are likely to misperceive stimuli in unfamiliar domains, or to have difficulty responding to them. Since different parts of an organization have experience with different domains, organizational perceptions interact with politics and control structures. Starbuck, Greve, and Hedberg (1978) observed that some top managers prevent their organizations from dealing effectively with serious crises, either because they do not understand the situations faced by their firms or because they fear losing their high statuses. Thus, organizations typically welcome the small 'variations' on their recent activities but they resist dramatic 'reorientations' (Normann 1971; Starbuck 1983).

Organizations find it especially difficult to recognize and confront failure. Not seeing and not acting can result from slow sense-making processes or from ineffective information systems (Hodgkinson 1997). Slow sense-making processes and ineffective information systems make it more difficult for organizations to make sense of early warning signals and to recognize gradual transitions.

Overall, the evidence justifies caution about the accuracy of learners' perceptions. Although some people have accurate perceptions of some variables, most people have inaccurate perceptions of most variables, and an observer cannot distinguish accurate perceivers from inaccurate ones by their behaviors. As a result, theories of learning need to explain how learning can occur despite large perceptual errors.

Theories of learning fall into two broad classes that make very different assumptions about human capabilities and the complexity of learning processes. One of these approaches, behavioral learning, places little reliance on the perceptions of decision-makers. The second approach, cognitive learning, emphasizes the perceptions of decision-makers. Each approach has weaknesses, and each approach explains some phenomena that the other cannot. Using both approaches together gives a more complete picture, as the two approaches complement each other (Leroy and Ramanantsoa 1997).

One Framework: Behavioral Learning

An ancient debate in social science echoes an ageless philosophical debate about free will. Must models of human behavior allow for choice, or is choice merely an illusion that disguises environmental control? Do organizations control their destinies, or do environments compel certain behaviors?

Theorists on the behavioral side of this debate seek to explain as much behavior as possible without injecting conscious thought or decision processes as controls. According to this approach, learning arises from automatic reactions to performance feedback, and learn-

ers' cognitions have weak effects. Figure 14.1 diagrams such a loop.

Behavioral approaches portray learning as a mechanistic and involuntary process over which learners can exert little control. Behavioral psychologists assume that actions are determined by hypothetical Stimulus–Response links. Pleasant outcomes (rewards, successes) strengthen the Stimulus–Response links and make the corresponding actions more likely to recur. Unpleasant outcomes (punishments, failures) weaken the Stimulus–Response links and make the corresponding actions less likely to recur. Behavioral organization theorists sometimes speculate about decision makers' rationales, but they do not obtain data about these rationales and they do not study changes in perceptions or thought processes. They are satisfied to assume that good outcomes allow behaviors to persist or organizations to survive, that bad outcomes provoke behavioral changes or organizational failures.

One great advantage of behavioral theories is that they can explain how behaviors can improve even though learners misunderstand their environments or misunderstand the causal relations between actions and outcomes. Learners' erroneous perceptions do not become barriers to improved performance because learning is involuntary and noncognitive.

Behavioral theories can also explain why people and organizations may learn elaborate routines in which many components seem to have no instrumental effects. Over time, simple Stimulus–Response links aggregate into complex repertoires of habits that evolve, generalize, lose relevance, grow dysfunctional, and so forth. Since the behavioral theories do not require people or organizations to appraise the rationality of their behaviors, repertoires can include irrelevant behaviors that persist as long as rewards continue.

Because behavioral theories emphasize repetition of the same stimuli, they are less persuasive as descriptions of behavior in changing environments. Indeed, many psychologists refuse to apply the term learning to behavioral

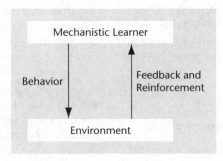

Fig. 14.1. Behavioral learning

changes that occur in response to environmental changes; they restrict the term learning to performance improvements in response to the same or similar stimuli (Weick 1991). Thisio restriction cannot be enforced strictly, as learning experiments always begin by presenting learners with new stimuli, but environmental change does obscure the notion of performance improvement (Levinthal 1994). An unstable environment makes it difficult to evaluate consequences of behavior, and one must evaluate consequences before judging whether performance has improved. Weick (1991) submitted that changing stimuli are so pervasive in organizations that there is need for a different definition of learning in organizations.

Similarly, behavioral theories cannot explain how people and organizations suddenly act in dramatically novel ways. Successes reinforce prior behaviors, failures inhibit prior behaviors, and actions do not reflect learners' global understanding, so exploration and innovation remain mysterious and inexplicable.

Another problem is that a purely behavioral approach becomes difficult to sustain because rewards and punishments are subject to interpretation. When does a learner find an outcome rewarding? Different people find pleasure in different results. Different organizations have different standards for success.

As the ensuing subsections explain, behavioral studies have concentrated on learning by individual people or by populations of organizations. They have said little about learning by individual organizations.

Learning by Individual People

Much organizational learning involves learning by people within the organizations. Countless studies have applied behavioral-learning frameworks to individual people (Estes 1975–8; Hilgard 1948). These studies generally show that pleasant outcomes (successes) reinforce Stimulus–Response links whereas unpleasant outcomes (failures) break Stimulus–Response links. As a result, pleasant outcomes are much more effective at teaching new behaviors, whereas unpleasant outcomes are much more effective at discouraging existing behaviors. Also, extremely unpleasant outcomes often evoke aggression toward others.

Reinforcement frequency affects the speed of learning and the retention of learned behaviors. Reinforcements that occur after every repetition of a specific behavior produce fast learning but the learned behaviors are readily unlearned. Reinforcements that occur randomly after some repetitions but not all produce slow learning but the learned behaviors are difficult to unlearn later.

Complexity Theory (Schroder, Driver, and Streufert 1967) says the quality and sophistication of an individual's responses depend on the frequency of problematic stimuli. However, very high frequencies may produce information overload. Streufert (1973) later showed that negative feedback tends to make the performance peak earlier and at a lower level. Thus, negative feedback (failure) fosters simpler, less improved, responses than positive feedback (success) does.

Learning by Individual Organizations

Although organizations may learn when their members learn, it is possible for learning by individual members to have no effect on organizational behavior, as occurs when new members learn to follow established routines. Also, organizations can add new behaviors to their repertoires by adding new members without either the new or continuing members learning new behaviors.

Industrial learning curves afford one analog to behavioral learning by organizations. These curves describe how production costs decline when a manufacturing process is repeated. For example, the BCG Matrix, developed by the Boston Consulting Group and used globally as a prescriptive strategic model, relies heavily on the assumption that a production line becomes more efficient with the number of repeats and that overall efficiency depends on the number of items sold. The cost decreases have many sources that include both learning by individual workers and learning by the organization as an entity (Epple, Argote, and Devadas 1991; Levitt and March 1988). Possibly because industrial learning curves have been studied from macroscopic perspectives, theories about them say that improvements come from repetition alone, and the theories have not distinguished between successes and failures.

Evolutionary studies resemble behavioral learning theories insofar as they examine the results of change without describing processes inside learners. Although they acknowledge that organizations make choices, they do not describe choice processes or communications between people within an organization. They seek to relate the properties of behaviors to their survival or disappearance. However, most modern evolutionary theories do not assume that change implies improvement; beha-

viors that survive are not necessarily 'better' than those that disappear. In this respect, evolutionary theories differ from the behavioral theories of psychologists.

A very few evolutionary studies have focused on changes within or by one organization. However, Miner (1991) analyzed turnover of jobs in a university. Some jobs disappeared soon after they had appeared; others lasted for decades. Jobs created in larger departments lasted longer. Jobs created for specific people tended to disappear quickly.

Learning by Populations of Organizations

Most evolutionary studies have looked at populations of similar organizations in similar environments (Miner and Haunschild 1995). For instance, Milliken, Lant, and Batra (1992) interpreted data about two industries as showing that most poorly performing firms persist in their strategic orientations.

Nelson and Winter (1982) characterized organizational change as an evolutionary process in which standardized routines survive or disappear. The routines are not confined to single organizations because organizations imitate each other. Many studies have examined how managerial practices spread through interorganizational networks (Burns and Wholey 1993; Davis 1991; Haunschild 1993; Ingram and Baum 1997a; Powell, Koput, and Smith-Doerr 1996; Spender 1989). Such evolutionary theories have not, however, incorporated interorganizational communication processes. As Winter (1994: 100) stated the position, 'Evolutionary theory emphasizes that much of the knowledge that underlies organizational capabilities is tacit knowledge; it is not understood or communicable in symbolic form.'

Prevalent theories make drastic failure the main mechanism for learning in organizational populations. Organizations disappear if they act inappropriately or ineffectively, so the surviving organizations act appropriately and effectively. Miner et al. (1996) reviewed more subtle effects on an organizational population of failure by one organization or possibly a few. One effect can be the freeing of resources for other uses, either within the same population or in others. Other effects can include changes made to prevent additional failures, such as changes in government policies, industry practices, and organizational structures. Still another effect can be more experimentation by the surviving organizations, which makes the population more heterogeneous.

In a study of decisions to hire investment banks, Haunschild and Miner (1997) observed that firms were more likely to imitate more frequent events rather than less frequent events, to imitate larger and more profitable firms rather than smaller and less profitable firms, and to imitate successes rather than failures. However, although firms were more likely to hire investment banks that had been involved in more profitable acquisitions, they seemingly did not avoid hiring banks that had been involved in less profitable acquisitions.

Learning across a population of competing organizations creates the Red Queen effect. Barnett and Hansen (1996: 139) summarized this effect as follows: 'An organization facing competition is likely to engage in a search for ways to improve performance. When successful, this search results in learning that is likely to increase the organization's competitive strength, which in turn triggers learning by its rivals—consequently making them stronger competitors and so again triggering learning in the first organization.' They inferred that historical data about some banks are consistent with the Red Queen effect. Ingram and Baum (1997b) inferred that hotel chains grew less likely to fail as they observed (a) more other hotel chains and (b) more failures by other hotel chains. Barnett (1997) argued that data on breweries and telephone companies say smaller firms need more competitive strength to survive than do larger firms; larger firms can survive without being as effective as smaller firms. As a result, large firms become increasingly vulnerable over time.

A few researchers have modeled learning across organizational populations as races in which organizations that learn a new method sooner gain greater advantages. For instance, Amburgey, Dacin, and Singh (2000) analyzed strategic alliances among biotechnology firms in such a framework.

Thus, behavioral approaches interpret learning as being strongly dependent on rewards or punishments that arise in the environment. For learning to occur, a learner and an environment must be tightly linked, but the environment exerts much more influence on a learner than vice versa. This asymmetric interdependence creates a puzzle at the population level, where the environment is largely composed of learners who are all learning from each other.

A Second Framework: Cognitive Learning

The second approach describes learners as cognitive beings that perceive, analyze, plan, and choose. According to this approach, learning modifies cognitive maps that form the bases for analysis, and analysis guides action. Figure 14.2 diagrams such a loop.

Cognitive learning incorporates perception, analysis, and choice. Learners' mental processes integrate and interpret perceptions, analyze situations, and propose alternative behaviors. Schroder, Driver, and Streufert (1967) described how people build increasingly complex cognitive structures to analyze situations and to form responses to recurring problems. To varying degrees, learners can choose what to perceive, how to interpret perceptions, and which actions to take. Thus, the effectiveness of their behaviors depends on how well they read their environments and upon how rapidly they discover changes. Reading environments and rapidly discovering changes, in turn, depend upon factors such as curiosity, playfulness, willingness to experiment, and analytic skill (March 1973).

A great advantage of cognitive theories is that they can explain how people and organizations are able suddenly to act in dramatically novel

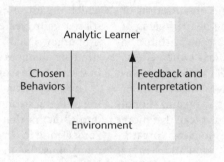

Fig. 14.2. Cognitive learning

ways. Cognitive maps allow people and organizations to predict the results of behaviors they have never tried. Thus, they can find opportunities, threats, and shortcuts, and they can conceive innovations.

The weak spots of cognitive learning theories are the degrees to which behaviors depend upon realistic understanding and the theories' inability to explain how learners can improve even though they misunderstand their environments or misunderstand the causal relations between actions and outcomes. Because learners' perceptions form the bases for analysis, choice, and interpretation, erroneous perceptions become barriers to improvement. March and Olsen (1979) reported a case in which the 'solutions' that an organization considered adopting were very weakly related to the 'problems' the organization had identified. They applied the label 'superstitious learning' to changes that are based on very precarious interpretations of environmental events (p. 32).

Rapid environmental changes create a paradox for cognitive theories. On the one hand, rapid changes stimulate cognitive processes. Because people are likely to notice more events and to engage in more sense-making while they are adapting to changes, they tend to think they are doing more problem-solving and to credit themselves with any ensuing benefits. On the other hand, rapid changes amplify perceptual errors and foster more innovation. While they are adapting to changes, people tend to make worse choices, to create poorer solutions, and

to learn inferior behaviors than they would in stable environments. As various authors remarked, successful use of inferior behavior reinforces use of that behavior even though much more effective behaviors would be possible (Ginsberg and Baum 1994; Levitt and March 1988). Horvath (1996) argued that rapid environmental changes and uncertainty about future conditions lead managers to rely on their memories and to deemphasize the significance of new data, to refine their knowledge rather than to reformulate it.

When learners model their situations, their models include noticed phenomena and omit unnoticed phenomena (Zebrowitz 1990). Learning usually changes what is noticed (Starbuck and Milliken 1988a). Noticing may be either involuntary or volitional. Voluntary noticing tends to depend on mental models that say some phenomena have relevance or importance; small stimuli or unimportant ones generally escape notice. For instance, people are more likely to notice words that relate to succeeding or failing immediately after they find out that they have succeeded or failed than at other times (Postman and Brown 1951).

Sense-making frameworks categorize data, fill in data that should exist, and edit out dissonant data. For instance, Milliken (1990) surmised that managers are less likely to interpret environmental changes as threatening when they perceive their organizations to be performing well than when they perceive their organizations to be performing poorly. Krull and Anderson (1997) reviewed some ways people's goals influence their choices among alternative sense-making frameworks. Watzlawick, Weakland, and Fisch (1974) pointed out that all perceptual frameworks have blind spots that prevent people from solving problems and that link behaviors into self-reinforcing cycles. When blind spots make problems unsolvable, people need new sense-making frameworks that portray situations differently. Watzlawick *et al.* proposed various strategies for reframing such situations.

Because social processes typically incorporate opposing effects, learning is much more likely to add sense-making frameworks than to eliminate them. Starbuck and Milliken (1988a: 59) remarked, 'A process that tends to displace a social system from its current state gets offset by processes that tend to restore the current state; a process that tends to eliminate some characteristics gets offset by processes that tend to preserve the existing characteristics or to add new ones.' Thus, people and organizations face complex, contradictory environments, and they need enough, diverse sense-making frameworks to allow them to make sense of almost any situation.

Cognitive studies have concentrated on learning by individual people or organizations. They have paid little attention to learning by organizational populations. As is the case for behavioral learning, it is possible for learning by individuals and learning by organizations to link weakly: Individual members of organizations can develop new perceptions without changing their actions or communicating their new perceptions to other members. When this occurs, individuals learn without their organizations also learning. Nonaka (1994) argued that individuals often acquire knowledge tacitly and this tacit knowledge does not become organizational knowledge until it becomes explicit. As well, organizations can add new personnel who have distinctive expertise that they do not communicate to other members, so that the organizations learn in the sense that they add new expertise without individual members learning.

Learning by Individual People

Cameron (1984) remarked that people find it easier to establish criteria for ineffectiveness than criteria for effectiveness. However, a large body of research indicates that people set 'levels of aspiration' for successful performance (Starbuck 1963a, b). Performance above a level of aspiration elicits pleasure; performance below a level of aspiration elicits disappointment. Levels of aspiration reflect experience, but people avoid setting them either too low or too high. Goals elicit the most effort if they are difficult but achievable, and performances produce the most satisfaction when they exceed difficult goals (Locke and Latham 1990). People are also more likely to feel satisfaction with their performances when they have devoted more effort to the tasks (Conway and Ross 1984).

Staw (1976) and colleagues (Staw and Fox 1977; Staw and Ross 1978) studied the tendency for college students to increase their commitments to unsuccessful courses of action in simulated tasks. That is, indications of failure may induce people to allocate more effort or resources to their current behavioral strategies rather than to adopt new behaviors. Milliken and Lant (1991: 131) argued that 'a number of forces push managers toward persistence after experiences of both success and failure' although these forces are stronger after success than after failure. The forces fostering persistence include the self-serving bias.

Some theorists have represented thought with computer programs that implement decision rules (Newell and Simon 1972). Some of these programs have accurately reproduced habitual routines, and some programs have learned in two senses: (a) they have searched for action alternatives and (b) they have adapted their response frequencies to match the frequencies of stimuli. They have not, however, shown holistic understanding or an ability to adapt to new circumstances, and they have been quite blind to their own limitations (Dreyfus and Dreyfus 1986; Stanfill and Waltz 1986). That is, programs have not been able to recognize that circumstances have changed in ways that make entrenched responses inappropriate.

Another, more prevalent approach portrays thought as mainly computational processes for choosing among already visible alternatives (Hogarth 1987; Mitchell 1974). These theories support three types of learning: (a) changes in perceived likelihoods of events, (b) changes in valuations of outcomes, and (c) changes in ability to discriminate among stimuli. However, their predictive accuracy has been low, partly because people do not always behave in logically consistent ways.

Cognitive phenomena vary across organizations and cultures. For instance, Dutton and Starbuck (1971) told how the problem-solving of a scheduler reflected the sense-making framework used by the scheduler's colleagues. If the scheduler had joined a different workgroup, his problem-solving would have reflected an alternative sense-making framework. Berthoin Antal, Dierkes, and Hähner (1997) described the effects of a company culture on the firm's perceptions of its environment and its readiness to respond to perceived issues. A company with a different culture would have different perceptions, would have perceived different issues, and would have responded differently to perceived issues. Nam (1991) presented evidence that Korean managers tend to take personal responsibility for poor performances by the groups they lead. Managers in a different society might blame poor performances on their subordinates or on uncontrollable external forces.

Learning by Individual Organizations

Dunbar, Garud, and Raghuram (1996a) argued that managers should manage the processes by which their firms acquire new sense-making frameworks. Porac and Rosa (1996: 35) contested this assertion, arguing that firms succeed without adapting to their environments: 'A frame's fit with the external environment is largely irrelevant' because a firm succeeds by imposing its frame on its environment. 'Success,' they (1996: 40) said, 'is more a function of energy and persistence than of the repeating cycles of belief and discrediting proposed by Dunbar et al.' Dunbar, Garud, and Raghuram (1996b) answered by saying that merely adhering to consistent strategies without attempting to adapt leaves survival up to natural selection.

Hedberg (1981: 10) emphasized the choices implicit in organizational learning: 'Reality is only the provider of potential inputs to a learner. Reality offers ranges of alternative environments from which an organization selects and enacts one from time to time.'

Some cognitive learning theories explicitly acknowledge communication within organizations. For instance, Clark (1972) wrote about shared 'sagas' that help colleges develop and preserve distinctive cultures, and Jönsson and Lundin (1977) described the waves of enthusiasm for successive business models pursued by politicians and administrators in city councils.

Other studies consider the use of communication to explicate tacit knowledge (Polanyi 1966; Weick 1995). These theories assert that organizations contain much more knowledge than people can express. Some knowledge is explicit and available; other is impossible to access or articulate at the moment. Thus, latent knowledge is waiting to be transformed, voiced, and interpreted. Processes of socialization, externalization, infusion, and diffusion transform tacit knowledge into explicit knowledge, and knowledge in individuals into knowledge in groups. For instance, Nonaka and Takeuchi (1995: 45–6) asserted: '[Knowledge-creating] organizations continuously create new knowledge by reconstructing existing perspectives, frameworks, or premises on a daily basis. In other words, the capacity for double-loop learning is built into the knowledge-creating organizations without the unrealistic assumption of the existence of a "right" answer.'

Baumard (1995, 1996, 1999), on the other hand, argued that knowledge need not be explicit to be useful. Not only can organizations exploit knowledge that has not been made explicit, but explication may fossilize knowledge, especially in turbulent settings. He interpreted four case studies as examples of how managerial groups can understand and manage tacit knowledge by experimenting with its borders.

On the ground that people are better able to generate appropriate responses to moderate successes and failures, Weick (1984) urged people to define problems in ways that will allow 'small wins' and 'small flops'.

Moderate Success

Cyert and March (1963) laid out a behavioral model in which decision rules govern actions, and successes and failures change the parameters in these decision rules. When actions yield apparently good results, organizations tend to repeat them, and repeated actions eventually become standard operating procedures. Starbuck (1983, 1985) observed that standard operating procedures frequently induce organizations to act unreflectively and automatically, and that they may invent 'problems' to justify their actions. Weick (1991) too argued that organizations tend to emit the same responses despite unstable and changing stimuli.

Success does not always induce organizations to standardize operating procedures, however. To explain firms' slowness in adapting to environmental changes, Cyert and March (1963: 36–8) introduced the concept of 'organizational slack', which is the difference between the resources available and the resources necessary to keep a firm in existence. Successes increase slack, which encourages risk taking and experimentation. The experiments can become launch platforms for new strategies, proactive actions, and market leadership. Furthermore, there are industries and professional cultures where creativity norms prohibit repetition of past successes. For example, a well-reputed advertising agency is unlikely to repeat a successful ad campaign twice. IKEA, the worldwide chain of furniture stores, has a strong culture (Salzer 1994) that seems to foster renewal. Whenever a product line, or a way of organizing, becomes routine, they change it. A similar culture of change seems to be present in the 3M Company, which creates 'garage projects' to foster new ideas. 3M employees can use 15 per cent of their working hours to develop new ideas, to challenge present practices, and to innovate.

Success provides discretion and it facilitates fine-tuning and elaboration of strategies, but it also diverts attention from the environment and from the future. It makes organizations confident and homogeneous (Sitkin 1992). Levinthal and March (1993) emphasized the short-sightedness of organizational learning and the subjectivity of performance evaluations. They said, 'Organizational learning oversamples successes and undersamples failures' because successes and failures are defined by the organizations (p. 109). Because learning appears to eliminate failures, it fosters optimistic expectations. Because organizations promote people who participated in successful activities, leaders are optimistic people.

During periods of repeated success, evolutionary learning in small steps seems to work better than does revolutionary learning. Continuous improvement, the daily challenging of status quo, supports the notion that everything can be improved. For instance, Asea Brown Boveri used simple bench-marks to challenge workers to cut lead times in half despite many years of success. The Japanese tradition of continuous improvement has demonstrated viability through long periods of daily-learning-at-work, particularly in manufacturing. Numerous Japanese companies, successful and not so successful, have implemented continuous improvement as a way of working life.

Nonaka and Takeuchi (1995) maintained that Japanese companies have considerably greater ability to learn, improve, and restructure in spite of success than do Western companies. Japanese shop-floor management has been very successful in supporting everyday learning and continuous improvement, mainly in manufacturing firms, but there seems to be no evidence that these principles have been applied successfully on management levels and to strategy reformulation. Indeed, Barker and Duhaime (1997) presented evidence that continuous improvement has little potential to drive organizational learning towards strategic turnarounds. They found that a few turn-arounds succeed while most do not, and that substantial strategic changes, often CEO changes, must occur before reorientations begin.

Chronic Success

Empirical research suggests that long-term success weakens the ability to unlearn radically and to reorient strategically (Grinyer and Norburn 1975; Starbuck and Hedberg 1977; Hedberg and Jönsson 1977; Sitkin 1992). Chronically successful organizations develop introverted complacency and they tell stories about victories and heroes of the past. They elaborate and reinforce their cognition structures. They expect success to continue and stop scanning their environments for signals that they believe to be irrelevant (Hedberg, Nystrom, and Starbuck 1976; Sitkin 1992). On the other hand, Dougherty and Hardy (1996) studied sustained product innovation in 15 firms that averaged 96 years of age and that had been quite successful. They concluded that a major obstacle to organizational change lay in innovators' inability to access power and to restructure resource flows rather than their inability to discover environmental threats and to exploit strategic opportunities. What product innovation did occur happened in spite of mature industrial organization, not because of it.

Miller (1990: 3) likened chronically successful organizations to Icarus, who flew so near the Sun that his wings melted: 'Success leads to specialization and exaggeration, to confidence and complacency, to dogma and ritual. . . . Robust, superior organizations evolve into flawed purebreds; they move from rich character to exaggerated caricature, as all subtlety, all nuance, is gradually lost.' He described four prototypic developmental trajectories corresponding to four formulas for success. After analyzing the histories of 36 firms, Miller (1993, 1994) inferred that lengthy periods of success foster (a) structural and strategic inertia, (b) extreme process orientations, (c) inattention, and (d) insularity. Success breeds simplicity and purity, not complexity. A focus on core

competence and competitive edge, which initially make an organization successful, tends to grow even more narrow and specialized over time. Positive feedback reinforces simplicity to a point where the organization loses requisite variety. Thus, simplicity yields benefits during the first phases of success, but turns into a liability.

Moderate failure

In their model, Cyert and March (1963) said actual or expected failures induce a firm to make parameter changes. If these parameter changes prove inadequate to allow forecasts of success, the firm searches its environments for new alternatives. Similarly, Sitkin (1992) argued that moderate levels of failure draw attention to potential problems and stimulate searches for potential solutions. He set forth criteria for 'intelligent failure' (p. 243). People should plan their actions (a) to yield diagnostic information, (b) to limit the costs of failure, (c) to generate feedback quickly, and (d) to focus on familiar domains so that they will be able to analyze what happened. He also listed organizational properties that foster intelligent failure.

The proposition that failure fosters experimentation contrasts with the findings from studies of individual people, which indicate that unpleasant consequences can stop existing behaviors without stimulating learners to try new behaviors. Also, Hedberg (1981) pointed out that organizational inertia often delays or counteracts problem-solving.

Burgelman (1994) portrayed moderate failure as a source of information. In a study of Intel Corporation, he analyzed the development of strategies as evolutionary processes. Top managers, he said, create 'an internal selection environment' of rules for choosing among courses of action. For such selection rules to be effective, they have to match prevailing pressures in the firm's environment. This match depends, in turn, on middle managers' generating appropriate strategic initiatives and on top managers' having 'strategic recognition capability'. Failure in a line of business gives top managers better understanding of the relations between the firm's 'distinctive competence' and 'the basis of competition in the industries in which they remain active' (p. 52).

Chronic failure

Organizations' resistance to dramatic reorientations creates a need for explicit unlearning. Organizations, especially older ones, find it hard to ignore their current knowledge and their current operating procedures because they build up explicit justifications for their actions and they associate specific people with specific policies (Hedberg 1981). As one result, organizations integrate their knowledge and procedures into rigid, coherent structures in which ideas and politics buttress each other. External attributions for failure prevent organizations from questioning their key assumptions (Virany, Tushman, and Romanelli 1992). Before attempting radical changes, they must dismantle parts of their current ideological and political structures. Before they will contemplate dramatically different procedures, policies, and strategies, they must lose confidence in their current procedures, policies, strategies, and top managers. Several authors have argued that change in top management may be a prerequisite for strategic change (Starbuck 1983; Virany, Tushman, and Romanelli 1992).

Chronic organizational failure is painful and destructive (Starbuck, Greve, and Hedberg 1978). Co-workers depart, and those who remain wonder if everyone with job options and ambition is going. Those remaining are working harder and shouldering unfamiliar tasks, they may be receiving less pay, and their promotion chances seem dim. Budgets decline. As departments fight to preserve their shares, trust erodes. Central control exposes the top managers' inability to produce success: If the top managers knew what to do, their organizations would not remain in such serious trouble. Moreover, the top managers have probably declared many times over that better times are at hand. When the better times do not appear, such declarations underline the top managers' impotence and unreliability. In many cases,

morale drops to such a low state that the organizations cannot go on. Like punishment, unlearning ends behavior without substituting new behavior, so many organizations discover that their procedures, policies, and strategies do not work and they lack the ability to replace them.

Learning by Populations of Organizations

Organizations transmit knowledge to each other via joint ventures, educational institutions, consultants, lawyers, venture capitalists, trade and popular periodicals, conventions, and personnel who change jobs (Levitt and March 1988, Miner et al. 1996). Hodgkinson (1997: 922) observed 'over time, strategists from rival firms develop highly similar (or "shared") mental models of the competitive arena due to the fact that they share similar technical and material problems and frequently exchange information.' Spender (1989) showed how recipes that had proven successful in one company spread to become industry-wide recipes. Sahlin-Andersson (1996) pictured such imitation as a process of 'editing success' (p. 82). Firms can imitate with or without communicating with each other, with or without sharing a common rationale. As a result, the perceptual errors of each individual firm have less impact and shared misperceptions become even more powerful.

Tripsas (1997) portrayed imitation as partial and inefficient when she described three waves of change in the global typesetter industry from 1886 to 1990. She found that most of the established firms invested heavily in new, competence-destroying technologies even though their ability to implement these technologies profitably was hampered by their previous experience. The incumbents mostly survived change and managed to prevent new invaders from taking over. The incumbents had the advantage of specialized complementary assets such as team skills and strong sales and service networks, which served to buffer performance and to give time for slow learning processes.

Other studies have considered how perform-ance affects learning. Miner *et al.* (1996) pointed out that failure by one organization often makes other organizations in the same popula-tion more alert to environmental changes. They also remarked that no such effect oc-curred in the Swiss watch industry. Miller and Chen (1994) analyzed data about U.S. airlines and inferred that, on average, high-revenue periods are followed by periods of inertia, and vice versa. Also, diversity of markets discour-aged inertia. Later, they (1996) also inferred that, on average, high-revenue periods are fol-lowed by periods in which firms take fewer types of competitive actions, and vice versa. They (1996: 434) remarked:

Success may drive managers to whittle down their repertoires—to zero in on what they believe is the path to success. But the simplicity of that path may be at least in part a product of 'extrarational' factors such as a munificent environment, the compla-cency born of size, and perhaps even the attribution of merit to practices of little consequence.

Thus, cognitive approaches allow learning to depend only weakly on rewards or punish-ments that arise in the environment. A learner and an environment can be loosely linked, a learner has much influence on the learning process, and indeed a learner can exert much influence on the environment.

The next two sections of this chapter describe illustrative cases of learning in real life. The first case shows the complexity of learning pro-cesses within both of two interdependent organizations. The second case broadens the horizon to an organizational population. Both cases indicate how greatly organizations de-pend on each other and how the slowness of learning influences what is learned. Both cases suggest that cognitive and behavioral learning occur at the same time.

Through Evolutionary Learning to the Challenger Disaster

NASA, the National Aeronautics and Space Administration, coordinates a coalition of aerospace firms that operate the U.S. space pro-gram. In the mid-1970s, this coalition began building space shuttles. Their efforts illustrate some common properties of organizational ef-forts to learn from feedback. Development efforts generated incremental changes that took place in a noisy and complex environ-ment. In each of two key organizations, some people interpreted the feedbacks from these changes as reassuring and others saw them as ominous. People misperceived events, they disagreed about interpretations, and they com-peted for control; communications were in-complete and biased by political agendas.

The space shuttles have rocket engines, but these do not have enough power for launch. The shuttles receive added lift during launch from Solid Rocket Boosters (SRBs). NASA chose Thiokol to build the SRBs. The SRBs are com-posed of interlocking cylinders. When SRBs ignite, they fill with fiery gases that must not leak through the joints between cylinders. Two O-rings in each joint were supposed to seal it tightly.

During the second shuttle launch in 1981, hot gases eroded an O-ring. The NASA personnel who saw this damage judged it so minor that they did not report it upward. Launches in 1982 produced no more evidence of problems.

During 1982, Thiokol proposed small changes to make the SRBs lighter and more powerful. After tests showed that these changes increased the probability of leakage, NASA reclassified the joints as more dangerous. However, Thiokol judged the threat to be small, and in 1983, NASA started using the modified SRBs.

During 1983, a static test and one launch dam-aged O-rings. In response, NASA changed the method for testing joints when it assembled SRBs. After another launch damaged an O-ring in February 1984, engineers from NASA and Thiokol speculated that the new test proced-ures were making the O-rings more vulnerable. A review commission ran laboratory tests that suggested the O-rings would seal tightly even if eroded as much as 0.241 centimeters, and it ran a computer simulation that implied the erosion would not exceed 0.229 centimeters. 'There-fore,' concluded the review commission, 'this is not a constraint to future launches' (Presidential Commission 1986: I-128-32). At this point, the NASA manager in charge of SRBs proposed that some damage was 'acceptable' because the O-rings embodied a safety factor. NASA's top managers approved this idea (Presidential Commission 1986: II-H1).

After a launch in April 1984 produced more O-ring damage, NASA's second-in-command asked for a thorough study of the O-rings. NASA gave this assignment to Thiokol, which proposed tests but did not make them and did not submit a report.

SRB joints were damaged during three of five launches in 1984, during eight of nine launches in 1985, and during the first launch in 1986. Two test firings also produced damage. Furthermore, the damage became more serious over time. The erosion grew larger and sometimes both O-rings in a joint suffered damage.

After the fifteenth launch in January 1985 produced especially severe damage, Thiokol proposed that a low ambient temperature during launch might have made the joints more vulnerable. But even more serious damage occurred during a launch in April 1985 when the ambient temperature was moderate, so the temperature hypothesis lost plausibility. In that April launch, one O-ring was eroded 0.434 centimeters, nearly twice the maximum predicted by NASA's earlier simulation.

On the evening before the Challenger launch in January 1986, managers and engineers from NASA and Thiokol confronted each other about the desirability of launching. Two Thiokol engineers argued that the launch should be postponed because low ambient temperatures existed at the launch site and low ambient temperatures were very probably a factor in O-ring erosion. Other Thiokol engineers advocated caution, but without fervor. The chief NASA engineer said he thought the Thiokol engineers were being excessively cautious. NASA's managers argued that the evidence about low ambient temperatures was unclear and that, since low ambient temperatures were common in winter, postponing this launch would imply that they should postpone all launches until spring brought warmer weather. Worried

about maintaining amicable relations with NASA, Thiokol's managers overruled their engineers and endorsed launching.

The next day, Challenger disintegrated, killing its crew and shattering America's confidence in NASA's competence.

Cognitive Learning

The gradually escalating damage convinced engineers at NASA and Thiokol that the SRBs posed risks, but the engineers disagreed about the degree of risk. In July 1985, Thiokol ordered new SRB cases with three O-rings in each joint, but the supplier was given three years to produce these SRBs. In August 1985, Thiokol at last created a task force to make the study that NASA had requested 16 months earlier; this task force proposed numerous studies but it had few resources. In January 1986, engineers from NASA and Thiokol assembled to discuss hypotheses about O-ring damage. There were many hypotheses and much ambiguity, as the engineers debated the alternative hypotheses.

The events that were causing engineers to worry were leading key managers at NASA and Thiokol to infer that the SRB joints posed only small risks. These managers observed that the SRBs had suffered no serious harm even though O-rings had been damaged in almost every recent launch. Indeed, the joints had sealed adequately even when the O-rings had sustained damage that greatly exceeded the direst forecast. Not only did the engineers seem to have overstated the risks but 'O-ring erosion was accepted and indeed expected' (Bell and Esch 1987: 43). After a briefing in August 1985, NASA's top management concluded, 'it is safe to continue flying' (Presidential Commission 1986: I-140).

An investigation after the disaster found much to blame in the behavior of NASA and Thiokol managers, but it did not yield a definitive explanation for the disaster. Indeed, the investigators introduced two hypotheses about causes for the disaster that no one had posed earlier. Many hypotheses remain plausible to this day (Starbuck and Milliken 1988b).

Two years after the disaster, an astronaut observed that the disaster had taught lessons that NASA would probably have to learn again and again. Although the astronaut did not explain what lessons he thought NASA had learned, different people, inside and outside NASA, might deem different lessons to be the appropriate ones.

Behavioral Learning

The Challenger disaster halted much of the behavior that preceded it, and it instigated widespread changes in NASA, in Thiokol, and in the space shuttle. Many managers were replaced in both organizations, including almost everyone who participated in the decision to launch Challenger. The replaced personnel may have behaved differently in their new jobs or in retirement but no data are available. NASA changed many procedures.

NASA made no further launches until Thiokol received new SRB cases; these were the cases that had been ordered in July 1985 except that they had three O-rings in each joint. During the launch hiatus, suppliers modified many components of the space shuttle, seeking to make them safer.

Later, NASA solicited SRB-design proposals from potential suppliers other than Thiokol. As is generally true of behavioral changes that follow failures, changes in design or supplier could introduce unforeseen problems or yield unexpected benefits.

Building Inertia in the Swedish Construction Industry

Events in the Swedish construction industry illustrate population-level learning. As the industry went through a cycle of success, crisis, and recovery, there was change in the kinds of firms in the population and in their interdependencies. Mainly, the industry lost diversity. The surviving firms had behaved differently from those that failed. They had had more financial resources initially and had remained financially stronger throughout the changes, partly because they had been slower to adopt changing industry recipes.

The construction industry, consisting of construction firms, real-estate firms, and combinations thereof, was a favorite at the Stockholm Stock Exchange during the 1980s. Deregulation of rents and of the banking system, an oversupply of credit from an expanding service industry, and low interest rates fueled a boom. Between 1983 and 1988, the property index increased more than 1,500 per cent, property prices grew an average of 25 per cent per annum, and the 35 listed firms increased their joint market value enormously. In 1988, several listed firms hit all-time highs, and more than half of them increased their adjusted net asset value by more than 50 per cent during that year alone.

Malmström (1995) and Hedberg and Malmström (1997) traced the histories of the listed firms over 1982–1992. They gathered economic indicators, strategies, and CEOs' statements in annual reports. Initially, the industry had subgroups with distinct performances and strategies. Some firms were mainly construction firms whereas others focused on ownership, maintenance, and rental of apartments and commercial buildings. However, as the boom developed, the firms elaborated their core businesses and imitated each other's strategies. Towards the end of the period, most firms focused on a few industry recipes and the industry exhibited much less heterogeneity. The CEOs expressed similar values and expectations in annual reports. The firms linked through interlocking ownership, and they formed a network that encompassed real-estate firms, construction firms, and the independent institutes that assessed and certified property values. Assuming that the Swedish market was becoming saturated, 23 of the 29 firms began to invest in Brussels, Amsterdam, Antwerp, and London during 1988–9. By these firms' standards, these markets were undervalued and offered good bargains.

Warning signals of oversupply, boosted valuations, and sagging rental development arrived in 1987 and 1988. These signals were first neglected, then recognized but not acted upon. For a short period also, firms attributed growing turbulence to 'the Saddam effect' in connection with the Gulf invasion. House rentals began stagnating early in 1989, but investments continued and the price index of commercial property increased by another 15 per cent during 1989. Seeing but not acting might have been a result of slow sense-making or of difficulties unlearning previously successful behaviors. Even when firms acted, time delays and inertia led to the initiation of new building projects at a time when property could not be sold or rented.

In September 1990, a once-highly-successful real-estate firm declared bankruptcy. This triggered an unprecedented crisis in the Swedish real-estate markets, and the crisis spread to the banks and to the financial institutions. Some 50 firms went bankrupt each month during the fall of 1990 and the property index declined by 50 per cent by year's end. The firms' total market value, which had more than quintupled between 1985 and 1990, fell one-third in less than two years and then continued to decline until it reached half of its peak value. Sweden struggled with economic turmoil for several years, as the crisis shattered financial institutions.

In retrospect, one can see clear and strong warning signals that might have heralded the approaching crisis. The warning signals that construction firms neglected include: (1) growing vacancy rates that signaled oversupply of commercial property, (2) reports showing that Swedish property yields were very low in comparison with yields in other countries, (3) a severe real-estate crisis in Norway that caused turbulence in banking, (4) construction costs that continued to rise dramatically, (5) a halt in new construction of commercial buildings by the Swedish government to cool down the economy, (6) two consecutive deregulations of the Swedish currency system, and (7) Sweden's application to join the European Union and beginning attempts to harmonize the Swedish economy with that of the EU. True enough, some CEOs did predict as early as 1987 and 1988 that their industry would stagnate, but even these firms continued to expand and invest. None of these CEOs predicted that property values would be cut in half and that almost all business activities would stop.

Cognitive Learning

As the industry grew and prospered, the firms shared their cognitive models; most firms focused on a very few industry recipes. With few exceptions, the firms' annual reports described similar expectations about the future. Firms developed and changed their assessment and accounting criteria with striking coordination. They also identified promising investment opportunities in the United Kingdom, in Holland, and in Belgium at about the same time. In short, their cognitive models became more and more homogeneous.

It took several years of mounting crises to reframe these mental models. When warning signals appeared they were first overlooked and then recognized, but the firms were slow in changing their strategies. The changing stimuli did not elicit behavioral change until very late, and the firms' public statements and analyses of the crisis bore weak relations to their behaviors.

There were no distinctly better learners. There were no firms that discovered early warning signals and reacted in timely fashion. The survivors may have had less-than-average propensities to imitate others.

Behavioral Learning

Success led to repeated behavior and, later, to unification of industry recipes. An initial population of quite diverse firms became much more homogeneous as firms imitated each other. This homogeneity, in turn, contributed to a build-up of organizational inertia across the industry. Inertia arose partly from complexity, as the firms integrated via interlocking ownership and created a network that spanned real-estate firms, construction firms, and property-valuation institutes.

Learning did not prepare the firms for a market downturn; instead it led to unfortunate delays and a collapsing market. Inertia in production systems made it difficult to halt new investments. Organizational inertia made strategic changes very difficult. Many construction firms went bankrupt, most firms suffered badly, and only a few firms came out of the turbulence with adequate performance. The firms that survived were ones that had had initial financial strength, that ran diverse operations, and that adopted industry recipes slowly; they may have reacted to warning signals more rapidly, although not rapidly enough. The survivors that have continued to do well subsequently have maintained diversity of operations and have focused on well-defined geographic regions and on certain types of housing projects. They have also sold most of their foreign investments.

Integrating Behavioral and Cognitive Learning

The foregoing cases suggest that cognitive and behavioral learning occur in combinations that are difficult to disentangle. Perhaps this mutual entanglement is why theories of learning are filled with ironic contradictions. Extreme advocates of behavioral learning have asserted that cognition plays an unimportant role in behavioral change, whereas extreme advocates of cognitive learning have asserted that all behavioral change follows cognitive dictates. Yet each approach seems to find it difficult to ignore the other. Those who study behavioral learning often explain hypotheses in terms of peoples' motives and thoughts; the fundamental concepts of success and failure cannot be separated from people's interpretations of outcomes. Those who study cognitive learning often speak of reinforcement effects or of unconscious processes; the routines that people use when perceiving or deciding may be established through mechanistic processes.

Loose Links

Although people perceive that their thinking controls their behavior, neither theory nor empirical evidence is consistent with tight cognitive control. The links between behavior and cognition must be loose. Even cognitive theories assert that learning can be occurring while outsiders can see no behavioral changes. For instance, in their study of a merger, Leroy and Ramanantsoa (1997) noted that cognitive changes both began and ended before observable changes in behavior.

Behaviors have many determinants in addition to cognitive ones. Firstly, many behaviors occur automatically without continuing reflection, which implies that cognitive controls operate intermittently if at all. Secondly, external forces dictate many behaviors. For instance, in hierarchical organizations, subordinates have to obey orders and rules, and their compensation and promotions depend on their conformity. Thirdly, people sometimes imitate successful behaviors or the behaviors of respected people even though they do not know why their models acted as they did. Some imitated behaviors yield benefits solely or mainly because they conform to societal norms.

There is abundant evidence that cognitions adapt to actual behavior (Kiesler 1971). Involuntary perceptual changes make behaviors seem more rational, and these changes occur even when external forces have compelled the behavior. Festinger (1962) theorized that forced compliance generates less and less cognitive dissonance as rewards or punishments grow larger. That is, people's actions cause little dissonance for them when their actions seem to promote enormous success or to prevent dreadful failure. Festinger also suggested that perceptions of successes and failures change to reduce the dissonance created by forced compliance (see also Conway and Ross 1984). Sproull (1981) conjectured that cognitions correlate with behaviors in situations that appear familiar, but that novel situations induce people to innovate and subsequently to revise their cognitions to match the new behaviors.

Causal theories that people construct from their experience may be so erroneous that they afford no useful bases for behavioral control (Anderson, Krull, and Weiner 1996). That is, they may lead to very inaccurate predictions about the effects of actions on outcomes. As a result, behavior that appears optimal on the basis of cognitions can be foolhardy.

The hypothesis that cognitions determine behaviors has shown such weak predictive power that some psychologists regard it as having been disconfirmed (Broadbent 1961; Skinner 1974). For instance, people's stated perceptions of their leaders predict poorly their actions with respect to their leaders (Kerr and Slocum 1981). Nystrom and Starbuck (1984) concluded that, in general, behaviors exert stronger influence on cognitions than cognitions exert on behaviors. They (1984: 284) prescribed: 'Change beliefs by changing peoples' behaviors rather than by ideological education, propaganda, or structural interventions. Focus on behaviors as causes of beliefs rather than the other way around.'

Festinger (1962) framed the issue of behavioral control versus cognitive control in terms of the difficulty of making different kinds of changes. Some behaviors are easy to change and others hard to change; and likewise, some cognitions are easy to change and others hard to change.

Organizations tend to have looser connections between behaviors and cognitions than do individual people. Firstly, organizations frequently concretize their cognitions as stable behavior programs that continue even as environmental and social conditions evolve. Starbuck (1982, 1983, 1985) asserted that organizations often amend their cognitions to fit with actions that they have already taken or that they take programmatically and nonreflectively. Secondly, organizational political processes loosen the connections between specific cognitions and specific behaviors.

March and Olsen (1979: 26) likened organizational decision settings to 'garbage cans' filled with diverse actors, diverse problems, and diverse potential solutions. Starbuck, Greve, and Hedberg (1978) said top managers' efforts to retain their positions often prevent their organizations from taking actions needed to deal with crises. Thirdly, organizations often wait too long to respond to external forces, then make dramatic responses. Fourthly, most organizations follow institutionalized rituals in order to win societal support (Meyer and Rowan 1977).

Duality

Studies of learning by individual organizations show a puzzling imbalance. Almost all of these studies have taken a cognitive approach and very few a behavioral one. Yet the theories arising from these studies emphasize the importance of standard operating procedures, as well as behavior programs that are not formalized.

Likewise, studies of learning by populations of organizations show an imbalance of a different sort. Most of these studies have taken a behavioral approach and very few a cognitive one. The latter have focused on imitation and they have de-emphasized rational thought. The former have often explained their theories in cognitive terms even though they did not gather evidence about cognitions.

That such incongruities not only exist but also exist without bothering researchers poses yet another puzzle. Perhaps the distinction between behavior and cognition is an abstraction that does not exist in the realities of daily life?

. . . we are only able to perceive the environment as composed of separate things by suppressing our recognition of the nonthings which fill the interstices.—Edmund Leach (1964: 37)

References

Amburgey, T. L., Dacin, T., and Singh, J. V. (2000). *Racing to Learn and Learning to Race: Cooperation and Competition in Biotechnology.* Unpublished manuscript, University of Toronto.

Anderson, C. A., Krull, D. S., and Weiner, B. (1996). 'Explanations: Processes and Consequences', in E. T. Higgins and A. W. Kruglanski (eds.), *Social Psychology: Handbook of Basic Principles*. New York: Guilford Press, 271–96.

Barker, V. L., III and Duhaime, I. M. (1997). 'Strategic Change in the Turnaround Process: Theory and Empirical Evidence'. *Strategic Management Journal*, 18: 13–38.

Barnett, W. P. (1997). 'The Dynamics of Competitive Intensity'. *Administrative Science Quarterly*, 42: 128–60.

——and Hansen, M. T. (1996). 'The Red Queen in Organizational Evolution'. *Strategic Management Journal*, 17: 139–57.

Baumard, P. (1995). *Organisations déconcertées: La Gestion stratégique de la connaissance*. Paris: Masson.

——(1996). 'Organizations in the Fog: An Investigation into the Dynamics of Knowledge', in B. Moingeon and A. Edmondson (eds.), *Organizational Learning and Competitive Advantage*. London: Sage, 74–91.

——(1999). *Tacit Knowledge in Organizations*. London: Sage.

Bazerman, M. H. (1997). *Judgment in Managerial Decision Making* (2nd edn). New York: Wiley.

Bell, T. E. and K. Esch (1987). 'The Fatal Flaw in Flight 51-L'. *IEEE Spectrum*, 24/2: 36–51.

Berthoin Antal, A. B., Dierkes, M., and Hähner, K. (1997). 'Business Perception of Contextual Changes: Sources and Impediments to Organizational Learning'. *Business and Society*, 36/4: 387–407.

Broadbent, D. E. (1961). *Behaviour*. London: Eyre & Spottiswoode.

Burgelman, R. A. (1994). 'Fading Memories: A Process Theory of Strategic Business Exit in Dynamic Environments'. *Administrative Science Quarterly*, 39: 24–56.

Burns, L. R. and Wholey, D. R. (1993). 'Adoption and Abandonment of Matrix Management Programs: Effects of Organizational Characteristics and Interorganizational Networks'. *Academy of Management Journal*, 36: 106–38.

Cameron, K. S. (1984). 'The Effectiveness of Ineffectiveness', in B. M. Staw and L. L. Cummings (eds.), *Research in Organizational Behavior: An Annual Series of Analytical Essays and Critical Reviews* (Vol. 6). Greenwich, Conn.: JAI Press, 235–85.

Clark, B. (1972). 'The Organizational Saga in Higher Education'. *Administrative Science Quarterly*, 17: 178–84.

Conway, M. and Ross, M. (1984). 'Getting What You Want by Revising What You Had'. *Journal of Personality and Social Psychology*, 47: 738–48.

Cyert, R. M. and March, J. G. (1963). *A Behavioral Theory of the Firm*. Englewood Cliffs, NJ: Prentice-Hall.

Davis, G. F. (1991). 'Agents Without Principles? The Spread of the Poison Pill through the Intercorporate Network'. *Administrative Science Quarterly*, 36: 583–613.

Dougherty, D. and Hardy, C. (1996). 'Sustained Product Innovation in Large, Mature Organizations: Overcoming Innovation-to-Organization Problems'. *Academy of Management Journal*, 39: 1120–53.

Downey, H. K., Hellriegel, D., and Slocum, J. W., Jr. (1975). 'Environmental Uncertainty: The Construct and Its Application'. *Administrative Science Quarterly*, 20: 613–29.

Dreyfus, H. L. and Dreyfus, S. E. (1986). *Mind over Machine*. New York: Free Press.

Dunbar, R. L. M., Garud, R., and Raghuram, S. (1996a). 'A Frame for Deframing in Strategic Analysis'. *Journal of Management Inquiry*, 5: 23–34.

————(1996b). 'Run, Rabbit, Run! But Can You Survive?' *Journal of Management Inquiry*, 5: 168–75.

Dutton, J. M. and Starbuck, W. H. (1971). 'Finding Charlie's Run-Time Estimator', in J. M. Dutton and W. H. Starbuck (eds.), *Computer Simulation of Human Behavior*. New York: Wiley, 218–42.

Edwards, W. (1968). 'Conservatism in Human Information Processing'. In B. Kleinmuntz (ed.), *Formal Representation of Human Judgment*. New York: Wiley, 17–52.

Epple, D., Argote, L., and Devadas, R. (1991). 'Organizational Learning Curves: A Method for Investigating Intra-plant Transfer of Knowledge Acquired through Learning by Doing'. *Organization Science*, 2: 58–70.

Estes, W. K. (1975–8). *Handbook of Learning and Cognitive Processes*. Hillsdale, NJ: Erlbaum.

Festinger, L. (1962). *A Theory of Cognitive Dissonance*. Stanford, Calif.: Stanford University Press.

Ginsberg, A. and Baum, J. A. C. (1994). 'Evolutionary Processes and Patterns of Core Business Change', in J. A. C. Baum and J. V. Singh (eds.), *Evolutionary Dynamics of Organizations*. New York: Oxford University Press, 127–51.

Glynn, M. A., Lant, T. K., and Milliken, F. J. (1994). 'Mapping Learning Processes in Organizations'. *Advances in Managerial Cognition and Organizational Information Processing*, 5: 43–93.

Grinyer, P. H. and Norburn, D. (1975). 'Planning for Existing Markets: Perceptions of Executives and Financial Performance'. *Journal of the Royal Statistical Society,* Series A, 138819: 70–9.

Haunschild, P. R. (1993). 'Interorganizational Imitation: The Impact of Interlocks on Corporate Acquisition Activity'. *Administrative Science Quarterly*, 38: 564–92.

—— and Miner, A. S. (1997). 'Modes of Interorganizational Imitation: The Effects of Outcome Salience and Uncertainty'. *Administrative Science Quarterly*, 42: 472–500.

Hedberg, B. L. T. (1981). 'How Organizations Learn and Unlearn', in P. C. Nystrom and W. H. Starbuck (eds.), *Handbook of Organizational Design*: Vol. 1. *Adapting Organizations to Their Environments*. New York: Oxford University Press, 3–27.

—— and Jönsson, S. (1977). 'Strategy Formulation as a Discontinuous Process'. *International Studies of Organization and Management*, 7/2, Summer: 88–109.

—— —— (1978). 'Designing Semi-confusing Information Systems for Organizations in Changing Environments'. *Accounting, Organizations and Society*, 3: 47–64.

—— and Malmström, L. (1997). *Building Organizational Inertia: How the Swedish Real-Estate Industry Turned Tents into Palaces in the Decade of 1982–1992*. Stockholm: Stockholm University, School of Business, Research series.

—— Nystrom, P. C., and Starbuck, W. H. (1976). 'Camping on Seesaws: Prescriptions for a Self-designing Organization'. *Administrative Science Quarterly*, 21: 41–65.

Heider, F. (1958). *The Psychology of Interpersonal Relations*. New York: Wiley.

Hilgard, E. R. (1948). *Theories of Learning*. New York: Appleton-Century-Crofts.

Hodgkinson, G. P. (1997). 'Cognitive Inertia in a Turbulent Market: The Case of the UK Residential Estate Agents'. *Journal of Management Studies*, 34: 921–45.

Hogarth, R. M. (1987). *Judgement and Choice: The Psychology of Decision*. New York: Wiley.

Horvath, J. A. (1996). *Managerial Learning: An Inductive Systems Perspective*. New Haven: Yale University, Department of Psychology.

Huff, A. and Schwenk, C. R. (1990). 'Bias and Sensemaking in Good Times and Bad', in A. Huff (ed.), *Mapping Strategic Thought*. New York: Wiley, 98–108.

Ingram, P. and Baum, J. A. C. (1997a). 'Chain Affiliation and the Failure of Manhattan Hotels, 1898–1980'. *Administrative Science Quarterly*, 42: 583–613.

—— —— (1997b). 'Opportunity and Constraint: Organizations' Learning from the Operating and Competitive Experience of Industries'. *Strategic Management Journal*, 18: 75–98.

Jönsson, S. and Lundin, R. (1977). 'Myths and Wishful Thinking as Management Tools'. *TIMS Studies in the Management Sciences*, 5: 157–70.

Kerr, S. and Slocum, J. W., Jr. (1981). 'Controlling the Performances of People in Organizations', in P. C. Nystrom and W. H. Starbuck (eds.), *Handbook of Organizational Design*: Vol. 2. *Remodeling Organizations and Their Environments*. New York: Oxford University Press, 116–34.

Kiesler, C. A. (1971). *The Psychology of Commitment*. New York: Academic Press.

Krull, D. S. and Anderson, C. A. (1997). 'The Process of Explanation'. *Current Directions in Psychological Science*, 6/1: 1–5.

Lawrence, P. R. and Lorsch, J. W. (1967). *Organization and Environment: Managing Differentiation and Integration*. Boston: Division of Research, Graduate School of Business Administration, Harvard University.

Leach, E. R. (1964). 'Anthropological Aspects of Language: Animal Categories and Verbal Abuse', in E. H. Lenneberg (ed.), *New Directions in the Study of Language*. Cambridge, Mass.: MIT Press, 23–63.

Leroy, F. and Ramanantsoa, B. (1997). 'The Cognitive and Behavioral Dimensions of Organizational Learning in a Merger: An Empirical Study'. *Journal of Management Studies*, 34: 871–94.

Levinthal, D. (1994). 'Surviving Schumpeterian Environments: An Evolutionary Perspective', in J. A. C. Baum and J. V. Singh (eds.), *Evolutionary Dynamics of Organizations*. New York: Oxford University Press, 167–78.

—— and March, J. G. (1993). 'The Myopia of Learning'. *Strategic Management Journal*, 14: 95–112.

Levitt, B. and March, J. G. (1988). 'Organizational Learning'. *Annual Review of Sociology*, 14: 319–40.

Locke, E. A. and Latham, G. P. (1990). *A Theory of Goal Setting and Task Performance*. Englewood Cliffs, NJ: Prentice Hall.

Loftus, E. F. (1979). 'The Malleability of Human Memory'. *American Scientist*, 67: 312–20.

Malmström, L. (1995). *Lärande organisationer? Krisen på den svenska fastighetsmarknaden* (Learning Organizations? The Crisis in the Swedish Real-Estate Market). Ph.D. thesis, Stockholm University, School of Business, Stockholm, Sweden.

March, J. G. (1973). 'The Technology of Foolishness', in H. J. Leavitt and L. R. Pondy (eds.), *Readings in Managerial Psychology* (2nd edn). Chicago: University of Chicago Press, 628–39.

—— and Olsen, J. P. (1979). *Ambiguity and Choice in Organizations* (2nd edn). Bergen: Universitetsforlaget.

Meindl, J. R. and Ehrlich, S. B. (1987). 'The Romance of Leadership and the Evaluation of Organizational Performance'. *Academy of Management Journal*, 30: 91–109.

—— —— and Dukerich, J. M. (1985). 'The Romance of Leadership'. *Administrative Science Quarterly*, 30: 78–102.

Meyer, J., and Rowan, B. (1977). 'Institutionalized Organizations: Formal Structure as Myth and Ceremony'. *American Journal of Sociology*, 83: 340–63.

Miller, D. (1990). *The Icarus Paradox: How Exceptional Companies Bring about Their Own Downfall*. New York: HarperBusiness.

—— (1993). 'The Architecture of Simplicity'. *Academy of Management Review*, 18: 116–38.

—— (1994). 'What Happens after Success: The Perils of Excellence'. *Journal of Management Studies*, 31: 325–58.

—— and Chen, M.-J. (1994). 'Sources and Consequences of Competitive Inertia: A Study of the U.S. Airline Industry'. *Administrative Science Quarterly*, 39: 1–23.

—— —— (1996). 'The Simplicity of Competitive Repertoires: An Empirical Analysis'. *Strategic Management Journal*, 17: 419–39.

Milliken, F. J. (1990). 'Perceiving and Interpreting Environmental Change: An Examination of College Administrators' Interpretations of Changing Demographics'. *Academy of Management Journal*, 33: 42–63.

—— and Lant, T. K. (1991). 'The Effect of an Organization's Recent Performance on Strategic Persistence and Change'. *Advances in Strategic Management*, 7: 129–56.

—— —— and Batra, B. (1992). 'The Role of Managerial Learning and Interpretation in Strategic Persistence and Reorientation: An Empirical Exploration'. *Strategic Management Journal*, 13: 585–608.

Miner, A. S. (1991). 'Organizational Evolution and the Social Ecology of Jobs'. *American Sociological Review*, 56: 772–85.

—— and Haunschild, P. R. (1995). 'Population Level Learning', in L. L. Cummings and B. M. Staw (eds.), *Research in Organizational Behavior: An Annual Series of Analytical Essays and Critical Reviews* (Vol. 17). Greenwich, Conn.: JAI Press, 115–66.

Miner, A. S., Kim, J.-Y., Holzinger, I. W., and Haunschild, P. (1996). 'Fruits of Failure: Organizational Failure and Population Level Learning'. *Best Papers Proceedings, Academy of Management*, 239–43.

Mitchell, T. R. (1974). 'Expectancy Models of Job Satisfaction, Occupational Preference, and Effort: A Theoretical, Methodological, and Empirical Appraisal'. *Psychological Bulletin*, 81: 1053–77.

Nam, S. (1991). *Cultural and Managerial Attributions for Group Performance*. Unpublished doctoral dissertation, University of Oregon, Eugene.

Nelson, R. R. and Winter, S. G. (1982). *An Evolutionary Theory of Economic Change*. Cambridge, Mass.: Belknap Press.

Newell, A. and Simon, H. A. (1972). *Human Problem Solving*. Englewood Cliffs, NJ: Prentice Hall.

Nisbett, R. E. and Wilson, T. D. (1977). 'Telling More Than We Can Know: Verbal Reports on Mental Processes'. *Psychological Review*, 84: 231–59.

Nonaka, I. (1994). 'A Dynamic Theory of Organizational Knowledge Creation'. *Organization Science*, 5: 14–37.

——and Takeuchi, H. (1995). *The Knowledge-Creating Company: How Japanese Companies Create the Dynamics of Innovation*. New York: Oxford University Press.

Normann, R. (1971). 'Organizational Innovativeness: Product Variation and Reorientation'. *Administrative Science Quarterly*, 16: 203–15.

Nystrom, P. C. and Starbuck, W. H. (1984). 'Managing Beliefs in Organizations'. *Journal of Applied Behavioral Science*, 20: 277–87.

Payne, R. L. and Pugh, D. S. (1976). 'Organizational Structure and Climate', in M. D. Dunnette (ed.), *Handbook of Industrial and Organizational Psychology*. Chicago: Rand McNally, 1125–73.

Polanyi, M. (1966). *The Tacit Dimension*. London: Routledge & Kegan Paul.

Porac, J. and Rosa, J. A. (1996). 'In Praise of Managerial Narrow-Mindedness'. *Journal of Management Inquiry*, 5: 35–42.

Postman, L. and Brown, D. R. (1951). 'The Perceptual Consequences of Success and Failure'. *Journal of Abnormal and Social Psychology*, 47: 213–21.

Powell, W. W., Koput, K. W., and Smith-Doerr, L. (1996). 'Interorganizational Collaboration and the Locus of Innovation: Networks of Learning in Biotechnology'. *Administrative Science Quarterly*, 41: 116–45.

Presidential Commission (1986). *Report of the Presidential Commission on the Space Shuttle Challenger Accident*. Washington, DC: U.S. Government Printing Office.

Rotter, J. B. (1966). 'Generalized Expectancies for Internal versus External Control of Reinforcement'. *Psychological Monographs*, 80: 1–28.

Sahlin-Andersson, K. (1996). 'Imitating by Editing Success: The Construction of Organizational Fields', in B. Czarniawska-Joerges and G. Sévon, (eds.), *Translating Organizational Change*. Berlin: de Gruyter, 69–92.

Salzer, M. (1994). *Identity across Borders: A Study in the 'IKEA-World'*. Ph.D. thesis, Linköping University, Department of Management & Economics, Linköping, Sweden.

Schroder, H. M, Driver, M. J., and Streufert, S. (1967). *Human Information Processing*. New York: Holt, Rinehart, and Winston.

Singer, B. and Benassi, V. A. (1981). 'Occult Beliefs'. *American Scientist*, 69: 49–55.

Sitkin, S. B. (1992). 'Learning through Failure: The Strategy of Small Losses', in B. M. Staw and L. L. Cummings (eds.), *Research in Organizational Behavior: An Annual Series of Analytical Essays and Critical Reviews* (Vol. 14). Greenwich, Conn.: JAI Press, 231–66.

Skinner, B. F. (1974). *About Behaviorism*. New York: Knopf.

Spender, J.-C. (1989). *Industry Recipes—The Nature and Sources of Managerial Judgement*. Oxford: Basil Blackwell.

Sproull, L. S. (1981). 'Beliefs in Organizations', in P. C. Nystrom and W. H. Starbuck (eds.), *Handbook of Organizational Design*: Vol. 2. *Remodeling Organizations and Their Environments*. New York: Oxford University Press, 203–24.

Stanfill, C. and Waltz, D. (1986). 'Toward Memory-based Reasoning'. *Communications of the ACM*, 29: 1213–28.

Starbuck, W. H. (1963a). 'Level of Aspiration'. *Psychological Review*, 70: 51–60.

——(1963b). 'Level of Aspiration Theory and Economic Behavior'. *Behavioral Science*, 8: 128–36.

——(1982). 'Congealing Oil: Inventing Ideologies to Justify Acting Ideologies Out'. *Journal of Management Studies*, 19: 3–27.

——(1983). 'Organizations as Action Generators'. *American Sociological Review*, 48: 91–102.

Starbuck, W. H. (1985). 'Acting First and Thinking Later: Theory versus Reality in Strategic Change', in J. M. Pennings and Associates, *Organizational Strategy and Change: New Views on Formulating and Implementing Strategic Decisions*. San Francisco: Jossey-Bass, 336–72.

—— Greve, A., and Hedberg, B. L. T. (1978). 'Responding to Crises'. *Journal of Business Administration*, 9/2: 111–37.

—— and Hedberg, B. (1977). 'Saving an Organization from a Stagnating Environment', in H. B. Thorelli (ed.), *Strategy + Structure = Performance*. Bloomington: Indiana University Press, 249–58.

—— and Mezias, J. (1999). *The Mirrors in Our Funhouse: The Distortions in Managers' Perceptions.* Unpublished manuscript, New York University.

—— and Milliken, F. J. (1988a). 'Executives' Perceptual Filters: What They Notice and How They Make Sense', in D. C. Hambrick (ed.), *The Executive Effect: Concepts and Methods for Studying Top Managers*. Greenwich, Conn.: JAI Press, 35–65.

—— —— (1988b). 'Challenger: Changing the Odds until Something Breaks'. *Journal of Management Studies*, 25: 319–40.

Staw, B. M. (1976). 'Knee-deep in the Big Muddy: A Study of Escalating Commitment to a Chosen Course of Action'. *Organizational Behavior and Human Performance*, 16: 27–44.

—— and Fox, F. V. (1977). 'Escalation: Some Determinants of Commitment to a Previously Chosen Course of Action'. *Human Relations*, 30: 431–50.

—— and Ross, J. (1978). 'Commitment to a Policy Decision: A Multi-Theoretical Perspective'. *Administrative Science Quarterly*, 23: 40–64.

Streufert, S. (1973). 'Effects of Information Relevance on Decision Making in Complex Environments'. *Memory and Cognition*, 1: 224–8.

Tosi, H., Aldag, R., and Storey, R. (1973). 'On the Measurement of the Environment: An Assessment of the Lawrence and Lorsch Environmental Uncertainty Subscale'. *Administrative Science Quarterly*, 18: 27–36.

Tripsas, M. (1997). 'Unraveling the Process of Creative Destruction: Complementary Assets and Incumbent Survival in the Typesetter Industry'. *Strategic Management Journal*, 18 (Special Issue, Summer): 119–42.

Virany, B., Tushman, M. L., and Romanelli, E. (1992). 'Executive Succession and Organization Outcomes in Turbulent Environments: An Organization Learning Approach'. *Organization Science*, 3: 72–91.

Wagner, J. A., III and Gooding, R. Z. (1997). 'Equivocal Information and Attribution: An Investigation of Patterns of Managerial Sensemaking'. *Strategic Management Journal*, 18: 275–86.

Watzlawick, P., Weakland, J. H., and Fisch, R. (1974). *Change*. New York: Norton.

Weick, K. E. (1984). 'Small Wins: Redefining the Scale of Social Problems'. *American Psychologist*, 39/1: 40–9.

—— (1991). 'The Nontraditional Quality of Organizational Learning'. *Organization Science*, 2: 116–23.

—— (1995). *Sensemaking in Organizations*. Thousand Oaks, Calif.: Sage.

Winter, S. G. (1994). 'Organizing for Continuous Improvement: Evolutionary Theory Meets the Quality Revolution', in J. A. C. Baum and J. V. Singh (eds.), *Evolutionary Dynamics of Organizations*. New York: Oxford University Press, 90–108.

Zebrowitz, L. A. (1990). *Social Perception*. Pacific Grove, Calif.: Brooks-Cole.

15 The Role of Time in Organizational Learning

Christiana Weber and Ariane Berthoin Antal

Time is an omnipresent component of social life and generally represents one of the most fundamental concepts of the world as people experience it (Wendorff 1989). Nevertheless, a review of the literature suggests that a wide range of writers in philosophy, natural sciences, mathematics, economics, the social sciences, and history have avoided producing a clear and unambiguous definition of time. Instead, specific aspects of time have been explored (Hassard 1996), questions about time have been studied from different research angles and disciplinary perspectives (McGrath and Rotchford 1983), and metaphors have been used to describe time (Schoeller 1998). Generally speaking, time is universal (Bieri 1972), relational, and multidimensional. 'Time is a muddle of many kinds of observations' (de Goeje 1949: 37). Concepts of time develop in a constant process of interaction between humans and their environment and are therefore first and foremost mental constructs (Berger and Luckmann 1966; Bluedorn and Denhardt 1988; Cohen 1981). Depending on the worldview and culture that people share, the way time is understood varies tremendously between and within societies (Bluedorn and Denhardt 1988; Rifkin 1989). Using the term 'pluritemporalism', Nowotny (1992: 484) proposed the existence of a multitude of different modes of times within societies. Hall (1983) went so far as to say that at the microlevel of analysis, 'there are as many different kinds of time as human beings on this earth' (p. 13). Similarly, everything on this earth was considered by Nowotny (1989) to have an *Eigenzeit*, its own perception of time.

Considering the ever shorter life cycles of many things in contemporary societies, be they products, services, or management concepts, and the resulting pressure on organizations to adapt or change radically, the time required for organizational learning or unlearning processes is an increasingly important research question. For the purpose of this chapter, learning is defined as a process of knowledge creation (Nonaka and Takeuchi 1995), and unlearning is taken to mean the process of discarding obsolete and misleading knowledge (Hedberg 1981). Unlearning therefore is seen as part of the knowledge-creation process. The learner arrives at the insight that the knowledge he or she created earlier is no longer appropriate. The basic assumption in this chapter is that organizational learning processes can vary in the amount of time they require and that under certain conditions it is possible to speed up or slow down learning processes, depending on the kind of learning needed. To a certain extent, the management of an organization can influence these conditions. The question then becomes which processes or factors in the overall process of organizational learning require time and which processes or factors can reduce the amount of time needed for organizations to learn and unlearn. This chapter is an attempt to answer this fundamental question. We begin by identifying the key dimensions of time in the process of organizational learning. The first section deals with general concepts of time in the social sciences and organizations. In the second section this general approach is focused on time and learning processes—particularly in organizations—

having to do with the question how learning processes can be accelerated or slowed down. In the third section a number of dimensions of time that can be relevant for organizational learning are described. In the fourth section the interaction of these dimensions is illustrated in a case study of the *Treuhandanstalt*, the agency set up by the German government in 1990 to sell off or close down the businesses owned by the government of the former German Democratic Republic (GDR). The chapter closes with a discussion of how management can choose to accelerate or slow down organizational learning processes.

The Concept of Time in the Social Sciences and in Organizations

Strikingly little has been written about the role of time in organizational learning processes. To the extent any mention of time is made, it is usually as a general statement about the fact that learning requires time (Dierkes 1990, 1994; Garvin 1993). Maier, Prange, and Rosenstiel (Ch. 1 in this volume) point out that knowledge about the learning process, particularly the how of learning, facilitates corrections that un-complicate or shorten learning time. In an analysis of behavioral learning, Starbuck and Hedberg (Ch. 14 in this volume) explain that the frequency of reinforcement affects the speed of learning and the retention of learned behaviors. To compensate for the dearth of published insights into the role of time in organizational learning, the search has to be expanded to include social sciences in general, where numerous treatises on time have been published (e.g. Bergmann 1983; Bleicher 1985; Bluedorn and Denhardt 1988; Child and Kieser 1981; Clark 1985; Gherardi and Strati 1988; McGrath and Rotchford 1983; Moore 1963*a*, *b*; Perich 1992; Zerubavel 1982). Nevertheless, even they offer few comprehensive treatments of time in organizations.

A key distinction in conceptualizations of time is that between an 'objective' view, which corresponds closely to external units (e.g. the minutes, days, weeks, etc., of chronological time) as measured by such instruments as clocks and calendars, and a 'subjective' view, in which time is attributed 'a specific and largely individual dimension resulting from the values held by the actors, from the significance ascribed to a situation, from limiting factors, from attendant circumstances, and so forth' (Perich 1992: 245). To characterize these two different conceptualizations, Clark (1985) used the terms 'even time' (p. 41), which is characterized by divisibility into equalized, cumulating units, and 'event time' (p. 41), which refers to the meaningful events that frame life. Gherardi and Strati (1988) explained that time is very much a relative concept. According to Hauser (1955), objective time is largely standardized and separate from individual experiences; it is uniform, randomly divisible, mathematically and numerically expressible, linear, and irreversible. By contrast, subjective time is not randomly divisible, and its component parts have different meanings (Heath 1956; McGrath 1990). Thus, units of time that appear to be completely identical from a quantitative and formal (i.e. 'objective') perspective can have totally diverging meaning and experiential content when seen from a qualitative and human (i.e. 'subjective') perspective. 'What goes into an hour . . . differs greatly from hour to hour, from place to place, from person to person, from age to age, from day to night, from weekday to weekend, and across all of the other dimensions of human variation and experience' (McGrath and Rotchford 1983: 59).

The way time is experienced reflects subjective senses of time (Cohen 1981). The 'self' represents the frame of reference, which reflects the temporal elements of the experience, particularly the assessment of duration. Situational factors (e.g. mood, alertness, motivation, and physical condition) and constitutive factors (e.g. level of experience and age) give the feeling that periods of time can pass at different speeds. Every individual's subjective sense of the duration of time is subject to constant variations. Accordingly, periods of time are experienced along a continuum from calm to frenzy, from fullness to emptiness. Time tends to appear to pass more rapidly when it is 'filled' with many activities or stimuli (Pöppel 1983). Organizations are social systems, and they are embedded in a multifaceted environment. Therefore, the concept of organizational time is a subset of social time (Hassard 1996). The way time is seen and worked with in an organization is something that the organization has learned and developed over time (Clark 1982). It is therefore one of the elements that constitutes the uniqueness of an organization (Frost, Moore, Louis, Lundberg, and Martin 1991; Schein 1991). Every organization, like every society, develops its own, and hence subjective, ideas about time. Organizational time cannot be isolated as an entity, for it is embedded in multiple parallel and superordinate time structures such as 'economic time', 'societal time', and 'world time' (Perich 1992: 252). Organizational time 'is a plurality of internal and particular times within each organization' (Gherardi and Strati 1988: 149).

Operating in ever more dynamic environments, organizations are coming under increasing time pressure because the environment usually accords them only limited reaction time. The latitude they have to dispose over their own time is shrinking. Organizations have to respond quickly and flexibly in order to meet the deadlines (Perich 1992: 260; Weber 1996).

Learning Processes and Time

A key question is how long organizational learning processes take and whether the duration can be externally influenced. What is the time frame for the process of knowledge creation described by Nonaka and Takeuchi (1995)—socialization, externalization, combination, and internationalization—and how long does it take to store what has been learned and make it available to all members of the organization? Despite the variability in the

time required for social activities and processes, many of them are accorded the amount of time that is considered appropriate (Hassard 1996; Moore 1963a; Perich 1992). This fact once more underscores the subjective aspect of time. In terms of organizational learning, it means that individuals entering into a learning process in an organization are likely to have certain expectations about the length of time the learning process will take, creating a self-fulfilling prophecy that might influence the speed of the learning process. However, not much has been written about which learning processes and which elements thereof require more or less time under what conditions. The scant literature that does exist on these questions refers to individual or group learning (Futoran, Kelly, and McGrath 1989; Gersick 1984; McGrath 1990). Moreover, the transferability of these findings to organizational learning has not yet been studied.

When learners draw incorrect conclusions from the consequences of their behavior and when they are slow or unable to perceive changes in their environment, learning processes take longer than they otherwise might. Learning is also slowed when it occurs via negative feedback, for such communication only tells learners which behavior does not work, not which behavior would be more appropriate (Gagliardi 1986). In addition, behavior associated with a negative experience of fear or pain has a further disadvantage for learning because such behavior is perpetuated only by fear of reexperiencing the pain or negative response. It slows down learning because the learners do not test whether the sanction they fear will or might occur under changed environmental conditions (Schein 1993).

Learning processes that require practice take more time than those that do not require practice, for the former must be repeated until they are done correctly (Wiegand 1996). Starbuck and Hedberg (Ch. 14 in this volume) explain that learning is slow when reinforcements in a learning process occur randomly. Socialization, the process of learning to become a member of any kind of community, generally takes time, for it is necessary for different people to come together and exchange, compare, and adjust their views of reality. It is only then that 'an individual acquires the social knowledge and skills necessary to assume an organizational role' (Van Maanen and Schein 1979: 211). Ironically, repeated success can slow down a learning process by reinforcing current behavior and diverting attention from the environment and from environmental changes that might require new behavior (Levitt and March 1988; Nevis, DiBella, and Gould 1995; Sitkin 1992).

Learning processes are accelerated when learners interpret the consequences of their actions correctly and perceive changes in their environment quickly (Wiegand 1996). This acceleration is particularly pronounced when past behavior has always been positively responded to and hence reinforced. In such cases learners immediately notice when the positive reinforcement is missing, and they adjust their behavior quickly to the new conditions (Schein 1993). Starbuck and Hedberg (Ch. 14 in this volume) explain that 'reinforcement after every repetition of a specific behavior produces fast learning'.

Learners can accelerate their discovery and acquisition of 'correct' behavior if they themselves need not take the time required for trial-and-error learning processes but can benefit from the learning of others. This possibility arises, for example, with learning by observing (Bandura 1976, 1986). Though negative emotional experiences can slow down learning processes, it is also true that learning is accelerated if the behavior is generated by negative emotional experiences or through sanctions, for no repetition is usually needed for such processes (Schein 1993). In other words, the context in which those negative emotional experiences are made is what determines whether learning is accelerated or slowed down. In general one could state that in the short run those negative emotional experiences accelerate the process of learning and slow it down in the long run.

Socialization can be speeded up when the quality and quantity of social interactions are high, that is, when a relatively large number of different people come together and compare and contrast their various perspectives within a given period of time. 'When people live or work in close proximity to one another, they can communicate frequently on a face-to-face basis about how they view their world and how they cope with it' (Homans 1950: 126). The socialization of the community's new members is accelerated when the process takes place in such a way that they receive consistent information and signals from the organization. If the organizational code corresponds closely to what the new members learned in their primary socialization process, they will learn it more quickly than they otherwise would.

Moderate failure can speed up learning because it draws attention to potential problems (Sitkin 1992). It stimulates learners to observe their environment, for alternative behaviors are then experimented with (Levitt and March 1988).

Dimensions of Time in Organizational Learning Processes

In this section six key dimensions of time that affect the temporal dimension of organizational learning processes are explored: (a) the organization's prevailing time perspective and orientation to time, (b) the time pressure that is either generated internally by the organization or imposed upon it by external forces, (c) the simultaneity of events and the attendant time scarcity and restrictions on an organization's autonomy in its use of time, (d) the synchronization of responses to multiple events and the resulting windows of opportunity for an organization, (e) the cyclical nature of time in learning and organizations, and (f) history as an aspect of time and organizational learning. These six dimensions subsume most of the aspects relating to the role of time in organizational learning.

Time Perspective and Orientation to Time

The time perspective of an organization defines the temporal boundaries that its main actors apply to their decision-making and actions in the context of the reality they perceive. This time perspective establishes the framework for organizational thinking and action (Bleicher 1985; Gherardi and Strati 1988). The time perspective is thereby a clear expression of the subjective rationality of organizational time (Perich 1992). An event is seen differently, depending on the time perspective from which it is considered. This assessment, in turn, implies different ideas about what needs to be done. The time perspective of an organization therefore functions as a behavioral filter (Bleicher 1985; Gherardi and Strati 1988).

Within an organization different actors, groups, or divisions can hold very different time perspectives. Organizations or groups need a consensus on the appropriate understanding of time for a given situation (Schein 1995). Bleicher (1985) therefore recommended that a generally accepted 'organization time' (p. 102) be established to guide behavior in order to ensure that the different time perspectives are harmonized and related to one another. According to him, 'the time orientation that determines the course of organizational development is that of the top management team' (Bleicher 1985: 66; my translation). It shapes the organizational time, enters into the functional symbols of organizational culture, guides strategic decision-making processes, and thereby influences organizational change and learning processes.

What matters is the dominant orientation to time within a time perspective. Is an organization more oriented to the future, the past, or the present? The typology established by Miles and Snow (1978) revealed that organizations oriented to the future tend to think ahead, anticipate future changes, and act accordingly. They are likely to be more open to learning than are organizations oriented to the past. Thus, one can say that organizational learning processes would take place more rapidly in future-oriented organizations than in organizations that are oriented to the past, heavily conscious of tradition, and reluctant to change.

Time Pressure

Time pressure can be built up in an organization, usually top-down, although bottom-up is also possible. Time pressure can also be applied from diverse external sources, such as customers, political actors, competitors, or grassroots initiatives. However, it has an impact on behavior only if it is also perceived by members of the organization. The external pressure experienced by members of an organization to perform, meet expectations, or take action for example, can lead to time pressure to change a given situation. The visibility of an organization plays a significant role in this process. The more visible an organization and its behavior are in the organization's environment, the greater and more critical the attention they are likely to receive from the environment, and the more the organization will feel pressure to respond (Weber 1996).

Time pressure can both accelerate and slow down learning processes. Learning is accelerated when time pressure is experienced as motivating or threatening. If the sense of threat becomes excessive, however, learning can be slowed or made impossible altogether. Gersick (1984, 1988) built on this observation by differentiating temporal patterns of group performance within various degrees of time pressure. As summarized by McGrath (1990) 'the temporal patterning of group performance [which includes learning processes] is relative to the task and to the time constraints under which the group is operating. In other words, there are temporal patterns in how groups go about their work, but those temporal patterns are not fixed in time' (p. 26). That is to say, group performance, too, can be speeded up or slowed down.

Kelly and McGrath (1985) found that groups working under a tight deadline work faster than groups that have long lead times or no specific deadline. But the two researchers also reported that time pressure often causes groups to produce a product of inferior quality. By contrast, Peters, O'Connor, Pooyan, and Quick (1984) found that perceived time pressure not only leads to an increased rate of work but to an increased level of performance as well. These findings are therefore inconclusive, and the research to date has been conducted only on individuals and groups, so their transferability to organizations remains unclear.

Simultaneity

Simultaneity refers to the parallel occurrence of events, which often leads to a scarcity of time for responding to these events and to the concomitant danger that an organization will lose its ability to control the time frame of its own activities in light of time pressures from the environment. The quantity and diversity of knowledge existing in an organization, the numerous potential learning options, and the limited (albeit variable) capacity of individuals to assimilate and process information restrict the number of learning processes that can occur simultaneously in an organization. In other words, the numerous and often complex learning options within an organization put limits on the pace of its learning.

An organization will rarely, if ever, have enough resources to respond appropriately to all available learning options. The result is time scarcity, which can call into question an organization's ability to control the time frames of its own activities. According to Perich (1992), an organization totally determined by its environment would completely lose that ability. An organization's capacity for selective response and self-determination is a precondition for successful learning processes because once learners have perceived and analyzed a situation, they want to choose an appropriate course of action.

Synchronization and Windows of Opportunity

Synchronization refers to the act of coordinating events, that is, of recognizing when something should or must be done (Corazza 1985) and then doing it. A significant factor in synchronization is the constellation of events, that is, the events or sequence of activities that come together at a given point in time or within a defined time frame (Perich 1992). These specific constellations establish the basis for attempts to coordinate one's own action with that of others.

Within the multilayered and ever changing flow of events, it is crucial for organizations to 'seek out and aim for the constellation of events conducive to achieving their goals and then to "hook into" the stream of events at the "right time"' (Perich 1992: 274). Building on the Greek concept of *kairos*, of historical, or favorable, moment, modern management theory recognizes the existence of specific points in time or limited periods during which an organization can successfully initiate action. Such terms as 'strategic windows' (Abell 1978) or 'windows of opportunity' (p. 21) refer to optimal moments for action. The key difficulty is that such windows are usually easier to identify after they have shut than when they are open.

Windows of opportunity are relevant for organizational learning because there are times during which an organization is particularly open to learning and therefore able to learn faster. In this context, windows of opportunity are potential learning situations that can occur both inside an organization (say, through an exchange or rotation of employees, the introduction of new communication technologies, or a change of organizational structure) and through interactions with the organization's environment (e.g. the recruitment of new employees in order to acquire new knowledge, the observation of the environment, or the launch of a new product). If an organization recognizes its windows of opportunity and has the resources needed to respond to them, it can learn a great deal in a short time. Unsuccessful synchronization can mean that an organization has to wait for the next favorable constellation. This delay would slow the learning process down, a hypothesis supported by Gersick's (1988) findings that a group is more likely to adapt to a changing environment during a period of transition than during a period of stability, for transition is a powerful opportunity for change and, particularly, a unique time that should be used well.

Learning Cycles and Life Cycles

The concept of cycles has a long tradition in learning theories (see Kolb 1984). Describing cognitive learning cycles, Lewin (1947, cited by Kim 1993), for example, stated: 'A person continually cycles through a process of having a concrete experience, making observations and reflections on that experience, forming abstract concepts and generalizations based on those reflections, and testing those ideas in a new situation, which leads to another concrete experience' (p. 38). The literature contains many variations on this basic idea of a learning cycle. Most of them involve individual learning: Argyris and Schön (1978) spoke of a discovery–invention–production–generalization cycle; Kofman (1992, as adapted in Kim 1993: 39), of an observe–assess–design–implement (OADI) cycle; Kolb (1984), of a concrete experience–reflective observation-abstract conceptualization–active experimentation cycle; and Schein (1985), of an observation–emotional reaction–judgment–intervention cycle. Other researchers, too, have tried to develop organizational learning models (see Kim 1993). Socialization processes are particularly interesting in this context of time and learning cycles because new members have to learn whole ranges of time patterns and rhythms when they enter an organization. Individuals start learning these time disciplines early through membership of different kinds of formal organizations such as the family and the school. Eventually they are also learned at the workplace (Hassard 1996; Elias 1984).

The regular recurrence of individual cycles provides the mooring for temporal patterns of events and activities and thereby contributes significantly to a sense of security among the actors in the system. It is a prerequisite for the routinization of social processes. This routinization through repetition is precisely what harbors both danger and the potential for success in the process of organizational learning. The frequent repetition of a behavior generally leads to the acceleration and increased accuracy of the behavior's execution. The organization thereby develops standard operating procedures and habits. They work well, however, only as long as the organizational conditions under which the behavior is produced remain unchanged. When the conditions change, the cycles anchored in the organizational culture slow down the learning process. The organization is then forced to unlearn and learn as quickly as possible. Hedberg (1981) explains that 'it seems as if slow unlearning is a crucial weakness of many organizations' (p. 3).

The life cycle of an organization as a whole seems to be important, too. It is widely assumed that organizations go through an irreversible, gradual cycle analogous to the basic phases of human biological development: birth, growth, maturity, degeneration, and death (Adizes 1979; Gray and Ariss 1985; Kimberly and Miles 1980; Miller and Friesen 1983, 1984; Mintzberg 1984; Quinn and Cameron 1983). 'Time provides the metaphor for the life of the organizations and its stages of development (birth, maturity, decline)' (Gherardi and Strati 1988: 151). Even if one does not concur with this narrow idea of a predetermined, endogenous developmental logic of organizations, certain phases related to their age and size are discernible. In contrast to biological life cycles, however, the development process of organizations does not have one fixed and predetermined starting point. Nor does it always go through the whole range of possible stages. Also, the duration of each stage of this process seems to be determined more by the length of the process on the whole (Gersick 1988) than by its own inherent time limit. Because there are several possible starting points for organizational development and because some stages might be skipped, the process of change and organizational learning is flexible and can be accelerated.

In general, the time likely to be required for an organization's learning processes thus depends on both age and size and hence on the life phase of an organization, not to mention many other factors pointed out by Berthoin Antal, Dierkes, and Marz (1999), such as organizational structures, strategies, cultures, management styles, information and communication systems, and external constellations. It seems that it is easier for younger and smaller organizations to learn and unlearn than it is for older and larger ones because the development of routines and standard operating procedures becomes ever more deeply embedded over time. In younger organizations they are less deeply engrained than in older ones (Starbuck and Hedberg, Ch. 14 in this volume; Hassard 1996).

History

The history of an organization, what happened in its past, can be used to orient present and future actions. Continuity is ensured by referring to the past and the learning experiences it contains. History has an identity-building effect. But which identity emerges? Remembering, the process of drawing on past events for the present, is subject to selective processes and interpretation (Koselleck 1979). Different organizational members can interpret shared experiences differently and can therefore draw different conclusions from it for their future behavior. In addition, every organization has its own history, which refers to the birth and continued development of the organization. Organizational time, then, is 'the interpretative dimension of history employed by organizational actors to give a social structure to reality' (Gherardi and Strati 1988: 152).

The specific history of an organization, which is shaped by many organizational learning processes, is manifested in diverse forms of memory in an organization (Levitt and March 1988; March 1991; Walsh and Ungson 1991). Organizational culture, which has been defined as 'a pattern of basic assumptions—invented, discovered, or developed by a given group as it learns to cope with its problems of external adaptation and internal integration—that has worked well enough to be considered valid and,

therefore, to be taught to new members as the correct way to perceive, think, and feel in relation to those problems' (Schein 1991: 9), is considered to be one of the prime storage mediums of organizational learning. It plays a key role in the further development of the organization. The reason is that organizational culture has not only shaped the organization in the past, it also has a significant influence on organizational perception (Berthoin Antal, Dierkes, and Hähner 1997) and on future-oriented behavior and decision-making (Frost, Moore, Louis, Lundberg, and Martin 1985; Kilman, Saxton, and Serpa 1985; Martin 1992; Schein 1985). Elements of the organizational culture, such as an organization's rules, procedures, conventions, strategies, technologies, structure of beliefs, codes, paradigms, time perspective, and time orientation, are therefore not only the outcome of past organizational learning but also the basis for future organizational learning (Cook and Yanow 1993; Fiol and Lyles 1985; Normann 1985).

The influence of history on the organization can be positive as well as dysfunctional (Schein 1994). The identity-forming, accumulated, learned, and stored knowledge is its source of potential competitive success. But if that knowledge becomes obsolete, it can lead to organizational inertia, for organizations tend to conserve what exists and to act automatically according to standard operating procedures. As a 'legacy of a firm's history' (Child and Smith 1987: 568), accumulated knowledge can thereby slow processes of organizational learning (Starbuck and Hedberg, Ch. 14 in this volume; Schein 1985; Weber 1996), especially when the changes to be made require radical deviations from the functional knowledge that has been stored in the past.

In summary, although the various dimensions of time have been discussed separately in this section, it is clear that they are closely related to one another, that they form a kind of web or net because an organization's perspective on and orientation to time result largely from past, shared history. They are anchored in the organization through learning processes and learning cycles. The time perspective, as much as the organization's shared history in the form of organizational culture, also influences an organization's ability to recognize windows of opportunity, for it defines the segments of reality that are perceived. The time scarcity and time pressure that arise from simultaneity usually condition each other. The need to do several things at once leads to time scarcity and hence usually to time pressure if the problem of time scarcity cannot be efficiently solved in some other way. As a result, time pressure eventually makes it necessary to do even more things at the same time. The simultaneity of events and tasks also usually results in the need to synchronize responses in order to reduce temporal uncertainty as much as possible and to obtain the greatest possible certainty for planning and predicting. Lastly, the position of an organization in its life cycle says something about the amount of history that the members have shared. It also implies the extent and depth of routinization and bureaucratization achieved in the organization, two factors that influence the organizations's potential learning speed. The way these different dimensions of time interact to influence organizational learning are illustrated in the following case study.

The Case of the Treuhandanstalt

On 1 July 1990, about eight months after the fall of the Berlin Wall, the German government established the Treuhandanstalt (THA) to transform East Germany's state-owned holdings as rapidly as possible into market-oriented structures—or liquidate them. From the outset, the agency's existence was limited to four and a half years. This stipulation makes the THA a particularly interesting case for study of the relation between time and organizational learning, for the THA had to establish itself, the instruments it needed to complete its complex task, and its relation to its social and economic environment in very little time. No comparable organization or charter had ever existed to which the THA could look to see

how to function effectively. Moreover, the THA began its task in 1990 at a time of deepening crisis in the East German economy, an unprecedented situation unknown in recent economic history. In short, the learning challenge facing the THA was enormous.

Time Perspective

From the start, time played a key role in the THA and the minds of its members (Weber 1996). The prevailing time perspective in the organization was clearly determined by its successive presidents, both of whom were widely viewed as charismatic, dominant, action-oriented individuals with their eyes clearly on the future. Time pressure stemming from the economic exigencies that the THA had to address, together with the strict deadline for completion of its work, meant that the organization's mottoes were 'when in doubt, act quickly rather than well' and 'better rough and rapid than detailed and slow'. All the members of the organization knew these mottoes and worked accordingly, giving the THA enormous dynamism and shaping its emerging organizational culture. The spirit of these mottoes implied that mistakes could be made in the learning process, an attitude that was formulated explicitly by the presidents in both internal and external communication. They, too, lived by them.

Not only was the perceived external pressure on the THA extremely high, the THA was also confronted by numerous and varied problems and expectations from different quarters (Albach 1995). The organization therefore soon went through an enormous number of formative critical events, each of which can be said to have represented a potential learning experience. Among the most dramatic were the assassination of the first THA president in April 1991 and the failure of major privatization processes, such as Interflug (the erstwhile airline of the GDR) and Interhotel (the former GDR's most prestigious hotel chain). These events generated numerous shared learning experiences, which significantly accelerated the overall organizational learning process. The failure of some particularly important privatization negotiations led to vast improvements in subsequent privatization processes, such as the introduction of sanctions in cases where commitments to jobs or investments were broken.

Time Pressure

Generally, time pressure was considered by the employees of the THA as motivating and was therefore beneficial to an accelerated learning process. The experience in the THA clearly confirms Gersick's (1988) findings that temporal patterns concerning how groups go about their work are not fixed in time. At an organizational level the experience in the THA also confirmed the finding reported by Kelly and McGrath (1985) for groups, namely, that groups that have been assigned a tight deadline for a production task work faster than groups that have been given more time. Contrary to Kelly and McGrath's thinking, however, time pressure both in and on the THA did not result in the elimination of much of the organization's communication activity, nor did it lower the level of well-being and member support inside the organization. Instead, time pressure showed that communication activity was particularly high under the given circumstances and that an organizational culture developed within a very short time (Weber 1996). It is not possible to assess the impact of time pressure on the quality of work done in the THA, for there is no way to compare it to work that would have been achieved under less severe time constraints.

Windows of Opportunity

Given the enormous scale of changes in conditions during the unification of Germany, windows of opportunity played a significant role in the organizational learning process of the THA. The very constellation that led to the fall of the Berlin Wall can be seen as a unique window of opportunity that made the creation of the THA

possible. It opened learning possibilities for all organizations and institutions in Germany that were involved in the process of unification. In the course of the THA's privatization efforts, there was at least one window of opportunity for each of the East German companies that could be privatized. (About one-third of all East German companies were found to be unsalvageable from the outset.) Particularly during the first three years of the THA's operations, these windows of opportunity were almost always recognized and it was possible to take advantage of them thanks to the organization's great flexibility, which worked in favor of organizational learning. In some cases, however—as in the case of Interflug—time pressure caused bottlenecks in the THA, impasses that made it impossible to use the windows of opportunity and thereby prevented learning experiences. The process of organizational learning was thus sometimes delayed.

Simultaneity, Time Scarcity, and Control over Time Frames

Both time pressure and the simultaneous emergence of windows of opportunity meant that time scarcity became one of the THA's biggest problems. The primary response to this problem was an extreme acceleration of action and decision-making. For example, formal approval processes were dispensed with, and decision-making responsibilities were delegated within the organization, even at the risk of making mistakes. This approach permitted the THA to generate a large number of shared learning experiences in a very short period. The THA managed to sustain autonomous control over its action and the time frames thereof, particularly during the first two phases of its existence, because the presidents recognized early that the organization's success would hinge largely on freedom of movement in both respects.

Cycles

The development of standard operating procedures (SOPs) via the repetition of learning cycles occurred automatically, but it was not one of the primary reasons for rapid learning in the THA. The conditions in the political and economic environment changed too rapidly for the establishment of SOPs to seem a priority. In addition, the time horizon within which the THA was operating meant that dedicating scarce time to this process did not appear appropriate.

In 1990 a more significant point was that the THA had only just begun its brief and compressed life cycle as an organization that was specifically established for the transformation process. According to Weber (1996), the life cycle of the THA is divisible into three phases: (a) a founding, pioneer phase (1 July 1990 to the assassination of the THA's first president in spring 1991); (b) an implementation phase (spring 1991 through December 1992); and (c) a maturity phase, in which the members' accumulated experience was applied and closure of the organization was initiated (January 1993 through 31 December 1994).

The THA started off as a small, relatively agile, flexible organization in which the employees were highly motivated and open to learning. These conditions were ideal for rapid organizational learning. The East German employees, partly out of enormous fear for their jobs, were particularly willing to unlearn old ways and learn new ones (Rost 1994; Weber 1996).

History

Initially, the THA could draw neither on knowledge it had already acquired nor on standard operating procedures to fulfill its mission, for the organization's task was greater than anything any member of the organization had ever had experience with. On the one hand, this uniqueness made the task more difficult because almost all learning proceeded by trial-and-error in the early phase. Still, the employees were able to learn a great deal by observing their superiors, with whom they shared the THA's scant office space, an arrangement that accelerated organizational learning. On the

other hand, the absence of shared experience meant that the organization did not suffer from the burden of obsolete knowledge, entrenched structures, or other learning obstacles. As a result, unlearning was not necessary in the beginning; there was no shared knowledge that needed to be unlearned. As the employees gained experience in privatization, restructuring, and closing down companies, they developed routine and confidence. The knowledge that was acquired and tested in practice during the short history of the THA was stored in the organization's culture, handbooks, data banks, rules, and standard operating procedures and was passed on to new members of the organization.

In summary, the example of the THA illustrates how the various dimensions of time interact in organizational learning processes. Different constellations in each of the phases of the THA can be said to have different consequences for learning.

Phase 1

- No shared time perspective existed because the perceptions of East and West Germans differed significantly, but the THA's president ensured that the institution's time orientation was clearly focused on the future.
- There was a lack of shared history.
- Unlearning was not an issue.
- Time was scarce, but the organization had the ability to control its own activities and the time frames in which they took place.
- The organization initially had a very small staff. The small number of staff members, combined with time scarcity led to a rigorous delegation of responsibility. The small staff grew rapidly from 100 to 2,000 employees within the first nine months.
- A great amount of new knowledge was brought into the organization from outside.
- There were enormous external expectations, most of them resulting in time pressure.
- There was a very large number of windows of opportunity for individual decisions, a very

good seller's market, and keen perception of and great response to these windows.

Phase 2

- Some shared history existed.
- The size of the organization increased from 2,000 to 4,000 employees, growth that brought large amounts of new knowledge into the organization.
- The socialization of new employees proceeded more slowly than in phase 1 because the organization continued to grow rapidly. The knowledge that the employees had acquired and found useful could no longer be diffused as rapidly throughout the organization as had been the case at the outset.
- A future-oriented time perspective came to be more widely shared within the organization, than had been the case in phase 1, but it was marked increasingly by the awareness that the THA's operations would be ending.
- External pressure increased mainly because of the first significant mistakes made by the THA and because of rising unemployment in Germany. Time pressure persisted.
- Time scarcity developed, but the THA maintained its ability to control its own activities and the time frames in which they took place.
- Windows of opportunity kept opening and continued to be perceived at a high rate.
- Toward the end of this phase, the first signs of bureaucratization appeared: an increased number of structural layers and hierarchies and a formalization of processes.

Phase 3

- The history of the institution continued to build up. The staff shared more and more experiences, mostly positive ones. The organization continued to employ a large staff. Later in this phase, however, the first cutbacks in personnel occurred. Anxiety about unemployment was especially apparent among East German staff members.
- Bureaucratization increased; the speed of decision-making and learning slowed down.

- Time orientation remained forward-looking, but the time horizon of East German employees differed greatly from that of West German employees. The East Germans were worried about the approaching end of the THA's activities.
- The THA was subject to time scarcity and lost some of its ability to control its own activities and their time frames because the influence of Germany's federal government and *Länder* increased.
- Windows of opportunity declined significantly in number mainly because a buyer's market had developed. In other words, the THA could no longer choose its potential investors but rather had to attract them. This change in the market was due to the deteriorating economic situation in western Germany and to the realization by potential investors that many of the companies for sale in eastern Germany were in dismal condition and had lost contact with their markets (Tiedge 1998).
- External pressure and time pressure remained high, particularly as the THA's closure date of 31 December 1994 approached.

Breaking down the life cycle of the THA into phases shows that the constellation of factors had a significant impact on the speed of learning in the organization. It appears that the THA learned extremely fast during its first two and one-half years in comparison to the third phase and to the pace considered realistic in the literature on organizational learning. Neither the time pressure that existed throughout the organization's existence nor time scarcity was able by itself to sustain these rapid learning processes. Equally interesting is that it was apparently unnecessary for the organization to have a shared history as a key ingredient to a common culture in order to learn quickly. Of greater importance were the number of windows of opportunity; the flat hierarchies; the rapid decision-making processes; a rigorous delegation of responsibility, including decision-making; and the other factors characterizing the early phase of the THA's organizational life cycle.

Management's Influence on Time in Organizational Learning

The comparison between the THA case and the cases as well as the theoretical approaches reported in the literature on the role of time in organizational learning shows that the time needed for organizational learning processes can vary significantly. In this section we explore how management can influence the speed of learning. Depending on the organization and its learning needs, management has some influence over how to accelerate or slow down the learning process. Both options may be appropriate, according to the situation. Rapid learning is generally seen to be desirable, but March's (1991) warning should be heeded:

Slow learning on the part of individuals maintains diversity longer, thereby providing the exploration that allows the knowledge found in the organization code to improve . . . . The fact that fast individual learning from the code tends to have a favorable first-order effect on individual knowledge but an adverse effect on improvement in organizational knowledge and thereby on long-term individual improvement suggests that there might be some advantage to having a mix of fast and slow learners in an organization. (p. 76)

Building on this idea, we believe that it is useful not only to have a mix of fast and slow learners in an organization but also to include, as far as possible, fast and slow learning processes. There are many situations in which it is appropriate and helpful to accelerate the learning processes in an organization. Yet there are also constellations under which it appears advisable to consciously slow down certain selected learning processes and to really take enough time for them.

By slowing a learning process down, it is possible to improve its quality. Deceleration could therefore have been helpful to the THA. In the spirit of 'less is more', it can also be better to focus on the quality rather than the quantity of learning processes so that fewer, but well conceived, learning processes are completed instead of initiating many processes and cycles of learning that cannot be completed for lack of time or other resources. This approach could help avoid superficial and superstitious learning, which 'occurs when the subjective experience of learning is compelling, but the connections between actions and outcomes are misspecified' (Levitt and March 1988: 325).

Rapid development of organizations can also be disadvantageous to their processes of socialization. March (1991) pointed out that 'a major threat to the effectiveness of such learning is the possibility that individuals will adjust to an organizational code before the code can learn from them. Relatively slow socialization of new organizational members and moderate turnover sustain variability in individual beliefs, thereby improving organizational and average individual knowledge in the long run' (p. 85). Carley (1992) explained that 'a crucial irony in a fast changing world, then, is that slow individual learners accelerate organizational learning' (p. 27).

How can and should management intervene to accelerate or slow down learning processes? Given the realities of organizational life, it seems to be more often necessary to accelerate learning than to slow it down. Because social learning, by eliminating the need for individual trial-and-error processes (Bandura 1977), is, by definition, a form of rapid learning, it is advisable for management to create the necessary conditions for learning to occur from models.

Trial-and-error learning is by nature a slower learning process (Weber 1996; Wiegand 1996; and see above) than social learning. It can only be productive when errors are not treated as taboo in an organization but instead, as in the case of the THA, are considered a part of learning and are responded to constructively. Management can greatly help accelerate learning by giving more than mere lip service to the notion of accepting mistakes as a necessary part of learning. Acceptance of mistakes must be integrated into organizational practice, say, by means of remuneration and incentive systems and internal communication.

A common way to accelerate learning processes is for management to create time pressure. To a certain degree, this approach can be effective, as shown by the case of the THA. However, after a certain point time pressure has a counterproductive effect on people and can lead to paralysis, fear, or aggression. The exact point at which the negative rather than the positive effect of time pressure is reached depends on the individual personality, the culture of an organization, or both. McGrath and Rotchford (1983) suggested that it is possible to delay the point at which a person feels overly stressed or overloaded by too many stimuli in a certain period of time. To accelerate learning, one 'gradually increases the stimulus rate at a rate that lets adaptation wash out the impact of the changes' (p. 94). This approach seems to be applicable as a management technique not only in the individual case but also in an organization.

The time scarcity that often results from time pressure forces an organization to use time economically and rationally. There are different ways to achieve this end. Time can be used more intensively, say, by speeding up decision-making and action (Perich 1992), a change that, in turn, speeds up organizational learning processes. Leberl (1988) referred to this approach as a reduction of 'throughput-time' (p. 131) in an organization. It clearly corresponds to the strategy that was pursued by the THA. McGrath and Rotchford (1983) suggested denying the culture's one-thing-at-a-time conception of time and urged management to 'seek ways to do more than one thing in at least some segments of time' (p. 96)—increasing the potential organizational learning opportunities.

Another management approach is to assign priorities to actions and responses. This practice is possible when the potential learning situations do not involve extremely pressing problems or crises, which would result in the external imposition of priorities. The fact that an organization faces multiple learning options and that it requires clear priorities forces management to select learning processes consciously. If these two variants do not cover all alternatives, then time scarcity can preclude the use of learning options and block opportu-

nities to gain experience. Such obstacles slow the organizational learning process.

A further way to deal with time scarcity is through planning. Decisions in the planning process can be 'regarded as representing the moment of present time that ensures coherence and continuity between past and future' (Gherardi and Strati 1988: 151). Management's primary roles in planning are anticipating and preparing (Albach 1978; Kreikebaum 1991; Perich 1992; Staehle 1991). These two roles imply two kinds of errors: incorrect expectations and inadequate preparation. Anticipation can be improved by a well-known, but rarely well-applied, technique: focused and systematic environmental scanning and the creation of a 'catalogue of consequences' (Kreikebaum 1991: 94). An organization does not have to be completely surprised by all future developments; presumably, some of them can be anticipated through such techniques as scenario planning (Geschka and Hammer 1990; see also Galer and van der Heijden, Ch. 38 in this volume). Possible future developments are extrapolated and thereby anticipated on the basis of present conditions, and potential organizational responses are worked out. The procedure allows the organization to prepare the learning process for this situation. In other words, it enables the organization to begin learning before enormous time pressure builds up. The organization thereby gains the chance to—

(1) step through windows of opportunity in time and respond to them appropriately;
(2) reduce its time pressure by preparing a plan by which to deal with changed circumstances;
(3) maintain the autonomy of action needed for its learning processes;
(4) circumvent sudden bottlenecks in resources and thereby maintain an ability to use the greatest possible number of learning opportunities; and
(5) avoid inappropriate and poorly conceived responses.

By using learning cycles, management can exert considerable influence on the speed of learning. It can consciously create and pursue cycles (i.e. routines) by means of multiple repetitions in order to achieve the effect of learning curves and thereby build or alter standard operating procedures. Management can and should identify and root out obsolete cycles and routines. In so doing, management can prompt unlearning.

Another key way in which management can influence the speed of learning in the organization is to take into account the different time horizon(s) within which management and other members think, choose, decide, and behave. The same event has several meanings when perceived at various levels and in various subcultures. A single event can lead to very different decisions and different learning outcomes. Management therefore should attempt to harmonize the multitude of time perspectives in an organization and must attempt to establish a dominant time perspective to guide decisions and actions.

In summary, if the various dimensions of time and their impact on organizational learning processes are taken into consideration by management, they can help an organization—

(1) realistically assess the amount of time needed for desired organizational learning processes under given conditions;

(2) reduce frustrations or exaggerated expectations; and

(3) create the conditions necessary for shaping the processes of organizational learning and anticipating the time they require.

This review of the literature relating to the role of time in organizational learning reveals that there is a significant need for both theoretical work and empirical research in the area. One particularly important aspect that remains to be explored is the degree to which the results and insights of available research on time in individual and group learning can be transferred to organizational learning. Equally critical is the need for comparative studies on time and learning in organizations, for such work would help determine the extent of variance in the speed of organizational learning.

References

Abell, D. F. (1978). 'Strategic Windows'. *Journal of Marketing*, 42/3: 21–6.

Adizes, I. (1979). 'Organizational Passages: Diagnosing and Treating Life Cycle Problems in Organizations'. *Organizational Dynamics*, 8: 3–24.

Albach, H. (1978). 'Strategische Unternehmensplanung bei erhöhter Unsicherheit'. *Zeitschrift für Betriebswirtschaft*, 48: 702–15.

—— (ed.) (1995). *Transformationsprozesse in ehemals volkseigenen Betrieben*. Final Report. Koblenz: Wirtschaftshochschule für Unternehmensführung.

Argyris, C. and Schön, D. A. (1978). *Organizational Learning: A Theory of Action Perspective*. Reading, Mass.: Addison-Wesley.

Bandura, A. (1976). 'Die Analyse von Modellierungsprozessen', in A. Bandura (ed.), *Lernen am Modell: Ansätze zu einer sozial-kognitiven Lerntheorie*. Stuttgart: Klett-Cotta, 9–68.

—— (1977). *Social Learning Theory*. Englewood Cliffs, NJ: Prentice Hall.

—— (1986). *Social Foundations of Thought and Action: A Social Cognitive Theory*. Englewood Cliffs, NJ: Prentice Hall.

Berger, P. L. and Luckmann, T. (1966). *The Social Construction of Reality: A Treatise in the Sociology of Knowledge*. Garden City, NY: Doubleday.

Bergmann, W. (1983). 'Das Problem der Zeit in der Soziologie: Ein Literaturüberblick zum Stand der "zeitsoziologischen" Theorie und Forschung'. *Kölner Zeitschrift für Soziologie und Sozialpsychologie*, 35: 462–504.

Berthoin Antal, A., Dierkes, M., and Hähner, K. (1997). 'Business Perception of Contextual Changes: Sources and Impediments to Organizational Learning'. *Business and Society*, 36: 387–407.

Berthoin Antal, A., Dierkes, M., and Marz, L. (1999). 'Organizational Learning in China, Germany and Israel'. *Journal of General Management*, 25/1: 63–88.

Bieri, P. (1972). *Zeit und Zeiterfahrung: Exposition eines Problembereichs*. Frankfurt am Main: Suhrkamp.

Bleicher, K. (1985). *Zeitkonzeptionen der Entwicklung und Gestaltung von Unternehmungen*. Diskussionsbeiträge des Instituts für Betriebswirtschaft, No. 11. University of St. Gallen, Switzerland.

Bluedorn, A. C. and Denhardt, D. B. (1988). 'Time and Organizations'. *Journal of Management*, 14: 299–320.

Carley, K. (1992). 'Organizational Learning and Personnel Turnover'. *Organization Science*, 3: 20–46.

Child, J. and Kieser, A. (1981). 'Development of Organizations Over Time', in P. C. Nystrom and W. H. Starbuck (eds.), *Handbook of Organizational Design* (Vol 1). New York: Oxford University Press, 28–64.

——and Smith, C. (1987). 'The Context and Process of Organizational Transformation: Cadbury Limited in Its Sector'. *Journal of Management Studies*, 24: 565–93.

Clark, P. (1982). *A Review of the Theories of Time and Structure for Organizational Sociology*. Working paper, Aston University, Birmingham, UK.

——(1985). 'A Review of the Theories of Time and Structure for Organizational Sociology', in S. B. Bacharach and S. M. Mitchell (eds.), *Research in the Sociology of Organizations* (Vol. 4). Greenwich, Conn.: JAI Press, 35–79.

Cohen, J. (1981). 'Subjective Time', in J. T. Fraser (ed.), *The Voices of Time* (2nd edn). Amherst: University of Massachusetts Press, 257–78.

Cook, S. D. N. and Yanow, D. (1993). 'Culture and Organizational Learning'. *Journal of Management Inquiry*, 2: 373–90.

Corazza, R. (1985). *Zeit, Social Time und die zeitliche Ordnung des Verhaltens: Grundlagen einer Sozialzeitforschung und Sozialzeitpolitik*. Unpublished doctoral dissertation, University of St. Gallen, Switzerland.

de Goeje, J. (1949). *What Is Time?* Leiden: E. J. Brill.

Dierkes, M. (1990). 'Veränderung von Unternehmenskultur durch Organisationsentwicklung', in H. Merkens and F. Schmidt (eds.), *Strategie, Unternehmenskultur und Organisationsentwicklung im Spannungsfeld zwischen Wissenschaft und Praxis*. Waldmannsweiler: Pädagogischer Verlag, 13–46.

——(1994). 'Ständige Anpassung und Weiterentwicklung: Organisationslernen—eine ständige Herausforderung'. *Blick durch die Wirtschaft*, 12 January: 7.

Elias, N. (1984). *Über die Zeit*. Frankfurt am Main: Suhrkamp.

Fiol, C. M. and Lyles, M. A. (1985). 'Organizational Learning'. *Academy of Management Review*, 10: 803–13.

Frost, P. J., Moore, L. F., Louis, M. R., Lundberg, C. C., and Martin, J. (eds.) (1985). *Organizational Culture*. Beverly Hills, Calif.: Sage.

——————————(eds.) (1991). *Reframing Organizational Culture*. Newbury Park, Calif.: Sage.

Futoran, G. C., Kelly, J. R., and McGrath, J. E. (1989). 'TEMPO: A Time-based System for Analysis of Group Interaction Process'. *Basic and Applied Social Psychology*, 10: 211–32.

Gagliardi, P. (1986). 'The Creation and Change of Organizational Cultures: A Conceptual Framework'. *Organization Studies*, 7: 117–34.

Garvin, D. A. (1993). 'Building a Learning Organization'. *Harvard Business Review*, 71/4: 78–91.

Gersick, C. J. G. (1984). *The Life Cycles of Ad Hoc Task Groups: Time, Transitions, and Learning in Teams*. Unpublished doctoral dissertation, Yale University, New Haven, Conn.

——(1988). 'Time and Transition in Work Teams: Toward a New Model of Group Development'. *Academy of Management Journal*, 31: 9–41.

Geschka, H. and Hammer, R. (1990). 'Die Szenario-Technik in der strategischen Unternehmensplanung', in D. Hahn and B. Taylor (eds.), *Strategische Unternehmensplanung—Stand und Entwicklungstendenzen* (5th edn). Heidelberg: Physica, 238–63.

Gherardi, S. and Strati, A. (1988). 'The Temporal Dimension in Organization Studies'. *Organization Studies*, 9: 149–64.

Gray, B. and Ariss, S. A. (1985). 'Politics and Strategic Change across Organizational Life Cycles'. *Academy of Management Review*, 10: 707–21.

Hall, E. T. (1983). *The Dance of Life: The Other Dimension of Time*. Garden City, NY: Anchor Press.

Hassard, J. (1996). 'Images of Time in Work and Organization', in S. R. Clegg, C. Hardy, and W. R. Nord (eds.), *Handbook of Organization Studies*. London: Sage, 581–98.

Hauser, A. (1955). 'Der Begriff der Zeit in der neueren Kunst und Wissenschaft'. *Merkur*, 9: 803–11.

Heath, L. R. (1956). *The Concept of Time*. Chicago: University of Chicago Press.

Hedberg, B. L. T. (1981). 'How Organizations Learn and Unlearn', in P. C. Nystrom and W. H. Starbuck (eds.), *Handbook of Organizational Design*: Vol. 1. *Adapting Organizations to Their Environments*. Oxford: Oxford University Press, 3–27.

Homans, G. C. (1950). *The Human Group*. New York: Harcourt Brace.

Kelly, J. R. and McGrath, J. E. (1985). 'Effects of Time Limits and Task Types on Task Performance and Interaction of Four-person Groups'. *Journal of Personality and Social Psychology*, 49: 395–407.

Kilmann, R. H., Saxton, M. J., and Serpa, R. (eds.) (1985). *Gaining Control of the Corporate Culture*. San Francisco: Jossey-Bass.

Kim, D. H. (1993). 'The Link between Individual and Organizational Learning'. *Sloan Management Review*, 35/1: 37–50.

Kimberly, J. R. (ed.) (1980). *The Organizational Life Cycle: Issues in the Creation, Transformation, and Decline of Organizations*. San Francisco: Jossey-Bass.

Kofman, F. (1992). Lecture Slides. Cambridge, Mass.: MIT Sloan School of Management.

Kolb, D. A. (1984). *Experiential Learning: Experience as the Source of Learning and Development*. Englewood Cliffs, NJ: Prentice Hall.

Koselleck, R. (1979). *Vergangene Zukunft: Zur Semantik geschichtlicher Zeiten*. Frankfurt am Main: Suhrkamp.

Kreikebaum, H. (1991). *Strategische Unternehmensplanung* (4th edn). Cologne: Kohlhammer.

Leberl, D. (1988). *Systemkomplexität und Zeitautonomie: Ein systemtheoretischer Beitrag zur Aufrechterhaltung der Zeitautonomie in Unternehmungen*. Unpublished doctoral dissertation, University of St. Gallen, Switzerland.

Levitt, B. and March, J. G. (1988). 'Organizational Learning'. *Annual Review of Sociology*, 14: 319–40.

Lewin, K. (1947). 'Frontiers in Group Dynamics'. *Human Relations*, 1: 2–38.

March, J. G. (1991). 'Exploration and Exploitation in Organizational Learning'. *Organization Science*, 2: 71–87.

Martin, J. (1992). *Cultures in Organizations*. New York: Oxford University Press.

McGrath, J. E. (1990). 'Time Matters in Groups', in J. Galegher, R. E. Kraut, and C. Egido (eds.), *Intellectual Teamwork*. London: Lawrence Erlbaum, 23–61.

—— and Rotchford, N. L. (1983). 'Time and Behavior in Organizations', in L. L. Cummings and B. M. Staw (eds.), *Research in Organizational Behavior: An Annual Series of Analytical Essays and Critical Reviews* (Vol. 5). Greenwich, Conn.: JAI Press, 57–101.

Miles, R. E. and Snow, C. C. (1978). *Organizational Strategy, Structure, and Process*. New York: McGraw-Hill.

Miller, D. and Friesen, P. (1983). 'Successful and Unsuccessful Phases of the Corporate Life Cycle'. *Organization Studies*, 4: 339–56.

—— —— (1984). *Organizations: A Quantum View*. Englewood Cliffs, NJ: Prentice Hall.

Mintzberg, H. (1984). 'Power and Organizational Life Cycles'. *Academy of Management Review*, 9: 207–24.

Moore, W. E. (1963a). 'Temporal Structure of Organization', in E. A. Tiryakian (ed.), *Sociological Theory, Values, and Sociocultural Change*. London: Collier-Macmillan, 161–9.

—— (1963b). *Man, Time, and Society*. New York: Wiley.

Nevis, E. C., DiBella, A. J., and Gould, J. M. (1995). 'Understanding Organizations as Learning Systems'. *Sloan Management Review*, 36/2: 73–85.

Nonaka, I. and Takeuchi, H. (1995). *The Knowledge-creating Company: How Japanese Companies Create the Dynamics of Innovation.* New York: Oxford University Press.

Normann, R. (1985). 'Developing Capabilities for Organizational Learning', in J. M. Pennings (ed.), *Organizational Strategy and Change: New Views on Formulating and Implementing Strategic Decisions.* San Francisco: Jossey-Bass, 217–48.

Nowotny, H. (1989): *Eigenzeit: Entstehung und Strukturierung eines Zeitgefühls.* Frankfurt am Main: Suhrkamp.

——(1992). 'Time in the Social Sciences—Theoretical and Empirical Approaches', in M. Dierkes and B. Biervert (eds.), *European Social Science in Transition.* Frankfurt am Main: Campus, 481–525.

Perich, R. (1992). *Unternehmungsdynamik: Zur Entwicklungsfähigkeit von Organisationen aus zeitlich-dynamischer Sicht* (2nd edn). Stuttgart: Haupt.

Peters, L. H., O'Connor, E. J., Pooyan, A., and Quick, J. C. (1984). 'The Relationship between Time Pressure and Performance: A Field Test of Parkinson's Law'. *Journal of Occupational Behavior,* 5/5: 293–9.

Pöppel, E. (1983). 'Erlebte Zeit und Zeit überhaupt: Versuch einer Integration', in A. Peisl and A. Mohler (eds.), *Die Zeit: Schriften der Carl-Friedrich-von-Siemens-Stiftung* (Vol. 6). Munich: Oldenburg, 364–82.

Quinn, R. E. and Cameron, K. S. (1983). 'Organizational Life Cycles and Shifting Criteria of Effectiveness: Some Preliminary Evidence'. *Management Science,* 29/1: 33–51.

Rifkin, J. (1989). *Time Wars.* New York: Touchstone.

Rost, D. (1994). *Innenansichten der Treuhandanstalt: Ergebnisse einer qualitativen Befragung von Führungskräften* (Research Report 43). Free University of Berlin, Department of Sociology.

Schein, E. H. (1985). 'How Culture Forms, Develops, and Changes', in R. H. Kilmann, M. J. Saxton, and R. Sherpa (eds.), *Gaining Control of the Corporate Culture.* San Francisco: Jossey-Bass, 17–43.

——(1991). *Organizational Culture and Leadership: A Dynamic View.* San Francisco: Jossey-Bass.

——(1993). 'How Can Organizations Learn Faster? The Challenge of Entering the Green Room'. *Sloan Management Review,* 34/2: 85–92.

——(1994). *Organizational and Managerial Culture as a Facilitator or Inhibitor of Organizational Learning.* Script No. 10.004. Boston: MIT, Sloan School of Management.

——(1995). *Unternehmenskultur: Ein Handbuch für Führungskräfte.* Frankfurt am Main: Campus.

Schoeller, W. F. (1998). 'Kampf der Uhren'. *Tagesspiegel,* 26 April: 14.

Sitkin, S. B. (1992). 'Learning through Failure: The Strategy of Small Losses', in B. M. Staw and L. L. Cummings (eds.), *Research in Organizational Behavior: An Annual Series of Analytical Essays and Critical Reviews* (Vol. 14). Greenwich, Conn.: JAI Press, 231–66.

Staehle, W. H. (1991). *Management: Eine verhaltenswissenschaftliche Perspektive* (6th edn). Munich: Franz Vahlen.

Tiedge, J. (1998). *Systemtransformation und Wettbewerbsentwicklung.* Wiesbaden: Gabler.

Van Maanen, J. and Schein, E. H. (1979). 'Toward a Theory of Organizational Socialisation', in B. M. Staw (ed.), *Research in Organizational Behavior: An Annual Series of Analytical Essays and Critical Reviews* (Vol. 1). Greenwich, Conn.: JAI Press, 209–64.

Walsh, J. P. and Ungson, G. R. (1991). 'Organizational Memory'. *Academy of Management Review,* 16: 57–91.

Weber, C. (1996). *Treuhandanstalt—Eine Organisationskultur entsteht im Zeitraffer.* Wiesbaden: Gabler.

Wendorff, R. (ed.) (1989). *Im Netz der Zeit: Menschliches Zeiterleben interdisziplinär.* Stuttgart: Hirzel, Wissenschaftliche Verlagsgesellschaft.

Wiegand, M. (1996). *Prozesse organisationalen Lernens.* Wiesbaden: Gabler.

Zerubavel, E. (1982). 'The Standardization of Time: A Sociohistorical Perspective'. *American Journal of Sociology,* 88: 1–23.

16 Effects of Emotion on the Process of Organizational Learning

Klaus R. Scherer and Véronique Tran

Emotions in Organizations

For decades a somewhat narrow interpretation of Max Weber's emphasis on the rational nature of the bureaucratic organization (Albrow 1992; Putnam and Mumby 1993) has led organization theorists to keep their theorizing and research sterile—uncontaminated by the unsavory mention of emotion or affect. One of the reasons for avoiding affect is the long-standing philosophical tradition in which anything emotional is considered 'passion' and hence a threat to rationality. Traces of these deep-seated attitudes can still be found in the rationalistic currents of the literature on organizational behavior and organizational learning (Flam 1990a, b). Ashforth and Humphrey (1995) argued that rationalist thought has led to institutionalized mechanisms for regulating the experience and expression of emotion in the workplace, mechanisms such as neutralizing, buffering, prescribing, and normalizing emotion. Attacking these persistent beliefs, these authors showed that emotionality and rationality are interdependent, that emotions are an integral and inseparable part of organizational life, and that emotions are often functional for the organization.

The discovery of emotion as an important factor in organizational processes is fairly recent. One of the first milestones was the description of organizational feeling rules that require individuals to engage in elaborate 'emotion' work (Hochschild 1979, 1983) and the management of affect in the interest of the organization's aims. In the last decade, a number of authors writing about the role of emotion in specific work settings have highlighted both outward expression and inner feeling as determined by role requirements or organizational and cultural norms (see Fineman 1996; Waldron 1994 for detailed reviews). In the following section, the implication that this literature has for organizational learning is summarized.

Tactical Manipulation of Emotion in Work Settings

Most empirical studies in this area have dealt with ways in which the work role of an employee more or less explicitly requires that person to artificially fabricate emotions seen as supportive of the work activity or to suppress real emotions considered harmful. Not surprisingly, many of these studies have focused on service industries in which flight attendants, waiters, and sales clerks are routinely expected to express positive emotions toward their customers and to suppress any negative emotions they might feel about their work or interaction with the customer (Hochschild 1979, 1983; Rafaeli 1989; Rafaeli and Sutton 1991; Sutton and Rafaeli 1988; Van Maanen and Kunda

Work on this chapter was supported by a grant from the Gottlieb-Daimler-und-Karl-Benz-Stiftung to Klaus Scherer. The authors thank Christina Prange, Ursula Scherer, Susan Schneider, and the editorial team for valuable comments and suggestions.

1989). For people in other occupations different types of emotions, such as sadness for funeral directors, pity and sympathy for nurses, and controlled anger for bill collectors or policemen, may be regarded as useful for interaction with customers or clients. In some cases the required emotion may depend on the behavior of the client or the specific work context. For example, the emotions that bill collectors are expected to show depend on the reactions of the debtor (Rafaeli and Sutton 1991; Sutton 1991). Whereas some writers in this tradition have highlighted the effort and potential alienation involved in this emotion work, others have emphasized the functionality of the tactical use of emotion displays (Rafaeli and Sutton 1987). For example, Staw, Sutton, and Pelled (1994) reviewed evidence showing how positive emotions can help employees to obtain favorable outcomes at work. Conversely, Morris and Feldman (1996) hypothesized that frequency of emotional display, attentiveness to display rules, variety of emotions to be displayed, and emotional conflict would eventually increase 'emotional exhaustion' and, consequently, decrease job satisfaction.

The debate about the use of tactical emotion displays, especially in customer contact situations, illustrates an interesting aspect of organizational learning. Organizations, particularly in the service industry, first learned that success in sales and product delivery heavily depended on their employees' appropriate emotional behavior toward the customer. They learned not only that customer satisfaction depends to a large extent on smooth emotion management but also that the company image is greatly enhanced by such efforts. Public organizations have been much slower to learn the same lesson, probably because of their monopoly on dispensing public-service goods. However, the rapidly deteriorating image of government and public-service bureaucracies has led, in many countries, to an effort to improve the social skills of civil servants in dealing with clients (see Kaufmann 1979). It seems, however, that both companies and public organizations may have learned only half the lesson. Expression management can actually backfire if clients be-

come aware of being manipulated. If the interactive behavior of an employee is artificially changed (e.g. through courses centered on the adage 'keep smiling') without changing fundamentally negative attitudes about dealing with clients (an aversion often found in civil service settings; see Scherer, Scherer, and Klink 1979), negative affect may leak through the smiles, and clients may be negatively affected (Scherer and Scherer 1980). Thus, strategic emotion management can be a double-edged sword, and organizations need to learn to carefully evaluate the effects on employees and clients alike.

Emotion in the Service of Motivational Support of Work Activities

In the literature on motivation in organizational behavior, researchers and theorists often neglect to acknowledge the powerful motivational effects that are generated by emotional reactions. According to Frijda (1986), specific action tendencies may be the most important consequences of emotional arousal. Various types of emotional arousal in an organization may create powerful motivational tendencies that can help or hinder organizational goals. In fact, much of the literature on organizational behavior implicitly acknowledges that emotions such as satisfaction, enthusiasm, and pride can be important motors for work performance (see Frese 1990; Hackman and Wageman 1995; Isen and Baron 1991; Pekrun and Frese 1992). Although the role of motivational factors, such as incentives, is often highlighted, the important issue of the *emotional* reactions of employees to rewards and punishments (involving appraisals of adequacy, deservingness, interpersonal justice, and timeliness, for example) is frequently overlooked. Obviously, although the intention of giving an incentive may be a very good one, it is the motivation generated by the emotional reaction to this incentive that will affect work performance. In other words, what is important is the way the receiver affectively perceives the incentive. In many cases, self-esteem is an emotionally much more powerful determinant than material advantages are, so the timeliness or the delivery of the incentive may be much more important than its actual value. Organizations still have much to learn about emotion management in the context of motivating their employees.

Other areas of interest include the emotional regulation of relationships in the workplace (Erera 1992; Waldron 1994), the role of emotion in leadership (Mizuno, Matsubara, and Takai 1994), the importance of affect in building trust (McAllister 1995), effects of emotion on judgment (Park, Sims, and Motowidlo 1986), emotional aspects of decision-making and negotiation (Donahue and Ramesh 1992; Kumar 1997), and emotional reactions to restructuring (Astrachan 1995; Callan 1993; Dolan and Renaud 1992; LaFarge 1994).

The renewed interest in emotion is starting to affect the field of organizational learning. In one of the first contributions on this topic, Fineman (1997) emphasized that emotion is an inevitable feature of learning, both as a product and as part of the process. He illustrated the need for a more complete integration of emotion into the framework of organizational learning by criticizing the modular approach that treats the tactical use of emotion as just another management competency to be learned. So far, there has not yet been a systematic effort to describe the effects of emotion on different aspects of the process of organizational learning. The purpose of this chapter, which is focused on the role of emotion in various types of learning processes in organizational settings, is to provide such a description. We demonstrate in detail how emotions contribute to efficient learning, both individual and organizational. In this context, we introduce the notion of 'emotional climate' in organizations, suggesting that emotions and emotional climate can be expected to be of central importance to successful organizational learning.

A Definition of Emotion and Emotional Climate

Emotions are functional for the adaptation to the environment. Nesse and Berridge (1997) summarized this key point:

Emotions are coordinated states, shaped by natural selection, that adjust physiological and behavioral responses to take advantage of opportunities and to cope with threats that have recurred over the course of evolution. Thus, the characteristics and regulation of basic emotions match the requirements of specific situations that have often influenced fitness. Emotions influence motivation, learning, and decision and, therefore, influence behavior and, ultimately fitness. (p. 64)

Apart from their long-term adaptational functions, emotions are relevance detectors. They alert the individual to important changes in the environment, focus attention on these situations, prepare the appropriate response strategies, and anchor events of great importance in the individuals' long-term memory.

Emotion psychologists view emotions as episodes in time (Ekman 1992; Frijda, Mesquita, Sonnemans, and Van Goozen 1991; Scherer 1993) that involve a noticeable change in the functioning of the organism, a change brought about by some triggering event that can be external (e.g. behavior of others, changes in the state of affairs, or an encounter with novel stimuli) or internal (e. g. thoughts, memories, or sensations). Most current theorists postulate a multicomponential definition of emotion that includes physiological arousal, motor expression, subjective feeling, and often also action tendencies and cognitive processes. Cognitive processes are involved in the evaluation or appraisal of the eliciting stimuli or events and in the regulation of ongoing emotional processes. There is now a strong consensus in the literature that the type of emotion elicited by an event and the intensity of the reaction depend on the outcome of this *appraisal process*, which can occur very rapidly and automatically at low levels of central nervous system processing or in a more controlled, conscious fashion involving the cortical association regions (Frijda 1986; Lazarus 1991; Scherer 1984, 1993).

Emotions not only play a major role in preparing the individual's behavior, they also have powerful effects on social interaction. Emotions serve to inform the individual's social surroundings of his or her reactions to certain events. Because of this communicative relevance, emotions are often used tactically to deceive others about one's true reactions and behavioral intentions (Frank 1988).

In addition to differentiating between individual and organizational learning (see Maier, Prange, and Rosenstiel, Ch. 1 in this volume), one needs to make the parallel distinction between individual emotions and emotional climate in groups and organizations. Emotions have been regarded as individual, private experience and the collective occurrence of emotion is generally seen as an exceptional event during which many individuals tend to have very similar emotions (sports contests, riots, catastrophes). Yet, one can easily think of more mundane examples of 'collective emotions' in organizations: joy in celebrating good results, sadness when layoffs occur, or anger during strikes. Increasingly, the concept of emotional climate is suggested in order to cover these cases of shared or convergent emotions in groups, organizations, and even society at large. Coming from a social-interactionist perspective, De Rivera (1992) proposed a definition of the concept by focusing on emotional climate in nation-states. He argued that the concept of emotional climate not only refers to collective feelings and behaviors but also to the way in which all members of a society emotionally relate to each other. (For example, an emotional climate can be labeled as fear or joy but also as hostility, caring, or solidarity.) In a similar vein, Paez, Asun, and Gonzalez (1995) proposed that emotional climate be defined as

a state of collective mood, characterized by the predominance of certain emotions (for instance, happiness and anger versus sadness and fear), by the predominance of a social representation or group of beliefs held about the world (positive, trust versus negative, mistrust) and of the future (optimistic, hope versus pessimistic, despair) shared by a specific subculture; and by the predominance of certain action tendencies that will permeate the network of social interactions. (p. 144)

Both De Rivera and Paez and his colleagues agree that an emotional climate is a collective phenomenon and not the mere sum of individual emotions. One can identify a common theme in these two definitions: the notion that a certain number of prevalent emotions (e.g. joy or anxiety) or emotional attitudes (e.g. hostility or solidarity) are shared and the claim that these emotions determine the behavior and the interactions of the members of a group or an organization.

Adopting the definition of emotion outlined at the beginning of this section, we propose to use the concept of emotional climate (understood as a collective phenomenon in the sense used by Paez, Asun, and Gonzalez 1995) to describe emotional phenomena at the organizational level. Specifically, in line with an appraisal-based explanation of the elicitation and differentiation of emotion (see Scherer 1998), we suggest that the generating conditions (or determinants) of an organization-specific emotional climate are the shared dispositions of its members to evaluate events in a similar fashion and, in consequence, to react in a common way. This suggestion is based on the assumption that members of an organization, because of a shared social environment (e.g. structure of the organization, type of leadership, nature of the networks, and physical working conditions) and common experiences, develop similar values, motivations (goals and needs), and beliefs and attitudes. These similarities, in turn, are responsible for the members' shared appraisal dispositions, which tend to produce similar emotions in response to specific events. Obviously, such shared dispositions are essential components of what is generally called organizational culture (e.g. Schein 1992) or organizational climate (e.g. Reichers and Schneider 1990). Given the increasing convergence of these approaches (Denison 1996), it seems futile to define these concepts differentially with respect to the notion of emotional climate. Rather, it is important to stress that the psychological commonalities in the way members of an organization perceive and evaluate events (commonalities that are in large part due to organizational culture and climate) produce common tendencies in emotional reactions to specific events and are thus a precondition for the generation of an emotional climate in an organization.

Further generators of emotional climate are emotional contagion and shared information-processing. Hatfield, Cacioppo, and Rapson (1992) defined primitive emotional contagion as 'the tendency to automatically mimic and synchronize facial expressions, vocalizations, postures, and movements with those of another person and, consequently, to *converge* emotionally' (pp. 153–4, emphasis in the original). Elaborating on that definition, Ashforth and Humphrey (1995) stated that 'people "catch" emotions through conscious information processing (e.g. feeling sad upon reading about a tragedy) and/or nonconscious or automatic imitation (via facial, postural, and vocal cues, e.g. a person sensing and feeling his co-worker's distress)' (p. 113). Applied to organizational settings, research on emotional contagion tends to indicate that contagion emerges when interaction and cohesion are high within a given group (i.e. when the group shares values, goals, and beliefs), when a leader expresses a particular emotion, when the emotion felt is congruent with feeling rules (i.e. social rules about the way one expresses emotions) or when a certain event is interpreted in an ambivalent manner (Ashforth and Humphrey 1995).

The notion of the group as an information processor is relevant to the occurrence of both collective emotions and learning. Cognitive research on group performance suggested that 'some basic level of shared or common knowledge is necessary for (any) group to operate' and that 'at the group level, information processing involves the degree to which information, ideas, or cognitive processes are shared, and are being shared, among the group members and how this sharing of information affects both individual- and group-

level outcomes' (Hinsz, Tindale, and Vollrath 1997: 43).

Most important, an emotional climate is characterized by the convergent feelings of organizational members. Internal or external events that occur during the activities of an organization or any of its subgroups elicit either brief, but intense, emotional episodes or more enduring, less focused moods. The important difference between emotional climate and individual emotions is that emotional climate affects all or most members of a unit, department, or division in a uniform manner. That is, the affective reactions of all members are comparable because of shared evaluative dispositions. In consequence, the result of this affective convergence is not just the aggregation of individual emotions; rather, a collective emotion emerges. As one might expect, such collective emotions have important effects on group dynamic processes such as conformity (Tran 1998).

The Nature of the Learning Process and the Role of Emotions

Although learning, both individual and organizational, has been defined in many ways, most authors agree that one can identify a number of aspects or phases of the learning process (see the introduction and various other chapters in this volume, see also Berthoin Antal 1998). In this chapter we examine the effects of emotion on the following component phases: (a) readiness to learn, (b) the search for and processing of new information, (c) conferral of significance, (d) storage in memory, (e) transfer and generalization, and (f) disposition to reproduce. For each of these processes we discuss, first, how emotions can be expected to affect individual learning and, second, how emotional climate is likely to influence organizational learning. Both positive and negative aspects of the role of emotion in learning are highlighted (see also overview in Strongman 1986).

Readiness to Learn

A frequently neglected precondition for learning to take place reliably is the readiness of the individual to learn, including the nature of the processing structures, such as personality, cognitive style, speed of habituation, and goal conflicts. It has been demonstrated that the processing characteristics of the central nervous systems may differ across individuals. For example, at a very basic level, individuals operate with very different cognitive processing speeds (see Hale and Jansen 1994). Clearly, faster processing is likely to be more efficient in cases where a large amount of highly variable information needs to be processed. Some individuals habituate rapidly to new input and others take much longer to assimilate new information. Similarly, the efficiency of inhibition is a major variable of individual difference. Some individuals are adept at inhibiting competing impulses, emotions, or motives while pursuing a goal or being involved in a learning process; others are much less able to do so and are therefore far more subject to interference, so their learning results are suboptimal. Many different factors of the individual's learning history may play a role. For example, prior exposure to rich learning contexts or constant reinforcement of learned performances will enhance readiness to learn. Of course, readiness to learn also involves the perception of the need to learn.

Another major aspect of readiness to learn in individuals is the underlying affective attitude toward novelty, acquisition of new information, and change. Individuals who are convinced that they have reached a stage of perfection and superior knowledge are notoriously slow to learn because of low motivation to do so. The problem in these cases is an exaggeratedly high self-esteem, which often goes hand in hand with the conviction that acquiring knowledge or learning new procedures is threatening the valued status quo. Another personality trait likely to drastically reduce the readiness to learn is rigidity, which is often associated with low cognitive complexity (see Schroder, Driver, and Streuffert 1967).

Such individuals use rather wide categories, often in a very undifferentiated way, when perceiving, classifying, and judging people and events. In addition, they are slow to change a judgment or decision once it has been made.

Like individuals, organizations differ widely in their readiness to learn, and there are many parallels with respect to the underlying factors. For example, communication and decision structures, internal processing and transmission speeds can be highly variable across organizations, and such dissimilarity will strongly affect how well they are prepared to learn. In organizations, habituation and prior learning experiences play a role analogous to the one they have in individuals. Some organizations habituate rapidly to novel conditions and react accordingly; others may take much longer to adapt to new input. The perception of the need to learn and consistent reinforcement of prior learning will create favorable conditions for any kind of learning activity.

Just as at the individual level, the efficiency of learning in organizations is also strongly affected by the capacity to inhibit competing or even conflicting goals or concerns. Concretely, this issue is linked to the existence of internal mechanisms that help organizations focus on central, important goals rather than allowing them to be side-tracked by a multitude of unrelated or less urgent issues. Partly, learning efficiency involves the capacity for vision and leadership of upper management levels and thereby helps to actively inhibit potentially irrelevant or untimely activities. However, another major factor is the sharing and enforcement of values, goals, and priorities all across the organization. It, too, helps inhibit nonpertinent input at the source.

Finally, the organizational level shows evidence also of personality variables such as rigidity and cognitive simplicity. Much of the rigidity in organizations stems from the existence and enforcement of rules and regulations that are ill adapted to flexible, learning-based adaptive strategies. Clearly, the danger of rigidifying structures and procedures increases in close relation to the size of an organization and the degree of its hierarchization or compartmentalization.

How can emotions affect the readiness to learn? Clearly, transitory emotions are unlikely to change stable structural characteristics or personality dispositions of either individuals or organizations in the short run. However, some emotions may reinforce existing dispositions and thus lead to a vicious circle. For example, rigid and undifferentiated processing of information, because of its inefficiency in dealing with novel and unusual situations, often engenders emotions such as fear or anxiety. Such emotions tend to reduce learning efficiency further because they tend to decrease the propensity to expose oneself to new experiences (see below, and Fineman 1997: 15; Child and Heavens, Ch. 13 in this volume). In other cases, emotions may positively influence the readiness to learn. For example, emotions such as interest and hope can help focus attention on important issues and foster inhibition of goals that compete with a learning task at hand. In an analysis of management processes for knowledge generation, Nonaka and Takeuchi (1995: 136–9) provided an interesting example of how the bottom-up management structure and the high value placed on individualism provided an optimal readiness to learn at 3M. Individuals like Art Fry, the inventor of the Post-It sticker, were able to pursue their interests and visions, unhampered by conflicting constraints and driven only by their emotional involvement (a description that implies a complex mix of emotions: enthusiasm, interest, hope, enjoyment, and pride).

Processing New Information: Attention, Filtering, and Searching

The readiness or disposition of an individual to learn heavily influences the likelihood that learners will expose themselves to new information and procedures. But the most decisive precondition for learning to take place is the actual exposure to novel information, knowledge, or procedures. If the learner finds himself or herself in a rich, diverse, dynamically evolving environment, chances are that new information to be learned may present itself almost continually. Under such conditions there may even be the problem of too much input ('information overload') for the individuals who filter or select the information that provides learning material relevant to a given person's needs and goals. One of the major devices for making the massive influx of information manageable is the focusing of attention, the homing in on those parts of the continuous stimulation that appear to be pertinent at a particular point, the blending out of everything else. The ability to tune out irrelevant stimulation and to focus attention differs greatly from one person to the next.

Expectations can also help structure information-processing. Learning does not occur in a vacuum; it is always integrated into existing schematic and propositional knowledge that facilitates the selection of the pertinent information and the integration of the newly learned content into existing knowledge or skills. This feature of the learning process is responsible for the exponential increase in learning efficiency as one proceeds into a new subject area. The more elaborate the existing schemata or knowledge structures, the more efficiently expectations about the utility of new information steer the learning process.

Expectations are also essential when new information is not easily available. In such instances, active search strategies guided by expectations are required in order to guarantee a continuous learning process. Single cases or events with a dramatic emotional impact play an important role in this context, for the emotional arousal produced by such events serves to maintain the circumstances in memory and to set up expectations for future events. This phenomenon, as exemplified by the fact that most people older than 50 years of age vividly remember the situation in which they learned of President Kennedy's assassination, is often called 'flashbulb memory' (see Brown and Kulik 1977). The description of the ways in which organizations learn from single cases (see March, Sproull, and Tamuz 1996: 4) suggests a similar mechanism of emotional enhancement.

Emotions, as relevance detectors (Frijda 1986; Scherer 1984) play a major part in this process of information filtering and searching. People become excited—and emotionally involved—when something seems important to their well-being or their values. Emotional arousal is a good indicator that the source of this arousal is of great concern, even if one thinks that it is not. Relevance detection automatically focuses attention on each source and increases the probability that information will be processed. It is this unconscious operation of the emotion system—which forces the individual to attend to fundamentally important issues, often despite presumably rational considerations—that is part of the 'wisdom of the body'.

But emotions are not only reactions to events; they often have proactive functions, triggering active relevance search. One of the most proactive emotions, largely determining whether and what kind of exploratory behavior will occur, is interest. Interest provides the most important motivational underpinning of the active search for new information and of the purposeful filtering of incoming information (Izard 1993). Interest focuses attention on information related to pertinent values and goals of the individual and thus can be expected to increase the efficiency of the information search and to facilitate assimilation.

These mechanisms operate in organizational learning in much the same way that they do in individual learning. As with individuals, organizations need to structure the way in which the mass of available information is attended to and processed. Individuals and organizations alike meet this need by focusing attention and filtering or channeling information. Much of this filtering is based on prior schemata and the resulting expectations. What is important in knowledge creation is not having specific information but knowing which information is pertinent and where to find it quickly (see Nonaka 1994; Nonaka and Takeuchi 1995). Efficient search strategies and preexisting schemata form an essential part of such capacity, but the motivational motor of affectively determined interest is likely to be decisive for knowledge generation. As in individual learning, interest at the level of the organization (as part of the emotional climate) implies not only a general openness to things encountered but also an existence of the active, directed search for material that is perceived as pertinent to the specific goals.

What about situations in which it is impossible to assimilate new information or accommodate existing schemata to divergent observations? Argyris and Schön (1978, 1996) suggested that such cases require double-loop learning, which requires a fundamental change in shared assumptions and theories of action in order to bring them into line with the adaptive behavior patterns required by the situation. Emotions play a major role in this process, too. In individual learning, new information that is incompatible with existing schemata will produce consternation, surprise, and often irritation. It is the strength of these emotions that determines whether major changes in existing knowledge and opinion structures will occur. Because there is an inherent tendency for existing mental structures to persist, minor instances of surprise are often not sufficient to trigger changes in schemata. For example, it is well known that attempts to change attitudes exclusively on the basis of conflicting information (as is often the case in many public-service campaigns) are doomed to failure because the emotional states created by the discrepant information are weak and very transient. The individual will, generally in an unconscious fashion, mobilize defence strategies that allow the existing mental structures to persist. Only continuous exposure to discrepant information (as when prejudiced individuals are compelled to interact with the objects of their prejudice and thus continuously invalidate their beliefs through direct observation) will produce emotions of sufficient strength to bring about schemata transformation (Hewstone 1994).

It is not surprising, then, that Argyris and Schön (1978, 1996) predicted that double-loop learning would require intensive contact and often conflict among the members of an organization in order to forge new shared assumptions and theories of action. This prerequisite is equivalent to the need for strong emotions to overcome the inertia of existing interpretative structures. Under special circumstances it actively fosters an emotional climate characterized by uncertainty, consternation, doubt, and irritation in organizations where one would normally tend to avoid these kinds of emotions. Unless this type of emotional climate is sufficiently strong and enduring, the natural defense strategies that exist at both the group and the individual levels (e.g. denial, compartmentalization, avoidance, de-emphasis) will hamper changes in established assumptions and theories of action and thus prevent double-loop learning from occurring.

Similarly, an emotional climate characterized by satisfaction, contentment, or even pride can have equally negative consequences for learning in an organization. Although such a positive climate is obviously conducive to job satisfaction and an agreeable organizational atmosphere, it may discourage the development of interest and the active search for new information. Even more problematic, it is unlikely to encourage massive modification of cherished mental structures and patterns of interpretation (see section on 'Different Types of Emotion in Organizational Learning', below).

Conferral of Significance

Very few objects or situations have 'built-in' significance due to their intrinsic agreeableness or painfulness. The vast majority of the things one learns have their significance or pertinence *conferred* on them by a process of association, reinforcement, or appraisal that makes the facts or events important because of actual or perceived conduciveness or obstructiveness to people's needs or goals. This phase of the learning process, because of its powerful motivational aspect, has a strong affective component. In the following pages, some of these mechanisms—association and classical conditioning, reinforcement learning, imitation learning, and cognitive learning—are reviewed

for the role that emotion plays in their operation.

Classical Conditioning

Classical conditioning, which is based on the pairing of an unconditional stimulus that is intrinsically agreeable (such as good food) or painful (such as an electrical shock) with a conditioned stimulus (see Maier, Prange, and Rosenstiel, Ch. 1 in this volume for details), is the simplest form of significance conferral in individual learning. The powerful, often unconscious, processes involved can have a lasting impact on an individual's behavior precisely because the emotion generated by an unconditioned event is transferred to the conditioned event or situation. The strong behavioral component of emotion—avoidance or approach—is thereby activated, and it influences behavior each time the conditioned stimulus occurs. Conditioned fear can make someone avoid places, people, and things for long periods—without any objective justification, and possibly to the individual's detriment. Similarly, conditioned hope, based on a single success, may make someone pursue completely unrealistic courses of action.

Can companies be compared to salivating dogs (Pavlov's famous experiments in which dogs were conditioned to associate food with the ringing of a bell)? The answer is yes for cases in which a collective emotion is automatically generated whenever a conditioned event occurs. Assume that a company profits several times, by chance, from windfall gains in periods after particular economic policy constellations, such as countercyclic government spending. The company will most likely learn the contingency and upon the next instance of the conditioned stimulus may 'salivate', may prepare to 'digest' the expected increase in activity and gain. Such reactions are based on affect (hope in the case of positive conditioning, fear in the case of negative conditioning) rather than 'cold' cognitive analysis (see also Levitt and March 1996: 523).

The example shows the potential problems with conditioned emotional responses, which are largely unconscious or undeliberate in individuals. In a similar fashion, implicit, uncritical, shared expectations and the resulting collective emotions among the decision-makers in an organization may influence their decisions. If earlier pairings of economic policy decisions and sales development for the company's product were based on chance, the implicitly conditioned, affectively mediated expectations may well provoke suboptimal decision-making.

Reinforcement Learning

Reinforcement learning is another instance of classical association learning (see Maier, Prange, and Rosenstiel, Ch. 1 in this volume for details) in which emotions play a major role. If an organism is rewarded or punished (e.g. receiving unconditioned stimuli such as food that is intrinsically pleasurable or disagreeable, respectively) immediately after having exhibited a particular type of behavior, the frequency of that type of behavior will increase (with rewards) or decrease (with punishments). This mechanism is so pervasive that it often operates completely outside awareness, both for the 'teacher' and the 'learner'. In this type of learning, too, the mechanism strongly depends on the association between emotional responses and a particular class of behaviors.

It is not necessary to belabor the significance of reinforcement and punishment for the organizational behavior of individuals—the examples abound: praise, bonuses, and incentives for good work, and various types of sanctions for unwanted behavior. However, numerous examples exist of reward systems that fail to reinforce the desired behavior. Company policy for instance, may discourage behaviors that are informally rewarded by the system and may fail to reward desired behaviors at all (Kerr 1975). For example, it is currently fashionable to talk about the need for teamwork, but employees' investments in team-building are rarely formally rewarded. On the contrary, rewards are generally distributed according to individual performance. Similarly, the complexity of the use of punishment in management has been well documented in a study showing that this form of negative reinforcement may often have unintended emotional outcomes, particularly if it is seen as unfair (Butterfield, Trevino, and Ball 1996). In fact, it has been shown in a large-scale cross-cultural study that perceived injustice is one of the most powerful factors for eliciting negative emotions, especially anger (Mikula, Scherer, and Athenstaedt 1998).

The effect of emotion on mechanisms of reinforcement learning at the *organizational* level has been rarely addressed in the literature. Let us take the case of a company that brought in new heads of sales in rapid sequence, with sales volume increasing each time because of chance fluctuation. Chances are that a process of reinforcement learning will produce among decision-makers implicit shared expectations of that behavior's efficacy. These expectations, in turn, may well produce an increase in its frequency—with potentially disastrous results. The emotional underpinnings of such accidental learning processes are very powerful, particularly in the case of negative emotions. For example, if fear or anxiety has been established through a series of accidental mishaps, the false attributions about the potential danger of certain courses of action may never be rectified, for the avoidance behavior produced by the fear responses will effectively inhibit any positive experiences in the future.

Similarly, learning psychologists have described interesting cases of 'superstitious behavior' in animals and humans, who after a series of accidental reinforcements, kept up rather nonsensical behavior in the hope of further reinforcements (or avoidance of punishment). One of the reasons for the extraordinary stability of even very haphazardly reinforced behavior is the effect of intermittent reinforcement that prevents the disappearance (extinction) of the learned contingencies or expectations. Given that these processes operate largely below the level of conscious awareness, they are often insulated against rational analysis of the real contingencies. Such superstitious behavior, preventing extinction, also occurs at the level of the organization, where accidentally rewarded strategies may be pursued even if the corresponding actions fail to cause the response that members of the organization expect (Levitt and March 1996; March and Olsen 1988). Thus the fact that our fictitious company finds itself repeatedly punished by severe losses after having fired heads of sales may not affect its superstitious behavior as long as the originally learned contingency (i.e. firing a head of sales will sometimes make sales rise) is intermittently reinforced. The problem is aggravated by the fact that implicit expectations, based on accidentally established reinforcement chains, are often explicitly motivated by myths or apparent justifications (e.g. 'our company thrives on new blood').

At this point one may ask, given the strength of such 'apparent' associations of causality based on emotional reactions, whether superstitious behavior of organizations is likely to be the rule rather than the exception. Luckily, a special set of conditions needs to be present in order to produce strong expectations elicited by chance association. First, chance operates, by definition, in an unsystematic or random fashion. Although a sufficient number of systematic reinforcements for a particular type of policy decision may occur by chance, such happenstance is rare (such as obtaining a six for each of ten consecutive throws on the dice). Second, implicit expectations are less likely to be established if the consequences of particular actions can be clearly attributed to specific causal factors independent of the accidental reinforcement. For example, if our fictitious company had realized that the sales increases after the initial replacements of sales directors had all occurred during an economic upswing, implicit expectations might not have been established. Thus, a systematic analysis of the causal factors underlying certain consequences of organizational decisions constitutes an antidote for these implicit expectations based on accidental reinforcement.

One of the organization's major tasks of organizational learning is to learn to avoid succumbing to the vagaries of the reinforcement learning or conditioning process. Unfortunately, the emotional nature of reinforcement learning often prevents such analysis. To understand why, one needs to examine the role of emotion in reinforcement learning more closely.

The major function of emotion in reinforcement learning is the conferral of significance to a previously innocuous stimulus or situation, thereby acquiring signal value. Obviously an intrinsic reward (preferred food) received several times in a row by a rat for showing a novel type of behavior (e.g. pressing a red bar in an experimental cage) will confer on this random behavior a significance that it did not initially have. This significance is bestowed by the effects of the positive emotion experienced after the unexpected reward. Similarly, a company that finds itself repeatedly rewarded—let us say, by huge sales increases—after the introduction of what seemed routine personnel decisions will see such actions in a new light, imbued with fresh significance. Repetition of the rewarded behavior, or in the case of classical conditioning, the appearance of a conditioned stimulus, will lead to the expectation of further rewards, a response that creates a state of contentment and complacency. For example, a company that has, because of a stroke of luck, succeeded in selling products that are very innovative at a particular moment in time may indulge in unrealistic expectations that sales will continue. This type of positive emotional climate may prevent essential adaptations in the company's strategy from occurring in a timely fashion. A classic case is IBM, which, having long been considered the prime example of growth and success, faced serious difficulties in the early 1990s. Market analysts concluded: 'Instead of responding to the market need for cheap PCs and practical business applications, IBM stubbornly stuck with mainframes' (MSN Investor Report, 7 March, 1999). The results of this complacency based on past reinforcement were severe: IBM's CEO, John Akers, announced a cutback in the R&D budget of $1 billion in 1993, and 25,000 jobs were cut worldwide (Greyser and Langford 1993).

Because of the strong negative emotions elicited by the punishment or the withdrawal of expected reward, negative reward or punishment likewise confers significance to previously innocuous behavior. The signal value of these stimuli or events is quite different: Recurrence of the behavior or of a negatively conditioned stimulus will produce fear and, consequently, avoidance behavior. Schein (1993) argued that if an organization wants to learn well and fast, it has to overcome the fear of punishment that may have become engrained over the years, generating the type of anxiety that makes one unwilling to learn because it appears to be too difficult or too disruptive of 'the good old way of doing things'. He proposed inducing a different type of anxiety, one that motivates learning and change and helps override previous conditioning. In a context of strongly encouraged organizational learning, leaders could, for example, elicit shame or guilt in people who do not learn. The ensuing perception of potential threat to their job security might produce a more constructive type of anxiety. It is, of course, essential for the success of such a change initiative. It permits the formation of new attitudes and behaviors, ones conveying the message that employees can safely engage in trial-and-error behavior and make occasional mistakes.

The signaling system provided by the emotions is quite flexible. It allows for the fact that chance may play a major role in conditioning or reinforcement chains and that the environment may change dramatically, suddenly reinforcing behavior that used to be punished. Thus, the 'signal emotions' known as fear and hope affect the likelihood that certain behaviors will be exhibited but do not completely preclude or automatically produce the respective responses. Once a previously reinforced behavior is no longer rewarded, 'extinction' or, in a sense, 'unlearning' will take place (subject, however, to the strong stabilizing effects of intermittent reinforcement, as described above). Similarly, a previously punished behavior may reassert itself once punishment stops.

However, as Schein (1993) pointed out, unlearning is emotionally difficult. Indeed, it requires constant testing of the validity of previously acquired reinforcement or punishment contingencies (see also Hedberg 1981). In an analysis of learning from single cases, March, Sproull, and Tamuz (1996: 5) illustrated how the analysis of outcomes centrally depends on the interpretation of events. A more appropriate interpretation or reappraisal of an event that first produced anxiety will effectively change the emotion and thus the consequent behavior. The flexibility of the emotion mechanism is the reason that organisms and companies do things despite of a certain amount of fear—for many different reasons (e.g. spite, recklessness, rational analysis of change, and conviction). Acting in spite of fear, allows one to test the continued existence of certain contingencies. This mechanism is aided by the enormous variability of stimuli, events, and behaviors and by a process called stimulus generalization (see section on 'Storage of Learned Knowledge' below, p. 381), that is the transfer of learned associations to new stimuli or events.

Imitation Learning

In addition to the two major types of learning based on associative conditioning, which are both based on significance conferral via positive or negative emotions, a third variety can be distinguished: imitation learning. In this case, the learner observes and then imitates a model, learning both the nature of the required behavior and the appropriate contingencies purely by the cognitive activity of information acquisition (see Maier, Prange, and Rosenstiel, Ch. 1 in this volume for further details).

The evidence shows that the conferral of significance in imitation learning seems to be brought about by the attention value, prestige, and perceived success of the model. 'Prestige suggestion' is a household word in advertising, with companies marketing many brand names by using the names and photos, if not live TV-spot appearances, of famous actors or sports stars. The same practice is used in the sponsorship of sports or musical events. The association between the well-known, and often liked, image of the star and the product confers significance upon the latter that it might never gain on its own.

What is the role of emotion in this process? Obvious candidates are admiration, even envy, of a successful model. Admired or envied models are likely to be observed very closely, making it highly likely that learning will occur. But because any kind of attentive observation can yield some kind of learning (if there is anything to be learned), the model does not have to instill positive emotions as long as it is able to draw attention. Thus, even anger-inducing models can be sources of learning if they can muster the observer's attention. Of course, it is yet another question whether learned behaviors are then imitated.

Interorganizational and network-based imitation plays a major role in organizational learning (see Wiegand 1996; Tsui Auch, Ch. 32 in this volume). As in the case of individual learning, emotions play a major role. An emotional climate of widespread admiration or envy for the exploits of another company, such as the market leader, might easily produce, even unintentionally, processes of imitation learning and knowledge transfer through a variety of means. There is a clear danger, however, of fostering an emotional climate of self-denigration and glorification of a competitor's achievement: If imitation learning is encouraged, self-reliance and creativity might suffer.

Cognitive Learning

For acquiring new knowledge and behaviors rather than changing response probabilities, one of the most important kinds of learning is cognitive learning. This heading subsumes much of what the word *learning* is understood to mean: The acquisition of language, ideas, skills, tastes, strategies, and so forth. Simplifying an extremely complex process, one could argue that cognitive learning consists of being exposed to new concepts, ideas, scripts, and behaviors, paying attention to these inputs, seeing their relevance, and storing them in memory (see Maier, Prange, and Rosenstiel, Ch. 1 in this volume for further details).

Much research has been conducted on the effect of emotion, mood, or both on cognitive

processes. Thus, affect has been empirically related to the negotiation process (Carnevale and Isen 1986; Kumar 1997) and to biases in information-processing (Alloy and Abramson 1988). Positive affect seems to enable people to perform more complex tasks (Isen and Means 1983) and to solve problems more creatively than negative affect does (Estrada, Isen, and Young 1994). Although most of this research has been conducted at the individual level, the results can be easily generalized to the organizational level. For example, an emotional climate of hope or interest is better than frustration or anxiety as a basis for conveying a CEO's new strategic vision to all levels of the organization. It is suggested, then, that emotions have a strong impact on organizational cognition (Schneider and Angelmar 1993), particularly its outcomes such as decision-making and learning.

Storage of Learned Knowledge

In order to have lasting impact, any objects, events, facts, or associations that have acquired significance for the organism in a learning process need to be stored in long-term memory (Phillips and Baddely 1989). In individual learning, this storage is a highly complex process whose neuropsychological mechanisms are still imperfectly understood. However, it has been amply demonstrated that emotion plays a major role in storage (see Christianson 1992). One of the phenomena that have been firmly established through a large number of empirical studies is mood-dependent recall. The pertinent research has shown that individuals are more likely to recall an object or fact if they are in the same emotional state as they were when first presented with the new information (Bower 1992). For example, new stimuli that have been learned when paired with highly pleasant stimulation (e.g. positive emotional responses) may be stored in memory together with affective markers that are very different from those used when the material is originally paired with negative expressions of affect (e.g. critical remarks from an authoritarian, disapproving teacher). Obviously, this mood dependency of recall has both positive and negative aspects. In a positive sense, an individual in an anxious mood is more likely to recall important details about events that presented a danger to his or her well-being than about innocuous events. This recall may help the individual to be better prepared for eventual emergencies than would otherwise be the case. On the other hand, the person may be overwhelmed by negative affect and paralyzed by fear, responses that impede adaptive behavior. This possibility is particularly salient in cases in which traumatic experiences have been encountered. The learning that takes place in such situations may lead to constant recall of the events and to ruminations that may not only preclude adaptive responses but also drain large amounts of energy.

The processes whereby learned facts and associations are stored in some kind of collective memory system in organizational learning have been treated extensively in the literature. According to Huber (1996), organizational learning heavily depends on organizational memory because learning processes such as information acquisition, information distribution, and information interpretation are all anchored in memory. Levitt and March (1996) suggested that rules, beliefs, experiences, procedures, and cultures are shared and circulated inside an organization and then stored within a memory structure. Senge (1990) talked about shared mental models in terms of internal mental images of how the world works. Nonaka's five-phase model of organizational knowledge creation (Nonaka and Takeuchi 1995: 83–9) highlighted the central importance of shared mental models and their externalization in this process. The important role of memory for organizational learning is also emphasized in the chapters by Pawlowsky, Forslin, and Reinhardt, Ch. 35; and by Kieser, Beck, and Tainio, Ch. 27 (in this volume).

Clearly, both written records and individual memories of members of the organization are involved. To the extent that collective memory rests on an assembly of individual memories, one can expect to find that the strength of emotion effects and their positive or negative consequences in organizational learning is similar to that in individual learning (see Christianson 1992 for an overview). One of the potential effects of emotion on learning is the repression of information recall. As Rapaport (1971) showed, individuals may unconsciously extinguish their memory of information associated with negative events that threaten self-esteem. Heuer and Reisberg (1992) demonstrated that such emotion-induced information repression could produce serious errors in judgment and decision-making. Although literature on organizational learning contains few empirical studies of this phenomenon, one may surmise that emotion-induced information repression is likely to have a powerful effect on collective memory. One of the mechanisms involved is probably the decrease in the tendency of memory rehearsal of such events. Nobody likes to recall—and particularly to superiors—events associated with unpleasant emotional experiences.

Although emotions can weaken or even eradicate memories, they can also sharpen and enhance them. What is remembered about emotion-producing events seems to be remembered with great accuracy. This mechanism has a powerful effect on organizational learning: Conflicting interpretations of events may lead to diverging memories and biases maintained by subcultures and subgroups (Levitt and March 1996). For example, if certain facts or associations, such as the effects of particular types of restructuring, have been learned by members of an organization under conditions of anxiety and/or frustration, the onset of a generalized emotional climate of anxiety or frustration in the organization may then trigger a preferential recall of these earlier memories. Such memory enhancement may have positive effects. It may, for example, indicate unwanted consequences of certain actions or make the members of an organization wary of specific courses of action that may not have worked well in the past. In other cases, however, the effects of memory enhancement can be very negative, as when an emotional climate of anxiety (possibly due to cyclical downswings in demand) generates traumatic memories of more serious structural changes. Such effects may paralyze the organization just as they do an individual and may prevent adaptation from occurring.

Transfer and Generalization

One of the most important aspects of learning is the capacity to generalize from an initial learning experience, to transfer knowledge and associations from a particular instance to a class of objects or events. For example, a child who has burnt his or her tongue with a hot beverage is likely to generalize from this experience and be more circumspect when drinking steaming fluids. Both the extent to which learning will show transfer and the conditions determining that extent have been intensively studied by learning psychologists (see Maier, Prange, and Rosenstiel, Ch. 1 in this volume for further details).

To illustrate the major, even fundamental mechanism that emotions constitute in many cases, let us return to the example of the child whose tongue has been burned by hot chocolate. This person has experienced pain associated with a certain stimulus. Upon a similar occasion later, the child will experience fear or apprehension. The emotion of fear is the most direct consequence of the transfer of learning. Its effect is generally highly adaptive: The behavior of sipping and swallowing will not be initiated unless extensive prior checking has revealed the absence of danger. As in other cases mentioned above, the transfer of learning via emotion elicitation may also have negative consequences, leading to dysfunctional behavior. For example, if the generalization gradient is too flat, that is if even highly dissimilar objects, such as nonliquid matter in a similar container, evoke fear and require elaborate checking procedures, the behavioral responses will obviously be slowed down and inappropriate behavior may occur. Interestingly, habitual tendencies to over- or undergeneralize in learning may become part of an individual's personality. Thus, overgeneralizing from danger stimuli can be seen as part of an anxiety syndrome. Conversely, chronic anxiety can lead to overgeneralization of perceived danger. In this fashion, these processes reinforce each other.

To what extent can one observe effects of transfer and generalization in an organizational learning context? Are there 'anxious' organizations that see risks and dangers everywhere because of some traumatic learning experience? Although 'learning by mistakes' or 'learning through failure' is an appealing concept for organizational learning (Sitkin 1992/1996), some organizations have to analyze the situation carefully before they decide what and how they want to learn from their mistakes. For example, trial-and-error learning could easily be detrimental to survival in high-reliability organizations such as aircraft carriers (see LaPorte and Consolini 1991) and nuclear power stations (see Perrow 1984). As Weick and Roberts (1996) pointed out, however, high-reliability organizations can be learning organizations if their team members have a sufficiently high degree of interrelatedness keeping fear at bay.

Whereas transfer generally occurs unconsciously in individuals, it may be quite explicit, at least in part, in organizational learning. The Walkman provides a good illustration. SONY introduced the first Walkman—the TPS-L2—in response to a complaint in 1978 from its honorary chairman, who considered the traditional tape-recorder too heavy for easy use (Cooper 1994). Despite the new product's negative ratings from dealers, it was launched in 1979, and over 1.5 million units were sold within two years. A climate of hope and interest must have prevailed at SONY, facilitating transfer, because the company continued to develop and launch innovative, high-risk products.

In the case of negative experiences, excessive transfer can become dysfunctional if fear, which is based on experiences of punishment in the past, becomes the dominant emotion, blocks all impulses of exploratory behavior, and thus hampers creativity (see above). In some cases one may even speak of 'corporate traumas' comparable to anxiety disorders treated as affective disorders. For this reason Sitkin (1992/1996) insisted that failure—and the experience of successfully dealing with it—is essential to organizational learning. Failure makes for systemic resilience in confronting future unknown changes. The relentless efforts of Jack Welch, the CEO of General Electric, to make GE a 'boundaryless' company (Hirschhorn and Gilmore 1992: 30; Nonaka and Takeuchi 1995: 131–5) might be interpreted as an attempt to break through such corporate trauma: 'getting ideas to flow means thawing out those parts of the company still frozen by fear' (Webber 1992: 16).

The Production of Learned Behavior Patterns

The components of the learning process that have been dealt with so far have all concerned changes that the behavior of organisms and organizations undergo because of new motivational tendencies, knowledge of strategies or skills, or insight into cause–effect relationships. The probability that the results of these learning processes actually change observable behavior has been referred to only in passing. In fact, one of the important limitations of learning is that it serves adaptation but does not guarantee it. Thus, adaptation to changing environmental conditions not only implies the learning of new contingencies and strategies but also requires the execution of appropriate behaviors. There are a multitude of factors that may encourage or prevent the realization of behaviors that correspond to earlier learning (see Maier, Prange, and Rosenstiel, Ch. 1 in this volume for further details). For example, the prestige or perceived success of an observed model company can encourage the actual imitation of behavior learned by observation, particularly because long-range negative effects of such imitation (e.g. a law suit) often may occur at a much later time and may be less visible.

Emotional responses, especially interest, jealousy, or envy, can play a major role in the effects of models that incite imitative behavior. One process to note in particular is emotional contagion: A model that is seen to enjoy strong positive affect following an observed action may engender positive feelings in the learner and increase the likelihood of imitation.

The fact that the learning of contingencies or behavioral strategies is independent of the execution of the corresponding behaviors is particularly evident from the inhibition of learned behaviors. In many cases, this inhibition is due to anxiety stemming from actual or imagined punishment or to moral principles. Thus, learning processes continuously increase the behavioral repertoire and the knowledge base of organisms and organizations, but the actual behavior is often subject to stringent control and regulation by factors that depend on the individual, the organization, or the larger social context. In consequence, the study of organizational learning needs to distinguish clearly between the failure to acquire appropriate knowledge or skills and the failure to execute the behavior reflecting such learning. It is highly likely that both individuals and organizations have an enormous reserve of 'unactualized' learning. In many cases the inhibition of asocial or amoral behavior is highly desirable. Sometimes, however, the nonactualization of valuable learning is due to false conceptions of moral principles and thus to inadequate feelings of shame and guilt. In organizational learning, it may often be that the organizational units that have learned are too weak or timid to influence decisions on actual behavior. In some cases, learning at a given level in the power structure may be suppressed by higher units in order to stabilize the status quo and the privileges that go with it (see also discussion of the effect of power on organizational learning in Gherardi and Nicolini, Ch. 2; and Rothman and Friedman, Ch. 26 in this volume).

Although emotions like shame and guilt may often be appropriate to prevent the organism or organization from engaging in high-risk or legally or morally dubious activities, high levels of anxiety (e.g. as part of the emotional climate in a company) can interfere with the full utilization of learning processes. In many cases, attempts at disinhibiting learning-based behaviors may have important adaptational effects without requiring great effort. On the whole, then, attention should be directed not only to the learning process and the acquisition of knowledge but also to the issues of how emotions and emotional climate can affect the transfer and the production of behavior that prior learning may have made available. Many of these effects have been illustrated in literature dealing with group dynamics in organizations (see contributions in Hare, Blumberg, Davies, and Kent 1994). Although few studies on such topics as conformity, power, and coalition formation have explicitly analyzed the role of emotion and emotional climate in reinforcement learning, classical conditioning, imitation learning, extinction, mood-dependent recall, and other phenomena described in this chapter, it is reasonably safe to say that many of these phenomena's effects are, in fact, due to emotion. For example, a climate of anxiety in a group can increase conformity among its members.

Different Types of Emotion in Organizational Learning

We have explored the nature of the learning process in both individuals and organizations, reviewing the effects of emotion and emotional climate on each aspect of this process. Drawing on the insights gained from the review of the effects that emotion has on the different components of the learning process, we conclude by summarizing and synthesizing the role of different kinds of emotions and their relative functionality or dysfunctionality in organizational learning. It seems appropriate to group the various emotions into five major classes: approach emotions, achievement emotions, deterrence emotions, withdrawal emotions, and antagonistic emotions. Each of these classes has both positive and negative effects on organizational learning. This classification scheme is based on both a synthesis of the effects of emotion on learning—one that emerges from the survey of the literature presented in the preceding sections— and on general theoretical considerations of the functions that different emotions have.

We suggest the label of 'approach emotions' for affective states like interest, hope, joyful anticipation, or other states that are likely to fuel the investment of energy into new activities of exploration and development, focusing the attention on areas of major significance to the learner and providing the necessary drive to overcome obstacles. Obviously, such motivational-emotional contexts provide optimal conditions for the acquisition of new skills and competencies. Although approach emotions are generally among the most functional states for organizational learning, there can be drawbacks when they are too intense or unrealistic. For example, ill-founded hopes and anticipations that channel much energy and attention into directions unlikely to yield the expected profits can be highly dysfunctional. Similarly, interest that is fueled mostly by fashion or blind imitation of others may also disperse energy and attentional capacity rather than focus them on what is pertinent to the learner.

Another class of generally positive emotions, such as satisfaction, happiness, and pride, can be labeled 'achievement emotions'. They mark the celebration of success based either on one's achievement or on unexpected luck and reinforce the contingencies in which the emotion-producing experience is rooted. This class of emotions has rather paradoxical effects on individual and organizational learning. Although these emotions have very agreeable consequences for both individuals and organizations and serve the highly positive function of reinforcing positive contingencies, they do present dangers, in particular stagnation. Satisfaction, happiness, elation, and pride all mark reactions to achievement and success. They capitalize on past investments. This relation is particularly obvious in the case of pride when the success is attributed exclusively to internal sources, that is, when one's own contribution is seen as the most important factor in the success under consideration. Self-attribution of this kind does not necessarily lead to an impartial analysis of a situation or to ever-increasing efforts to improve and learn. Only if the emotions potentially leading to stagnation are paired with other types of motivations, such as wanting to always be the best or worrying about losing a privileged position, is the learner propelled from the state of rejoicing in past achievements to the state of making new efforts. An instructive illustration of the dangers of success and the accompanying achievement emotions for organizational learning is provided by the existence of 'competence traps' (see Dierkes, Marz, and Teele, Ch. 12; Kieser, Beck, and Tainio, Ch. 27 in this volume).

March, Sproull, and Tamuz (1996) discussed the balance between the exploitation of old certainties and the exploration of new possibilities in organizational learning. Clearly, an emotional climate marked by achievement emotions in an organization is likely to shift the balance to the exploration of old certainties. In particular, achievement emotions may prevent learning if they bring about a failure to routinely reinterpret specific outcomes or explore alternatives to them (see March, Sproull, and Tamuz 1996).

We suggest using the term 'deterrence emotion' to denote anxiety, fear, distress, pessimism, and all other varieties of affective states that all keep the learner from engaging in particular activities or seeking out places or markets. Emotions of this type can have quite deleterious effects on learning because they often prevent learners from even exposing themselves to new information and experiences, thus vitiating the potential for learning. Excessive worry and anxiety can be a formidable block to acquiring new skills, competencies, or opportunities. At most, an emotional climate dominated by deterrence emotions guarantees the maintenance of the status-quo, for it will not encourage innovation or creativity. On the other hand, the effect of deterrence emotions is not entirely negative, either for an individual or an organization. They prevent the learner from repeating mistakes, from entering into overly risky strategies or behaviors, and from disregarding potential threats. Thus, judiciously blending deterrence emotions with approach emotions could provide the proper balance for cautious advancement into new learning environments.

The class of states called 'withdrawal emotions', including sadness, resignation, shame, and guilt, generally provides a negative context for learning activities. The reason is that the individual or organization characterized by these emotions tends to focus on the inside rather than the outside and lacks the necessary energy to pursue a learning process vigorously or to invest in new ventures. Periods of resignation are typically accompanied, for instance, by severance of contacts, a slackening of efforts and an avoidance of new investments, phenomena generally not conducive to learning. On the other hand, their effects are not only negative. For an individual, periods of withdrawal are generally considered healing periods. Sadness, for example, is often seen as grief work to help the mourner readapt to changes in his or her world after a loss of a relationship. Similarly, in an organizational context, one could conceive of a period of resignation and of focus on intraorganizational matters as a phase of restructuring and regeneration requiring all the organization's energies to be directed inward.

Finally, one can distinguish 'antagonistic emotions' such as anger, irritation, hate, and aggression. Hindrances to achieving one's goals and interests universally trigger antagonistic emotions (Scherer 1997). The evolutionary function of these emotions is to overcome such obstacles and reassert the interests of the organism or the organization. These emotions obviously have positive consequences, such as enabling one to get what one wants. (They thereby also provide learning experiences in how to overcome obstacles.) But antagonistic emotions may also divert focus from what is pertinent, may limit attentiveness, and may have other similarly deleterious effects on essential ingredients of learning. As the popular saying goes, anger often makes one blind. The angry individual is driven by an overriding concern with surmounting the obstacle or with punishing the agent responsible for the frustration. In this sense, antagonistic emotions set up new aims and goals such as revenge, which may be quite alien to a productive learning process (see Bies and Tripp 1996).

Antagonistic emotions within an organization often represent friction between its members. Being detrimental to a positive emotional climate, antagonistic emotions seriously hamper the organizational learning process. Obviously, this interference will lead members to block each other and will prevent the development of synergy between the members of the organization.

Table 16.1 summarizes the functions and potential effects that different kinds of emotions have on the behavior and performance of individuals and organizations. This review has demonstrated that there is no simple answer to the question of what might be ideal emotions for individual or organizational learning. Each class of emotions has advantages and drawbacks for the learning process. Often, a blend of the various classes of emotions is what seems to foster optimal learning. Clearly, the optimal blend depends on the nature of the situation in which an organization finds itself. If readaptation and reorganization are needed, it may well be necessary for withdrawal emotions to dominate (although not exclusively, for it is also important to continue seeking the necessary external input into the reorganization process). In periods of rapid development and environmental change, an optimal climate seems to require a predominance of approach emotions—coupled with deterrence emotions in order to avoid overshooting. With such analysis, it might be possible in the future to increase the precision of the mix of emotions necessary in order to optimize the emotional climate for learning organizations.

Conclusion and Outlook

The general theme of this chapter has been the strong adaptive function of emotions. Just as in the case of individuals, emotions in organizations are powerful determinants of the organization's fitness in the modern market place. Contrary to what was believed for a very long period of time when notions of rationality pervaded management science, organizations, like individuals, cannot behave rationally without emotions. In individuals and organizations alike, emotions constitute organized, coordinated states rather than, as has always been believed, chaotic or disorganized states. Emotions focus the energies of an organization on events, provide the organization with crucial learning opportunities, and produce the motivational underpinning necessary for a sustained effort to learn about adapting to changing environments. However, the adaptive function of emotion in evolutionary terms does not imply that effects are always positive in the short run. On the contrary, emotions can have negative impacts—both the chaotic, disorganized effects feared by the rationalists and the stagnation that may result from the consistency and orderliness characterizing achievement emotions. Thus, it is only through careful consideration of the different potential effects of emotion and emotional climate on organizational learning processes that organizational performance can be optimized. The complex effects of different types of emotion make it difficult to establish simple recipes specifying the type of emotion or emotional climate that is optimal for organizational learning. Rather, it seems that different blends of emotions at different points in time in the activity of a company can be described as optimal for organizational learning. Furthermore, different, partly incompatible emotions may occur at the same time, producing emotional conflict. This complication is particularly common at the organizational level, where the emotional climate may be characterized by the simultaneous emergence of incompatible emotions shared by different subgroups in an organization. Such a situation is especially likely if the goals and interests of these subgroups start to diverge (see Rothman and Friedman, Ch. 26 in this volume).

In this chapter a number of ways in which emotions impinge on different phases of the learning process were reviewed. These effects can be helpful or harmful, depending on the kind of emotion and the respective context involved. It is therefore to the advantage of the learning organization to monitor emotions

Table 16.1. Major classes of emotion and their effects on organizational learning

Functional class	Representative emotions	Effects on organizational learning
Approach emotions	Interest, hope, joyful anticipation	Foster exploration and development, provide motivational underpinning for sustained goal-directed activity
Achievement emotions	Relief, satisfaction, contentment, joy, pride, elation	Positively reinforce achievement, are responses to positive chance outcomes, may imply overattribution of personal merit and encourage stagnation
Deterrence emotions	Anxiety, fear, distress, pessimism	Serve as warnings of imminent danger or negative consequences based on generalizations from past experiences; may prevent further development, block exploration, and generally inhibit learning
Withdrawal emotions	Sadness, resignation, shame, guilt	Serve to facilitate restoration of forces and internal adaptation after an uncontrollable loss or the discovery of a major personal shortcoming requiring dissimulation, re-pair, or both in oneself; may deprive organism of energy and drive it to vigorous pursuit of learning or acting on knowledge
Antagonistic emotions	Irritation, anger, hate, aggressiveness	Serve to forcefully overcome obstacles to goal achievement and assert individual or organizational interest and status; may lead to self-assertion becoming aim in itself and conflict hampering or permanently damaging normal relations and interactions

and emotional climate in the organization and to assess potential effects on learning as well as on other important factors of an organization's effectiveness, such as efficiency, productivity, and creativity. With improvement in the understanding of emotion and the processes that enhance learning and performance in organizations, there are interesting parallels to be drawn. Janis (1989), for example, took emotions into account in his research on the 'Groupthink' phenomenon—the tendency for top-level decision-makers to conform closely to the leader's or majority's decision. He specifically considered anger, hostility, fear, anxiety, elation, shame, and guilt to be detrimental to decision-making. Emotional climate based on this class of states may also be detrimental to learning and the company's general performance because such emotions may inhibit the generation and or the thorough evaluation of

alternatives, as when a 'group emotion' leads to Groupthink. On the other hand, an emotional climate of interest and hope (approach emotions) will enhance learning through exploration and creativity (generation of alternatives). In this case, group emotion based on shared appraisals from the group members is actually beneficial and is likely to prevent the development of Groupthink.

Research on the determinants and dynamics of organizationally relevant emotions is still in its infancy. High potential for rapid development exists, however, for the conceptual and theoretical foundations are being laid and methodological tools are being developed. Such emotions are clearly not only triggered by eliciting events but also shaped by the larger organizational context, such as power and communication structures and organizational culture. Consequently, the role of emotions in organizations and their effects on learning need to be addressed in comprehensive inter-disciplinary research at both the individual and organizational levels.

References

Albrow, M. (1992). 'Sine Ira et Studio—Or Do Organizations Have Feelings?' *Organization Studies*, 13: 313–29.

Alloy, L. B. and Abramson, L. Y. (1988). 'Depressive Realism: Four Theoretical Perspectives', in L. B. Alloy (ed.), *Cognitive Process in Depression*. New York: Guilford, 223–65.

Argyris, C. and Schön, D. A. (1978). *Organizational Learning: A Theory of Action Perspective*. Reading, Mass.: Addison-Wesley.

——— (1996). *Organizational Learning*: Vol. 2. *Theory, Method, and Practice*. Reading, Mass.: Addison-Wesley.

Ashforth, B. E. and Humphrey, R. H. (1995). 'Emotions in the Workplace: A Reappraisal'. *Human Relations*, 48: 97–125.

Astrachan, J. H. (1995). 'Organizational Departures: The Impact of Separation Anxiety as Studied in a Mergers and Acquisitions Simulation'. *Journal of Applied Behavioral Science*, 31: 31–50.

Berthoin Antal, A. (1998). 'Die Dynamik der Theoriebildungsprozesse zum Organisationslernen', in H. Albach, M. Dierkes, A. Berthoin Antal, and K. Vaillant (eds.), *Organisationslernen—institutionelle und kulturelle Dimensionen. WZB Jahrbuch 1998*. Berlin: edition sigma, 31–52.

Bies, R. J. and Tripp, T. M. (1996). '"Getting Even" and the Need for Revenge', in R. M. Kramer and T. R. Tyler (eds.), *Trust in Organizations: Frontiers of Theory and Research*. Thousand Oaks, Calif.: Sage, 246–60.

Bower, G. H. (1992). 'How Might Emotions Affect Learning?', in S.-A. Christianson (ed.), *The Handbook of Emotion and Memory: Research and Theory*. Hillsdale, NJ: Erlbaum, 3–31.

Brown, R. and Kulik, J. (1977). 'Flashbulb Memories'. *Cognition*, 5: 73–99.

Butterfield, K. D., Trevino, L. K., and Ball, G. A. (1996). 'Punishment from the Manager's Perspective: A Grounded Investigation and Inductive Model'. *Academy of Management Journal*, 39: 1479–512.

Callan, V. J. (1993). 'Individual and Organizational Strategies for Coping with Organizational Change' (Special issue: Coping with Stress at Work). *Work and Stress*, 7: 63–75.

Carnevale, P. J. D. and Isen, A. M. (1986). 'The Influence of Positive Affect and Visual Access on the Discovery of Integrative Solution in Bilateral Negotiation'. *Organizational Behavior and Human Decision Processes*, 37: 1–13.

Christianson, S.-A. (ed.) (1992). *The Handbook of Emotion and Memory: Research and Theory*. Hillsdale, NJ: Erlbaum.

Cooper, R. (1994). *Sony Corporation: The Walkman Line*. Case No. 9–195–076. Boston: Harvard Business School Press.

Denison, D. R. (1996). 'What IS the Difference between Organizational Culture and Organizational Climate? A Native's Point of View on a Decade of Paradigm Wars'. *Academy of Management Review*, 21: 619–54.

De Rivera, J. (1992). 'Emotional Climate: Social Structure and Emotional Dynamics'. *International Review of Studies of Emotion*, 2: 197–218.

Dolan, S. L. and Renaud, S. (1992). 'Individual, Organizational and Social Determinants of Managerial Burnout: A Multivariate Approach'. *Journal of Social Behavior and Personality*, 7: 95–110.

Donahue, W. A. and Ramesh, C. R. (1992). 'Negotiator–opponent Relationships', in L. L. Putnam and M. Roloff (eds.), *Communication and Negotiation*. Thousand Oaks, Calif.: Sage.

Ekman, P. (1992). 'An Argument for Basic Emotions'. *Cognition and Emotion*, 6/3–4: 169–200.

Erera, I. P. (1992). 'Social Support under Conditions of Organizational Ambiguity'. *Human Relations*, 45: 247–64.

Estrada, C. A., Isen, A. M., and Young, M. J. (1994). 'Positive Affect Improves Creative Problem-Solving and Influences Reported Source of Practice Satisfaction in Physicians'. *Motivation and Emotion*, 18: 285–99.

Fineman, S. (ed.) (1996). *Emotion and Organising*. London: Sage.

——(1997). 'Emotion and Management Learning'. *Management Learning*, 28: 13–25.

Flam, H. (1990a). 'Emotional "Man": I. The Emotional "Man" and the Problem of Collective Action'. *International Sociology*, 5: 39–56.

——(1990b). 'Emotional "Man": II. Corporate Actors as Emotion-motivated Emotion Managers'. *International Sociology*, 5: 225–34.

Frank, R. H. (1988). *Passions within Reason*. New York: Norton.

Frese, M. (1990). 'Arbeit und Emotion', in F. Frey and I. Udis (eds.), *Das Bild der Arbeit*. Bern: Huber, 285–301.

Frijda, N. H. (1986). *The Emotions*. Cambridge: Cambridge University Press.

——Mesquita, B., Sonnemans, J., and Van Goozen, S. (1991). 'The Duration of Affective Phenomena or: Emotions, Sentiments and Passions', in K. T. Strongman (ed.), *International Review of Studies on Emotion* (Vol. 1). New York: Wiley, 187–225.

Greyser, S. A. and Langford, N. (1993). *IBM: When the Numbers Failed to Compute*. Case No. 9–593–079. Boston: Harvard Business School Press.

Hackman, J. R. and Wageman, R. (1995). 'Total Quality Management: Empirical, Conceptual, and Practical Issues'. *Administrative Science Quarterly*, 40: 309–42.

Hale, S. and Jansen, J. (1994). 'Global Processing-time Coefficients Characterize Individual and Group Differences in Cognitive Speed'. *Psychological Science*, 5: 384–9.

Hare, A. P., Blumberg, H. H., Davies, M. F., and Kent, M. V. (eds.) (1994). *Small Group Research: A Handbook*. Norwood, NJ: Ablex.

Hatfield, E., Cacioppo, J. T., and Rapson, R. L. (1992). 'Primitive Emotional Contagion', in S. C. Margaret (ed.), *Review of Personality and Social Psychology*: Vol. 14. *Emotion and Social Behavior*. Thousand Oaks, Calif.: Sage, 151–77.

Hedberg, B. L. T. (1981). 'How Organizations Learn and Unlearn', in P. C. Nystrom and W. H. Starbuck (eds.), *Handbook of Organizational Design*: Vol. 1. *Adapting Organizations to Their Environments*. Oxford: Oxford University Press, 3–27.

Heuer, F. and Reisberg, D. (1992). 'Emotion and Detail Memory', in S.-A. Christianson (ed.), *The Handbook of Emotion and Memory: Research and Theory*. Hillsdale, NJ: Erlbaum, 3–31.

Hewstone, M. (1994). 'Revision of Stereotypic Beliefs', in W. Stroebe and M. Hewstone (eds.), *European Review of Social Psychology* (Vol. 5). Chichester: J. Wiley, 69–110.

Hinsz, V. B., Tindale, R. S., and Vollrath, D. A. (1997). 'The Emerging Conceptualization of Groups as Information Processors'. *Psychological Bulletin*, 121: 43–64.

Hirschhorn, L. and Gilmore, T. (1992). 'The New Boundaries of the "Boundaryless" Company'. *Harvard Business Review: The Emerging Organization*, Set No. 49303: 30–41.

Hochschild, A. R. (1979). 'Emotion Work, Feeling Rules, and Social Structure'. *American Journal of Sociology*, 85: 1–75.

——(1983). *The Managed Heart*. Berkeley: University of California Press.

Huber, G. P. (1996). 'Organizational Learning: The Contributing Processes and the Literatures', in M. D. Cohen and L. S. Sproull (eds.), *Organizational Learning*. Thousand Oaks, Calif.: Sage, 124–62.

Isen, A. M. and Baron, R. A. (1991). 'Positive Affect as a Factor in Organizational Behavior', in L. L. Cummings and B. M. Staw (eds.), *Research in Organizational Behavior: An Annual Series of Analytical Essays and Critical Reviews* (Vol. 13). Greenwich, Conn.: JAI Press, 1–53.

——and Means, B. (1983). 'The Influence of Positive Affect on the Unusualness of Word Associations'. *Journal of Personality and Social Psychology*, 48: 1413–26.

Izard, C. E. (1993). 'Four Systems for Emotion Activation: Cognitive and Noncognitive Processes'. *Psychological Review*, 100: 68–90.

Jains, I. L. (1989). *Crucial Decisions: Leadership in Policymaking and Crisis Management*. New York: Free Press.

Kaufmann, F. X. (ed.) (1979). *Bürgernahe Sozialpolitik*. Frankfurt am Main: Campus.

Kerr, S. (1975). 'On the Folly of Rewarding A, while Hoping for B'. *Academy of Management Journal*, 18: 49–58.

Kumar, R. (1997). 'The Role of Affect in Negotiations: An Integrative View'. *Journal of Applied Behavioral Science*, 33: 84–100.

LaFarge, V. V. S. (1994). 'The Ambivalence of Departing Employees: Reactions of Involuntary and Voluntary Exiters'. *Journal of Applied Behavioral Science*, 30: 175–97.

LaPorte, T. R. and Consolini, P. M. (1991). 'Working in Practice but Not in Theory: Theoretical Challenges of High-reliability Organizations'. *Journal of Public Administration Research and Theory*, 1: 19–47.

Lazarus, R. S. (1991). *Emotion and Adaptation*. New York: Oxford University Press.

Levitt, B. and March, J. G. (1996). 'Organizational Learning', in M. D. Cohen and L. S. Sproull (eds.), *Organizational Learning*. Thousand Oaks, Calif.: Sage, 516–40.

March, J. G. and Olsen, J. P. (1988). 'The Uncertainty of the Past: Organizational Learning under Ambiguity', in J. G. March (ed.), *Decisions and Organizations*. New York: Oxford University Press, 335–8.

—— Sproull, L. S., and Tamuz, M. (1996). 'Learning from Samples of One or Fewer', in M. D. Cohen and L. S. Sproull (eds.), *Organizational Learning*. Thousand Oaks, Calif.: Sage, 1–19.

McAllister, D. J. (1995). 'Affect- and Cognition-based Trust as Foundations for Interpersonal Co-operation in Organizations' (Special issue: Intra- and Interorganizational Cooperation). *Academy of Management Journal*, 38: 24–59.

Mikula, G., Scherer, K. R., and Athenstaedt, U. (1998). 'The Role of Injustice in the Elicitation of Differential Emotional Reactions'. *Personality and Social Psychology Bulletin*, 24: 769–83.

Mizuno, S., Matsubara, T., and Takai, J. (1994). 'Influences of Emotional Reaction and Personal Power on the Leadership Process: An Examination of Moderating and Mediating Effects'. *Japanese Journal of Experimental Social Psychology*, 33/3: 201–12.

Morris, J. A. and Feldman, D. C. (1996). 'The Dimensions, Antecedents, and Consequences of Emotional Labor'. *Academy of Management Review*, 21: 986–1010.

MSN Investor Report. (1999). *Benetton Group, S.p.A. Report*, 7 (7 March). Available: http//:www.investor.msn.com

Nesse, R. M. and Berridge, K. C. (1997). 'Psychoactive Drug Use in Evolutionary Perspective'. *Science*, 278: 63–6.

Nonaka, I. (1994). 'A Dynamic Theory of Organizational Knowledge Creation'. *Organization Science*, 5: 14–37.

—— and Takeuchi, H. (1995). *The Knowledge-creating Company: How Japanese Companies Create the Dynamics of Innovation*. New York: Oxford University Press.

Paez, D., Asun, D., and Gonzalez, J. L. (1995). 'Emotional Climate, Mood and Collective Behavior: Chile 1973–1990', in H. Riguelme (ed.), *Era in Twilight*. Hamburg/Bilbao: Foundation for Children/Horizonte Ed., 141–82.

Park, O. S., Sims, H. P., Jr., and Motowidlo, S. J. (1986). 'Affect in Organizations: How Feelings and Emotions Influence Managerial Judgement', in H. P. Sims, Jr. and D. A. Gioia (eds.), *The Thinking Organization*. San Francisco: Jossey-Bass, 215–37.

Pekrun, R. and Frese, M. (1992). 'Emotions in Work and Achievement'. *International Review of Industrial and Organizational Psychology*, 7: 153–200.

Perrow, C. (1984). *Normal Accidents: Living with High-risk Technologies*. New York: Basic Books.

Phillips, W. A. and Baddeley, A. D. (1989). 'Learning and Memory', in A. D. Baddeley and N. O. Bernsen (eds.), *Research Directions in Cognitive Science: European Perspectives*: Vol. 1. *Cognitive Psychology*. Hillsdale, NJ: Erlbaum, 61–83.

Putnam, L. and Mumby, D. K. (1993). 'Organizations, Emotion and the Myth of Rationality', in S. Fineman (ed.), *Emotions in Organizations*. London: Sage, 36–57.

Rafaeli, A. (1989). 'When Clerks Meet Customers: A Test of Variables Relating to Emotional Expression on the Job'. *Journal of Applied Psychology*, 74: 385–93.

Rafaeli, A. and Sutton, R. I. (1987). 'Expression of Emotion as Part of the Work Role'. *Academy of Management Review*, 12: 23–37.

Rafaeli, A. and Sutton, R. I. (1991). 'Emotional Contrast Strategies as Means of Social Influence: Lessons from Criminal Interrogators and Bill Collectors'. *Academy of Management Journal*, 34: 749–75.

Rapaport, D. (1971). *Emotions and Memory*. New York: International Universities Press.

Reichers, A. E. and Schneider, B. (1990). 'Climate and Culture: An Evolution of Constructs', in B. Schneider (ed.), *Organizational Climate and Culture*. San Francisco: Jossey-Bass, 5–39.

Schein, E. H. (1992). *Organizational Culture and Leadership* (2nd edn). San Francisco: Jossey-Bass.

—— (1993). 'How Can Organizations Learn Faster? The Challenge of Entering the Green Room'. *Sloan Management Review*, 34/2: 85–92.

Scherer, K. R. (1984). 'On the Nature and Function of Emotion: A Component Process Approach', in K. R. Scherer and P. Ekman (eds.), *Approaches to Emotion*. Hillsdale, NJ: Erlbaum, 293–318.

—— (1993). 'Neuroscience Projections to Current Debates in Emotion Psychology' (Special issue: Neuropsychological Perspectives on Emotion). *Cognition and Emotion*, 7: 1–41.

—— (1997). 'The Role of Culture in Emotion-antecedent Appraisal'. *Journal of Personality and Social Psychology*, 73: 902–22.

—— (1998). 'Appraisal Theories', in T. Dalgleish and M. Power (eds.), *Handbook of Cognition and Emotion*. Chichester: Wiley, 637–63.

—— Scherer, U., and Klink, M. (1979). 'Determinanten des Verhaltens öffentlich Bediensteter im Publikumsverkehr', in F. X. Kaufmann (ed.), *Bürgernahe Sozialpolitik*. Frankfurt am Main: Campus, 408–51.

Scherer, U. and Scherer, K. R. (1980). 'Psychological Factors in Bureaucratic Encounters: Determinants and Effects of Interactions between Officials and Clients', in W. T. Singleton, P. Spurgeon, and R. B. Stammers (eds.), *The Analysis of Social Skill*. New York: Plenum, 315–28.

Schneider, S. C. and Angelmar, R. (1993). 'Cognition in Organizational Analysis: Who's Minding the Store?' *Organization Studies*, 14: 347–74.

Schroder, H. M., Driver, M. J., and Streufert, S. (1967). *Human Information Processing: Individuals and Groups Functioning in Complex Social Situations*. New York: Holt, Rinehart and Winston.

Senge, P. M. (1990). *The Fifth Discipline: The Art and Practice of the Learning Organization*. New York: Doubleday Currency.

Sitkin, S. B. (1996). 'Learning through Failure: The Strategy of Small Losses', in M. D. Cohen and L. S. Sproull (eds.), *Organizational Learning*. Thousand Oaks, Calif.: Sage, 541–77.

Staw, B. M., Sutton, R. I., and Pelled, L. H. (1994). 'Employee Positive Emotion and Favorable Outcomes at the Workplace'. *Organization Science*, 5: 51–71.

Strongman, K. T. (1986). *The Psychology of Emotion* (3rd edn). Chichester: Wiley.

Sutton, R. I. (1991). 'Maintaining Norms about Expressed Emotions: The Case of Bill Collectors'. *Administrative Science Quarterly*, 36: 245–68.

—— and Rafaeli, A. (1988). 'Untangling the Relationship between Displayed Emotions and Organizational Sales: The Case of Convenience Stores'. *Academy of Management Journal*, 31: 461–87.

Tran, V. (1998). 'The Role of the Emotional Climate in Learning Organizations'. *Learning Organization*, 5: 99 103.

Van Maanen, J. and Kunda, G. (1989). ' "Real Feelings": Emotional Expression and Organizational Culture', in L. L. Cummings and B. M. Staw (eds.), *Research in Organizational Behavior: An Annual Series of Analytical Essays and Critical Reviews* (Vol. 11). Greenwich, Conn.: JAI Press, 43–103.

Waldron, V. R. (1994). 'Once More, with Feeling: Reconsidering the Role of Emotion at Work', in S. A. Deetz (ed.), *Communication Yearbook* (Vol. 17). London: Sage, 388–428.

Webber, A. M. (1992). 'What's so New about the New Economy?' *Harvard Business Review: The Emerging Organization*, Set No. 49303: 9–18.

Weick, K. E. and Roberts, K. H. (1996). 'Collective Mind in Organizations: Heedful Interrelating on Flight Decks', in M. D. Cohen and L. S. Sproull (eds.), *Organizational Learning*. Thousand Oaks, Calif.: Sage, 330–58.

Wiegand, M. (1996). *Prozesse organisationalen Lernens*. Wiesbaden: Gabler.

PART IV

AGENTS OF ORGANIZATIONAL LEARNING

Introduction

Whereas Part III focused on structure and context, this section deals with agency. Agents of organizational learning are identified as individuals or groups—whether inside or outside the organization—whose actions facilitate or inhibit organizational learning. Each chapter in this part focuses on the role of a particular agent, broadening the still relatively narrow scope of research in the field. A central message is that the process of organizational learning occurs through the complex web of relationships created among the various agents as they carry out their organizational roles. Thus, no single group can be seen to be the primary agent or source of organizational learning. The actions of one set of agents can support or hinder the contribution that other agents make to organizational learning, a possibility suggesting that much more attention needs to be paid to the dynamics of relationships.

Friedman's chapter reveals a striking gap in the literature on organizational learning. Whereas scholars agree that organizational learning is based on individual learning, the actual process whereby individuals act as agents of organizational learning has received little attention. Friedman seeks to close this gap and thereby complements the other chapters in this section by focusing on the individuals in middle or lower management functions. He uses three short case studies to explore the behavior, skill, and motivation of individuals as agents of organizational learning and to highlight the barriers they face in the organization. Although Friedman locates individual actions in the context of social and material circumstances and recognizes that both internal and external factors of organizations constrain individuals' options, he seeks to avoid the pitfall of structural determinism. He illustrates how individuals can play a more proactive role in enlarging their space of free movement if they recognize their own construction of their reality images and their role in shaping the organizational context.

Sadler succinctly reviews the voluminous literature on leadership over the past century and links it with theories and practices of organizational learning. In so doing, he reveals the limitations of most available models of leadership: an explicit or implicit assumption that the initiative for organizational learning lies primarily with senior managers. He argues that leadership committed to continuous learning is needed at all levels in organizations if they are to adapt successfully to heightened environmental change. He shows how the responsibility of top management becomes one of creating the conditions for distributed leadership and active learning by employees. Sadler recognizes that leaders cannot choose their styles at will and discusses how cultures influence the roles leaders can play in different countries, depending on the norms and expectations of employees. He provides examples from diverse organizations in Europe and the United States to illustrate the characteristics of 'learning leaders' and the opportunities they have to embed learning into the structure and culture of organizations.

The chapter by Tainio, Lilja, and Santalainen explores another agent of organizational learning, boards of directors, and challenges the assumption that they become involved in organizational learning only in times of crisis. Boards with a high proportion of external members are boundary-spanning institutions and can therefore provide vital links between companies and their environment by contributing to knowledge available to top management in strategic decision-making. Although recognizing that corporate governance is subject to different cultural norms, institutions, and regulations around the world, the authors point out that boards have the capacity to be active in different phases of the life cycle and at different points in the performance path of an organization. Boards have the possibility of supporting single-loop as well as double-loop learning. They can stimulate organizational learning strategies of exploitation that are designed to keep small difficulties from turning into large problems and to trigger experimentation with fresh ideas in the search for genuinely new alternatives for the organization. The extent to which boards actually use their possibilities for active engagement in organizational learning depends on the performance of the firm and the power relations with management. Accordingly, the relationship between the board and top management is both complementary and conflicting, and there exists a 'creative tension' between them. The authors propose a typology with which to characterize four conceivable relationships with management in learning processes, emphasizing that in practice the line between the responsibilities can be a fine one that needs to be negotiated carefully by the various actors involved.

Labor unions are usually characterized as resisting and impeding changes in organizations rather than contributing positively to learning processes. Drinkuth, Riegler, and Wolff recognize that organized labor is generally not regarded as having the necessary qualities or even the potential for becoming a constructive and effective partner in organizational learning. In other words, in order to become an agent of learning in public and private organizations, organized labor must first redefine its role and undertake its own organizational learning. The authors argue that organized labor needs to shift from a reactive to a proactive stance in its interaction with employers and must develop new competencies if it is to remain an effective force in society. They then show that in a number of countries change is indeed underway in the self-concept, behavior, and structure of labor unions and works councils, enabling them to become unique agents of organizational learning. Three very different case studies from Sweden and Germany illustrate the factors that promote and hinder organized labor's learning about how to shape processes of change effectively at the national, regional, and local levels. The authors show how such learning entails the reconstruction of many relationships, both within organized labor (e.g. between union headquarters and local unions) and between unions and employers, requiring new processes of trust-building and leading to an altered sharing of responsibilities for agenda-setting and decision-making.

Consultants are yet another kind of boundary-spanning agent of organizational learning. They are usually brought in specifically in order to achieve organizational change, although clients do not necessarily associate this purpose with learning. In their chapter, Berthoin Antal and Krebsbach-Gnath explore the relationship between learning and change. By applying phase models of learning and knowledge creation to process models of consulting interventions, the authors indicate how consultants can either stimulate or impede the ability of the client organization to learn from an intervention. The chapter illustrates that each role a consultant plays entails a counterpart role for the client. Berthoin Antal and Krebsbach-Gnath argue that the distribution of roles is subject to tension between marginality and centrality: The more central the role taken by or assigned to the consultant, the less the organization is likely to learn from an intervention.

The chapters in this part reflect an awareness of how the actions of agents are shaped and constrained by the organizational, institutional, legal, and cultural contexts that are particular to their situation. The multiplicity of changes that these contexts are undergoing requires organizational learning on the part of all the actors. As a result, the agents' roles are constantly evolving and cannot be characterized by a fixed, general model. A common theme throughout the chapters in this part is that organizational learning is a reflexive process. The authors in this part stress that the willingness and ability to learn is a key quality required of all types of agents of organizational learning.

17 The Individual as Agent of Organizational Learning

Victor J. Friedman

By definition, organizational learning is a process that can be fully understood only at the group or organizational level. Nevertheless, seminal theorists on the subject have tended to agree that organizational learning begins, and often ends, with the individual (Argyris and Schön 1978, 1996; March and Olsen 1976; Nonaka and Takeuchi 1995; Senge 1990). Although it makes good sense to analyze individual learning within the context of organizational conditions and processes, this approach often obscures the critical role of the individual as an agent of organizational learning. In fact much subsequent theory and research has all but ignored the role of the individual, focusing on the organization as the unit of analysis (Huber 1991; Levitt and March 1988; Shrivastava 1983) or on the structural and cultural features that promote organizational learning (Cook and Yanow 1993; Garvin 1993; McGill, Slocum, and Lei 1993).

The objective of this chapter is to examine the role of the individual as agent of organizational learning. Because other contributors to this volume discuss the role of leaders (Sadler, Ch. 18 in this volume) and the board of directors (Tainio, Lilja, and Sautalainen, Ch. 19 in this volume), this chapter is focused on individuals who are not necessarily in the position to institute the structural and cultural conditions conducive to the 'learning organization'. I illustrate the role of the individual by presenting three brief case studies: one about an engineer in a manufacturing firm, one about a department manager in a retail store, and one about a department manager in a publishing firm. I draw primarily on the existing theory

and research in order to address four questions: What does it mean for an individual to be an agent of organizational learning? What characterizes the agents' behavior? What special skills are necessary in order to be an effective agent of organizational learning? What motivates people to take on this role despite the considerable risks?

The Link between Individual and Organizational Learning

The link between individual and organizational learning occupies a critical position in theories of organizational learning. Simon (1969, 1991) defined organizational learning as the insights and successful restructuring of organizational problems by individuals as reflected in the structural elements and outcomes of the organization itself. He rejected the notion that organizations themselves learn, claiming that 'all learning takes place inside individual human heads' (Simon 1991: 125) and that organizations learn either through the learning of their members or by taking in new members with new knowledge.

The idea that organizational learning is simply the sum of individual learning has not been widely accepted by other theorists of organizational learning (Fiol and Lyles 1985). March and Olsen (1976) conceived of organizational learning as a cyclical process that links individual belief to individual action to organizational action to environmental response and back to individual belief. Levitt and March (1988) suggested that learning by individuals and groups becomes organizational when inferences drawn from their experiences are encoded into routines (e.g. rules, standard operating procedures, policies, structures) that guide behavior. March and Olsen (1976), and to a somewhat lesser extent Levitt and March (1988), took a rather pessimistic view of an organization's ability to complete the learning cycle. They attributed the limits of organizational learning partly to the limited .cognitive capacity and mixed motivations of individuals.

Nonaka and Takeuchi (1995), who framed the organizational learning process in terms of knowledge creation, clearly emphasized the role of the individual. In their scheme, knowledge creation occurs out of an ongoing process of conversions between tacit and explicit knowledge, conversions that are performed by individuals and not by the organization.

As we have stated repeatedly, an organization cannot create knowledge by itself. Since tacit knowledge held by individuals is the basis of organizational knowledge creation, it seems natural to start the process by focusing on tacit knowledge, which is the rich, untapped source of new knowledge. But tacit knowledge cannot be communicated or passed onto others easily, since it is acquired primarily through experience and not easily expressed in words. Thus, the sharing of tacit knowledge among individuals with different backgrounds, perspectives, and motivations becomes the critical step for organizational knowledge creation to take place. (p. 85)

Thus, the behavior of individuals is necessary, but not sufficient, for organizational learning. In order to make their tacit knowledge explicit and to generate organizational knowledge creation, individuals need to work within groups or teams that facilitate the process by forcing individuals to share their knowledge and by bringing together different knowledge sources.

In a detailed account of the links between learning at the individual, group, departmental, and organizational levels, Argyris and Schön (1996) represented individual knowledge as 'theories of action' (p. 4), which include strategies of action, the values that govern the choice of strategies, and the assumptions on which those strategies and values are based. The authors also posited the existence of group and organizational theories of action that account for the patterned way in which groups and organizations perform their tasks (Argyris and Schön 1978, 1996). On both the individual and the organizational levels, Argyris and Schön (1974: 6–7) made a critical distinction between 'espoused' theory, which represents what people or organizations say about their behavior, and theories-in-use, which are implicit in that behavior. Argyris and Schön (1974, 1978, 1996) not only found contradictions between the two kinds of theories, they also found that individuals were unaware of the contradictions.

According to this approach, one can understand organizational learning only by examining the ways in which individual and interpersonal inquiry are linked to organizational patterns of both action and learning that are characteristic of subunits and the organization as a whole. Argyris and Schön (1996) drew on Dewey's (1938) concept of 'inquiry' as the process that links the individual and organizational learning:

Organizational learning occurs when individuals within an organization experience a problematic situation and inquire into it on the organization's behalf. They experience a surprising mismatch between expected and actual results of action and respond to that mismatch through a process of thought and further action that leads them to modify their images of the organization and their understandings of organizational phenomena and to restructure their activities so as to bring outcomes and expectations into line, thereby changing organizational theory-in-use. In order to become organizational, the learning that results from organizational inquiry must become embedded in the images of organization held in its members' minds and/or in the epistemological artifacts (maps, memories, and programs) embedded in the organizational environment. (Argyris and Schön 1996: 16)

This account of inquiry describes a chain of events that begins with surprise and ends with changes in both individual and organizational theories-in-use. According to this approach, individual learning does not necessarily precede organizational learning, but individuals do play the critical role of setting learning processes in motion. Individuals act as agents of organizational learning when their inquiry is on behalf of the organization, the implication being that this role is either explicitly or implicitly sanctioned by the organization.

Kim (1993) defined 'individual learning as increasing one's capacity to take effective action' (p. 38) and 'organizational learning as increasing an organization's capacity to take effective action' (p. 43). At both levels learning means improving either the conceptual or operational components of mental models. Organizational learning is accomplished when individuals make their mental models explicit and mutually modify them to create shared organizational mental models. Kim (1993) went even further, stating that a group can be viewed as a 'collective individual with its own set of mental models' and that groups can be treated as if they were 'extended individuals' (p. 43).

The conceptual jump from the idea of learning by individuals within organizations to the view that organizations themselves actually learn has raised 'the problem of anthropomorphism' (Kim 1993; Lipshitz, Popper, and Oz 1996). Learning is generally associated with living, biological entities that have some form of intelligence and nervous system that process and store information. Attaching the 'organization' as a subject to the verb 'learn' attributes to organizations an inherent capacity that is not self-evident (Lipshitz, Popper, and Oz 1996). Or, as Argyris and Schön (1978, 1996) asked: 'What is an organization that it may learn?'

One way of answering this question is to use individual learning as a model or metaphor for understanding organizational processes that constitute learning. This approach draws on theories that view organizations as 'systems of interpretation' whose very essence is the ongoing making of meaning and its enactment in organizational behavior (Daft and Weick 1984; Weick 1979). Just as individuals have brains and beliefs, organizations have 'cognitive systems and memories . . . world views and ideologies' (Hedberg 1981: 6). Theorists in

this tradition have applied concepts such as theory-of-action (Argyris and Schön 1974, 1978, 1996) and mental models (Senge 1990) to both the individual and organizational levels.

The foregoing discussion reflects a potential confusion between two common uses of individual learning in discussions about organizational learning (Tsang 1997). In certain contexts discussions of individual learning focus on the roles individuals play as agents of the organizational learning process (Argyris and Schön 1978, 1996; March and Olsen 1976; Nonaka and Takeuchi 1995; Senge 1990). At other times individual learning is used as a model or metaphor for understanding organizational learning itself (Argyris and Schön 1978, 1996; Kim 1993). Because there is a close relationship between individual learning as it occurs in an organizational context and organizational learning itself, confusion may arise about whether the individual is being referred to as an agent of organizational learning or as a metaphor for organizational learning (Tsang 1997). The focus of this chapter is on the individual as agent of, not as a metaphor for, organizational learning.

Who Are Agents of Organizational Learning?

The discussion so far has provided the theoretical justification for focusing on individuals as agents of organizational learning. The following minicases describe the activities of three agents of organizational learning: Dave, Peter, and Marc. The first minicase is drawn from a study by Frohman (1997); the second and third are based on case studies written by participants in courses I have taught on organizational learning.

Minicase #1. Dave, a 42-year-old engineer, had spent his entire career with the company. . . . He had always worked on development projects and . . . was seen as a competent, but not spectacular, performer.

In creating the design for a new vehicle model . . ., Dave realized that substituting lighter weight plastics for metal would be more cost-effective and would improve the vehicle's performance considerably. However, the organization had little experience with plastics and thus provided little support for the idea. Dave took it upon himself to call on potential suppliers to learn more about the benefits of plastics. He performed preliminary analysis of both the technical performance and the economic parameters of substituting plastics for metal.

Because no one in the organization strongly supported his activity, Dave pursued it in a way that was visible but did not produce an enormous amount of attention. After establishing in his own mind that substituting plastic for metal could be very beneficial, Dave worked through organizational channels to propose a series of projects to support-testing plastic components and, if the tests proved successful, their introduction. After persisting for more than nine months, Dave received some support and an opportunity to develop and test plastic parts in trial vehicles.

After two more years of development and testing, the plastic parts were introduced as standard in several of the vehicles Dave had been working on. Meanwhile, Dave was promoted to another project and continued to work enthusiastically for the organization. (Frohman 1997: 42)

Minicase #2. Peter was hired as a department manager in the flagship store of a new autoparts 'superstore' chain. The chain's strategy was 'selling knowledge', not just equipment, so it hired department managers with a high degree of technical expertise and offered them a bonus plan for surpassing sales quotas. Peter, however, soon discovered that his management responsibilities kept him so busy that he had little time to interface with customers. The salespeople, on the other hand, had no expertise and little motivation to sell because they did not receive a bonus.

In order to address this problem, Peter reorganized his department into a team in which the salespeople shared responsibility for management duties such as inventory, ordering, and arranging displays. As a result, Peter found more time to both serve customers and support his salespeople on technical issues. In addition, he sent his salespeople for technical training so that they could serve customers more effectively. Peter's department consistently outperformed other departments, both in the flagship store and in the chain as a whole. After considerable effort, he persuaded top management to include his salespeople in the bonus plan. Even when Peter was promoted and became a purchasing agent for the entire chain, his former department maintained its high performance.

The chain's overall performance had fallen far short of expectations, and Peter felt strongly that the experience of his department could be applied to the entire chain to make a significant improvement. He brought the issue up in a number of management meetings and was asked by the CEO (and his eventual successor) to submit a proposal. Although Peter felt that he had the CEO's personal support, the CEO never acted on Peter's advice even though the chain was struggling to maintain its competitiveness. The CEO admired Peter's accomplishments but attributed them to his unusual talent and rejected Peter's claim that his approach could be applied elsewhere, even though his department continued to outperform all others two years after his promotion to another position. Because Peter enjoyed his work and felt loyal to the company, he stayed on despite a deep sense that the company had missed an important opportunity.

Minicase #3. Marc was a middle manager for the U.S. division of a large European publishing company. With no forewarning the middle managers received a memo announcing top management's decision to shut down three of the eight editorial departments in the organization, instantaneously firing all of their employees. Shortly afterwards another unexpected memo announced, with no explanation, the promotion of two editors to top management. Middle managers had no idea what to tell their employees, who were feeling very insecure, and morale was plummeting. Many of them shared their concerns with Marc, who was known to have close relations with top management. Marc sensed that trust had broken down and that middle management believed that top management did not really want to communicate with them.

Some time after the changes, the CEO called a special meeting in which he presented a very general picture of what had taken place and asked for middle management's support. Marc, however, felt that the real issues were not being addressed by top management, and he was surprised that none of the middle managers were saying what was on their minds. He believed that the meeting ought to be a channel for two-way communication. He wanted to understand top management's actions and to have top management address middle management's concerns.

Finally, Marc stood up and asked the CEO, 'How does top management expect us to respond to the promotion of these two editors in view of the recent, unexplained, sudden firings of our colleagues?' Marc's question was followed by a long silence, after which the CEO addressed his question in general terms. After the meeting the CEO summoned Marc, who felt sure that he was going to be fired. Instead, the CEO demanded an apology and asked Marc what he had meant to accomplish by posing the question as he had. Marc apologized but also described the problems caused by top management's way of communicating its decisions. Although the CEO defended his actions and scolded Marc for putting him on the spot, he did not outwardly reject Marc's criticisms.

Marc then added that, despite the CEO's open-door style of management, many of the managers did not feel free to come speak with him. The CEO was surprised to hear that many of his managers found him inaccessible, but he did not reject Marc's claim. Finally, the CEO told Marc that he would have expected him to come to him personally before confronting him in a meeting. The CEO also warned him that he would 'suffer the consequences' if it happened again. Marc was not fired and continued working with the company for two more years.

The stories of Dave, Peter, and Marc illustrate what it means to be an agent of organizational learning in the realms of product development, organization, and behavior. Dave was an innovator who came up with an idea for improving the product he was working on. By working quietly, but persistently, he was able to bring his idea into fruition and was eventually rewarded. Peter was an innovator in managing the human resources of a retail sales organization. On the local level he was given the freedom to experiment and was rewarded for his success. Although he succeeded in bringing his knowledge to the attention of the organization, he was unable to get them to act on this knowledge. Marc perceived that top management's strategy for communicating its decisions was creating serious problems for its remaining employees. He brought his concerns to top management's attention in a way that he later felt was inappropriate. Nonetheless, he succeeded in providing the CEO with important information that might otherwise have been withheld.

Each example indicates that some organizational learning occurred, though it may have been limited and perhaps even ephemeral. As a result of Dave's efforts, the organization began to incorporate new materials within its production processes. Peter created a department that realized the organization's espoused strategy of selling knowledge and that maintained this strategy even after Peter was promoted to a corporate position. However, he was unable to disseminate this learning throughout the organization. In Marc's case the learning involved norms and perceived violations of norms governing communication, trust, and leadership in the organization. Although these vignettes are not meant to represent a typical or comprehensive sample of the activities of agents of organizational learning, they do provide a basis for illustrating some important characteristics.

All three individuals underwent a similar process that can be analyzed in terms of the four steps in the experiential learning cycle (Argyris and Schön 1978; Kolb 1976). In the first step, all three recognized a gap, contradiction, or mismatch (Argyris and Schön 1996) between the status quo and the standard by which they judged performance. Dave had a hunch that substituting plastic for metal would improve their product's performance. Peter recognized the gap between the company's strategy of selling knowledge and what was actually happening in the stores. Marc saw a contradiction between the kind of relationships that members of top management espoused and their actual behavior in the reorganization process. He was also bothered by the contradiction between what his peers were saying privately and what they were willing to say in public.

The second step was engagement in a process of inquiry in order to make sense of the perceived mismatch. Each individual collected some data and developed a tacit 'theory' of the situation. Dave learned as much as he could about the use of plastics, ran some experiments, and performed an economic analysis in order to determine whether his hunch was correct. Peter analyzed the problem and came to the conclusion that the gap stemmed from a management structure and reward system that did not support the organization's espoused strategy. By talking with peers, Marc diagnosed the problem as one-way communication and a breakdown of trust between top and middle management. He did not at first share his peers' belief that top management avoided discussion with them, but the CEO's behavior in the meeting seemed to confirm this belief. In this sense Marc ran a private test of his theory.

The third step was the development of some idea or proposal designed to produce a significant change. Dave developed a series of projects that could confirm his theory about plastics. Peter rethought the design of the department's task and came up with an idea for a new way of organizing the work. Marc envisioned a two-way process in which both sides could address problems by explaining their concerns and trying to understand each other.

Finally, all three acted on their ideas. Dave introduced his ideas through organizational channels and received authorization to implement them. Peter simply exercised his authority to organize his department as he saw fit. At a later stage he wrote a formal proposal for the CEO in an attempt to disseminate his ideas at the organizational level. Trying to stimulate two-way communication, Marc confronted the CEO, though in retrospect Marc felt that he had not been very competent in performing the intervention itself.

Contradictory Characteristics

Who is likely to take on the role of agent of organizational learning, and what are the attributes of such a person? Nonaka and Takeuchi (1995) offered a profile of 'knowledge practitioners', that is, front-line employees and line managers who 'accumulate, generate, and update both tacit and explicit knowledge' (p. 152). These qualifications include high intellectual standards, a strong sense of commitment to recreating the world according to their own perspectives, a wide variety of experience both inside and outside the company, skills in communicating with customers and colleagues, and an openness to carrying on candid discussions and debates with others. Peter seemed to fit this profile perfectly. Dave appeared to fit most of this profile, though it is questionable whether he had a wide variety of experience outside the company. Marc fitted most of the profile as well, but in this particular case he failed to display skill in carrying on a dialogue with his colleagues and superiors.

Dave and Peter could also be described as 'intrapreneurs'—individuals who 'champion' new ideas and turn them into completely profitable reality (Pinchott 1985). In studies of corporate entrepreneurship (and intrapreneurship), researchers have tried to identify the distinguishing attributes of internal entrepreneurs (using profiles of external entrepreneurs as their model), and the organizational conditions that facilitate their activities (Burgelman and Sayles 1986). For example, Hornsby et al. (1993) hypothesized that internal entrepreneurs are characterized by features such as risk-taking, desire for autonomy, need for achievement, goal orientation, and internal locus of control. Stopford and Baden-Fuller (1994) suggested that entrepreneurship is characterized by proactiveness, attempts to move beyond current capacity, team orientation, ability to resolve dilemmas, and learning ability. Bazeal (1993) pointed out that corporate entrepreneurship requires securing the loyalty and long-term commitment of innovation-minded individuals who might more naturally pursue their ventures on the outside. Miner (1997) found that there is no single set of attributes but rather four types of internal entrepreneurs with four distinct, and to some extent, contradictory profiles.

In this light it is interesting to compare studies of intrapreneurs with the findings of Frohman (1997), who conducted one of the few empirical studies of initiators of organizational change. Many of these initiators of change, such as Dave, were also agents of organizational learning in that their initiation stimulated a process of inquiry into some facet of the organization's operations. In certain ways Frohman's findings clearly contradict the image of intrapreneurs. For instance, these internal change agents were seen as competent people but not as the performers with the highest potential in the company. Furthermore, they were driven more by a desire to meet the needs of the organization than by a personal need for achievement or autonomy. They were internally driven to 'make a difference'.

These studies suggest that a single set of attributes may be insufficient for characterizing agents of organizational learning. These agents are complex individuals who may be driven by mutually opposed forces. It is precisely the complexity and constructive tension of such contradictory attributes that lead these persons to take on the role of agent despite the potential costs.

Thus, if a profile for agents of organizational learning can be identified, it is likely to reflect characteristics that themselves are somewhat contradictory. On the basis of the studies cited above and my own research (Friedman and Lip-shitz 1992) I would like to suggest the following pairs of attributes, using the minicases discussed above to illustrate them:

1. *Proactive but reflective*. In each of the minicases, the agents took action rather than wait for the organization to solve problems. They were not complainers who simply sat back and judged others; they did something. At the same time, they were all thinkers who invested time and energy into inquiring and analyzing the situation rather than simply 'shooting from the hip'. They liked ideas and concepts. Although Marc was reflective, his intervention was impulsive, motivated by the need to do something in the face of the puzzling passivity of his peers. In this case his proactiveness got the best of him. However, afterwards he was reflective rather than defensive about the incident.

2. *High aspirations but realistic about limitations*. All three agents of organizational learning were driven by values that they took seriously and held dear. Each tried to live up to these values and expected others and the organization as a whole to live up to the values they espoused. At the same time, the three agents of organizational learning were realistic about the complexity of organizational life and the forces that limit effectiveness. As a result, they were appreciative of small gains, and they persisted in the face of resistance, setbacks, and failures, without becoming cynical. Their strength seemed to stem from realistic naivete.

3. *Critical but committed*. In all three cases the agents of organizational learning were quite aware that something was wrong. Peter and Marc were particularly critical of the organization (and each of himself as well). At the same time, all three agents were deeply committed and loyal to the organization. Neither Peter nor Marc needed to act as agents of organizational learning in order to advance their careers. In fact, taking on the role of an agent could have even interfered with their career advancement. However, they strongly identified with the organization and wanted to improve it.

4. *Independent but very cooperative with others*. Dave, Peter, and Marc saw what they thought

had to be done and acted on their own sense of what was right. They did not first seek support, approval, or consensus. At the same time, they all appeared to like other people and work well with them. They were not abrasive characters who pushed relentlessly to get what they wanted. Rather, they tended to be sensitive to the needs of others and kept their own objectives clearly in mind. Dave was able to enlist the cooperation of others in developing and testing his idea. Peter was able to maintain a good relationship with top management while being open and persistent about his ideas for change. Marc was a natural leader among his peers and had a good relationship with the CEO, situational factors that he was able to draw on after making his intervention.

Technical and Nontechnical Problems

Dave, whose ideas came to be tested, accepted, and ultimately integrated into the organization's 'instrumental theory-in-use' (Argyris and Schön 1996: 14), was more successful than Peter and Marc were in getting the organization to learn. One of the important factors may have been the nature of the problem and the learning itself. Dave's idea of replacing metal components with plastic ones can be viewed as a response to the problem of reducing the weight of the vehicle without compromising its performance. This problem could be considered 'technical', for (a) it was clearly defined, (b) most of Dave's colleagues probably agreed that it was a problem, (c) its causes were easily identifiable, (d) there existed a body of science-based knowledge (theory and research) upon which to base a solution, (e) a set of specific criteria and measures for a successful solution could be determined in advance, (f) potential solutions could be designed and tested before implementation, and (g) attempts to solve the problem involved little interpersonal conflict, threat, or embarrassment. Technical problems are relatively unambiguous and lend themselves to rational solutions.

The use of plastics represented an area of uncertainty for the organization, but this uncertainty was overcome through thorough research and systematic testing. Both the research and the testing were consistent with the organization's theory-in-use for product innovation. Existing criteria and standards for performance were maintained. There is no indication from the case study that the change to plastics required other significant changes in the product or the production process. Nor does it seem that the innovation was particularly threatening to any party within the organization. Thus, the organization was able to assimilate the change yet remain fundamentally unchanged. When individuals face technical problems, they tend to take the ends, or goals and values, as givens and focus their efforts on finding the best means to achieve those ends. In this sense Dave could be considered an agent of organizational single-loop learning (Argyris and Schön 1996).

Peter faced a problem that can be defined as relatively 'nontechnical' in the sense that there was little a priori agreement among the parties about the definition and causes of the problem, which were somewhat ambiguous. Both top management and Marc agreed on the desired ends (profitability), but Peter saw top management's solution (e.g. cheap labor) as a fundamental cause of the problem. It took all of Peter's powers of persuasion to overcome top management's opposition to providing bonuses for salespeople, resistance that was based on the fear that these bonuses would have to be offered to salespeople in other departments as well. In addition, Peter encountered top management's deeply held beliefs about who was responsible for performance and who should be rewarded.

There is considerable theory and research on participatory management, but Peter based his solution on hunches and beliefs, not on scientific evidence. Essentially, Peter performed an experiment in his own department, and when it proved successful he suggested implementing it elsewhere in the chain of superstores. However, there was no way of knowing in advance whether wider implementation would be successful or whether top management was correct in attributing the success to Peter's exceptional leadership abilities.

Peter's experimentation did not present a significant threat or source of embarrassment to others in the organization as long as it remained within his own department. Peter had the advantage of implementing his innovation in a new store that had not yet solidified its theory-in-use, so he was less restricted by a set way of doing things. Although his way of managing was radically different from that found in other departments, it was simply a more effective way of carrying out the organization's espoused strategy of selling knowledge. Furthermore, he was functioning within his own area of authority, and his changes were consistent with the organization's criteria and standards for performance.

On the other hand, when Peter attempted to disseminate his learning beyond the boundaries of his own department, he was implicitly bringing to the surface a contradiction between the organization's espoused theory of selling knowledge and its theory-in-use, which increasingly put an emphasis on selling products that required little technical knowledge. Peter attributed this contradiction to the fact that many of the top managers had come from retail businesses in which the workers' knowledge about the products and their use played almost no role. Thus, Peter's proposal was potentially embarrassing to top management because it contradicted their mental models of human resource management within retail business and called into question their expertise.

There was also a subtle difference between Peter and top management in their criteria for a successful outcome. Peter's proposal required investment and a long-term perspective on improving performance. Top management was under heavy pressure to produce short-term improved performance in the face of intense competition. They preferred to focus on merchandising and cutting personnel costs in order to gain as much as they could from the current system. In Peter's view this strategy was self-defeating in the long run because it led to a drop in customer satisfaction and drove customers to the competitors. Both the short-term and long-term perspectives were valid and needed to be taken into account in any solution. These conflicting demands made the problem much less technical and pointed to the need for 'double-loop learning' (Argyris and Schön 1996: 22) in which underlying values, goals, and standards for performance become the objects of inquiry and change.

In Marc's case the problem was located even closer to the nontechnical end of the continuum. Middle managers did not know what was going on. They were extremely anxious and uncertain about top management's intentions. Members of top management appeared to be defensive, secretive, and apparently unaware of the effects of their behavior on middle management. They wanted middle management's support for their decisions, whereas middle management felt betrayed. According to Marc's perception of the situation, there was a clear contradiction between top management's espoused theory of open communication and the way in which it had handled the reorganization. On the other hand, Marc also perceived a gap between what his peers were saying privately and what they were willing to say in public. Marc wanted to do something that would cut through the game-playing, but he knew that his intervention was touching on very sensitive and threatening issues for all the parties concerned. Under these conditions it would have required considerable work simply to arrive at a common definition of the problem, much less its causes and possible solutions.

The closer a problem lies to the nontechnical end of the continuum, the greater the difficulties and threats that it presents to the agent of learning. Although Marc apparently succeeded in getting important messages through to the CEO, Marc had little effect on the game itself. Given the complex, ambiguous, and highly sensitive situation, it is not surprising that Marc experienced only limited success as an agent of organizational learning.

Pushing Back the Walls: A Constructionist Approach

Nonaka and Takeuchi (1995) have pointed out that knowledge-creating companies 'amplify' (p. 72) and 'synthesize' (p. 236) the knowledge of individuals. As illustrated above, however, organizations sometimes impede rather than amplify individual contributions. Although Frohman (1997) found many examples of successful agents of organizational learning, agents of organizational learning may encounter seemingly insurmountable obstacles, particularly when facing nontechnical problems that require double-loop learning.

The experience of Peter and Marc may be typical for individuals who come to an organization at first believing that hard work and achievement will advance both the organization's goals and their own. Individuals encounter 'walls', or obstacles to effective task performance. Attempts to break through or work around these obstacles often engender even higher walls, which seem to be built by the organization itself. Argyris and Schön (1996) called these obstacles organizational 'defensive routines' (p. 101), actions and policies that are intended to protect individuals from experiencing embarrassment or threat but that at the same time prevent individuals and organizations from identifying and correcting the problems causing embarrassment or threat. The harder people push against these walls, the more the walls push back until they seem to be closing in on the protagonists. As a result, the organization may become an increasingly frustrating and even dangerous place. Some members escape by leaving the organization; others escape to an inner world of self-protectiveness and cynicism.

What can be done to 'push the walls back'? Argyris and Schön (1974, 1978, 1996) advocated 'Model II', a normative model of reasoning and behavior that can promote double-loop learning. The basis of Model II is a set of governing values that consists of valid information, free and informed choice, internal commitment to a particular choice, and the monitoring of the implementation of that choice. When individuals act according to Model II, they attempt to produce action that will realize or maximize these values. However, Argyris and Schön's research (Argyris 1982; Argyris and Schön 1996) demonstrated that Model II behavior is extremely rare, if it exists at all, particularly in situations involving a high degree of psychological threat. Under these conditions people are 'programmed' with 'Model I' reasoning, which is based on governing values—unilateral control, self-defense, and rationality—that tend to inhibit inquiry and a willingness to deal with ambiguity and uncertainty. Furthermore, Argyris (1993) advocated a top-down process, reflecting his skepticism about the ability of relatively low-ranking individuals to influence organizational defensive routines.

I propose that individuals at any level of the organization are capable of pushing back these walls if they adopt a constructionist approach (Friedman and Lipshitz 1992). This approach draws on the assumption that human behavior is based not on objective reality but on a perception, or image, of reality that people construct in their minds (Kim 1993; Searle 1995). Images of reality are not perceived whole; rather, they are actively constructed out of the 'materials' of a situation and mediated by cognitive structures such as schemata (Neisser 1976), cognitive maps (Weick and Bougon 1986), frames (Bateson 1972), theories of action (Argyris and Schön 1974), and mental models (Senge 1990). The constructionist approach does not necessarily imply that there is no such thing as objective reality. However, people can never really know objective reality; they can only know what they make of it.

People develop constructs, or 'theories', that order the world, make it predictable, and guide action (Kelly 1955). These theories are often powerful tools for explaining behavior and making sense of a situation. However, any given theory represents only one of many possible interpretations of a situation. It is the very indeterminacy of these theories that presents opportunities for pushing back the walls. The problem is that people tend to develop powerful explanatory theories that may stifle inquiry and blind them to other possibilities.

In very simple terms, people tend to act as if their constructions of reality are facts and not theories. This tendency is also true for people who cognitively understand the constructionist approach, particularly in the face of threat or conflict. As a result, they become more deeply entrenched in their views and less aware of other viable possibilities. Yet, if what people know is a theory, or hypothesis, about reality, the logical strategy would be to find ways of testing it.

Peter's case, for instance, raises a fascinating puzzle. What prevented top management from consistently copying the experience of the most successful department in the chain? Peter had very reasonable explanations for top management's behavior. He also had a number of evaluations of and attributions about top management (e.g. their previous conceptions of retail sales, pressure from the board of directors to achieve quick results, and influence from managers of other stores). Although these explanations may have been perfectly valid, they constituted Peter's theory of the situation, not reality itself. His theory of the situation was clearly based on a number of questionable inferential leaps and interpretations. Peter had picked up his information from a wide variety of sources, but he never tested it directly with top management.

Testing a theory does not simply mean asking for confirmation or disconfirmation. Rather, it means helping the organization inquire into the puzzle itself. Engaging in such an inquiry process might include the following steps:

1. *Describing as concretely as possible one's perception of the current problem and of the events or conditions that have created it*. This step provides the basic information that is to be tested and from which the organization might learn.

2. *Asking members of top management and members of middle management whether this description accurately reflects the situation as they perceive it*. This step is intended to identify and correct significant distortions, gaps, or errors in the individual's image of reality.

3. *Attempting to inquire into the source of significant differences (e.g. different data or different interpretations) in perception among the different actors or groups involved*. This step leads to the discovery of deeper discrepancies that lead to ineffectiveness. When important differences arise, this step requires a process of negotiating reality, which one hopes will lead to sufficient perceptual common ground for dealing with the problem.

4. *Critically inquiring into the reasoning behind action*. Peter could have asked top management what led them to employ strategies that seemed so obviously counterproductive from the standpoint of middle management. This step assumes that organizational actors generally do not act in ways that are intentionally counterproductive. An attempt to comprehend the sense in the actions of others can increase the insight that all parties have into the complexity, uncertainty, ambiguity, and dilemmas of the problem involved. Critically inquiring into the reasoning behind action does not necessarily mean accepting it. On the contrary, it implies a search for gaps, contradictions, inconsistencies, and alternative interpretations. Critical inquiry means struggling openly with conflicting goals and engaging with uncertainty in order to discover new ways of thinking about and acting on the problem.

5. *Designing strategies for dealing with the current situation and for dealing more effectively with similar situations when they arise*. This step is intended to move from an understanding of the problem to the design, implementation, and monitoring of a solution.

It would be foolishly overoptimistic to assume that an individual can always push back the walls. Clearly, there are situations in which other organizational members are not open to learning or in which organizational defensive routines present insurmountable obstacles. Nonetheless, people can always look for a potential point of leverage for pushing back the wall. Senge (1990: 114) defined leverage as small, well-focused actions that produce significant, enduring improvements. For agents of learning in any social system, leverage means identifying a feature of the system that is open to influence and that, if changed, might interrupt vicious cycles or even transform them into benevolent ones.

The most promising source of leverage is one's own behavior. Rothman (1997) defined this kind of leverage as *reflexivity*: 'When pointing a finger at an opponent, we might stop ourselves, count to ten, notice the three fingers pointing back at ourselves, and ask first: Why do I care so much? then, What have I done to contribute to this situation? and finally, What might I do to contribute to its creative resolution?' (p. 37). Discovering points of leverage means discovering one's causal responsibility for creating an undesired outcome, that is, discovering features of one's perception, strategy, or objectives that can at least partially account for the undesired outcome. An individual can apply leverage at these points because they are under his or her own control. Applying leverage changes the conditions, and these changed conditions may then influence the behavior of others.

Marc's case illustrates the use of leverage. It would have been easy enough for Marc to walk away from the incident feeling as though he had been right and the CEO wrong. In fact, many of his peers congratulated him for his courage in confronting the CEO. Marc, however, was not happy with his behavior. In retrospect he became aware of the fact that he had unilaterally appointed himself to represent middle management. By doing so, he became caught up in a game in which his peers blamed top management for not communicating while they themselves were not communicating with top management. Rather than mobilize the group to channel these feelings into constructive action, he became filled with negative emotions (Hirschhorn 1988). He expressed these feelings, which were not necessarily his own, in the form of a rhetorical question ('How do you expect . . .?') that communicated strongly antagonistic feelings toward top management and left out the substance of the problem itself. Given the way Marc crafted his intervention, the CEO's

defensive reaction was highly predictable, even if he had been open to learning (and the subsequent discussion indicated an openness to learning).

Marc confused his image of reality with the reality of the situation. He acted as though his interpretations of the situation and of his role were facts. If he had reflected on his image of reality and had treated it as a hypothesis to be tested rather than as a fact, he could have acted more effectively as an agent of organizational learning. For Marc, the first step in testing his image of reality would have been to recognize certain signs that he had distorted his perception of the situation, of his role, or of both (e.g. emotions that were not his own and the sense of having to take action). When Marc finally recognized his own causal responsibility, he felt shame and embarrassment, but that recognition enabled him to keep the inquiry going and to help the CEO.

Marc's case also points to the role of emotions in acting as an agent of organizational learning. In reflecting on his case, Marc described his strategy as bordering on 'professional suicide' or 'martyrdom':

I was quite oblivious at the time to what I said or did. I didn't care at that point in time what happened. I remember thinking he could have fired me and I gave him the tools at that point . . . I was all charged up and felt that if I got fired over this issue, it was the right issue to get fired over.

Marc was also puzzled by his thoughts and feelings during the subsequent discussion with the CEO. Although he held the CEO in very high regard and later felt that the CEO had been extremely fair toward him, Marc realized that his thoughts and actions at the time reflected utter disrespect toward his superior.

In retrospect Marc began to realize that his intervention had been motivated by a complex mix of emotions. On the one hand, he shared his peers' anger and uncertainty. In addition, he experienced feelings of betrayal because he strongly identified with top management and enjoyed a close, personal relationship with the CEO. On the other hand, he was disappointed and angry at his peers for not stating publicly what they had confided to him. Most of all, he felt an intense sense of responsibility to repair a situation that he felt had gone wrong.

On the surface there may appear to be a contradiction between emotional intensity (or emotionality) and detachment or reflectiveness a person needs in the role as agent of organizational learning. Taking a constructionist stance requires one to step outside of oneself in order to test one's image of reality (Schön 1983). However, this detachment does not necessarily mean that one has to ignore or repress emotions. Marc's sense of responsibility was an extremely important emotion that could have led him to be more effective had he handled it better. In other cases, emotions such as interest or doubt provide the most important motivational underpinning to inquiry and the active search for new information. Both 'positive' emotions (e.g. interest, enthusiasm, excitement, and love) and 'negative' emotions (e.g. anger, fear, aggression, and shame) may be required to overcome both individual and organizational inertia (Hirschhorn 1988; Schein 1969; Scherer and Tran, Ch. 16 in this volume).

From a constructionist standpoint emotions are important data for the agent of organizational learning. Rather than blindly acting on his emotions, Marc might have attempted to become aware of his emotions, where they were coming from, and what they meant. In doing so he could have asked himself whether these emotions were appropriate for the given 'reality' (depending upon how that reality is interpreted). In retrospect he was able to see that his sense of self-sacrifice and his feelings toward the CEO were highly distorted. Nevertheless, there are times when emotions such as enthusiasm, anger, aggression, or shame are called for. Then the question becomes whether to express them and how to do so in a way that is likely to help others learn. As illustrated by Marc's case, grappling with these questions on the spot is very difficult and requires a great deal of skill and self-awareness.

Agents of Organizational Learning: An Endangered Species?

As Frohman (1997) has observed, agents of organizational change go far beyond their job requirements. The same is even more true for agents of organizational learning. To the extent that their job descriptions do not explicitly include such a role, they are likely to experience role ambiguity, role conflict, or both (Kahn et al. 1964). Taking on such a role is likely to involve frustration and unmet expectations, both of which often lead to cynicism and burnout (Andersson 1996; Meyerson 1990). Thus, there are considerable risks and disincentives for taking on such a role in organizations, and one might expect that agents of organizational learning are a rare and endangered species.

In some organizations this problem has been solved through the creation of organizational learning mechanisms (Lipshitz, Popper, and Oz 1996) with the specific purpose of drawing on individual knowledge in order to improve organizational performance. Furthermore, programs such as total quality management (TQM) and reengineering are intended to transform employees at all levels into agents of organizational learning.

In many cases, however, TQM has been limited or not seriously applied, a situation creating considerable cynicism among employees. Similarly, process reengineering has sometimes become a way of involving employees in their own 'downsizing'. Finally, there are many organizations that do not have any formal mechanisms for organizational learning. How, then, does it benefit the individual to act as an agent of organizational learning, and what is the likelihood that individuals will take on this role?

The imagery of walls and barriers suggests that individuals experience organizational life as restricting them and closing them in. Kurt Lewin (1948) introduced the concept of the 'lifespace of the individual' (p. 86) in an attempt to describe sociopsychological experience in topographical terms. At the heart of this concept is the principle of movement:

By movements, we have to understand not only bodily locomotions but, above all social and mental 'locomotions'. These three kinds of locomotion are somewhat different, but all three are to be recognized in psychology and sociology as real events. (p. 5)

One of the most important facts for all social life is probably the amount of what one may call 'space of free movement'. (p. 150)

According to Lewin, restricting the space of free movement leads to a high state of tension and pathologies, particularly when an individual is prevented from reaching desired goals. In addition, Lewin pointed out that individual action is dependent upon the individual's perception of a situation and that the individual's subjective view of a situation is what counts most.

The constructionist approach combines these two insights. When individuals act as agents of organizational learning, they are trying to expand their space of free movement. Many internal and external factors define an individual's space of free movement. However, the more that individuals recognize their own role in creating their images of reality and in shaping the context in which learning occurs, the more proactive they can be in determining their space of free movement.

When individuals act as agents of organizational learning in this way, they also empower themselves. Conger and Kanungo (1988) have defined 'empowerment' as 'enhancing the feelings of self-efficacy among organizational members through the identification of conditions that foster powerlessness' (p. 474). Models of empowerment generally focus on intrinsic motivation, internal justification for decision-making, shared responsibilities, and integration for problem-solving (Thorlakson and Murray 1996). Most models, case studies, and research of empowerment focus on employee participation and other ways in which organizations transfer authority from one level to another (Thorlakson and Murray 1996). This

chapter suggests that the constructionist approach offers a powerful source of empowerment that is within the grasp of every individual.

There are real risks in acting as an agent of organizational learning. Frohman (1997) found that such people are generally not considered to be on an organization's list of 'high potential' personnel. Similarly, Spreitzer and Quinn (1996) studied the career tracks of Ford Company middle managers before and after they underwent a special training program designed to stimulate the initiation of fundamental changes. Although innovation per se was positively correlated with advancement, the most upwardly mobile managers were the ones who made the most conservative changes, whereas the plateaued managers were the ones most likely to make the most radical changes. In effect, the Ford Company, which has been an industry leader in espousing and investing in the development of middle managers into agents of 'transformational' change, failed to reward such agents (and sometimes even punished them) for actually taking on this role.

An even more surprising finding in the Spreitzer and Quinn (1996) study was that the plateaued managers expressed very little bitterness and cynicism about the price that they had paid for their initiative. On the contrary, they expressed a deep sense of satisfaction about what they had done:

Many talked of how [the training program] served as an important wake-up call for them as middle managers, explaining how [it] stimulated them to break out of a rut. Through participation in the program and their own introspection, they chose, in their own words, to 'do the right thing' rather than the 'political thing' or the 'easy thing' as in the past. To the present day, participants approach the second author, recounting stories that reflect this rationale. (p. 255)

Spreitzer and Quinn (1996) hypothesized that the training program might have led plateaued middle managers to redefine the risk–reward ratio. Feeling less constrained by the need to play political games in the race for promotion, they may have felt more comfortable challenging organizational assumptions and practices.

Although organizational learning begins and ends with individual behavior, few researchers have focused on the role of individuals as agents of organizational learning. Furthermore, growing interest in creating 'learning organizations' may create the impression that learning is a formal, top-down process. The fact is, however, that individuals at every level of every organization encounter new ideas, errors, puzzles, or other opportunities for learning every day. People who choose to act on these discoveries and to bring them to the attention of the organization as-sume the role of agents of organizational learning. This role may be risky and requires a particular set of attributes and skills for dealing with the conflict and resistance that learning often engenders. However, this role is not necessarily assumed for the benefit of the organization alone. It may also enable people 'to push back the walls' of helplessness, stagnation, and cynicism that frequently characterize organizational life. Given the proper training and support, individuals who act as agents of organizational learning can experience increased satisfaction and a greater sense of integrity in their professional lives.

References

Andersson, L. M. (1996). 'Employee Cynicism: An Examination Using a Contract Violation Framework'. *Human Relations*, 49: 1395–418.

Argyris, C. (1982). *Reasoning, Learning, and Action: Individual and Organizational.* San Francisco: Jossey-Bass.

——(1993). *Knowledge for Action: A Guide to Overcoming Barriers to Organizational Change.* San Francisco: Jossey-Bass.

——and Schön, D. A. (1974). *Theory in Practice: Increasing Professional Effectiveness.* San Francisco: Jossey-Bass.

————(1978). *Organizational Learning: A Theory of Action Perspective.* Reading, Mass.: Addison-Wesley.

————(1996). *Organizational Learning*: Vol. 2. *Theory, Method, and Practice.* Reading, Mass.: Addison-Wesley.

Bateson, G. (1972). *Steps to an Ecology of Mind: A Revolutionary Approach to Man's Understanding of Himself.* New York: Ballantine Books.

Bazeal, D. V. (1993). 'Organizing for Internally Developed Corporate Ventures'. *Journal of Business Venturing*, 8: 75–90.

Burgelman, R. and Sayles, L. (1986). *Inside Corporate Innovation: Strategy, Structure, and Managerial Skills.* New York: Free Press.

Conger, J. A. and Kanungo, R. N. (1988). 'The Empowerment Process: Integrating Theory and Practice'. *Academy of Management Review*, 13: 471–82.

Cook, S. D. N. and Yanow, D. (1993). 'Culture and Organizational Learning'. *Journal of Management Inquiry*, 2: 373–90.

Daft, R. L. and Weick, K. E. (1984). 'Toward a Model of Organizations as Interpretation Systems'. *Academy of Management Review*, 9: 284–95.

Dewey, J. (1938). *Logic: The Theory of Inquiry.* New York: Holt.

Fiol, C. M. and Lyles, M. A. (1985). 'Organizational Learning'. *Academy of Management Review*, 10: 802–13.

Friedman, V. J. and Lipshitz, R. (1992). 'Teaching People to Shift Cognitive Gears: Overcoming Resistance on the Road to Model 2'. *Journal of Applied Behavioral Science*, 28/1: 118–36.

Frohman, A. L. (1997). 'Igniting Organizational Change from Below: The Power of Personal Initiative'. *Organizational Dynamics*, 25/3: 39–53.

Garvin, D. A. (1993). 'Building a Learning Organization'. *Harvard Business Review*, 71/4: 78–91.

Hedberg, B. L. T. (1981). 'How Organizations Learn and Unlearn', in P. C. Nystrom and W. H. Starbuck (eds.), *Handbook of Organizational Design*: Vol. 1. *Adapting Organizations to Their Environments*. Oxford: Oxford University Press, 3–27.

Hirschhorn, L. (1988). *The Workplace Within: The Psychodynamics of Organizational Life*. Cambridge, Mass.: MIT Press.

Hornsby, J. S., Naffziger, D. W., Kuratko, D. F., and Montago, R. V. (1993). 'An Interactive Model of the Corporate Entrepreneurship Process'. *Entrepreneurship Theory and Practice*, 18/2: 29–37.

Huber, G. P. (1991). 'Organizational Learning: The Contributing Processes and the Literatures'. *Organization Science*, 2: 88–115.

Kahn, R., Wolfe, D., Quinn, R., Snoek, J., and Rosenthal, R. (1964). *Organizational Stress: Studies in Role Conflict and Ambiguity*. New York: John Wiley.

Kelly, G. A. (1955). *The Psychology of Personal Constructs*. New York: Norton.

Kim, D. H. (1993). 'The Link between Individual and Organizational Learning'. *Sloan Management Review*, 35/1: 37–50.

Kolb, D. A. (1976). 'Management and the Learning Process'. *California Management Review*, 18/3: 21–31.

Levitt, B. and March, J. G. (1988). 'Organizational Learning'. *Annual Review of Sociology*, 14: 319–40.

Lewin, K. (1948). *Resolving Social Conflicts: Selected Papers on Group Dynamics*. New York: Harper & Row.

Lipshitz, R., Popper, M., and Oz, S. (1996). 'Building Learning Organizations: The Design and Implementation of Organizational Learning Mechanisms'. *Journal of Applied Behavioral Science*, 32: 292–305.

March, J. G. and Olsen, J. P. (1976). 'Organizational Learning and the Ambiguity of the Past', in J. G. March and J. P. Olsen, *Ambiguity and Choice in Organizations*. Bergen: Universitetsforlaget, 54–68.

McGill, M. E., Slocum, J. W., and Lei, D. (1993). 'Management Practices in Learning Organizations'. *Organizational Dynamics*, 22/1: 5–17.

Meyerson, D. E. (1990). 'Uncovering Socially Undesirable Emotions: Experiences of Role Ambiguity in Organizations'. *American Behavioral Scientist*, 33: 296–307.

Miner, J. B. (1997). 'The Expanded Horizon for Achieving Entrepreneurial Success'. *Organizational Dynamics*, 25/3: 54–67.

Neisser, U. (1976). *Cognition and Reality: Principles and Implications of Cognitive Psychology*. San Francisco: Freeman.

Nonaka, I. and Takeuchi, H. (1995). *The Knowledge-creating Company: How Japanese Companies Create the Dynamics of Innovation*. New York: Oxford University Press.

Pinchott, G., III (1985). *Intrapreneuring: Why You Don't Have to Leave the Corporation to Become an Entrepreneur*. New York: Harper & Row.

Rothman, J. (1997). *Resolving Identity-based Conflict in Nations, Organizations, and Communities*. San Francisco: Jossey-Bass.

Schein, E. H. (1969). 'The Mechanisms of Change', in W. G. Bennis, K. D. Benne, and R. Chin (eds.), *The Planning of Change*. New York: Holt, Rinehart and Winston, 98–108.

Schön, D. A. (1983). *The Reflective Practitioner*. New York: Basic Books.

Searle, J. R. (1995). *The Construction of Social Reality*. New York: Free Press.

Senge, P. M. (1990). *The Fifth Discipline: The Art and Practice of the Learning Organization*. New York: Doubleday Currency.

Shrivastava, P. (1983). 'A Typology of Organizational Learning Systems'. *Journal of Management Studies*, 20: 7–28.

Simon, H. A. (1969). *The Sciences of the Artificial*. Cambridge, Mass.: MIT Press.

—— (1991). 'Bounded Rationality and Organizational Learning'. *Organization Science*, 2: 125–34.

Spreitzer, G. M. and Quinn, R. E. (1996). 'Empowering Middle Managers to Be Transformational Leaders'. *Journal of Applied Behavioral Science*, 32: 237–61.

Stopford, J. M. and Baden-Fuller, C. W. F. (1994). 'Creating Corporate Entrepreneurship'. *Strategic Management Journal*, 15: 521–36.

Thorlakson, A. J. H. and Murray, R. P. (1996). 'An Empirical Study of Empowerment in the Work-place'. *Group and Organization Management*, 21/1: 67–84.

Tsang, E. W. K. (1997). 'Organizational Learning and the Learning Organization: A Dichotomy between Descriptive and Prescriptive Research'. *Human Relations*, 50: 73–89.

Weick, K. E. (1979). *The Social Psychology of Organizing* (2nd edn). Reading, Mass.: Addison-Wesley.

—— and Bougon, M. G. (1986). 'Organizations as Cognitive Maps: Charting Ways to Success and Failure', in H. P. Sims, Jr. and D. A. Gioia (eds.), *The Thinking Organization: Dynamics of Organizational Social Cognition*. San Francisco: Jossey-Bass, 102–35.

18   Leadership and Organizational Learning

Philip Sadler

The Key Issues

In the context of increasingly rapid environmental change, the research interests of social scientists from a range of disciplines and schools of thought have converged in the study of the processes by which organizations adapt and change in the face of uncertainty. One stream of research has focused on the role of organizational leadership in these processes; another stream has been concerned with the analysis of the processes involved in organizational learning. The purpose of this chapter is to attempt some integration of these two approaches. Relevant literature and research findings in each field are drawn upon, with special attention being given to the relatively small number of studies that focus specifically on the role of leadership in facilitating organizational learning.

Leadership Defined

The literature abounds with definitions of leadership. Analyzing what they have in common, one may find that the concept breaks down into the following components:

(1) Leadership is a social process.
(2) The defining quality of the process is influence, which can be exercised in a variety of ways, such as persuasive eloquence or exemplary behavior.
(3) The process involves interaction between actors who are both leaders and followers. This interaction leads to the creation of a relationship between leaders and followers that involves a two-way process of influence.
(4) The process has various outcomes—most obviously the achievement of the organization's goals but also such intermediate consequences as the commitment of individuals to organizations and their objectives, the enhancement of group cohesion, and the reinforcement or changing of organizational culture.

From these observations it follows that the study of leadership cannot be validly carried on from a purely psychological perspective. It must include study of the interactive and decision-making processes and other aspects of the functioning of organizations, including the processes by which organizations can be said to learn.

The Development of Leadership Theory

Various attempts have been made to trace the development of thinking and research about leadership since their origins in the late nineteenth century. For example, Van Seters and Field (1990) produced a highly detailed analysis of the stages through which leadership theory has evolved. The first phase they described as the Personality Era, dating, in terms of serious scientific work, from the work of Galton (1869) in particular. They subdivided this era into two periods—the Great Man Period and the Trait Period. The approach in the former period was focused on great men and women leaders in history and on their personalities, on the assumption that the route to becoming an effective leader was to study their lives and emulate them. In the approach during the Trait Period, the attempt to link leadership qualities with particular individuals was abandoned in favor of listing a number of traits. Although empirical studies have failed to establish a link between effective leadership and any single trait or group of traits, traits are still believed in general to relate to effective leadership, and the trait approach is still very much favored in popular treatments of the subject.

The second phase in the development of leadership research and theory was characterized as the Influence Era. This term conveys the recognition that leadership is a process involving relationships between individuals and that one cannot understand leadership by focusing solely on the leader.

The third phase with its focus on what leaders actually do, set out in a fresh direction. Researchers examined typical leader behavior patterns and differences in behavior between effective and ineffective leaders. The best known work in this phase was carried out at Ohio State and Michigan Universities and led to the identification of two important dimensions of leader behavior: Initiating Structure (or concern for the task) and Consideration (concern for individual satisfaction and group cohesion). These findings were adapted and applied in industry, most notably by Blake and Mouton (1964), whose Managerial Grid was adopted as a tool in leadership development by industrial enterprises in several countries.

Phase four has been styled the Situation Era, in which researchers turned their attention to the context in which leadership is exercised. The fifth phase, the Contingency Era, has been described by Van Seters and Field (1990) as a major advance in the evolution of leadership theory. 'For the first time it was recognized that leadership was not found in any of the pure, unidimensional forms discussed previously but rather contained elements of them all. In essence, effective leadership was contingent or dependent on one or more of the factors of behavior, personality, influence, and situation' (p. 35). Among the most important contributors to this advance was Fiedler (1971).

The sixth phase, the Transactional Era, added to the previous insights the idea that 'leadership resided not only in the person or the situation but also, and perhaps rather more, in role differentiation and social interaction' (Van Seters and Field 1990: 35).

Phase seven is known as the Anti-Leadership Phase. The idea grew that there might not be a valid concept called leadership, that leadership existed only as a perception in the mind of the observer.

In the eighth phase, the Culture Era, the idea was adopted that if a leader can create a strong culture in an organization, then people will, in effect, lead themselves. The key role of the leader was to recognize the need for culture change and to bring about the necessary changes. The work of such writers as Schein (1992) and Peters (1992) falls into this group.

The ninth era, as termed by Van Seters and Field (1990) is the Transformational Era, 'the latest and most promising phase in the evolutionary development of leadership theory' (p. 37). Leader behavior during periods of organizational transition is examined, as are processes such as creating visions of a desired future state and obtaining employee commitment to change. The emphasis is on strong executive leadership, which both creates the vision and empowers subordinates to carry it out. This perspective is exemplified in the work of Tichy and Devanna (1986).

This survey of the development of thinking and research about leadership is useful in that it provides a framework into which the various approaches can be fitted.

The Process of Organizational Learning and the Concept of the Learning Organization

Organizations need to acquire and store a body of knowledge that individual members can draw upon and need to use that knowledge to improve performance—a process increasingly referred to as knowledge management. Organizations need, too, to develop what are currently termed 'core competences', or sets of skills that are critical for the successful accomplishment of the organization's tasks. Both processes involve learning on the part of individuals and teams. Organizations also need to learn how to build and maintain internal cohesion, how to build and maintain relationships with external stakeholders, and, not least, how best to manage the learning process itself.

Any lingering doubts that whole organizations, as well as individuals and small groups, are capable of learning in a real and meaningful sense should be dispelled by the study by Collins and Porras (1995), which gave a detailed account of a number of companies that have remained successful over at least fifty years and, in some cases more than a century. Consistent market leadership of this kind implies that knowledge, competences, and other learned practices are passed successfully from one generation of employees to another as the organization adapts successfully to an environment characterized by an accelerating rate of change. One of the findings of this study was that leadership played an important role in this process of adaptation.

Of the many definitions of the learning organization, perhaps the most apt is that by Pedler, Boydell, and Burgoyne (1989): 'An organization which facilitates the learning of all its members and continually transforms itself' (p. 2). To describe a company as a learning organization implies that the activities of the organization as a whole are more or less continually monitored to provide feedback, which is then used as a basis for learning how to improve performance. The concept is applicable to a range of contexts extending from discrete events involving a single actor (e.g. conducting an employment interview) at one extreme, through more complex processes involving many actors (launching a new product), to the achievement of strategic objectives by the organization as a whole.

Key research questions about the learning organization are: By what processes do organizations learn, as distinct from individuals or face-to-face groups, and what part can and does leadership play? These processes are many and complex. They include the following aspects:

(1) Inputs. Inputs include scenarios, designs, research results, employee and customer surveys, feedback mechanisms of various kinds, and benchmarking. The list is endless; the sources are both internal and external.

(2) Processing of inputs. To process inputs is to filter them. The outcome is essentially acceptance (and possible adoption) or rejection of the utility and validity of the inputs as a basis for future decision-making.

(3) Arrangements for the storage and retrieval of accepted inputs. These inputs can be recorded and made available in documents, manuals, computer discs, files, blueprints, programs, and sometimes just peoples' heads.

(4) Dissemination and ongoing reinforcement of what has been learned. This process takes place, for example, via mission statements, prescriptions for behavior, appropriate performance management and reward systems, and training programs and communications of all kinds. Information technology has an obvious role to play in organizational learning, facilitating the development of networks that act as channels for the transfer of learning from one part of an organization to others.

The link between the study of the processes by which organizations learn and the study of leadership is, as previously noted, the need for organizations to adapt to environmental change and the part to be played by leaders in facilitating organizational learning. The leader's role is exemplified by the actions of George Fisher when he was Chairman of Motorola. Milmer and Sadler (1993) described how Fisher applied organizational learning to help the company solve a key strategic problem. Today, the key talent for Motorola is the ability to write software. Until the mid-1980s, however, the design skills involved in Motorola products lay in the fields of electrical and mechanical engineering.

Efforts at retraining engineers from these disciplines proved largely unsuccessful because software expertise called for divergent thinkers, whereas successful engineers tended to be convergent thinkers. So Motorola set out to recruit large numbers of software people. The company soon discovered two things: first, that there was a world shortage of first-class talent and, second, that the expertise in software specific to the communications industry was largely held captive by companies such as Ericsson and AT&T, which had moved into software creation earlier.

This issue was designated as one of the five key strategic problems facing Motorola. The approach that Fisher adopted to solve the problem was to utilize the company's top-executive development program, redesigning it along action-learning lines, following the model developed by Revans (1980), in which learning takes place through analysis of real problems facing organizations, development of workable solutions, and then the implementation of these solutions. The problem was defined as how to create within Motorola an environment that would attract best-in-class software people. The program began in 1991. Fisher personally invited 25 top-level executives to participate. In inviting them, he gave them the following objectives:

- to become fully informed and educated about what would be a best-in-class work environment for software people and to come up with a plan for achieving it;
- to invent a process for the realization of this plan;
- to learn how to make these changes inside the corporation, to document how these changes were made, and to begin to leave a legacy of the new model for organizational change.

Transformational Leadership and Its Critics

Burns (1978) drew a distinction between *transactional* and *transformational* leadership.

Although he was writing about political leadership, the distinction has been applied in the sphere of business leadership, where it is seen as equally relevant. Transactional leadership occurs when managers take the initiative in offering some form of need satisfaction in return for something valued by employees, such as pay, promotion, improved job satisfaction, or recognition. The manager/leader sets clear goals; adeptly understands the needs of employees; and selects appropriate, motivating rewards. Transformational leadership, by contrast, is defined as the process of engaging the commitment of employees in the context of shared values and a shared vision. It is, therefore, particularly relevant in the context of managing change. Bass and Avolio (1990) suggested that transformational leadership has four components:

- Idealized influence. Having a clear vision and sense of purpose, such leaders are able to win the trust and respect of followers. By showing followers that they can accomplish more than they believed possible, leaders build a base for future missions that enables them to obtain extra efforts from followers.
- Individual consideration. This component means paying attention to the needs and development potential of their individual followers. It includes delegating, coaching, and giving constructive feedback.
- Intellectual stimulation. Leaders must actively solicit new ideas and new ways of doing things.
- Inspiration. Leaders must motivate people, generate enthusiasm, set an example, and be seen to share the load.

Tichy and Devanna (1986), having observed a number of successful leaders of change or transformational leaders in action, drew the conclusion that such people shared a number of common characteristics that differentiated them from transactional leaders. Transformational leaders—

- clearly see themselves as change agents. They set out to make a difference and to transform the organization for which they are responsible;

- demonstrate courage. They can deal with re-sistance, take a stand, take risks, and confront reality;
- believe in people. They have well-developed beliefs about motivation, trust, and empow-erment;
- draw inspiration from a strong set of values;
- pursue life-long learning. They view mis-takes, their own as well as other people's, as learning opportunities;
- can cope with complexity, uncertainty, and ambiguity;
- show themselves to be visionaries.

Tichy and Devanna linked the concept of transformational leadership to the process of organizational learning in the context of organ-izational change and adaptation to a changing environment.

Frequently cited examples of transforma-tional leaders are Jack Welch of GEC, Percy Barnevik of ABB, Lee Iacocca of Chrysler, and John Harvey Jones of ICI.

Critiques of Transformational Leadership

A recurring theme from the late 1980s onwards is the importance of the relations between lead-ers and followers. Nicoll (1986), for example, argued that the 'hero' or 'savior' leader is large-ly mythical. The myth rests on the wish for leaders to be 'higher, stronger, and better than we ourselves are—our saviors' (p. 31). This de-sire, he pointed out, places huge burdens on leaders. The myth also implies a passive follow-ership role for everyone else. It causes one to underestimate the importance of the interac-tive aspects of leader–follower relations. Nicoll suggested that direction and goals are 'not dreamed up and delivered to us by a leader' but rather 'created within and through our in-teraction with a leader' (p. 32).

Distributed Leadership

The process of transformational leadership is commonly linked with the role or roles at the apex of the organization—the chairman, the chief executive, or both. Needless to say, people in such positions, by virtue of the position power they can deploy as well as their own personal vision and values, are uniquely placed to influence for good or bad the long-term fu-ture of their organizations. Nevertheless, in practice many others at all organizational levels can and do contribute to the processes of creating a sense of common purpose and a sense of belonging. Sayles (1993), for example, drew attention to the important role of the 'working leader'. Senge (1996) described a simi-lar distributed leadership role, which he termed the 'local line leader' (p. 46).

The Myth of Charisma

Collins and Porras (1995) concluded, that 'a high profile, charismatic style is absolutely not required to successfully shape a visionary company' (p. 32). They cited William Mc-Knight, who served 3M successively as general manager (15 years), CEO (20 years), and chair-man (17 years)—a soft-spoken, gentle, man; humble, modest, and unobtrusive. Others lack-ing obvious charismatic qualities included Bill Hewlett of Hewlett Packard, Bill Allen of Boe-ing, and George W. Merck of Merck Inc.

Pascale (1990), in his account of Petersen's period of stewardship as president of Ford dur-ing its recovery from near disaster in the 1980s, argued that most of what had been written about leadership in recent years had missed the point. He pointed out that whereas the tendency had been to emphasize the leader as the heroic figure whose actions lead to success, Petersen's approach had been to look at the interplay between the leader, the followers, and the situation. Petersen, stated Pascale, did not believe he had all the answers but set out to act as the catalyst that enabled Ford's employees to come up with the answers them-selves.

Stewardship

Block (1993) was deeply critical of the transfor-mational leader concept. He argued the case for replacing current ideas of leadership with a new concept: 'stewardship'. Most theories about making changes, he asserted, are clustered around the idea of leadership and the role of the leader in achieving the transformation of organizational performance either as an output of organizational learning or as an objective of it. In his view, this pervasive and almost religious belief in the power of leaders actually slows the process of genuine transformation.

Block (1993) drew a basic distinction between 'good parenting' as an approach to the governance of organizations and 'partnership'. The former is based on the belief that the people at the top are responsible for the success of the organization and the well-being of its members. Partnership is based on the principle of placing control close to where the work is done.

Another distinction relating to corporate governance and hence to organizational learning is between dependency and empowerment. Dependency rests on the belief that the people in power know what is best and that it is their job to create a safe and predictable environment for others. Empowerment reflects the belief that the ability to get things right lies within each person and in his or her willingness to make the organization work well, with or without the sponsorship of those above. It follows that the leader as steward recognizes that he or she does not know the solutions to the problems facing the organization but enables people to find the solutions themselves through learning and empowerment.

The assumptions underlying the transformational school of thought have also been challenged on the grounds that they reflect a particularly masculine approach to the leadership process (Simmons 1996) and that they reflect the values of Western culture, particularly that of the United States (Bennis 1997).

Gender Issues

The assumption that the leader is in control and knows the answers is frequently construed as a particularly masculine notion. To test the assumption for gender bias, Morrison, White, and Van Velsor (1987) studied the careers of 78 of the most senior women in corporate America. The popular literature and some earlier social science research had prepared the researchers to expect to find a distinctive feminine style of leadership, that, in comparison with men's style of leadership, would be characterized by greater willingness to listen, greater empathy and orientation to people, and less aggressiveness in the pursuit of goals. However, Morrison, White, and Van Velsor did not find any significant differences between men's and women's styles. It is not clear just how conclusive these findings are. According to Hooijberg and DiTomaso (1996), who have summarized the main research findings on differences in leadership style between men and women, a number of researchers have found little dissimilarity (Bass 1990: 725; Dobbins and Platz 1986: 118).

Others, however, *have* found differences (Eagly and Johnson 1990). In the latter studies, women were seen to use a more democratic, participative approach, compared with a more autocratic, directive style used by men. Rosener (1990), for example, found that women not only encouraged participation and shared power and information to a greater extent than men did but also practiced what she called *interactive leadership* (p. 120), which involves enhancing others' feelings of self-worth and believing that high levels of performance result from people's feeling excited about their work and feeling good about themselves.

Cultural Differences

In view of the impact that leadership has on organizational learning, knowledge about cultural differences and their implications for the contexts and styles of leadership can enhance the ability to shape and guide such learning. Hofstede (1991) has pioneered research on precisely this topic by contrasting national cultures in terms of four dimensions:

(1) Power distance—the extent to which a society accepts the fact that power in organizations is distributed unequally;
(2) Uncertainty avoidance—the extent to which a society feels threatened by uncer-

tain and ambiguous situations and tries to avoid these by establishing rules and believing in absolute truth;

(3) Individualism versus collectivism—the extent to which people see themselves as living in a loosely knit social framework in which people are supposed to take care of themselves and their immediate families only (individualism) or in a tight social framework in which people can expect to be looked after by the community, to which, in return, they give their loyalty and commitment (collectivism);

(4) Masculinity versus femininity—the extent to which the dominant values in society are masculine (e.g. assertiveness, acquisitiveness, and disregard for quality-of-life issues).

Hofstede pointed out that leadership theories current in the management literature have largely originated in the United States, a country characterized by an average level of power distance, extremely strong individualism, slightly below-average uncertainty avoidance and slightly above-average masculinity. He argues that many U.S.-based theories of leadership have adherents who advocate that leaders should encourage their subordinates to participate in decision-making but on the basis that the leader takes the initiative towards participation. This viewpoint makes sense from the intermediate position of the United States on the scale of power distance. A stronger power-distance culture would have produced theories in which the use of power and manipulation are emphasized. Hofstede exemplified this point by citing French management writing, in which participation is paid little attention and the exercise of power is heavily stressed. On the other hand, in countries like Sweden, Norway, and Israel, which have low power-distance scores, there is greater acceptance of models of leadership behavior in which subordinates take the initiative.

It can therefore be argued that leaders are more likely to be able to act as agents of organizational learning in cultures where power distance is low and tolerance of uncertainty

is high, as in Scandinavia, than in cultures where power distance is high and tolerance of uncertainty is low. Hampden-Turner and Trompenaars (1993), in their study of cultural differences, reached the conclusion that Swedish companies, particularly the large ones, were able to draw on extraordinary qualities of leadership. They cite Gyllenhammar of Volvo, Barnevik of ABB, Svedberg of Ericsson, and Carlzon of SAS, among others, as examples. Hampden-Turner and Trompenaars presented three league tables, one on managerial initiative, one on the extent to which leaders delegate, and one on the capacity of leaders to take a long-term view. Sweden was given the highest score in the first two tables and came in third place, behind Japan and Germany, in the third.

Hofstede (1991) emphasized that leaders cannot choose their styles at will. The style that is feasible depends to a large extent on the cultural conditioning of the leader's subordinates. U.S. writers such as McGregor (1960), Likert (1967) and Blake and Mouton (1964) have tended, nevertheless, to be prescriptive, favoring a leadership style that fits the culture of the United States and centers such as Canada and Australia but not national cultures featuring power distance greater than that. One leadership theorist singled out by Hofstede as allowing for a certain amount of cultural relativity is Fiedler (1971), who argued that different leadership styles are needed for 'difficult' and 'easy' situations and that a cultural gap between superiors and subordinates is one of the factors that make for difficulty.

Binney and Williams (1995) described how the vice-president in charge of a major division of the European Patent Office (EPO) with 1,500 employees sought to help his organization adjust to a changing environment by facilitating learning through experimentation, the exchange of ideas, and encouragement of employee initiative. The trigger in this case was the need for the organization to change in response to a number of trends in the environment. Among them were the rapid development of information technology, the emergence of worldwide patents, and competitive pressure on prices. He identified a number of internal issues needing to change, including a high-cost structure, bureaucratic procedures, and inflexibility.

This case illustrates how a senior executive, a man named Michel who was working with employees from a range of national cultures, some of which were characterized by high power distance, set out to transfer responsibility for the organization's response to change from the leader and seat of authority to the employees. One of the first things he did was to think through the nature of the organization and its culture. Most of the employees were highly qualified engineers and scientists drawn from various European countries, and the nature of their work meant that they worked as individuals in relative isolation. The vice-president saw the necessity of alerting them to the changes in the environment, but of doing so in such a way as to engage their intellectual curiosity. He engaged Hervé Serieyx, a leading French thinker on the future of organizations, to lead a seminar, after which a working party known as the 'change group' was formed.

The vice-president understood the need for change and could see some of the things that needed changing. Operating as he was, in a multicultural organization, many of his employees expected that he would take a strong lead and let them know what was expected of them in terms of changed behaviors and new structures. He did not, however, allow himself to be drawn into making explicit statements about the future form of the organization, nor did he issue five-year plans with firm objectives laid out. Instead, in the words of Binney and Williams (1995), he 'pushed and prodded' (p. 77) and asked awkward questions. At the same time he listened attentively to peoples' ideas, provided space for people to experiment and gave support when problems arose.

It was clear to the vice-president that he alone could not bring about change and that it required the people working in the EPO to take ownership of the problem and to work through the needed changes. As the authors concluded:

[The EPO] is in the process of a major change. A number of differences are clearly obvious to people who knew it three years ago. There is a greater responsiveness to new ideas, a willingness to experiment, and people are picking up responsibility for actions outside their specific job accountabilities. A process of learning and transferring ideas is flourishing. The increase in energy is almost tangible. (Binney and Williams 1995: 77)

Other Influences

The scope for leaders to act as agents of organizational learning is influenced not only by expectations created by gender or national culture but also by such contextual factors as organizational structure and organizational culture (see also Child and Heavens, Ch. 13 in this volume). Handy (1996), for example, commented on the role of leaders in a typical modern organization that works on a 20/80 basis, with only 20 per cent of the work force being employed full time, the rest consisting of a mix of temporary, casual, and part-time employees, and with the employees of contractors supplying outsourced services. In such a context the task of top-level leadership is to provide what he called 'the soft glue that holds this virtual community together' (p. 7). The leader's approach to creating a learning environment in such a 'virtual' organization will be different from that in a more traditional structure (see Hedberg and Holmquist, Ch. 33 in this volume).

The influence of corporate culture may well be even more significant than that of structure. When an organization has gradually developed a culture characterized by avoidance of risk-taking, deep respect for traditional hierarchical authority, and procedural rules that have been elevated into ends in themselves, the first task facing leadership will be to change the culture. Schein (1992) asserted that

the most intriguing leadership role in culture management is one in which the leader attempts to develop a learning organization. The learning leader must portray confidence that active problem-solving leads to learning and, thereby, set an appropriate example for other members of the organization. . . . The toughest problem here for learning leaders is to come to terms with their own lack of expertise and wisdom. . . . The only way to build a learning culture that continues to learn is for leaders themselves to realize that they do not know and must teach others to accept that they do not know. The learning task is then a shared responsibility. (pp. 366–7)

New Models—Leaders as Learners and Teachers

Although there is nothing about leadership in the title of Senge's 1990 book, *The Fifth Discipline: The Art and Practice of the Learning Organisation*, the work is essentially about leadership as the process of nurturing people's commitment to and capacity for learning at all levels of the organization. The first of Senge's five disciplines is Personal Mastery, which involves a commitment to life-long learning and is about 'clarifying the things that really matter to us [and] . . . living our lives in the service of our highest aspirations' (p. 8). The second discipline is Mental Models. It is about learning to become conscious of one's own mental models and subjecting them to rigorous scrutiny so as to get closer to reality. The third discipline is Building a Shared Vision. Senge stressed the value of a genuine vision, as distinct from a vision statement. The leader's role is to unearth a picture of an attainable future that is capable of fostering real commitment. To try to dictate a vision is usually counterproductive, but to offer one for consideration and debate can start a very powerful process (see also Dièshes, Marz, and Teele, Ch. 12 in this volume). Team Learning is the fourth discipline. It is vital because teams rather than individuals are the 'fundamental learning unit in modern organisations . . . [,] unless teams learn the organisation cannot learn' (p. 10). Systems Thinking is the fifth discipline. It is essential if one is to see the interactions between things that make up the whole and if one is to be able to manage change effectively. Systems thinking involves the most difficult learning.

In the learning organization, the leaders have three functions. He or she is designer, steward, and teacher. The design work of leaders is about creating an organization's policies, strategies, and systems and making them work. It is about integrating parts into a cohesive whole. The leader's first task lies in the field of vision, mission, and values. The essence of leadership in this first function is to design the learning processes. The leader's role as steward links directly with the ideas of Block (1993). Stewardship has to do with the long-term survival of the organization and with its contribution to the wider society. It provides an ethical foundation to the leader's role. The leader as teacher is continually helping people to see 'the big picture'—how the different parts of the organization interact, how apparently different situations have things in common, and what implications today's decisions have for the future. Leaders who are designers, stewards, and teachers see their core task as that of bringing about creative tension by highlighting the gap between reality and the vision.

A leader whose approach provides a good fit with Senge's (1990) model of designer, steward, and teacher is John Neill, chief executive of the U.K.-based automotive components manufacturer and distributor, Unipart. The company was created in 1987 by a management buyout of the parts division of former state-owned British Leyland (now Rover, a BMW subsidiary.) Neill, who led this buyout, is an entrepreneurial and charismatic figure. In many ways he conforms to the stereotype of the transformational leader. One of his first actions was to derecognize trade unions, which, in his view, were partly responsible for the low productivity of the British automotive industry (for an analysis of traditional and changing roles of unions in processes of organizational learning, see Drink, Riegler, and Wolff, Ch. 20 in this volume).

In an interview published in *Strategy*, the newsletter of the Strategic Planning Society (1997), Neill told how he turned around a company struggling to meet quality and delivery requirements with a third-rate manufacturing operation. The turning point came when the company won a contract with Honda because of the learning that Honda was willing to share with its new supplier. He sent a team of six people to study with Honda's fuel tank supplier in Japan. The result of this learning was a complete change in both management and production methods at the supplier's main factory. There was a change in the roles of engineers and supervisors, who were subsequently incorporated into autonomous teams, each with its own leaders and team bonuses supplementing monthly salaries. All the operatives henceforth wore spotless white overalls as a visible sign of quality.

In 1993 Neill established Unipart U, the company university. It now offers some 180 different courses, which have been developed and are taught by Unipart staff. The courses are designed to be practical, so that attendees train for work and can apply the morning's learning to that afternoon's job. The U's direction is in the hands of a Deans' Group, comprising the directors of each of the divisions within the company and chaired by the principal, Professor Dan Jones of Cardiff University Business School. Within the U is the Leading Edge, a state-of-the-art technology showroom and training center where all employees can drop in at any time of the day to work out new ways in which technology can help them unlock their creative potential. There is also the Learning Curve, a Learning Resource Center, which acts as a lending library for books, periodicals, on-line information, and even laptop computers that employees can use at home.

A feature of Neill's approach to learning is that he has not confined his attention to facilitating learning on the part of the work force but rather has embraced other stakeholder groups such as suppliers and customers (see also Lane, Ch. 31 in this volume). For example, he has collaborated with suppliers in a mutually beneficial learning process that has reduced peaks and troughs in deliveries. Guided by a clear vision of what it would involve to build a world-class organization, Neill has designed a learning organization. Despite the considerable market value that his success has created in the global market for top executive talent, he has stayed with Unipart for more than a decade, clear evidence of his stewardship

approach. As a member of Unipart U's faculty, he plays the part of teacher.

Binney and Williams (1995) concluded from their study of business leaders that successful leaders in change combine leading *and* learning. They lead in such a way that learning is encouraged; they learn in a way that informs and guides their actions as leaders. By combining leading and learning, individuals make possible the development of a genuine, shared understanding of current reality to provide the energy for change. They know the importance of learning by doing, reflecting, and learning in the context of real-life priorities and tasks. They look at best practices in other organizations in order to improve their understanding of themselves. They are not perturbed by the tension between leading and learning but rather work with it and exploit it.

Just as a sailor tacking into the wind steers first one way, then another, in order to reach an objective, so individuals who handle change effectively steer a winding course between leading and learning, first emphasising one objective, then the other. They do so in such a way that their success in leading encourages learning and their effectiveness in learning fosters leading. (Binney and Williams: 8–9)

Binney and Williams quote the group managing director of Grundfos, who spends twenty days each year in workshops with managers from all levels in an open-ended review of the company's core objectives and recent developments. The time he devotes to this purpose sends signals throughout the organization. It shows that he is willing to learn and to this end encourages openness in reviewing company operations. This commitment acts as a powerful example to others (for similar examples in Japan, see Nonaka, Reinmöller, and Toyama, Ch. 37 in this volume).

De Geus (1997), writing of his experience as a senior executive with Shell, pointed out that most managers do not think of their jobs in terms of learning: 'They still feel that their leadership depends on their "knowing" their ability to project self-assured confidence in their own information. . . . Even the phrase "I learned" was inadmissible in many Shell circles' (pp. 92–3).

White Water Leadership and 'Difficult Learning'

White, Hodgson, and Crainer (1996) stressed the need for future leaders to be able to cope with uncertainty and turbulence. Leadership used to be about certainty. Now, the most strategically important aspects of an organization's future lie in the area of uncertainty. So, the first component that a leader has to learn is to move toward uncertainty rather than away from it.

Among the five key skills essential to White Water Leadership is difficult learning. The things that are most difficult to learn are also the things that competitors will also find it difficult to learn; hence, such things are the sources of competitive advantage. Pfeffer (1994) argued that the supreme example of such a learning difficulty is learning how to create and sustain an internally consistent human resource strategy. Kay (1993) referred to the difficulty of learning how to create what he described as the organization's architecture, the network of relationships within and external to the organization.

Leadership and the Organization's Stakeholders

Ronald A. Heifetz is Director of the Leadership Education project at the John F. Kennedy School of Government, Harvard University. In one of the most challenging books on leadership of recent times (Heifetz 1994), he set out the case for the leader as a particular kind of educator. In his view, real leaders 'influence the community to face its problems [rather than] influence the community to adopt the leader's vision' (p. 14). He offers five principles to guide leaders:

- identify the problem and the need for change; make clear to all the stakeholders the issues and values involved;

- recognize that change results in stress and that without stress it is unlikely that real change can take place. The leader's task is to contain the stress and keep it within tolerable limits;
- concentrate on the key issues and do not be distracted by such things as personal attacks. Leaders should not accept attempts to deny the problem exists;
- give people responsibility at the rate they can stand, and put pressure on the people with the problem to contribute to its solution;
- protect those who contribute leadership even though they have no formal authority. People who raise tough questions and thereby create stress should not be silenced. They can often provoke the rethinking of issues in ways that leaders with formal authority cannot.

For Heifetz, strategy begins with asking which stakeholders have to adjust their ways in order to make progress in solving this problem. How can the leader strengthen the bonds that link the stakeholders, focusing on their community of interests, so that they can stand the stress of problem-solving?

Facing up to conflict and to the realities of the situation is critical to leadership (see Rothman and Friedman, Ch. 26 in this volume). Heifetz's (1994) ideas tie in with the concept of the learning organization and the need to expose underlying problems rather than treating immediate symptoms. Exercising leadership from a position of authority in change situations involves going against the grain: Instead of meeting people's expectations that the leader will supply the answers, the leader asks pertinent questions. Rather than shielding people from external threats, the leader lets people feel the threat so as to stimulate a thirst for change. Rather than suppressing conflict, the leader generates it; instead of maintaining and defending the status quo, the leader challenges it.

Conclusion

The current interest in the role of leadership in organizational behavior reflects two trends.

The first is the observed importance of processes of influence in the context of achieving adaptation and change in response to changes in the organization's environment. The second is the growing recognition that traditional heroic and charismatic styles of leadership may, with today's relatively sophisticated and educated employees, be less effective in creating an effective influence process than are styles of leadership that encourage learning, teamwork, and participation.

This is not to say that organizational learning is absent in organizations that have charismatic or heroic transformational leaders. When learning does occur in such a context, however, it results from the leader's acting as teacher or parent, with followers taking a relatively passive learning role. In organizations with leaders who act more like the learning leader described by Binney and Williams or who conform to Block's (1993) stewardship model, the leader acts as a facilitator of active learning on the part of others and serves as a role model by being seen to be learning as well as leading.

Organizations that face intense levels of environmental turbulence, need such learning leaders at *all* levels, from the chief executive to the leaders of shop-floor groups. The role of the learning leader in the learning organization has several aspects that are illustrated in the various examples given in the course of this chapter:

- a willingness not only to keep learning but also to be open about learning, encouraging others to follow the leader's example and making it clear that there is no use sitting around and waiting for the leader to come up with the answers;
- the encouragement of learning by asking challenging, awkward questions, by stimulating intellectual curiosity;
- the ability to facilitate the learning of others by acting as coach or mentor;
- the institutionalization of learning by putting in place appropriate incentives, commissioning training and development programs, and establishing facilities such as learning resource centers or even company 'universities';
- the fostering of a pro-learning culture, including such principal characteristics as tolerance of mistakes and avoidance of blame, absence of 'not-invented-here' attitudes, a high level of cross-functional and interdisciplinary integration, encouragement of active membership in professional bodies, and strong emphasis on authority based on competence and expertise rather than on rank or position power;
- the development of mechanisms for the transfer of learning from individuals and teams into the organization's store of knowledge and experience.

References

Bass, B. M. (1990). *Bass and Stogdill's Handbook of Leadership: Theory, Research, and Managerial Application* (3rd edn). New York: Free Press.

——and Avolio, B. J. (1990). 'Developing Transformational Leadership—1992 and Beyond'. *Journal of European Industrial Training*, 14: 21–7.

Bennis, W. (1997). *Organizing Genius*. Reading, Mass.: Addison-Wesley.

Binney, G. and Williams, C. (1995). *Leaning into the Future*. London: Nicholas Brealey.

Blake, R. R. and Mouton, J. S. (1964). *The Managerial Grid: Key Orientations for Achieving Production through People*. Houston: Gulf Publishing.

Block, P. (1993). *Stewardship*. San Francisco: Berrett Koehler.

Collins, J. C. and Porras, J. I. (1995). *Built to Last: Successful Habits of Visionary Companies*. London: Century.

de Geus, A. (1997). *The Living Company: Growth, Learning and Longevity in Business*. London: Nicholas Brealey.

Dobbins, G. H. and Platz, S. T. (1986). 'Sex Differences in Leadership: How Real Are They?' *Academy of Management Review*, 11: 118–27.

Eagly, A. H. and Johnson, B. T. (1990). 'Gender and Leadership Style: A Meta Analysis'. *Psychological Bulletin*, 108: 233–56.

Fiedler, F. (1971). *Leadership*. New York: General Learning Press.

Galton, F. (1869). *Hereditary Genius*. New York: Appleton.

Hampden-Turner, C. and Trompenaars, F. (1993). *The Seven Cultures of Capitalism*. New York: Doubleday.

Handy, C. (1996). 'The New Language of Organizing and Its Implications for Leaders', in F. Hesselbein, M. Goldsmith, and R. Beckhard (eds.), *The Leader of the Future*. San Francisco: Jossey-Bass, 3–9.

Heifetz, R. A. (1994). *Leadership without Easy Answers*. Cambridge, Mass: Harvard University Press.

Hofstede, G. H. (1991). *Cultures and Organizations*. New York: McGraw-Hill.

Hooijberg, R. and DiTomaso, N. (1996). 'Leadership in and of Demographically Diverse Organizations'. *Leadership Quarterly*, 7/1: 1–19.

Kay, J. (1993). *The Foundations of Corporate Success: How Business Strategies Add Value*. Oxford: Oxford University Press.

Likert, R. (1967). *The Human Organization: Its Management and Value*. New York: McGraw-Hill.

McGregor, D. (1960). *The Human Side of Enterprise*. New York: McGraw-Hill.

McGregor Burns, J. (1978). *Leadership*. New York: Harper & Row.

Milmer, K. and Sadler, P. (1993). *The Talent-intensive Organisation*. London: Economist Intelligence Unit.

Morrison, A. M., White, R. P., and Van Velsor, E. (1987). *Breaking the Glass Ceiling*. Reading, Mass.: Addison-Wesley.

Nicoll, D. (1986). 'Leadership and Followership', in J. D. Adams (ed.), *Transforming Leadership: From Vision to Results*. Alexandria, Va.: Miles River Press, 29–38.

Pascale, R. (1990). *Managing on the Edge*. London: Penguin Books.

Pedler, M., Boydell, T., and Burgoyne, J. (1989). 'Towards the Learning Company'. *Management Education and Development*, 20/1: 1–8.

Peters, T. (1992). *Liberation Management*. London: Macmillan.

Pfeffer, J. (1994). *Competitive Advantage through People: Unleashing the Power of the Work Force*. Boston: Harvard Business School Press.

Revans, R. W. (1980). *Action Learning: New Techniques for Management*. London: Blond and Briggs.

Rosener, J. B. (1990). 'Ways Women Lead'. *Harvard Business Review*, 68/6: 119–25.

Sayles, L. R. (1993). *The Working Leader: The Triumph of High Performance over Conventional Management Principles*. New York: Free Press.

Schein, E. H. (1992). *Organizational Culture and Leadership* (2nd edn). San Francisco: Jossey-Bass.

Senge, P. M. (1990). *The Fifth Discipline: The Art and Practice of the Learning Organisation*. London: Century Business.

—— (1996). 'Leading Learning Organizations: The Bold, the Powerful and the Invisible', in F. Hesselbein, M. Goldsmith, and R. Beckhard (eds.), *The Leader of the Future*. San Francisco: Jossey-Bass, 41–57.

Simmons, M. (1996). *New Leadership for Women and Men*. Aldershot: Gower.

Strategic Planning Society (1997). *Strategy* (April).

Tichy, N. M. and Devanna, M. A. (1986). *The Transformational Leader*. New York: Wiley.

Van Seters, D. A. and Field, R. H. G. (1990). 'The Evolution of Leadership Theory'. *Journal of Organizational Change Management*, 3/3: 29–45.

White, R., Hodgson, P., and Crainer, S. (1996). *The Future of Leadership: A White Water Revolution*. London: Pittman.

19   The Role of Boards in Facilitating or Limiting Learning in Organizations

Risto Tainio, Kari Lilja, and Timo J. Santalainen

Boards as Agents of Organizational Learning

Research on organizational learning has traditionally focused on top management teams (Child and Heavens, Ch. 13 in this volume) and leadership (Senge 1996; Sadler, Ch. 18 in this volume). It is the management that has the main responsibility for directing and controlling companies. By contrast, a board of directors meets only a few times a year, also includes outsiders, and works mostly on a part-time basis. It is fair to question the extent to which a body of this kind can contribute to organizational learning with such limited involvement in and knowledge of a company.

In most countries, however, corporate laws vest considerable power in boards of directors. Boards are responsible for corporate leadership without actually interfering in day-to-day operations, which are the responsibility of top management. In general, boards represent the interests of the firm's shareholders, and they are at the apex of the internal control system that monitors managerial and company performance. They have the power to hire, fire, and compensate senior executives and to provide high-level counsel and advice to top management (Baysinger and Hoskisson 1990; Zahra and Pearce 1989). By performing these tasks, boards can facilitate or limit organizational learning and consequently, corporate development.[1]

In the 1990s interest in boards of directors surged all over the world. Much of this growing interest has been due to mismanagement of companies, the widespread problems that shareholders have in governing managers in different institutional settings, and the activation of owners regarding corporate affairs in general.

In large part, the activation of owners and the rise of shareholder's influence stem from the growth in power of large U.S. institutional investors during the last few decades (Drucker 1991; Useem 1996). The institutional shareholders—public and private pension funds, bank trusts, insurance companies, and endowment funds—built up massive stakes in American corporations during the 1970s and early 1980s. By the late 1980s, they had learned how to convert these stakes into active influence through buyout threats, proxy fights, and quiet negotiations. During the 1990s institutional investors moved outside the United States in search of new investment opportunities. Aided by developments of new information technology, they have become key players in global, real-time capital markets and have invested in most of the national and regional economies in the world.

Institutional investors raised their aggregate ownership stakes in U.S. equity markets from 16 per cent in 1965 to 57 per cent by 1994 (Useem 1996). In the United Kingdom, they currently

[1] In different countries there are different kinds of boards through which owners channel their influence. In the United States, for example, a board of directors chaired by the CEO is the prevailing form (Lorsch 1995), whereas in Germany supervisory boards are the major channel.

hold more than 60 per cent of the stock in the largest companies (Monks 1999). In other parts of the world, the trend has been similar, although the process has been even faster (see Tainio 1999).

Shareholders who used to be quite passive and individually oriented on the whole have become active, professional, and more collective. Unlike individual shareholders, institutions invest 'other people's money', and they have a legal fiduciary obligation to take action to protect their investments against the erosion of value (David, Kochhar, and Levitas 1998). Although individual institutional investors may not have large block holdings, they have gained power from coordinated action through their joint holdings and collective institutions (Davis and Thompson 1994).

As a result, the Anglo-American 'shareholder view' of corporate management spread rapidly around the world during the 1990s. According to this view, shareholders have priority over all the other stakeholders of a company. Distant shareholders seek to initiate change and influence corporate governance through various channels (Carleton, Nelson, and Weisbach 1998), with one of the key channels being the board of directors. In corporate governance, therefore, boards have therefore risen in significance at the expense of CEOs and supervisory boards. But the role of supervisory boards in particular, and the 'stakeholder view' it represents, has recently been criticized as inefficient at adding value to the company and at providing an effective channel to monitor and secure shareholders' interests (Veranen 1996).

Boards have become significant agents for organizational restructuring and renewal (Hoskisson, Johnson, and Moesel 1994). There is a growing need to improve the understanding of how boards actually contribute to organizational learning and how this contribution is made in different management–board relationships, business conditions, and institutional contexts.

The traditional view on the role of boards in organizational learning is primarily that boards monitor and control the firm's performance and align the CEO and shareholder interests behind corporate renewal (Walsh and Seward 1990). From this perspective it is assumed that top management keeps boards passive and uninvolved in corporate development and organizational learning. Boards mainly respond when crisis erupts (Mizruchi 1983). Boards are thereby portrayed primarily as reactive agents, and their influence on organizational learning is mainly restricted to managerial and organizational failures (see Herman 1981).

Recent studies on the functions and tasks of boards have, however, underlined the significance of various proactive roles that boards have adopted in corporate governance (Lorsch 1995; McNulty and Pettigrew 1999; Zahra and Pearce 1989). Beside exercising control and supervision, boards have been increasingly engaged in helping top management to reduce environmental uncertainty through boundary-spanning, to secure critical resources for a company, and to review and ratify strategic initiatives (Pfeffer and Salancik 1977; Westphal 1999). Boards work typically at the interface between firms and their external environment. In this capacity boards are central to the organizational learning processes of transferring information and knowledge into a firm and between firms (see Child and Heavens, Ch. 13 in this volume).

In short, companies around the world have become more actively owned and more owner-driven than they used to be (Jensen 1993; Shleifer and Vishny 1997; Veranen 1996). The rise of investor power and intensified shareholder competition for returns on investments have focused attention on, and raised the relevance of boards in, advising and evaluating managerial action, initiating change in organizations, and facilitating or limiting organizational learning (Baysinger and Butler 1985; Gomez-Meija and Wiseman 1997; Johnson, Daily, and Ellstrand 1996).

In this chapter we address both the reactive and proactive roles of boards in organizational learning. The major questions are how and when do boards of directors facilitate or limit learning in organizations: in what way do they intervene and influence action by top management, build a context for organizational learning, and modify organizational routines and practices?

Organizational learning, in both its senses as a process and an outcome, is regarded in this chapter mainly as routine-based, history-dependent, and target-oriented (Levitt and March 1988). As a process, organizational learning occurs when inferences from history are encoded into organizational routines that become a foundation for future rule-driven experimentation and monitoring of targets and a catalyst for modifying behavior. As an outcome, organizational learning appears, for example, when old organizational routines are replaced by new ones and when new competencies are acquired and developed in organizations (Child and Heavens, Ch. 13 in this volume). Critical to this process is an organization's ability to mobilize uncodified, experience-based, 'tacit' knowledge and foster its interaction with 'explicit', articulated, and codified knowledge (see Nonaka and Takeuchi 1995).

Another important distinction in this chapter is that between single-loop learning (a changing of collective action within the existing norms, values, and structures) and double-loop learning (a critical inquiry into and changing of the underlying interpretative mechanisms, goals, and assumptions) (Argyris and Schön 1978; see also Rothman and Friedman, Ch. 26 in this volume).

Traditional View of the Role of Boards in Organizational Learning

A traditional view of the role of boards in organizational learning is based on observations that boards are mostly passive and distant when companies are doing well but that they start to intervene and respond when corporate performance begins to deteriorate and reaches an unacceptable level. The notion that boards remain passive until there is a crisis implies that members of boards are like 'firefighters' who sit around and wait for fire before going

into action (Lorsch 1995). In addition, a company's failure is assumed to be due to an inability of top management, not of the board, to create internal mechanisms for recognizing early warning signals, to start self-correcting action, or to facilitate organizational learning.

In order to understand the prevailing relevance of this traditional role of boards, it is important to see how organizational decline occurs and how managerial failures evolve. In an extensive literature review, Weitzel and Jonsson (1989) identified a five-stage model of organizational decline (see Figure 19.1). It summarizes a typical path leading organizations into crisis and failure. Each stage is characterized by particular organizational difficulties, various conditions for organizational learning, and opportunities for corrective action.

At the start of the decline process, management tends to become 'blinded'. At this 'blinded stage', operational difficulties start to emerge in an organization, but the signals are still weak and not yet apparent in the company's financial indicators of performance. This lack of perceptible evidence may be due to the supportive environment, the availability of sufficient resources within the organization, or a time lag before the change for the worse becomes directly visible. The managerial action against seemingly minor problems is weak and routine. The focus is still on the current line of action. Sometimes the opportunity for temporary belt-tightening is recognized. Cognitively, management tends to deny the problems, regards them as temporary, and makes no efforts to inform the board about them (see also Lorange and Nelson 1987). At this stage boards are typically left as outsiders. They have little chance to intervene and facilitate learning, for the managers do not provide them with information about the conditions of the firm or about the growing challenges of management.

During the 'inaction stage' the signs of crisis have become visible and undeniable to the management. At first, however, management typically underestimates the need for change. Its response is either inaction or the repetition of past practices, both of which mean delays in effort to start reorientation and learning in the

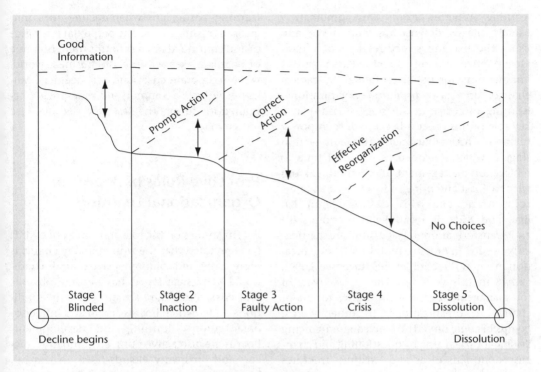

Fig. 19.1. Widening performance gap as decline deepens

Reprinted from 'Decline in Organizations: A Literature Integration and Extension', by W. Weitzel and E. Jonsson, published in *Administrative Science Quarterly* (34/1) by permission of *Administrative Science Quarterly*. © 1989 Cornell University.

organization. Past successes are used to justify present policies and procedures. A wait-and-see mentality, a cognitive commitment to the present course of action, and its active legitimation tend to increase the isolation of top management. If the company's decline is rapid or sudden, autocratic and rigid managerial behavior tends to increase as a way of coping with the confusion and chaos in the organization (Starbuck, Greve, and Hedberg 1978). The challenges are still construed as 'managerial' at this stage. Top management is regarded as having the major responsibility to initiate corrective action and start organizational learning. Boards are still treated as bystanders uninvolved in day-to-day operations and too distant to intervene.

At the stage of 'faulty action', the visibility and severity of the problems with several indicators increases. It becomes indisputable that the organization is in trouble. Uncertainty escalates in the organization, and the frequency and intensity of the power struggles within the dominant coalition increase. Under these conditions, management action tends to look both reactionary and experimental. Management defends itself, asks for loyalty, and tries to retain existing status and power structures even as it acts impulsively (Hambrick and D'Aveni 1988; Miller and Friesen 1980). The best people start to leave, and those who stay have to work harder for fewer rewards than used to be the case. Faulty actions are the result of rising time pressure, which tends to favor quick and expedient solutions (see also Weber and Berthoin Antal, Ch. 15 in this volume). Decisions made under stressful conditions are likely to lead to first-order incremental change and single-loop learning (Whetten 1980). This combination usually means downsizing work force and using the existing structures and dominant ideas (Weitzel and Jonsson 1989). Paradoxically, 'momentum' for major reorientation, radical change, and fast, profound organizational learning also exists at this stage. Boards play a key role in this process because of their power to hire and fire management. This faulty-action stage is widely regarded as the ideal time to replace top management in order to break ties with the past and bring in fresh ideas and new competencies and skills (Castrogiovanni, Baliga, and Kidwall 1992). Reorientation skills and transformational leadership are particularly needed in order to mobilize the organization in a new direction at this stage (see Sadler, Ch. 18 in this volume). The replacement of top management creates conditions for major change in organizations. In other words, boards become directly involved in enhancing double-loop learning by questioning and changing dominant ideas and existing structures (see Grinyer, Mayes, and McKiernan 1988; Pettigrew 1985).

During the 'crisis stage', an organization faces the problems that have the greatest bearing on its survival. The management is beset by aggravating internal problems and external pressures. Revolutionary changes in organization are necessary but extremely difficult to invent and implement. Lack of time and scarcity of both financial and human resources are critical factors limiting managerial action. At this stage boards mostly support the new management in firefighting in order to help gain time, to find enough financial resources to avoid bankruptcy, and to back up management in their efforts to reorganize the firm and turn it around (Weitzel and Jonsson 1991). The board, together with the new management, tries to combine short-term solutions and preparations for 'frame-breaking' change and double-loop learning for the future (see Tushman, Newman, and Romanelli 1986).

The traditional, mostly passive and reactive role of boards in organizational learning is generalized from special circumstances. Boards do indeed play a central role in organizational learning, particularly when decline turns into crisis in organizations. The perpetual relevance of and continued interest in this firefighter role of boards makes sense in the business world, where corporate crises and management failures have been a common and widespread phenomenon during the last few decades (see Jensen 1993).

Proactive Roles of Boards in Organizational Learning

Recent studies on the role and action of boards have revealed that the work done by boards is more active and comprehensive than the traditional view suggests. It has become obvious that crisis and failure are not the only conditions under which boards act on and influence organizational learning and development. Boards are also active during a company's success and prosperity. Boards have, in general, been found to be more and more future-oriented in anticipating environmental changes, in exploring new possibilities, and in developing new skills and competencies (Christensen and Westenholz 1998; Lorsch 1995; McNulty and Pettigrew 1999).

In light of these new circumstances and expanded task profiles, it has become important to redefine the roles and relationships between top management and a board. There is actually a fine line between managing a company and contributing ideas for managing a company. When boards increase their active role in corporate governance, it does not mean that they become active in actually managing companies but that boards intensify their active supervision of companies, keep top management to high performance standards, scrutinize strategic plans, and take responsibility for management succession ('Best and Worst Boards' 1997).

Zahra and Pearce (1989) identified two proactive roles of boards that extend their traditional roles of monitoring and control. They are called the roles of service and strategy. In their service role, boards are typically boundary spanners who provide vital links between companies and their environment. They play a critical role in the process of transferring information and knowledge across boundaries of organizations and thereby make timely knowledge available to top management (see Child and Heavens, Ch. 13 in this volume). Board members enhance information exchange through their external connections to other companies, research organizations, trade associations, and government agencies. In particular, their membership in other companies' boards makes it possible to 'bench mark' current operations and business practices, to diagnose managerial problems in different contexts, and to enhance learning from others' experience. In order to transfer experience and knowledge from other companies, however, board members need access to rich knowledge about their own company and about management's strategic thinking. If this tacit knowledge is lacking, outside explicit knowledge (e.g. best practices and model cases) becomes difficult to internalize, reflect upon, and turn into new knowledge (Nonaka, Toyama, and Byosière, Ch. 22 in this volume). In this service role, the ability of boards to facilitate learning therefore greatly depends on the quality of the knowledge they receive from management.

There is less controversy over the nature of this service role of boards than over their strategic role. The early work on boards reveals especially great skepticism of the board's active involvement in strategy (e.g. Andrews 1981; Lorsch and MacIver 1989). Harrison (1987), however, argued that boards using audit and compensation committees had become increasingly involved in examining strategic issues. As the strategic role of boards has expanded, their capacity to be more deeply involved in organizational learning has also increased. Most of the work on strategic issues requires inquiries that question current norms, goals, and structures. Boards' involvement in these matters has made them one of the key agents in double-loop learning in their organizations.

Lorsch and MacIver (1989) found that the primary role of boards in the strategy-formation process was advising and evaluating the management rather than initiating strategy. Recently, however, boards of a growing number of companies have created new ways to be involved in strategy work. They have, for example, utilized one- or two-day strategic retreats to deepen their strategic role. Instead of simply approving or rejecting major proposals by the management, the retreats have been used for open discussion and debate of the changes in the industry and the strategic directions and options available (Lorsch 1995). This practice, however, seldom means that boards demand approval of their own genuine alternatives. Rather, they contribute to organizational learning by debating and questioning suggestions and initiatives proposed by management (see Lainema 1997).

In their study about the actual behavior of boards in the United Kingdom, McNulty and Pettigrew (1999) conceptualized boards' role in strategy by distinguishing between three levels of possible involvement: taking strategic decisions; shaping strategic decisions; and shaping the content, context, and conduct of strategy. In taking strategic decisions, boards accept, reject, or request modifications for management's proposals. All boards take strategic decisions, indicating that the traditional firefighter role of boards in organizational learning is only rudimentary. Empirical evidence, however, suggests that boards that take strategic decisions are not very deeply involved in organizational learning. Boards have been found to approve the majority of proposals put forward by top management, although not all boards function like a rubber stamp all the time (McNulty and Pettigrew 1999).

'Shaping strategic decisions' refers to boards' activities before they take strategic decisions. In that preliminary phase boards can shape strategies through two kinds of process. First, top management can consult board members while preparing proposals either formally or informally. Second, management may be able to anticipate the response of the board and self-regulate the proposals. These processes enable board members to contribute quite extensively to organizational learning. They can test ideas, raise issues, question assumptions, give advice and hence caution, or offer encouragement for organizational learning.

When speaking of shaping the context, content, and conduct of strategy, McNulty and Pettigrew (1999) refer to boards' influence on the processes and methodologies through which new ideas and strategies evolve. Board members construct arenas where strategy and corporate development is debated and even formulated. Boards may thus enlarge the basis of managerial expertise, force management to consider a wide range of options, and persuade managers to diverge from their previous ways of thinking. In this way boards actively promote organizational learning by extending the range of options available for management. The greatest impact on organizational learning is achieved when boards are active at the three levels of strategic involvement simultaneously.

In performing their proactive roles, boards are likely to spot problems in advance, even in apparently good times. This capacity extends their involvement and influence beyond crisis and failures to turnarounds and successes (see Stopford and Baden-Fuller 1990; Tainio and Valpola 1996). Recent studies have provided empirical evidence that, during prosperous times, boards also serve as a sounding board for management (Lorsch and MacIver 1989), suggest new ideas, continuously follow and evaluate managerial proposals (Lorsch 1995), make and shape current courses of action (McNulty and Pettigrew 1999), and even become involved in initiating strategies (Demb and Neubauer 1992).

In their service roles, boards engage mostly in exploitation of existing strategies and knowledge. As a form of organizational learning, 'exploitation' means short-term improvements and refinements that leave underlying values and norms unchanged (March 1991). Proactive exploitation in fact means active involvement in preventive maintenance. Boards support and encourage management to make incremental changes in order to keep small difficulties from turning into large problems.

In their strategy roles, boards extend their efforts from exploitation of existing practices to exploration of new ones. Exploration means experimentation with new ideas, knowledge, paradigms, and strategies in order to find genuinely new alternatives. This kind of learning is mainly thought to be risky and to be stimulated by failures (see March 1995).

Performance Path, Organizational Life-cycle and the Role of Boards in Organizational Learning

The role of boards in organizational learning in successful companies differs from that in less successful ones (Zahra and Pearce 1989) and also differs from one phase of a company's life cycle to the next (Lainema 1997). A common observation is that board members in companies with poor financial performance have a greater desire to be involved in management's decision-making than do board members in well-performing companies (Lorsch 1995). Moreover, boards' role in new business organizations tends to be different from that in well-established, mature corporations (Zahra and Pearce 1989).

The role of boards in organizational learning can therefore be expected to vary in two different, but related, cycles: a company's performance path and its life cycle. A performance path is a historical trajectory describing the economic outcome of organizations. It represents variations in the results of an organization, and it can be described in terms such as a turnaround, an improving trend, a downturn, an oscillation, or a downward slope. By contrast, the life cycle of a company is conceptualized in terms of birth, growth, maturity, degeneration, and revival or death (e.g. Kimberly and Miles 1980; Miller and Friesen 1983). Organizations are assumed to go gradually and irreversibly through phases similar to those of people in their personal development. The phases are therefore mostly related directly to the age of organizations and only indirectly to performance and size.

As for organizational learning, it is useful to turn attention first to the various stages of a performance path and thereafter to briefly discuss the ways in which it occurs at the different phases of organizational life cycles.

There is an obvious asymmetry between a path of declining performance and a path of growing performance. The seeds of decline are often sown at times of success and growth (Jensen 1993). When members of management experience that an activity appears to succeed, they tend to increase its frequency, standardize it, and specialize in it. The success recipe becomes programmed (Starbuck, Greve, and Hedberg 1978), an outcome that leads organizations to specialize further and to accumulate experience primarily mainly with old routines (Cyert and March 1963). Repeated success therefore tends to slow down and stagnate learning in organizations (Weber and Berthoin Antal, Ch. 15 in this volume) and is likely to lead to a decrease in the search for new alternatives. The members of an organization become increasingly removed from other types of experience and knowledge and ever more dependent on existing skills and competencies. Specialized routines work well only as long as conditions remain unchanged. When the change occurs, the organization tends to do the wrong things well. Superior, but useless, practices have developed and even become dominant, leading the organization into the competency trap (Levitt and March 1988; Levinthal and March 1993). The organization has to unlearn and relearn as quickly as possible (Weber and Berthoin Antal, Ch. 15 in this volume). The favorable performance of a company is also related to tendencies toward complacency and overconfidence. Together, specialization and overconfidence tend to make management conservative and routinized. Organizations develop standard operating procedures, which improve the accuracy of execution (Kieser, Beck, and Tainio, Ch. 27 in this volume).

The role of boards in organizational learning varies, depending on the phase of the performance path. To facilitate discussion of this contingency, Figure 19.2 presents a stylized description of a hypothetical path.

After a turnaround and during the emerging success (phase A), boards are likely to adopt a service role. They tend to support managerial efforts to complete a turnaround and tend to avoid disturbing a positive trend. When success continues and accelerates (phase B), top management gains strength and power and its success recipe becomes more and more dominant, routinized, and repeated. Management becomes risk-averse, emphasizing its reliance on tested practices and stressing the importance of eliminating errors. This behavior often makes a company dangerously stable, that is, it excludes critical opinions, brave guesses, and deviant initiatives. In this phase, when the rate of routinization of managerial practices accelerates, the role of a board is to bring in critics and question the existing course of action. The strategy role of a board gains strength at the expense of its service role. Management needs to be prepared to assimilate change and to become sensitized to problems in advance. In phase B′, the strategy role of the board becomes even more obvious. This period is when it is difficult for both top management and the board to identify and interpret the early warning signals of a possible downturn. It becomes important for the board to become actively involved in the strategy process in order to stimulate a search for new ideas and to outline alternative courses of action. It is the time when management typically emphasizes the virtues of old certainties, whereas the board seeks to encourage management to explore new possibilities. This approach prepares the ground for double-loop learning and fundamental changes in the organization.

In the next phase C, the signs of organizational decline multiply. In this situation, management tends to act both experimentally and conservatively (Hambrick and D'Aveni 1988). Management is sorely tempted to make quick solutions as time pressure worsens. If time pressure becomes excessive, it can slow down the learning processes and paralyze the organization (see Weber and Berthoin Antal, Ch. 15 in this volume). In a crisis, however, an organization is also ready for change and open for learning and renewal. Under these conditions, the

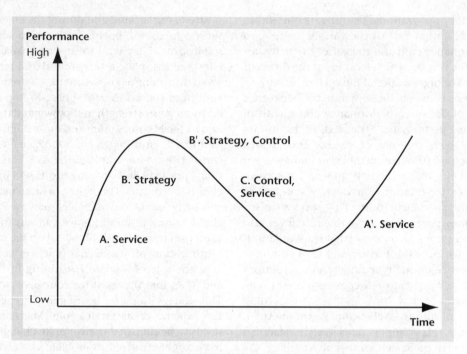

Fig. 19.2. The changing role of a board at the various stages of a performance path

board has two major options for building the necessary managerial skills and competencies for a turnaround. First, it may support the existing management by opening 'windows of opportunities' (Abel 1978: 21; see also Weber and Berthoin Antal, Ch. 15 in this volume) for future reorientation. Second, it may replace current management in order to unlock new organizational learning (Child and Heavens, Ch. 13 in this volume). If bankruptcy can be avoided, the service role can again be adopted and nurtured by the board (phase A').

In the stylized description above, the role of boards in organizational learning depends mainly on the performance of the firm and the content of the managerial work involved. The better the performance and the less routinized the managerial work, the more one expects a board to collaborate creatively with management. The worse the performance and the more routinized the managerial work, the more probable it is that creative tension exists between the board and management. In this sense management and the board act as

countervailing powers in companies. Their roles are complementary but often also conflicting.

These different performance conditions may occur at each stage of the organizational life cycle. It has been proposed that the stages of birth, growth, maturity, and degeneration all shape learning processes in organizations, although the evidence is mostly anecdotal (Weber and Berthoin Antal, Ch. 15 in this volume). It has, for example, been found that learning and unlearning is easier for young and small organizations than for old and large ones (Starbuck and Hedberg, Ch. 14 in this volume). During the phase of maturity, when organizational practices and routines are established and institutionalized, organizational learning is mainly slow and conservative by nature (Weber and Berthoin Antal, Ch. 15 in this volume).

In the early phases of the life cycle, the role of boards is based predominantly on the service function (Zahra and Pearce 1989). The board provides the owner–manager with advice and counsel that enhance the firm's legitimacy. To provide help for an entrepreneur at this stage, board members need rich inside information about the dynamics of the company, and preferably about growth companies in general as well. When an organization approaches maturity, boards become more involved in inquiries and debates about strategic directions and allocation of resources (Lainema 1997).

Different Types of Boards, their Internal Dynamics, and Organizational Learning

In order to be steered, a sailing boat needs a keel. It becomes especially important when a storm hits the boat. I would have needed a 'keel', the counterforce of the board, to succeed in steering my company in a turbulent business environment. (The personal learning experience of the CEO of a bankrupt firm)

In order to learn, any modern company needs an active and competent management and an active and competent board. The balance of power between them is important for understanding differences among the boards and for grasping the varied ways in which they contribute to organizational learning.

Pearce and Zahra (1991) have distinguished between four types of boards according to the relative power of CEOs and boards. The types of boards are the caretaker, statutory, proactive, and participative. These types reflect important board attributes: characteristics, internal processes, decision-making styles, and processes of organizational learning (see Figure 19.3).

Caretaker boards are characterized by low board power and low CEO power. These kinds of boards are legal necessities and do not contribute significantly to corporate development or organizational learning. Outsiders' representation is limited, and the proceedings tend to be informal and superficial. Decision-making is passive and weak. Caretaker boards do not

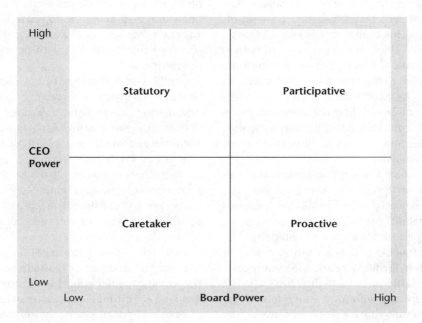

Fig. 19.3. The types of boards

Adapted from 'The Relative Power of CEOs and Boards of Directors: Associations with Corporate Performance', by J. Pearce, II and S. Zahra, *Strategic Management Journal*, 12 (1991), 137. © 1991 John Wiley & Sons Limited. Reproduced with permission.

facilitate organizational learning. They do not enhance discussion about the nature of dominating ideas. Managers might be passive because they either do not have alternatives for the current strategy or cannot agree upon several alternatives. The members of a caretaker board tend to be passive or indifferent to organizational learning if they have only a small stake in the company or have a lack or overload of knowledge about the company. They also tend to have other personal interests that receive a higher priority than their professional lives.

Statutory boards resemble boards 'taking strategic decisions' (see McNulty and Pettigrew 1999: 56–8). The CEO is the central figure in decision-making, and the action of the board greatly depends on management's efforts and initiatives. This type of board usually follows the CEO's proposals, a practice perhaps due to board members' lack of expertise, interest, or time. CEOs mostly regard statutory/strategy-taker boards as nuisances. They do not treat the members of this kind of board as true partners in shaping the future of corporations. The impact that such board members have on organizational learning occurs mainly through their approval of management's initiatives and proposals. The CEO controls the information provided to the board and often selects its members. Organizational learning is generally management-driven, and the board members have only a minor role in it. Normally, they offer advice and counsel to the management only when asked.

Proactive boards command powers that surpass those of their CEOs. This powerful position may be based, for example, on increased director liability and shareholder activism or, on poor performance by the company. The strength of such boards is accentuated by their composition. Proactive boards are usually composed primarily of outside directors, who are independent and who have a high level of expertise. They also have time to meet frequently in order to ensure the dissemination of information and effective decision-making. Proactive boards have the power and ability to influence top management to change the stra-

tegic direction of the company if necessary and, in extreme cases, to replace management. Hence, they are likely to have strong and direct instruments to bring about fundamental changes in corporate governance and organizational routines. These boards typically represent shareholders' interests. If disagreements and conflicts arise, proactive boards will tend to rely on their formal powers to resolve the dispute. This proclivity can easily hinder dialogue or debate between the board and the CEO.

Participative boards are characterized by high board power and high CEO power. The board meetings are full of discussion, debate, and confrontation. Extensive negotiations take place on building and reaching consensus among directors themselves and with top management. Participative boards and top management are likely to redefine their relationship and review it regularly. Both the board and the management have their own active role to play in company development. This development is based on mutual trust among board members and between board members and top management, on access to the same information, and on willingness and time to share knowledge with one another. For organizational learning, this type of a board seems to be particularly interesting.

Conflicts and debate within a participative board, and between that type of board and top management are regarded as a major source of opportunity for organizational learning (see Rothman and Friedman, Ch. 26 in this volume). Argyris and Schön (1978) have also argued that conflicts have a central part in generating double-loop learning: 'Double-loop learning, if it occurs, will consist of the process of inquiry by which the group of managers confront and resolve their conflict' (p. 23).

Although conflicts are potentially destructive, in the context of participative boards they appear to offer opportunities for 'reflexive dialogue'—legitimate expression of differences in opinions and the inquiry into the values, interests, and goals of its members (Rothman 1997: 38; Rothman and Friedman, Ch. 26 in this volume). Hence, conflicts between two powerful parties in corporate governance may enrich the learning process by increasing the number of alternatives to be considered, broadening the range of options, and expanding definitions of organizational reality.

This possibility suggests that the diversity of voices and the acceptance of pluralism among members of the board and between them and top management enlarges the basis for expertise and facilitates organizational learning. Conflicts become part of the process through which board members and managers can critically read signals of performance and utilize multiple logics in developing a company.

In participative boards, deliberations are based on intense and profound negotiations. In other words, both formal and informal channels of communication are used extensively. From formal channels it is possible to get explicit knowledge about the company, such as financial data about its history, its present, and its plans for the future. The informal channels, on the other hand, provide knowledge about the insights of managerial practice, about its routinization or power of regeneration, and about minor emerging difficulties in business operations. This knowledge may help a board spot problems in advance, keep it alert, and maintain its involvement. Knowledge from informal channels may also serve as an early warning of failures in organizational learning. For example, management may stymie organizational learning by overemphasizing exploitation of old certainties. At that point the role of a board is to encourage and bring in a new mode of exploration to legitimate and catalyze a search for new ideas and prospects. Management may also overemphasize the exploration of new opportunities and may routinely initiate continuous experimentation in the company. Under these conditions, boards apply brakes and restrain the speed with which new knowledge is pursued.

Companies commonly note a strong tendency toward unanimity and wishful thinking in board–management relations and within boards themselves (Jensen 1993; Johnson, Daily, and Ellstrand 1996). For different reasons this tendency is typical of caretaker, statutory, and proactive boards. When this unanimity overrides motivation to appraise alternative courses of action realistically, the phenomenon is called 'Groupthink' (Janis 1982; Whyte 1989). The outcome of this process is politeness and courtesy at the expense of truth and frankness. It makes members of the board and management team hesitant to raise controversial issues, to question weak arguments, and to admit their ignorance. This response can block organizational learning by closing information flows and limiting the assimilation of new information.

A strong, one-sided power position, as found in the statutory and proactive boards, often silences divergent voices, creates self-censorship, and hinders criticism and debate. Organizational success further accentuates unanimity, especially in statutory boards. First, success tends to augment the relative power of top management at the expense of the board (Lainema 1997). During the years of success and growth, it becomes rewarding and flattering to be a part of a winning team, which creates the illusion of invulnerability. Second, the success of some businesses covers the losses of a few others, a tradeoff that creates the debts of gratitude. Success also tends to entail specialization, which makes it difficult for a board to intervene in 'expert debates'.

During a period of apparent decline or crisis, unanimity is common in all four types of boards. Under these conditions, it is mostly a result of outside pressures and hierarchical rigidities. During the crisis, it is assumed that an organization cannot afford the luxury of internal disputes. It is easy to justify that an organization needs to be united to confront common enemies. Several studies have also indicated that reduced performance and crisis lead to tightened controls, centralization of authority, and enforced unity (e.g. Czarniawska and Hedberg 1985). This search for concurrence in crisis stems partly from fear and defensiveness and partly from a lack of time to respond to rapid external changes and aggravated internal problems.

Participative boards seem to have potential to avoid the Groupthink phenomenon, but it does not occur automatically. It needs, at least to some extent, to be designed. Extensive negotiations and differences in opinions necessitate forums of open criticism and debate, where managers and board members meet each other regularly. These forums of debate play a significant part in creating a 'learning board' (Garratt 1999: 33). In addition, the board sets up a regular and strict rhythm of critical review for its own conformance and performance and utilizes external feedback and peer reviews to improve its performance and activate group learning.

Of course, it is also necessary to have board members and managers who are willing to use these arenas, and actually provide a multiplicity of voices to companies. This need creates particular demands on the composition of boards and top management teams alike. They all require diverse expertise, experience, and worldviews. It is, therefore, important to pay particular attention to the processes of recruitment and replacement of board members and top managers so that people from different specialties and backgrounds can be brought together in order to enrich collective learning. Maintaining a multiplicity of voices requires mechanisms to break down the defensiveness and insecurities of individuals, to build their mutual respect, and to raise tolerance of different and often contradictory opinions. Paradoxically, open and frank communication may also lead to wide and unbridgeable gaps between members (Rothman and Friedman, Ch. 26 in this volume).

Future Tendencies in the Role of Boards in Organizational Learning

In recent years, large U.S.-based institutional investors in particular have expressed increased concern about the influence of boards of directors over corporate affairs (Westphal 1999). They have strongly criticized CEO-dominated, statutory, strategy-taker boards, asserting that such boards are weak and ineffective at looking out for shareholders' interests. It is argued that these boards lack independence from top management and that this dependence has made them passive and uninvolved in strategic decision-making and organizational renewal. Shareholders, especially institutional investors, have been particularly active in pressing for change in board structures and in strengthening the role of these rejuvenated boards at the expense of CEOs and supervisory boards.

These reproaches are especially understandable with respect to the United States, where the CEO still holds a board chair in more than 80 per cent of the publicly held corporations (Lorsch 1995). In the European context, the role of boards has also been somewhat controversial when powerful CEOs and supervisory boards are involved.

The calls for board reform have emphasized the need to reconstitute boards. The proposed changes include increasing the independence of board members and of board leadership structure, improving the quality of board members, raising the level of board members' accountability to shareholders, and widening the demographic diversity of the board ('Best and Worst Boards' 1997; Westphal 1998).

The independence of board members is one of the essential principles in current board reforms. It is preferable to have a majority of board members who have no relationship with the CEO or the company. This arrangement minimizes the number of insiders on the board and bars members of the board from doing consulting or other work for the company. Avoidance of interlocking directorships is favored as well.

Another change being urged is improvement in the quality of board members. They are supposed to have experience with and expertise in a range of businesses and business conditions so that they understand the issues and problems faced by the company. Board members also required to have time to attend meetings and provide active, critical stands on and evaluations of management's plans and strategies.

The role of boards in organizational learning in the future will depend to a large extent on the knowledge that their members have about their companies (Lorsch 1995). Board members need both explicit knowledge about the company's financial and product-market performance and tacit knowledge about the managerial practices, work contents, and development of the company. For members of the board, board meetings have become one of the major sources of all this knowledge and a main opportunity to learn about the company from those who have been with the organization longer than the board members themselves. Hence, the questions put to management during the board meetings are at least as important as the answers or solutions provided.

A current trend is that the board needs to be small enough to be a cohesive group ('Best and Worse Boards' 1996, 1997). In practice, the power of boards in relation to top management depends greatly on their solidarity and unity as a group (Lorsch 1995). But as discussed in the previous section, a strongly unified board may prevent its own renewal and may restrain the creation of a learning board.

The above change tendencies mean that the principles of what make a good board are subject to redefinition and reconstruction. They mainly reflect shareholders' interests and pressures to transform CEO-driven strategy-taker boards into empowered 'proactive' boards. If this board reform is accomplished, it is likely that the consequences for organizational learning are likely to be somewhat contradictory. On the one hand, this particular board reform facilitates organizational learning by increasing the diversity of expertise and experience, outside evaluations, and critical questioning within the top echelons of companies. Moreover, the strong power enjoyed by proactive boards endows them with the capacity to make fundamental changes and stimulate double-loop learning. On the other hand, board reform may limit organizational learning. The emphasis on the principle of independence tends to restrict boundary-spanning, and having only a minimal number of insiders on the board does not enhance utilization of tacit knowledge. The formal power of a proactive

board may also silence voices, hinder dialogue, and underutilize the opportunities that conflicts provide for organizational learning.

There seems to be less discussion of the nature of participative boards and of a possible transition from strategy-taker boards to participative boards. In the light of the preceding description of the different types of boards, it could be argued that the creation of participative boards would have even more far-reaching consequences for organizational learning than the emergence of proactive boards would.

The rapid rise of shareholder activism and the spread of a shareholder view on corporate management has brought in new professional groups whose role in organizational learning also needs to be taken seriously in the future. Shareholders' influence on companies and their management is channeled through networks of financial professionals (e.g. financial analysts and portfolio managers), investor-relations specialists, and CEOs. Especially important are financial professionals who play a crucial role in the intensified corporate, regional, and international competition for capital and investors. They produce the actual and potential knowledge that shareholders have about companies as investment targets. They rate and evaluate the quality of companies and their prospects, and they influence criteria for sound governance structures and desirable characteristics of boards. To the management, financial professionals bring information about shareholders' preferences and demands. They may also advise management on how to enhance its company's attractiveness to investors.

It seems evident that the importance of the role that financial analysts play in processes of organizational learning is also destined to grow. As mediators between shareholders and managers, financial analysts monitor and challenge the routines and practices of boards as well as those of top management. Financial professionals will be influential in determining what kind of knowledge is produced about and in companies and what kinds of learning and innovations are going to be valued and respected.

Conclusions

At the moment, managers and boards represent two major agents at the apex of corporate control. A board of directors is one of the major bodies through which owners channel their impact on corporate development and renewal. In this capacity a board, together with top management, has a central role in facilitating or limiting organizational learning.

There exists, however, a boundary between the tasks of the management and the tasks of the board. Although this boundary is a fine line, whose course may vary according to conditions, in most cases the management is responsible for actually managing the company, and the board's role is to monitor the management and be of service to it. A more controversial issue is the extent to which the board has become involved in strategic issues and processes and hence in double-loop learning. Whereas management is involved full-time in company affairs and has rich and deep knowledge about the organization, the board has only limited involvement in and comparatively remote knowledge of the company.

In recent decades the activation of owners has increased all over the world. Accordingly, the role of the boards has grown in scope and scale. In general, it has shifted from reactive to proactive, enhancing the viability of organizations and shareholders' interest in a highly volatile environment.

Organizations have a tendency 'to fight to remain the same' (Schön 1971: 32) even when they experience unexpected internal developments or perceive alarm signals from the changing environment. Organizational learning is jeopardized if there is no discussion or debate about existing strategies, dominating ideas, or operational routines or if such discussion is not allowed. Confrontations and conflicts between a board and top management are often required to facilitate organizational learning, especially double-loop learning (Argyris and Schön 1978).

The effects of boards on organizational learning depend on two major factors: the nature of the knowledge and information available to the board and the power relations between the board and the management. A board needs in-depth knowledge about management practices, company development, and environmental change. In addition to coded, explicit knowledge about the history and presence of the company, a board needs tacit knowledge, which is highly personal, company specific, and organizationally embedded (Nonaka, Toyama, and Byosière, Ch. 22 in this volume). One of the great challenges to boards is to create knowledge in order to sensitize and identify excessive and routinized exploitation of old certainties or excessive exploration of new opportunities in managerial practice (March 1991). These modes of organizational learning have been found effective in the short run but problematic in the long run. A board may succeed in balancing the modes of exploitation and exploration by providing modes that run against the grain of managerial thinking and action over time.

The great challenge to a board is to reach out for tacit knowledge and to foster its own interaction with explicit knowledge. This task makes it necessary to generate and maintain diversity in organizational thought, voice, and action. Such diversity, however, will not necessarily prevent failures or disasters or enhance organizational learning, but it may nevertheless help a board identify threats and problems in advance, expand top management's understanding about early warning signals, and prevent small difficulties from accumulating and turning into large crises.

The different power relations between boards and management generate different types of boards. They tend to produce, mobilize, and diffuse knowledge in different ways. It is suggested in this chapter that a participative type of board tends to have the most potential to facilitate organizational learning. The type gives both the board and top management relatively great power, and informal and formal networks are utilized in knowledge creation. The conflicts, debates, and extensive discussions that boards and top management engage in help reveal the tacit dimension of organizational knowledge and practice. From this starting point the board may further encourage and legitimate inquiry and debate about existing managerial practices and organizational work procedures and may thus facilitate double-loop learning in organizations.

The current board reforms to strengthen and 'empower' boards at the expense of CEOs will make boards more rather than less significant agents of organizational learning than they used to be. This change will create new demands for future research. There is a need to specify further the conditions under which the relative power and, consequently, the effects of boards are likely to increase or decrease. In this chapter we have briefly illustrated the importance that the phases of a firm's performance path and organizational life cycle have in this respect. The tentative links established by anecdotal evidence require empirical investigation that is more systematic and comparative than in the past. In addition, there is a need to devote increased attention to the effects that institutional and national differences and the fragmentation of firms' ownership structures have on the nature of boards as agents of organizational learning.

References

Abell, D. F. (1978). 'Strategic Windows'. *Journal of Marketing*, 42/3: 21–6.

Andrews, K. R. (1981). 'Corporate Strategy as a Vital Function of the Board'. *Harvard Business Review*, 59/6: 174–84.

Argyris, C. and Schön, D. (1978). *Organizational Learning: A Theory of Action Perspective*. Reading, Mass.: Addison-Wesley.

Baysinger, B. and Butler, H. (1985). 'Corporate Governance and the Board of Directors: Performance Effects of Changes in Board Composition'. *Journal of Law, Economics, and Organization*, 1: 101–24.

—— and Hoskisson, R. (1990). 'Composition of Boards of Directors and Strategic Control: Effects on Corporate Strategy'. *Academy of Management Review*, 15: 72–87.

'Best and Worst Boards, The'. (1996). *Business Week*, 25 November: 62–8.

—— (1997). *Business Week*, 8 December: 46–52.

Carleton, W., Nelson, J., and Weisbach, M. (1998). 'The Influence of Institutions on Corporate Governance through Private Negotiations: Evidence from TIAA-CREF'. *Journal of Finance*, 53: 1335–62.

Castrogiovanni, G., Baliga, B. R., and Kidwall, R. (1992). 'Curing Sick Business: Changing CEOs in Turnaround Efforts'. *Academy of Management Executive*, 6/3: 26–41.

Christensen, S. and Westenholz, A. (1998). 'The Role of the Board of Directors in Danish Companies'. *Reports on the Research Project*, No. 8. Department of Organization and Industrial Sociology, Copenhagen Business School.

Cyert, R. and March, J. G. (1963). *A Behavioral Theory of the Firm*. Englewood Cliffs, NJ: Prentice Hall.

Czarniawska, B. and Hedberg, B. L. T. (1985). 'Control Cycle Responses to Decline'. *Scandinavian Journal of Management Studies*, 2: 19–39.

David, P., Kochhar, R., and Levitas, E. (1998). 'The Effect of Institutional Investors on the Level and Mix of CEO Compensation'. *Academy of Management Journal*, 41: 200–8.

Davis, G. F. and Thompson, T. A. (1994). 'A Social Movement Perspective on Corporate Control'. *Administrative Science Quarterly*, 39: 141–73.

Demb, A. and Neubauer, F. (1992). *The Corporate Board*. New York: Oxford University Press.

Drucker, P. (1991). 'Reckoning with the Pension Fund Revolution'. *Harvard Business Review*, 69/2: 106–14.

Garratt, B. (1999). 'Developing Effective Directors and Building Dynamic Boards'. *Long Range Planning*, 32/1: 28–35.

Gomez-Meija, L. and Wiseman, R. (1997). 'Reframing Executive Compansation: An Assessment and Outlook'. *Journal of Management*, 23: 291–374.

Grinyer, P. H., Mayes, D. G., and McKiernan, P. (1988). *Sharpbenders: The Secrets of Unleashing Corporate Potential.* Oxford: Blackwell.

Hambrick, D. and D'Aveni, R. (1988). 'Large Corporate Failures as Downward Spirals'. *Administrative Science Quarterly*, 33: 1–23.

Harrison, J. (1987). 'The Strategic Use of Corporate Board Committees'. *California Management Review*, 30/1: 109–25.

Herman, E. (1981). *Corporate Control, Corporate Power.* New York: Cambridge University Press.

Hoskisson, R., Johnson, R., and Moesel, D. (1994). 'Corporate Divestiture Intensity in Restructuring Firms: Effects of Governance, Strategy, and Performance'. *Academy of Management Journal*, 37: 1207–51.

Janis, I. L. (1982). *Groupthink: Psychological Studies of Policy Decisions and Fiascoes* (2nd edn). Boston: Houghton Mifflin.

Jensen, M. (1993). 'The Modern Industrial Revolution, Exit, and the Failure of Internal Control Systems'. *Journal of Finance*, 48: 831–73.

Johnson, J. L., Daily, C., and Ellstrand, A. (1996). 'Boards of Directors: A Review and Research Agenda'. *Journal of Management*, 22: 409–38.

Kimberly, J. R. (ed.) (1980). *The Organizational Life Cycle: Issues in the Creation, Transformation, and Decline of Organizations.* San Francisco: Jossey-Bass.

Lainema, M. (1997). *Hallitus yrityksen menestystekijänä* (A Board as a Success Factor in a Firm). S. A. M. I Ernst & Young Year Book 1998. Helsinki: Libris Oy.

Levinthal, D. A. and March, J. G. (1993). 'The Myopia of Learning'. *Strategic Management Journal*, 14 (Winter special issue): 95–112.

Levitt, B. and March, J. G. (1988). 'Organizational Learning'. *Annual Review of Sociology*, 14: 319–40.

Lorange, P. and Nelson, R. (1987). 'How to Recognize—and Avoid—Organizational Decline'. *Sloan Management Review*, 28/3: 41–8.

Lorsch, J. (1995). 'Empowering the Board'. *Harvard Business Review*, 73/1: 107–17.

——and MacIver, E. (1989). *Pawns and Potentates.* Boston: Harvard Business School Press.

March, J. G. (1991). 'Exploration and Exploitation in Organizational Learning'. *Organization Science*, 2: 71–87.

——(1995). 'The Future, Disposable Organizations, and the Rigidities of Imagination'. *Organization*, 2/3–4: 427–40.

McNulty, T. and Pettigrew, A. (1999). 'Strategists on the Board'. *Organization Studies*, 20: 47–74.

Miller, D. and Friesen, P. (1980). 'Momentum and Revolution in Organizational Adaption'. *Academy of Management Journal*, 23: 591–614.

—— ——(1983). 'Successful and Unsuccessful Phases of the Corporate Life Cycle'. *Organization Studies*, 4: 339–56.

Mizruchi, M. (1983). 'Who Controls Whom? An Examination of the Relation between Management and Boards of Directors in Large American Corporations'. *Academy of Management Review*, 8: 426–35.

Monks, R. (1999). 'What Will Be the Impact of Active Shareholders? A Practical Recipe for Constructive Change'. *Long Range Planning*, 32/1: 20–7.

Nonaka, I. and Takeuchi, H. (1995). *The Knowledge-creating Company: How Japanese Companies Create the Dynamics of Innovation.* New York: Oxford University Press.

Pearce, J., II and Zahra, S. (1991). 'The Relative Power of CEOs and Boards of Directors: Associations with Corporate Performance'. *Strategic Management Journal*, 12: 135–53.

Pettigrew, A. M. (1985). *The Awakening Giant: Continuity and Change in Imperial Chemical Industries.* Oxford: Blackwell.

Pfeffer, J. and Salancik, G. (1977). *The External Control of Organizations: A Resource Dependency Perspective.* New York: Harper & Row.

Rothman, J. (1997). *Resolving Identity-based Conflict in Nations, Organizations, and Communities.* San Francisco: Jossey-Bass.

Schön, D. A. (1971). *Beyond the Stable State.* London: W. W. Norton.

Senge, P. M. (1996). 'The Leader's New Work: Building Learning Organizations', in K. Starkey (ed.), *How Organizations Learn*. London: International Thomson Business Press, 288–315.

Shleifer, A. and Vishny, R. (1997). 'A Survey of Corporate Governance'. *Journal of Finance*, 52: 737–83.

Starbuck, W. H., Greve, A., and Hedberg, B. L. T. (1978). 'Responding to Crises', in C. F. Smart and W. T. Stanbury (eds.), *Studies on Crisis Management*. Montreal: Institute for Research on Public Policy, 117–37.

Stopford, J. M. and Baden-Fuller, C. W. F. (1990). 'Corporate Rejuvenation'. *Journal of Management Studies*, 27: 399–415.

Tainio, R. (1999). *Ulkomaalaisomistuksen vaikutus suomalaisten yritysten johtamiseen ja rakenteeseen* (Impact of Foreign Stock Ownership on Finnish Management and Corporations). Academia Scientiarum Fennica. Year Book 1998. Vammala: Vammalan kirjapaino.

—— and Valpola, A. (eds.) (1996). *Johtajana muutoksissa* (A Manager under Conditions of Change). Porvoo: Werner Söderström OY.

Tushman, M. L., Newman, W., and Romanelli, E. (1986). 'Convergence and Upheaval: Managing the Unsteady Pace of Organizational Evolution'. *California Management Review*, 29/1: 29–44.

Useem, M. (1996). *Investor Capitalism: How Money Managers Are Changing the Face of Corporate America*. New York: Basic Books.

Veranen, J. (1996). *Tuottoa vaativat omistajat* (Yield Demanding Owners). Porvoo: Werner Söderström OY.

Walsh, J. P. and Steward, J. (1990). 'On the Efficiency of Internal and External Corporate Control Mechanisms'. *Academy of Management Review*, 15: 421–58.

Weitzel, W. and Jonsson, E. (1989). 'Decline in Organizations: A Literature Integration and Extension'. *Administrative Science Quarterly*, 34: 91–109.

—— (1991). 'Reversing the Downward Spiral: Lessons from W. T. Grant and Sears Roebuck'. *Academy of Management Executive*, 5/3: 7–20.

Westphal, J. D. (1998). 'Board Games: How CEOs Adapt to Increases in Structural Board Independence from Management'. *Administrative Science Quarterly*, 43: 511–37.

—— (1999). 'Collaboration in the Boardroom: Behavioral and Performance Consequences of CEO–Board Social Ties'. *Academy of Management Journal*, 42: 7–24.

Whetten, D. (1980). 'Sources, Responses, and the Effects of Organizational Decline', in J. Kimberly (ed.), *The Organizational Life Cycle: Issues in the Creation, Transformation, and Decline of Organizations*. San Francisco: Jossey-Bass, 342–74.

Whyte, G. (1989). 'Groupthink Reconsidered'. *Academy of Management Review*, 14: 40–56.

Zahra, S. and Pearce, J., II (1989). 'Boards of Directors and Corporate Financial Performance: A Review and Integrative Model'. *Journal of Management*, 15: 291–334.

20   Labor Unions as Learning Organizations and Learning Facilitators

Andreas Drinkuth, Claudius H. Riegler, and Rolf Wolff

Why Labor Unions and Organizational Learning?

Labor unions are democratic organizations that were created to represent workers' demands for fair wages, an adequate working environment, and a social safety net. In some countries the participation of labor unions in business decisions has been an important issue. These objectives are still relevant in Europe, but with the industrialized world on the threshold of the new Internet economy, the way of organizing workers' interests has to be adapted to the evolving economic and sociopolitical structure. As a counterforce to capital, unions traditionally thrived on the differences between labor and capital, but in a world where capital is the mind of the knowledge-worker, such historical class differences are eliminated.

Unions organize their actions in democratic processes, whereas business organizations organize themselves in rather nondemocratic ways. This mismatch has considerably influenced the repertoire with which unions may or may not represent their members' interests. The basic repertoire is reactive, so unions have had restricted influence on companies' strategic business decisions.

At first glance the concept of labor unions as agents of organizational learning might therefore be considered an oxymoron. Organized labor is generally not regarded as having the necessary qualities or even the potential for becoming a constructive and effective partner

in organizational learning. The common wisdom seems to be that organized labor has tended to resist and impede changes in organizations. This view is reflected in many publications on unions in the United States (for useful reviews, see Pasmore 1988, 1994) and other parts of the world (e.g. Brilman 1995; Hertog and Huizenga 1998; Schneider 1996). Given this generally negative perception of the stance that unions take on change, it is probably unsurprising that scholars of organizational learning have not focused on the role organized labor plays in such processes. The purpose of this chapter is to start closing this gap in the literature and thereby not only help improve the understanding of the conditions under which organized labor can act as an agent of organizational learning but also contribute to substantiated theory-building in this field of research.

A look at recent developments and experiments involving organized labor reveals that the purely negative view of unions as obstacles to change needs to be overhauled. Significant changes are taking place in the self-concept and behavior of unions and works councils in different countries. These changes suggest that organized labor can become an important force for organizational learning at the local, regional, and national levels of societies. The possibility to act as boundary-crossing organizations may make organized labor a unique agent of organizational learning. Whereas other actors (such as individuals, management, and boards) operate primarily, if not exclusively, as agents of organizational learning within the boundaries of the organization to which they belong, unions seek to represent the interests of their members beyond the interests and performance of the single enterprise. Organized labor can influence organizational learning at the microlevel through plant representatives and works councils (Rogers and Streeck 1995). It can also have an impact on organizational learning at the meso- and macrolevels of societies through its industry-wide collective bargaining and its input into policies and programs initiated by governments and by supranational organizations such as the European Union. Studying unions as agents of organizational learning can therefore help expand the understanding of levels of action beyond the currently dominant focus on the single company (Berthoin Antal 1998; Tsang 1997).

From the perspective of theory-building, an exploration of labor unions as agents of organizational learning is relevant for another reason as well. It offers the opportunity to build bridges between bodies of literature that have been quite separate. The literature on organizational learning has focused on top management, whereas the literature on organized labor has focused primarily on strategic action and democratic bargaining. There is growing recognition that organizational learning is dependent on the commitment of all employees involved (Hertog, Hart, and Riegler 1997) and that effective communication processes are therefore needed between different types of actors with different and often conflicting interests (Gustavsen 1992).

To set the context for the possibly growing role of unions as agents of organizational learning, we first outline some of the trends that are triggering changes in the self-concept and strategies of unions. Recognizing that unions operate in a variety of sociopolitical environments and that unions therefore differ in their learning arenas from country to country, we present case studies illustrating new conditions under which unions have been involved more or less effectively as agents of organizational learning. The practical and theoretical implications of these examples are then discussed, and ideas for further exploration are suggested.

Labor Unions as Learning Organizations

Trends and Obstacles

It would be naive to assume that unions are discovering the topic of organizational learning and taking on a new role simply for the intellectual pleasure of change. A number of pressures for change in society are challenging unions to reconsider their self-concept and their strategies. The three most important challenges for unions in western Europe in particular are (a) the restructuring of the welfare state (Trentin 1997); (b) the globalization of national economies (Altvater and Mahnkopf 1997; Fricke 1997; Group of Lisbon 1995; Howells and Wood 1993; Kapstein 1996; Muldur and Petrella 1994); and (c) the formation of a universal language of management and management techniques (Carr, Hard, and Trahant 1996; Ghoshal and Bartlett 1997; Hamel and Prahalad 1994; McHugh, Merli, and Wheeler 1995), a development that is tending to abolish the legitimacy of historically developed national systems of industrial relations (Nutzinger 1999: 7).

These trends have significant consequences for the organization of labor and for the labor market. The profound changes in the welfare state are revitalizing the historic roles and importance of unions as bargaining organizations for fair wages and labor contracts. Because of globalization processes, companies in western Europe are having to undergo structural changes in order to deal with differences in cost structures in different locations. These changes are leading to unemployment and shifts from blue- and white-collar industries to the growth of knowledge-intensive work. Knowledge-intensive industries are different from the institutionalized structures that created industries until the 1960s and 1970s (Schreyögg and Conrad 1996; Stewart 1997). The questioning of traditional concepts of job security and the rapidly changing quests for new qualifications and competencies (Andréasen, Coriat, and Hertog 1995; Behr and Hirsch-Kreinsen 1998; Bender and Luig 1995; Drexel 1994; Frei 1993; Matthies, Mückenberger, Offe, Peter, and Raasch 1994; Mückenberger, Schmidt, and Zoll 1996; Commissariat au plan 1995; Sitter, Hertog, and Dankbaar 1997) have an impact on how unions can represent the interests of their members at both a local and a societal level.

These changes require union representatives themselves to develop new competencies that go beyond their traditional repertoires. Product and process innovations (Lippert, Jürgens, and Drüke 1996) are constantly driving all organizations, public and private. As Sperling (1994: 8) pointed out, these developments, which are a result of the combined efforts of organizational and structural changes and changed options of the actors involved, are leading to new constellations of participation in economic, technological, and sociopolitical structural change. We are probably witnessing a transition from centralized bureaucratic organizational forms to decentralized, flatter, self-managing units. Such organizational structures appear to be desirable not only because they function more efficiently than those they replace but also because they could contribute to meeting the demands of employees for more participation. Empowerment covers some of these aspects.

Although high levels of unionization remain in some countries, such as Sweden (see Kjellberg 1997: 18), the confluence of these various trends has decreased the degree of unionization in many industrialized countries. From the perspective of the individual employee, labor unions and firms are competing for his or her engagement and commitment. The concurrent trends toward pluralization and individualization in societies have far-reaching consequences for the ability of unions to aggregate the interests of their members. The life situations and plans of employees have become more heterogeneous as the differentiation between the models of employment and professional activity has increased (Andersson

and Sylwan 1998; Ghoshal and Bartlett 1997; Gustavsen 1992; Hirschhorn 1997; Matthies et al. 1994; Willke 1996).

In addition to losing members, unions are further weakened by shifts in the locus of policy-making. For example, there is a trend toward moving the regulation of working conditions from the sectorial level down to the company level. Industrial relations are increasingly being shaped by individual companies rather than by entire industries, a development one might call a 'Japanization' of industrial relations (Brulin and Victorin 1992; Kjellberg 1998; Sasajima 1995).

Confronted with such deep and constant structural changes, unions are discovering that learning is not only relevant but even necessary for their credibility and survival. One type of learning can be seen in restructuring, specifically in abolishment of the separate unionization of blue-collar and white-collar employees (see Mahon 1994). The quest for trustful cooperation between unions and works councils as a basis for active and innovative works is another response that has been observed (Rogers and Streeck 1995). Yet another form of learning is the questioning of traditional tactics in labor relations and the search for new strategies. For example, wage strikes are coming to be seen as an inadequate way to achieve union objectives, for the symbolic function of wages has been weakened by widespread high unemployment in Europe since 1990. Strikes play a role primarily in questions of principle, such as the introduction of the thirty-five-hour work week in Germany (Coriat 1990: 254).

Traditional union structure is hierarchical, and its institutional mechanism has been the subject of extensive research. The basic structure, though, has been maintained, and the democratic architecture of unions as organizations shape their specific logic and process of legitimization. Although unions tend to describe themselves as democratic organizations, they have a propensity for centralized decision-making and ideological rigidity. However, the centralized structure of unions was disrupted in the 1990s because ever more frequently company-related issues at union headquarters tended to overrule issues that are ideologically defined. The decoupling of business companies from their national domestic markets has induced changes that the traditional union structure cannot cope with (Beckérus and Edström 1995; Elvander and Seim Elvander 1995). New ways of coordinating local initiatives and processes at headquarters are called for.

These processes for generating and modifying policy can be characterized as mutual adjustments between the local union and the union headquarters. Headquarters define ideologies and themes. These themes are transformed into rules and codes, which create frameworks for action at the company level. The actions are then locally developed into practices, which slowly change the character of the ideologies and themes that are legitimized throughout the union organization. Ultimately, the new practices are incorporated into new ideologies.

Institutional Context: Culture and Industrial Relations

In Europe, labor unions have been deeply involved in regional and national programs aimed at supporting various areas of development (see Alasoini, Kyllönen, and Kasvio 1997; Gustavsen *et al.* 1996; Oehlke 1998; Riegler 1998). A European strength in strategies for reforming work life and sharing responsibility for the productivity and economic prosperity of firms has been laid down in programs covering organization, efficiency, leadership, and code-termination. In Germany, unions that have actively pursued these efforts are in so-called future congresses, which are arenas for broad labor-union debate about renewal and innovation (Bahnmüller 1998; Martin 1997). In Italy, the works councils in FIAT and similar enterprises have strategies for developing comanagement (Cattero 1998). Unions also participate in vitalizing regional districts (Brusco and Solinas 1997; Brutti 1992; Brutti and Calistri 1990; Cossentino, Pyke, and Sengenberger

1996; Putnam 1993: 106) and conducting in work-life research programs and institutes such as the Institute for Labor created by the regional government of Emilia-Romagna in Bologna in 1998. In France, unions have been engaged in innovative process of product development in the automotive industry and have taken an active role in public-sector modernization (Bartoli 1997: 279). In Sweden, union commitment to public-sector reforms, as in the municipality of Stockholm (see Wallenberg 1996), has been crucial for joint learning by the main actors. The implementation of the labor unions' concept of 'good work' (Berggren and Brulin 1997; Svenska 1998) is another example of union initiative for renewal and innovation. In Japan, union commitment to the knowledge-intensive processes in companies is traditionally high, a fact that has often led to attempts to imitate Japanese practice (Berggren, Björkman, and Hollander 1991; Nonaka and Tacheuchi 1995; Yutaka 1998).

So far, we have treated labor unions as a rather uniform category of more or less powerful agents in the organization. Union members, however, take on different roles in the everyday work process. For example, individual members of a union can be activists or, like members of the works councils, can be representatives with an official status. In all these roles there are factors facilitating or impeding the ability of individuals to contribute to organizational learning (see Friedman, Ch. 17 in this volume). Furthermore, there are national differences based on specific traditions and institutional forms of industrial relations (for an overview of the state of the characteristics of industrial relations at workplaces in the United States, Japan, the United Kingdom, France, and Italy, see Ferner and Hyman 1998 and Rogers and Streeck 1995; for Japan, see Yutaka 1998). As this chapter's two case studies show, these national differences can be significant for the role that unions can play in organizational learning processes. In both institutional settings that are described—Sweden and Germany—unions are comparatively strong and well entrenched at the sectorial and plant levels.

The System of Industrial Relations and Works Councils in Germany

The dual system of industrial relations in Germany consists of two institutions: The right to engage in free collective bargaining (a process in which employer federations and national unions are actors) and labor–management relations at the workplace (which regulate the activities of works councils and management at the company level). The works council is a legal body, and its members are elected by the employees of a company. Approximately 85 per cent of all members of the works councils in the metal-working sector are also members of the Metalworkers' Union. Works councils are usually regarded by employees as their labor union's representation in the company (Jacobi, Keller, and Müller-Jentsch 1998; Müller-Jentsch 1995, 1999). Admittedly, the capacity of the works councils and certain committees to have a say in corporate decision-making is limited under the Workplace Labor–Management Relations Act of 1971. The committees do, however, have extensive rights of information. They have to be consulted in due time on any important structural changes. Their recommendations should be taken into consideration whenever possible. Such industrial relations afford opportunities for development activities and organizational learning in work organization and new technologies (Müller-Jentsch, Sperling, and Weyrather 1997). The works councils have been guarantees for a culture of consensual codetermination that explicitly emphasizes organizational learning. According to Müller-Jentsch (1999), employer representatives and unions in Germany are both conscious of a 'general lack of innovation' (p. 295; our translation), the reason that learning for innovation in, say, regional policies has high priority in regions such as the Ruhr District, Bremen, and eastern Germany (Gerlach 1999).

The System of Industrial Relations in Sweden

Collective bargaining in Sweden is characterized by decentralization and 'increased activities of the state in coordinating national agreements and in making them compatible with low inflation and other economic policy goals' (Kjellberg 1998: 92). Several examples from the metal-working industry show that the implementation of the labor unions' concept of 'good work' has led to an increased use of teams 'combined with pay systems that might contribute to learning' (Kjellberg 1998: 112). Sweden has 'no workplace-based arrangements for the representation of employees independent of trade unions' (Brulin 1995: 189). The model of representation is based on strong labor unions at both the local level and at headquarters. The Codetermination Act of 1976 in Sweden requires management to negotiate any major restructuring plans with the unions in the company, and it allows unions to engage outside consultants for the purpose at the company's expense. These external experts also investigate possible alternatives to management's plans. The final decision on a restructuring plan cannot be taken before the external experts have concluded their investigation and their proposal has been considered in union–management negotiations.

Keenly aware of the changes being induced by globalization and the new economy, labor unions in both Germany and Sweden are seeking to respond to them. But the unions are facing a fundamental issue. Whereas they have traditionally been a countervailing power to capital, there is increasing recognition at the company level in both countries that the works councils (in Germany) and the local union 'clubs' (in Sweden) must have a say in issues related to developing businesses. The new challenges require learning in different ways and at different levels: within union headquarters, within the local unions, and in relation to stakeholders of industrial development (at both levels). One learning strategy involves building on historically successful strategies and redefining the nature of countervailing power. Another learning strategy, in which systems boundaries are transcended, is the adoption of new roles for which new competencies have to be acquired. In the case of the IG Metall labor union, for example, local members of works councils must learn new skills because they do not usually have the ones needed in order to participate in business decisions. Seen as a counterpart to single-loop and double-loop learning as conceived of by Argyris and Schön (1978), it constitutes a third type of organizational learning. Serving as a countervailing power and participating in decisions with management may be contradictory functions, but both are essential for the survival of unions, and perhaps even for businesses.

From reactive gatekeeping to comanagement: A Swedish longitudinal case study

Inköpscentralernas AB

Phase I

In 1990 the management team of Sweden's largest retail grocery chain, Inköpscentralernas AB (ICA), decided to restructure its logistics, distribution chain, and network. The analysis and implementation plan was presented to the two unions (blue- and white-collar) in the group. Of eighteen distribution centers, nine were to be closed, and approximately 500 people were to lose their jobs. The plan was a milestone in the organization's transition from a warehouse-dominated distribution structure to logistics based on information technology (IT) and just-in-time deliveries.

Work groups organized in the company by the unions and supported by outside consultants developed a modified plan and presented it to the management. A solution was negotiated whereby the number of warehouses and distribution centers to be closed was reduced from nine to seven. The unions and management then negotiated a severance package for the employees who were to leave the organization.

For the local unions, this process was a turning point after a postwar period of continuous growth, prosperity, and the security of life-long

employment in the company. For the management team, too, this conflict presented a new situation. It was the largest restructuring it had ever conducted, and the whole process of not just presenting a plan for decision but also having to defend and negotiate its details and ramifications openly contradicted a traditional culture of strictly defined authority. Recognizing the unprecedented nature of the circumstances for both sides, the local unions and management met to discuss the implications for their relationship. The unions' feeling of exclusion from important considerations affecting the company's future coincided with management's wish to avoid such conflicts in the future, a combination that led to an agreement to find new ways of dealing with structural changes in the company.

Phase II

From 1992 through 1993 a new structural decision to merge the retail and wholesale arms of the company was proposed by top management. Despite the earlier agreement on a new way of negotiating structural changes, almost the same approach was taken as in 1990. But the CEO comforted the organization with the message that radical changes of the kind experienced in the previous three years were not probable in the near future.

Phase III

In 1994 the CEO nevertheless announced that three distribution centers were to be closed, an intention affecting a total of 590 people. This time, the investigation, implementation, and handling of the employee-related problems was entrusted to a project group consisting of representatives from management, the local unions, and union headquarters, as well as outside consultants. After a two-year process, the number of employees to lose their jobs had been reduced from the original projection of 590 to 97.

After extensively reflecting on the experiences of this period, both the management and the unions agreed in 1995 on a new model for dealing with change. Four 'future teams' were created to explore strategic changes continually. In every team the blue- and white-collar unions had at least one representative each. In addition, the management agreed on an elaborate education plan including subjects such as management theory, management accounting, and logistics in order to equip union representatives to participate effectively in negotiations with management.

Phase IV

In September 1997, ICA announced yet another major restructuring decision involving four distribution centers. This decision affected some 800 employees. The local unions again called for external expert help. In this phase, too, little could be done to reverse the board's strategic plan; only minor changes in the affected employees' social security package were achieved. The principal decision was implemented as soon as the consultants had left the company.

Phase V

In August 1998 it was announced that ICA would merge its business-to-business part with the Norwegian Hakon Group in order to improve effectivity in distribution. The question of union involvement reappeared on the agenda. The codetermination agreement allowed for external consultants, but, again, nothing could really be changed in the structural proposal presented by the board of directors.

Analysis of Organizational Learning: ICA

What outcome did the eight-year restructuring of ICA's logistics, distribution chain, and network have in terms of organizational learning? In principle, the likely learning situations for unions and management, respectively, were those shown in Table 20.1.

In single-loop learning in each step of the changes in the company, the unions might be expected to try to preserve their status quo, whereas management might be expected to force through the intended changes as quickly and smoothly as possible. Deadlocks and conflicts arise, and formal rules of negotiation are followed. Usually the result is a win–lose situation, with management winning and the unions and the members losing.

In double-loop learning both partners abandon some of their traditional positions. A give-and-take situation develops, and both partners start to gain some understanding of their constraints. The union representatives accept that structural changes are necessary for the business to survive; the management understands the needs of the unions to secure employment and demonstrate gains in a bargaining process.

Lastly, a third situation is possible, a new ball game in which unions and management develop a partnership on strategic issues. Depending on the consequences, roles have to be divided between strategists and negotiators. Still, a strategy process open to union participation would have different qualities than a

Table 20.1. Union and management learning in ICA

Learning Agent	Single-loop learning	Double-loop learning	'New ball game'
Unions	Preservation of employment levels	Active involvement in structural change discussion	Proactive partnering with management
Management	Implementation of planned change	Opening up of process for participation	Cooperation with unions as equal partners in business strategy development

closed process, in which management itself prepares, decides, and reduces the participatory aspect to informing other agents of a decision that has already been made.

In the ICA case, both unions and management seemed at each step to want to learn from the experience and tried to develop new structures and processes to ensure greater union involvement in restructuring plans. In effect, however, they repeated the same process whereby management presented its decision to the unions and the unions pressed for a revised plan (single-loop learning). What happened within ICA examplifies the inertia of systems and the iteration of old patterns more than it demonstrates successful organizational learning. Despite apparently good intentions to learn and change, the participants failed to exploit the opportunities that each program of structural change offered for the emergence of new processes and strategies. ICA is thus an example of single- and double-loop learning, but not of the follow-up that could have led to the creation of a new culture for strategically developing the business. The negotiations followed the traditional legal forms, and the new future groups remained mainly symbolic in character. The established pattern—structural decision followed by renegotiation, external consultants, modification of details, and implementation of the original plan—was preserved and perpetuated.

Cross-boundary learning—A German Case

IG Metall

The Krupp-Rheinhausen Case

In December 1987 tens of thousands of steelworkers, their families, and others blocked busy highways and the bridge over the Rhein River in Duisburg. An industrial dispute over the continuation of the Krupp steel company's Rheinhausen foundry in Duisburg had escalated. It lasted 160 days. The clash received nationwide attention.

What had happened? Krupp's CEO had announced plans to close the highly modern foundry in order to undertake 'structural straightening-out' within the group. Such closures were nothing new. Since the 1960s, several hundred thousand jobs had been phased out of western Germany's steel industry in a socially acceptable manner despite fierce opposition from the steelworkers and their labor union, IG Metall. But this time more than 6,000 employees were to lose their jobs in one fell swoop.

The initial demand made by the steelworkers and IG Metall was to keep all the steelworks going and preserve as many jobs as possible. With industrial action and subsequent activities, they wanted to ensure that at least the steelworks in Duisburg-Rheinhausen stayed open. During the dispute, which lasted for weeks, it became clear that Krupp would insist on closing these steelworks, and with the regional government of North-Rhine–Westphalia steering the course, the objectives of the steelworkers and IG Metall were modified. The new demand was for Krupp to create new jobs by locating new industries to that area. An agreement to create 1,500 new jobs in this way and to include generous social benefits finally settled the dispute. The whole discussion about the steelworks in Duisburg-Rheinhausen severely eroded a paradigm that IG Metall had embraced for more than a decade. The demand to preserve all steelworks was a call for support from steelworkers in other areas. The aim was to prevent competition between companies from turning into competition between workers. IG Metall and its works councils were therefore prepared to make concessions on personnel reduction as long it was socially tolerable.

By demanding the creation of new jobs through location of new industries to the Duisburg area, IG Metall more or less consciously entered the sphere of regional politics. Initially, it remained unclear just what jobs in which branches of industry were to be created. From the remains of the old apprentices' workshop, Krupp and the government of the state of North-Rhine–Westphalia established a company-nonaffiliated training center, which in

1997—ten years later—had a staff of almost 1,000 employees, most of whom were involved in further training. Paradoxically, there were initially no industrial sites available for the location of new industries. Persuaded by IG Metall's reasoning and by public pressure, the government of North-Rhine–Westphalia has released more and more and more unused sites for development. Within ten years after the city of Duisburg founded a company for the promotion of trade, the organization has managed to introduce approximately 7,500 new jobs.

At the same time however, 22,500 jobs in the steel and metal-working industry have been lost, and it has gradually become apparent that the policy of locating new industries to an area can have only limited success if the traditional range of jobs decreases simultaneously. The choice was difficult for employees and unions. They had to reorient themselves to changed realities in markets and business. And the Krupp crisis in Rheinhausen was not to be the last, either.

The Ruhrort Shipyard Case

In summer 1993 workers and others active within IG Metall occupied 'their' shipyard. Bankruptcy was threatening, 108 jobs were to be cut, and wages and salaries were to be reduced by 15 per cent. Just six months earlier, sixty jobs had been eliminated after an initial agreement on a severance package because the shipyard had decided to stop all business related to the building of new ships for inland waterways. Because of high unemployment in Duisburg (more than 15 per cent) and because the average age of the shipyard's workforce was almost 50, few of the workers were likely to find work with any other company.

This conflict of the local branch of IG Metall and the workers led to a new strategy. The works council chairman of the shipyard, representatives of IG Metall, and two former senior members of staff formed a Workers' Initiative with the aim of refounding the company in order to continue work at the shipyard. Public pressure, political support, and, above all, the determination of the workers and IG Metall made the plan succeed in early 1994.

The Workers' Initiative developed a concept for a service called the Center for Inland Waterways Shipping. A qualifying period for the employees who could not immediately be given work was introduced. By 1995 it was possible to integrate another shipyard into the service concept. After a period of two years, a comprehensive marketing and controlling concept and corresponding corporate reorganization was accomplished with support from IG Metall. The shipyard survived. Only four of the 108 employees at the time of bankruptcy still had no jobs two and one-half years later. The rest had found work again, 60 per cent of them are with the newly founded shipyard. At the end of 1997, the shipyard employed 120 people, including those with limited contracts.

Subsequently, IG Metall has supervised twelve similar reorganization projects, of which nine have been successful. It has established cooperation between companies in their regions. (Duisburg, being situated on the Rhine, has the largest inland waterway shipping harbor in Europe.) The union has participated in the development of traffic and logistic concepts for the city of Duisburg. Bringing together the employment agency, the chamber of commerce, the city of Duisburg and the local university, the union has encouraged and initiated a joint project in which company projects and further potential for employment are being explored, in order to prevent future unemployment. In short, IG Metall has begun to redefine its role as a representative of interests.

Cross-boundary Learning within IG Metall

Throughout these processes, mainly in cooperation with a host of external partners such as those involved in the project for developing company resources, IG Metall has learned that representatives of interests must have their own vision. The union understands that its traditional repertoire of responses to repetitive crisis management has to be broadened to include a policy of fostering a regional structure policy, that absorbs traditional strengths and expands them. For this purpose, IG Metall in Duisburg carried out a survey on the future sustainability of fifty-five companies located in its operating area. It wanted to gain an understanding about which companies have the chance of surviving the next ten to twenty years given their current profile of products and services, management, qualification potential, R&D, and marketing and corporate structures such as work organization and supply of capital. The results were disturbing. Only five of the companies had sufficient innovative potential to ensure long-term survival. IG Metall responded with a two-track strategy. While Thyssen Stahl AG and Thyssen Edelstahl AG were being merged, a task force for the creation and security of new jobs was formed. It created three innovative subgroups. The model for regional economic cycles, which IG Metall had been actively promoting since 1990, was adopted. This model did provide orientation for further innovative development of the region and tapped the historical assets of the region.

Analysis of Organizational Learning: IG Metall

The types of organizational learning that occurred in the IG Metall cases are summarized in Table 20.2. Some of the major issues that these cases raise are the relationship between union headquarters and local branches of the union and the relationship between unions and management in the respective companies. The other issue raised, related to the roles of

unions, is the question of competence. What competencies are needed in order to meet with the new challenges triggered by new economic structures? Lastly, the Duisburg case shows that the traditional view of unions—that local issues are related to individual companies—is broadening into a regional and even a national perspective.

Despite many differences, one common feature of the Swedish and German cases described in this chapter is that recent changes in firm structure, management strategy, and the market have brought about a rethinking of union structures and strategies. Above all, the relationship between national union headquarters and plant-level representation has changed in character. The case of ICA illustrates a shift in the role and potential influence of local unions. Until recently, Swedish unions have focused on traditional issues such as wages, occupational safety, and other issues related to the workplace. Since the early 1990s, structural changes triggered by both globalization and IT-induced developments have affected entire industries. The unions have therefore had to search for a role in these processes that enables them to foresee the changes that will impinge on them and their members. Two key factors in this transition are competence and responsibility. Are local unions able to acquire the competence they need in order then to take on responsibilities for business development?

A change from a gatekeeper role to active involvement in business-related processes requires an understanding of the rhetoric of management and the underlying conceptions. Moreover, IT issues, especially in the retail business, accelerate speed and increase complexity, making it even more complicated to

Table 20.2. From single-loop learning to boundary-transcending

Single-loop	Double-loop	Boundary-transcending
Negotiation on existing level of employment (preserve)	Assumption of active responsibility for replacing existing industries	Creation of new institutions for shaping of new futures

understand underlying rationales and patterns of change. In the ICA case the union's local branch and union headquarters did not succeed at any point in acquiring the competencies necessary for reversing the proposed structural changes. In addition, the unions entered the decision-making process so late that they could no longer participate in defining the problems.

Active involvement in business-related decision-making opens important opportunities for the unions. But by participating in these processes, where solutions emerge successively, unions suddenly also discover that they are part of a process that continuously changes the basic structure of their operations and has profound impacts on their members. Unions did not take on a proactive role in ICA, especially when structural changes occurred with negative effects on employment. When it came to the point of agreements on future structures, which the union representatives had been discussing and developing together with the management in the future teams, the unions withdrew, leaving management without a counterpart. In other words, involvement required shared responsibility for the decisions at hand. Communication gaps, and probably gaps in competencies, could not be bridged.

In the Duisburg case, the local branch of IG Metall modified its own structures and its political self-perception. Its new slogan—'Not more, but different, ways of working'—became a reflection of the new challenges to act. IG Metall realized that 'job security' had to be created primarily through proactive development strategies. In order to act on this new philosophy, the union reorganized its own administrative procedures. Within ten years it developed a reputation as a moderator and facilitator of changes within the companies. Whereas this union used to see itself ideologically mostly as an opponent of capital and whereas it used to declare that capital owners alone were responsible for creating jobs, it has assumed wide responsibility for designing the future in its region. It has understood that strategic alternatives require convincing programs of change. The union has succeeded in integrating the effects of union headquarters and the local branch, for representatives from both joined forces in an effort to further regional business development.

Unions as Facilitators of Learning

Transcending Institutional Boundaries

Our case studies indicate two major obstacles that unions meet when organizational learning is concerned: an ideology of conflict, which creates a unified institution intent on perpetuating its legitimacy through strategies of opposition, and a perspective according to which power is based on control over capital. In short, unions have a traditionally reactive action repertoire of strategies for action. This repertoire has limited the ways in which unions have been able to adapt to and influence economic development at the national, regional, and company levels.

One of the outcomes of the ideology of conflict has been the centralized decision-making by which union authorities have acquired the right to define policies that restrict options for local action. The relation between union headquarters and local union branches is about to change because company decisions are now taken with global rather than just national considerations in mind. The national structure of unions simply cannot adapt to this change. Unions therefore have to find new ways in which they can influence business development within a company network, a quest that is bound to invert traditional union hierarchy, in which union headquarters is at the top.

Unions have, by definition, emerged as institutions that handle conflicts (see also Rothman and Friedman, Ch. 26 in this volume). Their legitimacy has been grounded in their relative success at representing members' interests. As these interests shift, the processes by which unions gain legitimacy among their members and in society at large are changing. Many issues now emerge within a specific company and, therefore, witness a specific cultural context. They are interpreted at the local level within an industry and are based on professional judgments. New organizational forms, structure, and rules are institutionalized, they penetrate organizational life and require the union's interpretation and translation into action. Slowly, unions are changing their functional orientation from specific issues to processes of understanding and sense-making (Weick 1995). It may be that unions are developing loosely coupled forms of organization in order to adapt a formerly standardized way of responding to changes in society. Unions that have been 'infused with values' as 'ends in themselves' (Selznick 1957: 17) have embarked on a journey of discovering new values, new organizational structures, and hence new theories of action. This view of unions as organizations of discovery also calls for a new way of describing unions as institutions, for a description reflecting acceptance of the notion that the knowledge of everyday life is no longer taken for granted and that 'objective facticities' (Berger and Luckmann 1966/67: 44) are shaped through continually changing subjective meanings. Seen in this manner, unions appear to be transcending their own institutions and boundaries and to be reshaping themselves in the process of shaping the new economy. Perhaps these processes are transitional, but who knows; 'only what moves is visible' (Czarniawska and Sevón 1996: 1). Unions follow the paradoxes of organizational life. They will undergo change and seek stability at the same time. Their challenge, though, is to construct meaning in a highly deconstructed economic reality.

Translating Knowledge

In times of transition, old practices are destroyed and new ones are constructed, a process implying a deconstruction of the old order (see also Merkens, Geppert, and Antal, Ch. 10 in this volume). The national state has lost some of its unifying power; other institutions, too, are losing theirs. Corporations and managerial rhetoric set the agenda for how welfare is to be produced. Shareholder value creation is offered as the most successful way of creating welfare for society (Copeland 1994: 3). Management concepts are being produced and communicated ever more rapidly, and firms are imitating business strategies, policies, organizational structures, technologies, and products. This production and communication has been described as 'institutionalisation of fashions' (Røvik 1996: 141), and the process of imitation has been described as 'something that is created and transformed by chains of translators' (Czarniawska and Sevón 1996: 51).

We believe that unions should intensify their active engagement in the process of 'translating'. Management ideas travel, and the professionalization of management tends to create a particular worldview of appropriate organizational solutions. To understand these dynamics—and to transform a reactive action repertoire into a proactive one—unions have to learn at three levels: (a) the linguistic understanding of these managerial constructs, (b) the processes in which these concepts are translated into practices, and (c) the mechanism by which constructs are created, shipped around the world, and given legitimacy in specific contexts. If unions do engage and learn in these ways the concept of emancipation as it has been adapted through the labor movement will be transformed into a continuous reflection of values, norms, and traditions. Emancipation will no longer be formulated in terms of organizational ideology or a set of institutionalized beliefs. Instead, unions as learning organizations will have to offer platforms for everyday reflection on life styles and opportunities. These processes are local in practice, but they are shaping a world of global competition.

In a society where traditions are reconstructed in everyday life, personal and social responsibility depends on active trust (Giddens 1994). Active trust has to be won in day-to-day action and discourse, not being offered by existing traditions and positions. In the context of unions, active trust implies commitment to others and to emerging values. The rhetoric of economics and management thought is a focus of reflection rather than a framework for action. Dialogue on these issues should afford platforms for action. Learning in these terms is an outcome of continuous reconstruction of trust and personal and social responsibility; it is social reflexivity (see also Gherardi and Nicolini, Ch. 2 in this volume).

National and union policy are only two of many arenas in which references to individuals' lives are shaped. 'Generative politics is a politics which seeks to allow individuals and groups to make things happen, rather than have things happen to them, in the context of overall social concerns and goals' (Giddens 1994: 15). Generative politics is not politics between state and market. Rather, it provides conditions and frameworks for interpreting the life decisions of individuals, groups, and organizations within the social order shaped by the state and global community. Even though individuals might basically keep in touch with it, many other political influences shape everyday life. In this context the use and adaptation of language is a crucial point, for it is connected at a deep level with the sensitization to everyday life as a process of knowledge development. Through language a learning organization becomes 'identical to an organization which can continuously develop and transform its linguistic resources' (Gustavsen 1992: 119).

In the global economy representation of interests as an inherent part of democracy has to be accompanied by the creation of arenas where controversial issues can be handled through dialogue rather than through preestablished formalized institutions. A new welfare system will be created in arenas, locally, and will shape macrochanges. In such a political culture, unions will not act as mere gatekeepers in the distribution of wages and welfare benefits. Constantly striving for legitimacy, unions will act instead as organizers of political arenas and translators of economic rhetoric for the benefit of their members.

References

Alasoini, T., Kyllönen, M., and Kasvio, A. (eds.) (1997). *Workplace Innovations: A Way of Promoting Competitiveness, Welfare and Employment.* Report No. 3. Helsinki: Ministry of Labour/National Workplace Development Programme.

Altvater, E. and Mahnkopf, B. (1997). *Grenzen der Globalisierung: Ökonomie, Ökologie und Politik in der Weltgesellschaft.* Münster: Westfälisches Dampfboot.

Andersson, Å. E. and Sylwan, P. (1998). *Framtidens arbete och liv* (Work and Life in the Future). Stockholm: Natur och Kultur.

Andréasen, L.-E., Coriat, B., and Hertog, J. F. den (1995). *Europe's Next Step: Organisational Innovation, Competition and Employment.* Ilford: Frank Cass.

Argyris, C. and Schön, D. A. (1978). *Organizational Learning: A Theory of Action Perspective.* Reading, Mass.: Addison-Wesley.

Bahnmüller, R. (1998). *Tarifpolitik und Beteiligung: Innergewerkschaftliche Willensbildung und zwischenverbandliche Kompromissbildung am Beispiel der 'Tarifreform 2000' der IG Metall in Baden-Württemberg.* Münster: Westfälisches Dampfboot.

Bartoli, A. (1997). *Le Management dans les organisations publiques.* Paris: Dunod.

Beckérus, Å. and Edström, A. (1995). *Den europeiska rockaden: Svenska företag väljer ny strategi* (The European Castling: Swedish Companies Choose a New Strategy). Stockholm: Svenska Dagbladet and FA-rådet.

Behr, M. von and Hirsch-Kreinsen, H. (eds.) (1998). *Globale Produktion und Industriearbeit: Arbeitsorganisation und Kooperation in Produktionsnetzwerken.* Frankfurt am Main: Campus.

Bender, C. and Luig, M. (1995). *Neue Produktionskonzepte und industrieller Wandel: Industriesoziologische Analysen innovativer Organisationsmodelle.* Opladen: Westdeutscher Verlag.

Berger, P. L. and Luckmann T. (1967). *Die gesellschaftliche Konstruktion der Wirklichkeit: Eine Theorie der Wissenssoziologie* (M. Plessner, trans.). Frankfurt am Main: Fischer. (Original work published 1966)

Berggren, C., Björkman, T., and Hollander, E. (1991). *Are They Unbeatable? Report from a Field Trip to Study Transplants, the Japanese-owned Auto Plants in North America*. Stockholm: The Royal Institute of Technology.

—— and Brulin, G. (1997). *Goda arbeten—starka regioner: Dags för Metall att gå på två ben!* (Good Work—Strong Regions: Time for the Metalworkers' Union to Walk on Two Legs!). Stockholm: Metall.

Berthoin Antal, A. (1998). 'Die Dynamik der Theoriebildungsprozesse zum Organisationslernen', in H. Albach, M. Dierkes, A. Berthoin Antal, and K. Vaillant (eds.), *Organisationslernen—institutionelle und kulturelle Dimension. WZB Jahrbuch 1998*. Berlin: edition sigma, 31–52.

Brilman, J. (1995). *L'Entreprise réinventée: Organisation par processus, structures plates, équipes en réseaux*. Paris: Les Éditions d'organisation.

Brulin, G. (1995). 'Sweden: Joint Councils under Strong Unionism', in J. Rogers and W. Streeck (eds.), *Works Councils: Consultation, Representation, and Cooperation in Industrial Relations*. Chicago: University of Chicago Press, 189–216.

—— and Victorin, A. (1992). 'Improving the Quality of Working Life: The Swedish Model', in P. Tergeist and L. O'Leary (eds.), *New Directions in Work Organisation: The Industrial Relations Response*. Paris: OECD, 149–67.

Brusco, S. and Solinas, G. (1997). *Competitività e partecipazione: Una proposta di politica del lavoro*. Bologna: Il Mulino.

Brutti, P. (1992). 'Industrial Districts: The Point of View of the Unions', in F. Pyke and W. Sengenberger (eds.), *Industrial Districts and Local Economic Regeneration*. Geneva: International Institute for Labour Studies, 251–4.

—— and Calistri, F. (1990). 'Industrial Districts and the Unions', in F. Pyke, G. Becattini, and W. Sengenberger (eds.), *Industrial Districts and Inter-firm Co-operation in Italy*. Geneva: International Institute for Labour Studies, 134–41.

Carr, D. K., Hard, K. J., and Trahant, W. J. (1996). *Managing the Change Process*. New York: McGraw-Hill.

Cattero, B. (1998). *Lavorare alla Fiat—Arbeiten bei VW: Technologie, Arbeit und soziale Regulierung in der Automobilindustrie*. Münster: Westfälisches Dampfboot.

Commissariat au plan (1995). *Le Travail dans vingt ans* (J. Boissonat, rapporteur). Paris: Éditions Odile Jacob.

Copeland, T. E. (1994). *Valuation: Measuring and Managing the Value of Companies*. New York: Riley.

Coriat, B. (1990). *L'Atelier et le robot: Essai sur le fordisme et la production de masse à l'âge de l'électronique*. Paris: Christian Bourgois.

Cossentino, F., Pyke, F., and Sengenberger, W. (1996). *Local and Regional Response to Global Pressure: The Case of Italy and Its Industrial Districts*. Research Series No. 103. Geneva: International Labour Office.

Czarniawska, B. and Sevón, G. (1996). 'Introduction', in B. Czarniawska and G. Sevón (eds.), *Translating Organizational Change*. Berlin: de Gruyter, 1–12.

Drexel, I. (ed.) (1994). *Jenseits von Individualisierung und Angleichung: Die Entstehung neuer Arbeitnehmergruppen in vier europäischen Ländern*. Frankfurt am Main: Campus.

Elvander, N. and Seim Elvander, A. (1995). *Gränslös samverkan: Fackets svar på företagens internationalisering* (Co-operation without Frontiers: The Answer of the Unions to Business Internationalization). Stockholm: Studieförbundet Näringsliv och Samhälle.

Ferner, A. and Hyman, R. (eds.) (1998). *Changing Industrial Relations in Europe* (2nd edn). Oxford: Blackwell.

Frei, F. (1993). *Work Design for the Competent Organization*. Westport, Conn.: Quorum Books.

Fricke, W. (ed.) (1997). *Jahrbuch Arbeit und Technik: Globalisierung und institutionelle Reform*. Bonn: Dietz.

Gerlach, F. (1999). 'Transformation und Partizipation: Praktische Erfahrungen in Ostdeutschland', in H. G. Nutzinger (ed.), *Perspektiven der Mitbestimmung: Historische Erfahrungen und moderne Entwicklungen vor europäischem und globalem Hintergrund*. Marburg: Metropolis, 249–66.

Ghoshal, S. and Bartlett, C. A. (1997). *The Individualized Corporation: A Fundamentally New Approach to Management*. New York: Harper Collins.

Giddens, A. (1994). *Beyond Left and Right: The Future of Radical Politics.* Stanford, Calif.: Stanford University Press.

Group of Lisbon (1995). *Limits to Competition.* Cambridge, Mass.: MIT Press.

Gustavsen, B. (1992). *Dialogue and Development: Theory of Communication, Action Research and the Restructuring of Working Life.* Assen: Van Gorcum.

—— Hofmaier, B., Ekman Philips, M., and Wikman, A. (1996). *Concept-driven Development and the Organization of the Process of Change: An Evaluation of the Swedish Working Life Fund.* Amsterdam: John Benjamin.

Hamel, G. and Prahalad, C. K. (1994). *Competing for the Future: Unleashing the Power of the Workforce.* Boston: Harvard Business School Press.

Hertog, J. F. den, Hart, H., and Riegler, C. H. (1997). *Building the Knowledge Enterprise: Learning Organizations as the Source of Growth and Employment.* European Work & Technology Consortium, Commission of the European Communities, DG-V, Brussels.

—— and Huizenga, E. (1998). *The Knowledge Enterprise.* London: Imperial Press.

Hirschhorn, L. (1997). *Reworking Authority: Leading and Following in the Post-modern Organization.* Cambridge, Mass.: MIT Press.

Howells, J. and Wood, M. (eds.) (1993). *The Globalisation of Production and Technology.* London: Belhaven.

Jacobi, O., Keller, B., and Müller-Jentsch, W. (1998). 'Germany: Facing New Challenges', in A. Ferner and R. Hyman (eds.), *Changing Industrial Relations in Europe* (2nd edn). Oxford: Blackwell, 190–238.

Kapstein, E. B. (1996). 'Workers and the World Economy'. *Foreign Affairs,* 75/3: 16–37.

Kjellberg, A. (1997). *Fackliga organisationer och medlemmar i dagens Sverige* (Labor Unions and Members in Modern Sweden). Lund: Arkiv.

—— (1998). 'Sweden: Restoring the Model?', in A. Ferner and R. Hyman (eds.), *Changing Industrial Relations in Europe* (2nd edn). Oxford: Blackwell, 74–117.

Lippert, I., Jürgens, U., and Drüke, H. (1996). 'Arbeit und Wissen im Produktentstehungsprozess', in G. Schreyögg and P. Conrad (eds.), *Wissensmanagement.* Berlin: Walter de Gruyter, 235–61.

Mahon, R. (1994). 'Wage Earners and/or Co-workers? Contested Identities', in C. Wallace and R. Mahon (eds.), *Swedish Social Democracy: A Model in Transition.* Toronto: Canadian Scholars' Press, 347–72.

Martin, T. (1997). *Produktion 2000: Trying to Jointly Improve Technology, Organisation and Qualification.* Preprint of paper presented at the 6th IFAC Symposium on Automated Systems Based on Human Skill, Kranjska Gora, Slovenia, 17–19 September (Mimeograph).

Matthies, H., Mückenberger, U., Offe, C., Peter, E., and Raasch, S. (1994). *Arbeit 2000: Anforderungen an eine Neugestaltung der Arbeitswelt.* Hamburg: Rowohlt.

McHugh, P., Merli, G., and Wheeler, W. A., III (1995). *Beyond Business Process Reengineering: Towards the Holonic Enterprise.* Chichester: John Wiley and Sons.

Midler, C. (1995). 'Organizational Innovation in Project Management: The Renault–Twingo Case', in L.-E. Andréason, B. Coriat, and J. F. den Hertog (eds.), *Europe's Next Step: Organisational Innovation, Competition and Employment.* Ilford: Frank Cass, 131–50.

Mückenberger, U., Schmidt, E., and Zoll, R. (eds.) (1996). *Die Modernisierung der Gewerkschaften in Europa.* Münster: Westfälisches Dampfboot.

Muldur, U. and Petrella, R. (eds.) (1994). *Science and Technology Policy: The European Community and the Globalization of Technology and the Economy.* Luxembourg: Office for Official Publications of the European Communities.

Müller-Jentsch, W. (1995). 'Germany: From Collective Voice to Co-management', in J. Rogers and W. Streeck (eds.), *Works Councils: Consultation, Representation, and Cooperation in Industrial Relations.* Chicago: University of Chicago Press, 53–78.

—— (1999). 'Die deutsche Mitbestimmung: Ein Auslaufmodell im globalen Wettbewerb?', in H. G. Nutzinger (ed.), *Perspektiven der Mitbestimmung: Historische Erfahrungen und moderne Entwicklungen vor europäischem und globalem Hintergrund.* Marburg: Metropolis, 287–304.

—— Sperling, H. J., and Weyrather, I. (1997). *Neue Technologien in der Verhandlungsarena: Schweden, Grossbritannien und Deutschland im Vergleich*. Schriftenreihe Industrielle Beziehungen No. 12. Munich: Rainer Hampp Verlag.

Nonaka, I. and Takeuchi, H. (1995). *The Knowledge-creating Company: How Japanese Companies Create the Dynamics of Innovation*. New York: Oxford University Press.

Nutzinger, H. G. (ed.) (1999). *Perspektiven der Mitbestimmung: Historische Erfahrungen und moderne Entwicklungen vor europäischem und globalem Hintergrund*. Marburg: Metropolis.

Oehlke, P. (1998). 'Innovation as a Social Process: The Shift from Design to Employment Strategies within German Work and Technology Policies', in T. Alasoini and M. Kyllönen (eds.), *The Crest of the Wave: Finnish National Workplace Development Programme*. Report 5, Yearbook 1998. Helsinki: Ministry of Labour, 77–110.

Pasmore, W. A. (1988). *Designing Effective Organizations: The Sociotechnical Systems Perspective*. New York: Wiley.

—— (1994). *Creating Strategic Change: Designing the Flexible, High-performing Organization*. New York: Wiley.

Putnam, R. D. (1993). *Making Democracy Work: Civic Traditions in Modern Italy*. Princeton: Princeton University Press.

Riegler, C. H. (1998). 'Learning from Experiences of the Swedish Working Life Fund: New Public Policy Initiatives', in T. Alasoini and M. Kyllönen (eds.), *The Crest of the Wave: Finnish National Workplace Development Programme*. Report 5, Yearbook 1998. Helsinki: Ministry of Labour, 46–76.

Rogers, J. and Streeck, W. (eds.) (1995). *Works Councils: Consultation, Representation, and Cooperation in Industrial Relations*. Chicago: University of Chicago Press.

Rovik, K.-A. (1996). 'Deinstitutionalization and the Logic of Fashion', in B. Czarniawska and G. Sevón (eds.), *Translating Organizational Change*. Berlin: de Gruyter, 139–72.

Sasajima, Y. (1995). 'Japan: The Case of the Metal Manufacturing Industry', in P. Tergeist (ed.), *Flexible Working Time: Collective Bargaining and Government Intervention*. Paris: OECD, 63–81.

Schneider, U. (ed.) (1996). *Wissensmanagement: Die Aktivierung des intellektuellen Kapitals*. Frankfurt am Main: Frankfurter Allgemeine Zeitung, Edition Blickbuch Wirtschaft.

Schreyögg, G. and Conrad, P. (1996). *Wissensmanagement*. Berlin: de Gruyter.

Selznick, P. (1957). *Leadership in Administration: A Sociological Interpretation*. New York: Harper & Row.

Sitter, L. U. de, Hertog, J. F. den, and Dankbaar, B. (1997). 'From Complex Organizations with Simple Jobs to Simple Organizations with Complex Jobs'. *Human Relations*, 50: 497–534.

Sperling, H. J. (1994). *Innovative Arbeitsorganisation und intelligentes Partizipationsmanagement*. Marburg: Schüren Presseverlag.

Stewart, T. A. (1997). *Intellectual Capital: The New Wealth of Organizations*. New York: Doubleday.

Svenska Metallindustriarbetareförbundet [Swedish Metalworkers' Union] (1998). *Projekt 2001: Det goda arbetet* (Project 2001: The Good Work). Several Reports, Stockholm: Metall.

Trentin, B. (1997). *La città del lavoro: Sinistra e crisi del fordismo*. Milan: Feltrinelli.

Tsang, E. W. K. (1997). 'Organizational Learning and the Learning Organization: A Dichotomy between Descriptive and Prescriptive Research'. *Human Relations*, 50: 73–89.

Wallenberg, J. (1996). 'Kommunala förnyelsekrafter: Formellt medbestämmande eller informella utvecklingsprocesser?' (Forces of Innovation in Local Government: Formal Codetermination or Informal Development Processes?). *Arbetsmarknad och Arbetsliv*, 2: 247–57.

Weick, K. E. (1995). *Sensemaking in Organizations*. Thousand Oaks, Calif.: Sage.

Willke, H. (1996). 'Dimensionen des Wissensmanagements: Zum Zusammenhang von gesellschaftlicher und organisationaler Wissensbasierung', in G. Schreyögg and P. Conrad (eds.), *Wissensmanagement*. Berlin: de Gruyter, 263–304.

Yutaka, N. (1998). 'Japanese-style Industrial Relations in Historical Perspective', in H. Harukiyo and G. D. Hook (eds.), *Japanese Business Management: Restructuring for Low Growth and Globalization*. London: Routledge, 195–216.

21 Consultants as Agents of Organizational Learning: The Importance of Marginality

Ariane Berthoin Antal and Camilla Krebsbach-Gnath

Considering the growing emphasis that organizational scholars place on embeddedness and open systems, it is striking that theory-building about organizational learning has focused almost exclusively on the role of internal agents of the organization. This narrow scope is all the more surprising at a time when ever more consultants are being hired to help companies solve a variety of problems and improve or stabilize their market position through such initiatives as reengineering, total quality, cultural change, and lean management. The trend toward globalization has only intensified the need for organizations to review their strategies, structures, and processes. All such initiatives require organizations to engage in significant learning processes, which range from increasing the efficiency of current procedures to introducing radically new structures and ways of thinking about the organization and its markets. In order to contribute to closing the gap in theory building, we explore the many roles that consultants play in either promoting or hindering organizational learning and discuss how consultants and clients alike shape the conditions for both kinds of impact.

There is very little research explicitly on how consultants contribute to or impede organizational learning (for overviews, see Delany 1994; Ginsberg and Abrahamson 1991; Steyrer 1991). It is therefore necessary to look in neighboring fields of inquiry—organizational development and change management—to find studies that explore the roles of consultants in these related processes. Although that work rarely treats organizational learning as such, it often implicitly relates to learning. Many consultants in organizational development seek to provide clients with help for self-help (French and Bell 1999; Ibelski and Küster 1993; Thom 1992), a commitment that entails an engagement in learning processes.

In order to add detail to the picture of the roles of consultants in organizational learning, we have enlarged this research base by analyzing reports on management consultants in the business press and management journals and by studying publications by some of the major consultancies.[1] We also drew on interviews with managers who have worked with consultants[2] and on our own experience with a variety of clients over the past twenty years. With combined resources we sought to understand how consultants and their clients conceive of organizational learning, how they define the roles to be played in the process, and how they analyze their experiences to date.

Defining the Population

Reaching back to soothsaying by high priests and court jesters, the consulting profession has

[1] The authors thank Victor Friedman and Hedwig Rudolph for comments on earlier versions of this chapter as well as Ekmel Cizmecloglu, John Gaynor, and Kristina Vaillant for their assistance in obtaining and analyzing the material from consultancies.

[2] The interviews, in which managers reflected on the use and usefulness of consultants, were conducted during a

a long tradition of helping organizations prepare for the future (Turner 1995: 155; for an overview of the history of management consulting and of types of consultancies today, see Kubr 1996: 27–40). The population of consultancies today ranges from individual experts or part-time academic consultants to large multinational companies providing services to smaller, focused consultancies. Some organizations—such as the German trade organizations and industrial associations that, in addition to their primary roles, provide consultancy to their members—also advise companies.

A small, but growing, group within the population of consultants can be found inside organizations (Burgmaier and Reischauer 1998). For example, companies are designating some employees as 'change agents' and some senior managers as 'Chief Learning Officers' or 'Chief Knowledge Officer', and they are developing their human resource managers to take on roles as internal consultants (Berthoin Antal and Lange 1997). There are strong business reasons for developing internal consultants and clear advantages for organizational learning. Compared to outside consultants, internal consultants know their organization better, can read its politics more effectively, generally identify more strongly with the interests of the organization, and often are better accepted by lower level managers. However, there is a downside. Internal consultants usually have the same blind spots as do the managers of their organization and cannot bring in as much experience with other ways of seeing and doing things as external consultants can. Being a part of the existing culture and structure, they are rarely in a position to conceive of introducing major changes (Staehle 1994: 918). Our experience in numerous organizational change projects is consistent with reported findings suggesting that these limitations can sometimes be compensated for if a team of internal and external consultants is formed (Block 1989; Newstrom and Davis 1993: 296).

study of how companies have learned how to downsize (Berthoin Antal 1997a, b).

Not only does consulting have a long tradition, it is a very large and growing business (Bierach 1996a: 162; Jackson 1996: 8; Kurbjuweit 1996; Staute 1996: 9; Voss 1999). The most visible, and probably dominant, members of the population are the big international management consultancies. Although there are no reliable statistics on the population of the smaller and individual consultancies, neither their scope nor their creativity should be underestimated.

For the purpose of understanding the dynamics of consultants as actors in processes of organizational learning, this chapter focuses on management consulting,[3] a wide category that includes a range of organizational change and strategic development work. Formulating a generally accepted definition that encompasses the generic purposes of management consulting, Kubr (1996) described it as an 'independent professional advisory service assisting managers and organizations in achieving organizational purposes and objectives by solving management and business problems, identifying and seeing new opportunities, enhancing learning and implementing changes' (p. 8). The most rapidly growing fields for management

[3] This category does not include such consulting services as executive search, consulting on information technologies (IT), and other special expertise. The outcome of executive searches may have an impact on organizational learning, in that newly recruited members of management can be expected to influence learning processes (Carley 1996; Virany, Tushman, and Romanelli 1996). However, the actual process of working with an executive search firm is not central to organizational learning. Consideration of IT consulting is also excluded in this chapter because, as Jackson (1996) pointed out, the growth of consulting activities corresponds to a kind of outsourcing in which the consultancy companies are 'buying the company's IT staff and running the process because they are better at it, . . . and that's not consulting as I understand it' (Jackson 1996: 8). The focus on management consulting avoids the Pandora's box of equating training with organizational learning. Training, whether for individuals or, more recently, for teams and units in organizations, is dedicated to learning, but its relevance for organizational learning remains indirect at best. The concern is that 'training programs, regardless of how personally powerful, do not change organizational behavior . . . [because] these programs simply do not affect enough elements in the system—roles and responsibilities at work, the boss, rewards, and structure, for example—to change organizational behavior' (Beer, Eisenstat, and Spector 1990: 33 also provides an overview of the literature).

consultants are strategy and knowledge management. The growing significance of strategy consulting is illustrated by a study conducted by Customer Satisfaction Surveys (CSS) of 1,559 top managers in twelve European countries. More than 60 per cent of the respondents reported that their company had brought in consultants on at least one strategic project in the past year, compared to 48 per cent two years earlier (Bierach 1996b: 132; see also Voss 1999). Consulting on knowledge management as a business process is a newer field than strategic management, and it is requiring both consultancies and their client organizations to learn rapidly (Sarvary 1999).

The clients of management consultants are diverse. Although the prime candidates remain large companies, the pressures of change and globalization are broadening the client base. Companies of all sizes are turning to consultants to strengthen themselves for international competition and rapid technological change (Kurbjuweit 1996). As pointed out by the European director of management consultancy at Price Waterhouse, Peter Davis, 'clients are asking us to work on strategic partnerships, alliances, and projects in ways they didn't before. And the global requirement will take in south-east Asia and eastern Europe, which the global player will have to respond to' (see also Byrne 1996; Jackson 1996: 8). Furthermore, it is not only in the private sector that consultancies are engaged. In Germany, for example, McKinsey has been called on by clients as diverse as the Bremer Theater, the city of Ludwigshafen, the football club of Bayern München, St. Georg's hospital in Hamburg, Deutschlandfunk (a major nationwide public radio station), and the Protestant church in Munich (Kurbjuweit 1996).

How Consultants Conceive of Learning

As reflected in this volume, the academic literature has generated many definitions of organizational learning (for recent overviews and critiques, see also Krebsbach-Gnath 1996; Marriott and Morrison 1996; and Moingeon and Edmondson 1996). It would not be surprising if consultants have produced an equally wide spectrum of definitions. Before exploring the roles consultants play in organizational learning processes, one will therefore find it useful to look at how they conceive of these processes.[4] What key elements from the academic literature should one look for in consultants' representations? The following three questions may guide the way to relevant answers.

1. *To what extent do consultants convey an awareness of both a behavioral and a cognitive dimension to learning?*
Psychological theories of individual learning fall into two broad categories, behavioral and cognitive (see Maier, Prange, and Rosenstiel, Ch. 1 and Starbuck and Hedburg, Ch. 14 in this volume). The definitions by such scholars of organizational learning as Huber (1991), who suggested that 'an entity learns if, through its processing of information, the range of its potential behaviors is changed' (p. 89), stress change in behaviors as an outcome of learning but do not limit such outcomes to observable behavioral change (Cook and Yanow 1993: 377). Huber's definition does not explicitly include a perceptual dimension in learning processes but does enable it to be subsumed in information-processing, for perceptions play a significant role in organizational learning by filtering the information considered relevant for processing (Berthoin Antal, Dierkes, and Hähner 1997).

2. *How do consultancies distinguish between individual and organizational learning?*
There is broad consensus in the academic literature that individuals are key agents of organizational learning (Friedman, Ch. 17 in this volume) but that organizational learning is more than the sum of individual learning

---

[4] Seven major international consultancies were asked to provide materials, including brochures on products and services, newsletters, and publications describing experiences with learning processes in client organizations. The range of publications of smaller or individual consultancies are not systematically accessible, and no known representative surveys of them have been undertaken.

(Argyris and Schön 1978). Organizational learning is not simply a matter of diffusing existing information. It entails the continual creation of new knowledge through the interaction between individuals (Gherardi and Nicolini, Ch. 2 in this volume). Researchers (and consultants) therefore need to understand the processes of interaction between individuals that lead to the generation of shared knowledge (Nonaka 1994), to collective framing and sense-making (Büchel and Raub, Ch. 23 in this volume; Daft and Weick 1984), and to the integration of individual learning into an organization's memory in such forms as routines (Kieser, Beck, and Tainio, Ch. 27 in this volume) and structures (Kim 1993). It is also important to note that research on organizational learning has highlighted 'communities of practice' as learning entities that cut across departmental and interfirm boundaries and that are therefore usually not immediately visible (Brown and Duguid 1991; Stopford, Ch. 11 in this volume).

3. *What kind of process model do the consultancies assume?*

Much of the literature on organizational learning treats the process in terms of phases and steps that can be initiated and planned. It is usually conceived of as iterative, with feedback loops to facilitate adjustments for unforeseen developments (Daft and Weick 1984; DiBella, Nevis, and Gould 1996). There is also a competing view of organizational learning as a continuous dynamic, illustrated by Nonaka and Takeuchi (1995) as a spiral and by Choo (1998) as concentric circles. In this conception, organizational learning can be channeled or unblocked but not planned (Schreyögg and Noss 1995).

The definitions of organizational learning used by the consultancies in their publications are quite consistent. They all emphasize learning as an ongoing process and as an outcome of the acquisition of knowledge and the review of experience. Price Waterhouse, for example, has defined a learning organization as 'one that has the willingness and capacity to acquire knowledge and leverage it to modify behavior in the pursuit of enhanced organizational effectiveness. The ultimate goal should not be the

pursuit of a precise answer, but rather the stimulation of new thinking that leads to productive action' (Pederson and Dickinson 1995: 7). Arthur D. Little has contended that organizational learning is 'an organization's capacity to learn from its experience, to examine its own processes, and change itself' (Lancaster 1995: 45). Boston Consulting Group has written that 'learning occurs when the requirements of knowledge, will, and ability are continually realized in many small steps' (von Oetinger 1994: 2, our translation).

The process of organizational learning as outlined by Arthur D. Little occurs in five classical stages: 'awareness, understanding, action, review, and reflection' (Lancaster 1995: 19, 59). The other consultancies do not specifically identify steps in learning processes, but they do describe steps in change processes. For example, Schitag Ernst and Young (1996) specified '1. strategy/problem analysis; 2. organization; 3. analysis; 4. design; and 5. realization' (p. 6, our translation). They also accentuated the need to analyze the willingness and ability to change, which would presumably precede their first step. Booz Allen and Hamilton do not mention organizational learning specifically but do describe their approach to reengineering in terms that are relevant for learning:

Understand the process as it exists, rather than how we believe it works.
Listen to and solicit input from employees who actually do the work.
Redesign processes from the customers' perspective.
Look for innovative ideas and model against the best companies.
Deploy all new processes and systems at a test site before rolling them out company-wide. (Lee 1996: 59)

Boston Consulting Group, too, conceives of a process but emphasizes that 'the sequential progression of analysis, discovery, and implementation must be abandoned. The development of strategy and its implementation must occur simultaneously' (Habgood 1986: column 1, our translation).

In summary, these definitions indicate, first, that these consultancies are aware of both cognitive and behavioral dimensions to organizational learning. They appear to have avoided the trap of becoming locked into one of these two academic traditions and have succeeded in bridging them, as academics are currently being encouraged to do (e.g. Starbuck and Hedberg, Ch. 14 in this volume).

The second conclusion from this review is less positive, however. The consultancies do not elaborate on the distinctions or links between individual and organizational learning. Rather, they anthropomorphize the organization as a unitary actor. A lack of differentiation and clarity on this matter augurs badly for role specification in learning processes. If consultants and their clients are not clear about the key characteristics of organizational learning as distinct from individual learning, it is very likely that insufficient attention will be paid to the dynamics of embedding individual learning into the organization. The concept of communities of practice does not appear in the consultancy materials, probably because communities of practice do not coincide with formal organizational structures. Therefore, these valuable units of organizational learning are likely to be particularly at risk during consultancy interventions, for their invisibility in the formal organization makes them vulnerable to unwitting dismantling in change processes.

Third, the materials suggest that the consultants equate learning and change, which they see as processes that progress through definable steps. These steps are treated as plannable, and usually as sequential. Mention is made of simultaneous processes, but the iterative and unplannable dimensions of learning and change processes treated in the academic discussion are not reflected in the consultants' publications. This is not surprising. First, a consultancy engagement is usually based on a contract stipulating an assignment with a clear beginning and a clear end (although the actual relationship between the client and the consultancy begins before the contract and can last beyond it). When writing about organizational learning, consultancies therefore find it easier to communicate to a client that this process, too, has a clear beginning and a clear end point to sell a client a process that appears unplannable and

messy. Second, the logical consequence of the view of organizational learning as a continuous dynamic is that agents who are not full members of the system have a relatively limited contribution to make because they are not constantly present and able to participate from day to day (Schreyögg and Noss 1995). It appears to contradict basic principles of marketing to expect consultants to underscore the marginality of their potential contributions (Kieser 1998). It is unfortunate that marketing materials lend themselves badly to communicating messiness and marginality, for the way in which they position their expertise is precisely where the crucial tension between the roles of consultants and the expectations of their clients lies. In order for consultants to contribute effectively to organizational learning, they need to manage this tension in the relationship with their clients.

As March (1991) pointed out, it is on the margin that consultants[5] can ideally contribute to organizational learning. He meant that consultants should 'attempt to complement, rather than duplicate' what members of organizations have already learned through their own experiences (p. 26). The concept of marginality can usefully be expanded to include several dimensions: marginality of (a) perspective, (b) influence, and (c) action. External consultants can offer their clients a marginal perspective in the sense that they can add value to the client's learning process by bringing an outside view to the organization. During an intervention, consultants can choose to exert influence over the client's choice of actions in a directive or nondirective manner, whereby nondirective approaches imply that the consultants play a rather marginal role in the client's decision (Kubr 1996). Marginality in action means that the client is more central than the consultant in undertaking steps during the intervention. A core thesis of this chapter is that the balance

---

[5] March (1991) introduced the concept of marginality in an article exploring the contributions of consultants and researchers to the experiential knowledge of managers. Empirical research by Hofmann (1995) revealed a similar phenomenon in the positioning of the expertise that academics and consultants offer to small and medium-sized firms.

between the marginality of the consultant and that of the client must be appropriate on all three of these dimensions in order to assure that learning is generated and retained in the organization.

Roles that Consultants Play in Organizational Learning

Consultants are very rarely, if ever, brought into organizations specifically with the charge of 'improving organizational learning'. They are generally called upon to solve problems and help improve the performance of an organization. There is, however, an implicit learning agenda behind the task of solving problems and improving performance (see Ch. 3 for a review of organizational learning as a problem-driven search), for that task is based on the assumption that things must be done differently or that new things must be done. Learning is required in either case. According to Argyris and Schön's (1978) typology of learning, the solving of problems by doing things differently represents single-loop learning, and solving problems by doing new things represents double-loop learning.

Defining consultants only as problem-solvers, however, is both too broad to be useful and too narrow to capture reality. Consultants play a wide range of roles in organizations, and these roles vary in their potential impact on learning, depending on how they are played.

Typology of Consultants' Roles

The most common categorizations distinguishing between the roles of consultants are (a) content versus process and (b) directive versus nondirective (e.g. Kubr 1996; Schreyögg and Noss 1995). Content-focused consulting roles involve the provision of expertise (e.g. information) and the delivery of a specific service to the client (e.g. design of a new system). Process consulting, by contrast is 'a set of activities on the part of the consultant that help the client to perceive, understand, and act upon the process events that occur in the client's environment' (Schein 1987: 34). There is a strong trend toward recognizing the complementarity of content and process consulting, and consultants are finding it necessary to develop skills in both modes (Kubr 1996: 58). Some observers believe that 'the basic model of management consulting has changed' (Sarvary 1999: 97). Instead of delivering 'smart people to solve the client's problem' (p. 97) or offering process consulting for the clients to find their own solutions, consultancies are moving toward providing 'access to the knowledge that emerges from . . . experience' (p. 97).

As illustrated in Fig. 21.1, the types of activities that management consultants can provide to organizations can be distributed along the directive/nondirective continuum. Figure 21.1 also shows how the consulting activities at the nondirective end of the continuum place the client in the position of primary actor and the consultant on the margin. The activities toward the directive end of the continuum assign far greater presence to the consultant than to the client, whose level of activity is marginalized.

Although the boundary between content and process approaches to management consultancy are blurring in practice, their 'pure' modes imply different assumptions about learning. The content mode of consulting rests on the assumption that learning is a process of transforming information and skills from expert to student. In the process mode of consulting, learning is treated as a participative experiential process that the consultant can facilitate for the client. This distinction highlights the fact that the consultant and the client are counterparts. For example, if in the content mode of consulting a client organization is not a willing recipient of the information that the consultant is capable of providing, learning is not likely to result from the intervention. Similarly, if in the process consulting mode the consultant attempts to facilitate a participative learning experience whereas the client is seeking an input of information or clear directions

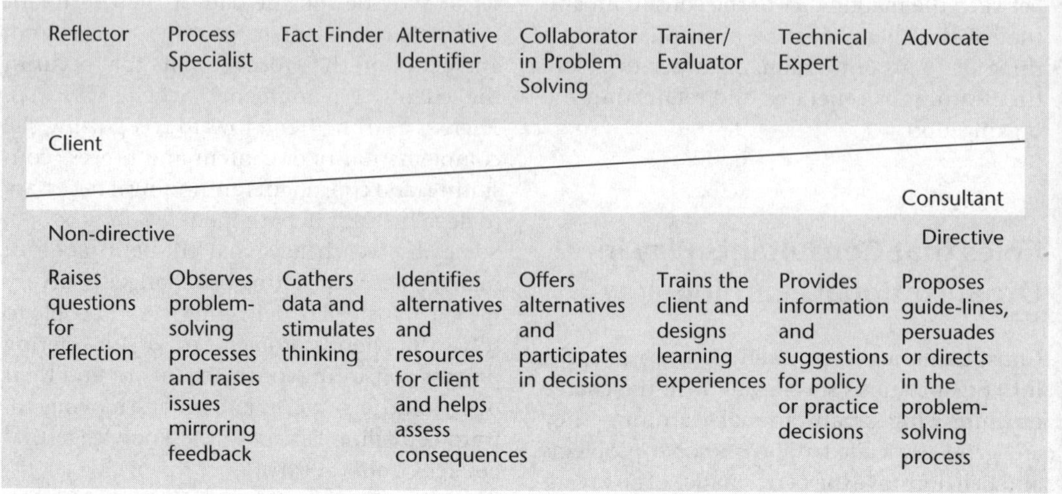

Reflector	Process Specialist	Fact Finder	Alternative Identifier	Collaborator in Problem Solving	Trainer/ Evaluator	Technical Expert	Advocate
Client							
							Consultant
Non-directive							Directive
Raises questions for reflection	Observes problem-solving processes and raises issues mirroring feedback	Gathers data and stimulates thinking	Identifies alternatives and resources for client and helps assess consequences	Offers alternatives and participates in decisions	Trains the client and designs learning experiences	Provides information and suggestions for policy or practice decisions	Proposes guide-lines, persuades or directs in the problem-solving process

Fig. 21.1. Type and level of consultant activity *vis-à-vis* the client

From *Management Consulting: A Guide to the Profession*, edited by M. Kubr, 3rd edn. (Geneva: International Labour Office, 1996), 61. © 1996 International Labour Organization. Original source: University Associates, La Jolla, Calif.

on what to do, the learning process will be impeded. In order for the consultant to contribute effectively to meeting the client's needs, the client must play the role of counterpart appropriately.

Categorizing Clients

Much less work has been done to differentiate client roles than consultant roles (Hoffmann and Hlawacek 1991: 419; Strasser 1993), and although the need to look at the match in roles and expectations has been recognized for a number of years (Gattiker and Larwood 1985: 127). A preliminary categorization that offers connections to organizational learning uses two axes: the willingness of the client to learn and cooperate with the consultant, and the level of urgency or pressure caused by the problem that has led the client to the consultant (Carqueville 1991: 271; Fleischmann 1984 cited in Hoffmann and Hlawacek 1991: 420). Figure 21.2 illustrates the four types of clients defined by these two dimensions. A typology of this kind is a snap-shot of a client dealing with a specific problem at a particular time rather than

a permanent label. Clients can move from one cell to the next, depending on the situation they are facing.

The matrix suggests that two kinds of clients can be found when there is urgent pressure to solve a problem: those who want the consultant to solve the problem for them (the Driven) and those who are interested in learning and participating in solving the problem themselves (the Crisis Managers). When the pressure generated by the problem is low, clients may feel that they can afford to take the time to learn (the Cooperative Problem-Solvers), or they can be quite uninterested in learning (the Image Managers). These categories were used in a study of 62 consulting cases in Austria and revealed a distribution that appears quite promising for organizational learning: 16 per cent of the clients were categorized as Driven, 23 per cent as Crisis Managers, 52 per cent as Cooperative Problem-Solvers, and only 9 per cent as Image Managers. In other words the overwhelming majority (75 per cent) were considered willing to learn and to take an active role in solving their particular problems (Hoffmann and Hlawaceck 1991: 421).

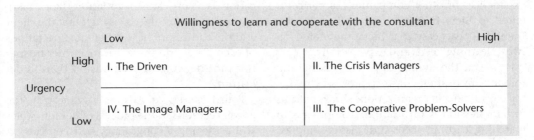

Fig. 21.2. Typology of clients

Source: Based on Fleischmann (1984); our translation of figure found on p. 420 of Hoffmann and Hlawacek (1991).

Matching Consultant Roles with Client Roles

There have been theoretical and empirical efforts to match the four very rough categorizations of client types presented in Fig. 21.2 with consultants using the content/process and the directive/nondirective typologies (Carqueville 1991: 270–2; Hoffmann and Hlawacek 1991: 419–23). These studies suggest that Driven clients will seek to use only the content input a consultant can provide and that they are not likely to be interested in participative learning processes. Crisis Managers are in principle more willing to engage with the consultant in a learning process but still have a high focus on using the consultant's input in order to solve the immediate problem. Cooperative Problem-Solvers are the ideal clients for consultants skilled in stimulating participative learning processes. Lastly, the Image Managers are the most likely to bring in consultants as a symbolic gesture, with little or no intention of learning from the intervention. Consequently the consultant will be asked to provide content input, but no process is put in place for the input to be used. The researchers concluded that, in practice, the directive modes of consulting dominated for all four client types, with a fair degree of nondirective consulting reported only for Cooperative Problem-Solvers (Hoffmann and Hlawaceck 1991: 422–3). Because directive modes of consulting tend to put the consultant rather than the client at the center position, the consultant marginality

that is needed for effective organizational learning appears difficult to achieve.

These categorizations are appealing, as labels in management research often are, but they have drawbacks. The most important weakness is that the labels suggest a monolithic client organization, whereas in practice a consultant deals with numerous actors in an organization. These actors tend to have their own agendas and are therefore likely to have a different stake in the consulting relationship. For example, one of us was involved in a major change project at a European agency and had to deal with a mix of client roles. The senior manager who commissioned the project was an Image Manager, the personnel manager and several middle managers and staff members were Cooperative Problem-Solvers, and a unit director who was experiencing difficulties was a Crisis Manager.

These factors indicate that it is useful to look closely at the process of role clarification. The clearer the consultants and their clients are about the type of learning sought and about their respective expectations in the process, the greater the likelihood that organizational learning will result from the interaction. Market research suggests that clients are quite clear about what they expect from consultants. According to an international study by CSS, for example, senior managers have cited three primary reasons for engaging consultants: (a) lack of in-house know-how (66 per cent), (b) 'objectivity' of external perspective (49 per cent), and (c) the benefit of learning from experiences of other companies (48 per cent) (cited in Bierach 1996b: 131). At first glance, then, it appears easy to achieve the match between learning needs and expectations.

However, the dynamics of role-taking and role-making (Carqueville 1991) processes involving consultants in organizations show that this first impression is misleading. The process of matching learning needs and roles is complex, and the outcome is often not conducive to maximizing the use of learning opportunities. First, the official or stated reason why a client chooses to bring in a consultant does not necessarily correspond exactly to the actual needs in the organization. For example, the CEO of a company called one of us in to help redesign business processes so that the company could deliver more quickly than it was at that time. During interviews and observation, we discovered that the problem lay not in the design of the business process but rather in how leadership was understood and implemented in the organization. The discovery of the needs is in fact one of the major initial tasks of the consultancy and can result in roles different than those that appeared to flow from the first definition of the problem. The role originally given to the consultant by the client therefore frequently has to be revised, a change implying that the role the client originally expected to play in the process should be revised as well.

Second, consultants tend to play several roles over the course of an assignment, not just one. While working on a project, consultants 'make' their own roles, say, as a result of their professional style and their perceptions of the changing needs in each phase of an assignment, and they 'take' the roles given to them by their counterparts in the client organization. Furthermore, consultants deal with numerous counterparts in an organization during any given intervention, so they are likely to have different roles in these relationships.

Third, much of the role-taking and role-making process is handled implicitly rather than explicitly. Even in the contractual phase some roles are left unspoken by both the consultant and the client (Carqueville 1991: 263), although experts have long advised role clarifi-cation as a conscious negotiation (Block 1981). In such situations the risk is high that the client and the consultant have different expectations of each other and therefore encounter frustrations in the working relationship that hinder learning.

Fourth, and possibly most significantly, the power relations in the process of defining roles and achieving a congruency between the expectations of the consultant and the client are skewed. Critics of the consulting industry tend to position clients as being at the mercy of consultants' expert rhetoric (for a review, see Fincham 1999). Such representations overlook that the client has the power to hire and fire the consultant and is therefore in the driver's seat in determining expectations and roles. Although the consultant can exert a certain amount of influence on the client to achieve a mutually acceptable congruence, the consultant must ultimately either modify his or her own expectations to match those set by the client or not accept the task. In this regard, too, however, the client is not a monolithic organization but rather a political system in which some actors have more power than others. Although some senior actors in the client organization can fire the consultant, the latter has greater influence in determining the roles to be played in relationships with many other internal actors who have less power than senior management. This is not to say that people who are lower in the hierarchy are powerless. They may not have the power to fire consultants, but they can actively boycott or passively resist consultants' attempts to fulfill the role designations established with top management.

These four complicating factors preclude a guarantee that client roles and consultant roles are well matched for organizational learning. As a result, learning obstacles deeply embedded in the organization's culture are likely to remain untouched. When one of us was asked by a multinational company some years ago to help identify problems with cross-cultural communication in relationships between headquarters in one country and subsidiaries in four other countries, the roles appeared clear. The consultant (working in process-oriented and nondirective mode with a strong background in cross-cultural issues) was to provide insights through interviews abroad in order to enable the client (a Co-operative Problem-Solver) at headquarters to make necessary changes. The managers interviewed in the subsidiaries were generally extremely open because they welcomed this opportunity to express their frustrations with the arrogant behavior of managers and the bureaucratic controls at headquarters. They saw in the consultant an expert and a person close to the seat of power at headquarters, able to 'get them to listen to us', as several local managers put it. The report fascinated the client at headquarters, who decided to have the results presented to his boss and other colleagues. The senior manager, however, turned out to be an 'Image Manager', he found the results of the study excessively critical. The report was filed, and no further action was taken. To the extent that organizational learning can be said to have occurred, it is likely that the managers in the subsidiaries felt confirmed in their opinion that managers of headquarters were arrogant and unwilling to learn, even with information provided by an expert.

How Consultants Support or Impede Organizational Learning Processes

Consultants can play various roles in various ways during the organizational learning process. For the sake of clarity, the following discussion is structured according to phase models of organizational learning because they correspond largely to the episodic nature of consultancy interventions. We return later to the competing conceptions of organizational learning as ongoing processes.

Four- and five-phase models have been suggested (Berthoin Antal 1998: 41; see also Büchel and Raub, Ch. 23 in this volume). They tend to start with knowledge acquisition and proceed to information interpretation and

diffusion, then to translation into action, and lastly to storage in organizational memory. The iterative nature of organizational learning processes is explicitly recognized in some of these models, so the presentation of stages should not be seen as a simple linear approach (see also Pawlowsky, Ch. 3 in this volume).

Although the current stage models of organizational learning start with knowledge acquisition, examination of the roles consultants play in practice reveals that additional early phases become visible: the generation of an awareness of the need to learn and the definition of the problem to be dealt with. Consultants can be involved directively and nondirectively in both content and process dimensions during these phases. They can share levels of activity with their clients to greater or lesser degrees of marginality and centrality.

Generating the Awareness of Need to Learn

As Scherer and Tran (Ch. 16 in this volume) imply, willingness to learn is a key variable that supports learning processes in organizations. A precondition for learning is the awareness of a need to learn to do or see things differently. Consultants exert influence in this phase directly in interaction with specific clients, and indirectly through publications and other means of communication with the community of potential clients.

Direct Impact

The generation of the awareness of the need to learn to do or see things differently is actually a primary, but unofficial, function of consultants, particularly when a client has the unrealistic expectation that the consultants can take over the problem and 'make it go away'. In order to put the client into the center of activity, consultants often have to awaken that need to learn. Some consultants seek to do so by combining a content and process approach in a directive manner that involves confronting the client with very different realities. Wilhelm Rall of McKinsey reported shaking up his

German clients by showing them production sites in Japan. They 'experience an existential uprooting. At first they think they have no chance, that it is totally hopeless. Then, after analyzing the situation, they usually come to the conclusion: "I can do that, too." It is then that change becomes conceivable for them' (Kurbjuweit 1996: 10, our translation). In this case the consultant takes on the role of generating both the awareness of a need to learn and a willingness to learn in the client organization by exposing a group of opinion-makers and decision-makers in the organization to new information and challenging them to change their mindsets about what is possible. The clear message in this approach is that the client must learn—the consultant can help only by creating the conditions for the client to learn; the consultant's role is marginal compared to that of the client in the learning process.

Generating the awareness of a need to learn often requires challenging existing recipes for success in solving problems that have built up in the organization (Phills 1996; see also Starbuck and Hedberg, Ch. 14 in this volume). In other words, the consultant must bring the client to accept greater levels of complexity and discomfort to solve the problem than the client probably originally expected. Generating a need to learn also often means dealing with discrepancies between espoused theories and the client's actual behavior, a process that can be painful for the client and frustrating for the consultant (Argyris 1991; see also Rothman and Friedman, Ch. 26 in this volume for additional discussion of conflict in organizational learning). Not surprisingly, consultants who tackle such difficult issues face a high risk of being rejected by the organization. External consultants are fired, and internal consultants are assigned to other projects. We have experienced an interesting variation on the theme of unwillingness to learn. When consultants who work as a team engage with an issue that the client finds uncomfortable but cannot totally deny, there is a tendency to split the team by rejecting one of the consultants. Nevertheless, such challenging of assumptions and reframing of past solutions as inappropriate for

current problems is a key role consultants play to trigger learning processes.

Indirect Influence

Consultants generate the awareness of a need to learn in another way as well. It is not included in the existing role typologies, for the typologies focus on the roles consultants play once they have been brought into the organization. The indirect ways in which consultants influence organizations remain invisible in these typologies, but they are very significant in both stimulating and impeding the ability of the organization to learn.

The past decade has witnessed a parade of management techniques and processes under various headings, published in books, seen on videos, and heard in speeches by consultants (Pascale 1990; Shapiro 1995). The diffusion of concepts has had an agenda-setting impact for organizational learning. 'By ushering in new conceptualizations and jargon, consultants act like fashion-setters who create new frames of reference that force top managers to recognize the antiquated nature of previous strategic orientation and the "fashionability" of the new' (Ginsberg and Abrahamson 1991: 177). The diffusion process has become international in scope. Many of the bestsellers in the United States and the United Kingdom are translated into other languages and attract a business readership abroad even if they are sharply criticized for their superficiality and weaknesses (e.g. Benders, van den Berg, and van Bijsterveld 1998; Gloger 1996; Kieser 1997).

This agenda-setting function can, however, also impede organizational learning. The danger with the agenda-setting role is that the speed with which new topics are put on to the management agenda can leave too little time for organizational learning processes to take hold. 'Employees have barely had the time to understand lean management before the wave of reengineering washes over them' (Shapiro 1996: 170, our translation). Agenda-setting can then degenerate to fad-setting. As Fincham (1999) has pointed out, it would be wrong to cast managers as passive victims of consultancy fads. The process is an interactive one, whereby consultancies have developed a 'capacity to roll over their techniques and renew their language, feeding off the constant demand from clients for new techniques' (Fincham 1999: 336).

Organizational learning is impeded if each concept is presented as a totally new and different solution, for members of organizations then easily become cynical about the value of learning and engaging in any change process. We have encountered this phenomenon frequently when working with European subsidiaries of U.S.-based multinational companies. Managers in subsidiaries who have witnessed the rapid introduction of one change initiative after another do not, as the managers in the U.S. headquarters probably hope, develop the ability to 'learn how to learn'. Instead, they learn that it is better to wait, for, as our respondents have told us, 'this new big idea, too, will pass'.

The major consultancies do seem to be aware of the dangers of their role in launching fads, and they actively caution companies not to undertake an initiative for the wrong reasons. Emphasizing the need to 'care for the human dimension of change', for example, the Boston Consulting Group gave the following advice to the readers of its 1993 report, *Re-engineering and Beyond*, 'Don't reengineer simply to reduce costs. . . . Excessive cost-cutting can destroy value' (cited in Mumford and Hendricks 1996: 23). Similarly, McKinsey was among the first large consultancies to express serious doubts about reengineering, skepticism based on the firm's published accounts of its experiences in projects in more than a hundred companies (Mumford and Hendricks 1996: 24). This additional cautionary role of consultants can, of course, be interpreted cynically as a strategy that some consultants use simply to generate more business for themselves (Kieser 1998).

Problem Definition

A correct diagnosis of the problem for which the consultant has been called in is usually seen as the first and most important task in an assignment, not only by consultants themselves but also by researchers in the field. 'No amount of sophistication in the execution of an intervention can overcome an error in problem definition,' warn Krantz and Gilmore (1991: 308; see also Mitroff and Featheringham 1974). The external view that consultants can bring to the situation from their position on the margin of organizations and from their experience in many other comparable situations enables them to generate a definition of the problem that is not hampered by the culturally determined perceptions shared by members of the organization. Consultants have the additional advantage of being relative outsiders to organizational politics. It would be naive, however, not to recognize that the problem definition offered by consultants is at least partly influenced by political interests of the factions within the organization with whom the consultants come to identify themselves or with whom they are seen to be identified.

On the other hand, the very fact that consultants bring a different frame of reference to a situation can raise barriers for organizational learning. Phills (1996) distinguished between two types of barriers to learning in this context: cognitive and motivational. Cognitive barriers can emerge in client organizations because consultants use different (and often complex) concepts to define problems. Motivational barriers are the resistance that is generated when the definition of the problem implies assessments of past performance. In other words, members of an organization are likely to resent and reject problem definitions that detract from the way they are seen in the organization and that could endanger their future status (for insights into defensive routines that impede organizational learning in such situations, see Argyris 1991, 1993). The position of consultants as relative outsiders to the organizational politics may enable them to voice problems that are difficult for insiders to bring up (e.g. Voss 1999: 68), but it does not mitigate the issue's political sensitivity. Micropolitics can therefore continue to block learning (Coopey 1995).

Some critics see the problem definition phase as yet another point at which consultants can play a central role in order to generate business rather than to foster learning. 'Consulting is a contrived-demand business; you may not be sick, but a consultant's diagnosis will convince you that you are. . . . Problem defining is really where all the action is. There was always a huge opportunity for us to spin the business our way,' confessed a former consultant after leaving the profession (Anonymous 1996: 71). This statement is a particularly cynical view of a trap associated with the role that consultants have in defining the problem. Although suspicion that consultants engage in self-enrichment may not be totally unfounded, the phenomenon may be greater in theory than in practice, for many client organizations have become experienced in assessing marketing jargon from consultancies. They are increasingly aware of the possibility that consultants might come in with a predefined notion of the problem in order to apply their preferred solution. Experienced managers, having learned to be much more challenging of consultants' definitions of problems and solutions, probe behind the logic and the calculations more intensely than they need to do.

A more frequent and insidious danger in this stage stems from the overreliance by less experienced and less critical clients on the ability of the consultant to define the 'real' problem because the consultant is attributed the gift of objectivity. This potentially ill-placed confidence shifts the consultant from the margin to the center of the process. As we have observed from our own consulting and from the experiences of colleagues, if clients do not participate actively in defining the problem, they will not own the problem enough to learn from the process. The intervention will come to be seen as an exercise in solving the consultants' problem.

Knowledge Acquisition

Consultants can help their clients acquire knowledge from both external and internal sources.

External Knowledge Acquisition

When organizations are faced with situations they have not managed before, they are likely to have consultants bring in knowledge in order to learn vicariously rather than relying exclusively on their own trial-and-error experimentation (Huber 1991). The competitive pressures of globalization, downsizing, and IT, for example, are experienced as new by many companies and therefore require information not yet available in-house (or not perceived to be available). Consultants are seen as bearers of the needed knowledge because they have developed an expertise in these areas and because they can bring in their experience from other companies when managing similar challenges. As we were told by a German personnel manager in an international company that had downsized for the first time, 'the consultancy knows what the best practice is, without giving us the names of the competitors. . . . They tell us how the process could be performed better. This is one of the best arguments for the consultancy.' Such managers evidently place a value on maximizing their knowledge and see consultants as a useful resource to tap into.

There are obstacles and limits to the effectiveness of consultants as importers of information and experience for organizational learning. The first blockage is that some members of a client organization may not believe that the consultants can add any information of value. Many managers who were interviewed about their ways of acquiring knowledge in preparation for downsizing processes stated: 'The consultants usually tell you what you exactly know. . . . We don't need consultants.' To these managers, no external information could be valid. Consultants had no intimate knowledge of the company and its workforce, so they were not considered able to add value. (For an insightful analysis of the symbiosis that consultants and clients can cultivate in order to achieve the necessary intimate knowledge of the companies' business, and for the drawbacks this strategy has for learning, see Lilja, Penn, and Tainio 1993.) As March (1991) pointed out with his concept of marginality, unless the consultants succeed in positioning their knowledge as complementary to and relevant for the organization, they cannot serve as useful contributors to internal learning processes.

A second blockage that is related to, but distinct from, the first is fueled by the emotional rejection of unwelcome data. A Dutch manager we interviewed reported that 'consultants came and gave us comparisons with the competition, and at first we did not believe them. We rejected their information and recommendations. After a while we decided to look into it and see whether a cost gap really existed.' In this case the managers did not reject all external data on principle (as they would have if they had been prone to the first blockage) but rather slipped into immediate denial of the problem indicated by the data provided by these consultants.

These obstacles can be overcome by drawing the clients into a more central role during knowledge acquisition. The more consultants can activate their clients in the process of knowledge acquisition, the more useful and acceptable the information will be perceived to be in the organization. One can activate members of the client organization by involving them, for example, in external benchmarking exercises in scenario development (see Galer and van der Heijden, Ch. 38 in this volume). Other techniques include coaching managers in organizational inquiry and in action learning sets (e.g. Friedman, Lipshitz, and Overmeer, Ch. 34 in this volume; Mumford 1995; Reason 1997; Senge 1990).

Internal Knowledge Acquisition

The familiar specter of 'armies of young MBAs [who] . . . fan out throughout the company, carrying clipboards and laptops' (Mumford and Hendricks 1996: 24) is a diagnostic service the client expects to pay for. The learning function it can fulfill for the organization may be far more significant than the formal role assigned to the young consultants. In the course of collecting data in the organizations, consultants tap into knowledge and experience that otherwise tend to remain unrecognized in the members at all levels. The consultants thereby activate internal knowledge. For example, Jim Down, a partner at Mercer Management Consulting, tells his clients 'we know that you have already dreamed up the best ways to improve your business. But if you're like every other company, those great ideas are probably not being acted upon' (Lieber 1996: 75). It is therefore not the consultants' external knowledge but rather the internal knowledge that has center stage. Thinking that has been going on among organizational members who do not have direct access to top management is brought to the surface and legitimated as useful and relevant by consultants who facilitate the acquisition of this internal knowledge.

Information Interpretation and Diffusion

In organizational learning the crucial step between the acquisition and application of knowledge is to interpret that knowledge and adapt it to the needs of the organization. As Levinson (1991: 58) pointed out, the mere communication of the consultants' knowledge is not sufficient justification for the statement that learning has occurred. The knowledge imported from external sources, whether it be the 'best practices' from other companies or complex concepts from academic theories, needs to be translated, integrated, and anchored within the organization. This process of translating external ideas so that they make sense in a new context requires active cooperation between consultants and clients (von Alemann and Vogel 1996; see also Czarniawska, Ch. 5 in this volume).

The danger is great, however, that new knowledge will be treated in an additive fashion, without regard for how it contradicts existing practices in the organization, or it might not be processed at all. Several writers call attention to the function of consultants as external agents for challenging the organization's existing cognitive order and traditional views to which members are acculturated (Staute 1996: 24). Consultants can 'state the obvious, ask foolish questions, and doubt—all of which helps organizational members get outside of themselves' (Smircich and Stubbart 1985: 731). They are seen as 'quite useful in helping to reframe managerial perspectives regarding the external environment' (Ginsberg and Abrahamson 1991: 181).

The process of interpreting information and making sense of it prepares the ground for agreement on ways of dealing with whatever problems have been identified. The difficulty that consultants must manage with their clients in this phase is that many clients, when faced with uncertainty and complexity, are more likely to want quick solutions than circumspection. It is precisely in such situations that consultants need to stimulate their clients to open up to unfamiliar ways of tackling the problems.

An obstacle to organizational learning during this phase can stem from the positioning of the consultant as the dominant figure and expert interpreter working in the interests of top management. If the consultant is not seen to be helping the members understand their organization, they are likely to have an interest in impeding the consultant's work. A German manager reported to us that 'people tend to be proud that the consultant didn't find out how they hid the lack of efficiency. "What can I do in order to make the consultants shut up?" All sorts of games.' This kind of response is also to be expected when the consultants are seen to be acting in the interests of one group in the organization at the expense of other groups. 'Information is distorted and efforts toward change are often undermined by implicit and unrecognized forces that emerge in the course of an intervention' (Krantz and Gilmore 1991: 307). Clearly, if consultants cannot break through such barriers to achieving a solid analysis of the problem, they cannot contribute much to organizational learning.

A key factor that emerges as a precondition for consultants to support learning is trust in the relationship with members of the client organization. Whereas trust between members within an organization is closely linked to their perceived level of integration within the organization (Kieser, Beck, and Tainio, Ch. 27 in this volume), the trust placed in consultants is endangered if they are seen as too integrated or too closely allied to particular interests within the organization. Probably the most common blockage to organizational learning with which consultants have tended to collude is the focus on working with a small elite group (Staehle 1994: 864). Managers too often assume that this group can learn for the organization, rather than regarding elites as being responsible for creating learning environments in which the broad membership can learn (Sadler, Ch. 18 in this volume). There are few examples of consultants facilitating broad-based learning processes that enjoy wide participation of the organizational membership (for exceptions, see Dierkes, Marz, and Teele, Ch. 12; Hedberg and Wolff, Ch. 24; and Krebsbach-Gnath, Ch. 40 in this volume).

Equally dangerous for trust-building, however, is a position so far outside the organization that the consultant is perceived to be disinterested or pursuing self-interested goals at the expense of the client. Clients and consultants need to establish an appreciation of each other's interests and values as a basis for a trusting relationship. In our work as international consultants, we have experienced various approaches, ranging from the direct approach used by Finnish managers to the indirect exploration of common values engaged in by French managers over long meals (see Trompenaars and Hampden-Turner 1997 for a discussion of different cultural strategies in trust-building). Appropriate marginality for the skilled consultant therefore means attaining a position of multipartisanship, whereby trust is based on the ability to communicate to different groups in the client organization that their interests and values are understood and taken seriously.

Translation into Action

The issue of the centrality and marginality of consultants in the implementation phase is a particular source of tension. Traditionally, consultants have been seen as the people who 'produce theories and methods that promise to solve problems' (Shapiro 1996: 176, our translation), but they have not usually been involved in the application of their recommendations. As a senior manager in Audi noted, it was evident from the report they produced that 'the authors would not be responsible for the implementation' (Kurbjuweit 1996: 10, our translation). Even in cases where consultants had been positioned in the center rather than on the margin for the other phases of organizational learning, there has been general agreement that the responsibility for action lies squarely with the client by the phase of implementation. In recent years, however, consultants have come to participate more frequently in the implementation phase (Ittermann and Sperling 1998: 19–40). In some cases consultants have even become 'interim managers' (Wimmer 1991: 63–5).

This shift is largely due to problems that emerged because the role in which consultants had been positioned during the implementation phase was not even marginal—they were absent altogether, and their analyses and recommendations turned out to be too theoretical to implement. The negative cliché has been that consultants fly in, make an analysis, and afterwards tell people what to do. Axel Leeb, Partner in Boston Consulting Group in Munich, has explained the implications of the current shift for his company: 'BCG used to be a pure ideas factory and produced highflying plans for the CEO. Since the middle of the 1980s, we have emphasized the implementation of our projects' (Bierach 1996a: 164, our translation). The close involvement of consultants in the implementation process seems to improve the results of their work with organizations. Studying degrees of innovativeness in a number of policy areas in companies, for example, Beer, Eisenstat, and Spector (1990) found that companies on the leading edge of innovations commonly had a higher level of active consultancy participation in the implementation phase than did companies they labeled as 'lagging' (p. 167).

There are marginal ways in which consultants can support organizational learning processes through catalytic roles during the implementation phase. Consultants can enable change to happen in the organization because they come into the company under different rules. They are not bound by the hierarchical structures or cultural taboos that limit the scope of action experienced by members of the organization. 'We are good catalyzers', summarized Herbert Henzler, Chairman of McKinsey Germany (Kurbjuweit 1996: 9, our translation). In a similar vein, the head of central controlling in the German multinational company BASF believes that consultants can be useful change agents because they are 'effective communicators, who can overcome barriers in the company' (Bierach 1996a: 163, our translation). In addition, their contribution may lie in the pressure they create for action. As one observer comments, 'maybe the value of consultants is the speeding up of agreement to act and the pressure to implement decisions' (Staute 1996: 30, our translation).

There are, however, also ways that consultants can impede organizational learning in the implementation phase. These pitfalls are due to the consultants, the clients, and the organizational situation.

Inappropriate Behavior by Consultants

The ability of consultants to contribute to organizational learning during the implementation phase can be torpedoed by a lack of interpersonal skills and credibility. Such skills are particularly needed, considering that 'consultants embody the uncertainty that change brings, and this may cause some skepticism or outright hostility' (Lieber 1996: 75). Problems can emerge in this domain because consulting companies tend to send in young people to do the legwork in projects. 'When the consultants are young and inexperienced, insult can be added to injury' (Mumford and Hendricks 1996: 26). Age and level of experience are important in being credible and effective change agents, but arrogance and insensitivity are features that can also characterize older consultants. 'I've had to kick individual consultants out who were brutalizing my people, ones who didn't realize that they shouldn't be critical or were talking over the heads of my employees' reported a manager of Kaiser Permanente (Lieber 1996: 75). All the knowledge that consultants can bring to an organization is useless if their behavior does not support learning.

Inappropriate Behavior by Clients

Companies have found that blaming the consultant is a way of relieving tension and deflecting anger from other internal actors when problems arise in a process (Shapiro 1996: 176). As the CEO of a German corporation explained, 'the consultants did not need to tell him how to restructure his company. He knew that himself. But with the external report from the consultants, which recommended cutting several thousand jobs, he had a lightning rod to which to direct the anger of the employees' (Kurbjuweit 1996: 10, our translation; for other examples, see Behrens and Bierach 1996: 138). Using the consultant as a lightning rod may be a useful technique to manage anger and frustration, but it can also become a barrier to learning. If all the problems of a process are blamed on the consultants, then members of the organization might assume that getting rid of the consultants will solve the problem. The actual problems inherent in the organization will most probably not be grappled with if failure is 'outsourced' to the consultants. The extent to which consultants can help their clients face up to problems and learn from failures indicates how successfully they can contribute to organizational learning processes.

Inappropriate Organizational Assignments

The increased involvement of consultants in the implementation phase has resulted not only from the experience that this role shift improves the quality of the consultants' service but also from the fact that downsizing and lean management have significantly reduced the number of people available to implement projects in organizations. 'The downsizing of middle management means that companies use consultants to staff one-off projects, where previously they could rely on their own pool of talent' (Jackson 1996: 8).

The raised profile of consultants during the implementation phase has several negative implications for organizational learning. It points to a questionable trend toward management's abdication of responsibility for running the company (Krantz and Gilmore 1991: 312). It is alarming that the *Financial Times* ('Gurus under Fire' 1999) has found it necessary to admonish managers to remember that 'consultants . . . should be treated as an adjunct to management and not, as is too often the case, a substitute for it' (p. 11). Another drawback of the trend toward involving consultants in the implementation phase of interventions is that it blurs the distinction between the perspectives of consultants as outsiders and the perspectives of organizational members as insiders. This obfuscation could compromise the future usefulness of consultants as a source of 'objective' perspectives for organizational learning processes of reframing and questioning internal mindsets. The costs of relying too much on consultants during the implementation phase become especially apparent in the storage stage of organizational learning.

Storage in Organizational Memory

Knowledge and experience with new processes need to be stored in the organization's memory. The contribution of consultants has tended to be limited to storage in the form of reports and new policies or systems that grow out of consultancy interventions. As a way to store knowledge and experience, reports are potentially far less effective than coherent policies and systems that are accepted by the members of the organization (Kieser, Beck, and Tainio, Ch. 27 in this volume).

There are, however, several ways in which consultants can negatively affect organizational memory. First, not all learning can be stored in reports and procedures, so the more central the role of external consultants is during an intervention, the more likely it is that much of the experiential knowledge they gained will be lost to the organization when they leave at the end of their assignment. This risk grows with the current trend toward increased involvement of consultants during the implementation phase. Second, a valuable component of organizational memory may be lost through layoffs due to restructuring or downsizing exercises recommended by consultants without regard for the wealth of tacit organizational knowledge held by the employees (as individuals and as 'communities of practice'). (Sometimes, of course, a conscious choice is made to 'lose' memories of old practices so that new ways of thinking and behaving can take hold in the organization, see Berthoin Antal 1997*b*.)

Conclusions for Practitioners

This review shows that consultants can contribute to organizational learning in a number of significant ways. It is the commitment to the adoption of 'marginal' roles by consultants and 'central' roles by clients throughout the process that maximizes each's contribution to organizational learning. The consultant cannot learn 'for' the client, both of them must play their own roles. 'Unless the client collaborates in the assignment, he is unlikely to learn from it. Learning does not occur by defining terms of reference and accepting or rejecting a final report, but by joint work at all stages of the assignment, starting with problem definition and diagnosis, and ending with the implementation and assessment of the results actually obtained' (Kubr 1996: 42).

There are, however, a number of factors that conspire to pull and push the consultant into the center of the process and thereby marginalize the actors in the organization itself. The client can pull the consultant from the margin. When organizations are faced with problems that have to be resolved under pressure, the tendency is to 'get someone to fix it quickly', and the trend toward leaner organizations has increased the likelihood that the 'fixer' will be

sought outside, particularly when new skills are required. In addition to the pull that results from scarce in-house human resources, there are political and psychological factors that lead members of an organization to shift responsibility to the consultant. Carver Johnson, a Sears systems executive, offers fellow managers useful advice against falling into a number of traps.

Using consultants as a rubber stamp for your decisions is generally a waste of time. If your management is sound and well-versed in the issues at hand, you rarely need to hire someone to validate a strategy everyone agrees is correct. Consultants should not act as corporate referees, either. If two competing factions are fighting over strategy, you're asking for trouble by hiring a consultant to throw up a jump ball. If you're calling in consultants to second-guess your people, that's not smart either. If your people are inefficient, you fix that by getting better people, not by trying to circumvent the problem with consultants. (Lieber 1996: 74)

There are also undoubtedly 'push' factors that lead consultants to propel themselves onto center stage. The need to market themselves as indispensable emanates from their primary interest in their own survival and growth as a business. A certain amount of such behavior is exhibited by consultants who hope to maintain a demand for their support by feeding a sense of dependence on the part of their clients (Kieser 1998). Another 'push' factor is more psychological than economic. Studies suggest that there is a 'tendency for consultants to overfunction. . . . The overfunction consultant often takes on a kind of executive staff role that unintentionally reinforces fantasies of internal incompetence and efforts to sidestep responsibility for difficult actions' (Krantz and Gilmore 1991: 326). However, not only is such dependence-generating behavior contrary to the ethic of 'help for self-help' that underlies the work of organizational development consultants (Block 1981; Thom 1992), it is generally recognized to be a short-term business strategy. Consultants find that they are more likely to remain credible partners for future business if they do not overextend their stay in any one project.

These push and pull factors that shift consultants to the center and marginalize the role of the client not only diminish the potentially very positive contributions that consultants can make to organizational learning. If consultants play too central a role, they can also create lasting blockages to learning. It is therefore in the interest of both partners to be acutely aware of the roles they are taking and thereby giving each other.

Implications for Organizational Learning Theories

This exploration of the roles that consultants can play in organizational learning processes has several implications for theory-building. First, the episodic nature of consulting interventions lends itself well to a detailed examination of phase models of organizational learning. It reveals that significant phases, namely, the development of a willingness to learn and the phase of problem definition, are overlooked in current models that start with knowledge acquisition. The exploration of consultancy interventions in organizational learning processes highlights the limitations of phase models and the need to understand organizational learning as being embedded in ongoing processes.

It is evident that organizational learning does not occur only when consultants enter and that it does not stop when they leave. Nevertheless, theories of organizational learning in which a constant and unplannable process is postulated rather than a phase model may be based on overly optimistic assumptions that members of organizations are always highly willing and able to learn. There is a definite need for events or people as catalysts or triggers of organizational learning, and their interventions can be studied as episodes in a continual dynamic of organizational learning. It would therefore seem fruitful to combine these two currently competing streams of theory-building.

Second, the analysis of the roles of consultants and their clients underlying the importance of studying organizational learning as an interpersonal process and of having the field of observation include actors who are not permanent members of the organization. The dynamics discussed in this chapter point to the fact that there are numerous roles in learning processes and that those played by the members of the organization shape, and are shaped by, the counterpart roles played by external actors, such as consultants. This role-based analysis facilitates a differential exploration of hitherto largely ignored dimensions of interaction: emotions, power, and trust. Future research could explore other sets of dynamics of 'taking' and 'making' roles, both within the organization and with other actors based outside the organization. Such studies could examine the transferability of the concepts of 'marginality' and 'centrality' in other learning relationships and could generate additional concepts to characterize the dynamics that promote or obstruct processes of organizational learning.

References

Anonymous (1996). 'Confessions of an Ex-consultant'. *Fortune*, 134/7, 14 October: 69–72.

Argyris, C. (1991). 'Teaching Smart People How to Learn'. *Harvard Business Review*, 69/3: 99–109.

——(1993). *Knowledge for Action: A Guide to Overcoming Barriers to Organizational Change*. San Francisco: Jossey-Bass.

——and Schön, D. A. (1978). *Organizational Learning: A Theory of Action Perspective*. Reading, Mass.: Addison-Wesley.

Beer, M., Eisenstat, R., and Spector, B. (1990). *The Critical Path to Corporate Renewal*. Boston: Harvard Business School Press.

Behrens, B. and Bierach, B. (1996). 'McKinsey: Kehrwoche in Stuttgart'. *Wirtschaftswoche*, 43, 17 October: 138.

Benders, J., van den Berg, R.-J., and van Bijsterveld, M. (1998). 'Hitchhiking on a Hype: Dutch Consultants Engineer Re-engineering'. *Journal of Organizational Change Management*, 11/3: 201–15.

Berthoin Antal, A. (1997*a*). *Organizational Learning Processes in Downsizing*. Discussion paper No. FS II 97–113, Wissenschaftszentrum Berlin für Sozialforschung.

—— (1997*b*). 'Organisationslernen in Restrukturierungsprozessen'. WZB Mitteilungen, No. 78: 22–5.

—— (1998). 'Die Dynamik der Theoriebildungsprozesse zum Organisationslernen', in H. Albach, M. Dierkes, A. Berthoin Antal, and K. Vaillant (eds.), *Organisationslernen—institutionelle und kulturelle Dimensionen. WZB Jahrbuch 1998*. Berlin: edition sigma, 31–52.

—— Dierkes, M., and Hähner, K. (1997). 'Business Perception of Contextual Changes: Sources and Impediments to Organizational Learning'. *Business and Society*, 36: 387–407.

—— and Lange, A. (1997). 'The Live Case Method for Management Development'. *Forum*, 97/3: 43–6.

Bierach, B. (1996*a*). 'Der leise Riese'. *Wirtschaftswoche,* 10, 29 February: 162–5.

—— (1996*b*). 'Von der Stange'. *Wirtschaftswoche*, 47, 14 November: 130–2.

Block, P. (1981). *Flawless Consulting*. San Francisco: Jossey Bass-Pfeiffer.

Brown, J. S. and Duguid, P. (1991). 'Organizational Learning and Communities of Practice: Toward a Unified View of Working, Learning, and Innovation'. *Organization Science*, 2: 40–57.

Burgmaier, S. and Reischauer, C. (1998). 'Unbequeme Fragen'. *Wirtschaftswoche*, 17, 16 April: 164–6.

Byrne, J. (1996). 'Strategic Planning'. *Business Week*, 2 September: 46–9.

Carley, K. (1996). 'Organizational Learning and Personnel Turnover', in M. P. Cohen and L. S. Sproull (eds.), *Organizational Learning*. Thousand Oaks, Calif.: Sage, 230–66.

Carqueville, P. (1991). 'Rollentheoretische Analyse der Berater-/Klientenbeziehung', in M. Hofmann (ed.), *Theorie und Praxis der Unternehmensberatung: Bestandsaufnahme und Entwicklungsperspektiven*. Heidelberg: Physica, 247– 80.

Choo, C. W. (1998). *The Knowing Organization: How Organizations Use Information to Construct Meaning, Create Knowledge, and Make Decisions*. New York: Oxford University Press.

Cook, S. D. N. and Yanow, D. (1993). 'Culture and Organizational Learning'. *Journal of Management Inquiry*, 2: 373–90.

Coopey, J. (1995). 'The Learning Organization: Power, Politics, and Ideology'. *Management Learning*, 26: 193–214.

Daft, R. L. and Weick, K. E. (1984). 'Toward a Model of Organizations as Interpretation Systems'. *Academy of Management Review*, 9: 284–95.

Delany, E. (1994). *The Role and Effectiveness of Strategy Consultants*. Working paper, Henley Management College, Henley-on-Thames, UK.

DiBella, A. J., Nevis, E. C., and Gould, J. M. (1996). 'Understanding Organizational Learning Capability'. *Journal of Management Studies*, 33: 361–79.

Fincham, R. (1999). 'The Consultant–Client Relationship: Critical Perspectives on the Management of Organizational Change'. *Journal of Management Studies*, 36: 335–51.

Fleischmann, P. (1984). *Prozessorientierte Beratung im strategischen Management*. Unpublished doctoral dissertation, University of Munich.

French, W. L. and Bell, C. H., Jr. (1999). *Organization Development* (6th edn). Upper Saddle River, NJ: Prentice Hall.

Gattiker, U. and Larwood, L. (1985). 'Why Do Clients Employ Management Consultants?' *Consultation*, 4/1: 119–29.

Ginsberg, A. and Abrahamson, E. (1991). 'Champions of Change and Strategic Shifts: The Role of Internal and External Change Advocates'. *Journal of Management Studies*, 28: 173–90.

Gloger, A. (1996). 'Bis an die Basis'. *Wirtschaftswoche*, 42, 10 October: 233–7.

'Gurus under Fire' (1999). *Financial Times*, 19 August: 11.

Habgood, A. J. (1986). 'Die selbstentdeckte Strategie'. *Perspektiven*, No. 68 (Company brochure), The Boston Consulting Group, Munich.

Hoffmann, W. and Hlawacek, S. (1991). 'Beratungsprozesse und -erfolge in mittelständischen Unternehmen', in M. Hofmann (ed.), *Theorie und Praxis der Unternehmensberatung: Bestandsaufnahme und Entwicklungsperspektiven*. Heidelberg: Physica, 403–36.

Hofmann, J. (1995). 'Implicit Theories in Policy Discourse: An Inquiry into the Interpretations of Reality in German Technology Policy'. *Policy Sciences*, 28: 127–48.

Huber, G. P. (1991). 'Organizational Learning: The Contributing Processes and the Literatures'. *Organization Science*, 2: 88–115.

Ibielski, D. and Küster, N. (1993). *Handbuch der Unternehmensberatung* (24th edn). Berlin: Schmidt.

Ittermann, P. and Sperling, H.-J. (1998). 'Unternehmensberatung in Deutschland: Ein Überblick', in U. Pekruhl (ed.), *Unternehmensberatung: Profil und Perspektiven einer Branche*. Gelsenkirchen: Institut Arbeit und Technik, 19–40.

Jackson, T. (1996). 'Well Fed and Growing Fast'. *Financial Times*, 16 December: 8.

Kieser, A. (1997). 'Myth and Rhetoric in Management Fashion'. *Organization*, 4: 49–74.

—— (1998). 'Unternehmensberater—Händler in Problemen, Praktiken und Sinn', in H. Glaser, A. von Werder, and E. F. Schroeder (eds.), *Organisationsgestaltung in sich wandelnden Märkten*. Wiesbaden: Gabler, 192–225.

Kim, D. H. (1993). 'The Link between Individual and Organizational Learning'. *Sloan Management Review*, 35/1: 37–50.

Krantz, J. and Gilmore, T. N. (1991). 'Understanding the Dynamics between Consulting Teams and Client Systems', in M. Kets de Vries (ed.), *Organizations on the Couch*. San Francisco: Jossey-Bass, 307–30.

Krebsbach-Gnath, C. (1996). *Organisationslernen: Theorie und Praxis der Veränderung*. Wiesbaden: Deutscher Universitäts-Verlag.

Kubr, M. (ed.) (1996). *Management Consulting: A Guide to the Profession* (3rd edn). Geneva: International Labour Office.

Kurbjuweit, D. (1996). 'Die Propheten der Effizienz'. *Die Zeit*, 1 January: 10.

Lancaster, K. L. (ed.) (1995). 'The Learning Organization: Making It Happen, Making It Work'. *Prism* (Entire issue), Third Quarter: Arthur D. Little Consultants.

Lee, C. R. (1996). 'Milestones on a Journey Not Yet Completed'. *Strategy and Business* [Newsletter], 5, Fourth Quarter: 58–67. (Published by Booz·Allen & Hamilton Consultants)

Levinson, H. (1991). 'Diagnosing Organizations Systematically', in M. Kets de Vries (ed.), *Organizations on the Couch*. San Francisco: Jossey-Bass, 45–68.

Lieber, R. B. (1996). 'Controlling Your Consultants'. *Fortune*, 134/7, 14 October: 74–5.

Lilja, K., Penn, R., and Tainio, R. (1993). *Dimensions of Consulting Knowledge: The Symbiotic Relationship of Leading Consulting and Manufacturing Firms in the Global Pulp and Paper Industry*. Paper presented at the 11th EGOS Colloquium on 'The Production and Diffusion of Managerial and Organizational Knowledge', Paris, July.

March, J. G. (1991). 'Organizational Consultants and Organizational Research'. *Journal of Applied Communication Research*, 19/1–2: 20–31.

Marriott, F. and Morrison, M. (1996). *In Search of Organizational Learning: Polishing the Signpost*. Paper presented at the Symposium on 'Organizational Learning and the Learning Organization', Lancaster University, UK, 1–3 September.

Mitroff, I. and Featheringham, T. R. (1974). 'Systematic Problem Solving and the Error of the Third Kind'. *Behavioral Science*, 19: 383–93.

Moingeon, B. and Edmondson, A. (eds.) (1996). *Organizational Learning and Competitive Advantage*. London: Sage.

Mumford, A. (1995). 'A Review of Action Learning Literature'. MCB University Press: 1–14. Available: http//www.mcb.co.uk/services/conferen/nov95/ifal/paper3.htm

Mumford, E. and Hendricks, R. (1996). 'Business Process Re-engineering RIP'. *People Management*, 2/9: 22–9.

Newstrom, J. W. and Davis, K. (1993). *Organizational Behavior: Human Behavior at Work*. New York: McGraw-Hill.

Nonaka, I. (1994). 'A Dynamic Theory of Organizational Knowledge Creation'. *Organization Science*, 5: 14–37.

——and Takeuchi, H. (1995). *The Knowledge-creating Company: How Japanese Companies Create the Dynamics of Innovation*. New York: Oxford University Press.

Pascale, R. T. (1990). *Managing on the Edge*. London: Viking.

Pederson, P. and Dickinson, J. (1995). *Benchmarking: A Best Practice for the Learning Organization*. Dallas: Price Waterhouse White Paper.

Phills, J. A. (1996). 'The Epistemology of Strategic Consulting: Generic Analytical Activities and Organizational Learning', in B. Moingeon and A. Edmondson (eds.), *Organizational Learning and Competitive Advantage*. London: Sage, 202–23.

Reason, P. (1997). 'Revisioning Inquiry for Action: A Participatory View'. Invited Address at the Academy of Management Annual Conference, Boston, 9–12 August.

Sarvary, M. (1999). 'Knowledge Management and Competition in the Consulting Industry'. *California Management Review*, 41/2: 95–107.

Schein, E. H. (1987). *Process Consultation*: Vol. 2. *Lessons for Managers and Consultants*. Reading, Mass.: Addison-Wesley.

Schitag Ernst and Young (1996). 'Business Change Implementation: Management des Wandels'. *Erfolgskonzepte* (Corporate brochure by Schitag Ernst and Young Consultancy).

Schreyögg, G. and Noss, C. (1995). 'Organisatorischer Wandel: Von der Organisationsentwicklung zur lernenden Organisation'. *Die Betriebswirtschaft*, 55: 169–85.

Senge, P. M. (1990). *The Fifth Discipline: The Art and Practice of the Learning Organization*. New York: Doubleday Currency.

Shapiro, E. (1995). *Fad Surfing in the Boardroom*. Reading, Mass.: Addison-Wesley.

——(1996). Interview. *Manager Magazine*, 26/12: 170–6.

Smircich, L. and Stubbart, C. (1985). 'Strategic Management in an Enacted World'. *Academy of Management Review*, 10: 724–36.

Staehle, W. H. (1994). *Management* (7th edn). Munich: Vahlen.

Staute, J. (1996). *Der Consulting Report* (2nd edn). Frankfurt am Main: Campus.

Steyrer, J. (1991). 'Unternehmensberatung: Stand der deutschsprachigen Theoriebildung und empirischen Forschung', in M. Hofmann (ed.), *Theorie und Praxis der Unternehmensberatung: Bestandsaufnahme und Entwicklungsperspektiven*. Heidelberg: Physica, 1–44.

Strasser, H. (1993). *Unternehmensberatung aus Sicht der Kunden: Eine resultatorientierte Gestaltung der Beratungsbeziehung und des Beratungsprozesses*. Zürich: Schulthess.

Thom, N. (1992). 'Organisationsentwicklung', in F. Czaika, S. Gagsch, and L. Theursen (eds.), *Handbuch der Organisation*. Stuttgart: Poeschel, 1478–91.

Trompenaars, F. and Hampden-Turner, C. (1997). *Riding the Waves of Culture* (2nd edn). London: Nicholas Brealey.

Turner, J. R. (1995). *The Commercial Project Manager*. London: McGraw-Hill.

Virany, B., Tushman, M. L., and Romanelli, E. (1996). 'Executive Succession and Organization Outcomes in Turbulent Environments: An Organization Learning Approach', in M. D. Cohen and L. S. Sproull (eds.), *Organizational Learning*. Thousand Oaks, Calif.: Sage, 302–29.

von Alemann, H. and Vogel, A. (eds.) (1996). *Soziologische Beratung: Praxisfelder und Perspektiven: IX Tagung für angewandte Soziologie*. Opladen: Leske + Buderich.

von Oetinger, B. (1994). 'Organisation neu andenken: Bausteine einer lernenden Organisation'. *Industrie und Handelskammer Report*, Siemens AG, 2 April.

Voss, M. (1999). 'Die Besserwisser'. *Capital*, 9: 64–8.

Wimmer, R. (1991). 'Organisationsberatung', in M. Hofmann (ed.), *Theorie und Praxis der Unternehmensberatung: Bestandsaufnahme und Entwicklungsperspektiven*. Heidelberg: Physica, 45–136.

PART V

PROCESSES OF ORGANIZATIONAL LEARNING AND KNOWLEDGE CREATION

Introduction

To analyze and describe the diverse processes involved in organizational learning and knowledge creation, the authors of the chapters in this section draw on widely differing concepts. Whereas some of the contributors understand learning processes in terms of a linear sequence, others express doubt about the possibility and advantage of conceptualizing learning processes in this way. Rather, these skeptics focus on uncovering the informal, interactive behavioral dimensions of these processes, the role of implicit knowledge, the media, power, conflict, and rules. To enhance the explanatory power of these aspects some authors link different conceptions of organizational learning and argue that the commensurability of contending theories depends on the particular learning situation under study.

Nonaka, Toyama, and Byosière provide an overview and detailed description of the theory of knowledge creation. Drawing on pragmatist philosophical tradition and Eastern philosophy, the authors emphasize the contextual dependency of knowledge and the unity of cognition and action. Furthermore, departing from the traditional view of an organization as a passive and static information-processing machine, they take a dynamic view of an organization as an entity that creates and utilizes knowledge continuously and dynamically. To Nonaka *et al.* an organization is not the sum of individual learning; it can learn and create knowledge through interactions among individuals. The authors view an organization as a collection of various *ba*, that is, of spaces where such interactions take place. Using examples from Japanese companies, Nonaka *et al.* postulate the knowledge-creating process and the role of the leadership in fostering and shaping the process. They especially stress the role of middle managers in bridging the skills of frontline workers and the vision of top management. This view of knowledge and learning helps fill many of the gaps left by conventional organizational learning theories and has been adopted by many scholars and practitioners in the field.

The role of communication media in organizational learning has been given much attention because the potential to increase access to information is expected to improve corporate performance. Büchel and Raub's review of the literature on communication media and organization centers on the inherent features of different forms of media. The authors reject technocentric views, which emphasize communication technology as a determinant of organizational success. Instead, they propose the application of media choice theory for identifying the most crucial dimensions to consider when selecting the media to be used in processes of organizational learning. Key concepts of this theory are media richness, media scope, and media perception. The authors attempt to identify how the learning sequence is shaped by the media, as theorized in phase models of organizational learning. They suggest that an organization's context, culture, and structure play an important role in determining the effects of media. Building on Part IV's discussion of the factors and conditions that shape organizational learning, Büchel and Raub go a step further by linking factors and conditions to ways in which media can process information to communicate and promote learning.

In order to gain a full understanding of how knowledge and learning processes are conceptualized and communicated within organizations, it is important to describe the interplay between organizing, learning, and strategizing. In a comprehensive review of literature linking organizational learning and strategy formulation, Hedberg and Wolff suggest it is in interactive processes that knowledge and strategies are 'discovered' and made sense of, often retrospectively. Examining the learning cycle, the authors explore not only the programming of behaviors but also the barriers encountered along the way. When organizations have difficulty unlearning and relearning, they enter a state that the authors label as organizational inertia. The authors attribute this problem to incomplete learning cycles and a time lag between organizing knowledge, strategizing, and learning. They show how organizations strive to find a balance between information and opportunities for learning; between strategy, organizing, and performance; between planning and experimentation; and between environmental determinism and choice in shaping outcomes. They argue that leaders need to be both constructors and prospectors of knowledge because organizations, by exploiting learning and stretching their capabilities, can significantly increase their competitiveness and security in turbulent environments.

The exercise of power as vested in organizational hierarchy has generally been treated as legitimate, functional, and nonproblematic in traditional organizational behavior and organizational studies. In the chapter on 'Power and Politics in Organizations: Public and Private Sector Comparisons', LaPalombara compares the relationship between power and learning in the public sphere to that in the private sphere in order to examine the implications for the overall field of organizational learning. In this context he discusses different types of power distribution in the public sector and explores the structures of pluralism, monocratic systems, and federalism to examine what characteristics distinguish organizations in this sector from those in the private sector. He recognizes that private-sector organizations are under enormous pressure to engage in learning and that their learning processes are influenced by power and politics just as the learning processes of public-sector organizations are. Leaders often engage in power struggles and disagree over strategies and budgets, but LaPalombara argues that organizational conflict is not a zero-sum game and that constructive conflicts can actually trigger learning. Consequently, he suggests that organizations need to find the right leader, someone who will exploit conflicts as a learning strategy.

In general, studies on organizational behavior and research on organizational learning tend to emphasize the need for consensus and order rather than for conflict and domination, reflecting the influence of functionalism or rational–utilitarian paradigms. The chapter by Rothman and Friedman represents a different voice, for they advocate cross-fertilization between organizational learning theory and newer approaches to conflict resolution. Drawing insights from literature in the field of international relations, functional sociology, and conflict management, the authors delineate conflicts in terms of three categories: resource-, interest-, and identity-based conflicts. The authors propose that conflict should not be seen as an obstacle to learning but rather as an essential part of the learning process itself. Deep conflicts in organizations are rooted, they say, more in concerns about identity than in struggles over resource. Hence, Rothman and Friedman consider the framing of identity-based conflicts to be especially relevant to organizational learning. It promotes inquiry into deep concerns, interests, needs, and perceptions of individuals and groups within organizations. Rather than eradicating or suppressing conflicts, organizations might, as the authors suggest, wish to use a transformational learning approach to engage in and manage identity-based conflicts.

In the final contribution to this part, Kieser, Beck, and Tainio discuss the relationship between rules and organizational learning. Like the authors of Chapters 22 through 26, Kieser *et al.* realize that people as well as organizations operate with limited rationality, that rules are imposed because they bring an element of stability by reducing complexity and increasing the efficiency and legitimacy of organizations. In the view of the authors, rules enable members of an organization to perform consistently under changing conditions. These rules are derived from a consensus on ideas that individuals and groups have about the types of behavior that are appropriate under certain conditions. The cumulation of experience with creating rules is what the authors call organizational learning. In general, they view organizational learning as an evolutionary process in which organizations learn from the experience of individuals or from other organizations. More specifically, rule-based organizational learning is the process whereby rules are gradually replaced in a trial-and-error process. The formalized rules that emerge serve as storage places of organizational knowledge. However, the relationship between rules and learning is not always clear or easily managed. As Kieser *et al.* point out, rules can influence organizational learning both positively and negatively because the behavior of individuals depends on their perception and reaction to the rules themselves. Following this behavioral approach to organizational learning, the authors argue that the main challenge for organizations is to monitor and alter rule systems to fit changing contexts and environments.

The common denominator of the six chapters presented in this part is the detailed description of the multiple processes that have an impact on organizational learning. The creation of knowledge, the means of communicating, and the issues of power, conflict, and rules represent three important aspects of organizational learning. The authors do not use these concepts to provide a method or model for organizations to follow. Instead, they suggest the need for organizations to be flexible and open in their learning strategies. This approach is partly a response to the intangible and tacit nature of knowledge and organizational learning, but it is also a reaction to the fluctuations of today's environment. The authors in this part recognize that knowledge creation and learning can occur under diverse conditions and settings and that organizations must therefore be prepared to exploit whatever opportunities for them arise.

A Theory of Organizational Knowledge Creation: Understanding the Dynamic Process of Creating Knowledge

Ikujiro Nonaka, Ryoko Toyama, and Philippe Byosière

In recent years many researchers have argued that knowledge and the capability to create and utilize it are the most important sources of a firm's sustainable competitive advantage (Cyert, Kumar, and Williams 1993; Drucker 1993; Nonaka 1990, 1991, 1994; Nonaka and Takeuchi 1995; Quinn 1992; Sveiby 1997; Teece, Pisano, and Shuen 1997; Toffler 1990; Winter 1987). In a world where markets, products, technologies, competitors, regulations, and even entire societies change very rapidly, continuous innovation and knowledge that enables such innovation have become important sources of sustainable competitive advantage. Quinn (1992) observed that a company's competitive advantage increasingly depends on such knowledge-based intangibles as technological know-how and an in-depth understanding of customers. Drucker (1993) argued that knowledge has become the only meaningful resource in business today. Toffler (1990) claimed that knowledge is the source of the highest quality power and the key to the shifts in power that lie ahead. Knowledge accumulated through organizational learning is an important source of a firm's sustainable competitive advantage because it is nontradable and difficult to imitate (Edvinsson and Malone 1997; Grant 1996a; Nelson 1991; Prahalad and Hamel 1990). This kind of knowledge has a strong tacit dimension, is embedded in local organizational skills and routines, and is tailored to a firm's specific needs (Dierickx and Cool 1989; Henderson and Cockburn 1994; Leonard-Barton 1992, 1995).

Yet, despite all the attention that leading observers have devoted to organizational knowledge creation, and despite all the talk about intellectual capital and knowledge-based management, very few people understand how organizations create and manage knowledge. Management scholars recognize the need for new knowledge-based theory that differs 'in some fundamental way from the kinds of explicit abstract theories which have characterized both economics and organizational theory' (Spender and Grant 1996: 8).

Such a theory, however has yet to be established, partly because the theory of the organization has long been dominated by the information processing paradigm. In this paradigm, which is deeply ingrained in the traditions of Western management from Taylor (1911) to Simon (1947, 1973), the organization is viewed as an information-processing machine that takes and processes information from the environment in order to solve a problem and adapt to the environment. For example, Choo (1998) still relied on this view of the organization in his 'knowing organization' model, treating knowledge creation as a mere part of the process in which an organization processes information in order to reach rational decisions based on a given goal. The problem with this paradigm is that its view of the organization and of knowledge creation is static and passive, characteristics that preclude an adequate explanation of the dynamic process of innovation.

Although the terms 'information' and 'knowledge' are often used interchangeably, there is a clear distinction between them. Information is a flow of messages, whereas knowledge anchored in the beliefs and commitment of its holder is created by that flow of information. Information provides a new point of view for interpreting events or objects. As Bateson (1979) put it, 'information consists of differences that make a difference' (p. 5). Thus, information is a necessary medium or material for eliciting and constructing knowledge. Information affects knowledge by adding something to it or restructuring it (Machlup 1983).

When organizations innovate, they do not merely process information. Rather, they create new information and reshape the environment through interactions with their environments (Cyert and March 1963; Levinthal and Myatt 1994; March 1991). Instead of merely solving problems, organizations create and define problems, develop and apply new knowledge in order to solve these problems, and then further develop new knowledge through problem-solving activities. An organization is not a mere information-processing machine, but an entity that creates knowledge through action and interaction. An organization actively interacts with its environment, reshaping this environment and even itself through the process of knowledge creation. Hence, the most important aspect in understanding the dynamic knowledge-related capabilities of a firm is the focus on how it can continuously create new knowledge from its existing capabilities and not on the stock of knowledge, such as a particular technology, that a firm possesses at one point in time (Barney 1991; Lei, Hitt, and Bettis 1996; Nelson 1991; Teece, Pisano, and Shuen 1997; Wilkins 1989).

Organizational learning theories have long dealt with the issue of continuous change in organizations (Dodgson 1993). Organizations cope with changes in their environments and change themselves through learning. To con-

vey this concept, Senge (1990) proposed a model of what he called the 'learning organization', that is, an organization that has the capacity for both passive, adaptive learning and active, generative learning as sustainable sources of competitive advantage.

However, there are still some critical limitations in the existing studies of organizational learning. First, organizational learning theories basically lack 'the view that knowledge development constitutes learning' (Weick 1991: 122). The majority of studies in organizational learning are based on behaviorism; they focus on stimulus and response. The behaviorist paradigms treat all learning subjects as black boxes, leaving the learning processes existing therein largely unexplained. Second, most of the studies in organizational learning are still based on the paradigm of individual learning (Dodgson 1993; Weick 1991). A comprehensive view of what constitutes organizational learning has yet to be established. Third, most of the studies have failed to address not only the active and generative side of learning but also the knowledge creation that results from that learning. With few exceptions, such as Brown and Duguid (1991), Daft and Weick (1984), and Duncan and Weiss (1979), organizational learning theories have focused excessively on the passive aspect of learning, on how organizations adapt to change. Fourth, organizational learning theorists implicitly or explicitly assume that double-loop learning, which is the questioning and rebuilding of existing perspectives, interpretation frameworks, or decision-making premises (Argyris and Schön 1978), is difficult to implement and that organizations need special instruments to trigger this type of learning. However, organizations question and reconstruct existing perspectives, frameworks, or premises on a daily basis through a continuous process of knowledge creation. Creating knowledge is a continuous, self-transcending process in which one reaches beyond the boundaries of one's own existence (Jantsch 1980); it is not a special kind of learning at one point in time.

Building on this view of the organization as an entity that creates knowledge continuously, our goal in this chapter is to understand the dynamic process whereby an organization creates and manages knowledge. In the following sections we discuss the basic concepts of the knowledge-creation process in organizations, the ways in which the process is managed, and the organizational issues involved.

The Knowledge-creation Process

In our theory of knowledge-creation process, we adopt the traditional definition of knowledge as justified true belief. However, our focus is on the 'justified', rather than on the 'true' aspect of belief. In traditional Western epistemology, 'truthfulness' is the essential attribute of knowledge. It is an absolute, static, and nonhuman view of knowledge. This view, however, fails to address the relative, dynamic, and human dimensions of knowledge. As Whitehead stated, 'there are no whole truths; all truths are half-truths' (Whitehead 1954: 16). Knowledge is context-specific and relational. It depends on the situation. Knowledge is dynamic, for it is dynamically created in social

interactions between individuals both within and across organizations. Knowledge is also human and has an active and subjective nature conveyed by such terms as 'commitment' and 'belief', which are deeply rooted in individuals' value systems. Knowledge is essentially related to human action and emotion (Scherer and Tran, Ch. 16 in this volume). In this study we consider knowledge to be 'a dynamic human process of justifying personal belief toward the "truth"' (Nonaka and Takeuchi 1995: 58).

To understand how organizations create knowledge dynamically, we propose a multi-layered model of knowledge creation (Nonaka, Konno, and Toyama 1998). In this model the three layers of knowledge creation must interact with each other in order to form the knowledge spiral that creates knowledge (see Fig. 22.1). The three layers are (a) the process of knowledge creation through socialization, externalization, combination, and internalization (SECI), the knowledge-conversion processes between tacit and explicit knowledge; (b) *ba*, the platforms for knowledge creation; and (c) knowledge assets, or the inputs, outputs, and moderator of the knowledge-creation process.

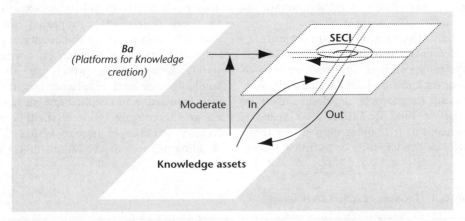

Fig. 22.1. Three layers of the knowledge-creation process, including *ba* (platforms for knowledge creation) and SECI (socialization–externalization–combination–internalization processes)

Adapted from 'Leading Knowledge Creation: A New Framework for Dynamic Knowledge Management', by I. Nonaka, N. Konno, and R. Toyama, paper presented at the Second Annual Knowledge Management Conference, Haas School of Business, University of California Berkeley, 22–24 September 1998.

The SECI Process: Four Modes of Knowledge Conversion

There are two types of knowledge: explicit knowledge and tacit knowledge. Table 22.1 summarizes the qualities of these two types of knowledge. Explicit knowledge can be expressed in formal and systematic language and can be shared in the form of data, scientific formulae, specifications, manuals, and so forth. It can be easily 'processed', transmitted, and stored. Explicit knowledge is about past events or objects 'there and then', and it is oriented to a context-free theory. It is sequentially created by digital activity. Tacit knowledge, on the other hand, is highly personal and hard to formalize. As Polayni (1966) put it, 'we can know more than we can tell' (p. 4). Subjective insights, intuitions, and hunches fall into this category of knowledge. Tacit knowledge is deeply rooted in action, procedures, routines, commitment, ideals, values, and emotions (Cohen and Bacdayan 1994; Schön 1983; Winter 1994). In addition, tacit knowledge is often 'here and now' in a specific, practical context of time and space (Hayek 1945). It entails an analog quality. It is difficult to communicate tacit knowledge to others because it is an analog process that requires a kind of simultaneous processing.

Tacit knowledge includes technical and cognitive elements. The technical elements of tacit knowledge encompass informal and hard-to-pin-down know-how, crafts, and skills. Master artisans, for example, develop a wealth of expertise 'at their fingertips' after years of experience. But it is often difficult for them to articulate the scientific or technical principles behind their knowledge. On the other hand, the cognitive elements center on what Johnson-Laird (1983) called 'mental models', through which human beings create working models of the world. Mental models, such as schemata, paradigms, perspectives, beliefs, and viewpoints, help individuals perceive and define their world by enabling them to make and manipulate analogies in their minds. It is important to note that the cognitive elements of tacit knowledge reflect an individual's images of reality (i.e. what is) and his or her visions for the future (i.e. what ought to be). As discussed later in this chapter, the articulation of tacit mental models is a key factor in creating new knowledge.

Westerners tend to view knowledge as explicit. Japanese, on the other hand, tend to regard knowledge as primarily tacit. In reality, these two types of knowledge are complementary, and both are crucial to knowledge creation. Excessive focus on explicit knowledge can easily lead to 'paralysis by analysis', whereas exaggerated valuation of tacit knowledge tends to foster overreliance on past successes. Without experiences, one has difficulty gaining understanding. And unless one goes beyond experiences, universality cannot be achieved. If one does not analytically reflect on experiences, the same things will be repeated over and over, with no increase in the quality of knowledge. By analyzing experiences, one understands their meaning, which can then be applied to the next experience. In this way, tacit knowledge and explicit knowledge interact and interchange with each other in the creative activities of human beings. Understanding this reciprocal relationship is the key

Table 22.1. Tacit and explicit knowledge

Tacit knowledge (subjective)	Explicit knowledge (objective)
Knowledge of experience (body)	Knowledge of rationality (mind)
Simultaneous knowledge (here and now)	Sequential knowledge (there and then)
Analog knowledge (practice)	Digital knowledge (theory)

to understanding the knowledge-creation process.

We call the interaction of the two types of knowledge 'knowledge conversion'. This conversion is a social process *between* individuals; it is not confined *within* an individual. Knowledge is created through interactions between individuals with different types and contents of knowledge. Through this process of social conversion, the quality and quantity of both tacit and explicit knowledge expand (Nonaka 1990, 1991, 1994; Nonaka and Takeuchi 1995).

There are four modes of knowledge conversion: (a) socialization (from tacit knowledge to tacit knowledge), (b) externalization (from tacit knowledge to explicit knowledge), (c) combination (from explicit knowledge to explicit knowledge), and (d) internalization (from explicit knowledge to tacit knowledge). Table 22.2 lists the factors that characterize the four knowledge conversion modes. We discuss each of these four modes in detail below.

Socialization

Socialization is the process of bringing together tacit knowledge through shared experiences. Because tacit knowledge is context-specific and difficult to formalize, the key to acquiring tacit knowledge is to share the same experience through joint activities. The quintessential example of socialization is traditional apprenticeship. Apprentices learn their craft not through spoken words or written textbooks but through observation and imitation of the works of their masters and through practice. Another example of socialization is the use by Japanese companies of informal meetings outside the workplace. Participants talk over meals and drinks, creating common tacit knowledge, such as a worldview, and mutual trust. Socialization also occurs outside organizational boundaries. Organizational members interact with customers or suppliers in order to share and take advantage of their tacit knowledge. Such socialization often takes place during a new product's development process.

Socialization is difficult to manage because it is the conversion of tacit knowledge. In order to promote socialization, the members first should be provided with high-quality physical experiences so that their tacit knowledge can accrue. The richness of tacit knowledge promotes the creation of knowledge, and it also becomes the motivating force for the generation of high-quality knowledge. Second, love, care, and trust must be cultivated among members so that they can transcend the individual boundaries and share tacit knowledge.

Externalization

Externalization is the process of articulating tacit knowledge as explicit knowledge. Of the four modes of knowledge conversion, externalization is the key to knowledge creation because it creates new, explicit concepts from tacit knowledge. When tacit knowledge is made explicit, knowledge becomes crystallized, at which point it can be shared by others and can be made the basis for new knowledge. Externalization comes about, for example, when a research and development (R&D) team tries to clarify the concept for a new product or when a skilled worker attempts to set down his or her embodied technical skills in a manual.

The successful conversion of tacit knowledge into explicit knowledge depends on the sequential use of metaphors, analogies, and models. Metaphor is a way of perceiving or intuitively understanding one thing by imagining it symbolically as another thing. Metaphor is an important tool for creating a network of new concepts. Using metaphor makes it possible to continually relate concepts that are far apart in one's mind, even to relate abstract concepts to concrete ones. The imbalance, inconsistency, or contradiction that is brought about by the association of two unlike concepts through metaphor often leads to the discovery of new meanings and even to the formation of a new paradigm. The contradictions inherent in a metaphor are then harmonized by analogy, which throws light on the unknown by highlighting the similarities of two different things. Analogy helps one understand the unknown through the known and bridges the gap

Table 22.2. The factors constituting the knowledge-conversion process in companies

Factor	Description
Socialization: from tacit knowledge to tacit knowledge	
Accumulation of tacit knowledge	Managers gather information from sales and production sites, share experiences with suppliers and customers, and engage in dialogue with competitors
Extrafirm collection of social information	Managers wander about outside their firms, gathering ideas for corporate strategy from daily social life, interacting with external experts, and meeting informally with competitors
Intrafirm collection of social information	Managers find new strategies and market opportunities by wandering inside the firm
Transfer of tacit knowledge	Managers create a work environment that allows peers to observe demonstrations by and the practice of master craftsmen in order to understand the expertise that their work involves
Externalization: from tacit knowledge to explicit knowledge	
	Managers facilitate creative and essential dialogue, 'abductive thinking', the use of metaphors to foster concept creation, and the inclusion of industrial designers in project teams
Combination: from explicit knowledge to explicit knowledge	
Acquisition and integration	Managers plan strategies and operations, drawing on published literature, computer simulation, and forecasting in order to assemble internal and external data
Synthesis and processing	Managers create manuals, documents, and databases for products and services and gather management figures, technical information, or both throughout the company
Dissemination	Managers plan and make presentations in order to transmit newly created concepts
Internalization: from explicit knowledge to tacit knowledge	
Personal experience, acquisition of real-world knowledge	Managers engage in 'enactive liaisoning' activities with functional department through members of cross-functional development teams, overlapping product development. Managers search for and share new values and thoughts, share and try to understand management visions and values by communicating with fellow members of the organization
Simulation and experimentation; acquisition of virtual-world knowledge	Managers facilitate prototyping and benchmarking and foster a spirit of challenge within the organization. Managers form teams as a model, conduct experiments, and share results with the entire department

Note: Adapted from Nonaka *et al.* 1994: 344. © 1994 Elsevier Science Ltd.

between an image and a logical model. Once explicit concepts are created, they can then be modeled. Models are usually generated from metaphors when new concepts are created in the business context.

Combination

Combination is the process of connecting discrete elements of explicit knowledge into a set of explicit knowledge that is more complex and systematic than any of its parts. Knowledge is exchanged and combined through such media as documents, meetings, telephone conversations, and computerized communication networks. The reconfiguration of existing knowledge through sorting, adding, combining, and categorizing can create new knowledge. When a comptroller of a company collects information from the entire organization and puts it together in a financial report, that report is new knowledge in the sense that it synthesizes information from many different sources.

Combination can also include the 'breakdown' of concepts. For example, middle managers analyze and break down a concept, such as a company vision or a new product concept, into workable action plans, such as operationalized business plans or design tasks.

In practice, combination entails three processes. First, explicit knowledge is collected from inside or outside the organization and then combined. Second, the new explicit knowledge is disseminated among the organizational members. Third, the explicit knowledge is edited or processed in the organization in order to make it more usable. Creative use of computerized communication networks and large-scale databases can facilitate this mode of knowledge conversion.

Internalization

Internalization is the process of embodying explicit knowledge as tacit knowledge. It is closely related to learning-by-doing. Through internalization, knowledge that is created is shared throughout an organization. Internalized knowledge is used to broaden, extend,

and reframe organizational members' tacit knowledge. When knowledge is internalized in individuals' tacit knowledge bases through shared mental models or technical know-how, it becomes a valuable asset. This tacit knowledge accumulated at the individual level is, in turn, shared with other individuals through socialization, and it sets off a new spiral of knowledge creation.

In practice, internalization entails two dimensions. First, explicit knowledge must be embodied in action and practice. The process of internalizing explicit knowledge actualizes concepts about or methods for strategy, tactics, innovation, or improvement. For example, training programs help trainees understand the organization and themselves. Second, explicit knowledge can be embodied through simulations or experiments in order to trigger learning-by-doing. Thus, new concepts or methods can be learned in virtual situations.

Knowledge is created through a continuous and dynamic interaction between tacit and explicit knowledge. This interaction is shaped through the SECI process, that is, through the shifts from one mode of knowledge conversion to the next: socialization, externalization, combination, and internalization. Figure 22.2 illustrates the four modes of knowledge conversion and the evolving spiral movement.

The SECI process is not confined to one ontological level, that is, the level of knowledge-creating entities (e.g. individual, group, organizational, and interorganizational actors). The organization must tap into the tacit knowledge created and accumulated at the individual level, for tacit knowledge of individuals is the basis of organizational knowledge creation. The tacit knowledge created is organizationally amplified through four modes of knowledge conversion and is crystallized at higher ontological levels. We refer to this amplification as the 'knowledge spiral'. It represents a dynamic process in which the scale of the interaction between tacit knowledge and explicit knowledge increases as it moves up the ontological levels. Starting at the individual level, the spiral ascends through expanding communities of interaction that spans sectional, departmental,

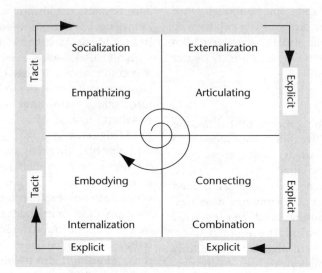

Fig. 22.2. The four modes of knowledge conversion and the evolving spiral movement

Adapted from *The Knowledge-Creating Company: How Japanese Companies Create the Dynamics of Innovation* by Ikujiro Nonaka and Hirotaka Takeuchi, copyright © 1995 by Oxford University Press, Inc. Used by permission of Oxford University Press, Inc.

divisional, and even organizational boundaries.

The process of organizational knowledge creation is not confined to the organization; it includes many interfaces with the environment as well. Not only does the environment receive the explicit knowledge created by the organization (e.g. technologies, products or services, values, and so on), it also supplies knowledge to be brought into a new cycle of organizational knowledge creation. Firms acquire knowledge from outside sources such as customers, suppliers, and competitors and utilize such knowledge to create their own knowledge (see Child, Ch. 29; and Hedberg and Holmqvist, Ch. 33 in this volume). For example, many dimensions of customer needs take the form of tacit knowledge that customers cannot articulate by themselves. A product works as a trigger to articulate such tacit knowledge. Customers give meaning to the product by purchasing, adapting, using, or not purchasing it. This mobilization of the tacit knowledge of customers will be reflected back to the organization, and a new process of organizational knowledge creation will be initiated.

Organizational knowledge creation is a never-ending process that upgrades itself continuously. A spiral emerges when the interaction between tacit and explicit knowledge is elevated dynamically from a lower ontological level to higher ontological levels. This interactive and spiral process, which we call the cross-leveling of knowledge, takes place both intra- and interorganizationally. Through the cross-leveling of knowledge, new spirals of knowledge creation are triggered. For example, when created knowledge is presented to other departments, it can lead to the internalization of this knowledge by individuals, who thus gain tacit knowledge. Thus, an entire new SECI process can begin. In short, the continued dynamism of turning ideas into words, words into forms is a main characteristic of organizational knowledge creation.

Ba: *The Foundation for Knowledge Creation*

The foundation of the SECI process described above is *ba* (roughly meaning 'place'). Based on a concept that was originally proposed by the Japanese philosopher Kitaro Nishida (1933/1970) and that was further developed by Shimizu (1995), ba is defined in this chapter as a context in which knowledge is shared, created, and utilized, in recognition of the fact that knowledge needs a context in order to exist. In the process of knowledge creation, the generation and regeneration of ba is key (Nonaka and Konno 1998; Nonaka, Konno, and Toyama 1998). Ba does not necessarily mean a physical space. It can be a physical space (e.g. an office or multilocation business space), virtual space (e.g. E-mail, teleconference), mental space (e.g. shared experiences, ideas, ideals), or any combination of these kinds of spaces. The most important aspect of ba is interaction. As discussed above, the power to create knowledge is embedded not just within an individual but also within the interactions with other individuals or with the environment. Ba is a space where such interactions take place. Knowledge held by a particular individual can be shared, recreated, and amplified when that person participates in ba.

Ba as an interaction means that ba itself is knowledge rather than a physical space containing knowledge or individuals who have knowledge. Interactions between individuals, interactions between individuals and the environment, and ba that contains such interactions are a dynamic form of knowledge. Therefore, the knowledge-creation process is also the process of creating ba, of creating a boundary of new interaction.

Ba is also conceived of as the framework in which knowledge is activated as a resource. Because knowledge is intangible, without boundaries, and dynamic, and because it cannot be stocked, the use of knowledge requires the concentration of knowledge resources in a certain space and at a certain time. For example, when knowledge is created, the personnel possessing knowledge and the knowledge base of a company are brought together at a defined space and time, that is, ba. Ba works as the platform for the concentration of the organization's knowledge assets, for it collects the applied knowledge of the area and integrates it. Thus, ba can be thought of as being built from a foundation of knowledge.

The concept of ba seems to have some similarities with the concept of a 'community of practice', where members of a community learn by participating in the community and practicing their jobs (Brown and Duguid 1991; Lave and Wenger 1991; Wenger 1998). However, there are important differences between the concepts of community of practice and ba. Whereas a community of practice is a place where members learn knowledge that is embedded in the community, ba is a place where new knowledge is created. Whereas learning occurs in any community of practice, ba needs energy in order to become an active ba where knowledge is created. Whereas the boundary of a community of practice is firmly set by the task, culture, and history of the community, the boundary of ba is set by its participants and can be changed easily. Instead of being constrained by history, ba has a here-and-now quality. It is created, it functions, and then it disappears, all as needed. Whereas the membership of a community of practice is fairly stable and whereas new members need time to learn about the community of practice and become fully participatory, the membership of ba is not fixed, for participants come and go. Finally, whereas members of a community of practice belong to the community, participants of ba relate to the ba.

Figure 22.3 illustrates the four types of ba, that is, originating ba, dialoguing ba, systemizing ba, and exercising ba. Each ba supports a particular mode of knowledge conversion and offers a platform for a specific step in the knowledge spiral process. Understanding the different characteristics of ba and how they interact with each other can facilitate successful knowledge creation.

Originating Ba

Originating ba is the place where individuals share feelings, emotions, experiences, and mental models. It is primarily in this ba that the sharing of tacit knowledge (i.e. socialization) occurs and where the knowledge-creation process begins. Knowledge creation that takes

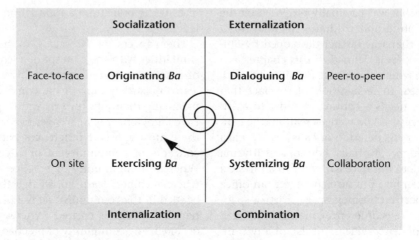

Fig. 22.3. *Ba,* the shared space for interaction

From 'Leading Knowledge Creation: A New Framework for Dynamic Knowledge Management', by I. Nonaka, N. Konno, and R. Toyama, paper presented at the Second Annual Knowledge Management Conference, Haas School of Business, University of California Berkeley, 22–24 September 1998.

place in originating *ba* is characterized by physical, face-to-face interaction, for this kind of interaction is the only way to capture the full range of physical senses and psychoemotional reactions (e.g. ease or discomfort), which are important elements in transferring tacit knowledge.

Originating *ba* is an existential space in the sense that it is the world where an individual sympathizes or empathizes with others, removing the barrier between the self and others. From originating *ba* emerges care, love, trust, and commitment, which form the basis for knowledge conversion among individuals.

Dialoguing Ba

Dialoguing *ba* is the place where individuals' mental models and skills are converted into common terms and concepts. It is where the conversion of tacit knowledge into explicit knowledge (i.e. externalization) occurs.

Dialogue and reflection are key in the knowledge creation of dialoguing *ba*. Individuals share their mental models of others through dialogues and reflect on and analyze their own mental models at the same time. To participate in a *ba* is to become involved and to transcend

one's own limited perspective or boundaries. Yet, one remains analytically rational in order to apply the acquired knowledge to one's own knowledge or perspective. Thus, in dialoguing *ba,* the individual can profit from the creativity-producing synthesis of rationality and intuition.

Dialoguing *ba* is more consciously constructed than originating *ba* is. Selecting individuals with the right mix of specific knowledge and capabilities is the key to managing knowledge creation in dialoguing *ba,* where knowledge is created through peer interactions.

Systemizing Ba

Systemizing *ba* is a virtual world rather than real time and space. It is where new systemic, explicit knowledge is created through a combination of various elements of explicit knowledge. This combination of elements of explicit knowledge is most efficiently supported in a collaborative environment utilizing information technology, such as on-line networks, groupware, documentation, and databanks. The rapid advances in information technology over the last decade have enhanced this conversion process. Because explicit knowledge can be transmitted to a large number of people relatively easily, the interaction that takes place in systemizing *ba* is group-to-group.

Exercising Ba

Exercising *ba* is the place where the conversion of explicit knowledge into tacit knowledge (i.e. internalization) is facilitated. Rather than teaching based on analysis, it is continuous learning and self-refinement through on-the-job training or peripheral and active participation that are stressed in exercising *ba* in order to communicate knowledge. Through such activities, certain patterns of action and thinking are continually stressed so that organizational members internalize them. The internalization of knowledge is constantly enhanced through the use of explicit knowledge in real life or in simulated applications. Exercising *ba* synthesizes transcendence and reflection through action, whereas dialoguing *ba* achieves this synthesis through thought. The interaction that takes place in exercising *ba* is on-site, which means that it shares both time and space.

The knowledge generated in each *ba* is eventually shared and forms the knowledge base of organizations. Moreover, *ba* exists at many ontological levels, and these levels may be connected to form a greater *ba*. Individuals form the *ba* of teams, which, in turn, form the *ba* of an organization. The market environment then becomes the *ba* for the organization. The organic interactions between these different levels of *ba* can amplify the knowledge-creation process.

These *ba* have to be strategically coherent within the organization's vision of knowledge. In this context coherence means the organic relationships in which each part interacts with each other part, not a mechanistic concentration in which the center dominates. This interactive, organic coherence of various *ba* and the individuals who participate in them has to be supported by trustful sharing of knowledge and constant exchange between all units involved

in order to create and strengthen the relationships.

Knowledge Assets

Knowledge assets, which are inputs and outputs of the knowledge-creation process, form the basis of organizational knowledge creation. Knowledge assets also influence how *ba* functions as a platform for the knowledge-creation process. We define assets as firm-specific resources that are indispensable to the creation of values for the firm, and many researchers today agree that knowledge is precisely such an asset.

However, an effective system and set of tools with which to evaluate and manage knowledge assets does not exist yet. Because of the tacit nature of knowledge, the current accounting system cannot adequately capture the value of knowledge assets. There is a need to build a system for evaluating and managing the knowledge assets of a firm more effectively.

In order to understand how knowledge assets are created, acquired, and exploited, we categorize knowledge assets into four types: experiential knowledge assets, conceptual knowledge assets, systemic knowledge assets, and routine knowledge assets (see Fig. 22.4).

Experiential Knowledge Assets

Experiential knowledge assets are the shared tacit knowledge that is built through hands-on experiences that are shared between organizational members; between organizational members and customers, suppliers, or affiliated firms, or both. Individual skills and know-how that are acquired and accumulated through experiences in a particular context at work are examples of such knowledge assets.

The tacit nature of experiential knowledge assets makes them difficult to grasp, evaluate, or trade. Because of this tacit nature, experiential knowledge assets are firm-specific, difficult-to-imitate resources that give a firm sustainable, competitive advantage. Firms must build their own knowledge assets through their own experience in their own context.

Experiential knowledge assets	Conceptual knowledge assets
Tacit knowledge shared through common experiences	Explicit knowledge articulated through images, symbols, and language
• skills and know-how of individuals • care, love, trust, and security • energy, passion, and tension	• product concepts • design • brand equity
Routine knowledge assets	**Systemic knowledge assets**
Tacit knowledge routinized and embedded in actions and practices	Systemized and packaged explicit knowledge
• know-how in daily operations • organizational routines • organizational culture	• documents, specifications, manuals • database • patents and licenses

Fig. 22.4. Four categories of knowledge assets

From 'Leading Knowledge Creation: A New Framework for Dynamic Knowledge Management', by I. Nonaka, N. Konno, and R. Toyama, paper presented at the Second Annual Knowledge Management Conference, Haas School of Business, University of California Berkeley, 22–24 September 1998.

Experiential knowledge assets are built through a process of socialization. Therefore, an important characteristic of experiential knowledge assets is that they are human. Examples of such knowledge assets are emotional knowledge, such as care, love, and trust, physical knowledge, such as facial expressions and gestures, energetic knowledge, such as the sense of existence, enthusiasm, and tension, and rhythmic knowledge, such as improvisation and entrainment.

Conceptual Knowledge Assets

Conceptual knowledge assets are explicit knowledge articulated as concepts through images, symbols, and language. Brand equity, product concepts, or product designs are examples of such knowledge assets. Because they are explicit, conceptual knowledge assets are easier to grasp than experiential knowledge assets are. Conceptual knowledge assets are built through a process of externalization. The experiential knowledge assets, which are shared tacit knowledge built through socialization, are articulated through externalization and turned into conceptual knowledge assets.

Systemic Knowledge Assets

Systemic knowledge assets are systematized and packaged explicit knowledge. Explicitly stated technologies, patents, licenses, product specifications, manuals, and documented information about customers and suppliers are examples of such knowledge assets. When academics and practitioners talk about knowledge assets, they often mean systemic knowledge assets.

A characteristic of systemic knowledge assets is that they are made explicit as documents or data through a process of combination and therefore are transferable. This transferability means that conceptual knowledge assets can be purchased or sold. It also means that they can be stolen. Protecting these assets through legal and other means is an important and urgent issue for a firm that bases its competitive advantage on this type of knowledge asset.

Routine Knowledge Assets

Routine knowledge assets are the tacit knowledge that is routinized and embedded within the actions and practices of an organization. Know-how, organizational routines, and organizational culture in carrying out the daily business of the organization are the examples of such knowledge assets. Routine knowledge assets are created and shared by the organization through a process of internalization. Through continuous exercises, certain patterns of thinking and action are reinforced and shared among organizational members. Hence, routine knowledge assets are practical knowledge. Sharing the backgrounds and 'stories' of the company also helps form routine knowledge.

Knowledge assets form the basis of the knowledge-creation process. Hence, to manage the creation and exploitation of knowledge effectively, a company needs to 'map' its stocks of knowledge assets (Reinhardt, Bornemann, Pawlowsky, and Schneider, Ch. 36 in this volume). However, cataloging existing knowledge is not enough. It is important to understand that knowledge assets are dynamic, for new knowledge assets can be created from existing ones. Knowledge assets are both inputs and outputs of an organization's knowledge-creation activities. For example, experiential knowledge about customers' needs, through socialization and externalization, may become explicit conceptual knowledge about a new product concept. Such conceptual knowledge then turns into systemic knowledge through combination. For example, a new product concept guides the combination phase, in which newly developed and existing component technologies are combined in order to build a prototype. Systemic knowledge, such as a simulated production process for the new product, turns, through internalization, into routine knowledge for mass production. The routine knowledge then triggers a new spiral of knowledge creation. For example, the routine tacit knowledge that line workers have about the new production process can be socialized and can thereby initiate a new spiral of knowledge creation for improving the process.

Managing the Knowledge-creation Process

In the previous section, we presented a model of the organizational knowledge-creation process, illustrating and explaining its constituents: SECI, *ba*, and knowledge assets. An organization, building on its existing knowledge assets, creates new knowledge through the SECI process that takes place in *ba*. The knowledge created then becomes part of the knowledge assets of the organization and the basis for a new cycle of knowledge creation. The key to engaging in this dynamic process of knowledge creation is to manage the three layers effectively. For this reason we now turn our attention to the question of how such knowledge creating task can be accomplished.

The knowledge-creation process cannot be managed in the traditional sense of 'management', which centers on controlling the information flow (von Krogh, Nonaka, and Ichijo 1997; Nonaka and Takeuchi 1995). The management process that fits organizational knowledge creation differs decidedly from traditional management models such as the top-down and the bottom-up models. But the top-down model, with its foundation in bureaucracy, and the bottom-up model, with its emphasis on autonomy, fail to grasp the dynamic dimension of organizational knowledge creation. In these models, knowledge is seen as something to be created by individuals, and the creation of knowledge through interactions between individuals or between individuals and the environment is ignored (Child and Heavens, Ch. 13 in this volume). In order to capture the dynamic nature of organizational knowledge creation, we propose another model, the middle-up-down model.

The middle-up-down management model is suitable primarily to promoting the efficient creation of knowledge within business organizations. It is neither top-down nor bottom-up. In middle-up-down management, middle managers, who are often leaders of a team or a task force, play a key role in facilitating the process of organizational knowledge creation. The process puts middle managers at the very center of knowledge management, positioning them at the intersection of the vertical and horizontal flows of information and knowledge within the company. It also puts top management in the role of 'leading' rather than 'managing' the knowledge-creation process.

Two Types of Traditional Management Models: Top-down and Bottom-up

In this section we describe the characteristics of top-down and bottom-up models as conceptualized by management scholars. Top-down management is basically the classic, hierarchical model. In this model, the organization is viewed as a bureaucratic information-processing machine, which functions through division of labor and hierarchy (Simon 1947, 1983; Taylor 1911) rather than through a knowledge-creating entity. Simple and select information is passed up the pyramid to top managers, who then use it to create plans and orders, which are passed back down the hierarchy. Top managers create basic managerial concepts and break them down hierarchically so that they can be implemented by subordinates. Top managers' concepts become operational conditions for middle managers, who then decide how to put the concepts into practice. Middle managers' decisions, in turn, constitute operational conditions for lower managers, who implement the decisions of the middle managers. If this model is to work, the concepts held by top management should not be ambiguous or equivocal; they should be strictly functional and pragmatic.

This traditional model is based on an implicit assumption that information and knowledge are processed most efficiently through a tree structure. The division of labor within this kind of bureaucratic organization is associated with a hierarchical pattern of information-processing. Moving from the bottom to the top, information is processed selectively, so that people at the top only receive simple, processed information. Moving in the reverse direction, information is processed and transformed from the general to the particular. It is this deductive transformation that enables human beings, with their limited information-processing capacity, to deal with a mass of information. In this model information-processing by middle and lower members of the organization is of minor relevance to knowledge creation. Only top managers are allowed to and supposed to be able to create information. Moreover, information created by these top managers exists for the sole purpose of implementation. In this model, information is a tool rather than a product.

In the bottom-up model, on the other hand, information is typically created by middle and lower managers, not top managers. In this model, top managers give few orders and instructions, serving rather as sponsors for individual employees who function as intra-company entrepreneurs (Nonaka and Kiyosawa 1987; Pinchot 1985). Knowledge is created by these individual employees at the frontline of business. However, as in the top-down model, this model is also anchored to the critical role of the individual as an independent, separate actor. There is little direct dialogue with other members of the organization, either vertically or horizontally. Autonomy, not interaction, is the key operating principle in this model.

As pointed out in the previous section, intense interactions among organizational members are a key to organizational knowledge creation. However, such interactions hardly take place in the military-like hierarchy of the top-down model or between the autonomy-driven individuals of the bottom-up model. Furthermore, notions such as fluctuation and chaos are not permitted in the top-down model and are incarnated only within individuals in the bottom-up model.

The fact that individuals, not teams or groups, are the primary knowledge creators is potentially problematic. In the top-down model, there is the danger of depending too much on a few top managers. In the bottom-up model, because knowledge creation depends on the patience and talent of a particular individual, knowledge creation tends to be much more time-consuming than in the top-down model.

Another limitation of the two models is the lack of recognition and relevance given to middle managers. In the top-down model, top managers are the ones who create knowledge. Middle managers process information but do not create knowledge. In the bottom-up model, the knowledge creator is the entrepreneur-like individual at the frontline of business. Small headquarters, a flat organizational structure, and a propensity for top managers to serve as direct sponsors characterize a typical bottom-up model and the autonomy granted to individuals. In neither model do middle managers seem to have a role. Hence, many business scholars have looked upon middle managers as employees whose roles and usefulness have been disappearing, as employees to be shed (Dopson and Stewart 1990; Peters 1987; Quinn 1992). However, such a view overlooks the important role played by middle managers in creating knowledge, as shown by de Haën, Tsui-Auch, and Alexis (Ch. 41 in this volume).

Middle-up-down Management for Knowledge Creation

Given the limitations of the top-down and bottom-up models, we suggest a third kind, the middle-up-down management model, as the most suitable for knowledge creation. Unlike the two models discussed above, the middle-up-down model portrays all members of the organization as important actors who should work together horizontally and vertically (Nonaka 1988, 1990; Nonaka and Takeuchi 1995). The model is characterized by the wide scope of cooperative relationships and interactions between top, middle, and lower managers. Especially important in this model is the role of middle managers, who work as knowledge-producers, in facilitating the process of organizational knowledge creation. Table 22.3 provides a summary comparison of the three models in terms of their knowledge creator, resource allocation, structural characteristics, process characteristics, knowledge accumulation, and inherent limitations.

In the middle-up-down model, top management articulates visions, which provide direction. Middle managers, working as knowledge-producers, translate these visions into more concrete concepts, which are to be realized in the fields. Whereas top management articulates the dreams of the firm, frontline employees and low-level managers look at its reality. The gap between these two perspectives is narrowed by and through middle managers. In other words, top management's role is to create a grand theory, whereas middle management, as knowledge-producers, create a mid-range theory that can be empirically tested within the company with the help of frontline employees. Knowledge is created through such interactions and then disseminated throughout the company.

Top and middle management take up a leadership role in knowledge creation by working on all three layers of the knowledge-creation process. They provide knowledge vision, develop and promote the sharing of knowledge assets, create and energize *ba*, and enable and promote the continuous spiral of knowledge creation (see Fig. 22.5). Especially important is the provision of the knowledge vision, which affects all three layers of the knowledge-creation process.

Providing Knowledge Vision

In order to create values through knowledge-creation activities, an organization needs a vision that orients the entire organization to the kind of knowledge it must acquire and wins spontaneous commitment by the individuals and groups involved in knowledge creation (Dierkes, Marz, and Teele, Ch. 12; Stopford, Ch. 11 in this volume). To create knowledge, organizations should foster the commitment of its organizational members by formulating the organizations' intention, for commitment underlies human knowledge-creating activity (Polanyi 1958). It is top management's role to articulate this knowledge vision and communicate it throughout and beyond the company.

Table 22.3. Comparison of three management models of knowledge creation

Dimension	Management model		
	Top-down	Bottom-up	Middle-up-down
Who			
Agent of knowledge creation	Top management	Entrepreneurial individual	Team (with middle managers as knowledge-producers)
Top management role	Commander	Sponsor/mentor	Catalyst
Middle-management role	Information-processor	Autonomous intrapreneur	Team leader
What			
Accumulated knowledge	Explicit	Tacit	Explicit and tacit
Knowledge conversion	Partial conversion focused on combination and internalization	Partial conversion focused on socialization and externalization	Spiral conversion of the SECI[a] process
Where			
Stage of knowledge	Computerized database and manuals	Embodied in individuals	Organizational knowledge base
How			
Organization	Hierarchy	Project team and informal network	Hypertext
Communication	Orders and instructions	Self-organizing principle	Dialogue and use of metaphor and analogy
Chaos/fluctuation	Not permitted	Permitted	Create and amplify
Weakness	Great dependence on top management	Time-consuming process, costs of coordinating individuals	Physical exhaustion, redundancy costs

[a] Socialization–externalization–combination–internalization.

Source: Adapted from *The Knowledge-Creating Company: How Japanese Companies Create the Dynamics of Innovation* by Ikujiro Nonaka and Hirotaka Takeuchi, copyright © 1995 by Oxford University Press, Inc. Used by permission of Oxford University Press, Inc.

A knowledge vision defines what kind of knowledge the company should create in what domain. It gives direction to the knowledge-creation process and to the knowledge created by it. In short, it is a vision that determines how an organization and its knowledge base will evolve in the long term. Because knowledge is without boundaries, any form of new knowledge can be created regardless of the company's business structure. It is therefore important for top management to articulate a knowledge vision that transcends the boundaries of existing products, divisions, organizations, and markets.

A knowledge vision also defines the value system according to which one evaluates, justifies, and determines the quality of knowledge that the company creates. Together with

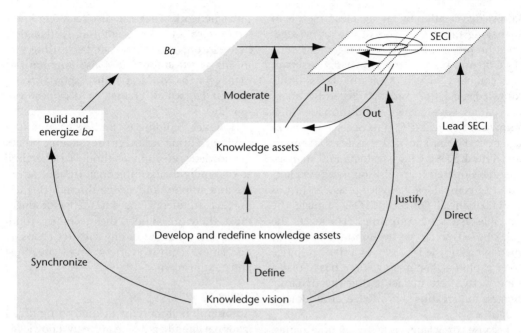

Fig. 22.5. Leading the knowledge-creation process with *ba* (platforms for knowledge creation) and SECI (socialization–externalization–combination–internalization processes)

From 'Leading Knowledge Creation: A New Framework for Dynamic Knowledge Management', by I. Nonaka, N. Konno, and R. Toyama, paper presented at the Second Annual Knowledge Management Conference, Haas School of Business, University of California Berkeley, 22–24 September 1998.

organizational norms, routines, and skills, the value system determines what kinds of knowledge are needed, created, and retained (Leonard-Barton 1995; Nonaka 1985).

Serving as a bridge between the visionary ideals of the top management and the chaotic reality of organizational members on the frontline, middle management then has to take the values and visions created by top management and break them down into concepts and images that can effectively guide the knowledge-creation process. Middle managers work as knowledge-producers in order to remake reality, or produce new knowledge according to a particular company's vision.

Researching on visionary companies, Porras and Collins (1994) found that an excellent and clear vision gives a company a sustainable competitive advantage. Many of the visionary companies have values that are closely related to thought and activity principles that relate to

knowledge creation. For example, at 3M, the evaluation standard 'Thou shall not kill ideas for new products' has been established as a fundamental part of company ideology and an essential part of company culture. Motorola continues to focus on the value 'stimulate the latent creativity of the employees.' Kao emphasizes the 'pursuit of the truth' beyond the pursuit of profit. Honda bases its management on the 'respect for theory' and firmly denies that there is any value attached to great effort unless it is grounded in 'a correct theory'. The value articulated by Sharp—'Do not imitate. Create Products that are imitated'—harks back to its founder, who recognized the importance of creativity.

Developing and Promoting the Sharing of Knowledge Assets

Building on the knowledge vision of the company, top management must facilitate dynamic knowledge creation by taking a leading role in managing the three layers of the knowledge-creation process. First, top management must develop and manage the knowledge assets of the company, which form the basis of its knowledge-creation process. Recently, many companies have created a position of Chief Knowledge Officer (CKO) to oversee the management of their knowledge assets (Davenport and Prusak 1998). CKOs evaluate and manage the development, acquisition, and exploitation of companies' knowledge assets, just as Chief Financial Officers (CFOs) manage the tangible assets of companies. However, the role of CKOs so far has been limited mostly to managing knowledge assets as a static resource to be exploited. Top management has to play a more active role in facilitating the dynamic process of creating knowledge from knowledge.

Because knowledge is without boundaries, top management has to redefine its organization in terms of the knowledge it owns rather than in terms of existing definitions, such as technologies, products, and markets. Top management and knowledge-producers can take an 'inventory' of their knowledge assets and then form a strategy based on the knowledge vision to build, maintain, and utilize these knowledge assets effectively and efficiently.

Knowledge assets, especially routine knowledge assets such as organizational routines and organizational culture, could hinder knowledge creation as well (Berthoin Antal, Lenhardt, and Rosenbrock, Ch. 39 in this volume; Leonard-Barton 1992; Levit and March 1988). Inertia makes it difficult for an organization to diverge from the course set by its previous experiences (Hannan and Freeman 1984). Hence, leaders should be careful not to let a firm's knowledge assets become hindrances.

Building and Energizing Ba

Ba can be spontaneously created, or it can be built consciously. Top management and knowledge-producers can facilitate knowledge creation by providing physical space, such as meeting rooms, or cyber space, such as a computer network. They can also facilitate knowledge creation by promoting interactions between organizational members, using such means as a task force. It is also important for managers to find and utilize spontaneously formed *ba*, which change or disappear very quickly.

However, building or finding *ba* is not enough for a firm to manage the dynamic process of knowledge creation. *Ba* should be 'energized' so that individuals or the organization can create and amplify knowledge through the SECI process. To energize *ba*, knowledge-producers must therefore supply the necessary conditions, including autonomy, creative chaos, redundancy, requisite variety, love, care, trust, and commitment.

Autonomy

Autonomy is important in motivating organizational members to create new knowledge. Autonomy can be a source of unexpected knowledge as well. By allowing the members of an organization to act autonomously, the organization may increase the chance of accessing and utilizing the knowledge held by its members (Grant 1996a, b; Wruck and Jensen 1994).

Self-organizing teams can be used as powerful tools with which to create autonomy within firms. The use of cross-functional teams that involve members from a broad cross-section of different organizational activities is very effective in the process of innovation (Clark and Fujimoto 1991; Imai, Nonaka, and Takeuchi 1985). At NEC, autonomous teams have been used to foster the expansion of NEC's technology program. To develop strategically important products, Sharp uses the 'Urgent Project System', in which the team leader is given sole responsibility for the project and the power to recruit any necessary personnel.

Fluctuation and Creative Chaos

Fluctuation and creative chaos stimulate the interactions between the organization and its environment. Fluctuation is characterized by 'order without recursiveness', which is different from complete disorder. It is order whose pattern is initially hard to predict (Gleick 1987). Examples include changes in market needs, the growth of competing companies, and challenges given by top management.

When fluctuation is introduced into an organization, its members face a 'breakdown' of routines, habits, or cognitive frameworks. Such breakdowns, or unlearning, are important, for they give one an opportunity to reconsider one's own fundamental thinking and perspective (Hedberg 1981; Hedberg and Wolff, Ch. 24 in this volume; Winograd and Flores 1986). The continual process of questioning and reevaluating existing premises, of unlearning by individual members of the organization fosters organizational knowledge creation. Thus, an environmental fluctuation often triggers breakdown within an organization, a situation out of which new knowledge can be created. Some have called this phenomenon the creation of 'order out of noise' or 'order out of chaos' (Prigogine and Stengers 1984; von Foerster 1984).

Chaos is generated naturally when an organization faces a real crisis, such as a declining market. It can also be generated intentionally when the organization's leaders try to evoke a sense of crisis among organizational members by proposing challenging goals or ambiguous visions. For example, Wal-Mart encourages its employees 'to oppose fashion and to overthrow common thinking'. This intentional chaos, referred to as 'creative chaos', increases tension within the organization and focuses the attention of organizational members on defining the problem and resolving the crisis situation.

Redundancy

The term 'redundancy' may sound like something to avoid because of its connotations of unnecessary duplication, waste, and information overload. However, redundancy is absolutely essential if the knowledge spiral is to take place organizationally. Redundancy here means the existence of information that goes beyond the immediate operational requirements of organizational members. In business organizations, redundancy refers to *intentional* overlapping of information about business ac-

tivities, management responsibilities, and the company as a whole.

Redundancy of information promotes the knowledge-creation process in two ways. First, sharing redundant information fosters the sharing of tacit knowledge because one's sense of what others are trying to articulate better is often improved if a great amount of information is shared in the effort to form the basis for common understanding. Redundancy is especially important in the concept-development stage, when it is critical to articulate images rooted in tacit knowledge. Redundant information enables individuals to invade each other's functional boundaries and to offer advice or provide new information from different perspectives. In short, redundancy of information brings about 'learning by intrusion' into each individual's sphere of perception.

Second, redundancy of information helps organizational members understand their position in the organization by letting them see themselves from the outside. Thus, redundancy of information influences their direction of thinking and action and provides the organization with a self-control mechanism that keeps it heading in a certain direction.

Redundancy of information is also a prerequisite for the 'principle of redundancy of potential command' (McCulloch 1965), according to which each part of an entire system has the same degree of importance and has the potential to become the leader of the system. Even within a strictly hierarchical organization, redundant information helps build unusual communication channels. Thus, redundancy of information facilitates the interchange between hierarchy and nonhierarchy. At Maekawa Seisakusho, different people take turns in leadership during the course of a project. The member who best fits the issues or problems steps into the center of the team and drives the project forward, guaranteeing the right person in the right place for each phase of the project. These handovers are possible because team members have overlapping information and thus are well able to recognize the strengths of their colleagues. By rotating specialists between different positions and roles within the team (leader, support, and so forth), specialists gain both additional knowledge in related fields and management skills and knowledge specific to different roles in teams and leading functions. In short, redundancy is created in order to support innovation by sharing knowledge and hence by generating highly specialized generalists in technical areas and highly generalized specialists in management and leadership.

There are several ways to build redundancy into an organization. One is to have different functional departments work together in a 'fuzzy' division of labor (Takeuchi and Nonaka 1986). Another way is to foster internal competition. Some companies divide the product development team into competitive groups that develop different approaches to the same project. Competing groups then argue over the advantages and disadvantages of each of their approaches so that they eventually develop a common understanding of the 'best' approach. Internal competition encourages the team to look at a project from a variety of perspectives. Yet another way to build redundancy into an organization is the 'strategic rotation' of personnel. This kind of rotation helps members of an organization understand its business from multiple perspectives, making organizational knowledge more 'fluid'. It also enables each employee to diversify his or her skills and information sources. This additional information held by individuals across different functions helps the organization expand its knowledge-creating capacity.

Redundancy of information does have its costs. It increases the amount of information to be processed and can lead to information overload. It also increases the cost of knowledge creation, at least in the short run. One way to deal with these possible problems is to make clear where necessary knowledge and information can be located.

Requisite Variety

Requisite variety helps a knowledge-creating organization strike a balance between order and chaos that is necessary for knowledge creation to take place. In order to deal with challenges posed by the environment, the internal diversity of an organization has to match the variety and complexity of the environment (Ashby 1956). To cope with environmental changes, which are impossible to predict completely, an organization must possess requisite variety, or minimax internal diversity, which should be at a minimum for organizational integration (order) and at a maximum for effective adaptation to environmental changes (chaos).

Requisite variety can be enhanced by combining information differently, flexibly, and quickly and by providing equal access to information throughout the organization. When information differentials exist within an organization, organizational members cannot interact on equal terms. That inequality hinders the search for different interpretations of new information. Organizational members should be able to know where information is located, where knowledge is accumulated, and how information and knowledge can be accessed at the greatest speed. Kao Corporation, Japan's leading maker of household products, utilizes a computerized information network to give every employee equal access to corporate information, which then serves as the basis for exchanges of opinion between various organizational units.

Love, Care, Trust, and Commitment

In order for knowledge (especially tacit knowledge) to be shared and for the knowledge-creation process to occur, there needs to be strong love, caring, and trust among organizational members, for these qualities are the foundation of knowledge creation (von Krogh 1998; von Krogh, Nonaka, and Ichijo 1997). To foster such love, care, trust, and commitment, knowledge-producers need to be highly inspired and committed to their goal. They also need to be selfless and altruistic. If a manager tries to monopolize the knowledge created by an organization or take credit for other members' achievements, it destroys the love, care, trust, and commitment among organizational members. Knowledge-producers should also be positive thinkers and should avoid having or showing negative thoughts and feelings. Creative and positive thoughts, imagination, and a drive to act are important characteristics of a good knowledge-producer.

Promoting the SECI Process

Taking the direction given by the knowledge vision, knowledge-producers must facilitate organizational knowledge creation by furthering all four modes of knowledge conversion, although their most significant contribution is made in externalization. An empirical study has shown that middle managers of high-performing firms spend more hours in externalization than middle managers of low-performing firms (Shakai Keizai Seisansei Honbu 1998). Middle managers synthesize the tacit knowledge of both frontline employees and top management, make it explicit, and incorporate it into new technologies, products, or systems. To do so, knowledge-producers need to create their own concepts and express them in their own words. One effective method of concept creation is 'reflection in action'. As Schön (1983) explained, when a person reflects while in action, he or she becomes independent of established theory and technique and is able to construct a new theory about the unique case.

The effective use of language is another way to facilitate knowledge conversion processes. Language includes tropes (such as metaphor, metonymy, and synecdoche); the 'grammar' and 'context' of knowledge; and nonverbal, visual language, such as design. Each of the four modes of knowledge conversion requires different kinds of language in order for knowledge to be created and shared effectively. For example, nonverbal language, such as body language, is essential in the socialization process, for tacit knowledge cannot be expressed through articulated language. Conversely, clear, articulated language is essential in the combination process, for in this process knowledge has to be disseminated and understood by many people. In externalization, tropes such as metaphor, metonymy, and synecdoche are effective for creating concepts out of vast amounts of tacit knowledge. Hence, knowledge-producers need to carefully choose and design language to promote the SECI process.

Another important task for knowledge-producers is to facilitate the knowledge spiral across the different conversion modes and across the different organizational levels. It is the middle managers who facilitate the cross-leveling of knowledge to other departments of organizations. In order to facilitate the creation of knowledge effectively, knowledge-producers need to improvise and facilitate improvisation by all the people participating in the process. Improvisation is an important factor in dynamic knowledge creation, especially when it is focused on tacit knowledge (Weick 1993).

The Organizational Structure for Knowledge Creation

In the previous sections, we discussed how knowledge is created through a dynamic knowledge-creation process and that process can be best managed through middle-up-down management style. For effective knowledge creation, we need an organizational structure that can support this knowledge-creation process. We propose that a new organizational structure, called 'hypertext' organization, is best suited to creating knowledge efficiently and effectively (Nonaka, Konno, and Kosaka 1993; Nonaka and Takeuchi 1995).

For most of the twentieth century, organizational structures oscillated between two basic types: bureaucracy and task force. Bureaucratic structure is based on the division of labor and a hierarchical distribution of authority and responsibility (Simon 1947; Weber 1922). It is a highly formalized, specialized, centralized structure and is largely dependent on the standardization of work processes for organizational coordination. Bureaucracy is suited to conducting routine work efficiently on a large scale when conditions are stable. However, it does not work well when it faces uncertainty and radical, rapid change. Hence, firms with bureaucratic organizational structures

encounter difficulties in creating new knowledge when they face 'radical uncertainty', for
they 'do not, they cannot, know what they
need to know' (Tsoukas 1996: 22). Other costs
of bureaucracy include intraorganizational resistance, red tape, tension, sectionalism, the
hobbling of individual initiative, the shrinking
of employees' sense of responsibility, and the
problem of means becoming objectives (Gouldner 1954; Merton 1940; Selznik 1949).

The task force, conversely, is a flexible, adapt-
able, dynamic, and participatory organizational
structure. The task force is an institutionalized team or group that brings together representatives from a number of different units
for intense work on a flexible basis, in many
cases to deal with a temporary issue. However,
the task-force organizational structure has its
own weaknesses as well. Because of its *ad hoc*
nature, the task force is not appropriate for exploiting and transferring knowledge continuously and widely throughout an entire
organization. When composed of many different small-scale task forces, an organization be-

comes incapable of setting and achieving its
goals or vision at the corporate level.

Thus, bureaucracy is more efficient and
effective in implementing, exploiting, and
accumulating new knowledge, whereas the
self-organizing task force is more effective in
generating new knowledge. A knowledge-
creating organization should pursue both the
efficiency of a bureaucratic organization and
the flexibility of a task-force organization. In
short, some combination or synthesis of the
two is needed to provide a solid basis for knowledge creation. We refer to such an organizational structure as a hypertext organization.

The critical factor for the design of the hypertext organization lies in coordinating time,
space, and resources in such a way as to achieve
requisite variety. As illustrated in Fig. 22.6, the
hypertext organization can be visualized as an
organization with three layers: the knowledge
base, business system, and project team. The
bottommost layer of the hypertext organization is the knowledge-base, which embraces
both tacit knowledge associated with organiza-

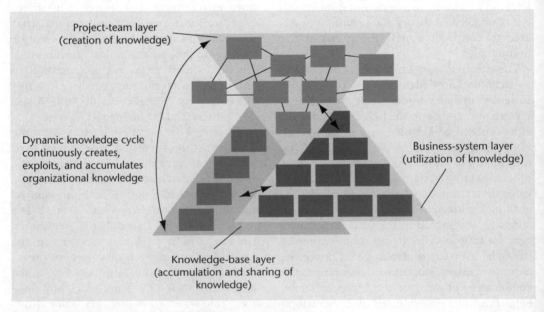

Fig. 22.6. The hypertext organization

Adapted from 'Chisiki Beesu Sosiki' [The Knowledge-based Organization], by I. Nonaka and H. Takeuchi, *Business Review*, 41/1 (1993), 71. © 1993 Adapted with permission.

tional culture and procedures and explicit knowledge in the form of documents, filing systems, computerized databases, and so on. This layer functions as an archive, or corporate university, for the knowledge creation of the company. The second layer is the business system, where normal, routine operation is carried out by a formal, hierarchical, bureaucratic organization. The topmost layer, the 'project team', relates to the area where multiple, loosely interlinked self-organizing project teams share in the joint creation of knowledge through a common corporate vision. Thus, the hypertext organization takes different forms, depending on the perspective from which it is observed.

Organizational knowledge creation is a dynamic cycle of knowledge and information traversing the three layers. Members of project teams on the top layer are selected from diverse functions and departments across the business-system layer. Based on the corporate vision presented by top management, they engage in knowledge-creation activities interacting with other project teams. Once the task of a team is completed, members move 'down' to the knowledge-base layer and inventory the knowledge acquired and created in the project. After categorizing, documenting, and indexing the new knowledge, they return to the business-system layer and engage in routine operation until they are called for another project. A key design requirement for the hypertext organization is the forming of this kind of circular movement of organization members.

Conclusion

In this chapter, we have discussed how organizations manage the dynamic process of knowledge creation. We have proposed a new, multilayered model of knowledge-creation in order to understand the dynamic nature of knowledge creation and to manage the process effectively. Three layers of knowledge assets,

ba, and the SECI process must interact with each other organically and dynamically. The knowledge assets of a firm are mobilized and shared in *ba*, where the tacit knowledge held by individuals is converted and amplified by the knowledge spiral through the socialization, externalization, combination, and internalization of knowledge.

We have also discussed the role of managers in facilitating the knowledge-creation process. Creating and understanding the knowledge vision of the company, understanding the knowledge assets of the company, facilitating and utilizing *ba* effectively, and managing the knowledge spiral are all important tasks that managers have to perform. Especially important is the role of the knowledge-producers, the middle managers who are at the center of this dynamic knowledge-creation process. We have proposed middle-up-down management and hypertext organization as the effective management system and organizational structure that can support this knowledge-creation process.

In focusing mainly on the organizational knowledge-creation process that takes place in companies, we have described it as the dynamic interaction not only between organizational members but also between organizational members and the environment. The latter dimension of this interaction underlines the fact that the knowledge-creation process is not confined within the boundaries of a single company. The market, where social interaction brings together the knowledge held by companies and that held by customers, is also a place for knowledge creation. In addition, the aggregated creation of knowledge by groups of companies is possible. If we were to raise the level of analysis further, we would arrive at the discussion on how so-called national systems of innovation can be built. The next step, then, is to examine how companies, governments, and universities might intertwine in order to facilitate knowledge creation in the future.

References

Argyris, C. and Schön, D. A. (1978). *Organizational Learning: A Theory of Action Perspective*. Reading, Mass.: Addison-Wesley.

Ashby, W. R. (1956). *An Introduction to Cybernetics*. London: Chapman & Hall.

Barney, J. B. (1991). 'Firm Resources and Sustained Competitive Advantage'. *Journal of Management*, 17: 99–120.

Bateson, G. (1973). *Steps to an Ecology of Mind: A Revolutionary Approach to Man's Understanding of Himself*. London: Paladin.

—— (1979). *Mind and Nature: A Necessary Unity*. New York: Bantam Books.

Brown, J. S. and Duguid, P. (1991). 'Organizational Learning and Communities-of-Practice: Toward a Unified View of Working, Learning, and Innovation'. *Organization Science*, 2: 40–57.

Choo, C. W. (1998). *The Knowing Organization: How Organizations Use Information to Construct Meaning, Create Knowledge, and Make Decisions*. Oxford: Oxford University Press.

Clark, K. B. and Fujimoto, T. (1991). *Product Development Performance: Strategy, Organization, and Management in the World Auto Industry*. Boston: Harvard Business School Press.

Cohen, M. D. and Bacdayan, P. (1994). 'Organizational Routines Are Stored as Procedural Memory: Evidence from a Laboratory Study'. *Organization Science*, 5: 554–68.

Cyert, R. M., Kumar, P. K., and Williams, J. R. (1993). 'Information, Market Imperfections and Strategy'. *Strategic Management Journal*, 14 (Winter special issue): 47–58.

—— and March, J. G. (1963). *A Behavioral Theory of the Firm*. Englewood Cliffs, NJ: Prentice Hall.

Daft, R. L. and Weick, K. E. (1984). 'Toward a Model of Organizations as Interpretation Systems'. *Academy of Management Review*, 9: 284–95.

Davenport, T. H. and Prusak, L. (1998). *Working Knowledge: How Organizations Manage What They Know*. Boston: Harvard Business School Press.

Dierickx, I. and Cool, K. (1989). 'Asset Stock Accumulation and Sustainability of Competitive Advantage'. *Management Science*, 35: 1504–14.

Dodgson, M. (1993). 'Organizational Learning: A Review of Some Literatures'. *Organization Studies*, 14: 375–94.

Dopson, S. and Stewart, R. (1990). 'What Is Happening to Middle Management?' *British Journal of Management*, 1: 3–16.

Drucker, P. (1993). *Post-capitalist Society*. London: Butterworth Heinemann.

Duncan, R. and Weiss, A. (1979). 'Organizational Learning: Implications for Organizational Design', in B. M. Staw (ed.), *Research in Organizational Behavior: An Annual Series of Analytical Essays and Critical Reviews* (Vol. 1). Greenwich, Conn.: JAI Press, 75–123.

Edvinsson, L. and Malone, M. S. (1997). *Intellectual Capital: Realizing Your Company's True Value by Finding Its Hidden Brainpower*. New York: Harper Business.

Gleick, J. (1987). *Chaos*. New York: Viking Press.

Gouldner, A. W. (1954). *Patterns of Industrial Bureaucracy: A Study of Modern Factory Administration*. Glencoe, Ill.: Free Press.

Grant, R. M. (1996a). 'Prospering in Dynamically-competitive Environments: Organizational Capability as Knowledge Integration'. *Organization Science*, 7: 375–87.

—— (1996b). 'Toward a Knowledge-based Theory of the Firm'. *Strategic Management Journal*, 17 (Winter special issue): 109–22.

Hannan, M. T. and Freeman, J. H. (1984). 'Structural Inertia and Organizational Change'. *American Sociological Review*, 49: 149–64.

Hayek, F. A. (1945). 'The Use of Knowledge in Society'. *American Economic Review*, 35: 519–30.

Hedberg, B. L. T. (1981). 'How Organizations Learn and Unlearn', in P. C. Nystrom and W. H. Starbuck (eds.), *Handbook of Organizational Design*: Vol. 1. *Adapting Organizations to Their Environments*. Oxford: Oxford University Press, 3–27.

Henderson, R. and Cockburn, I. (1994). 'Measuring Competence: Exploring Firm-Effects in Pharmaceutical Research'. *Strategic Management Journal*, 15 (Winter special issue): 63–84.

Imai, K., Nonaka, I., and Takeuchi, H. (1985). 'Managing the New Product Development Process: How Japanese Companies Learn and Unlearn', in K. B. Clark, R. H. Hayes, and C. Lorenz (eds.),

The Uneasy Alliance: Managing the Productivity–Technology Dilemma. Boston: Harvard Business School Press, 337–81.

Jantsch, E. (1980). *The Self-organizing Universe*. Oxford: Pergamon Press.

Johnson-Laird, P. N. (1983). *Mental Models*. Cambridge: Cambridge University Press.

Kogut, B. and Zander, U. (1996). 'What Firms Do? Coordination, Identity, and Learning'. *Organization Science*, 7: 502–18.

Lave, J. and Wenger, E. (1991). *Situated Learning: Legitimate Peripheral Participation*. Cambridge: Cambridge University Press.

Lei, D., Hitt, M. A., and Bettis, R. (1996). 'Dynamic Core Competences through Meta-learning and Strategic Context'. *Journal of Management*, 22: 549–69.

Leonard-Barton, D. (1992). 'Core Capabilities and Core Rigidities: A Paradox in Managing New Product Development'. *Strategic Management Journal*, 13: 363–80.

——(1995). *Wellsprings of Knowledge: Building and Sustaining the Sources of Innovation*. Boston: Harvard Business School Press.

Levinthal, D. and Myatt, J. (1994). 'Co-evolution of Capabilities and Industry: The Evolution of Mutual Fund Processing'. *Strategic Management Journal*, 15 (Winter special issue): 45–62.

Levit, R. and March, J. G. (1988). 'Organizational Learning'. *Annual Review of Sociology*, 14: 319–40.

Machlup, F. (1983). 'Semantic Quirks in Studies of Information', in F. Machlup and U. Mansfield (eds.), *The Study of Information*. New York: John Wiley & Sons, 641–71.

March, J. G. (1991). 'Exploration and Exploitation in Organizational Learning'. *Organization Science*, 2: 71–87.

McCulloch, W. (1965). *Embodiments of Mind*. Cambridge, Mass.: MIT Press.

Merton, R. K. (1940). 'Bureaucratic Structure and Personality'. *Social Forces*, 18: 560–8.

Nelson, R. R. (1991). 'Why Do Firms Differ, and How Does It Matter?' *Strategic Management Journal*, 12 (Winter special issue): 61–74.

Nishida, K. (1970). *Fundamental Problems of Philosophy: The World of Action and the Dialectical World* (D. Dilworth, trans.). Tokyo: Sophia University. (Original work published 1933)

——(1990). *An Inquiry into the Good* (M. Abe and C. Ives, trans.). New Haven: Yale University. (Original work published 1921)

Nonaka, I. (1985). *Kigyo Shinka-ron* (Corporate Evolution: Managing Organizational Information Creation). Tokyo: Nihon Keizai Shumbun-Sha.

——(1988). 'Toward Middle-up-down Management: Accelerating Information Creation'. *Sloan Management Review*, 29/3: 9–18.

——(1990). *Chishiki-Souzou no Keiei* (A Theory of Organizational Knowledge Creation). Tokyo: Nihon Keizai Shimbun-sha.

——(1991). 'The Knowledge-creating Company'. *Harvard Business Review*, 69/6: 96–104.

——(1994). 'A Dynamic Theory of Organizational Knowledge Creation'. *Organization Science*, 5: 14–37.

——Byosière, P., Borucki, C. C., and Konno, N. (1994). 'Organizational Knowledge Creation Theory: A First Comprehensive Test'. *International Business Review*, 3: 337–51.

——and Kiyosawa, T. (1987). *3M no Chousen* (The Challenge of 3M). Tokyo: Nihon Keizai Shinbunsha.

——Konno, N., and Kosaka, S. (1993). 'Chisiki Beesu Sosiki' (The Knowledge-based Organization). *Business Review*, 41/1: 59–73.

—— ——(1998). 'The Concept of "Ba": Building a Foundation for Knowledge Creation'. *California Management Review*, 40/3: 40–54.

—— ——and Toyama, R. (1998). *Leading Knowledge Creation: A New Framework for Dynamic Knowledge Management*. Paper presented at the 2nd Annual Knowledge Management Conference. Haas School of Business, University of California at Berkeley, 22–24 September.

——and Takeuchi, H. (1995). *The Knowledge-creating Company: How Japanese Companies Create the Dynamics of Innovation*. New York: Oxford University Press.

Peters, T. J. (1987). *Thriving on Chaos*. New York: Alfred A. Knopf.

Pinchot, G., III (1985). *Intrapreneuring: Why You Don't Have to Leave the Corporation to Become an Entrepreneur*. New York: Harper & Row.

Polanyi, M. (1958). *Personal Knowledge*. Chicago: University of Chicago Press.

——(1966). *The Tacit Dimension*. London: Routledge and Kegan Paul.

Porras, J. I. and Collins, J. C. (1994). *Built to Last: Successful Habits of Visionary Companies*. New York: Harper Collins.

Prahalad, C. K. and Hamel, G. (1990). 'The Core Competence of the Corporation'. *Harvard Business Review*, 68/3: 79–91.

Prigogine, I. and Stengers, I. (1984). *Order out of Chaos: Man's New Dialogue with Nature*. New York: Bantam Books.

Quinn, J. B. (1992). *Intelligent Enterprise: A Knowledge and Service Based Paradigm for Industry*. New York: Free Press.

Schön, D. A. (1983). *The Reflective Practitioner*. New York: Basic Books.

Selznik, P. (1949). *TVA and the Grass Roots: A Study in the Sociology of Format Organization*. Berkeley: University of California Press.

Senge, P. M. (1990). *The Fifth Discipline: The Age and Practice of the Learning Organization*. London: Century Business.

Shakai Keizai Seisansei Honbu (1998). *Shin Nihon-gata Sangyou, Kigyou Keiei Saikouchiku heno Teigen* (New Japanese-type Industries: A Proposal for Reconstruction of Corporate Management). Tokyo: Shakai Seisansei Honbu.

Shimizu, H. (1995). 'Ba-principle: New Logic for the Real-time Emergence of Information'. *Holonics*, 5: 67–79.

Simon, H. A. (1947). *Administrative Behavior: A Study of Decision-making Processes in Administrative Organization*. New York: Macmillan.

——(1973). 'Applying Information Technology to Organization Design'. *Public Administration Review*, 33: 268–78.

——(1983). *Reason in Human Affairs*. Stanford, Calif.: Stanford University Press.

Spender, J. C. and Grant, R. M. (1996). 'Knowledge and the Firm: Overview'. *Strategic Management Journal*, 17 (Winter special issue): 5–9.

Sveiby, K. E. (1997). *The New Organizational Wealth: Managing and Measuring Knowledge-based Assets*. San Francisco: Berret-Koehler.

Takeuchi, H. and Nonaka, I. (1986). 'The New New Product Development Game'. *Harvard Business Review*, 64/1: 137–46.

Taylor, F. W. (1911). *The Principles of Scientific Management*. New York: Harper.

Teece, D. J., Pisano, G., and Shuen, A. (1997). 'Dynamic Capabilities and Strategic Management'. *Strategic Management Journal*, 18: 509–33.

Toffler, A. (1990). *Powershift: Knowledge, Wealth, and Violence at the Edge of the 21st Century*. New York: Bantam Books.

Tsoukas, H. (1996). 'The Firm as a Distributed Knowledge System: A Constructionist Approach'. *Strategic Management Journal*, 17 (Winter special issue): 11–25.

von Foerster, H. (1984). 'Principles of Self-organization in a Socio-managerial Context', in H. Ulrich and G. J. B. Probst (eds.), *Self-organization and Management of Social Systems*. Berlin: Springer, 2–24.

von Krogh, G. (1995). *Organizational Epistemology*. New York: St. Martin's Press.

——(1998). 'Care in Knowledge Creation'. *California Management Review*, 40/3: 133–53.

——Nonaka, I., and Ichijo, K. (1997). 'Develop Knowledge Activists!' *European Management Journal*, 15: 475–83.

Weber, M. (1922). *Wirtschaft und Gesellschaft*. Tübingen: Mohr.

Weick, K. E. (1991). 'The Nontraditional Quality of Organizational Learning'. *Organization Science*, 2: 116–24.

——(1993). 'The Collapse of Sensemaking in Organization: The Mann Gulch Disaster'. *Administrative Science Quarterly*, 38: 628–52.

Wenger, E. (1998). *Communities of Practice: Learning, Meaning, and Identity*. Cambridge: Cambridge University Press.

Whitehead, A. N. (1954). *Dialogues of Alfred North Whitehead* (Recorded by L. Price). Boston: Little, Brown and Company.

Wikstrom, S. and Normann, R. (1994). *Knowledge and Value: A New Perspective on Corporate Transformation*. London: Routledge.

Wilkins, M. (1989). *The History of Foreign Investment in the United States to 1914*. Cambridge, Mass.: Harvard University Press.

Winograd, T. and Flores, F. (1986). *Understanding Computers and Cognition: A New Foundation for Design*. Reading, Mass.: Addison-Wesley.

Winter, S. G. (1987). 'Knowledge and Competence as Strategic Assets', in D. J. Teece (ed.), *The Competitive Challenge: Strategies for Industrial Innovation and Renewal*. Cambridge, Mass.: Ballinger, 159–84.

——(1994). 'Organizing for Continuous Improvement: Evolutionary Theory Meets the Quality Revolution', in J. A. C. Baum and J. V. Singh (eds.), *Evolutionary Dynamics of Organizations*. New York: Oxford University Press, 90–108.

Wruck, K. H. and Jensen, M. C. (1994). 'Science, Specific Knowledge, and Total Quality Management'. *Journal of Accounting and Economics*, 18: 247–87.

23 Media Choice and Organizational Learning

Bettina Büchel and Steffen Raub

A growing number of companies rely on new media[1] to improve their performance (Davenport 1997). This trend can be observed across various countries and in companies of different size. There are two major reasons for the increased attention given to media within organizations. The first is that managers spend 70 to 80 per cent of their time managing information by using a wide range of media (Mintzberg 1973). The time allotted to managing information has been validated for both industrialized (Kurke and Aldrich 1983; Mintinko and Gardner 1990) and developing countries (Montgomery 1986). In addition, with the introduction of computer-mediated media, the effective and efficient use of media has become an ever more difficult task. As Davenport, Eccles, and Prusak (1992) state, 'broadening information access and usage and enhancing the quality are key to improving business performance' (p. 53). Although this argument sounds convincing, the efficiency and effectiveness of information management through media usage has improved little despite the fact that U.S. companies have invested $1 trillion in information technology (Malhotra 1997).

The ineffective management of information has been attributed to different factors, such as the misinterpretation of information because of different values, information overload, and politics related to information activities. The most frequently stated cause, however, is the inappropriate use of information technology. With the emergence of new information technologies, organizations have come to believe that all situations may be dealt with by optimizing the technology necessary to deal with various information tasks (Davenport 1997). Technocrats commonly focus on the development of new hardware and software in order to address all the organization's information problems. 'Their goal is to plan a technology infrastructure that can deliver information to each individual's desktop and then to build databases with the correct structure to store this information without redundancy' (Davenport, Eccles, and Prusak 1992: 55). The underlying assumptions of such an approach are that technology will resolve all problems and that behavioral issues are nonexistent or unmanageable.

Empirical research indicates that these assumptions deserve to be challenged. A study by Fulk and DeSanctis (1995) showed that an increase in the number of different media within an organization does not necessarily lead to improved performance. The mere availability of media for distributing information within organizations does not seem sufficient to improve performance. Rather, we argue that media choice and usage behavior play an important role in information-processing and, ultimately, in organizational learning.

Managers have to perform a multitude of information-processing tasks that constitute the ability of an organization to learn (Huber 1991). Without media to acquire, distribute, interpret, or store information, the options for communicating within organizations would be

[1] Whereas old media traditionally refer to media that have been extensively used within organizations, such as written letters, memos, and the telephone, new media are usually computer-mediated. Computer-mediated communication includes any kind of human communication involving the transmission of electronic signals between computers (Rudy 1996: 198).

significantly reduced. Media are options for communication, for they are pipelines, or carriers of information (Trevino, Daft, and Lengel 1990: 87). Because media facilitate information-processing, they are necessary for learning organizations. Nonaka, Reinmöller, and Toyama's discussion (Ch. 37 in this volume) of conversion-support tools (CSTools) supports this view by describing this particular media as 'fuel for the engine' (p. 833, below). As a result, media choice becomes an important managerial task in attempting to stimulate and enhance organizational learning. The goal of this chapter is to look at the role of communication media in processing information. Based on a match between communication media and organizational learning processes, a framework of media choice will be proposed.

Organizational Learning and Information Processing

A rising number of articles in the area of organizational learning and a lack of integration among the theoretical perspectives has produced a variety of terms relating to the organizational learning construct. As pointed out by several authors (Huber 1991; Berthoin Antal and Krebsbach-Gnath, Ch. 21 in this volume), organizational learning encompasses several tasks: the acquisition, distribution, interpretation, and storage of information. Information acquisition is the process by which information is obtained from the environment. Information distribution is the sharing of different information sources by organizational members. Information interpretation refers to the process of establishing a common understanding based on distributed information. Storing information plays a critical role in organizational learning because the reusability of learning depends on the effectiveness of the organization's memory. Essentially, an organization learns when it increases its knowledge of action–outcome relationships by obtaining information that it recognizes as potentially useful. As Huber

(1991) suggested, 'an entity learns if, through the processing of information, the range of its potential behaviors is changed' (p. 89). The advantage of this framework is that it breaks the overall learning phenomenon down into a number of relatively small and observable processes. Although these processes are distributed in time and space, they are more readily identifiable than when they are not situated in this framework (Pentland 1995). The constituent tasks of learning help to isolate problems for which practical solutions can be found.

To understand the nature of information-processing, which is at the heart of learning, it is necessary to examine its origins. Research within the field of organization theory and communication suggests that there are two influences on information-processing: uncertainty and ambiguity (Daft and Macintosh 1981; Tushman and Nadler 1978; Weick 1979, 1995; Weick 1995 used the terms equivocality and ambiguity interchangeably). Galbraith (1974) proposed that organizational members process more information as levels of uncertainty increase. According to him, uncertainty is the difference between the amount of information required to perform a task and the amount of information already possessed by the organization. Organizations acquire additional data in order to reduce uncertainty. In contrast to uncertainty, ambiguity refers to the existence of multiple and conflicting interpretations about a situation within the organization (Weick 1979). When managers observe the environment, they often find external information cues to be ambiguous. This ambiguity may be a result of diverse interpretations by different organizational members, or it may be due to the inability of individuals to make sense of the confusing information. As a result of ambiguity, managers are unsure about the consequences that a particular observation has on organizational action. If the ambiguity surrounding the information is to be resolved, minimal shared interpretations must be developed in order to produce organized action (Donnellon, Gray, and Bougon 1986). Development of these shared interpretations may be achieved through negotiation of a solution based on accumulated experience in order to establish mutual understanding.

A major difference between uncertainty and ambiguity is the required information-processing response.[2] Acquiring additional information through the process of search reduces uncertainty. The exchange of individual constructions of reality among organizational members in order to facilitate a joint decision on a solution reduces ambiguity. In order to arrive at a shared understanding, organizational members resolve disagreements that are based on ambiguity. To reduce ambiguity, individuals within the organization must thus jointly define information.

Media vary in their capacity to reduce uncertainty or ambiguity. Therefore, media need to be matched to the type of information-processing task in order to make organizational learning possible. Various media available to organizational members are discussed in this chapter in order to deepen the understanding of the role that media have in fostering information acquisition, information distribution, information interpretation, and organizational memory and thereby to support learning tasks proposed by Huber (1991). Because the information-processing context connected with each learning process varies, managers need to match the context, be it one of uncertainty or of ambiguity, with the appropriate medium. This notion is consistent with Nonaka, Reinmöller, and Toyama's contention (see Ch. 37 in this volume) that computer supported tools regulate different modes of knowledge conversion through sustaining platforms of knowledge work, called *ba*.

Media Choice

Various information-processing contexts demand different types of media. Media choice

is the selection of channels of communication, e.g. written text, voice, or visual transmission. For example, one medium for communication is E-mail, with the channel being electronic transmission based on written text. Yet the term 'media' goes beyond channels, for it embodies a constellation of features. 'Features of a medium are both the objective and psychosocial characteristics of a medium that result from communication channel selection' (Griffith and Northcraft 1994: 273). Objective features of media include the speed of information transmission, the synchronicity, and the ability to provide feedback (Nass and Mason 1990). Psychosocial features are a result of collectively developed perceptions of contextually efficient media use (Fulk, Steinfield, Schmitz, and Power 1987).

In the growing literature on media choice, the discussion about objective and psychosocial features results from various theoretical approaches. Whereas media richness theory (Daft and Lengel 1984; Daft, Lengel, and Trevino 1987), social presence theory (Short, Williams, and Christie 1976), and situational theories (Rice 1992; Straub and Karahanna 1998) focus primarily on objective features of media, social influence theory (Fulk 1993; Schmitz and Fulk 1991), media symbolism (Daft, Lengel, and Trevino 1987; Trevino, Lengel, and Daft 1987), and critical mass theory (Markus 1987) pay more attention to the psychosocial features of media. In summary, media choice involves the selection of a medium based on two factors: invariant features and socially constructed features based on their context of use (Sitkin, Sutcliffe, and Barrios-Choplin 1992). In the following section, the most frequently mentioned concepts of media choice concepts are discussed.

Media Richness

Lengel (1983) introduced the media richness concept. He suggested that media exhibit features that vary in the richness of information processed. According to Lengel (1983), the term 'richness' refers to the ability of media to

---

[2] When we refer to information-processing, information is perceived to be dependent on the context and human values. This perspective is rather closely related to the concept of knowledge and, differs from Nonaka, Reinmöller, and Toyama's discussion of information and knowledge (Ch. 37 in this volume).

change human understanding by clarifying ambiguous issues. According to Daft and Lengel (1984), a mechanism's distinct features for richness are (a) the ability to provide rapid feedback, (b) the ability to communicate multiple cues, (c) the ability to convey personal feelings, and (d) the ability to use natural language. With these four features of media richness in mind, Daft and Lengel proposed a scale that denotes face-to-face communication as the richest medium, followed by telephone, personal written text (letters or memos), formal written text (documents or bulletins), and formal numeric text (data). In general, oral media are believed to be richer than written media, for they provide for immediate feedback and convey multiple cues.

Because ambiguity is key to understanding the amount and kind of interaction appropriate for delivering a message (Daft and Macintosh 1981; Trevino, Lengel, and Daft 1987), tasks with a high degree of ambiguity require organizational members to choose media that are rich. In essence, matching the information-processing task with the appropriate media choice leads to the most effective outcome. In support of this theory, Daft, Lengel, and Trevino (1987) demonstrated that managers who match medium to message content are rated as better performers than managers who do not. In addition, a meta-analysis of empirical research showed twice as many supportive as nonsupportive studies for the proposition that rich media are used for tasks characterized by a high degree of ambiguity (Straub and Karahanna 1998).

Although empirical support for media choice theory has been growing (Markus 1994; Schmitz and Fulk 1991; Steinfield and Fulk, 1987; Trevino, Lengel, and Daft 1987), new information technologies have challenged the original scale developed by Daft and Lengel. With the introduction of media such as electronic communication, teleconferencing, and voice mail, new technologies that have entered organizational life have features that go beyond the richness concept (Evans and Wurster 1997; Fulk and DeSanctis 1995; Zmud 1990). The first feature is the increased speed of communication, which leads to high volumes of information moving between people. The second is the reduction of costs of communication as the use of communication technology spreads. The third is the increased connection between people and machines, an interface that may eventually give people in organizations widespread access to information. The fourth is the rise in communication bandwidth, with more information moving simultaneously to different people and in a combination of text, voice, and graphics. The fifth is the integration of various computing technologies allowing information to be stored so that organizational members can retrieve the information from the collective database. Altering communication patterns and enabling organizations to process information in unprecedented ways, these features of computer-mediated media can make important contributions to organizational learning.

Based on these features, computer-mediated media have challenged the ranking of media that is based on the media richness concept. Empirical research has contested the relatively low ranking—somewhere between the telephone and nonelectronic written communication—that electronic communication has on in the richness scale (Fulk *et al.* 1987; Markus 1994; Saunders and Jones 1990). Markus (1994) found that electronic communication and voice mail are used more frequently and for different purposes than originally proposed by Daft and Lengel (1984). According to Markus (1994), electronic mail is used as a primary medium for internal work-related communication and is particularly important in situations involving time pressure. These various perspectives show that computer-mediated media, specifically electronic communication, have been used for purposes beyond the traditional explanations of media richness.

If the media richness scale does not explain media choice in its entirety, and if new technologies are increasingly being used, then there is a need to review the richness concept. This review can be pursued in two ways: by enlarging the traditional list of features proposed by Daft and Lengel (1984) or by adding a new concept separate from the richness concept, one that enhances the theoretical perspective on media choice. If the traditional list of features proposed by Daft and Lengel (1984) is enlarged, no clear ranking of the various media emerges. Table 23.1 shows the most frequently used media for daily communication, arranged by the number of frequently mentioned features. Electronic communication, for example, is high on the ability to record messages and to address multiple people, yet it is low in the ability to convey multiple cues. The opposite applies to face-to-face communication. Because no clear ranking emerges, there is a need to enhance the theoretical perspective by adding a separate concept, that of media scope.

Media Scope

Media scope involves two additional features: storage, referring to the ability to keep messages in memory, and reach, referring to the ability to address multiple people simultaneously. Although rich media reduce ambiguity, organizational members need to use media that are high in scope in order to reduce uncer-

tainty. The demand for more information increases as organizational members work together on interrelated tasks, across organizational levels and across time and space. The higher the demand for information by organizational members across organizational levels, time, and space, the more relevant a medium's scope is. The accessibility of another person in a different time zone (Swanson 1987) and the ability to finish a task by sending the same message to several people instead of talking to them individually (Markus 1994) may become as important as the ability of a medium to reduce ambiguity. These considerations highlight the importance of media scope as a criterion for selecting media. A manager may communicate via electronic mail, a medium high in scope, because it is more important to reach a person in a different location within a short period of time than it is to communicate face to face. It can therefore be argued that media scope represents an additional concept in determining media choice. The ability to keep messages in memory and the ability to address multiple recipients simultaneously reduce uncertainty by providing organiza-

Table 23.1. Media and their features

Medium	Features					
	Feedback	Channel	Source	Language	Storage	Reach
Face-to-face communication	Immediate	Visual, audio	Personal	Body, natural	Limited	Limited
Videoconferencing	Almost immediate	Visual, audio	Personal	Body, natural	Limited	Moderate
Telephone	Fast	Audio	Personal	Natural	Limited	Limited
Voice mail	Moderate	Limited audio	Personal	Natural	Possible	Moderate
Fax	Moderate	Text	Personal	Natural	Possible	Moderate
Electronic communication	Moderate	Text	Personal, impersonal	Natural	Possible	Wide
Formal letter	Slow	Text	Personal, impersonal	Natural	Possible	Wide
Numeric output	Slow	Text	impersonal	Numeric	Possible	Wide

tional members with wide access to information. The distinction between media richness and scope has been implicitly mentioned by Boisot (1995), who suggested that (a) information abstraction or codification and (b) information diffusion are separate concepts that demand different types of support. Information diffusion increases the population to which information is available. For this purpose, media high in scope are useful. Information abstraction and codification demand cognitive investment and therefore require rich media.

Figure 23.1 shows the tradeoff between rich media and media high in scope. Based on analysis of the situation's degree of ambiguity and uncertainty, media choice involves the selection of a medium that matches the information-processing task. Because there is no ideal medium, which combines media richness and scope, media choice entails consideration of the type of information task—ambiguous versus uncertain tasks—and a tradeoff between the two concepts.

Media Perception

The inability of the richness theory to explain the confounding empirical evidence has led to the search for broader collective variables. These theories are not based on object-centered media choice. They are a 'collective behavioral response to a socially constructed definition of the medium's appropriateness' (Markus 1994: 522). Richness is viewed not as a cause of behavior but rather as an outcome of social behavior. The most comprehensive theory in this regard is the social influence model of technology use (Fulk 1993; Fulk et al. 1987). It posits that the perception of an individual medium perception is not just a function of objective, rational choice but is partly a social construction. Because communication arises in social contexts, the perception of and attitudes and behavior toward media influence the choices made by managers (Rice and Shook 1990; Webster and Trevino 1995). Perceptions of media attributes are socially constructed through information exchange. This construction may result from

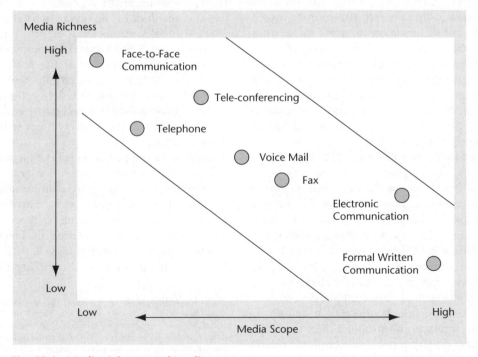

Fig. 23.1. Media richness and media scope

social patterns of use, co-worker influences, organizational norms, or the culture of media use. These factors determine media selection within organizations. Because the environment of organizations and social interactions vary between companies, media selection differs depending on the context. As far as social influence is concerned, technology will not be adopted because of its invariant features but rather because of individual attitudes toward or group norms applying to various communication technologies.

Variables influencing media choice are characteristics of the organization, personal attitudes, job demands, and one's level in the organization's hierarchy (Rice and Aydin 1991). For example, the more experienced a manager is with a medium, the more likely he or she is to have a positive attitude toward that medium and therefore the more likely that person is to use it. Different jobs may also imply various levels and types of technology use and may thereby influence attitudes toward media. An individual's level in the organization can also influence his or her attitudes about the information requirements and participation in the decision-making process. For example, executives may require more strategic information than their subordinates do and may therefore demand increased use of monthly updates through reports. All these influences result in differing perceptions about appropriate media use. Media use that is adapted to the needs of the organization is likely to foster organizational learning.

Social-influence theorists (Fulk 1993; Fulk *et al.* 1987) have argued that patterns of use of established media persist over time even when more efficient communication media become available. This argument contrasts with the object-centered perspective, according to which patterns of media use change as new technologies are adopted. For example, telex has been replaced by fax machines, and electronic mail is likely to replace phone calls or meetings for tasks that do not require a high amount of social interaction. Although Rice and Bair (1984) and Markus (1994) substantiated this assumption about the substitution process, evidence also suggests that established media are not completely supplanted. The influence of social norms within organizations explains the additional situations in which new, more efficient media continue to be under- or over-utilized. Computer-mediated media, such as electronic mail, video conferencing, or voice mail, will be adopted depending on the organizational context of use. If key managers within organizations do not readily use electronic mail, then the introduction of this medium is likely to take longer than if those managers did readily use it. If, however, key managers champion the use of electronic mail, then this medium is likely to replace other media. In addition, a critical mass of users[3] exist before a medium becomes effective (Markus 1987; Markus 1994; Rudy 1996). According to the theory of critical mass, an individual's media choices are interdependent with the organizational context. It is beneficial to use a medium to which everyone has access, for that medium reduces the costs of using multiple media to convey information decline (Markus 1987). Electronic mail, a universal access medium, requires that nearly everyone in the organization agree to use this medium on a regular basis (Markus 1994). If social patterns for widespread use of electronic mail have not been established within an organization, then the match between the medium (e.g. electronic mail) and the information-processing task (e.g. information distribution) will not necessarily enhance learning, for the information will not arrive at all destinations.

Social influence theorists take the social context of behavior into consideration and focus on the informal, emergent communication processes. From this point of view, the informal communication processes are seen as both antecedents and consequences of behavior and attitudes toward technology. Rather than looking at the features of media to determine

[3] In the anthropological literature, the idea of critical mass has been expanded with the term 'diffusion', or 'translation', referring to the idea that through interaction of people information is mediated and a link created that did not exist before (Czarniawska, Ch. 5 in this volume).

media choice, social influence theorists high-light the importance of media perception as a criterion for media use within organizations. Although media choice based on media percep-tion or media richness and scope may diverge initially, Markus (1994) has argued that media selection will converge over time because the most effective media will socially dominate within an organization.

Media Richness, Media Scope, Media Perception, and Organizational Learning

For media to foster organizational learning, they must support the processes of information acquisition, distribution, interpretation, and storage. Media richness, media scope, and media perception are all important factors to consider when choosing a medium to process information. Therefore, it is important to con-sider what media features or attitudes contrib-ute to the various learning processes. We propose that a match between information-processing tasks and media richness, scope, and perceptions contributes to learning organ-izations.

Information Acquisition and Media

Information acquisition refers to the incorpora-tion of external information into the organ-izational knowledge base (MacDonald 1995). Information is acquired from outside the boundaries of the firm and is integrated with existing information. The organization 'must bring home this new information to be mixed with resident information to shape a novel pattern of knowledge into a package that can be used' (MacDonald 1995: 562). This process focuses on the breadth of organizational learn-ing that is achieved by acquiring a large pool of external information (Huber 1991).

One of the challenges of information acqui-sition lies in the need to capture weak signals in the environment (Ansoff 1975). Capturing weak signals involves the identification of threats and opportunities and is crucially important in double-loop learning processes, for which the organization has to look for long-term options beyond existing strategies. Through increased information-gathering from the environment, the organization is able to shar-pen its awareness of the threats and opportu-nities in the environment and thereby increase its 'absorptive capacity' (Cohen and Levinthal 1990). Absorptive capacity, a firm's ability to recognize the value of new external informa-tion, assimilate it, and apply it to commercial ends, is a function of a firm's existing know-ledge. Information acquisition, which involves awareness of threats and opportunities in stra-tegically ambiguous environments, demands the use of rich media. In ambiguous situations, 'personal sources may provide the direct under-standing needed by senior executives to inter-pret unclear issues' (Daft, Sormunen, and Parks 1988: 126). When acquisition involves under-standing the information, the use of rich media is necessary to make sense of the envir-onment in order to be able to detect threats and opportunities. In this context, face-to-face communication, teleconferencing, and the telephone provide multiple cues and allow for rapid feedback.

Task analyzability is an additional factor to be considered for media choice. Task analyz-ability is the way that individuals are able to respond to problems that arise in the process of task completion. 'Analyzable tasks are those for which predetermined responses to potential problems and well-known procedures, are available and useful, because outcomes are well understood' (Rice 1992: 478). Unanalyzable tasks are those for which no suitable solution is already known. Because the analyzability of a task is related to the degree of task ambiguity, it determines the type of media required for learning based on information acquisition. In situations involving unanalyzable tasks, Rice (1992) found some support for the hypoth-esis that rich media are used to acquire information. The unanalyzability of a task de-mands information-processing that is relat-ively 'personal, less linear, more *ad hoc* and improvisional' (Daft and Weick 1984: 287). This kind of information-processing requires the use of rich media if one is to understand the nature of the task. In situations involving analyzable tasks, media high in scope are suitable, for organizational members know how to respond if the type of problem is known. Under these circumstances managers search for more information in order to be able to solve a problem characteristic of an uncertain, but not ambiguous, situation.

For information acquisition, media perception may not be as important as for the other learning processes—information distribution, interpretation, and storage—because one has more autonomy in using various media to acquire outside information than to distribute, interpret, or store it. This autonomy enables managers to make choices with a relatively high degree of independence from the internal organizational context. However, managers need to be aware of the patterns of media usage among their communication partners outside the organization. Obtaining a report through electronic mail from an industry association, for instance, requires knowledge about the availability of electronic mail within the association. Therefore, knowledge about external patterns of media use is important for information acquisition.

In summary, it is suggested that different types of media are appropriate for learning through information acquisition (Daft and Lengel 1984; Jones, Saunders, and McLeod 1988). Because ambiguous situations demand rich media whereas uncertain situations demand media high in scope, one can conclude that effective media use for information acquisition depends on the perceived nature of the environment or type of task.

Information Distribution and Media

Development of organizational knowledge requires a certain amount of consensus between individuals on the content of knowledge. Yet organizational learning also implies that the development of different interpretations leads to an increase of the organizational knowledge base (Huber 1991; Fiol 1994). Through expansion of the variety of interpretations, new ideas enter the organization, increasing its stock of knowledge. As Huber (1991) argued 'it seems reasonable to conclude that more learning has occurred when more and more varied interpretations have been developed, because such development changes the range of the organization's potential behaviors, and this is congruent with the definition of learning' (p. 102). Information distribution can foster the existence of both homogeneous and varied interpretations of information by allowing information to be shared between organizational members.

The main challenges for information distribution and sharing are spatial and hierarchical barriers between various functional groups or subcultures. Media high in scope may help overcome hierarchical and spatial barriers by increasing the likelihood of reaching organizational members across organizational levels, time, and space. Sending a fax, letter, or electronic mail to the CEO for his or her information allows all organizational members to reach the CEO and avoids the spatial constraints entailed by face-to-face communication or a telephone call.

Media high in scope may also overcome hierarchical barriers by overcoming the inhibiting factors of hierarchical differences and thereby allowing organizational members from different levels to participate equally in information-sharing (Griffith and Northcraft 1994: 277). Tan, Wei, and Watson (1999) found that when groups are engaged in activities in which authority differentials matter, group support systems, a medium high in scope, can remedy the problem by allowing groups to substitute verbal with textual cues. This substitution process was found to reduce status differentials. Anonymity and simultaneity are the features of group support systems that can alter status differentials (Dennis and Gallupe 1993). Anonymity gives lower-status individuals opportunities to contradict higher-status individuals without fear of being identified. Simultaneity does not allow higher-level individuals to dominate group discussions. The reduction of inhibited behavior is needed in order to facilitate the exchange of information (Griffith and Northcraft 1994). Fostering the exchange of ideas across organizational levels by reducing inhibited behavior is likely to lead to varied interpretations of information and can thus contribute to organizational learning.

Given high levels of interdependence between organizational members, electronic communication, a medium high in scope, reduces coordination costs by obviating the need for physical proximity. This contribution allows the widespread distribution of information and thereby fosters organizational learning. Feldman (1987) found that the greater the spatial distance between communication partners, the higher the proportion of messages that have been sent (or received) by electronic mail. By loosening the constraint of spatial proximity, electronic communication reduces the costs of signaling one's interest, so people who otherwise would not know that they share common interests can now discover and communicate with each other (Feldman 1987: 95). By communicating with groups of people distant from one's close network, one has access to more ideas and information than would otherwise be the case. According to Scherer and Tran (Ch. 16 in this volume), emotions can play a major role in the process of filtering and searching because they act as 'relevance detectors'. These relevance detectors allow organizational members to filter distribution lists and at the same time allow people to broadcast their problems and potential solutions to others with similar interests. Once a common interest has been identified, the exchange of ideas is likely to increase. If it does, the exchange can foster the development of both varied and shared interpretations of information and, hence, learning.

For information distribution, media perception plays an important role, for the reception of information depends on factors influenced by the social environment of the organization. Two factors influencing the reception of information are organizational usage patterns and compatibility of media infrastructures. If there is a high degree of divergence in media infrastructures between sender and receiver, the sender cannot use all the media at his or her disposal in order to distribute information. A similar argument applies patterns of media to usage. A critical mass of users must exist within the organization if a manager is to be reasonably sure that the information will arrive at most destinations. In addition, symbolic cues attached to media may influence the type of media chosen for distributing information. Symbolic cues influence media choice because the medium itself is considered to be a symbol or carrier of meaning (Trevino, Lengel, and Daft 1987). When the CEO of an organization announces the best-employee-of-the-year award, a medium that is low in richness may not be sufficient to signal to other organizational members the significance that the company attributes to personal achievements. Electronic mail may suffice to report on the unambiguous decision to reward an employee, yet it may not have enough symbolic value to motivate other employees to strive for similar recognition.

Although media high in scope may serve the purpose of widely distributing information, the repeated use of the same type of medium may also be ineffective. According to Tourish and Hargie (1998), the main source of the National Health Service staff's dissatisfaction with the reception of information from managers was a lack of face-to-face contact and too much written information. Overusing certain media may focus attention on issues that are less relevant than others and can thereby confuse organizational members about where the organization is headed. Because the medium of communication can be selected for symbolic purposes, repetitive use of the same medium may send an unintended message to the organization. Relying solely on electronic communication even when congratulating a manager for his or her achievement in the organization may signal lack of appreciation. Thus, media selection based on media perception is not the only factor critical to learning; so is the degree to which those media are used.

Information Interpretation and Media

Interpretation is the 'process through which information is given meaning' (Daft and Weick 1984: 294). As a part of the learning process, information interpretation requires a certain amount of agreement on shared knowledge. Adding to this point, Huber (1991) argued that there is a need for a common or shared understanding among the organization's units that various interpretations exist, a multiplicity that requires consensus on interpretations.

One of the challenges for developing shared interpretations of information is the need for social interaction and collective sense-making (Weick 1995). As Starbuck and Milliken (1988) mentioned, sense-making consists of understanding 'incongruous events, events that violate perceptual frameworks' (p. 52). In these situations, organizational members perceive ambiguity because of a lack of clarity or high complexity of information, making multiple interpretations possible (Martin 1992). Because organizational members need to take action, contradictory conclusions about events require communication in order to arrive at a minimum shared understanding.

Huber (1991: 102) suggested that the extent to which interpretations of new information are shared is likely to be affected by the richness of the media used to convey information. Media richness plays a crucial role in developing shared interpretation because rich media allow for both the sender and the receiver of a message to develop common meaning. Meaning is primarily created and negotiated as individuals retain cues from others and obtain feedback to help interpret information. This process is aided by the use of natural language, rapid feedback, and multiple cues, all of which are characteristics of rich media. Anthropologists have provided similar findings, pointing out that the establishment of cultural patterns requires continuous first-hand contact (Czarniawska, Ch. 5 in this volume).

Face-to-face communication, a rich medium, can change organizational members' frames of reference within a specific time interval. For example, Nonaka, Toyama, and Byosière and Nonaka, Reinmöller, and Toyama (Chs. 22 and 37 in this volume) speak of the dialoguing *ba*, the process of face-to-face interactions among a group of people. This assessment of face-to-face communication is supported by Weick (1995), who concluded that 'people need to meet more often' (p. 185). Through feedback and multiple cues in meetings, understanding can be checked and interpretations corrected. Daft, Lengel, and Trevino (1987) found that effective managers use rich media when developing a common understanding and thereby lend credence to the notion that richness has a bearing on the establishment of shared interpretations. In addition, Hedlund, Ilgen, and Hollenbeck (1998) found that face-to-face, rather than computer-mediated, communication can increase awareness of necessary information and raise the accuracy of group decision-making on tasks demanding consensus. This finding bears out the need to use rich media for ambiguous situations. The use of rich media facilitates the development of shared interpretations within the organization. According to Donnellon, Gray, and Bougon (1986), a minimum degree of shared interpretation within the organization is necessary to produce organized action and hence organizational learning.

Although empirical work has confirmed that media richness is an important criterion for media selection in ambiguous situations (Carlson and Davis 1998), other criteria may intervene to undermine the selection of a rich medium. Such interference may come from users' perceptions about the organizational context, communication partners, or the type of relationship between communication partners. Other contextual factors influencing media selection are job and time pressures, geographic dispersion, individual media experience, and attitudes of colleagues. If, for example, a task must be completed when the other person is not available for face-to-face contact, geographic dispersion combined with job and time pressure may demand the use of a medium that is low in richness.

Organizational Memory and Media

Organizational memory refers to stored information drawn from an organization's history information that can be brought to bear on present decisions (Walsh and Ungson 1991). Organizations continually store information as standard operating procedures (March and Simon 1958) routines, rules,[4] and scripts (Nelson and Winter 1982; see also Kieser, Beck, and Tainio, Ch. 27 in this volume). Memory involves the retention of information in various storage sites, ranging from individuals to organizational routines and archives.

According to Huber (1991: 106), organizational memory plays a critical role in organizational learning because the effectiveness of an organization's memory affects the other learning processes. When past information is stored within an organization, it may not have to be acquired from the outside. It may be readily retrievable and available for distribution, and comments on the stored information may facilitate interpretation. We propose that media choice for organizational memory depends on the type of storage site.

Individuals retain information based on their own experiences with and observations about action–outcome relationships. Czarniawska (Ch. 5 in this volume) suggests that the change in individual action patterns is reinforced by interaction. This process enables individual action patterns to be stored as information in the organization's memory. Walsh and Ungson (1991) complemented this behavioral perspective by proposing that individuals have the cognitive capability of understanding the 'why' of a decision. Because the why of a decision 'will distort and decay as it is passed over time' (Walsh and Ungson 1991: 68), it is important to use rich media for storing information with individuals. Rich media enable the communication of contextual information. Face-to-face communication, a rich medium, minimizes the amount of distortion and makes it possible

to store information in the cognitive repositories of individuals. The degree to which these cognitive repositories serve learning depends on the interconnectedness, integration, and trust of individuals within the organization (Kieser, Beck, and Tainio, Ch. 27 in this volume).

Culture has been defined as learned ways of perceiving, thinking, and feeling about problems that are transmitted to members of the organization (Schein 1985). Routines are one of the forms in which cultural information is stored. Organizational routines reduce transaction costs associated with search and experimentation. They can facilitate learning by providing information on how to deal with the occurrence of typical problems, by increasing transparency through the provision of contextual information, by ensuring the analysis of deviations, and by allowing organizational members to participate in their establishment (Kieser, Beck, and Tainio, Ch. 27 in this volume). Organizational members develop routines over time through the process of sharing interpretations. For this purpose, rich media are required because a shared definition of information is primarily created through natural language, rapid feedback, and multiple cues. Rich media can also help enhance people's commitment to and involvement in a collective learning process, hence the interest in teams as an organizational mechanism with which to promote learning. One of the dangers of using rich media is the creation of conflicting interpretations of events, discrepancies that would lead to deviant memories and biases maintained by subcultures. This outcome could lead to preferential recall of previous memories or to the repression of information from memory (Scherer and Tran, Ch. 16 in this volume).

When the memory of individuals fails, organizational members may also turn to archives as sources for retention. Organizations use various forms of archival systems, such as annual reports, performance indicators, benchmarking reports, or database systems that chronicle an organization's past. Storing information in a universally accessible manner in archival

---

[4] After an extensive review of the literature, Kieser, Beck, and Tainio (Ch. 27 in this volume) define rules as ideas shared by a number of people about which behavior is appropriate under certain conditions. Routines link behavior to rules.

systems, increases the likelihood that a large number of organizational members will retrieve and use this information. Because media high in scope support the archiving of information and thereby help keep track of the organization's past, organizational memory can be enhanced.

The archival storage of information also enables organizational members to follow the pattern of their negotiation with others over time. As a result, the identification of common interests among organizational members is facilitated. This identification process may lead to jointly defined solutions (Griffith and Northcraft 1994) based on the shared interpretations that develop. Stored information can contribute to the development of shared understanding by making it possible to trace individual frames of reference over time and thereby to build on existing knowledge. Electronic communication and written letters allow organizational members to trace their messages over time. Therefore, media high in scope seem to be appropriate for storing information in archival systems.

In summary, whether learning based on organizational memory demands the use of media high in scope or media high in richness depends on the type of storage site. The use of media high in scope fosters learning by storing information within database systems or archives. If individuals or organizational routines are storage sites for organizational memory, then rich media are necessary to facilitate learning. The use of rich media enhances learning by helping people keep track of past decisions, cognitive maps, or frames of references.

Media perception plays a critical role in storage sites where rich media are appropriate. If individuals are the storage site, media perception has an important impact on media choice because the symbolic message of media influences the way information is stored in the minds of individuals. For organizational routines, media perception is important because consistency of information-sharing can be guaranteed only if the way information is shared is consistent with the symbolic impact of the medium. Media perception may not be as important for storing information in archival systems as it is for storing information in the minds of people, for the social context of the organization has a smaller influence on storing information in documented form than in other forms.

Table 23.2 summarizes the relationship between learning processes, learning context, and media choice. Information distribution primarily calls for the selection of media high in scope, whereas information interpretation generally requires the selection of rich media. For information acquisition and organizational

Table 23.2. Match between learning processes, learning context, and media choice

Learning process	Factors influencing learning context	Media choice based on media richness and scope	Importance of media perception
Information acquisition	Capturing weak signals Unanalyzable tasks	Media richness	Medium
	Analyzable tasks	Media scope	Low
Information distribution	High interdependence	Media scope	High
	Hierarchical and spatial barriers		
Information interpretation	Consensus	Media richness	High
Organizational memory	Individuals, routines	Media richness	High
	Database systems, archives	Media scope	Low

memory, the appropriate choice of a medium depends on a number of different factors. In order to identify opportunities and threats in the environment or to find solutions to unanalyzable tasks, rich media are appropriate for information acquisition. For analyzable tasks, media high in scope ought to be chosen for information acquisition. Storing information in individuals or organizational routines demands the use of rich media, whereas storing information in archival or database systems involves using media high in scope. In addition to choosing media according to their invariant features, managers need to pay attention to the organizational context within which the media are used. Organizational norms for various media may have developed over time, an outcome that may undermine the use of certain media. It would therefore be appropriate to consider the organizational context before setting on a particular medium. Media perception has the most important impact not only on information distribution and interpretation but also on the storage of information in individuals or organizational repositories.

Conclusion

We have proposed that media be selected according to the type of information-processing task associated with learning. Because the underlying information-processing task for each learning process is fundamentally different, a match between learning process and media richness and scope is necessary in order to foster learning within organizations. Although media richness and media scope are considered to be the two most important criteria of selection, these variables are sometimes overridden by the presence of other needs, such as media accessibility, ease of use, or need for symbolic impact. Therefore, the role that media perception has in each learning process depends on the social context of their use. For information distribution, interpretation, and organizational memory stored in individuals or organizational routines, media perception is

crucial, for human interaction is more prominent during these processes than in any other.

The framework for media choice has implications for both managers and architects of information systems. This framework allows managers to make more informed information-processing decisions about the appropriate use of media for various learning tasks. In studying the situation before selecting a medium, a manager may improve his or her performance because the appropriate match between medium and information task can be found. And in understanding the features of available media, information system architects are able to make informed implementation decisions once they are aware of the learning purpose of new technologies. Managers' sharpened awareness of media features and media perception increases the likelihood that informed media choices will be made in the future. Raising the degree to which the architects of information systems are aware of the user context will facilitate the implementation of new information technology within organizations.

The proposed framework also has implications for further research. Because media vary in their capacity to reduce uncertainty or ambiguity, enhancing organizational learning means matching media to the type of information-processing task involved. Table 23.2 outlines propositions in which media choice concepts and organizational learning processes are matched according to the type of information-processing task at hand. For example, can one empirically confirm the propositions that information interpretation relies exclusively on rich media and that information distribution relies exclusively on media high in scope? Is media perception more important in situations where rich media should primarily be used? Although theoretical arguments have been provided to support the framework developed in this chapter, it is necessary to validate these propositions empirically.

Given the frequency and importance of media choice in the everyday communication of managers, both descriptive and prescriptive investigations of media choice are important.

Research is needed to support the findings that media choice is related to managerial effectiveness (see Daft, Lengel, and Trevino 1987). If this relationship can be empirically supported, then it will be crucial for managers to be able to match the types of media with information-processing tasks. In prescriptive terms, a sound match between media and information-processing task is expected to lead to improved managerial performance.

References

Ansoff, H. I. (1975). 'Managing Strategic Surprise by Response of Weak Signals'. *California Management Review*, 17/3: 21–33.

Boisot, M. (1995). *Information Space: A Framework for Learning in Organizations, Institutions and Culture*. London: Routledge.

Carlson, P. and Davis, G. (1998). 'An Investigation of Media Selection among Directors and Managers: From "Self" to "Other" Orientation'. *Management Information Systems Quarterly*, 22: 335–62.

Cohen, W. M. and Levinthal, D. A. (1990). 'Absorptive Capacity: A New Perspective on Learning and Innovation'. *Administrative Science Quarterly*, 35: 128–52.

Daft, R. L. and Lengel, R. H. (1984). 'Information Richness: A New Approach to Managerial Behavior and Organization Design', in B. M. Staw and L. L. Cummings (eds.), *Research in Organizational Behavior: An Annual Series of Analytical Essays and Critical Reviews* (Vol. 6). Greenwich, Conn.: JAI Press, 191–233.

—— —— and Trevino, L. K. (1987). 'Message Equivocality, Media Selection and Manager Performance: Implications for Information Systems'. *Management Information Systems Quarterly*, 11: 355–66.

—— and Macintosh, N. B. (1981). 'A Tentative Exploration into the Amount and Equivocality of Information Processing in Organizational Work Units'. *Administrative Science Quarterly*, 26: 207–24.

—— Sormunen, J., and Parks, D. (1988). 'Chief Executive Scanning, Environmental Characteristics, and Company Performance: An Empirical Study'. *Strategic Management Journal*, 9: 123–39.

—— and Weick, K. E. (1984). 'Toward a Model of Organizations as Interpretation Systems'. *Academy of Management Review*, 9: 284–95.

Davenport, T. H. (1997). *Information Ecology*. New York: Oxford University Press.

—— Eccles, R. G., and Prusak, L. (1992). 'Information Politics'. *Sloan Management Review*, 34/1: 53–65.

Dennis, A. and Gallupe, R. (1993). 'A History of Group Support Systems Empirical Research: Lessons Learned and Future Directions', in L. Jessup and J. Valacich (eds.), *Group Support Systems: New Perspectives*. New York: Macmillan, 59–77.

Donnellon, A., Gray, B., and Bougon, M. G. (1986). 'Communication, Meaning, and Organized Action'. *Administrative Science Quarterly*, 31: 43–55.

Evans, P. B. and Wurster, T. S. (1997). 'Strategy and the New Economics of Information'. *Harvard Business Review*, 75/5: 71–82.

Feldman, M. S. (1987). 'Electronic Mail and Weak Ties in Organizations'. *Office, Technology and People*, 3: 83–101.

Fiol, C. M. (1994). 'Consensus, Diversity, and Learning in Organizations'. *Organization Science*, 5: 403–20.

Fulk, J. (1993). 'Social Construction of Communication Technology'. *Academy of Management Journal*, 36: 921–50.

—— and DeSanctis, G. (1995). 'Electronic Communication and Changing Organizational Forms'. *Organization Science*, 6: 337–49.

—— Steinfield, C., Schmitz, J., and Power, J. (1987). 'A Social Information Processing Model of Media Use in Organizations'. *Communication Research*, 14: 529–52.

Galbraith, J. R. (1974). 'Organization Design: An Information Processing View'. *Interfaces*, 4/3: 28–36.

Griffith, T. L. and Northcraft, G. B. (1994). 'Distinguishing between the Forest and the Trees: Media, Features, and Methodology in Electronic Communication Research'. *Organization Science*, 5: 272–85.

Hedlund, J., Ilgen, D., and Hollenbeck, J. (1998). 'Decision Accuracy in Computer-mediated versus Face-to-face Decision-making Teams'. *Organizational Behavior and Human Decision Processes*, 76: 30–47.

Huber, G. P. (1991). 'Organizational Learning: The Contributing Processes and the Literatures'. *Organization Science*, 2: 88–115.

Jones, J. W., Saunders, C., and McLeod, R. (1988). 'Information Media and Source Patterns across Management Levels: A Pilot Study'. *Journal of Management Information Systems*, 5/3: 71–84.

Kurke, L. and Aldrich, H. (1983). 'Mintzberg Was Right: A Replication and Extension of the Nature of Managerial Work'. *Management Science*, 29: 975–83.

Lengel, R. H. (1983). *Managerial Information Processing and Communication Media Source Selection*. Unpublished doctoral dissertation. Texas A & M University, College Station.

MacDonald, S. (1995). 'Learning to Change: An Information Perspective on Learning in the Organization'. *Organization Science*, 6: 557–68.

Malhotra, Y. (1997). *Knowledge Management for the New World of Business*. Available: www.brint.com/km/whatis.html

March, J. G. and Simon, H. A. (1958). *Organizations*. New York: Wiley.

Markus, M. L. (1987). 'Toward a "Critical Mass" Theory of Interactive Media'. *Communication Research*, 14: 491–511.

—— (1994). 'Electronic Mail as the Medium of Managerial Choice'. *Organization Science*, 5: 502–27.

Martin, J. (1992). *Culture in Organizations*. New York: Oxford University Press.

Mintinko, M. and Gardner, W. (1990). 'Structured Observation of Managerial Work: A Replication and Synthesis'. *Journal of Management Studies*, 3: 329–57.

Mintzberg, H. (1973). *The Nature of Managerial Work*. New York: Harper & Row.

Montgomery, J. (1986). 'Life at the APEX: The Functions of Permanent Secretaries in Nine Southern African Countries'. *Public Administration and Development*, 6: 211–21.

Nass, C. and Mason, L. (1990). 'On the Study of Technology and Task: A Variable-based Approach', in J. Fulk and C. Steinfield (eds.), *Organizations and Communication Technology*. Newbury Park, Calif.: Sage, 46–67.

Nelson, R. R. and Winter, S. G. (1982). *An Evolutionary Theory of Economic Change*. Cambridge, Mass.: Belknap Press.

Pentland, B. (1995). 'The Social Epistemology of Organizational Learning Systems'. *Accounting, Management and Information Technology*, 5/1: 1–21.

Rice, R. E. (1992). 'Task Analyzability, Use of New Media, and Effectiveness: A Multi-site Exploration of Media Richness'. *Organization Science*, 3: 475–500.

—— and Aydin, C. (1991). 'Attitudes toward New Organizational Technology: Network Proximity as a Mechanism for Social Information Processing'. *Administrative Science Quarterly*, 36: 219–44.

—— and Bair, J. (1984). 'New Organizational Media and Productivity', in R. Rice (ed.), *The New Media*. Beverly Hills, Calif.: Sage, 185–216.

—— and Shook, D. E. (1990). 'Relationships of Job Categories and Organizational Levels to Use of Communication Channels, Including Electronic Mail: A Meta-analysis and Extension'. *Journal of Management Studies*, 27: 195–229.

Rudy, I. A. (1996). 'A Critical Review of Research on Electronic Mail'. *European Journal of Information Systems*, 4: 198–213.

Saunders, C. and Jones, J. W. (1990). 'Temporal Sequences in Information Acquisition for Decision-Making: A Focus on Source and Medium'. *Academy of Management Review*, 15: 29–46.

Schein, E. H. (1985). *Organizational Culture and Leadership: A Dynamic View*. San Francisco: Jossey-Bass.

Schmitz, J. and Fulk, J. (1991). 'Organizational Colleagues, Media Richness, and Electronic Mail'. *Communication Research*, 18: 487–523.

Short, J., Williams, E., and Christie, B. (1976). *The Social Psychology of Telecommunication*. London: Wiley.

Sitkin, S. B., Sutcliffe, K., and Barrios-Choplin, J. (1992). 'A Dual-capacity Model of Communication Media Choice in Organizations'. *Human Communication Research*, 18: 563–98.

Starbuck, W. H. and Milliken, F. J. (1988). 'Executives' Perceptual Filters: What They Notice and How They Make Sense', in D. C. Hambrick (ed.), *The Executive Effect: Concepts and Methods for Studying Top Managers*. Greenwich, Conn.: JAI Press, 35–65.

Steinfield, C. W. and Fulk, J. (1987). 'On the Role of Theory in Research of Information Technologies in Organizations'. *Communication Research*, 14: 479–90.

Straub, D. and Karahanna, E. (1998). 'Knowledge Worker Communications and Recipient Availability: Toward a Task Closure Explanation of Media Choice'. *Organization Science*, 9: 160–75.

Swanson, B. E. (1987). 'Information Channel Disposition and Use'. *Decision Sciences*, 18: 131–45.

Tan, B., Wei, K., and Watson, R. (1999). 'The Equalizing Impact of a Group Support System on Status Differentials'. *ACM Transactions on Information Systems*, 17/1: 77–100.

Tourish, D. and Hargie, O. (1998). 'Communication between Managers and Staff in the NHS: Trends and Prospects'. *British Journal of Management*, 9: 53–71.

Trevino, L. K., Daft, R. L., and Lengel, R. H. (1990). 'Understanding Media Choices: A Symbolic Interactionist Perspective', in J. Fulk and W. Steinfield (eds.), *Organizations and Communication Technology*. Newbury Park, Calif.: Sage, 71–94.

——Lengel, R. H., and Daft, R. L. (1987). 'Media Symbolism, Media Richness, and Media Choice in Organizations'. *Communication Research*, 14: 553–74.

Tushman, M. L. and Nadler, D. A. (1978). 'Information Processing as an Integrating Concept in Organizational Design'. *Academy of Management Review*, 3: 613–24.

Walsh, J. P. and Ungson, G. R. (1991). 'Organizational Memory'. *Academy of Management Review*, 16: 57–91.

Webster, J. and Trevino, L. K. (1995). 'Rational and Social Theories as Complementary Explanations of Communication Media Choices: Two Policy-capturing Studies'. *Academy of Management Journal*, 38: 1544–72.

Weick, K. E. (1979). *The Social Psychology of Organizing* (2nd edn). Reading, Mass.: Addison-Wesley.

——(1995). *Sensemaking in Organizations*. Thousand Oaks, Calif.: Sage.

Zmud, R. W. (1990). 'Opportunities for Strategic Information Manipulation through New Information Technology', in J. Fulk and C. Steinfield (eds.), *Organizations and Communication Technology*. Newbury Park, Calif.: Sage, 95–116.

24 Organizing, Learning, and Strategizing: From Construction to Discovery

Bo Hedberg and Rolf Wolff

A reader of contemporary management books might conclude that organizational learning is the normal state of affairs. Students of the Fifth Discipline (Senge 1990) learn to handle tools in order to implement learning procedures in their companies, and Japanese companies excel in continuous learning, or *Kaizen*. Consultants sell learning through total quality management (TQM) in an ongoing and rather low-key effort, or through business process reengineering (BPR), promising radical restructuring of strategic business processes. Who dares admit that they run narrow-minded (although profitable) enterprises with little intention of learning? Still, inability to learn characterizes many organizations. Successful organizations find it difficult to unlearn and relearn when times change and failures occur. Organizational inertia stabilizes organizational development both when stability is functional and when it is dysfunctional. To unlearn previously successful strategies and to learn new ways to direct behavior is often very difficult. What Argyris and Schön (1978) called double-loop learning is often referred to, but rarely reported, at least not as far as learning at strategic levels in organizations is concerned.

Strategies that prolong success are easier to formulate than strategies that create success. But learning that affects strategy is particularly important when organizations face uncertainty and encounter 'crossroads.' Strategizing is supported by organizing, and restrategizing is often subject to organizational inertia. Attempts to change are blocked by existing organizational structures and processes. Thus, it is important to describe the interplay between organizing, learning, and strategizing in order to understand how these processes interact and sometimes interlock.

This chapter traces research on interfaces between organizing, learning, and strategizing. It starts out from a perspective in which organizations, knowledge, and strategies are seen as *constructed* by people, particularly by managers, and in which structures dominate. It ends up with a different perspective in which interactive processes dominate and organizations, knowledge, and strategies are *discovered* and made sense of, sometimes retrospectively and often as a result of reframing.

Organizing, Organizational Learning, and Strategizing: Patterns of Development

Organizing

Early organization theories were predominantly normative. Through them readers were told how to build a successful organization. They discussed and prescribed lines of command, spans of control, and line-and-staff interaction. With Barnard (1938) came an ambition to begin understanding and predicting organizational behavior.

The behavioral approach to organizations (the Carnegie School) focused on how the handling of information flows and decision flows shape organizational behavior. Early models, in which organizations were pictured as close-to-perfect goal-oriented systems (thermostats), were replaced by models such as the behavioral theory of the firm (Cyert and March 1963), where purely rational decision-making mechanisms were enriched by assumptions about human motivation, cognitive constraints, goal conflicts, and politics. Organizations emerged as purposive, but only partly manageable, sociotechnical systems.

Images of organizations as goal-seeking systems with slack were eventually replaced by images of organizations as organized anarchies (Cohen, March, and Olsen 1972), action generators (Starbuck 1983), or systems with rational irrationality (Brunsson 1985). In less than forty years, organization theories went from reassuring models of management as the art of control, through images of science muddling through, to models of management as hypocrisy and of decision centers as 'garbage cans'. In his book *Images of Organizations* Morgan (1986) showed how various perspectives on organizations coexist and how several of these images help people understand how to manage, or simply survive, in organizations.

The growing notion of organizations as combinations of processes (Nystrom, Hedberg, and Starbuck 1976; Weick 1979; Wolff 1982) stimulated the understanding of organizations as self-designing systems and as temporary systems in which sets of processes, in interaction, constitute the organization from time to time. It was a rather small step to go from that idea to approaches in which organizations were seen as time-dependent combinations of customer bases, delivery systems, core processes or core competencies (Hamel and Prahalad 1989), and partner systems in which markets were perceived as interactive networks (Håkansson and Snehota 1995). The advent of advanced information technology reduced transaction costs and facilitated lateral communication so that flat organizations—permanent or temporary constellations of rather independent actors—could be set up swiftly to meet market needs on nongeographical markets such as the Internet. The virtual enterprise emerged as a new role model (Davidow and Malone 1992; Hedberg *et al.* 1997).

Johansen and Swigart (1994) used the term 'fishnet organization' (pp. 10–15) to describe how components on markets are interrelated, as nodes in passive networks, and how a leader with a business idea can grab hold of the fishnet, raise the level of one particular node, and create a temporary hierarchy for a special purpose.

Hedberg *et al.* (1997) developed a framework based on imaginary systems to describe how new enterprises are created as combinations between leader units with visions, business ideas, certain core competencies, customer bases, delivery systems, systems for market communication and payment, and production systems based on coordinated partnerships. Descriptions of such imaginary systems made it easier to discover the activity systems behind many existing businesses.

In retrospect, the perspective on organizing has been shifting from a focus on building and constructing to a focus on discovering and interpreting, a development in which a multitude of basic processes exist to be combined rather than to be designed. Organizations were initially seen as perfect or nearly perfect, then as equally defective, whereas in the emerging perspective they are pictured as potentials to be discovered. Similar patterns of development can be read into both the body of knowledge on organizational learning and the understanding of strategy formulation.

Organizational Learning

Most theories of organizational learning developed out of cognitive psychology and were built upon the then current understanding of how individuals learn through their cognitive systems. These cognitive models were mostly based on stimulus–response mechanisms, whereby individuals, interacting with their environment, learned to discriminate within repertoires of stimuli and to connect these stimuli to repertoires of behavior. Successful couplings were reinforced by feedback, strengthened and perhaps refined, and then turned into action programs (standard operating procedures—SOPs).

When the computer came along as a practical research tool, there was a notable interaction between the development of computer architecture and the simultaneous development of new models in cognitive psychology. The computer served, however, not only as an image of human cognition but also as a tool for simulating organizational behavior. Elaborate models of organizational behavior began to emerge in the early 1960s, most notably with the behavioral theory of the firm (Cyert and March 1963), Bonini's (1963) simulations of information and decision systems, and Forrester's (1961, 1968, 1971) various studies of industrial and urban dynamics.

Computer models of the firm could fairly easily be programmed to learn. A simulation model is able to react to inputs (stimuli) and to store performance information in memory, making it relatively easy to represent organizational learning in a structure of interrelated programs. Such representation is exactly what is being done in the behavioral theory of the firm and, to some extent as well, in the various computer simulations that Cohen, March, and Olsen (1972) performed in order to demonstrate certain features of their garbage can model. This achievement, however, does not prove that *organizations* learn.

When organizations learn, they learn through individuals, and these individuals may form groups, departments, subsidiaries, or other organizational arrangements (Kim 1993). They may be employed now, or they may have been employed in the past. Thus, even if individuals learn on behalf of organizations, *organizations* may memorize, and such memories make up the groundwork for the future. 'This is the way we do things in this bank', says the experienced banker. 'The IKEA spirit' tells new employees a good deal about behavior and attitudes and passes on previous learning to future generations of employees in the worldwide IKEA empire (Salzer 1994). New leaders often make a point of departing from prevailing strategies and behaviors,

and change of leadership often facilitates unlearning.

Most theories of organizational learning develop models about the interaction between an organization and its environment. Organizations react to organizational conditions, but they also attempt to bring about favorable outside conditions. Repeated cycles of interaction form the basis for learning, programming, and reinforcement. Observing, reflecting, and acting are the three basic processes of the genuine learning cycle. However, much learning within organizations takes place through imitation (Bierly and Hämäläinen 1995; Sahlin-Andersson 1995).

The cycle implies that learning requires both change and stability in the relationship between organizations and their environments. If there is too much turbulence, the learning system will have difficulties in mapping anything. By the time observations are translated into actions, these actions may well be obsolete. Too much stability, on the other hand, is also dysfunctional. If established and functional behaviors almost never grow obsolete, there is marginal interest in learning and improving. Situations with much stability offer little information and few opportunities for learning; situations with much turbulence may produce much data but poor grounds for learning. The people responsible for the viability and efficiency of organizations should therefore be especially concerned about these balances to the extent that they can be designed and determined (Hedberg, Nystrom, and Starbuck 1976).

Noting the tendency toward cognitive programming in organizations, Argyris and Schön (1978) distinguished between single-loop and double-loop learning. The former is adaptive and takes place within the structure and processes of the learning system. This system is, in turn, framed within a theory of action. In double-loop learning this theory of action is replaced, a rare occurrence that results in radical reorientation. Double-loop learning implies a model with metalevels in which rules that define situations, analyze stimuli, assemble responses, and replace action programs are changed. Beer (1972) concluded that such me-talevel learning mostly lies outside the reach of managers and other policy-makers in complex organizations. These actors, he argued, mostly lack the language in which to express and change these metarules, so they are not able to implement new modes of behavior in their organizations. The result is that organizational change typically is restricted to shifts within modes of behavior and theories of action (Argyris 1992). When these theories become obsolete, survival is threatened. Figure 24.1 portrays a simple model of organizational learning with options for single-loop adjustments or double-loop changes. The model shows how the learning system (e.g. an organization) enacts and reacts in relation to its environments. Adjustments in this learning cycle take place through single loops, which improve the way problems are defined, modeled, and reacted to. Double-loop learning requires metalevel changes, such as reframing which allow new ways of formulating problems. Double-loop learning might also involve radical remodeling or innovative responses that go beyond the existing repertoire of behaviors.

Models of organizational learning were later enriched when the learning cycles often were found to be blocked, and hence incomplete, as observed by March and Olsen (1976). They outlined a sequence of models based on the interaction between individual action, organizational action, environmental response, and the forming of individual beliefs. When individual learning has little or nothing to do with individual behavior, learning is role-constrained (the first model in the sequence). When the link between organizational action and environmental response is weak, there is room for superstitious learning (the second model). When individual action does not affect organizational action, the learner sits in the audience (the third model). When the mapping of environmental responses onto individual beliefs is vague, learning takes place in conditions of ambiguity (the fourth model).

If the notion that successful organizations develop action programs is combined with the notion that many learning cycles are incomplete, fail to help the organization fully understand what is happening, and/or fail to affect organizational behavior directly, there is an obvious potential for delays and other imperfections in the learning cycle. It takes time for organizations to learn. It takes time for them

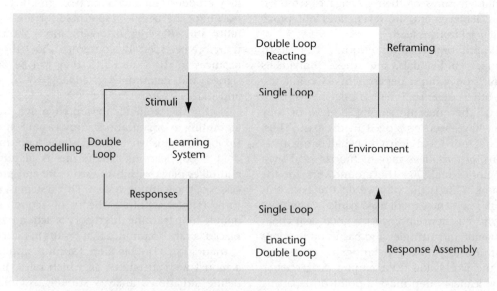

Fig. 24.1. Single-loop and double-loop learning

to establish action programs, and it takes even more time for them to eliminate and replace these action programs when they fail to work because they are obsolete. The result is organizational inertia. Hedberg and Ericson (1997) distinguished between insight inertia and action inertia. The former denotes the inertial forces that cause time lags between important changes in the environment and the organization's discovery and insights about the implications of that change. The latter denotes the forces that result in additional time lags between managerial insight and the implementation and results of actions taken. For example, it took several years for the management of Facit, a successful multinational manufacturer of electromechanical office machines, to gain insight into the full implications of the invasion of electronics into the calculator business (Hedberg 1974). It then took some years more (too many to survive) to reorient and reorganize the production systems for a new reality in technologies and in the market.

Delays due to incomplete learning cycles are one factor behind organizational inertia; the programming of behaviors during auspicious and successful periods is another. Before new learning can take place, unlearning has to happen. The more established and integrated the cognitive structures are, the more difficult unlearning becomes. Miller (1990) described how exceptional companies work their success programs to the point that Icharus' wings are melted by the sun. Spender (1989) used the term 'industrial recipes' to describe how successful SOPs spread from one company to others in developing industries. Industrial recipes are also a reminder that strategies in organizations result at least as much from imitation (Sahlin-Andersson 1995) and cross-industrial influences (e.g. consultants) as from organizational problem-solving.

Triggers, or cues, play important roles in S–R models of organizational learning. They are the initiators of both learning and unlearning. They build up action programs, and they tear them down. However, the latter process may well be delayed because of organizational inertia. Learning is not always easy, but unlearning is almost always difficult.

The current surge of interest in learning organizations has almost equated learning and flexibility. But the meaning of organizational learning is then restricted to incremental improvements at operative levels, such as those accomplished through *kaizen* and TQM. Important as these activities may be, they have little relevance for strategic reorientations and turnarounds in problem-ridden companies. Thus, although there is reason for optimism with respect to organizational learning as a widespread, daily activity in healthy companies, there is little reason for optimism about organizational learning that changes strategies when such changes are badly needed.

Attempting to trace the development of concepts pertaining to organizational learning, one finds a pattern similar to that characterizing the development of theories on organizing. Organizational learning was initially seen as perfect (or nearly perfect) interaction between and mapping of a learning organization and its environment. These early models were later enriched to include more and more defects in this interactive learning. As with the case of organizing, described above, a paradigm in which learning is seen as knowledge creation was confronted with an emergent perspective from which knowledge is discovered rather than produced and from which much more potential knowledge exists than what is known.

Before returning to this topic in the last section of this chapter, we first trace patterns of development in strategizing.

Strategizing

Jelinek (1979) has described the historical routes by which the management of operations and the management of strategy diverged. She rightly claimed that the use of formal systems is necessary for the institutionalization of strategy formation. Planning, by virtue of its powers of formalization, becomes the means both to create and operationalize strategy. Since the 1960s, the field of strategy research has gone through various more or less distinct stages of development and ups and downs. According to Andrews (1980) and Ansoff (1965), strategy concerns careful setting of objectives, systematic analysis, and techniques for evaluation and planning.

The focus of these approaches was on planning and the development of adequate techniques for analysis. Systematic analysis of past events and their extrapolations into the future was expected to provide the basis for product and market-related tactics and strategies. An assumption was that development over three to five years could be fairly well estimated. The business environment for these approaches can be characterized by companies in their first phase of internationalization. The political environment was relatively stable and economic growth was treated as a proxy. But when the environment changed in the 1970s—slowed rates of growth along with acceleration in internalization and in the pace of political crises—a new skepticism about planning and analysis emerged.

Whereas previous research had focused on planning, the decade of the 'fit' (the 1970s) was the period of an attempt to identify the 'strategic fit' between strategy, organization, and performance. 'The best strategy' suited to specific market conditions, 'the balanced portfolio', and 'the match of strategy and structure' were some of the major themes in the field. In retrospect, it is therefore no coincidence that Mintzberg's notion of 'emergent strategies' (Mintzberg, Ahlstrand, and Lampel 1998: 189–95) was introduced as a counter model during that same period. It was a rejection of planning and analysis, because empirical evidence showed that companies' processes of strategy formation and implementation were loosely coupled to formalized plans and budgets. There was also growing concern about the orientation of portfolio models to mass production, a concern that reflected a new competitive situation in global business.

The strategy field subsequently fell dormant until publication of work by Porter (1980, 1985), to whom a renaissance of interest in the strategy field was largely due. His work had an in-

tegrative and pedagogical power, merging the strategy field with industrial economics and opening it up for organization research (Porter 1998). His writing also had a strong conceptual influence on business practice, for he presented the nature of competition in a pedagogical way, introduced and explained the structure of value chains and value systems, and differentiated and related strategy types to the life cycles of industries.

The early 1990s marked a growing dominance of approaches in which strategy was examined from a process perspective (Mintzberg 1994; Mintzberg, Ahlstrand, and Lampel 1998). Simultaneously the organization perspective gained ground in the strategy field, not just through the contribution of 'implementation' of strategy but through the examination of processes of knowledge diffusion in organizations. In addition, the dimension of leadership started influencing the field as researchers began looking at the interplay between how strategies are developed and how they are constantly renewed. 'Strategy emerges under the influence of the driving force of a strategic vision in an ever-changing and uncertain business environment' (van der Heijden 1993: 137). The strategic visions of top managers were connected to corporate success (Hamel and Prahalad 1989).

According to the traditional approach to corporate policy (Andrews 1980), strategies were designed at the corporation's apex by top management and implemented by the members of the organization. Hampden-Turner (1993: 328) argued, on the contrary, that strategies frequently emerge from various parts of the organization, especially those interacting with customers in the field, and are later picked up by management. Mintzberg (1994) also pointed out the incremental character of strategy as formation processes: 'Strategies can form without being formulated . . . not because strategies have to be purely emergent but simply to allow for the fact that they can be, or more realistically, almost inevitably *partially* are' (p. 26). The controversy has been a variant of the top-down versus bottom-up conflict. But given the way organizations are structured and managed today, it is more plausible that strategies emerge in a constant dialogue between top management and other areas in the organized network. In view of flatter hierarchies and flatter process and project organization, the employees of an organization are an important strategic resource for those managing the organization.

Hampden-Turner (1993) suggested that we researchers should 'not get carried away in our adversarial enthusiasm', but instead see designed versus emergent strategies 'less as a debate or social case than a dilemma within strategic learning loops' (p. 328).

The 'new institutionalism' (Powell and Di-Maggio 1991) is an organizational-theory complement to Mintzberg's process approach. In new institutionalism, irrationality is located in formal structures, whereby the diffusion of certain departments and operating procedures is attributed to interorganizational influences and the persuasiveness of cultural accounts rather than to the functions they are intended to perform (Meyer and Rowan 1977). New institutionalism also focuses on organizational sectors and fields roughly coterminous with the boundaries of industries, professions, or the national society (Scott and Meyer 1994). Institutionalization occurs at the sectorial level. Organizational forms, structural components, and rules—not specific organizations—are institutionalized. For the strategy field new institutionalism implies a formulation of strategy as an interplay within loosely coupled, but rela-

tively stable, elements of organization. In this approach, norms of a sector or an industry have an important impact on the institutionalization of both the content of strategy and the rules for formulating strategy.

Decisions are strongly influenced by the shared visions of managers involved, and rational strategic analysis is by no means the only determinant of the outcome (Hitt and Tyler 1991). The term 'strategic vision' is used with many different connotations. Van der Heijden (1993) defined it as 'a view of the future of the company in terms of its business idea, size, scope, success formula . . . In this sense vision is an entrepreneurial notion, something that will indicate direction for action' (p. 140).

Often designed as cultural artifacts within a company, visions provide a unifying concept (Campbell and Yeung 1991). Terms used in this context are 'values', 'credo', 'code of conduct', 'ideals', 'dreams', and they are often used with ethical overtones. Hamel and Prahalad (1989) introduced the notion of 'strategic intent', which they contrasted with 'fit' (see Table 24.1). In other words, when developing strategic visions one should avoid the traditional concepts and thus the conceptual restrictions that strategic fit produces. Instead, the emphasis is on inventing entrepreneurial concepts that eventually lead to competitive advantages. Hamel and Prahalad (1989) claimed to have empirical evidence that companies with clear 'strategic intents' succeed better than others do.

Table 24.1. From 'strategic fit' to 'strategic intent'

Strategic fit	Strategic intent
Search for niches	Search for new rules
Offer a portfolio for businesses	Offer a portfolio of competencies
Identify products/channels/customers	Identify core competencies/relationships
Find sustainable advantages	Accelerate learning
Trim ambitions to resources	Leverage resources to reach goals
Concentrate on financial targets	Concentrate on strategic challenges

Capabilities, Competencies, and Knowledge as Integrating Themes

In recent years competencies and knowledge creation have received a good deal of attention in the strategy field. The basic line of thought is that competitive battles are won by organizational capability rather than by new products, resources, or market position. Competitive advantages result from the capability to cultivate, mobilize, and create distinct competencies and to integrate specialized inputs into the exploitation of new business opportunities (Doz and Prahalad 1988; Porter 1998). Observations of and data from relatively new global competitors show that they have overcome a number of disadvantages in a relatively short time. According to Doz and Thanheiser (1993), these companies—

(1) have ambitions well beyond the reach of their current means. Management in these companies has been directed toward 'constantly stretching the capabilities of the organization and building new capabilities over time';

(2) have focused their resource commitments on core competencies, thereby accelerating learning in areas that could be applied across many competitive arenas, a strategy that makes it difficult for competitors to imitate these companies' strategies;

(3) have a unique ability to bring together markets and technologies in their domestic and global markets;

(4) succeed in managing complex processes (and tradeoffs) creatively and in coordinating and integrating opportunities in their network; and

(5) effectively manage new product development, ensuring that their R&D is efficiently controlled and conducted in a timely manner.

Doz and Thanheiser also stated that many of these relatively new global competitors rely on alliances, partnerships, and collaboration as a means for acquiring competencies that they do not possess. They therefore learn faster and with fewer resources than their competitors.

The organizational ability to mobilize people and other resources and to learn is central to the strategic pursuit of these companies. They innovate, integrate, and learn.

Such processes characterize the growing mutual influence of the strategy field and organization research. The shared factor is leadership and organizational learning, defined—not as bases for making better choices—but as basis for accumulating competencies. The focus of this common factor is on the quality of the strategy process rather than on form. Constant communication of visions is its means. Change is managed in networks of internal subunits with distinct competencies and in networks of external stakeholders with varying demands. Strategy is a complex process of leadership at all levels in the network, a view that reflects the growing complexity of the institutional web of which organizations are a part.

The development of both the strategy and the organizational field includes similarities in themes and a growing potential for mutual enrichment (see Table 24.2). Strategy research is primarily normative in character. As stated by Schendel (1996), 'work in strategy does revolve around the central notion of the search for competitive advantage. Competitive advantage implies that an abnormal return is (or is not) earned and is the explanation for organizational performance differentials' (p. 1). Schendel's notion of creation of abnormal returns is based mainly on two theoretical perspectives: models and frameworks. Models are an attempt to separate the causes of superior performance in a given period, whereas frameworks address the dynamic processes by which competitive advantages are created. Frameworks require longitudinal research and are less developed in theory. Porter (1990) claimed that the purpose of a dynamic theory of strategy ought to be to improve understanding of the balance between environmental determinism and company/leader choice in shaping competitive outcomes (p. 115). In the following section, we develop a conceptual model that enables us to discuss the relationship between strategizing and learning.

Table 24.2. Organizing, strategizing, and organizational learning—A historical simplification

Period	Organizing	Strategizing	Organizational learning
1960s	Structural behavior	Focus on plans	Behavioral theory, Tavistock group learning
1970s	Organizational anarchies	Planning	Weick: Enactment, Selection, Re-enactment
	Processes	Emergent strategies	Focus on discovery of organizational learning theory
1980s	Action generators, Irrationality images	'Fit' between strategy and organization	Focus on discovery of organizational learning praxis
1990s	Cultural institutions	Strategic vision	Leadership
Post-1990s	Networks, Virtual/ imaginary organizations	Core competencies (resource view)	Tacit knowledge-producing systems

A Conceptual Model: Learning Levels and Organizational Transition

The Logical Structure of Learning

In Weick's (1991) view of organizational learning, it is more typical for responses to stimuli to be the same than for them to be different. This quality of being the same results from routines and practices such as division of labor, formalization, and socialization. Although stimuli tend to change, and although organizational environments present a variety of information, response systems are designed to respond rather routinely and to neglect certain degrees of variety in stimuli.

Traditional learning theory defines learning as the change in the response made to the same stimulus: 'The sign of learning is not a shift of response or performance as a consequence of change in stimulus-situation or in motivation, but rather a shift in performance when the stimulus-situation and the motivation are essentially the same' (English and English 1958: 289).

The pattern of different stimulus–same response is very common in organizations and is probably the reason for theorists' interest in strategic learning. Although the stimulus might be different from previous stimuli, it is usually transformed into a framework of established routines or ways of seeing. This process entails the mechanism of socialization, power structures, and hence legitimization. Previous research has demonstrated that the pattern of different–same actually can involve dynamics that intensify the efforts to undo or manipulate new and deviating stimuli (Hedberg, Nystrom, and Starbuck 1976).

One part of the literature on strategy formation is occupied with the traditional learning sequence of same–different. To achieve 'abnormal returns', companies tend to copy themselves and previously successful routines. These dynamics can be regarded as automorphism (Schwartz 1992). The companies develop new strategies based on old theories or frameworks that rest, in turn, on old successes. Non-learning is thus just as important an aspect of strategy theories as learning is. Confirmation of established truths often dominates the search for new frameworks. History becomes a constraint that prohibits seeing.

It is often claimed in organization theory that stimulus situations tend to be changing and unstable. 'When there is flux, there is both no stimulus and a changing stimulus, but there is seldom the same stimulus' (Weick 1991: 117). What business organizations do or do not perceive as 'stimulus' could be called 'the theory of business' (Drucker 1994):

The assumptions that shape any organization's behavior dictate its decisions about what to do and what not to do, and define what the organization considers meaningful results. These assumptions are about markets. They are about identifying customers and competitors, their values and behavior. They are about technology and its dynamics, about a company's strengths and weaknesses. These assumptions are about what a company gets paid for. They are what I call a company's theory of business. (p. 95)

The theory of business that a company develops influences its perception and shapes its culture and memory. 'Seeing' determines which stimuli are processed and which are not. The theory of business is the filtering mechanism that opens or closes the organization's interpretation of information. The responses that a company chooses for particular stimuli tend to be copies of previous responses (Schwartz 1992). Nonetheless, there are situations in which responses change dramatically, in which mismatches occur between the stimulus and the chosen response. Mismatches become visible because of failures or near failures. New responses may be characterized as 'single-loop learning cycles' (Argyris and Schön 1978). 'Whenever an error is detected and corrected without questioning or altering the underlying values of the system (be it individual, group, intergroup, organizational or interorganizational), the learning is single-loop' (Argyris 1992: 8).

Organizations deal with many different stimuli and responses. Which ones imply strategic learning, and which ones signal operative and routine learning? We define 'strategic stimuli and responses' as those that contribute substantially to the short-term and long-term survival of the company (although we are aware of the fact that, from an organizing and learning perspective, it may be quite difficult to distinguish strategic events from nonstrategic ones).

'Strategic stimuli' are those that disturb the established order. They may tend to increase variety rather than homogeneity.

Cyert and March (1963) labeled adaptation as 'organizational learning' and described three different phases of the decision-making process: adaptation of goals, adaptation in attention rules, and adaptation in search rules. Adaptation in attention refers to the selective attention that the organization bestows on different parts of the environment. In a study on 'ecological demands' Dobers and Wolff (1995) showed that organizations are influenced by conflicting external demands and that they therefore develop processes and institutional arrangements that enable them to deal with these conflicting demands, even simultaneously.

Usually, an organization responds to external signals by correcting its core theories-in-use incrementally. The basic assumptions of these theories are rarely questioned. Continual and concerted sharing and meshing of individual assumptions, of individual images of self and others, and of one's activities in the context of collective interaction maintain the organization's theories-in-use (Shrivastava 1983). The construction and modification of these theories through individual and collective inquiry is what Argyris and Schön (1978) labeled organizational learning.

The effectiveness of organizations depends on their long-term strategic choices, choice of transformation processes, and the administrative structure that supports these processes (Duncan and Weiss 1978). Organizational choices are based on the knowledge base incorporated in the organizational mind, which is the accumulation of the experiences and knowledge of the organization's individual members. However, the organizational mind is more than the sum of its individual minds. Knowledge endures even though individuals join and leave the organization.

Duncan and Weiss (1978) defined organizational learning 'as the process within the organization by which knowledge about action–outcome relationships and the effects of the environment on these relationships is developed' (p. 84). This knowledge is distributed across the organization, is communicable to its members, has consensual validity, and is integrated into the working procedures and administrative structures of the organization. Threats to learning exist as a consequence of organizational ideologies, rigid structures, historical standards of performance, and established legitimating standards.

If one discards the traditional definition of learning mentioned above and examines instead the dynamics of perception and action in organizations, the simple, logical structure of learning situations makes it possible to explore learning and nonlearning in a more elaborate way. For example, a simple stimulus–response structure inspired by Weick (1991) enables one to distinguish between four learning situations: 'S' represents the organization's mechanism for 'seeing' or 'perceiving'. Perception and filters are based on the theory of business. Responses are the organization's instrumental answers to the theory of business and represent the 'action portfolio' a company possesses. The four learning situations that emerge from this conceptual structure contain initiators of change, the organizational learning mode, and the principal role that strategy development plays.

Type I Learning: Same Perception and Same Response

When the theory of business is unchallenged, the overall responses typically follow from the existing repertoire. Learning within this framework takes the form of fine tuning, such as continuous improvement and refinement of quality (TQM).

Organizations are typically stabilizers, and standardization breeds efficiency (Weick and Westley 1996). Therefore, organizations strive to maintain and develop established S–R pairings. The dynamics of these relationships are sometimes rather intricate, however. Although an outsider may view patterns of behavior as consistent with previous patterns, 'sameness' may be a result of power and legitimization processes, which are reflected in control routines of a company. SOPs and routines are the fundamental basis for interpreting new and old stimuli and transform these stimuli into legitimized frames of behavior.

Similar or identical responses also require an in-depth analysis of reality. Similar or identical actions or outputs may evolve from new routines, although the outside observer may evaluate only the learning relationship based on the organization's performance. For example, a manufacturer of refrigerators may produce the same refrigerators as in the past, but in less time and with optimized logistics. Neither the framework nor the output of the company has changed, but internal routines have changed considerably.

Type II Learning: Same Perception and Different Response

The theory of business remains the same, but new responses are needed. For example, new market segments are exploited with old products and services. However, the changes needed are implemented within the previous frame of

Table 24.3. Four learning situations

Learning situations	Stimulus (S)	Response (R)
I	Same	Same
II	Same	Different
III	Different	Same
IV	Different	Different

reference. Therefore, this situation may be characterized as 'single-loop learning'. This learning sequence is a dominant theme in the literature on positioning-oriented strategy, for that body of work is related to the search for superior strategies. Developing new responses is one way to outperform competitors. The basic parameters for a business are not reversed, but the related strategies are reevaluated in order to exploit the dominating theory of business even more than in the past. New regional markets are exploited with old products, old products and services are repackaged for new customer segments, or new products and services are developed in accordance with es-tablished business ideas.

Type III Learning: Different Perception and Same Response

This type of learning occurs when a company's actions fail to match the perceived business situation. Companies continue to apply old measures and strategies, although the basis for business has changed. The result may well be a deadlock, and at best a new theory can be de-veloped to define new strategies. At worst, the company disappears from the market.

Many organizations encounter times when established truths and routines are questioned. The dynamics of these situations may have various results. Organizations may respond by ignoring the new stimuli, by denying them, or by readapting to a new situation. For example, a company might readapt by taking old produc-tion facilities that are not acceptable in a Euro-pean context and moving them to Asia. The processes of denying and ignoring have re-sulted in numerous organizational crises and have therefore occupied management re-searchers and consultants for decades. More often than readapting, companies must refor-mulate their theory of business in order to sur-vive on the market.

Type IV Learning: Different Perception and Different Response

A genuine situation of 'double-loop-learning' arises when both the theory of business and the behavioral repertoire are perceived to be obsolete. The company has to start a radical process of discovering its future basis for sur-vival, and an intensive search for a new theory of business and related strategies is needed. Although cognitive psychologists may argue that double-loop learning is rare among indi-viduals and that only individuals who forget can develop totally new frames and responses, organizations are different in the sense that the groups of people who shape and establish frames in organizations can be replaced. Un-learning is not a trivial challenge, but it is clearly possible.

Normative literature on strategic manage-ment has focused in recent decades on double-loop learning in order to discover heretofore unoccupied niches for organizations. These niches are supposed to create the abnormal returns that strategists are interested in. Cre-ativity, innovation, and change are the catch-words for these efforts, and renewed interest in organizational learning is related to these themes.

Learning Level 1: Refinement

Much of what organizations do aims at improv-ing existing processes, procedures, and prod-ucts. There are countless models of how to handle this type of change. The quality move-ment is a recent example. TQM has resulted in continuous improvement, customer orienta-tion, and so on. Some attempts at TQM, how-ever, have been superficial. 'A sad observation of the last decade is that many employees and managers, confronted by the implementation of such programs, view them as add-ons, over-lays, or "programs of the month". In most cases these pessimists are right' (Pearson and Wilson 1995: 149). TQM programs have a tendency to preserve existing procedures and standards. Either standards are set too high, making them unattainable, or they function as devices of legitimization. TQM also focuses on the cus-tomer expectations but tends to forget about the empowerment of employees by either their organization or their customer (Pearson and Wilson 1995: 149).

Statistical controls and the goal of zero defects were established for what might be considered 'simple' problems—ones that have easily measurable errors. Corrective action for those problems often flows almost naturally from the measured results. But in a situation where exploration and experimentation are necessary to achieve quality, SOPs for measuring quality restrict or thwart learning.

In describing the difference between 'operational effectiveness' and strategy, Porter (1996) pointed out that operational efficiency (in terms of productivity, quality, and speed) has spawned, since the early 1990s, a large number of management techniques in addition to TQM, time-based competition, benchmarking, outsourcing, partnering, reengineering, and change management. 'Bit by bit, almost imperceptibly, management tools have taken the place of strategy. As managers push to improve on all fronts, they move farther away from viable competition' (p. 40).

This process partly explains why management techniques create disappointment. For example, Hammer and Champy (1993) claimed that 'business process reengineering [BPR] is not about fixing anything, it means starting all over, starting from scratch' (p. 2) and that 'it is no less than a reversal of the Industrial Revolution' (p. 2). Why are so many BPR projects a failure or disappointment? According to Rothschild (1992), it appears that the majority (70%) of reengineering projects fail. This failure, though, can be qualified in terms of sameness, because its implementation in praxis is limited to efficiency.

Learning Level 2: Single-loop Learning

Single-loop learning occurs when decisions made about new responses are based on old stimuli and interpretations of stimuli. Because learning is traditionally defined as a change in the response to a stimulus situation that has remained essentially unchanged, single-loop learning is identical with that learning situation.

Single-loop learning situations are similar to 'strategic positioning' (Porter 1996), which means 'performing *different* activities from rivals or performing similar activities in *different ways*' (p. 40; Porter's emphasis).

The limitations of the 'productivity frontier' have led to competitive convergence among companies. As said before, the prescriptive management literature on strategy is occupied with the efficient use of existing capabilities and the extension of these competencies into new markets, with new combinations of products and services, or what Porter called differentiation. On rare occasions, these strategic approaches transcend existing theories of business and they challenge the underlying assumptions about *how* success is accomplished, but they do not raise the question *'why'*? Same–different learning is single-loop learning. It is often positioning and is the most common aspiration in business. It is also similar to what Weick (1991) referred to as the traditional concept of cognitive learning.

Learning Level 3: The Organizational Mind as a Prison

Traditional planning is based on the assumption that tomorrow's environment will be pretty much the same as today's. The forecasts on which plans are based often provide unrealistic pictures about the future. Today's planning culture should be open to and incorporate the unpredictable and should help organizations prepare for dramatic, rapid, and unanticipated changes. Planning must be designed as a journey of discovery.

Two approaches to planning, scenario planning and contingency planning, are designed for discovery. Contingency planning focuses on single critical events, whereas scenario planning is about exploring possible roads for future developments. If such planning procedures are to contribute substantially to exploration of opportunity, they have to create surprises and may allow space for challenging the established theories of the business.

Learning Level 4: Learning as Discovery

The vast bulk of the management literature on strategy emphasizes that organizations learn from success and repeat effort that leads to desired outcomes. Corporate performance improves by repeating successes. Some organization researchers have started to recognize the importance of unusual events for learning. They have seen that crises (Shrivastava 1995), failures (Sitkin and Pablo 1992), and potential dangers (Chess, Tamuz, and Greenberg 1995) create opportunities for learning and may even contradict the established theories of action.

By definition, organizational learning does not imply that learning always leads to improvement (Levitt and March 1988). Organizations learn in an attempt to make sense of what they and others experience. They can be guided by their own incremental patterns of trial and error, by lessons from single unusual events, or by failures that others suffer.

In conclusion, learning is inherent in the organizational culture. Only when the basic assumptions, beliefs, and success formulae are made conscious and visible do they become testable and open to experimentation (Normann 1984).

Conceptualization of the Learning Model

Having begun by exploring the possible interfaces between organization theory, organizational learning, and the management literature on strategy, we conclude this discussion with an attempt to integrate the various perspectives and levels in a conceptual model. The aim is to be able to identify the properties of learning that specific strategic approaches have and the manner in which they relate to change, learning, and to each other.

Learning to Prospect and Discovering How to Learn

Our attempts to describe how the scholarly understanding of organizing, organizational learning, and strategizing has developed over time have a common theme: Normative ideas about the perfect state of affairs in the highly manageable organization have gradually given way to mounting empirical evidence of organizational imperfection. At worst, organizations have been described as 'organized anarchies' (March and Olsen 1976); strategies, as reconstructions; and organizational learning, as either a lure into trivial, almost mechanical, minor adjustments or an outright obstacle to an organization's reorientation. The results have raised doubt about anyone's ability to design efficient organizations, develop and implement excellent strategies, or supply organizational memory with well-founded, timely, and adequate knowledge resulting from learning.

Table 24.4. A conceptual model of organizational learning

Type	Focus		Initiators of change	Mode of organizational learning	Strategy formation
	Perceiving (stimulus)	Acting (response)			
I	Same	Same	*Kaizen*, BPR,[a] TQM[b]	Refinement	Planning as reproduction
II	Same	Different	Strategic planning	Single loop	Planning as technology
III	Different	Same	Failure, crisis	Deadlock	Planning as defense
IV	Different	Different	Learning strategy	Double loop	Planning as discovery

[a] Business process reengineering.
[b] Total quality management.

But perhaps the primary challenge is not to construct organizations, formulate strategies, or produce knowledge. Perhaps organizations, strategies, and knowledge are already there to be *discovered*. Organizing takes place in a mindscape rather than in a landscape. The main purpose of strategizing is to make sense of ongoing flows of events (Mintzberg 1994). Moreover, the body of tacit knowledge exceeds the body of explicit knowledge in many organizations. Much more is known than can be expressed (Baumard 1996) and retrieved. If only organizations knew what they know, they would vastly improve their competitive strength, claim the proponents of knowledge management tools.

Discovering Organizing: The Power of Imagination

Organizing is the activity of bringing various organizational processes to bear upon common tasks and goals. Basic organizational processes exist, actors are available, markets are there and may perhaps be improved, and systems for market communication, service delivery, payment, and so on often can be copied or bought. The building blocks are present, waiting for the architect.

Some systems are already assembled to behave in a regulated fashion. They are institutions, and they behave, or shape behaviors, in rather predictable ways. The business entrepreneur, or social entrepreneur for that matter, can move in with a blueprint and a sense of mission and try to coordinate actors and processes for that mission. They can establish imaginary organizations (Hedberg *et al.* 1997), networks of actors and assemblies of interacting processes that make up organizations operating far beyond their borders and relying on membership well beyond the relationship entailed by employment contracts.

Modern information technology has greatly facilitated such arrangements. With the rapid growth of networks and markets on the Internet, the virtual enterprise and a number of other temporary organizations have been attracting increasing interest and attention. In addition, modern information technology has clearly the potential to greatly reduce transaction costs and to facilitate coordination in organizations where markets are interpreted as networks and production systems are set up as partnerships.

Normann and Ramirez (1993) described how successful service companies achieve evolutionary growth through interactive strategies that make it possible for competencies and customer bases to profit from value creation and for combinations of values (value constellations, not value chains) to be packaged and offered. The authors prescribed a normative strategy in which the development of competencies and the growth of customer bases go hand in hand (see Fig. 24.2).

The model above inspires an alternative way of thinking about business development. Instead of evolutionary growth within one company, an entrepreneur can move in and bring together competencies and customers from various actors and markets. He or she can articulate activity systems with the same components but with a different perspective on organizing. The visionary entrepreneur provides the vision for the whole system, communicates a mission and a sense of belonging to a number of scattered actors, facilitates communication, builds the necessary infrastructures, and makes sense and builds trust throughout the system.

The notion of imaginary organizations can be positioned in a space of existing knowledge, mechanisms, and processes. The notion of organizations as interactive processes draws attention to the necessary connectedness of activity systems. Some of these processes represent core competencies, whereas others are important but more peripheral, processes that can be supplied by partners outside the core system. Processes produce transactions. Some of these transactions are best coordinated through hierarchies, whereas others are more efficiently dealt with through market mechanisms. Coase (1937) and Williamson (1981) developed the principles of transaction-cost theory, and recent developments in information technology have put these theories to the test. In addition to these subsystems, there are interactions with

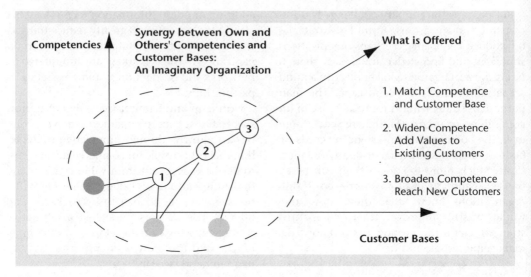

Fig. 24.2. Evolutionary growth of competencies and customer bases

Interpretation by Normann and Ramirez 1993. The imaginary organization (dotted circle) denotes activity systems of these components.

clients or consumers. These forces are spelled out in great and intriguing detail in relationship marketing (Gummesson 1995). Finally, there is a clear connection to the major theme of this chapter, the theme of organizational learning. A thoughtful and visionary manager can combine these mechanisms and proclaim an imaginary organization where others merely see competition, conflict, or stagnating industries.

Discovering Strategies: Retrospect as a Promising Prospect

The oil crisis of 1973 put an end to a period of growing trust in corporate strategy and in the predictive power of long-range planning. After a few years of turmoil, companies that had been guided by their planning departments adopted a lower profile and emerged with alternative scenarios and a portfolio of possible strategies.

Almost simultaneously Mintzberg, Raisinghani, and Théorèt (1976) concluded that strategies were rather reconstructions of flows of decisions in organizations than the guiding

lights that they earlier were described as. In further effort Weick (1979) began research that eventually resulted in several articles about sense-making in organizations and that later was summarized in a major work bearing the same title (Weick 1995). In that book Weick characterized sense-making as grounded in identity construction, retrospective, intended to provide intelligible interpretation of an organization's environments, social, ongoing, focused on extracted cues, and driven by plausibility.

The sense-making cycle may look something like the model in Figure 24.3, which depicts sense-making as a retrospective process. Events ultimately fall into patterns. They are organized into frames of reference (mental maps), and reframing is needed mostly in order to accommodate surprising events. Sense-making is, of course, also a process in which power is exercised. Management of meaning, albeit *ex post*, is a powerful way to shape actions for both the present and the future.

With sense-making, too, the problem of finding a balance arises. Unlike the previously mentioned need to balance between information and opportunities for learning; between

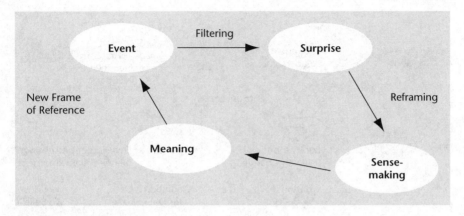

Fig. 24.3. The sense-making cycle
Interpretation of Weick 1995.

strategy, organization, and performance; or between environmental determinism and company/leader choice in shaping outcomes, sense-making involves the issue of balancing between planning, experimentation, and what is known about the future. If the future is known and distinct, then managers should make plans and follow strategies. If the future is uncertain, they should instead experiment and evaluate. When forecasts are unreliable, then 'aftercasts' are useful. Plan little and evaluate much.

Jönsson and Lundin (1977) used the concept of myth and myth cycles to describe how organizations form theories of action (i.e. make sense of 'reality') and how sequences of myths follow each other (see Fig. 24.4). Hedberg and Jönsson (1977) described the interplay between myths and strategies and applied the model to studies of crises in organizations. Strategy formulation is a discontinuous process, they concluded.

If strategies are difficult or impossible to construct and implement, then perhaps they can be discovered. They can be discovered retrospectively through processes by which companies make sense of and find patterns in what they do (Mintzberg, Raisinghani, and Théorèt 1976). Alternatively, strategies of others can be imitated. Industrial recipes (Spender 1989) fall into the latter category. They are sec-

torial patterns of imitation. The danger with industrial recipes, though, is the reduction of variance and the obvious risk of a poor fit between that which is imitated and the system to which it is imported. As with organizing, a dichotomy may develop. Strategies can be constructed, or they can be discovered. Behavior patterns can be prescribed, or they can be described.

Prospecting Knowledge: Making the Known Known

As shown in this chapter, organizational learning that produces knowledge and adapts to changing circumstances has several limitations. Producing knowledge for continuous, small improvements is easier than establishing the knowledge that might be necessary for turning a company around. Studies of crises in businesses provide sample evidence.

But organizations are seldom left to learn on their own. They can learn from others, including customers, partners, and competitors, and can transfer knowledge between their own internal functions and levels, as Bierly and Hämäläinen (1995) demonstrated.

Nonaka (1991) and Nonaka and Takeuchi (1995) developed the theme of the knowledge-producing enterprise and emphasized both the

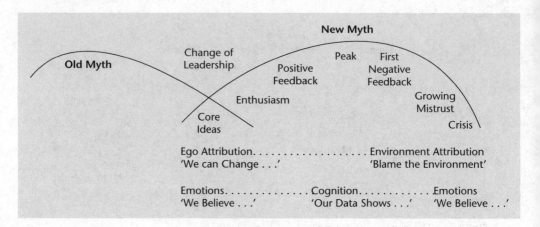

Fig. 24.4. Myth cycles as sense-makers and bases for action in organizations

richness of tacit knowledge and the importance of 'intensive outside–inside interaction' in the knowledge-production process. Learning, stated Nonaka and Takeuchi, 'runs counter to the basic premises in Western thinking of the modular, or vertical, enterprise . . . learning must be internalized' (Nonaka and Takeuchi 1995: 6). Nonaka (1991) saw no particular difficulties in strategic learning in the Japanese companies he studied, but concluded: 'creating new knowledge is not simply a matter of "processing" objective information. Rather, it depends on tapping the tacit and often highly subjective insights, intuitions, and hunches of individual employees and making those insights available for testing and use by the company as a whole' (p. 97). In order to facilitate the eradication of existing mental maps and to encourage problem detection in earlier successful organizations, Nonaka and Takeuchi (1995) and Morgan (1986) suggest that the use of metaphors and analogies be increased in attempts at organizational learning and that ambiguity and redundancy be recognized as playing important roles in knowledge production by organizations. This approach is the theme of Hedberg and Jönsson's (1977) design for semi-confusing information systems.

But metaphors, ambiguity, and redundancy may also serve the purpose of enabling organizations to discover tacit and individual know-

ledge and to facilitate the transformation of such knowledge into explicit and collective organizational knowledge by means of processes of group interiorization. Baumard (1995) studied several such strategic learning processes in French international companies. He produced convincing evidence for the hypothesis that organizational learning has more to do with modes of knowing in a world where much more is known than can be expressed and where the art of making the already-known explicit is more important than producing or constructing new knowledge. Baumard found companies that deliberately induced hypothetical information into communities of knowledge and then waited to see if induced knowledge would turn tacit knowledge into explicit knowledge and make individuals come out in the open through group processes. The members of one company in the intelligence industry used this strategy very successfully in order to verify or falsify certain information on the market. They crystallized knowledge through discovery processes rather than building it through traditional intelligence.

In addition to thinking of knowledge production in learning organizations as the construction of new knowledge, one might therefore also consider the case where organizational learning is more like mining in individual or collective depositories of tacit knowledge, of knowledge that for one reason or another is not, or cannot be, expressed. Reframing should then be seen as prospecting, and sense-making as authorization to treat what is known as known. Legitimacy, in the latter perspective, is a resource that can be allocated in order to determine what can be said.

If organizational learning is primarily a matter of moving organizations into new modes of knowing, then processes of sense-making (Weick 1995), outside–inside interaction (Nonaka 1991), and isolation-hypocrisy (Brunsson 1992) deserve increased emphasis both in practice and in further research. Management's attempts to encourage organizational learning should focus on strategies to transfer individual insights into multiple collective sights. 'Management of meaning' should then primarily involve activities designed to articulate what is known rather than efforts to speculate around the unknown. If knowledge is plentiful, but hidden, then managers should focus more on reframing and reproblematizing and less on problem-solving.

Conclusions

The concept of organizational learning has mainly been used in recent years to refer to adaptive and incremental learning at the operative and administrative levels. Learning for strategizing is much more difficult. Few successful companies manage to unlearn old strategies and to relearn new ones without serious delays. Organizational inertia is perhaps most noticeable, and certainly most dangerous, when it delays urgent strategy-prospecting.

We have shown how organizations, knowledge, and strategies can be seen and understood as the results of a management's endeavors. Skilled and energetic managers design organizations, create knowledge, and formulate strategies. We have also shown how organizing, learning, and strategizing can be seen and dealt with as interacting processes, and how managers then take on roles as catalysts, destabilizers, sense-makers, and trust-builders.

The *constructor* of knowledge that leads to successful strategies faces a difficult task and is given low odds by researchers. The *prospector* of strategy has a somewhat easier task, and probably more fun, though sometimes neither the constructor nor the prospector manages to connect organizational learning to strategy formulation. Whereas the constructor often makes use of large data bases, impressive time series, and highly developed analytical skills and manages to delineate and formulate elaborate strategies, the prospector takes pride in an open mind, associative skills, networks, and balanced training of both the left side and the right side of the human brain. The constructors probably still dominate the scene. But repeated failures to foresee change and limited ability to take advantage of opportunities have undermined trust in these professionals and given way to more experimental and evolutionary forms of strategizing.

If organizational learning is going to contribute to strategizing in turbulent environments, fast-moving industries, or companies that go from success to crisis, managers will probably see themselves as both prospectors and constructors.

References

Andrews, K. R. (1980). *The Concept of Corporate Strategy*. Homewood, Ill: Erwin.
Ansoff, H. I. (1965). *Corporate Strategy*. New York: McGraw-Hill.
Argyris, C. (1992). *On Organizational Learning*. Cambridge, Mass.: Blackwell.
——and Schön, D. A. (1978). *Organizational Learning: A Theory of Action Perspective*. Reading, Mass.: Addison-Wesley.

Barnard, C. I. (1938). *The Function of the Executive*. Cambridge, Mass.: Harvard University Press.

Baumard, P. (1995). *Organisations déconcertées: La Gestion stratégique de la connaissance*. Paris: Masson.

——(1996). 'Organizations in the Fog: An Investigation into the Dynamics of Knowledge', in B. Moingeon and A. Edmondson (eds.), *Organizational Learning and Competitive Advantage*. London: Sage, 74–91.

Beer, S. (1972). *Brain of the Firm*. New York: Herder and Herder.

Bierly, P. E. and Hämäläinen, T. (1995). 'Organizational Learning and Strategy'. *Scandinavian Journal of Management*, 11: 209–24.

Bonini, C. P. (1963). *Simulation of Information and Decision Systems in the Firm*. Englewood Cliffs, NJ: Prentice Hall.

Brunsson, N. (1985). *The Irrational Organization: Irrationality as a Basis for Organizational Action and Change*. Chichester: Wiley.

——(1992). *The Organization of Hypocrisy: Talk, Decisions and Actions in Organizations*. Chichester: Wiley.

Campbell, A. and Yeung, S. (1991). 'Creating a Sense of Mission (Management Technique/Model)'. *Long Range Planning*, 24/4: 10.

Chess, C., Tamuz, M., and Greenberg, M. (1995). 'Organizational Learning about Environmental Risk Communication—The Case of Rohm-and-Haas Bristol Plant'. *Society and Natural Resources*, 8/1: 57–66.

Coase, R. H. (1937). 'The Nature of the Firm'. *Econometrica*, 4, New Series: 386–405.

Cohen, M. D., March, J. G., and Olsen, J. P. (1972). 'A Garbage Can Model of Organizational Choice'. *Administrative Science Quarterly*, 17: 1–25.

Cyert, R. M. and March, J. G. (1963). *A Behavioral Theory of the Firm*. Englewood Cliffs, NJ: Prentice Hall.

Davidow, W. H. and Malone, M. S. (1992). *The Virtual Corporation*. New York: Harper Collins.

Dobers, P. and Wolff, R. (1995). 'Managing Ecological Competence'. *Greener Management International*, 11: 32–48.

Doz, Y. L. and Prahalad, C. K. (1988). 'Quality of Management: An Emerging Source of Global Competition?', in N. Hood and J. E. Vahlne (eds.), *Strategies in Global Competition*. London: Croom Helm, 345–69.

—— and Thanheiser, H. (1993). 'Regaining Competitiveness: A Process of Organisational Renewal', in J. Hendry, G. Johnson, and J. Newton (eds.), *Strategic Thinking: Leadership and the Management of Change*. Chichester: Wiley, 293–310.

Drucker, P. (1994). 'The Theory of Business'. *Harvard Business Review*, 72/5: 95–104.

Duncan, R. and Weiss, A. (1979). 'Organizational Learning: Implications for Organizational Design', in B. M. Staw (ed.), *Research in Organizational Behavior: An Annual Series of Analytical Essays and Critical Reviews* (Vol. 1). Greenwich, Conn.: JAI Press, 75–123.

English, H. B. and English, A. C. (1958). *A Comprehensive Dictionary of Psychological and Psychoanalytical Terms: A Guide to Usage*. New York: Longmans Green.

Forrester, J. W. (1961). *Industrial Dynamics*. New York: Wiley.

——(1968). *Urban Dynamics*. New York: Wiley.

——(1971). *World Dynamics* (2nd edn). Cambridge, Mass.: Wright-Allen.

Gummesson, E. (1995). *Relationsmarknadsföring* (Relations Marketing). Malmö: Liber Hermods.

Håkansson, H. and Snehota, I. (1995). *Developing Relationships in Business Networks*. London: Routledge.

Hamel, G. and Prahalad, C. K. (1989). 'Strategic Intent'. *Harvard Business Review*, 67/3: 63–76.

Hammer, M. and Champy, J. (1993). *Reengineering the Corporation*. London: Nicholas Brealey.

Hampden-Turner, C. (1993). 'Dilemmas of Strategic Learning Loops', in J. Hendry, G. Johnson, and J. Newton (eds.), *Strategic Thinking Leadership and the Management of Change*. Chichester: Wiley, 327–46.

Hedberg, B. L. T. (1974). *Reframing as a Way to Cope with Organizational Stagnation*. Working paper, International Institute of Management, Berlin.

—— Dahlgren, G., Hansson, J., and Olve, N.-G. (1997). *Virtual Organizations and Beyond: Discover Imaginary Systems*. Chichester: Wiley.

—— and Ericson, A. (1997). 'Insiktströghet och manövertröghet i organisationers omorientering' (Insight Inertia and Action Inertia in Organizational Reorientation), in B. L. T. Hedberg and S.-E. Sjöstrand, *Från företagskriser till industripolitik* (From Organizational Crises to Industrial Politics). Malmö: Liber, 54–66.

—— and Jönsson, S. A. (1977). 'Strategy Formulation as a Discontinuous Process'. *International Studies of Organization and Management*, 7/2: 88–109.

—— Nystrom, P. C., and Starbuck, W. H. (1976). 'Camping on See-saws: Prescriptions for a Self-designing Organization'. *Administrative Science Quarterly*, 21: 41–65.

Hitt, M. A. and Tyler, B. B. (1991). 'Strategic Decision Models: Integrating Different Perspectives'. *Strategic Management Journal*, 12: 327–51.

Jelinek, M. (1979). *Institutionalizing Innovation: A Study of Organizational Learning Systems*. New York: Praeger.

Johansen, R. and Swigart, R. (1994). *Upsizing the Individual in the Downsized Organization: Managing in the Wake of Reengineering, Globalization, and Overwhelming Technological Change*. Reading, Mass.: Addison-Wesley.

Jönsson, S. A. and Lundin, R. A. (1977). 'Myths and Wishful Thinking as Management Tools'. *TIMS Studies in Management Sciences*. Amsterdam: North Holland, 157–70.

Kim, D. H. (1993). 'The Link between Individual and Organizational Learning'. *Sloan Management Review*, 35/1: 37–50.

Levitt, B. and March, J. G. (1988). 'Organizational Learning'. *Annual Review of Sociology*, 14: 319–40.

March, J. G. and Olsen, J. P. (1976). *Ambiguity and Choice in Organizations* (2nd edn). Bergen: Universitetsforlaget.

Meyer, J. W. and Rowan, B. (1977). 'Institutionalized Organizations: Formal Structure as Myth and Ceremony'. *American Journal of Sociology*, 83: 340–63.

Miller, D. (1990). *The Icarus Paradox: How Exceptional Companies Bring about Their Own Downfall*. New York: Harper Business.

Mintzberg, H. (1978). 'Patterns in Strategy Formation'. *Management Science Quarterly*, 24: 934–48.

—— (1994). *The Rise and Fall of Strategic Planning*. Hemel Hempstead: Prentice Hall.

—— Ahlstrand, B., and Lampel, J. (1998). *Strategy Safari: A Guided Tour through the Wilds of Strategic Management*. New York: Free Press.

—— Raisinghani, D., and Théorèt, A. (1976). 'The Structure of "Unstructured" Decision Processes'. *Administrative Science Quarterly*, 21: 246–61.

Morgan, G. (1986). *Images of Organization*. Beverly Hills, Calif.: Sage.

Nonaka, I. (1991). 'The Knowledge-creating Company'. *Harvard Business Review*, 69/6: 96–104.

—— and Takeuchi, H. (1995). *The Knowledge-creating Company: How Japanese Companies Create the Dynamics of Innovation*. New York: Oxford University Press.

Normann, R. (1984). *Service Management*. Chichester: Wiley.

—— and Ramirez, R. (1993). 'From Value Chain to Value Constellation: Designing Interactive Strategy'. *Harvard Business Review*, 71/4: 65–77.

Nystrom, P. C., Hedberg, B. L. T., and Starbuck, W. (1976). 'Interacting Processes as Organization Designs', in R. H. Kilmann, L. R. Pondy, and D. P. Slevin (eds.), *The Management of Organization Design*: Vol. 1. *Strategies and Implementation*. New York: North Holland, 209–30.

Pearson, R. D. and Wilson, P. F. (1995). *Performance-based Assessments: External, Internal, and Self-assessment Tools for Total Quality Management*. Milwaukee: ASQC Quality Press.

Porter, M. E. (1980). *Competitive Strategy*. New York: Free Press.

—— (1985). *Competitive Advantage*. New York: Free Press.

—— (1990). *The Competitive Advantage of Nations*. London: Macmillan.

—— (1996). 'What Is Strategy?' *Harvard Business Review*, 74/6: 61–78.

—— (1998). *On Competition*. Boston: Harvard Business School Press.

Powell, W. W. and DiMaggio, P. J. (eds.) (1991). *The New Institutionalism in Organizational Analysis*. Chicago: University of Chicago Press.

Rothschild, M. (1992). 'How to Be a High IQ Company'. *Forbes*, 150/13 (Supplement, 7 December): 17–21.

Sahlin-Andersson, K. (1996). 'Imitating by Editing Success: The Construction of Organizational Fields', in B. Czarniawska and G. Sevón (eds.), *Translating Organizational Change*. Berlin: de Gruyter, 69–92.

Salzer, M. (1994). *Identity across Borders: A Study in the IKEA-World*. Doctoral dissertation, Department of Management and Economics, Linköping University, Sweden.

Schendel, D. (1996). 'Editor's Introduction to the 1996 Winter Special Issue—Knowledge and the Firm'. *Strategic Management Journal*, 17 (Winter special issue): 1–4.

Schwartz, P. (1992). *The Art of the Long View*. London: Doubleday.

Scott, W. R. and Meyer, J. W. (1994). *Institutional Environments and Organizations: Structural Complexity and Individualism*. Thousand Oaks, Calif.: Sage.

Senge, P. (1990). *The Fifth Discipline: The Art and Practice of the Learning Organization*. New York: Doubleday Currency.

Shrivastava, P. (1983). 'A Typology of Organizational Learning Systems'. *Journal of Management Studies*, 20: 7–28.

——(1995). 'Environmental Technologies and Competitive Advantage'. *Strategic Management Journal*, 16: 705–26.

Sitkin, S. B. and Pablo, A. L. (1992). 'Reconceptualizing the Determinants of Risk Behavior'. *Academy of Management Review*, 17: 9–30.

Spender, J. C. (1989). *Industry Recipes: An Inquiry into the Nature and Sources of Managerial Judgement*. Oxford: Basil Blackwell.

Starbuck, W. H. (1983). 'Organizations as Action Generators'. *American Sociological Review*, 48: 91–102.

van der Heijden, K. (1993). 'Strategic Vision at Work: Discussing Strategic Vision in Management Teams', in J. Hendry, G. Johnson, and J. Newton (eds.), *Strategic Thinking: Leadership and the Management of Change*. Chichester: Wiley, 137–50.

Weick, K. E. (1979). *The Social Psychology of Organizing* (2nd edn). Reading, Mass.: Addison-Wesley.

——(1991). 'The Nontraditional Quality of Organizational Learning'. *Organization Science*, 2: 116–24.

——(1995). *Sensemaking in Organizations*. Thousand Oaks, Calif.: Sage.

——and Westley, F. (1996). 'Organizational Learning: Affirming an Oxymoron', in S. R. Clegg, C. Hardy, and W. R. Nord (eds.), *Handbook of Organization Studies*. London: Sage, 440–58.

Williamson, O. E. (1981). 'The Economics of Organization: The Transaction Cost Approach'. *American Journal of Sociology*, 87: 548–77.

Wolff, R. (1982). *Der Prozeß des Organisierens: Zu einer Theorie des organisationalen Lernens*. Spardorf: Wilfer.

25 Power and Politics in Organizations: Public and Private Sector Comparisons

Joseph LaPalombara

Political Organizations and Their Milieu

Organizational learning derives most of its knowledge from research on organizations in the private sector, particularly from the study of the firm. Its rich interdisciplinary quality is reflected in the range of social sciences that have contributed to the field's robust development. The contribution from political science, however, has been minimal (reasons are suggested by LaPalombara, Ch. 6 in this volume).

The mutual failure of political scientists to pay more systematic attention to organizational learning and of organizational learning specialists to extend their inquiries into the public/political sphere is unfortunate in at least three senses. First, a general theory of organizational learning is unlikely to emerge unless and until what is claimed to be known about this phenomenon is shown to be the case (or not) in the public/political sphere as well. Second, sufficient evidence in political science—even if not gathered with organizational learning as the central focus—shows that organizations in the public/political sector do differ in significant ways from those in the private sphere. And third, considerations of power and its exercise are so ubiquitous in public/political-sector organizations, indeed they are so central to an understanding of these bodies, that one wonders why such meager attention has been paid to this concept in the literature on organizational theory and organizational learning.

The present chapter is intended to show that the integration of political science into the field of organizational learning will be improved and that knowledge about organizational learning itself will be deepened if increased attention is focused on two general questions: What characteristics of organizations in the public/political sector distinguish them from organizations in the private sector? And what are some of the implications of these differences for the overall field of organizational learning?

The Normative Dimension

The answer to the first question must be that one and perhaps the most salient distinguishing characteristic of public/political-sector bodies is that they are normative at their core. For organizations in the private sector, utility and efficiency are universally accepted as primary values. Theories about them are naturally based on the assumption that these bodies are organized and behave according to rational principles that reflect these values and not other considerations. This assumption, however, remains so central to writing about management that, as shown below, it actually serves to impede almost any serious attention to power and politics in private-sector, for-profit entities.

To be sure, any portrayal of private-sector, for-profit entities as monolithic structures exclusively and rationally oriented to the market and the so-called bottom line is much too stark and oversimplified. Even when this flaw is recognized or conceded, however, organizations in the public/political sector are quite different, so the logic and rationality that may apply to a private-sector body cannot easily be extrapolated to them. These differences are also reflected in the ways in which public-sector organizations relate to the learning process. The fact that they typically carry very heavy and distinctive normative baggage is only one of many dimensions along which differences may be assessed.

Normative considerations are endemic to public/political-sector organizations, first because they are directly or indirectly involved in what Easton (1953) once called 'the authoritative allocation of values' (p. 129). This phrase is a shorthand way of describing a government's vast organizational apparatus that engages in a wide range of activities over people. These activities typically include matters over which even the meekest of persons affected will argue and fight with each other, sometimes violently. These contrasts, or differences in preferences (i.e. what government should do or not do), apply not just to the ends of government but also to the means chosen to bring these ends to fruition. In Lasswell's (1936) brutally unvarnished observation, politics is about 'Who Gets What, When, How'.

Where organizations are constrained or hemmed in by normative considerations, appeals to logic and rationality do not travel far or reach many receptive ears. Even when political issues appear to be settled and consensus is reached, say, on the desirability of a given policy, normatively driven questions will arise over the mode or method of policy achievement. Because these policies involve things that happen (or do not happen) to human beings, considerations of expediency and efficiency will often take a backseat to normative ideas about goal achievement. In Etheredge's (1981) words, such normative matters also raise the issue of 'what should government learn and what should government not learn' (p. 86). To put it bluntly, learning things about goal-setting or policy implementation that may be rational and efficient but that are palpably un-

feasible politically is not only a waste of resources but also a one-way ticket to political bankruptcy.

This and other aspects of public/political-sector organizations to be discussed below make for a good deal of messiness—in organizational boundaries; in the specification of organizational missions and authority; in the functional, territorial, and hierarchical division of labor that relates to policy-making and policy execution; and so on. This messiness cautions against a too-easy extrapolation to the public sphere of agency theory or concepts such as principal–agent relationships. These theoretical frameworks may work quite well for the private sector, where one finds much clearer statements of purpose or of means and ends and where the boundaries demarcating organizations, their authority, and their responsibility are much more unambiguously delineated than in the public political sphere.

To cite the most obvious example (see Mayntz and Scharpf 1975, for example), in the public sphere it is not easy to separate, say, the legislature (as 'principal') and the bureaucracy (as 'agent') for the simple reason that in many circumstances the bureaucrats not only administer policies but also *de facto* make policies. In fact, the fabric of public policy-making and its administration is typically a seamless admixture of official and unofficial bodies interacting together in ways that make it next to impossible to distinguish principals from agents. This aspect is in part what I mean by messiness.

Other Dimensions of Differentiation

It will help clarify the above exposition if one considers some of the additional dimensions that differentiate organizations in the public/political sphere from those in the private sector. The distinctions drawn are not a matter of black or white but rather one of degree. In every instance, however, differentiation is at least a caution against thinking that differences between the private and public/political spheres are superfluous, misleading, irrelevant, or nonexistent. The dimensions are the organization's

(a) purposes or goals, (b) accountability, (c) autonomy, (d) orientation to action, and (e) environment.

Purposes and Goals

Political organizations are typically multipurpose. The public policies they are expected to make or administer will often be quite vague, diffuse, contradictory, and even in conflict with each other (Levin and Sanger 1994: 64–8). What governments do is so vast and touches on so many different aspects of organized society that it would be astonishing if these policies did not have such characteristics. Even where single agencies of government are concerned, their purposes, goals, specific marching orders —to say nothing of their procedures and actual behavior—will rarely be coherent or logically consistent.

Not only are the mandates of government normally quite vague and diffuse (Leeuw, Rist, and Sonnichsen 1994: 195; Palumbo 1975: 326), they may not be known to many of the people who make up the organizations designated to carry them through. It is not unusual for such organizations to have no goals at all (Abrahamsson 1977), or to have goals that appear to be quite irrational (Panebianco 1988: 204–19; 262–74). For this reason rational-actor models, in which it is assumed that preferences are 'exogenous' to the organizations themselves, rightly draw criticism when applied to public/political organizations (Pfeffer 1997).

Accountability

In the private sector, a timeworn cliché is that those who manage publicly held firms are accountable to their shareholders. As Berle and Means (1933) long ago established, this claim is largely a myth. If the ensuing decades have changed this situation at all, it is only in the influence now exercised over the firm by some of the rather large institutional investors as well as by some stock analysts. Occasionally, even the mass media may influence what a corporation does.

The corporate community's relatively recent references to management's accountability to stakeholders does not make the publicly held firm similar to public/political organizations. In comparison with those who are in public office or who manage governmental and other political organizations, corporate managers live in splendid freedom. Paying attention to stakeholders is, like many other aspects of corporate policy, a matter of management's choice. In the public/political sphere, accountability to a wide spectrum of individuals and organizations is an inescapable fact of organizational life. People in the public/political sphere who fail or refuse to understand this fact spend very little time there.

Public-sector officials, especially those who occupy governmental office, whether appointive or elective, wisely pay attention to and worry about many constituencies, all of which are more or less ready and able to apply sanctions if their wishes or advice are not followed. The vaunted autonomy of the executive branch is much more limited than one supposes (Levin and Sanger 1994: 17). In all democratic systems, what the executive does is subject to oversight by legislatures and to challenge in the courts. And the latter two institutions are themselves subject to checks by still others. All of them are under continual scrutiny by outsiders prepared to intervene. In addition, many activities that are considered legitimate, and even praiseworthy, in the private sphere would subject public office-holders to arrest, prosecution, and possible imprisonment were they to practice them (Gortner, Mahler, and Nicholson 1987: 60–4). Consider, for example, the public's quite different reactions to words like 'broker' and 'influence peddler'—or the variety of meanings ascribed to a term like 'corruption'.

As noted by Child and Heavens (Ch. 13 in this volume), the universal condition of governmental and other public-sector organizations is that they are subject to constitutions, laws, administrative regulations, judicial decisions, executive orders, and so on. The actions of those persons called upon to manage these organizations are constrained by external and internal *de facto* rules and limitations (Rainey and Milward 1981). Comparable examples of accountability in the private sector are rare.

Public/political-sector organizations are also far more 'porous' than private firms are. The former are easily permeated by organized outside interest groups determined to pull these organizations, and therefore their leaders and managers, in different policy directions. The mass media (often the instruments of powerful interests in civil society) also often make quite explicit and sometimes contradictory demands on them. Because these organizations are presumably representatives of the public and are expected to behave in its interest, the press is expected to be especially vigilant on behalf of the public.

Above all, public-sector organizations in democracies are subject to the influence of political parties. These parties have their own preference orderings of issues and their own sense of the public policies required to deal with them. Their agendas are essentially normative; rarely do they brook qualification or interference on grounds of efficiency or similar considerations (Gortner, Mahler, and Nicholson 1987: 65–9). Members of governmental organizations, even when protected by civil service laws, defy political parties at considerable risk. This exposure may be extreme in the United States, but it is endemic to European and other parliamentary systems as well.

Autonomy

This condition of multiple accountability, formal and informal in nature (Cohen and Axelrod 1984), implies that political organizations are considerably less autonomous than private-sector organizations. Not only are the formal chains of command multiple and complex, but informal influences and pressures often limit, sometimes drastically, the degrees of freedom open to persons in these organizations. Although managers in the private sector are also not free to act exactly as they might prefer, their organizations (as long as they operate within the law) are immensely more autonomous than public/political sector organizations are.

Two additional characteristics relating to autonomy are worth noting. First, not only the goals of these organizations may be dictated from the outside, they may also be dependent on other external bodies to achieve them. Lawmakers need the executive branch, as do the courts, to have their policies enforced. Central governments need regional or local governments. A single policy may require the coordination and collaboration of different governmental bodies, many of which are in competition or conflict with each other. And, as I noted earlier, successful goal achievement may in part also lie in the hands of political parties and interest groups.

Furthermore, governmental bodies or agencies often disagree about goals and policies. Evaluations of how well or poorly organizations are doing will be driven not by objective criteria (assuming they are available) but rather by political ideology and partisanship. Even within the same government, existing organizations will be in conflict over policies, such as in the case of ministries and departments that spend money while others have to worry about deficits, exchange rates, inflation, and so on. Even in highly authoritarian or dictatorial political systems, such factors make organizations in the public/political sphere, if not radically different in kind from their counterparts in the private sector, then certainly different in the valence of the factors that I have been enumerating.

To summarize, the missions of these public/political bodies, their membership, the resources provided for operations, the rewards and punishments for good or bad goal achievement, and often the sheer survival of the organization itself are all matters that typically lie outside the organization. Hence, before taking initiatives, persons in political and governmental organizations will make careful internal and external assessments. First, they seek to discover how their superiors or immediate colleagues may feel about a policy or mode of policy implementation. Second, they look to how this policy or mode of implementation will sit with those internal or external forces that can impinge on their professional careers, their economic well-being, or the welfare of the organization. Third, they make assessments about what will lie in the way of their ambitions, including, perhaps, their desire to make and enforce given policies.

This basic pattern suggests that these organizations are under enormous pressure to engage in learning. Attention will certainly be paid to other governmental agencies, political parties, labor unions, trade associations, religious or ethnic groups, the courts, the mass media, professional associations, the corporate community, and other political and governmental jurisdictions at home or abroad that may affect the organization's well-being. The list is very long of constituencies that wield enough power, formal or otherwise, to either dictate or veto certain policies or facilitate or nullify their successful implementation (Dean 1981: 133). Failures to perform calculations of this kind and to learn about these things—and at a reasonably high level of competence—will hobble or defeat the persons or organizations involved.

The corporate community has taken to engaging in somewhat similar scanning in recent years, largely because of the internationalization of the firm. When managers extend their operations abroad, they come to appreciate the value, indeed the necessity, of scanning these new environments for aspects that are not, strictly speaking, directly related to the market. As noted above this scanning has also been practiced at home, for national and local governments have come to exercise jurisdiction over matters that affect the life and particularly the profit or loss of private enterprise. One can generalize this tendency by noting that managers are increasingly impelled to engage in scanning whenever gaps begin to appear between a corporation's policies and its actual performance. Failure to catch sight of such gaps before the media do can carry severe consequences.

Orientation to Action

The conditions described above do not encourage much initiative by public/political-sector organizations. Action tends to be reactive, not proactive, and prophylactic, not innovative. Fresh ideas are typically viewed as threats to a delicate equilibrium between internal and external forces. Few people wish to risk taking steps that might trigger chain reactions with unknown consequences. Conservatism, not risk-taking, becomes the modal orientation to action. Persons in the private sector, and the mass media, lament this attitude, sometimes stridently. They overlook, perhaps, that they themselves are partly responsible for the shortcomings that they criticize.

Conservatism also grows out of the fact that these organizations are much more tied to tradition and more deeply institutionalized than is true in the private sector. These traits, too, make them extremely resistant to change. Whether legislatures (Cooper 1975), political parties (Panebianco 1988), or bureaucratic agencies (Powell and DiMaggio 1991; Scott 1995) are meant, the length of time they have been around will greatly condition what the organization is capable of doing, including its capacity to learn and, on this basis, to change. Max Weber's (1958) reference to bureaucracy's 'dead hand' (p. 228) suggests that this type of conservatism is brought about by the very same characteristics that he associated with legal-rational authority systems.

Some writers have labeled this phenomenon 'strong institutionalization' (Panebianco 1988: 53). Others have called it the embeddedness of values, or norms, that affect the cognitive systems of organizations (Herriott, Levinthal, and March 1985). In the governmental sphere, therefore, endless examples show that efforts to reform these organizations fail more often than not (Destler 1981: 167–70). This pattern does not mean that the bureaucrats who run these organizations are beyond anyone's control or that change is impossible (Wood and Waterman 1994). It does mean, however, that organizational change is extraordinarily difficult to carry off, given the magnitude of inertial forces (Kaufman 1981).

The budget process and goal displacement in the public/political sphere are additional factors that impinge on an orientation to action.

For instance, not only are public budgets controlled from outside the organizations that depend on these allocations, in the short and medium terms, they can be modified and redirected only minimally, and at the margins. This circumstance is one reason why political scientists who wish to identify the most powerful groups and organizations, within government itself and within civil society, will profile public budgetary allocations over fairly long periods of time.

Goal displacement occurs when the personal interests and expediency of organizational leaders and members come to dominate and replace the purpose(s) of the organization itself. This tendency is ubiquitous in the political sphere. Cooper (1975) nicely summed it up in his observation on the U.S. Congress: he found that institution 'quite vulnerable to the deleterious effects the pursuit of residual goals [of its members] involves. [These self-regarding goals] distort policy orientations and block institutional reforms by making individual self interest or collective partisan advantage the focus of attention and the criterion of action' (p. 337). Mayhew (1974) found that the best explanation for the action orientation of members of Congress is the strength of each member's desire to be reelected. In extreme form, and in many different types of organizations, these characteristics actually result in a transformation of the organization itself (Perrow 1972: 178–87).

The Environment

Because the environment of organizations in the public/political sphere is so strongly normative, the policies enacted there are not only temporary but also contested in their implementation every step of the way both inside and outside government. Knowing about these aspects of their environment, the managers of public/political organizations engage in a predictable type of environmental scanning and learning. For example, they learn whether to pay more attention to the legislature or to the executive office (Kaufman 1981). In order to be at least minimally effective in their environments, the organizations involved must learn the ways and means of overcoming the kinds of constraints that I have been summarizing (Levin and Sanger 1994: 66–8, 171–6). Indeed, considerations of organizational efficiency may be and often are entirely irrelevant to decision-making and choice in the political sphere. Successful 'entrepreneurs' in this context are the ones who learn how to survive and/or help their policies survive in an environmental landscape full of dangerous surprises and subject to frequent and radical change. The basic knowledge to be internalized is that this struggle will remain continuous and that space for freedom of action will not last long.

It is these qualities—ambiguity, messiness, and continuous struggle and conflict—in the political and governmental environment that lead political scientists to give considerable attention to power and its distribution both among and within organizations. That attention remains intense, notwithstanding that power is an elusive concept invariably laden with all sorts of normative claims about what type of power is legitimate and what type is not. In political science there is fairly broad agreement (Dahl 1968) that power is the ability, through whatever means, of one person to make another do his or her bidding, even and particularly in circumstances in which doing so is not what the other person wishes or prefers.

Power and Organizations

The Role and Anatomy of Power Struggles

Power, and the struggle over it, describe the essence of the political process. Rothman and Friedman (Ch. 26 in this volume) note that scholars writing on organizational learning rarely take conflict and conflict resolution into consideration. They add that organizational conflict, even in the hands of authors as skilled as March and Olsen (1976), is not mentioned as one of the factors that may inhibit the successful development of a learning cycle (see also March 1966). This neglect stems in part from the tendency, widespread in both the corporate community and management literature, to consider conflict itself as something highly undesirable and potentially pathological and, therefore, as something to be defeated (Hardy and Clegg 1996: 627–8; Pfeffer 1981: 2–9). It cannot be without negative consequences, either for the theory of organizational learning or for attempts to apply it in the workplace, that such organizations are almost never studied from the vantage point of power and of the competition that takes place to create and maintain control of it or wrest it from others (Berthoin Antal 1998; Dierkes 1988; Hardy and Clegg 1996: 631).

One author (Kotter 1979: 2) noted that the open seeking of power is widely considered a sign of bad management. Indeed, the authors of management literature not only skirt the behavior associated with power struggles but also condemn it as 'politicking', which is seen as parochial, selfish, divisive, and illegitimate (Hardy and Clegg 1996: 629). Kotter (1979) found, for example, that in 2,000 articles published by the *Harvard Business Review* over a twenty-year period, only five of them included the word 'power' in their titles. This finding is astounding. It suggests that power is treated like a dirty little family secret: Everyone knows it's there, but no one dares come right out to discuss it.

One might imagine, though incorrectly, that the situation has changed for the better in recent decades. An examination of the *Harvard Business Review* with Kotter's same question in mind shows that less than fifteen of over 3,000 items published in the period from 1960 to mid-1999 contained the word 'power' in their titles and that three contained the word 'conflict'. 'Leadership' appeared in nine titles. In a sample of abstracts of these articles, one finds, as expected, the term 'power' somewhat more often than in the article's titles. But the term is almost never treated as a central concept that orients the way the researcher looks at an organization or develops propositions about its internal life.

This finicky, keep-it-in-the-closet attitude toward power is puzzling. For political scientists, the question of power in organizations is central for many reasons: because power is held unequally by its members, because there is a continuous struggle to change its distribution, because these inequalities and efforts to change them inevitably lead to internal tensions. A persistent quest in political science, therefore, is to illuminate the structural aspects of public/political management that permits those involved to confront and handle power confrontations without defeating the purpose of the organization itself.

Is There a Power Struggle?

The puzzle of inattention to power in the fields of organizational theory and organizational learning is all the more intriguing given that leading organizational theorists, such as Argyris and Schön (1978, 1996) and Perrow (1972), have certainly addressed this matter. For example, Perrow treated organizational traits such as nepotism and particularism as means by which leaders of economic and noneconomic organizations maintain their power within them. Because these organizations are the tools of those who lead them and can be used to accumulate vast resources, a power struggle typically occurs over their control (pp. 14–17). And because of goal displacement that may accompany such power struggles, organizations may well become 'things-in-themselves' (pp. 188–9).

It is possible that leading theorists such as Argyris and Schön (1978, 1996) and Senge (1990) have themselves been excessively reticent in treating phenomena such as power struggles within the firm (Coopey 1995). It may be that corporate managers are in denial and therefore loath to acknowledge that even they, like their counterparts in politics, are playing power games. Firms, and the literature about them, stress the beauty of teamwork and team players. Plants are organized around work teams and quality circles. Mission statements are endlessly reiterated. Human resource managers expend enormous energy instilling the firm's culture as a distinctive way of doing things. People who excel at the approved traits are rewarded with promotions and stock options. All these practices might be cited as evidence that corporate behavior is instrumentally rational and that the search for power, especially for its own sake, is alien to the firm.

This way of thinking and describing things leaves little room for attention to the power games that lie at the center of most organizational life. Thus, making decisions about corporate strategic plans and the budgetary allocations that go with them; defining of core businesses and the shedding of what is not 'core'; effecting mergers, acquisitions, and alliances; and carrying out radical corporate restructuring that may separate thousands of persons from their jobs and yet dazzlingly reward others would typically be seen by political scientists as behavior that is quite similar to the kind of power struggles that take place every day in public-sector organizations.

Behind the veil of corporate myth and rhetoric, managers obviously know about this aspect of their environment as well. So do writers for the financial newspapers, where words such as 'power struggle' appear much more frequently than they do in the management journals. How could it be otherwise when the efforts at leveraged buyouts, struggles to introduce one product line and abolish others, and differences over where and how best to invest abroad take on the monumental dimensions reported in the press? It would be astonishing if the persons involved in these events were found actually to believe that considerations of personal and organizational power are not germane to them. Nevertheless, as Hardy and Clegg (1996) noted, 'the hidden ways in which senior managers use power behind the scenes to further their position by shaping legitimacy, values technology and information are conveniently excluded from analysis. This narrow definition obscures the true workings of power and depoliticizes organizational life' (p. 629).

Attempts to correct the queasy orientation to the reality of conflict and power struggles have been relatively rare. One reason is that not just the actors in the corporate community but also students of such things come to believe in the mythologies about empowered employees, concern for the stakeholders, the rationality of managerial decisions, and the pathology of power-seeking within organizations. Their belief is a pity in that, without doubt, the structure of power, explicit or implied rules about its use, and the norms that attach to overt and covert power-seeking will deeply affect the capacity of the organization to learn (Coopey 1995). In any case, there can be no doubting the fact, however much it may continue to be obscured in the corridors of corporate power, that struggles of this kind deeply affect corporate life—its external behavior and who gets what, when, and how within these institutions (Coopey 1995: 202–5).

The Benefits of Power Struggle

Power struggle, of course, is not the only aspect of organizations worth study, and the world of politics is not just Hobbesian in nature. Cooperation is the obverse of conflict. How power is defined and whether the definition reflects left-wing or right-wing bias makes a difference in thinking about or conceptualizing the salience of power in organizations (Hardy and Clegg 1996: 623–5). In particular, it is essential that one avoid any definition or relatively broad conceptualization that does not take into account that in any organization the existing 'rules of the game', even if they are considered highly rational and 'legitimate', constitute in themselves the outcome of an earlier (and typically ongoing) struggle over control of an organization's resources (Hardy and Clegg 1996: 629).

When the ubiquitous existence of power struggle within organizations is acknowledged and put into proper perspective, when power-seeking (even when the impulse is entirely ego-centered and not driven by organizational needs) is accepted as normal behavior, and when it is recognized that no existing organizational structure is entirely neutral, only then can one hope to clarify what kind of single-loop or double-loop learning is likely to occur. For example, Coopey (1995) argued, correctly in my view, that where the distribution of power within an organization is hierarchical and asymmetrical, the type of organizational learning that proceeds in such contexts will tend to buttress the status quo. Their reasoning makes sense not just because, for example, the learning process tends to favor senior managers but also because the kind and quality of information to which those managers have access becomes, in itself, an instrument for exercising and preserving one's favorable position in the power hierarchy.

In the public sector, double-loop learning is even more impeded and therefore rarer than in the private sphere. The reason is that politics, in both the organizational environment and political organizations, actually infuses every aspect of what public-sector organizations are and what they do. The more important the sphere of action or the issues treated by these bodies and the more public attention they draw, the more difficult it will be to reach consensus. And once consensus is reached, the more improbable it will be that anyone will either want to modify it or succeed in doing so—no matter what the feedback about the policies and their efficacy may turn out to be (Smith and Deering 1984: 263–70).

Double-loop learning in the public sphere is impeded also by the formal separation of policy-making and policy implementation, as for example between legislative and administrative bodies. As noted earlier, policies are infrequently the choices of the organizations called on to implement them. In this setting, endemic to governmental systems, certain types of impediments to organizational learning tend to materialize. On the principal's side, there may not be sufficient time, or technical competence, or interest to learn what is actually going on with policy implementation. The probability is low, therefore, that those who make policy and set organizational goals will ever get information that might encourage a realistic articulation of goals and a rational specification of the means to be used in goal achievement. Organized interest groups are well aware of this gap. As a consequence, their typical strategy is to keep fighting for what they want, not only when alternative policies are up for consideration but also (sometimes particularly) after an unwanted policy has formally been adopted but must still face the vagaries of being carried out.

On the agent's side, whatever is learned about policy implementation that might urge a change of methods or of the policy itself may never be articulated at all, for to do so might upset an existing political equilibrium. Not only are these equilibria difficult to obtain in the first place, they often also involve an unspoken, symbiotic relationship—often dubbed the 'Iron Triangle' (e.g. Heclo 1978: 102)—between a specialized legislative committee, a bureaucratic agency responsible for administering the specialized policies, and the organized interests that benefit from particular policies, particular ways of implementing these policies, or both. Potential learning that would upset this balance of forces finds very rough sledding. The treatment of whistleblowers, who sometimes go public with revelations of misguided or distorted policies or of bad methods used in their administration, is eloquent evidence of this problem.

One way to overcome the stasis implied by these tendencies is to encourage power struggles, not to obscure them (Lindblom 1971: 21–42, 64–7). Nothing will galvanize the attention of politicians and bureaucrats more than learning that organized groups with a vested interest in a given policy and large numbers of faithful voters are unhappy about a particular aspect of public policy. When these groups lie outside the Iron Triangle, they are far less inhibited by considerations of equilibria than when they are inside it. This single-issue focus is indeed one of the reasons why even small and not well-financed public advocacy groups can sometimes be very effective in bringing about change (Heclo 1978).

The trick is to maximize transparency, to encourage more group intervention as well as prompt the media to provide more, and more responsible, investigative reporting than they usually offer. Today it appears that the Internet is quickly becoming an important instrument for the timely, accurate, and detailed exposure, now on a global scale, of conditions that require correction. The organizational learning implications of this development are potentially enormous. Increased transparency implies, if nothing else, a more democratic, capillary diffusion and sharing of information (see also Friedman, Lipshitz, and Overmeer, Ch. 34 in this volume). In an organizational context, whether in the private or the public sphere, this fact alone modifies the form, quality, and spread of learning; it also brings about a modification of the organizational power structure itself.

Such modifications also mean that the structure and configuration of conflict will change. In political science this kind of transformation, which widens and deepens competition, is considered to have healthy implications for the overall political system in which competition takes place. That is, benefits are expected to derive from the fact that the 'market' becomes, in comparison to the more *dirigiste* state, more Smithian, less concentrated, and less dominated by a handful of competitors who, rhetoric aside, rarely pursue the general welfare but rather much narrower considerations. At the very least, increased transparency and the broadening of the competitive sphere clearly require that political managers develop a set of skills that permit them to meet such challenges and function well within these constraints.

New Signals from the Private Sector

Something similar to this attitude about encouraging conflict may be developing in the private sector. Gortner, Mahler, and Nicholson (1987) lamented that theories of the organization 'simply do not deal with the issue of politics, and . . . [that these theories] interpret power as an internal phenomenon usually related to the area of leadership' (p. 76). But change may be afoot in this respect for at least two reasons. Contributors to this volume as well as writers such as Pfeffer (1981, 1997),

Coopey (1995), and Hardy and Clegg (1996) may well succeed in their efforts to raise self-consciousness and broaden and refine theories of the organization and organizational learning to include attention to power and politics. Second, variations and abrupt changes in the environment of business are ubiquitous today and likely to intensify tomorrow. It could not be otherwise in an era of globalization of the firm, in which, more than ever before, firms venture into a wide variety of cultural settings. In addition, managers increasingly come from quite different cultures and professional backgrounds where values and norms are not necessarily carbon copies of each other. An organization's capacity to read signals about politics and power distributions, outside as well as inside the firm, and to make quick, constructive adaptations to them will represent not just a luxury but also a necessary condition for establishing a competitive advantage in the global marketplace. In limiting cases, this capacity may actually become a necessary condition for survival.

Power-driven behavior within the firm not only is endemic to such organizations but remains salient irrespective of the degree to which the firm succeeds in creating an internal environment that is homogeneous, harmonious, and collaborative—an environment peopled by those who share corporate values and a corporate culture and who stress collective over individual goals (Handy 1993: 123–49). By definition, the firm is typically an organization that places high value on the competitive spirit. That spirit is an aspect of human behavior everywhere, and it can scarcely be divorced from the impulse to obtain and hang on to disproportionate shares of power. Improved understanding of the structure of such internal competition also illuminates the relationship between these kinds of patterns and corporate learning (Coopey 1995: 197–8; Hardy and Clegg 1996: 633–5; Kotter 1979: 9–39).

Increased attention to power (even if the term itself is not used) is implicit in the corporate community's recent encouragement of internal open expression of objections to existing policies and of open competition between units of the company and between its members. Bringing these universal underlying conditions to the surface may be inevitable, given how much more variegated today's large-scale companies are from those in the past, not just in technology, product lines, and personnel but above all in the great diversity of markets and cultures in which they now operate. The less homogeneous the international firm becomes, the more difficult it will be to mask the fact that corporate life, like political life, involves a good deal of organizational and individual struggle over power.

Power Linkages and Networks

Because conflict and power struggle in public-sector organizations are both internal and external, their managers are impelled to search the environment for opportunities to form alliances. Sometimes such alliances are of the Iron Triangle variety, but they are certainly not limited to this form. The idea is to create structural linkages that will improve one's chances of prevailing.

As public policies become more salient for the firm, the firm too will experience increased need to expand its own networks beyond those that already exist in the marketplace. Linkages with public bodies, for example, cannot be optimized (as once may have been the case) through the use of consultants and lobbyists. Structures and capabilities consonant with the establishment of direct networks come to replace or supplement these older approaches. Multinational corporations that operate abroad, where public policies represent new risks for the firm as well as new opportunities, have often moved in exactly this networking direction. One indicator of this change is the proliferation not just of equity joint ventures (as opposed to the once-dominant fetish of the wholly owned subsidiary) but also all manner of other interfirm alliance, designed to optimize, in overseas local markets, the use of firms and their managers who have extensive experience there.

In the case of U.S. companies, this type of change was also spurred by the passage of the Foreign Corrupt Practices Act a generation ago. At home, one immediate consequence of this legislation was a sharp increase in the number of in-house attorneys employed by American firms. Overseas, it led to a much more intense search for the ways and means of finding arrangements that can somehow enable overseas U.S. firms to engage in corporate behavior that was unexceptional abroad but suspect or even outright unacceptable at home.

The globalization of enterprise, the growth of networks in which the firm becomes involved at home and abroad, also brings about a considerable extension of learning methods and horizons, if not a new type of organizational learning in the private sector. The international firm becomes more sensitized to power configurations and power equilibria. The search is broadened as well as intensified in order to identify aspects of the environment that might impinge on corporate success. The quality of intelligence relevant to business operations at home and abroad is improved, as is the knowledge about the location and means of access to points in the decision-making process that relate to public policies affecting the foreign investor. A keen sense that each environment has its unique aspects as well as dimensions that are general to any environment impels the firm to sharpen its analytical instruments and thereby try to improve its learning. Efforts to create a total quality system come to include not just the production, distribution, and servicing of a firm's products but also the firm's ability to recognize power and power struggles for what they are and to attune its learning methods to profit from this new capability.

Types of Power Distributions and Equilibria

Although power equilibria are never permanent, they tend to last for a long time. The reform of governmental bodies tends to be greatly resisted because, even when reforms are relatively mild, they threaten existing equilibria (Seidman 1977). As a rule, unless quick and deep change is the goal, it is better for an organization (inside or outside the public/political sphere) to learn how to operate within an existing equilibrium than to make efforts to change it. Indeed, it is almost axiomatic that, where a radical departure in public policy is intended, creating a new organization is far preferable to seeking achievement of these new goals through the existing system (Levin and Sanger 1994: 172–3). Events of this kind, though rare, provide highly fluid opportunities to achieve first-mover advantages as new networks and a new equilibrium are established.

In this regard, it makes a difference whether the overall configuration of the political system is monocratic or pluralist, unitary or federal, highly centralized or characterized by broad delegation or devolution of powers. That is, power equilibria at the microlevels will be influenced in no small measure by the configuration of the larger system in which these equilibria are embedded.

Pluralism

Pluralist systems tend to maximize not only the number of individuals and organizations able to intervene in the policy-making and policy implementation processes but also the number of channels through which the interventions occur. Pluralism implies minute and fragmented representation of interests. The underlying assumption is that equality of opportunity, central to democratic theory, should also apply to the policy-making process. It will obviously make a difference which groups prevail in these efforts to exercise influence. It is equally important whether and what kinds of groups can bring some order to the process by aggregating a number of small groups under a single organizational umbrella.

Pluralism also invites much debate. In theory, when consensus is achieved, it is expected to be very strong, precisely because of widespread opportunities that interested parties have for being consulted and hearing the views of others. Again in theory, this system of broad participation should also optimize the discovery both of best solutions and of innovative ideas about public policies and how best to achieve them. It is behind such policies, according to pluralist democratic theory, that one can expect the strongest collective effort to emerge. And given all of these assumptions, consensual policies are likely to be well administered and widely accepted as long as they achieve expected aims. Within this rich mosaic of interactive participation, organizational learning is presumably optimized, as are the efficacious making and implementation of public policies.

There are also negative sides to pluralism, and they are well known to organizational theorists. A plethora of communication channels easily degenerates into information overload. This overload in turn can lead to never-ending debates that wind up in stalemates or paralysis. There may be too much talk, too many options raised, and little inclination, or indeed ability, to reach closure. An even more notable objection to this mode of decision-making is the raised probability that it will produce only lowest-common-denominator outcomes. The need to balance competing forces and to find acceptable compromises implies that only in extreme emergencies can pluralist systems adopt radical measures. Pluralism and the forceful, timely management of issues do not sit easily side by side. Hence, it seems valid to presume that such systems will not work well within a corporate structure that, almost by definition, is expected to be hierarchical and unitary (Hardy and Clegg 1996: 622–6).

Monocratic and Unitary Systems

Monocratic and unitary systems are highly centralized. If they permit a broad representation of interests, it is likely to be within a framework that is much more disciplined than that of pluralist systems. Monocratic and unitary systems are able to act even when broad consensus may be wanting or impossible to bring about. Participation from the ground up, so to speak, is not so loose or permissive as to tie the hands of or paralyze those at the center.

Compared to pluralist systems, monocratic arrangements tend to be less democratic (not to be confused with undemocratic). They may involve broad, well-articulated participation in policy-making and implementation, but within limits. They tend to be more intolerant of inputs that are judged to be dysfunctional. They are immensely more suspicious of interventions in the formal decision-making and policy implementation process by groups and organizations that are not official, or not officially approved by the government.

The tensions between pluralistic/democratic and unitary/monocratic arrangements are not unlike those found within corporations that move in the direction of empowerment of those located toward the bottom of the pyramidal hierarchy. As I have suggested, this pyramid is not just one of positions and authority but also of command and control. That is, as long as the pyramid remains a pyramid, even slightly, it is a power arrangement governed by rules that, with rare exceptions, are themselves the outcome of a power struggle. Serious efforts to empower persons who have not had very much power, or who through empowerment will come to exercise more of it than in the past, clearly imply a widening and deepening of participation in decision-making both in the making of corporate policies and in their implementation. It is no wonder that changes of this kind, as well as those designed to bring stakeholders meaningfully into such processes, are fraught with complications and that they usually degenerate into not much more than lip-service platitudes (Coopey 1995).

Monocratic and unitary political systems, such as those typically found in Europe and elsewhere outside the United States (and to some extent outside Great Britain), accord very high status to the state writ large. Those who manage the state are more inclined to redirect, minimize, and, if necessary, override interference from civil society when this interference threatens to paralyze government. Reasons of state, as the justification is often called, will lead to closure of debate and then to public action, presumably in favor of the community as a whole. In monocratic systems, popular sovereignty and broad participation by the masses or by organized groups will not be permitted to place the state and its overriding welfare at risk. This attitude is similar to the posture of senior corporate managers who are not at all likely to tolerate modes of empowerment or participation that might cast serious doubt on the company's mission, the rationality of its basic long-term strategy, or the company's very survival. Nevertheless, in the corporate sphere, as in the sphere of the state, the powers available to managers must be and often are used to lend an aura of legitimacy not just to existing rules and policies but also to the outcomes that derive from them (Hardy and Clegg 1996: 630).

Federalism

Federalism adds another facet to this discussion. As a political concept that stands in opposition to that of unitary structures, federalism implies a division of power on the basis of territory. A much-touted advantage of federalism is that it permits the bringing together, under one central authority, of territorial units that differ quite markedly from each other in many ways, including, say, the size of their population or territory; racial or linguistic make-up; and a wide range of social, economic, and even political conditions.

Federal systems represent ways of organizing and managing diversity. In the realm of politics, experience has shown that these systems are therefore much more viable means of managing large nations than are highly centralized unitary systems. In fact, most of these nations are of the federal, not the unitary, variety—even the Soviet Union and the People's Republic of China in their so-called totalitarian heyday. Federalism also maximizes the amount of experimentation (with different laws, institutions, electoral arrangements, administrative organizations, and the like) that can take place under a common political roof. This umbrella-like structure permits, indeed encourages, the search for best practice in institutional form and relationships and in policy-making and implementation.

This feature of federalism permits and, indeed, encourages self-conscious learning. In the United States, for example, there are formal organizations designed to provide the individual states and major cities with information about the potentially innovative or effective approaches that each may be taking to organizational procedures or public policy. Similar information-sharing institutions also exist at the international level. This institutionalized learning is designed in the broadest sense to raise the quality and lower the cost of governmental services.

In a federal setting the political center shares a number of powers with other territorial units. Except in restricted areas, it cannot pretend to be the exclusive holder or exerciser of power and authority. Even where in formal terms the political center's authority may be exclusive and where policies are expected to be uniformly administered throughout the system's territories and subunits, considerable local variation must be permitted. Unitary systems, by contrast, permit much less flexibility of this type. The central authority within such systems exercises nearly exclusive powers to make system-wide policies, and it is also expected that these policies will be uniformly administered everywhere. Any deviation from centrally established policies, indeed any policy-making within subnational units, proceeds only with some sort of authorization by the center. As often said in France, if one wishes to know exactly what children might be doing at a certain hour of any school day, it is sufficient to consult the manual issued by the appropriate ministry in Paris.

The unitary form is highly analogous to the worldwide business firm, including firms organized by product group or division, in which authority and control are concentrated in a single, central organization. The postwar development of the multinational corporation, at least in the United States, proceeded for the most part on the basis of this model. It was thought that the revolutions in jet travel and electronics made such centralized control both desirable and feasible. That is, these changes in the speed and facility of travel and communication were said to make possible the global extension of the so-called Sloan model of the corporation, a model that had worked so well within the United States.

Feedback and Learning

No matter whether the basic structure is pluralistic or monocratic, federal or unitary, the need for feedback from which the center can presumably learn is universal. Federal systems, because they produce many streams of information, may be more open but less efficient than unitary systems. Unitary systems, although in theory narrower and easier to control than federal systems are in terms of information-producing channels, are at high risk of having information delayed, distorted, or misdirected. It is apparent, however, that the center often deludes itself into believing that, with a highly disciplined and centralized organizational weapon at its disposal (like the Communist party under Stalin in the USSR or the Chinese Communist party under Mao), it can both learn and control what transpires at the periphery (Hough 1969). The fallacious assumption in this instance is that a centralized and highly disciplined organizational instrument, such as the Communist party, can prevail irrespective of whether the overall system is of the federal or unitary configuration.

Pluralism and Federalism in the Firm?

A pluralist and federal model of the polity ill fits the generally held image of the firm and of other private-sector organizations. Decision-making of the kind represented by the typical firm can scarcely follow a pluralist model to the letter, at least not without a rethinking of a great many well-established notions of what a world-scale company should be and how it should be run. Within the firm great emphasis is placed on clear lines of authority, both horizontal and vertical. The global firm still tries to instill a single corporate culture so that the hierarchy of values, the operational norms, and the *modus operandi* will be essentially the same wherever its branches and units may be located. This model leaves little room for pluralist inputs and local diversity.

Pluralist democracies and federal systems thrive (most of the time) on their multicultural dimensions. Rather than eliminate diversity, it is honored and encouraged. In the corporate world, much of what is claimed about decentralization, 'planning from the bottom up', and individual empowerment often is spurious. Senior managers in the corporate world are rarely able or inclined to practice the decentralization or the broad and deep participation that they may preach. More often than not they use the considerable powers at their disposal not to encourage debate that leads to consent but rather to mobilize consent itself (Hardy and Clegg 1996: 626).

In the public/political sector, a key test of how seriously the center wishes to encourage diversity and favor empowerment lies in the practice of devolution, as opposed to decentralization. Devolution, typically practiced on a territorial basis, substantially reduces the powers of the center over the periphery, sometimes drastically. The strongest indicator of this reduction is the empowerment of the periphery not only to make policies but also to tax or otherwise raise capital in connection with these policies. Such transfers, in turn, encourage high levels of competition between the subnational units of federal systems, sometimes creating very difficult problems at the center. Devolution increases pluralism. When hierarchy is replaced by something composed of rather free-acting units, managers need to develop skills that are germane to these changed circumstances. It is one thing when a person's position makes it possible to mobilize consent and conforming behavior; it is quite another story when both of these things must be generated within the context of a relatively open, participatory, and fluid system of reaching consensus on what should be done and how best to do it.

It is possible that the globalization of enterprise will force an increase in genuinely federal arrangements on the firm, a shift that would certainly imply moving away from a strict unitary, hierarchical model and award one that is genuinely more participatory, even if more difficult to manage. Charles Handy (1996) stated

that such a change may be taking place (pp. 33–56), although even he suggested that the application of federal principles to the corporate world will, perhaps inevitably, be imperfect (pp. 109–12). The creation of similar federal structures, even ones remaining distant from devolution, requires a new look at many of the most canonical ideas about how best to organize and manage the profit-seeking enterprise. On close inspection, the sometimes spectacular downsizing and other changes in corporate structures since about 1990 do not appear to have brought about radical operational changes in hierarchical structure. In both the public and the private sectors, centralized control of organizations dies hard.

Nevertheless, the federal thrust in many of today's global firms should not be underestimated. In the truly global firm, where multinationality is not just a label, traditional arrangements for strategic plans, corporate finance, and capital budgeting—which are still basically monocratic and unitary in nature—will gradually be revised. It is misleading to think, as so many corporate managers still do, that the continuing electronic and information technology revolutions will permit efficient global control from a single, geographically distinctive center. Experiences with joint ventures, as well as the corporation's growing need to sharpen its attention to local markets and their customers and to local politics, have led to heightened interest in federal arrangements. In fact, as cross-border arrangements, especially nonequivalent ones, continue to multiply, there is some speculation that the future global firm will be confederal and not just federal. This formula implies that increased autonomy among the far-flung units of such firms is better than monocratic, unitary structures as a way of organizing for tomorrow's global enterprise. If devolution is indeed the configuration destined to characterize the truly global firms, then the earliest and most telling signs of it are likely to come from the megamergers that began to accelerate as the twentieth century drew to a close.

An important concomitant of any such transformation would be changes in both the ways in which these corporate bodies learn and the kinds of information they seek. These changes, if and when they occur, will perhaps decrease the universal lament among regional or local units that the center does not take variations in local conditions sufficiently into consideration in its decision-making. Managers are likely to experience a marked improvement in their ability to make salutary adaptations to a marketplace that, in the years ahead, will be increasingly characterized by rapidly mutating conditions that not only mark or reflect diversity but actually create it. Global firms, well-organized to deal with such challenges, are the ones that will have tomorrow's competitive advantages.

Any such transformation should also encourage attention to the concept of power within the organization. Ongoing and endemic power struggles can be glossed over and even concealed when organizations are hierarchical and monolithic, particularly when they operate within a single or highly similar cultural context. When the firm expands geographically and begins to move in a pluralistic or federal direction, a fundamental rethinking of the place of power and of power-struggle considerations in the organization and management of enterprise will inevitably attract the attention it obviously deserves.

Lessons in Learning from the Public/Political Sector

Public/political-sector organizations experience not only thorny problems with learning but also rather strong pressure to endow themselves with capabilities particular to this sphere. The main pressure is to develop the kind of leadership that the public/political milieu requires (Fairholm 1990: 153). That such leadership does develop is an important indicator of instrumental learning. This kind of learning can also bring about changes in policy (Bennett and Hawlett 1992). As Heclo (1974) noted, alongside conflict within and between bureaucratic agencies, a good deal of collective attention to

nagging problems also is the rule (pp. 1–16). This in turn brings about a great deal of political learning on the part of all concerned—bureaucrats as well as those with whom they interact (Heclo 1974: 284–326). As a further consequence, high levels of cooperation and collaboration, often across vast spatial distances, are reached in finding solutions to common problems.

Both inter- and intranational diffusion of this type of learning has long been known to exist among functional specialists in public administration. As noted earlier, it is even more distinctive in federal systems than in unitary systems, in part because of the experimentation and competition that this form encourages between governmental units. There may be less of this type of learning in the private sector than in the public sector, no matter how the firm is organized, because so many discoveries, including those involving management know-how, have proprietary and potential rent-producing characteristics. For this reason, information is typically stringently guarded rather than shared.

The Question of Leadership

Like power, the concept of leadership remains elusive (Sadler, Ch. 18 in this volume). Nevertheless, much corporate learning effort centers on the search for the right man or woman to assign to the tasks at hand at every level, beginning at the top. In the public/political sphere, the right person is in general one who can operate effectively within organizations that display such characteristics as the following:

(1) they are nonhierarchical;
(2) they do not produce or control their own internal resources;
(3) they have, at best, limited control over their personnel, especially those people located at the most senior levels;
(4) their mission is defined and imposed from outside;
(5) the lines that separate them from other organizations that are involved in and sometimes essential to their mission are unclear;

(6) their actions are subject to continual official and unofficial scrutiny, objection, and potential reversal for nonobjective, politically motivated reasons.

As I have shown, these and similar constraints define the existential condition of most organizations in the public/political sphere. If neither neat, clear, and widely accepted organizational boundaries nor hierarchical instruments of command and control are feasible, how does one lead?

Leadership Qualities

There is a high premium on the ability to handle horizontal relationships within the organization as well as among other bodies with which the organization interacts (Kettl 1988). The effective leader must understand and be able to exploit the differences between hierarchy and equality, between formal and informal methods of communication.

More than ever before, horizontal relations challenge the manager to transcend formal rules (Barnard 1938). In informal channels, many of which lie outside the organization itself, the status of an individual on an organizational chart does not count for much and provides little guidance (Bailey 1988: 52–9). Anyone who has worked in government or in large-scale organizations in the private sector comes to appreciate the critical importance of the 'back-channel' aspect of organizational behavior. In the public/political sector these channels are more complex, less encapsulated, and potentially more explosive than in the private sector—and they require delicate and refined qualities of managing interpersonal relationships.

Highly desirable in this milieu are individual qualities such as perception, empathy, discretion, subtlety, flexibility, and decisiveness, which are translated as needed into acts of mediation, diplomacy, negotiation, advocacy, opposition, and persuasion. Implicit in these latter skills is a mastering of myriad modes of direct and indirect communication. This mastery in turn requires an acute and refined capacity to read the environment and learn from it (Rose 1993: 77–117). Myths about the man at the top actually being in control are almost useless. Ideas that derive from overly simplified principal–agent models are even worse. The leader must know and learn the productive exploitation of the distinction between having power and exercising it (Coopey 1995; Dahl 1968: 413; Gross 1964: vol. 1, pp. 49–72).

Bureaucrats sometimes do respond as though, for example, they are the agents of legislative bodies. Wood and Waterman (1994: 77–102, 150–4) bore this statement out, but they also illustrated the complexities that accompany environmental scanning and adaptation by governmental bodies involved in given policy areas. The legislature may wish to dictate policy as well as to control its administration. The bureaucrats have minds of their own, and they are inclined to exercise considerable discretion whenever they can. As the authors put it, 'Bureaucracies also have powers in their own right, and sometimes use that power to alter outcomes in their relations with other actors' (pp. 126–7).

Whether based on the formal distribution of power and authority or on the definition of roles, expectations about these interactions may cause one to miss the point completely. As one leading American political scientist observed, the essence of leadership in politics is to bring about group cohesion directed toward goal achievement through the exercise not of power but of influence (Burns 1978; Handy 1993: 133–49).

Ability to Mediate

Where conflict is the norm, the shrewd mediator is unusually endowed. The ability to encourage a search for balance among conflicting interests and to locate a point of equilibrium that will bring a working truce into being is as valued in the political sphere as it tends to be rare. For leaders of political organizations, finding the ways and means to mediate conflict among the outside groups that I have mentioned may well be a necessary condition for being able to operate at all. Without this leadership capacity, contention over the organization's policies can easily lead to paralysis (Gross 1964: vol. 1, pp. 49–72; Sandole and van der Merwe 1993: 131–57, 176–93).

Ability to Compromise

Horizontal power relations also require the leader to be flexible and to have a propensity to compromise. Both the fragmentation of power implicit in horizontal relationships and the myriad agencies and other organizations that make up the realm of government and politics, represent *de facto* pluralism. The notion that in this setting one can have one's way or impose a 'one best way' is entirely unrealistic. Rather, one must search for compromise that will not involve lowest-common-denominator agreements or place at risk the organization's goals. These dangers complicate problem-solving, but they also can and do impel a search for the type of organizational learning that such complicated circumstances require (Kriesberg 1998; Wise 1994).

Ability to Give Minorities a Voice

The need for compromise, however, also underscores that in essentially all political organizations it is prudent, indeed essential, to give minorities a continuing voice in the making and execution of policy. Majorities are rarely permanent, and the more durable they become, the more they tend to stagnate or atrophy. Today's power holders may be replaced, sometimes abruptly, by those over whom they exercise power. Leaders soon learn that only fools treat organizational conflict as a zero-sum game or ride roughshod over today's minorities. It is more than prudent to assure minorities a 'voice' option. This arrangement will encourage a required minimum amount of loyalty to the system (Hirschman 1970).

Thus, in well-run public/political-sector organizations, those in power go to some pains to guarantee not only that minorities will be heard but also, and perhaps above all, that they will share in the distribution of privileges and benefits that the organization controls. This collaboration in the sharing of material and symbolic rewards often goes under such derisive names as 'pork barrel' and 'log-rolling' and is frowned upon. Leaders of public/political-sector organizations that engage in such practices fully appreciate that, without it, life would be immensely more complicated and that failure would always be a short step away.

It is also arguable that the treatment of minorities in this way not only is essential to organizational equilibrium but also may serve to improve the performance of the organization itself. Minority roles can be arranged so that they provide a stream of information that may often be at odds with the kind of information the majority is getting. Aspects of misguided policies or inappropriate or counterproductive methods of policy implementation may be brought to the attention of the majority. This kind of learning raises the probability that corrective single-loop or double-loop learning will ensue, for organizational actions that incorporate inputs from the minority are likely to be much more consensual than otherwise.

Something similar to providing minorities with the voice option occurs when the firm introduces new or improved procedures that permit criticism of existing policies. Adversary styles of decision-making create a distinctive format for structured learning. Such learning, it might be recalled, is likely to work optimally in situations where the overall organization is more federal than unitary in character.

Ability to Mobilize Support

Diplomacy, skill at negotiation, willingness to compromise, and due care for the interests of minorities may not be enough, however. Leaders must also be adept at mobilizing support, outside as well as inside the organization. In the political realm, this quality is considered the *sine qua non* of effective leadership. It implies that one has learned to transcend negotiations and mediation and reached a higher level of leadership that brings about fundamental change (Burns 1978). The ability to mobilize, when needed, the appropriate constituencies is an essential aspect of this leadership quality. In political power struggles, the stakes are often such that competitors will take high risks in order to prevail. In these moments one's well-nurtured constituencies must be called upon to lend support. Such mobilization requires planning. It cannot be activated at a moment's notice, as needed, without such preparation (Wood and Waterman 1994: 104–7, 145–54).

Ability to Build Coalitions

Mastering this type of complexity also raises the need for yet another leadership skill, namely, that of consciously and systematically building coalitions (Levin and Sanger 1994: 76–8). This capability is especially desirable where sharply diverse interests, including territorial ones, must be reconciled. One sees this need unfold dramatically in national parliaments composed of many political parties. The more diverse the interests or territories involved, the more skillful the leadership must be at creating at least a minimum-winning coalition (Levin and Sanger 1994: 76–8).

Coalition-building implies cooperation with allies but on occasion with competitors or enemies as well (Axelrod 1984). This orientation to conflict can produce remarkably useful forms of single-loop learning, which bring about changes in collective action—but without necessarily requiring a relinquishment of long-term goals (M. Deutsch 1994). The prospect is particularly attractive in the political sphere, where the abandonment of such goals by leaders almost always creates major problems for them.

Learning in the Future

Similarities and Differences

Many of these characteristics of leadership and patterns of organizational behavior will be found in the private sector as well. People who see similarities in organizations, in whatever sphere they may be found, are basically correct in their perceptions. The point is to look for the nuances that may be distinctive in both the private and the public/political spheres and to weave these nuances into what someday may become a robust general theory of organizations and of organizational learning.

Evidence from both spheres shows the types of benefits that organizational learning can bring. They include cost reductions in the delivery of public services (Levin and Sanger 1994: 90) and increased effectiveness of goal attainment, a product of learning that has been documented in the public-administrative sector many times since the appearance of Selznick's (1949) landmark study of the Tennessee Valley Authority. It is also known that, where governmental bodies are concerned, a great deal of copying takes place which by definition means that the quest to learn is both deliberate and instrumentally motivated. This transfer of knowledge, for better but sometimes also for worse, encompasses the widest range of institutions and organizations in the public/political sphere: from constitutional conventions, executive offices, legislatures, regulatory agencies, judicial bodies, and bureaucracies to political parties, interest groups, and other organizations that make up the polity in civil society.

Evidence of beneficial learning in the governmental sector comes from both sides of the Atlantic (Furubo 1994). One overall conclusion from this work is that single-loop learning far outpaces the double-loop variety. Government organizations may be eager to improve policy implementation but may hesitate to do so where double-loop learning might be indicated, for they might not have sufficient freedom to act on the substance of policies. It is one thing to tinker with or change the methods used in the implementation of public policies but quite another to attempt a shift in substance. The literature on public administration and policy studies provides ample evidence that such tinkering does occur in many different political settings. Despite the array of obstacles I have reviewed, it remains true that creative leaders indeed manage to effect changes, particularly when it comes to improvement in the methods of delivering certain public services. And this kind of single-loop learning should continue apace as some of these services are privatized.

A problem mushrooms in the public/political sector when a policy change of the double-loop type is indicated. Of course, this predicament is also true of the private sector: It is universally more difficult to modify ends than to modify means. In the public sphere, however, changing the goals of an organization typically, often instantly, triggers debate over the ends of government because, as I have shown, these ends are what public policies reflect. Debates over such questions immediately bring into play the messiness that leaders of public-sector organizations are called upon to decipher and manage.

There is an additional nuance worth repeating. For reasons already explored, bureaucrats in the public/political sector may have learned very well, and they may know exactly what should be modified, either in method or in the content of policy. But they are handicapped not just because control over policy may lie outside their capacity to act. The mosaic that is almost always the public policy realm may well imply that those who administer given public policies are unable to assess the tradeoffs that would be involved were either single-loop or double-loop learning to be applied (Wilson 1989: 349).

Before the benefits of organizational learning can reach optimal levels in the public/political sector, learning activities must be more self-consciously pursued than they are at present (Hedberg 1981; Rose 1993: 7–12, 16–18, 19–49). Both principals and agents in the public sector should shun practices that displace their energies when it is learned that something needs changing because methods are wrong or because the policy is misguided. Energy displacement is guaranteed, for example, when errors lead those involved to try to fix blame or to find scapegoats as opposed to working for amelioration (LaPorte 1975: 348–52).

Ways need to be found to lower the valence of three additional and ubiquitous factors that impinge on public-sector organizations and perhaps on the private-sector organizations as well. One is the hostility that is certain to be directed against any information, however objective it may be, that threatens existing distributional arrangements. This problem places a high premium on the ability to show that the application of single-loop or double-loop learning will have positive-sum effects—no easy task!

The second problem, which poses great difficulties as well, is the necessity of reducing the probability, very high in large-scale organizations of all kinds, that those who need and could most productively learn from and use information will fail to get it (K. Deutsch 1963: 146–62). Information is knowledge and, as so many experts on organizations have pointed out, knowledge is also power (Hardy and Clegg 1996: 622–4, 633–7). In any organization the people who control the kind of information that is produced and, equally important, determine who see this information and when, wield enormous *de facto* power within such structures. The ability to ration and direct information is the obverse of information glut or overkill, but it is no less potentially inimical to organizational health.

The third problem carries some irony for the field of organizational learning. It is that the evaluation of programs, the search for additional information, may become a way of delaying the adoption of a policy or stopping it in its tracks at the implementation stage (Henry 1990: 122–4). The old saying about the appointment of committees being the best means to organizational paralysis applies to information-gathering and evaluations as well.

Prospects for Learning

Charles Handy has pointed out that 'in an uncertain world . . . we are going to need organizations that are continually renewing themselves, reinventing themselves, reinvigorating themselves. These are the learning organizations, the ones with the learning habit' (Handy 1995: 45). If private-sector organizational trends of recent years persist, the structure of the firm is also likely to be 'flatter' than it has been, with fewer layers of management separating those at the apex from those at the bottom of the pyramid. This reduction of hierarchy implies and probably even requires, broadened participation in decision-making. Participation, in turn, should vastly enhance system transparency, increasing the diffusion of information and therefore reducing the chances of its being used narrowly as an instrument of power. Widened sharing of information should also reduce problems of span of control, the almost certain and highly unwanted outcome of reforms that make organizations 'leaner' and 'flatter' than in the past. Any restructuring of enterprise that moves in this general organizational direction will require much more attention than is currently given to developing the kind of leaders and leadership that the 'learning organization' requires (Coopey 1995).

According to Pinchot and Pinchot (1993: 39–50), such basic change supports the notion that the future belongs to the 'intelligent organization', which is more sensitively attuned to the market and less attached to and encumbered by outmoded bureaucratic practice than are other kinds of organizations. This change implies, indeed it requires, the withering away of the kinds of public/political-sector organizations that I have been describing. Examples in the United States, Europe, and Latin America of governmental functions that have been radically changed through their 'privatization' lend credence to this expectation.

I have a slightly different sense of the future. In my view the truly intelligent organization in the private sector will have abandoned some of the mythologies that persist in management journals and corporate boardrooms. The omnipresence of power within organizations and the struggle over its exercise (Pfeffer 1992; Pfeffer and Salancik 1974) will be more widely acknowledged than it is today. Power-seeking in the corporate sphere, recognized as indeed a form of politics (Coopey 1995), will no longer be considered deviant or pathological managerial behavior. When this change in attitude comes about, more of what has been learned in the public sector about the management of complex organizations will perhaps find its way into theory and practice in the private sector as well. Among the benefits of revealing the struggle over power will be the recognition that it is nothing more than the reciprocal of the exercises of leadership.

Some of the trends now apparent in the corporate sphere give mild reason for thinking that this transformation is already under way. Pinchot and Pinchot (1993: 64–74), for example, predicted that tomorrow's intelligent organization will consist of many smaller ones, perhaps tied together in a federal or confederal structure. If this prediction holds true of the global firm, then these authors are correct in saying that styles of management will have to change, though not necessarily in the traditional market-centered direction. Managers will have to learn to scan the environment differently, work hard on horizontal relationships, and hone their skills at coalition-building and compromise.

Above all, these managers of the future will construct different information and learning networks inside and outside the firm, ones designed to bolster their own organizational capacity. In short, comparative advantage will be in part the result of incorporating and rendering operational some of the leadership qualities reviewed in this chapter. This observation may be just another way of saying that the intelligent firm and its managers will have to become much more political in their perceptions and other sensibilities than their predecessors have been. The intelligent firm and its managers will also have to be much more willing than in the past to recognize that all such networks, indeed all organizations at their core, are really about who gets how much of what is valued and scarce—about how and when this distribution happens and to what effect.

These considerations also imply a research agenda for political science. The testing of organizational theory and of theories and hypotheses of organizational learning needs to be expanded and accelerated in the realm of public/political-sector organizations, where it is only barely under way. This testing will not only provide needed modification and deepening of knowledge in this area. It will also decrease the descriptive or anecdotal nature of the knowledge that political scientists have about organizations. And will make that knowledge more systematic than it currently is and easier to integrate into the field of organizational learning than it has been.

This new research can especially be encouraged in such constituent fields of political science as policy studies and public administration, which are already to some degree interdisciplinary and integrated into the literature on organizational theory and organizational learning. But these efforts should not stop there. In the era of the globalized firm, these giant organizations will be, indeed they already are, major actors in the international sphere. Knowing how and what they learn and then comparing such insight with how and what is learned on the public/political side of the international organizational sphere should have the highest priority for the academic community and policy-makers alike.

Other subfields, such as political parties and interest groups, should also be on this future research agenda. There is simply not enough systematic knowledge about the kinds of things these organizations learn, about whether or not such learning proceeds in a self-conscious way, and about the uses to which such knowledge is put. Illumination of any of these dimensions might also be fruitfully utilized by those nations (still growing in number) said to be in transition. They are not necessarily headed toward democracy or, for that matter, toward market economies as they are traditionally understood. If experts can teach these nations something about the economic marketplace and about how the organizations found in the marketplace learn and utilize knowledge, then why not recognize that this effort is both needed and possible in the political sphere as well.

Attention to organizational learning will, I believe, also help improve the understanding not only of the emergence and spread in Western politics of the so-called Third Way, but also of the future implications of this momentous change. Adopted by many former left-wing political parties and more or less accepted by a number of key interest groups associated with them, this new departure promises to bring major transformations in the political systems of many countries. This phenomenon would not have spread as it has without a good deal of learning that is centered in organizations. It goes without saying that the particular configuration that the Third Way takes on in each country will be organizationally centered. It will also bring into existence dynamic interactions, some of them perhaps brand new, among the kinds of organizations that are found in the public/political as well as the private spheres.

In order to look at these phenomena more systematically than in the past, we should use the concepts and theoretical questions that derive from work in the fields of organizational theory and organizational learning. They encourage more of the cross-fertilization and interdisciplinary knowledge that presumably represents a widely shared ambition.

References

Abrahamsson, B. (1977). *Bureaucracy and Participation: The Logic of Organization*. London: Sage.

Argyris, C. and Schön, D. A. (1978). *Organizational Learning: A Theory of Action Perspective*. Reading, Mass.: Addison-Wesley.

——— (1996). *Organizational Learning*: Vol. 2. *Theory, Method, and Practice*. Reading, Mass.: Addison-Wesley.

Axelrod, R. (1984). *The Evolution of Cooperation*. New York: Basic Books.

Bailey, F. G. (1988). *Humbuggery and Manipulation: The Arts of Leadership*. Ithaca, NY: Cornell University Press.

Barnard, C. (1938). *The Functions of the Executive*. Cambridge, Mass.: Harvard University Press.

Bennett, C. J. and Hawlett, M. (1992). 'The Lessons of Learning: Reconciling Theories of Policy Learning and Policy Change'. *Policy Studies*, 25: 275–94.

Berle, A. A. and Means, G. C. (1933). *Modern Corporation and Private Property*. New York: Macmillan.

Berthoin Antal, A. (1998). 'Die Dynamik der Theoriebildungsprozesse zum Organisationslernen', in H. Albach, M. Dierkes, A. Berthoin Antal, and K. Vaillant (eds.), *Organisationslernen—institutionelle und kulturelle Dimensionen. WZB Jahrbuch 1998*. Berlin: edition sigma, 31–52.

Burns, J. M. (1978). *Leadership*. New York: Harper & Row.

Cohen, M. D. and Axelrod, R. (1984). 'Coping with Complexity: The Adaptive Value of Changing Utility'. *American Economic Review*, 74: 30–42.

Cooper, J. (1975). 'Strengthening the Congress: An Organizational Analysis'. *Harvard Journal of Legislation*, 12: 307–68.

Coopey, J. (1995). 'The Learning Organization: Power, Politics, and Ideology'. *Management Learning*, 26: 193–213.

Dahl, R. A. (1968). 'Power'. *International Encyclopedia of Social Sciences* (Vol. 12). New York: Macmillan, 405–15.

Dean, A. L. (1981). 'General Propositions of Organizational Design', in P. Szanton (ed.), *Federal Reorganization: What Have We Learned*. Chatham, NJ: Chatham House, 131–54.

Destler, I. M. (1981). 'Implementing Reorganization', in P. Szanton (ed.), *Federal Reorganization: What Have We Learned*. Chatham, NJ: Chatham House, 155–70.

Deutsch, K. (1963). *The Nerves of Government*. Glencoe, Ill.: Free Press.

Deutsch, M. (1994). *The Resolution of Conflict*. New Haven: Yale University Press.

Dierkes, M. (1988). 'Unternehmenskultur und Unternehmensfuhrung—Konzeptionelle Ansätze und gesicherte Erkenntnisse'. *Zeitschrift für Betriebswirtschaft*, 58: 554–75.

Easton, D. (1953). *The Political System*. New York: Knopf.

Etheredge, L. S. (1981). 'Government Learning: An Overview', in L. S. Long (ed.), *The Handbook of Political Behavior* (Vol. 2). New York: Plenum, 73–161.

Fairholm, G. W. (1990). 'Leadership', in M. L. Whicker and T. W. Areson (eds.), *Public Sector Management*. New York: Praeger, 153–79.

Furubo, J. E. (1994). 'Learning from Evaluation: The Swedish Example', in F. L. Leeuw, R. C. Rist, and R. C. Sonnichsen (eds.), *Can Governments Learn? Comparative Perspectives on Evaluation and Organizational Learning*. New Brunswick, NJ: Transaction, 45–63.

Gortner, H. F., Mahler, J., and Nicholson, J. B. (1987). *Organizational Theory: A Public Perspective*. Chicago: Dorsey.

Gross, B. M. (1964). *The Managing of Organizations* (2 vols.). Glencoe, Ill.: Free Press.

Handy, C. (1993). *Understanding Organizations*. New York: Oxford University Press.

——(1995). 'Managing the Dream', in S. Chawla and J. Renesch (eds.), *Learning Organizations: Developing Cultures for Tomorrow's Workplace*. Portland, Ore.: Productivity Press, 45–55.

——(1996). *Beyond Certainty: The Changing World of Organizations*. Boston: Harvard Business School Press.

Hardy, C. and Clegg, S. R. (1996). 'Some Dare to Call it Power', in S. R. Clegg, C. Hardy, and W. R. Nord (eds.), *Handbook of Organization Studies*. London: Sage, 622–41.

Heclo, H. (1974). *Modern Social Politics in Britain and Sweden*. New Haven: Yale University Press.

——(1978). 'Issue Networks and the Executive Establishment', in A. King (ed.), *The New American Political System*. Washington, DC: American Enterprise Institute, 87–124.

Hedberg, B. L. T. (1981). 'How Organizations Learn and Unlearn', in P. C. Nystrom and W. H. Starbuck (eds.), *Handbook of Organizational Design*: Vol. 1. *Adapting Organizations to Their Environments*. Oxford: Oxford University Press, 3–27.

Henry, G. (1990). 'Program Evaluation', in M. L. Whicker and T. W. Areson (eds.), *Public Sector Management*. New York: Praeger, 113–28.

Herriott, S. R., Levinthal, D. A., and March, J. G. (1985). 'Learning from Experience in Organizations'. *American Economic Review*, 75: 298–302.

Hirschman, A. (1970). *Exit, Voice, and Loyalty: Responses to Decline in Firms, Organizations and States*. Cambridge, Mass.: Harvard University Press.

Hough, J. B. (1969). *The Soviet Prefects: The Local Party Organization in Decision-Making*. Cambridge, Mass.: Harvard University Press.

Kaufman, H. (1981). *The Administrative Behavior of Federal Bureau Chiefs*. Washington, DC: Brookings Institution.

Kettl, D. E. (1988). *Government by Proxy*. Washington, DC: CQ Press.

Kotter, J. B. (1979). *Power in Management*. New York: Amacom.

Kriesberg, L. (1998). *Constructive Conflict from Escalation to Resolution*. London: Rowan and Littlefield.

LaPorte, T. (1975). *Organized Social Complexity: Challenge to Politics and Policy*. Princeton: Princeton University Press.

Lasswell, H. D. (1936). *Politics: Who Gets What, When, How*. London: McGraw-Hill.

Leeuw, F. L., Rist, R. C., and Sonnichsen, R. C. (eds.) (1994). *Can Governments Learn? Comparative Perspective on Evaluation and Organizational Learning*. New Brunswick, NJ: Transaction.

Levin, M. and Sanger, M. B. (1994). *Making Government Work: How Entrepreneurial Executives Turn Bright Ideas into Real Results*. San Francisco: Jossey-Bass.

Lindblom, C. E. (1971). *The Policy-making Process*. Englewood Cliffs, NJ: Prentice Hall.

March, J. G. (1966). 'The Power of Power', in D. Easton (ed.), *Varieties of Political Power*. Englewood Cliffs, NJ: Prentice Hall, 39–70.

—— and Olsen, J. P. (1976). *Ambiguity and Choice in Organizations* (2nd edn). Bergen: Universitetsforlaget.

Mayhew, D. (1974). *Congress: The Electoral Connection*. New Haven: Yale University Press.

Mayntz, R. and Scharpf, F. W. (1975). *Policy-making in the German Federal Bureaucracy*. New York: Elsevier.

Palumbo, D. J. (1975). 'Organization Theory and Political Science', in F. I. Greenstein and N. W. Polsby (eds.), *Handbook of Political Science* (Vol. 2). Reading, Mass.: Addison-Wesley, 319–89.

Panebianco, A. (1988). *Political Parties: Organization and Power*. Cambridge: Cambridge University Press.

Perrow, C. (1972). *Complex Organizations: A Critical Essay*. Glenview, Ill.: Scott Foresman.

Pfeffer, J. (1981). *Power in Organizations*. Marshfield, Mass.: Pittman.

—— (1992). 'Understanding Power in Organizations'. *California Management Review*, 35/1: 29–50.

—— (1997). *New Directions for Organizational Theory*. New York: Oxford University Press.

—— and Salancik, G. (1974). 'Organizational Decision Making as a Political Process'. *Administrative Science Quarterly*, 19: 135–51.

Pinchot, C. and Pinchot, E. (1993). *The End of Bureaucracy and the Rise of the Intelligent Organization*. San Francisco: Berrett-Koehler.

Powell, W. W. and DiMaggio, P. J. (eds.) (1991). *The New Institutionalism in Organizational Analysis*. Chicago: University of Chicago Press.

Rainey, H. G. and Milward, H. B. (1981). 'Public Organizations, Policy Networks, and Environments', in R. A. Hall and R. E. Quinn (eds.), *Organization Theory and Public Policy*. Beverly Hills, Calif.: Sage, 133–46.

Rose, R. (1993). *Lesson Drawing in Public Policy*. Chatham, NJ: Chatham House.

Sandole, D. J. D. and van der Merwe, H. (eds.) (1993). *Conflict Resolution Theory and Practice*. Manchester: Manchester University Press.

Scott, R. W. (1995). *Institutions and Organizations*. Thousand Oaks, Calif.: Sage.

Seidman, H. (1977). *Politics, Position, and Power* (2nd edn). Oxford: Oxford University Press.

Selznick, P. (1949). *TVA and the Grass Roots: Study of the Sociology of Formal Organization*. Berkeley: University of California Press.

Senge, P. M. (1990). *The Fifth Discipline: The Art and Practice of the Learning Organization*. New York: Doubleday.

Smith, S. S. and Deering, C. J. (1984). *Committees in Congress*. Washington, DC: CQ Press.

Wilson, J. Q. (1989). *Bureaucracy: What Government Agencies Do and Why They Do It*. New York: Basic Books.

Wise, C. R. (1994). 'The Public Service Configuration Problem: Designing Public Organizations in a Pluralistic Public Service', in A. Farazmand (ed.), *Modern Organizations: Administrative Theory in Contemporary Society.* Westport, Conn.: Praeger, 81–103.

Wood, B. D. and Waterman, R. W. (1994). *Bureaucratic Dynamics: The Role of Bureaucracy in a Democracy.* Boulder, Colo.: Westview.

26 Identity, Conflict, and Organizational Learning

Jay Rothman and Victor J. Friedman

Conflict is ubiquitous. It has been a major concern of every social science discipline, from political science to psychology and from sociology to economics. Conflict has also been a central feature of all professions, from law and diplomacy to social work and management. Organizational theory, too, has taken up the subject of conflict since its inception as a field. Indeed, 'few aspects of formal organizations have been visited and revisited as much as conflict' (Morrill 1995: 7). Since the early 1990s, however, when organizational theory began undergoing significant changes in emphasis and priority, the contribution of conflict and conflict resolution as a field to this evolution has been disappointingly small. A review of the literature reveals little cross-fertilization between cutting-edge developments in conflict and conflict resolution as a field and organizational behavior (De Dreu and Van de Vliert 1997).

The objective of this chapter is to present a framework for bridging the gap between organizational learning theory and conflict intervention theory and practice. The following analysis of conflict theory is based on three conceptual frames: resources, interests, and identities. These frames will be used to examine the role that conflict has played in organizational theory generally and in organizational learning in particular. The analysis of these frames of conflict suggests that the identity frame may be much more relevant to organizational learning than are the resource and interest framings because it promotes inquiry into the concerns and motivations of organizational members and learning.

The role of conflict in organizational learning

The literature on organizational learning theory and practice does not present a uniform approach to the role of interpersonal and intergroup conflict. Conflict was not an explicit element in March and Olsen's (1976) theory of incomplete learning cycles, nor was it mentioned as a significant factor in reviews by Fiol and Lyles (1985), Huber (1991), Levitt and March (1988), or Shrivastava (1983). Conflict has also been conspicuously absent from discussions of organizational learning aimed at practitioners (see Prokesh 1997; Garvin 1993; McGill, Slocum, and Lei 1993).

This silence about conflict starkly contrasts with the treatment of conflict in the theory of organizational learning developed by Argyris and Schön (1996), for whom conflict is central to the process of 'double-loop learning':

In such an example of organizational double-loop learning, incompatible requirements in organizational theory-in-use are characteristically expressed through a conflict among members and groups of members. One might say that the organization becomes a medium for translating incompatible requirements into interpersonal and intergroup conflicts (p.23). . . . In this type of organizational double-loop learning, individual members resolve interpersonal and intergroup conflicts that express incompatible requirements for organizational performance. (p. 25)

According to this perspective, organizational conflict is an expression of critical contradictions within an organization's system of goals, values, and criteria for performance. Rather than being an obstacle to learning, conflict offers opportunities for engaging in learning. Double-loop learning is a form of conflict resolution in which organizational members inquire into the reasoning behind the positions they take and the meaning of these positions for them.

Conflict is also an integral part of 'team learning' and 'creating shared vision', two of the five disciplines in Senge's (1990) 'learning organization':

Contrary to popular myth, great teams are not characterized by an absence of conflict. On the contrary, . . . one of the most reliable indicators of a team that is continually learning is the visible conflict of ideas. In great teams conflict becomes productive. There may, and often will, be conflict around the vision. The essence of the 'visioning' process lies in the gradual emergence of a shared vision from different personal visions. Even when people share a common vision, they may have many different ideas about how to achieve that vision. The free flow of conflicting ideas is critical for creative thinking, for discovering new solutions. . . . Conflict becomes, in effect, part of the ongoing dialogue. (p. 249)

This conflict of ideas involves the clash among different personal visions about the team's goals, values, and means for achieving them. In this sense, too, conflict is not seen as an obstacle to learning but rather as a means through which learning occurs. In fact, conflict is essential for creativity and innovative problem-solving.

Conflict also plays a prominent role in the dialogue approach to organizational learning described by Isaacs (1993) and Schein (1993). Isaacs defined dialogue as 'a sustained collective inquiry into the processes, assumptions, and certainties that compose everyday experience' (p. 25). He illustrated the centrality of conflict in dialogue by citing a case involving a steel mill with a history of intense union–management conflict (Isaacs 1993). In this example, the steel mill and the crucible for heating ore provide imagery for describing the dialogue process, which, like steel-making, involves intense heat and pressure under control. Through the dialogue process, intense conflict

is 'contained' so that organizational members can 'step deliberately into their anger and . . . step back from their collective (and hopelessly stuck) reasoning' (p. 33). According to Isaacs, dialogue transforms conflict from divisive blaming into a process of open disagreement and inquiry in which organizational members challenge 'one another to think together, rather than separately' (p. 34).

The creative role of conflict in organizational learning is also evident in the 'knowledge-creating companies' described by Nonaka and Takeuchi (1995). For example, members of a new product development team, who have to satisfy demands for both high reliability and low cost, play out this conflict among themselves in intensive, overnight 'camp sessions'. One of the team members described the process as follows:

To solve a fundamental question like the 'seesaw' between cost and reliability requires a reorientation of the mind. First, one needs to ask, 'What is the essence?' Then, the available approaches to deal with it are enumerated and diffused. . . . Often, conflicts occur when people have rhythms that do not agree with each other. Attempts to bring them together don't succeed when they are diverging. If the rhythms are in unison from the beginning, we can hardly have good results. . . . Creating the rhythms of divergence and convergence is the trick of conducting a successful camp session. (pp. 142–3)

In this approach, the issue is not resolving conflict but rather making sure that it occurs. The team members solved a dilemma in product design by first creating a conflict among themselves (divergence) and then working to resolve it (convergence).

Nonaka and Takeuchi (1995) described a similar process, but on a much larger scale, in a multinational joint venture company created by Mitsubishi Heavy Industries Ltd. of Japan and Caterpillar Inc. of the United States. At the beginning, the partnership between these two organizations was characterized by misunderstanding and conflict over different approaches to product development. The U.S. and Japanese engineers were fundamentally at odds over issues such as the relative value of performance criteria (cost, quality, performance, and safety), project leadership, the development process, and the level of standardization in production. Not surprisingly, cultural differences and different approaches to problem-solving made communication over these matters particularly difficult.

Rather than backing off from or smoothing over the conflict, however, the two organizations actively engaged each other's differences through a variety of mechanisms such as interplant meetings and the pairing of engineers. As a result, the U.S. engineers developed tacit knowledge about Japanese methods through contacts with their Japanese colleagues (socialization) and Japanese engineers learned how to make their tacit knowledge more explicit to their U.S. colleagues (externalization). This process was not easy and involved heated debate, discomfort, and a great deal of time, but it led to a synthesis of Japanese and U.S. approaches to both product development and knowledge creation.

This brief analysis points to a number of surprising propositions about the role of conflict in organizational learning:

- Conflict is essential for organizational learning.
- Conflict is a process through which organizational learning occurs.
- These conflicts tend to involve deeply held goals, values, performance criteria, and beliefs about how to get things done.
- Conflict leads to creative thinking and innovation.
- Conflict leads to greater self-awareness and understanding of others.
- Conflicts not only need to be resolved, they also need to be created, engaged, or both.

Although these propositions reflect a highly positive attitudes toward conflict, they say very little about the nature of conflict or the conflict processes themselves. Interesting questions arise about the meaning of conflict and why it plays such an important role in organizational learning. These questions are even more puzzling given the conventional

wisdom of managers and other organizational members, many of whom dislike conflict and tend to avoid it whenever possible (Eisenhardt, Kahwajy, and Bourgeois 1997; Tjosvold 1991).

Framing Conflict

These puzzles of conflict and organizational learning need to be examined within the context of conflict theory, especially that of organizational conflict. Although labor and industrial relations (Follett 1942) and the group dynamics movement (Lewin 1948) are wellsprings of conflict resolution theory, much work in the field of conflict and conflict resolution has grown out of developments in diplomacy, law, and community relations. As a result, conflict resolution theory and the study of conflict in organizations have often developed along parallel tracks.

In order to simplify the analysis, we have attempted to categorize the great many treatments of conflict into three major frames, which we call resource conflict, interest conflict, and identity conflict (see Table 26.1). The term 'frame' signifies that each of these perspectives acts as a kind of window to the world of conflict. Frames set phenomena within a conceptual and cognitive context that delineates their components and imposes upon them a particular organization and meaning (Bateson 1972; Schön 1983; Schön and Rein 1994). Frames focus the attention of both theorists and practitioners on particular aspects of the conflict situation, shape the definition of the problem, and guide conflict intervention (Bolman and Deal 1984; Friedman and Lipshitz 1994). Frames may also be limiting and lead to selective perception (Dearborn and Simon 1958). Applied to any given conflict situation, each of the three frames will point to different causes, different issues, and different ways of intervening. The three frames will also show that different ways of viewing conflict influence the way researchers and practitioners see its relationship to organizational learning.

Table 26.1. The frames of conflict and organizational learning

Frame	Issue	Intervention	Outcomes	Implications for Learning
Resource	Material goods Economic benefits Territory	Distributive or positional bargaining	Settlement Win/lose (zero sum)	Limited Single loop
	Coercive power		Compromise	Short term at expense of long term
Interest	Motives Goals	Integrative or interest-based bargaining	Agreement	Single-loop learning
	Values Needs		Win/win	Integrative solutions
	Concertive power		Mutual gains	Leaves goals unchanged
Identity	Purpose Meaning	Inquiry	Mutually defined perceptions of reality	Double-loop learning
	Definition of self and group	Studied unknowing		Changes in definition of values, goals, and needs
	Relational power	Reflexive dialogue	Growth and moral development Changed self and relationships	
				'Good dialectic'

The Resource Frame of Conflict

Within the resource frame, conflict is viewed as 'a struggle over values and claims to scarce status, power, and resources in which the aims of the opponents are to neutralize, injure, or eliminate rivals' (Coser 1967: 8). This definition reflects the dominant Western approaches to conflict since antiquity (Hocker and Wilmot 1995: 20). From the perspective of the resource frame, life is viewed in Hobbesian terms as nasty, brutish, and short, and human existence is seen as a competitive process in which conflict may be contained or ameliorated but never eliminated.

The resource frame of conflict is inherent in the power-politics approach to international relations, which focuses on the preservation and promotion of national interest. National interest is defined in terms of economic and territorial resources and military power, though it may also be laden with ideological meaning, such as capitalism or communism. Within this perspective, which has also been called 'political realism' (Morgenthau 1948: 4), national interests, or resources, are both ends and means. The state exists to promote its interests, its interests are promoted so the state can exist.

Domestic conflict, as seen through the resource frame, is the natural outcome of competition among individuals and groups over material goods, economic benefits, property, and power. Power, which we briefly examine through the lens of each frame, is viewed in this frame as a scarce resource, as something to be sought and protected in competitive and often coercive ways. It is, in the classic definition of power, the ability to force others to do what they would otherwise not do (Dahl 1957). The resource frame also draws on the perspective of sociologists, such as Parsons (1960), who regard equilibrium or harmony as the state of a healthy society. According to this view, conflict represents a disease that threatens equilibrium and should be prevented or cured. In a classic study of conflict, Coser (1956) pointed out that, despite a relatively positive attitude toward conflict among early sociologists, the field (at least in the United States) became dominated by this disease model (e.g. Parsons). (For a more thorough discussion of sociological approaches to conflict, see Gherardi and Nicolini, Ch. 2 in this volume.)

Within the resource frame, the alternatives to violence or brute force for settling conflicts are either mechanisms for social control or bargaining or negotiation processes, which are essentially war by other means. However, for bargaining to occur there needs to be a tacit agreement that it is in the best interests of each party to find a satisfactory solution. The bargaining game is one of distribution of resources with all sides jockeying at the starting line to set the agenda, give up the least, and gain the most. The means is persuasion, gentle or otherwise. If negotiation and settlement are to be effective in resource conflicts, the parties involved must determine the true goals and bottom line of their opponents and must identify common ground. If they are able to do so, agreement may not be that difficult to reach, despite the subterfuge. Within the resource frame, each party's interests are generally assumed to be nonnegotiable, but compromise is viewed as an acceptable outcome when total domination is viewed as unnecessary or impossible to win or sustain. From the perspective of the resource frame, reaching an agreement in which resources have been redistributed to the mutual satisfaction of all sides means that the conflict has been resolved.

The resource frame is implicit in many treatments of organizational conflict. The work of early organizational theorists reflected the disease model of conflict, which was regarded as undesirable and detrimental to the organization (e.g. Fayol 1949; Taylor 1911). These theorists believed that conflict could be eliminated by strong social control mechanisms inherent in features of rational organizational design, such as proper division of labor, careful and specific job definitions, specification of relationships among positions, hierarchy, and the exercise of authority through a clear and unitary chain of command. The founders of the human relations school of management also viewed conflict as wholly undesirable and symptomatic of the irrationality of workers. Their claim, however, was that conflict could be eliminated through increased consideration and improved leadership on the part of management (Roethlisberger and Dickson 1939).

After World War II, organizational theorists began to accept that conflicts over goals, resources, and power were a built-in feature of organizational life and could not be done away with through proper management (Tjosvold 1991). Simon (1947) recognized inherent contradictions between classical management principles, the tendency toward suboptimization, and the inevitability of boundary disputes over authority. From this perspective, conflicts were still seen as ailments that needed to be resolved by management as quickly and efficiently as possible through bargaining and negotiation. In the context of bureaucratic design, March and Simon (1958) described inner contradictions that led to interdepartmental conflict, suboptimization of goals, and other unintended, negative consequences. They noted that perceived conflict in an organization motivated organizational actors to reduce it and restore equilibrium.

The resource frame of conflict is most strongly reflected in the work of researchers who have focused on the fundamentally political nature of organizations (Bolman and Deal 1984). In a classic study of the Tennessee Valley Authority, Selznick (1949) showed how organizational goal-setting was itself a political process and that goals emerged from a clash of the commitments, interests, and belief systems of various organizational stakeholders. Cyert and March (1963) viewed organizations as coalitions, and regarded organizational objectives as something arising from an ongoing process of bargaining among coalition members attempting to maximize their individual objectives. According to Cyert and March's model, goal conflicts can be ameliorated (but never entirely resolved) through local rationality, acceptable decision rules, or sequential attention to goals (Cyert and March 1963). Subsequent researchers have portrayed conflict as the natural result of competition over scarce resources and fundamental conflicts of interest between groups (Baldridge 1971; Gamson 1968; Pettigrew 1973; Pfeffer 1978). From the political perspective, conflict is neither good nor bad; it is simply inevitable. The central focus is on strategy and tactics because only those organizational actors (i.e. not just managers) who know how to increase and wield power will achieve their objectives. In either case the outcome of conflict is win, lose, or compromise.

The resource frame offers very little insight into the potentially positive role of conflict in organizational learning because conflict is viewed as something that needs to be managed rather than engaged with as a vehicle for learning and development. From the perspective of Cyert and March (1963), who defined organizational learning as the process through which organizations adapt and change their goals through experience, organizations learn strategies for resolving goal conflict. To the extent that formal attempts at organizational learning or change create conflict between different levels of the organization or between organizational units, the resource frame suggests that cooperation will have to be regained through bargaining, tradeoffs, and compensation. To the extent that negotiation processes lead to acceptable ways of dividing resources, resource-frame conflict resolution may represent a limited form of 'single-loop learning', in which 'strategies and assumptions are modified . . . to keep organizational performance within the range set by existing organizational values and norms' (Argyris and Schön 1996: 20).

The resource frame strongly reflects what Argyris and Schön (1974: 66, 1996) described as a Model I theory-in-use, or mental model, which informs human behavior, particularly under conditions of embarrassment and threat.

Model I means that individuals (and organizations) are 'programmed' to achieve values such as exercising control, winning and not losing, avoiding expression or generation of negative feeling, and being rational. The resource frame focuses on each side's attempts to gain control of the bargaining situations so as to maximize its predefined outcomes. From the perspective of this frame, raising doubts or questioning one's own position represents a weakness that should be avoided.

Acting from a resource frame of conflict, partners may clear the way for change, but they are unlikely to discover errors in their own thinking and action. They may have a lot to 'teach' each other but would be foolish or naive to be open to learning from the other side. Thus, resource-based conflict resolution may enable conflicting parties to coexist and function as members of a common coalition, but it is unlikely to lead to joint inquiry or creativity.

Another problem with the resource-based framing is that it leads to interventions that emphasize short-term, material fixes that leave underlying causes untouched. When the focus on resources is paramount in organizations, as in the scientific management practices of Taylor (1911) and his disciples (and in the origins of organizational development as a field), it is not surprising that the human side of enterprise was often neglected. A reaction against this approach is at the core of the trend that led to the subfield of organizational learning in which 'human capital' has been increasingly viewed as the most valuable resource in organizations (see McGregor 1960; for a full review of the history of the human dynamics movement and its evolution into modern organizational development and learning, see Kleiner 1996). As a result, deeply held conflicts that threaten people's sense of self and efficacy tend to recur with added intensity. Each time a conflict recurs, it may become more difficult and threatening to handle, and the cost of resolution may rise for disputants. Moreover, to the extent that the underlying causes remain unaddressed, resource-based framing may leave deeper problems ignored until they explode as full-blown crises.

The Interest Frame and Conflict Management

Conflict management as a field has been dominated by an interest frame of conflict. It was popularized by Fisher and Ury (1981) and by others in the fields of international diplomacy, law, environmental mediation and community relations (Carrbonneau 1989; Goldberg, Green, and Sander 1985; Raifa 1982; Rubin and Brown 1975; Susskind and Cruikshank 1987) as a way to get away from competitive resource framing. These approaches reject the view of conflict as a zero-sum competition over scarce resources and power. Although conflicts may appear to hinge upon incompatible demands for power, territory, or material resources, Fisher and Ury (1981) suggested that such demands, or bargaining positions, are simply concrete expressions of interests, which they defined as 'needs, desires, concerns, and fears' (p. 42). This approach suggests that such interests, when brought to the surface and scrutinized, can often be reconciled. It focuses on clarifying what is really at stake, the assumption being that such a clarification will increase the parties' common ground and improve resolutions of conflicts. Rather than haggling over ways to divide limited resources, parties explore ways in which their core concerns can be redefined in mutual terms and functionally linked through what Follett referred to as 'integrative' bargaining (p. 32) rather than through domination or compromise.

The interest frame of conflict and conflict resolution evolved largely as an alternative to coercive power-based, legalistic, and litigious means of addressing disputes, particularly in labor relations. Fisher and Ury (1981) argued that resource-focused bargaining is often inadequate. It regularly produces unwise and unstable agreements, incurs high costs to both sides (inefficiency), and endangers the ongoing relationship between the parties to a conflict. Instead, Fisher and Ury, and other advocates of 'alternative dispute resolution', developed a process of interest-based bargaining, which focuses upon articulating what each party is really seeking and upon employing creative methods for maximizing the degree to which the interests of both sides can be satisfied.

The interest frame is implicit in the treatment of conflict in certain theories of organizational design. Lawrence and Lorsch (1967), for instance, introduced the idea that interdepartmental conflict is a natural outcome of the ways in which departments adapt to their different environments. Differentiation creates the need to design appropriate integration mechanisms for managing these differences and conflicts. Similarly, the emergence of the matrix structure, which is based on the concept of two bosses, turned the classical model of organization on its head and created the conditions for built-in conflict (Argyris 1967; Galbraith 1973). Janis's (1972) study on 'Groupthink' highlighted the danger of suppressing conflict in order to maintain group cohesion. Subsequent empirical studies found that high levels of conflict led to the consideration of additional alternatives, improved the understanding of the choices, and significantly increased the effectiveness of decision-making (Eisenhardt, Kahwajy, and Bourgeois 1997).

These organizational conflicts are not merely an expression of competition over resources, territory, or power. Rather, they are an expression of conflicting demands made upon the organization by its technology and the external environment. These conflicts become translated into the worldviews and objectives of different groups and individuals within an organization. Implicit in these organizational designs is the need to forge integrative solutions from fundamental conflicts of interest. Groups and individuals within an organization, in playing out their conflicts, find ways of reconciling incompatible demands and solving complex problems. Thus, conflict plays an important role in organizational effectiveness and adaptation. The interest-based approach is a search for an alternative 'concertive power' wherein actors voluntarily accept a kind of conformity based on, for example, a mission statement, shared values, or commitments to goals. The tendency toward competition is then constrained, or at least redirected outward, by the creation of a form of social contract that can forge a functionally integrated organization based on the alignment or reconciliation of self (or collective) interests. In the interest frame, power indeed is to be functionally shared, or at least apparently so, such that organizational actors find it in their self-interest to embrace conformity and obedience to authority voluntarily, if not enthusiastically.

The interest frame, with its more optimistic view of conflict, is strongly reflected in intervention theories that focus on 'managing' conflict (Blake, Shepard, and Mouton 1964; Likert and Likert 1976; Thomas 1976; Tjosvold 1991; Walton 1987; Walton and McKersie 1965). Conflict management implies that certain levels of social or organizational conflict (or tension) are necessary and functional. Conflict is like a soup that must be kept boiling if it is to cook but that cannot be allowed to boil over. From this perspective the job of the manager or the intervener is to control conflict and parties in conflict —sometimes reducing or resolving it, sometimes even stimulating it (Walton 1987). For the most part, these approaches to conflict management promote collaborative, integrative, and participatory approaches to dealing with organizational problems.

Unlike the resource frame, through which conflict is seen as something to be externally controlled or ameliorated, the interest-based approach suggests that the procedures used should enable parties to adjust to each other's concerns and then to work together on achieving mutually acceptable outcomes (i.e. problem-solving), efficiency, and good relationships (Rahim 1986; Thomas 1976; Walton 1987) in part by employing conflict as a vehicle for such ends. Interest-based conflict management also draws on contingency models for matching conflict styles or strategies with the conflict situation (Thomas 1976). The essence of conflict management is to create conditions and communication processes that enable conflicting parties to hear and understand each other so that they can ultimately arrive at cooperative solutions. This process may lead parties to a conflict to clarify their interests so that they discover areas where no real conflict exists or

even that no real conflict exists at all. Furthermore, they may generate cooperative or superordinate goals that facilitate cooperation or circumvent divisive issues. Conflict management shares the resource frame's emphasis on bargaining strategies and tactics but has a strong bias toward replacing competitive strategies with cooperative or collaborative ones and for producing win/win outcomes (Axelrod 1984; Deutsch 1973, 1994; Walton 1987).

The interest frame is useful for understanding the role of conflict in organizational learning. The conflict of ideas and the need to satisfy conflicting demands for performance (Argyris and Schön 1996; Nonaka and Takeuchi 1995) may be seen as an expression of fundamental differences in the needs, desires, and concerns of different individuals within the organization. Engaging in conflict may help organizational members clarify their own interests and perceptions and understand those of the other side. Through conflict, they attempt to produce creative and innovative solutions that take the interests of both sides into account. Similarly, the interest approach focuses on managing or controlling negative emotions, such as anger, so that they can be used to help achieve cooperative agreements rather than derailing them and escalating the conflict (Tjosvold 1991).

Conflict management, however, harbors a rarely discussed paradox. When parties communicate with each other more forthrightly than in the past, they might easily discover that the gap between them appears even harder to bridge than they thought. The emphasis on cooperative rather than competitive strategies does not necessarily mean that a solution will emerge. Despite good will and a desire to find solutions, parties to a conflict may find themselves even more at odds than ever. One source of the paradox is that needs and interests are implicitly regarded as more or less sovereign in interest-based conflict management. In other words, the interest frame leads conflicting parties to clarify their interests, but only rarely does it lead those parties to question them or ask why these interests are so important.

Smith (1987) pointed out that many interveners associated with the interest frame see themselves as agents of social change. However, by focusing primarily on agreements and fostering improved working relationships, they may actually reinforce the status quo of the systems even though they espouse fundamental system change (Smith 1987). Because of an emphasis on controlling conflict and promoting cooperative strategies, conflict management lends itself to single-loop learning, which focuses on changing individual and collective action strategies but leaves the underlying values and norms unchanged. As a result, the interest frame may be of limited help, or even counterproductive, in producing double-loop learning, which involves critically inquiring into and changing underlying goals, values, and standards for performance as well as strategies and assumptions (Argyris and Schön 1996).

As with the resource frame, the interest frame's focus on solutions may leave the roots of a conflict undiscussed and undiscussable. Even when the interest frame appears to be successful in forging at least temporary agreements, interest-based conflict management can lead to blindness about the true or underlying nature of a conflict. As a result, cooperation may be fostered on the basis of what in diplomatic terms is called 'constructive ambiguity', where each side has fundamentally different understandings of the reasons for the conflict and the purposes of the solution they have forged. If the underlying problems are not addressed, an omission that may often occur in interest-based conflict management, the deeper conflicts will persist, resurfacing again and again around different issues and exacerbating distrust, cynicism, and hopelessness. Thus, the opportunity to learn and grow from such conflicts is subverted as they become increasingly debilitating and pernicious.

The Identity Frame and Double-loop Learning

In the identity frame of conflict, too, conflict is seen as stemming from needs, desires, concerns, and fears. However, this point of view suggests that the most intractable conflicts are really about the articulation and confrontation of individual and collective identities (Rothman 1997). These conflicts may be expressed and negotiated in terms of resources or interests, but they really involve people's individual and collective purposes, sense of meaning, and definitions of self. According to the identity frame, conflicts are rooted in threats to or the frustration of deeply rooted human needs such as dignity, recognition, safety, control, purpose, and efficacy (Azar 1990; Burton 1990). They involve threats and frustrations to disputants' sense and expression of self. At the same time, identity conflicts are formative because people and groups tend to forge their own sense of self in opposition to others.

Within the identity frame conflicts are not viewed primarily as problems to be resolved, or even managed. In this regard it differs from the other two conceptual frames of conflict. Although the destructive potential of conflict is acknowledged, the contention is that conflict offers opportunities for growth, adaptation, and learning (Bush and Folger 1995; Lederach 1995; Rupesinghe 1995). Conflict can lead all parties 'to clarify for themselves their needs and values, what causes them dissatisfaction and satisfaction' (Bush and Folger 1995: 82). Instead, conflicts in this frame are viewed as opportunities for engagement for the purpose of learning and development.

Gurevitch (1989) suggested that true dialogue and learning occurs when disputants learn how not to understand each other instead of continually imposing their own mental models on the other. This 'studied unknowing' involves inquiring fundamentally into the way in which individuals and groups have constructed their reality. It can lead to expanding definitions of reality. From this perspective, the desired outcome of conflict is not just a settlement, but also growth, moral development, and fundamental changes in perception of truth or reality.

The identity frame of conflict emerged largely from attempts to deal with intractable ethnic conflict (Rothman 1992, 1997) and alternative approaches to the static power-politics model of international diplomacy (Banks 1984). It emphasizes the role of human needs in international conflict and conflict resolution. It builds largely on the small-group dynamics movement (Lewin 1948) and a new view of cybernetics or self-steering and internal feedback systems of decision-making in international relations. In this approach, also known as the analytical (or interactive) problem-solving approach, conflict is viewed as a result of threatened or frustrated needs that must be brought to the surface, fully analyzed, and addressed before any kind of bargaining, settlement, or negotiation can succeed (Azar 1990; Burton 1990; Fisher 1996; Kelman 1982).

The identity frame focuses on the process of engaging conflict rather than simply reaching a particular settlement. Conflict engagement means creating 'reflexive dialogue' (Rothman 1997: 38), in which parties to a conflict speak about their needs and values in the presence of their adversaries. However, rather than treating each party's interests or needs as sovereign, the identity frame leads parties to inquire into their own needs, values, and goals (Why is this so important to me?). It also aims explicitly at change both within individual parties (Who am I? What do I really want? Why?) and between parties (How is it that we create conditions that prevent us from achieving our needs, goals, and values?). Having first expressed themselves and heard each other in this way, they can then frame disputes in ways that articulate an overlapping of goals and values. Upon this common foundation, a process of cooperative solution-seeking may begin such that disputants become partners in setting new goals and restructuring their relationship on the basis of changes in and more positive definitions of themselves.

In the organizational sphere, the identity frame of conflict is implicit in the work on the psychological dynamics of interpersonal and intergroup conflict inspired first by Lewin (1948) and Bion (1961). The work of the Tavistock Institute and the National Training Laboratory focused largely on the interplay between deep intrapsychic and interpersonal conflicts and organizational processes and design. The centrality of identity to organizational conflict, particularly in the face of organizational change, was foreshadowed in studies of participation and sociotechnical systems. In a study of worker participation in corporate governance, Emery and Thorsrud (1969) pointed to the following contradiction between two kinds of power:

When people talk about industrial democracy, they are usually referring to the sharing of independent power, but when they come to the practice of industrial democracy, they tend to assume that steps to increase the effective application of independent power (and hence their ability to get what they define as a fair deal) will automatically lead to a greater sharing of managerial power (and presumably responsibility). In the cases we have examined, there is no evidence that this happens.... In so far as industrial democracy means more than extended negotiations and consultations, there is a need for the transfer of some real managerial power to the employees. (pp. 85–6)

Independent power, which refers to the kind of advantages gained by employee participation in the corporate governance structure, reflects the perspective of the resource frame. By placing representatives within these structures, employees strengthen their bargaining position in negotiating their differences with management and are more likely to get a fair deal. Emery and Thorsrud (1969), however, pointed to a confusion between this kind of power and managerial power, which involves responsibility and decision-making in the work itself. Managerial power cannot be obtained by placing employee representation on the board but rather requires a fundamental change in the roles of employees at every level. In other words, it involves fundamental changes in what it means to be a worker or a manager (Emery and Thorsrud 1976). Boulding (1989) wrote of relational power, or the power with, instead of over, others. This notion is a distinction of and key to the identity frame. Through the articulation and assertion of self (including one's group)—that is, of needs, values, identities—and through the recognition of others' articulation and assertion of self, conflict provides the opportunity for mutual transformation and empowerment (Bush and Folger 1995).

Morrill (1995) indicated that the identity frame is beginning to take hold among both managers and researchers of organizational conflict:

Personal, social and group identities may have as much to do with how people accomplish and frame basic activities within organizations (such as communication, evaluation, innovation, change, and routine indigenous conflict management) as with the substantive goals of action. Because conflict management often ritualizes and brings into relief basic assumptions and action about how people go about their daily lives, it in turn may be a key factor in establishing, maintaining, and dissolving personal and social identities. (p. 225)

Morrill used the term 'conflict management' to describe a process through which individuals and groups create and change their basic identities and work together to forge relational power. Because this process goes far beyond cooperation and the achievement of integrative settlements, we refer to it as conflict engagement rather than conflict management.

A study of twelve top management teams by Eisenhardt, Kahwajy, and Bourgeois (1997) found that the highest performing teams were all characterized by a very high level of 'substantive' conflict, whereas the low performing teams were lower in conflict. By substantive conflict the researchers meant conflict centered on alternative courses of action and the interpretation of facts rather than on interpersonal friction and dislike. However, these conflicts went far deeper than bargaining over concrete positions:

Conflict is dynamic in that it unfolds as executives gain a deeper grasp of their business and their preferences for action through constant immersion in alternative viewpoints. Conflict is not a static reflection of fixed self-interests among senior executives. Rather, conflict reflects a continuously evolving understanding of the world that is gained through interaction with others around alternative viewpoints. (p. 60)

According to this view, conflict is not a discrete event that ends in a resolution but rather a continuous process that unfolds as an integral part of management. Conflict is like the progressive peeling of an onion—as one problem is solved, a new one emerges to be engaged and mined for its creative potential. Furthermore, top managers should engage in conflict not just to settle disputes or conflicts of interest but to understand the world around them, their business, and especially themselves. Thus, conflict is not only a means of adjustment but also a means of learning and increased awareness of self and other.

The identity frame of conflict represents a way of understanding the approaches to organizational learning described earlier in this chapter. Rather than focusing on resolving conflicting interests, it provides a way of thinking about conflict as an opportunity for double-loop learning. Unlike single-loop learning, which focuses on changing strategies, double-loop learning inquires into the fundamental goals, values, needs, standards, and assumptions which underlie those strategies (Argyris and Schön 1996). Interests are not sovereign but rather objects of inquiry because parties to a conflict must ask themselves 'why' their goals, values, needs, and assumptions are so important to them.

Unlike the resource or needs frames of conflict, the identity frame does not focus on bargaining or negotiation as a means of intervening in or resolving conflict. Although agreements or solutions represent important ends, inquiry takes precedence over cooperation, promoting the process that Nonaka and Takeuchi (1995) described as the 'rhythms of divergence and convergence' (p.143). From the perspective of the identity frame, the goal of intervention is not just to reach agreements or solutions. Rather, the process of engaging conflict is seen as an opportunity for challenging the status quo (including the parties themselves). From the perspective of the identity frame, conflict promotes what Argyris and Schön (1978: 42) call 'good dialectic' in the context of organizational learning. Agreements may emerge not through a change of strategies from competition to cooperation but through inquiry and fundamental changes in thinking.

The identity frame is particularly important when organizational learning means overcoming the institutionally embedded nature of organizational practices (see Child and Heavens, Ch. 13 in this volume). If conflict is conceived of primarily in terms of resources, interests, or needs, parties will attempt to find compromises or integrative solutions that take both sets of interests into account. However, as Child and Heavens point out, these solutions will be constrained by what organizational members conceive of as possible or legitimate in the institutional context. Conflict will then likely produce single-loop learning but leave the deeper context unchanged (or even reinforced). The identity frame, with its emphasis on having parties to a conflict consider the meanings behind their needs and interests, offers an approach to conflict and conflict engagement that can go deeper than single-loop learning and make the formative context an object of inquiry as well.

Conflict, Identity, and Organizational Learning

Because the emphasis of the interest-based approach to conflict is focused on the question of how conflict may be best managed so that disputing parties can reach practical agreement about concrete interests, it is not surprising that it offers little guidance on the positive use of conflict to promote organizational learning. On the other hand, even those organizational learning theorists who recognize the importance of conflict have not gone far enough in conceptualizing how conflict can lead to learning. The uses of conflict by organizational learning theorists referred to at the beginning of this chapter provide little concrete help for practitioners who wish to engage conflict for the purposes of learning. In the conclusion of a highly detailed description of a long-term process of organizational learning in a single firm, Argyris (1993) admitted that he lacked an adequate theory for describing and explaining what he actually did:

The least developed part of our theory concerns how to get from here to there. We believe that we are quite strong at the empirical level in helping people move from here to there. We are less strong in being able to specify a priori what goes on during the intervention and change process. (p. 253)

We wish to suggest that this gap is derived from the limited perspectives offered by the interest frame of conflict and from the limited ways in which organizational learning researchers and practitioners frame and deal with conflict. Argyris (1993), for instance, presented a detailed description, including a transcript, of what became a highly charged emotional conflict between two organizational members, a clash whose escalation nearly led to the breakdown of the relationship. Although the parties involved with Argyris's assistance, effectively handled the disagreement, there was little analysis of the conflict and what enabled them to transform it into an opportunity for learning. If organizational learning is to move beyond the domain of exceptionally skilled practitioners, sound theory for engaging conflict within the context of organizational learning is needed.

The three-frame analysis suggests that the resource and interest frames of conflict continue to dominate the thinking of practitioners and many researchers and may thus limit new thinking and applications in this area. The absence of conflict in most theoretical or prescriptive discussions of organizational learning practice (e.g. Garvin 1993; McGill, Slocum, and Lei 1993; Prokesh 1997) may reflect the abiding tendency toward conflict avoidance, or reductionism, in organizational practice (Eisenhardt, Kahwajy, and Bourgeois 1997; Tjosvold 1991).

Pondy (1967) pointed out early that organizational members tend to value conflict negatively and to engage in it only when there is no escape from the relationship or when the costs of not resolving conflict are excessive. As Tjosvold (1991) has noted, however, the problem for organizations is not conflict but conflict avoidance:

The idea that conflict is destructive and causes misery is so self-evident that it is seldom debated.

Employees fight about many issues, but the wisdom of avoiding conflict is too often not one of them. . . . people work hard to avoid conflict. . . . Avoiding conflict does not make problems disappear, but allows them to linger and fester, and then emerge in more divisive ways. . . . [People] assume the way to strong relationships is through harmony and avoiding conflict. However, avoiding conflict makes it very difficult to deal realistically with the inevitable frustrations and difficulties. (p. 5)

If organizational members view conflict through the resource or even the interest frames, they are likely to avoid approaches to organizational learning that engage conflict (see Gherardi and Nicolini, Ch. 2; as well as Kieser, Beck, and Taino, Ch. 27 in this volume). As Argyris and Schön (1978, 1996) have pointed out, enlightened managers and organizational members may fervently espouse the language of organizational learning or the learning organization while producing the kinds of conflict-avoiding behaviors that keep change from occurring.

One of the reasons for the lasting dominance of the resource frame may be a deep skepticism or disappointment with conflict management. Interest-based conflict management was meant to provide a constructive alternative to the narrow, negative approach of the resource frame. However, cooperative strategies and win/win solutions are extremely difficult to achieve when the issues involved are deep, complex, and identity-driven. Parties to a conflict may clarify the interests underlying their positions only to discover that the conflict seems even more intractable than ever. The identity frame, which draws its inspiration from the study of deeply entrenched or intractable ethnic and international conflicts is better than the resource frame at capturing what is at stake in many organizational conflicts, particularly where double-loop learning is concerned. It also provides a more useful map for anticipating and working through the seemingly insurmountable obstacles and resistance to a resolution.

Major trends in organizations and their environment make it likely that conflicts appearing to be resource-based or interest-based are actually rooted in deep identity issues. The rapid move toward globalization and multinational strategic alliances means that the identity of organizations and organizational members will increasingly be attacked and doubted. Revolutions in information technology, downsizing, changes in organizational structure, and changes in the nature of work and careers threaten what Schön (1971) called the 'anchors for identity' that were once found in relatively stable institutions. This loss of the stable state raises questions not only about one's sense of security but also about one's sense of self.

Individuals and groups may resist fundamental organizational learning because it both involves conflict and threatens their own sense of identity. Both conflict and learning may require changes in some of the ways individuals and groups understand themselves and relate to the world. Identity-based conflicts cannot be adequately addressed by interest-based conflict management even when it aims at win/win outcomes and empowerment. In order to exploit the potential of conflict for organizational learning, or at least to test this potential in a significant fashion, there needs to be a fundamental change in the attitude of organizational members toward conflict. Approaches to conflict engagement that make identity issues an object of inquiry, critical reflection, and change may provide useful means for the promotion and study of organizational learning.

References

Argyris, C. (1967). 'Today's Problems with Tomorrow's Organizations'. *Journal of Management Studies*, 4: 31–55.

——(1993). *Knowledge for Action: A Guide to Overcoming Barriers to Organizational Change*. San Francisco: Jossey-Bass.

—— and Schön, D. A. (1974). *Theory in Practice: Increasing Professional Effectiveness*. San Francisco: Jossey-Bass.

—— —— (1978). *Organizational Learning: A Theory of Action Perspective*. Reading, Mass.: Addison-Wesley.

—— —— (1996). *Organizational Learning*: Vol. 2. *Theory, Method, and Practice*. Reading, Mass.: Addison-Wesley.

Axelrod, R. (1984). *The Evolution of Cooperation*. New York: Basic Books.

Azar, E. (1990). *The Management of Protracted Social Conflict: Theory and Cases*. Aldershot: Dartmouth.

Baldridge, J. V. (1971). *Power and Conflict in the University*. New York: Wiley.

Banks, M. (ed.) (1984). *Conflict in World Society: A New Perspective on International Relations*. Sussex: Wheatsheaf Books.

Bateson, G. (1972). *Steps to an Ecology of Mind: A Revolutionary Approach to Man's Understanding of Himself*. New York: Ballantine Books.

Bion, W. (1961). *Experiences in Groups, and Other Papers*. London: Tavistock.

Blake, R. R., Shepard, H., and Mouton, J. S. (1964). *Managing Intergroup Conflict in Industry*. Houston: Gulf.

Bolman, L. and Deal, T. (1984). *Modern Approaches to Understanding and Managing Organizations*. San Francisco: Jossey-Bass.

Boulding, K. (1989). *Three Faces of Power*. Thousand Oaks, Calif.: Sage.

Burton, J. (ed.) (1990). *Conflict: Human Needs Theory*. New York: St. Martin's Press.

Bush, R. and Folger, J. (1995). *The Promise of Mediation: Responding to Conflict through Empowerment and Recognition*. San Francisco: Jossey-Bass.

Carrbonneau, T. (1989). *Alternative Dispute Resolution: Melting the Lances and Dismounting the Steeds*. Chicago: University of Chicago Press.

Coser, L. A. (1956). *The Functions of Social Conflict*. New York: Free Press.

—— (1967). *Continuities in the Study of Social Conflict*. New York: Free Press.

Cyert, R. M. and March, J. G. (1963). *A Behavioral Theory of the Firm*. Englewood Cliffs, NJ: Prentice Hall.

Dahl, R. (1957). 'The Concept of Power'. *Behavioral Science*, 2: 201–15.

Dearborn, D. and Simon, H. (1958). 'Selective Perception: A Note on the Department Identifications of Executives'. *Sociometry*, 21: 284–95.

De Dreu, C. and Van De Vliert, E. (eds.) (1997). *Using Conflict in Organizations*. London: Sage.

Deutsch, M. (1973). *The Resolution of Conflict*. New Haven: Yale University Press.

—— (1994). 'Constructive Conflict Management for the World Today'. *International Journal of Conflict Management*, 5: 139–55.

Eisenhardt, K. E., Kahwajy, J. L., and Bourgeois III, L. J. (1997). 'Conflict and Strategic Choice: How Top Management Teams Disagree'. *California Management Review*, 39/2: 42–62.

Emery, F. E. and Thorsrud, E. (1969). *Form and Content in Industrial Democracy: Some Experiences from Norway and Other European Countries*. London: Tavistock.

—— —— (1976). *Democracy at Work: The Report of the Norwegian Industrial Democracy Program*. Leiden: Martinus Nijhoff.

Fayol, H. (1949). *General and Industrial Management* (C. Stours, trans.). London: Pittman. (Original work published 1919)

Fiol, C. M. and Lyles, M. A. (1985). 'Organizational Learning'. *Academy of Management Review*, 10: 802–13.

Fisher, R. (1996). *Interactive Conflict Resolution*. Syracuse, NY: Syracuse University Press.

—— and Ury, W. (1981). *Getting to Yes: Negotiating Agreement without Giving in*. Boston: Houghton Mifflin.

Follett, M. P. (1942). 'Constructive Conflict', in H. C. Metcalf and L. Urwick (eds.), *Dynamic Administration: The Collected Papers of Mary Parker Follett*. New York: Harper Collins, 30–49.

Friedman, V. J. and Lipshitz, R. (1994). 'Human Resources or Politics: Framing the Problem of Appointing Managers in an Organizational Democracy'. *Journal of Applied Behavioral Science*, 30: 438–57.

Galbraith, J. R. (1973). *Designing Complex Organizations*. Reading, Mass.: Addison-Wesley.

Gamson, W. A. (1968). *Power and Discontent*. Homewood, Ill.: Dorsey.

Garvin, D. A. (1993). 'Building a Learning Organization'. *Harvard Business Review*, 71/4: 78–91.

Goldberg, S., Green, E., and Sander, F. (1985). *Dispute Resolution*. Boston: Little Brown.

Gurevitch, Z. D. (1989). 'The Power of Not Understanding: The Meeting of Conflicting Identities'. *Journal of Applied Behavioral Science*, 25: 161–73.

Hocker, J. and Wilmot, W. (1995). *Interpersonal Conflict* (4th edn). Dubuque, Ia.: Wm. C. Brown.

Huber, G. P. (1991). 'Organizational Learning: The Contributing Processes and the Literatures'. *Organization Science*, 2: 88–115.

Isaacs, W. (1993). 'Dialogue, Collective Thinking, and Organizational Learning'. *Organizational Dynamics*, 22/2: 24–39.

Janis, I. L. (1972). *Victims of Groupthink*. Boston: Houghton Mifflin.

Kelman, H. (1982). 'Creating Conditions for Israeli–Palestinian Negotiations'. *Journal of Conflict Resolution*, 26: 39–75.

Kleiner, A. (1996). *The Age of Heretics: Heroes, Outlaws, and the Forerunners of Corporate Change*. New York: Doubleday.

Lawrence, P. R. and Lorsch, J. W. (1967). *Organization and Environment: Managing Differentiation and Integration*. Cambridge, Mass.: Harvard University, Graduate School of Business Administration.

Lederach, J. P. (1995). *Preparing for Peace: Conflict Transformation Across Cultures*. Syracuse, NY: Syracuse University Press.

Levitt, B. and March, J. G. (1988). 'Organizational Learning'. *Annual Review of Sociology*, 14: 319–40.

Lewin, K. (1948). *Resolving Social Conflicts: Selected Papers on Group Dynamics*. New York: Harper & Row.

Likert, R. and Likert, J. (1976). *New Ways of Managing Conflicts*. New York: McGraw-Hill.

March, J. G. and Olsen, J. P. (1976). 'Organizational Learning and the Ambiguity of the Past', in J. G. March and J. P. Olsen (eds.), *Ambiguity and Choice in Organizations*. Bergen: Universitetsforlaget, 54–68.

—— and Simon, H. A. (1958). *Organizations*. New York: Wiley.

McGill, M. E., Slocum, J. W., and Lei, D. (1993). 'Management Practices in Learning Organizations'. *Organizational Dynamics*, 22/1: 5–17.

McGregor, D. (1960). *The Human Side of Enterprise*. New York: McGraw-Hill.

Morgenthau, H. (1948). *Politics among Nations: The Struggle for Power and Peace*. New York: Knopf.

Morrill, C. (1995). *The Executive Way: Conflict Management in Corporations*. Chicago: University of Chicago Press.

Nonaka, I. and Takeuchi, H. (1995). *The Knowledge-creating Company: How Japanese Companies Create the Dynamics of Innovation*. New York: Oxford University Press.

Parsons, T. (1960). *Structure and Process in Modern Society*. New York: Free Press.

Pettigrew, A. M. (1973). *The Politics of Organizational Decision-Making*. London: Tavistock.

Pfeffer, J. (1978). *Organizational Design*. Arlington Heights, Ill.: AHM Publishing.

Pondy, L. R. (1967). 'Organizational Conflict: Concepts and Models'. *Administrative Science Quarterly*, 12: 296–320.

Prokesh, S. (1997). 'Unleashing the Power of Learning: An Interview with British Petroleum's John Browne'. *Harvard Business Review*, 75/5: 146–68.

Rahim, M. A. (1986). *Managing Conflict in Organizations*. New York: Praeger.

Raifa, H. (1982). *The Art and Science of Negotiation*. Cambridge, Mass.: Harvard University Press.

Roethlisberger, F. J. and Dickson, W. J. (1939). *Management and the Worker*. Cambridge, Mass.: Harvard University Press.

Rothman, J. (1992). *From Confrontation to Cooperation: Resolving Ethnic and Regional Conflict*. Newbury Park, Calif.: Sage.

—— (1997). *Resolving Identity-based Conflict in Nations, Organizations, and Communities*. San Francisco: Jossey-Bass.

Rubin, J. and Brown, B. (1975). *The Social Psychology of Bargaining and Negotiation*. New York: Academic Press.

Rupesinghe, K. (ed.) (1995). *Conflict Transformation*. New York: St. Martin's Press.

Schein, E. H. (1993). 'On Dialogue, Culture, and Organizational Learning'. *Organizational Dynamics*, 22/2: 40–51.

Schön, D. A. (1971). *Beyond the Stable State*. New York: Norton.

——(1983). *The Reflective Practitioner*. New York: Basic Books.

——and Rein, M. (1994). *Frame Reflection: Toward the Resolution of Intractable Policy Controversies*. New York: Basic Books.

Selznick, P. (1949). *TVA and the Grass Roots: A Study in the Sociology of Formal Organization*. Berkeley: University of California Press.

Senge, P. M. (1990). *The Fifth Discipline: The Art and Practice of the Learning Organization*. New York: Doubleday Currency.

Shrivastava, P. (1983). 'A Typology of Organizational Learning Systems'. *Journal of Management Studies*, 20: 7–28.

Simon, H. A. (1947). *Administrative Behavior: A Study of Decision-making Processes in Administrative Organization*. New York: Macmillan.

Smith, D. (1987). *Stalking Conflict*. Unpublished Qualifying Paper, Cambridge, Mass.: Harvard Graduate School of Education.

Susskind, L. and Cruikshank, J. (1987). *Breaking the Impasse: Consensual Approaches to Resolving Public Disputes*. New York: Basic Books.

Taylor, F. W. (1911). *The Principles of Scientific Management*. New York: Harper & Row.

Thomas, K. (1976). 'Conflict and Conflict Management', in M. Dunnette (ed.), *Handbook of Industrial and Organizational Psychology*. Chicago: Rand McNally, 889–935.

Tjosvold, D. (1991). *The Conflict-positive Organization: Stimulate Diversity and Create Unity*. Reading, Mass.: Addison-Wesley.

Walton, R. E. (1987). *Managing Conflict: Interpersonal Dialogue and Third-party Roles* (2nd edn). Reading, Mass.: Addison-Wesley.

——and McKersie, R. B. (1965). *A Behavioral Theory of Labor Negotiations: An Analysis of a Social System*. New York: McGraw-Hill.

27 Rules and Organizational Learning: The Behavioral Theory Approach

Alfred Kieser, Nikolaus Beck, and Risto Tainio

How Can Complex Organizations Learn Despite the Bounded Rationality of Individual Members?

Imagine a clerk in an outlet of a manufacturing organization. His or her task entails monitoring the stocks of materials and parts on hand. As soon as the stock of a material or part reaches its reorder point, the person has to fill out an order form and send it to the purchasing department. Such a simple organizational rule solves a number of problems. It ensures that the probability of interruptions in the production process remains low, keeps inventories small, and thereby avoids tying up capital unnecessarily. The clerk does not need to know about pending orders or stocks of finished products. He or she can 'produce' acceptable solutions just by applying the rule. Of course, the solutions resorted to by the clerk are appropriate only if the reorder points have been set in a way that minimizes production halts and inventories. Momentarily leaving aside the question of how these reorder points are determined, we assert that the rule is a repository for organizational knowledge. The clerk does not have to calculate solutions by taking into consideration developments of demand, delivery times of suppliers, finished products on stock and so forth. It is not even necessary to understand the formula behind the rule. The clerk only has to apply the rule reliably. Rules also retain organizational knowledge beyond the tenure of individuals.

One changes such rules, to some extent, by applying rules for change. For example, the organizational member responsible for determining the level at which items or materials must be reordered may have developed a formula indicating how to adjust that level if demand rises at a certain rate or if the flexibility of production is increased.

Similarly, rules for changing rules can themselves be altered, to some extent, by means of still other rules, as happens when the organizational member in charge sets up departmental guidelines specifying which consultant to turn to if problems with inventories arise or stipulating which general methods (e.g. reengineering) to apply. These search rules facilitate organizational learning. Thus, it is possible to distinguish between levels of rule-based organizational learning processes. There are rules for the changing of change rules and rules for the changing of the rules that change those change rules, and so forth.

However, rules not only facilitate organizational learning, they can also impede it. This aspect of rules is usually subsumed under the concept of bureaucratization. Organizational rules have functional and dysfunctional aspects, an issue discussed in more detail later in this chapter. In general, no organization of any complexity can exist without rules.

Support from the Deutsche Forschungsgemeinschaft, SFB 504, at the University of Mannheim, and the Daimler-Benz Foundation, Ladenburg, is gratefully acknowledged.

Organizational learning is always influenced—positively and negatively—by organizational rules.

Although researchers in organizational theory broadly agree on the importance of rules for the functioning of organizations, the role of organizational rules in processes of organizational learning tends to be neglected or underestimated in most theories of organizational learning. One important exception is James G. March and his colleagues. Cyert and March (1963) developed a theory of organizational learning long before this concept became fashionable in management. Since 1963, he and his group have continually revised and developed this theory. Their concepts, though not yet duly recognized in popular management literature, afford fundamental insights into processes of organizational learning. It is assumed in these concepts that complex organizations learn from the ways in which individuals experiment, draw inferences, and code the lessons of history into rules. Organizational learning is based on routines. It is history-dependent and target-oriented. It is largely a function of the relation between observed organizational outcomes and the aspirations set for these outcomes (Levitt and March 1988: 320).[1]

This chapter presents an introduction to the learning theories of the March school and links them with our own conceptual and empirical work. We begin by analyzing the role that the inception, development, functions, and dysfunctions of rules has for organizations and members of organizations. An attempt is then made to reconstruct the development of

organizational learning theories within the school of thought associated with March. We conclude by applying these theories to specific processes of organizational learning.

Rules as Basic Elements of Organizations

Organizational Rules and Related Constructs

Behavior in organizations in general and organizational learning in particular are largely based on rules and routines. However, most authors have made little effort to properly define the construct of organizational routines and to analyze its relationship to similar constructs. For example, Winter (1986) used 'the word *routine* as the generic form for a way of doing things' (p. 165). To him, this construct 'is . . . the counterpart of a wide range of terms employed in everyday life and in various theoretical languages . . . ; among the terms are decision rule, technique, skill, standard operating procedure, management practice, policy, strategy, information system, information structure, program, script and organization form' (p. 165).

March and Simon (1958) were more precise, for they regarded a set of activities as routinized 'to the degree that choice has been simplified by the development of a fixed response to defined stimuli. If search has been eliminated, but a choice remains in the form of a clearly defined and systematic computing routine, we will still say that the activities are routinized' (p. 142). They pointed out that the link between the stimulus and the response lies in the perceptions and reactions of the individuals in the organization. According to them, certain stimuli trigger a fixed sequence of activities.

This conceptualization places routine in the neighborhood of concepts such as the 'script' (Ashforth and Fried 1988; Schank and Abelson 1977). A script is defined as a cognitive structure that specifies a typical sequence of occurrences

---

[1] Regarded as behavioral, the approaches within the March school of organization studies stand in contrast to the neoclassical concepts of organizing. In March's notion of 'behavioral', members of an organization are seen as having only limited rational abilities, whereas in the neoclassical approach humans are thought of as being able to find optimal decisions willfully through rational search. March's meaning of 'behavioral' differs from the interpretation of the term in the psychology of learning, where, as an antonym of *cognitive*, it denotes automatic responses to a stimulus from the environment. (See Starbuck and Hedberg, Ch. 14 in this volume, on behavioral theories of organizational learning that match the psychological meaning of behavioral studies.)

in a given situation, such as a formal meeting or an employment interview. Thus, scripts extend formal rules: Containing information on how to behave when certain rules apply, scripts extend formal rules into the minds of individuals.

Drawing on Giddens (1984), Pentland and Rueter (1994) stated that even interactions commonly thought to be highly routinized are not automatic responses, that they exhibit considerable variety and require effort from anyone intent on engaging in them successfully. They argued 'that organizational routines frequently require the participation of multiple individuals; as complex interactional products, they are unlikely to unfold the same way every time' (p. 488). Consequently, Pentland and Rueter conceptualized routines as 'grammars of action' (p. 489). Just as the grammar of a language enables individuals to engage in conversations that change in content, the grammar of rules or routines enables individuals to perform complex tasks under changing conditions.

March's (1994b) concept of a 'rule' does not seem to diverge greatly from Pentland and Rueter's concept of a routine. He argued that

[t]housands of observations are summarized in the rules of physics and economics and transferred to novices who do not know and cannot reproduce that experimental and evidential base for the rules. Similarly, experiences with technologies or marketing strategies are transferred to new technicians and new product managers in the form of rules that reflect but do not reproduce the experiences on which they are based. (p. 33)

Rules, as defined by March, store and provide knowledge that enables individuals to solve problems in a highly flexible fashion. Rules therefore support individual learning. March (1994a) also stated that

[r]ule-based behavior is freighted with uncertainty. Situations, identities, and rules can all be ambiguous. Decision makers use processes of search and recall to match appropriate rules to situations and identities. The processes are easily recognized as standard instruments of intelligent human behavior. They require thought, judgment, imagination, and care. They are processes of reasoned action, but they are quite different from the processes of rational analysis. (p. 61)

Thus, rules do not have to be formalized (written down). But in what way do routines and rules that reside in the minds of organizational members relate to formalized organizational rules? Formalized organizational rules (e.g. standard operating procedures) can be interpreted as a kind of protocol through which organizational members who are entitled to formulate those rules can effectively communicate what behavior they expect from organizational members in certain situations. A codification of rules, even if it is detailed, is only an incomplete description of the behavior that major actors consider appropriate. Since the designers of formal rules can never foresee all eventualities, they themselves have only limited ideas of what behavior will actually be induced by the rule (Johnson 1977). The formalized rules give organizational members relevant information but do not determine their behavior. In a similar vein Giddens (1984) argued that formal rules are 'codified interpretations of rules rather than rules as such' (p. 21). The rule designers conceive of ambiguous rules, which they can only formulate imperfectly in writing. In order to become effective, rules have to be constantly interpreted during interactions. Actors agree to characterize a particular behavior as conforming to or deviating from formalized rules. Formalized rules structure the intraorganizational communication processes that lead to the formation of appropriate rules in the minds of organizational members (Johnson 1977). Formalized rules necessarily draw on rules that persons have acquired during their socialization processes. Most persons, for instance, have internalized rules on how to behave as, say, an accountant or how, in principle, to deal with a superior or a subordinate. German and British employees know how to handle 'job descriptions'. Some of their specific routines are activated by this term. A Japanese employee, by contrast, probably does not handle them as well, for job descriptions are not a regular element of Japanese organizations. Formalized rules 'do not determine behavior, they rather structure possibilities for behavior about which actors negotiate' (Friedberg 1995: 151).

Routines, whose development and application by organizational members is facilitated by written rules, not only confine the activities of individuals but also enable them (Adler and Borys 1996). This duality is one of Giddens's (1984) core concepts. Routines cannot always be made explicit, for they also encompass 'tacit knowledge' (Nonaka and Takeuchi 1995). This aspect was touched upon when Nelson and Winter (1982) argued that

[r]outines are the skills of an organization. The performance of an organizational routine involves the effective integration of a number of component subroutines (themselves further reducible) and is ordinarily accomplished without 'conscious awareness'—that is, without requiring the attention of top management. This sort of decentralization in organizational functioning parallels the skilled individual's ability to perform without attending to the details. (pp. 124–5)

In summary, rules are widely shared notions about which behavior is appropriate under certain conditions. Rules can be societal (the majority of people in a society agree on what constitutes the appropriate behavior expected of a statesman) or organizational (organizational members agree on specific behavior expected of their salespeople). Individuals and groups have routines that link behavior to rules. When a certain rule applies, the person or the group activates a number of specific routines. These routines should not be perceived as automatic responses but rather as grammars that allow flexible response patterns. Therefore, effective organizational learning entails changes of formalized rules. A rule that is written down in clear language attracts notice and can set off a focused discussion on how it should be interpreted and what kind of behavior is the most fitting under given circumstances.

The Inception and Development of Formal Organizational Rules

In the Middle Ages the idea that rules can be rationally constructed for certain purposes was completely unknown (Weber 1922/1978). Rules existed, of course, but they were seen as being handed down by forefathers and legitimized by religion. It was not possible to change

them by rationally arguing that certain ends could be achieved better with new or changed rules. The only way to change or create rules was to interpret or reinterpret the tradition. The dominant institutions at that time were social ones such as the guilds, the clergy, and the nobility, which were all-encompassing for their respective members (Kieser 1989, 1998). It was impossible to change these rules merely for the sake of increasing the institution's effectiveness or efficiency. Guild members who changed the rules of production in their shops were imprisoned. In modern organizations, formal rules specify tasks, decision-making competencies, hierarchical relationships, and work procedures more or less precisely for organizational members. Organizational members who are entitled to introduce or change formal rules can do so at their discretion.

Originally there was a complete absence of the notion that rules of conduct possessing the character of 'law', i.e., rules which are guaranteed by 'legal coercion', could be intentionally created as 'norms'. . . . But where there had emerged the conception that norms were 'valid' for behavior and binding in the resolution of disputes, they were at first not conceived as the products, or even the possible subject matter, of human enactment. Their 'legitimacy' rather rested upon the absolute sacredness of certain usages as such, deviation from which would produce either evil magical effects, the restlessness of spirits, or the wrath of the gods. As 'tradition' they were, in theory at least, immutable. They had to be correctly known and interpreted in accordance with established usage, but they could not be created. (Weber 1922/1978: 760)

Formal rules enable individuals to be members of several organizations at the same time. In each organization in which a person is a member, he or she only invests finite resources (such as the willingness to work a certain number of hours per week, to pay membership fees, to invest capital) or entitles other organizational members to act on his or her behalf (Kieser 1989). Without formal rules that define organizational roles, it would be impossible for individuals to manage such a multitude of organizational memberships or identities (March 1994a). Rules that define organizational roles also decouple organizational goals from personal goals of the members. In order to join an organization, one need not identify with its goals. A person need only accept the membership conditions and regard the organization's incentives—pay, opportunities for advancement, and so forth—as fair compensation for his or her contributions to the organization (Barnard 1968; Luhmann 1972).

Within the confines of their formally defined roles, members cannot refuse to respond to organizational expectations without risking their membership. Consequently, the organization can require its members to adopt highly 'artificial roles', roles that the members are not necessarily able or willing to identify with. In principle, this means that organizations today can achieve greater flexibility than they could earlier. They do not have to arrive at a consensus; the motivation to carry out the rules suffices. Formal rules also allow internal differentiation of the organization into specialized departments. A person who works in a specialized department needs only cursory knowledge of the tasks performed in other departments. The clerk in the book-keeping department knows very little of work processes in sales or production. Nevertheless, all the work is coordinated both intra- and interdepartmentally with the organization's goals in mind. This harmonization is accomplished by formal rules that keep the activities of the different departments within certain bounds. A 'superrational' organizational designer of rules who is an expert in all the functions of the organization is not required in order to construct rules that ensure this coordination. As discussed in more detail below, formal rules evolve and thereby bring about organizational learning. Through trial and error, rules that do not fit together are gradually replaced by ones of greater mutual compatibility.

Functions and Dysfunctions of Formalized Organizational Rules

Gouldner (1955) was persuaded that Weber 'thought of bureaucracy as a Janus-faced organization, looking two ways at once' (p. 22). Gouldner explained his conviction with the statement that '[bureaucracy] was administration based on discipline' (p. 22) and that 'an individual obeys because the rule of order is felt to be the best known method of realizing some goal' (p. 22). As Adler and Borys (1996) noted, subsequent research on bureaucracy has either concentrated on the enabling aspects of formal rules or on the coercive ones. The insight that formal rules can be simultaneously restraining and enabling has hardly been discussed.

One of the enabling functions of formal organizational rules is that they reduce complexity and uncertainty for individuals. This argument derives from the fact that the rationality of individuals is bounded (March 1994a; March and Simon 1958; Simon 1958). When making decisions, individuals cannot know all the alternatives, cannot anticipate the consequences of alternatives, and cannot anticipate the utilities they would attach to possible consequences. In everyday life, individuals deal with their bounded rationality by satisfying instead of maximizing, by basing their decisions on drastically simplified models of the real world, and by relying heavily on routine behavior.

But how can individuals equipped with only limited cognitive capabilities cope with the highly complex decisions required in modern organizations? According to Simon (1979), 'organizations . . . can only be understood as machinery for coping with the limits of man's abilities to comprehend and compute in the face of complexity and uncertainty' (p. 501). A central function of formal rules is to reduce complexity and uncertainty for individual decision-makers:

Individual choice takes place in an environment of 'givens'—premises that are accepted by the subject as bases for his choice; and behavior is adaptive only within the limits set by these 'givens.' . . . One function that organization performs is to place the organizational members in a psychological environment that will adapt their decisions to the organization objectives, and will provide them with the information needed to make these decisions correctly. (Simon 1958: 79)

The premises consist of five organizational devices, all of which are based on organizational rules (Simon 1979).

1. Departmentalization. As noted above, formal rules also make it possible for the organization to be differentiated into specialized departments. It reduces the number of criteria that a decision-maker within a department has to take into consideration. For example, the personnel manager only has to consider criteria relevant to personnel and can abstract from problems of accounting, production, or marketing. In this sense, organizations are 'loosely coupled systems' (Orton and Weick 1990; Weick 1976).

2. Standard operating procedures. If standard operating procedures are a solution to a certain problem, there is no need for the individual to develop solutions creatively each time the problem comes up. The program or standard operating procedure, in conjunction with the routine that has developed in executing this procedure, yields the solution. As long as this solution is appropriate, it is possible to give difficult tasks to persons who are not able to develop adequate solutions on their own. Thus, standard operating procedures reduce the need to collect information; the 'condensed' experience of the organization with regard to the respective problem is stored in programs. Knowledge on how to create and revise lower-order programs is stored in higher-order programs (March and Simon 1958: 149, 190).

3. Indoctrination. Organizational indoctrination encompasses organization-specific priorities and norms that the members have internalized (Smircich 1983). To a certain extent, internalized norms can replace written standard operating procedures. The advantage of norms is that they allow a higher degree of flexibility than written rules do. It is also assumed that identification and motivation is increased by cultural norms.

4. Communication. Organizational members do not have to find out what kind of information is important for the decisions they have to make. The organization, through its information system, communicates preselected information to the members. Decision-makers do not have to define and characterize their environment themselves; the organization defines it for them, narrowing their focus.

5. Hierarchy. Some premises are set by members at senior levels of the organization. The organizational members normally cannot and need not question the decisions made at those levels. Hierarchy, too, therefore reduces complexity and uncertainty.

A second enabling function of formal rules is that formal rules increase efficiency. Weber (1922/1978) observed that bureaucracies or organizations based on formal rules achieve greater efficiency and adaptability than other forms of administration do. They are efficient, according to Weber, because their rules can be constructed in such a way as to interlock smoothly like the cogwheels of a machine. Rules also make organizational responses highly predictable, a result that makes it possible to increase efficiency in the interactions between organizations (pp. 973–6).

Formal rules also make it easier for new organizational members to integrate themselves into the work processes; or, seen from the organization's viewpoint, organizations make themselves independent of specific individuals by applying formal rules. Of course, by enabling individuals to perform complex tasks in a coordinated fashion, organizational rules also contribute to the efficiency of the organization and to its learning capabilities.

A third enabling function is that organizational rules serve as organizational memories. Organizations store knowledge in formalized rules. However, organizational rules have to be interpreted. And most of them are useless if not combined with the specific knowledge of organizational members who apply them (Mills and Murgatroyd 1991). Thus, the notion of organizational rules as stores of organizational knowledge denotes the use of rules by trained individuals, of rules and cognitive dispositions of individuals in their interconnectedness. Organizational rules therefore constitute the medium through which the individual's learning is coordinated so that it results in organizational learning.

Fourth, organizational rules erect façades of rationality and thereby afford legitimacy. Proponents of the neoinstitutional school (DiMaggio and Powell 1983, 1991; Meyer and Rowan 1977; Scott 1987, 1992; Zucker 1986) argue that organizations often adopt rules that are 'institutionalized', that is, rules that represent 'good practice' in the eyes of important stakeholders. Generally, institutionalized norms define how a 'rational organization' should look—which departments it should have, how it should calculate the profitability of investment projects, which methods it should implement in order to determine the salaries of its employees, and so forth. By adopting institutionalized rules, organizations demonstrate and acquire legitimacy. Legitimacy, in turn, stabilizes internal and external relationships and increases the likelihood that the organization will secure the resources it needs for survival (Meyer and Rowan 1977).

If an organization has to adopt organizational rules that are at odds with the expectations of stakeholders and that therefore do not contribute to the organization's legitimacy, it applies decoupling devices in order to separate the façade from the technical core. The organization pays lip service, it tries to avoid control by the environment by, say, weakly formulating organizational goals or by ritualizing control exerted by the outside and by statements of account. This behavior also constitutes a kind of organizational learning: Organizations adapt by erecting façades and decoupling their internal processes.

Having analyzed the functions of organizational rules, we now turn to their dysfunctions, including those pertaining to organizational learning. One of them is coercive effects. Critics of bureaucracy often claim that formal rules that are linked to positive and negative sanctions for conforming or deviating behavior are the essence of coercive systems, which force organizational members to behave in ways that do not reflect their true aspirations. This interpretation is supported by empirical studies in which positive correlations have been established between formalization on the one hand and absences; the propensity to leave; physical and psychological stress; job dissatisfaction; and feelings of powerlessness, self-estrangement, and alienation on the other hand (Arches 1991; Bonjean and Grimes 1970; Kakabadse 1986; Rousseau 1978). The fact that highly formalized organizational structures undermine employees' commitment; increase dissatisfaction; and reduce creativity, self-management, and the ability to innovate is a common theme addressed in management texts on organizational change (e.g. Mintzberg 1979) and by management gurus (e.g. Peters and Waterman 1983). The gurus perceive a fundamental conflict between 'empowerment' and the degree of formalization.

A second dysfunction of organizational rules is that they impede organizational change. According to Weber (1904–5/1958), organizations eventually become an 'iron cage' (p. 181), by which he meant that the machinery of the organization becomes inescapable. It develops its own dynamics, which members or external stakeholders cannot entirely control (Ritzer 1996). The organizational members are therefore not able to change rules of the organization that contradict their personal ideas of an appropriate treatment of problems (Weber 1923/1961).

Formal rules that were originally designed as means for certain ends become ends in themselves (Merton 1940). When organizational members perceive that a program no longer solves problems adequately, they realize that it will probably come under attack. Because their possibilities for changing the rules are restricted, they prefer to leave such programs unchanged and decide instead to follow them to the letter in order to immunize themselves against criticism, which is very likely to be sparked by the low quality of the solutions that are generated (Crozier 1964). The conflicts that are provoked by inadequate solutions to problems within the organization often do not result in effort to improve the programs but rather in power struggles between groups and departments, and these conflicts detract from effort to solve the original problems (Crozier 1964: 187–94).

The existence of programs reduces the motivation to develop creative solutions. Organizational members develop a tendency to solve problems by applying standard operating procedures mechanically. They are not used to taking responsibility and risks, so when they discover that they have freedom of choice in some details they tend to ask superiors to install more detailed rules. Members with these characteristics tend to confound precision in applying rules with the quality of solutions to problem. In the words of Sims, Fineman, and Gabriel (1993): 'Rules can become the opium of bureaucratic officials. Without the rules, they are lost, paralyzed' (p. 31). In this way, rules can impede organizational learning.

From the above analysis it follows that formal rules are both coercive and enabling; they impede organizational learning and facilitate it. Which one of these aspects prevails depends on the way in which rules are established (Adler and Borys 1996). The enabling characteristics of formal rules surface if the implementation process includes certain things:

1. Information on repair. It is important that rules not only prescribe a sequence of activities but also convey information on how to deal with the occurrence of typical problems so that the organizational members can help themselves when encountering these problems.

2. Transparency. Enabling rules give organizational members a wide range of contextual information, which helps them interact creatively with the organization and environment as a whole. Procedures are designed to convey to organizational members an understanding of how their own tasks fit into the whole.

3. Flexibility. Enabling procedures have built-in flexibility. Not only do rules allow for different courses of action, they are embedded in an organizational culture in which departures from formalized rules are predominantly regarded as learning opportunities. An analysis of the reasons for deviations can point to necessary improvements or other changes in rules or to the need for a thorough revision of formalized rules.

4. Participation. Organizational members have the opportunity to participate in designing rules. Not only does participation improve acceptance and motivation, it can also increase the effectiveness of the rules because the organizational members regularly have to contribute valuable experience. A formalized procedure that is designed in cooperation with experts, or even completely by the organizational members themselves, is not perceived as coercive.

If processes of formalization bear these four characteristics, then processes of organizational learning are likely to take place. The basic point is that formalized rules enable individuals to design complex organizational processes. Formalized rules increase the effectiveness of intraorganizational communication about which behavior is appropriate under certain organizational conditions. Moreover, written procedures help focus the discussion about necessary changes of rules. One can forge consensus that the formalized rules describe the status quo. It can also be ensured that the interpretations of these rules by different organizational members are fairly similar. Starting from such consensus makes it easier to discuss alternative approaches, choose between these alternatives, and retain the new agreement in new formalized rules. In this context, the slogan 'You can't improve a process that hasn't been standardized' (Adler 1993: 169) becomes a philosophy of collaborative learning.

Rule Evolution as Organizational Learning

Recognition that rule-following characterizes much of the behavior in organizations has directed attention to the processes by which rules emerge, change, and develop over time (March 1981). In the literature of the behavioral theory, rules are generally seen as reflecting history.

Three major processes by which rules develop are commonly considered (Cyert and March 1963: 231).

First, in the rational paradigm it is assumed that rules are created in an intentional, calculated process by rational actors. The actors design rules after analyzing the current situation. The differences between organizations in terms of the rules they follow can be attributed to differences between their environments. Specific decision rules dominate because they entail advantages (Cyert and March 1963). By contrast, behavioral theory, underscoring the inefficiencies of history, emphasizes how slow and indeterminate the match between environment and organizational rules often is.

The second process of rule development is learning from experience. According to this approach, organizational rules emerge and are modified incrementally on the basis of feedback from the environment either through the organization's own experience or through imitation. This view is in keeping with the concept of organizational rules and routines as stores of organizational knowledge (some of which is tacit). One prompts organizational learning by scrutinizing the existing rules with the aim of identifying opportunities for improvement (Nelson and Winter 1982). A firm identifies and selects new rules by focusing on idiosyncrasies of processes founded on unique aspects of its history. Thus, the elicitation and representation of knowledge embedded in organizational rules and routines is crucial in the process of learning.

The third process that can lead to changes in organizational rules is the process of selection among invariant rules. As with experiential learning, rules are a function of history, but the mechanism is different. Individual rules are seen as invariant, but it is claimed that the population of rules changes over time (McKelvey and Aldrich 1983).

These approaches to describing the way in which less effective routines are replaced by more effective ones can be classified as early attempts to explain rule-based organizational learning.

By conceptualizing organizational routines as equivalents to genes in biological evolution, Nelson and Winter (1982: 135) also underlined the function of routines as organizational memories. Integrating this function into an evolutionary concept, they assumed that the future behavior of organizations, being based on routines, will resemble behavior that would be produced if organizations were simply to follow their past routines. In other words, the evolution of organizations does not occur in leaps. Expansion of capacity is normally manifested as 'faultless replication' of routines. According to Nelson and Winter, imitation of effective routines within the organization can be seen as a powerful mechanism through which effective routines spread more quickly in a given organization than less effective ones do. New routines come about when scientists, engineers, or managers bring their problem-solving creativity to bear. Ultimately, the success or failure of their attempts to solve problems is decided by environmental selection.

McKelvey and Aldrich (1983), in their version of population ecology theory, also took organizational routines—they called them 'comps', an expression derived from competencies—as the basic units of organizational evolution. Variations in comps occur when organizational designers err when trying to copy comps from other organizations or when trying to improve comps rationally. Since organizational designers are not able to adapt comps rationally to changing conditions of the environment, the variations that they produce in their attempts at improvement are essentially 'blind'. It is not the designer who makes the important choices, it is the environment via 'natural selection'.

As conceptualized in McKelvey and Aldrich's version of the population ecology approach, natural selection raises the chances that superior comps will be reproduced in an organizational population. This notion is similar to the basic mechanism in biological evolution. For example, antelopes that have been endowed through mutation with the ability to outrun their predators live longer and have more opportunity to reproduce than they would otherwise. The ability to run fast—or more precisely, the genes responsible for this ability—can therefore spread in the population. Analogously, successful organizations necessarily have a higher percentage of successful comps than less successful organizations do. The comps of successful organizations also have a higher chance of being copied by other organizations, for other organizations prefer to hire employees who bring in experience from successful organizations. Moreover, business magazines, management bestsellers, university textbooks, and management seminars communicate the solutions of successful organizations more often than they do the solutions of less successful ones. Solutions—comps—pass from successful organizations to less successful ones through consultants as well. In short, effective comps have a higher chance to spread in the population than less effective ones do.

Hayek (1973), too, developed an evolutionary concept of routine-based organizational learning. His basic thesis was that 'spontaneous order' is preferable to 'planned order'. Spontaneous order implies tacit knowledge. In order to explain the emergence of rules as the result of evolutionary processes, Hayek assumed an interaction of two processes (Vanberg 1986): (a) variation, in which new transmittable variance—patterns of behavior—are continuously generated, and (b) selection, whereby the only kinds of generated variance (patterns of behavior) that are systematically selected are those that are actually transmitted, that is, the ones that become behavioral regularities (routines) in social systems. Hayek stressed the role of individuals who, by deviating from traditional rules and by experimenting with new practices, act as innovators. These individuals generate 'new variance', which, through ever wider imitation by organizational members, may prevail over both traditional and alternative new behaviors and become new behavioral regularities within the social community (Hayek 1979: 167). This argument obviously suggests a process of variation based on innovations by individuals and a process of selection based on imitation by individuals. Thus, Hayek's concept is in essence an individualistic, invisible-hand conception of cultural evolution.

Vanberg (1986) criticized Hayek's basic assumptions of an evolution of routines:

> When Hayek . . . refers to cultural evolution as a process by which adaptations to changing circumstance and solutions to new problems, faced by a group, are brought about, it is obvious that, according to an individualistic, invisible-hand notion, only the individual actors are the ones who perceive 'problems' and who respond to changing circumstances by choosing those practices which they expect to serve their interests. It cannot be simply postulated that from a process of variation and selection, based on *individual* imitation, rules will emerge that benefit the group. Rather, one would have to show *why* and *under what conditions* the process of individual innovation and individual imitation can be expected to generate socially beneficial rules—just as the theory of spontaneous social order does not simply *postulate* that all spontaneously generated social outcomes are necessarily beneficial, but *explains* why this can be expected, given certain 'appropriate' conditions. (p. 82; Vanberg's emphasis)

Variations in group behavior can be brought about not only by a spontaneous interplay of separate individual actions—the process favored by Hayek—but also by planning. Two modes of planning can be distinguished: (a) planned self-organization, whereby the group members agree to accept certain rules, and (b) planned external organization, whereby new rules are imposed on the group by one or more external persons.

It is impossible to imagine the emergence of sizeable, complete, formal organizations out of a spontaneous interplay of discrete actions. Complex organizational designs for companies such as ABB, General Motors, or Daimler-Benz do not emerge from processes of that sort. There are simply too many individuals whose actions have to form a pattern from spontaneous interaction. What works for tribes does not necessarily work for large formal organizations. It is also hard to imagine that spontaneous individual actions give rise to accounting systems or information systems (Kieser 1994).

This criticism does not apply to McKelvey and Aldrich's (1983) concept. They did not exclude planning as a source of variation of comps but rather only assumed that planning is essentially 'blind', that it is impossible for planners to construct solutions that fit the environment. The planners plan, and the environment selects.

McKelvey and Aldrich (1983) did not analyze which factors move individuals to change rules or introduce new ones. That question was pursued by Schulz (1993), a student of March. Schulz analyzed changes in a university administration's rules over time, asking whether rule changes are positively or, rather, negatively affected by the knowledge that organizational members have acquired in the application of rules. His most central hypothesis stated that the probability of a rule change diminishes with rule age because of habitualization effects. He argued that the use of rules increases the competence with which this rule is used. The development of alternative rules, he reasoned, would devalue this knowledge, so the organizational members' motivation to change the rules declines as the age of the rules increases. Levitt and March (1988) called this dilemma a 'competency trap', a concept we explore in more detail later.

Acceptance of rules by organizational members is a second variable that contributes to the increasing stability of rules. Rules become institutionalized over time. New rules are perceived as preliminary attempts to solve certain problems. This perception invites changes. The longer a rule exists, the more the members become used to it. However, Schulz presented a contradictory hypothesis as well: The older a rule becomes, the higher the probability is that environmental changes necessitate its revision because it no longer fits the changed conditions. Hence, rules become obsolete if they are not adapted to environmental changes.

Schulz's (1993) data showed that the probability of rule change decreased with rule age. However, the age of a rule *version*—the time that has elapsed since the last modification of the rule—increases the probability of further change

in the rule. Explaining these results, Schulz pointed out that rules have stable and unstable elements. The unstable elements, he stated, become obsolete after a modification (see also Schulz 1998a). Other elements of rules, according to Schulz, remain stable because they mean security and an accumulation of competencies for the members of the organization. Because of this staying power, rule age reduces the probability of rule change.

Schulz (1998b) also analyzed the inception of rules. He found that an increasing density of rules tended to slow the rate at which they are conceived. He explained this result with the absorptive capacity of rules, stating that the impetus for change—the inception of new rules—is eliminated once problems are codified into rules.

Another project about rule histories and organizational learning extended the concept of the age dependence of rule changes and suspensions by taking environmental and organizational changes into account (Beck and Kieser 1998). Analysis of the development of a German bank's personnel rules revealed that the processes of rule change differed from those of rule suspension. Although it was shown that the rate of rule change strongly decreased as the age of rule versions increased (indicating the habitualization process mentioned above), the rate of rule suspension increased (perhaps because of a process of obsolescence). One conclusion from this finding was that the contents of the rules became obsolete because the older the version of the rules became, the less likely their contents was to be changed. The two processes seem to be complementary. The growing reluctance to change a rule the older a rule version becomes necessitates increased pressure to suspend that rule because an additional modification might no longer be the appropriate measure to adapt the rule to the changed situation. These complementary, yet different, patterns of influence underline the need to differentiate between rule change and rule suspension when processes of organizational learning are analyzed for the life cycles of organizational rules. Another important result is that organizational learning depends not only on cumulated experience in dealing with rules but also on experience in creating rules. The older a given mode (or system) of creating rules, the less likely it becomes that a version of a newly established rule will be changed or suspended. Rule suspension, in particular, declines with each additional year between the rule book's introduction and the point at which a new rule is made.

Organizational Learning in the March School

Our analysis shows that the creation and revision of rules or programs can be regarded as a basic outcome of organizational learning. Thus, it is not at all surprising that these processes also play a major role in organizational learning concepts of the March school, one of the most important behavioral approaches to organizational learning. However, March and his colleagues have taken the idea of organizational learning beyond the processes of creating and modifying rules. The purpose of this section is to examine the major aspects of the organizational learning concepts in their school of thought.

In the first of several highly influential models of organizational learning, Cyert and March (1963) assumed that a search for better problem solutions is stimulated as soon as existing programs no longer guarantee the achievement of the organization's goals, which are formulated as aspiration levels. The search is also controlled by programs or rules. At first, an organizational search proceeds on the basis of a simple model of causality. The model becomes more complex if this initial search is not successful. Solutions that are identified during this search and that appear adequate are stored in new programs that replace the old ones. However, organizations learn not only by replacing programs as just described but also by adapting goals and attention rules. Two ways of adapting attention rules are conceptualized: (a) over time, organizations learn to define more appropriate performance criteria, and (b) they

also learn to identify those parts of the environment that are important for them. The basic assumption in this concept of organizational learning is that a rule, be it a decision rule, an attention rule, or a goal-formulation rule, that leads at some point to a preferred state is more likely to be used in the future than it was in the past, and a rule that leads at some point to a nonpreferred state is less likely to be used in the future than it was in the past.

A fundamental problem of this model was that it defined whole organizations or organizational subunits as the units of analysis, meaning that the link between individual learning and organizational learning is neglected. March and Olsen (1975) overcame this problem by explicitly including the roles of individuals in processes of organizational learning. They conceptualized a complete learning cycle and identified barriers able to interrupt learning at different points in this cycle. The complete cycle consists of four stages (see Fig. 27.1): (a) individual actions are based on certain individual beliefs; (b) these actions lead to organizational actions that produce certain outcomes; (c) these outcomes are interpreted in terms of environmental response, with success being distinguished from failure, and links being drawn between actions and perceived outcomes; (d) this reasoning leads to beliefs.

The creation or modification of rules that lead to actions are results of experimentation. In this respect, organizational learning consists of three steps: variation through experimentation, selection based on inferences drawn from experiments, and retention through the formulation of rules that produce successful actions and that thus can be passed on to other organizational members.

The barriers that can interrupt this cycle are indicated in Figure 27.1 by boldface type and pairs of parallel bar lines. The first interruption occurs when individuals are prevented by certain organizational conditions—especially by prevailing role definitions or standard operating procedures—from adapting their behavior to their beliefs. March and Olsen (1975) called this impediment 'role-constrained experiental learning' (p. 158; March and Olsen's emphasis).

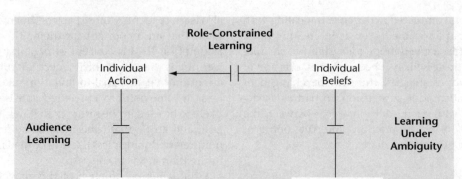

Fig. 27.1. The cycle of organizational learning and its interruptions
Adapted from March and Olsen 1975.

Organizational members are convinced that new actions have to be initiated because environmental conditions have changed, but they are not able to change their actions. Their roles within the organization are so fixed by the organizational structure that they have no way of acting as they think they should. The second interruption of the learning cycle is labeled '*audience* experiential learning' (p. 159; March and Olsen's emphasis). It occurs when individuals are able to change their own behavior but are unable to affect rule-guided actions of others (see also Gherardi and Nicolini, Ch. 2 in this volume). A third interruption of the learning cycle is caused by a misinterpretation of the consequences of organizational actions. The organizational members cannot evaluate correctly which impact the executed organizational actions have on the environment and on the results. They tend to interpret data as justifying the actions taken in response to certain problems that were identified. In other words, '*superstitious* experiential learning' (p. 158; March and Olsen's emphasis) takes place. The last interruption is called 'learning under *ambiguity*' (p. 159; March and Olsen's emphasis). It occurs when changes in the environment cannot be correctly identified. The

organizational members are not able to make sense of the environment or to explain why certain changes happened at all.

A few examples can illustrate the interruptions of organizational learning. Assume that a controller of a company's profit center comes to the conclusion one day that the existing transfer price system is seriously flawed. She asks herself whether she can at least modify the respective rules for the profit center she is working in. On the one hand, appropriate modification would mean that she can submit better data for the manager of this profit center. On the other hand, she runs the risk of her 'correction' being detected and disapproved by the controllers in the headquarters. If she decides not to implement what she thinks is a necessary correction of the rules of the transfer price system, she gives in to role-constraint learning.

Next, assume that this controller implements new transfer prices in her profit center and that she tries to convince the central controlling department to change the system of transfer pricing for the whole company. In doing so, she has to keep in mind that organizational members who point out weak spots may compromise their reputations in the organization, especially when the weaknesses being criticized are those of other departments or higher hierarchical levels. She cannot be sure that she will be able to convince others with her arguments. Failure to do so will harm her career at some point. It is therefore possible that our controller will decide to keep to herself what she has learned. This response would then be an example of audience learning. As shown in our analysis of the dysfunctions of organizational rules, it is often difficult to change existing standard operating procedures.

Now assume that our controller did succeed at convincing the people in the central controlling department to change the transfer price system for the whole company. Everybody in the organization is eager to find out whether this idea was good or not. However, it is extremely difficult to establish the effects that changes in the transfer price system have on the performance of the company. Have results improved because of the changes in the transfer price system? The proponents of the change are generally in favor of an optimistic interpretation, whereas the opponents try to achieve agreement that the new transfer price system has no positive effect on the performance of the company. There is always the danger that the interpretations are biased, that they reflect superstitious learning. If the organizational members are uncertain about how to interpret environmental changes at all, apart from the question of how they were influenced by the action of the organization, then they face the situation of learning under ambiguity.

Kim (1993) extended this model. In particular, he reconceptualized the starting point of the March–Olsen learning cycle: the connection between the 'states of the world' and the ways in which individuals interpret them. Individuals, according to Kim, interpret the world on the basis of 'mental models'. (Other authors, such as Argyris and Schön 1978, have spoken of subjective theories.) A mental model represents a person's view of the world, including his or her explicit and implicit understandings. It furnishes the context in which the person views and interprets new information. 'Mental models not only help us make sense of the

world we see, they can also restrict our understanding to that which makes sense within the mental model' (Kim 1993: 39).

Kim distinguished between two levels of learning—operational and conceptual. Operational learning concerns learning at the procedural level: learning of the steps that are necessary to complete a task. This know-how is stored in routines. Thus, operational learning leads to changes in routines. Conceptual learning concerns the thinking about 'why things are done in the first place, sometimes challenging the very nature or existence of prevailing conditions, procedures, or conceptions and leading to new frameworks in the mental model' (Kim 1993: 40). Mental frameworks set the context in which events are analyzed and interpreted. Frameworks change when the individual routines that are shaped by the frameworks no longer appear suitable for solving a specific problem. In this way a complete individual learning cycle is generated. Certain routines of action are implemented and tested because of individual beliefs (frameworks) that these actions have positive effects on the organization. Unsatisfactory results, however, eventually lead to a revision of the mental frameworks that are responsible for the implementation of the routines.

According to Kim (1993), mental models exist not only at the level of the individual but, as 'shared mental models', at the organizational level as well. They represent, on the one hand, the organization's consensual view of the world—what Kim calls the organization's 'weltanschauung' (p. 42). Organizational shared mental models also contain the organization's routines that are individuals' former routines that have proven successful in the organization and have been adopted by others. As a result, the full organizational learning cycle encompasses changes in the shared mental models, which, in turn, presuppose changes in the individual beliefs and routines.

This reasoning led Kim (1993) to add three additional interruptions in the March–Olsen model. The first is situational learning. It occurs when an individual solves a new problem by improvised action but does not store the solution in his or her individual mental model for later use. The learning is coupled to one solitary event only. Another kind of friction in the learning cycle is called fragmented learning. This interruption occurs when individual learning takes place but does not succeed in changing the shared mental models. The organizational view of the world remains the same. The difference between this form of interrupted learning and audience learning in the March–Olsen model is not easy to make out. It might be that March and Olsen (1975) concentrated solely on the missing link between individual and organizational action, whereas Kim (1993) took the link between individual and organizational worldviews into consideration as well. Kim's third addition to interruptions of the learning cycle is opportunistic learning. It occurs when organizational members want to take advantage of a rather unique and promising chance but the standard operating procedures or the shared mental models are not yet adapted to the new situation. This mismatch between initiative and organizational or mental frameworks then makes it necessary for the organizational actors to circumvent the existing rules in order to preserve the chance.

In other words, how do individuals arrange their way of learning in these ambiguous situations and by which factors are they influenced in their attempts to draw inferences from what they perceive? March and Olsen (1975) argued that the behavior of an organizational member is influenced by different patterns of interaction with other organizational members, varying levels of trust, and different degrees of integration into the organization. Depending on these variables, patterns of perception of organizational events differ from individual to individual. The more integrated into the organization an individual is, the greater that person's tendency is to perceive mainly those events that confirm his or her state of integration. It is more likely that what one sees is what one likes and that what one likes is what one sees. Conversely, an alienated person will mainly perceive things that he or she does not like and will dislike what he or she sees, for this individual will tend to find as much evidence as possible for the differences between him- or herself and other organizational members. Similar to this pattern of influences on attention is the way in which trust among organizational members affects the way individuals perceive organizational events. The more an organizational member trusts colleagues, the more likely it is that he or she will like what they like. The more the member distrusts those colleagues, the more likely it is that he or she will dislike what they like. In an atmosphere of trust, an individual will be more likely to perceive what other organizational members perceive. The more the person distrusts colleagues, the more likely it is that he or she will not see what they see.

Individual learning that can contribute to the whole organization is therefore strongly affected by integration and trust. The sources of information afforded by interactions and discussions are assessed in different ways, depending on the degree of integration and trust that exists. The organizational code—the organizational mental model—is adopted only slowly, if at all.

However, slow adoption of the organizational code does not necessarily deprive the organization of benefit from deviating members. In a simulation study, March (1991) found that organizational actors who are slow learners—persons who socialize into the organizational code at a relatively slow pace—benefit the organization a great deal. The slow learner does not take the prevailing beliefs of the other participants for granted but rather explores the outside world for new possibilities of acting instead of just exploiting previous experience. Such exploration enables the organization to augment its store of accepted knowledge about the 'real' states of the world. The organizational code thereby adapts to the additional knowledge of the deviating organizational member. 'Slow learning on the part of individuals maintains diversity longer, thereby providing the exploration that allows the knowledge found in the organizational code to improve' (p. 76).

An organization can benefit from a deceleration not only of individual learning but also of the overall rate of organizational adaptation to environmental shifts (Lounamaa and March 1987; see also Levinthal and March 1981). Organizations that change too quickly to adapt to new situations might be unsuccessful because they have not gathered enough experience to judge the new situation reliably. In turbulent environments frequent and continual adjustment to misleading signals can lead an organization to learn false lessons. In order to avoid questionable adaptation, it is more intelligent for the organization to wait until it has a fairly large sample of environmental signals, making it easier to draw valid inferences about the 'real' events in the environment. Furthermore, a high rate of adaptation often indicates simultaneous learning in different parts of the organization, a process that may curtail the adaptability of organizations because the different adaptations might not be compatible.

Personnel turnover, too, can contribute to organizational learning (March 1991), as when mid-level turnover accompanies rapid socialization into the organizational code. What has to be learned by the organization is quickly adopted by its individual members. However, because there are always a number of newcomers in the organization, the tendency to explore yet-unknown possibilities and to implement this new knowledge in the organization does not vanish. Excessively high turnover, on the other hand, distorts both individual learning of the organizational code and the action taken on new insights offered by nonconformists. As a result, the organizational knowledge code cannot be improved.

In their attempt to learn from experience, organizations not only take their new or old certainties into account but also survey the experience of other comparable organizations. Hence, another major aspect of the behavioral theory of organizational learning is the observation of learning in ecologies of other learning organizations. Levitt and March (1988) looked at processes of information diffusion among organizations, a phenomenon that is also of interest in neoinstitutional theory (DiMaggio and Powell 1983). The first process, which can be called 'coercive', is the recommendation of a

new rule by a single agent, such as a professional association or a union. Different organizations are affected by this recommendation to different degrees. Another process of knowledge diffusion, labeled 'mimetic', occurs when new organizational routines are communicated from organizations that have already adopted them to organizations that have not. The third process, called 'normative', is the teaching of new routines by a small group of influential persons or institutions, such as management experts or educational institutions.

In keeping with proponents of neoinstitutional theory (Meyer and Rowan 1977), Levitt and March (1988) argued that organizations copy routines from other organizations not only in order to increase their own technical efficiency but also in order to retain their legitimacy. Such imitation has two different consequences for organizations whose practices are copied. Organizations whose experience with technological efficiency is transferred to other organizations mainly suffer from this diffusion, for their competitive advantage disappears. By contrast, an organization whose routines are copied in order to gain legitimacy basically benefits from the diffusion, for the greater the number of other organizations that follow these routines, the more its own legitimacy increases.

Organizational learning is an interactive process. Competitors learn similar technologies at the same time, and the learning of one organization depends on the learning of other organizations because knowledge often diffuses among competitive learners. This diffusion has a severe impact on the outcomes of organizational actions that are learned. The returns of learning new strategies or technologies—the competitive advantage of new organizational routines that are implemented—depend not only on the quality of these technologies and the quality of learning but also on the ability and effort of competitors to deal with the new technologies (Levitt and March 1988: 332; Herriott, Levinthal, and March 1985).

The interactive process of learning in ecologies of competing organizations has a second effect that contributes to the overall development of technology. Innovations are necessary for making technological progress and meeting the needs for change in systems of organizations. However, the introduction of new technological elements is risky because it is not possible to foresee whether these innovations will have positive results. Nevertheless, the ideology of good management holds that it is necessary to bring new ideas into the shared world of organizational perception. This maxim leads to situations that March (1981) called 'unwitting altruism', for one organization runs experiments with uncertain outcomes while other organizations have the chance to see whether these innovations are successful before they decide to copy them. However, drawing conclusions from observations is also subject to superstitious learning and to ambiguity, especially because of the rhetoric used in reports about these experiments (Kieser 1997).

Levitt and March (1988) pointed to a third consequence of the competitive situation of learning organizations in ecologies of other learning organizations. The ability to adapt to experience that has accumulated in changing environments must itself be learned. Powerful organizations that are able to create their own environment normally do not have to learn how to learn. As a result, their ability to adapt to an environmental shift that even they cannot significantly influence is less than that of weaker organizations, which are used to having to adapt to changing situations.

The different approaches to organizational learning that we have discussed so far are all based on the single assumption that organizations learn from their experience. However, sometimes it is imperative that organizations learn even though there are few, if any, cases from which they can draw inferences (March, Sproull, and Tamuz 1991). A striking example of this predicament is an airline that wants to reduce the probability of future accidents. Because no airline has experienced a large number of fatal accidents, the amount of experience from which to learn is small indeed. Organizations have developed different strategies to en-

large their bases of experience. The first is to take more aspects of experience into account. For instance, they register the outcomes of a decision as well as the experiences they had while making that decision. In other words, organizational decisions on a certain issue depend on the outcomes of previous decisions on this issue. However, it often takes too much time to wait for the outcomes of previous decisions, or the outcomes turn out to be ambiguous. In these cases, organizational members tend to make a decision that resembles an earlier one if they experienced positive consequences (e.g. a friendly atmosphere) when making it (March, Sproull, and Tamuz 1991).

Another possibility for broadening the experiential base from which to draw inferences that will support learning is to attend to the different interpretations of the outcome of one organizational action. Conflicting opinions about what has happened in the past lead to a variety of lessons that can be learned. Furthermore, preferences are not fixed. By learning and interpreting the past, organizations modify their opinions of what a success is and what a failure. This process also improves their comprehension of history. When there are no events at all to learn from, organizations have to draw inferences from events that almost happened, or they have to create hypothetical histories. Both approaches are techniques for simulating experience. Because the differences between the condition of occurrence and the conditions of nonoccurrence are very small, 'near histories' of events that—sometimes only out of sheer luck—did not take place are often regarded as though they had. If an air-traffic accident is avoided thanks only to a fortunate circumstance, airlines can learn about the conditions of an accident by pretending that the lucky circumstance had not existed.

Hypothetical histories are quite similar to near histories. However, they represent not one possible alternative plot of events but rather a whole range of histories that might have happened if circumstances had changed only slightly. The construction of hypothetical histories is based on theories developed from the sample of events actually experienced. Thus, an actual incident leads to reflection on the background variables of this incident. These background variables are then used to construct an enlarged sample of histories of which the actual plot was only one possible manifestation. One could say that organizations increase the number of lessons from experience by creating histories that are not actually observable and might never even have happened.

In addition to the costs of constructing hypothetical histories and the fact that simulated events are never as compelling as real ones, the problem with simulated histories is that their interpretation is often very ambiguous. Judging that an accident is very likely if a particular source of failure is not neutralized tends to be regarded as too pessimistic in the presence of success. Conversely, optimistic interpretations of what could have happened if the outcome had just barely missed the goal tend to be regarded as too optimistic and unrealistic. Generally, it is possible to argue that '[i]t is not clear whether the learning should emphasize how close the organization came to a disaster, thus the reality of danger in the guise of safety, or the fact that disaster was avoided, thus the reality of safety in the guise of danger' (March, Sproull, and Tamuz 1991: 10).

Summarizing the development of concepts within the group around March, we note that the initial units of analysis were organizations that adapted to experience in response to environmental changes. The question of how this adaptation is brought about was neglected at first. March and his colleagues then extended their theory of organizational learning by analyzing interactional processes. Organizations can benefit from individual insights but can also make it impossible to transfer individual knowledge to the organizational level. An important result of this school is the evidence that deviant behavior of an organization's members can substantially contribute to organizational welfare because their divergent interpretations of reality increase the chances that new possibilities of action will be explored. Having taken a close look at the micromechanisms of inter-

action, March and his colleagues focused their analysis next on the macrolevels of organizational interaction, the learning of organizations within ecologies of other learning organizations. 'Unwitting altruism' and different effects of being copied were some of the results that they have come to. How to learn in the absence of experience was another important issue taken up within this school of theory. Creating hypothetical histories is a strategy that organizations can pursue in order to cope with this problem. The construction of scenarios is a systematic way to create hypothetical histories (see Galer and van der Heijden, Ch. 38 in this volume).

Limits of Rule-based Learning

Just as there are well-known limits of rationality, there are also limits of rule-based learning (Levinthal and March 1993). A close examination of the relationship between organizational success (or failure) and organizational learning suggests that it is difficult for organizations to learn. It is only in certain circumstances that organizational learning appears to be a route to intelligence and success.

The literature from the March school of thought showed early on how the same mechanisms of organizational learning and rule-following that lead to improvements could also destroy them (Cyert and March 1963; March and Simon 1958). In particular, the short-term effectiveness of organizational learning related to current experience has been shown to interfere with learning in the long run (Levinthal and March 1993; see also Starbuck and Hedberg, Ch. 14 in this volume).

How Success Breeds Failure

The most commonly cited example of limited learning is the process leading to the so-called competency trap. The process starts from the propensity of successful organizations to accumulate slack in the form of surplus resources. These resources become a buffer against the dangers of unpredictable outside shocks but may also become a source of organizational inefficiencies. When managers find that certain activities appear to be successful, they tend to perform them with increasing frequency, to standardize them, and to specialize in them. The 'success recipe' becomes programmed. A program generates activities resembling those that have led to good results in the past.

However, organizational slack allows management to reduce dependence, and that change eventually diminishes the organization's sensitivity to outside events. Management becomes blind to environmental changes, and if it does perceive them, it becomes unable to respond to them beyond the recipes that its programs offer. Organizational autonomy, together with overconfidence in a successful programmed recipe, leads management to accumulate experience mainly with the routines that provide success and to stick to existing rules of operation. Competence in an activity leads to success, which leads to greater competence. The organizational members increase their skill with a technology and the programs surrounding it. Efficiency in using one alternative makes experimentation with other alternatives unlikely and locks organizational members into their competencies. Success fosters programming, and programming facilitates success, but mainly in the short run (Starbuck, Greve, and Hedberg 1978; see also Starbuck and Hedberg, Ch. 14 in this volume). 'A competency trap occurs when favorable performance with an inferior procedure leads to an organization to accumulate more experience with, thus keeping experience with a superior procedure inadequate to make it rewarding to use' (Levitt and March 1988: 322).

Organizations pursue routines and procedures that have produced success too often and too long. It is difficult to escape the competency trap because the exploration of alternatives becomes less certain, more time-consuming, and more remote from present actions than returns on exploitation of present technologies are. When conditions change, organizations find themselves in trouble and suffer from obsolescence. The competency trap is a potentially self-destructive product of organizational learning.

Students of organizational decision-making have found that the repeated use of given rules has additional consequences that are quite similar to competency traps. Whenever the context resembles a familiar situation, the recurrent use of a particular rule can lead to fixed responses even though a superior response is available through reasoned analysis of the situation (Cohen 1991: 138). At a more general level, the routine behavior that organizational members become accustomed to might produce habits that are highly inappropriate under some circumstances. During the Cuban missile crisis, for example, Russian soldiers who were supposed to behave like civilians were easy to spot upon their arrival at Cuban docks because they formed up into ranks of four and moved away in truck convoys (Allison 1971: 109). Automatic execution of action was so deeply engraved in their cognitive structures that they were unable to deviate from it even when the context demanded.

Another consequence of repetitive automatic responses to rules is the reduced ability to react quickly to changed situations. Organizational programs have tolerances built in, and as long as environmental shifts do not exceed these tolerances, the programs are not changed (Hedberg, Nystrom, and Starbuck 1976). Therefore, learning opportunities are often ignored. Moreover, radical changes in environmental conditions often do not trigger the development of radically new unorthodox programs, for the existence of many old programs prompts the organization to try out modes of response to which the organizational members are accustomed. Under these conditions it is necessary to initiate a time-consuming process in which all existing programs are tested to see whether they contribute satisfying solutions for the new situation. It is only after such a process that old routines are gradually unlearned and new activity programs are introduced (Hedberg 1981; Hedberg, Nystrom, and Starbuck 1976).

However, competency traps are not inevitable. One can reduce the danger of their occurrence by reorienting aspirations to performance, altering ideologies, and rewarding experimentation (Levinthal and March 1993). To avoid the competency trap, exploratory activities and systematic evaluation of the results have to be encouraged; experimentation has to become attractive to organizational members. Large rewards for successful explorations are necessary, and members of the organization must not be punished for exploratory mistakes.

The degree of exploration also depends on the relation between performance and aspirations. Unless the organization's survival is threatened, the likelihood of exploration is higher when the absolute difference between performance and aspiration grows than when it shrinks or remains unchanged (March and Shapira 1992). With equal absolute difference between performance and aspiration among the members of the organization, a greater tendency toward exploration can be expected with failure than with success. Normally, aspirations do not lie far above or below past performance. This constellation leads, at best, only to modest experimentation with refinements in an organization's rules. If aspirations are stable or only slowly changing, performance would markedly diverge—positively or negatively—from aspirations, and this divergence would spark exploration of a more substantial nature. Therefore, a policy of slowing down the adaptation of organizational aspirations can help encourage experimentation. One achieves the same effect by linking levels of organizational aspiration to the performance of other organizations that do much better or much worse than one's own.

Creating ideologies (visions) can also help reduce the dangers of the competency trap. 'Ideology is a buffer to experience. It shapes interpretations of experience. For example, it allows failure to be interpreted as a sign that beliefs are right (though perhaps not adequately pursued). These buffers make risk taking less a matter of experiental-based estimations or aspirations than of ideology.' (March 1994b: 26). New ideologies systematically change the mental models and thereby encourage experimentation.

Thus, success does not 'deterministically' bring about inferior rules or organizational failures. According to some observations made in the behavioral literature, success that leads to slack resources enables management to become less vulnerable to its environment, relax its controls and existing rules, increase experimentation, reduce fears of failure, and improve performance. Occasionally, success enhances the self-confidence of managers and thereby increases risk-taking (March and Shapira 1987). Slack generates maneuvering space and creates an 'experimenting atmosphere' that may result in unintended innovations (Levitt and March 1988: 334; March 1981). Usually, however, success seems to be the enemy of experimentation. Lastly, Nystrom and Starbuck (1984) recommended that organizations set up a *regular* process of unlearning old routines in order to prevent a struggle to find new solutions when old answers no longer meet environmental challenges.

How Failure Breeds Failure

Organizations in a crisis tend to avoid rules and procedures that have led to failures. Several studies have indicated that organizational crises tend to lead to a tightening of controls, a centralization of authority, and a low level of risk-taking (Czarniawska-Joerges and Hedberg 1985; Staw, Sandelands, and Dutton 1981). As a result, organizational rigidity as well as competition within the organization tend to increase. Under these conditions it is likely that resistance against stricter controls will mount and that the internal conflicts will increase (Tainio, Korhonen, and Santalainen 1991). These responses will spread fear and defensiveness around the organization, exacerbating the organizational crisis, inducing managerial paralysis, and propelling the organization further toward failure. Thus, the failure often becomes accentuated and results in an endless cycle of failure and unrewarding change.

This 'failure trap' can also emerge from another process (Levinthal and March 1993). Attempts to avoid existing procedures often spur a search for change. However, this failure-driven search is often found to be relatively narrow, focused mainly on the improvement of productive efficiency with known technologies and procedures (Cyert and March 1963). A genuine overhaul of routines is rare. The organizations in which it does occur often suffer from the difficulties of reaping the returns on continuous experimentation and innovations. An organization heavily engaged in experimentation often has trouble exploiting the results of this experimentation, for not enough time or energy is left.

Failure leads to search and change, which lead to failure, which leads to more search, and so on. This pathology of abortive new rules and procedures stems from three pervasive features of organizational life (Levinthal and March 1993): (a) most new ideas are bad, and most innovations are unrewarding; (b) innovations, even those that eventually prove to be successful, are likely to perform poorly until experience in using them has accumulated; (c) aspirations are adjusted downward more slowly than they are adjusted upward, and they exhibit a consistent optimistic bias. However, this failure trap can also be broken (Levinthal and March 1993). Failure may lead to search and change, by which an exceptionally effective new alternative can be found and introduced. Failure-driven searching may therefore still be critical in stopping the deterioration process and turning an organization around.

In general, success seems to decrease search and to increase rule-following, and failure tends to increase search and the questioning of old rules and procedures. Reverse tendencies are possible, but they require special effort. The same learning mechanism that leads to improvements also limits them.

Concluding Remarks

Behavioral theories of the firm, as represented by James G. March and his collaborators over the last four decades, portray organizations as target-oriented and rule-based systems that adapt incrementally to past experience. This view is sharply distinct from the conventional doctrine of rational choice, in which it is assumed that organizational action is based on preferences, expectations about future outcomes, and choices based on these expectations (March 1988: 2–3).

In the tradition of the behavioral approach, organizational learning is viewed as a continuous process involving experimentation, the monitoring of results, and the modification of behavior on the basis of those results. Routines and rules are developed as experience with different contingencies accumulates. These routines become a foundation for future rule-driven behavior and learning. This view of history-dependent learning processes has posed a serious empirical and theoretical challenge to the notion of anticipatory choice as a foundation for organizational intelligence. Behavioral theories of organizational learning also challenge a traditional psychological view of learning, where the sign of learning is defined as a change in response or performance when the stimulus situation and the motivation of an individual are essentially the same (Weick 1991).

Behavioral theorists of organizational learning note that stimulus situations in organizations are mostly unstable and subject to change. Moreover, the centrality of routines in organizational life tends to make responses of organizations relatively consistent. The routines themselves encode and perpetuate what has been learned in the past, but individual routines are slow to change. When they do change, the shift typically consists in the addition of new subroutines, suggesting that the portfolio of routines is an important seat of organizational learning (Weick 1991).

Organizational learning is a process rather than an outcome. From this perspective organizations and their environments are both in constant flux, and a variety of stimuli can be identified at different levels (Cohen, March, and Olsen 1972). Under these conditions organizational learning is essentially rooted in bounded rationality. Individual agents are not fully able to process information in uncertain and continuously changing environments. The search for satisfying solutions tends to emphasize either refinements of existing knowledge or exploration of new knowledge, depending largely on the relation between organizational performance and achieved targets.

The behavioral perspective highlights the fact that organizational learning need not be conscious and intentional. Numerous and varied subprocesses contribute to changing an organization's intelligence. Organizational learning may often result in new and significant insights and awareness of different alternatives that dictate no behavioral change. This new self-reflection may not result in observable changes in short-term behavior (Huber 1991).

According to the rule-based view of organizational learning, the major challenge organizations have to cope with in order to learn is the monitoring of the rule system for identifying which rules must be altered and in which ways they are to be altered. The processes by which organizations bring about routine and incremental adaptation have been unexplored terrain on the map of knowledge about organizations; organization researchers prefer to analyze dramatic, fundamental organizational change. However, effective incremental change partly substitutes for this much riskier fundamental change. Research is therefore needed on the processes through which organizations interpret environmental change, find out which rules no longer fit, and incorporate new solutions into the rule system. Researchers also know very little about how competency traps and failure traps develop in organizations and which activities can help an organization avoid or escape them.

Most studies on organizational learning rest on the assumption that, in order for an organization to learn, as many of its members as possible have to learn as much as possible from each other. As Grant (1996) and Kogut and Zander (1992, 1996) have rightly pointed out, it is essential that there be possibilities for organizational learning to take place across organizational departments in a way that preserves the advantages of job and departmental specialization. Coordination mechanisms that effectively integrate specialized knowledge have to

be developed and applied. The system of codified rules is such a mechanism. It provides a frame within which the departments can effectively manage their interfaces without having to learn many details from each other. A qualitative study by Koch (1999), for example, showed that the members of different departments who participated in the process of rule change were able to combine their specialized knowledge without having to gain a common understanding of the problems at hand or to generate deep insights into each other's specialized experience.

Additional quantitative research is needed on the influence that experience or rule obsolescence has on the rate at which rules are created and modified. Such inquiry is necessary in order to find out whether the empirical results of Beck and Kieser (1998), Schulz (1993, 1998a, b), and Zhou (1991, 1993) are generalizable or whether they apply only to the specific organizations that were studied. It is also important to find out whether the results of quantitative studies on rule creation and rule modification hold for different cultural contexts. Comparative studies are needed that search for general patterns of rule-making and rule-changing activities across cultures.

Our analysis suggests that practice-oriented studies on organizational learning should focus more on organizational rules than they have thus far. A research program along these lines would have to address several questions, including:

1. What kind of rules facilitate individual learning? Empirical results indicate that such rules (a) tend to concentrate on goals and methods and less on fixed procedures; (b) constitute a clear hierarchy, with the most general rules on the top level and increasing specification at each successive lower level; and (c) are easy to understand by using simple language and diagrams (Adler and Borys 1996).

2. Which procedures are appropriate for creating and modifying rules?

3. Is it effective to screen rules regularly in order to identify ones that need revision or that can be deleted?

In summary, the behavioral theories re-describe the phenomenon of organizational learning by specifying processes by which the range of organizations' potential behaviors are changed (Huber 1991). They clarify some of the fundamental issues in understanding human behavior in modern organizations.

References

Adler, P. S. (1993). 'The "Learning Bureaucracy": New United Motors Manufacturing Incorporated', in L. L. Cummings and B. M. Staw (eds.), *Research in Organizational Behavior: An Annual Series of Analytical Essays and Critical Reviews* (Vol. 15). Greenwich, Conn.: JAI Press, 111–94.

——and Borys, B. (1996). 'Two Types of Bureaucracy: Enabling and Coercive'. *Administrative Science Quarterly*, 41: 61–89.

Allison, G. (1971). *Essence of Decision: Explaining the Cuban Missile Crisis*. Boston: Little, Brown.

Arches, J. (1991). 'Social Structure, Burnout, and Job Satisfaction'. *Social Work*, 36: 202–6.

Argyris, C. and Schön, D. A. (1978). *Organizational Learning: A Theory of Action Perspective*. Reading, Mass.: Addison-Wesley.

Ashforth, B. E. and Fried, Y. (1988). 'The Mindlessness of Organizational Behaviors'. *Human Relations*, 41: 305–29.

Barnard, C. J. (1968). *The Functions of the Executive*. Cambridge, Mass.: Harvard University Press.

Beck, N. and Kieser, A. (1998). *Rule-based Organizational Learning*. Working paper, Sonder-forschungsbereich 504: Rationalitätskonzepte, Entscheidungsverhalten und ökonomische Modellierung, University of Mannheim, Germany.

Bonjean, C. M. and Grimes, M. D. (1970). 'Bureaucracy and Alienation: A Dimensional Approach'. *Social Forces*, 48: 356–73.

Cohen, M. D. (1991). 'Individual Learning and Organizational Routine: Emerging Connections'. *Organization Science*, 2: 135–9.

——March, J. G., and Olsen, J. P. (1972). 'A Garbage Can Model of Organizational Choice'. *Administrative Science Quarterly*, 17: 1–25.

Crozier, M. (1964). *The Bureaucratic Phenomenon*. London: Tavistock.

Cyert, R. M. and March, J. G. (1963). *A Behavioral Theory of the Firm*. Englewood Cliffs, NJ: Prentice Hall.

Czarniawska, B. and Hedberg, B. L. T. (1985). 'Control Cycle Responses to Decline'. *Scandinavian Journal of Management*, 2: 19–39.

DiMaggio, P. J. and Powell, W. W. (1983). 'The Iron Cage Revisited: Institutional Isomorphism and Collective Rationality in Organizational Fields'. *American Sociological Review*, 48: 147–60.

————(1991). 'Introduction', in W. W. Powell and P. J. DiMaggio (eds.), *The New Institutionalism in Organizational Analysis*. Chicago: University of Chicago Press, 1–38.

Friedberg, E. (1995). *Ordnung und Macht: Dynamiken organisierten Handelns*. Frankfurt am Main: Campus.

Giddens, A. (1984). *The Constitution of Society: Outline of the Theory of Structuration*. Cambridge: Polity Press.

Gouldner, A. W. (1955). *Patterns of Industrial Bureaucracy*. London: Routledge and Kegan Paul.

Grant, R. M. (1996). 'Toward a Knowledge-based Theory of the Firm'. *Strategic Management Journal*, 17 (Winter special issue): 109–22.

Hayek, F. A. v. (1973). *Law, Legislation and Liberty*: Vol. 1. *Rules and Order*. London: Routledge and Kegan Paul.

——(1979). *Law, Legislation and Liberty*: Vol. 3. *The Political Order of a Free People*. London: Routledge and Kegan Paul.

Hedberg, B. L. T. (1981). 'How Organizations Learn and Unlearn', in P. C. Nystrom and W. H. Starbuck (eds.), *Handbook of Organizational Design*: Vol. 1. *Adapting Organizations to Their Environments*. Oxford: Oxford University Press, 3–27.

—— Nystrom, P. C., and Starbuck, W. H. (1976). 'Camping on See-saws: Prescriptions for a Self-designing Organization'. *Administrative Science Quarterly*, 21: 41–65.

Herriott, S. R., Levinthal, D. A., and March, J. G. (1985). 'Learning from Experience in Organizations'. *American Economic Review*, 75: 298–302.

Huber, G. P. (1991). 'Organizational Learning: The Contributing Processes and the Literatures'. *Organization Science*, 2: 88–115.

Johnson, B. M. (1977). *Communication: The Process of Organizing*. Boston: Allyn and Bacon.

Kakabadse, A. (1986). 'Organizational Alienation and Job Climate'. *Small Group Behavior*, 17: 458–71.

Kieser, A. (1989). 'Organizational, Institutional, and Societal Evolution: Medieval Craft Guilds and the Genesis of Formal Organizations'. *Administrative Science Quarterly*, 34: 540–64.

—— (1994). 'Fremdorganisation, Selbstorganisation und evolutionäres Management'. *Zeitschrift für betriebswirtschaftliche Forschung*, 46: 199–228.

—— (1997). 'Myth and Rhetoric in Management Fashion'. *Organization*, 4: 49–74.

—— (1998). 'From Freemasons to Industrious Patriots: Organizing and Disciplining in 18th Century Germany'. *Organization Studies*, 19: 47–72.

Kim, D. H. (1993). 'The Link between Individual and Organizational Learning'. *Sloan Management Review*, 35/1: 37–50.

Koch, U. (1999). *Rule Change Processes: A Link between Individual Expertise and Organizational Knowledge Bases*. Paper presented at the 15th EGOS Colloquium, Warwick, U.K., 4–6 July.

Kogut, B. and Zander, U. (1992). 'Knowledge of the Firm, Combinative Capabilities, and the Replication of Technology'. *Organization Science*, 3: 383–97.

—— —— (1996). 'What Firms Do? Coordination, Identity, and Learning'. *Organization Science*, 7: 502–18.

Levinthal, D. A. and March, J. G. (1981). 'A Model of Adaptive Organizational Search'. *Journal of Economic Behavior and Organization*, 14: 95–112.

—— —— (1993). 'The Myopia of Learning'. *Strategic Management Journal*, 14 (Winter special issue): 95–112.

Levitt, B. and March, J. G. (1988). 'Organizational Learning'. *Annual Review of Sociology*, 14: 319–40.

Lounamaa, P. H. and March, J. G. (1987). 'Adaptive Coordination of a Learning Team'. *Management Science*, 33: 107–23.

Luhmann, N. (1972). *Funktionen und Folgen formaler Organisation* (2nd edn). Berlin: Duncker und Humblot.

March, J. G. (1981). 'Footnotes to Organizational Change'. *Administrative Science Quarterly*, 26: 563–77.

—— (1988). *Decisions and Organizations*. Oxford: Basil Blackwell.

—— (1991). 'Exploration and Exploitation in Organizational Learning'. *Organization Science*, 2: 71–87.

—— (1994a). *A Primer on Decision-Making: How Decisions Happen*. New York: Free Press.

—— (1994b). *Three Lectures on Efficiency and Adaptiveness in Organizations*. Helsingfors: Swedish School of Economics and Business Administration.

—— and Olsen, J. P. (1975). 'The Uncertainty of the Past: Organizational Learning under Ambiguity'. *European Journal of Political Research*, 3: 147–71.

—— and Shapira, Z. (1987). 'Managerial Perspectives on Risk and Risk Taking'. *Management Science*, 11: 1404–18.

—— —— (1992). 'Variable Risk Preferences and the Focus of Attention'. *Psychological Review*, 99: 172–83.

—— and Simon, H. A. (1958). *Organizations*. New York: Wiley.

—— Sproull, L. S., and Tamuz, M. (1991). 'Learning from Samples of One or Two'. *Organization Science*, 2: 1–13.

McKelvey, B. and Aldrich, H. E. (1983). 'Populations, Natural Selection, and Applied Organizational Science'. *Administrative Science Quarterly*, 28: 101–28.

Merton, R. (1940). 'Bureaucratic Structure and Personality'. *Social Forces*, 18: 560–8.

Meyer, J. W. and Rowan, B. (1977). 'Institutionalized Organizations: Formal Structure as Myth and Ceremony'. *American Journal of Sociology*, 83: 340–63.

Mills, A. J. and Murgatroyd, S. J. (1991). *Organizational Rules: A Framework for Understanding Organizational Action*. Milton Keynes: Open University Press.

Mintzberg, H. (1979). *The Structuring of Organizations: A Synthesis of the Research*. Englewood Cliffs, NJ: Prentice Hall.

Nelson, R. R. and Winter, S. G. (1982). *An Evolutionary Theory of Economic Change*. Cambridge, Mass.: Belknap Press.

Nonaka, I. and Takeuchi, H. (1995). *The Knowledge-creating Company: How Japanese Companies Create the Dynamics of Innovation*. New York: Oxford University Press.

Nystrom, P. C. and Starbuck, W. H. (1984). 'To Avoid Organizational Crisis, Unlearn'. *Organizational Dynamics*, 12/4: 53–65.

Orton, J. D. and Weick, K. E. (1990). 'Loosely Coupled Systems: A Reconceptualization'. *Academy of Management Review*, 15: 203–23.

Pentland, B. T. and Rueter, H. H. (1994). 'Organizational Routines as Grammars of Action'. *Administrative Science Quarterly*, 39: 484–510.

Peters, T. J. and Waterman, R. H. (1983). *In Search of Excellence*. New York: Harper & Row.

Ritzer, G. (1996). *The McDonaldization of Society* (2nd edn). New York: McGraw-Hill.

Rousseau, D. M. (1978). 'Characteristics of Departments, Positions, and Individuals: Contexts for Attitudes and Behavior'. *Administrative Science Quarterly*, 23: 521–40.

Schank, R. C. and Abelson, R. P. (1977). *Scripts, Plans, Goals and Understanding: An Inquiry into Human Knowledge Structures*. Hillsdale, NJ: Lawrence Erlbaum.

Schulz, M. (1993). *Learning, Institutionalization, and Obsolescence in Organizational Rule Histories*. Doctoral dissertation, Stanford University, Calif. (Ann Arbor: University Microfilms International, No. 9317814)

——(1998a). 'A Model of Obsolescence of Organizational Rules'. *Computational & Mathematical Organization Theory*, 4: 241–66.

——(1998b). 'Limits to Bureaucratic Growth: The Density Dependence of Organizational Rule Births'. *Administrative Science Quarterly*, 43: 845–76.

Scott, W. G. (1992). *Chester I. Barnard and the Guardians of the Managerial State*. Lawrence: University Press of Kansas.

Scott, W. R. (1987). 'The Adolescence of Institutional Theory'. *Administrative Science Quarterly*, 32: 493–511.

Simon, H. A. (1958). *Administrative Behavior: A Study of Decision-making Processes in Administrative Organization* (2nd edn). New York: Macmillan.

——(1979). 'Rational Decision-Making in Business Organizations'. *American Economic Review*, 69: 493–513.

Sims, D., Fineman, S., and Gabriel, Y. (1993). *Organizations and Organizing: An Introduction*. London: Sage.

Smircich, L. (1983). 'Concepts of Culture and Organizational Analysis'. *Administrative Science Quarterly*, 28: 339–58.

Starbuck, W. H., Greve, A., and Hedberg, B. L. T. (1978). 'Responding to Crises', in C. F. Smart and W. T. Stanbury (eds.), *Studies on Crisis Management*. Montreal: Institute for Research on Public Policy, 111–37.

Staw, B. M., Sandelands, L. E., and Dutton, J. E. (1981). 'Threat-rigidity Effects in Organizational Behavior: A Multilevel Analysis'. *Administrative Science Quarterly*, 26: 501–24.

Tainio, R., Korhonen, P., and Santalainen, T. (1991). 'In Search of Explanations for Bank Performance'. *Organization Studies*, 12: 425–50.

Vanberg, V. (1986). 'Spontaneous Market Order and Social Rules: A Critical Examination of F. A. Hayek's Theory of Cultural Evolution'. *Economics and Philosophy*, 2: 75–100.

Weber, M. (1958). *The Protestant Ethic and the Spirit of Capitalism* (T. Parson, trans. [1930], with an introduction by A. Giddens). New York: Charles Scribner's Sons. (Original work published 1904–5)

—— (1961). *General Economic History* (F. H. Knight, trans.). New York: Collier-Macmillan. (Original work published 1923)

—— (1978). *Economy and Society: An Outline of Interpretive Sociology* (2 vols., E. Fischoff, H. Gerth, A. M. Henderson, F. Kolegar, C. W. Mills, T. Parsons, M. Rheinstein, G. Roth, E. Shils, and C. Wittich, trans.). G. Roth and C. Wittich (eds.). Berkeley: University of California Press. (Original work published 1922)

Weick, K. E. (1976). 'Educational Organizations as Loosely Coupled Systems'. *Administrative Science Quarterly*, 21: 1–19.

—— (1991). 'The Nontraditional Quality of Organizational Learning'. *Organization Science*, 2: 116–24.

Winter, S. (1986). 'The Reason Program of the Behavioral Theory of the Firm: Orthodox Critique and Evolutionary Perspective', in B. Gilad and S. Kaish (eds.), *Handbook of Behavioral Economics*. Greenwich, Conn.: JAI Press, 151–88.

Zhou, X. (1991). *The Dynamics of Organizational Rules, Stanford University, 1891–1987*. Doctoral dissertation, Stanford University, Calif. (Ann Arbor: University Microfilms International, No. 9206893)

—— (1993). 'The Dynamics of Organizational Rules'. *American Journal of Sociology*, 98: 1134–66.

Zucker, L. G. (1986). 'Production of Trust: Institutional Sources of Economic Structure, 1840–1920', in B. M. Staw and L. L. Cummings (eds.), *Research in Organizational Behavior: An Annual Series of Analytical Essays and Critical Reviews* (Vol. 8). Greenwich, Conn.: JAI Press, 53–111.

PART VI

INTERORGANIZATIONAL LEARNING AND KNOWLEDGE IN A GLOBAL CONTEXT

Introduction

In research on organizational learning, corporations have quite often been treated as monolithic, self-contained systems that have fixed boundaries and that operate relatively independently from other actors in the external environment. Central themes have been environmental adaptation, information acquisition, rule development, collective sense-making, and intraorganizational memory. Today, the emergence of global networks confronts researchers of organizational learning with new issues, such as the role of interorganizational relations, trust, and coordination and the competing notions of competition, cooperation, diffusion of innovation, and imitation. Network analysis of knowledge creation and diffusion elaborates on these issues as well as on the structural characteristics of interorganizational ties, determinants, and mutual effects of the execution of power by partners, and on the role that national cultures play in shaping construction of and relations between networks. To foster the cross-fertilization of these ideas, the authors of this section provide detailed analyses and reviews of different forms of network relations and their implications for organizational learning.

Macharzina, Oesterle, and Brodel analyze organizational learning in multinational corporations (MNCs), which they define as geographically dispersed interorganizational groupings connected by forms of ownership. The authors suggest that MNCs are capable not only of exploiting existing knowledge internationally but also of using several strategies to capitalize on the potential systemic knowledge-related advantages inherent in the international network of their subsidiaries. The authors review different schools of thought, such as the theory of the multinational firm and the behavioral theory of the firm, as they explore the challenges of knowledge transfer in an international environment marked by increasing complexity and diversity. They also address how firm-specific knowledge contributes to this internationalization. Drawing on the notion that knowledge is socially constituted and that learning is always mediated by social processes, Macharzina, Oesterle, and Brodel propose that firms operating in different countries have a unique opportunity to exploit a wide variety of market conditions and learning forms in order to improve, consolidate, and sometimes even completely change their own knowledge base. Effective management of multinationals requires a decentralized and flexible approach to learning and knowledge transfer. The authors suggest that the key to success is to maintain a delicate balance between differentiation and integration and between change and stability.

The chapter by Child opens with an analysis of one of the most pervasive forms of international cooperation—strategic alliances. Companies have increasingly sought strategic alliances, often with competitors, to jointly develop products, gain synergies, penetrate new markets, acquire new knowledge and skills, and, importantly, to realize the potential for inter-organizational learning. Yet, like multinational organizations, strategic alliances pose a formidable challenge to management because of their hybrid nature. The chapter offers an overview of the salient issues that pertain to learning through strategic alliances. The author uses examples ranging from equity and contractual joint ventures to consortia and in-formal collaborations in order to highlight collaborative and competitive learning motives among partner organizations and to stress the implica-tions those motives have for the process of learning and the evolution of alliances. This account helps discern both the requirements for learning through alliances and the barriers to such learning. Child offers sugges-tions on how to manage learning through strategic alliances and proposes measures for overcoming cognitive, emotional, and organizational bar-riers, which hamper the diffusion, internalization, and joint development of knowledge.

Complementing Child's chapter on strategic alliances, the contribution by Lyles explores organizational learning in joint ventures. Lyles focuses on the downward flow of knowledge and learning from foreign parent organizations to international joint ventures (IJVs) in the context of transitional economies, specifically Hungary. Given the environment of high uncertainty and constant change in which transitional economies operate, IJVs are attractive because they can provide an element of stability and build long-term relationships and trust. They also present several opportunities to learn and improve competitiveness. Firms in transitional economies are confronted with tremendous change: altered organiza-tional structures, shifts in the role of state-owned enterprises, and the emergence of a viable private sector. The author suggests many IJVs that were successful at adapting to these changes relied heavily on the acquisition of knowledge from foreign firms. Lyles points out that the learning capability of joint ventures depends largely on the ability and intent of the firms involved, their knowledge acquisition and absorptive capacities, the involvement of the foreign parent, and the business relat-edness of the firms. She draws attention to specific skills and characteristics that maximize learning opportunities.

The vertical dimension of cooperative arrangements is addressed by Lane in her analysis of supplier networks. She identifies major organiza-tional learning concepts in supplier networks, namely, the relationship between individual and organizational learning, operational learning ver-sus conceptual learning, and national learning styles. She reviews literature on networks in order to identify the peculiarities of interorganizational learning as compared to intraorganizational learning. Providing research evidence of the learning experience in manufacturing networks organized by British, German, and Japanese firms in traditional industries, Lane then discusses how national industrial structures and cultures shape the trust relations and learning of supplier networks. She argues that, in order to understand vertical networks, it is particularly important to focus on the organization's environmental scanning strategy and on structural and cultural mechanisms (including the role of trust) that facilitate the coordination of mental models and learning styles. Lane suggests that managers should identify the type of learning they wish to encourage and should construct networks accordingly. Trust-building that helps preserve the dynamic nature of the overall network should, in her view, also be encouraged.

To start correcting the bias toward large Western organizations in the existing organizational literature, Tsui-Auch provides a review of the experience of Chinese manufacturing firms in Hong Kong, Taiwan, and Singapore. Her analysis is based on small and medium-sized enterprises, which are characterized by personal trust, power centralization, volatile labor relations, and loosely coupled network relations with local and global players. The learning strategy of these firms generally revolves around the objective of achieving incremental improvements by importing technology and imitating production skills from global corporations. At the same time, however, these businesses preserve their local networking and organizing strategies rather than adopt Western and Japanese models. The Chinese network model of imitation and innovation lends support to the notion that learning is an active social process that extends beyond information-processing or passive behavioral adaptation. But, as Tsui-Auch comments, imitation learning has intended and unintended consequences alike. Although it reinforces the ability of firms to spot niches, generate quick profits, and pursue constant renewal, it also creates an environment of success, which may lead firms to forget the importance of technological upgrading and hence to lose their competitiveness. The chapter thus echoes the discussion about the paradoxes of organizational learning in Part IV.

Most recently, there has been a growing trend of cooperation between organizations without ownership ties. For this reason the handbook contains a chapter on exploring how organizations collaborate through virtual connections and how organizational learning is thereby facilitated or impeded. This chapter, written by Hedberg and Holmqvist, explores the concept of 'virtual', or 'imaginary', organizations and describes how learning takes place within these networks. Modern technology, say the authors, provides partners with constant patterns of interaction that enable them to relate to each other and that facilitate their creation and explanation of possible synergies. As Hedberg and Holmqvist point out, the role of trust becomes particularly important, and a high degree of transparency is needed in order to shape learning conditions and disseminate knowledge in virtual organizations. The chapter uses two case studies to illustrate how knowledge is created and shared in imaginary organizations. The authors suggest that imaginary organizations have a potential for innovation and organizational learning that goes beyond conventional relationships and alliances. Their chapter reinforces the main theme explored throughout the section—the contention that interorganizational learning in a global context challenges organizations to develop new skills and structures, including new and multiple forms of learning.

28　Learning in Multinationals

Klaus Macharzina, Michael-Jörg Oesterle, and Dietmar Brodel

Research in the field of international business has provided a rich and diverse picture of the factors underlying and shaping the internationalization of business operations. Among the analyzed determinants, or 'drivers', of cross-border operations, knowledge and organizational learning have long attracted the attention of scholars from diverse schools of thought, such as the theory of the multinational firm (e.g. Buckley and Casson 1976; Caves 1971; Hymer 1976) and the behavioral theory of the multinational firm (e.g. Aharoni 1966; Johanson and Vahlne 1977). The creation of knowledge-related advantages through the synergistic expansion of organizational-knowledge bases across borders has also become a focus of international strategy research and research on organizational behavior (e.g. Bartlett and Ghoshal 1989; Gupta and Govindarajan 1991; Porter 1990). This chapter reviews these strands of research. Four key questions are addressed: How does firm-specific knowledge contribute to the internationalization of business operations? What is special about international knowledge transfers? How do multinational firms go about mastering the challenges of increased complexity and diversity in international environments? And, which avenues can multinational firms take in order to create knowledge-related advantages over national firms?

We are indebted to the editors of this volume for their suggestions on the first and second drafts of this chapter.

Similarities and Peculiarities of Organizational Learning in National and International Contexts

Since World War II, firms have increasingly committed themselves to international markets and international operations. An indication of this trend toward internationalization is the growth of trade between nations, which has expanded at a greater rate than the growth of the global economy as a whole. In addition, a rapidly rising proportion of economic activity is now performed by firms that conduct their international transactions within a network of subsidiaries distributed around the globe.

International firms operate simultaneously in many different environments. To do business abroad is to enter into relations with customers, employees, suppliers, governmental agencies, and other actors who may have quite incongruous claims and perceptions. Consequently, international firms face the issue of understanding and adapting to the conditions in foreign environments. Unlike firms operating in a purely national context, firms operating abroad require additional information-processing and, therefore, additional organizational learning as well. At the same time, however, there are also potential benefits associated with internationally dispersed operations. Doing business in different countries offers the opportunity to exploit a variety of market conditions by gathering information about individual markets, condensing this information into organizational knowledge (see also Nonaka, Toyama, and Byosière, Ch. 22; as well as Reinhardt, Bornemann, Pawlowsky, and Schneider, Ch. 36 in this volume), and using it for similar cases within a multinational setting. If this learning process is managed successfully, it will generate a substantial competitive advantage over nationally operating firms.

In order to deal successfully with the challenges and potential benefits of market diversity, multinationally operating business organizations, i.e. multinational corporations (MNCs) must strike a balance between fragmentation and unity, between local adaptation and international integration (Fayerweather 1960; Perlmutter 1969). Thus, although the problem of increased diversity originates at the local level, its effects are systemic, for they also involve the characteristics of cross-border processes. It is not only foreign subsidiaries that are faced with the need to decipher their local environment and respond accordingly; the impact of local conditions is potentially relevant for the design and management of the entire international or multinational system as well. The implication is that the diversity and complexity of managing a geographically dispersed system of value-added activities is greater than—and hence qualitatively different from—that of managing operations within a single national market.

Internationality, in particular, adds a new layer of complexity to the tasks of creating, transferring, applying, and exploiting knowledge. Because knowledge is essentially related to human action (Nonaka and Takeuchi 1995), and because all sorts of business activities are shaped by and are a reflection of deeply rooted, culture-bound knowledge structures (see also Czarniawska, Ch. 5 in this volume), one can even define the international firm in terms of its distinct knowledge-generating and knowledge-utilizing mechanisms (Kogut 1993). Building on a characterization formulated by Vicari (1994: 342), we define international firms as instruments through which individuals or groups achieve their objectives in a process of creating and applying knowledge about efficient international operations. This process involves the use of internally available knowledge across borders in order to generate new knowledge internationally.

Taking this definition as a starting point, we are able to identify several issues to be addressed for the purpose of analyzing the special features of organizational learning in international firms. As depicted in Fig. 28.1, we distinguish between three interrelated sets of issues. First, firm-specific assets are necessarily connected with some kind of knowledge. Hence, the question arises as to how firms can exploit their proprietary knowledge internationally (see also Stopford, Ch. 11 in this volume). Second, international firms are confronted with a higher level of external and internal complexity than national firms are. Consequently, one can investigate the impact of these complexities on international operations and ask how firms can go about acquiring the capabilities they need in order to use and exploit their proprietary knowledge internationally. Lastly, firms are not only instruments of knowledge exploitation; they are also institutions capable of generating knowledge. In other words, information and subsequent behavioral changes that have raised the degree of corporate efficiency and effectiveness will be added to the body of the firm's organizational knowledge or will at least lead to the restructuring of that knowledge. Through this process, information is transformed into knowledge.

Van Maanen and Laurent (1993) noted that 'in the very process of doing business internationally, a firm may also discover new ways of doing things and new things to do' (p. 275). Important issues to be addressed, then, are how internationality can help to improve the existing knowledge base and which measures can facilitate the creation of knowledge within a network of transborder activities under common governance. As indicated by the two feedback-loops in Fig. 28.1, these issues are intertwined. Although the international exploitation of firm-specific assets requires certain capabilities before a firm can successfully engage in international activities, an important means of improving the capability of exploiting advantages abroad is international experience gained through international activities. In

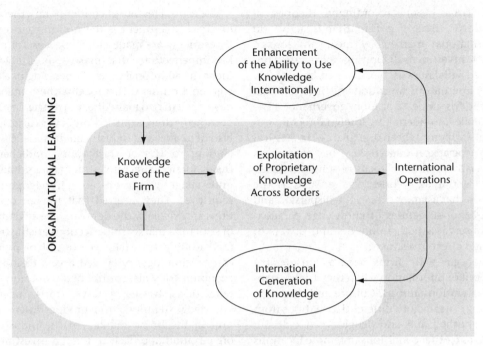

Fig. 28.1. Double-feedback model of knowledge generation and knowledge exploitation in multinational corporations

addition, in the course of undertaking international activities, firms have the chance to enhance their knowledge base, an opportunity that, in turn, lends itself to cross-border exploitation. In short, there is the problem of what comes first: the chicken or the egg.

Despite such interconnections and feedback loops, we will treat knowledge exploitation and knowledge generation in MNCs separately. In the following section we focus on the rationale for international knowledge exploitation and on the kinds of knowledge and organizational learning required in order to exploit knowledge-related advantages in international contexts. We also describe the specific problems associated with internationalization processes. It is shown that the international transfer of organizational knowledge such as organizational routines (see also Kieser, Beck, and Tainio, Ch. 27 in this volume), is not only a management task involving a transmission of knowledge 'as is' from an advanced unit to a less advanced, foreign unit. Rather, we argue that effective knowledge transfer may, in addi-

tion, require a change of context (Brannen, Liker, and Fruin 1997). In the third section of this chapter, we investigate how internationalization can contribute to the expansion of the firm's knowledge base. We also discuss models for the development of capabilities needed to manage internationalization processes effectively (Johanson and Vahlne 1977).

Evolution of International Operations: Organizational Learning and Knowledge as Facilitators of Internationalization Processes

Knowledge as a Factor in the Theory of the MNC

Theories of the firm address the questions of why firms exist and what determines their scale and scope (Connor 1991; Holmstrom and Tirole 1989). Accordingly, theories of the MNC, that is, a firm that is active on international markets by means of foreign direct investment (Dunning 1993), are concerned with issues of the existence, boundaries, and internal organization of international operations under common governance. The rationale for undertaking foreign direct investments, which has been unexplained in classical and neoclassical trade theory, has become an especially prominent focus of scholarly interest. Central to theories of the MNC is the notion that asymmetries in the dispersion and transactional features of knowledge paradoxically serve as both inhibitors and drivers of foreign direct investment.

To begin with, firms need a considerable amount of information when they try to establish operations abroad. Culture and language, among other factors, differentiate nations from one another, and knowledge about cultural, legal, and other conditions in remote locations is usually not available at zero cost. As stressed by Hymer (1976) 'national firms have the general advantage of better information about their country: its economy, its language, its law, and its politics. To a foreigner, the cost of acquiring this information may be considerable' (p. 34).

Because foreign firms do not possess the same knowledge about local conditions as indigenous competitors, operating abroad is more difficult and more costly than operating at home. Because the foreign firm must incur costs for what the indigenous firm has acquired either more cheaply or at no cost, the question arises as to which factors drive firms to expand internationally through direct investments. From an economic point of view, the answer to that question is obvious. The foreign investor has to possess an advantage over local firms that offsets the additional costs of running operations abroad. Otherwise, given the competitive nature of markets, that investor would have no chance to succeed. Moreover, the characteristics of the asset that the firm intends to exploit across borders has to be such that market transactions, that is, international trade, would otherwise yield suboptimal results.

The central feature of contemporary theories of direct investment is the notion that direct investments are made chiefly because of market imperfections that make it profitable to incur the additional costs of operating in a foreign environment. Historically, these theories developed in two main directions. The first line of thought drew explicitly on Bain's (1956) analysis of market and industry characteristics. According to Hymer (1976) and Kindleberger (1969), foreign direct investments are primarily undertaken by firms operating in oligopolistic industries. They asserted that foreign operations are driven by the desire to take advantage of structural market imperfections arising from (and leading to) exclusive control of proprietary technology, privileged access to inputs, economies of scale, control of distribution systems, or as stressed by Caves (1971), superior knowledge stemming from product differentiation in the home market. In the industrial-organization approach to foreign investment, it is suggested that competition and free market entry will eliminate advantages stemming from superior knowledge, making the persistence of such advantages an indication of market power and impeded entry. Compared to the Pareto optimality offered by perfect markets in an ideal world, foreign direct investment and the activities of MNCs hence appear to be socially undesirable, for they imply a social loss.

Despite the valuable contribution of the industrial-organization approach to the understanding of internationalization processes, it is by no means complete or without limitations. In particular, the industrial-organization approach does not account for the fact that there are imperfections other than those grounded in the specific structure of markets. As acknowledged by Hymer (1968), market imperfections of a second type exist as well. They come about because the implicit neoclassical assumptions of perfect knowledge and perfect enforcement of contracts frequently do not hold. As stressed by Coase (1937), market transactions come at a cost. Economic agents have to bear information costs as well as the costs of defining property rights and negotiating, monitoring, and enforcing contracts (Williamson 1975). Such costs, referred to as transaction costs, lead to 'natural' market imperfections (Hennart 1982).

Transaction-cost theories of the MNC hold that MNCs represent an institutional arrangement that is able to bypass the 'natural' imperfections of international markets (Brown 1976; Buckley and Casson 1976; Hennart 1982; McManus 1972). According to the transaction-cost approach, firms are prone to exploit the assets under their own governance if market transactions involve higher costs than the administrative cost of running a hierarchical system. Thus, from a transaction-cost perspective, the primary issue is not the use of structural market imperfections and the maximization of monopoly power through the international exploitation of firm-specific assets, such as managerial knowledge or technology (Hymer 1976), but rather the avoidance of market failure by means of internalization. As opposed to the Hymer–Kindleberger tradition, this conception implies a very positive outlook on MNC activities. If some international transactions are indeed coordinated more efficiently within organizations than through markets, then MNCs allow for both increased private profits and enhanced social welfare.

Most applications of transaction-cost theory to the MNC stress the benefits of internalizing the market for knowledge (Buckley and Casson 1976; Casson 1979; Caves 1982; Hennart 1982; Magee 1977; Teece 1981; Rugman 1981). The reason for this emphasis is that knowledge is characterized by a number of features that hinder its exploitation through market transactions (Casson 1987). A buyer of knowledge, for instance, experiences considerable uncertainty about the quality of the product. In order to reduce the buyer's uncertainty, the seller could disclose his or her knowledge. The problem with this approach is that the supply of knowledge is irreversible. By revealing the information, the seller would, in effect, transfer it free of charge. In essence, because knowledge has properties of a public good, the firm that created it faces the difficulty of appropriating a return for its use (Arrow 1962).

Patents, which are officially granted property rights to knowledge, may offer a solution to this problem. Such property rights, however, are frequently difficult to define and codify. In addition, patents are costly to enforce. A firm that fears the cost of protecting its patent rights will keep its knowledge secret and tend to exploit it itself. The choice between international licensing and foreign direct investment is therefore dependent on the relative efficiency of the relevant market for knowledge (Davidson and McFertridge 1982). If limitations of the patent system make it difficult to market know-how internationally, foreign direct investment is typically chosen as a way to exploit knowledge internationally. The need for internalization is especially acute with experiential knowledge about the production of goods and with managerial know-how, where codification is difficult and internal exploitation is practically the only way to appropriate rents.

International exploitation through cross-border operations under common governance is further enhanced by the fact that knowledge is usually costly to produce but relatively easy to reproduce. For instance, firms whose competitive edge in the home market is based on 'created assets', such as a firm's own technologies or experiential knowledge, can internationally exploit their proprietary ownership assets fairly easily by complementing the transfer of capital with the transfer of skilled and experienced managers and engineers. The economic rationale for such exploitation of domestic knowledge through horizontal foreign investments, has been explained by Caves (1971: 4): 'Any advantage embodied in knowledge, information or technique that yields a positive return over direct costs in the market where it is first proven can potentially do the same in other markets without need to incur again the sunk costs associated with its initial discovery.'

Implicit in this statement is the notion that the international knowledge transfer that usually accompanies foreign direct investments is primarily a 'one-way' knowledge transmission from one organizational unit to another. In general, economic models of the

MNC employ a positivist conception of knowledge. This conception is characterized by the assumption that knowledge is a universal constant, that is, that it has objective validity and that it will be seen the same way by all economic actors. Accordingly, it is assumed that knowledge can be transferred easily within and between organizations and can be applied uniformly across cultural contexts. In addition, it is implicitly assumed that knowledge can be created in its complete form by a single organizational unit. The only task then is to communicate this knowledge so that foreign organizational units can put it to productive use.

If the assumption that knowledge is objective, universally applicable, and complete were true, international organizational learning would be less of a problem than it is. In fact, it would be reduced to technical knowledge transfers. As noted in the following section, however, there are several indications that international knowledge transfers and internationalization processes are not so simple and that the assumptions about knowledge that are inherent in the economic theory of the MNC may not be accurate.

In sum, although the different approaches constituting the theory of the MNC provide an answer to the question of why firms exploit their assets through foreign direct investment, they have little to say about how firms manage the process of transferring knowledge internally or which requirements have to be met if knowledge is to be transferred successfully between diverse cultural settings. This lack of guidance indicates the need to identify and utilize related theories in order to explain the processes and problems of international knowledge transfers.

Social Features of International Knowledge Transfers

In contrast to the assumption that knowledge is something objective, social theories, from symbolic interactionism (Denzin 1994; Mead 1934) to postmodernism (Boje, Gephart, and Thatchenkery 1996; Kilduff and Mehra 1997), maintain that knowledge is based on individual interpretations that in turn, are shaped by socially determined classifications of reality (see also Child and Heavens, Ch. 13 in this volume). Barnes (1983), for instance, underscored the social nature of knowledge and learning. He argued that knowledge is socially constituted and that learning is always mediated by a social process. To learn is to classify, and to classify is to employ the specific classifications particular to a given social entity. It is through socially situated judgments of reality that individual and social knowledge are constituted. Hence, what counts as valuable knowledge does not appear to be fixed but rather derives at least in part from social conventions that differ from one social context to the next.

According to constructionist theories, social entities develop specific cognitive repertoires that guide their interpretations. These interpretative repertoires are characterized by two aspects. First, the social entity's 'fund of knowledge', or what is known, and second, their 'systems of meaning', or how it is known. These domains are linked by language (or other symbolic representations). On the one hand, language is embedded in systems of meaning, of which it is also a reflection. On the other, the specific classifications that social entities employ in order to structure their funds of knowledge and make sense of external or internal stimuli are framed by language (Berger and Luckmann 1966). In short, language goes hand in hand with socially determined ways of perceiving and interpreting, that is, with ways of knowing (Kilduff 1993; Kilduff and Mehra 1997; von Krogh, Roos, and Yip 1996).

One implication of this assertion is that knowledge can be transmitted effectively between and within organizational units if they employ the same coding scheme (Kogut and Zander 1992) and, conversely, that attempts to transfer knowledge effectively will prove difficult to the extent that language boundaries (e.g. functional, organizational, and national) are to be crossed. If the respective language patterns of social entities refer to different systems of meaning, then knowledge may have to be reconfigured or 'recontextualized' (Brannen *et al.* 1997) to fit the interpretative repertoire of the receiving organizational unit. Giddens's (1974, 1984) theory of structuration provides insights into the process of reconfiguration. Central to structuration theory is the notion of an ongoing, reciprocal interaction between social structure and human action. In structuration theory, the essential argument is that human understanding and behavior are contextual in the sense that knowledge, cognition, and behavior are guided and constrained by the contextual rules and resources resident in social structures. Actors use these rules to make sense of their own acts and those of other individuals. The structurational conventions that condition human understanding and behavior are constituted by interpretative schemes, norms, and power relationships. External knowledge is appropriated within the context of these structurational conventions. Knowledge that conflicts with or is antithetical to a system's structurational conventions will trigger what Argyris (1985, 1993) called 'defensive routines' and hence will likely be rejected. The task thus becomes one of reconfiguring the knowledge or technology so that it fits the contextual requirements or of changing the structurational conventions of the recipient unit.

Adaptations may be particularly necessary if institutional rules are to be transferred across culturally defined borders (see also Child and Heavens, Ch. 13 in this volume). Institutional rules such as management techniques or organizational routines can be conceived of as social practices that incorporate structurational conventions on how to organize, how to work, or how to manage people (see also Kieser, Beck, and Tainio, Ch. 27 in this volume). An examination of the inherent structurational conventions in light of the foreign units' contextual background can help prevent an improper transfer of social technologies.

Attempts to transfer organizational procedures and management practices from one cultural context to another are likely to yield suboptimal results unless the governing philosophy—the system of underlying structurational conventions—fits the system of meaning of those expected to implement these procedures from day to day, or unless the organizational routines are transformed so that they conform to existing cultural expectations. Case study evidence (Brannen, Liker, and Fruin 1997; Kenney and Florida 1993; Thompson and Rehder 1996) as well as conceptual (Kilduff 1992, 1993) and broad empirical research (Newman and Nollen 1996) have provided evidence supporting the proposition that international business performance is dependent on 'correct' adaptation of transferred management practices and organizational routines, in other words, on a suitable fit with culturally determined structurational conventions. Research on the international diffusion of lean management, for instance, has shown that the adaptive activities of Japanese firms that have established transplants in the United States and Europe have in fact resulted in multiple hybrids of the lean management system (Kenney and Florida 1993; Thompson and Rehder 1996).

Learning and Knowledge in the Behavioral Theory of the International Firm

Learning is a key concept in behavioral theories. From a behavioral point of view, an entity learns if its information-processing activities lead to a change in the range of its actual or potential behavior (Huber 1991). If they do, then the knowledge base of the entity has been changed. In other words, it has been expanded or restructured through addition of new information and, eventually, through deletion of old information. Behavioral theories of the firm focus on individual and interpersonal characteristics that influence the applied pattern of problem-solving—the selection of issues that require attention, the setting of goals, the design of suitable courses of action, and actual decision-making, that is the choice of appropriate measures (see also Hedberg and Wolff, Ch. 24; as well as Kieser, Beck, and Tainio, Ch. 27 in this volume). Thus, the study of internationalization processes from a behavioral perspective implies a focus on individual and collective problem-solving and decision-making activities that precede and accompany the evolution of cross-border operations.

The behavioral approach to the study of internationalization processes has been strongly influenced by the works of Penrose (1959/1980), Simon (1947), and Cyert and March (1963). The foundations laid by these scholars improved the understanding of how knowledge is acquired and how decisions are made in complex organizational settings.

With her seminal theory of the dynamics of the growth of the firm, Penrose (1959/1980) offered a tool that could be used to analyze the prerequisites of successful geographical diversification. Her discussion of organizational knowledge-bases in particular led to the assumption that knowledge about foreign business must be acquired over a lengthy period through direct experience. The concept of bounded rationality (Simon 1947) became another building block for theoretical explanation of internationalization processes that transcends purely economic reasoning. According to this line of thought, managers tend to be risk-avoiders rather than risk-takers, and the decisions made are based on knowledge acquired through previous experience. Simon's work was extended by Cyert and March (1963).

Aharoni (1966) was the first scholar to apply these concepts to the field of international business. Aharoni sought to analyze the ways in which U.S. firms made decisions about their foreign investments. In his study of thirty-eight manufacturing firms, he found that internationalization decisions were rarely based on rational decision-making processes. Instead, he found that opportunistic behavior, previous experiences, and coincidence played an important role. For instance, an international outlook of high-ranking executives and the effects of an international image were strongly associated with attempts by firms to grow through international operations.

Drawing on his empirical findings, Aharoni (1966: 172) concluded that experiential learning-by-doing played a pivotal role once the decision to internationalize operations had been made. In order to reduce uncertainty, decision-makers 'prefer to "test the market" by exporting to it before any investment program begins' (Aharoni 1966: 150).

The notion that the internationalization of business operations is a process of sequential experiential learning was further elaborated by a group of Swedish scholars from Uppsala University. Development models similar to the Uppsala concept have been introduced (Barrett and Wilkinson 1986; Bilkey 1978; Bilkey and Tesar 1977; Cavusgil 1980, 1984; Crick 1995; Czinkota 1982; Lim, Sharkey, and Kim 1991; Moon and Lee 1990; Rao and Naidu 1992; Reid 1983). But they deal only with the process of internationalization through exports and therefore appear to be applicable primarily to small firms. Because exports are treated in these models as an innovation for the firm, these concepts have been termed I-models (Andersen 1993).

The Uppsala internationalization process model (U-model), on the other hand, is less bound to the earliest stages of internationalization (Andersen 1993). It portrays the internationalization process as an overarching pattern of growth. It is based, as Aharoni's study is, on behavioral theories of the firm and includes assumptions about lack of information and the importance of perceived risk and uncertainty.

In the U-model, internationalization processes are not conceptualized as a sequence of deliberately planned steps founded on rational analysis and conscious calculations by well-informed executives. Instead, it is maintained that the major characteristic of internationalization processes is their incremental nature of successive learning through stages of increased commitment to diverse foreign markets. In this respect, the model postulates an unpredictable interplay between commitment to the market and development of knowledge about the market. Nevertheless, Johanson and Vahlne (1977, 1990) proposed that internationalization processes proceed along certain stages. Each firm must go through a number of predetermined steps of international involvement, with successful passage being based on the 'gradual acquisition, integration and use of knowledge about foreign markets and operations, and on its successively increasing commitment to foreign markets' (Johanson and Vahlne 1977: 23).

The U-model suggests that the internationalization of firms proceeds along two dimensions: the establishment chain and psychological distance. The establishment chain pertains to transborder operations. The process by which firms gradually increase their international resource commitments within given settings is seen as sequential; the firms move from engagement in sporadic export activities to the establishment of foreign production units. The incremental and sequential nature of internationalization is attributed to the fact that acquiring knowledge, especially experiential knowledge, about foreign market conditions is difficult and time-consuming.

Building on the work by Penrose (1959/1980), the U-model distinguishes between objective and experiential knowledge. Although the former is relatively easy to acquire through standardized methods, it is assumed to be of minor relevance only. According to Johanson and Vahlne (1977, 1990), internationalization processes are primarily driven by experiential knowledge. Learning through the development and accumulation of experiential knowledge about foreign markets is necessary in order to overcome the psychological distance to these markets, that is, in order to understand the differences between any two countries in terms of culture, business practice, and the actual execution of legislation. Experiential knowledge about foreign countries' conditions reduces both the uncertainty and the transaction costs of operating in a foreign market (Eriksson, Johanson, Majkgård, and Sharma 1997), but it is fairly costly to acquire.

According to Johanson and Vahlne (1977, 1990), and in line with the arguments presented in the previous section, the perceived psychological distance between the domestic and the foreign culture is likely to have an adverse impact on the flow of knowledge and information between geographically dispersed units. In a recent contribution, Eriksson et al. (1997) went so far as to suggest that 'experiential knowledge

is country-specific and cannot be transferred between firms or business units' (p. 340). However, firms can learn to acquire experiential, country-specific knowledge. Each step in the dimension called psychological distance may be considered a learning cycle that provides an opportunity to improve the ability to absorb the relevant information from the external environment and to process it (Cohen and Levinthal 1990). Over time, firms can at least learn what knowledge is necessary in order to enter new markets successfully (Eriksson et al. 1997). Because national firms do not possess such a knowledge base, they will most likely start their internationalization process in markets having low psychological distance and a low degree of perceived market uncertainty, in other words, in markets that can be understood rather easily. Firms will subsequently enter markets with greater psychological distance.

The U-model is based on empirical research on the internationalization of Swedish firms, but it is supported by several other studies conducted in other settings (Davidson 1980; Denis and Depelteau 1985; Erramilli 1991; Erramilli and Rao 1990; Johanson and Nonaka 1983; Li 1994). Nevertheless, as Johanson and Vahlne (1990) admitted, the model suffers from a number of shortcomings. For instance, the deterministic, sequential nature of the internationalization process as depicted in the model excludes other options, such as that of initiating local production in a foreign country without having gone through the steps of exporting or establishing local sales subsidiaries. Indeed, the leapfrogging of stages seems to be quite common (McKiernan 1992; Nordström 1991). In addition, the option of acquisition as a route to internationalization is not considered in the U-model (for an approach to differentiate start-ups from acquisitions in a learning perspective, see Barkema and Vermeulen 1998). Furthermore, the model's significance is limited to the early stages of international operations. The model does not elucidate the internationalization and reconfiguration processes taking place in multi-subsidiary companies that have learned through decades of international activities.

Multinational Learning Networks: Knowledge Creation in International Contexts

A firm in the early stages of internationalization must possess firm-specific advantages that are accrued through activities in its home country. However, these advantages are not always created first at home and subsequently exploited abroad. Empirical research has provided sufficient evidence to suggest that experienced MNCs can invest abroad in order to take advantage of regional or national leadership in technology (Cantwell 1989; Cantwell and Santangelo 1999; Papanastassiou and Pearce 1997; Pearce 1989; Pearce and Papanastassiou 1996; Pearce and Singh 1992). Moreover, scholars of international business and international management have identified several advantages and synergies that are unique to multinational operation networks. Accordingly, an internationally experienced firm with an extended network of international operations has the opportunity to create and defend firm-specific advantages by virtue of its multinationality. For instance, it has been suggested that MNCs with extensive networks of subsidiaries can benefit from their international operating flexibility in arbitraging institutional restrictions as well as exploiting joint production economies (Kogut 1983; Kogut and Kulatilaka 1995), can utilize portfolio effects in order to balance exchange rate fluctuations and other macroeconomic swings (Rugman 1975), can outdo local firms through cross-subsidization (Hamel and Prahalad 1985), and can benefit from their enhanced power in negotiations with governmental representatives and labor unions (Vernon 1971).

Another type of advantage associated with multinational operations is the synergies created through the cross-border creation, accumulation and sharing of knowledge (Bartlett and Ghoshal 1989; Gupta and Govindarajan 1991; Kogut and Zander 1993). MNCs can do several things to benefit from cross-border 'synergies of knowledge' (Nonaka 1994: 31). They can, for example, formally structure themselves according to their intended strategic direction, use modern information and communication technologies (see Büchel and Raub, Ch. 23 in this volume); and pursue a creative synthesis of meaning systems, such as cross-border socialization and the enhancement of international personal communication. These levers are discussed in subsequent sections of this chapter.

Global Organizational Structures as Levers in the Enhancement of Organizational Learning

In the vast body of literature on the history of and changes in the international economy, the globalization of industries is viewed as the key parameter in the sense that it has been and continues to be the cause and consequence of MNCs' tendency to realign the balance between differentiation and integration (Lawrence and Lorsch 1967). Before the globalization of industries, MNCs could afford to view their subsidiaries from a portfolio perspective. Though empirical research (e.g. Macharzina 1993) provided evidence that MNCs rarely embarked on a purely 'multinational' or 'multidomestic' path of international activities (Bartlett and Ghoshal 1989)—which leads to a structure in which subsidiaries are granted a great deal of autonomy and maintain the whole range of value-added activities—the level of international integration remained fairly low in general. Although transfers of tangible and intangible assets necessarily occurred from headquarters to foreign subsidiaries so that firm-specific assets could be exploited, and although subsidiaries occasionally provided raw materials, intermediate goods, and knowledge to the parent company, efforts to integrate subsidiaries with one another were typically not perceived to be necessary (Egelhoff, Gorman, and McCormick 1996). Because foreign subsidiaries primarily played an exploitative role in the preglobalization era, which lasted until the early 1950s (Porter 1986), the dominant concern was the tailoring of 'hard' and 'soft' technologies to fit local conditions and subsidiary performance in local markets (Birkinshaw and Ridderstråle 1996).

Increasing intercountry interdependence, a phenomenon that began in the mid-1950s (Porter 1986) and that usually is referred to as globalization, went hand in hand with a gradual, yet fundamental, change in the management of MNCs. Globalization at the corporate level pertains to the cross-border integration of strategies and value-added activities (Porter 1990; Yip 1992). Instead of using international operations as instruments of purely domestic asset exploitation and profit optimization, or instead of treating foreign activities as important in their own right, the internationally dispersed value-added activities of global firms tend to be means of serving the global effectiveness of the entire firm (von Krogh, Roos, and Yip 1996).

Whereas the cross-border integration of value-added activities has been fostered by a number of exogenous factors, such as changed government policies (e.g. removal of trade barriers), improved infrastructures (e.g. cheaper and quicker transportation and telecommunications), shifts in technology (e.g. modularization of components), changed individual preferences (e.g. homogenization of demand patterns), and altered buyer needs (e.g. internationalization of industrial customers), globalization in itself is a dynamic element in the sense that it appears to be a self-reinforcing process. For one, it intensifies competition among MNCs and thereby reinforces pressure to enhance effectiveness and efficiency. At the level of individual firms, efforts to create system-based advantages may involve both a redefinition of the roles assigned to corporate units and a tightening of linkages between subsidiaries. These efforts, in turn, are likely to intensify competitive pressures at the sectorial level, which then drive other firms to the limits of their efficiency. Moreover, in institutional theory (DiMaggio and Powell 1983) it is suggested that processes for designing international strategy and structure are not guided solely by rational, well-informed deliberation. Rather, it is argued that, under conditions of uncertainty, decision-makers are likely to mimic the behavior of other organizations in their environment. This disposition may lead to a specific type of organizational learning: the emergence of strategic norms at the sectorial level. These strategic norms can supersede 'objective', exogenous globalization forces. Thus, even if the globalizing activities of single firms are not justified by exogenous globalization forces, and even if these activities produce economically suboptimal results in the long run, they are likely to intensify perceived competitive pressures and may lead to imitative behaviors (see Hedberg and Wolff, Ch. 24 in this volume) by other firms within the same industry (Birkinshaw and Morrison 1995).

Although the degree to which corporate strategies and the structure of international value-added activities should become globalized is a matter of debate, there is broad consensus on Vernon's (1979) assertion that multiple flows of intraorganizational knowledge between international units are an important source of competitive advantage in global industries. The question, then, is how MNCs should organize in order to optimize the learning-related payoffs from international operations. Sölvell and Zander (1995) identified two lines of reasoning that address the structural options available for upgrading the effectiveness of creative and innovative learning processes within global, integrated MNCs.

The first line of thought originated from a strategic perspective on innovations that are triggered or made possible by the characteristics of the external environment. From this perspective, the issue of coordinating and configuring MNCs is addressed primarily in light of comparative differences between countries and between the distinct opportunities offered by regional contexts. Porter (1986, 1990), in particular, highlighted the importance that the home base of MNCs has in the process of upgrading competitive advantage. Even though he stressed that global firms' competitiveness stems from their ability to 'combine advantages drawn from their home base with those resulting from locating particular activities in other nations and those emerging from the overall worldwide network' (Porter 1990: 60), his diamond model suggests that the capabilities of MNCs are strongly shaped by the competitive and institutional conditions of the countries from which they originated.

The second set of models is rooted in systems theory. According to that theory organizations that decentralize decision-making by delegating it to self-regulating subsystems are more adaptive, innovative, and capable of dealing with complex environments than organizations that maintain centralized decision-making and coordination. From the perspective of systems theory, a key asset of MNCs is their potential to learn from and through their activities in foreign environments. Researchers adopting this point of view as opposed to the home-base model, therefore claim that MNCs enjoy the opportunity to capitalize on local knowledge and skill regardless of location (Ghoshal 1987; Van Maanen and Laurent 1993). They also emphasize the systemic advantages of combining geographically dispersed external and internal knowledge sources (Nonaka 1990). In order to turn these opportunities into a distinct advantage, sophisticated organizational structures and management processes as well as strong informal ties between the subsidiaries are advocated (Ensign 1999; Ghoshal and Nohria 1989). Normative models that are geared to the combination of geographically dispersed competencies on a global scale include the geocentric firm (Chakravarthy and Perlmutter 1985; Heenan and Perlmutter 1979; Perlmutter 1969), the multifocal firm (Doz 1986), the diversified multinational corporation (Doz and Prahalad 1993; Prahalad and Doz 1987), the transnational firm (Bartlett 1986; Bartlett and Ghoshal 1989), the horizontal firm (White and Poynter 1990), and the heterarchical MNC (Hedlund 1986, 1993; Hedlund and Rolander 1990). In general these models can be labeled as network-oriented modes of doing multinational business under common governance (on the problems of learning and knowledge acquisition within external networks, that is, international strategic alliances, see Inkpen 1998).

Center-oriented Modes of International Activities

Business research on innovation often builds on the implicit assumption that the sources of innovation are to be found at the firm level rather than at the country level. Because the impact of country-specific conditions on firms' ability to improve performance and to innovate has become a prominent focus of scholarly inquiry, this assumption has been increasingly questioned. In particular, the work on national systems of innovation has significantly added to the understanding of factors that go beyond the scope of an individual firm—ones that determine the speed and direction of technological change within distinct geographical areas (e.g. Dosi, Pavitt, and Soete 1990; Freeman 1995; Kogut 1991; Nelson 1993; Nelson and Winter 1977, 1982; Porter 1990). Within this line of research, the technological development at the country or regional level is conceived of as a cumulative, path-dependent phenomenon rooted in interactive and collaborative learning. Accordingly, national economies are thought to develop along certain technological trajectories that vary cross-nationally. Moreover, knowledge-related advantages of nations appear to be relatively persistent. In the design of semiconductors, for example, the United States for many years enjoyed a quasi-monopoly, or at least a significant comparative advantage in the deployment of relevant skills. Several authors have argued that such advantages are likely to be transient because increasing price competition forces firms to relocate to low-cost countries (e.g. Vernon 1966) and that technological differences among countries will become less significant as the multitude of national economies is replaced by a 'borderless world' with a single, interlinked economy (Ohmae 1990). However, proponents of new growth economics (e.g. Krugman 1991) hold that knowledge-based local advantages are likely to become even more pronounced in the age of globalization because dynamic industrial environments attract skilled workers and, more important, foreign direct investment. The latter is attracted by the opportunity to tap local fields of scientific and technological expertise. The inflow of resources then amplifies those agglomerative advantages that made the location an attractive site for business and research in the first place (Cantwell 1995). The dynamic upgrading of local knowledge-related advantages facilitates the creation of advanced products and applications that will probably give rise to the emergence of new industries. The evolution of Silicon Valley is a well-known case that exemplifies the ability of regional networks to create persistent, dynamic advantages. Despite the increasing globalization of computer hardware and software production, Silicon Valley has been able to defend its position as a gravitational center of technological development.

The concept of national systems of innovation applies to regions and nations alike. As indicated above, however, companies have the opportunity to take advantage of the regional expertise that emerges within local networks of competitors, customers, suppliers, and research institutes. By being spatially grouped in clusters of related activities, firms are able to benefit from positive externalities (Porter 1990). More precisely, intended and unintended knowledge spillovers—above all 'thick' spillovers of tacit and proprietary knowledge—among organizations located in close proximity to one another give rise to competitive advantages at the firm level (e.g. Bartholomew 1997).

The question of how MNCs should be organized if knowledge generation and innovation are indeed context-bound and dependent on local conditions has been addressed by Porter (1990). He suggested that MNCs should focus on home bases as global platforms for their knowledge-generating processes. In its simplest form, the home country of the parent organization serves as the company's home base. In the home base, the firm has strong formal or informal links to other organizations (e.g. suppliers, rivals, customers, local research and education facilities, and governmental bodies). These linkages provide channels for the rapid dissemination of information and knowledge. Because the cost of transferring tacit knowledge is usually positively related to distance (Audretsch and Feldman 1996; Krugman 1991), the home base is considered crucial for corporate innovation and learning. Consequently, core functions such as strategic decision-making and R&D should be performed in these locations. Corporate entities situated in the home base serve as sources of skills and capabilities that can be leveraged throughout the corporation. These entities are therefore assumed to take responsibility for the management of knowledge outflows to other internationally dispersed units (Gupta and Govindarajan 1991, 1993). Likewise, foreign subsidiaries mainly serve as units that help commercialize firm-specific assets generated in the home base through sales, service, and local adaptations. Thus, it is recommended that the MNC be structured as a spatial hierarchy in which supporting functions and upstream activities are centralized and only downstream activities are geographically dispersed.

In a role alternative to that of operational implementers and commercializers, foreign subsidiaries may also serve as supporting units that perform upstream activities. This kind of 'selective tapping' into the sources of advantage in other nations is referred to in the literature as global rationalization (Negandhi and Welge 1984). In the case of global rationalization, foreign subsidiaries are parts of a system that is rationalized worldwide, with headquarters being responsible for system coordination. Each foreign subsidiary performs only a subset of the value-adding processes that the system comprises. Subsidiaries are linked to each other on an operational level, but core competencies and the specialized knowledge for managing the entire system remain concentrated at the headquarters. Similarly, the degree of managerial discretion is low at the subsidiary level, given that the responsibilities for the coordination of decision-making reside at headquarters.

Porter's diamond model suggests that a diversified MNC may run several home bases, one for each segment of the industry in which it operates. This case is referred to as lateral centralization. With lateral centralization, global decision-making is not necessarily located at headquarters. Rather, the responsibilities can be dispersed laterally throughout the organization. As with global rationalization, however, strategic and operational responsibilities are centralized and coordinated worldwide, with foreign home bases having worldwide responsibility for a complete set of value-added activities associated with a specific product or product line. However, the performance of subsidiaries with global mandates, as opposed to the performance of single home-based MNCs, becomes multifaceted, defined by both local and worldwide corporate objectives. Although these subsidiaries remain accountable for market- or country-based performance, they must also contribute to the competitive position of the corporation as a whole.

Lateral centralization requires subsidiary management to have specialized knowledge about the product or market and about cross-unit linkages. Knowledge is managed globally by each home base. The subsidiary needs this information in order to facilitate decision-making on the coordination of activities of other subsidiaries located in more than one country. Thus, the global firm becomes a multi-local innovator rather than a global innovator, as is the case of the transnational firm or heterarchy.

Network-oriented Modes of International Activities

Network-oriented modes of international collaboration within MNCs are rooted in a very different organizational logic and hence are fundamentally different from center-oriented modes. In sharp contrast to the assertion that 'the knowledge and capability to design and upgrade the product and to improve and operate the complete production process must be maintained at home' (Porter 1990: 609), the assumption underlying network-oriented modes of international collaboration is that the knowledge required for the production of complex goods is, unlike capital, difficult to accumulate at a single location and to allocate according to the evaluation of strategic need.

Thus, with respect to the process of developing and transmitting knowledge, the centrality of parent headquarters and home countries is questioned. Proponents of the network mode of international organization maintain instead that global MNCs face the challenge of absorbing and creating information and knowledge at many locations (Bartlett and Ghoshal 1989; Ghoshal and Nohria 1989; Ghoshal and Westney 1993). Moreover, as stressed by Bartlett (1986), transnational firms in particular must cope with the conflicting challenges of maintaining internal efficiency and allowing for organizational responsiveness to diverse local conditions. In consequence, it appears that neither strategies in which subsidiaries function as quasi-independent entities nor strategies with tight, centralized management and control are suited to dealing with these challenges at the same time. Rather, it is assumed that MNCs operating as an integrated network of interdependent, tightly coupled organizational units have the highest potential to outperform competitors (Bartlett 1986).

Whereas highly centralized decision-making processes are proposed in center-oriented models because the linkages of organizational units located in industrial centers with their environments are assumed to be of overriding importance, network-oriented models are rooted in both a philosophy of radical decentralization and a philosophy of strong interdependence. These philosophies are best reflected in the heterarchical model of the MNC (Hedlund 1986, 1993; Hedlund and Rolander 1990), which elaborates on previous frameworks developed by Perlmutter (1969) and Bartlett (1986). The heterarchical model stresses the organizational consequences of attempting to develop systemic firm-specific advantages through multinational operations. These advantages are expected to stem from the transmutation of subsidiaries' accumulated knowledge into an asset of the entire organization.

Unlike center-oriented MNCs, the heterarchical MNC employ many centers that are coordinated in various ways. This multifaceted approach is based on the assumption that specialized knowledge and expertise reside in frontline units, such as research laboratories, marketing groups, and engineering departments. In order to achieve competitive advantage by drawing on these scattered sources of knowledge, the traditional functions of headquarters are geographically dispersed but organizationally integrated. None of the dimensions of country, product, or function is assumed to be uniformly superordinate in the process of formulating and implementing strategy. Moreover, quite different from the rather clear, abiding, and holistically defined responsibilities of the global platforms and international implementers in center-oriented models of the MNC, the tasks of subsidiaries in network models are said to be more flexible and more interrelated to the tasks of other units.

In general, flexible nonbureaucratic and nonhierarchical structures and approaches are expected to foster rapid information and knowledge diffusion and, hence, are expected to be positively associated with a high absorptive capacity (Cohen and Levinthal 1990; Dodgson 1993). Whereas hierarchical processes in the home-based MNC tend to dampen local absorptive capacities, decentralized initiatives, and innovation, the heterarchical model is designed to promote opportunities for acquiring knowledge provided by an established network of subsidiaries. Such networks, or heterarchies, which are characterized by dispersed assets, specialized operations of subunits, and interdependent relationships between virtually all units, are exemplified by Philips Electrics N.V. and Matsushita Electrics Industrial Co. Ltd. (Bartlett and Ghoshal 1989). Both organizations have managed to reduce their degree of centralized activities and decision-making by delegating specific functions and tasks to subsidiaries that use their competencies not only for local issues but also for the organization as whole. Because foreign subsidiaries may draw on the competencies of other units of the firm, especially fulfilling decentralized, but actually corporate-wide, management functions, knowledge about the whole company should be embedded in all parts of the multinational system (Hedlund and Rolander 1990). Thus, a central feature of the heterarchi-

cal model is a strong orientation to the global acquisition and use of knowledge by means of information redundancy.

By decentralizing assets and resources, heterarchical MNCs try to create an organizational environment that nurtures the global development and application of that scarce resource, knowledge. However, decentralization creates a great need to ensure, through horizontal integration, that the entire organization benefits from the specialized resources and expertise developed in geographically dispersed organizational units. Consequently, there is a need for using complex structural integrative mechanisms such as liaison positions, cross-unit committees, and matrix relationships (Gupta and Govindarajan 1991; Lawrence and Lorsch 1967).

Moreover, the role of top management in heterarchical MNCs tends to be different from the functions of top managers in center-oriented MNCs. The most significant difference and the biggest challenge is to move from an attitude of control to an attitude of enabling. More precisely, the dominant task of top management in heterarchical MNCs is to strengthen both the competence of decentralized units and interunit coordination rather than dictate processes and outcomes. Thus, its functions are more systemic than direct. Instead of being designers of strategies and architects of formal structures, members of top management in heterarchical MNCs are the ones primarily responsible for communicating a corporate vision that provides direction and for enhancing organizational processes that create supportive relationships between the diverse units.

Horizontal integration is further enhanced by system-wide information-sharing. For instance, computer-based information and communication systems are essential in facilitating on-line, instant and coordinated information flows within an organization. Rotation of personnel in order to transfer knowledge and information within an organization is another mechanism by which the organization's memory, learning, and capacity for rapid transfer of information can be ensured. Rotation also allows for horizontal integration through normative means, that is through corporate culture and a shared sense of organizational identity (Gupta and Govindarajan 1991).

Information Technology and Telecommunications as Levers for the Enhancement of International Organizational Learning

The diffusion of information and knowledge is an important part of international learning processes. The ability to transfer knowledge internationally is largely determined by the characteristics of international corporate infrastructures for communication (see Büchel and Raub, Ch. 23 in this volume). During the last decade, new communication technologies, such as electronic mail, voice mail, and teleconferencing, have proliferated in the workplace. They enable individuals to communicate despite great spatial distance between them. In addition, information and telecommunication technologies are changing the work processes within MNCs. They enhance the potential for more transparency and allow for tighter control and coordination of the activities in geographically dispersed units (Roche 1992). Modern information technologies facilitate decision-making by enabling people to store and retrieve large amounts of information quickly and inexpensively, to create new information through the recombination of existing information, and to make the assessment and decision models of experts broadly available (Huber 1990).

Particularly interesting is that modern information and communication technologies tend to change the ways in which internationally dispersed funds of explicit knowledge are gathered and appropriated. The recent technological development of electronic knowledge databases, for instance, helps to transform scattered knowledge into a corporate knowledge account. The more that electronic knowledge-management tools are used, the less geography interferes with knowledge accumulation. These tools allow one to pull together interna-

tionally dispersed knowledge, map it, and make it easy to use, enhancing the process of turning human capital into a firm-specific asset. Electronic tools for knowledge management keep one from reinventing the wheel. In particular, MNCs that have knowledge as their major asset (e.g. international consulting companies) are increasingly using electronic knowledge tools.

Limiting the issue of corporate communication infrastructures to the quality of electronic information and communication systems would, however, miss the point. For one, technology appears to be less important than its management. For instance, companies that are enchanted by the technical possibilities of knowledge databases run the risk of creating a chaotic and expensive data cemetery. Knowledge databases require professional knowledge management that keeps the database orderly. In addition, without a culture of teamwork—and compensation and rewards that support such a culture—it is unlikely that employees will share their individual knowledge with the corporate community.

Moreover, in spite of the rapid development and pervasive impact of new information and communication technologies, there is ample evidence that efficient exchange of information often depends heavily on opportunities for personal, face-to-face communication. For instance, in seminal work on engineers' information-seeking behavior, Allen (1977) found that their major source of information was direct contact and communication with colleagues. The implication is that computer-based communication can substitute for personal contacts only to a limited extent. In general, there does not seem to be much confidence in electronic communication as more than an imperfect alternative to direct, face-to-face contact. For instance, by its very nature, the transfer of tacit know-how involves demonstrations, negotiations, and collective problem-solving—activities that frequently require immediate, personal contact. In addition, significant new technical developments may be transferred between units because of *ad hoc* personal contacts, and new ideas and unexpected synergies may emerge as different competencies and technical skills meet.

Sociocultural Dimensions of International Organizational Learning

A key asset of MNCs is their ability to leverage the creativity and skills located in different parts of the world. Both multicenter and network modes of international operations are geared to this end. At the same time, these models imply an increased international interdependence within firms (Bartlett and Ghoshal 1989; Gupta and Govindarajan 1991; Kobrin 1991; Roth, Schweiger, and Morrison 1991). As decision-making processes are tightly coupled and as resources are interchanged on a regional or worldwide basis, extensive collaboration and mutual adjustments become necessary (Ghoshal and Westney 1993). The effect is that multinational systems are likely to lose flexibility, especially if technocratic measures of coordination, such as plans or standard operating procedures, are employed. We therefore conclude that internationality adds another dimension not only to the difficult task of managing the delicate balance between differentiation and integration but also to the task of finding an optimal tradeoff between stability and change. In order to benefit from international diversity, MNCs must allow for local learning and decentralized initiatives. Yet, at the same time, MNCs must provide for closely coordinated strategies and system-wide organizational routines (see Kieser, Beck, and Tainio, Ch. 27 in this volume) in order to allow for concerted action and the use of internationally dispersed knowledge on a global scale.

These difficulties are amplified by cultural barriers and even nationalistic issues. For one, the issue of loyalty is likely to result in further local–global tensions. Host-country nationals are likely not only to identify with the local subunit in which they are working but also to have stronger rapport with the immediate sociocultural environment than with people in other parts of the world. Yet, for internationally integrated foreign subsidiaries, a high level

of commitment to the entire corporation is necessary, for they may need to accept decisions or adjustments that are suboptimal at the subsidiary level (Gupta and Govindarajan 1991). Consequently, MNCs face the challenge of dealing with the tensions between the loyalties that individuals have to domestic goals and those they have to corporate goals (Simon 1994).

In addition, MNCs face the possibility of a culture-induced conflict between the process of developing knowledge and the process of sharing and implementing knowledge across national boundaries. As noted by Forsgren (1997), 'the greater the variation in the different subsidiaries' business contexts, the higher the prospects for creating new knowledge somewhere within the MNC. But the greater the variation in the business contexts, the more difficult it will be to exploit this new knowledge on a more general basis' (p. 72). Several factors can lead to difficulties in sharing and implementing knowledge across borders. First, innovations developed by dispersed units might be highly culture-specific and hence of little value in other settings. Second, subsidiaries might have little incentive to share their local knowledge with other units. And third, the difficulties of transferring knowledge across organizational units are exacerbated by the 'not-invented-here' syndrome (Allen 1977). Ethnocentrism, skepticism of the credibility of remote sources, suspicion of the unknown, and resistance to change can lead organizational units to reject proposals. Empirical research suggests that headquarters are especially prone to reject proposals from international subsidiaries (Birkinshaw and Ridderstråle 1996).

Moreover, according to the structurational perspective (Giddens 1974), it is difficult to transfer tacit knowledge or achieve a creative synthesis of several knowledge bases in MNCs. The underlying problem is that the members of geographically dispersed organizational units are likely to filter information and insights according to their culturally influenced systems of meaning and their different funds of knowledge. For this reason, organizational members tend to ignore information that is of low relevance to the local task but that might be essential to the global task.

Grappling with these problems, scholars have suggested that the notion of a world-oriented, geocentric mind-set among top executives (Perlmutter 1969) needs to be extended to include the entire corporation (Bartlett and Ghoshal 1989; Prahalad and Doz 1987). To the extent that members in dispersed organizational units are able to develop and share a pattern of thinking and perceiving, a common worldview becomes a constitutive element of the corporate culture and makes it possible to abandon restrictive, formal coordination (Martinez and Jarillo 1989; Westney 1993).

The establishment of an integrative corporate culture requires realignments of the attitudes and perception of employees, particularly those who have professional and managerial responsibilities. Despite the fact that 'research on the cultural side of MNCs still remains largely on the science fiction side of the house' (Van Maanen and Laurent 1993: 306), and although it is certainly questionable to conceptualize corporate culture as 'the superglue that connects structural elements of a firm to its economic, political and social strategies' (Van Maanen and Laurent 1993: 276), it is probably appropriate to hypothesize that mutual understanding can help maintain an atmosphere in which organizational members at different locations are able and willing to work together and accept a common way of doing things (Galbraith and Edström 1976).

Because managerial values, assumptions, and beliefs in a MNC are strongly shaped by the divergent national cultures it comprises (Adler and Jelinek 1986; Laurent 1983, 1986), it is impossible to form a monolithic global culture. There are, however, several approaches that appear to be suited for reducing differences among managerial cultures and enhancing the development of an internationally shared core set of beliefs and assumptions. The first approach to the creation of an internationally shared normative framework is aimed primarily at the socialization of foreign personnel (see Nonaka, Toyama, and Byosière, Ch. 22 in this volume). Building on the fact that socialization

requires exposure to reference individuals or groups (Lyles and Salk 1996), companies can staff top managerial positions with expatriates from the parent organization. As reported by Kamiyama (1994) and McKern (1994), Japanese firms, in particular, tend to rely on managers imbued with parent-company cultures, obliged to report through a strong formal hierarchy, and interconnected through informal relationships. Expatriates who have internalized the parent-company's culture and whose adherence to these normative standards is constantly monitored are less likely than 'non-internalized' expatriates to monitor the appropriateness of their own behavior toward divergent social expectations in foreign settings. Thus, although socialization is always an interactive process—people exposed to a foreign culture over a lengthy period tend to internalize at least part of the foreign value- and knowledge-system—the primary target of the socialization approach is local personnel, who are expected to adapt to and internalize the meaning system of the foreign parent organization. The interaction of local personnel with 'low self-monitors' who lack sensitivity to local expectations, combined with the local personnel's exposure to ideas, concepts, and procedures from the foreign parent, is likely to result over time in a partial replication of the parent culture (Kilduff 1993).

It is quite obvious that a one-way transfer of managers is likely to foster the development of an ethnocentric corporate culture opposed to a global or 'geocentric' (Perlmutter 1969) culture. Although the socialization of foreign personnel can enhance integration and thereby lower the barriers to international knowledge transfers, attempts to impose elements of a foreign culture on a domestic work force can trigger defensive routines (Argyris 1985, 1993). In addition, ethnocentric company cultures may have a negative impact on innovation because they limit the propensity for 'outside the box' thinking (Forsgren 1997: 77).

By contrast, the opportunity to benefit from a greater variety of knowledge bases and perspectives is enhanced by global corporate cultures. Such cultures characteristically have organizational members with a broad scope of thought that allows for systemic solutions going beyond those arrived at through nationally defined perspectives. In order to move to the direction of a global corporate culture, companies can try to promote international collaborative learning. Such learning can be described in terms of Learning II (Bateson 1972), double-loop learning (Argyris and Schön 1978), or second-order learning (Ciborra and Schneider 1992). It is the learning that leads one to question the appropriateness of locally framing the situation, to recognize the subjectivity of local meaning, and to reframe the situation according to the circumstances in the international context (see Hedberg and Wolff, Ch. 24 in this volume).

From the perspective of symbolic interactionism, the basis of collaborative learning is the process of taking each other's perspective (Mead 1934). In this process the distinctive knowledge, values, meanings, assumptions, and beliefs of individuals are exchanged, evaluated, and integrated with the knowledge values, meanings, assumptions, and beliefs of others (Duncan and Weiss 1979; Shrivastava 1983). This mutual perspective-taking, however, is a complex process because at least some of the knowledge, beliefs, meaning systems, and norms that form structurational or interpretative conventions are tacit in nature. For example, Giddens (1974) explained that every social system has at least two levels of consciousness—discursive and practical. Discursive consciousness involves knowledge that actors are able to express at the level of discourse. Practical consciousness involves tacit stocks of knowledge that actors are normally not able to formulate discursively but draw upon in their social conduct. Mutual understanding, therefore, involves a great deal that is not explicit or explicable. That content is framed and embedded in structurational conventions, and one is not aware of it in daily operations. Because meaning systems usually operate outside the bounds of consciousness, there is a tendency to automatically assume that other people's views are more similar to one's own than they actually are. Effective cross-cultural collaborative learning is difficult to achieve because the process of taking each other's perspective is hampered by such assumptions. In order to allow for mutual understanding and to bring these meaning systems to the surface, actors must become involved in a lengthy period of personal interaction.

Measures suited to fostering international collaborative learning include foreign assignments, visits by personnel both to and from foreign subsidiaries, management development programs that involve participants from several units, and extensive cross-border communication (Galbraith and Edström 1976). In addition to the fact that the basis for mutual understanding is international personal interaction, frequent horizontal contacts between employees lead to the development of personal networks. These networks promote the spontaneous transfer of knowledge and expertise as well as their recombination. Besides international management development programs, foreign assignments and visits to or from foreign subsidiaries, MNCs can use structural devices, such as international boards, steering committees, and project teams, all of which serve not only as channels for the transfer of knowledge but also as platforms for negotiations of differences and the resolving of conflicts (Kets De Vries 1999).

Conclusions

Internationality adds a number of important new dimensions to the issue of organizational learning. First, in the course of internationalizing their operations, firms must learn how to exploit firm-specific assets acquired at their home base. Second, the source of continuing success in generating innovations is variety of skills and diversity of knowledge, not homogeneity of skills. Obviously, what differentiates MNCs from organizations operating more locally is that MNCs have the opportunity to take advantage of international variations of skills.

Third, there is little doubt that MNCs can benefit from cross-border fertilization, for knowledge creation is closely bound up with the notions of synergy, interdependence, and interactive organizational learning. The implication is that a firm's capacity to innovate is not simply the sum of discrete capabilities. Rather, this capacity is the result of an interplay between diverse units. In order to be successful, MNCs must be able to transfer locally generated know-how in an adaptive manner within its relatively broad range of cultural and political settings.

Fourth, international firms must be able to integrate people from a wide spectrum of national cultures. However, internationally operating firms are confronted not only with the need to accommodate people from different cultures but also with the critical task of balancing the conflicting demands of channeling, promoting, and harnessing international diversity. Put in another way, international firms must find strategic, organizational, and social concepts that allow them to prevent variety from becoming disruptive and enable them to turn it into a distinct advantage.

This necessity is closely related to a fifth aspect. Because organizational learning in MNCs can exceed the contributions of single local units, it is useful for MNCs to adopt a broad, cosmopolitan perspective and to develop a non-ethnocentric mind-set. The management of MNCs, in particular, faces the challenge of creating an atmosphere in which people treat each other as part of a solution rather than as part of a problem. If it does not meet that challenge, it is unlikely that MNCs will be able to take full advantage of their multinational operations.

To increase the chances that MNCs will be capable of optimizing their operations, specific research topics related to organizational learning must be emphasized and intensified in international management as an applied science. There is a need to deepen insights into the relationship between contextual factors, different informational and communicational structures and techniques, the utilization of information, and a firm's effectiveness. The subdisciplines of international management that deal with organizational learning and knowledge have contributed an immense number of descriptive statements but only a small number of explanatory ones, and those of the latter type are, by their very nature, isolated from each other. The most important research task ahead is to develop an integrative theoretical framework that could subsequently serve as a platform for empirical investigations into the effects that specific information and communication situations have on the efficiency and effectiveness of MNCs. The contribution would enable the researchers to accomplish their mission—the creation of applied knowledge.

References

Adler, N. and Jelinek, M. (1986). 'Is "Organizational Culture" Culture Bound?' *Human Resource Management*, 25: 73–90.

Aharoni, Y. (1966). *The Foreign Direct Investment Process*. Boston: Harvard Graduate School of Business Administration.

Allen, L. (1977). *Managing the Flow of Technology*. Cambridge, Mass.: MIT Press.

Andersen, O. (1993). 'On the Internationalization Process of Firms: A Critical Analysis'. *Journal of International Business Studies*, 24: 209–31.

Argyris, C. (1985). *Strategy, Change, and Defensive Routines*. Boston: Pittman.

——(1993). *Knowledge for Action: A Guide to Overcoming Barriers to Organizational Change*. San Francisco: Jossey-Bass.

——and Schön, D. (1978). *Organizational Learning: A Theory of Action Perspective*. Reading, Mass.: Addison-Wesley.

Arrow, K. J. (1962). 'Economic Welfare and the Allocation of Resources', in R. R. Nelson (ed.), *The Rate and Direction of Inventive Activity*. Princeton: Princeton University Press, 609–26.

Audretsch, D. B. and Feldman, M. P. (1996). 'R&D Spillovers and the Geography of Innovation and Production'. *American Economic Review*, 86: 630–40.

Bain, J. S. (1956). *Barriers to New Competition: Their Character and Consequences in Manufacturing Industries*. Boston: Harvard University Press.

Barkema, H. G. and Vermeulen, F. (1998). 'International Expansion through Start-up or Acquisition: A Learning Perspective'. *Academy of Management Journal*, 41: 7–26.

Barnes, B. (1983). 'On the Conventional Character of Knowledge and Cognition', in K. D. Knorr-Cetina and M. Mulkay (eds.), *Science Observed: Perspectives on the Social Study of Science*. Thousand Oaks, Calif.: Sage, 19–51.

Barrett, N. I. and Wilkinson, I. F. (1986). 'Internationalization Behavior: Management Characteristics of Australian Manufacturing Firms by Level of International Development', in P. W. Turnbull and S. J. Paliwoda (eds.), *Research in International Marketing*. London: Croom Helm, 213–33.

Bartholomew, S. (1997). 'National Systems of Biotechnology Innovation: Complex Interdependence in the Global System'. *Journal of International Business Studies*, 28: 241–66.

Bartlett, C. A. (1986). 'Building and Managing the Transnational: The New Organizational Challenge', in M. E. Porter (ed.), *Competition in Global Industries*. Boston: Harvard Business School Press, 367–401.

—— and Ghoshal, S. (1989). *Managing across Borders: The Transnational Solution*. Boston: Harvard Business School Press.

Bateson, G. (1972). *Steps to an Ecology of Mind: A Revolutionary Approach to Man's Understanding of Himself*. New York: Ballantine Books.

Berger, P. L. and Luckmann, T. (1966). *The Social Construction of Reality: A Treatise in the Sociology of Knowledge*. Garden City, NY: Doubleday.

Bilkey, W. J. (1978). 'An Attempted Integration of the Literature on the Export Behavior of Firms'. *Journal of International Business Studies*, 9/1: 33–46.

—— and Tesar, G. (1977). 'The Export Behavior of Smaller Wisconsin Manufacturing Firms'. *Journal of International Business Studies*, 8/1: 93–8.

Birkinshaw, J. M. and Morrison, A. J. (1995). 'Configurations of Strategy and Structure in Subsidiaries of Multinational Corporations'. *Journal of International Business Studies*, 26: 729–53.

—— and Ridderstråle, J. (1996). 'Fighting the Corporate Immune System: A Process Study of Peripheral Initiatives in Multinational Corporations', in *Innovation and International Business: Proceedings of the 22nd Annual EIBA-Conference Stockholm* (Vol. 1), 15–17 December. Stockholm: Institute of International Business, 103–28.

Boje, D. M., Gephart, R. P., and Thatchenkery, T. J. (eds.) (1996). *Postmodern Management and Organization Theory*. Thousand Oaks, Calif.: Sage.

Brannen, M. Y., Liker, J. K., and Fruin, M. (1997). *Recontextualization and Factory-to-Factory Transfer from Japan to the U.S.: The Case of NSK*. Paper presented at the 1997 AIB Annual Meeting, Monterrey, Mexico, 8–12 October.

Brown, W. B. (1976). 'Islands of Conscious Power: MNCs in the Theory of the Firm'. *MSU Business Topics*, 24/1: 37–45.

Buckley, P. J. and Casson, M. (1976). *The Future of the Multinational Enterprise*. London: Macmillan.

Cantwell, J. A. (1989). *Technological Innovation and Multinational Corporations*. Oxford: Basil Blackwell.

—— (1995). 'The Globalisation of Technology: What Remains of the Product Cycle Model?' *Cambridge Journal of Economics*, 19: 155–74.

—— and Santangelo, G. D. (1999). 'The Frontier of International Technology Networks: Sourcing Abroad the Most Highly Tacit Capabilities'. *Information Economics and Policy*, 11: 101–23.

Casson, M. (1979). *Alternatives to the Multinational Enterprise*. London: Macmillan.

—— (1987). *The Firm and the Market: Studies in Multinational Enterprise and the Scope of the Firm*. Oxford: Basil Blackwell.

Caves, R. E. (1971). 'International Corporations: The Industrial Economics of Foreign Investment'. *Economica*, 38: 1–27.

Caves, R. E. (1982). *Multinational Enterprises and Economic Analysis*. Cambridge: Cambridge University Press.

Cavusgil, S. T. (1980). 'On the Internationalization of Firms'. *European Research*, 8: 273–81.

——(1984). 'Differences among Exporting Firms Based on their Degree of Internationalization'. *Journal of Business Research*, 12: 195–208.

Chakravarthy, B. S. and Perlmutter, H. V. (1985). 'Strategic Planning for a Global Business'. *California Journal of World Business*, 20/3: 3–10.

Ciborra, C. U. and Schneider, L. S. (1992). 'Transforming the Routines and Contexts of Management, Work and Technology', in P. S. Adler (ed.), *Technology and the Future of Work*. Cambridge, Mass.: MIT Press, 269–91.

Coase, R. H. (1937). 'The Nature of the Firm'. *Economica*, 4, New Series: 386–405.

Cohen, W. M. and Levinthal, D. A. (1990). 'Absorptive Capacity: A New Perspective on Learning and Innovation'. *Administrative Science Quarterly*, 35: 128–52.

Connor, K. R. (1991). 'A Historical Comparison of Resource-based Theory and Five Schools of Thought within Industrial Organization Economics: Do We Have a New Theory of the Firm?' *Journal of Management*, 17: 121–54.

Crick, D. (1995). 'An Investigation into the Targeting of U.K. Export Assistance'. *European Journal of Marketing*, 29/8: 76–94.

Cyert, R. M. and March, J. G. (1963). *A Behavioral Theory of the Firm*. Englewood Cliffs, NJ: Prentice Hall.

Czinkota, M. R. (1982). *Export Development Strategies: U.S. Promotion Policy*. New York: Praeger.

Davidson, W. H. (1980). *Experience Effects in International Transfer and Technology Transfer*. Ann Arbor: UMI Research Press.

——and McFertridge, D. (1982). *International Technology Transactions and the Theory of the Firm*. Working paper No. 106, Amos Tuck School of Business Administration, Hanover, NH.

Denis, J. E. and Depelteau, D. (1985). 'Market Knowledge, Diversification and Export Expansion'. *Journal of International Business Studies*, 16/3: 77–89.

Denzin, N. K. (1994). *Symbolic Interactionism and Cultural Studies*. Oxford: Blackwell.

DiMaggio, P. J. and Powell, W. W. (1983). 'The Iron Cage Revisited: Institutional Isomorphism and Collective Rationality in Organizational Fields'. *American Sociological Review*, 48: 147–60.

Dodgson, M. (1993). 'Organizational Learning: A Review of Some Literatures'. *Organization Studies*, 14: 375–94.

Dosi, G., Pavitt, K., and Soete, L. (1990). *The Economics of Technical Change and International Trade*. New York: New York University Press.

Doz, Y. L. (1986). *Strategic Management in Multinational Companies*. Oxford: Pergamon.

——and Prahalad, C. K. (1993). 'A Search for a New Paradigm', in S. Ghoshal and D. E. Westney (eds.), *Organization Theory and the Multinational Corporation*. New York: St. Martin's Press, 24–50.

Duncan, R. and Weiss, A. (1979). 'Organizational Learning: Implications for Organizational Design', in B. M. Staw (ed.), *Research in Organizational Behavior: An Annual Series of Analytical Essays and Critical Reviews* (Vol. 1). Greenwich, Conn.: JAI Press, 75–123.

Dunning, J. H. (1993). *Multinational Enterprises and the Global Economy*. Wokingham: Addison-Wesley.

Egelhoff, W. G., Gorman, L., and McCormick, S. (1996). 'The Relationship between Technical Knowledge Flows, Technological Similarity and Change, and Subsidiary Performance', in *Innovation and International Business: Proceedings of the 22nd Annual EIBA-Conference Stockholm* (Vol. 1), 15–17 December. Stockholm: Institute of International Business, 229–50.

Ensign, P. C. (1999). 'The Multinational Corporation as a Coordinated Network: Organizing and Managing Differently'. *Thunderbird International Business Review*, 41: 291–322.

Eriksson, K., Johanson, J., Majkgård, A., and Sharma, D. D. (1997). 'Experiential Knowledge and Cost in the Internationalization Process'. *Journal of International Business Studies*, 28: 337–60.

Erramilli, M. K. (1991). 'The Experience Factor in Foreign Market Entry Behavior of Service Firms'. *Journal of International Business Studies*, 22: 479–501.

—— and Rao, C. P. (1990). 'Choice of Foreign Market Entry Modes by Service Firms: Role of Market Knowledge'. *Management International Review*, 30: 135–50.

Fayerweather, J. (1960). *Management of International Operations: Text and Cases*. New York: McGraw-Hill.

Forsgren, M. (1997). 'The Advantage Paradox of the Multinational Corporation', in I. Björkman and M. Forsgren (eds.), *The Nature of the International Firm*. Copenhagen: Copenhagen Business School Press, 69–85.

Freeman, C. (1995). 'The "National System of Innovation" in Historical Perspective'. *Cambridge Journal of Economics*, 19: 5–24.

Galbraith, J. R. and Edström, A. (1976). 'International Transfer of Managers: Some Important Policy Considerations'. *Columbia Journal of World Business*, 11/2: 100–12.

Ghoshal, S. (1987). 'Global Strategy: An Organizing Framework'. *Strategic Management Journal*, 8: 425–40.

—— and Nohria, N. (1989). 'Internal Differentiation within Multinational Corporations'. *Strategic Management Journal*, 10: 323–37.

—— and Westney, D. E. (1993). 'Introduction and Overview', in S. Ghoshal and D. E. Westney (eds.), *Organization Theory and the Multinational Corporation*. New York: St. Martin's Press, 1–23.

Giddens, A. (1974). *Positivism and Sociology*. London: Heinemann.

—— (1984). *The Constitution of Society: Outline of the Theory of Structuration*. Berkeley: University of California Press.

Gupta, A. K. and Govindarajan, V. (1991). 'Knowledge Flows and the Structure of Control within Multinational Corporations'. *Academy of Management Review*, 16: 768–92.

—— —— (1993). 'Coalignment between Knowledge Flow Patterns and Strategic Systems and Processes within MNCs', in P. Lorange, B. Chakravarthy, J. Roos, and A. Van de Ven (eds.), *Implementing Strategic Processes: Change, Learning and Cooperation*. Oxford: Basil Blackwell, 329–46.

Hamel, G. and Prahalad, C. K. (1985). 'Do You Really Have a Global Strategy?' *Harvard Business Review*, 63/4: 139–48.

Hedlund, G. (1986). 'The Hypermodern MNC—A Heterarchy'. *Human Resource Management*, 25: 9–35.

—— (1993). 'Assumptions of Hierarchy and Heterachy, with Applications to the Management of the Multinational Firm', in S. Ghoshal and D. E. Westney (eds.), *Organization Theory and the Multinational Corporation*. New York: St. Martin's Press, 211–36.

—— and Rolander, D. (1990). 'Action in Heterarchies: New Approaches to Managing the MNC', in C. A. Bartlett, Y. Doz, and G. Hedlund (eds.), *Managing the Global Firm*. London: Routledge, 15–46.

Heenan, D. A. and Perlmutter, H. V. (1979). *Multinational Organization Development*. Reading, Mass.: Addison-Wesley.

Hennart, J.-F. (1982). *A Theory of the Multinational Enterprise*. Ann Arbor: University of Michigan Press.

Holmstrom, B. R. and Tirole, J. (1989). 'The Theory of the Firm', in R. Schmalensee and R. D. Willig (eds.), *Handbook of Industrial Organization*. Amsterdam: North Holland, 61–133.

Huber, G. P. (1990). 'A Theory of the Effects of Advanced Information Technologies on Organizational Design, Intelligence, and Decision-Making'. *Academy of Management Review*, 15: 47–71.

—— (1991). 'Organizational Learning: The Contributing Processes and the Literatures'. *Organization Science*, 2: 88–115.

Hymer, S. H. (1968). 'La Grande Firme multinationale'. *Revue Economic*, 19: 949–73.

—— (1976). *The International Operations of National Firms: A Study of Direct Investment*. Cambridge, Mass.: MIT Press.

Inkpen, A. C. (1998). 'Learning and Knowledge Acquisition through International Strategic Alliances'. *Academy of Management Executive*, 12/4: 69–80.

Johanson, J. and Nonaka, I. (1983). 'Japanese Export Marketing: Structures, Strategies, Counterstrategies'. *International Marketing Review*, 1/1: 12–25.

Johanson, J. and Vahlne, J.-E. (1977). 'The Internationalization Process of the Firm: A Model of Knowledge Development and Increasing Foreign Commitments'. *Journal of International Business Studies*, 8/2: 23–32.

——— (1990). 'The Mechanisms of Internationalization'. *International Marketing Review*, 7/4: 11–24.

Kamiyama, K. (1994). 'The Typical Japanese Overseas Factory', in T. Abo (ed.), *Hybrid Factory: The Japanese Production System in the United States*. Oxford: Oxford University Press, 58–81.

Kenney, M. and Florida, R. (1993). *Beyond Mass Production: The Japanese Lean System and Its Transfer to the U.S.* Oxford: Oxford University Press.

Kets De Vries, M. F. R. (1999). 'High-performance Teams: Lessons from the Pygmies'. *Organizational Dynamics*, 27/3: 66–77.

Kilduff, M. (1992). 'Performance and Interaction Routines in Multinational Corporations'. *Journal of International Business Studies*, 23: 133–45.

—— (1993). 'The Reproduction of Inertia in Multinational Corporations', in S. Ghoshal and D. E. Westney (eds.), *Organization Theory and the Multinational Corporation*. New York: St. Martin's Press, 259–74.

—— and Mehra, A. (1997). 'Postmodernism and Organizational Research'. *Academy of Management Review*, 22: 453–81.

Kindleberger, C. P. (1969). *American Business Abroad: Six Lectures on Direct Investment*. New Haven: Yale University Press.

Kobrin, S. J. (1991). 'An Empirical Analysis of the Determinants of Global Competition'. *Strategic Management Journal*, 12 (Summer special issue): 17–31.

Kogut, B. (1983). 'Foreign Direct Investment as a Sequential Process', in D. B. Audretsch (ed.), *The Multinational Corporation in the 1980s*. Cambridge, Mass.: MIT Press, 38–56.

—— (1991). 'Country Capabilities and the Permeability of Borders'. *Strategic Management Journal*, 12 (Summer special issue): 33–47.

—— (1993). 'Learning, or the Importance of Being Inert: Country Imprinting and International Competition', in S. Ghoshal and D. E. Westney (eds.), *Organization Theory and the Multinational Corporation*. New York: St. Martin's Press, 136–54.

—— and Kulatilaka, N. (1995). 'Operating Flexibility, Global Manufacturing, and the Option Value of a Multinational Network'. *Management Science*, 40: 123–39.

—— and Zander, U. (1992). 'Knowledge of the Firm, Combinative Capabilities, and the Replication of Technology'. *Organization Science*, 3: 383–97.

——— (1993). 'Knowledge of the Firm and the Evolutionary Theory of the Multinational Corporation'. *Journal of International Business Studies*, 24: 625–46.

Krugman, P. (1991). *Geography and Trade*. Cambridge, Mass.: MIT Press.

Laurent, A. (1983). 'The Cultural Diversity of Western Conceptions of Management'. *International Studies of Management and Organization*, 13/1–2: 75–96.

—— (1986). 'The Cross-cultural Puzzle of International Human Resource Management'. *Human Resource Management*, 25: 91–102.

Lawrence, P. R. and Lorsch, J. W. (1967). *Organization and Environment: Managing Differentiation and Integration*. Boston: Harvard University Press.

Li, J. (1994). 'Experience Effects and International Expansion: Strategies of Service MNCs in the Asia-Pacific Region'. *Management International Review*, 34: 217–34.

Lim, J. S., Sharkey, T. W., and Kim, K. I. (1991). 'An Empirical Test of an Export Adoption Model'. *Management International Review*, 31: 51–62.

Lyles, M. A. and Salk, J. E. (1996). 'Knowledge Acquisition from Foreign Parents in International Joint Ventures: An Empirical Examination in the Hungarian Context'. *Journal of International Business Studies*, 27: 877–903.

Macharzina, K. (1993). 'Rahmenbedingungen und Gestaltungsmöglichkeiten bei Umsetzung von globalen Strategieansätzen', in Schmalenbach-Gesellschaft/Deutsche Gesellschaft für Betriebswirtschaft e.V. (ed.), *Internationalisierung der Wirtschaft: Eine Herausforderung an Betriebswirtschaft und Unternehmenspraxis*. Stuttgart: Poeschel, 29–55.

Magee, S. P. (1977). 'Information and the Multinational Corporation: An Appropriability Theory of Foreign Direct Investment', in J. N. Bhagwati (ed.), *The New International Economic Order*. Cambridge, Mass.: MIT Press, 317–40.

Martinez, J. and Jarillo, J. C. (1989). 'The Evolution of Research on Coordination Mechanisms in Multinational Corporations'. *Journal of International Business Studies*, 20: 489–514.

McKern, B. (1994). *International Network Corporations in a Global Economy*. Working paper No. 94-9. Pittsburgh: Carnegie Bosch Institute.

McKiernan, P. (1992). *Strategies of Growth: Maturity, Recovery and Internationalization*. London: Routledge.

McManus, J. (1972). 'The Theory of the Multinational Firm', in G. Paquet (ed.), *The Multinational Firm and the Nation State*. Don Mills, Ontario: Collier-Macmillan, 66–93.

Mead, G. H. (1934). *Mind, Self, and Society: From the Standpoint of a Social Behaviorist*. Chicago: University of Chicago Press.

Moon, J. and Lee, H. (1990). 'On the Internal Correlates of Export Stage Development: An Empirical Investigation in the Korean Electronic Industry'. *International Marketing Review*, 7/5: 16–26.

Negandhi, A. R. and Welge, M. K. (1984). *Beyond Theory Z: Global Rationalization Strategies of American, German and Japanese Multinational Companies*. Greenwich, Conn.: JAI Press.

Nelson, R. R. (ed.) (1993). *National Innovation Systems: A Comparative Analysis*. New York: Oxford University Press.

—— and Winter, S. G. (1977). 'In Search of a Useful Theory of Innovation'. *Research Policy*, 6: 36–76.

—— —— (1982). *An Evolutionary Theory of Economic Change*. Cambridge, Mass.: Belknap Press.

Newman, K. L. and Nollen, S. D. (1996). 'Culture and Congruence: The Fit between Management Practices and National Culture'. *Journal of International Business Studies*, 27: 753–79.

Nonaka, I. (1990). 'Managing Globalization as a Self-renewing Process: Experiences of Japanese MNCs', in C. A. Bartlett, Y. Doz, and G. Hedlund (eds.), *Managing the Global Firm*. London: Routledge, 69–94.

—— (1994). 'A Dynamic Theory of Organizational Knowledge Creation'. *Organization Science*, 5: 14–37.

—— and Takeuchi, H. (1995). *The Knowledge-creating Company: How Japanese Companies Create the Dynamics of Innovation*. New York: Oxford University Press.

Nordström, K. A. (1991). *The Internationalization Process of the Firm: Searching for New Patterns and Explanations*. Stockholm: Institute of International Business.

Ohmae, K. (1990). *The Borderless World*. New York: Harper Business.

Papanastassiou, M. and Pearce, R. D. (1997). 'Technology Sourcing and the Strategic Roles of Manufacturing Subsidiaries in the UK: Local Competences and Global Competences'. *Management International Review*, 37: 5–25.

Pearce, R. D. (1989). *The Internationalization of Research and Development by Multinational Enterprises*. London: Macmillan.

—— and Papanastassiou, M. (1996). 'Overseas R&D and the Strategic Evolution of MNEs: Evidence from Laboratories in the UK', in *Innovation and International Business: Proceedings of the 22nd Annual EIBA-Conference Stockholm* (Vol. 2), 15–17 December. Stockholm: Institute of International Business, 609–37.

—— and Singh, S. (1992). *Globalizing Research and Development*. New York: St. Martin's Press.

Penrose, E. T. (1980). *The Theory of the Growth of the Firm*. London: Basil Blackwell. (Original work published 1959)

Perlmutter, H. V. (1969). 'The Tortuous Evolution of the Multinational Corporation'. *Columbia Journal of World Business*, 4/1: 9–18.

Porter, M. E. (1986). 'Competition in Global Industries: A Conceptual Framework', in M. E. Porter (ed.), *Competition in Global Industries*. Boston: Harvard Business School Press, 15–60.

—— (1990). *The Competitive Advantage of Nations*. London: Macmillan.

Prahalad, C. K. and Doz, Y. L. (1987). *The Multinational Mission*. New York: Free Press.

Rao, T. R. and Naidu, G. M. (1992). 'Are the Stages of Internationalization Empirically Supportable?' *Journal of Global Marketing*, 6/1–2: 147–70.

Reid, S. D. (1983). 'Firm Internationalization, Transaction Costs and Strategic Choice'. *International Marketing Review,* 2/1: 44–56.

Roche, E. M. (1992). *Managing Information Technology in Multinational Corporations.* New York: Macmillan.

Roth, K., Schweiger, D. M., and Morrison, A. J. (1991). 'Global Strategy Implementation at the Business Unit Level: Operational Capabilities and Administrative Mechanisms'. *Journal of International Business Studies,* 22: 369–402.

Rugman, A. M. (1975). 'Motives for Foreign Investment: The Market Imperfection and Risk Diversification Hypotheses'. *Journal of World Trade Law,* 9: 567–73.

—— (1981). *Inside the Multinationals: The Economics of Internal Markets.* London: Croom Helm.

Shrivastava, P. (1983). 'A Typology of Organizational Learning Systems'. *Journal of Management Studies,* 20: 7–28.

Simon, H. A. (1947). *Administrative Behavior: A Study of Decision-making Processes in Administrative Organization.* New York: Macmillan.

—— (1994). *Is International Management Different from Management?* Working paper No. 94-1. Pittsburgh: Carnegie Bosch Institute.

Sölvell, Ö. and Zander, I. (1995). 'Organization of the Dynamic Multinational Enterprise'. *International Studies of Management and Organization,* 25/1–2: 17–38.

Teece, D. J. (1981). 'The Multinational Enterprise: Market Failure and Market Power Considerations'. *Sloan Management Review,* 22/3: 3–17.

Thompson, J. K. and Rehder, R. R. (1996). 'The Gap between the Vision and the Reality: The Case of Nissan UK'. *Journal of General Management,* 21/3: 74–92.

Van Maanen, J. and Laurent, A. (1993). 'The Flow of Culture: Some Notes on Globalization and the Multinational Corporation', in S. Ghoshal and D. E. Westney (eds.), *Organization Theory and the Multinational Corporation.* New York: St. Martin's Press, 275–312.

Vernon, R. (1966). 'International Investment and International Trade in the Product Life Cycle'. *Quarterly Journal of Economics,* 80: 481–94.

—— (1971). *Sovereignty at Bay: The Multinational Spread of U.S. Enterprises.* New York: Basic Books.

—— (1979). 'The Product Life Cycle Hypothesis in a New International Environment'. *Oxford Bulletin of Economics and Statistics,* 41: 255–67.

Vicari, S. (1994). 'Acquisitions as Experimentation', in G. von Krogh, A. Sinatra, and H. Singh (eds.), *The Management of Corporate Acquisitions.* London: Macmillan, 337–58.

von Krogh, G., Roos, J., and Yip, G. (1996). 'A Note on the Epistemology of Globalizing Firms', in G. von Krogh and J. Roos (eds.), *Managing Knowledge: Perspectives on Cooperation and Competition.* Thousand Oaks, Calif.: Sage, 203–17.

Westney, D. E. (1993). 'Institutionalization Theory and the Multinational Corporation', in S. Ghoshal and D. E. Westney (eds.), *Organization Theory and the Multinational Corporation.* New York: St. Martin's Press, 53–76.

White, R. and Poynter, T. (1990). 'Organizing for World-wide Advantage', in C. A. Bartlett, Y. Doz, and G. Hedlund (eds.), *Managing the Global Firm.* London: Routledge, 95–113.

Williamson, O. E. (1975). *Markets and Hierarchies: Analysis and Antitrust Implications.* New York: Free Press.

Yip, G. (1992). *Total Global Strategy: Managing for World-wide Competitive Advantage.* Englewood Cliffs, NJ: Prentice Hall.

29   Learning Through Strategic Alliances

John Child

This chapter provides an overview of salient issues concerning learning through strategic alliances. The term 'strategic alliance' refers to cooperation between firms for the purpose of improving the partners' ability to achieve their strategic objectives. Such alliances can range from equity and contract-based joint ventures to consortia and less formal collaborations (see Child and Faulkner 1998; Lorange and Roos 1992). Some strategic alliances are between firms occupying similar positions in a value chain, where the prime motivation often is to achieve scale economies or reduce the financial risk of costly new projects rather than to acquire knowledge. Other strategic alliances are formed between firms that occupy different positions in a value chain; in this case the acquisition of new competencies may be an important motive behind their cooperation (Garrette and Dussauge 1996). The distinction between alliances along the value-chain and long-standing supplier–customer relationships is that the former normally involve a degree of shared management and formal technology transfer (e.g. through licensing agreements), whereas the latter usually do not. Lane's chapter (Ch. 31 in this volume) addresses learning through customer-supplier networks; they are not included within the scope of the present discussion.

Organizations are increasingly forming alliances with the specific intention of acquiring new knowledge and know-how. Even when alliances are formed for reasons other than learning and knowledge acquisition, such acquisition can be a desirable by-product of their collaboration. As Inkpen (1998) commented, 'in bringing together firms with different skills and knowledge bases, alliances create unique learning opportunities for the partner firms' (p. 69). The prospect of acquiring relatively advanced technology and management expertise is a major reason firms from emerging countries favor alliances with those from developed countries. The partners from developed countries often view such alliances as an opportunity to learn about unfamiliar business environments (Child and Czeglédy 1996; Steensma and Lyles 2000). In sectors like biotechnology, which have a rapidly expanding but dispersed knowledge base, alliances form part of wide 'networks of learning' (Powell, Koput, and Smith-Doerr 1996). Successful cooperation between firms requires a learning process by the partners (Inkpen 1995a). Yet, despite its undoubted importance, rather little is known about learning through alliances or other forms of interorganizational cooperation (Choi and Lee 1997; Larsson, Bengtsson, Henriksson, and Sparks-Graham 1994; von Krogh and Roos 1996).

Two defining dimensions position strategic alliances in relation to the other forms of interorganizational cooperation considered in Part VI of this handbook. The first dimension is the extent to which the cooperation is managed through formalized contractual provisions that

The author wishes to acknowledge the Daimler-Benz Foundation's support of the production of this paper and the funding of case study investigations that have informed its content. He is also very grateful to Sally Heavens, his coworker in this research, for the insightful comments she provided on a previous draft.

may be market- or hierarchy-based as opposed to implicit relationships usually heavily dependent on interpersonal trust. The second dimension is the extent of the transactional reach involved in the cooperation between organizations, namely, the extensiveness and spread of such transactions. Transactional reach is highest in the case of global business dealings, whether through markets or multinational corporations. By contrast, it can be quite limited in local networks or in the case of focused links between strategic alliance partners. These distinctions give rise to the framework set out in Fig. 29.1, which compares the subject of this chapter with the subjects of the other chapters in Part VI. This positioning is very approximate; some forms of interorganizational cooperation, such as customer–supplier networks, can vary considerably in their transactional reach. The level of trust is also a variable factor and one that tends to increase in importance the longer the experience that partners have of working together (Gulati 1995; Inkpen 1996). The framework can also help one appreci-

ate that there are different forms of strategic alliance, such as contract-based alliances like licensing, and equity joint ventures that have their own management systems and involve interpersonal and implicit relationships as well as contractual provisions. Equity joint ventures have been found to be more effective vehicles for the acquisition of knowledge from partners than are contract-based alliances, especially when knowledge is complex and tacit in nature (Kogut 1988; Mowery, Oxley, and Silverman 1996).

The nature of learning through strategic alliances is considered next in this chapter. I then discuss collaborative and competitive learning motives among partner organizations and the implications these motives have for the process of learning and alliance evolution. This treatment informs the understanding of the requirements for learning through alliances and of the barriers that may stand in the way of this learning. In the concluding section, I note implications for the practical management of learning through strategic alliances.

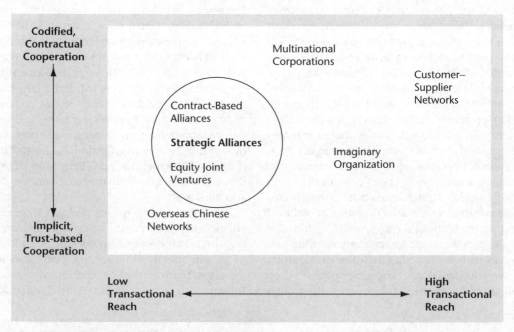

Fig. 29.1. A framework for comparing strategic alliances with other forms of interorganizational cooperation

The Nature of Learning through Strategic Alliances

Strategic alliances are hybrid arrangements for they combine the strategic objectives and cultures of the partner organizations. When they are achieved through the establishment of a new joint venture, alliances may also have to combine elements of the partners' management structures and systems (Borys and Jemison 1989). The hybrid nature of alliances has a number of implications for the possibilities of learning through them; these implications are explored in later parts of this chapter. A positive feature is that the complementary expertise and knowledge brought to an alliance by partners can promote learning both through transfer and through the dynamic synergy that may be stimulated by the coming together of experts from different corporate, and perhaps national, backgrounds. Alliances between comparatively small, research-intensive biotechnology firms and rather large pharmaceutical companies with expertise in development, production, and marketing serve as one example (Schacht 1999). A problematic feature lies in the barriers to knowledge-sharing between alliance partners, barriers that can arise for a number of reasons. The underlying relationship between the partners may remain fundamentally competitive. It may prove difficult to reconcile the different corporate or social identities of their staff. The members of an organization may assume that they have nothing to learn from their partners. Companies may not have the experience or capacity to acquire and absorb the knowledge available from their alliance partners.

Lindholm (1997) categorized three different processes through which learning can take place in international joint ventures. The first is the *transfer of knowledge* by the partners to the joint venture, much of it in the form of technology transfer. A similar transfer of knowledge may take place directly between partners who collaborate by means other than setting up a separate joint venture. This form of transfer involves the movement of existing technology, knowledge, or management practice into an organizational setting for which such transfer represents a new knowledge input. The second learning process is different because it involves the creation of *new* knowledge, or at least a *substantial transformation* of existing knowledge, within the ambit of the cooperative venture. This process implies that mutual learning occurs through a constructive integration of the different inputs offered by the partners and their members. This type of learning is qualitatively different from learning through knowledge transfer, and its realization presents a correspondingly greater challenge (see Child and Markóczy 1993). It is, nevertheless, one of the potential prizes of cooperation between organizations that can offer one another valuable complementary knowledge. The third learning process, which Lindholm (1997) termed 'harvesting' (p. 141), involves the retrieval of knowledge that has been generated in the joint venture or other collaborative unit and its internalization within the parent firms so that they can use it in other areas of operation. These processes indicate that strategic alliances can provide a means to acquire or generate knowledge that might otherwise not be available. Alliances can also be an important vehicle for the incorporation of new knowledge into practice, particularly through the medium of joint ventures or cross-partner teams that work on the necessary adaptation and application of knowledge drawn from the partners.

The type of learning to which strategic alliances aspire will depend on their purpose and the involvement and needs of their partners. For this reason, it is useful to distinguish the levels of knowledge being transferred between alliance partners and between them and their joint venture. Knowledge can be classified into different levels of intrinsic composition and scope of organizational application: technical, systemic, and strategic. Each level has equivalent learning processes. The *technical* level refers to the acquisition of new, specific techniques, such as those for quality measurement, for systematic market research, or for personnel selection. This level broadly corresponds to single-loop or routine learning (see Argyris and Schön 1978; Pawlowsky 1992). The *systemic* level of knowledge pertains to organizational systems and procedures. The focus here is on an integrative type of learning that involves the restructuring of relationships and the creation of new roles. This notion parallels that of organizational reframing or double-loop learning. The *strategic* level of knowledge concerns the mind-sets of senior managers, especially their criteria of organizational success and their mental maps of the factors significant for achieving that success. The type of learning associated with the strategic level of knowledge involves reflexive cognitive processes that may generate new insights and promote strategic proactiveness. This type of learning is likely to be the most difficult of the three to achieve (Child and Rodrigues 1996), a point to which I return later.

In several frameworks learning processes are conceived of in terms of three or four stages (see Berthoin Antal 1997: 16). Following Kolb (1984), one can express these stages in terms of an organizational learning cycle: data $\longrightarrow$ information $\longrightarrow$ knowledge $\longrightarrow$ wisdom. According to this scheme, data become available to an organization in raw form; the data are not categorized or standardized. At a further stage these data are categorized and analyzed in a manner that permits inferences to be drawn: They become information. Once the information is considered and reviewed critically in terms of the context of its applicability, the information becomes knowledge. Experience with applying the knowledge leads to wisdom; that is, an appreciation is built up of when and how the knowledge can be applied, especially to new and unfamiliar circumstances, and what its limits are. The limits to knowledge become apparent through problems in its application. The problems generate fresh data, and an awareness of the limits to knowledge may prompt a search for further data. The learning cycle thus moves on again over time (see also Weber and Berthoin Antal, Ch. 15 in this volume).

Within strategic alliances, even the transfer of *existing knowledge* or practice may involve movement around much of this organizational learning cycle. Abstract and codified knowledge reverts to the status of data for people receiving it for the first time, if they are not in a position to validate it immediately. Members of alliances will be unable to validate such knowledge if it is not structured in a manner familiar to them. Technical knowledge *qua* knowledge should be easier to absorb if it is already classified and codified according to widely accepted and known standards, but this characteristic is less likely to be true of systemic and strategic knowledge. The creation of *new knowledge* through mutual learning within a strategic alliance may involve several passes through the organizational learning cycle. In this case the alliance is used to draw upon a number of different knowledge systems, none of which may have been applied previously to the specific circumstances faced by the alliance. A number of attempts may be required to arrive at acceptable and effective schemes of classification and codification, and at least one pilot project may be necessary to demonstrate the wisdom of the emerging approach for the new circumstances.

For present purposes, two features of the organizational learning cycle are particularly significant. The first is that within the cycle information passes through various levels of abstraction, codification, and diffusion (Boisot 1998). When information is presented in a form that is abstract enough to possess meaning for a variety of situations and codified enough as to be easy to articulate in a precise manner, then one could say that the information was in an explicit rather than a tacit form.[1] However,

[1] Polanyi (1966) distinguished between tacit knowledge and explicit knowledge. The former is usually regarded as personal, intuitive, and context-specific. It is therefore difficult to verbalize, formalize, and communicate to others. Explicit knowledge, by contrast, is specified and codified. It can therefore be transmitted through formal, systematic language. To make tacit knowledge available in a form that permits its retention for future use by an organization at large and, even more, that enables it to be shared among several cooperating organizations, it must be converted into a codified or programmable form. This conversion may not be possible, either for technical reasons or because the people with tacit knowledge do not wish to lose their control over it.

although the explicitness of information *within* the terminology of one organization assists its diffusion and wide use within that organization, it does not necessarily do so *between* organizations. A problem can arise in learning through strategic alliances when there is a desire to transfer knowledge based on experience grounded in the specific concrete situation of one partner to the situation of the other partner or when there is a desire to meld the two together as a basis for mutual learning. This knowledge may well have become codified in routines of one organization that do not match those of the other partner organization(s). These routines will almost certainly require an abstraction of the underlying principles, followed by the experimental application of these principles to the different circumstances of the partner organization (Lillrank 1995). Hence, initial decodification of the knowledge and its recontextualization are necessary before the knowledge can be recodified into a form that suits the other partner(s) or their joint activity. This process may take time, effort, and commitment to achieve and therefore it constitutes a potential barrier to inter-organizational learning. It is likely to pose a problem in particular for systemic and strategic learning, because there will have developed systems and policies that are very specific to the circumstances of each organization and that are couched in its unique language and culture.

In addition to the problem of translation from the milieu of one alliance partner to that of another, the passage of information and knowledge between different actors or groups in the learning cycle implies that constructive relationships must exist between them for the process to be effective. Knowledge is socially constituted because it is created or compiled by social groups who have a sense of ownership over it. This sense of ownership means that the groups will attribute value to the knowledge and will assume the right to arbitrate over this value (see Child and Heavens, Ch. 13 in this volume). In other words, social identity is vested in different systems and bodies of knowledge. When knowledge is transferred between organizations, or when the members of different organizations pool their knowledge resources, the question of how these organizations perceive the validity of what is, for them, novel knowledge will impinge on the extent to which they are prepared to accept and work with this knowledge (Child and Rodrigues 1996).

The issue of validity is likely to be more sensitive for systemic and strategic knowledge and practice than it is for knowledge of a primarily technical nature. Although technical knowledge is also socially constituted, several of its characteristics reduce its sensitivity to being transferred or shared between different organizations. One of these characteristics is that technical knowledge is often expressed in a widely accessible, standardized form, some of it in the form of international standards. Another is that technical knowledge is accepted as valid by trained specialists who have a relatively cosmopolitan identity that can bridge discrete organizational identities. Problems can arise, of course, when knowledge generation requires the collaboration of people from different specialties, for then presence of widely validated technical standards can increase the problem of integration.

Competitive and Collaborative Learning between Organizations

Strategic alliances face a tradeoff between the opportunities they offer for generating and sharing knowledge and the possibility that the partner may act opportunistically (Mody 1993). This question comes down to whether the partners' learning goals are complementary or competitive, either in terms of the cost–benefit calculus for forming and maintaining a specific alliance or, more fundamentally, in terms of their location within industry or market structures. Khanna, Gulati, and Nohria (1998) identified two qualitatively different kinds of benefit that are available to partners in alliances in which their primary objective is to learn from each other. The first kind is private benefits, which a firm can unilaterally acquire through learning from its partner and apply to its operations in areas not related to the alliance's activities. In this case, the partners have divergent goals for learning through an alliance. The presence of private benefits is likely to encourage a race between the partners to exploit opportunities to learn from each other. Once they have done so, there is little incentive for the winner to continue the cooperation. Even out-and-out competitors may collaborate in order to benefit from learning opportunities, but they will be wary about sharing their knowledge. A fundamentally competitive relationship will render the balance between the contributions each partner makes to the alliance, and the benefits each is able to extract from it, a sensitive issue. Such a relationship encourages opportunism. In this kind of situation, the co-operation is often relatively short-lived, and the partners may well revert to competing with each other if and when their alliance breaks up.

The second kind is common benefits, which arise from mutual learning within the scope of the alliance and applies to the alliance's own operations. Common benefits foster continued cooperation and investment in the use of alliances as vehicles for mutual learning. Many strategic alliances are formed between organizational partners who perceive that they can benefit from their complementarities (Geringer 1991). This perception gives them a common interest in learning how to extract the potential synergies between their respective competencies. An absence of fundamental competition between the partners will also promote their sharing of knowledge and its accumulation as an alliance asset over time (Bleeke and Ernst 1993).

There are therefore two possible learning situations within a strategic alliance. One, competitive learning, is based on an underlying attitude of competition between the partners; the other, collaborative learning, is based on an underlying spirit of collaboration between them.

Competitive Learning

Competitive learning is a situation in which one alliance partner intends to learn as much as possible from the other rather than adopt mutual learning as the priority. Larsson et al. (1994) noted that the endeavor by partners to maximize their appropriation of the joint outcomes of collective learning undermines the very conditions, particularly mutual trust, for the generation of learning between them. Reporting on his investigations of international strategic alliances, Hamel (1991) described this dilemma as 'competition for competence':

[M]anagers often voiced a concern that, when collaborating with a potential competitor, failure to 'outlearn' one's partner could render a firm first dependent and then redundant within the partnership, and competitively vulnerable outside it. The two premises from which this concern issued seemed to be that (1) few alliances were perfectly and perpetually collusive, and (2) the fact that a firm chose to collaborate with a present or potential competitor could not be taken as evidence that that firm no longer harbored a competitive intent *vis-à-vis* its partner. (p. 84)

Hamel pointed to the possibility that asymmetric learning between alliance partners derives from the fact that they have failed, or are unwilling, to transform their partnership into a fully cohesive organization. The lack of perfect collusion is a failure by the partners to achieve total integration of their operations within the joint venture. A race develops between the partners to learn from the other, for their own advantage rather than for the benefit of the alliance as an organization in its own right. Performance in this race is associated with interpartner bargaining power. The partner with the most bargaining power can, during the formation of the alliance, establish conditions favorable for it to achieve asymmetric learning by, for instance, insisting that the other partner's technology be made fully available. A projected alliance between one of the world's largest software producers and a smaller European computer systems firm with strong niche positions gave rise to considerable fears within the latter that it would be 'sucked dry' by the dominant partner (J. Child, personal interview, 28 May 1997). Successful asymmetric learning during the life of the alliance will, in turn, enhance the more effective partner's bargaining power *vis-à-vis* the other to the point where the former dominates the alliance or where the alliance breaks up under the strains that asymmetry generates (Makhija and Ganesh 1997). Indeed, Bleeke and Ernst (1995) claimed that nearly 80 per cent of joint ventures ultimately end up in a sale by one of the partners, and they urged partner CEOs to plan for this outcome.

Pucik (1991), referring to technology transfer in strategic alliances, maintained that the partners should approach the matter in a planned, rather than haphazard, manner. He argued that 'not providing a coherent strategy for the control of invisible assets in a partnership is a sure formula for failure' (p. 127). However, if alliance partners adopt a competitive view of one another, they may be encouraged to hold back their knowledge as a defensive measure. This tactic was used within a collaboration between a Norwegian microbiology company and a U.K. water company with responsibility for sewage treatment. After some eighteen months of joint work, it was discovered that the Norwegians were misleading their U.K. partner by not releasing full information on certain technical issues because they believed that withholding this information would preserve their unique value. 'They were protecting their company's independence', one informant remarked (J. Child and S. Heavens, personal interviews, 2 February 1998). Another example is when a company in a developing country holds back its tacit knowledge of local networks from a multinational partner because of the often justified fear that the latter, once it has acquired this knowledge, will have no further need for genuine cooperation. If both or all partners adopt this tactic, they are likely to face major difficulties in converting each partner's tacitly and/or covertly held knowledge into a form usable for cooperative activities. Such behavior can, obviously, become counterproductive to the success of the cooperative venture, which almost certainly requires some mutual learning

in order to achieve other strategic objectives as well.

The prisoner's dilemma applies to learning within a competitive strategic alliance. That is, opportunism between partners is encouraged when an individual partner can gain considerably by reneging on the other. Yet such behavior destroys the potential for all partners to gain (Axelrod 1984). The prisoner's-dilemma paradigm, however, also indicates that alliance partners are likely to learn the most together when they all choose collaborative learning strategies, which involve high levels of openness (transparency) and receptivity to new knowledge. This model of being a 'good partner' in strategic alliances (Larsson *et al.* 1994: 16) points to the benefits of collaborative learning.

Collaborative Learning

Collaborative learning can occur when alliance partners do not regard themselves as fundamentally in competition or as having irreconcilable long-term interests. Alliances between organizations can enhance learning on this basis in two main ways (Inkpen 1995a: 53–4). One involves learning *from* a partner; the other involves learning *with* a partner.

In the first case, collaboration provides access to the partner's knowledge and skills, which can include product and process technology, organizational skills, and knowledge about new environments (among other things, an introduction to key relationships within them). Transfer can be achieved in several ways, such as through the exchange of data sets and secondment of key personnel, with the intention of grafting new knowledge onto, or even having it transform, existing activities (Huber 1991). If the alliance takes the form of a new unit, such as a joint venture established for a specific purpose, the knowledge sought from partners may be relevant only to and embodied only in the outputs of that unit. Such learning may not have any general value outside the scope of the particular collaboration. There is, however, always a danger of underestimating that value for the partner's overall organization of knowledge acquired in this way. Moreover, there is a risk that imported new knowledge, like any graft, will be rejected.

Although the transfer of knowledge held by a partner is a frequent and important motive for entering into a strategic alliance, it can also be an unexpected benefit of collaboration that is undertaken primarily for other reasons. Olivetti Corporation's experience demonstrates how alliances can open up important organizational learning opportunities that were not envisaged or given much importance when the alliance was first formed. Olivetti's main strategic alliance during the 1980s was its partnership with AT&T Corporation between 1983 and 1989. The alliance had a range of goals, many related to controlling the environment, such as forming a defense against IBM's dominance, introducing a new operating system (UNIX) in Europe as well as in the United States, and easing both companies' access to each other's markets. Although only a few of the alliance's stated goals were achieved, it had some positive, if unexpected, results for Olivetti as an exercise in learning. One was the acquisition and absorption of new knowledge through the broadening of Olivetti's management horizons. As a supplier to AT&T, Olivetti was also transformed rapidly into a major vendor of personal computers. Ciborra (1991: 66) observed of this and other Olivetti alliances that 'what seems to be particularly significant here is that in each alliance the elements of surprise and tinkering seem to have played a role in learning at least as important as the specific contractual arrangement'.

The second mode of collaborative learning in a strategic alliance involves learning with a partner. One example is the accumulation of mutual experience with and knowledge about how to manage interorganizational cooperation *per se*. This benefit is becoming increasingly significant in a world where business activity is coming to be organized through strategic alliances, including those whose management has to cope with cultural differences and unfamiliar environments. This mode of learning falls primarily into the category of systemic learning, although for a successful collaboration it is also important that its members learn how to learn together (deutero-learning). Collaborative know-how might be used later in the design and management of other collaborations. Lyles (1988), for instance, found unanimous agreement among managers and staff of two U.S. and two European firms, all of them with a successful history of operating joint ventures in an international context, that there was a valuable transference of experience from previous ventures. This transference took place largely through the sharing of experiences, the continuity of top management's oversight, and the development of management systems. The companies were also able to use their experience as a credential, an advantage that facilitated their efforts to form new joint ventures.

The alliance between the Royal Bank of Scotland and the Banco Santander of Spain, launched in October 1988, provides examples of collaborative learning both from and with each partner. Senior officials from both partners perceive the alliance as having promoted organizational learning of mutual benefit. Each partner was able to learn about and absorb improvements in banking operations as well as learn over time how to deepen the process of working together. Initially, the major areas of cooperation between the two banks included access to branches, shared ownership of German and Belgian banks, offshore banking in Gibraltar, merchant banking, technology development, and acquisitions. As an act of faith and demonstration of commitment, the two companies exchanged a small percentage of their equity.

Comments by senior managers in both banks illustrate the learning that has been achieved with the alliance partner, again, not all of it anticipated. The chief executive of the Royal Bank commented:

We have been surprised by the intangible benefits from the alliance, as each side has got to know and observe the working practices of the other. Simple things like the differing ways in which we prepare and organize meetings; the nature and content of papers presented to internal audiences; and differences in structures and reporting relationships have all provided ample food for thought. (Faulkner 1994: 168)

With reference to business lending, the Royal Bank's alliance manager remarked:

Santander have put a huge amount of time and expertise into that area. And there is a huge amount of money that can be saved in terms, not just of cost, but also of time. So I think that is learning from what they have learned . . . it's the capability of the other organization, it's being prepared, both ways, to help out. (J. Child, personal interview, 2 May 1997)

The director of the alliance for Banco Santander remarked:

We have learnt best how to launch an interest bearing current account after having learnt what RBS's experience has been. We admire how they develop business by phone, even selling loans. At top management level we are exchanging views on how best to handle credits, and geographical risks. On the Royal side, they look at our branch network with five people or less per branch, and compare it with their average of nine. Probably they will centralize the back office more. Also they are very good at serving customers, and we are very good at developing profitable customers . . . those are processes that are on going and enriching on both sides. (Faulkner 1994: 173)

The same Banco Santander director noted that 'Selling is one thing that very definitely, and from the top down, the Royal Bank has incorporated from our culture' (J. Child, personal interview, 16 June 1997).

Alliance Evolution and Learning

A cooperative alliance develops as a relationship over time. This realization leads to the notion of thinking about the evolution of strategic alliance in terms of a life cycle, just as one refers to the concepts of product or technology life cycles (Lorange and Roos 1992; Murray and Mahon 1993). Over time, a collaboration moves from initial contact, through negotiations and start-up, to a phase of managed cooperation. This development may, in turn, lead to an extension of the cooperation, a drift toward separation, or a rather abrupt decision to divorce. Extension and deepening of the cooperation, based partly on learning how to work together and achieve synergies between complementary competencies, might eventually lead to a free-standing entity with a sense of its own identity and independent management. Faulkner (1995), drawing from over sixty case studies, identified a direct link between organizational learning and the alliance life cycle. He concluded that an underlying learning philosophy is one of several conditions necessary for successful alliance evolution, along with strong bonding and regular new projects. To prevent the collaboration from becoming dormant because of operational mismatches or overdependence on one partner, constant adjustments are needed.

Others have similarly explored the role of learning in alliance evolution. Doz (1996), for example, conducted longitudinal case studies of six projects in three strategic alliances. He found that successful alliances were highly evolutionary and went through a sequence of interactive cycles of learning, reevaluation, and readjustment. By contrast, unsuccessful projects were characterized by little learning or by a failure to carry through learning at the cognitive level to behavioral adjustment in organizational routines (see also Kieser, Beck, and Tainio, Ch. 27 in this volume). Makhija and Ganesh (1997) postulated that the learning process introduces subtle changes over time in the relationship between alliance partners, especially in their need for each other and, hence, their relative bargaining power. These changes must be managed if the alliance is not to come under strain and fail.

Schacht (1995) explored the evolution of three international strategic alliances entered into by Hoechst AG and the association of this evolution with the learning they achieved. He found that the rates of technical, systemic, and strategic learning over time varied between the three cases. For example, in two of the cases the rate of learning about new strategic opportunities increased over time as the collaboration deepened, but in the third case it appeared to remain rather low. The third case was a collaboration that Hoechst had with Bayer AG on the development and promotion of an anti-AIDS drug. Although close, informal communication developed between the companies' research scientists, which led to a rising rate of technical learning, the static rate of strategic learning appeared to result from the persistence of purely formal communication at relatively high organizational levels where goals were set for the collaboration and strategic issues discussed.

In a subsequent, more extensive study of strategic alliances between biotechnology and pharmaceutical firms, Schacht (1999) found that there is a clear relationship between the evolution of alliances in terms of their scale, scope, and intensity and the degree of organizational learning achieved. Technical learning showed the greatest association with alliance evolution, followed by systemic learning and strategic learning. The adoption of a highly collaborative, trust-based, integrated approach to learning-related activities within the alliances was most effective in promoting learning. Schacht concluded that awareness, and active management, of strategic alliance life cycles and of their implications for organizational learning is vital for the future of biopharmaceutical cooperation. His assessment was that the degree to which strategic alliances evolve has more impact on the organizational learning that they produce than do the value-chain elements combined in the alliance or the relative size of the partners.

The evolution of collaborative relationships is itself also affected by the learning objectives that alliance partners attach to their cooperation. If they are committed to the idea of mutual learning within the partnership for an indefinite period, their relationship is likely to evolve progressively. If, on the other hand, they regard the cooperation as a one-off opportunity to access knowledge that they may subsequently turn to competitive advantage against their partners—an attitude of competitive learning—then clearly the scope for alliance evolution is limited. The partners' rates of learning need to be kept in equilibrium, or at least in a mutually acceptable balance, if an alliance is to evolve through the intensification of a cooperative relationship.

Requirements for Learning through Strategic Alliances

Even when partners undertake to collaborate with a view to mutual benefit and learning, certain requirements must be met in order for it to take place. One is that learning is included in a partner's intentions when that partner enters into a cooperative relationship, or at least that the partner is willing to take the opportunities for learning that arise. Another is that the partner must have the necessary capacity to learn. This capacity includes an ability to internalize within its core organization the knowledge that it acquires through an alliance so that this knowledge becomes a collective organizational property. Although all these requirements appear to be rather obvious, they are not easy to achieve in practice.

Partner Intentions

In a detailed study of nine international alliances, Hamel (1991) found that the partners varied considerably in the extent to which they viewed the collaboration as a learning opportunity and that this variation was an important determinant of what they actually learned. For instance, several of the Western firms had not intended to absorb knowledge and skills from their Japanese partners when they first entered alliances with them. The Western firms initially appeared to be satisfied with substituting their partner's competitive superiority in a particular area for their own lack in this area. In every case where this intent of substitution was maintained, the partners failed to learn in any systematic way from their collaboration.

Other companies, including many of the Japanese partners, entered into alliances regarding them as transitional devices in which their primary objective was to capture their partner's skills. In several cases, partners undertook cooperative strategies for the purpose of learning the business (especially to meet international requirements), mastering a technology, and establishing a presence in new markets. These cases illustrate the intention of a company to use collaborative learning opportunities to enhance its competitive position and internalize its partners' skills rather than collaborate over the long term and be content merely with accessing instead of acquiring a partner's skills. The threat that this strategy poses to an unwitting partner is obvious and does not foster an enduring long-term cooperative relationship. When learning *from* a partner is the goal, the termination of a cooperation agreement should not necessarily be seen as a failure, nor should its stability and longevity be seen as evidence of success. Hamel (1991) noted that one partner's ability to outstrip the learning of the other(s) contributes to an enhancement of that partner's bargaining power within the cooperative relationship, reducing its dependence on the other partner(s) and hence providing a gateway to the next stage of internalizing those partners' knowledge and skills. For these reasons, Hamel concluded that, in order to realize the learning opportunities offered by an alliance, a partner must both give priority to learning and consciously consider how to go about it.

To illustrate a clear intention to learn from interorganizational cooperation, Inkpen (1995a) cited the case of an American automotive supplier [referred to as 'Beta Corporation'] that, like many others in its sector, was losing market share to Japanese companies in the early 1980s (p. 92). The formation of a joint venture with a Japanese company that was closely linked to one of the largest Japanese car manufacturers was seen by the American company's management as an excellent opportunity to learn about Japanese management.

Learning Capacity

A partner's capacity to learn will be determined by a combination of factors: the transferability of the knowledge, the receptivity of the partner's members to new knowledge, members' competencies to understand and absorb the knowledge, and their incorporation of the lessons from previous experience.

Transferability

Unlike the other three factors listed, transferability refers to a quality of the knowledge itself rather than to a feature of the would-be learning partner. Transferability concerns the ease with which a type of knowledge can be transferred from one party to another. Explicit knowledge, such as technical product specifications, is relatively easy to transfer and be absorbed. Not so with tacit knowledge, which is less codified than explicit knowledge. I discussed earlier, with reference to the organizational learning cycle, the technical problems of transferability.

Receptivity

The more receptive people are to new knowledge, the more likely they are to learn. When the members of a collaborating partner organization adopt the attitude of students toward their counterparts in the other partner organization, they are being more receptive to insights from that partner than if they assume that they already possess superior techniques, organizing abilities, and strategic judgment. For example, some Chinese partners in joint ventures with foreign companies make the mistake of assuming that they cannot learn useful motivational practices from their foreign collaborators because they already have a superior knowledge of Chinese workers. To an equal degree, some foreign partners unwisely disdain advice from their Chinese collaborators on the best ways to relate to external governmental authorities that wield an unusual degree of influence over the conditions for doing business (Child 1994).

Hamel (1991) found several factors that influence a partner organization's receptivity. Firms that had entered an alliance as laggards, in order to access an easy way out of a deteriorating competitive situation, tended to possess little enthusiasm for learning from the other partner or little belief that they could achieve it. They tended to be trapped by deeply embedded cultures and behaviors, which made the task of opening up to new knowledge all the more difficult. In clinging to the past, they were not capable of unlearning, a necessary prerequisite to learning (Hedberg 1981).

Receptivity also depends on the availability of time and resources for engaging in the processes of gathering knowledge and embedding it within the organization's own routines through staff training and investment in new facilities. The paradox of deteriorating competitiveness as both a pressure to learn and a constraint on being able to achieve learning becomes critical for poorly performing partners. In some alliances, this paradox may be resolved through the additional cash and other resources that are injected by the other partner. If a collaborator has, however, slipped far behind its partner(s) in the skills and competencies necessary for it to absorb new knowledge, it may find it extremely difficult to close the gap.

Competence

Cohen and Levinthal (1990) argued that a firm's 'absorptive capacity' is a crucial competence for its learning and innovative capabilities. Absorptive competence is a firm's ability to recognize the value of new, external information, to assimilate it, and to apply it to commercial ends. This competence is largely a function of the firm's level of prior related knowledge. Hence, existing competence favors the acquisition of new competence, which implies that a partner entering an alliance with learning objectives should ensure that it does so with not only a positive attitude toward learning but also at least a minimal level of skills. If those skills are not available, the training of staff to acquire them should be an immediate priority.

Competence is required at all three levels of knowledge—strategic, system, and technical— if a partner is to take advantage of the opportunities for learning offered through cooperation with other organizations. At the strategic level, collaboration that is perceived as peripheral to a partner's overall strategy will probably yield relatively few opportunities for the transfer of learning from the collaboration back into the partner's main organization. This tendency emerges because the lack of perceived strategic

importance is likely to reduce the level of interaction between the partner and the cooperative venture. A related problem arises from a partner's failure to appreciate that it can derive broad strategic lessons from the cooperation rather than ones restricted to comparatively narrow issues. General Motors Corporation, for example, approached its NUMMI joint venture with Toyota Motor Corporation with the expectation that what it could learn from Toyota would be confined to production skills in the manufacturing of small cars. As a consequence, although the lessons to be learned were actually of general relevance, they were not applied to General Motors as a whole (Inkpen 1995a: 63).

Competence at the systemic level is required in order to make the most innovative use of new knowledge or technology that is acquired. For example, the introduction of mill-wide computerization in the paper and pulp industry opened up radical, new possibilities for the constructive redesign of mill organization and the combined empowerment and enrichment of mill workers' jobs. This new technological development came about through close cooperation between paper manufacturers and system suppliers. The ability of U.K. paper manufacturers to take full advantage of the potential offered by the new systems depended on their organizational vision and competence in terms of being able to envisage and accept radically changed roles and relationships (Child and David 1987).

It is self-evident that a partner needs to possess adequate skills that enable it to absorb and use new technical knowledge. With the complex nature of many modern technologies, and with the importance of deploying them in conjunction with the 'human' skills and motivations of employees, multidisciplinary technical competence is required. In particular, inadequate competence in the partner's language can cause problems in international alliances. As Hamel (1991) noted, the fact that almost all employees in Western firms lacked Japanese language skills and cultural experience in Japan limited their access to their Japanese partners' know-how. Their Japanese partners did not suffer from a lack of language competence to the same degree, and they benefited from the access that their linguistic skills gave them to their partners' knowledge. Similarly, Villinger (1996) found that in eastern central European firms acquired by Western companies, both Eastern and Western managers perceived language and communication deficiencies to be the main barriers to learning between the two parties, even though for the most part rather little priority was given to improving language competencies.

Previous Experience

Two aspects of experience can facilitate learning through strategic alliances. The first is experience of having formed and managed previous alliances. The second is experience of having collaborated with the same partner.

Previous experience of alliances is a double-edged sword for subsequent learning capacity. Previous alliance experience might well enhance a partner's capacity to learn through subsequent alliances. Such an outcome depends, however, on the lessons of that experience being passed on to the persons involved in a subsequent alliance and on the relevance of the experience. If the circumstances of a subsequent alliance are very different, the formalization of experience gained from a previous alliance into an organization's routines can actually create a barrier to further learning. Being good at single-loop learning may therefore constitute a handicap for double-loop learning (Argyris and Schön 1978). These observations are prompted by research such as Inkpen's (1995a: 65–6), which found that previous joint venture experience of partners with Japanese companies did not lead to improvements in their learning process. Simonin (1997) found that firms do not always capitalize on their previous alliance experience in order to develop their collaborative know-how, and that the experience was not always relevant. Barkema, Shenkar, Vermeulen, and Bell (1997) found that previous experience with domestic joint ventures and international subsidiaries contributed to the longevity of international joint ventures as long as that experience was relevant in the sense that it related both to the firm's core business and to a similar context: that is, developed versus developing country.

If there is an intention to collaborate for mutual benefit on a long-term basis, the experience of working together should in itself create relationship assets for the partners. They will acquire some understanding of each other's capabilities, and they are likely to have established a degree of mutual confidence and trust (Gulati 1995). The fact that they have already got through the initial period of working together will have generated a degree of commitment to one another (Fichman and Levinthal 1991). For these reasons, previous direct alliances between organizations increase the probability of new alliances between them (Gulati and Gargiulo 1999). The benefits of their previous joint experience are expected to encourage partners to be open toward each other, and this openness increases the chances that they will learn through their new alliance. Again, however, this expectation needs to be treated with caution, for previous experience of working together has been found to not affect the learning efforts of joint venture parent companies (Simonin 1997). Inkpen (1998) qualified 'the logical notion that prior partner relationships is a factor in learning effectiveness' (p. 76). As he pointed out, a lack of familiarity between the partner firms does complicate the creation of a learning relationship, but if that lack means a considerable difference between the partners, then the learning opportunity is enhanced because of the potential new knowledge bases that they offer each other.

Barriers to Organizational Learning in Strategic Alliances

Many barriers to learning arise from the internal differentiation within organizations and the external differentiation between them (Child and Heavens, Ch. 13 in this volume).

Differentiation forms the basis for distinct social identities and perceptions of competing interests. When two or more organizations form an alliance, such barriers are typically augmented by their different corporate cultures and, in the case of international alliances, their different national cultures. If the organizations regard each other competitively, the barriers will be raised even further. These barriers reduce what Hamel (1991) termed 'transparency', namely, the openness of one partner to the other(s), and its willingness to transfer knowledge. Hamel found that some degree of openness was accepted as a necessary condition for carrying out joint tasks in an alliance, but that managers were often concerned about unintended and unanticipated transfers of knowledge—transparency by default rather than by design (p. 93).

Obstacles to the necessary transference of knowledge, identified by Nonaka and Takeuchi (1995), are liable to arise because of the divergent ways of sense-making associated with the social identities of the different parties that make up the collaboration. When the members of different organizations come together to collaborate, they bring their own social identities with them. These social identities are sets of substantive meanings that arise from a person's interaction with different reference groups during his or her life and career. They derive from belonging to particular families, communities, and work groups within the context of given nationalities and organizations. Social identities are therefore based on social identifiers such as nationality, ethnicity, occupation, education, and family and are enhanced by differences in language and acquired behavioral norms (Giddens 1991; Tajfel 1982).

The receptivity of the members of a strategic alliance to knowledge transfer from their partners, and their ability to learn collaboratively from the knowledge resources they bring to the alliance, is bound up with their social identities (Child and Rodrigues 1996). Social identities are likely to create the greatest difficulties for collaborative learning in alliances that are socially constituted by partners that are distinct organizationally, nationally, and in terms of the economic development level of the society from which they come. Just as with knowledge that is offered in the learning process by one organizational specialty to others, so knowledge and practice transferred from a partner to the alliance impinges on the other members' mental constructs and norms of conduct. Their social identity derives from a sense both of sharing such ways of thinking and behaving and of knowing how these ways contrast with those of other groups. The process of transferring practical knowledge between different managerial groups will be interdependent on the degree of social distance that is perceived between the parties involved. Thus, if initially this distance is high, the transfer is likely to be impeded. If the transfer is conducted in a hostile manner or in threatening circumstances, then the receiving group is likely to distance itself from those initiating the transfer.

International strategic alliances present a particular challenge for learning that is intended to draw upon knowledge transferred between the partners, or between the partners and the cooperative venture, and to build upon the potential synergies between their complementary competencies (Child and Rodrigues 1996). Although alliances provide extremely important means for international knowledge transfer and synergistic learning, they introduce special sensitivities into the process. It may not be easy to accommodate the interests of their constituent groups and to manage the cultural contrasts among them. These differences contribute to a sense of separate social identity between staff who are attached or beholden to the respective partners.

Some types of internationally transferred knowledge impinge on group social identity more than others. This observation is particularly true of knowledge relating to new systems and strategic understanding. Resistance to the transfer of such knowledge is likely to heighten the separate identities of the partner groups, including those groups transferring the knowledge, for whom persuading their recalcitrant colleagues may take on the nature of a crusade.

The relation between social identity and international knowledge transfer is a dynamic one, in which contextual factors such as the performance of the joint venture also play a part through inducing changes in factors that condition the process, such as partner dominance and compatibility. By contrast, the sharing and transfer of technical knowledge are normally less socially sensitive and, indeed, are likely to benefit from the common engineering or other occupational identity shared by the staff directly involved.

The cooperation of Western multinational companies with firms in eastern Europe provides an instructive instance of the problem. Western companies are expected to make a significant contribution to the transformation of the former Communist countries of eastern Europe, not only as financial investors but also as agents of organizational learning (EBRD 1995; Lyles and Steensma 1997; see also Lyles, Ch. 30; and Merkens, Geppert, and Antal, Ch. 10 in this volume). This collaboration often takes the form of joint ventures that dramatically illustrate how social identities, stemming from the mixed social constitution of such ventures, have an impact on the learning process. For example, Simon and Davies (1996) described barriers to learning by local managers working in international joint venture companies located in Hungary. They drew upon the self-reported experience of the managers and upon their own experience as process consultants in the Hungarian operation of a major multinational. They argued that managerial learning is concerned basically with the acquisition of new roles both in terms of changing individual behavior and in terms of acting as agents for the implementation of new practices brought in by the multinational partners. Roles and the willingness or confidence to assume them are frequently linked to the social identities people hold within a particular cultural setting. The authors concluded that a major barrier to learning among Hungarian managers stemmed from the vulnerability of their social identities. In the threatening conditions of radical organizational change, and with expatriate managers often being perceived as arrogant and control-

ling, the learning that occurred mostly amounted to compliance, which was a strategy for survival. Their study illustrates how the sociopsychological conditions affecting learning are informed by the overall context of meanings that Hungarian managers ascribe to the evolving conditions of transformation in which they find themselves.

The members of an organization are reluctant to give up the beliefs and myths that constitute important supports for their social identity. Jönsson and Lundin (1977) wrote that the prevailing myth is one that guides the behavior of individuals in organizations and at the same time justifies their behavior to themselves, hence sustaining their identity. Beliefs and myths form an important part of the cultural web that sustains an existing paradigm and set of practices against the possibility of their replacement through organizational learning (Johnson 1990). The social identities of joint venture employees are likely to be tied up in this way with their distinctive and separate beliefs, rigid adherence to which may be sustained by their very proximity to their partners who comprise an 'other' or out-group. This proximity reinforces the sense of difference on which social identity thrives.

It is perhaps therefore not surprising to find that Inkpen and Crossan (1995) concluded from their study of organizational learning in forty North American–Japanese joint ventures that a rigid set of managerial beliefs associated with an unwillingness to cast off or unlearn past practices tended to severely constrain the learning process within the ventures. For example, American managers often failed to appreciate their Japanese partner's areas of competency. In line with the American belief in the appropriateness of formalization, these managers commonly expected that the knowledge associated with differences in skills between the Japanese and American partners would be visible and easily transferable (p. 608). Nonaka and Takeuchi (1995: 95) illustrated from Japanese cases how, if senior architects of an alliance recognize this problem, they may be able to undermine this rigid and blinkered thinking by deliberately injecting a sense of crisis and engendering 'creative chaos'.

Implications for the Management of Learning through Strategic Alliances

Pucik (1991) ascribed many of the problems in learning through strategic alliances to managerial failures to plan and provide for such learning. Problems can arise from (a) misplaced strategic priorities, such as short-term objectives and low priority given to learning activities; (b) unfocused organizational control systems, for example when little or no reward is given for contributions to the accumulation of learning as an invisible asset, and the responsibilities for learning are not clear; and (c) inconsistent human resource management policies, such as surrendering responsibility for staffing to the alliance partner. Pucik was particularly concerned lest, because of these failings, firms should lose valuable knowledge to a partner that is more aggressive and skillful in its learning efforts than they are.

This closing section outlines a number of provisions that can be made toward facilitating the process of learning through strategic alliances. I assume the alliances are learning-oriented in the sense that the partners' attitude is that mutual long-term benefit can only be achieved through a win–win approach (Büchel, Prange, Probst, and Ruling 1998: 222). Although Hamel (1991) and Pucik (1991) reminded their readers that this assumption does not always apply, it is constructive to make it in order to concentrate on positive measures that are aimed at achieving the full learning potential that alliances can offer. I first look at overcoming the cognitive and emotional barriers to learning, then at reducing organizational barriers, and finally at fostering the intensive communication and circulation of information required for effective learning. These issues are to a considerable extent interdependent, and

the provisions for tackling them should therefore be mutually supportive.

Overcoming Cognitive and Emotional Barriers

A lack of intent to learn can be an important cognitive barrier to realizing the learning potential of collaboration with other organizations. This obstacle can arise because a partner enters into an alliance for reasons other than learning, such as to spread the risks of R&D or to achieve production economies of scale, and does not appreciate that it has something valuable to learn until it increases its familiarity with its partner's capabilities. Inkpen (1995b: 13) found several examples of American firms that did not have a learning intent when they entered upon a collaboration with a Japanese partner and that developed this intent only when they became aware of their inferior levels of skill. Ways of reducing lack of intent to learn due to inadequate prior knowledge include programs of visits, and (even better) secondment, to prospective cooperation partners and close examination of their products and services. The Korean *Chaebol* (conglomerates), for example, have learned a great deal through reverse engineering of other companies' products, and investigations along such lines can enhance an intent to learn through collaboration by signaling technical and other skill deficiencies.

Drummond (1997) studied projects or programs involving Japanese and local participants within Toshiba Corporation's consumer products subsidiary in the United Kingdom and within the joint venture between Toshiba and Semp in Brazil. Each project succeeded in creating new organizational knowledge. A high level of managerial commitment to the projects, signifying an intention to generate knowledge through them, was one of the consistently important factors facilitating the learning process.

The emotional barriers to learning within a collaboration often boil down to a problem of mistrust. Although there is no shortcut to establishing trust, one can identify conditions that promote it and therefore can derive practical guidelines that foster it. Commitment to the relationship and a degree of direct personal involvement by the partners' senior managers are important in this regard, too. If the principals take the time and trouble to establish a close, personal relationship, their effort promotes confidence and signals that each partner regards the other in a positive light. A British packaging-printing company, for example, succeeded in moving from ink-jet to laser-based technology through an innovation project that depended on three other partners (a laser equipment producer, a supplier of special marking chemicals, and a large U.S. brewery that was a potential customer) entirely on the basis of personal contacts and friendships between individuals in the firms, without any formal contracts being signed between them. Senior managers of the British printing firm asserted that they consciously sought to establish mutual trust on this basis in order to remove barriers to cooperation in the creation of the new technical knowledge. An indication of this process is that the CEO of the printing firm was sharing family holidays with the vice president of procurement for the brewery after only eighteen months of meeting with him (J. Child, personal interview, 23 May 1997). In short, a reduction of the emotional barriers to learning within an alliance requires the parties to take a long-term view of their cooperation and to generate sufficient managerial commitment, especially from the top (Faulkner 1995).

Both cognitive and emotional barriers can manifest themselves in a low motivation to engage in activities that promote learning. One important way to enhance this motivation, which at the same time will provide a clear sign of high-level learning intent, is to create material and nonmaterial incentives to achieve learning objectives. Staff appraisals can include, as one of the performance criteria taken into account, efforts made to secure and disseminate new information within the alliance. It is more straightforward to implement a procedure of this kind if the alliance and its partners actively manage knowledge so that contribu-

tions to their formalized knowledge bases can readily be measured. Individual progress in competence acquisition can be rewarded through upgrading when relevant qualifications are attained, and pay raises can be given for knowledge-creating projects that are completed by teams. It may be more difficult in alliances than in unitary firms to secure top management agreement on what constitutes relevant competence and knowledge creation, especially if the partner firms' learning objectives and organizational practices differ, but it is usually well worthwhile to investigate the possibility of securing agreement on a learning-oriented motivational policy.

Reducing Organizational Barriers

Serious organizational barriers are created if the senior managers of alliance partners do not know how to benefit from the opportunity to learn from their collaboration. Inkpen found that a major problem arose because the American parents of joint ventures with Japanese partners were unable to go beyond recognition of potential learning opportunities to exploitation of these opportunities. They did not establish organizational mechanisms to assist this exploitation. In some cases they even resisted the idea that there was something to learn from the collaboration, thereby contributing to a situation of blocked learning where joint venture managers could not get their improved understanding carried over into practical actions (Inkpen 1995b; Inkpen and Crossan 1995).

The role of senior managers in an alliance is again critical, this time as a lever for reducing organizational barriers to learning. Managers and staff will take their cue from the senior levels. Senior managers are in a position to establish organizational procedures and provisions that foster the learning process within their cooperative ventures. Inkpen and Crossan (1995) identified ways in which senior managers can design provisions, or encourage practices that facilitate interorganizational links in support of the learning process. In the case of joint ventures, these possibilities include '(1) the rotation of managers from the JV [joint venture] back to the parent; regular meetings between JV and parent management; (2) JV plant visits and tours by parent managers; (3) senior management involvement in JV activities; and (4) the sharing of information between the JV and the parent' (p. 609). A successful and expanding catering consortium, with partners from four European countries, has adopted some of these boundary-breaking methods in an attempt to maximize its intellectual capital as a core competitive competence. It is also backing up personal information exchange with an IT-based 'knowledge highway' that records and disseminates information about best practice (Heavens and Child 1999).

Control is a further organizational feature that facilitated learning in the Toshiba experience. There are two main aspects to this control: the establishment of limits to the actions of participants in the learning process and the assessment of outcomes. Control is not usually regarded as a facilitator of learning. Indeed, learning is normally associated with autonomy and creativity, to which control is considered to be antithetical. However, as Drummond (1997) pointed out, this view of organizational politics is naive: a belief that those participating in learning projects will not try to direct their process toward their own objectives rather than those that benefit the alliance as a whole. Control, then, seems to be a very important condition for giving clear direction to a learning intention. Second, the systematic assessment of outcomes should ensure that they are recorded and thereby entered into the organization's memory. Assessment also provides feedback on the effectiveness of the learning process, which should enable the alliance and its partners to improve their capacity to promote learning.

When the strategic alliance takes the form of a separately established joint venture, the leadership provided by its CEO in terms of building trust and a shared identity between the staff of the two partners is critical (on leadership, see Sadler, Ch. 18 in this volume). In other words, the CEO should forcefully articulate a long-term view of the collaboration and its develop-

ment. Among more specific provisions, the venture's CEO must establish adequate communications between staff who need to work together in order to pool their knowledge and skills and must ensure that meetings are held to discuss views, including differences, openly. He or she must also ensure that there is an adequate circulation of information, sufficient personal contact between managers and staff seconded by the partners, and adequate resources of time and funding invested in activities oriented toward learning. The formation of teams, with learning and innovation goals and comprising participants drawn from the alliance partners' staff, can be a powerful means of sharing knowledge constructively, breaking down barriers to interpersonal trust, and ensuring that time and effort are devoted to learning activities (Heavens and Child 1999). Not least, the CEO must generate a sense of common learning objectives through a shared identity with the collaboration, based, among other things, on an understanding that its members enjoy real possibilities for career progression within it.

This focus on the facilitation of learning by the people who are placed in charge of alliances or joint ventures derives from their critical position in the middle of the vertical system between the partners, on the one hand, and the staff working within the alliance, on the other hand. It echoes the conclusion reached by Nonaka and Takeuchi (1995: 130) that what they termed the 'middle-up-down' style of management can make a crucial contribution to fostering knowledge creation. Managers in the middle can reduce the gap that often otherwise exists between the broad vision coming down from top management and the hard reality experienced by employees. The alliance CEO is the key manager in the middle, for he or she must achieve agreement between the partners on the alliance's learning objectives and at the same time create the conditions for these objectives to be achieved. As noted, this achievement depends on both the partners and the alliance personnel themselves.

The aim of the organizational provisions just mentioned is to promote the conditions for integrated learning within alliances. Another requirement, which the techniques of organization development can facilitate, is to break down the hostile stereotypes that partner groups may have of one another and that, if allowed to persist, will militate against the development of trust and bonding. Many of the techniques first developed by practitioners of organization development can be used to advantage in this situation, though one must remain sensitive to the cultural mix when deciding on specific methods. The confrontation-meeting approach, which often works well with North American personnel, could, for instance, cause grave offence if tried with staff from East Asia (Beckhard 1969). Once stereotypes are recognized and diffused, various techniques for team-building are available to promote a collaborative approach to learning between members of the alliance.

Open Communication and Circulation of Information

A climate of openness can also facilitate organizational learning. It involves the accessibility of information, the sharing of errors and problems, and acceptance of conflicting views. Drummond (1997) found that Japanese managers particularly stressed the need to share problems and make information accessible in their U.K. subsidiary. They insisted on the importance of documenting problems when they occurred in order to avoid them in the future. The availability of information also stimulates an awareness of new needs and concepts. It requires mechanisms to encourage the circulation of such information to the persons or groups who need it. These mechanisms are obviously more effective when the barriers to learning just described are not a serious impediment.

The idea of redundancy expresses an approach to information availability which is positive for organizational learning. Redundancy is 'the existence of information that goes beyond the immediate operational requirements of organizational members. In business organizations, redundancy refers to intentional overlapping of information about business activities, management responsibilities, and the company as a whole' (Nonaka and Takeuchi 1995: 80).

For learning to take place, information or a concept available to one person or group needs to be shared by others who may not need it immediately. It may, for example, be information on how a particular problem was tackled creatively in another one of a partner's alliances. If that information is circulated, it is accessible to others should a comparable problem arise. Redundancy also helps build unusual communication channels, and it is indeed fostered through the melding of horizontal channels with the more usual vertical channels for reporting information. In this way it is associated with the interchange between hierarchy and nonhierarchy or heterarchy (Hedlund 1986), which helps promote learning on the basis of procedures that are different from those officially specified by the organization and, hence, based on solutions to old problems (Nonaka and Takeuchi 1995).

Modern information technology makes a very significant contribution to the promotion of information redundancy through its capacity for information storage and, more important, through its ability to transmit that information to virtually all points within an organization. Electronic mail (E-mail), in particular, offers access to information and the facility to communicate in ways that are not constrained by boundaries of time, geography, or formality. As long as the partners to an alliance link up their E-mail and other information technology, these systems provide an excellent vehicle for circulating information and encouraging creative commentary around it (Karahannas 1998). Information technology is, of course, only a tool. The extent to which its potential to assist learning through alliances is realized depends on factors such as role modeling by leaders and a sense of cross-organizational and cross-cultural understanding (Büchel and Raub, Ch. 23 in this volume).

PepsiCo, Inc. combines information redundancy and modern information technology in order to promote learning within the company and within its cooperative ventures. Open and fast communication is coupled with the encouragement of local managers to act upon the information circulated to them, including initiatives to contact others within the company worldwide from whom they might usefully learn (J. Child, personal interviews in the USA and Hong Kong, 23 August and 16 November 1995). PepsiCo operates through many local alliances and stresses the value of open communication both within its corporate systems and with its partners. An illustration of open communication with its partners is the fact that in PepsiCo's joint ventures in China, all general managers speak Mandarin Chinese, and its Asia-Pacific budget meetings are conducted entirely in Mandarin. Despite its size and scope, PepsiCo does not operate with organization charts or many formal procedures, but instead prefers to encourage informal communication flows and to promote the empowerment of its constituent units.

PepsiCo circulates information within its corporate network to the point of redundancy. Its internal E-mail system is an important vehicle for this circulation. This form of communication overcomes international time differences, permits simultaneous communication with several people, is very fast, and encourages an open, informal expression of views. Consolidated reports for different countries and regions are also widely circulated. If, as a result of the circulation of these reports, managers wish to learn more about developments elsewhere in PepsiCo's worldwide operations, they have access to all of the company's telephone numbers and are encouraged to make direct contacts and decide whether to travel to the location, subject only to their travel and entertainment budgets. Many examples are told of how this rich circulation of information, and the ability to act upon it, have promoted learning and the transfer of beneficial practices throughout the corporation. For instance, it facilitated the transfer, from their Hungarian operation to their Chinese joint ventures, of knowledge about ways of curbing theft on distribution runs.

Conclusion

Strategic alliances can foster learning both by facilitating knowledge transfer and by promoting knowledge creation on the basis of complementary competencies. They are relatively efficient in transferring technical knowledge between partners, as long as restrictions are not placed on the release of such knowledge. The joint venture form of alliance, which brings alliance partner staff into a close working relationship, can be effective in transferring tacit knowledge and fostering innovation.

There are, however, certain basic requirements for learning to take place through alliances. Alliances are not necessarily undertaken with learning objectives in mind, though such objectives are becoming more common than they used to be. The first requirement, therefore, is that the partners must have an intention to use the alliance as a learning opportunity. Second, they must have the capacity to learn, which involves, *inter alia*, receptivity to new knowledge on the part of their members, the necessary competencies to understand and absorb the knowledge, and an ability to manage the process of knowledge acquisition in an alliance informed by previous experience.

There are likely to be even more barriers to organizational learning in the hybrid forms that alliances take than in unitary organizations. The main conclusion that arises from this chapter is that managers can take identifiable steps to realize the learning potential offered by alliances. They must combine a demonstrated commitment to achieving organizational learning with know-how of facilitating the process through overcoming the various barriers that stand in the way of its accomplishment (see Berthoin Antal, Lenhardt, and Rosenbrock, Ch. 39 in this volume).

Although I have demonstrated in this chapter that useful knowledge about the process of learning through strategic alliances has already been accumulated, a number of questions deserve further investigation. One of them is the form an alliance takes. Little is known about the impact that the constitution of alliances has on learning. Equity joint ventures, for instance, can be constituted in terms of different partner shares in their ownership, and this difference, in turn has been found to have a significant impact on the participation that the partners enjoy in joint venture control (Child, Yan, and Lu 1997). Dominance by one partner may well inhibit the opportunities for any of the partners to learn through their collaboration. The dominant partner may well discount the value of its junior partner's knowledge and not be prepared to listen to it. The junior partner may not be in a sufficiently influential position to acquire new knowledge through participation in key managerial or technological processes. For this reason, a balanced partnership within a strategic alliance may provide the best opportunities for mutual learning to take place. The possibility that alliance form has an impact on the process of learning is a specific case of the more general proposition, explored in the chapter by Child and Heavens (Ch. 13 in this volume), that learning is affected by the way that organizations are constituted.

The ways in which the evolution of strategic alliances is associated with their learning is another subject deserving further investigation.

Strategic alliances are potentially fragile types of organization in which cooperation requires considerable nurturing. One would expect that the evolution of alliances, if achieved, from an initially contract-based relationship between partners toward a trust-based relationship would create conditions in which their mutual learning process can correspondingly evolve from the sharing just of explicit knowledge to a willingness to share tacit knowledge as well. The potential for exchanging and building upon tacit knowledge is held to be a distinctive advantage of alliances in contrast to arm's length market relations. The experience of mutually beneficial learning should, in turn, promote trust between alliance partners and thus itself foster further strengthening of the alliance. Ongoing work by Doz, Schacht, and others mentioned in this chapter is exploring how different forms of learning can have a positive impact on the evolution of alliances. Thus, technical learning can strengthen alliances' resource bases, systemic learning can enhance their capability to organize complementary assets, and strategic learning can align their partners' goals more closely than in the past. Such insights are opening up a new and very important field for future research.

References

Argyris, C. and Schön, D. A. (1978). *Organizational Learning: A Theory of Action Perspective*. Reading, Mass.: Addison-Wesley.

Axelrod, R. (1984). *The Evolution of Cooperation*. New York: Basic Books.

Barkema, H. G., Shenkar, O., Vermeulen, F., and Bell, J. H. J. (1997). 'Working Abroad, Working with Others: How Firms Learn to Operate International Joint Ventures'. *Academy of Management Journal*, 40: 426–42.

Beckhard, R. (1969). *Organization Development: Strategies and Models*. Reading, Mass.: Addison-Wesley.

Berthoin Antal, A. (1997). *Organizational Learning Processes in Downsizing*. Discussion paper No. FS II 97-113, Wissenschaftszentrum Berlin für Sozialforschung.

Bleeke, J. and Ernst, D. (eds.) (1993). *Collaborating to Compete*. New York: Wiley.

————(1995). 'Is Your Strategic Alliance Really a Sale?' *Harvard Business Review*, 73/1: 97–105.

Boisot, M. H. (1998). *Knowledge Assets: Securing Competitive Advantage in the Information Economy*. Oxford: Oxford University Press.

Borys, B. and Jemison, D. B. (1989). 'Hybrid Arrangements as Strategic Alliances: Theoretical Issues in Organizational Combinations'. *Academy of Management Review*, 14: 234–49.

Büchel, B., Prange, C., Probst, G., and Ruling, C.-C. (1998). *International Joint Venture Management: Learning to Cooperate and Cooperating to Learn*. Singapore: Wiley.

Child, J. (1994). *Management in China during the Age of Reform*. Cambridge: Cambridge University Press.

——and Czeglédy, A. P. (1996). 'Managerial Learning in the Transformation of Eastern Europe: Some Key Issues'. *Organization Studies*, 17: 167–79.

——and David, P. (1987). *Technology and the Organization of Work*. London: National Economic Development Office.

——and Faulkner, D. (1998). *Strategies of Cooperation*. Oxford: Oxford University Press.

——and Markóczy, L. (1993). 'Host-country Managerial Behavior and Learning in Chinese and Hungarian Joint Ventures'. *Journal of Management Studies*, 30: 611–31.

——and Rodrigues, S. (1996). 'The Role of Social Identity in the International Transfer of Knowledge through Joint Ventures', in S. R. Clegg and G. Palmer (eds.), *Producing Management Knowledge*. London: Sage, 46–68.

——Yan, Y., and Lu, Y. (1997). 'Ownership and Control in Sino-foreign Joint Ventures', in P. W. Beamish and J. P. Killing (eds.), *Cooperative Strategies: Asian Pacific Perspectives*. San Francisco: New Lexington Press, 181–225.

Choi, C. J. and Lee, S. H. (1997). 'A Knowledge-based View of Cooperative Interorganizational Relationships', in P. W. Beamish and J. P. Killing (eds.), *Cooperative Strategies: European Perspectives*. San Francisco: New Lexington Press, 33–58.

Ciborra, C. U. (1991). 'Alliances as Learning Experiments: Cooperation, Competition and Change in High-tech Industries', in L. K. Mytelka (ed.), *Strategic Partnerships: States, Firms and International Competition*. London: Pinter, 51–77.

Cohen, W. M. and Levinthal, D. A. (1990). 'Absorptive Capacity: A New Perspective on Learning and Innovation'. *Administrative Science Quarterly*, 35: 128–52.

Doz, Y. L. (1996). 'The Evolution of Cooperation in Strategic Alliances: Initial Conditions or Learning Processes?' *Strategic Management Journal*, 17: 55–83.

Drummond, A., Jr. (1997). *Enabling Conditions for Organizational Learning: A Study in International Business Ventures*. Unpublished doctoral dissertation, Judge Institute of Management Studies, University of Cambridge, U.K.

EBRD (European Bank for Reconstruction and Development) (1995). *Transition Report*. London: EBRD.

Faulkner, D. (1994). 'The Royal Bank of Scotland and Banco Santander of Spain', in J. Roos (ed.), *European Casebook on Cooperative Strategies*. Hemel Hempstead: Prentice Hall, 157–73.

——(1995). *International Strategic Alliances: Cooperating to Compete*. London: McGraw-Hill.

Fichman, M. and Levinthal, D. A. (1991). 'Honeymoons and the Liability of Adolescence: A New Perspective on Duration Dependence in Social and Organizational Relationships'. *Academy of Management Review*, 16: 442–68.

Garrette, B. and Dussauge, P. (1996). 'Contrasting the Evolutions and Outcomes of "Scale" and "Link" Alliances: Evidence from the Global Auto Industry'. *Cahiers de Recherche*, CR580/1996, Jouy-en-Josas: Groupe HEC.

Geringer, J. M. (1991). 'Strategic Determinants of Partner Selection Criteria in International Joint Ventures'. *Journal of International Business Studies*, 22: 41–62.

Giddens, A. (1991). *Modernity and Self-identity: Self and Society in the Later Modern Age*. Oxford: Polity Press.

Gulati, R. (1995). 'Does Familiarity Breed Trust? The Implications of Repeated Ties for Contractual Choice in Alliances'. *Academy of Management Journal*, 38: 85–112.

——and Gargiulo, M. (1999). 'Where Do Interorganizational Networks Come from?' *American Journal of Sociology*, 104: 1439–93.

Hamel, G. (1991). 'Competition for Competence and Interpartner Learning within International Strategic Alliances'. *Strategic Management Journal*, 12 (Summer special issue): 83–103.

Heavens, S. and Child, J. (1999). *Mediating Individual and Organizational Learning: The Role of Teams and Trust*. Paper presented at the Third International Conference on Organizational Learning, Lancaster, U.K., 6–8 June.

Hedberg, B. L. T. (1981). 'How Organizations Learn and Unlearn', in P. C. Nystrom and W. H. Starbuck (eds.), *Handbook of Organizational Design*: Vol. 1. *Adapting Organizations to Their Environments*. Oxford: Oxford University Press, 3–27.

Hedlund, G. (1986). 'The Hypermodern MNC—A Heterarchy'. *Human Resource Management*, 25: 9–35.

Huber, G. P. (1991). 'Organizational Learning: The Contributing Processes and the Literatures'. *Organization Science*, 2: 88–115.

Inkpen, A. C. (1995a). *The Management of International Joint Ventures: An Organizational Learning Perspective*. London: Routledge.

—— (1995b). *The Management of Knowledge in International Alliances*. Working paper No. 95–1, Carnegie Bosch Institute, Pittsburgh: Carnegie Mellon University.

—— (1996). 'Creating Knowledge through Collaboration'. *California Management Review*, 39/1: 123–40.

—— (1998). 'Learning and Knowledge Acquisition through International Strategic Alliances'. *Academy of Management Executive*, 12/4: 69–80.

—— and Crossan, M. M. (1995). 'Believing Is Seeing: Joint Ventures and Organizational Learning'. *Journal of Management Studies*, 32: 595–618.

Johnson, G. (1990). 'Managing Strategic Change: The Role of Symbolic Action'. *British Journal of Management*, 1: 183–200.

Jönsson, S. A. and Lundin, R. A. (1977). 'Myths and Wishful Thinking as Management Tools', in P. C. Nystrom and W. H. Starbuck (eds.), *Prescriptive Models of Organizations*. Amsterdam: North Holland, 157–70.

Karahannas, M. V. (1998). *Interorganizational Systems within Strategic Alliances: Power, Risk and Trust*. Unpublished paper, Judge Institute of Management Studies, University of Cambridge, U.K., February.

Khanna, T., Gulati, R., and Nohria, N. (1998). 'The Dynamics of Learning Alliances: Competition, Cooperation, and Relative Scope'. *Strategic Management Journal*, 19: 193–210.

Kogut, B. (1988). 'Joint Ventures: Theoretical and Empirical Perspectives'. *Strategic Management Journal*, 9: 319–32.

Kolb, D. A. (1984). *Experiential Learning: Experience as the Source of Learning and Development*. Englewood Cliffs, NJ: Prentice Hall.

Larsson, R., Bengtsson, L., Henriksson, K., and Sparks-Graham, J. (1994). *The Interorganizational Learning Dilemma: Collective and Competitive Strategies for Network Development*. Working paper 22, Institute of Economic Research, School of Economics and Management, Lund University, Sweden.

Lillrank, P. (1995). 'The Transfer of Management Innovations from Japan'. *Organization Studies*, 16: 971–89.

Lindholm, N. (1997). 'Learning Processes in International Joint Ventures in China'. *Advances in Chinese Industrial Studies*, 5: 139–54.

Lorange, P. and Roos, J. (1992). *Strategic Alliances: Formation, Implementation and Evolution*. Oxford: Blackwell.

Lyles, M. A. (1988). 'Learning among Joint Venture-sophisticated Firms', in F. Contractor and P. Lorange (eds.), *Cooperative Strategies in International Business*. Lexington, Mass.: Lexington Books, 301–16.

Makhija, M. V. and Ganesh, U. (1997). 'The Relationship between Control and Partner Learning in Learning-related Joint Ventures'. *Organization Science*, 8: 508–27.

Mody, A. (1993). 'Learning through Alliances'. *Journal of Economic Behavior and Organization*, 20: 151–70.

Mowery, D. C., Oxley, J. E., and Silverman, B. S. (1996). 'Strategic Alliances and Interfirm Knowledge Transfer'. *Strategic Management Journal*, 17 (Winter special issue): 77–91.

Murray, E. and Mahon, J. (1993). 'Strategic Alliances: Gateway to the New Europe'. *Long Range Planning*, 26/4: 102–11.

Nonaka, I. and Takeuchi, H. (1995). *The Knowledge-creating Company: How Japanese Companies Create the Dynamics of Innovation*. New York: Oxford University Press.

Pawlowsky, P. (1992). 'Betriebliche Qualifikationsstrategien und organisationales Lernen', in W. H. Staehle and P. Conrad (eds.), *Managementforschung* (Vol. 2). Berlin: de Gruyter, 177–237.

Polanyi, M. (1966). *The Tacit Dimension*. London: Routledge and Kegan Paul.

Powell, W. W., Koput, K. W., and Smith-Doerr, L. (1996). 'Interorganizational Collaboration and the Locus of Innovation: Networks of Learning in Biotechnology'. *Administrative Science Quarterly*, 41: 116–45.

Pucik, V. (1991). 'Technology Transfer in Strategic Alliances: Competitive Collaboration and Organizational Learning', in T. Agmon and M. A. von Glinow (eds.), *Technology Transfer in International Business*. Oxford: Oxford University Press, 121–38.

Schacht, O. (1995). *The Evolution of Organizational Learning in International Strategic Alliances*. Unpublished M.Phil. dissertation, Judge Institute of Management Studies, University of Cambridge, U.K.

——(1999). *The Evolution of Organizational Learning in International Strategic Alliances in Biopharmaceuticals*. Unpublished doctoral dissertation, Judge Institute of Management Studies, University of Cambridge, U.K.

Simon, L. and Davies, G. (1996). 'A Contextual Approach to Management Learning: The Hungarian Case'. *Organization Studies*, 17: 269–89.

Simonin, B. L. (1997). 'The Importance of Collaborative Know-how: An Empirical Test of the Learning Organization'. *Academy of Management Journal*, 40: 1150–74.

Steensma, H. K. and Lyles, M. A. (2000). 'Explaining IJV Survival in a Transitional Economy through Social Exchange and Knowledge-based Perspectives'. *Strategic Management Journal*, 21: 831–51.

Tajfel, H. (ed.) (1982). *Social Identity and Intergroup Relations*. Cambridge: Cambridge University Press.

Villinger, R. (1996). 'Post-acquisition Managerial Learning in Central East Europe'. *Organization Studies*, 17: 181–206.

von Krogh, G. and Roos, J. (eds.) (1996). *Managing Knowledge: Perspectives on Cooperation and Competition*. London: Sage.

30 Organizational Learning in International Joint Ventures: The Case of Hungary

Marjorie A. Lyles

This chapter addresses the downward flow of knowledge and organizational learning from foreign parents to international joint ventures (IJVs) in the context of transitional economies, in particular Hungary. It draws heavily on the research work on Hungarian joint ventures done by Lyles, which includes three data collection periods during the 1990s. Organizational learning is the embodied know-how resulting from absorptive capacity, receptivity of the firm to new knowledge, and the firm's ability to develop knowledge utilization skills (Cohen and Levinthal 1990; von Krogh, Lyles, Mahnke, and Rogulic 1999). Thus, organizational learning is not only the capabilities of the firm to learn and to acquire knowledge but also the firm's capabilities to transfer this knowledge into useful skills and end products over time.

The case of transitional economies is special and important for practitioners and academics for several reasons. First, the transitional economies represent almost half of the world's population, for they include countries such as China, Russia, Vietnam, and the recently liberalized countries of central Europe. Kornai (1992) referred to them as socialist-system countries in which Communist party rule and classical socialism distinguished them for their command economies. Other transitional economies include countries that have colonial pasts and that are now also trying to overcome centralized controls, develop skills for local competitiveness, and move toward open-market economies (Peng 2000).

Second, these firms have traditions and organizational structures that differ from the multinationals of developed economies in that the multinationals have leeway to determine how they are structured and how they shall make strategic decisions. Merkens, Geppert, and Antal (Ch. 10 in this volume) described the transformation as one that involves the restructuring of the firms and the development of learning processes. In the transitional economies, such as Hungary, state-owned enterprises (SOEs) controlled the majority of economic activity and were subject to planning, pricing, and production goals determined by centralized planning. Hungary was in many aspects a typical socialist economy in which, for the most part, the SOEs were hierarchical, authoritarian, bureaucratic, and inefficient (Marer 1998). The state typically funded money-losing SOEs, soft budgets were common, and meeting specific profit goals was unusual (Kornai 1992; Peng 2000). With changing economic conditions, the transitional economies have had to face tremendous change regarding the structure of their firms, the role of SOEs, and the emergence of a viable private sector.

Third, firms within the transitional economies face the challenge of becoming

The author would like to thank the Carnegie Bosch Institute, Indiana University, and U.S. A.I.D. for their assistance and funding.

internationally competitive and have great opportunities to develop new capabilities and to learn from (and to teach) multinationals. Either because it is forced upon them by their foreign partners or because it is seen as advantageous, Hungarian firms rely in part upon knowledge acquisition from foreign firms in order to improve important skills and decision-making processes (Czeglédy 1996). At the same time, for multinationals learning is frequently aimed at gaining both market information and knowledge about local customs and cultures (Makino and Lau 1998). Multinationals typically have firm's specific advantages, such as marketing expertise, product development skills, or specialized distribution networks that need to be adapted in order to develop specific host-country advantages. This adaptation typically involves transferring knowledge to the local IJV or subsidiary. Unfortunately, foreign parents may have difficulty sharing their knowledge because of misunderstandings and cross-cultural difficulties (Dörr and Kessel 1996; Makino and Lau 1998). The foreign parents may have varying skill levels for interacting with the local managers and for teaching, just as the local IJV may have varying skill levels for recognizing, acquiring, and utilizing knowledge transferred from the foreign parent.

In this chapter, the goal is to discuss one aspect of this learning process, namely the learning that flows downward from the foreign parents to local IJVs, in this case Hungarian IJVs. Certainly, horizontal and upward knowledge flows deserve equal time, but my purpose is first to evaluate the factors affecting the downward flow of knowledge. This direction of knowledge flow is viewed as particularly important in light of economic reform and the movement toward market economies (Peng and Tan 1998). As a theoretical explanation of the special context of transitional economies, this chapter examines the nature of transitional economies, the role of the foreign parent and of knowledge transfer to local firms, and the nature of successful IJV knowledge-acquirers in transitional economies.

Transitional Economies

The trend toward downsizing SOEs; the development of new legal environments addressing issues such as civil codes, property rights, and intellectual property; the movement toward market-based systems; and the significant role of the private sector in industrial development make the development of the private sector increasingly important to transitional economies. Foreign direct investment and IJVs are means to counterbalance the loss of jobs at SOEs and play a role in stimulating economic stability and growth. Indeed, foreign direct investment and IJVs have been triggers for organizational learning in the transitional economies (Hooley et al. 1996; Merkens, Geppert, and Antal, Ch. 10 in this volume).

Many of the managers of the newly formed enterprises and IJVs came from a firm that had been centrally controlled and applied their skills and knowledge to firms competing in the private sector. Under the socialist system, the SOE managers acted as order-takers, whereas the bureaucrats made the primary decisions on pricing, investment, technology, and foreign trade (Child 1994; Merkens, Geppert, and Antal, Ch. 10 in this volume; Peng 2000). So, although the former SOE managers brought much in the way of useful skills and knowledge to the new private firms and IJVs, there were still whole arenas in which the managers needed to learn and acquire new knowledge and skills.

The challenges to the managers of private enterprises and IJVs are daunting because of the lack of protection, previous training, available capital and infrastructure supporting a market economy (Peng 2000). New ways of thinking, decision-making, and competitive behavior are required of the managers. However, Markoczy (1993) has suggested that many times the foreign parents of IJVs attempted to shelter the local managers from strategic decision-making, so that these skills and new knowledge would not be transferred.

Merkens, Geppert, and Antal (Ch. 10 in this volume) documented that, by the early 1990s, the countries in transition were in varying states of reform and that this varied state would influence their abilities to implement financial, fiscal, and managerial reforms. Some of the countries were more prepared than other countries to address the transformation of their economies (Marer 1998), and Hungary possibly because of its earlier attempts at reform, was deemed as a country with a sense of willingness and readiness for future reform. Ernst, Alexeev, and Marer (1996) stated:

[E]conomic reforms [in Hungary] became cumulatively significant because by the late 1980s they created an environment that provided considerable independence for SOEs, a sizable private sector, and certain comfort with nondirigiste methods of influencing economic activity. This legacy gave Hungary a head start and permitted more gradual transformation policies than either in Poland or in Czechoslovakia. (p. 161)

Hungarian Context

Hungary's economic reform has been under way since the 1960s, with some forward and backward swings (Marer 1993). Much of the growth within industries has been due not to the restructuring of the SOEs but rather to the growth of new private business (Lane 1995). Indeed, Hungary allowed quasi-legal and quasi-private enterprises in its informal economy even before the well-known transition of 1989 (Marer 1998; Webster 1992). As early as 1968, Hungary began to support attempts at economic reform that spread throughout the 1970s.

In Hungary there was dynamic growth of foreign capital between 1992 and 1996. At the beginning of the transition from 1988 to 1992, the number of joint ventures in Hungary had increased from about 100 in 1988 to over 3,000 in 1992. In 1992, U.S. $1.47 billion in foreign capital was registered, and in 1996 the figure was up to U.S. $11.2 billion, having reached a high in 1995 and then declined in 1996. The major foreign investors were the United States, Germany, and Austria. There was a greater number of foreign firms investing in Hungary

than in any of the other transitional economies of eastern Europe. Foreign direct investment was mostly in medium-sized to large-sized firms, which included about 124,000 active limited-liability companies by 1997.

Hungary has been widely regarded as a leader in the development of a market economy, with its managers most prepared for the change to a market orientation (Hooley et al. 1996; Marer 1998). It was expected that Hungarian managers would be open to new ways of competing and to recognizing the value of knowledge to be gained from foreign firms.

Webster (1992) reported that the Hungarian managers of private enterprises at the beginning of the 1990s were mostly middle-aged men with technical backgrounds. Most of them had come from SOEs. They were in a better position to manage the new businesses than their counterparts in Poland or in other countries with transitional economies because they frequently had travel experience and experience at negotiating contracts and analyzing foreign markets. Webster (1992) also reported that most of the early managers were one of three types: '(1) new entrants with little experience in business; (2) ex-managers of state enterprises; and (3) pre-reform managers of private enterprises' (p. 2). It was the third group that was able to perform best in creating new firms.

Thus, the setting for the following discussion of knowledge transfer from foreign parents to IJVs is Hungary in the 1990s. Hungary exhibited characteristics typical of the former socialist economies, such as an informal economy, inaccurate reporting, slow decision-making, little market knowledge, and an economic slowdown from 1988 to 1995. In 1993 the development of infrastructure for the business environment was poor but in the process of change. The legal environment had changed considerably during this period, too, and much of the legislation in effect in 1995 dated from 1990 (Hungarian Foundation for Enterprise Promotion 1996). GDP growth was quite slow to negative, and the rate of unemployment increased from 1.9 per cent in 1990 to 9.5 per cent in 1995 (Hungarian Foundation for Enterprise Promotion 1996).

The private sector was increasing its share of economic activity during this period, and its contribution was significant in industrial manufacturing and the service sector by 1995 (Lane 1995). The number of IJVs was also rapidly increasing, with most foreign parents coming from western European countries.

For these reasons, Hungary in the 1990s represented an ideal natural laboratory for the study of knowledge acquisition and downward knowledge transfer in transitional economies. Hungary's relatively long history of tolerance for market conditions suggests that the experiences of Hungarian managers in the 1990s may presage what is in store for other transitional economies in the future. Despite being an 'ideal' setting, Hungary's relationship with foreign firms did not lead to dynamic growth as expected, and this discrepancy can be partly explained by the difficulties encountered with knowledge transfer and with achieving mutual respect between the foreign and local managers.

Acquisition of Knowledge in Transitional Economies

IJVs play several essential roles in countries making the transition from monopolistic industries to market-based industries. Because many transitional economies faced massive costs related to development of infrastructure and education and social reform, the domestic funds were not available to make the large investments in the modernization of technology and human capital that were necessary to catch up with the developed countries. Discussing Hungary in particular, Marer (1998) explained the importance of the relationship with foreign firms: 'The ingenuity and dedication of Hungary's vaunted engineers, scientists and skilled work force notwithstanding, few domestic producers would have a good chance to obtain—by relying mainly on domestic resources—the finance, the technology, the management know-how, and the market access that, in combination, are required to be successful

in the increasingly competitive global market place' (p. 33).

The foreign firms are seen as reservoirs of vital technical and managerial knowledge (Child and Markoczy 1993; Hisrich and Szirmai 1993; Lyles and Baird 1994) as well as sources of foreign direct investment. This viewpoint is mutual both because the foreign firms regard local partners as having resources that are necessary to them, for local knowledge is useful and too costly to replicate (Hennart 1991; Makino and Delios 1996), and because they utilize IJVs to establish a viable long-term presence (Parkhe 1991; Yan and Gray 1994). Domestic firms view foreign partners as sources of needed knowledge about technology, decision-making processes, marketing, global support, and managerial know-how (Lyles and Salk 1996; Pearce and Branyiczki 1997; Yan and Gray 1994). The flow of knowledge is regarded as important. However, it is also important to recognize that the flow of knowledge may not result in exactly the same skill sets between the foreign parent and the IJV because of the differences in context and cultures (Child and Czeglédy 1996).

The flow of knowledge within an IJV can be horizontal between the two parents, downward between the parents and the IJV, or upward from the IJV to the parents. Given the context of transitional economies, it is appropriate to discuss the downward flow of knowledge but recognize that there are important aspects of knowledge flow that may flow upward, such as local market knowledge, cultural adaptations, and technical expertise.

Knowledge Acquisition from Foreign Parents in Transitional Economies

The premise is that reduction of transaction costs is not always why firms forgo arm's length arrangements (e.g. licensing) and pursue joint equity ventures. Another reason is that high levels of integration are more effective than arm's length arrangements when it comes to transferring know-how that is tacit, difficult to imitate, and likely to lead to above-normal returns (Kogut and Zander 1993). Transferring knowledge between organizations is always difficult (Szulanski 1996), and the disparity between firms in developed economies and firms in transitional economies adds to the challenge. For the foreign firm, forming an IJV facilitates learning by providing the expectation of a stable, long-term relationship that allows trust and knowledge-sharing to develop (Beamish and Banks 1987).

Although learning from foreign parents is important to the ultimate success of IJVs and subsidiaries, surprisingly little is known about the structures and processes needed to support it. In one of the first studies of this type of learning in Hungary, Lyles and Salk (1996) found articulated goals for the IJV and the provision of training, technology, and managerial assistance by foreign parents to be associated with acquiring knowledge from the foreign parent. One important issue is that those

Hungarian IJVs that had the greatest knowledge acquisition from their foreign parents also showed a positive relationship with their performance ratings. This finding is also supported by a case study of a Japanese–Hungarian joint venture, in which Woodside and Somogyi (1994) suggested that the Japanese firms were not willing to transfer knowledge downward and thus had IJVs that failed. Understanding the process of knowledge acquisition, the characteristics of the foreign parents that enable knowledge transfer, and the characteristics of the IJV that encourage knowledge acquisition, assimilation, and utilization are important for improving the performance of the IJV.

Lane and Lubatkin (1998) proposed that 'the ability of a firm to learn from another firm is jointly determined by the relative characteristics of the two firms, particularly the relationship between their knowledge-processing systems' (p. 473). Figure 30.1 lists the foreign-parent and joint-venture characteristics that facilitate the transfer and acquisition of new

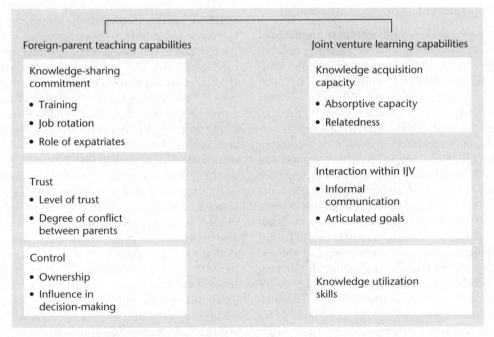

Fig. 30.1. Capabilities affecting high knowledge acquisition in international joint ventures (IJVs) in transitional economies

Adapted from Lyles, Aadne, and von Krogh 1998.

knowledge. It is assumed that the foreign parent takes on the role of teacher and has situational aspects that support this role. These aspects include trust and control, both of which can ensure stability within the IJV. Foreign-parent teaching capabilities require a desire by the foreign parent to transfer knowledge and then to communicate both tacit and explicit knowledge to the IJV. They depend upon the foreign parent being reassured through the development of trust, through the IJV's stability, and through the ownership structure and decision-making process. The term 'joint-venture learning capabilities' expresses the assumption that the IJV has the capacity to recognize new knowledge, disseminate it, and utilize it. Although the capabilities identified in Figure 30.1 may be applicable to developed economies, the research supporting this model is based on data from Hungary (Lane, Lyles, and Salk 1998; Lyles, Aadne, and von Krogh 1998; Lyles and Baird 1994; Lyles and Salk 1996).

Foreign-parent Teaching Capabilities

A key to knowledge acquisition in transitional economies is foreign-parent teaching capabilities, which facilitate the foreign partner's sharing of knowledge and technology. For the most part, all subsidiaries or IJVs require some knowledge transfer from the foreign parent in terms of managerial tasks, technological activities, administrative activities, or a combination thereof. High levels of integration provide an effective means of transferring tacit know-how and information-sharing (Barkema and Vermeulen 1998). Of particular importance are (a) the foreign parent's willingness and ability to assume teaching activities in the IJV involving a transitional economy, and (b) the foreign parent's underlying motives for sharing knowledge and technology. In order for the IJV to absorb tacit knowledge, such as administrative and managerial skills, it is likely to require the active involvement of the foreign partner(s) so that local managers can learn from such exposure to new ideas, concepts, and processes over time (Nonaka 1994). Active

participation is also commonly associated with having parents with equal or nearly equal equity participation (Killing 1983; Salk 1992).

Knowledge-sharing Commitment

Knowledge-sharing commitment facilitates the bestowing of new knowledge and technology on the IJV. This type of commitment is part of a general commitment from the foreign partner's management to the subsidiary (Johnson 1997). Commitment, in turn, reveals itself in contributions to the IJV, such as managerial time and management training (Yan and Gray 1994).

A knowledge-sharing commitment manifests itself in the foreign parent's caring behavior (von Krogh, Ichijo, and Nonaka 1996). The foreign partner can exercise care in at least two ways. First, it can engage in extensive training of IJV managers. Training shows caring behavior because it demonstrates respect and confidence in the learning capabilities of the IJV. It shows that the foreign parent is willing to take the time necessary to share its knowledge, and it sets the expectation that knowledge will be shared. It also indicates that the foreign parent is interested not only in the performance of the IJV but also in the skills and intellectual development of the IJV managers. In Hungarian IJVs, Lyles and Salk (1996) found empirical support for the linkage between training of local employees by a foreign parent and knowledge acquisition in IJVs. Training can comprise foreign partner values and leadership principles, technical and administrative skills, foreign partner routines and practices, marketing skills, financial and accounting principles, and so forth. Second, the foreign partner's design of job rotation programs for local employees also represents caring behavior, for reasons similar to those given above. Job rotation is found to have a high impact on the internal transfer of knowledge within a corporation (Hedlund and Nonaka 1993; Inkpen 1997). In particular, job rotation allows employees to acquire tacit knowledge and skills in various disciplines, business areas, or both, and it can be a new source of reflection and improved dialogue among organizational members.

Role of Expatriates

Expatriates can be an effective vehicle for knowledge acquisition and, in turn, a mechanism for enhancing performance (Berthoin Antal and Böhling 1998; Inkpen and Beamish 1997; Lyles and Salk 1996). Tacit knowledge is typically organization-specific and often based on shared experiences, which makes it difficult to transfer and understand. Explicit know-how that can be codified and documented in written form can be readily communicated and transferred between individuals or organizations. Expatriates thus become important vehicles for the transfer of tacit knowledge because of their relationships and networking capabilities (Berthoin Antal and Böhling 1998). Lyles and Salk (1996) found that Hungarian IJVs with relatively high levels of knowledge acquisition from foreign parents employ significantly more expatriates than do Hungarian IJVs with low knowledge acquisition.

Trust

According to transaction-cost theory, foreign parents should be cautious in providing technology and knowledge to IJVs (Hamel 1991; Hennart 1991). This view is supported by several stories about unintended leakage and opportunistic behavior among IJV partners (Hamel 1991).

Theoretically, individuals and groups that have established personal relations of trust tend to avoid information distortion, to dismantle emotional barriers that could prevent the free flow of information and knowledge (Ashford and Humphrey 1995), to avoid keeping secrets from one another (Krackhart and Hanson 1993; Simmel 1959), and to share information in an effort to mutually help each other solve internal tasks (von Krogh et al. 1996). When trust increases, confidence about future expectations grows, and the partners tend to act as though their certainty about the future has risen (Aadne, von Krogh, and Roos 1996).

Protective behavior and suspicion of local partners or the local unit can jeopardize knowledge acquisition and performance in IJVs. Trust between IJV partners has been highlighted as

one of the factors having a fundamental impact on the success of cooperative relationships (Smith, Carroll, and Ashford 1995). Lack of trust often causes a serious breakdown in communication and cooperation (Borys and Jemison 1989).

Several aspects of trust are important in assessing knowledge transfer in Hungarian IJVs. The first is trust within the IJV. As discussed earlier, when there is no atmosphere of trust and sharing, managers will withhold information from each other, and each individual will act opportunistically (von Krogh et al. 1999). This behavior limits the building of long-term trust and the sharing of tacit knowledge. The second aspect is interorganizational trust between the foreign parent and the local parent and trust between the parents and the IJV. Concern about opportunism and self-protecting behaviors may greatly limit the willingness to share information between the foreign parent and the IJV and knowledge transfer (Hamel 1991). Czeglédy (1996) and Markoczy (1993) found evidence that foreign parents lack trust in Hungarian managers. Although the effects of this finding were not tested directly, this lack of trust may be reasonably assumed to affect the ability of the local managers to assimilate new knowledge and building innovative solutions to problems. Czeglédy (1996) suggested that trust is necessary in order to help local managers stretch themselves and demonstrate their skills.

Thus, not surprisingly, knowledge acquisition in IJVs has mostly been found to be dependent upon high levels of trust and mutual respect (Dörr and Kessel 1996; Inkpen and Currall 1997; Wathne, Roos, and von Krogh 1996). In contrast, Lane, Lyles, and Salk (1998) found no significant statistical evidence of a relationship between trust and knowledge acquisition in Hungarian IJVs, but they did find a direct relationship between trust and the performance of Hungarian IJVs. Their study showed that trust is highly correlated with IJV flexibility and adaptability and with management support from the foreign parents—variables that do have an impact on knowledge transfer. In a study of buyer–supplier relationships, Zaheer,

McEvily, and Perrone (1998) also found a direct relationship between trust and performance, and they suggested that this relationship can influence the exploration of new information and technologies.

Conflict is closely related to trust, for the existence of conflict may mean there is less trust (Anderson and Narus 1990). Conflict inhibits the development of norms of fair exchange and reciprocal trust that are necessary to support an enduring relationship (Buckley and Casson 1988; Lane and Beamish 1990). Disagreement over goals is a difficult and pervasive conflict issue in IJVs and foreign subsidiaries (Shenkar and Zeira 1992) and has been reported to be a major cause for the failures of IJVs (Petterson and Shimada 1978). When the cooperating partners agree on goals, conflict is minimized and trust can develop (Anderson and Weitz 1989). Agreement on goals provides some degree of stability (Inkpen and Beamish 1997). Thus, under conditions of minimal conflict, the foreign parent's ability to assess future knowledge needs improves, increasing the parent's willingness to provide the IJV or subsidiary with necessary technology, experience, and knowledge.

Some interesting results arose when Steensma and Lyles (2000) integrated a social exchange and knowledge-based perspective and examined how the level of foreign parent support provided to the Hungarian IJV influenced the level of conflict between the parents. Support in terms of technical know-how reduces the level of conflict between the parents, which, in turn, increases the likelihood of survival. Such technical know-how support may indicate a high level of commitment from the foreign partner to the local partner, a commitment that the local firm may not want to jeopardize with friction that could end continued support and training from the multinational firm.

Control

The degree of control that a parent firm has may influence the knowledge transferred and the performance of the IJV (Killing 1983;

Makhija and Ganesh 1997; Mjoen and Tallman 1997). It would be quite risky for the parent to transfer valuable knowledge to an IJV when the parent has little say over strategic decisions. In IJVs in transitional economies, there are many decisions that need to be made about the operation and strategic direction, all of which may entail some transfer of knowledge from the foreign parent to the IJV. Indeed, a determinant of IJV performance is thought to be the nature of control that the parents exercise over the venture (Killing 1983). Because of the dual ownership of an IJV, the ability of a parent firm to exercise control over an IJV can be conceptualized as its *relative* influence in comparison with the other parents involved with the IJV (Child, Yan, and Lu 1997). Control has typically been represented by the relative degree of ownership, the amount of bargaining power, the disposition of resources, or a combination thereof.

Supporting the premise that the relative degree of ownership is important, Kogut and Zander (1993) found that the greater the perceived complexity of the know-how, the more likely a multinational company is to transfer its know-how internally through subsidiaries or IJVs rather than through licensing agreements. They suggested that internal knowledge transfer, such as that from the foreign parent to the IJV, is the more effective mode of communicating complex technology because of the difficulty involved in codifying and teaching such knowledge through an arm's length contract. Whereas explicit knowledge can be viewed as a public good and is readily transferred via market contracts, the transfer of tacit know-how is highly contact-dependent and requires extensive interaction between those possessing the knowledge and those wishing to internalize the knowledge.

There is evidence that shared or split control leads to positive knowledge acquisition and performance in Hungarian IJVs. In Hungarian joint ventures, Lyles and Salk (1996) found that 50/50 IJVs had significantly higher levels of knowledge acquisition from the foreign parent than did majority-controlled IJVs. The IJVs with Hungarian majority control had the least amount of knowledge transferred by the foreign parents to the IJV. Ownership was not significantly related to other measures of performance.

Joint-venture Learning Capabilities

The extent to which any IJV is capable of learning may vary. Causes for this variation may be attributed to both the *ability* and the *intent* of the IJV. Not all IJVs have similar capabilities for assimilating knowledge. Within Hungary, IJVs and local experience with IJVs is relatively new, for most IJVs were formed only since 1989. Merkens, Geppert, and Antal (Ch. 10 in this volume) suggested that local firms may have to demonstrate their capabilities to foreign firms in order to develop working relationships with foreign firms. Thus the local Hungarian managers may need to demonstrate their capabilities for operational issues but also their willingness to be flexible, to learn, and to be innovative in decision-making (Feher and Bonifert 1998).

Knowledge Acquisition Capacity

The knowledge acquisition capacity of the Hungarian IJV is based on its ability to recognize, assimilate, and utilize new knowledge. Its absorptive capacity and the degree of business-relatedness to its foreign parents are important determinants of its knowledge acquisition capacity.

Absorptive Capacity

Each organization has a certain ability to learn from other organizations, or what Cohen and Levinthal (1990) termed that 'absorptive capacity' (p. 128), the ability 'to recognize the value of new, external knowledge, assimilate it, and apply it to commercial ends' (p. 128). They showed that some organizations have a greater capacity to absorb knowledge than do other organizations. The premise is that prior knowledge is related to a firm's facility in identifying and understanding new knowledge. The more a firm knows about a particular knowledge base, the more easily it can absorb new knowledge

about this area of knowledge. The firm's previous learning serves as a base for new learning to develop. The social and mental barriers to accepting the new knowledge and technology will be considerably lower when the knowledge or technology is familiar (Berger and Luckmann 1966; Kogut and Zander 1992) than when it is unfamiliar. Thus, the absorptive capacity of the IJV or subsidiary in relation to the parent firm becomes important.

Research on Hungarian IJVs shows that absorptive capacity is indeed important to knowledge acquisition from the foreign parent. Lyles and Salk (1996) indicated that the capacity to learn, in particular to learn flexibility, creativity, and knowledge, is a significant indicator of knowledge acquisition from the foreign parent. Lane, Lyles, and Salk (1998) tested the explanatory power of relative absorptive capacity measures with learning structure and process measures, using hierarchical regression analyses. The hierarchical regression incorporating learning structures and process variables is significant. The relative absorptive capacity variables are significant and explain most of the variance in knowledge acquired from the foreign parents in the Hungarian IJVs.

Degree of Business-relatedness to Foreign Parent

Cohen and Levinthal (1990) suggested that it is easier to learn when learning domains are similar and that it is more difficult to learn when learning domains are novel. In the organizational context discussed in this chapter, their idea means that the knowledge acquisition of an IJV is likely to be affected by the degree of similarity between its own business areas, objectives, and strategic resources and those of its foreign parent. This similarity is what I refer to as the business-relatedness of the IJV and its parent. The greater this business-relatedness is between the two firms (i.e. the more similar their learning domains are), the more common ground they are assumed to have for discussing managerial issues, technology, marketing, and product development, and therefore the easier it is assumed to be for the IJV to acquire knowledge.

Using a variety of measures, some researchers have looked at relatedness and performance or survival rather than knowledge acquisition. In an early study, Lyles (1991) tested the effect of parent–IJV business-relatedness on the performance and risk reduction of the parent firm and found no systematic relationships. Yan and Gray (1994) suggested that there should be an overlap and similarity of expertise. Mjoen and Tallman (1997) showed that the higher the relatedness of the IJV with the parent, the stronger the positive effect on control over specific activities and the higher the perceived IJV performance. Kogut (1988) found a positive relationship between relatedness and IJV survival.

Only a few studies have directly addressed the relationship of the relatedness of the IJV and knowledge acquisition with the parent firms. Mowery, Oxley, and Silverman (1996) provided empirical support to show that convergent development increases interfirm transfer of knowledge and technological capabilities. Furthermore, Inkpen (1997) suggested that 'if the IJV is involved in an unrelated business, it is unlikely that the primary rationale for collaboration will be knowledge creation' (p. 354). Steensma and Lyles (in press) showed a direct relationship between learning, managerial support from the foreign parents, and survival of Hungarian IJVs.

Although relatedness is important, it does not appear to be a sufficient explanation for the effectiveness of knowledge acquisition by the IJV. Although communication and knowledge transfer may be easier among competitors in similar lines of business than between competitors in dissimilar ones, relatedness may not guarantee effective knowledge transfer, for factors such as firm-level differences in idiosyncratic skills, capabilities, and cultural orientations can negatively affect the transfer of knowledge.

The opportunities for mutual gains in knowledge are greater if the activities of the Hungarian IJV are closely related to the foreign parent's main line(s) of business than if the IJV operates in relatively peripheral areas. The first kind of IJV may receive from the parent more attention, greater substantial parent–IJV interaction,

and a larger commitment of resources than the second kind of IJV is likely to get (Inkpen 1997). Besides increasing exposure to parent knowledge, similarities of learning domains also influence knowledge acquisition because they enhance the usefulness of both explicit and tacit knowledge (Hedlund 1994).

Support for the importance of relatedness in Hungarian IJVs is provided by Lane, Lyles, and Salk (1998), who showed that prior knowledge and relatedness are positively associated with knowledge acquisition. They suggested that an IJV whose activities are related to those of its foreign parent has similarities in problem-solving skills, in the technology base, and in the orientation toward the operation of the business that improves understanding of tacit and explicit knowledge.

Interaction within the IJV

Knowledge flows within the IJV are equally important for diffusing knowledge and making it available to many people within the IJV.

Informal Communication

Brown and Duguid (1991) found that informal communication channels allow new knowledge about technical problems and remedies to be widely acquired throughout the organization. Informal communication can help avoid misunderstanding (Donnellon 1996), which aids the organization in integrating or making use of new knowledge (Fiol and Lyles 1985; von Krogh, Roos, and Slocum 1994). Informal communication channels are also important when individuals and groups search for expertise. The transmission of a person's reputation through informal channels decreases the time and efforts needed to locate an expert. Increased interaction can also minimize some of the negative factors affecting knowledge transfer such as low transparency, poor timing, and high levels of noise (Miner and Mezias 1996).

Yet within transitional economies, traditions of withholding information and hoarding resources sometimes remain (Kornai 1992; Peng and Heath 1996). Feher and Bonifert (1998) observed that Western managers frequently characterized Hungarian managers as having poor collaboration skills, low-level horizontal communication, and a defensive attitude. In their study of Hungarian IJVs that were the most successful at acquiring knowledge from their foreign parents, Lyles, Aadne, and von Krogh (1998) found that informal communication is a significant variable in predicting which IJVs will be high knowledge-acquirers.

Articulated Goals

Articulated goals and milestones can also facilitate knowledge acquisition (Child, Ch. 29 in this volume; Hill and Hellriegel 1994; Nonaka and Takeuchi 1995). It is crucial to direct attention to and set priorities for the most important aspects of acquiring strategic capabilities (Nonaka and Takeuchi 1995). Organizational learning occurs when strategic goals are guiding the learning process. Articulated goals advance knowledge acquisition by drawing the attention of the members upon the same vision or mission (von Krogh, Roos, and Slocum 1994). Articulated goals and plans provide a common measure against which to assess and adjust individual and collective actions and their outcomes while at the same time giving IJVs the flexibility to create their own implementation plans and subordinate goals. Likewise, different types of articulated strategies might have different implications for the amount and type of knowledge transfer to the IJV. Having an explicit, written framing or IJV organizational goals and plans should selectively focus IJV employees on acquiring potentially useful knowledge from the foreign parent.

In Hungarian IJVs, an articulated strategy provides mechanisms for evaluating (a) the state of collective understanding and the efficacy of action, (b) the discrepancies between explicit goals and plans, and (c) the new knowledge needed to correct deficiencies or difficulties (Lyles and Salk 1996). Lyles and Salk (1996) found that in 50/50 Hungarian IJVs articulation of goals had a positive effect on the transfer of knowledge from the foreign parents.

Knowledge Utilization Skills

An important element of acquiring knowledge is learning how and when to utilize the new knowledge. Knowledge utilization may lag behind knowledge acquisition (Cohen and Levinthal 1990), complicating the effort to discern if something has been learned. Child and Czeglédy (1996) suggested that such knowledge is tacit and will be modified to become a context-specific competency. In addition, knowledge may be acquired but not well utilized. So the challenge is in understanding how to recognize both that knowledge utilization has occurred and what skills are involved.

Several kinds of knowledge utilization skills have been identified. Lyles (1994) identified discrimination skills, which represent the ability to discern differences between situations and to choose the appropriate course of action. Past success programs, the amount of time available, the number of people involved, and the ways in which past experiences have been encoded into the organizational memory, affect discrimination. Discrimination entails a diversity of experience that can enhance the ability to make distinctions. Nelson and Winter (1982) suggested that focusing on one way of doing things can diminish an organization's ability to discriminate and innovate. It can also limit the organization's capacity to recognize the need for new solutions. Little research has been done in this area, but Lyles (1988) did suggest that firms that accumulate a great deal of experience in an area are better able to make discriminating decisions than less experienced firms are.

Another type of knowledge utilization skill is unlearning, which involves the process of reframing past success programs in order to fit them with changing environmental and situational conditions (Lyles 1988; Lyles and Schwenk 1992). Mistakes, failures, organizational change, or poor performance triggers unlearning. Under any circumstances, unlearning is difficult. It seems that unlearning and discrimination skills would be especially important in transitional economies, such as Hungary, where the IJV managers are learning which of their existing management and decision-making processes are appropriate and which need to be unlearned.

A third skill is translating the knowledge into innovations or product development. Lane,

Lyles, and Salk (1998) suggested that knowledge utilization skills are evident through the performance and strategy of the Hungarian IJVs. The strategic context in which the knowledge is used as well as the IJV's ability to internalize and adapt that knowledge to its own needs will also influence firm performance. Lane, Lyles, and Salk (1998) found that performance in Hungarian joint ventures is influenced by high levels of learning combined with effective training to disseminate the learning and an appropriate business strategy for the IJV's environment.

Successful Knowledge Acquirers

In order to evaluate the different knowledge-transfer competencies of high versus low knowledge-acquirers, Lyles and Salk (1996) divided a sample of Hungarian IJVs into two groups. The high knowledge-acquirers consisted of the IJVs that had scored more than one standard deviation above the mean on their measure of learning acquired from the foreign parents; the low knowledge-acquirers were those that scored one or more standard deviations below the mean.

The results reported by Lyles and Salk (1996) indicated that Hungarian IJVs classified as high knowledge-acquirers had greater absorptive capacity, clearer goals, and more active managerial and technical involvement of the parent firm than did the IJVs classified as low knowledge-acquirers. Lyles and Salk (1996) found no differences between the high and low knowledge-acquirers in terms of characteristics or backgrounds of the top management of the IJVs. The high knowledge-acquirers employed significantly more expatriates from the foreign parent working than did the low knowledge-acquirers, a difference that means increased opportunity for interaction, trust-building, and knowledge transfer with the parent.

Their study revealed a significant difference between the two-parent 50/50 Hungarian IJVs and dominant two-parent firms: 50/50 IJVs had the highest percentage of high knowledge-acquirers. There were some differences between the two-parent high and low knowledge-acquirers in terms of types of ownership structure. For most of the low knowledge-acquirers, the largest partner was the local parent (Lyles and Salk 1996). In only about one-third of the high knowledge-acquirers was the local parent the largest equity holder. This finding suggests the possibility that the relative power of the local parents might affect the propensity of an IJV to draw on information and knowledge from the foreign parent.

In Hungary, tacit, managerial knowledge acquisition had a greater positive impact on performance than did technical knowledge acquisition (Lyles and Salk 1996). This circumstance may be particularly important in Hungary, where many managers have very good technical training and there would be a greater need to learn managerial knowledge. Moreover, placing emphasis on competency-based, managerial know-how may facilitate other exchanges of knowledge.

Using a categorization technique similar to that of Lyles and Salk (1996), Lyles, Aadne, and von Krogh (1998) showed that informal communication was significant in predicting the high knowledge-acquirers among Hungarian IJVs. The importance of informal communication suggests that knowledge is being shared within the firm in a context in which tacit knowledge can be taught and explained (Kogut and Zander 1992). In formal settings, it might not be possible to discuss misunderstandings, explain concepts, or discuss politically sensitive knowledge. Because formal channels of communication may become bottlenecks, informal communication can increase the rapidity of knowledge transfer. It allows for increased interaction, iteration, and speed of knowledge discussions (Nonaka and Takeuchi 1995).

Longitudinal Perspective of Knowledge Management in Transitional Economies

IJVs will vary in their ability to internalize knowledge from the foreign parent, and some

IJVs may operate successfully without the on-going support and knowledge transfer from the parents. Over time, it is hoped that the Hungarian IJV would acquire enough knowledge from the foreign parent to begin to innovate and to function well on its own. Lane, Lyles, and Salk (1998) showed in their longitudinal study of Hungarian IJVs that some IJVs acquire less knowledge from the foreign parent over time but at the same time are able to maintain creativity and high performance. The importance of learning from the foreign parent may wane over time, even though learning still may be necessary in order to maintain the relationship, to learn new managerial techniques or technologies, and to continue to receive support from the foreign parent.

Discussion

Knowledge acquired from the foreign parents plays a key role in Hungarian IJVs. Discussion in this chapter has focused on the internal organizational mechanisms that influence knowledge acquisition and utilization capabilities. This chapter has also offered the opportunity to contrast findings from traditional economic models of organizational learning and knowledge acquisition with those based on factors thought to play a fairly large role in transitional economies.

Because of the continued importance of the state and SOEs, even in transition, SOE linkages might facilitate organizational learning and IJV performance. These linkages could provide soft-budget opportunities, supplier credits, access to government officials, or informal networks. Past research in Hungary and eastern Europe has recognized the importance of institutions, particularly in transitional environments (Antal-Mokos 1998; Kornai 1992; Peng and Heath 1996). The results of studies of Hungarian IJVs do not fully support the institutional viewpoint. Neither former SOE experience nor SOE involvement as a supplier or customer significantly affected organizational learning or the performance of the IJVs (Lyles

and Salk 1996; Steensma and Lyles in press). Some of these linkages may be difficult to document in research studies.

From the perspective of institutional economics, one would argue that, as transitional economies evolve from hierarchical to market structures, transaction costs will increase because of the disaggregation of the value chain. Following this logic, managers of IJVs with industry or SOE experience could minimize the increases in transaction costs. Theoretically, they could leverage contacts with SOEs in order to build trust, gain credibility, and decrease information asymmetries typical of market transactions. Research has provided no significant empirical evidence to show that experience with SOEs influences organizational learning. The conclusions that can be drawn from these findings are limited because the nature of the data does not allow for further fine-grained analysis of the exact background of the respondents and the firms involved.

Alternatively, the research presented supports a socially derived resource-dependence view. The Hungarian IJVs studied operate in an environment characterized by legal, social, and cultural change. The IJVs are free to create new relationships, and their owners or managers are capable of developing new networks. The nurturing relationship with the foreign parent becomes critically important to enhancing knowledge acquisition but also to enhancing the performance of the IJVs (Lane, Lyles, and Salk 1998; Lyles and Salk 1996).

Consistent with the literature, there is a positive relationship between the active involvement of the foreign parent and organizational learning in the IJV. This issue is particularly relevant for transitional economies whose institutional structure is evolving. In such an environment, it is often difficult for local firms and IJVs to obtain training, technology, financing, and market knowledge on their own. This complication also emphasizes the importance of linkages, for these IJVs frequently need to rely upon their foreign parents for new knowledge and for help in finding the means to improve their performance. The alignment of an

IJV to the changing transitional environment is critical to its success, for IJVs need to learn quickly.

Knowledge acquisition from the foreign parents plays a major role in driving or facilitating a transition from state control to a market-based economy (Ernst, Alexeev, and Marer 1996; Marer 1998). Broadening the understanding of what drives this behavior and performance is a research imperative. This chapter set out to advance the literature on transitional economies by examining factors affecting organizational learning in IJVs in Hungary. The focus on IJVs, the empirical nature of the literature cited, the longitudinal nature of the data, and the inclusion of alternative mechanisms affecting organizational learning offer a unique contribution to the literature. The research demonstrates that IJVs do indeed learn from their foreign parents even in environments of high uncertainty. This observation should not be minimized. The findings suggest that capabilities, including knowledge-sharing commitment, trust, control, knowledge-acquisition capacity, interaction within the IJV, and knowledge utilization skills, can help enhance downward knowledge transfer and IJV performance.

The context of Hungary makes it possible to examine these factors at a critical time in its transition, and these results may presage what is in store for other countries that are not as far along in transition. How relationships are structured among organizational stakeholders (e.g. the division of labor, control, training) and the intraorganizational factors contributing to the knowledge acquisition and knowledge transfer capabilities of an organization operate as distinct influences on what and how much is learned by an IJV organization.

Organizational learning provides an important framework for thinking of the processes and capabilities that are necessary for the exchange of knowledge. Yet the degree to which firms and managers are willing to adapt new ways to approaching knowledge and innovation will depend upon their histories and institutions. Accessing know-how through ongoing parental support may be sufficient for survival in the short run, but longitudinal studies need to address the impact of knowledge acquisition and parental support for the long term.

References

Aadne, J. H., von Krogh, G., and Roos, J. (1996). 'Representationism: The Traditional Approach to Cooperative Strategies', in G. von Krogh and J. Roos (eds.), *Managing Knowledge: Perspectives on Cooperation and Competition*. London: Sage, 9–31.

Anderson, E. and Weitz, B. (1989). 'Determinants of Continuity in Conventional Industrial Channel Dyads'. *Marketing Science*, 8: 310–23.

Anderson, J. C. and Narus, J. A. (1990). 'A Model of Distributor Firm and Manufacturer Firm Working Partnerships'. *Journal of Marketing*, 54/1: 42–58.

Antal-Mokos, Z. (1998). *Privatization, Politics, and Economic Performance in Hungary*. Cambridge: Cambridge University Press.

Ashford, B. E. and Humphrey, R. H. (1995). 'Emotions in the Workplace: A Reappraisal'. *Human Relations*, 48: 97–125.

Barkema, H. G. and Vermeulen, F. (1998). 'International Expansion through Start-up or Acquisition: A Learning Perspective'. *Academy of Management Journal*, 41: 7–26.

Beamish, P. W. and Banks, J. C. (1987). 'Equity Joint Ventures and the Theory of the Multinational Enterprise'. *Journal of International Business Studies*, 18/2: 1–16.

Berger, P. L. and Luckmann, T. (1966). *The Social Construction of Reality: A Treatise in the Sociology of Knowledge*. New York: Penguin.

Berthoin Antal, A. and Böhling, K. (1998). 'Expatriation as an Underused Resource for Organizational Learning', in H. Albach, M. Dierkes, A. Berthoin Antal, and K. Vaillant (eds.), *Organisation-*

slernen—institutionelle und kulturelle Dimensionen. WZB Jahrbuch 1998. Berlin: edition sigma, 215–36.

Borys, B. and Jemison, D. B. (1989). 'Hybrid Arrangements as Strategic Alliances: Theoretical Issues in Organizational Combinations'. *Academy of Management Review*, 14: 4–49.

Brown, J. S. and Duguid, P. (1991). 'Organizational Learning and Communities-of-Practice: Toward a Unified View of Working, Learning, and Innovation'. *Organization Science*, 2: 40–57.

Buckley, P. J. and Casson, M. (1988). 'A Theory of Cooperation in International Business', in F. Contractor and P. Lorange (eds.), *Cooperative Strategies in International Business*. Lexington, Mass.: Lexington Books, 31–53.

Child, J. (1994). *Management in China during the Age of Reform*. Cambridge: Cambridge University Press.

—— and Czeglédy, A. (1996). 'Managerial Learning in the Transformation of Eastern Europe: Some Key Issues'. *Organization Studies*, 17: 167–79.

—— and Markoczy, L. (1993). 'Host-country Managerial Behavior and Learning in Chinese and Hungarian Joint Ventures'. *Journal of Management Studies*, 30: 611–31.

—— Yan, Y., and Lu, Y. (1997). 'Ownership and Control in Sino-foreign Joint Ventures', in P. W. Beamish and J. P. Killing (eds.), *Cooperative Strategies: Asian Pacific Perspectives*. San Francisco: New Lexington Press, 181–225.

Cohen, W. and Levinthal, D. A. (1990). 'Absorptive Capacity: A New Perspective on Learning and Innovation'. *Administrative Science Quarterly*, 35: 128–52.

Czeglédy, A. P. (1996). 'New Directions for Organizational Learning in Eastern Europe'. *Organization Studies*, 17: 327–41.

Dörr, G. and Kessel, T. (1996). 'Transformation as a Learning Process: Experiences with Joint Ventures in the Czech Republic and an Example for a New Modern Form of Organizing Production'. *EMERGO*, 3/2: 44–57.

Donnellon, A. (1996). *Team Talk*. Boston: Harvard Business School Press.

Ernst, M., Alexeev, M., and Marer, P. (1996). *Transforming the Core: Restructuring Industrial Enterprises in Russia and Central Europe*. Boulder, Colo.: Westview.

Feher, J. and Bonifert, M. S. (1998). *The Application of Change Management Methods at Business Organizations Operating in Hungary: Challenges in the Business and Cultural Environment and First Practical Experiences*. Working paper No. 198, the Davidson Institute Working Paper Series, University of Michigan, Ann Arbor.

Fiol, C. A. and Lyles, M. A. (1985). 'Organizational Learning'. *Academy of Management Review*, 10: 803–13.

Hamel, G. (1991). 'Competition for Competence and Interpartner Learning within International Strategic Alliances'. *Strategic Management Journal*, 12 (Summer special issue): 83–103.

Hedlund, G. (1994). 'A Model of Knowledge Management and the N-Form Corporation'. *Strategic Management Journal*, 15: 73–90.

—— and Nonaka, I. (1993). 'Models of Knowledge Management in the West and Japan', in P. Lorange, B. Chakravarthy, J. Roos, and A. Van de Ven (eds.), *Implementing Strategic Processes: Change, Learning and Cooperation*. Oxford: Basil Blackwell, 117–44.

Hennart, J. (1991). 'A Transaction Costs Theory of Equity Joint Ventures: An Empirical Study of Japanese Subsidiaries in the United States'. *Management Science*, 37: 483–97.

Hill, R. C. and Hellriegel, D. (1994). 'Critical Contingencies in Joint Venture Management: Some Lessons from Managers'. *Organization Science*, 5: 594–607.

Hisrich, R. D. and Szirmai, P. (1993). 'Developing a Market-oriented Economy: A Hungarian Perspective'. *Entrepreneurship and Regional Development*, 5: 61–71.

Hooley, G., Cox, T., Shipley, D., Fahy, J., Beracs, J., and Kolos, K. (1996). 'Foreign Direct Investment in Hungary: Resource Acquisition and Domestic Competitive Advantage'. *Journal of International Business Studies*, 27: 683–709.

Hungarian Foundation for Enterprise Promotion, Institute for Small Business Development (ed.) (1996). *State of Small and Medium Sized Business in Hungary: 1996 Annual Report*. Budapest: Institute for Small Business Development.

Inkpen, A. C. (1997). 'An Examination of Knowledge Management in International Joint Ventures', in P. W. Beamish and J. P. Killing (eds.), *Cooperative Strategies: North American Perspectives*. San Francisco: New Lexington Press, 337–69.

—— and Beamish, P. W. (1997). 'Knowledge, Bargaining Power, and the Instability of International Joint Ventures'. *Academy of Management Review*, 22: 177–202.

—— and Currall, S. C. (1997). 'International Joint Venture Trust: An Empirical Examination', in P. W. Beamish and J. P. Killing (eds.), *Cooperative Strategies: North American Perspectives*. San Francisco: New Lexington Press, 308–34.

Johnson, J. P. (1997). 'Procedural Justice Perceptions among International Joint Venture Managers: Their Impact on Organizational Commitment', in P. W. Beamish and J. P. Killing (eds.), *Cooperative Strategies: North American Perspectives*. San Francisco: New Lexington Press, 197–226.

Killing, P. (1983). *Strategies for Joint Venture Success*. New York: Praeger.

Kogut, B. (1988). 'Joint Ventures: Theoretical and Empirical Perspectives'. *Strategic Management Journal*, 9: 319–32.

—— and Zander, U. (1992). 'Knowledge of the Firm, Combinative Capabilities, and the Replication of Technology'. *Organization Science*, 3: 383–97.

—— —— (1993). 'Knowledge of the Firm and the Evolutionary Theory of the Multinational Corporation'. *Journal of International Business Studies*, 24: 625–46.

Kornai, J. (1992). *The Socialist System: The Political Economy of Communism*. Princeton: Princeton University Press.

Krackhart, D. and Hanson, J. (1993). 'Informal Networks: The Company behind the Chart'. *Harvard Business Review*, 71/4: 104–11.

Lane, H. W. and Beamish, P. W. (1990). 'Cross-cultural Cooperative Behavior in Joint Ventures in LDCs'. *Management International Review*, 30 (Special issue): 87–102.

Lane, P. J. and Lubatkin, M. (1998). 'Relative Absorptive Capacity and Interorganizational Learning'. *Strategic Management Journal*, 19: 461–77.

—— Lyles, M. A., and Salk, J. E. (1998). 'Relative Absorptive Capacity, Trust and Interorganizational Learning in International Joint Ventures', in M. A. Hitt, J. E. Ricart, I. Costa, and R. D. Nixon (eds.), *Managing Strategically in an Interconnected World*. New York: Wiley, 373–98.

Lane, S. J. (1995). 'Business Starts during the Transition in Hungary'. *Journal of Business Venturing*, 10: 181–94.

Lyles, M. A. (1988). 'Learning among Joint Venture Sophisticated Firms'. *Management International Review*, 28 (Special issue): 85–98.

—— (1991). 'A Study of the Interaction of Firm Business Area Relatedness and the Propensity to Joint Venture'. *Journal of Global Marketing*, 5/1: 91–106.

—— (1994). 'The Impact of Organizational Learning on Joint Venture Formations'. *International Business Review*, 3: 459–67.

—— Aadne, J. H., and von Krogh, G. (1998). *The Making of High Knowledge Acquirers: Understanding the Nature of Knowledge Catalysts in International Joint Ventures and Their Foreign Parents*. Working paper presented at the Informs Meeting, Seattle, Wash., 25–26 October.

—— and Baird, I. S. (1994). 'Performance of International Joint Ventures in Two Eastern European Countries: The Case of Hungary and Poland'. *Management International Review*, 34: 313–30.

—— and Salk, J. E. (1996). 'Knowledge Acquisition from Foreign Parents in International Joint Ventures'. *Journal of International Business Studies*, 27: 877–904.

—— and Schwenk, C. R. (1992). 'Top Management, Strategy, and Organizational Knowledge Structures'. *Journal of Management Studies*, 29: 155–74.

Makhija, M. V. and Ganesh, U. (1997). 'The Relationship between Control and Partner Learning in Learning-related Joint Ventures'. *Organization Science*, 8: 508–27.

Makino, S. and Delios, A. (1996). 'Local Knowledge Transfer and Performance: Implications for Alliance Formation in Asia'. *Journal of International Business Studies*, 27: 905–27.

—— and Lau, C. M. (1998). *The Road to MNE of Firms from Newly Industrialized Economies*. Paper presented at National Academy of Management, San Diego, Calif., August.

Marer, P. (1993). 'Economic Transformation in Central and Eastern Europe', in S. Islam and M. Mandelsbaum (eds.), *Making Markets: Economic Transformation in Eastern Europe and the Postsoviet States*. New York: Council of Foreign Relation Press, 53–98.

—— (1998). 'Economic Transformation, 1990–1998', in A. Braun and Z. Barany (eds.), *Dilemmas of Transition: The Hungarian Experience*. New York: Roman and Littlefield, 157–202.

Markoczy, L. (1993). 'Managerial and Organizational Learning in Hungarian–Western Mixed Management Organizations'. *International Journal of Human Resource Management*, 4: 277–304.

Miner, A. S. and Mezias, S. J. (1996). 'Ugly Duckling No More: Pasts and Futures of Organizational Learning Research'. *Organization Science*, 7: 88–99.

Mjoen, H. and Tallman, S. (1997). 'Control and Performance in International Joint Ventures'. *Organization Science*, 8: 257–74.

Mowery, D. C., Oxley, J. E., and Silverman, B. S. (1996). 'Strategic Alliances and Interfirm Knowledge Transfer'. *Strategic Management Journal*, 17: 77–92.

Nelson, R. R. and Winter, S. G. (1982). *An Evolutionary Theory of Economic Change*. Cambridge, Mass.: Belknap Press of Harvard University Press.

Nonaka, I. (1994). 'A Dynamic Theory of Organizational Knowledge Creation'. *Organization Science*, 5: 14–37.

—— and Takeuchi, H. (1995). *The Knowledge-creating Company: How Japanese Companies Create the Dynamics of Innovation*. New York: Oxford University Press.

Parkhe, A. (1991). 'Interfirm Diversity, Organizational Learning, and Longevity in Global Strategic Alliances'. *Journal of International Business Studies*, 22: 579–602.

Pearce, J. L. and Branyiczki, I. (1997). 'Legitimacy: An Analysis of Three Hungarian–Western European Collaborations', in P. W. Beamish and J. P. Killing (eds.), *Cooperative Strategies: European Perspectives*. San Francisco: New Lexington Press, 300–22.

Peng, M. W. (2000). *Business Strategies in Transition Economies*. Thousand Oaks, Calif.: Sage.

—— and Heath, P. S. (1996). 'The Growth of the Firm in Planned Economies in Transition: Institutions, Organizations, and Strategic Choice'. *Academy of Management Review*, 21: 492–528.

—— and Tan, J. J. (1998). 'Toward Alliance Postsocialism: Business Strategies in a Transitional Economy'. *Journal of Applied Management Studies*, 7/1: 145–8.

Petterson, R. B. and Shimada, J. Y. (1978). 'Sources of Management Problems in Japanese–American Joint Ventures'. *Academy of Management Review*, 3: 796–804.

Salk, J. E. (1992). *Shared Management Joint Ventures: Their Developmental Patterns, Challenges and Possibilities*. Unpublished doctoral dissertation, Sloan School of Management, Massachusetts Institute of Technology, Cambridge, Mass.

Shenkar, O. and Zeira, Y. (1992). 'Role Conflict and Role Ambiguity of Chief Executive Officers in International Joint Ventures'. *Journal of International Business Studies*, 23: 55–75.

Simmel, G. (1959). *The Sociology of George Simmel*. New York: Free Press.

Smith, K. G., Carroll, S. J., and Ashford, S. J. (1995). 'Intra- and Interorganizational Cooperation: Towards a Research Agenda'. *Academy of Management Journal*, 38: 7–23.

Steensma, K. and Lyles, M. A. (2000). *Explaining IJV Survival in a Transitional Economy through Social Exchange and Knowledge-based Perspectives*. Working paper, Smeal College of Business Administration, Pennsylvania State University, University Park.

Szulanski, G. (1996). 'Exploring Internal Stickiness: Impediments to the Transfer of Best Practice within the Firm'. *Strategic Management Journal*, 17 (Winter special issue): 27–43.

von Krogh, G., Ichijo, K., and Nonaka, I. (1996). *Bringing Care into Knowledge Development of Business Organizations*. Paper presented at the International Comparative Study of Knowledge Creation: Implications for the Business Enterprise of the 21st Century, 12–15 December, Hawaii.

—— Lyles, M. A., Mahnke, V., and Rogulic, B. (1999). 'Preparing the Organization for New Competencies: A Process Perspective of Integrating Knowledge and Competence', in R. Garud and J. Porac (eds.), *Advances in Managerial Cognition and Organizational Information Processing: Knowledge, Cognition and Organizations* (Vol. 6). New York: JAI Press, 57–78.

—— Roos, J., and Slocum, K. (1994). 'An Essay on Corporate Epistemology'. *Strategic Management Journal*, 15 (Summer special issue): 33–71.

Wathne, K., Roos, J., and von Krogh, G. (1996). 'Towards a Theory of Knowledge Transfer in a Cooperative Context', in G. von Krogh and J. Roos (eds.), *Managing Knowledge: Perspectives on Cooperation and Competition*. London: Sage, 55–81.

Webster, L. (1992). *Private Sector Manufacturing in Hungary: A Survey of Firms*. Report for Industry Development Division, Industry and Energy Department, World Bank. Washington, DC: World Bank.

Woodside, A. G. and Somogyi, P. (1994). 'Creating International Joint Ventures: Strategic Insights from Case Research on a Successful Hungarian–Japanese Industrial Enterprise', in P. J. Buckley and P. Ghauri (eds.), *The Economics of Change in East and Central Europe*. London: Academic Press, 169–83.

Yan, A. and Gray, B. (1994). 'Bargaining Power, Management Control, and Performance in United States–China Joint Ventures: A Comparative Case Study'. *Academy of Management Journal*, 37: 1478–517.

Zaheer, A., McEvily, B., and Perrone, V. (1998). 'Does Trust Matter? Exploring the Effects of Interorganizational and Interpersonal Trust on Performance'. *Organizational Science*, 9: 141–59.

31 Organizational Learning in Supplier Networks

Christel Lane

The literature on organizational learning is now voluminous, and the topic has been explored from a variety of different angles (Albach, Dierkes, Berthoin Antal, and Vaillant 1998; Edmondson and Moingeon 1996; Starkey 1996). Most accounts, however, have focused on learning *within* organizations, whereas learning in networks has received much less consideration. The few studies that cover external learning either deal with diffusion of information in a highly general way (Levitt and March 1988) or focus only on strategic alliances (Child, Ch. 29 in this volume) and learning in relation to R&D activity (e.g. Ciborra 1991; Dodgson 1993). The rather mundane and fairly widespread customer–supplier networks (hereafter, supplier networks), in contrast, have received hardly any in-depth study. Although the work of Nonaka (e.g. Nonaka and Reinmöller 1998) does not leave supplier networks unconsidered, it does not reflect sufficient appreciation of the distinctive problems they pose for organizational learning. This general lack of systematic study in this area is particularly surprising because gaining access to new knowledge is widely seen to be an important reason why supplier networks have developed in many industries (Grabher 1993a; Miles and Snow 1992; Nohria 1992; Powell 1987; Ring and van de Ven 1992; Semlinger 1993). In this chapter I therefore examine existing theories of organizational learning and accounts of supplier networks and identify mutually relevant features of networks and processes of organizational learning. The resulting observations will then be used to amend or expand existing theory of organizational learning so that it can be applied to the analysis of supplier networks as well. In the following theoretical analysis and its application to specific empirical cases I adopt a comparative perspective. Different styles of organizational learning are assumed to have been shaped by different cultural and institutional environments, both of a national and, to a lesser extent, an industrial kind. In this context, the notion of trust and of the institutional production of trust is a special focus, but some consideration is given also to power as a mechanism of coordination.

Part I presents an examination of theoretical work on supplier relations and supplier networks. In a review of the literature on organizational learning, theoretical propositions that also have implications for the analysis of vertical interfirm relations are pointed out. At the end of the section, insights drawn from both bodies of theory are combined in order to render existing organizational learning theory more relevant to the study of supplier networks than it has been.

In Part II case data are cited in order to illustrate how organizational learning occurs and how knowledge is transferred in supplier networks. The focus is specifically on different processes of acquiring and institutionalizing knowledge and on the mechanisms used to coordinate the mental maps of network firms. The final section of Part II provides a comparison of different mental maps and learning styles in advanced economies and relates them to divergent forms of supplier networks. The concluding section of the chapter offers a summary of the argument and draws some general lessons that might be useful to the business and policy-making communities.

Part I. Supplier Networks and Organizational Learning: Theoretical Approaches

Network Analysis

The term 'network', understood as 'two or more firms involved in a long-term relationship' (Thorelli 1986: 37), became prominent during the 1980s, when the ascendency of a new way to coordinate economic transactions was recognized, a way based on 'neither market nor hierarchy' (Powell 1991). Whether networks should therefore be viewed as a hybrid (e.g. Thorelli 1986; Williamson 1985) or a unique organizational form (e.g. Grabher 1993a; Powell 1987, 1991; Semlinger 1993) is still being debated. In either case, a network is said to combine relatively loose coupling with complex reciprocal, cooperative, and relatively stable relations between legally independent units. It is designed to acquire competitive advantage for network members. Network relations, which are closer and longer term than market relations, are seen to facilitate greater information density and a more reliable information exchange than markets do. At the same time, the autonomy of network firms permits exits and entries that can reshape the network and thus generates greater flexibility than hierarchy does (Alter and Hage 1993; Grabher 1993a; Powell 1987, 1991; Sydow 1992a, b; Thorelli 1986).

These loosely coupled, but cooperative, relationships between enterprises take a variety of forms and stimulate the exchange of a range of different goods. This study focuses only on vertical networks in which an important customer company (the hub firm) is at the center of a network of supplier firms. Although such networks have been identified as existing both within and between industrial sectors (Sydow 1992a) and have exchanged goods, services, and knowledge, the literature has focused mainly on networks in the manufacturing sector and

the outsourcing of development and production tasks. Supplier networks that crossnational boundaries have hardly been explored at all. Hence, this chapter concentrates on the manufacturing sector and on networks within countries.

Subcontracting production tasks in order to augment capacity, enter new niches, or reduce costs (Holmes 1986) is not a new business practice, but developments in the last two decades have both increased the scale of outsourcing and changed the quality of these relations. It is this changed quality that underlies the network character. Responding to new competitive pressures on international markets—particularly pressures to expand product variety, enhance quality, shorten production cycles, and decrease costs—large vertically integrated firms have increasingly begun to concentrate on 'core business' and have externalized activities that can be performed more cheaply, better, or both by more specialized supplier companies. Most important, increased outsourcing has been designed to provide the customer firm with greater flexibility to respond to more volatile markets (Harrison and Kelley 1993). As outsourcing has changed from a fairly peripheral activity to a strategic one, the network form of organization has assumed a proportionate degree of importance.

Relations between the firm at the center of the network and its suppliers are said to have become closer, more stable, and more cooperative (Sydow 1992a, b). This change, in turn, has encouraged both sides to make investments in the relationship. Customer firms have imposed a range of new demands on supplier firms. In return, supplier firms are said to receive longer contracts and more technical assistance than in the past (Sydow 1992a, b). To facilitate these closer and multiplex relations, customer firms have reduced the number of their supplier firms and have introduced a number of practices to bind supplier firms more closely than has hitherto been the case. Among the latter, technical links, such as just-in-time (JIT) delivery, computerized links with suppliers, and openbook accounting by suppliers, stand out. Additionally, social links, such as personnel exchanges, technical assistance, and increased frequency of mutual visiting, have been noted (Deakin, Lane, and Wilkinson 2000; Sydow 1992b: 40–1). This synchronization of processes between customer and supplier firms and the accompanying scrutiny of supplier companies clearly make rapid, intensive information exchange one of the distinguishing features of networks and have strong implications for organizational learning. 'Hybrid organizational forms represent a fast means of gaining access to sources of know-how located outside the organization' (Powell 1987: 81). Relations in supplier networks involve both an exchange of a large volume of fairly routine information and improved access to complementary, but different, bodies of knowledge.

But perspectives on supplier networks have not uniformly shared this sanguine emphasis on cooperation and trust. Many theoretical analyses present an overdrawn contrast between old-style arm's length supplier relations and the new reciprocal and cooperative network relations based on trust. Power and conflict are underplayed, and the way in which the resultant withholding of information becomes an impediment to organizational learning receives insufficient note (Grabher 1993a; Semlinger 1993; see also Tsui-Auch, Ch. 32 in this volume). The objectives of customer and supplier firms are only partially in agreement, and the danger that the more powerful firm will impose its objectives on its more dependent trading partner is ever present. It is particularly acute in highly globalized industries marked by intense competition, such as the automobile and computer industries.

Power in interfirm relations may be defined as the ability to influence other firms' sets of opportunities. It usually results from greater size, superior resources, and related market power. Thus, although autonomy of network firms is one condition of learning, the dominant position of the hub firm often permits only limited autonomy. But power may also be based on the possession of knowledge indispensable to the trading partner, and suppliers may enjoy greater power than their customers and may carefully guard tacit knowledge.

The perpetually changing competitive environment in which supplier networks are now situated means that organizational learning now receives more external stimuli than it used to, has become less intermittent than in the past, and occurs at an accelerated pace. It is also claimed that the knowledge transferred no longer consists of merely operational knowledge but frequently also of conceptual knowledge (see Kim 1993, discussed below). Learning styles have had to become coordinated between network members. On the one hand, closer and more stable ties, particularly in trust-based relationships, encourage greater openness and hence both multiply opportunities for learning and encourage the disclosure of previously confidential knowledge. 'Security and stability encourage the search for new ways of accomplishing tasks' (Powell 1987: 82). On the other hand, however, uneven power resources among network firms and constant pressure on suppliers to reduce costs have resulted in conflict and distrust and a consequent decline in learning opportunities. Both the increased importance that supplier networks have for competitiveness and the much enhanced status of various kinds of knowledge and associated learning processes within supplier networks make it imperative for scholars of organizational learning to sharpen their awareness of the specificity of learning in networks and to adjust their theories accordingly.

Organizational Learning Theory: A Selective Review

This overview of selected theories is intended to pinpoint the limits of current theory for the analysis of supplier networks and to highlight the insights that provide a point of departure for making organizational learning theory more widely applicable to new organizational forms. Some of the most recent work in this field includes external learning in general and learning in supplier networks in particular (Dodgson 1993; Nonaka, Toyama, and Byosière, Ch. 22 in this volume; Nonaka and Reinmöller 1998). The authors of this research appreciate the importance of external learning for innovation, but they do not fully recognize that the adjustment problems involved in the transfer of mental maps between groups become magnified when those groups are located in different organizations that do not share all the same goals and interests.

One prominent focus of organizational learning theory is the exploration of the relation between individual learning and organizational learning (Kim 1993). In order to understand how individual learning is transformed into organizational learning, Kim analyzed the various stages of the learning process, concentrating particularly on the transfer from individual to organizational memory, or what others have termed the diffusion of individual knowledge within the organization (Nonaka 1996) or the encoding of inferences from history into organizational routines (Levitt and March 1988). Organizational routines are transmitted and improved upon through socialization, education, imitation, problem-solving, and personnel movement (Levitt and March 1988: 320). Additionally, processes of social control are necessary in order to sustain organizational learning, particularly when there are conflicting normative orientations held by different organizational groups. Such conflicts are much more likely to occur in interfirm relations than within firms, and social control in networks is a more problematic undertaking than within firms. There is no systematic coverage of this aspect in the literature on organizational learning.

A related aspect of the process of learning is a view of the organization as an embodiment of past learning. The concept of memory as the storehouse of either individual or organizational knowledge is further explicated by reference to the term 'mental models', which contain both explicit and implicit worldviews and, in turn, guide the acquisition and organization of new knowledge. Mental models, by providing interpretive schemes, may both open up certain learning processes and block others. Organizational mental models exist when individual actors orient themselves to shared models (Argyris and Schön 1978). Such shared models constitute an organization's worldview. Important research questions then become how the sharing of models is accomplished and how much sharing is necessary for an organization to be cohesive but still flexible. This question has so far been framed mainly with reference to learning *within* organizations. That framework, however, is not entirely adequate for grappling with the related, but more complex, issues raised by the mutual adjustment of mental models *between* organizations in order to facilitate learning in vertical networks. Processes of mutual adaptation may involve not only technical matters, such as standardization of components and routines, but also business ethics, technical philosophy, and organizational culture.

Another preoccupation of organizational learning theory is the elaboration of a distinction between different levels of learning: between operational and conceptual learning (Kim 1993), single- and double-loop learning (Argyris and Schön 1978), or Learning I and Learning II (Edmondson and Moingeon 1996). Although there are slight differences of emphasis between the various terms, the basic distinction refers to very similar circumstances. Whereas the first term in each conceptual pair refers to the learning of sets of routines that consist of imitation and error-correcting behaviors, the second term indicates that taken-for-granted assumptions are being challenged. Learning I is bound up with improving existing skills and routines; Learning II involves the questioning of existing goals and the attempt to reframe the situation (Edmondson and Moingeon 1996).

Organization theory in which organizational memory is regarded as organizational routines (e.g. Levitt and March 1988; Powell and DiMaggio 1991) implies a view of actors as habit-driven and imitative and is therefore prone to stress the obstacle that organizational memory presents to learning. Although this view is well supported by evidence of the ways in which organizations function, the negative view of operational routines may be excessive, and their importance in some learning contexts is perhaps underestimated.

Because networks open access to various sources of information and offer a broader learning interface than hierarchies do, operational learning is viewed as being easier to promote in hierarchies than in networks, whereas networks are held to be more conducive to conceptual learning than hierarchies are (Kogut, Shan, and Walker 1993: 77; Lundvall 1993: 56). Lundvall (1993) therefore referred to conceptual learning as 'interactive learning', that is, learning which is particularly likely to take place in customer–supplier collaboration. (Similar points are made by Nonaka, Toyama, and Byosière, Ch. 22 in this volume.) The ease of conceptual learning is related to the extent of loose coupling in networks, for the extent of loose coupling preserves identity and uniqueness of supplier firms and potentially retains a greater number of solutions than is possible in tightly coupled systems (Grabher 1993a: 10). Conversely, learning is inhibited if mutual negotiation and reciprocity are replaced by one-sided domination.

Whereas some definitions of organizational learning concentrate mainly on operational learning (e.g. Levitt and March 1988), others give prime emphasis to conceptual learning (e.g. Lundvall 1993). The type of learning varies with the type of transaction and the context in which it occurs. To achieve the right balance between the two types of learning is particularly important in supplier networks. Huber (1991) and Nonaka, Toyama, and Byosière (Ch. 22 in this volume) have pointed out that it is not even clear whether the sharp analytical distinction between operational and conceptual learning can be sustained in real-life learning. In this chapter, I work on the assumption that, in supplier networks, both types of learning are important and should not be viewed in dichotomous terms. As shown by Tsui-Auch (Ch. 32 in this volume), the two types of learning are not necessarily mutually exclusive, and learning through imitation, in certain contexts, can become the first stage of innovation.

But the above broad-brush observations about suitable institutional contexts for conceptual learning are largely hypothetical, and few have been supported by systematic empir-

ical studies (Huber 1991). Despite recent advances by Nonaka, Toyama, and Byosière (Ch. 22 in this volume), there is insufficient detailed information about whether and how conceptual learning in supplier networks can be systematically fostered. The only detailed empirical analysis of conceptual learning is Nonaka's work (1988, 1996; Nonaka, Toyama, and Byosière, Ch. 22 in this volume). According to Nonaka (1988: 60), chaos, in the form of freedom, redundancy, and ambiguity, is conducive to conceptual learning. His examples of conceptual learning illustrated that management's encouragement of experimentation, free communication flows in all directions, and tolerance of redundancy, that is, the conscious overlapping of information, activities, and responsibilities, fosters such learning (Nonaka 1996; Nonaka, Toyama, and Byosière, Ch. 22 in this volume). In networks, in Nonaka's view, creative chaos may result from collaboration with customers, suppliers, or both. Overall, there is little recognition of how difficult it has become to cultivate redundancy in the face of pressure toward cost-cutting and 'lean production', which, moreover, introduce conflict into supplier relations and thus may inhibit knowledge transfer between organizations. Clearly, more work on conceptual learning in supplier networks is needed.

Another type of learning discussed in the literature (e.g. Nonaka 1996; Spender 1996) is the acquisition of tacit knowledge, that is, knowledge intimately tied to the knower's experience. To Nonaka, Toyama, and Byosière (Ch. 22 in this volume), capturing individual, intuitive knowledge by converting it into explicit knowledge for the benefit of the organization is the central activity of the knowledge-creating company. Spender pointed out that the idiosyncratic and rare nature of tacit knowledge makes it difficult to transfer and hence particularly likely to give comparative advantage (Spender 1996: 56). But again, insufficient attention has been given to the fact that the conversion of implicit learning into explicit learning across organizational boundaries may be much more problematic than such conversion within organizations.

One basic assumption of most organizational learning theory is that learning is socially constructed, that is, what is learned and how learning occurs are fundamentally connected to the context in which that learning occurs (for greater detail on this aspect, see Macharzina, Oesterle, and Brodel, Ch. 28 in this volume). Presumably, a firm's organizational mental models, or maps, modes of interaction, and organizational structures are shaped at least to some extent by the philosophical traditions and social institutions of the society in which the firm is located. Philosophical traditions and societal ideologies influence the degree of individualism or collectivism in a society and affect attitudes toward uncertainty, risk, and trust, all of which are highly important to how knowledge is acquired, shared, and transferred between organizations. Societal institutions, such as government agencies, trade associations, and standard-setting bodies, may diffuse information among firms through coercive and normative processes that, in turn, affect both network structure and the ease of coordination within networks. The mode of financing and of human resource development also have a crucial bearing on what kind of knowledge is produced, how easily it is produced, and how smoothly one type of knowledge is converted into another (Nonaka, Toyama, and Byosière, Ch. 22 in this volume). Hence, the issue of differing organizational mental maps, or, in the words of DiBella, Nevis, and Gould (1996), organizational learning styles, has particular relevance for the comparative cross-national study of supplier networks.

For DiBella, Nevis, and Gould (1996), variations in learning style are based on learning orientations that, in turn, are composed of different attitudes toward and policies on sources and modes of learning, the question of how to organize the learning process, and the organizational activities that are selected as foci for learning. These learning orientations then form the basis for the development of a typology of learning styles that can be useful in intersectorial or cross-national comparisons of supplier networks.

Organizational Learning in Supplier Networks

The review of theory on supplier networks and organizational learning has demonstrated that, although many of the basic concepts of organizational learning theory are applicable to learning within supplier networks, this body of theory needs to be amended in order to accommodate the special features and requirements of supplier networks. Network analysis, in turn, must take on board some of the findings of theory on organizational learning. Whereas theory of learning *within* organizations has focused mainly on the transfer of learning from the individual to the organization, an amended theory has to direct consideration to the coordination of learning *between* organizations and must raise awareness of the problems entailed in this process.

Several specific dimensions that have not received adequate attention in theories on learning in networks can be readily identified. First, it is now widely realized that extensive external interorganizational relations may be a more important source of capacity and capability than are many aspects of internal relations (Clegg and Hardy 1996: 9; Lundvall 1993; Nonaka, Toyama, and Byosière, Ch. 22 in this volume), and dense flows of information are connected with superior performance (Barney and Hansen 1994; Helper and Sako 1995; Ring and van de Ven 1992). Hence, scanning of the organizational environment may have to become a more important part of organizational learning theory.

Second, the foremost learning problem in networks is the transfer of various kinds of information and knowledge *between* legally and economically independent organizations. Because such transfer is seldom contractually regulated and because it involves relinquishing potentially valuable resources, network-building and maintenance necessitate the creation of the conditions that make such transfer possible. The impediments to openness and reciprocity in network relations are still not sufficiently considered in either network or organizational learning theory.

Network construction entails devising structural and cultural mechanisms to facilitate the coordination of mental models and learning styles between network firms in order to smooth information exchange and synchronize operating procedures. Going beyond building good channels of communication, network construction is also about coordination of goals and of ways to achieve them. Given that network organizations have some shared and some opposing goals, such coordination amounts to a difficult balancing act. The hub firm, which in many cases is more powerful than the other organizations in its network, may impose its priorities on supplier firms, but the use of power precludes the possibility of capturing implicit knowledge and inhibits conceptual learning.

The most important task in network construction is to coordinate mental maps or learning styles on the basis of mutual trust (Lane and Bachmann 1998), but the problematic aspects of building and maintaining trust have received insufficient consideration in the literature on interorganizational learning (e.g. Nonaka, Toyama, and Byosière, Ch. 22 in this volume). Only when exchange partners trust each other, when they believe or expect that the other party will not take advantage of their vulnerability to opportunism, will the relationship open up enough to foster a free and dense exchange of information (Ring and van de Ven 1992). Definitions of trust vary widely, depending on whether trust is regarded as being based on rational calculation, common values, or common cognitions (for an extended discussion of definitional problems, see Lane 1998). One theoretical distinction highly relevant in the context of interorganizational learning is that between personal trust and institutionally based trust (Zucker 1986).

The creation and maintenance of trust between network firms is usually reliant on some form of institutionally based trust, that is, mutually known and accepted institutionalized rule systems, which are more durable than personal relations. This reliance may substitute for or reinforce personal trust, that is, trust embedded in the social relations between boundary-spanning personnel of network firms. Once trust has been established, hub firms may need to sustain it by devising incentive systems and modes of control that secure a lasting and reliable coordination of routines and worldviews. Finally, flexibility on the part of the buyer firm is required in order to adjust its internal relations and capabilities to take advantage of what the network has to offer.

Third, given the importance of conceptual knowledge for innovation (Lundvall 1993), network relations have to be organized so that they encourage such learning. At the same time, care must be taken to ensure that already accumulated knowledge does not become an obstacle to radical change (Miles and Snow 1992). Hence, network construction for conceptual learning poses particularly difficult problems for the hub firm. They relate both to the building of the network and to relations with individual supplier firms in the network (Semlinger 1993: 326–30). The hub firm has to retain enough freedom to introduce new firms and new bodies of knowledge into the network. However, this freedom cannot be retained at the expense of the stability and security of firms in the network. Relations between the customer and supplier firms have to be coupled loosely enough to afford supplier firms the autonomy that encourages learning; at the same time, network relations have to be close and stable enough to establish trust.

Fourth, unlike the three preceding points, which deal with learning in networks, this one focuses on the notion of 'network as knowledge', developed by Kogut, Shan, and Walker (1993: 76–7). They argued that networks represent a stock of knowledge for participating firms and that a firm's knowledge of the network is itself an important organizational resource. Such knowledge is about how to harness the capabilities of network firms through cooperation, and it becomes an important determinant of the firm's competitive strength. A similar point is developed by Ciborra (1991: 66). Thus, firms have to build up experience in network management before they commit themselves to the transfer of valuable strategic capabilities.

Fifth, the issue of divergent mental maps is revealed particularly starkly in cross-national comparisons of supplier networks. Organizations vary from country to country in the form they assume for balancing the need for freedom with the need to promote the stability and security of firms in their networks. This variability results from the presence of different worldviews and interpretative schemes. It leads to a diversity of structural and cultural attributes: maintenance of differing balances between loose and tight couplings between network firms; varying role definitions within network firms, with consequences for redundancy of knowledge; different conceptions of knowledge, such as knowledge as individual property and knowledge as collective property; and varying degrees of codification and formalization of knowledge. For comparative network analysis, the impact that the diversity of institutions has on the synchronization of the mental models and learning styles of network firms is another area where research must increase. Whenever a particular national learning style has become associated with competitive advantage, companies from less competitive nations have engaged in learning through imitation. Despite problems with learning through imitation, in which the social embeddedness of learning is largely disregarded, such learning has nevertheless led to some moderate convergence in learning styles (Cooke 1993; Helper and Sako 1995; Jürgens 2000a).

Part II. Learning in Networks: Diversity among Industries and Countries

Building Networks and Organizational Learning

The much increased use of outsourcing in all advanced economies has not universally been associated with the building of network structures and a heightened propensity for external learning. Although suppliers have become more and more closely linked to and even dependent on customer firms, this change has not necessarily promoted trust, openness, and willingness to exchange knowledge. Most scholars studying networks overestimate the readiness of firms to share knowledge and underestimate the many obstacles that prevent knowledge transfer (Hardy, Phillips, and Lawrence 1998). Such obstacles are particularly formidable when exchange is coordinated by means of power rather than trust. Even if mutual trust is present, the sheer volume of new knowledge and competencies now demanded of suppliers in leading-edge industries often overtaxes their capabilities. The result has been the disappointment of customer expectations and even severe failure in communication (Jürgens 2000a). Additionally, the increasing internationalization of such networks has led to a 'walling off' (an erection of barriers), which is indicative of the problem of establishing trust across spatial and cultural distances (Hirsch-Kreinsen 1997: 4–5).

Where networks have been built, one finds marked differences between countries, industries, and firms. Networks are concentrated in industries that are highly internationalized and characterized by the assembly of a large number of parts. Within industries, enduring networks are more commonly developed by customer firms that make customized rather than standardized products. In these industries, of which the automotive industry is prototypical, the transfer of both operational routines and conceptual knowledge has been intense (Helper 1991; Helper and Sako 1995; Imrie and Morris 1992; Jürgens 2000b; Semlinger 1993). In the automotive and electronics industries, network-building and reshaping have been of a strategic character, and access to conceptual knowledge has been a vital part of the strategy.

In more traditional industries, by contrast, network relations have remained more loosely coupled, information flows less dense, and the quest for conceptual knowledge more muted (e.g. Arrighetti, Bachmann, and Deakin 1997; Lane and Bachmann 1996, on the mining machinery and kitchen furniture industries).

Networks mainly have been utilized to gain complementary capacity, cost advantage through specialization, and, in some cases, incremental improvement of products. Networks are not constantly reshaped in order to increase competitive advantage but rather are often extremely stable (Arrighetti, Bachmann, and Deakin 1997).

Lastly, in industries exposed to intense global competition, pressures to achieve cost reduction have been strong and have often been incompatible with open and trusting relations, which are conducive to organizational learning. Practices such as lean production, which involves the elimination of redundancy, are in some respects even fundamentally at odds with conceptual learning. In rather traditional industries, this dilemma has not been as acute, although the managerial ideology of lean production has begun to encroach even on these industries.

Coordinating Mental Maps: Facilitators and Obstructions

The coordination of mental maps, as argued in the preceding sections of this chapter, requires the building of trust relations, which can be based on either interpersonal trust or institutional trust. Comparative research on trust between organizations has shown that the building of trust relations is influenced by the institutional framework in which networks are situated. For example Lane (1997a) established that, in Germany, where institutional systems of legal, technical, and market rules are dense, mutually reinforcing, and legitimated by common membership in rule-making associations, mutual trust and cooperation were more frequently established than in Britain, where the reverse conditions pertained. The development of interpersonal trust heavily depends on geographical proximity, and the overall opportunity for face-to-face relationships, and the stability of the network relationship. Although British firms placed greater emphasis on interpersonal contact when establishing trust relations, the conditions for durable face-to-face relations were generally more fragile in Britain than in Germany because of greater instability in both large companies (more take-overs) and smaller firms (higher bankruptcy rates) (Lane and Bachmann 1996).

Mutual trust is only the first and basic condition for fostering interorganizational learning. Other structural arrangements have to be made in order to stimulate and maintain the different kinds of learning that take place. The most common type of learning in supplier networks is operational learning and the mutual acceptance of common organizational routines. Operational learning has found its highest development in systems of JIT production and delivery and associated measures of quality control, and the importance of operational learning for the smooth functioning of supplier networks should not be underestimated. Without the constant detection and correction of error, tight synchronization of production processes between organizations could not function at all. Synchronization is achieved through the adoption of supplier rating systems, quality control measures, close inspection of suppliers' premises, and, above all, through computerized links between customer and supplier firms.

The presence of such arrangements is, however, still uneven among industries and countries. It is most developed in the automotive industry and only patchily adopted in more traditional industries (Arrighetti, Bachmann, and Deakin 1997; Lane and Bachmann 1996). In more traditional industries, German firms have advanced further than their British counterparts in the adoption of JIT delivery, rating systems, and quality audits, and German firms are also more prone to strengthen commercial ties through other means, such as giving suppliers purchase guarantees or technical assistance and exchanging engineering staff (Deakin, Lane, and Wilkinson 2000; Lippert 1997).

It is clear, however, that during the 1990s greatly intensified competition and increased vulnerability to cost pressures among British and German firms began to undermine previously consensual relations and the willingness of suppliers to disclose knowledge (Cooke 1993; Jürgens 2000b; Semlinger 1993). In globalized industries, such as the automotive and the machine-tool industries, cooperation between German firms has become more strained than it used to be, and knowledge transfer is being impeded through the worsening obstruction of the mobility of technical staff between contracting firms (Hirsch-Kreinsen 1997: 4). Nevertheless, supplier relations are still more consensual in Germany than, say, in the United States (Hirsch-Kreinsen 1997; Lippert 1997).

To capture implicit knowledge, supplier networks have to encompass technological cooperation between customer and supplier firms based on common development and design activities. As noted above, such collaboration is unevenly developed. It is most common in technologically advanced industries and where either customization or 'whole-system' supply is common. It occurs mainly with first-tier suppliers or, outside the automotive industry, with technologically sophisticated suppliers of important components. Lane (1997a) found this kind of collaboration to be more frequent in machine-building than in the furniture industry and, within industries, more common in German networks than in British networks. The fact that boundary-spanning personnel in Germany includes persons with technical expertise far more often than is the case in Britain must also contribute to this more frequent exchange of technical knowledge. Such superior technological cooperation and access to implicit knowledge, particularly among German manufacturers of mining machinery, are linked to that industry's high degree of incremental innovation (Weber 1992), which is based on continual improvement through learning. Because of fierce competition between firms, technological collaboration and learning in horizontal network relationships between suppliers do not exist in either Britain or Germany.

The great significance that conceptual learning is accorded in the literature is not paralleled by eager embrace within organizations (Dodgson 1993; Huber 1991). The literature on supplier relations offers few insights into conceptual learning, into the questioning of established learning routines and their replacement with new frameworks. But a study of customer–supplier networks in the German engineering industry of the Ruhr District (Grabher 1993b) put forward a suggestive explanation of why conceptual learning has been blocked in local networks. The very same characteristics of networks that promote extensive operational learning, continual incremental improvement of products, and the updating of those products' technical features—the very stability and close linkage of networks—have also led to what Grabher termed cognitive lock-in and hence to an inability to think conceptually. High mutual commitment may result in a homogeneous worldview that precludes competing perceptions and interpretations of information (Grabher 1993a: 18; see also Lane and Bachmann 1996 on the industry for mining machinery and, more generally, Lippert 1997 on the machine-tool industry). Such cognitive lock-in also lends support to network theorists (Nohria 1992) who argue for promoting dynamic networks and wish to combine a constant reshaping of networks with stable, trust-based relations. Just how this precarious balance between organizational flexibility and stability can be created and maintained remains elusive, however.

National Learning Styles

In the notion of national learning styles, previously mentioned work that DiBella, Nevis, and Gould (1996) have done on learning orientation and styles is adapted and combined with Aoki's (1994) insights into communication and information flows. This elaboration of national learning styles within supplier networks conveys a stylized picture of differences that emerge in the manner and focus of learning as shaped by national, cultural, and institutional environments and by resulting divergence in organizational structures and understanding of the managerial role. Contrasts are drawn between the learning styles of Britain, the United States, Japan, and Germany.

In Japan, the comparatively high degree of vertical disintegration and network development and the close coupling of networks, including supplier networks, is reflected in references to Japan as a network economy or as alliance (or organized) capitalism (Aoki 1994; Gerlach and Lincoln 1992: 493; Imai and Itami 1984: 294; Nonaka and Reinmöller 1998). It is less well known that Germany's organized or coordinated capitalism also includes very stable, albeit less tightly coupled, supplier networks (Lane and Bachmann 1996; Porter 1990), although vertical integration has remained significantly higher in Germany than in Japan. The description of capitalism in Britain and the United States as 'atomized', in contrast, refers, among other features, to the more decentralized supplier structures and their more competition-oriented nature (Lippert 1997). Both comparative and individual-country studies of supplier networks in these four countries tend to confirm these labels although variation between industries is also emphasized (Helper and Sako 1995; Jürgens 2000a; Sako 1992). But such studies also indicate that network structures and processes in the Western capitalist countries are beginning to show some features of the Japanese pattern (Cooke 1993; Helper and Sako 1995; Imrie and Morris 1992; Jürgens 2000a; Oliver and Wilkinson 1988; Sako 1992).

The literature suggests that Japanese networks foster a high degree of both internal and external learning as well as a team approach (Nonaka and Reinmöller 1998). The Japanese view of knowledge as collective property has led to dense and relatively free information flows across organizational boundaries both within and between organizations (Aoki 1994; Nonaka and Byosière 1999). Although processes of dissemination have some formal characteristics, informal dissemination of knowledge is very prevalent. These learning orientations make it possible to capture implicit knowledge and convert it into explicit, conceptual knowledge (Nonaka and Byosière 1999). This learning style corresponds closely to what DiBella, Nevis, and Gould (1996) termed 'communal style' (p. 51).

Information on the conduciveness of Japanese networks for the generation of original conceptual knowledge, or the existence of platforms for dynamic conversion of types of knowledge (Nonaka and Reinmöller 1998) is ambiguous. On the one hand, the easy combination of different bodies of knowledge across horizontal and vertical boundaries (Aoki 1994; Nonaka and Reinmöller 1998) and the tolerance of redundancy (Nonaka and Reimöller 1998) are seen to be conducive to conceptual learning. On the other hand, single-sourcing and the fostering of strong interdependence between powerful hub firms and generally smaller suppliers in very hierarchically organized and pyramidic network structures may lead to domination and the blocking of conceptual learning. But this likely negative effect is mitigated by other measures. Competition between suppliers, both through ranking by the customer firm and through lateral communication in supplier associations (Sako 1992: 236), discourages routinization and complacency. Additionally, the encouragement of some suppliers to serve multiple customers may serve to prevent cognitive lock-in in tightly coupled networks.

The association by Imai and Itami (1984) of Japanese networks with strengths in incremental innovation is probably the most adequate typification, although Nonaka and Reinmöller (1998: 412, 418, 423) also highlight recent, more radical product innovation in fax machines, optical products, and bicycle components. Highly positive performance outcomes in manufacturing also suggest that operational routines are constantly improving through the continuous encouragement of operational learning and the integration of explicit knowledge into efficient systems. A prime example of this improvement is Toyota's perfection of the JIT process (Nonaka and Reinmöller 1998). The Japanese learning style is reflected in a pattern of supplier networks operating on the basis of long-term implicit contracts, close interdependence between customer and supplier firms, diffuse interpersonal relations, little formalization of interfirm contracts, high developed interdependence, and strong mutual obligation (Helper and Sako 1995; Sako 1992).

The organizational learning style DiBella, Nevis, and Gould (1996) termed 'rugged individualism' (p. 51) is closest to the pattern found in the two Anglo-Saxon countries. It entails an understanding of knowledge as personal property and an emphasis on individual development. According to these authors, knowledge is predominantly created internally, and dissemination of knowledge tends to be informal. Where knowledge is sought externally, network ties tend to be short term, and networks are fairly loosely coupled (see Sturgeon 1997: 15, on the computer industry) and hence more dynamic than their Japanese counterparts. Potentials of network linkages are often underutilized, because of the short-term efficiency considerations of final assemblers (Lippert 1997: 7). These features are summarized by the term 'competitive network'. In addition to such cultural orientations, institutional factors, such as antitrust legislation, also mitigate the construction of close and enduring networks. This learning style is said to be well adapted to conceptual learning and innovation (Imai and Itami 1984: 306; on the United States, see Kogut, Shan, and Walker 1993: 80) but less conducive to operational learning and continual incremental improvement. Mutual adaptation of learning orientations is not a top priority.

Rugged individualism is associated with a greater incidence of arm's length relations and decentralized supplier structures and with a lesser development of supplier networks than is the case with other styles of corporate interaction (Hirst and Zeitlin 1989; Imai and Itami 1984: 294; Imrie and Morris 1992; Kogut, Shan, and Walker 1993; Lippert 1997). The form of network organization is distinguished by a strong emphasis on loose coupling, competition between suppliers, continued emphasis on price over quality, the preservation of autonomy for all network participants, and the avoidance of long-term commitments. Despite recent changes in these supplier networks away from arm's length contracting, trust within networks remains more elusive and precarious in the United States and Britain than in Japan and Germany (Arrighetti, Bachmann, and Deakin 1997; Helper and Sako 1995; Lane and Bachmann 1996).

The German learning style contains a mixture of elements of the two styles already discussed and is partially captured by what DiBella, Nevis, and Gould (1996) referred to as a 'techno-analytic' style (p. 51). It favors internal and external learning, but external learning does not feature as prominently as in Japan and is confined to customer–supplier relationships with a strong emphasis on joint product development. Preparedness for the pooling of knowledge and the joint continual improvement of routines is undergirded by mechanisms to safeguard the interests of individual firms. Dissemination of knowledge within an industry occurs in a formal manner, although informality can flourish under the protective umbrella of formal procedures. Information flows tend to be denser in German networks than in Anglo-Saxon ones, but organizational flexibility to absorb new knowledge is often less developed in German network firms (Jürgens 2000a: 9). German firms place greater value on preserving autonomy than Japanese firms do, a priority meaning that knowledge does not cross boundaries in Germany with the same ease as in Japan. There is a strong emphasis on the perfecting of existing routines, and conceptual learning has failed to flourish in such networks (Audretsch 1995; Hirsch-Kreinsen 1997; Kern 1996).

The network organization corresponding to the German style of organizational learning is characterized by long-term and close relations and a high degree of reliance on institutionally based trust (Arrighetti, Bachmann, and Deakin 1997; Burchell and Wilkinson 1997; Lane and Bachmann 1996). Such trust relations are particularly developed between the buyers and suppliers of a whole 'system' of vital components (see Lippert 1997: 7, on the machine-tool industry). Networks do not have the same pyramidic form as in Japan, and single-sourcing is fairly rare. In Germany autonomy of network firms is defended by both sides, which is not the case in Japan. Network relationships in Germany are more formal, less diffuse, and less particularistic than they are in Japan. Legal regulation is ubiquitous, if only as a safety net that rarely comes into use (Arrighetti, Bachmann, and Deakin 1997). The main differences between German and Anglo-American networks are the greater stability, higher degree of reciprocity, and the risk-sharing in German interfirm relations (Arrighetti, Bachmann, and Deakin 1997; Lane and Bachmann 1996, 1997). Paradoxically, close, localized trust relations have obstructed the cultivation of openness toward new bodies of knowledge, which are considered essential for radical innovation (Hirsch-Kreinsen 1997: 7).

Such cooperative relations are not universal, however, and the automotive industry in Germany is singled out as being more conflictual. Paradoxically, intense global competition, which requires high levels of continuous innovation, has undermined the chances of establishing learning networks. The radical changes in this industry have not been conducive to relational contracting and collaborative learning (Jürgens 2000b: 279). Domination of smaller suppliers by powerful buyer firms in the automotive industry has become more common than it once was in Germany. Nevertheless, power inequality appears to be less pronounced in Germany than in the Anglo-American countries. This impression is due to Germany's pool of strong, medium-sized supplier firms, which is larger than that in Anglo-American countries, and to Germany's regulation of many aspects of supplier relations through social and technical norms within an industry and through contract law (Lane 1997b; Lane and Bachmann 1997). German contract law encourages risk-sharing and makes it more difficult to exploit power inequalities (Lane and Bachmann 1997).

Conclusions and Lessons for Network Management

This analysis of both supplier networks and organizational learning has revealed that, although each is currently a focus of academic and managerial attention, the two have rarely been linked. This gap in the literature is all the more surprising when one considers that knowledge creation is held to be one of the main reasons for building networks. Although work on organizational learning in hierarchies can be adapted so that it also becomes useful for the stimulation and management of learning in supplier networks, important theoretical and practical problems remain. Some of the impediments to organizational learning that have been identified in hierarchies are magnified in networks, where conflicts of interest loom much larger and competition is as important as collaboration. Hence, managers must systematically develop knowledge of and experience in networks in order to create and exploit learning opportunities. In addition to solutions to the more practical problems of operational synchronization, network management requires sensitivity to the different mental maps and learning styles of network firms. The problems with building dynamic networks conducive to knowledge-sharing and learning should not be underestimated.

For most aspects of organizational learning, it is problematic to extract any clear-cut and detailed lessons for managers. Analysts are still uncertain about whether and how organizations can intentionally create certain types of knowledge—particularly, implicit and conceptual knowledge (e.g. Nanda 1996: 98), the acquisition of which is often seen as serendipitous. Generalizations about the structural and cultural conditions that stimulate such learning remain broad. Simultaneous encouragement of operational and conceptual or implicit learning also remains problematic. The former requires close coordination and tight coupling, particularly when JIT production and delivery are practiced, whereas the latter flourishes particularly in dynamic networks with an emphasis on loose coupling and creative chaos. Hence, managers need to be clear about what type of learning they wish to encourage and need to construct networks accordingly. The development of organizational learning in networks reliant on mutual trust and openness toward new knowledge remains a formidable management challenge in a global economy based on intense competition and high levels of risk.

As for the development of trust, advice cannot go beyond counsel that trust-sensitive management of particular network firms must be combined with preservation of the dynamic nature of the overall network. Although it is easy to advise managers that interorganizational learning in networks requires the establishment of the right balance between competition, cooperation, and trust, between stability and dynamism, it would be extraordinarily difficult to supply detailed instruction on how to achieve that balance.

References

Albach, H., Dierkes, M., Berthoin Antal, A., and Vaillant, K. (eds.) (1998). *Organisationslernen— institutionelle und kulturelle Dimensionen. WZB Jahrbuch 1998.* Berlin: edition sigma.

Alter, C. and Hage, J. (1993). *Organizations Working Together.* Newbury Park, Calif.: Sage.

Aoki, M. (1994). 'The Japanese Firm as a System of Attributes: A Survey and Research Agenda', in M. Aoki and R. Dore (eds.), *The Japanese Firm: Sources of Competitive Strength.* Oxford: Clarendon Press, 11–40.

Argyris, C. and Schön, D. A. (1978). *Organizational Learning: A Theory of Action Perspective.* Reading, Mass.: Addison-Wesley.

Arrighetti, A., Bachmann, R., and Deakin, S. (1997). 'Contract Law, Social Norms and Interfirm Cooperation'. *Cambridge Journal of Economics,* 21: 171–96.

Audretsch, D. B. (1995). *The Innovation, Unemployment and Competitiveness Challenge in Germany.* Discussion paper FS IV 1995–6. Wissenschaftszentrum Berlin für Sozialforschung.

Barney, J. B. and Hansen, M. H. (1994). 'Trustworthiness as a Source of Competitive Advantage'. *Strategic Management Journal,* 15: 175–90.

Burchell, B. and Wilkinson, F. (1997). 'Trust, Business Relationships and the Contractual Environment'. *Cambridge Journal of Economics,* 21: 217–38.

Ciborra, C. U. (1991). 'Alliances as Learning Experiments: Cooperation, Competition and Change in High-tech Industries', in L. K. Mytelka (ed.), *Strategic Partnerships: States, Firms and International Competition.* London: Pinter, 51–77.

Clegg, S. R. and Hardy, C. (1996). 'Introduction: Organizations, Organization and Organizing', in S. R. Clegg, C. Hardy, and W. R. Nord (eds.), *Handbook of Organization Studies.* London: Sage, 1–28.

Cooke, P. (1993). 'The Experiences of German Engineering Firms in Applying Lean Production Methods', in International Institute for Labour Studies (ed.), *Lean Production and Beyond.* Geneva: International Institute for Labour Studies, 77–93.

Deakin, S., Lane, C., and Wilkinson, F. (2000). 'Performance Standards in Supplier Relations: Relational Strategies, Organisational Processes and Institutional Structures', in S. Quack, G. Morgan, and R. Whitley (eds.), *National Capitalisms, Global Competition and Economic Performance.* Amsterdam: John Benjamins, 53–78.

DiBella, A. J., Nevis, E. C., and Gould, J. M. (1996). 'Organizational Learning Style as a Core Capability', in B. Moingeon and A. Edmondson (eds.), *Organizational Learning and Competitive Advantage.* London: Sage, 38–55.

DiMaggio, P. J. and Powell, W. W. (1991). 'Introduction', in W. W. Powell and P. J. DiMaggio (eds.), *The New Institutionalism in Organizational Analysis.* Chicago: University of Chicago Press, 1–38.

Dodgson, M. (1993). 'Organizational Learning: A Review of Some Literatures'. *Organization Studies,* 14: 375–94.

Edmondson, A. and Moingeon, B. (1996). 'When to Learn How and When to Learn Why: Appropriate Organizational Learning Processes as a Source of Competitive Advantage', in B. Moingeon and A. Edmondson (eds.), *Organizational Learning and Competitive Advantage.* London: Sage, 17–37.

Gerlach, M. L. and Lincoln, J. R. (1992). 'The Organization of Business Networks in the United States and Japan', in N. Nohria and R. G. Eccles (eds.), *Networks and Organizations: Structure, Form, and Action*. Boston: Harvard Business School Press, 491–520.

Grabher, G. (1993a). 'Rediscovering the Social in the Economics of Interfirm Relations', in G. Grabher (ed.), *The Embedded Firm*. London: Routledge, 1–31.

—— (1993b). 'The Weakness of Strong Ties: The Lock-in of Regional Development in the Ruhr Area', in G. Grabher (ed.), *The Embedded Firm*. London: Routledge, 255–77.

Hardy, C., Phillips, N., and Lawrence, T. (1998). 'Distinguishing Trust and Power in Interorganizational Relations: Forms and Facades of Trust', in C. Lane and R. Bachmann (eds.), *Trust within and between Organizations*. Oxford: Oxford University Press, 64–87.

Harrison, B. and Kelly, M. (1993). 'Outsourcing and the Search for Flexibility'. *Work, Employment and Society*, 7: 213–36.

Helper, S. (1991). 'Strategy and Irreversibility in Supplier Relations: The Case of the U.S. Automobile Industry'. *Business History Review*, 65: 781–824.

—— and Sako, M. (1995). 'Supplier Relations in Japan and the United States: Are They Converging?' *Sloan Management Review*, 36/3: 77–84.

Hirsch-Kreinsen, H. (1997). *Machine Tool Industry: New Market Challenges and Problems of Innovation Networks*. Paper presented at the International Conference on 'New Product Development and Production Networks: Learning from Experiences in Different Industries and Countries', Wissenschaftszentrum Berlin für Sozialforschung, 20–22 March.

Hirst, P. and Zeitlin, J. (1989). *Reversing Industrial Decline?* Leamington Spa: Berg.

Holmes, J. (1986). 'The Organization and Locational Structure of Production Subcontracting', in A. Scott and M. Storper (eds.), *Production, Work, Territory*. Boston: Allen and Unwin, 80–106.

Huber, G. P. (1991). 'Organizational Learning: The Contributing Processes and the Literatures'. *Organization Science*, 2: 88–115.

Imai, K. and Itami, H. (1984). 'Interpenetration of Organization and Market: Japan's Firm and Market in Comparison with the U.S.'. *International Journal of Industrial Organization*, 2: 285–310.

Imrie, R. and Morris, J. (1992). 'A Review of Recent Changes in Buyer–Supplier Relations'. *Omega: International Journal of Management Science*, 20: 641–52.

Jürgens, U. (2000a). 'Restructuring Product Development and Production Networks: Introduction to the Book', in U. Jürgens (ed.), *New Product Development and Production Networks: Global Industrial Experience*. Berlin: Springer, 1–22.

—— (2000b). 'Toward New Product Development and Production Networks: The Case of the German Car Industry', in U. Jürgens (ed.), *New Product Development and Production Networks: Global Industrial Experience*. Berlin: Springer, 259–88.

Kern, H. (1996). 'Vertrauensverlust und blindes Vertrauen: Integrationsprobleme im ökonomischen Handeln'. *SOFI Mitteilungen*, 24: 7–14.

Kim, D. H. (1993). 'The Link between Individual and Organizational Learning'. *Sloan Mangement Review*, 35/1: 37–50.

Kogut, B., Shan, W., and Walker, G. (1993). 'Knowledge in the Network and the Network as Knowledge: The Structuring of New Industries', in G. Grabher (ed.), *The Embedded Firm*. London: Routledge, 67–94.

Lane, C. (1997a). 'The Social Regulation of Interfirm Relations in Britain and Germany: Market Rules, Legal Norms and Technical Standards'. *Cambridge Journal of Economics*, 21: 197–216.

—— (1997b). 'The Governance of Interfirm Relations in Britain and Germany: Societal or Dominance Effects?', in R. Whitley and P. H. Kristensen (eds.), *Governance at Work*. Oxford: Oxford University Press, 62–85.

—— (1998). 'Introduction: Theories and Issues in the Study of Trust', in C. Lane and R. Bachmann (eds.), *Trust within and between Organizations*. Oxford: Oxford University Press, 1–30.

—— and Bachmann, R. (1996). 'The Social Constitution of Trust: Supplier Relations in Britain and Germany'. *Organization Studies*, 17: 365–95.

—— —— (1997). 'Cooperation in Inter-firm Relations in Britain and Germany: The Role of Social Institutions'. *British Journal of Sociology*, 48: 226–54.

—— —— (eds.) (1998). *Trust within and between Organizations*. Oxford: Oxford University Press.

Levitt, B. and March, J. G. (1988). 'Organizational Learning'. *Annual Review of Sociology*, 14: 319–40.

Lippert, I. (1997). *Reorganizing Process Chains in the German and American Machine Tool Industry.* Paper presented at the International Conference on 'New Product Development and Production Networks: Learning from Experiences in Different Industries and Countries', Wissenschaftszentrum Berlin für Sozialforschung, 20–22 March.

Lundvall, B.-A. (1993). 'Explaining Interfirm Cooperation and Innovation: Limits of the Transactions-cost Approach', in G. Grabher (ed.), *The Embedded Firm.* London: Routledge, 52–63.

Miles, R. E. and Snow, C. C. (1992). 'Causes of Failure in Network Organizations'. *California Management Review*, 34/2: 53–72.

Nanda, A. (1996). 'Resources, Capabilities and Competencies', in B. Moingeon and A. Edmondson (eds.), *Organizational Learning and Competitive Advantage.* London: Sage, 93–120.

Nohria, N. (1992). 'Introduction: Is a Network Perspective a Useful Way of Studying Networks', in N. Nohria and R. G. Eccles (eds.), *Networks and Organizations: Structure, Form, and Action.* Boston: Harvard Business School Press, 1–22.

Nonaka, I. (1988). 'Creating Organizational Order out of Chaos: Self-renewal in Japanese Firms'. *California Management Review*, 30/3: 57–73.

—— (1996). 'The Knowledge-creating Company', in K. Starkey (ed.), *How Organizations Learn.* London: International Thomson Business Press, 18–31.

—— and Reinmöller, P. (1998). 'The Legacy of Learning: Toward Endogenous Knowledge Creation for Asian Economic Development', in H. Albach, M. Dierkes, A. Berthoin Antal, and K. Vaillant (eds.), *Organisationslernen—institutionelle und kulturelle Dimensionen. WZB Jahrbuch 1998.* Berlin: edition sigma, 401–32.

Oliver, N. and Wilkinson, B. (1988). *The Japanisation of British Industry.* Oxford: Blackwell.

Porter, M. E. (1990). *The Competitive Advantage of Nations.* London: Macmillan.

Powell, W. W. (1987). 'Hybrid Organizational Arrangements: New Form or Transitional Development?' *California Management Review*, 30/1: 67–87.

—— (1991). 'Neither Market nor Hierarchy: Network Forms of Organization', in G. Thompson, J. Frances, R. Levacic, and J. Mitchell (eds.), *Markets, Hierarchies and Networks.* London: Sage, 265–76.

Ring, P. S. and van de Venn, A. H. (1992). 'Structuring Cooperative Relationships between Organizations'. *Strategic Management Journal*, 13: 483–98.

Sako, M. (1992). *Prices, Quality and Trust: Interfirm Relations in Britain and Japan.* Cambridge: Cambridge University Press.

Semlinger, K. (1993). 'Effizienz und Autonomie in Zuliefernetzwerken—zum strategischen Gehalt von Kooperation', in W. H. Staehle and J. Sydow (eds.), *Managementforschung* (Vol. 3). Berlin: de Gruyter, 309–54.

Spender, J. C. (1996). 'Competitive Advantage from Tacit Knowledge? Unpacking the Concept and Its Strategic Implications', in B. Moingeon and A. Edmondson (eds.), *Organizational Learning and Competitive Advantage.* London: Sage, 56–73.

Starkey, K. (ed.) (1996). *How Organizations Learn.* London: International Thomson Business Press.

Sturgeon, T. J. (1997). *Turnkey Production Networks: The Organizational Delinking of Production from Innovation.* Paper presented at the International Conference on 'New Product Development and Production Networks: Learning from Experiences in Different Industries and Countries', Wissenschaftszentrum Berlin für Sozialforschung, 20–22 March.

Sydow, J. (1992a). 'On the Management of Strategic Networks', in H. Ernste and V. Meyer (eds.), *Regional Development and Contemporary Industrial Response.* London: Belhaven, 114–29.

—— (1992b). 'Enterprise Networks and Codetermination: The Case of the Federal Republic of Germany', in International Institute for Labour Studies (ed.), *Is the Single Firm Vanishing?* Geneva: International Institute for Labour Studies, 34–65.

Thorelli, H. B. (1986). 'Networks: Between Markets and Hierarchies'. *Strategic Management Journal*, 7: 37–51.

Weber, B. (1992). *Strukturwandel des Bergbaumaschinenbaus und innovative Beschäftigungs- und Qualylifizierungspolitik*. Research Report. Spezialstudie im Auftrag der Innovations- und Koordinierungsstelle der Metallindustrie an der Ruhr-IKS. Gelsenkirchen: Institut Arbeit und Technik.

Williamson, O. E. (1985). *The Economic Institutions of Capitalism: Firms, Markets, Relational Contracting*. New York: Free Press.

Zucker, L. G. (1986). 'Production of Trust: Institutional Sources of Economic Structure, 1840–1920', in B. M. Staw and L. L. Cummings (eds.), *Research in Organizational Behavior: An Annual Series of Analytical Essays and Critical Reviews* (Vol. 8). Greenwich, Conn.: JAI Press, 53–111.

32 Learning in Global and Local Networks: Experience of Chinese Firms in Hong Kong, Singapore, and Taiwan

Lai Si Tsui-Auch

The development of perspectives on organizational learning has been based primarily on the experience in large Western industrialized countries. The learning experience of enterprises in non-Western countries is underrepresented. This chapter presents a review of the learning processes of Chinese firms in Hong Kong, Taiwan, and Singapore, which have characteristics distinct from large Western and Japanese enterprises (see Macharzina, Oesterle, and Brodel, Ch. 28; Child, Ch. 29; Lane, Ch. 31; Nonaka, Toyama, and Byosière, Ch. 22 in this volume).

The chronic Asian economic downturn has prompted policy-makers in many countries in the region to rethink their strategies of development. This reassessment has directed a certain degree of attention to three Chinese-dominated economies—Taiwan, Hong Kong, and Singapore—which are seen as being more resilient than their chief export rivals, such as South Korea and Japan. This characteristic is attributed at least partly to the dominance of Chinese small and medium-sized enterprises, whose corporate flexibility and adaptability enables them to cope with market fluctuation. Within these three economies, however, academics and policy-makers are concerned about the capacity for innovation and competitiveness of small and medium-sized enterprises

in the face of both persistent regional economic downturn and economic as well as social structural transformation at the national and local level.

Since the English industrial revolution, the role of small and medium-sized enterprises in society has received far less attention than the role of large firms. Conflict sociology has traditionally focused on the study of the class struggle between capital and labor primarily in large corporations. By contrast, Calhoun (1982) pointed out that factory workers are not directly exposed to the market but rather are shielded by their organizations, in which they can seek a higher level of security and income than craft workers, self-employed artisans, and owners of small domestic enterprises who are directly exposed to flagging economic activity and market fluctuations. Further interest in the role of small and medium-sized enterprises has built in light of several other realities as well, including the indigenous economic development of non-Western countries since the end of the World War II era (Kumar 1981; Lall 1980); the growing competitiveness of industrial districts in Germany, Italy, and Japan (Piore and Sabel 1984; Sayer 1986; Semlinger 1994), and the rise of small high-tech start-ups in technopolis since the 1970s (Saxenian 1994). Whole fields of social science, such as industrial

The author wishes to thank Mark Auch, Dietmar Brodel, John Child, Meinolf Dierkes, Ute Hoffmann, Christel Lane, Klaus Macharzina, and Kristina Vaillant for their suggestions on earlier versions of this chapter. The present revised version benefits particularly from detailed comments of Barbara Czarniawska and an exchange of ideas with Christoph de Haën.

sociology, development sociology, and the macroeconomic approach to development, now deal with the impact that history and the international and national politicoeconomic environment have on the organization of global, regional, and local production systems (Bello and Rosenfeld 1990; Fujita and Hill 1997), a major topic being technological development, transfer, and learning among firms (Hobday 1994, 1995). Another stream of research, the study of Chinese business organizations[1] (Hamilton 1991; Redding 1990), has concentrated on uncovering cultural strengths and constraints of overseas Chinese enterprises and networks, based on which some phenomena of interorganizational learning can be discerned.

A review of the experience of Chinese small and medium-sized enterprises in Hong Kong, Singapore, and Taiwan can contribute to the field of organizational learning by informing researchers and policy-makers of the diversity in learning strategies and by providing insights for the evaluation of the various perspectives in this line of study. The perspectives of organizational learning can offer concepts to help improve the understanding of the learning processes these firms undergo. This chapter therefore represents an attempt to promote the cross-fertilization of ideas between a variety of research fields.

Perspectives of Organizational Learning

The contending perspectives on organizational learning are broadly categorized in this chapter as the conventional model and the pragmatist viewpoint, depending on the philosophical and theoretical traditions that underlie each.

[1] There is a strand of research on Chinese business organizations sited outside mainland China. It is focused on the business organizations run by overseas Chinese in Southeast Asian countries, Hong Kong, Taiwan, and Western countries. Some authors prefer to use 'overseas Chinese' business organizations or networks.

The Conventional Model of Organizational Learning

The conventional model of organizational learning is based on the traditional theory of organization, which draws insights from cognitive and behavioral theories, structural contingency theory, and ecological approaches (for an overview, see Baum 1996; Burrell and Morgan 1979; Donaldson 1996; Tenbrunsel, Glavin, Neale, and Bazerman 1996). Proponents of the traditional theory of organization conceptualize organizations as systems, as rather stable entities defined by a boundary separating them from the environment (Cyert and March 1963). Organizations need to learn to solve new problems in response to stimuli from the changing environment (Lawrence and Lorsch 1967). Hence, the central task of an organization is to process information in order to arrive at the right strategic decision and to design appropriate rules and procedures to effect changes in cognitive behavior. Leaders and top management are considered the agents responsible for the management of learning. Learning is distinguished largely in terms of dichotomous typologies, such as exploitation versus exploration (March 1991), operational learning versus conceptual learning (Kim 1993), tactical learning versus strategic learning (Dodgson 1993), and lower learning versus higher learning (Fiol and Lyles 1985). These typologies reflect the dichotomous distinction between imitation and innovation: the former being adaptive behavior; the latter, creative behavior.

There are three streams of views on the organizational learning process. The first stream is the information-processing approach, which conceptualizes the learning process as a linear sequence of information acquisition, diffusion, interpretation, and storage of information and experience in organizational memory (Huber 1991; Walsh and Ungson 1991). In this stream the roles of information technologies and written media are discussed in fairly great depth. Action is not taken into explicit account and is assumed to be a natural consequence of learning. The second stream focuses less on the linear sequence of information processing than on the development of shared views derived from different values and ideas of individuals and groups. To facilitate organizational learning, authors suggest ways to promote dialogue between the proponents of different mental models (Argyris and Schön 1996) or to evolve shared mental models (Kim 1993) or cognitive maps (Lee, Courtney, and O'Keefe 1992). In the third stream of views on the organizational learning process, learning is conceived of as stimuli-response patterns, a perspective that reflects a biologistic view of social life (Levitt and March 1988; March and Olsen 1976). Levinthal and March (1993), in line with the institutionalist tradition of organizational studies, discern the paradoxes of organizational learning by theorizing the learning traps of both success and failure. On the one hand, success reinforces excessive exploitation of the existing routine, reducing the organization's ability to cope with the changing environment. On the other hand, failure triggers an excessive exploration of new solutions, leading to neglect of the need for continuity and subjecting the organization to vulnerability in the long run.

Learning as Practice

Authors adopting the view that learning is rooted in practice make no distinction between cognition and interpretation or between knowledge and action (Czarniawska and Sevón 1996; Nonaka and Takeuchi 1995). They thereby suggest that learning stems primarily from action rather than from diffusion of information and training (Brown and Duguid 1991; Orr 1993). Other authors suggest that people learn through creative imitation anchored in specific time and space (Czarniawska 1997; Gherardi 1997). Much of the knowledge that helps people deal with actual problems or sparks innovation is tacit and informal, being spread through interaction, story-telling, and informal processes in action-nets or communal processes (Tyre and von Hippel 1997). From this standpoint learning is a daily process of individuals in groups. It is the accumulation of experience, the formation of skills, and the creation and development of knowledge through practice,

or action, rather than a specific, difficult task that needs to be designed and managed by leaders and top management. Although authors who view learning as practice do not disagree that knowledge is stored in human minds, they conceive of learning as inherently social. Learning, knowledge, and action are not freestanding; they are context-dependent. Knowledge can be formalized and made explicit in some ways, but primarily it is tacitly rooted in individuals' experience and spread through direct communication (for the concept of tacit knowledge, see Polanyi 1967).

Drawing on their research on large Japanese companies in comparison with large U.S. firms, Nonaka and Takeuchi (1995) attributed the success of Japanese firms to a focus on tacit, informal, on-the-job knowledge and informal processes of knowledge creation based on physical experience, intuition, and direct communication. Being unique to each company, such knowledge, they said, is difficult for competitors to copy and hence endows the company with a proprietary value all its own. However, Nonaka and Takeuchi did not dismiss the role of explicit knowledge, crisis excitement instilled by top leaders, knowledge management by top managers, and the role of organizational hierarchy (see also Nonaka and Konno 1998). They claimed to challenge dichotomies, and they aimed to build a universal model of management, linking the implicit and the explicit, the top-down and the bottom-up, bureaucracy and task force, and Eastern philosophy and Western thinking. Instead of following the U.S. trend of slashing the ranks of middle management in the downsizing era, Nonaka and Takeuchi (1995) identified middle management (e.g. knowledge engineers and line supervisors) as the key agent for bridging the ideals of top managers and the views of frontline workers. The theory of organizational knowledge creation is built on the experience that large Japanese corporations have had with product development processes and mirrors the specific organizational structure, corporate culture, and industrial relations of these enterprises in the era of economic boom. Its applicability to Japanese companies during the current economic debacle and to organizations in other countries remains to be explored.

In fact, the theory of knowledge creation has recently been extended to include three foci, reflecting an effort to widen its applicability. The first focus is on the inclusion of the concept of knowledge management, specifically the role of top management and leaders (Nonaka and Konno 1998). What distinguishes this approach from the prevalent models of information-processing and knowledge management is that it emphasizes the nurturing and cultivation of tacit knowledge and individual and collective experience more than it stresses the processing of information by means of advanced technologies. The second focus is on the spatial nature of knowledge creation, as seen in their development of *ba* (a concept originated by a Japanese philosopher and translated as 'shared space for emerging relationships'; see Nonaka and Konno 1998: 1). The authors have linked the intraorganizational focus of knowledge creation to the interorganizational context in a regional industrial district. The third focus of this extended theory of knowledge creation is 'regional endogenous creation', a concept explained by Nonaka, Reinmöller, and Toyama (Ch. 37 in this volume), who suggest that Asian companies go beyond product imitation to product innovation by harnessing the endogenous knowledge rooted in their cultural heritage.

The conception of imitation was regarded by Czarniawska (1997) as inherently creative and innovative. In order for a company or individual to learn from a context-dependent experience, the original experience must be recontextualized to fit a new context. Czarniawska and Sevón (1996) rejected the conventional negative image of imitation as mechanistic copying and borrowed the metaphor of 'translation' (which Latour 1986 proposed as a substitute for the metaphor of diffusion) in order to illuminate the creative nature of imitation. Translation is literally an act or process by which a text in one language is rendered in another, a way of expressing something in another medium or form. It involves transformation, modification, change, renovation, and identity construc-tion—a blending of the foreign and the local, the new and the old. Some authors argued that the recontextualization of ideas disembedded from their original context during processes of organizational imitation processes requires creativity, just as translation does (Sevón 1996). As shown by examples of city management in Warsaw during the 1990s (Czarniawska 1997), the legal and management philosophy of Western administrative systems must be translated into the post-Communist context of Poland before they are likely to result in new solutions to problems.

In illuminating the paradox of continuity and change, Czarniawska and Sevón (1996) stressed change stemming from action and power rather than from mistakes and thereby took a neoinstitutionalist approach to organization. According to them, learning changes individual action patterns that, when reinforced by the interaction of individuals, leads to a change in other people's action patterns. The two authors rejected the conventional definition of power as a fixed property or capacity possessed by particular actors or groups of actors and suggested that power stems from associations. As they stated, the more actors there are who associate with each other, the greater the power that the network creates to effect change (see also Coopey 1995). Nevertheless, Czarniawska and Sevón recognized that learning has both intended and unintended consequences, reflecting the paradox of organizational life.

The Learning Experience of Chinese Firms: A Review of the Literature

Characteristics of Chinese Firms in Hong Kong, Taiwan, and Singapore

This section focuses on Chinese manufacturing firms in light industries (such as electronics, textiles and garments, toys, and footwear) of Hong Kong, Taiwan, and Singapore. Most of the Chinese manufacturing firms in these economies have three characteristics in common. They are (a) small and medium-sized enterprises, (b) latecomers to product technology, and (c) subcontractors or suppliers tied to both global and local production networks. First, most of the small and medium-sized enterprises are owned by a single individual, family, relatives, or friends (Sit and Wong 1989). They are often managed by the owner and a few managers, and the organizational structure is rather flat (Kao 1993). Some authors argue that such a governance structure can enhance a firm's ability to respond quickly to market changes (Lee 1997; Tam 1990). However, given the relative dominance of state monopolies, government-linked companies, and multinational corporations (particularly in Singapore), small and medium-sized enterprises have encountered barriers to the financial market for credit, to the labor market for human resources, and to the product market for sales (Tong 1991; Wade 1990). As compared to the large enterprises, they are more likely to suffer from the vicious cycle of underfinancing, technological underdevelopment, vulnerability to market fluctuations, and bankruptcy.

Second, most of the overseas Chinese firms in Hong Kong, Taiwan, and Singapore are 'latecomers' in product technology (Hobday 1995). Latecomer firms have limited access to the main sources of advanced technology and markets of industrialized countries. They enter the production race not by innovating in the area of production but by performing standardized assembly of low- to medium-end products, traveling backwards along the product life cycle. They gradually catch up with leaders in their respective markets by learning to manufacture, to improve product designs and production processes, and to distribute products beyond domestic markets.

Third, most of these firms are incorporated into the regional production networks of global corporations based in the United States, Japan, western Europe, or their own countries. In the light consumer-goods industries, many brand name companies have given up manufacturing

and shifted to design and development and marketing and distribution. They subcontract firms in the catch-up economies to produce the finished products as specified, namely, on an original-equipment manufacturing contract. For products involving fairly sophisticated technology, corporations provide subcontractors core parts and components, production equipment, or know-how (often through licensing). By outsourcing, global firms do not need to bear the costs and risks of expanding their manufacturing facilities and work force or of taking equity in wholly owned subsidiaries and joint ventures.

Unlike the Japanese small and medium-sized firms, which are often tied to one larger firm, most subcontractors do not work for only one customer but rather constantly compete for contracts from various global corporations. The subcontractors seldom develop a high level of in-house backward integration for manufacturing numerous components and parts but rather procure them from local suppliers. Most of the subcontractors pursue cost-cutting strategies by relocating the manufacturing processes to neighboring countries with cheap labor and sufficient land. In summary, a Chinese firm in these economies is often tied to various global networks and local or regional networks.

The Learning Strategies and Processes of Chinese Firms in Hong Kong, Taiwan, and Singapore

Attention to the learning strategies of Chinese firms in Hong Kong, Taiwan, and Singapore (and other Southeast Asian countries) has been recent, reflecting the economic success of these countries during the past three decades. Both Western and Japanese-centered perspectives focus primarily on the transfer of technology and organizational or management systems to the catch-up economies. The modernization and diffusion of innovation paradigms emphasize the diffusion of advanced Western technology and management systems from the global corporations and prescribe a model of copying to the latecomers (Rogers 1962; for an overview, see Blomstrom and Hettne 1985). The metaphor of diffusion fits with the notion of learning as a stimulus-response pattern. In the Japanese-centered flying geese model it is assumed that Japan and Asia are in the catch-up product cycles. Japan is portrayed as the leading goose, diffusing appropriate technology and management practices to East and Southeast Asia, which constitute the following flock. They adapt to the changing product cycles and copy the Japanese strategy (Inoue, Kohama, and Urata 1993; Kojima 1977). This perspective embodies a biological metaphor, that posits a systemic relationship in which the parts function to support the whole. It fits with the notion of learning as adaptive and imitative action.[2]

Both the modernization approach and the flying geese model focus on the processes of diffusion and adaptation that are being driven from the center by Western and Japanese firms leading in technology but do not deal with the active, learning process of the local firms themselves. This gap is filled by studies on imitation and innovation strategies of Chinese business enterprises in networks.

Learning in Global Networks: A Review of Literature in Development Studies and Political Economies

Amsden (1989) was the first researcher to identify corporate learning by imitation as the key strategy by which latecomer firms may catch up with technological leaders. Taking into account the development experience of the newly industrialized Asian countries (Taiwan, Hong Kong, Singapore, and South Korea) in general and that of South Korea in specific, she argued that a learner, by definition, does not innovate and has to learn to manufacture and compete initially on the combined basis of imported technology, incremental productivity, qualitative improvement of existing

products, low wages, and state subsidies. (For a similar approach, see also writings of several development economists such as Lall 1992.)

Amsden's conceptualization of the imitation strategy is incorporated into Hobday's (1995) 'East Asian innovation approach'. In this study of the technological learning of firms in different industries in Taiwan, Singapore, Hong Kong, and South Korea, Hobday found that latecomer firms had improved their products and processes incrementally by accumulating daily production experience and internalizing the knowledge through interfirm cooperation. He argued that latecomer firms have entered the production race not by introducing new products and processes to the marketplace but by learning to manufacture products that have already entered the phase of their life cycle in which they have been standardized. These firms have gradually caught up by 'learning to imitate' and 'learning to innovate' (p. 47). Hobday argued that the experience of the latecomer firms refutes the standard Western model of the product life cycle, which suggests that corporate growth relies on product innovation in the marketplace. Hobday, instead, defined innovation as the introduction of a process or product new to the individual firm rather than to the marketplace. In other words, the incremental improvement of products or production processes is itself an innovation. Hobday rejected the view that imitation and innovation are dichotomous. He argued instead that learning to imitate, as with learning to innovate, requires creativity.

Hobday (1995) found that corporate learning, as with individual learning, is difficult to observe and analyze, for the process is often 'qualitative, informal, idiosyncratic in nature, cumulative in effect, and uncertain in outcome' (p. 33). He illustrated the institutional channels (forms of interfirm linkages) and determinants (especially the role of the state) that facilitate technological learning. In his conception, the institutional channels include wholly foreign-owned subsidiaries, joint ventures, licensing, subcontracting (original-equipment manufacturing or original-design

[2] The comparison between development perspectives and learning models is based on the comments of Barbara Czarniawska (19 March 1998).

manufacturing),[3] overseas acquisitions or equity investments, and strategic partnerships for technology. Hobday stated that a local, wholly foreign-owned subsidiary or joint venture partner learns to operate imported production equipment and to organize a production routine. He further observed that a local firm, in arranging for subcontracting or licenses, learns to develop full production capacities and to purchase material. Original design manufacturing by a local firm particularly demonstrates the firm's 'internalization' of design skills and knowledge.

Although imitative learning may enable latecomer firms to stay in the production race, it does not enable them to cooperate and compete on equal terms with technological leaders. Hobday (1995) revealed, for example, that subcontractors continued to depend on technological leaders for components, product technology, and market channels. He saw the establishment of own brand-name activity as the way to reduce this power asymmetry and he asserted that a firm could, through overseas acquisitions and strategic partnerships for technology tap the research and development knowledge of the partners, scan the environment of the markets in industrialized countries, and pave the way for bringing new products onto the global market. Acer (in Taiwan) is frequently cited as an example of the initial success and limitations of imitative learning and to show the way to strengthen a local firm's capability for product innovation (Engardio and Burros 1996; Hobday 1995; Wade 1990). Acer started with eleven engineers in 1976, mainly cloning IBM computer products. Original-equipment manufacturing deals enabled Acer to learn from technological leaders how to develop full production capacities, and the firm became the world's largest producer of

PCs, color monitors, keyboards, fax machines, and printers in the late 1980s. However, Acer was aware of its dependence on technological leaders for core technologies and market outlets. Given the limitation of the imitative learning strategy, Acer set out to create its own brand-name products. It employed a number of U.S.-trained Taiwanese engineers (who had worked for U.S. companies) to develop software behind the research and development frontier set by Intel, IBM, and AT&T. Acer designed the first Chinese operating system, 'Dragon', which became a standard in Asia. With IBM, Apple, and several Japanese companies, Acer helped define Asian computer standards (Hobday 1995). It also received royalties from NEC and several other U.S. companies for licensing its PC chipset designs. By 1988, Acer's own brand accounted for 60 per cent of the company's sales (Johnstone 1989: 51). Acer appears to be determined to continue developing and marketing its own brand names. It has licensed the know-how (a combination of semiconductor, optical, and liquid-crystal technologies) from IBM Japan and plans to introduce its first commercial state-of-the-art product, TFT-LCDs (thin-film-transistor liquid-crystal displays) (Lee 1999). In 1997, Acer's former customer, Hitachi, made an unprecedented move out of in-house product development in order to seek a strategic alliance with the company for joint development of multimedia home appliances so that the company could tap its fast prototype development (Morishita 1997). The decision reconfirms the existence of a 'reverse' flow of knowledge to traditional technological leaders in some niche product areas (Hobday 1995). As Acer has shown, expansion of a firm's size (which brings economies of scale) and financial base are preconditions for a company to learn to innovate, and these preconditions can be nurtured by the company itself, by the institutional environment or by both. Moreover, strategic alliances and joint ventures with traditional brand-name leaders continue to be an important mechanism of learning.

Some authors regard the state as a determinant of latecomers' technological learning (Amsden 1989; Hobday 1995; Lall 1992). They

---

[3] Undertaking an original-equipment manufacturing contract, a subcontractor is responsible for producing a finished product in compliance with the specification of the customer, who will be responsible for marketing under the customers' brand name. The term 'original design manufacturing' was first used in Taiwan (Johnstone 1989: 51) to refer to an arrangement whereby a subcontractor designs products according to a general design layout provided by a buyer.

have argued that the building of technological capabilities requires the development of new knowledge, skills, organizational forms, and interfirm linkages and that the associated high risks and learning costs often discourage individual firms from acquiring technological knowledge. These authors therefore reason that institutional support is badly needed to offset the costs and risks in knowledge acquisition. As evident in Taiwan, Singapore, and Hong Kong, the governments have created favorable conditions for learning by providing human resource training, spreading relevant production and marketing knowledge, setting regulations and standards, establishing science parks, or subsidizing research and development in strategic industries and in public institutions.

Learning in Local Networks: A Review of Literature on Overseas Chinese Business Organizations

In a study of the career histories of Hong Kong entrepreneurs, Tam (1990) constructed an ideal-type Chinese business system with which interorganizational learning, largely unintended, can be discerned. He posited that learning in Chinese enterprises is not firm-centered and that knowledge is not shared beyond the close circle surrounding the entrepreneur, the owner. In Tam's view, the most valuable knowledge is the formula for success. He regarded the learners as untrained excellent performers; they develop themselves, with or without facilitators. Their learning of entrepreneurship is 'essentially self-directed, self-structured, goal-driven, exploratory, experientially based, and continuous throughout life' (p. 173). A successful learner, he asserted, either breaks away from the existing firm to establish his or her own firm or takes over the original firm's leading position with a new vision. According to Tam, learning transcends an individual firm's boundary and existence, so it is futile to take an individual firm as a unit of analysis. Instead, he argued, one should analyze groups of firms, the 'Chinese Business system'.

Following Tam's argument, one should place the focus of study on the innovative capacity of the Chinese business system rather than on the organizational learning of individual firms. The conception of overseas Chinese firms as elements of networks built up by family, clans, former employer–employee relationships, and friendship is widely shared by a number of authors (Kao 1991; Wong 1991). The personal networks help internalize the costs of information exchange. They also provide an impetus for innovation because it is quicker to secure financial support from relatives and immediate family members than from banks (Hamilton 1991).

According to Tam (1990), the Chinese business system resembles the Japanese system only on the surface, diverging significantly from it because of the different institutional and cultural contexts involved. In contrasting the Hong Kong business system and the Japanese business system, he showed that the Japanese system is centripetal whereas that of Hong Kong is centrifugal. In Japan, he stated, supportive and protective government policies and the system's greater control over the market enable industrial groups to adopt a group corporate strategy and to sustain longer, more stable relationships with subcontractors than is usually the case in the Chinese business system. According to Tam, individual firms in Japan enjoy great stability and security, circumstances that enable them to develop mutually beneficial and prosperous interdependent relationships with each other for collective learning and innovation. Hong Kong firms, however, seek corporate survival in a context of uncertainty and insecurity stemming from their vulnerability to world market fluctuation and a lack of government support. Not having the safety nets provided in the Japanese business system, Hong Kong firms can hardly develop long-term orientation. Tam pointed out that their interorganizational bondage tends to be transient and unstable and that the relationships between firms is instrumental and utilitarian. Unlike Japanese corporate networks, which are characterized by a hierarchical structure, tight customer–supplier relationships, a focus on quality, and great stability, Chinese networks are decentralized, loosely coupled, cost conscious, and highly unstable (Tsui-Auch 1999a).

Within a Chinese enterprise, employees feel insecure (Tam 1990). This insecurity drives employees to learn to be self-reliant rather than to attain collective goals. Whereas Japanese firms practice egalitarian inclusion of their members, Chinese firms practice differential and discriminatory inclusion. Chinese firms, according to Tam, are characterized by high reward differentials between owners and employees, limited career opportunities, centralization of decision-making, and arbitrary dismissals. Employees who are related in one way or another to the owning family are nurtured on a fast track, eventually ending up in the ownership echelon. Employees who are not related to the owning family have only limited career movement and face a glass ceiling. Whereas employees in Japanese enterprises are socialized to take the company as their family and to work for the company, Chinese work in companies to earn a living for their own families, and their loyalty and commitment lie outside the firm. Japanese learn to depend on the company, while Chinese learn to depend on themselves. Japanese employees learn in a secure context, whereas Chinese work hard in a context of insecurity.

In Chinese firms the bifurcation of managerial career routes is paralleled by two layers of management development activities, with one being openly endorsed and the other closely concealed. There are two types of learners. The overt learners are those who have a 'relationship' with the owner and who are identified as the 'selected'. The covert learners do not have such a background and are left to develop their entrepreneurial skills and connections on their own within the company and the network, often without the awareness of the owner-manager. Analyzing the career histories of some 300 entrepreneurs drawn from a variety of industries, Tam found that some 71 per cent of them had gone the route of covert learners, moving from employee to employer status.

The spin-off of employees reinforces the employer's distrust of the work force and the strong belief in the loyalty of family members.

This combination, in turn, leads to an externalization of operational and administrative functions, which leads to the evolution of the subcontracting system. The balance of these forces produces a drive to reduce the internal complexity of firms, increases employees' determination to set up their own firms, and adds to the number of enterprises that are founded.

The path along which Chinese firms achieve constant renewal and innovation efficiency differs from that taken by U.S. and Japanese corporations. The corporate renewal of large U.S. enterprises depends on leadership replacement—the mechanism by which a new leader is substituted for the old one. The new leader is expected to introduce new vision and will adjust personnel, structure, and systems to reflect the new emphasis. Japanese firms achieve corporate renewal by means of crisis excitement. Instead of being replaced, the leader articulates the crisis and mobilizes the work force to respond to new situations and to share the fate of the 'community'. In Chinese firms, there is no separation of ownership and management (see also Redding 1990), an arrangement that makes it almost impossible to replace corporate leadership. Furthermore, the lack of a sense of belonging and of an integrative community makes crisis excitement impracticable. The articulation of crises might undermine the limited confidence that employees have in the owning family and might increase the firm's labor turnover. Instead, corporate renewal is achieved through the fission and refusion of firms. The business system is constantly revitalized when learners break away from the existing companies and strike out their own. The constant breaking-up of firms and the nonstandardization of employee behavior reduce the possibility of building bureaucracies and prevent ossification. Furthermore, Tam (1998) suggested that the Chinese business system provides a favorable context for the diffusion of innovation, that the entrepreneurial bent of the system makes it conducive to the cross-fertilization of ideas and to innovation. The system portrayed by Tam fosters rapid entry and exploitation of business opportunities. Tam concluded (p. 174) that the Chinese system offers a 'seedbed for learning and experimentation' given relatively free market entry and exit, and the readiness of entrepreneurial minded employees to establish spin-offs, and the spillover of success formulae. Hamilton (1991), who studied Chinese firms in Taiwan, observed that manufacturers cope with market fluctuations by keeping their firms small and develop a network of reliable firms by encouraging their employees to set up their own businesses as spin-offs. Employers supported the employees by granting them initial market access and supplying components to the new firms, and many of the former employees remained loyal to their former employers out of mutual self-interest. The constant fusion of firms, coupled with relatively free exit from and entry into networks, made it difficult for firms to keep new business formulae secret. In a local network, each firm was surrounded by a number of firms watching for new formulae, and each firm had potential entrepreneurs willing to set up their own business. Circulating stories of success and failure in networks encouraged organizational imitation. A firm that commenced the manufacture of wigs, plastic flowers, and electronic products would be imitated during the year by hundreds of firms, each locking into and expanding the core network.

The networking mode reflects heavy reliance on personal trust based on 'guanxi'—connections derived from family, clans, former employer–employee relationships, and friendship (Ichiro 1991; Kao 1991; Wong 1991). This reliance fosters fast learning and helps reduce the costs of learning and innovation. Rather than use impersonal channels such as advertising and sales promotion, Hong Kong textile manufacturers count on family members, relatives, friends, former employers, or employees to procure subcontracting orders (Leung 1993; Sit and Wong 1989; Wong 1988). Hamilton (1991) observed that manufacturers often entered into informal verbal agreements with local firms. For instance, computer firms in Taiwan based most of their transactions with local firms on personal trust instead of contracts (but they did close formal contracts with multinational corporations). Hamilton argued that reliance on

personal trust was not simply a kind of sentimental tie but rather a reflection of an instrumental rationality. First, it provided a degree of predictability for manufacturers. Reliance on personal trust has normative rules that people are obliged to follow; those who fail to fulfill their promise will find it difficult to reestablish connections. Second, such reliance offered manufacturers security. Manufacturers often passed on production and marketing knowledge to their family and friends free of cost at social gatherings in restaurants, festivals, and wedding dinners. Lastly, reliance on personal trust enhanced flexibility by making it possible to accelerate the mobilization of resources. A family often offered capital and credit for risk-taking ventures and thereby spurred innovation (see also Limlingan 1986). In these ways predictability, security, and flexibility help reduce risks and costs in knowledge acquisition and innovation.

Continuity Versus Change in the Learning Strategies

The organizing and networking modes of Chinese firms have fostered specific network-dependent learning processes, which generate both intended and unintended consequences. In global networks, Chinese firms succeed largely in imitative learning but, except for a few enterprises mainly in Taiwan, rarely develop their own brand-name products. In local contexts, the constant fusion of firms speeds up the flow of information and hence the imitation especially of product and investment strategies. Manufacturers imitate the business formulae of niche-spotting and quick profit-making and are successful in their pursuit of constant renewal. However, Chinese industrial networks maintain a short-term focus and do not engage in joint development and design as the Japanese do. Individual firms devote few resources to developing a skilled work force and strengthening their engineering capability. Firms produce standardized products in small lots, keeping minimum inventory and a small work force in neighboring countries that offer a cheap supply of labor. When the market expands, Chinese manufacturers subcontract their surplus orders to the other firms. When it contracts, they downsize their existing business and venture into more lucrative business such as real estate and stocks and shares. This business strategy enables firms to survive more than to innovate products. In fact, Chinese firms in Hong Kong, Taiwan, and Singapore are 'sandwiched' between the technological dominance of global corporations and stiff competition from their Southeast Asian imitators who can produce at even lower cost. The dependence on cheap labor and land available in China and Southeast Asian countries might pose high risks to manufacturers if social and political turmoil threatens these host countries (Wehrfritz 1995; Wyszomierski 1998).

Past success with interorganizational imitation, which has often meant neglect of intraorganizational learning, is not enough to sustain corporate survival and growth among enterprises in industries marked by rapidly increasing technological sophistication. In electronics and the associated supporting industries for metal and plastics, for example, Chinese manufacturing enterprises will eventually lose out if they resist organizational change. Firms in Taiwan and Singapore are increasingly stabilizing their subcontracting relationships with customers and suppliers in order to upgrade technologically, exchange information, and ensure high product quality and timely delivery (Tsui-Auch 2000). The institutionalization of quality control as exemplified in requirement 9002 of the International Organization for Standardization (ISO) has accelerated organizational learning and unlearning. The maintenance of ISO 9002 certification requires stringent quality control, systematic data analysis, documentation, storage, and retrieval. The learning of these new practices is also fostering a partial unlearning of the habit of relying purely on 'talk' or 'rough calculation' (Tsui-Auch 1999*b*).

Latecomer firms that are relatively isolated from markets and R&D bases in the traditional industrial center are initially unable to compete with leaders in the cutting-edge technologies. Instead of competing with the technological leaders head-on, latecomers might better concentrate on the niches where they enjoy comparative advantages. In the electronics industry, for example, firms should aim at developing electronics components for the Chinese market instead of competing with each other to supply similar consumer electronics products to the mature markets of the United States and western Europe (HKGID 1991). In the biotechnology industry, which is knowledge-intensive, Chinese firms in Hong Kong, Taiwan, and Singapore enjoy a competitive advantage in the development and manufacture of traditional Chinese medicine (Tsui-Auch 1997, in press). They are operating in a bilingual environment involving Chinese and English. Their home bases enjoy proximity to and affinity with China, which provides medical resources, human resources, and a potential market. The empirical knowledge of traditional Chinese medicine is available in the medical-research and health-care community. These factors pose a barrier to competition from the Western pharmaceutical companies (Berger and Lester 1997). In fact, the development strategy of creating endogenous knowledge and relying on local and regional markets has been proposed in dependency theory and the alternative development approach within development studies since the 1970s (Bello and Rosenfeld 1990; for a summary, see Blomstrom and Hettne 1985). Proponents of these theories and approaches have been criticized for leaning toward the politics of national and regional isolationism and for disregarding the advantage of combining exogenous and endogenous knowledge as a way to meet the needs of nations. Nevertheless, recent rediscovery of this strategy has come at a time when Asia is encountering economic stagnancy and crises and is seeking new paths for industrial development.

Whereas the strategy of creating regional endogenous knowledge may be the path in the long run, it may not be feasible in the short and medium term. It requires strong institutional support by a proactive state, a tradition characteristic of Taiwan and Singapore but not of Hong Kong (Tsui-Auch 1998). Nevertheless, the postcolonial Hong Kong government has recently made a paradigm shift toward supporting technological upgrading and organizational collaboration (personal interview with James Liu, Chairman, Hong Kong Industrial Technology Corporation, 15 October 1998). Hong Kong authorities have introduced policies to strengthen the industrial and R&D base, to upgrade human resources, and to help tap technical knowledge by facilitating the recruitment of ethnic Chinese to serve in industry. However, as necessary as the establishment of institutional mechanisms is for fostering learning and innovation, it is not sufficient. One must promote a cultural change—from one that fosters the pursuit of quick profit and tangible assets to one that encourages the pursuit of long-term development and tolerates risk and failure in new technological ventures. Such a change of industrial culture will take a long time. In the short and medium terms, there is little viable option other than striking strategic alliances with technological leaders by offering access to regional markets in exchange for technological and marketing knowledge. In other words, interorganizational learning, especially in global networks, remains crucial.

Cross-fertilization of Fields

The preceding review of the imitation and innovation strategies of Chinese firms in networks bears out support to the pragmatist perspective that learning is an active, social process more than it is a matter of information processing or passive behavioral adaptation. Manufacturers interact constantly with their customers in global networks and with suppliers in local networks. In the global networks, individual firms work with foreign partners through various interfirm linkages. Firms start with assembly processes based on the importation of simple tools and the testing of equipment. Their technological knowledge, production skills, and organizing routine are developed, accumulated, and improved in the production process. Manufacturers explore

business formulae largely through informal processes in local networks. The use of written media and information technologies for diffusion and storage of production and organizational knowledge is limited.

The learning experience of Chinese firms does not preclude information acquisition and diffusion processes. The use of foreign technology certainly involves the acquisition of information about licensing regulations and the diffusion of operational manuals. Exploring the possibility of establishing branch plants in neighboring countries requires information on regulations governing foreign investments, land use, labor employment, and taxation. Yet, these facets constitute only a small portion of the know-how required if Chinese firms are to operate successfully in global and local networks. Much of it is accumulated by manufacturers and engineers primarily through technological hardware and software and through interaction with local government officials, business persons, and relatives living in the target countries. Hence, the information-processing approach is inadequate for describing much of what is being learned in Chinese firms in Hong Kong, Singapore, and Taiwan. The approach has its strengths but serious weaknesses as well. It has an appeal of 'order' in that one assumes the organization to be an input–processing–output system; compresses the complex, social process of learning into a linear sequence of discrete processes; and disregards the concurrence of processes and likelihood of feedback loops between them. The 'usefulness' of the approach limits it to the function of accounting for the learning of abstract, formalized knowledge. The information approach can also be useful when it comes to prescribing recipes for building informational infrastructure in companies. As necessary as it may be to strengthen that infrastructure, however, such reinforcement alone cannot enhance learning, for as Weick (1979) might say, structure and process are only loosely coupled.

This review of the development experience of Chinese firms illuminates the imitative learning strategy of selectively adopting foreign technologies, organizational practices, and networking practices and then adapting them to fit into local production contexts without resorting to wholesale copying. The selective adoption of imported knowledge appears to be a creative and innovative process. In development studies, there are theses suggesting that the focus of this research be shifted from knowledge diffusion and adaptation to imitative learning and a reformation of imitation as an active, creative, innovative, and continual learning process. Indeed, the attention to learning-by-imitation reflects a gradual paradigm shift in social science research in general—from a view of the center to a view of the periphery, from the perspective of the provider to that of the adopter. The metaphor of 'translation' in the learning organizing perspective serves well to illuminate this new paradigm. The metaphor of translation has two advantages over that of diffusion and adaptation. First, it reflects learning as a dynamic, active process rather than a passive, behavioral adaptation to the environment. Second, it illuminates the action of the imitators rather than that of the providers or the source of knowledge. Future research on the learning of Asian, specifically Chinese, firms can benefit from using the metaphor of translation in exploring the learning processes involved.

The development experience of Chinese manufacturing networks indicates the difficulty in defining success and failure and in addressing the question of continuity and change in existing learning strategies. The identification of the success or failure of learning depends very much on the researcher's points of reference. Arguing that there is a success trap or exploitation trap, one can assert that the corporate success of given firms is due to their adoption of an imitative learning strategy, emphasis on network efficiency, and reliance on personal trust and that this success inspires other firms to follow suit. Imitation then becomes recognized as the most appropriate strategy or a norm, in the specified industry or business culture. The endorsement of the strategy or the norm allows most Chinese manufac-

turers to forgo exploration of alternatives for enhancing product innovation, economies of scale, and long-term development. However, a rejection of the theory of learning traps can also be justified. A review of the development experience of individual Chinese firms points to an incremental improvement of process and product technologies, a high degree of flexibility in operating different product lines, and constant renewal more than to mechanistic adaptation or excessive exploitation of existing routines. Especially in industries such as the electronics and the computer industry, where products require a fairly high level of technology and precision, there is evidence that firms are increasing the stability of their subcontracting networks and are employing professional managers and engineers. Overall, the learning strategy leads to at least small wins, if not 'quantum jumps' (Weick and Westley 1996: 455), revealing no success trap or exploitation trap. Even the shift of investment to real estate and the service industry despite the profit squeeze in those sectors can be said to reflect not a failure trap or exploration trap but rather a rational decision to redirect resources to profitable ventures.

Whereas it remains difficult to theorize about learning traps, it is safe to argue that there have been both intended and unintended consequences. One of the hazards of trying to illuminate the paradox of learning is the choice between the theory of learning traps and the conception of the duality of consequences. It is a decision that should be made on a case-by-case basis. The theory of learning traps, with its deterministic character, can be applied better to cases having a clear definition of success and failure (for an example that deals with learning how to implement regulations, see de Haën, Tsui-Auch, and Alexis, Ch. 41 in this volume) than to cases that lack such clarity. In most other instances, the concept of the duality of consequences is the more effective interpretive device. Yet, researchers interested in building theories and providing recipes will find the duality concept less useful for predicting change or continuity than the theory of learning traps is likely to be.

The original version of the theory of knowledge creation is more applicable to large Japanese firms, upon whose experience the theory was originally based, than to small and medium-sized Chinese enterprises, which often have unstable organizational structure, little or no middle management, and volatile labor relations. The knowledge creation and knowledge development demonstrated by such Chinese firms is split between the individual entrepreneurs, top managers, engineers, and scientists of the research complex organized by government, industry, and academia, which vary from country to country (more in Taiwan and Singapore than in Hong Kong). The theory of knowledge creation, which extends the focus of interest from the intraorganizational context to the interorganizational context in regional industrial districts, is highly applicable to the study of learning among Chinese firms, especially those pursuing product development and innovation. Nevertheless, the recent emphasis on the creation of endogenous knowledge needs to be combined with the translation of exogenous ideas into the local context in which firms operate. In the current context of regional Asian economic crises, the focus on exogenous ideas can help researchers and policy-makers avoid becoming trapped by regional and national isolationism in the process by which endogenous knowledge is created.

Lastly, the development experience of Chinese firms can provide insights on the study of power, learning, and knowledge distribution. In Chinese manufacturing firms, the process of knowledge creation centers on entrepreneurs, top management, and engineers; knowledge-sharing, collective sense-making, and the evolution of shared mental models or cognitive maps are virtually absent. Within a global manufacturing network, power is asymmetrically distributed between technological leaders and latecomers. The control of the former over resources often hinders the latter in learning to catch up. That asymmetry indicates that hierarchical structures within an organization or a vertical network empower leaders and tend to result in an unequal distribution of knowledge. The assumption that information diffusion and collective interpretation are processes of organizational learning in all human organizations is less inapplicable to the study of hierarchically structured organizations than to lean organizations. It remains unrealistic to prescribe the evolution of shared mental models in order to facilitate organizational learning. Instead of being fostered and managed by technological leaders, learning is initiated by the latecomers and facilitated by governmental policies to strengthen the pool of resources available to strategic industries and the industrial infrastructure as a whole. Improvement of the power base and resource base through individual and collective actions is a precondition to an enhancement of learning. The notion that power derives from association between actors as conceived in the learning organizing perspective, is applicable. Yet the power asymmetry and unequal distribution of knowledge within and between organizations need further analysis (Coopey 1995; Makhija and Ganesh 1997). To account for these phenomena, researchers developing theory may draw insights from one of the main sociological traditions, the conflict tradition (see Collins 1994: 47–120; Gherardi and Nicolini, Ch. 2 in this volume; Hardy and Clegg 1996).

References

Amsden, A. H. (1989). *Asia's Next Giant: South Korea and Late Industrialization*. New York: Oxford University Press.

Argyris, C. and Schön, D. A. (1996). *Organizational Learning*: Vol. 2. *Theory, Method, and Practice*. Reading, Mass.: Addison-Wesley.

Baum, J. A. C. (1996). 'Organizational Ecology', in S. R. Clegg, C. Hardy, and W. R. Nord (eds.), *Handbook of Organization Studies*. London: Sage, 77–114.

Bello, W. and Rosenfeld, S. (1990). *Dragons in Distress: Asia's Miracle Economies in Crisis*. San Francisco: Institute for Food and Development Policy.

Berger, S. and Lester, S. (eds.) (1997). *Made by Hong Kong*. Hong Kong: Oxford University Press.

Blomstrom, M. and Hettne, B. (1985). *Development Theory in Transition*. London: Zed Books.

Brown, J. S. and Duguid, P. (1991). 'Organizational Learning and Communities of Practice: Toward a Unified View of Working, Learning and Innovation'. *Organization Science*, 2: 40–57.

Burrell, G. and Morgan, G. (1979). *Sociological Paradigms and Organizational Analysis*. London: Heinemann.

Calhoun, C. (1982). *The Question of Class Struggle: Social Foundations of Popular Radicalism during the Industrial Revolution*. Chicago: University of Chicago Press.

Collins, R. (1994). *Four Sociological Traditions*. Oxford: Oxford University Press.

Coopey, J. (1995). 'The Learning Organization: Power, Politics, and Ideology'. *Management Learning*, 26: 193–214.

Cyert, R. M. and March, J. G. (1963). *A Behavioral Theory of the Firm*. Englewood Cliffs, NJ: Prentice Hall.

Czarniawska, B. (1997). 'Learning Organizing in a Changing Institutional Order: Examples from City Management in Warsaw'. *Management Learning*, 28: 475–95.

——and Sevón, G. (1996). 'Introduction', in B. Czarniawska and G. Sevón (eds.), *Translating Organizational Change*. Berlin: de Gruyter, 1–12.

Dodgson, M. (1993). 'Organizational Learning: A Review of Some Literatures' *Organization Studies*, 14: 375–94.

Donaldson, L. (1996). 'The Normal Science of Structural Contingency Theory', in S. R. Clegg, C. Hardy, and W. R. Nord (eds.), *Handbook of Organization Studies*. London: Sage, 57–76.

Engardio, P. and Burros, P. (1996). 'Acer: A Global Powerhouse'. *Business Week*, 1 July: 22–5.

Fiol, C. M. and Lyles, M. A. (1985). 'Organizational Learning'. *Academy of Management Review*, 10: 803–13.

Fujita, K. and Hill, R. C. (1997). 'Auto Industrialization in Southeast Asia: National Strategies and Local Development'. *ASEAN Economic Bulletin*, 13/3: 312–32.

Gherardi, S. (1997). *Learning in the Face of Mystery*. Paper presented at the conference on 'Modes of Organizing, Power/Knowledge Shifts'. Warwick, U.K.: 3–4 April.

Hamilton, G. (1991). 'The Organizational Foundations of Western and Chinese Commerce: A Historical and Comparative Analysis', in G. Hamilton (ed.), *Business Networks and Economic Development*. Occasional Papers and Monographs, No. 99. University of Hong Kong, Centre of Asian Studies, 48–65.

Hardy, C. and Clegg, S. R. (1996). 'Some Dare to Call it Power', in S. R. Clegg, C. Hardy, and W. R. Nord (eds.), *Handbook of Organization Studies*. London: Sage, 622–41.

Hobday, M. (1994). 'Innovation in East Asia: Diversity and Development', in M. Dodgson and R. Rothwell (eds.), *The Handbook of Industrial Innovation*. Aldershot: Edward Elgar, 94–105.

——(1995). *Innovation in East Asia: The Challenge to Japan*. Aldershot: Edward Elgar.

Hong Kong Government Industry Department (HKGID) (1991). *Techno-economic and Market Research Study on Hong Kong's Electronics Industry, 1988–1989*. Hong Kong: Hong Kong Government Industry Department.

Huber, G. P. (1991). 'Organizational Learning: The Contributing Processes and the Literatures'. *Organization Science*, 2: 88–115.

Ichiro, N. (1991). 'The Role of Personal Networks in the Making of Taiwan's Guanxiqiye (Related Enterprises)', in G. Hamilton (ed.), *Business Network and Economic Development*. Occasional Papers and Monographs, No. 99. University of Hong Kong, Centre of Asian Studies, 77–93.

Inoue, R., Kohama, H., and Urata, S. (eds.) (1993). *Industrial Policy in East Asia*. Tokyo: External Trade Organization.

Johnstone, B. (1989). 'Taiwan Holds Its Lead: Local Makers Move into New Systems'. *Far Eastern Economic Review*, 31 August: 50–1.

Kao, C. S. (1991). 'Personal Trust in the Large Businesses in Taiwan: A Traditional Foundation for Contemporary Economic Activities', in G. Hamilton (ed.), *Business Network and Economic Devel-*

opment. Occasional Papers and Monographs, No. 99. University of Hong Kong, Centre of Asian Studies, 66–76.

Kao, J. (1993). 'The Worldwide Web of Chinese Business'. *Harvard Business Review,* 71/2: 24–36.

Kim, D. H. (1993). 'The Link between Individual and Organizational Learning'. *Sloan Management Review,* 35/1: 37–50.

Kim, L. (1998). 'Crisis Construction and Organizational Learning: Capability Building in Catching-up at Hyundai Motor'. *Organization Science,* 9: 506–21.

Kojima, K. (1977). *Japan and a New World Economic Order.* Boulder, Colo.: Westview Press.

Kumar, K. (1981). *Multinationals from Developing Countries.* Lexington, Mass.: D. C. Health.

Lall, S. (1980). 'Vertical Interfirm Linkages in LDCs: An Empirical Study'. *Oxford Bulletin of Economics and Statistics,* 42/3: 203–26.

——(1992). 'Technological Capabilities and Industrialization'. *World Development,* 20/2: 165–86.

Latour, B. (1986). 'The Powers of Association', in J. Law (ed.), *Power, Action and Belief: A New Sociology of Knowledge?* London: Routledge and Kegan Paul, 264–80.

Lawrence, P. R. and Lorsch, J. W. (1967). *Organization and Environment: Managing Differentiation and Integration.* Cambridge, Mass.: Harvard University, Graduate School of Business Administration.

Lee, C. S. (1999). 'Headlong Plunge'. *Far Eastern Economic Review,* 10 June: 84–6.

Lee, K. M. (1997). 'The Flexibility of the Hong Kong Manufacturing Sector'. *China Information,* 12/2: 189–214.

Lee, S., Courtney, J. F., and O'Keefe, R. M. (1992). 'A System for Organizational Learning Using Cognitive Maps'. *International Journal of Management Science,* 20: 23–36.

Leung, C. K. (1993). 'Personal Contacts, Subcontracting Linkages, and Development in the Hong Kong-Zhujiang Delta Region'. *Annals of the Association of American Geographers,* 83/2: 272–302.

Levinthal, D. and March, J. G. (1993). 'The Myopia of Learning'. *Strategic Management Journal,* 14 (Winter special issue): 95–112.

Levitt, B. and March, J. G. (1988). 'Organizational Learning'. *Annual Review of Sociology,* 14: 319–40.

Makhija, M. V. and Ganesh, U. (1997). 'The Relationship between Control and Partner Learning in Learning-related Joint Ventures'. *Organization Science,* 8: 508–27.

March, J. G. (1991). 'Exploration and Exploitation in Organizational Learning'. *Organization Science,* 2: 71–87.

——and Olsen, J. P. (1976). 'The Uncertainty of the Past: Organizational Learning under Ambiguity', in J. G. March and J. P. Olsen, *Ambiguity and Choice in Organizations.* Bergen: Universitetsforlaget, 94–113.

Morishita, K. (1997). 'Electronics Giants Tighten Ties to Taiwan'. *Nikkei,* 17 April: 1, 3.

Nonaka, I. and Konno, N. (1998). 'The Concept of "Ba": Building Foundation for Knowledge Creation'. *California Management Review,* 40/3: 40–54.

——and Takeuchi, H. (1995). *The Knowledge-creating Company: How Japanese Companies Create the Dynamics of Innovation.* New York: Oxford University Press.

Orr, J. (1993). 'Sharing Knowledge, Celebrating Identity: War Stories and Community Memory among Service Technicians', in D. S. Middleton and D. Edwards (eds.), *Collective Remembering: Memory in Society.* Beverly Hills, Calif.: Sage, 169–89.

Piore, M. and Sabel, C. (1984). *The Second Industrial Divide: Possibilities for Prosperity.* New York: Basic Books.

Polanyi, M. (1966). *The Tacit Dimension.* Garden City, NY: Anchor Books.

Redding, S. G. (1990). *The Spirit of Chinese Capitalism.* Berlin: de Gruyter.

Rogers, E. M. (1962). *Diffusion of Innovations.* New York: Free Press.

Saxenian, A. (1996). *Regional Advantage: Culture and Competition in Silicon Valley and Route 128.* Cambridge, Mass.: Harvard University Press.

Sayer, A. (1986). 'New Developments in Manufacturing: The Just-in-time System'. *Capital and Class,* 30: 43–72.

Semlinger, K. (1994). *Industrial-District-Politik in Baden-Württemberg—zwischen Neubesinnung und Neuanfang.* Arbeitsbericht, No. 39 (November), Center of Technology Assessment of Baden-

Württemberg, Vaihingen, Stuttgart, Germany.

Sevón, G. (1996). 'Organizational Imitation in Identity Transformation', in B. Czarniawska and G. Sevón (eds.), *Translating Organizational Change*. Berlin: de Gruyter, 49–66.

Sit, F. S. and Wong, S. L. (1989). *Small and Medium-sized Industries in an Export-oriented Economy: The Case of Hong Kong*. University of Hong Kong, Centre of Asian Studies.

Tam, S. (1990). 'Centrifugal versus Centripetal Growth Processes: Contrasting Ideal Types for Conceptualizing the Development Patterns of Chinese and Japanese Firms', in S. R. Clegg and S. G. Redding (eds.), *Capitalism in Contrasting Cultures*. New York: de Gruyter, 153–84.

Tenbrunsel, A. E., Galvin, T. L., Neale, M. A., and Bazerman, M. H. (1996). 'Cognitions in Organizations', in S. R. Clegg, C. Hardy, and W. R. Nord (eds.), *Handbook of Organization Studies*. London: Sage, 313–37.

Tong, C. K. (1991). 'Centripetal Authority, Differentiated Networks: The Social Organization of Chinese Firms in Singapore'. *Business Networks and Economic Development*. Occasional Papers and Monographs, No. 99. University of Hong Kong, Centre of Asian Studies, 176–200.

Tsui-Auch, L. S. (1997). *Biotechnology Development in Asia: Government Policy, Industrial Infrastructure, Science and Technology Systems*. Report No. 84. Stuttgart: Center of Technology Assessment.

——(1998). 'Has the Hong Kong Model Worked? Industrial Policy in Retrospect'. *Development and Change*, 29/1: 55–78.

——(1999a). 'Regional Production Relationship and Developmental Impacts: A Comparative Study of Three Regional Networks'. *International Journal of Urban and Regional Research*, 23/2: 345–59.

——(1999b). *Beyond Western and Japanese Perspectives of Organizational Learning: An Inquiry into the Overseas Chinese Models*. Paper presented at the EGOS annual conference. Warwick, U. K., 4–6 June.

——(2000). 'The Applicability of Organizational Learning Perspectives to Chinese Business Organizations: A Comparative Study of Two Suppliers in Singapore'. Paper presented at Academy of Management Conference, Totonto, Aug. 4–9.

——(in press). 'Functional Versus Sectoral Industrial Policy: A Comparative Study of the Biotechnology Development in Hong Kong and Singapore', in D. Barben and G. Abels (eds.), *Biotechnologie–Globalisierung–Demokratie. Politische Gestaltung transnationaler Techonologie entwicklung*. Berlin: Edition Sigma.

Tyre, M. J. and von Hippel, E. (1997). 'The Situated Nature of Adaptive Learning in Organizations'. *Organization Science*, 8: 71–2.

Wade, R. (1990). *Governing the Market: Economic Theory and the Role of Government in East Asian Industrialization*. Princeton: Princeton University Press.

Walsh, J. P. and Ungson, G. R. (1991). 'Organizational Memory'. *Academy of Management Review*, 16: 57–71.

Wehrfritz, G. (1995). 'Is There Life in the Old Party?' *Far Eastern Economic Review*, 23 January: 36–7.

Weick, K. E. (1979). *The Social Psychology of Organizing* (2nd edn). Reading, Mass.: Addison-Wesley.

——and Westley, F. (1996). 'Organizational Learning: Affirming an Oxymoron', in S. R. Clegg, C. Hardy, and W. R. Nord (eds.), *Handbook of Organization Studies*. London: Sage, 440–58.

Wong, S. L. (1988). *Emigrant Entrepreneurs: Shanghai Industrialists in Hong Kong*. Hong Kong: Oxford University Press.

——(1991). 'Chinese Entrepreneurs and Business Trust', in G. Hamilton (ed.), *Business Networks and Economic Development*. Occasional Papers and Monographs, No. 99. University of Hong Kong, Centre of Asian Studies, 176–200.

Wyszomierski, T. (1998). 'Thinking Twice about Forcing Change in Asia'. *International Herald Tribune*, 20 January: 8.

33 Learning in Imaginary Organizations

Bo Hedberg and Mikael Holmqvist

Organizational learning has hitherto mainly been studied in formal, integrated organizations (e.g. Cyert and March 1992; March and Simon 1958; Nonaka, Toyama, and Byosière, Ch. 22 in this volume). The growing complexity of products and intense global competition have, however, made organizations increasingly dependent on organizational partnerships (Hagedoorn 1993; Inkpen and Crossan 1995; Larsson, Bengtsson, Henriksson, and Sparks 1998; Simonin and Helleloid 1993). As Powell, Koput, and Smith-Doerr (1996) noted: 'Sources of innovation do not reside exclusively inside firms; instead, they are commonly found in the interstices between firms, universities, research laboratories, suppliers, and customers' (p. 118).

In this respect partnerships represent one response to growing insights among organizations that competence-based alliances can be formed in order to facilitate organizational learning (Dodgson 1993; Hagedoorn 1993; Inkpen and Beamish 1997; Sanchez and Heene 1997). Though still rather modest, there is an increasing body of theoretical and empirical research that focuses on organizational learning as a major purpose for collaboration. Such endeavors are typically referred to as interpartner learning (Hamel 1991: 90), interorganizational learning (Larsson *et al.* 1998), or grafting (Huber 1991).

However, research on learning in organizational partnerships typically has two main problems. First, it does not stress the collectivity of actors as the unit of analysis, leaving unconsidered the question of how organizations and other actors jointly learn and create knowledge. Theories of interorganizational learning have typically focused on how single organizations learn by transferring knowledge between partners (e.g. Dodgson 1993; Hagedoorn 1993; Hamel 1991; Huber 1991; Inkpen and Beamish 1997), which leaves out the potential of organizational partnerships to create joint knowledge beyond the structures of any single entity. Interorganizational learning encompasses aspects of establishing a learning organization in a conventional sense. That is, it encourages intraorganizational learning (knowledge-sharing) and capacities for reactive and proactive responses to the environment. It also includes opportunities to learn with partners and from interaction with individual customers or communities of customers. Second, theories on organizational partnership typically start from the assumption that partnerships are integrated entities that can be distinctly separated from other organizations or other partnerships. The number of nodes or actors is, consequently, seen as limited, though value creation and learning in contemporary partner collaborations are in fact almost without boundaries.

When companies become allies in partnerships, a new platform for learning is added, the interorganizational one. When organizations

This chapter was made possible through the support provided by the Swedish Transport Communications Research Board (KFB Telematics Program), the Swedish Foundation for Research in Social Sciences and the Humanities, the Swedish National Board for Industrial and Technical Development, and the Daimler-Benz Foundation, Ladenburg, Germany.

begin to form larger networks, platforms for learning multiply. In this chapter we explore the opportunities for learning in imaginary organizations. Imaginary organizations (Hedberg, Dahlgren, Hansson, and Olve 1997) are systems of networking partners who coordinate their activities through shared missions, visions, and, in particular, shared platforms of information technology. Although they typically consist of a number of semi-independent legal units, they behave as one organization, and they exist and are manifested in the imagination of their leadership.

This rest of this chapter is divided into six sections. First, we describe imaginary organizations by contrasting them to virtual organizations and strategic alliances, two other common forms of partnership. In the second section we present a framework of learning and knowledge creation in imaginary organizations. The function of knowledge management in these knowledge-creation processes is discussed in the third section. We then describe knowledge creation in Scandinavian PC Systems (SPCS), Sweden's leading provider of administrative personal computer programs for small and medium-sized business. This example illustrates empirically the theoretical framework that is outlined in the second section. Building on the fourth section, the fifth focuses on knowledge management in Skandia Assurance and Financial Services, a subsidiary of the global insurance company Skandia. The chapter concludes with a brief exploration of knowledge creation and knowledge management in imaginary organizations.

Data for the case studies were collected through personal interviews, participant observation, and document analysis in 1992, 1998, and 1999, either directly by the authors or by members of our research program. More than 100 one-hour interviews were conducted with members of the organizations. In agreement with the CEOs of the respective companies, we and our team had complete autonomy in selecting respondents for the interviews and free access to internal documents and to facilities at each partner's working site.

Writing a handbook chapter normally involves the scanning of a range of research documents. However, research on imaginary organizations is still quite rudimentary, and part of the empirical research that has been conducted thus far comes from our own resources or related ones (for example Baumard 1999; Hedberg in press; Hedberg *et al.* 1997; Holmqvist 1999; Maravelias in press; Uggla in press). In addition, we must balance this presentation between recorded facts and qualified speculation because new forms of organizational partnerships are emerging and because the evaluation of how these new organizations learn must by necessity be based on fairly limited observations and on rather short time series.

Imaginary Organizations

Modern organizations are collaborating to an increasing extent, a practice that has resulted in a recognition among scholars that markets and formal organizations are not the only set of institutional forms to organize transactions (e.g. Astley and Brahm 1989; Borys and Jemison 1989; Collin and Larsson 1993; Thorelli 1986; Williamson 1991). Concepts such as virtual organizations, imaginary organizations, and strategic alliances are typically used to describe these patterns of organizing. What they all have in common is an interest in describing alternative forms of organizing that cannot be described as either hierarchies or as markets (Astley and Brahm 1989; Powell 1990). As Powell (1990) said:

When the items exchanged between buyers and sellers possess qualities that are not easily measured, and the relations are so long-term and recurrent that it is difficult to speak of the parties as separate entities, can we still regard this as a market exchange? When the entangling of obligation and reputation reaches a point that the actions of the parties are interdependent, but there is no common ownership or legal framework, do we not need a new conceptual tool kit to describe and analyze this relationship? Surely this patterned exchange looks more like marriage than a one-night stand, but there is no marriage license, no common household, no pooling of assets. In the language I employ . . . such an arrangement is neither a market transaction nor a hierarchical governance structure, but a separate, different mode of exchange, one with its own logic. (p. 301)

A strategic alliance (see, for example, Bengtsson, Holmqvist, and Larsson 1998; Hamel 1991; Harrigan 1988; see also Child, Ch. 29 in this volume) is a partner arrangement consisting of a limited number of organizations that are engaged in cooperation for a prolonged period and thus have clear organizational boundaries and obligations (Bengtsson, Holmqvist, and Larsson 1998). The joint venture (see, for example, Harrigan 1985), in which two or more companies create a third company over which they have joint control, is the most common and classical form.

Miles and Snow (1992) argued that alliances may be built around a core organization, which acts as an entrepreneur that pools various competencies and resources. Jarillo (1988) described such 'strategic networks' as being centered on a focal organization, 'which is the firm that, in fact, sets up the partnership, and takes a proactive attitude in the care of it' (p. 32). Both Miles and Snow (1992) and Jarillo (1988) stressed the need to analyze organizations as inescapably interwoven in complex arrays of partnership relations, potentially requiring a reconceptualization of the very essence of an organization. These scholars assumed, however, that the core-firm partnerships comprise distinct entities with ties that are formal and legally separable from their partners. A boundary was drawn between the organization and its partners and between the partnership and the environment.

Understanding partnerships in this way (i.e. as transactional relationships between semi-independent partners) has contributed to disciplinary knowledge of how firms use external sources to enhance their own performance and to learn. However, to regard partnerships as enterprises of coherently bounded entities engaging in cooperative relationships with other complete entities is a view that needs to

be developed and given nuance if organizational scholars are to fully appreciate the intricacies of how modern organizations interact in an increasingly interconnected world.

To an increasing extent, organizations rely on abilities to pool competencies and other resources from an infinitely large number of actors such as private customers, universities, research laboratories, competitors, and suppliers. Some actors are bound together through formal associations such as joint ventures and other forms of strategic alliances. This reliance, however, does not imply an absence of other actors who contribute to value creation. The value creation of contemporary firms largely depends on formal partnerships, but the partnership is hardly as static or integrated as is often assumed. In their value creation, organizations and their members use external sources that may not quite conform to what is formally acknowledged to be business partners but that are part of an overall 'community of practices' (Brown and Duguid 1991). When the organization itself is a partnership at the center of a multitude of relationships (see Badaracco 1991), it is no longer fruitful to speak of organizations as having distinct 'insides' and 'outsides'.

This approach to organizing is becoming increasingly recognized in the literature. The term 'virtual organizations' partly captures the notion of collective value-making in infinitely large partnerships. The expression is typically used to refer to systems that are interlinked by advanced information technology (Arnold 1998; Grenier and Metes 1995), and it mostly refers to temporary constellations (Goldman, Nagel, and Preiss 1995; Hale and Whitlam 1997). There is little agreement on the definition of a virtual organization, though some attempts to find common ground have been made (see, for example, Chesbrough and Teece 1996; Savage 1996). In an endeavor to define the 'virtual enterprise', Zimmermann (1997) stated:

The term 'virtual' usually stands for something that seem[s to exist] despite the lack of distinguishing attributes. Thus, for example, 'virtual reality' or 'virtual products' do not have any physical structure.

They exist only in computers. For the observer the reality product 'exists in the mind, especially as a product of imagination' . . . The term 'enterprise' generally associates a bounded and durable object, consisting of people and buildings and bas[ed] on a legal framework. Accordingly, a virtual enterprise is an enterprise [that] lacks some structural character-istics of real enterprises, but [that] nevertheless functions like an enterprise in the imagination of the observer. (p. 2)

In this formulation Zimmermann (1997) stres-sed a central characteristic of virtual organiza-tions. The number of nodes is not as statically defined as in the case of strategic alliances (cf. Bengtsson, Holmqvist, and Larsson 1998); instead, they can be infinite in number. The enterprise is bound together by the imagin-ation of either the observer or the organizer (see Grenier and Metes 1995).

In an attempt to avoid the overtones of in-formation technology and to counteract the temporary flavor of the term 'virtual', Hedberg *et al.* (1997) used the term 'imaginary organiza-tions' to refer to such partnerships. According to these authors, the concept of imaginary or-ganization is a particular perspective on organ-izations, one that both reveals new companies that organize and sustain boundary-transcend-ing activities and points out the significant re-sources and possible combinations of existing organizations. 'The perspective of the imagin-ary organization refers to a system in which assets, processes, and actors critical to the "focal" enterprise exist and function both in-side and outside the limits of the enterprise's conventional "landscape" formed by its legal structure, its accounting, its organigrams, and the language otherwise used to describe the enterprise' (Hedberg *et al.* 1997: 13).

Imaginary organizations have the market as their starting point (see Fig. 33.1). The market is where the most uncertainty is located, and scar-city of customers characterizes many industries today. Uncertainty in the market calls for flex-ibility in the production system. Thus, many parts of the production system are arranged as partnerships. Delivery systems and market communication are also often handled through partners. The leader of the imaginary

organization takes on the role of the director of a business play, manages the imaginary organ-ization, and typically faces the customers. In order to maintain leadership and power, the IO leader has to possess some strategically import-ant 'core competence' (Prahalad and Hamel 1990) that provides competitive edge.

The customer base rarely consists of passive customers (segments, target groups, and so forth) but rather increasingly of active custom-ers ('prosumers') or communities of interest with which the leader of the imaginary organ-ization seeks to establish dialogue and mutual value creation. This strategy is a way not only to co-opt important sources of uncertainty in the market but also to tap into valuable mechan-isms for knowledge creation and assist the enterprise in product development and cus-tomization.

Because all systems, particularly this kind of loosely coupled network, run the risk of disin-tegration and entropy, the leader of an imagin-ary organization must provide a source of consistency, a force that maintains and devel-ops the imaginary organization. A shared vi-sion, a strong brand, high-trust culture, and shared structural capital are examples of such sources of consistency. The business idea is expressed through the system that links the leader to the customers. The business idea is realized through the provision of resources for this core system by partners with other core competencies, who together develop the busi-ness idea.

The virtual organization is often described as a temporary organization and sometimes as a very opportunistic and short-lived arrange-ment. Our empirical data (Bay and Bäckius 1992; Hedberg *et al.* 1997; Holmqvist 1999; Mar-avelias in press; Uggla in press) suggest that imaginary organizations might be long-lived and that the market-sensitive network organ-ization is designed to provide robustness and longevity in a world where economic time zones (Williams 1999) tend to shorten. Virtual organizations may well deploy networks, but we would like to reserve the term 'imaginary organizations' for those organizations whose leaders have at least the same ambitions to

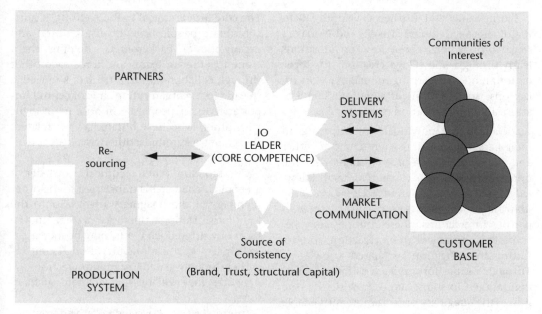

Fig. 33.1. The structure of an imaginary organization (IO)

grow and develop over time as their peers in traditional firms.

Knowledge Creation in Imaginary Organizations

All organizations are repositories of knowledge, but some organizations are more knowledge-intensive and knowledge-dependent than others. Knowledge is lodged in the brains of organizational members as well as in explicit rules, that is, artificial memories, which include files, records, and other documents (Cyert and March 1992; Simon 1997). Knowledge is also stored in organizational routines, that is, repetitive modes of acting, and standard operating procedures (Nelson and Winter 1982; see also Kieser, Beck, and Tainio, Ch. 27 in this volume).

Organizations learn when their knowledge (in the form of explicit rules and tacit routines) changes (Argyris and Schön 1996; Cyert and March 1992; Hedberg 1981), though this change hinges on altered states of individual knowledge. Only individuals can actively learn.

Thus, apart from learning among individuals in organizations, organizational learning is derived from transformations of individual knowledge into artificial memories and routines. Explicit rules, such as written regulations, blueprints, and memoranda, have a fairly obvious and 'objective' existence, whereas tacit routines exist only to the extent that individuals draw upon them and accept them in joint practices (Giddens 1984).

Creating and securing interorganizational knowledge is fundamental to the performance of imaginary organizations, for such knowledge can counteract sudden loss of knowledge due to partner turnover. Interorganizational knowledge thus consists of mutual knowledge, which is unique to collaboration and independent of any single organization's knowledge. Interorganizational knowledge represents a set of mental models shared by organizations (see Lane, Ch. 31 in this volume). In this sense imaginary organizations learn not only when partners' specific organizational knowledge changes but also, and primarily, when their interorganizational knowledge changes and develops.

Synthesizing and further developing Baumard's (1996), Hedlund's (1994), and Nonaka's (1994) propositions about how organizations learn through knowledge creation, we focus on four modes of learning in imaginary organizations: socialization, articulation, combination, and internalization (see Fig. 33.2).

Socialization: Individuals participating in imaginary organizations may come together and work closely on a project, thereby having opportunities to create mutual tacit knowledge, that is, joint routines (see Fig. 33.2). By drawing on organization-specific routines in partner interactions, these routines may become the routines of the interaction, too, resulting in a creation of shared knowledge. Through various forums such as formal meetings, apprenticeships, and teamwork, the core firm of the imaginary organization must enable people to meet and work together.

Articulation: In imaginary organizations the diverse backgrounds of the different actors involved will force people to articulate what they individually take for granted. The outcome may be stored in the imaginary organization's artificial memory (e.g. jointly written standard operating procedures and other formal rules).

The core firm is crucial to these efforts; it must coordinate people from diverse cultural and organizational backgrounds, helping them come together in teams and force each other through collaboration to articulate knowledge specific to the organization. It is of central importance to let people be in an environment with others who have unfamiliar, yet related, skills and backgrounds; otherwise, little articulation will take place.

Combination: When technical knowledge of an explicit character is transferred to the other members of the imaginary organization, the joint organizational memory system, in the form of written documents, may be increased. Imaginary organizations are often bound together through shared information technology networks that will further facilitate such efforts.

Internalization: Knowledge derived from another organization's memory and transmitted by individuals may be written down and specified in a joint memory store. Over time, however, people in the imaginary organization will refer to that knowledge in an intuitive manner if they find it to be important for working together. Internalization of values facil-

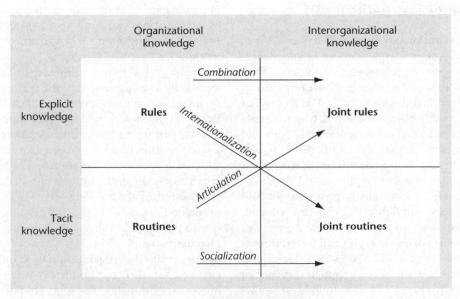

Fig. 33.2. Four models of learning in imaginary organizations

itates coordination of action, through enabling people to rely on an interorganizational knowledge.

In all these interorganizational learning activities, trust is fundamental. If partners do not trust each other's intentions, difficulty with socialization, articulation, and internalization will increase because these processes depend on the close interaction of partners. In this sense, the only option seems to be combination, a traditional knowledge transfer between the partners. But if learning activities are limited to combination only, interorganizational learning will be seriously inhibited.

One way for the leader of an imaginary organization to nurture interorganizational trust is to be highly transparent to the partners (see Friedman, Lipschitz, and Overmeer, Ch. 34 in this volume). The degree of transparency in organizational partnerships indicates how open or closed partners are to each other in sharing information and knowledge (Hamel 1991). Transparency thereby relates to the way in which the collaboration is structured, for example, whether it depends on following explicitly stated operations formally agreed on, or whether it is structured in a way that allows flexibility, openness to new tracks, and deviations. When the leader of an imaginary organization has an open attitude, emphasizes long-term relationships, and respects partners' autonomy, trust may develop to the benefit of all members of the imaginary organization.

Knowledge Management in Imaginary Organizations

As stressed by several scholars (e.g. Hedlund 1994; March and Simon 1958; Nonaka, Toyama, and Byosière, Ch. 22 in this volume), successful knowledge creation requires knowledge management. It is a basic requirement that the leader of an imaginary organization develops a vision (see Hedlund 1994; Nonaka, Toyama, and Byosière, Ch. 22 in this volume) around which partners unite. If this shared vision is provided, coordination of the imaginary

organization's learning improves. In addition, scholars assert that knowledge creation may be further facilitated through modern information technology (Büchel and Raub, Ch. 23; Nonaka, Reinmöller, and Toyama, Ch. 37 in this volume; Sanage 1996).

Development of a Shared Vision

Knowledge management in imaginary organizations tends to differ from traditional conceptualizations of knowledge management in that the elaboration of joint purposes and vision involves a multitude of autonomous players.

In formal organizations, learning can be a highly directed and controlled activity (Nonaka 1994; Simon 1997). Organizations devote considerable energy to developing collective understandings of experience. Obviously, not all experiences are recorded. 'The transformation of experience into routines and the recording of those routines involve costs' (Levitt and March 1995: 22), and ultimately those actors who have legal control over the organization have the final say, even though the decision-making processes are to a large extent decentralized. This selectivity will substantially influence the individual's propensity to accept some aspects of the learning process as given (Cyert and March 1992). In imaginary organizations, the traditional legal basis for control is absent, or at least substantially weakened.

Knowledge management in imaginary organizations is therefore primarily about inspiring and motivating people, many of whom are not employed by the leader of the organization and who are clearly not under the authority of the formal leadership. Leadership must therefore be lateral rather than vertical (Brousseau, Driver, and Larsson 1996; Mintzberg, Dougherthy, Jorgensen, and Westley 1996), and leaders must be able to trust the operations of partners and employees without having authority or full control over them. Certainly, the members are held together by contracts, giving a legal ground for the collaboration. Contracts have, however, proven to be a poor basis for coordination mechanisms in changing environments; their shortcomings in economics (Williamson 1975, 1985), sociology (Granovetter 1985), and organization theory (Ouchi 1980) are well known. The legitimacy that the leader of an imaginary organization has in formulating a joint vision does not come primarily from an official position but rather from the partners' trust in the leader to interpret the requirements of the broad community in which the imaginary organization operates.

Information Technology Networks

When intelligently used, information technology networks reduce distance, facilitate mind-to-mind contact, and help enable loosely coupled organizations bring available knowledge to bear on knowledge needs. By availing themselves of such networks, organizations may succeed at creating worldwide knowledge resources through jointly developed information-based products and processes and simultaneous design (Grenier and Metes 1995). Literature on virtual organizations typically stresses the importance of information technology in partnerships (e.g. Davidow and Malone 1992), leaving the reader with the impression that information technology is the decisive factor behind the virtual enterprise. Information technology is certainly important, but human networking (Ljungberg 1997) is the requisite. The challenge is to integrate information technology networks and human networking so that knowledge is both created and disseminated.

Knowledge Creation in Imaginary Organizations: The Case of Scandinavian PC Systems

To elaborate on the discussion in the previous section, we now use a study of Scandinavian Personal Computer Systems (SPCS) to illustrate how learning in an imaginary organization

may take place. This company has been researched during several periods by Bay and Bäckius (1992), Hedberg *et al.* (1997), and Holmqvist (1999).

In addition to being Sweden's leading manufacturer of standardized administrative personal computer programs (tax programs, salary administration programs, and the like) for small business, it is a major player in Norway as well. The company's highly competitive target market consists of companies with one to nineteen employees, a size that represents 98 per cent of all Swedish companies. The production of personal computer programs (e.g. a tax program), requires skills in a number of areas, not least because of constant technological changes.

First and foremost, knowledge of the market is crucial in small, often ownership-led companies such as SPCS. Second, advanced skills are needed in order to produce these programs according to specific programming techniques and systems design. Third, knowledge of the subject matter, such as tax law, tax regulation, tax deductions, and tax declaration is essential. Fourth, skills in writing manuals and handbooks that describe and explain the programs are needed. A number of other issues, such as distribution and marketing, are important as well.

In order to meet these demands, SPCS has chosen to work with external actors, resulting in an extended arena for value creation, an imaginary organization. Partners consist mainly of programmers and experts. In short, the programmers are programming companies that contribute their knowledge about how products shall be technically designed and programmed. They carry out the process of programming as well. The experts are companies that have specialist knowledge in, say, tax law or salary administration, that is needed for a certain program. They can be described as a knowledge support function for SPCS and the programmers.

SPCS works with other partners as well. For example, SPCS's news magazine, its main channel of communication with customers, is made by a partner company. During some projects customers, too, participate directly, as when SPCS led a project on developing a program for accounting firms. In that case, both new and old experts and programmers teamed up with a major accounting firm, KPMG, which possessed the needed knowledge about accounting techniques.

The system of actors is, however, never constant. Partners typically interact with other actors 'outside' the formal network core, who then become part-time members and contribute to the value-making, too. For instance, some of the programmers coordinating with SPCS were in continual contact with their 'own' partnerships, liaisons that resulted in a major innovation in one of the products developed during 1998. Likewise, the experts typically draw upon their respective partnerships. Overall, the actors interact freely with each other. Programmers have constant contact with other programmers, experts are in contact with programmers, SPCS has intense contact with all partners, and active customers are in contact with SPCS and directly with SPCS's partners. In addition, new partners are constantly joining the partnership in an effort to meet an ever-increasing demand for the partnership's products. Taken together, this network of contacts has resulted in a far larger organization than can be described formally, with a multitude of actors participating in the value-creation process.

Constant development of products is critical for SPCS and its partners if the company wants to remain competitive. The practical work of developing the programs is centered on various project groups. Typically, a revision of an existing product, or the development of an entirely new one, starts with brainstorming meetings, in which different ideas are ventilated and discussed. Members in a project group then meet. The initiative to hold such a meeting can come from anyone at SPCS or at one of the partner organizations, depending on the issue. Because of changes in the technological requirements, for example, programmers often prompt the others to initiate a modification, encouraging them to attend a meeting. Because of changes in legal requirements, experts push the others

to begin modifying products. Generally, these brainstorming meetings are characterized by a bandying of ideas with no other purpose than to discuss a more or less articulated idea evoked by either SPCS or some of the partners.

A series of telephone, e-mail, and face-to-face interactions between all actors follows as the product evolves. Continuous bargaining and compromising marks this period as specialists from different domains try to pursue their interests. Power in the bargaining process comes from the expectations of the others. If the matter is about a new technical function, the programmers jointly have more power than the experts and SPCS, who expect the programmers to be more knowledgeable about these issues than themselves. If, however, the matter is about how a tax declaration should be designed in order for it to be user-friendly, then experts and SPCS have an advantage. What is conspicuous about these interactions is that no party has the final say in all of the interactions. Even though SPCS clearly is the leading player, it constantly has to adapt its way of acting, as must the other actors as well. Leadership in imaginary organizations tends not to be as static as it is in more traditional alliances such as vertical supplier networks (see Lane, Ch. 31 in this volume).

For a more detailed analysis of how imaginary organizations learn through such interactions, consider the four modes of organizational learning outlined in Fig. 33.2.

Socialization: SPCS and the programming company with which it cooperates on a given product each has a person specifically responsible for that product. These two persons have daily contact with each other. On occasion, representatives from SPCS visit the programming company in order to watch the programmers in action. All partners and SPCS claim to have improved their understanding of each other's problems through such interactions. Moreover, the number of misunderstandings and the need to explain and clarify different standpoints have been substantially reduced. Having engaged in a great number of such interactions, SPCS maintains that it has enhanced its ability to think in programmers' terms. For example, programmers' tacitly held knowledge of how to design a program system has continually been conveyed to SPCS representatives who, in turn, now feel more knowledgeable about such issues than in the past and hence can communicate with the programmers more efficiently than they once could.

Articulation: When interacting with SPCS's partners, members of the company bring with them much tacitly held knowledge embedded in their firm-specific routines. An example is SPCS representatives' tacit assumptions about customer preferences. However, these assumptions are not always shared by some partners, who often lack contact with customers and thus have no regular knowledge of customer preferences and relations. SPCS's representatives are, therefore, constantly forced to articulate their tacit assumptions about and understandings of how SPCS as a company regards its customers' demands and requirements. Some of SPCS's knowledge is thereby made explicit to the partners. The results of such articulations are summarized in written protocols, which contribute to the explicit interorganizational knowledge of the entire imaginary organization.

Combination: Experts try to sharpen their skill at understanding the technical programming language of each program. In interacting with the experts, programmers show them how to write technical demand specifications in order to facilitate practical implementation. According to one of the expert companies, the programmers repeatedly state that they want the specifications 'simple and straightforward, without any need to make subjective interpretations' (our translation). By showing experts examples of programmers' specifications stored in files and computers and by letting the experts comment on them and combine them with their own explicit requirements, programmers and experts can jointly discuss how a solution should be constructed. This process leads to a joint foundation of explicit interorganizational knowledge that is satisfactory to both partners. The negotiated result is in writ-

ten form, typically in a demand specification that all partners have access to and, consequently, can benefit from.

Internalization: SPCS has developed an advanced customer database over the past several years. It gives SPCS important information on customer demands. Having received explicit customer feedback at meetings, some partners claim to have deepened their understanding of customer preferences. One of the programming companies said that nowadays it intuitively thinks more about the demands of customers than in the past and that its proposed solutions to SPCS are more focused on usability than they used to be. Thus, the two enterprises (i.e. SPCS and its partner) have closed some of the distance between them in terms of their knowledge, the result being an increase in tacit interorganizational knowledge.

The SPCS case illustrates an evolution of joint routines and norms for interaction that cannot be reduced to the intraorganizational level. These routines clearly facilitate the interactions between the parties involved. Experts have become more skilled in understanding both SPCS and the programmers than in the past and now interact with programmers in a different manner than in the past. Likewise, programmers have increased their awareness of the needs for usability and customer orientations in their proposals for product development.

The interorganizational knowledge of the actors involved is, however, constantly put under pressure as new actors enter the value-making process and as old ones leave. New actors, such as experts in a new market domain, bring with them new knowledge that gives them legitimacy in bargaining with the others. For example, KPMG through the legitimacy of its expertise, stressed perspectives of customer value creation other than the ones that the present routines were focused on, which triggered the other players to reconsider past truths and experiences and to shift their perspectives accordingly. Likewise, actors who did not formally belong to the partnership but who nevertheless contributed to major innovations enabled SPCS, the experts, and the programmers, to shift their focus to new demands in the market.

To sum up the above case, joint rules and routines as a basis for coordinated behavior are learned through bargaining processes in which no actor has the automatic final say. This process creates a need for compromise and fosters learning at both the intraorganizational and interorganizational levels. Interorganizational knowledge, not being grounded in a single authoritarian logic, may cause problems of short-term efficiency and increased costs in negotiating and bargaining, but it contributes to innovation. Learning and unlearning are natural ingredients in this highly dynamic organization of semiautonomous players.

Knowledge Management in Imaginary Organizations: Skandia Assurance and Financial Services

Whereas the SPCS case focuses on learning between partners, the case of Skandia Assurance and Financial Services (Skandia AFS), a subsidiary of the global insurance company, illustrates how the leader of an imaginary organization disseminates knowledge to participating actors and provides an infrastructure for knowledge-sharing in an effort to coordinate the learning process in a direction favorable to the core firm. Skandia AFS has been studied by Hedberg *et al.* (1997), Maravelias (in press), and Uggla (in press), among others. Skandia's attempts to manage the extended organization's growing intellectual capital was described by Edvinsson and Malone in 1997, when Edvinsson was the director of intellectual capital at Skandia AFS.

Skandia AFS is a group of companies within the leading Swedish-based insurance company, Skandia AB. Whereas the parent company was a fairly conventional insurance company until the early 1990s, Skandia AFS is a rapidly growing organization that totally redefined the Skandia Group in less than ten years. Skandia AFS now operates in twenty-nine countries on four continents outside Scandinavia. Some seventy people work at the headquarters, and they are mainly located in Sweden and in Shelton, Connecticut. An additional 2,600 Skandia employees run the national companies. The latter group of people engage some 91,000 partners in the various countries where AFS has established markets. The partners are money managers and financial advisers in the United States. Finally, some 1.5 million customers, or 'contracts', form the outer circle of the imaginary organization, Skandia AFS.

Skandia AFS prospers from the growing concern of people in many countries that retirement systems and other welfare arrangements are endangered and may not deliver what they once promised. Families and individuals are therefore increasing their savings, and Skandia is able to collect a portion of these savings and place them with fund managers who promise to beat inflation.

Learning in the entire imaginary organization of Skandia AFS heavily depends on the ability of the core organization (Skandia AFS) to manage and distribute knowledge. The company operates between a global market for savings and a global market for investments, with partners operating in each of these markets. Skandia AFS acts as an exchange system between these two markets, as shown in Fig. 33.3. Partners interact directly with clients (households) and investment opportunities.

We now briefly describe how Skandia AFS manages knowledge throughout the entire imaginary organization.

Development of Shared Vision

AFS's CEO, Jan Carendi, has stated that in order to lead the imaginary organization he has to realize that he is managing a voluntary organization. In this respect, he attempts to create a challenging vision, fast feedback on performance, and a high-trust culture (see Nonaka, Toyama, and Byosière, Ch. 22 in this volume). The concept of a high-trust culture is indeed a vision of how collaboration is to be

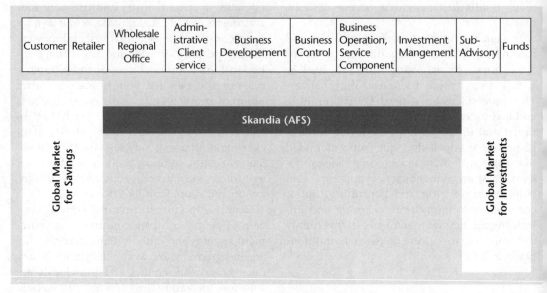

Customer	Retailer	Wholesale Regional Office	Administrative Client service	Business Developement	Business Control	Business Operation, Service Component	Investment Mangement	Sub-Advisory	Funds

Skandia (AFS)

Global Market for Savings

Global Market for Investments

Fig. 33.3. Skandia Assurance and Financial Services (AFS): A mediator between two global markets

sustained. Everyone in this organization should be a 'trustee' who deserves the trust of others and who trusts his or her collaborators.

To fulfill this ambition, Carendi and his fellow officers regularly write and distribute articles ('white papers') about AFS's industry, its strategic direction, core competencies, and so on. AFS was also one of the first companies to employ a director of its intellectual capital. His ambition is to develop a general terminology that depicts AFS and its partner network's hidden values, such as knowledge, skills, personal relations, and databases. By developing the necessary linguistic means to communicate and coordinate implicit and largely intangible values that had formerly lingered in the dark, the director of intellectual capital aims to facilitate a transfer of skills and knowledge within the AFS network. The writing of articles and the development of a general terminology that visualizes intellectual capital are examples of how AFS's management attempts to create interorganizational knowledge for the sake of establishing foundations upon which professional relations build on trust rather than on contracts and formalized procedures.

The enabling of face-to-face interaction is also regarded as important. Intraorganizational learning is encouraged through a number of platforms for face-to-face interaction (called 'Skandia Future Centers') and through attempts to establish knowledge markets where knowledge can be traded as free commodity or as a commercial product. In this way, the vision of a high-trust culture may be further nurtured.

IT Network

Information technology is a very important coordinator within both the inner system and the outer system of the imaginary organization of Skandia AFS. Partners and the national companies in twenty-seven countries are connected through a global area network and intranets that facilitate remote management and remote administration. A global management information system is another way to keep the worldwide organization together. The information technology infrastructure also allows existing national companies to provide, for example, back-office support for newly established subsidiaries. The back-office work for the pioneer companies in Mexico and Japan is thereby managed from American Skandia in Connecticut.

Another important ingredient of the glue for the AFS organization has been the provision of information technology support to partners on the market. The 'ASSESS' system helps partners make the financial products understandable and the investment experts human and trustworthy. The system also contains the embryo of a 'virtual university' with short courses for the continuing education that financial advisers in some countries are required to take, pass, and have recorded in order to remain authorized. The ASSESS system also contains a multimedia presentation of the extended Skandia enterprise. AFS experts and other sources of national expertise help the participating partners explain various savings programs and tax consequences to the client. In addition, the fund managers appear on the laptop screen and describe their business, their track record, and their investment policies.

ASSESS provides tens of thousands of partners in the field with supportive expertise on tax legislation, investment opportunities, and historic performance of various wealth-creating strategies. It provides access for the organization's members to shared information resources. The structural capital largely resides in data warehouses, application tools, and corporate intranets and extranets, and this structural capital is owned by the leader of the imaginary organization, Skandia AFS. ASSESS also serves as a trust-builder to the client, for it actually shows and introduces the investors who are going to handle the money and puts names and faces to a networking organization that otherwise could easily be called abstract and evasive.

Knowledge Creation and Knowledge Management in Imaginary Organizations

The preceding sections of this chapter give a broad, fairly detailed description of how im-

aginary organizations create and manage knowledge in two organizations. Summarizing that discussion now, we emphasize three factors that seem to determine imaginary organizations' capacity for knowledge creation, learning, and knowledge-sharing: (a) establishing multiple arenas for knowledge-creation, (b) continuous, driving innovation encouraged by diversity among the actors, and (c) establishment of trust and transparency in exchange mechanisms.

Multiple Arenas

Imaginary organizations have access to several interesting arenas for knowledge creation, arenas that offer rich sources for variation. The leader organization finds itself to be a knowledge manager in the midst of at least four arenas for knowledge creation (see Fig. 33.4). One is the customer relationship management (CRM) system, where interaction with customers takes place. Building relationships with numerous clients provides opportunities to tap into rich sources of knowledge and variation, especially if market communication truly follows a one-to-one concept. Another arena invites partners in the imaginary organization to share and develop useful knowledge, creating interorganizational knowledge. Interactive learning (see Lane, Ch. 31 in this volume) thereby becomes a conspicuous activity in imaginary organizations.

A third arena consists of intraorganizational communication systems where staff can create knowledge and value-added. This arena is improved when wide use of intranets develops. Intranets, combined with intelligent matching agents, have the potential to boost intraorganizational learning, especially because they can disseminate existing knowledge widely throughout the organization. The phrase 'imagine if we knew what we know' could be transformed from a hope to a reality. Of course, effective documentation routines, incentives to declare knowledge profiles among 'publishers' and 'subscribers' in the organization, and a culture of curiosity and sharing must be

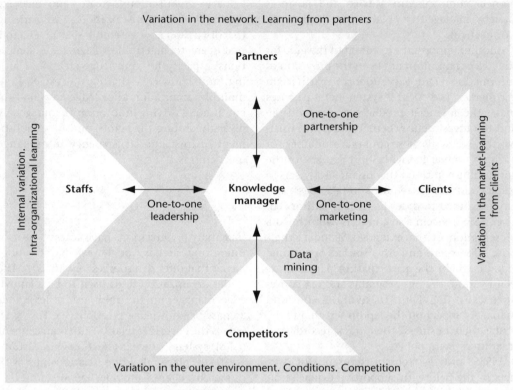

Fig. 33.4. Arenas for knowledge creation in imaginary organizations

properly combined in order to release the potential that new technologies can build. These possibilities are open to the core organization and can be extended to include other parts of the imaginary organization, such as partners, in a way that traditional organizations rarely can offer.

In addition to knowledge creation in and between these three arenas, imaginary organizations have the same opportunities as all other business organizations to explore their outer environments (e.g. competitors, economic developments, and technologies). Data-warehousing and applied data-mining are then the conventional solutions.

The modes for knowledge creation are closer to the models suggested by Baumard (1996), Hedlund (1994), and Nonaka (1994) than to traditional interactive models that are based on stimulus–response couplings (Cyert and March 1992; Hedberg 1981). Individual know-ledge is explicated and then socialized in the organizational arena. However, networks of partners or individual actors, rather than formal organizations, constitute the arenas for knowledge creation. Knowledge-creation processes are characterized by bargaining and compromising, and they are not coordinated by one party as consciously as they typically are in formal organizations. The result could be a more conflict-ridden learning process, but one with routines and rules that are better adapted to accommodate multiple realities and that thus meet new opportunities flexibly.

Continuous Innovation

In the research on knowledge creation in imaginary organizations—and much more is needed—perhaps the most intriguing aspect of imaginary organizations thus far is their potential to create arenas in which partners' tacitly held organizational knowledge can be brought to the surface. Through reflective conversation, tacitly held knowledge can be detected and articulated as explicit knowledge, a process that builds shared, interorganizational knowledge. By reflecting on habitual behavior, individuals can become aware of underlying knowledge that guides behavior. Dialogues between individuals belonging to various partner companies and living in different organizational cultures promise to increase these individuals' shared knowledge base. The outcome is mutual understanding and a joint body of knowledge. Reflective activities may enable business partners to discover their tacitly held assumptions and to articulate them as explicit knowledge; they may also help the partners share explicit knowledge with each other.

For SPCS and its partners, these reflective activities have resulted in major innovations. For example, one particular program was born of joint reflection between the programming company and its auditor. As the CEO (a programmer) of one of the partner companies explained: 'I discussed a lot of different things with my auditor when he was here, and then the idea was born that auditors ought to have a tool that would help them audit and maintain an overview of their clients. Suddenly something started to grow, which resulted in a fairly sophisticated program, the "client-integrator". It had not existed before' (our translation). The auditor's articulation of and reflection upon his routine behavior made the programmer aware of the basic needs for efficient auditing. This experience was the vehicle for transferring the knowledge to the programmer, who was then able to add to the interorganizational knowledge of their particular relationship and to that of the other actors as well.

The above example also illustrates how an imaginary organization makes use of blurred boundaries. The auditor did not formally belong to the partnership, yet he contributed meaningfully to the value creation of the imaginary organization. This arrangement contrasts with that of formal organizations, where membership is much more static and regulated through employment contracts, and that in strategic alliances, in which the number of members and usually also their roles are restricted by explicit contracts.

Trust and Transparency

Organization researchers have increasingly focused on the concept of trust in recent years, and there are strong indications that trust is especially important between actors in imaginary organizations (see Maravelias in press). Voluntary performance cannot be commanded through legal frameworks. Contracts are perhaps useful when people are about to part ways, but they are less useful when people are about to come together. When firms interact, strong cognitive and emotional ties may develop among individuals, laying the bases for the use of informal contracts rather than detailed and formal ones, which can result in high transaction costs (Gulati 1995). Trust may thus counteract fear of opportunism and can substitute for hierarchical solutions, such as contracts (Bradach and Eccles 1989).

In this regard, it seems that the interplay between four important factors, trust, respect, performance, and transparency (see Fig. 33.5), is what distinguishes imaginary organizations from conventional ones and what ideally, makes imaginary organizations develop and grow. Zand (1972) envisioned the first phases of a similar cycle when he described the interplay between trust, information, influence, and control within the context of early experiments on managerial problem-solving and effectiveness.

This interplay describes relationships to partners in the core organization, but it also describes relationships to customers and to the organization's own staff. Couplings are loose, trust is necessary in order to bridge gaps, and respect is required for trust to be an option. Performance, in order to live up to challenges and promises, is necessary for trust to survive, and even more for trust to grow, and transparency makes performance visible, nurturing trust. Trust may rapidly deteriorate when these interacting processes reverse.

Lastly this picture of the imaginary organization can be compared to formal organizations and strategic alliances. We find interesting differences in a number of dimensions that shape the opportunities for learning, especially in the dimensions of transparency, market communication, diversity, and trust (see Fig. 33.5). Imaginary organizations start in the market, and they typically treat the customer as a partner, sometimes even as a teacher. Most traditional organizations and most strategic alliances between such companies treat the customer as a target for sales pitches and advertisements. Today's production systems typically use in-house resources or contracted supply chains in the conventional organization. These production systems result from joint ventures in many strategic alliances and take the form of partner networks in imaginary organizations.

In general, internal variety is typically high in imaginary organizations, low to medium in strategic alliances, and comparatively low in the conventional, formal organization. Of coarse, variations within each group are considerable, but most traditional companies try to implement *one* corporate culture, strategic alliances blend a few such cultures, and imaginary organizations, even fairly small ones, may combine a host of company cultures, not least

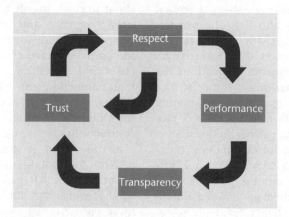

Fig. 33.5. Trust-building loops in imaginary organizations

Table 33.1. Comparison between three types of organizational framework

Property, function	Conventional organizations	Strategic alliances	Imaginary organizations
Market communication	Customer as target	Customer as target	Customer as partner
Production	In-house suppliers	Joint venture	Partnership network
Internal variety	Low	Low to medium	High
Intellectual capital	Marginal focus	Legal issue	Crucial focus Shared in network
Knowledge management	Passive to active	Negotiated	Very active
Dependence on trust	Low	Contract-based	All-important
Transparency	Low	Medium	High

because no player has the final say in all decisions. Similarly, the degree of transparency ranges from low to high. The distinctive feature in imaginary organizations is that market mechanisms reveal many of the coordinating arrangements that in traditional organizations are hidden by hierarchies.

The focus on intellectual capital and knowledge management has thus far been rather marginal in the formal organization (see Pawlowsky, Ch. 3 in this volume). Strategic alliances typically make the sharing and ownership of knowledge a contractual issue in the legal foundation of the alliance. Imaginary organizations, at least the ones that thus far have been described in research, share competence, know-how, and know-who in their networks and manage their knowledge-creating processes very explicitly.

Perhaps, the most distinguishing property in the comparison shown in Fig 33.5 is the dependence on trust. Trust is an all-important organizational glue in imaginary organizations, and that goes for all the learning arenas in which they are active: trust from the customers in the market, trust between partners in production and delivery systems, and trust inside the core organization. The leadership of Skandia AFS takes pride in the high-trust culture that binds actors around the world together in a loosely coupled system. Trust in strategic alliances rests on contracts, and mistrust is all too common because the allied partners ask themselves who gains what in detrimental learning races (see Larsson *et al.* 1998; Child, Ch. 29 in this volume).

The imaginary organizations familiar from experience or described and analyzed in current research are primarily those that are growing successfully. Little is known about how imaginary organizations will manage reorientation, turn-arounds, unlearning, and conflict resolution. How they cope with long-term success and avoid becoming complacent with it is not yet known either. This chapter can therefore at best be claimed to present fairly qualified speculations about learning in imaginary organizations. Much more research is needed and more time must pass before precise, and empirically well-based conclusions can be drawn. We therefore conclude this chapter by suggesting related areas in which further research is needed in order to improve understanding of the pros and cons of imaginary organizations:

- Empirically rich and detailed studies of learning in imaginary organizations
- Studies of knowledge integration and the presence of organizational memory in networks
- Modeling of the interplay between trust, knowledge creation, and knowledge-sharing in imaginary organizations
- Studies of the nature of knowledge-management and new demands on leadership
- The creation and measurement of intellectual capital in imaginary organizations and the related practices of monitoring performance through multidimensional scoring devices
- Studies of imaginary organizations in decline and crisis.

References

Argyris, C. and Schön, D. A. (1996). *Organizational Learning*: Vol. 2. *Theory, Method, and Practice*. Reading, Mass.: Addison-Wesley.

Arnold, O. (1998). Untitled (3 June). Available: http://www.teco.uni-karlsruhe.de/ITVISION/

Astley, W. G. and Brahm, R. A. (1989). 'Organizational Designs for Postindustrial Strategies: The Role of Interorganizational Collaboration', in C. C. Snow (ed.), *Strategy, Organization Design, and Human Resource Management*. Greenwich, Conn.: JAI Press, 233–70.

Badaracco, J. L. (1991). 'The Boundaries of the Firm', in A. Etzioni and P. R. Lawrence (eds.), *Socio-economics toward a New Synthesis*. London: ME Sharpe, 293–327.

Baumard, P. (1996). 'Organizations in the Fog: An Investigation into the Dynamics of Knowledge', in B. Moingeon and A. Edmondson (eds.), *Organizational Learning and Competitive Advantage*. London: Sage, 74–91.

——(1999). *Tacit Knowledge in Organizations* (S. Wauchope, trans.). London: Sage.

Bay, T. and Bäckius, P. (1992). *Imaginära organisationer* (Imaginary Organizations). Research Report, Stockholm University School of Business, Stockholm, Sweden.

Bengtsson, L., Holmqvist, M., and Larsson, R. (1998). *Strategiska allianser: Från marknadsmisslyckande till lärande samarbete* (Strategic Alliances: From Market Failure to Learning Cooperation). Malmö: Liber.

Borys, B. and Jemison, D. B. (1989). 'Hybrid Arrangements as Strategic Alliances: Theoretical Issues in Organizational Combinations'. *Academy of Management Review*, 14: 234–49.

Bradach, J. L. and Eccles, R. G. (1989). 'Price, Authority and Trust: From Ideal Types to Plural Forms'. *Annual Review of Sociology*, 15: 97–118.

Brousseau, K. R., Driver, M. J., Eneroth, K., and Larsson, R. (1996). 'Career Pandemonium: Realigning Organizations and Individuals'. *Academy of Management Executive*, 10/4: 52–66.

Brown, J. S. and Duguid, P. (1991). 'Organizational Learning and Communities-of-Practice: Toward a Unified View of Working, Learning, and Innovation'. *Organization Science*, 2: 40–57.

Chesbrough, H. W. and Teece, D. J. (1996). 'When Is Virtual Virtuous?' *Harvard Business Review*, 74/1: 65–73.

Collin, S.-O. and Larsson, R. (1993). 'Beyond Markets and Hierarchies: A Swedish Quest for a Tripolar Institutional Framework'. *International Studies of Management and Organization*, 23/1: 3–12.

Cyert, R. M. and March, J. G. (1992). *A Behavioral Theory of the Firm* (2nd edn). Cambridge, Mass.: Blackwell.

Davidow, W. H. and Malone, M. S. (1992). *The Virtual Corporation*. New York: Harper Collins.

Dodgson, M. (1993). 'Learning, Trust and Technological Collaboration'. *Human Relations*, 46: 77–95.

Edvinsson, L. and Malone, M. S. (1997). *Intellectual Capital: Realizing Your Company's True Value by Finding Its Hidden Brainpower*. New York: Harper Business.

Giddens, A. (1984). *The Constitution of Society: Outline of the Theory of Structuration*. Cambridge: Polity Press.

Goldman, S. L., Nagel, R. N., and Preiss, K. (1995). *Agile Competitors and Virtual Organizations*. New York: Van Nostrand Reinhold.

Granovetter, M. S. (1985). 'Economic Action and Social Structure: The Problem of Embeddedness'. *American Journal of Sociology*, 91: 481–510.

Grenier, R. and Metes, G. (1995). *Going Virtual: Moving Your Organization into the 21st Century*. Upper Saddle River, NJ: Prentice Hall.

Gulati, R. (1995). 'Does Familiarity Breed Trust? The Implications of Repeated Ties for Contractual Choice in Alliances'. *Academy of Management Journal*, 38: 85–112.

Hagedoorn, J. (1993). 'Understanding the Rationale of Strategic Technology Partnering: Interorganizational Modes of Cooperation and Sectorial Differences'. *Strategic Management Journal*, 14: 371–85.

Hale, R. and Whitlam, P. (1997). *Towards the Virtual Organization*. London: McGraw Hill.

Hamel, G. (1991). 'Competition for Competence and Interpartner Learning within International Strategic Alliances'. *Strategic Management Journal*, 12 (Summer special issue): 83–103.

Harrigan, K. R. (1985). *Strategies for Joint Ventures*. Lexington, Mass.: Lexington Books.

——(1988). 'Strategic Alliances and Partner Asymmetries'. *Management International Review*, 28: 53–72.

Hedberg, B. L. T. (1981). 'How Organizations Learn and Unlearn', in P. C. Nystrom and W. H. Starbuck (eds.), *Handbook of Organizational Design*: Vol.1. *Adapting Organizations to Their Environments*. Oxford: Oxford University Press, 3–27.

——(in press). 'Imaginary Organizations: New Enterprises Breed New Perspectives', in B. L. T. Hedberg, P. Baumard, and A. Yakhlef (eds.), *Investigating Imaginary Organizations: Contributions to a New Perspective on Business*. Amsterdam: Elsevier.

—— Dahlgren, G., Hansson, J., and Olve, N. G. (1997). *Virtual Organizations and Beyond: Discover Imaginary Systems*. London: Wiley and Sons.

Hedlund, G. (1994). 'A Model of Knowledge Management and the N-form Corporation'. *Strategic Management Journal*, 15: 73–90.

Holmqvist, M. (1999). 'Learning in Imaginary Organizations: Creating Interorganizational Knowledge'. *Journal of Organizational Change Management*, 12/5: 419–38.

Huber, G. P. (1991). 'Organizational Learning: The Contributing Processes and the Literatures'. *Organization Science*, 2: 88–115.

Inkpen, A. C. and Beamish, P. W. (1997). 'Knowledge, Bargaining Power, and the Instability of International Joint Ventures'. *Academy of Management Review*, 22: 177–202.

—— and Crossan, M. M. (1995). 'Believing Is Seeing: Joint Ventures and Organization Learning'. *Journal of Management Studies*, 32: 595–618.

Jarillo, J. C. (1988). 'On Strategic Networks'. *Strategic Management Journal*, 9: 31–41.

Larsson, R., Bengtsson, L., Henriksson, K., and Sparks, J. (1998). 'The Interorganizational Learning Dilemma: Collective Knowledge Development in Strategic Alliances'. *Organization Science*, 9: 285–305.

Levitt, B. and March, J. G. (1995). 'Chester I. Barnard and the Intelligence of Learning', in O. E. Williamson (ed.), *Organization Theory: From Chester Barnard to the Present and Beyond*. New York: Oxford University Press, 11–37.

Ljungberg, F. (1997). *Networking*. Report No. 11. Gothenburg Studies in Informatics. Gothenburg, Sweden.

Maravelias, C. (in press). 'Trust-based Control', in B. L. T. Hedberg, P. Baumard, and A. Yakhlef (eds.), *Investigating Imaginary Organizations: Contributions to a New Perspective on Business*. Amsterdam: Elsevier.

March, J. G. and Simon, H. A. (1958). *Organizations*. New York: Wiley.

Miles, R. E. and Snow, C. C. (1992). 'Causes of Failure in Network Organizations'. *California Management Review*, 34/2: 53–72.

Mintzberg, H., Dougherthy, D., Jorgensen, J., and Westley, F. (1996). 'Some Surprising Things about Collaboration: Knowing How People Connect Makes It Work Better'. *Organizational Dynamics*, 25/1: 60–71.

Nelson, R. R. and Winter, S. G. (1982). *An Evolutionary Theory of Economic Change*. Cambridge, Mass.: Belknap Press of Harvard University.

Nonaka, I. (1994). 'A Dynamic Theory of Organizational Knowledge Creation'. *Organization Science*, 5: 14–37.

Ouchi, W. G. (1980). 'Markets, Bureaucracies and Clans'. *Administrative Science Quarterly*, 25: 129–41.

Powell, W. W. (1990). 'Neither Market nor Hierarchy: Network Forms of Organization', in L. L. Cummings and B. M. Staw (eds.), *Research in Organizational Behavior: An Annual Series of Analytical Essays and Critical Reviews* (Vol. 12). Greenwich, Conn.: JAI Press, 295–336.

—— Koput, K. W., and Smith-Doerr, L. (1996). 'Interorganizational Collaboration and the Locus of Innovation: Networks of Learning in Biotechnology'. *Administrative Science Quarterly*, 41: 116–45.

Prahalad, C. K. and Hamel, G. (1990). 'The Core Competence of the Corporation'. *Harvard Business Review*, 68/3: 79–91.

Sanchez, R. and Heene, A. (eds.) (1997). *Competence-based Strategic Management*. Chichester: John Wiley and Sons.

Savage, C. M. (1996). *5th Generation Management: Cocreating through Virtual Enterprising, Dynamic Teaming, and Knowledge Networking*. Boston: Butterworth-Heinemann.

Simon, H. A. (1997). *Administrative Behavior* (4th edn). New York: Free Press.

Simonin, B. L. and Helleloid, D. (1993). 'Do Organizations Learn? An Empirical Test of Organizational Learning in International Strategic Alliances', in D. Moore (ed.), *Academy of Management Best Papers Proceedings*. Columbia, SC: Omnibus, 222–6.

Thorelli, H. B. (1986). 'Networks: Between Markets and Hierarchies'. *Strategic Management Journal*, 7: 37–51.

Uggla, H. (in press). 'Conceptualizing, Managing and Measuring Bases of Associations', in B. L. T. Hedberg, P. Baumard, and A. Yakhlef (eds.), *Investigating Imaginary Organizations: Contributions to a New Perspective on Business*. Amsterdam: Elsevier.

Williams, J. R. (1999). *Renewable Advantage: Crafting Strategy Through Economic Time*. New York: Free Press.

Williamson, O. E. (1975). *Markets and Hierarchies: Analysis and Antitrust Implications*. New York: Free Press.

——(1985). *The Economic Institutions of Capitalism: Firms, Markets, Relational Contracting*. New York: Free Press.

——(1991). 'Comparative Economic Organization: The Analysis of Discrete Structural Alternatives'. *Administrative Science Quarterly*, 36: 269–96.

Zand, D. E. (1972). 'Trust and Managerial Problem-Solving'. *Administrative Science Quarterly*, 17: 229–39.

Zimmermann, F. O. (1997). 'Structural and Managerial Aspects of Virtual Enterprises'. 29 June. Available: http://www.teck.uni-karlsruhe.de/IT-VISION/vu-e-teco-htm

PART VII

DEVELOPING LEARNING PRACTICES

Introduction

The growing interest in organizational learning concepts and theories has generated a rapid proliferation of approaches, tools, and techniques of learning. Thus, the common objective of all the authors in this part is to draw on theories, empirical research, and authors' practical experience to provide practitioners with an 'architecture' of organizational learning practices. Each chapter elaborates on this architecture and suggests corresponding tools and techniques of learning to develop and apply.

In their chapter on creating conditions for organizational learning, Friedman, Lipshitz, and Overmeer observe that organizational learning studies have produced compelling models for learning, but little guidance for action. The authors emphasize that organizational learning, or learning by the organization, requires both the appropriate structural mechanisms and the cultural conditions that promote habits of inquiry, experimentation, and reflection. Behavioral norms of transparency, inquiry, openness to disconfirmation, and accountability are important elements of this culture. These learning-oriented behaviors, which expose the reasoning of organizational members to public scrutiny, take a high degree of psychological safety. The authors argue that organizational learning requires relatively broad cultural norms that legitimate the open discussion of conflict and encourage the admission and candid examination of error. In order to create these conditions, managers must, according to the authors, suspend the need for control and predictability so that the above-mentioned habit of inquiry, experimentation, and reflection can be developed. The framework presented in the chapters represents a 'working theory' of organizational learning to be tested and refined through practice.

The chapter by Pawlowsky, Forslin, and Reinhardt is an attempt to bridge views of organizational learning theory and application by examining specific organizational learning practices grounded in a theoretical framework. The authors begin by drawing on theories of knowledge management in order to outline four stages of organizational learning: identification/generation, diffusion, integration/modification, and action. They then examine various practices and learning tools within these stages according to system level, learning mode, learning level, and process-phase application. In so doing, they provide a conceptual framework for categorizing intervention tools and for analyzing the points in the process at which they are likely to have the most impact. Such a theoretically derived classification scheme enables one to systematize organizational learning tools and test the effects of tools empirically. Experiment and analysis reveal that different tools demand different degrees of participation and that some tools are more appropriate than others for certain stages of learning and certain organizational goals. The authors argue that, with the appropriate tools, managers can overcome barriers to learning and can create an organizational environment conducive to innovation and the development of new knowledge. The authors offer helpful hints for facilitating these learning processes, but they also realize that the application of learning tools ultimately depends on the specific culture, leadership styles, and structural features of the organization.

Reinhardt, Bornemann, Pawlowsky, and Schneider, in the final chapter of this part, present a framework for operationalizing theories of intellectual capital. Like several other contributors in this handbook, the authors of this chapter regard knowledge as an economic resource, as an intangible asset that is becoming increasingly important for the performance of countries or companies. The authors follow a transdisciplinary approach to understanding knowledge, one in which intellectual capital is treated as a process, not merely as an object. They argue that the most important role of intellectual capital is not to raise new capital but rather to support organizational development. Thus, organizations should manage their intellectual capital by learning how to identify, generate, and deploy various forms of knowledge. Information technology, they assert, has an important role in the overall practice of knowledge management because it has enabled the integration and processing of large amounts of information independent of time and space. Human resource departments are now increasingly attempting to measure the value of a firm's intangible resources in order to improve decision-making related to these resources, to develop a universal human resource perspective, and, ultimately, to provide this information to investors. Yet the authors highlight that there still remains the challenge of how to account for, measure, and control intellectual capital. Measures of such capital, they explain, are strongly dependent on the strategy, culture, and goals of particular organizations; consequently, there are no universal measures for such assets.

By enriching discourses on organizational learning and knowledge and by pointing out the practical implications of theoretical work in this field, this section offers linkages between theory and action. The authors ground their analysis of learning practices in theory and show how the practices are dynamic processes shaped by conditions found within organizations. Although the chapters do not provide specific answers for how to develop these practices, they do highlight the role that culture, structure, leadership, and knowledge base play in developing learning tools and practices. Such an analysis allows for a greater understanding of learning processes, allowing practitioners to select and apply the appropriate tools and techniques of learning.

34 Creating Conditions for Organizational Learning

Victor J. Friedman, Raanan Lipshitz, and Wim Overmeer

Despite the rapidly growing interest in organizational learning, there remains a fundamental dichotomy between visionaries and skeptics regarding its practice. The visionaries (e.g. Garrat 1987; Howard and Haas 1993; Nonaka 1991; Senge 1990) advocate organizational learning as a process with the potential to transform organizations and organizational life. They take a prescriptive, normative stance, viewing organizational learning as both attainable and essential to meeting the need for continual innovation and change (Tsang 1997). The skeptics (e.g. Brehmer 1980; Levitt and March 1988; March and Olsen 1976; Weick and Westley 1996) focus on the limitations and failings of organizational learning, which they attribute to the relatively unchangeable features of people and organizations. Furthermore, the skeptics eschew a normative view of organizational learning, regarding it as a function of organizations that is neither good nor bad.[1]

Part of the problem may be that visionaries, though providing compelling models and illustrations of learning organizations, provide little guidance on how to 'get there from here'. The objective of this chapter is to further develop the question of how organizations 'learn to unlearn' (Hedberg 1981). Our aim is to help narrow the gap between visionaries and skeptics by providing a usable guide to creating conditions for organizational learning.

[1] This dichotomy also became apparent during a conference of the Strategic Management Society in Toronto in October 1992. After a keynote speech by P. Senge on 'the learning organization', an informal poll of participants pointed to the existence of two groups: academics who thought the address to have been mere 'preaching', and practicing managers and consultants who 'loved' it.

We define organizational learning as a process of inquiry (often in response to errors or anomalies) through which members of an organization develop shared values and knowledge based on past experience of themselves and of others. Furthermore, we are concerned with organizational learning processes that are conscious and systematic, that involve a critical and reflective attitude towards the information being processed, and that lead to actions to which organizational actors feel internally committed.

This definition of and our approach to organizational learning build largely on the pioneering work of Argyris and Schön (1978, 1996), who adopted an approach that was both skeptical and visionary, descriptive and prescriptive. On the one hand, they introduced the concepts of 'single-loop' and 'double-loop' learning in order to describe the processes through which individuals and organizations detect and correct errors in their behavioral strategies (single-loop learning) and in their underlying values, objectives, and standards for performance (double-loop learning). On the other hand, they focused on the ways in which individual and collective defenses make organizational double-loop learning unlikely, particularly under conditions of potential embarrassment or threat.

In order to make double-loop learning feasible, Argyris and Schön (1974) took the visionary step of prescribing a 'Model 2 theory-in-use' (p. 7), which is based on three simple values (or variables): valid information, free and informed choice, and internal commitment to the choice and monitoring of its implementation.

Individuals who internalize and act upon these values will produce action strategies such as combining advocacy with inquiry, making statements that are disconfirmable, openly testing their own inferences, inquiring into the reasoning of others, working with others to design means of protection, and jointly controlling tasks. According to Argyris and Schön (1996), these behaviors enhance those conditions for double-loop learning under which assumptions and norms central to an organization's theory-in-use can be brought to the surface, openly tested, and restructured.

The problems with Model 2 are that it does not come naturally and that it requires a complicated and lengthy learning process (Argyris 1982, 1993; Argyris, Putnam, and Smith 1985; Friedman and Lipshitz 1992). The difficulties entailed by Model 2 may explain why the concept of double-loop learning has become current in the literature on organizational learning whereas the concept of Model 2 (and its counterpart, Model 1) has largely been ignored. It is possible that Argyris and Schön greatly overstated the rarity of double-loop learning. However, it is also possible that many advocates of organizational learning prefer to remain vague about the potentially embarrassing question of how to get there from here.

From the standpoint of promoting learning practices, one of the great strengths of the approach taken by Argyris and Schön (1978, 1996) is its parsimony. Later advocates of organizational learning have tried to create more comprehensive models of the knowledge and skills necessary for generating learning practices. For example, Willard (1994) surveyed some thirty books and articles relevant to the promotion of organizational learning and came up with a list of no fewer than twenty-three required skills and attributes. Furthermore, many of these skills and attributes seem more like sound overall advice for management or organizational development (such as that found in Garvin 1993) than advice aimed specifically at organizational learning. A comprehensive model is likely to produce a complex, but hardly useful, guide to organizational learning. In addition, such models, though compelling, are often formulated at a high level of generalization that is difficult to translate into action.

Organizational actors require relatively clear milestones that can guide the process of trying to foster organizational learning, evaluate it, or both. Therefore, the approach we advocate for organizational learning is one in which parsimony and manageability of cognitive load is valued more than comprehensiveness. First, we describe the basic structural mechanisms necessary for systematic organizational learning. Second, we present a map that outlines the cultural conditions under which organizational learning is likely to occur. Third, we present three case studies that illustrate how systematic learning practices were developed in organizations. On the basis of these case studies, we then identify a number of strategies for creating conditions that promote organizational learning.

The Structural Element: Organizational Learning Mechanisms

A necessary, but not a sufficient, condition for systematically promoting organizational learning is the existence of organizational structures in which the learning process can be carried out. Dodgson (1993) defined learning organizations as 'firms that purposefully adopt structures and strategies to encourage learning'. Similarly, DiBella, Nevis, and Gould (1996) reported that 'learning capabilities and processes were identified in all the organizations . . . studied' and that these capabilities and processes took the form of 'formal and informal processes and structures . . . for the acquisition, sharing, and utilization of knowledge and skills in all these firms' (p. 372). Such structures have been labeled 'learning forums' (Garvin 1993: 91) and 'parallel learning structures' (Bushe and Shani 1991; Schein 1993: 90). Popper and Lipshitz (1997) used the term 'organizational learning mechanisms' (OLMs) to describe institutionalized structural and procedural arrangements that allow organizations to systematically collect, analyze, store, disseminate, and use information that is relevant to the performance of the organization and its members.

OLMs can be classified according to who carries out the learning and what the relationship of the OLM is to task performance. OLMs are 'integrated' to the extent that organizational members analyze their own and others' experience in order to improve their own performance. OLMs are 'nonintegrated' to the extent that members collect, analyze, store, and disseminate information primarily for the benefit of others. In addition, OLMs are 'designated' to the extent that they operate separately from task performance, and they are 'dual-purpose' to the extent that they operate in conjunction with task performance.

Strategic planning departments, for instance, are nonintegrated, designated OLMs because their form of learning is carried on separately from task performance and for the benefit of others. Because these OLMs are relatively remote from action and because they require a considerable transfer of knowledge, they are considered to be less powerful generators of organizational learning than those mechanisms in which participants analyze their own behavior as an integral part of the task. De Geus (1988), however, described how scenario-planning can be used to make the planning process more integrated and dual-purpose (see Galer and van der Heijden, Ch. 38 in this volume).

At Microsoft Corporation almost all project teams hold postproject discussion sessions, and more than half of them produce written post-mortem reports. As described by Cusumano and Selby (1995), these groups are integrated, designated OLMs, whose systematic reflection upon task performance is complemented by mechanisms for dissemination:

The postmortem documents are surprisingly candid in their self-criticism, especially because they are circulated to the highest levels of the company . . . Groups generally take three to six months to put a postmortem document together . . . The most common format is to discuss what worked well in the last project, what did not work well, and what the group should do to improve in the next project . . .

The functional managers usually prepare an initial draft and then circulate this via e-mail to the team members, who send in their comments. The authors collate these and create the final draft, which then goes out to team members as well as senior executives and directors of product development, and testing. The functional groups, and sometimes an entire project, will then meet to discuss the postmortem findings. Some groups . . . have also gotten into the habit of holding postmortem meetings every milestone to make midcourse corrections, review feature lists, and rebalance schedule. (pp. 331–2)

In order to distribute the lessons learned from one project to other units, Microsoft instituted a variety of dissemination OLMs that include formal and informal cross-group and cross-functional retreats and meetings.

Another example of an integrated and designated OLM is the Israeli Air Force's 'after-action reviews' (AARs), a process in which pilots and their commanders meet immediately after each mission to analyze both individual and group performances (Popper and Lipshitz 1997). Other examples include postproject appraisals at Boeing (Gulliver 1987) and retour d'expérience at Electricité de France (DiBella, Nevis, and Gould 1996). Because the learning in integrated, designated OLMs is carried out by people who are performing the task itself, it can be hypothesized that such OLMs will generate higher levels of organizational learning than other types of OLMs.

Dual-purpose, integrated OLMs fuse learning and task structures, creating a community of reflective practitioners (Schön 1983) who weave together work, learning, and the sharing of learning. Rayner (1993) provided an excellent illustration of this type of OLM in an interview of Arden C. Sims, the CEO of Globe Metallurgical Inc. Sims described what happened when a strike broke out in late 1986:

As the union workers left the plant, about 35 salaried workers and 10 company managers stepped in to take-over operation of two of the five furnaces. The strike was a time of great stress but also a time of great progress. We experimented with everything . . . A few weeks after management took over operating the plant, output actually improved by

20% . . . We were operating in a very fast, continuous improvement mode. Everyday people would suggest ways to improve the operation of the furnaces or the additive process or the way we transported material around the plant. I kept a pocket notebook, and if I saw something I'd note it down and discuss it with the team over coffee or during meals. I filled a notebook every day. . . . As we made more changes and as we settled in to the routine of running the plant we didn't need first-line supervisors. We could produce the product more effectively if everyone just worked together cooperatively—welders, crane operators, furnace operators, forklift drivers, stokers, furnace tapers, and taper assistants. (Rayner 1993: 287–9)

The integrated, dual-purpose OLM vividly described above emerged spontaneously in response to a crisis and a sudden flattening of the organization. Rayner did not specify whether this OLM persisted or whether other types of OLMs were instituted in the company after the strike.

As pointed out already, OLMs represent a necessary, but not a sufficient, condition for systematic organizational learning. To the best of our knowledge, no research has yet been done to test the hypothesis that levels of organizational learning rise with the level of integration and dual-purposeness of OLMs that are introduced. Furthermore, some anecdotal evidence raises doubts about the effectiveness of OLMs. For example, Dave Moore, Microsoft's director for development, noted that, despite the proliferation of project postmortems, the same errors kept occurring, a problem that he attributed to insufficient accountability for follow-up on the implementation of lessons learned (Cusumano and Selby 1995).

If an OLM is ineffective, it may be that learning has become ritualistic or may be limited by defensiveness, insufficient or distorted information, organizational politics, or many other 'learning disabilities' (Senge 1990: 18). Argyris (1991, 1994) has described how talented and well-intentioned professionals systematically inhibit learning when they experience psychological threat in the process of reflecting on practice. Thus, a map usable for guiding organizational learning needs to go beyond the structural element and address those features of an organization's culture that are likely to promote or inhibit organizational learning.

The Cultural Element: The Behavioral World

Several authors have noted that effective organizational learning requires a climate or culture that fosters inquiry, openness, and trust (Argyris and Schön 1978; Beer and Spector 1993; Davies and Easterby-Smith 1984; DiBella, Nevis, and Gould 1996; McGill, Slocum, and Lei 1993). If structures represent the relatively tangible 'hardware' of organizational learning, then organizational culture represents the 'software'. Organizational culture can be defined as the relatively stable ways of perceiving the world and the action strategies that an organization has learned from experience (Schein 1990). In this sense, culture is the output of organizational learning, but at the same time it constrains organizational learning as well as every other activity of the organization. Because culture is such an overarching and complex construct (Lundberg 1985), we have chosen to simplify matters by adopting the concept of the 'behavioral world' (Argyris and Schön 1996; 69), which focuses on the elements of an organization's culture that facilitate or inhibit learning.

Argyris and Schön (1996) defined the behavioral world as the 'qualities, meanings, and feelings that habitually condition patterns of interaction among individuals within the organization in such a way as to affect organizational inquiry' (p. 29). We suggest that the behavioral world can be mapped out in terms of contextual, psychological, and behavioral factors (see Fig. 34.1). Behavioral factors refer to the kind of observable actions that are likely to promote organizational learning. Psychological factors refer to the internal states that are likely to facilitate or motivate these actions. Contextual factors refer to those organizational norms or cultures that are likely to create and reinforce these psychological conditions. All these factors are linked by a causal loop.

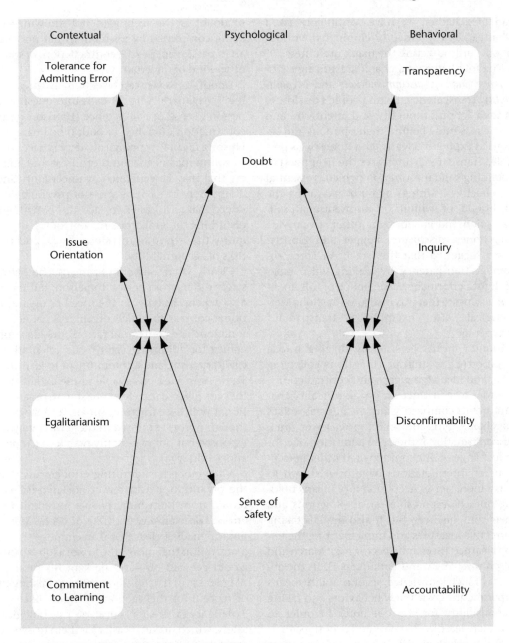

Fig. 34.1. Conditions for organizational learning

This map represents a heuristic model derived in part from Argyris and Schön's (1996) concept of a Model 2 theory-in-use and in part from our own research and practice (Friedman 1997; Friedman and Lipshitz 1992; Overmeer 1996; Popper and Lipshitz 1997). Parsimony was one of the main guiding principles in creating this map. To increase the map's practicability among practitioners and researchers, we have resisted the tendency to add more and more variables. Rather, we have continually asked what can be combined or eliminated without significantly affecting the map's usefulness.

The four behavioral characteristics are *transparency, inquiry, disconfirmation*, and *accountability*. Transparency means people's disclosure of their actions, thoughts, and intentions, and of the reasoning behind their opinions and actions as explicitly, clearly, and honestly as possible. Transparency increases the likelihood of obtaining valid information (which is essential for effective learning) by both decreasing the likelihood of willful or unintentional self-deception and encouraging others to provide full, honest disclosure. Popper and Lipshitz (1997) suggested that the Israeli Air Force encourage transparency by making video tapes of flight performance. The policy of full financial disclosure that was instituted at Globe Metallurgical also exemplifies transparency (Rayner 1993).

Inquiry means persistently digging into a situation (e.g. asking open questions, collecting data, and identifying gaps and contradictions) in order to construct an image of reality that captures its complexity and meaning as well as possible (Argyris and Schön 1996; Dewey 1938). Disconfirmation is the open admission of error or a change of one's mind when other perceptions or interpretations have been shown to make more sense. Accountability means holding oneself responsible for one's actions and their consequences, but it also implies taking corrective measures and implementing the lessons learned (Beer and Spector 1993; March and Olsen 1976; Shaw and Perkins 1992). In the absence of such knowledge, accountability means experimenting with new behaviors and taking responsibility for the outcomes in order to stimulate learning (Argyris and Schön 1996).

The psychological factors underlying these behaviors are doubt and a sense of psychological safety. Doubt is a psychological precondition for inquiry. Drawing on Dewey (1938), Argyris and Schön (1996) defined inquiry as 'the intertwining of thought and action that proceeds from doubt to the resolution of doubt' (p. 11). When people experience doubt, they are more likely to genuinely inquire into a situation. Part

of doubt is the feeling of not knowing—of being confronted by a situation that presents an impasse, gap, puzzle, contradiction, or some other kind of uncertainty.

Doubt, however, can be extremely threatening, particularly when it calls into question a person's sense of competence (Harrison 1962), construction of reality, or both (Friedman and Lipshitz 1992). Psychological safety is necessary to counterbalance feelings of threat and anxiety that may be generated by uncertainty and doubt (Schein 1969). A sense of psychological safety makes it easier to face the potentially disturbing or embarrassing outcomes of inquiry, the exposure of transparency, and the risks of accountability.

Clearly, what causes doubt and psychological safety differs from person to person, but it can also depend heavily on the social or organizational context in which organizational actors function. The contextual factors include a tolerance for admitting error, issue orientation, egalitarianism, and a commitment to learning. These norms are observable to the extent that they are given concrete expression in organizational policies, structure, rituals, and slogans, though norms expressed in these ways may be espoused but not necessarily practiced (Argyris and Schön 1974).

A tolerance for admitting error means that the organization will reward, or at least will refrain from punishing, people for admitting errors. For example, the CEO of Globe Metallurgical made it clear that if an employee made a suggestion that meant the loss of a job, no one would get laid off—and he kept his promise (Rayner 1993). If people do not fear punishment or reprisal for their actions, they are likely to experience a greater sense of psychological safety, which makes it easier for them to experiment and admit error (transparency and accountability) so that they and others can learn from the experience.

Issue orientation is the tendency to base judgments on substance rather than on political interests, status, or personal likes and dislikes. Eisenhardt, Kahwajy, and Bourgeois (1997) found that top management teams that engaged in a high level of conflict over substantive issues were more effective than teams that engaged in interpersonal conflict or low level of conflict. If people believe that they and others in the organization will base judgments on substantive criteria, their sense of psychological safety and fairness will increase, and they will be more willing to be transparent. An issue orientation also causes people to cast doubt on their attitudes and pre-judgments in light of substantive data.

Egalitarianism refers to the practices of power-sharing, participation, and equal responsibility for meeting performance standards regardless of formal status. Egalitarianism opens communication channels and thereby promotes innovation and learning (Kanter 1988; McGill, Slocum, and Lei 1993; Weisbord 1987). Egalitarianism reinforces people's sense of psychological safety, fairness, and commitment. For example, in the Israeli Air Force's after-action reviews, everyone—pilots and commanders, rookies and veterans—came under close scrutiny. Both egalitarianism and tolerance for admitting error were expressed in statements such as 'everybody is in the same boat' and 'all pilots make errors' (Popper and Lipshitz 1997). Egalitarianism can also stimulate doubt because people who hold positions of responsibility in organizations with egalitarian norms are more likely to be open about their own uncertainties.

Finally, the organization's commitment to learning plays an important role in creating psychological and behavioral conditions. An organization is committed to learning when it values collective learning either in itself or as an essential activity for survival or effectiveness. Commitment can be demonstrated through the investment of time and resources that take organizational learning beyond mere slogans. A no less important sign of commitment is the active involvement and openness of top management, whose behavior tends to become a standard against which organizational members judge the seriousness of a particular effort.

For the sake of clarity our map of a behavioral world that is conducive to organizational learning (see Fig. 34.1) has been drawn to show a series of causal links: The organizational context creates psychological conditions, which, in turn, generate behavioral conditions. In practice the links go both ways, and there are numerous causal connections within the categories themselves.

The purpose of this map is to provide a set of targets that managers or consultants could keep in mind if they wish to promote or evaluate organizational learning. The map is not intended to be a comprehensive model or theory of the conditions influencing organizational learning. For this reason it leaves out a number of factors, such as the degree of uncertainty in an organization's environment, the nature of its task, and the nature of its leadership (for a discussion of leadership in organizational learning, see Sadler, Ch. 18 in this volume; for a discussion of the role of top management, see Tainio, Lilja, and Santalainen, Ch. 19 in this volume). These factors may be crucial for understanding where and to what extent learning is likely to occur, but they are relatively fixed and not easily influenced by management or interventionists.

Although the map provides targets, it does not specify where to begin or how to hit those targets. In the following section we present three case studies that illustrate the development of learning processes within organizations. The three case studies represent a set of 'action experiments' (Argyris, Putnam, and Smith 1985: 118) carried out in very different settings and enable one to identify and illustrate a number of strategies for helping organizations learn to learn.

Three Case Studies

Case 1: Ordnance Corps of the Israel Defense Force

Lipshitz, Popper, and Oz (1996) described their attempt as consultants to foster organizational learning in the Ordnance Corps of the Israel Defense Force (IDF) through the design and implementation of organizational learning mechanisms (OLMs). Their prototype for such a mechanism was the Israeli Air Force's after-action review (AAR). The consultants knew that other parts of the IDF had growing interest in improving processes through which units were supposed to learn lessons from operational experience.

The consultants were invited to work with a task force that had been created to improve methods for learning from experience. The consultants had a vision of and belief in organizational learning, but they did not have a clear method for producing that vision. Rather, they based their intervention on a loose set of concepts involving both structural change (assimilating an organizational learning mechanism into project management) and cultural change (fostering the values and behaviors that facilitate organizational learning).

Although the consultants could not provide the task force with a recipe for generating organizational learning, they did attempt to convey their vision through familiar examples of an OLM (e.g. the Air Force's after-action review process) and of cultural change (the Unit 101 myth[2]). The consultants assumed that these 'metaphors', as they called them, would be easily grasped by the task-force members, and would subsequently fire their imaginations and stimulate them to think about how such processes could be applied to their own situation.

The consultants also devised a 'dual-track strategy' through which the task force, operating as a prototypical OLM, would devise a methodology for integrating after-action reviews into project management. On one track, the task force would work on specific problems involving the operational preparedness of Is-

raeli-made Merkava tanks, periodically conducting after-action reviews to look at their work. On the second track, it would simultaneously experiment with the format of after-action reviews themselves and reflect on the results.

Contrary to the consultants' expectations, the metaphors failed to inspire the task force members, and the dual-track process created considerable confusion over what was expected of them. The natural tendency of the task force was to focus on the concrete, operational objective (tank preparedness) and to subtly resist attempts to get them to focus on the 'second track' (after-action review development), which seemed of little inherent interest. At one point the project completely stalled for three months because the commander, who may have begun to lose interest, turned his attention elsewhere.

The commander turned his attention back to the project when he learned that he was going to be transferred and did not want to leave an unfinished project behind. A breakthrough was achieved when the consultants and the commander stumbled upon the fact that each of the units to which task-force members belonged used a different maintenance information system. The curious fact that each unit had developed its own unique system and the obvious value of learning from each others' experience stimulated the task-force members to focus attention and energy on this specific issue. The consultants thus invented a new OLM—an 'empirical seminar' in which each task-force member would present his unit's system, which the group would then study as a whole.

Gradually, the task-force underwent a marked change in both the clarity of the issues being discussed and the involvement of the members. Discussions were frank yet pleasant, and differences in rank came to play no role whatsoever. Members enjoyed a process that took them away from the daily routine but that remained extremely relevant to their work. The empirical seminar resulted in the development of a written guide for designing maintenance information systems, a manual that was based on the comparisons between

[2] In the early 1950s, Moshe Dayan (the then Chief-of-Staff of the IDF) wanted to improve the overall performance of the military by instilling three values: Accomplish your mission under all circumstances, physically lead your subordinates into combat, and never leave a wounded soldier behind in retreat. To do so, Dayan created Unit 101, a small elite commando that put these values into practice and became a legend through its daring, successful missions. Unit 101 became a vehicle for diffusing these values in two ways: It became a model for imitation, and its members, who were placed in key leadership positions throughout the IDF, instilled these values wherever they went.

the various systems. The participants also developed a guide for integrating after-action reviews into the Ordnance Corps's project management. This work concluded the first phase of the project. The second phase called for task-force members to follow the example of Unit 101, whose members had dispersed into various units of the IDF, and to disseminate in their individual units the lessons learned in the empirical seminar and the values behind it.

Case 2: The Mishlav Jaffa Vocational High School

Friedman (1997) described the process through which a team of teachers in a vocational high school developed and implemented an innovative approach to teaching secretarial studies. The project was initiated by two organizations, the Joint Distribution Committee—Israel (JDC —Israel, a nongovernmental social service organization) and the Israeli Ministry of Labor (which oversees vocational education), which joined together in order to develop an improved approach to providing 'girls at risk' with resources for social mobility.

For this purpose the initiators of the project wanted to enlist a school that would put together a team of teachers to study the problem and combine their field experience with the knowledge of experts. Five principals rejected the offer before the initiators secured the enthusiastic agreement of the principal of Mishlav Jaffa, a vocational school located in the center of Tel Aviv, Israel's largest city. For some time she had felt that the school's program failed to provide the students with a truly valuable education, and she saw the initiators' project as a way of addressing that problem and improving the school's image.

The principal put together a team of six teachers, herself, and a team coordinator, who was one of the outside initiators. The principal arranged the teachers' schedules so that they would all be free one full day each week for project work. The team began by meeting with experts, undergoing training, and visiting institutions that had developed innovative approaches to similar populations. After each visit the team members analyzed what they had seen and compared it to their students and their methods. The more they saw, the more they recognized the uniqueness of their own situation and the necessity for developing something new.

After about four months the team coordinator left the project, and the team was inactive until a new coordinator arrived a number of months later. In retrospect, team members attributed their passivity at that time to the feeling that it was the coordinator's project. The new coordinator immediately pressed the team to define its approach, opening a long period of discussion and conflict. Team members who taught skills (e.g. secretarial skills) felt the project should focus on concrete skill development, whereas those who taught more academic subjects (e.g. literature) wanted to focus on motivational and behavioral issues. The team eventually arrived at a consensus, deciding to focus the curriculum on skill-building while working informally on the development issues. This decision was based on the fact that (a) the team asked the students themselves what they wanted and (b) team members realized that they had a greater number of techniques for teaching skills than for encouraging development.

After a year and a half of development work, the project team presented a detailed, sixty-nine-page curriculum based on three main ideas: an integrative team approach to teaching, the development of cognitive skills, and the use of a simulated office laboratory. At the same time the members of the team envisioned the creation of a classroom environment in which students would take more responsibility and feel more freedom to express their needs than they had in the past. The team made an explicit decision not to expel problem students from the class, an act they saw as avoidance of responsibility, but to find a way of bringing out the potential of each student.

Within weeks of the program's implementation in a pilot class, some of the team members encountered serious behavioral problems;

others experienced 'lethargy' or 'inertia' in the class. Although these teachers were experienced in handling the toughest students, they had created a situation in which they could no longer rely on their old skills. As one of the teachers put it, in a regular classroom 'we wouldn't have put up with [such behavior, but that was] before we were aware of what we were actually doing.' Team members eventually decided to throw out the worst troublemakers, but they did not carry out their decision.

The team coordinator sensed that the discipline issue reflected deeper frustrations, so she invited the team members to freely express whatever was on their minds. Although they complained bitterly about the lack of support from the project initiators, they mostly expressed a deep sense of uncertainty about whether they themselves were doing the right thing. The coordinator believed that the teachers had made considerable progress but that they were somewhat blinded by the pressure, the fear of failure, and their sense of responsibility. The team coordinator assured the team members that no one would 'hang them from the public square' if they failed. She also brought in a social worker to help the teachers discuss their practice problems, the stress, and the emotional side of the change process. In this forum team members could get beyond the endless technical issues dealt with in regular team meetings. As these discussions continued and as the teachers gained experience, the behavioral issues ceased being a central problem.

The pilot year was considered a great success, and an attempt was immediately made to expand the project. However, members of the original team had difficulty explaining their ideas to their peers. Eventually, the original members realized that dissemination was not a matter of explanation or training and that newcomers had to undergo a learning process similar to theirs. Furthermore, the approach itself continued to change as the team took on new people, learned lessons from the past, and addressed new problems. The Mishlav Jaffa project has meanwhile become a change model for many other schools in Israel.

Case 3: The International Business Institute

The International Business Institute (IBI, a pseudonym) is a business school affiliated with a large telecommunications organization. The IBI offers an intensive one-year MBA program for an international group of twenty to thirty students per year. From its inception in the mid-1980s, the school has offered an 'organizational-learning-in-action' seminar based on the 'theory-of-action' approach (Argyris and Schön 1978). From the beginning, however, seminar instructors experienced strong negative reactions from the students. Even though the make-up of the visiting instructional team changed every year for the first few years, there was almost always an outburst aimed at the instructors, the IBI, or the students themselves.

During the fourth year of the program, the course was taught by an IBI faculty member and four visiting instructors. Early on, some of the students accused some of the instructors of attacking them. Later, some of the students spontaneously showed up at the instructors' hotel, where the two groups joined in drinks and a long informal discussion. From this exchange and from observations made during the seminar, the instructors were able to gather clues about what was causing the yearly outbursts.

In light of positive course evaluations, the same instructors were invited back the following year, and they were able to put more thought into designing the seminar. One of their central beliefs was that the students needed to experience and reflect upon organizational learning in order to really learn about it. For this purpose the instructors created simulations and exercises such as (a) an exercise in which small teams designed and built a real bridge, (b) the analysis of personal cases written by the students, and (c) a 'fishbowl' exercise in which the students could observe and participate in the instructors' evaluation and planning of the seminar.

The seminar seemed to move along very well until the final session, during which some of the students voiced angry criticisms of the instructors for not providing enough concrete skills and for having encouraged group members to be too open and to discuss threatening interpersonal issues that had been taboo until then. The instructors were at first surprised by this response, but the incident helped them develop a 'theory' of the situation. They hypothesized that the content of the seminar, which emphasized inquiry and transparency, acted as a catalyst for releasing whatever tensions and conflicts had been building up in the student group since the beginning of the year. For the instructors the central dilemma was allowing the real issues to surface while not violating the privacy of students who did not consider these issues appropriate for a regular classroom setting. At the beginning of the seminar, the instructors made their strategy explicit:

(1) The initiative to deal with the real issues had to come from the students themselves.
(2) The instructors would only act as consultants to the group if they were asked to do so.
(3) They would publicly or privately check the students' willingness to engage in such a process.
(4) Any student was free not to participate in such a process.

That year there was no outburst, but there was a key incident in which certain class members manipulated the formal class representative so as to neutralize him. Through an open, joint process of reflection, the class representative could see how his behavior was frustrating many of the students, and the students could see how their strategy perpetuated the very behaviors they found frustrating. The next year one of the students raised the issue of the group's difficulty in making decisions. This initiative led to an open, collective inquiry into the reasoning and behaviors that had brought the group to an impasse.

As a result of incidents like these, the seminar became a yearly forum in which the fundamental dilemmas and conflicts within the student group could be brought up and discussed. Most years the students came away from the seminar

feeling more capable of dealing with these issues than they had felt before the seminar. Furthermore, the IBI staff developed a clearer understanding of the students and how to relate to them.

Creating Conditions for Organizational Learning

An analysis of the three cases indicates that there were no discrete methods for creating each of the contextual, psychological, and behavioral factors. Rather, the conditions for organizational learning as a whole were fostered in each case by different combinations of six basic strategies: (a) combining learning with an instrumental objective, (b) generating optimal uncertainty, (c) controlling of the learning process jointly, (d) design conversations, (e) modeling, and (f) mapping.

Combining Learning with an Instrumental Objective

In all three cases the learning objective was coupled with an important instrumental objective, which was closely associated with the central task system of the organization. This combination helped generate sufficient organizational commitment to carry the learning process through.

At Mishlav Jaffa inquiry was not an end in itself but rather an important step toward developing a new educational program for a specific student population. As the team went from development to implementation, a passage that required intensive teamwork, its members discovered that an ongoing learning process was essential for overcoming unforeseen obstacles. Eventually, the project team functioned as an integrated, dual-purpose OLM.

In the initial stage of the Ordnance Corps case, assimilating an after-action review process into project management was defined as the central objective. However, this learning objective failed to stimulate the members of the task force, whose attention often drifted to concrete issues of project management. The breakthrough occurred when the learning objective was coupled with the objective of improving maintenance information systems. At that point, the task force evolved toward becoming a designated, partially integrated OLM because the officers were responsible for these systems.

Over the years the seminar at the IBI changed from being a purely academic course (its primary task) to offering an opportunity to address real organizational issues. Thus, it evolved into an integrated, dual-purpose OLM.

Coupling learning with instrumental objectives helped foster issue orientation by focusing attention on the task rather than on individuals, interpersonal relationships, or organizational politics. Although these factors often play a crucial role in organizational learning, they tend to be both threatening and complex. Focusing on them prematurely may create unnecessary defensiveness and cognitive overload, driving away potential learners. They are more likely to be dealt with effectively after organizational members have improved their skills and increased their appreciation for the learning process (Friedman and Lipshitz 1992).

Generating Optimal Uncertainty

Structural and cultural features that facilitate organizational learning are more likely to develop naturally in organizations functioning in high uncertainty environments than in organizations functioning in low-uncertainty environments (Lipshitz, Popper, and Oz 1996). However, all three organizations discussed in this chapter—a military unit, a public school, and a business school class—functioned in external and task environments generally considered to be relatively low in uncertainty. In all three cases outside interventionists stimulated learning by introducing uncertainty or by bringing latent uncertainties to the surface.

In the Mishlav Jaffa Project the outside agencies began the project by asking the team open-ended questions: Who are your students? What

are their needs? What is actually being done about them, and what leads these efforts to fall short? What other approaches are being tried with similar populations? These questions were not rhetorical, nor were they intended to lead the team to a predetermined answer or solution. They were intended to generate doubt about the basic beliefs and assumptions underlying teachers' practice and to stimulate inquiry into them. As it turned out, these questions simply enabled the teachers to openly express doubts that had long been on their minds. Team members made their beliefs, assumptions, and reasoning transparent and open to scrutiny. The process also fostered accountability, for the teachers began to perceive contradictions between what they believed in and what they were doing in practice.

During the development phase of the Mishlav Jaffa project, this process generated an 'optimal' level of uncertainty. It was stimulating enough to create doubt and inquiry while not being so threatening or challenging as to produce defensiveness. Furthermore, the team members had plenty of time to grapple with the uncertainty and to think together before making decisions. During the implementation phase, however, the members encountered a gap between the rejected former practices and their ability to put the new approach into practice. As one teacher put it, they could not fall back on old practices, for 'we were now aware of what we were doing'.

This situation created so much uncertainty and anxiety that the teachers were almost overwhelmed. However, the team coordinator reinforced the team members' sense of psychological safety by reassuring them that they were allowed to fail in the service of learning (i.e. tolerance for admitting error), by focusing on the practice problem itself (issue orientation) rather than on general complaints, and by creating a forum for working on that problem (an OLM that also expressed organizational commitment).

In the start-up phase of the Ordnance Corps project, the very task, inventing an appropriate procedure for organizational learning, generated considerable uncertainty. The officers did not really understand what the consultants wanted from them. The consultants were open about the fact that they did not have a clear method for guiding the task force. They tried to explain themselves and fire the imaginations of the task-force members by using familiar metaphors such as after-action review and the Unit 101 myth, but these attempts fell flat at first. The dual-track strategy added to the uncertainty by creating a high degree of cognitive complexity. In effect, the task-force members had to perform a complex task (managing tank maintenance projects), reflect on their performance (the continuous improvement of maintenance projects), and invent a better way of reflecting on performance (developing an after-action review for tank maintenance projects) all at the same time.

Uncertainty is necessary because organizational learning requires venturing beyond what is already known. The key challenge for consultants and managers is helping organizational members (and themselves) grapple with the uncertainty and experiment until they begin to make new sense of things. In the Ordnance Corps the consultants simply played with different ideas until they hit upon the right combination. However, other factors that counterbalanced the uncertainty were issue orientation (the focus on the maintenance information systems), organizational commitment (the commander's desire to complete the project), and, eventually, egalitarianism.

At both Mishlav Jaffa and the Ordnance Corps the OLM itself (i.e. the team and task force) was an important mechanism for keeping uncertainty within bounds. The fact that the team members faced the uncertainty together made it less threatening. The team functioned as a kind of holding environment that provided both information and psychological safety during the transition period (Heifetz 1994). Teams, however, do not guarantee that anxiety will be dealt with effectively. They may themselves facilitate the flight into basic assumptions (Bion 1959) or function as social defense systems that distort reality in order to guard team members from anxiety (Hirschhorn 1988). In both Mishlav and the Ordnance Corps

the groups appeared to have avoided this pitfall by keeping their attention focused on the task environment rather than fleeing inward.

In the IBI case the instructors discovered that their interventions raised latent doubts among the participants about their roles as students in a business school. At the beginning of the program, this role seemed too obvious to warrant any thought, but gradually it became clear that the students held different assumptions about this issue. In the seminar these doubts surfaced either directly or through confrontations with the instructors or other students. Acknowledging the uncertainty was viewed as a great opportunity by some of the students, but it raised the anxiety of those who were pessimistic about their ability to work these issues out. The challenge for the instructors was to keep this uncertainty within tolerable bounds in a heterogeneous group.

Controlling the Learning Process Jointly

Trying to foster a sense of psychological safety and accountability, the instructors in the IBI case implemented a strategy for involving the students in assessing the group's readiness for dealing with threatening issues and for giving them a choice about whether to participate in it. Joint control is also an important strategy for strengthening an organization's commitment to learning. It provides the organization with enough elbow room to adapt the learning process to its own particular situation. In the Ordnance Corps task force and the Mishlav Jaffa team the outside interventionists made it clear from the beginning that they viewed the organization, particularly the formal leader, as a partner and not as a client in the traditional sense. Gradually, however, the task-force team resisted assuming control over the process and preferred to be led by the outside consultants. In both cases the organizational members gradually took greater control and 'ownership' over the learning process and its products, enjoying considerable autonomy in defining, structuring, and pacing the task. By the end of this phase of the project, task-force members and team members were deeply committed to the process (as well as its products) and to its dissemination within the organization as a whole.

Joint control fostered egalitarianism within the Ordnance Corps task force. In the initial stages of the project, the commander played a dominant role, and obtaining his personal commitment was crucial to the success of the project. However, once the task force assumed more control over the process, differences of rank came to play no role whatsoever in substantive discussions, and the team was given extensive autonomy in decision-making. In the Mishlav Jaffa project the principal participated as a member of the project team, but team members reported that she never used her status to force a decision.

Design Conversations

Schön (1983), drawing on his study of architects and architectural education, used the concept of design, which he defined as a 'creative conversation with the situation', as a metaphor for the reflective practice of professionals. From the standpoint of the outside interventionists and organizational members, all three cases presented earlier in this chapter were examples of such conversations. The interventionists 'played' with objectives, tasks, and structures until a viable learning process emerged. Furthermore, the interventionists tried to provide the organizational members with a language and models for conducting such a conversation.

Design conversations often require more than verbal communication. Architects make drawings and models to express their ideas and test out possibilities. Practitioners trying to promote processes of organizational learning need special techniques for expressing ideas and experimenting in designing behavioral worlds.

Imagery, such as metaphors, similes, and exemplars, can be very useful tools for carrying on design conversations. Imagery enables people to envision a process and outcome that cannot be adequately described in technical terms.

Imagery guides sense-making and action in situations characterized by a high degree of complexity and uncertainty. Imagery conveys rich meaning through relatively simple and familiar language. When applied to a totally different situation, imagery provides relevant comparisons that suggest what might be going on, what actions might be taken, and what is likely to result.

As illustrated in the Ordnance Corps case, the consultants used imagery in lieu of concrete methods. They suggested to the task-force members that they assimilate after-action reviews into project management, though they do not actually engage in 'action' (i.e. combat), and that they function like Unit 101, even though their unit was entirely different. Although these metaphors did not speak to the officers at first, they became extremely powerful vehicles for expression at a later stage. Not only did the officers pick them up, they also used them to explain to others what they were doing.

Early in the learning process at IBI the consultants used the metaphor 'to skid' (the sliding or slipping that sometimes occurs when one drives on ice) to describe how individuals and groups automatically react to error and threat in ways that are counterproductive. This metaphor generally succeeded in stimulating the imaginations of the participants and giving them a new way of thinking about their experience. Later in the process both the consultants and the students used the metaphor to trigger transparency ('I think we are getting into a skid. What do I really intend to say and what do I honestly want to achieve?') and to stimulate inquiry ('What is getting me into the skid?') and accountability ('What might we do differently to get out of the skid?').

Personal case analysis drawn from the direct experience of organizational members is also a technique for creating design conversations. The empirical seminar of the Ordnance Corps task force was based on the practice of having each member present his unit's maintenance information system as a kind of personal case to be analyzed, critiqued, and compared with other systems. The writing and analysis of the cases generated 'data' for learning and opened information flows within the organization. The cases provided a concrete basis for learning lessons about current practice, determining best practices, and designing new systems.

At the IBI each student was required to write a case involving a difficult conflict or dilemma he or she had had to deal with in an organization (Argyris and Schön 1974). Simulations, such as the bridge-design exercise used at the IBI, can be used to create live cases. These cases provided a basis for generating inquiry into the reasoning, behavior, and the organizational dynamics that facilitate or inhibit learning. They also encouraged transparency because the students were asked to include unspoken thoughts and feelings. Lastly, the cases provided opportunities for the students to practice disconfirmation, by admitting error, and accountability, by redesigning reasoning and behavior in order to be more effective. These redesigns were then tested through role plays and in some cases actually attempted 'on-line'.

Modeling

Perhaps the most important strategy for creating conditions for organizational learning is modeling by outside interventionists and especially by organizational leaders. In the after-action review, the fact that veterans and commanders could publicly admit error played an important role in fostering disconfirmation as well as egalitarianism.

Both the consultants and the formal leaders in all three cases played by the same rules and remained open to criticism, fostering egalitarianism. In all the cases the consultants made their strategies explicit and were honest about their uncertainty (transparency) even though it was contrary to what is normally expected from a consultant. Criticism and disagreements between consultants and organizational members provided valuable opportunities for pursuing critical inquiry (rather than producing defensiveness). To the extent that the consultants (and group members, as in the IBI case) admitted their errors and took action to try to correct them, they also modeled disconfirmation and accountability.

Mapping

In the Mishlav Jaffa and the IBI case the consultants used diagnostic maps to help guide their interventions. Mapping, as illustrated in this chapter, can be used to capture a complex issue and make it accessible to intervention (Friedman and Lipshitz 1994). An organizational diagnostic map is an attempt to link the thinking of organizational members about a problem's causes with their thinking about its implications and solutions (Argyris, Putnam, and Smith 1985; Weick and Bougon 1986).

Maps can be generated through interviews, analysis of personal cases, and observation. Our diagnostic maps tend to focus on the causal links between the conditions under which a problem situation arises, perceptions of the problems, the action strategies of organizational members, and the consequences of those strategies. They identify the key dilemmas and how organizational members tend to address them, often illustrating how they collectively, but unintentionally, perpetuate and escalate problems.

Mapping fosters transparency because it captures knowledge that has been tacit and scattered among different individuals. Combining these perceptions into a single, more generalized map shifts the focus away from blaming individuals to the dynamics of the system as a whole, facilitating issue orientation. Mapping fosters accountability by helping people see their causal responsibility for a problem within the context of the system. The most important part is testing the map in order to confirm or disconfirm certain parts and stimulate further inquiry into the issue.

Organizational Learning as Ongoing Experimentation

Organizational learning is an inherently experimental, creative process because it pushes organizational members to the edge of their current state of knowledge. It imposes uncertainty on organizational members, either naturally or by design, so that they will critically inquire into and change their current practice. In many situations, particularly those involving double-loop learning, organizational members venture into learning without knowing what will come out of it.

Creating conditions for organizational learning means helping organizational members engage uncertainty rather than ignore or avoid it. Learning to learn requires suspending the need for control and predictability in order to acquire habits of inquiry and experimentation. Although skills and certainly skillfulness play a part in organizational learning, acquisition of these habits cannot be reduced to training or skills acquisition. In fact, training may actually impede learning by creating an impression of structure and certainty when participants should be experiencing uncertainty.

Acquiring habits of inquiry and experimentation is an 'experiential' process, not just in the sense of learning through activities but in a deeper sense of engaging the particular task-specific organizational experience of learners as individuals and as a group (Kolb 1983). For this reason it usually entails a strong emotional undercurrent. It also involves a process that is strongly influenced by the specific organizational context.

This chapter has focused on developing the habits of inquiry and experimentation among organizational members by introducing structural and cultural conditions that promote learning. Because every organization is different, it is difficult to predict or control exactly how organizational members will respond to these interventions. Although the three case studies presented above reveal patterns and commonalities in this process, unpredictability makes the development of a highly programmed, technical process for learning to learn highly unlikely at this stage.

Each of the three projects got stuck at some point, creating a puzzle for outside interventionists and organizational members. A skeptic might easily conclude that these impasses resulted from 'the realities of the world' or from 'human nature'. Conversely, a visionary might brush these moments aside and focus on instrumental issues or a new project. Such episodes often go unreported, yet they are critical to the learning of both organizational members and interventionists.

One of the ironies of this experience-based learning is that it is difficult to pass the lessons along to others. In Mishlav Jaffa and the Ordnance Corps the first group of learners found it difficult to explain themselves to their colleagues who joined them later. Instead, these colleagues had to undergo a process similar to the one that the first group had experienced. The necessity of such a process was encountered again and again in attempts to apply the lessons of the Mishlav Jaffa project to other schools (Cohen, Friedman, and Eran 1996, 1997). Although the interventionists developed a kind of map of where they were going and had provided catalysts for the learning process, the outcomes differed widely from one school to the next. These differences were attributable to differences in the student and teacher populations, leadership, organizational politics, and organizational culture.

The generalizability of these conclusions and of the map need to be qualified by the nature of the projects and of the organizations in which these projects were carried out. All of the projects involved either relatively small organizations or units within a larger organization. None of them represented comprehensive efforts to introduce organizational learning throughout a large organization. Furthermore, a similar theoretical approach with its own blinders was used by the interventionists conducting the project. The map is only a 'working theory' that needs to be continually tested and refined with each new project. It represents a repertoire of experience-based strategies for guiding organizational members and interventionists in making sense of situations and in designing their own strategies for moving the learning process forward.

References

Argyris, C. (1982). *Reasoning, Learning, and Action: Individual and Organizational*. San Francisco: Jossey-Bass.

—— (1991). 'Teaching Smart People How to Learn'. *Harvard Business Review*, 69/3: 99–109.

—— (1993). *Knowledge for Action: A Guide to Overcoming Barriers to Organizational Change*. San Francisco: Jossey-Bass.

—— (1994). 'Good Communication That Blocks Learning'. *Harvard Business Review*, 72/4: 77–85.

—— Putnam, R., and Smith, D. (1985). *Action Science: Concepts, Methods, and Skills for Research and Intervention*. San Francisco: Jossey-Bass.

—— and Schön, D. A. (1974). *Theory in Practice: Increasing Professional Effectiveness*. San Francisco: Jossey-Bass.

—— —— (1978). *Organizational Learning: A Theory of Action Perspective*. Reading, Mass.: Addison-Wesley.

—— —— (1996). *Organizational Learning*: Vol. 2. *Theory, Method, and Practice*. Reading, Mass.: Addison-Wesley.

Beer, M. and Spector, B. (1993). 'Organizational Diagnosis: Its Role in Organizational Learning'. *Journal of Counseling and Development*, 71: 642–50.

Bion, W. (1961). *Experiences in Groups, and Other Papers*. New York: Basic Books.

Brehmer, B. (1980). 'In One Word: Not from Experience'. *Acta Psychologica*, 45: 223–41.

Bushe, G. and Shani, A. (1991). *Parallel Learning Structures*. Reading, Mass.: Addison-Wesley.

Cohen, M., Eran, M., and Friedman, V. J. (1997). 'Evaluation of the "New Education Environment" Project in the "Amal" Technological School Network: An Interim Report on Student Characterics and Project Implementation during the 1996–1997 School Year'. Jerusalem: Joint Distribution Committee (JDC)–Brookdale Institute.

—— Friedman, V. J., and Eran, M. (1996). 'Evaluation of the "New Education Environment" Project in the "Amal" Technological School Network: An Initial Interim Report on School Characterics and Project Implementation during the Initial Phase (1995–1996)'. Jerusalem: Joint Distribution Committee (JDC)–Brookdale Institute.

Cusumano, M. A. and Selby, R. W. (1995). *Microsoft Secrets*. New York: Free Press.

Davies, J. and Easterby-Smith, M. (1984). 'Learning and Developing from Managerial Work Experiences'. *Journal of Management Studies*, 21: 169–83.

de Geus, A. (1988). 'Planning as Learning'. *Harvard Business Review*, 66/2: 70–4.

Dewey, J. (1938). *Logic: The Theory of Inquiry*. New York: Holt.

DiBella, A. J., Nevis, E. C., and Gould, J. M. (1996). 'Understanding Organizational Learning Capability'. *Journal of Management Studies*, 33: 361–79.

Dodgson, M. (1993). 'Organizational Learning: A Review of Some Literatures'. *Organization Studies*, 14: 375–94.

Eisenhardt, K. E., Kahwajy, J. L., and Bourgeois, L. J., III (1997). 'Conflict and Strategic Choice: How Top Management Teams Disagree'. *California Management Review*, 39/2: 42–62.

Friedman, V. J. (1997). 'Making Schools Safe for Uncertainty: Teams, Teaching, and School Reform'. *Teachers College Record*, 99/2: 335–70.

—— and Lipshitz, R. (1992). 'Teaching People to Shift Cognitive Gears: Overcoming Resistance on the Road to Model 2'. *Journal of Applied Behavioral Science*, 28: 118–37.

—— —— (1994). 'Human Resources or Politics: Framing the Problem of Appointing Managers in an Organizational Democracy'. *Journal of Applied Behavioral Science*, 30: 438–57.

Garratt, B. (1987). *The Learning Organization*. Aldershot: Gower.

Garvin, D. A. (1993). 'Building a Learning Organization'. *Harvard Business Review*, 71/4: 78–91.

Gulliver, F. R. (1987). 'Post-project Appraisals Pay'. *Harvard Business Review*, 65/2: 128–32.

Harrison, R. (1962). 'Defenses and the Need to Know', in R. T. Glomebiewski and A. Blumber (eds.), *Sensitivity Training and the Laboratory* (2nd edn). Itasca, Ill: Peacock, 117–22.

Hedberg, B. L. T. (1981). 'How Organizations Learn and Unlearn', in P. C. Nystrom and W. H. Starbuck (eds.), *Handbook of Organizational Design*: Vol. 1. *Adapting Organizations to Their Environments*. Oxford: Oxford University Press, 3–27.

Heifetz, R. A. (1994). *Leadership without Easy Answers*. Cambridge, Mass.: Harvard University Press.

Hirschhorn, L. (1988). *The Workplace Within: The Psychodynamics of Organizational Life*. Cambridge, Mass.: MIT Press.

Howard, R. and Haas, R. D. (eds.) (1993). *The Learning Imperative: Managing People for Continuous Innovation*. Boston: Harvard Business School Press.

Kanter, R. M. (1988). 'When a Thousand Flowers Bloom: Structural, Collective, and Social Conditions for Innovation in Organization', in B. M. Staw and L. L. Cummings (eds.), *Research in Organizational Behavior: An Annual Series of Analytical Essays and Critical Reviews* (Vol. 10). Greenwich, Conn.: JAI Press, 169–211.

Kolb, D. A. (1983). 'Problem Management: Learning from Experience', in S. Srivastva (ed.), *The Executive Mind: New Insights on Managerial Thought and Action*. San Francisco: Jossey-Bass, 109–43.

Levitt, B. and March, J. G. (1988). 'Organizational Learning'. *Annual Review of Sociology*, 14: 319–40.

Lipshitz, R., Popper, M., and Oz, S. (1996). 'Building Learning Organizations: The Design and Implementation of Organizational Learning Mechanisms'. *Journal of Applied Behavioral Science*, 32: 292–305.

Lundberg, C. C. (1985). 'On the Feasibility of Cultural Intervention in Organizations', in L. R. Pondy, P. J. Frost, G. Morgan, and T. Dandridge (eds.), *Organizational Symbolism*. Greenwich, Conn.: JAI Press, 169–85.

March, J. G. and Olsen, J. P. (1976). 'Organizational Learning and the Ambiguity of the Past', in J. G. March and J. P. Olsen, *Ambiguity and Choice in Organizations*. Bergen: Universitetsforlaget, 54–68.

McGill, M. E., Slocum, J. W., and Lei, D. (1993). 'Management Practices in Learning Organizations'. *Organizational Dynamics*, 22/1: 5–17.

Nonaka, I. (1991). 'The Knowledge-creating Company'. *Harvard Business Review*, 69/6: 96–104.

Overmeer, W. (1996). 'Strategy and Learning: Making Prescriptions Actionable', in C. Argyris and D. A. Schön, *Organizational Learning*: Vol. 2. *Theory, Method, and Practice*. Reading, Mass.: Addison-Wesley, 251–80.

Popper, M. and Lipshitz, R. (1997). *Organizational Learning Mechanisms: A Cultural/Structural Approach to Organizational Learning*. Working paper, University of Haifa, Haifa, Israel.

Rayner, B. (1993). 'Trial-by-fire Transformation: An Interview with Globe Metallurgical's Arden C. Sims', in R. Howard and R. D. Haas (eds.), *The Learning Imperative: Managing People for Continuous Innovation*. Boston: Harvard Business School Press, 277–97.

Schein, E. H. (1969). 'The Mechanisms of Change', in W. G. Bennis, K. D. Benne, and R. Chin (eds.), *The Planning of Change*. New York: Holt, Rinehart and Winston, 98–108.

——(1990). 'Organizational Culture'. *American Psychologist*, 45: 109–19.

——(1993). 'How Can Organizations Learn Faster? The Challenge of Entering the Green Room'. *Sloan Management Review*, 34/2: 85–92.

Schön, D. A. (1983). *The Reflective Practitioner*. New York: Basic Books.

Senge, P. M. (1990). *The Fifth Discipline: The Art and Practice of the Learning Organization*. New York: Doubleday Currency.

Shaw, R. B. and Perkins, D. N. T. (1992). 'Teaching Organizations to Learn: The Power of Productive Failures', in D. A. Nadler, M. S. Gerstein, and R. B. Shaw (eds.), *Organizational Architecture*. San Francisco: Jossey Bass, 175–91.

Tsang, E. W. K. (1997). 'Organizational Learning and the Learning Organization: A Dichotomy between Descriptive and Prescriptive Research'. *Human Relations*, 50: 73–89.

Weick, K. E. and Bougan, M. G. (1986). 'Organizations as Cognitive Maps: Charting Ways to Success and Failure', in H. P. Sims, Jr. and D. A. Gioia (eds.), *The Thinking Organization: Dynamics of Organizational Social Cognition*. San Francisco: Jossey-Bass, 102–35.

——and Westley, F. (1996). 'Organizational Learning: Affirming an Oxymoron', in S. R. Clegg, C. Hardy, and W. R. Nord (eds.), *Handbook of Organization Studies*. London: Sage, 440–58.

Weisbord, M. E. (1987). *Productive Workplaces*. San Francisco: Jossey-Bass.

Willard, R. (1994). *Ideas on Learning Organizations: The 'What', 'Why', 'How', and 'Who'*. IBM Corp. rgwilla@ibm.net

35 Practices and Tools of Organizational Learning

Peter Pawlowsky, Jan Forslin, and Rüdiger Reinhardt

Sooner or later the question arises as to how to implement organizational learning. On the one hand, conceptual models are of little use if they do not provide practical ways to develop and maintain a learning organization. On the other hand, the literature is full of 'how-to' articles and books, and the number of tools and instruments promising to foster a learning organization is overwhelming. Unfortunately, these resources do not offer criteria that help one know when to select which tool or instrument. Such criteria can only be derived from theory or from practical experience, that is from empirical patterns of evidence for making assumptions. On unclear and complex terrain, such as knowledge management, theories are the only compass that can be used in guiding the way to promising goals. The multitudes of practical tools and instruments in the ubiquitous training supermarkets in the fields of organizational learning may or may not be valuable. As long as there are no plausible assumptions about the effects that these tools and instruments have on organizational learning or knowledge management, their implementation is more akin to gambling than to reasoning. Assumptions, or at least fairly grounded hypotheses, enable one to observe these effects and to either alter the assumptions or to accept them with greater confidence than would otherwise be the case. Perhaps this lack of assumptions and hypotheses is why a practice-based orientation can sometimes be quite impractical and why theories can be quite practical (Lewin 1942).

There is evidently quite a gap between conceptual discussion of organizational learning and day-to-day managerial action within organizations. That gulf need not persist, however. Practical tools of organizational learning can be grounded in a theoretical framework that can facilitate their selection and appropriate use.

From Theory to Practices

Although an assessment of the literature on organizational learning reveals different theoretical perspectives, it also shows that most approaches share a number of similar dimensions (see Pawlowsky, Ch. 3 in this volume). Almost all approaches to organizational learning refer in one way or another to different system levels, especially the problem of how to transfer learning from the individual to the group level or organizational level. Most approaches also distinguish between various learning types, such as simple adaptive learning, and or higher-order reflective (double-loop and deutero-) learning. Further analysis of this literature shows that some authors either refer with their concepts to cognitive, cultural, and action approaches to learning or suggest an integration of these three learning modes, in their approaches to organizational learning. Lastly, one notices that most approaches to organizational learning entail a number of process phases along which organizational learning 'happens'. These observations plausibly lead to a theoretical framework for an integrative model of organizational learning. Its dimensions of the framework are (a) different system levels of learning (from individual to organizational network), (b) different learning types (single-loop, double-loop, and deutero-learning), (c) different learning modes (e.g. cognitive learning, cultural learning, and action learning), and (d) different phases of a collective learning process. The tools and instruments of organizational learning should therefore be derived from one or more of these dimensions.

Given the numerous practices called learning tools of knowledge management and organizational learning, what qualifies as such tools? The question seems almost unanswerable unless agreement is first reached about what they must accomplish. Keeping in mind the theoretical model outlined above, we define a learning tool as an instrument or intervention designed to bring about one or more of the process phases involving the various dimensions of organizational learning (system levels, learning types, and learning modes) (see Figure 35.1).

We can define tools as all intentional interventions that are directed at decreasing possible barriers, or inhibiting factors, between these process phases. With this working definition, interventions and instruments labeled as organizational learning tools can be classified according to the intention(s) behind them. What is the aim of a particular tool? What are its supposed effects on the dimensions of organizational learning?

One can begin answering these questions by examining a tool's range of effects. Is it to be used mainly with individuals or groups? Is it to be used instead at an organizational or even an interorganizational level? What learning modes does the tool focus on? For example, is it meant to support primarily cognitive learning, cultural learning, action learning, or some combination of these learning modes? Is it designed to give simple feedback about faults, or is it intended instead to develop higher types of learning, such as reflective learning and in-

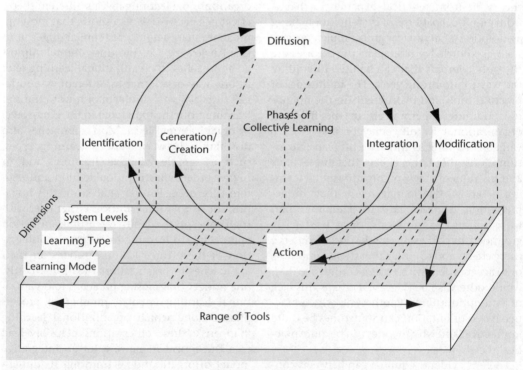

Fig. 35.1. Toolbox: Categorization of organizational learning tools

sights into problems and the learning experiences themselves? In addition, the tools can be classified according to the different phases of the learning process. So, for instance, is the instrument meant to support one phase of collective learning, such as identification, more than other phases, or does it potentially affect all process-phases equally?

The categories shown in Table 35.1 provide a framework that can be used for systematizing organizational learning tools according to the theoretical framework presented above. Into this scheme, one can classify the tools described in the organizational learning literature. Of course, even if each tool is rated by several persons in order to increase the validity of interrated comparisons, the scheme will still be questionable, for it currently rests only on judgments of plausibility, not on empirical support. At present, however, the probability that identified learning problems and deficits within organizations can be successfully matched with appropriate tools is higher than pure chance and higher than the probability of a successful match if ratings were based on the idiosyncratic beliefs of training departments. In other words, the selection of tools for organizational training and human resource development has only rarely been grounded in assumptions about organizational learning deficits and about the appropriate tools with which to surmount these shortcomings. Furthermore, this categorization opens up the possibility of empirically testing the effects of tools, for specific hypotheses can be derived. Thus, the key to the toolbox is the theoretical framework.

Practices of Organizational Learning

In this section we describe some or the organizational learning practices and tools discussed in the literature and categorize them according to the framework model presented above. There are several recent collections on organizational learning tools and practice-oriented publications, such as Bach, Vogler, and Österle

Table 35.1. Classification categories for organizational learning tools

Category	Evaluation
Learning level	• Individual • Group • Organization • Interorganizational
Learning type	• Single-loop learning • Double-loop learning • Deutero-learning
Learning mode	• Cognitive • Cultural • Behavioral
Learning process	• Identification • Generation/creation • Diffusion • Integration • Action

(1999); Böhmann and Krcmar (1999); Burgoyne and Reynolds (1997); Dixon (1994); Mabey and Iles (1994); Pearn, Roderick, and Romhardt (1998); Petkoff (1998); Mulrooney (1995); Pedler, Boydell, and Burgoyne (1989); Pedler, Burgoyne, and Boydell (1991); Probst, Raub, and Romhardt (1997); Ross (1994); Wilson (1996). On the basis of this literature and our own field research on learning instruments and interventions, we describe representative tools for each phase of the learning process.

Identification

The main intention of the identification phase is to facilitate the internal and external identification of knowledge by making internal knowledge visible, accessing external sources of new knowledge, or both, through boundary-spanning, establishment of contact with customers, and other activities. The identification of knowledge is certainly no simple task. In order to select what is relevant from the overwhelming amount of learning and information that is available, one needs criteria by which to identify the importance and value of knowledge. In the context of this chapter, we mean that one can evaluate the importance of knowledge by examining its relevance to the core business process. It, therefore makes sense first to describe the workflow of the core business process and then to add the 'knowledge' dimension by describing and evaluating the information-processing and knowledge inputs into this process. Petkoff (1998: 336) has explained how the ARIS Toolset (by IDS Scheer) can be used to describe knowledge processes that parallel the workflow in an organization. People involved in this knowledge process are prompted to judge the relevance of specific knowledge inputs, and their responses establish a yardstick against which to measure the importance of information and knowledge. This approach makes the identification of relevant knowledge less arbitrary than it would be otherwise. In the identification dimension a large number of activities and tools can be applied, including systematic Internet analysis

(through a growing number of sophisticated scanning tools), best-practice benchmarking, internal knowledge brokers, systematic boundary-spanning, participation in stakeholder group meetings, networking, the monitoring of information at the point of sale, promotion of dialogue with customers, and electronic customer care. We have chosen three examples from the literature and have classified them into the categories shown in Table 35.1.

Quick Market Intelligence

Originally developed by Wal-Mart Stores, Inc. Quick Market Intelligence (QMI; Dixon 1994: 96–7) is an instrument that is quickly spreading. The basic idea is to combine quick cycles of information-gathering, interpretation, decision-making, and communication. 'Regional managers spend from Monday to Thursday in the field visiting Wal-Mart and competitor stores. On Friday the regional managers come together in a town meeting, a large group of 80–100 people that includes key buyers, functional heads and Vice-Presidents, as well as selected representatives of the sales force' (Dixon 1994: 96). During this town meeting, financial information as well as qualitative impressions and anecdotal experiences are exchanged. The topics and the agenda depend partly on the information gathered during the field visits and observations and partly on other issues that the participants consider important. Strategies and action plans based on these discussions and problem analyses are designed and agreed upon. The groups decide on key persons responsible for implementation support. The action plans and results of the meetings are videotaped and transmitted via video broadcast to store managers. Dixon (1994) reported that the success of QMI is based on the fact that opportunities and direct responses are linked together. The main advantage of the tool is that multiple stakeholders come together, interpret information and data from different perspectives and positions, boil this information down into practical solutions to problems, decide on action to be taken, and then communicate the decisions to the people who can carry them out.

QMI involves either groups in organizations or entire departments as well as external experts. With respect to learning types, it depends on how the process is presented, but both single-loop and double-loop learning can be promoted if there is space and time to reflect on the problems presented. As far as learning modes are concerned, QMI addresses both the cognitive and cultural modes of learning. This tool focuses mainly on the identification of external and internal information and on the information-processing capabilities of internal knowledge.

Gamma: Interactive Modeling in Teams

Another tool that supports the identification and creation phases of organizational learning is Gamma, computer-based graphic software that aids the development of a holistic view of problem areas and thereby opens up various possibilities for collective reflection and discussion about problem-solving strategies. Gamma helps the user look at complex situations and problems in an overall context, identifying connections to other related areas and developing a feeling for interactional effects. Based on systems theory and system dynamics, this tool visualizes connections between decision fields in organizations and helps integrate different perspectives in the analysis of complex problems. Relations are described in network charts, and the effects of possible interventions can be simulated so that the user can see the effects on the complex problem as a whole. The power of Gamma is not so much that it gives realistic data on future developments but rather that it enables the construction of a collective cognitive map, a joint understanding of the organizational reality and its challenges. People construct their reality according to their naturally limited individual perception. With Gamma collective cognitive maps can be constructed through interactive modeling. This tool thereby makes it possible to develop a common understanding of the overall relation and interplay of activities, constraints, and possibilities of the social system that they are a part of (Dörner 1989; Eden, Jones, and Sims 1983; Ulrich and Probst 1991; Unicon 1990; Vester 1991).

Gamma is a tool intended for use in groups. It facilitates higher-order learning by bringing different perspectives to bear on one problem area and by helping people try to understand the systemic relations of the field in which the specific problem is embedded. The learning mode is primarily cognitive, but the in-depth discussions and the exchange of views among participants may well trigger cultural learning effects because mutual understanding is developed. The result may even be increased confidence in the activities of other groups' departments or functions. This tool can support knowledge creation and development. It also helps develop an understanding of the knowledge and perspectives of others in the organization (and, according to systems theory, even outside the organization). Gamma can therefore be seen as relevant to both the identification phase and the creation process of organizational learning.

Yellow Pages and Knowledge Maps

Another quite common tool that can help increase the transparency of the internal knowledge base is called the 'yellow pages', which takes its name from the common telephone book. Yellow pages systematize knowledge in a personnel handbook or dictionary, thereby giving all members of an organization information on the personal know-how. Hoffmann–La Roche has sampled the specific knowledge of its scientists the world over and summarized it in a dictionary. Typical problems that occur in product development processes, for example, were classified according to potential problem-solvers within the organization, thus affording people a degree of transparency with regard to the distribution of internal knowledge and opening up opportunities for linking internal knowledge bases (Probst, Raub, and Romhardt 1997: 107). Describing a project of the Swiss Banking Corporation, Romhardt (1998) stated that the intention in this case, too, was to increase the transparency of the knowledge held by organization's employees. The participants developed an electronic information system built on the content modules of projects, experts, documents, products, and instructions, bringing together information, documents, voice sources, and communication sources. Similarly, knowledge maps can increase internal transparency. Probst, Raub, and Romhardt (1997) distinguished between types of knowledge maps, such as knowledge-stock maps, knowledge-flow maps, knowledge-structure maps, and know-how bearer maps. Generally speaking, these maps are visualized lists of knowledge sources that are useful for identifying internal knowledge.

Within the theoretical framework outlined at the beginning of this chapter, yellow pages and knowledge maps are instruments that can support learning primarily at the departmental level or even throughout the organization, as the example of Hoffmann–La Roche shows. The instruments do not necessarily promote any specific learning type; the learning type depends on how the sources of knowledge are used within the organization. These tools can also be regarded as navigation instruments in the cognitive knowledge base of the organization; they therefore especially promote cognitive learning rather than cultural learning or the adoption of implicit knowledge.

When using these tools, one should keep their purpose in mind and not apply them for their own sake. The idea is to make internal knowledge visible and to access external sources of new knowledge through boundary-spanning, contacts with customers that promote processes such as 'originating *ba*' (Nonaka and Konno 1998), and 'emphatic design' (Cohen 1998: 26). The implementation of such tools raises certain questions that should be answered. For example: Which individuals or groups participate in boundary-spanning and the identification of external information? Which mental models guide the information-gathering process in the organization, and what are the filters like? Where do the members of the organization perceive knowledge weakness whose elimination could improve their understanding of the specific environments that are considered to be relevant external markets? What types of information are systematically gathered: simple feedback from suppliers and customers, or data that fosters reflection on the organization's theories? In other words, does the identification phase permit entry of information that can question the dominant assumptions and theories-in-use?

Generation/Creation

The second process phase of organizational learning—the creation of knowledge, the development of new ideas, and innovation in organizations—is regarded as vital to the competitiveness of firms. It is also quite complex, for as research on creativity and innovation shows, knowledge creation cannot be programmed (Koestler 1964). The question of how to generate knowledge cannot be answered with simple learning tools. However, there are reasons to believe that it is possible to create organizational environments that enhance the likelihood of innovations. Creativity is basically a result of processes that combine diverged information and sources of information and knowledge (Koestler 1964). The chances of developing new knowledge should therefore increase or decrease with the number of possibilities for combining explicit knowledge in organizations or for making the implicit knowledge of experts available to others. Four modes of such knowledge conversion—socialization, externalization, combination, and internalization (the SECI process, see Nonaka, Toyama, and Byosière, Ch. 22 in this volume)—have been derived by Nonaka and Takeuchi (1995: 62) from their studies of knowledge-creation processes in Japanese firms. A large variety of procedures, tools, and interventions, can support these modes of conversion, increasing the chances of knowledge creation. A central criterion is work organization. Group organization, teamwork, hypertext organization, matrix structures, and external knowledge links are important preconditions for cross-fertilization processes. Special learning laboratories, product clinics, and centers for competence building are other structural means of buffering innovative potential against daily routine. The intention behind them to allow new ideas to grow under protection from the chilly winds of cut-throat competition. Space and time, along with routines that promote the transfer of tacit knowledge (Nonaka and Konno's '*ba*' [1998] and Senge's *et al.* 'container' [1994: 360]), are important ingredients for knowledge development. Let us take a look at two examples of these tools.

Open Space Technology

Open Space is a new way of organizing conferences that gives space to participants. To gain an adequate understanding of the goals and process of Open Space, it is useful to look at the origins of this tool. The development of Open Space is based on two observations by its founder, Harrison Owen. The first is based on negative experience with traditional facilitating and consulting techniques.[1] The other is based on Owen's experience with a totally self-managed, large-group event.[2]

Open Space is an elaborate facilitation technique that has been used worldwide as a tool for enabling groups to address community and business issues. Open Space is best known for its use with groups of more than 1,000 people, but it can also be effective with groups as small as fourteen participants. Open Space creates an environment in which people are asked to take responsibility for what is truly on their minds and in their hearts. Results show that it leads to a qualitative improvement of organizational culture, increasing the capability of risk-taking, learning innovation, and the responsibility of the organization. Specific action plans are developed as well. A facilitator introduces and maintains a set of ground rules and invites participants to create their own agendas, based on predetermined topics. Small focus groups are convened in order to address specific issues raised by the participants.

Three kinds of applications for Open Space are described: assessment, consensus-building, and problem-solving. In assessment and consensus-building, the theme is likely to be, 'What are our issues and concerns about XY?' In problem-solving, the topic is likely to be, 'What can we do to achieve XY?' Because the intention of Open Space is to reveal what is on people's minds and in their hearts, the event will organize itself around people's true wants and needs no matter how a topic is set up. The process of Open Space can be briefly described as follows (Owen 1996; Petri 1996):

Phase 1: Planning/inviting

Top management invites organizational members to an Open Space meeting on challenging issues, such as reaching consensus between groups or within a group consisting of many stakeholders, developing a vision for the company, getting support from numerous people on a change process, or identifying business issues that are critical to the organization. This phase includes the complete planning steps for the Open Space sessions. The 'rest' is done by the participants however they like as the need arises.

Phase 2: Agenda-setting

Because all participants know the central issue to be worked on, no agenda has been set yet. Hence, the Open Space process starts with the development of the agenda. All participants sit in a circle, and some of them identify a topic related to an issue that they are passionate about. They place themselves in the middle of the circle, share their topic, formulate it on paper, and post the paper on the wall together with an announcement of a time and place for discussing it. Every participant decides where to participate and which topic to elaborate

---

[1] 'The only thing that everybody liked was the one thing I had nothing to do with: the coffee breaks. There had to be a message here. My question was a simple one. Was it possible to combine the level of synergy and excitement present in a good coffee break, with the substantive activity and results characteristic of a good meeting? And most of all, could the whole thing be done in less than a year?' (Owen 1996: 3).

[2] 'The actual celebration continued for four days with all sorts of rituals and other activities. Through it all there was amazingly nothing, so far as I could tell, that looked or acted like a planning committee, not during the event or prior to its occurrence. Nevertheless 500 people managed to manage themselves for four days in a highly organized, satisfactory, and I have to say, enjoyable fashion. How could that be?' (Owen 1996: 4).

upon. The agenda is not fixed, and changes in the topics to be discussed are welcome.

Phase 3: Elaborating in focus-group sessions

Every topic is discussed in focus groups, which also lead to action plans. To understand the learning processes that occur during these focus-group sessions, it is important to understand the rules of participation:

(1) Whoever shows up are the right people.
(2) Whatever happens is the only thing that could have happened.
(3) Whenever the discussion starts is the right time to start.
(4) When discussion is over, it is over. These rules are considered to be the basis on which people truly learn to become responsible for themselves and for the issue-related goals they seek to achieve.

Phase 4: Closing the conference and action-planning

The three-day process ends with a plenary session in which the learning results and action plans are shared.

Phase 5: Implementing and following-up

The identified action plans are ranked according to priority and implemented after the Open Space conference. Persons who identified the topics for the several focus-group sessions are often in charge of implementing the action plans.

A comparison between this description of Open Space and the conceptual framework for organizational learning shows that Open Space is conceived for the group level and the organizational level. In addition, double-loop learning and deutero-learning have a major effect. Participants learn to reflect on their own about collective theories of action and learn to develop action plans, which are at least partly based on new theories of action. People also learn to break down barriers in their thinking and acting. The related learning modes are cognitive, for people learn new rules and thereby become able to rethink and restructure their assumptions and actions. This cognitive learning also has a great impact on cultural and

behavioral issues, for people are supposed to see that the application of these rules leads to success, creativity, and innovation. A high degree of transfer of these new experiences to daily work is common. With respect to learning phases, the great impact that self-organized processes have on the participant's behavior shows that Open Space is a tool that allows one to identify new information or generate new knowledge. Both new information and new knowledge can be disseminated through the system and can lead either to their integration or to modification of the knowledge structures of the focus groups. In brief, Open Space is a powerful tool for fostering cultural and higher-level learning.

'Work Out'

'Work out' was developed by General Electric Company in the early 1980s during a phase of strategic reorientation aimed at changing the company's organizational culture (see Dixon 1994; Probst, Raub, and Romhardt 1997). According to Dixon (1994: 95), fifty or more people who share a common work process are brought together in a work-out meeting so that they can give thought to possible improvements. To begin the process, Human Resource professionals identify important issues by interviewing members of the organization and asking which questions should be addressed. Using these findings, management selects key issues and suggests participants for the work-out sessions. The core events are the two-and-a-half-day town meetings. At the outset of each town meeting, management acknowledges its commitment to the agreed-upon topics and procedure, and small groups start a team-building process by working as teams on these problems and questions. In these groups members discuss the problems from different perspectives, combining their knowledge in order to find new solutions. On the basis of this teamwork, the groups make recommendations to management on possible procedures. Management is required to respond to these recommendations immediately. Rejection of a recommendation must be justified. Dixon (1994) reported that at

General Electric over 90 per cent of the recommendations made were accepted. Once a solution is accepted, the team that proposed it is responsible for implementing it and checking up on it. This process of work-out sessions is considered to be a fast and effective procedure for generating creative new solutions, especially because the people who come up with the ideas are the ones who implement them and because there is a direct connection between the innovative idea and its translation into action.

We suggest that work-out meetings be classified primarily as a tool for use with groups, for its cornerstones are the team-building process and the work on solutions in small groups. Because the learning process grows out of reflection on the problems and the practice of looking at them from different perspectives, it is reasonable to assume that high-order learning processes, such as double-loop and deutero-learning, are likely to be triggered. The learning mode is cognitive at first, but both cultural and action modes of learning may result from the team-building process and the commitments made during implementation.

Diffusion

Diffusion—the intervention and process field of knowledge—is closely linked to the process phase of creation, for the exchange and distribution of relevant knowledge is a key prerequisite for the development and dissemination of new ideas and learning. Obstacles to diffusion may have very different origins. Structural causes include organizational hierarchies, functional differentiation and separation, dysfunctional workflow organization, and, in cases where related functions are not located together or near each other, poor space management. The frequency and radius of communication routines can be analyzed with netgraphing methods (Romhardt 1998: 222) in order to see whether communication flows are in line with business processes. If they are not, space management tools can help optimize these processes. Furthermore, the communica-

tion structure is vitally important. Which channels exist? Which are horizontal and which are vertical? Which channels are used in both ways? What are the dominant communication styles between important knowledge centers in the organization? What are the structural and personal barriers to communication flows? Are there specific places to communicate in the organization? Does information and knowledge flow one-way, or is there rather a reciprocal exchange with similar or different priorities for the parties involved? Are discussions, dialogues, or both a feature of the communication process?

One of the most important factors in the free flow of knowledge in organizations is socio-psychological dynamics. Knowledge diffusion requires not only the spatial distribution of knowledge but also a readiness to gather and share knowledge. Because this disposition depends greatly on a climate of mutual trust and a culture of sharing, tools for distributing knowledge are useless as long as the organization's culture and incentive systems do not promote the sharing of relevant knowledge.

Interventions and instruments that support the free flow of knowledge refer either to the implementation and improvement of the technical infrastructure of communication or the cultural climate in organizations and the motivation of their employees to share with and learn from one another. With respect to the technical infrastructure of knowledge distribution, the development of computer technology, networks, intranets, local area networks (LANs), and specialized groupware-based knowledge-management tools, such as Lotus Notes, grapeVINE, KnowledgeX, Soverign Hill, Live-Link, SemioTaxonomy, and Wincite, can greatly support the diffusion and filtering of knowledge within organizations. Consulting firms were among the first to implement information networks. McKinsey & Company, for instance, introduced the Rapid Response Network, Andersen Consulting did the same with the Knowledge Xchange System (Probst, Raub, and Romhardt 1997: 240), and Arthur D. Little, Inc. began using the ADL Link system. An important challenge posed by these systems is the filtering of stored information and continual updating needed in order to keep the database manageable. Two examples of tools supporting diffusion as a learning process are grapeVINE and learning histories.

grapeVINE

grapeVINE is a product designed to discover and route existing information stored in Lotus Notes databases or on the LAN, depending on the user's specific knowledge search-profiles. The first step in setting up the grapeVINE system is to build a knowledge chart (a database containing categories and subcategories of keywords) which serves as the outline of the organization's knowledge base. Building on these keywords, users define their personal search parameters, in which they outline knowledge areas of interest to them and then rank the priority of each area. By defining user profiles and requesting alerts (via Notes e-mail), users no longer need to scan the database continually. Rather, they are automatically informed about new entries. Furthermore, users can also see who else receives similar information and can select a topic from the knowledge chart to see who else is interested in that topic. Tools such as grapeVINE, Soverign Hill, Wincite, and KnowledgeX can track market conditions, competitors, and other information. These tools organize information and distribute it to employees within the organization. Having such features, tools such as grapeVINE and other groupware applications are ideal for identifying, disseminating, and sharing knowledge in organizations (Info World 1997).

Returning to our classification scheme, we assert that these tools facilitate organization-wide learning mainly in a cognitive mode. No distinct learning type is promoted by these tools. In terms of the learning process, they can provide powerful support for the identification, diffusion, and integration of knowledge in organizations.

In addition to technology-oriented support, there is a wide range of tools for facilitating the diffusion of knowledge. Among them are project-related learning histories, incentive sys-

tems that reward the filing of relevant knowledge in company networks, regular project workshops, cascade information on customer surveys, joint reflection on the results, and team-learning training. We shall now look more closely at one of these tools.

'Learning Histories'

According to George Roth (1996), a learning history is a tool that describes what happens in a process of learning and change. It documents 'hard' facts and events, and focuses on what people thought about events, how they perceived their own actions, and the differences between people's perceptions. By recreating the experience of 'being there', the learning history helps readers understand what happened in a way that helps them make more effective judgments than they would otherwise. The purpose of the learning history and of learning history projects in general is to produce documentation that provides context and information for others to learn from. Learning histories are a process for capturing, assessing, and diffusing pilot projects in organizations. They are in-depth oral histories, with commentaries, that help an organization increase its effectiveness at learning from deep changes that some parts of the company have been through. This tool has six major steps, which are summarized below (see Roth 1996). The range and scope of the document and of the audience that is seeking to learn from the organization's experience are delineated in a planning stage. The notable results of the improvement effort are specified at this time as well. The subsequent reflective, informal interviews focus on linking notable results with an effort to improve.

1. A series of retrospective, reflective informal interviews is conducted with participants in the learning effort (along with key outsiders) in order to gather perspectives from every significant point of view.

2. A small group of internal staff members and external learning historians takes the raw material from the reflective informal interviews, documents, observations, and other

sources and 'distills' it into a coherent set of themes relevant to the people seeking to learn from the effort. This analytic effort, based on techniques of qualitative data analysis and the development of grounded theory, builds up the capacity to make sense of improvement efforts and to evaluate them.

3. A written document based on a thematic orientation is prepared. This document draws extensively on edited narratives from the interviews. Even though the statements are anonymous in all drafts, they are checked for factual accuracy with participants before distribution as part of any written material.

4. A small, key group of managers, participants in the original effort, and others interested in learning from their efforts attend a validation workshop after reading the learning history prototype. This validation workshop allows those who participated in the improvement effort to reflect on the material and review it for accuracy.

5. The learning history document becomes the basis for a series of dissemination workshops. In the dissemination workshops, people throughout the company address the questions of what the company has learned so far from this program, how they are to judge the program's success (or lack of success), and how they—and the company—are to build on what can be learned in order to move forward best with other initiatives.

6. After a series of dissemination workshops, there is a review of the learning history effort itself. In this review the people in the organization develop their abilities to conduct learning history efforts, and they consider how they can improve upon the process and adapt it to their own specific needs in the future.

In terms of our theoretical framework, we see that this tool focuses on organization-wide learning. Although in some cases learning may encompass only certain departments or even only a core group, the purpose of learning history is to capture experiences with former learning processes in the entire company. The aim of this tool is to trigger deutero-learning, for learning from past learning and reflection

on these processes are the core principles of this method. When it comes to learning modes, the cognitive learning aspect clearly dominates, but certainly a reflection process that involves a large number of employees or an organization-wide dissemination workshop will also benefit a corporate learning culture. Lastly, learning histories relate primarily to the diffusion of knowledge, though they do involve all learning phases to a certain extent.

Integration and Modification

The integration and modification phase prompts the important question of how knowledge is kept, stored, and secured within the organization and how the organizational knowledge base is altered, modified, and renewed. Often, knowledge stored in organizational memories does not reflect current demands, for assumptions and norms have not been adapted to new learning and insights. What are the sociopsychological obstacles to the integration of new knowledge and to the modification of dominant mental models and their resulting standard operating procedures? Which of the mental models that are stored in the organizational memory function as strategy-guiding frames of reference for management or as the dominant coalition in top management? How differentiated and integrated are these mental models, and to what degree are they constantly being questioned and challenged with anomalous information? It might prove useful to have an inventory of different practices with which to challenge assumptions that are regarded as organizational 'truth'. Are there any barriers, such as fear of failure, that prevent new knowledge from being incorporated into these knowledge systems? To what degree do the existing incentive systems support experimental behavior and new thinking? Solutions can be found with a wide variety of tools.

For the integration and modification phase, there are a number of tools that help build the organizational knowledge base and thereby structure the organizational memory. Because lessons that have been learned are also forgotten and because knowledge-bearers leave the organization, this task is crucial in organizations where knowledge is a commodity and a core competency. Many consulting firms that sell knowledge have developed internal information systems (e.g. 'Global Best Practices' at Arthur Andersen or 'Power Packs of Knowledge' at Ernst & Young International, Ltd.) that capture and store important lessons that have been learned and provide later access to this learning. In order to encourage people to store information in these databases and to learn from them, organizations have come up with different incentives. To make sure all project results are stored in the knowledge base, McKinsey project managers must file a two-page abstract of their project before they receive the billing code necessary for preparing invoices. At the beginning of each project, Arthur D. Little nominates a project knowledge manager, who is responsible for the documentation of the corresponding knowledge. A number of companies have developed criteria for evaluating both the quality of stored information and its usefulness to other members of the organization. The results of the evaluations are then used as guides for offering incentives and granting rewards.

In addition to these technology-based tools that are useful for storing and retrieving information and knowledge that is in organizational databases, there are many tools that aid the critical questioning of assumptions within the organizational memory and that help modify, refine, or add new dimensions to the knowledge base of an organization. Examples of such tools are business-process awareness workshops, self-evaluation as developed by the European Foundation for Quality Management, dialogue sessions, external workshops on strategic outlook, and workshops on company-wide scenario-planning. Let us examine dialogue as a tool in this context.

Dialogue

One of the tools that can effect various learning phases is dialogue as advocated by Bohm and Edwards (1991) and especially by Senge (1990). The purpose of dialogue is to produce a shared environment of inquiry by refocusing the group's attention. These environments, which Senge *et al.* (1994) called 'containers', or fields of inquiry, emerge as a group moves through a process of dialogue. A container can be understood as the mental environment in which a joint construction of reality occurs, as 'the sum of the collective assumptions, shared intentions, and beliefs of a group' (p. 360). As the members of the group move through the dialogue, they gradually develop a collective understanding of a situation or problem. They begin to change their individual understandings, and a joint understanding begins to emerge. This method focuses mainly on the integration and modification of a knowledge system, but by allowing people to think and associate more freely than they otherwise might, it can have other effects, such as diffusion or the creation of new knowledge. The dialogue process has four phases (see Senge *et al.* 1994: 361–4).

Phase 1: Instability of the Container
The dialogue process confronts the participants with the necessity of communicating to each other their tacit, unexpressed differences in perspectives. Instead of merely trying to understand each other or reach a compromise that they can live with, the members of the group slowly perceive themselves as an entity of which they are part. They come to realize that they can suspend their views by examining them and their own assumptions. 'Gradually people recognize that they have a choice: they can suspend their views, loosening the grip of their certainty about all views' (p. 361). The group members thereby prepare for a dialogue.

Phase 2: Instability in the Container
Positions are no longer fixed, the members of the group are ready to live with chaos, and the members begin to oscillate between suspending views and engaging in discussion. 'At this stage people may find themselves feeling frustrated, principally because the underlying fragmentation and incoherence in everyone's thought begin to appear' (p. 362). In this phase,

a 'crisis of suspension' (p. 362) usually occurs, extreme views are stated and defended, and the common ground of the group is shaken. 'The members begin to feel as if they were in a giant washing machine' (p. 362). Disorientation and frustration surfaces, and fragmentation of views and beliefs destroys the cohesion of the group. At this point facilitation is very important. It can help show that group members do not need to fight over the stances they have taken and do not have to categorize assumptions as wrong or right. Rather, they can start to listen to others and to themselves and inquire about the meaning of these assumptions for both the group and themselves. At this point, the opportunity to learn becomes apparent.

Phase 3: Inquiry in the Container

The group develops joint space for thoughts. Communication begins to flow differently. Topics are not 'heated' anymore, and group members are no longer prisoners of views that they have to defend; instead, they begin to inquire together, as a whole. Often, new ideas begin to emerge as a result of joint inquiries. This freedom from being locked into standpoints is also perceived as painful because people gradually begin to sense their separateness from one another: 'It especially hurts to feel how you have created your own fragmentation and isolation, throughout your life' (p. 363). If groups move successfully through this critical phase, they will reach Phase four.

Phase 4: Creativity in the Container

'A distinction between memory and thinking becomes apparent in this phase. Thinking takes on an entirely different rhythm and pace. The net of words may not be fine enough to capture the subtle and delicate understandings that begin to emerge' (p. 364). The group no longer has meaning in its conversation, but rather the group *is* its meaning. According to Senge *et al.* (1994), this state can generate breakthrough creativity and collective intelligence.

A comparison of this description of the dialogue process with our conceptual framework shows that this tool is oriented to the group level and makes little sense at the organizational or individual level. We assert that a major effect of dialogue is a change in the learning culture, for the intention behind this instrument is to change the way people think and feel together. It is about 'freeing up rigidity and old habits of attention and communication' (Senge *et al.* 1994: 363). The tool involves the cognitive learning mode with respect to the assumptions that are being questioned and possibly altered. In terms of learning processes, dialogue focuses on the integration/modification phase. Use of the tool therefore seems promising if a reorientation of or a change in the organization's learning culture is intended. The tool may be valuable in developing a set of intersubjective meanings and values for the group members. Of course, the process of dialogue may have several effects on other dimensions of the model, but we argue that the most effective use of this tool is for achieving group-level learning goals that are cultural in nature and that have to do with integrating and modifying joint constructions of reality.

Action

In the action phase the perspective goes beyond the adoption of new learning and the integration of new knowledge into organizational databases and existing frames of reference. In this phase, the focus is on the behavioral consequences of learning. Guiding questions for this phase might be: What procedures translate new developments into action? How do action plans come about, and who attends to them? Are there specific, implicit social and behavioral norms that prevent the introduction of new behavioral patterns based on new insights or learning? Does the organization have enough platforms and sufficient latitude within for practical experimentation with new ideas? What type of experiential 'playgrounds' does the company have for developing new ideas and testing new patterns of behavior? To what degree does the daily work environment allow for questioning, reflection, and experiential acting (Kolb 1984)?

There are three major classes of tools related to the action phase. The first is based on action-learning research and focuses on the improvement of problem-solving through practical experiences (Pearn, Roderick, and Mulrooney 1995; Pedler, Burgoyne, and Boydell 1994; Revans 1982). This first class of tools includes learning contracts, mentoring, shadowing, learning accomplishment audits, and scenario planning (on scenario planning, see Galer and van der Heijden, Ch. 38 in this volume). The second group of action-related tools stems from large-group interventions (e.g. Search Conference, Emery 1969; Real Time Strategic Change-Conference, Future Conference, Weisbord 1992). The third group is closely related to system dynamics and includes such tools as micro worlds and learning laboratories. Let us now briefly examine two tools from class 1 and two from class 3, all of which link daily routines with learning experiences.

Learning Contracts

A learning contract is a formal agreement between a learner and a supervisor, trainer, or manager on specific learning objectives, on how and when these objectives will be achieved, and on how the learning shall be evaluated. The learning contract has three fundamentals: First, the learner is assigned an active role and responsibility for learning. Second, the learning objectives should be closely linked to the work situation, a principle that makes the learning highly relevant to the learner. Third, the functioning of the learning contract is based on the learning cycle (Kolb 1984): That is, the learner moves successively from action, to reflection, to knowledge, and to planning. According to Kolb's learning cycle, the movement from one of these learning activities to the next is crucial to the success of the learning experience. Two activities must precede negotiation of the learning contract: the learner's adequate preparation and the learner's self-audit, or self-assessment, of his or her learning needs. The learner's preparation involves the definition of the learning objectives, an understanding of how to move through the learning cycle, and a readiness to take responsibility and initiative for the negotiation of the contract. Once the assessment has been made and learning needs have been defined, the contract can be negotiated. As Pearn, Roderick, and Mulrooney (1995) pointed out, the elements of the contract have to be made explicit, and the role of the supervisor or trainer is to clarify the needs of the learner and to support him or her in developing an action plan and a realistic time frame. Before categorizing this tool, we turn to examine another one from the action-learning toolbox.

Shadowing

Shadowing, the process of learning from colleagues by observing them doing their work, also closely links work and learning. This learning instrument can facilitate the transmission of implicit knowledge from experienced employees to younger colleagues. Shadowing can be used in two ways. Either the learner observes the work process and joins the experienced colleague in reflecting from time to time on these activities and how they are performed or, in those cases where a work process is not easily observable, the learner engages in a new task from the beginning and follows the steps of its accomplishment by examining different stages of its development.

An example of this might be a design project. During the initial meeting to clarify the objectives and constraints of the project, the learner could observe his or her colleague; but the work resulting from the meeting cannot be observed easily. To shadow this type of task, the learner might be shown the design at various stages, and would take the opportunity to discuss the work with the experienced colleague. Alternatively, some of the work may be given to the learner, who . . . actually contributes to the project, and in this way gains first-hand experience of what is involved, but in a supportive environment which is conducive to learning. (Pearn, Roderick, and Mulrooney 1995: 130)

Learning contracts and shadowing are both applied at the individual level. In the examples presented above, they incorporate a reflective type of learning that can result in deutero-learning. Both tools focus on behavioral relevance and the relation between reflection and action, and they are rooted in an action-learning perspective. With respect to the learning phase, these tools clearly focus on the action phase of learning.

Learning Laboratories and Microworlds

According to Bergin and Prusko (1990), a learning laboratory can be defined as

a learning manager's equivalent to a . . . pilot's flight simulator. It is a place where managers cannot only accelerate time simulating a model . . . but also slow down the flow of time at each decision point to reflect on potential outcomes. The learning laboratory is a managerial 'practice field' where managers can test out new strategies and policies, reflect on the outcomes and discuss pertinent issues with others. (p. 5)

Computer-based simulations that meet this definition are referred to under different names, such as learning laboratories or microworlds (Morecroft 1988; Senge *et al.* 1994), or computer-based case studies. The major phases of the development and implementation of a learning laboratory can be described as follows:

1. Preparing the ground: Starting with a 'real problem'

Nick Zeniuk, the Ford Motor Company's business-planning manager responsible for launching the Ford Lincoln Continental in 1990 and 1994, described the initial ideas for implementing a learning laboratory as follows: 'But with that car [the 1990 Lincoln], we had depended a great deal on heroic effort at the last minute—we called it "managing by panic"—because somehow we weren't able to put the right processes in place early enough. I wanted to avoid that this time' (Senge *et al.* 1994: 555).

2. Ownership of the project: The core team

Zeniuk and his colleagues in the core team initially had problems convincing management and operations of the need to conduct an in-depth analysis of the closed project: 'There was a fear of being wrong that led to people not sharing information. People did not trust others to help them. . . . And there was the

bosses' need to control every detail' (Senge *et al.* 1994: 556). Nevertheless, this core team started practicing open communication and thereby was able to get a better understanding of prior problems: 'It's better that we know now . . . than when it's too late for us to do anything about it' (p. 557).

3. Transfer of learning: Creating the learning laboratory

The core group then wanted to spread their learning to the rest of the people working on the car. With the support of MIT researchers and consultants, this transfer problem was solved through the use of a learning laboratory, which included computer-based and noncomputer-based exercises:

We worked . . . to design the first two-day session, for a team of key people working on the interior of the car. . . . Working in pairs in front of the computer, team members would make decisions about (for instance) adding or removing engineers, changing deadlines, or resetting goals. By watching how the behavior of the system changed, they would see the underlying relationships. . . . But the noncomputer-based parts of the learning lab had the most impact. They gave us ways of talking more directly and effectively about our issues. (Senge *et al.* 1994: 557)

4. Involving the organization: Spreading the learning beyond the core team

Based on their success, the members of the core team decided to involve other teams:

In the last year or so, we've brought five or six more teams into the learning labs. We waited a long time before we conducted the second one. We wanted to convince ourselves that this process would work. We also needed our top management support in order to continue funding the project. They were reluctant initially, until we presented some of the results and benefits of the project to them. (Senge *et al.* 1994: 559)

Relating this description of the learning laboratory to our conceptual framework, one sees that this tool is aimed at the group level or, depending on the problem to be solved, at the organizational level. With regard to learning types, we argue that learning laboratories typically support the development of capabilities for double-loop learning and deutero-learning. The learning mode is action learning, for specific experiences are considered to be the triggers of the learning process. Decisions can be observed in relation to different consequences. One can also assume that cognitive learning occurs if these experiences mean that the mental models or other action–outcome assumptions of the learning individuals or learning group come to be replaced by other mental models or action–outcome assumptions. Generally speaking, learning laboratories can be applied to complex business issues, such as the reduction of development time and the effects of service quality and value-added services on customer satisfaction. Learning-laboratory projects have been or are being conducted at Ford, the Federal Express Corporation, Harley-Davidson, and the National Semiconductor Corporation, among others (http://www.mit.edu/XX). In practice, the use of learning laboratories may have effects on different dimensions of the learning model. Users may broaden their conceptual views of problems or become aware of possible relations that they had not previously thought of. Nevertheless, we argue that this tool has its greatest impact on the action phase, for behavior (i.e. decisions) is simulated, and possible effects can be studied and tested.

The tools described and categorized in this chapter are summarized in Table 35.2.

Conclusion

In examining the different theoretical perspectives on organizational learning, we proposed the existence of joint elements of thought that can be combined in an eclectic, basic model of organizational learning. Within this framework, questions can be formulated and indicators can be defined in order to investigate organizational 'learning' reality. By evaluating employees and assessing top management with this model's categories and criteria in mind, one can identify strengths and weaknesses and can select the interventions or activities most appropriate for promoting learning and overcoming difficulties. The advantage of this procedure is that it introduces a theoretical foundation for learning interventions within organizations. With the basic model of organizational learning, we have a blueprint that can guide the application of learning tools.

Not all tools are adequate for some learning objectives. If one finds a high frequency of suggestions for improvements in a company, yet discovers that few of these ideas have resulted in change, then it makes sense to operate with learning tools that aid the translation of ideas into practice. If an evaluation of organizational practices reveals that the same errors are repeatedly committed because a learning outcome has not spread throughout the company, tools that promote the diffusion of knowledge within the company might be useful. If much of an organization's core business depends on the knowledge of a few employees who might retire from the company soon, one might focus on tools that support the integration of knowledge within the company in order to reduce the company's dependence on the employees in question. Our theoretical framework and the categorization of learning tools may help in the exploration of the learning environment within an organization and may aid in the selection of tools that improve on weaknesses or deficits that have been found.

Our final note is that the usefulness of individual tools depends not only on the characteristics of the tool but also to a high degree on the culture of the organization, on the maturity of organizational members, on leadership styles, and on the organization's structural features. It may make little sense to use tools such as Open Space or the dialogue process in environments where people have little experience with participation, discretion, and self-organization. On this point, there are many open questions for future research. It remains to be seen if certain conditions (e.g. typical routines, behavioral norms, or the structural properties of the organizational system) are systematically linked to positive outcomes (e.g. economic indicators or a process-related success). This empirical question calls for an answer because systematic cultivation of organizations that are capable of

Table 35.2. Overview and categorization of learning tools

Tools	Learning level	Learning type	Learning mode	Learning process
Quick market intelligence	Groups, departments	Single- and double-loop learning	Cognitive and cultural learning	Identification
Gamma	Groups	Double-loop learning and deutero-learning	Cognitive learning with effects on cultural factors	Identification and generation
Yellow pages and knowledge maps (inventories)	Departments, organization-wide		Cognitive learning	Identification
Open space technology	Group, organization	Double-loop learning and deutero-learning	Cognitive and cultural learning	Identification and generation
Work-out	Groups	Double-loop learning and deutero-learning		Generation
grapeVINE	Organization-wide		Cognitive learning	Identification, diffusion, and integration
Dialogue	Group		Cognitive and cultural learning	Integration and modification
Learning histories	Organization-wide	Deutero-learning	Cognitive and cultural learning	Diffusion
Learning contracts	Individual	Deutero-learning	Cognitive and action-learning	Action
Shadowing	Individual	Deutero-learning	Action-learning	Action
Learning laboratories	Group	Double-loop learning and deutero-learning	Action-learning	Action

learning requires deepened understanding of the conditions that promote these capabilities. We hope that this chapter helps build the necessary bridge between improved theoretical understanding of organizational learning and its practical application.

References

Bach, V., Vogler, P., and Österle, H. (eds.) (1999). *Business Knowledge Management*. Berlin: Springer.

Bergin, R. S. and Prusko, G. F. (1990). 'System Thinking in Action: Learning Laboratories Give Hanover Insurance a Competitive Edge'. *System Thinker*, 1/1: 4–5.

Bohm, D. and Edwards, M. (1991). *Changing Consciousness: Exploring the Hidden Source of the Social, Political and Environmental Crisis Facing Our World*. San Francisco: Harper.

Böhmann, T. and Krcmar, H. (1999). *Spezialreport Wissensmanagement*. Düsseldorf: Symposium Publishing.

Burgoyne, J. and Reynolds, M. (1997). *Management Learning: Integrating Perspectives in Theory and Practice*. London: Sage.

Cohen, D. (1998). 'Toward a Knowledge Context: Report on the First Annual U.C. Berkeley Forum on Knowledge and the Firm'. *California Management Review*, 40/3 (Special issue on Knowledge and the Firm): 22–39.

Dixon, N. (1994). *The Organizational Learning Cycle: How We Can Learn Collectively*. London: McGraw-Hill.

Dörner, D. (1989). *Die Logik des Mißlingens: Strategisches Denken in komplexen Situationen*. Reinbek bei Hamburg: Rowohlt.

Eden, C., Jones, S., and Sims, D. (1983). *Messing about in Problems: An Informal Structured Approach to Their Identification and Management*. Oxford: Pergamon.

Emery, F. E. (1969). *Systems Thinking*. Harmondsworth: Penguin.

Info World (1997). *Knowledge Management Solutions*, 19/46 (17 November): 1–26. Available: www.ysiwyg://ddgnet_main.11/http://archive...splayArchive.pl?/97/46/ knownmana.dat.htm

Koestler, A. (1964). *The Act of Creation*. London: Hutchinson.

Kolb, D. A. (1984). *Experiential Learning: Experience as the Source of Learning and Development*. Englewood Cliffs, NJ: Prentice Hall.

Lewin, K. (1942). 'Feldtheorie und Lernen', in K. Lewin and D. Cartwright (eds.), *Feldtheorie in den Sozialwissenschaften: Ausgewählte theoretische Schriften*. Bern: Huber, 102–25.

Maybey, C. and Iles, P. (1994). *Managing Learning*. London: Open University.

Morecroft, J. D. W. (1988). 'System Dynamics and Microworlds for Policymakers'. *European Journal of Operational Research*, 35: 301–20.

Nonaka, I. and Konno, N. (1998). 'The Concept of "Ba"—Building a Foundation for Knowledge Creation'. *California Management Review*, 40/3: 40–54.

——and Takeuchi, H. (1995). *The Knowledge-creating Company: How Japanese Companies Create the Dynamics of Innovation*. New York: Oxford University Press.

Owen, H. (1996). *Open Space Technology: A User's Guide*. Potomac, Md.: Abbot.

Pearn, M., Roderick, C., and Mulrooney, C. (1995). *Learning Organizations in Practice*. London: McGraw-Hill.

Pedler, M., Boydell, T., and Burgoyne, J. (1989). 'Towards the Learning Company'. *Management Education and Development*, 20/1: 1–8.

——Burgoyne, J., and Boydell, T. (1991). *The Learning Company: A Strategy for Sustainable Development*. London: McGraw-Hill.

————(1994). *Das lernende Unternehmen: Potentiale freilegen—Wettberwerbsvorteile sichern*. Frankfurt am Main: Campus.

Petkoff, B. (1998). *Wissensmanagement: Von der computerzentrierten zur anwenderorientierten Kommunikationstechnologie*. Bonn: Addison-Wesley.

Petri, K. (1996). 'Let's Meet in Open Space'. *Organisationsentwicklung*, 2: 56–65.

Probst, G., Raub, S., and Romhardt, K. (1997). *Wissen managen: Wie Unternehmen ihre wertvollste Ressource optimal nutzen*. Frankfurt am Main: Frankfurter Allgemeine.

Revans, R. W. (1982). 'The Enterprise as a Learning System', in R. W. Revans (ed.), *The Origins and Growth of Action Learning*. Lund: Studentlitteratur, 280–6.

Romhardt, K. (1998). *Die Organisation aus der Wissensperspektive*. Wiesbaden: Gabler.

Ross, R. (1994). 'Tools for Discovering Learning Styles', in P. M. Senge, C. Roberts, R. B. Ross, B. J. Smith, and A. Kleiner (eds.), *The Fifth Discipline Fieldbook: Strategies and Tools for Building a Learning Organization*. New York: Currency Doubleday, 421–2.

Roth, G. (1996). 'Learning Histories: Using Documentation to Assess and Facilitate Organizational Learning'. Available: http://learning.mit.edu/wp/18004.html

Senge, P. M. (1990). *The Fifth Discipline: The Art and Practice of the Learning Organization*. New York: Bantam Doubleday.

——Roberts, C., Ross, R. B., Smith, B. J., and Kleiner, A. (1994). *The Fifth Discipline Fieldbook: Strategies and Tools for Building a Learning Organization*. New York: Currency Doubleday.

Ulrich, H. and Probst, G. J. B. (1991). *Anleitung zum ganzheitlichen Denken und Handeln: Ein Brevier für Führungskräfte*. Bern: Haupt.

Unicon (1990). *Das PC-Werkzeug für vernetztes Denken*. Meersburg: UNICON Management Systeme GmbH.

Vester, F. (1991). *Neuland des Denkens: Vom technokratischen zum kybernetischen Zeitalter* (7th edn). Stuttgart: Deutsche Verlags Anstalt.

Weisbord, M. R. (1992). *Discovering Common Ground*. San Francisco: Berrett-Koehler.

Wilson, D. A. (1996). *Managing Knowledge*. Oxford: Butterworth.

36 Intellectual Capital and Knowledge Management: Perspectives on Measuring Knowledge

Rüdiger Reinhardt, Manfred Bornemann, Peter Pawlowsky, and Ursula Schneider

Knowledge as an economic resource

There is one leitmotif reflected in many contributions to this handbook, namely, that intangible assets are rapidly becoming an important indicator of the future performance of a country or a company. In Germany, Sweden, the United Kingdom, and other countries, for example, the total investment in intangible assets since the mid-1980s has exceeded the investment in physical assets (BMFT 1996; Deiaco, Hörnell, and Vickery 1990; OECD 1996). In the United States, expenditures on information technology ($112 billion) surpassed expenditures for production technology ($107 billion; see Stewart 1997: 21) for the first time in 1991. These figures indicate a growing difference between the market value of a company and the cost of replacing its physical and financial assets.

With knowledge as one of the most important resources today, traditional factors of production have become secondary. This fact confronts economists and managers with a core problem (Drucker 1993): It is much more difficult to see and count ideas and expertise than to count money or products. Usually, the value-added knowledge embedded in goods and services cannot be identified. If knowledge is an essential resource for establishing competitive advantage, then management obvi-

ously should attempt to identify, generate, deploy, and develop knowledge. Hence, managers need more knowledge about knowledge (Drucker 1993: 43) and about how it can be managed, if it can be managed at all.

To outline the problems entailed by this task, we begin with a review of the relevant terms used much like synonyms in the actual discussion of intellectual capital (IC). First, a company's intellectual capital can be defined as 'the sum of the knowledge of its members and the practical translation of this knowledge' (Roos, Roos, Edvinsson, and Dragonetti 1997: 27), to which we add that it is translated into organizational action. From a financial perspective, the concepts of intellectual capital define the market value of a firm as the sum of its financial and intellectual capital (Edvinsson and Malone 1997; Roos *et al.* 1997; Stewart 1997; Sveiby 1997). An intangible asset, a term frequently used in accounting literature to refer to trademarks, copyrights, patents, and licenses, is defined as 'an identifiable nonmonetary asset without physical substance held for use in the production or supply of goods or services, for rental to others, or for administrative purposes' (International Accounting Standards Committee 1998: 14). Investment in information technology (IT) infrastructure can also be found on the balance sheet, as can goodwill. However, that kind of investment covers the asset's historical cost, not its current or market value. Traditionally, property rights and patents are recorded at their registration cost, not at their potential value; franchises are recorded at contract cost, not at their potential value; and goodwill is recorded only in the case of acquisition. In the field of knowledge management, the term 'intangible asset' is understood in a broader context. It includes, for example, employer–employee relations and databases on customers or technologies (see Petkoff 1998). Lastly, knowledge comprises both the stock aspect of intellectual assets and the flow aspect of interchange among those assets. This distinction also can be linked to the 'Western perspective', in which explicit knowledge is given prominent place, whereas the Japanese approach to knowledge tends to focus on the tacit dimension of knowledge in organizations (see Nonaka 1988, 1991; Nonaka and Takeuchi 1995).

Summarizing these brief definitions, we conclude that intellectual capital is typically intangible, includes tacit aspects, and therefore is not a focus of classic economic analysis. Hence, neither intellectual capital nor intangible assets is a synonym for knowledge, for using them as such would imply the reductionist interpretation that knowledge is an object. That viewpoint would leave the processes of knowledge and their partly tacit characteristics unaccounted for.

Understood in this way, the challenge posed by the IC perspective can now be briefly outlined. Unlike the scholars and researchers involved in the development of organizational learning theories, participants in the debate about intellectual capital are mainly managers. Their models of intellectual capital clearly reflect a vision of improved management of the resources regarded as essential in the knowledge economy. Such management entails development of internal reports on intellectual capital. In addition, the movement for measuring intellectual capital is nourished by a shareholder–value approach which requires increased transparency and information for external constituencies. It implies the need for external reporting of intellectual capital. Unfortunately, recent concepts of intellectual capital lack solid theoretical foundations. This weakness is not only unsatisfactory for aca-

demics but also highly problematic for practitioners of knowledge management because it contributes little to a clear understanding of intellectual capital, knowledge, and the management of these resources.

With this brief description in mind, we proceed in this chapter to elaborate on two interwoven aspects of intellectual capital: its overarching theoretical foundations and its operationalization and measurement in day-to-day management.

To provide an adequate framework of terms and models, we start by looking at currently discussed concepts of intellectual capital. In the second section we compare these concepts with their theoretical roots in order to identify major problems with the operationalization of intellectual capital. In the third section we show that the distinct character of knowledge, as opposed to that of classical economic resources, affords an adequate explanation of these theoretical problems. We conclude the chapter by identifying the distinct features of 'knowledge as a resource' and discussing the linkage between intellectual capital and knowledge management.

Concepts of Intellectual Capital

Dimensions and Categories of Intellectual Capital as Stock

The common understanding among the authors of the literature on intellectual capital is that the value of intellectual capital is to be calculated as the difference between the market value and the book value of a company (Brooking 1997; Edvinsson and Malone 1997; Roos *et al.* 1997; Stewart 1997; Sveiby 1997). Intellectual capital itself is subdivided into either two dimensions—human capital and structural capital (see Roos *et al.* 1997)—or three dimensions, such as human capital, organizational capital, and customer capital (Edvinsson and Malone 1997); competence, internal structure, and external structure (Sveiby 1997); or human capital, structural capital, and customer capital (Stewart 1997). The diversity of these names, however, belies the similarity of the three dimensions of intellectual capital as seen from an integrative perspective.

Human capital is seen as a company's total workforce and its knowledge about the business. It contains elements such as competence (skills), work attitude, intellectual agility, motivation, and seniority. It is seen as crucial for marshaling the company's assets, both tangible and intangible, for the purpose of generating value. Human resource managers are therefore customarily concerned with detailed information on trends and developments of this resource.

Organizational capital includes traditional intellectual assets (e.g. patents), intellectual property (brands), databases, information technology, and cultural phenomena (e.g. knowledge-sharing culture or employee cooperation as opposed to competition and 'mobbing'). It can be divided into process capital (the specific layout of company processes and the process intimacy of the employees) and innovation capital, or 'renewal-and-development' value.

Customer capital describes the long-term relations between the company and its key customers, including the knowledge about customers and their specific needs, standards, and values. There is a consensus that solid customer intimacy increases productivity (Reichheld 1996). The underlying hypothesis is that differentiation and adaptation based on customer needs avoids ruinous price competition and leads to higher quality for the customer and to value-added for the firm.

The interaction between human capital, organizational capital, and customer capital can produce financial capital that, over time, can turn into equity recognized by the capital market, a status that enables the equity to influence the market value of the company.

The Process Perspective on Intellectual Capital: From Stock to Flow

Concepts of intellectual capital that deal with the flow between stocks of intellectual capital are scarce. To our knowledge, the model of such flow has been developed by Roos and Roos (1997) and Roos et al. (1997). It provides one conceptualization of the change within stocks of intellectual capital and between those stocks and financial and physical assets. The authors have developed a matrix that includes variables describing the flow within and between specific stocks of intellectual capital (see Table 36.1).

Although Table 36.1 provides some insight into the conceptual basics of the flow perspective on intellectual capital, it remains unclear how this enumeration can do the same for the empirical measurement of the relationships between the different categories of intellectual capital and their changes. Furthermore, most of the interventions listed in Table 36.1 are related to behaviorally oriented management research. This association leads to the problem of theoretically describing changes in microeconomic indicators.

Measures of Intellectual Capital

Measures of intellectual capital can be divided into two major categories (North 1998): financial measures, which are derived deductively, and nonfinancial measures, which are derived inductively. In this section, we first describe three financial measures and then examine nonfinancial ones.

Financial Measures of Intellectual Capital

One device that can be used to measure intellectual capital is Tobin's ratio Q, which compares the market value of an asset with its replacement cost (book value). This ratio is interpreted as the intellectual capital of a company (Landsman and Shapiro 1995), as the company's knowledge intensity. Frequently cited examples of companies with high Q-values are software developers and pharmaceutical companies. Q's utility in this capacity stems from Tobin's (1969) demonstration that Q is able to predict corporate investment decisions independent of macroeconomic factors such as interest rates. Having originally been developed for purposes of financial accounting,

Table 36.1. Examples of the process perspective on intellectual capital

	Categories of intellectual capital				
	Competence value	Relationship value	Organizational value	Renewal and development value	Financial value
Competence value	Reflection on events and theories, conversations, training programs	Exchange of ideas and skills, reflection on assumptions	Encouragement of learning and reflections (vs. 'You are not paid to think')	Research and development, training	Training, hiring of key people
Relationship value	Assessment of quality of partners, contribution to the relations	Word-of-mouth, halo effects	Outside orientation (vs. inside)	New relations	Number of relations the company can manage, 'quality' of those relations
Organizational value	Creation of new structures and new solutions	New organizational forms (virtual organizations)	Only through human contribution	New structures, processes, and culture	Availability of alternative solutions, creation of 'cultural' events
Renewal and development value	New directions of discovery and exploration, and expansion, increased attractiveness as business partner	Suggestion of new alternatives	Cultural orientation towards the future, encouragement of free flow of information	New renewal	Investments in the future development of the company
Financial value	Added value in product and services, consulting	Customer satisfaction, improvement of sales influence, easy access to financing, cost savings	Reengineering, cost savings	New products	Traditional accounting/ financial flows

Source: Excerpts of Roos *et al.* 1997: 55.

Tobin's Q is known by a different name—'market-to-book value'—when borrowed for the measurement of intellectual capital. In management theory it has been applied in order to forecast market value in relation to investments in technology and human capital (Brigham and Gapenski 1988; Tenbrock 1997). The problem with interpreting Q as a measurement of intellectual capital is the bubble economy, the hazard of determining the market value from plain speculation of investors. For example, Bill Gates lost $5 billion during the 'Russia Crises' in August and September 1998 but all that 'intellectual capital' was hardly destroyed. Additional influences relating to speculation or to problems of Q come from money supply, interest rates, and cyclical shifts from bonds to shares and vice versa. Book values are influenced by accounting rules that lead to relatively low figures. If one keeps these restraints in mind, Q certainly is an indicator for shareholders' recognition of intellectual assets.

A second measure of intellectual capital is called value added intellectual potential (VAIP). VAIP is calculated from the ratio between value-added (pretax sales less all necessary inputs for the product generation, except personnel) and total expenses for personnel (Pulic 1998). A study involving 108 Austrian companies over a five-year period provided evidence supporting the hypothesis that the productivity of human capital, broadly measured by means of value-added (company performance) per total employees, is on average about 2.8 times higher than the productivity of financial assets. The results reported by Pulic and Bornemann (1998) suggest that demand is increasing for measures of soft indicators as a complement to measures of financial productivity.

A third way to measure intellectual capital is intellectual-capital accounting, a theoretically derived concept developed by Rennie (1998). She proposed the establishment of a 'statement of investments in the future' with which to buffer expenditures on intangible assets for a period of three to five years, until they prove to be either expenses (income statement) or investments (balance sheet). This concept of buffering seems to handle the problem of the long-term orientation of intellectual capital as opposed to the long-term orientation of financial capital. Cash outflows for intellectual capital are stored in the buffer until they turn out to be investments (ultimately booked as assets) or expenditures (ultimately booked as profit or

loss). This concept might prove to be useful for a future cost-accounting model, especially with regard to long-term and high-risk, knowledge-intensive research projects. The definition of buffer time seems somewhat questionable, however, for it depends on parameters whose use differs from country to country and sector to sector (for a practical perspective on this approach, see Stewart 1997: 232).

Nonfinancial Measures of Intellectual Capital

The oldest concept and intellectual root of intellectual capital accounting originated in Scandinavia. The concept was then in the late 1980s developed by Sveiby with models of the invisible balance sheet and what he referred to as the Intellectual Capital Monitor. The concept has since been applied in several companies (e.g. Celemi, WM-data). The most prominent concepts of intellectual capital accounting come from Skandia, an international insurance company based in Sweden, which started to document intellectual capital in 1991 and has published reports on it since 1996. Dow Chemical started to harvest its intellectual property rights systematically in 1993, when it turned 'a passive function—central record-keeping for their 29,000 in-force patents—into active management of the opportunities patents represented in their portfolio' (Stewart 1997: 62). Other companies have started to monitor their intellectual capital and have institutionalized a CKO (chief knowledge officer), a CLO (chief learning officer), or similar managerial position.[1]

[1] Established positions for knowledge management exist, for example, at Arthur Andersen Knowledge Enterprises (Managing Partner, Packaged Knowledge), British Petroleum (BP's Knowledge Management Team), Coca-Cola (Chief Learning Officer), Dow Chemical Company (Global Director, Intellectual Assets and Capital Management), General Electric (Chief Learning Officer), General Motors (Director, Knowledge Network Development), Hewlett-Packard Company (Program Manager, Knowledge Management Program), Nokia Telecommunications (Head of Knowledge Management Development), Shell International Exploration and Production (Manager of Learning and Development), and Skandia AFS: Vice President and Corporate Director, Intellectal Capital (cf. Grundstein 1998: 1–4).

Skandia does not claim that its approach is focused merely on accounting. The company tries to improve shareholder relations by increasing transparency of its stocks of intellectual capital. The company's tool for its task is the Skandia Navigator, a set of more than 160 indicators with which to measure stocks of intellectual capital. It condenses these qualitative, numerical, and financial parameters into an index of intellectual capital, allowing management to 'navigate' the company with a portfolio of highly aggregated knowledge assets, such as the qualifications and experience of employees and the value that these employees generate. The distinct parameters for the index of intellectual capital can be derived from corporate strategy.

The main idea of the Skandia Navigator is to define five key areas for the company's future success (financial, human, customer, process, and renewal and development focuses). The first area represents past achievements, the next three represent results, and the final area represents the future. Several measures used in the Skandia Navigator explained in Edvinsson and Malone (1997: 139–75) are presented in Table 36. 2. The Skandia intellectual capital accounts do not actually measure the company's intellectual capital flows thereof. Rather they represent a mere statement of intellectual capital stock and its changes from one period to another. If compiled regularly over some years, these accounts will signify a development process likely to influence the scenarios of Skandia's corporate future. According to Edvinsson (1997), the next step is to develop methods to visualize flows between these stocks.

Implementation of Intellectual Capital Accounts

Although research on intellectual capital is a very recent subject, there has been intense activity in implementing systems for managing and measuring intellectual capital. Drawing on case studies, Roos and Roos (1997) and Roos *et al.* (1997) published an implementation and process model for measuring intellectual capital. Its starting point is the corporate strategy and critical success factors prescribed by top management. With the help of a wide range of financial and nonfinancial indicators, this model establishes a link between operational actions (business processes) and long-term goals (strategy). The next step is to identify reliable indicators that capture these activities from a bottom-up perspective and to try to understand which indicators best reflect the key success factors.

Because most studies on intellectual capital are derived from consulting activities and can therefore be characterized as case studies (Edvinsson 1997; Roos *et al.* 1997; Sveiby 1997), there is need for systematic empirical research. In 1997 an empirical investigation was undertaken in ten Scandinavian companies (Danish Memorandum 1997). This study put major emphasis on a three-dimensional categorization of intellectual capital: human resources, customers, and, as a specific form of structural capital, processes and technology. The research showed two major findings on how intellectual capital is dealt with (Danish Memorandum 1997: 5):

1. The primary intention behind implementing intellectual capital accounts is *not* to raise new capital for the companies but rather to support organizational development. Intellectual capital accounts are meant to function as a communication tool for presenting and maintaining the corporate strategy and vision.

2. Though intellectual capital accounts are not used for raising capital, they are interesting to many investors. When it comes to corporate strategy, customers, products, and the knowledge base, there is evidence that intellectual capital accounts often deal with the nonfinancial elements that have proven to be interesting to the capital market (Danish Memorandum 1997: 7). Three of the companies explicitly state that their intellectual capital accounts have aroused the interest of the capital market.

Table 36.2. Intellectual capital: Examples of dimensions, categories, and measures based on the Skandia Navigator

Financial focus: (history)	Customer focus: (today)	Process focus: (today)	Human focus: (today)	Renewal and development focus (tomorrow)
Total assets	Market share (%)	Administrative expense as % of total revenues	Leadership index: % of competent leaders	Competence development (expense per employee)
Total assets per employee	No. of customers	Cost of administrative errors as % of management revenues	Motivation index: % of motivated staff	Satisfied employee index: % of satisfied employees
Revenues as % of total assets	Annual sales per customer	Processing time	Empowerment index: % of empowered staff	Investment per customer
Profits as % total assets	No. of customers lost	No. of contracts filled without error	No. of employees	Training hours as % of total working time
Revenues resulting from new business operations	Average duration of customer relationships	No. of function points per employee-month	Employee turnover as % of total work force	Development hours as % of total working time
Revenues per employee	Average customer size	No. of PCs & laptops per employee	Average no. of years of service with company	Opportunity share
Revenues from new customers as % of total revenues	Customers per employee	IT[a]-expense as % of administrative expense	Time in training (days per year)	Expenditures on IT development as % of total IT expenditures
Market value	No. of revenue-generating staff	Administrative expense as % of gross premium	No. of IT-literate staff members	Expenditures on IT training as % of total IT expenditures
Return on net asset value (%)	Average time from customer contact to sales response	IT capacity (megahertz, hard-disk space)	No. of full-time/ permanent employees	R&D[b] resources as % of total resources
Value-added per employee	Customer index: % of satisfied customers	Corporate quality performance as % of quality goals	Average no. of years with company for full-time/permanent employees	Average age of customers, average education of customers, average income of customers
Value-added per IT-employee	IT investment per salesperson	Discontinued IT inventory as % of IT inventory	No. of managers assigned to full-time/ permanent employees	Average customer duration with company (in months)
Value-added per customer	% of IT-literate customers	IT capacity per employee	% of company managers of nationality other than that of the company registry	Sharing of 'method-&-technology' hours as % of total working time

[a] IT: information technology.
[b] R&D: research and development.

Source: Table created from data on pages 139–75 from *Intellectual Capital* by Leif Edvinsson and Michael S. Malone. Copyright © 1997 by Leif Edvinsson and Michael S. Malone. Reprinted by permission of HarperCollins Publishers, Inc.

Discussion of Current Concepts of the Purposes of Intellectual Capital

Reviewing the pertinent literature, we can identify three major lessons for the measurement of intellectual capital. First, a theoretical interpretation of the approaches discussed above shows that dimensions of intellectual capital have no explicit link to theoretical schools of economic and managerial thought. With regard to the idea of stocks of intellectual capital, a major emphasis is placed on indicators derived from microeconomics (see Howitt 1996). By contrast, the not yet worked out flow perspective (see Table 36.1) advances the idea that managerial approaches should be taken into account. The overemphasis on highly aggregated measures (numbers, ratios, and financial terms) affords little insight into the relationships between cause and effect. Second, the flow model does not really overcome the traditional idea of stocks of knowledge and remains very vague. Even if one is willing to accept these problems, the time interval during which flows of intellectual capital are to be measured seems to be too short. If behavioral interventions are treated as investments in intellectual capital, then the time frame that has to be considered obviously has to be much greater than a traditional accounting period. Third, the productivity of intellectual capital cannot be disentangled from physical or financial capital as long as the drawbacks of the flow perspective remain unresolved.

Analysis of the measurement perspective indicates the seeming arbitrariness of basing the measurement of intellectual capital on differences between market-to-book values, for such measures are not theoretically grounded. In view of the dynamic, even chaotic, changes in the capital markets, those differences are not stable, either. The emphasis tends to be on the measurement of individual abilities and competencies instead of on collective knowledge and capabilities. Current research on organizational learning and knowledge management (see Pawlowsky, Ch. 3 in this volume) implies that concepts of intellectual capital pertain mainly to the learning of individuals and do not capture the group and organizational levels. In addition, measures focus on inputs, seldom on outputs. If output measures exist, then the relation to indicators of financial performance is weak. Productivity is generally defined by means of an output–input ratio, implying that researchers lack productivity measures related to intellectual capital. Finally, measurement scales for tangible assets differ from those for intellectual capital, so the two kinds of measures are not directly comparable.

Empirical results reveal two managerial perspectives on intellectual capital accounting: internal and external, with an emphasis on the former. Additionally, measures of intellectual capital depend heavily on strategy and mission. In other words, there seem to be no universal measures of intellectual capital. This point is crucial because it implicitly precludes legal regulations for reporting intellectual capital in the near future, say, within the corpus of generally accepted accounting procedures (GAAP). There may also be implications that measures of intellectual capital need to be developed within a top-down/bottom-up approach in order to ensure that they are relevant to the company involved. As mentioned earlier in this chapter, the endeavor to measure intellectual capital, especially for internal reporting purposes, is ultimately intended to facilitate knowledge management. Furthermore, intellectual capital measurement within knowledge management is only one step in a chain of activities that contains many feedback loops. Tools such as the Measurement Kit of the American Society for Training and Development (Bassi and MacMurrer 1999) can foster knowledge management initiatives by pointing to important variables and ratios and by providing benchmarks for those variables and ratios that can inspire action.

This interpretation seems to make the modeling and measurement of intellectual capital both a theoretical and practical challenge. A coherent theoretical framework for intellectual capital would offer a solution to the problems caused by unreliable indicators of intellectual capital and by lack of information about how to use measures of intellectual capital in order to improve the overall performance of the firm. An additional advantage of such a framework is that it would enable one to ensure that the measures are actually used as intended and not just because they are convenient and because the necessary data is available.

In the following sections we aim to identify lessons for conceptualizing intellectual capital. We do so by looking at the concept's theoretical and mensural roots and by examining approaches that are both rooted in 'microeconomic theory' and linked with behavioral theories and by focusing on approaches that take several functions of the firm into account.

Microeconomic Roots of the Concept of Intellectual Capital

Human Capital Theory

In 1768 the Swedish economist Westerman observed that the performance of the Swedish ship-building industry was significantly lower than that of Dutch and British companies. He explained that this phenomenon was due to a lack of 'industrial knowledge' in Sweden. Westerman understood industrial knowledge to include both the capacity to organize work flows and knowledge and the skills for working with modern machines (e.g. Eliasson and Ryan 1987). Systematic research on human capital started in the early 1960s with the work of Schultz (1961) and Becker (1964) and focused primarily on the impact of human capital on national economies. Because the development of national economies heavily depends on the performance of firms, human capital theory has been applied to private and public companies (Anderson and Bowman 1976; Becker 1983, 1993; Kuznets 1966; Schultz 1981). Regardless of the level of application, human capital theory has focused on investment in education—human resources—and returns on such investment. This investment was related to different classes of dependent variables such as economic growth, organizational profitability, and individual lifetime earning profiles.

According to the OECD (1996), 'Human capital is defined as the knowledge that individuals acquire during their lifetime and use to produce goods, services or ideas in market or non-market circumstances' (p. 22). Similarly, Becker (1964) stated in his well-known definition that the development of human capital generally can be defined as 'activities that influence monetary and psychic income by increasing the resources in people' (p. 1).

Because early organizational applications of human capital theory were focused on investment in human resources and returns on such investment, researchers have recently started to consider a similarly managerial approach to human capital. This perspective reflects attempts both to shed light on the processes generating human capital within the traditional black-box model (e.g. Carnevale 1991; Nordhaug 1993) and to link individual competencies with core competencies (Prahalad and Hamel 1990) on the basis of concepts such as competence stocks, competence portfolios, competence configurations, team and organizational competence, and strategic competence pools (e.g. Grønhaug and Nordhaug 1993; Naugle and Davies 1987).

Within the human capital approach, three central lessons for intellectual capital measurement can be drawn. First, Machlup (1980, 1984) showed in detail that economic theory has not adequately dealt with the problem of knowledge creation. Second, in the managerial approach to human capital, flows of human capital and the processes that generate and transform human capital are discussed from an individual and an organizational learning perspective (e.g. Hall 1989; Itami and Roehl 1987). Third, Machlup (1984) differentiated the concept of human capital by distinguishing three major classes of knowledge stocks: knowledge embodied in individual, physical tools; knowledge embodied in individual persons; and nonembodied knowledge. This general distinction between human-embodied knowledge (e.g. skills, qualifications) and nonembodied knowledge (which can be identified at either an outcome or product level) is central to current thinking about intellectual capital. It helps one understand the difference between human capital and organizational capital within the range of interpretations of intellectual capital.

Human Resource Accounting

Early attempts at human resource accounting focused on improving productivity and performance (Flamholtz 1974; Hermanson 1964) by integrating behaviorally oriented management research (e.g. Lawler 1971; Likert 1961, 1967, 1973) with microeconomic insights from human capital theory (see preceding section).

Broadly speaking, the primary purpose of implementing systems of human research accounting was to provide managers with a tool that performed at least four major functions (e.g. Flamholtz 1974, 1985, 1987; Sackmann, Flamholtz, and Lombardi Bullen 1989): (a) acquisition of quantitative and qualitative information about the value and cost of workforces as a firm's resource, (b) improvement of internal decision-making, (c) assistance with developing a human resource perspective, and (d) provision of information for investors.

Differentiating the cost perspective and the value perspective of human resources in general, one can identify four models of human resource accounting (e.g. Cascio 1987; Flamholtz 1974; Fitz-enz 1990; and Spencer 1986). With the first model, the financial value of the individual is estimated in terms of that person's anticipated value to the company. This value depends partly on the person's ability to perform his or her job with consistent productivity and flexibility. It also depends on the person's overall work satisfaction which is relevant when assessing the probability that a person will remain with the company. Thus, the realizable value is a function of the person's financial value and the person's motivation to stay with the company. The second model of human resource accounting is focused on the financial value of groups with regard to motivation, organization, and financial results. In this model the value of groups is primarily a function of work climate. The model, therefore, does not measure values but rather 'surrogate concepts' in the form of welfare and motivation. The third approach to human resource accounting is based on staff replacement costs, which are related to the expenses connected with acquisition, training, and separation. Acquisition costs include expenditures on recruitment and advertising. Training costs consist of expenditures on education and on-the-job training. Separation costs are the losses of production when a person leaves a job. In the fourth model, human resource accounting and balancing are treated as complete accounts of the company's human resources. This approach focuses on cost control, capitalization, and the depreciation of the company's past expenditures on its human resources. An advantage of this system is that it enables one to visualize the impacts that human resource management has on the 'numbers' of the traditional balance sheet.

In summary, concepts of human resource accounting provide for a more practical way to measure intellectual capital than models of human capital do. The latter are applied by researchers to describe the relationship between financial investment in human resources and the consequences that this investment has for various output variables. Systems of human resource accounting are relevant for managerial decision-making as well, for they provide information for personnel selection (Spiceland and Zaunbrecher 1977), personnel development (Harrell and Klick 1980), layoffs (Oliver and Flamholtz 1978; Tomassini 1977), turnover (Gul 1984), and cost–benefit analysis of human resource development programs (Swanson and Gradous 1988).

As can be seen from the findings reported by Acland (1976), Elias (1972), Hendricks (1976), and Schwan (1976), human resource accounting systems also have an important impact on investors' perceptions and decision-making, and, therefore, on the market recognition of intellectual capital. The problem with implementing such systems, however, blurs their impact on the improvement of performance and effectiveness. According to Schmidt (1982) and Marr

(1982), most of these problems are due to the unpopularity of human resource accounting among most managers, employees, and union representatives, for most of the systems focus on the cost of human resources, not their value. In order to make clear the impact that human resource accounting systems have on the improvement of performance and effectiveness, Flamholtz (1979, 1980) introduced an important differentiation of the function of measurement within a firm: The process function of measurement increases acceptance of human resource accounting; the informational function includes the application of the data that have been collected and calculated via the measurement process.

Other major issues, too, can be seen as sources of learning about the implementation of systems for managing and measuring intellectual capital (Flamholtz 1974: 329–40; Sackmann, Flamholtz, and Lombardi Bullen 1989: 236–7): (a) the adequacy of terms, (b) the reliability of measures, (c) process-oriented measures, (d) the utility of intellectual capital systems to management and/or investors, (e) behavioral change activities, and (f) the linking of opportunities to corporate financial accounting rules. In addition, the concept of corporate social reporting (Dierkes 1979; Preston, Rey, and Dierkes 1978), which deals with the assessment of a company's impact on its employees and society (whereas human resources accounting deals with an employee's impact on a company as perceived by the company), intimated that organizational policies should be focused on the needs of stakeholders, not only on the need of shareholders.

Summarizing these arguments and the distinction between cost accounting and value accounting, we conclude that quantitative and qualitative measures of intellectual capital are relevant for the development of a system for measuring and managing intellectual capital. At the same time, qualitative measures are being acknowledged on the market, recognition that, in turn, might foster managerial acceptance of nonfinancial information systems.

Organizational Capital

The development of the concept of organizational capital was triggered by the detailed observation that according to employers, employee effort typically seems to be suboptimal. This line of thinking was taken further by Tomer (1987). Drawing on Leibenstein's (1966, 1976) distinction between 'X-efficiency' and 'X-inefficiency', he integrated insights from organizational behavior and economic theories into a new and improved theory of economic productivity. Because the concept of organizational capital therefore contains organizational and behavioral variables, it can be understood as an extension of human capital theory. Organizational capital is defined as 'human capital in which the attribute is embodied in either the organizational relationships, particular organization members, the organization's repositories of information, or some combination of the above in order to improve the functioning of the organization' (Tomer 1987: 24).

By contrast, Sadowski's (1980) model of developing organizational capital started from a purely neoclassical argumentation of human capital, a line of thought that has been modified by institutional economic thinking. He defined human capital as a discounted net value of educational investments and defined organizational capital as long-term utilizable assets, which are not brought about through isolated educational investments but formed through day-to-day operations. Hence, organizational capital is based on the degree of willingness to share information, resolve conflicts, or show cooperative attitudes (Sadowski 1991: 136).

Tomer (1987, 1998) identified two types of organizational capital, pure organizational capital (e.g. a firm's organizational structure), which is independent of the attributes of individual workers; and hybrid organizational capital, which is embodied in individuals but is still firm-specific. With hybrid organizational capital, investment in the socialization of the employee leads to employee-related improvements that are specific to the firm.

Information-gathering allows the firm to improve the way in which the skills of these employees are used. This information may reside in the memory banks of individual managers, but it, too, is specific to the firm. In all of these cases, the firm invests in an organizational feature that then produces a stream of benefits in the form of improved worker productivity.

Investment in organizational capital generally may include changes of organizational structure, climate, procedures, the quality of socialization processes, and information systems for enhancing management's decision-making capabilities. Consequently, organizational capital is related to the organizational incentives that workers experience and that influence their level of effort and their output.

Because the formation of organizational capital may involve '(1) changing the formal and informal social relationships and patterns of activity within the enterprise or (2) changing individual attributes important to organizational functioning, or (3) the accumulation of information useful in matching workers with organization situations' (Tomer 1987: 24), it becomes clear that concepts of organizational capital can be interpreted as a central conceptual source of structural capital (Edvinsson and Malone 1997) or a structural concept (Sveiby 1997) within the discussion about intellectual capital. In addition, a large body of evidence (see Chatman 1991; Tomer 1998) shows that investment in human capital affects the stock of organizational capital and vice versa. For example, the investment in Total Quality Training programs enhances the individual ability to improve daily work and promotes the organizational ability to improve process performance (Zink 1995). Hence, Tomer's (1998) concept of organizational capital teaches that the distinction between human and organizational capital within the discussion about intellectual capital makes sense from an analytical point of view, though the flows between human capital and organizational capital as postulated in the concepts of intellectual capital must be made more explicit than they are.

Social Capital

The social sciences have a strong tradition of treating relations between individuals as a source of social action and hence of welfare (e.g. Bourdieu 1986; Coleman 1988, 1990; Putnam 1995). The concept of social capital is based on the assumption that core organizational capabilities can be developed through cooperating individuals. This assumption leads to the interpretation of organizations as social communities (Conner and Prahalad 1996; Kogut and Zander 1996; Nahapiet and Ghoshal 1998). It is an interpretation that originates in Barnard's (1956) definition of an organization: a system of cooperative activities of two or more persons—something intangible and impersonal, largely a matter of relationships (p. 75).

According to Nahapiet and Ghoshal (1998), social capital can be defined as 'the sum of the actual and potential resources embedded within, available through, and derived from the network of relationships possessed by an individual or social unit' (p. 243). There are three dimensions of social capital (Granovetter 1992; Nahapiet and Ghoshal 1998; Putnam 1995). Its structural dimension is the overall pattern of connections between actors. These linkages can be operationalized through measures such as density, connectivity, and hierarchy of the network (Coleman 1993). Relational social capital is the history of interactions of people who constitute the network. Adequate measures of relational social capital are, for example, trust and trustworthiness (Putnam 1995), norms and sanctions (Coleman 1990), expectations (Burt 1992), and identity and identification (Merton 1948/1968). Lastly, the cognitive dimension of social capital includes shared representations, interpretations, and systems of meaning among parties. As shown by concepts such as 'alignment' or 'shared mental models', this perspective has also been recognized within strategic management thinking (see Conner and Prahalad 1996; Grant 1996).

Three major conclusions for the conceptualization of intellectual capital may be drawn from these viewpoints. First, it is obvious that social capital is owned jointly by the parties in a relationship and that no member has, or is capable of having, exclusive claim to ownership of social capital (Burt 1992). Second, the use of social capital can facilitate the achievement of aims that would otherwise go unmet, at least without extra cost. Finally, social capital can be viewed as a source for the formation and development of intellectual capital, which is created by a combination and exchange of existing intellectual resources (Nahapiet and Ghoshal 1998). The discussion of social capital together with ongoing exploration of resource-based views of the firm, points to the issues of ownership of intellectual resources and to their capacity to be appropriated. In the knowledge economy with virtual organizations and an increase in cooperative arrangements, the concept of ownership might have to be reconsidered and complemented with concepts of availability and connectivity.

Discussion of Microeconomic Approaches to Intellectual Capital

Given the microeconomic roots of intellectual capital management, the essentials of the previous sections can be summarized in the following key observations about the measurement and management of intellectual capital. First, neither neoclassical nor institutional assumptions provide a satisfactory theoretical framework for modeling intellectual capital, especially for ways to measure it. Second, the development of methodologies that can solve this problem of measurement implies the need to retain a dual view of intellectual capital. Both financial and nonfinancial measures of intellectual capital should be provided. Accordingly, a behavioral perspective on the firm should be considered. Lastly, the utility that measures of intellectual capital have for internal and external stakeholders will certainly influence the degree to which the concept of intellectual capital is accepted by the business community.

Having explored the microeconomic roots of the conceptualization and measurement of intellectual capital, we now focus on its functional roots, which stem from a functional perspective of the firm.

Functional Approaches to Intellectual Capital

The Financial Roots of Intellectual Capital

There are three major links between the conceptualization of intellectual capital and the economic perspective of the firm: accounting, value management, and controlling.

Accounting

The basic idea of accounting is to provide true and fair information of a business in compliance with established conventions, concepts, and legal requirements. Like the measurement of intellectual capital, accounting concepts have grown largely out of accounting practice, which embraces different ways of achieving the purpose of this activity and of facilitating its functions. In the anthropological approach 'accounting is seen as a language for objective measurement which should not lend itself to manipulation' (Ijiri 1967: 19). According to this view, the function of accounting is to record, not to assess value. It deals with prices, not values (Hedlin 1996: 15). By contrast, the true-income approach is an attempt to express wealth and changes in wealth in monetary terms. Like the anthropological approach, it is universalistic. As Hedlin (1996) explained, 'information for a special purpose would not be tailor-made to that purpose' (p. 21). The decision-model approach focuses on the idea that different systems of accounting fit different purposes of internal decision-making, and the market approach is mainly concerned with the correlation between information disclosure to shareholders and shareholder reactions as reflected by stock prices. The information-economics approach goes beyond the hypothesis that information is available at no cost. It introduces cost–benefit analysis to the task of accounting and focuses on maximizing the system's utility to each user of an accounting system. Finally, the behavioral approach centers on the observation that 'accountants can deliberately design their systems so as to influence behaviour' (Hedlin 1996: 32).

These approaches have several links to the modeling of intellectual capital. First, it is argued in the behavioral approach that accounting systems shape organizational behavior—a notion that is completely in keeping with thinking on intellectual capital. With regard to market approach, it can be argued that communication of intellectual capital fosters investors' willingness to respond to companies with systems for reporting intellectual capital. Second, accounting assumptions and cross-national differences due to publishing conventions and legal constraints seem to block the implementation of systems for managing and measuring intellectual capital. Assets are defined as a controllable economic resource whose actual value is calculated according to past transactions that may yield future economic benefits. Third, several professional organizations of accountants, including the American Institute of Certified Public Accountants (AICPA), have also recognized the need to treat knowledge (intellectual capital) as an asset and have started to develop models that can incorporate intellectual capital into financial accounting (e.g. Lev 1997; McLean 1995; Vitale and Mavrinac 1995). One prominent example is the AICPA's (1994) framework of publishing principles. It includes nonmonetary data (e.g. on the performance of business processes) and improves the application of figures and numbers used by managerial and financial accountants. Another initiative, sponsored by the Securities and Exchange Commission, reveals the need to publish data about the competencies and integrity of members of boards of directors.

Financial and Value Management

Early indicators of economic success have been closely related to the value of physical and financial assets. They are measured by means of accounting-based indicators, such as book value, return on investment (ROI), and return on assets (ROA). Since the early 1980s, the gap between market value and book value has steadily increased. The divergence has led to an explicit recognition of market value by financial managers. This period has been accompanied by the development of indicators such as economic value-added (EVA)[2] and market value-added (MVA),[3] which are designed to express the cost of capital explicitly. This effort is based on the core assumption of value management concepts: that capital, like any other factor, is a cost. Hence, the main objective is to maximize total value, which is discounted net value, but not solely to maximize the rate of return on the capital, an idea that belongs to indicators such as ROI or ROA.

In addition to Rappaport's (1986) well-known shareholder-value approach, a number of stakeholder-oriented approaches to value management provide for consideration of both financial and nonfinancial measures (e.g. Gomez 1993; Höfner and Pohl 1994; Siegert 1994). According to Rappaport, the thrust of managerial decisions should be to increase a company's value for its owners. Because the capital market has become more important for managerial decisions than ever before, this stance has sparked intense discussion about the question of what the most appropriate way is to measure and report the 'true' financial value of a company. This response is explained by manager's increasing need for capital and by the fact that information technology interconnecting investors and stock markets enables investors to decide rapidly on investments and disinvestments.

Management's increasing dependence on capital markets calls for the information needs

---

[2] EVA is defined as a company's after-tax net operating profit minus its cost of capital (both borrowed and equity). Studies have shown that a firm that achieves positive EVA year after year will see its MVA soar, whereas negative EVA will drag down MVA as the market loses faith that the firm will ever provide a decent return on invested capital (Stern, Stewart, and Chew 1995).

[3] MVA is a market-generated number calculated by subtracting capital invested in a firm from the sum of the total market value of the firm's equity and the book value of its debt. If MVA is a positive number, then the firm has made its shareholders richer (Stewart 1997).

of investors to be analyzed more systematically than in the past. In order to equip key stakeholders with information on important nonfinancial areas and performance, reports on intangible assets, including intellectual capital, have also been published. The impact of nonfinancial performance indicators on analyst and investor decisions has been illustrated by Ernst and Young (1997), who reviewed 300 reports by analysts and interviewed 275 institutional investors. An essential finding was that 35 per cent of institutional portfolio management decisions were based on nonfinancial information, obviously meaning that investors rely heavily on nonfinancial indicators when making decisions (see Table 36.3).

'Quality of management' seems to have an overall impact on investors' perspectives of organizational performance, whereas the influence of the other measures varies, depending on the industry. Hence, Ernst and Young (1997) suggested that the relevance of measures of intellectual capital differs from one industry to the next and that such measures should therefore be derived from the perspective taken in the specific corporate strategy that is involved.

Controlling

As an organizational function for coordinating corporate planning and the monitoring of results, controlling has traditionally been finance oriented. The prime goal of optimizing financial performance was achieved through formulation of explicit and measurable tasks, supervision of operational activities, and resort to countermeasures if results diverged from goals. In order to expand the spectrum of traditional finance-oriented indicators of organizational behavior, which introduced qualitative measures of performance, Kaplan and Norton (1996) developed the balanced scorecard approach.

This approach shifted the focus of management from exclusively monetary key figures, such as sales or margins, to a more holistic view that included nonmonetary information, such as employee turnover and the cumulated experience of staff. With the balanced scorecard, the factors influencing performance are differentiated into four areas: the financial focus, the customer focus, the process focus, and the growth focus. These four areas are com-

Table 36.3. Investor valuation of nonfinancial performance improvement

	Computer systems	Pharmaceuticals	Food products	Oil & gas
Quality of management	7.6	2.6	1.4	4.2
Quality of products and services	2.4	0.9	1.4	5.8
Level of customer satisfaction	0.0	0.0	0.0	0.0
Strength of corporate culture	0.0	0.0	0.0	0.0
Quality of investor communications	0.8	0.5	0.3	0.9
Effectiveness of executive compensation policies	0.9	0.6	0.4	1.1
Effectiveness of new product development	0.0	5.3	0.9	1.6
Strength of market position	3.1	0.3	0.0	7.3

Note: Scores indicate equivalent percentage increase in a company's P/E ratio for a 1-point improvement in investor perceptions of nonfinancial performance.

Source: Ernst & Young 1997: 65.

bined with the corporate vision and corporate strategy in order to support the long-term orientation. The link to operational business is established by means of measures derived from strategy, short-term indicators, operational goals, and initiatives. According to Kaplan and Norton (1996), the balanced scorecard has to be customized to a company's unique corporate goals and then used explicitly by that company. The concept does not support a knowledge management system *per se*. However, such a system could be derived from a balanced scorecard, for any 'soft' indicator representing intangible assets or intellectual capital can be integrated.

Behavioral and Managerial Roots of Intellectual Capital

The conceptualization of intellectual capital has been considerably influenced by two lines of thinking that have their origins in the 1960s: human resource management and marketing. Most modern management concepts, such as total quality management and business process reengineering, and most strategy-implementation approaches are also directly relevant to the behavioral and managerial roots of intellectual capital, but lack of space precludes their elaboration in this chapter.

Human Resource Management

Early management scholars (e.g. Likert 1961; McGregor 1960) introduced the theoretical assumption that all organizational members can be treated as reservoirs of untapped resources that include not only manual skills and energy (motivation) but also creative ability and the capacity for responsible, independent, and self-controlled behavior. Hence, a manager's job is to create an environment in which these resources can be utilized. Since the early 1960s, the focus of management theorists has shifted from normative to empirical models of human resources, a change that can also be expected in the domain of intellectual capital.

Of the many conclusions that can be drawn from the overwhelming number of publications related to human resources, two are particularly pertinent to this chapter. First, there is increasing evidence that human resource management is having an impact on strategy and financial results (Arthur 1994; Delaney 1996; MacDuffie 1995; Ulrich 1997). Second, this relation helps managers interpret human resource management as a source of value generation, not just as a cost factor. This trend is documented and explained, for example, by answers to the questions about the assessment of and values attached to measure-based human-resource activities accepted by top management (Fitz-enz 1984, 1991; Ulrich 1997; Yeung and Berman 1997).

This body of research contains three major lessons for the conceptualization and measurement of intellectual capital. With regard to implementation, top management's role in human resources is still crucial (Beer 1997; Ehrlich 1997) and is strongly related to the existence and use of business-oriented measures, including mission, vision, strategy, and, most recently, market value (e.g. Becker, Huselid, Pickus, and Spratt 1997; Boudreau and Ramstad 1997; Ulrich 1997; Wintermantel and Mattimore 1997). With regard to the integrative perspective of strategic human resource management,[4] investment in human resources is investment in organizational capital as well, for many human resource policies can be linked to both of these categories of intellectual capital. Lastly, an overemphasis of the notion of 'resource' or capital, may increase the probability of a reductionist interpretation of human resources, and of intellectual capital in particular (Pfeffer 1997).

Marketing

With concepts such as 'total customer satisfaction' and 'key account management' (Bruhn

---

[4] For example, Beer, Spector, Lawrence, Mills, and Walton (1985) developed a strategic model of human resource management by integrating stakeholder interests, situational factors, policies of human resource management, human resource outcomes, and long-term consequences. Schuler (1992) integrated human-resource philosophy, policies, programs, practices, and processes.

and Homburg 1998; Miller and Heimann 1991; Reichheld 1996; Sidow 1991; Simon 1997; Töpfer 1999), marketers have developed systematic approaches to planning, developing, and controlling a firm's relationship to its current and potential customers. These marketing approaches focus on both quantitative, primarily financial measures (e.g. stock turnover, frequency of orderings, and percentage of stock turnover) and qualitative data taken from customer satisfaction questionnaires, case analysis of complaints, and general studies of value shifts (e.g. Kotler and Bliemel 1997; Whiteley 1991). Recent, data-mining software enables one to extract detailed, customer-specific data, revealing preferences of which the customer would probably not be aware if inquired about in a questionnaire.

Traditionally, customer relations (along with technological knowledge) have been one of the major factors accounting for goodwill in mergers and acquisitions (Mandl and Rabl 1997). Customer relations include qualitative indicators of a company's current and possible future ways of doing business, a kind of barometer of later economic performance. This awareness of the importance of customer relations led to the development of national customer satisfaction indices, first in Sweden, then in the United States, Canada, Australia, Korea, and, most recently, Switzerland. These indices rely on rather simple models of factors influencing customer satisfaction but have rather sophisticated statistical procedures with which to relate input variables (such as friendliness or promptness) to output variables (such as repurchases or articulated satisfaction) (Anderson 1999; Bruhn and Grund 1999; Bruhn and Homburg 1998). Employee and customer satisfaction surveys, however, are susceptible to all the pitfalls of qualitative social research. Reliability and objectivity often must be traded for validity (McColl-Kennedy and Schneider 1999).

Above all, managers tacitly know that these highly subjective, vague factors influence success (for an overview, see Wagner 1991; Wagner and Sternberg 1985). They can draw two lessons from the marketing roots of intellectual capital. First, marketing surveys provide yardsticks, albeit necessarily inaccurate, incomplete, and only partly valid ones, that can enable a company to identify its strengths and weaknesses *vis-à-vis* competitors. Second, the marketing roots of intellectual capital inspire discussion of the relative importance of the types of measurement available: monetary as opposed to nonmonetary and quantitative as opposed to qualitative.

The Technological Roots of Intellectual Capital

Approaches to capturing knowledge in databases and 'expert systems' have a long tradition. In approaches based on information technology, knowledge is treated as an object with defined relations to other objects. This treatment has resulted in research on artificial intelligence but has been restricted to an explicit view of knowledge. Analyses of attempts at knowledge management shows that it has a high percentage of activities driven by information technology (e.g. Haney in press). It is important to recognize and treat information technology as an important and perhaps independent function of knowledge management. Constant development of new capacities in information technology makes it possible to integrate and process large amounts of data in ways unavailable ten years ago. People exchange data, text, images, and even movies independent of space and time, sharing their experiences quickly and inexpensively, and—via desktop E-mail systems and intranets easily, for there are few entry barriers to the medium. But, there is also agreement within the literature (Kubicek 1999) that information technology (hard- and software) is only an enabling factor. Even the best networks and software packages will not be used if people do not feel an urge to share knowledge or if they experience such high levels of stress that knowledge-sharing is perceived as an imposition. Resistance to sharing knowledge could be overcome through organizational strategies and incentive systems. A more serious argument is that documentation of knowledge in electronic systems still depends on explicitness and high degrees of codification.

Companies that rely on information technology to diffuse all knowledge available in the organization are confronted by particular types of problems. First, the process of eliciting and structuring knowledge for electronic storage is cumbersome and costly. Because knowledge is often ephemeral, there are also high follow-up costs for the updating and maintenance necessary if the systems in place are to be used to their full potential. Without that investment no economies of scale will legitimate the investment in information technology. Second, newcomers will have difficulty 'exforming' the code, that is to translate the code back into a rich format (one that contains tacit knowledge) so that they can effectively use the data structures available to them. This complication may partially explain why many firms report disappointment with the use of their databases. Even Dr. Stanley J. Buckman (from Buckman Laboratories) had to introduce carrots and sticks to induce his people to use the intranet (for an in-depth discussion of information technology and knowledge management, see Petkoff 1998).

Managers of information technology have been confronted with different productivity paradoxes; indeed, investment in information technology has not resulted in improved business data (the productivity paradox pertaining to personal computers was followed by a network paradox and an emerging internet/ intranet paradox, see Schneider 1998). These managers have long taken the defensive stance that, without investment in information technology, results would have deteriorated or will only materialize in the long run. Their assertion has only recently been supported. Nowadays, technology configuration allows for radical change in the way business is done, sparking a revolution in results (Strassmann 1997).

Two lessons emerge from the struggle to legitimate investment in information technology and both are related to learning from human resource management. First, benefits of such investment are spread over long periods and have partly to do with opportunity costs (costs that would arise if investment were *not* made). Second, benefits do not result from isolated investments but rather from managerial efforts to interlink them in effective ways. The implication, once again, is that investments in information technology lead to increasing returns only if they are combined with human-centered competencies (Arthur 1996; Strassmann 1997).

Functional Approaches and Intellectual Capital

Summarizing the essentials of the previous sections on the functional approaches, we see a number of key lessons for the theory and measurement of intellectual capital. First, the theoretical analysis makes clear that measuring intangibles is not a new idea. There are many forerunners, such as accounting and company evaluation, strategic controlling, human resource management, and the management and marketing of information technology. Despite the absence of theoretical groundwork integrating finance concepts and concepts related to human resources, the gap between financially oriented approaches and qualitative approaches seems to be narrowing. For the measurement issue, this convergence implies the perspective on the operational costs of investment in intangibles in becoming integrated with (a) financial management's perspective on estimating the future outcomes of value drivers—calculated via net discounted cash flow—and (b) strategic controlling and general management driven by qualitative and process measures. Suggestions for implementing functional approaches include—

- the institutionalization of standardized measures for benchmarking purposes,
- the development of customized measures for internal decision-making, and
- delineation of the content that external reports must contain.

With the market systematically overvaluing mature companies and undervaluing pioneer companies with high R&D spending (Lev

1999), these measures and prescriptions are meant to fulfil the information needs of investors and to prevent insider trading.

Where to Go with the Concept of Intellectual Capital

To synthesize the arguments we have outlined so far, we call attention in this section to three lines along which the management, measurement, and research of intellectual capital can develop: (a) the universality of measures of intellectual capital and the implications for their legal status, (b) the notion of knowledge and its ontology and epistemology, and (c) an integrative framework for the measurement of intellectual capital.

Measures of Intellectual Capital and their Lack of Universality

The fact that measures of intellectual capital lack universality is linked to the level of standardization and to the voluntary nature of reports on intellectual capital: First, we believe that progress in the discussion about intellectual capital depends heavily on the use of terms that enable one to detect the heuristic value that the idea of intellectual capital possesses beyond accounting systems. For example, the concept of potential can be used as an overarching category, subsuming the concept of capital. After all, intangibles and tangibles alike are increasingly difficult to quantify, and financial capital only constitutes potential for generating future returns. If that potential remains idle or, even worse, if it hinders full exploration of the potential of other resources, then it is a burden, not an asset. The notion of intellectual potential may therefore be preferable to the notion of intellectual capital (or intellectual assets) (see Schneider 1998). Adoption of the term 'intellectual potential' would also imply that the measurement of intellectual capital, because of its idiosyncratic characteristics, would not be accorded the

same status as traditional accounting, which is grounded in law.

Enriching the IC Perspective: The Characteristics of Knowledge

The epistemological characteristics of intellectual capital are related to trivial and nontrivial approaches to knowledge management. We have already argued that a dynamic, flow-oriented approach to intellectual capital still needs to be developed. The differences between tangible assets and knowledge assets should therefore be explained (see Table 36.4; see also Bornemann, Knapp, Schneider, and Sixl 1999: 13; North 1998: 47; Rehäuser and Krcmar 1996: 11; Roos *et al.* 1997: 23; Sveiby 1997: 45).

If the differences between knowledge and tangible assets presented in Table 36.4 are considered in connection with the arguments outlined in the previous sections, it becomes evident that intellectual capital is treated more or less as an object (similar to tangible assets) rather than as a process (similar to knowledge assets). In order to overcome this weakness, we recommend that the understanding of knowledge assets be broadened to include characteristics such as tacitness (Nonaka and Takeuchi 1995) or stickiness (Teece 1998). They seem to contradict managers' and investors' needs for certainty in reporting systems and therefore may not be expected for legal based IC reporting systems.

Expanding the View: Linking the Management of Intellectual Capital with Knowledge Management

An integrative framework for measuring intellectual capital should be developed in order to link such measurement to knowledge management. This link would ensure that measurement does not turn into an end in itself and that it would indeed contribute to the efficiency and effectiveness of knowledge management. Having now dealt with internal and external goals of intellectual capital reporting

Table 36.4. Characteristics of knowledge assets and tangible assets

Criteria	Tangible assets	Knowledge assets
Underlying theories	Accounting theories and neoclassical theories of economics	Information theory and various behavioral theories, deficit of implementation and empirical evidence
Mechanisms of price formation	Well-known, specifiable functioning markets	Only partly known, unspecifiable, or not fully specifiable markets that are failing or only emerging
Ownership	Only with one/few natural persons or legal entities	Ephemeral ownership, possibly by many; problems with protecting intellectual property
Returns	Decrease	Possible increase
Costs of production	Fixed and variable costs distributed rather evenly over the asset's life cycle	High fixed costs before creation of a market, reproduction costs negligible
Value over time	Depreciation with use	Appreciation with use
Management	Control orientation	Learning processes at different learning levels

and with ways in which the rationale of intellectual capital is linked with several economic and managerial disciplines, we propose a three-point framework that integrates the management of intellectual capital with both general management and knowledge management (see Figure 36.1).

As shown in Figure 36.1 there exists within the general management a link between corporate objectives, knowledge objectives, and the implications of both for measurements of an organization's stock of intellectual capital (see North 1998; Reinhardt 1999). In addition, we assume that the relation between measures of financial assets and measures of intellectual capital differs depending on which of two distinct balance sheets is used. The major advantage of this conceptual framework is that it integrates the concept of stocks of intellectual capital with the process, or flow, concept of knowledge management. (For a detailed description of the knowledge management model in the center of Figure 36.1, see Pawlowsky, Ch. 3 in this volume.) The key purpose of integrating these aspects of knowledge management is to explain the changes in the knowledge stocks between the periods t_0 and t_1 by means of knowledge flows that are related to knowledge management projects, the goals of which, as stated earlier in this chapter, are related to corporate and knowledge objectives. Hence, a first step has been taken in the effort to systematically disentangle the productivity of intellectual assets from that of tangible assets on the balance sheet.

Lastly, there is the question of how to proceed with the proposed integrative view of intellectual capital and knowledge management. We think that the challenging task of integrating economic and behavioral theories of management, integrating distinct academic disciplines, and integrating theory and practice, can be accomplished only by changing traditional academic research paradigms to 'mode 2' of knowledge production on the basis of a transdisciplinary understanding of knowledge. As Gibbons et al. (1994) explained:

[Transdisciplinary knowledge] is generated and sustained in the context of application and is not developed first and then applied later to that context

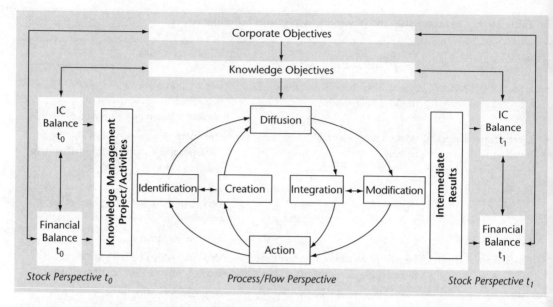

Fig. 36.1. Conceptual framework for integrating general management, the management of intellectual capital, and knowledge management

by a different group of practitioners; . . . [it] develops its own theoretical structures, research methods and modes of practice, though these may not be located on the prevailing disciplinary map; . . . [it] is communicated to those who have participated in the course of that participation and so, in a sense, the diffusion of results is initially accomplished in the process of their production; . . . [and, finally, it] is dynamic. It is problem-solving capability on the move. (p. 5)

First attempts at considering such a transdisciplinary perspective have been undertaken by scholars developing a knowledge-based theory of the firm, one that integrates both economic and behavioral assumptions and thinking from the economic and social sciences (Boisot 1998; Grant 1996; Kogut and Zander 1992; Spender 1996; Tsoukas 1996). It is to be hoped that continued integration of economic and behavioral concepts within a knowledge-based view of the firm will enhance the understanding the impact that 'knowledge' as a resource has on business performance.

References

Acland, D. (1976). 'The Effects of Behavioural Indicators on Investor Decisions: An Exploratory Study'. *Accounting, Organizations and Society*, 1/2–3: 133–42.

AICPA Special Committee on Financial Reporting (1994). *Improving Business Reporting: A Customer Focus: Meeting the Information Needs of Investors and Creditors*. New York: American Institute of Certified Public Accountants.

Anderson, C. A. and Bowman, M. J. (1976). 'Education and Economic Modernization in Historical Perspective', in L. Stone (ed.), *Schooling and Society: Studies in the History of Education*. Baltimore: Johns Hopkins University Press, 3–19.

Anderson, E. (1999). *Foundations of the American Customer Satisfaction Index*. Paper presented at the Vienna Conference on Customer Satisfaction: Theory and Measurement, 20–21 May.

Arthur, J. B. (1994). 'Effects of Human Resource Systems on Manufacturing Performance and Turnover'. *Academy of Management Journal*, 37: 670–87.

Arthur, W. B. (1996). 'Increasing Returns and the New World of Business'. *Harvard Business Review*, 74/4: 100–9.

Barnard, C. I. (1956). *The Functions of the Executive*. Cambridge, Mass.: Harvard University Press.

Bassi, L. J. and MacMurrer, D. (1999). *Indicators of Human Capital Investment and Outcomes from the American Society for Training and Development*. Paper presented at the OECD Conference on 'Measuring and Reporting Intellectual Capital: Experience, Issues, and Prospects'. Amsterdam, 9–11 June.

Becker, B. E., Huselid, M. A., Pickus, P. S., and Spratt, M. F. (1997). 'HR as Source of Shareholder Value: Research and Recommendations'. *Human Resource Management*, 36: 39–48.

Becker, G. S. (1964). *Human Capital*. Chicago: University of Chicago Press.

—— (1983). *Human Capital* (2nd edn). Chicago: University of Chicago Press.

—— (1993). *Human Capital* (3rd edn). Chicago: University of Chicago Press.

Beer, M. (1997). 'The Transformation of the Human Resource Function: Resolving the Tension between a Traditional Administrative and a New Strategic Role'. *Human Resource Management*, 36: 49–56.

—— Spector, B., Lawrence, P. R., Mills, D. Q., and Walton, R. E. (eds.) (1985). *Human Resource Management: A General Manager's Perspective*. New York: Free Press.

BMFT [Bundesministerium für Forschung und Technologie] (1996). *Zur technologischen Leistungsfähigkeit Deutschlands: Zusammenfassender Endbericht an das Bundesministerium für Bildung, Wissenschaft, Forschung und Technologie*. Hannover: Niedersächsisches Institut für Wirtschaftsförderung.

Boisot, M. H. (1998). *Knowledge Assets: Securing Competitive Advantage in the Information Economy*. New York: Oxford University Press.

Bornemann, M., Knapp, A., Schneider, U., and Sixl, K. I. (1999). *Holistic Measurement of Intellectual Capital*. Technical abstract for the OECD Conference on 'Measuring and Reporting Intellectual Capital: Experience, Issues, and Prospects'. Amsterdam, 9–11 June.

Boudreau, J. W. and Ramstad, P. M. (1997). 'Measuring Intellectual Capital: Learning from Financial History'. *Human Resource Management*, 36: 343–56.

Bourdieu, P. (1986). 'The Forms of Capital', in J. Richardson (ed.), *Handbook of Theory and Research for the Sociology of Education*. New York: Greenwood, 241–58.

Brigham, E. F. and Gapenski, L. C. (1988). *Financial Management: Theory and Practice*. Chicago: Dryden Press.

Brooking, A. (1997). *Intellectual Capital: Core Asset for the Third Millenium Enterprise*. London: Thompson.

Bruhn, M. and Grund, M. A. (1999). *Theory, Development and Implementation of National Customer Satisfaction Indices: The Swiss Index of Customer Satisfaction*. Paper presented at the Vienna Conference on Customer Satisfaction: Theory and Measurement, 20–21 May.

—— and Homburg, C. (1998). *Handbuch Kundenbindungsmanagement*. Wiesbaden: Gabler.

Burt, R. S. (1992). *Structural Holes: The Social Structure of Competition*. Cambridge, Mass.: Harvard University Press.

Carnevale, A. P. (1991). *America and the New Economy*. San Francisco: Jossey-Bass.

Cascio, W. (1987). *Costing Human Resources: The Financial Impact of Behavior in Organizations*. Boston: PWS-Kent.

Chatman, J. A. (1991). 'Matching People and Organizations: Selection and Socialization in Public Accounting Firms'. *Administrative Science Quarterly*, 36: 459–84.

Coleman, J. S. (1988). 'Social Capital in the Creation of Human Capital'. *American Journal of Sociology*, 94: 95–120.

—— (1990). *Foundations of Social Theory*. Cambridge, Mass.: Harvard University Press.

—— (1993). 'Properties of Rational Organizations', in S. M. Lindenberg and H. Schreuder (eds.), *Interdisciplinary Perspectives on Organization Studies*. Oxford: Pergamon Press, 79–90.

Conner, K. R. and Prahalad, C. K. (1996). 'A Resource-based Theory of the Firm: Knowledge versus Opportunism'. *Organization Science*, 7: 477–501.

Conti, T. (1993). *Building Total Quality.* London: Kluwer Academic.

Danish Memorandum (1997). *Intellectual Capital Accounts—Reporting and Managing Intellectual Capital.* The Danish Trade and Industry Development Council, May.

Deiaco, E., Hörnell, E., and Vickery, G. (eds.) (1990). *Technology and Investment: Crucial Issues for the 1990s.* London: Pinter.

Delaney, J. T. (1996). 'Unions, Human Resource Innovations, and Organizational Outcomes'. *Advances in Industrial and Labor Relations: A Research Annual* (Vol. 7). London: JAI Press, 207–45.

Dierkes, M. (1979). 'Corporate Social Reporting in Germany: Conceptual Developments and Practical Experience'. *Accounting, Organizations and Society,* 4: 87–107.

Drucker, P. (1993). *The Post-capitalist Society.* New York: Harper Collins.

Edvinsson, L. (1997). 'Developing Intellectual Capital at Skandia'. *Long Range Planning,* 30: 366–73.

—— and Malone, M. S. (1997). *Intellectual Capital: Realizing Your Company's True Value by Finding Its Hidden Brainpower.* New York: Harper Collins.

Ehrlich, C. J. (1997). 'Human Resource Management: A Changing Script for a Changing World'. *Human Resource Management,* 36: 85–90.

Elias, N. (1972). 'The Effects of Human Assets Statements on the Investment Decisions: An Experiment'. *Empirical Research in Accounting: Selected Studies,* 10: 215–33.

Eliasson, G. and Ryan, P. (1987). 'The Human Factor in Economic and Technological Change', in G. Eliasson and P. Ryan (eds.), *OECD Educational Monographs* (No. 3). Paris: OECD.

Ernst and Young (1997). *Enterprise Value in the Knowledge Economy—Measuring Performance in the Age of Intangibles.* Cambridge, Mass.: Ernst & Young Center for Business Innovation.

Fitz-enz, J. (1984). *How to Measure Human Resources Management.* New York: McGraw-Hill.

—— (1990). *Human Value Management: The Value-adding Human Resource Strategy for the 1990's.* San Francisco: Jossey-Bass.

Flamholtz, E. G. (1974). *Human Resource Accounting.* Encino, Calif.: Dickenson.

—— (1979). 'Towards a Psychotechnical Systems Paradigm of Organizational Measurement'. *Decision Sciences,* 10: 71–84.

—— (1980). 'The Process of Measurement in Managerial Accounting: A Psychotechnical Systems Perspective'. *Accounting, Organizations and Society,* 5: 31–42.

—— (1985). *Human Resource Accounting: Advances in Concepts, Methods, and Applications* (2nd edn). San Francisco: Jossey-Bass.

—— (1987). 'Valuation of Human Assets in a Securities Brokerage Firm: An Empirical Study'. *Accounting, Organizations and Society,* 12: 309–18.

Gibbons, M., Limoges, C., Nowotny, H., Schwartzman, S., Scott, P., and Trow, M. (1994). *The New Production of Knowledge.* London: Sage.

Gomez, P. (1993). *Wertmanagement: Vernetzte Strategien für Unternehmen im Wandel.* Düsseldorf: Econ.

Granovetter, M. S. (1992). 'Problems of Explanation in Economic Sociology', in N. Nohria and R. Eccles (eds.), *Networks and Organizations: Structure.* Boston: Harvard Business School Press, 25–56.

Grant, R. M. (1996). 'Toward a Knowledge-based Theory of the Firm'. *Strategic Management Journal,* 17 (Winter special issue): 109–22.

Grønhaug, K. and Nordhaug, O. (1993). 'Strategy, Competence, and Market Success'. *Proceedings American Marketing Association's Winter Conference,* 8: 111–17.

Grundstein, M. (1998). *Companies and Executives in Knowledge Management.* Available: http://www.brint.com/km/cko.htm

Gul, F. A. (1984). 'An Empirical Study of the Usefulness of Human Resources Turnover in Australian Accounting Firms'. *Accounting, Organizations and Society,* 9/3–4: 233–9.

Hall, R. (1989). 'The Management of Intellectual Assets: A New Corporate Perspective'. *Journal of General Management,* 15/1: 53–68.

Haney, D. S. (in press). 'Catching the Third Wave: Maximizing Knowledge Management through Culture and Leadership Engineering', in D. Moores (ed.), *Knowledge Management and Practice,* Cambridge, Mass.: MIT Press.

Harrell, A. M. and Klick, H. D. (1980). 'Comparing the Impact of Monetary and Nonmonetary Human Asset Measures on Executive Decision-making'. *Accounting, Organizations and Society*, 5: 393–400.

Hedlin, P. (1996). *Accounting Investigations*. Unpublished doctoral dissertation, School of Business, Stockholm University.

Hendricks, J. (1976). 'The Impact of Human Resource Accounting Information on Stock Investment Decisions: An Empirical Study'. *The Accounting Review*, 51: 292–305.

Hermanson, R. H. (1964). *Accounting for Human Assets*. East Lansing, Mich.: Bureau of Business and Economic Research, Michigan State University.

Höfner, K. and Pohl, A. (eds.) (1994). *Wertsteigerungs-Management: Das Shareholder-Value-Konzept: Methoden und erfolgreiche Beispiele*. Frankfurt am Main: Campus.

Howitt, P. (1996). 'On Some Problems in Measuring Knowledge-based Growth', in P. Howitt (ed.), *The Implications of Knowledge-based Growth for Microeconomic Policies*. Calgary: University of Calgary Press, 9–30.

Ijiri, Y. (1967). *The Foundations of Accounting Measurement*. Englewood Cliffs, NJ: Prentice Hall.

International Accounting Standards Committee (1998). *IAS 38*, September. London: IASC Publication.

Itami, H. and Roehl, T. (1987). *Mobilizing Invisible Assets*. Cambridge, Mass.: Harvard University Press.

Jacobs, J. (1965). *The Death and Life of Great American Cities*. London: Penguin Books.

Kaplan, R. S. and Norton, D. P. (1996). *The Balanced Scorecard: Translating Strategy into Action*. Boston: Harvard Business School Press.

Kogut, B. and Zander, U. (1992). 'Knowledge of the Firm, Combinative Capabilities, and the Replication of Technology'. *Organization Science*, 3: 383–97.

————(1996). 'What Firms Do? Coordination, Identity, and Learning'. *Organization Science*, 7: 502–18.

Kotler, P. and Bliemel, F. (1997). *Marketing-Management: Analyse, Planung, Umsetzung und Steuerung* (8th edn). Stuttgart: Schäffer-Poeschel.

Kubicek, H. (1999). *Erfordert die informationstechnische Entwicklung einen Funktionswandel im Management?* Paper presented at the 3. Berliner Kolloquium on 'Funktionswandel des Managements—Bestandsaufnahme und neue Perspektiven' organized by the Gottlieb Daimler- und Karl Benz-Stiftung together with the Institute of Management at the Free University Berlin, 6–7 May.

Kuznets, S. (1966). *Modern Economic Growth*. New Haven: Yale University Press.

Landsman, W. R. and Shapiro, A. C. (1995). 'Tobins's q and the Relation between Accounting ROI and Economic Return'. *Journal of Accounting, Auditing and Finance*, 10/1: 103–18.

Lawler, E. E. (1971). *Pay and Organizational Effectiveness: A Psychological View*. New York: Addison-Wesley.

Leibenstein, H. (1966). 'Allocative Efficiency vs. X-efficiency'. *American Economic Review*, 56: 392–415.

————(1976). *Beyond Economic Man: A New Foundation for Microeconomics*. Cambridge, Mass.: Harvard University Press.

Lev, B. (1997). 'The Old Rules No Longer Apply: Accounting Needs New Standards for Capitalizing Intangibles'. Available: http://www.forbes.com/asap/97/0407/034.htm

————(1999). 'R&D and Capital Markets'. *Journal of Applied Corporate Finance*, 11/4: 21–35.

Likert, R. (1961). *New Patterns of Management*. New York: McGraw-Hill.

————(1967). *The Human Organization: Its Management and Value*. New York: McGraw-Hill.

————(1973). 'Human Resource Accounting: Building and Assessing Productive Organizations'. *Personnel*, 4: 8–19.

MacDuffie, J. P. (1995). 'Human Resource Bundles and Manufacturing Performance: Organizational Logic and Flexible Production Systems in the World Auto Industry'. *Industrial and Labor Relations Review*, 48: 197–221.

Machlup, F. (1980). *Knowledge: Its Creation, Distribution, and Economic Significance*: Vol. 1. *Knowledge and Knowledge Production*. Princeton: Princeton University Press.

Machlup, F. (1984). *Knowledge: Its Creation, Distribution, and Economic Significance*: Vol. 3. *The Economics of Information and Human Capital*. Princeton: Princeton University Press.

Mandl, G. and Rabl, K. (1997). *Unternehmensbewertung*. Vienna: Ueberreuter.

Marr, R. (1982). 'Humanvermögensrechnung: Entwicklung von Konzepten für eine erweiterte Rechenschaftslegung in Unternehmen', in H. Schmidt (ed.), *Humanvermögensrechnung*. Berlin: de Gruyter, 45–50.

McColl-Kennedy, J. and Schneider, U. (1999). *Measuring Customer Capital: Why, What and How.* Paper presented at the Vienna Conference on Customer Satisfaction: Theory and Measurement, 20–21 May.

McGregor, D. (1960). *The Human Side of Enterprise*. New York: McGraw-Hill.

McLean, R. I. G. (1995). 'Performance Measures in the New Economy'. Toronto: *The Premier's Council*, March.

Merton, R. K. (1968). *Social Theory and Social Structure*. New York: Free Press. (Original work published 1948)

Miller, R. (1996). *Measuring What People Know: Human Capital Accounting for the Knowledge Economy.* Paris: OECD.

Miller, R. B. and Heimann, S. E. (1991). *Schlüsselkundenmanagement*. Landsberg am Lech: Verlag Moderne Industrie.

Nahapiet, J. and Ghoshal, S. (1998). 'Social Capital, Intellectual Capital and the Organizational Advantage'. *Academy of Management Review*, 23: 242–66.

Naugle, D. G. and Davies, G. A. (1987). 'Strategic-skill Pools and Competitive Advantage'. *Business Horizons*, 30/6: 35–42.

Nonaka, I. (1988). 'Creating Organizational Order out of Chaos: Self-renewal in Japanese Firms'. *California Management Review*, 30/3: 57–73.

——(1991). 'Managing the Firm as an Information Creation Process', in J. R. Meindl, R. L. Cardy, and S. M. Puffer (eds.), *Advances in Information Processing in Organizations: A Research Annual* (Vol. 4). Greenwich, Conn.: JAI Press, 239–75.

——and Takeuchi, H. (1995). *The Knowledge-creating Company: How Japanese Companies Create the Dynamics of Innovation*. New York: Oxford University Press.

Nordhaug, O. (1993). *Human Capital in Organizations*. Oslo: Scandinavian University Press.

North, K. (1998). *Wissensorientierte Unternehmensführung*. Wiesbaden: Gabler.

Oliver, J. and Flamholtz, E. (1978). 'Human Resource Replacement Cost Numbers, Cognitive Information Processing, and Personnel Decisions'. *Journal of Finance and Accounting*, 5/2: 137–53.

Petkoff, B. (1998). *Wissensmanagement: Von der computerzentrierten zur anwenderorientierten Kommunikationstechnologie*. Bonn: Addison-Wesley.

Pfeffer, J. (1997). 'Pitfalls on the Roads to Measurement: The Dangerous Liaison of Human Resources with the Ideas of Accounting and Finance'. *Human Resource Management*, 36: 357–66.

Prahalad, C. K. and Hamel, G. (1990). 'The Core Competence of the Corporation'. *Harvard Business Review*, 68/3: 79–91.

Preston, L. E., Rey, F., and Dierkes, M. (1978). 'Comparing Corporate Social Performance: Germany, France, Canada, and the U.S.' *California Management Review*, 20/4: 40–9.

Pulic, A. (1998). *Measuring the Performance of Intellectual Potential in the Knowledge Economy*. Paper presented at the 2nd World Congress on the Management of Intellectual Capital, McMaster University, Hamilton, Ontario, 21–24 January.

——and Bornemann, M. (1998). *Empirical Analysis of the Intellectual Potential of Value Systems in Austria*. Paper presented at the 2nd World Congress on the Management of Intellectual Capital, McMaster University, Hamilton, Ontario, 21–24 January.

Putnam, R. D. (1995). 'Bowling Alone: America's Declining Social Capital'. *Journal of Democracy*, 6/1: 65–78.

Rappaport, A. (1986). *Creating Shareholder Value: The New Standard for Business Performance*. New York: Free Press.

Rehäuser, J. and Krcmar, H. (1996). 'Wissensmanagement im Unternehmen', in G. Schreyögg and P. Conrad (eds.), *Wissensmanagement—Managementforschung* (Vol. 6). Berlin: de Gruyter, 1–40.

Reichheld, F. F. (1996). *The Loyalty Effect: The Hidden Force behind Growth, Profits, and Lasting Value*. Boston: Harvard Business School Press.

Reinhardt, R. (1999). *Management of Intellectual Capital: The Measurement Perspective of Knowledge*. Paper presented at the International Strategic Management Conference, Berlin, 3–6 October.

Rennie, M. (1998). 'Accounting for Knowledge Assets: Do We Need a New Financial Statement?' *International Journal of Technology Management*, 18: 648–60.

Roos, G. and Roos, J. (1997). 'Measuring Your Company's Intellectual Performance'. *Long Range Planning*, 30: 413–26.

Roos, J., Roos, G., Edvinsson, L., and Dragonetti, N. (1997). *Intellectual Capital: Navigating in the New Business Landscape*. London: New York University Press.

Sackmann, S., Flamholtz, E., and Lombardi Bullen, M. (1989). 'Human Resource Accounting: A State-of-the-Art Review'. *Journal of Accounting Literature*, 8: 235–64.

Sadowski, D. (1980). *Berufliche Bildung und betriebliches Bildungsbudget*. Stuttgart: Poeschel.

——(1991). 'Humankapital und Organisationskapital—Zwei Grundkategorien einer ökonomische Theorie der Personalpolitik in Unternehmen', in D. Ordelheide, B. Rudolph, and E. Büsselmann (eds.), *Betriebswirtschaftslehre und ökonomische Theorie*. Stuttgart: Metzlersche Verlagsbuchhandlung, 127–42.

Schmidt, H. (ed.) (1982). *Humanvermögensrechnung*. Berlin: de Gruyter.

Schneider, U. (1998). *Forming and Developing Intellectual Potential*. Paper presented at the 2nd World Congress on the Management of Intellectual Capital, McMaster University, Hamilton, Ontario, 21–24 January.

Schuler, R. S. (1992). 'Strategic Human Resources Management: Linking People with the Strategic Needs of Business'. *Organizational Dynamics*, 21/1: 18–32.

Schultz, T. W. (1961). 'Investment in Human Capital'. *American Economic Review*, 51/1: 1–17.

——(1981). *Investing in People: The Economics of Population Quality*. Berkeley: University of California Press.

Schwan, E. S. (1976). 'The Effects of Human Resource Accounting Data on Financial Decisions: An Empirical Test'. *Accounting, Organizations and Society*, 1/2–3: 219–37.

Sidow, H. (1991). *Key Account Management: Wettbewerbsvorteile durch kundenbezogene Verkaufsstrategien*. Landsberg am Lech: Verlag Moderne Industrie.

Siegert, T. (1994). 'Strategische Führung: Die finanzielle Dimension', in H. Siegwart, J. Mahari, and M. Abresch (eds.), *Meilensteine im Management: Finanzielle Führung, Finanzinnovationen und Financial Engineering*. Stuttgart: Schäffer, 63–79.

Simon, H. (ed.) (1997). *Kundenzufriedenheit: Konzepte, Methoden, Erfahrungen* (2nd edn). Wiesbaden: Gabler.

Spencer, L. (1986). *Calculating Human Resource Costs and Benefits*. New York: John Wiley and Sons.

Spender, J. C. (1996). 'Making Knowledge the Basis of a Dynamic Theory of the Firm'. *Strategic Management Journal*, 17 (Winter special issue): 45–62.

Spiceland, D. J. and Zaunbrecher, H. C. (1977). 'The Usefulness of Human Resource Accounting in Personnel Selection'. *Management Accounting*, 58/8: 29–40.

Stern, J. M., Stewart, G. B., and Chew, D. H. (1995). 'The EVA Financial Management System'. *Journal of Applied Corporate Finance*, 8/2: 32–46.

Stewart, T. A. (1997). *Intellectual Capital: The New Wealth of Organizations*. New York: Doubleday Currency.

Strassmann, P. A. (1997). *The Squandered Computer: Evaluating the Business Alignment of Information Technologies*. New Canaan, Conn.: Information Economics Press.

Sveiby, K. E. (1997). *The New Organizational Wealth: Managing and Measuring Knowledge-based Assets*. San Francisco: Berrett-Koehler.

Swanson, R. A. and Gradous, D. B. (1988). *Forecasting Financial Benefits of Human Resource Development*. San Francisco: Jossey-Bass.

Teece, D. J. (1998). 'Capturing Value from Knowledge Assets: The New Economy, Markets for Know-how and Intangible Assets'. *California Management Review*, 40/3: 55–79.

Tenbrock, C. (1997). 'Interview mit Alan Greenspan'. *Die Zeit*, 3 (10 January): 2.

Tobin, J. (1969). 'A General Equilibrium Approach to Monetary Theory'. *Journal of Money, Credit, and Banking*, 1: 15–29.

Tomassini, L. A. (1977). 'Assessing the Impact of Human Resource Accounting: An Experimental Study of Managerial Decision Preferences'. *Accounting Review*, 70/4: 1–17.

Tomer, J. F. (1987). *Organizational Capital: The Path to Higher Productivity and Wellbeing.* New York: Praeger.

——(1998). 'Organizational Capital and Joining-up: Linking the Individual to the Organization and to Society'. *Human Relations*, 51: 825–46.

Töpfer, A. (ed.) (1999). *Kundenzufriedenheit messen und steigern* (2nd edn). Neuwied: Luchterhand.

Tsoukas, H. (1996). 'The Firm as a Distributed Knowledge System: A Constructionist Approach'. *Strategic Management Journal*, 17 (Winter special issue): 11–25.

Ulrich, D. (1997). 'Measuring Human Resources: An Overview of Practice and a Prescription for Results'. *Human Resource Management*, 36: 303–20.

Vitale, M. R. and Mavrinac, S. C. (1995). 'How Effective Is Your Performance Measurement System?' *Management Accounting*, 77/2: 43–7.

Wagner, R. K. (1991). 'Managerial Problem-Solving', in R. J. Sternberg and P. A. Frensch (eds.), *Complex Problem Solving: Principles and Mechanisms.* Hillsdale, NJ: Erlbaum, 159–83.

——and Sternberg, R. J. (1985). 'Practical Intelligence in Real-world Pursuits: The Role of Tacit Knowledge'. *Journal of Personality and Social Psychology*, 48: 436–58.

Whiteley, R. (1991). *The Customer-driven Company: Moving from Talk to Action.* Reading, Mass.: Addison-Wesley.

Wintermantel, R. E. and Mattimore, K. L. (1997). 'In the Changing World of Human Resources: Matching Measures to Mission'. *Human Resource Management*, 36: 337–42.

Yeung, A. K. and Berman, R. (1997). 'Adding Value through Human Resources: Reorienting Human Resource Measurement to Drive Business Performance'. *Human Resource Management*, 36/3: 321–36.

Zink, K. (1995). *TQM als integratives Managementkonzept.* Munich: Hanser.

PART VIII

PUTTING LEARNING INTO PRACTICE

Introduction

This part is designed to complete the theoretical and practical framework that the editors of this handbook have sought to construct. The chapters present case studies that illustrate concepts from the theories and models presented in Parts I through VI and that demonstrate practices and tools described in Part VII. The cases are drawn from a variety of private- and public-sector organizations located in various European countries, Japan, and the United States. A clear message that emerges from the case studies is that the process of putting ideas into practice is a creative act. Organizational learning is not simply a matter of implementing a carefully thought-through plan or introducing a well-developed technique. Instead, it is a complex and interactive process that requires an understanding of the cultural and social embeddedness of organizations and an appreciation of barriers to organizational learning.

Information technology has the powerful potential to create and disseminate knowledge, but how can this potential be realized? Nonaka, Reinmöller, and Toyama illustrate how learning processes can be supported by information technology that enhances organizational interactions. Its possible role in knowledge creation is illustrated in examples from two retail companies, Seven-Eleven and Wal-Mart, that radically improved their retailing practices and knowledge management through the productive use of information technology systems. The authors conclude that organizations wishing to tap the potential of information technology must understand the general difference between information and knowledge and the difference between explicit and tacit knowledge. Information, they argue, is context free, whereas knowledge is grounded in value, experience, and action. Currently, knowledge management based on information technology focuses primarily on information or, at best, on explicit knowledge. Advancing the theory that knowledge is converted through processes of socialization, externalization, combination, and internalization, Nonaka, Reinmöller, and Toyama propose a framework for integrating information with both tacit and explicit knowledge through conversion-support tools (CSTools) and action–reflection-triggering (ART) systems. They illustrate that CSTools help support knowledge conversion, whereas ART systems trigger action or reflection to facilitate shifts between different modes of knowledge creation. They conclude that information technology needs to be complemented by CSTools and ART systems but that human insight is still the most important factor of knowledge management and organizational learning.

The contextual dimension of organizational learning is discussed in various chapters throughout the handbook, indicating that organizations must be aware of trends in their environments that may require the development of new knowledge, skills, processes, or structure. Scenario-planning is a specific approach that has been used and applied since the 1970s. It aims to prepare for changes in the sociopolitical, technological, and economic environment. The chapter by Galer and van der Heijden provides several case illustrations of how this technique can serve as a powerful form of experimental learning and process reflection. Scenario-planning, they argue, is a productive strategy for identifying indeterminate elements in the business environment and for specifying which factors can be predicted, thereby allowing organizations to perceive changes and potential discontinuities. They link scenario-planning to Kolb's cycle of experiential learning, in which learning is conceived of as a process of moving first from experiencing to reflecting, then on to conceptualizing and theory-building, to planning new action, and, finally, back to experiencing. Scenario-planning requires careful attention to both content and process, and it entails the ability to introduce multiple perspectives. Galer and van der Heijden differentiate between the perspectives of what they call the 'world of business' and 'the world of management'. They suggest that thinking in the world of business takes a strategic view and is particularly productive in theory development, integration, and reflection at the level of the organization in its environment, whereas thinking in the world of management focuses on the internal processes of the organization and change management, aiming at theory-sharing and joint action. The authors argue that it is only through the integration of these two worlds of thinking that the learning cycle can be completed.

An implicit assumption in much of the literature is that processes of organizational learning and knowledge creation progress smoothly along an anticipated trajectory once they have been set in motion. The chapter by Berthoin Antal, Lenhardt, and Rosenbrock challenges this assumption and presents four case studies to illustrate how organizational learning can be interrupted or blocked at different points in the process. The authors note that although barriers to organizational learning have received little attention in current theoretical literature, it is possible to generate propositions about where and why blockages to organizational learning might occur. They explore the propositions in four very different contexts (a community hospital, a chemical company, an automobile-parts manufacturer, and a privately owned transport company) and find that the risk of interrupted learning is high. In three of the four companies, learning processes lost their momentum. These case studies highlight the fact that organizational learning becomes blocked not only by the presence of certain conditions but also by the absence of other ones. In addition, the authors suggest that phase models of organizational learning processes do not adequately capture the dynamics of the learning processes and must be combined with the concept of interrupted learning cycles. A comparison of the four cases provides rich material for an analysis of how organizational culture and leadership can both obstruct and promote organizational learning. The empirical evidence presented by the authors reflects the overarching theme of this section: Putting learning theory into practice is not always smooth and predictable; management needs to be prepared to invest heavily in processes of organizational learning and knowledge creation.

The chapter by Krebsbach-Gnath offers a comprehensive analysis of the transformation of a retail fashion company in Germany, Adler Mode-märkte GmbH. The author examines tools, concepts, processes, and agents of organizational learning in order to illustrate the key variables and principles in the design and realization of a far-ranging transformation. The five-year process initiated with the arrival of a new managing director gave the organization a structure and culture in which the self-conception, future orientation, and leadership style fundamentally differed from the paradigm that used to dominate the organization. The longitudinal study offers the opportunity to explore the relationship between organizational learning and organizational change. The study shows how a participative process of developing a new organizational vision, coupled with the proactive diffusion of knowledge and significant investments in communication and training, serves to stimulate organizational learning. Krebsbach-Gnath traces how the organization achieved cognitive change that involved the transformation of tacit knowledge into explicit knowledge, enabling the organization to evaluate and create a new understanding of strategic options. The author suggests that constant monitoring of the change process and the publication of results promote learning from experience and lay the groundwork of a permanent capacity for organizational learning.

In order to illustrate how organizational learning occurs within and between organizations, the handbook features a case study that centers not on a specific company but rather an entire industry. The final chapter of this section, by de Haën, Tsui-Auch, and Alexis, provides a detailed case study on the development of good laboratory practices in the pharmaceutical industry. Drawing on first-hand experience, conversation, and interviews with numerous practitioners in the industry, the authors conclude that the learning of good laboratory practices takes more than just a cognitive understanding of the content of regulations, that it also requires a focus on the restructuring and rewriting of standard operating procedures within the organizations. Assessment of the various driving forces and stages of learning processes as well as of challenges to them leads to the finding that process implementation often demands both symbolic and material incentives. As de Haën, Tsui-Auch, and Alexis suggest, learning mechanisms, such as incentives, help introduce new norms and the unlearning of old habits. The authors also provide specific insights into organizational memory, a subject of which there is little systematic treatment in the field. The authors differentiate between the roles that written and oral communication play in the type of memory an organization has. Standard operating procedures constitute active memories of success, whereas individual experiences carry memories of failure. Thus, organizations with a high-loss or substitution rate of personnel will be less capable of learning from past failures than they could be. The authors suggest that, by including middle management, task forces, committees, and informal and interactive learning processes, organizations can strengthen and extend the practice of learning across time and space.

Case studies such as the ones presented in this part serve multiple purposes. They enable readers to explore the practical implications of theoretically derived concepts and models. They also illustrate how specific tools and techniques can actually be put into practice. These two purposes are rooted in the shift from the world of research to the domain of management practice. The reverse direction is equally important: Case studies also provide a forum in which to improve theory-building and generate new research questions. Detailed case analyses test the pertinence, explanatory power, and predictive ability of theories, the refinement of which can improve practice. This part suggests that organizational learning and knowledge creation can benefit a great deal from promoting the collaboration between academics with theoretical expertise and members of organizations undergoing change.

37 Integrated Information Technology Systems for Knowledge Creation

Ikujiro Nonaka, Patrick Reinmöller, and Ryoko Toyama

Because knowledge is considered an important source of firms' competitive advantage (Albert and Bradley 1997; Cohen 1998; Drucker 1994; Quinn 1992; Schendel 1995; Teece, Pisano, and Shuen 1997), today's firms are under increasing pressure to find a way to manage knowledge efficiently and effectively. In order to manage corporate knowledge strategically, many firms are employing the latest information technology (IT) as a set of knowledge-management tools. Papow and Papow (1998) estimated that 42 per cent of total U.S. investment capital in 1997 was spent on IT.

However, despite the continuing boom of and advances in IT, the productivity of knowledge-workers does not seem to have increased much (Drucker 1998a). Currently, IT is mostly used as a set of tools with which to improve efficiency in combining and disseminating existing information and explicit knowledge. These tools do not offer an integrated and holistic way of dealing with tacit and explicit knowledge in the context of the knowledge economy (Holsapple, Johnson, and Waldron 1996; Spender and Grant 1996). IT is not used to facilitate or trigger the creation of new knowledge. What is truly needed is an integrated system of information technology that elicits and supports knowledge creation.

In this chapter, we distinguish between information and knowledge and propose that conversion-support tools (CSTools) and action-reflection triggering (ART) systems be taken as the frameworks for such an integrated system. Drawing on the theory of knowledge creation (Nonaka 1990, 1994; Nonaka and Takeuchi 1995), we argue that CSTools and ART complement each other as an engine for knowledge-creating processes. The cases of Seven-Eleven Japan and Wal-Mart illustrate how these two internationally known companies, one Japanese and the other American, have come to be leading retailers. Though Wal-Mart and Seven-Eleven Japan are different in many respects, they both boast outstanding performance in turnover and profits. They have transformed retail competition and have sustained competitive advantage by using CSTools and ART systems in order to elicit and support their knowledge-creating processes.

Current Uses of IT by Firms

In today's business world, ITs, that focus on the efficient generation, accumulation, dissemination, utilization, and protection of information are becoming standard practice (Boisot 1998; Davenport, De Long, and Beers 1998; Ishida 1998; Schank 1997). Such IT tools are used to efficiently and effectively manage 'knowledge'. Many of them, however, actually deal with information management rather than knowledge management. Knowledge is fundamentally different from information. Information is indifferent to human values, context-free, and without intentions or commitment. Knowledge is grounded in values, experience, and purposeful action. Knowledge is meaningful; it is relational and context-specific, for it is continuously created in and justified in a changing environment. Like figure–ground relationships in Gestalt psychology, knowledge must be understood in its context in order to become meaningful. Knowledge is fragile, for it depends on beliefs and commitment. Mental models, perspectives, and intentions are essential to knowledge. Hence, knowledge can be defined as a meaningful set of information that constitutes a justified true belief and/or an embodied technical skill. Knowledge creation is a dynamic human process of justifying a personal belief directed toward the truth, of embodying a technical skill through practice, or both.

Despite the limitations of information-processing, there has been an increasing use of IT for intranets and data-warehousing in support of knowledge management in appropriating, connecting, disseminating, utilizing, and protecting information (Choo 1998; Churchill and Snowdon 1998; Ciborra 1993; Cohen 1998; Davenport and Pearlson 1998; Davenport and Prusak 1998; Earl 1996; Kelly and Allison 1999; Ruggles 1998). Information appropriating tools include software agents, browsers, search engines, and index tools. For example, Microsoft's software agents or voice-mail systems force customers to respond to questions structured like a decision tree and help a company appropriate information about its customers. Other examples are those free-service platforms (e.g. Microsoft's Hotmail.com®) and search engines (e.g. Yahoo® and Lycos®) that solicit and appropriate customer data automatically. However, the contexts of knowledge and their embeddedness in social relationships (Child and Heavens, Ch. 13 in this volume; Clancey 1997; Dyer and Singh 1998; Granovetter 1985; Lave and Wenger 1991; Wenger 1998) escape these tools; hence, such tools process information, not knowledge.

Second, databases, hyperlinks, and software discern relationships between documents from different sources and automatically connect dispersed information. For example, software that automatically tracks home-page traffic in order to evaluate Web performance by assessing the number and quality of visits (patterns of home-page use) creates elaborate transcripts of complex activities (e.g. path and access log analysis) that are difficult to observe otherwise. Home-pages that interact with visitors or databases of extensive user profiles such as Firefly.com (http://www.firefly.com), or Open Sesame (http://www.opensesame.com) have a wider media scope (see Büchel and Raub, Ch. 23 in this volume). They increase the amount of information on individuals by automatically connecting different data (Shout 1999; Turban, McLean, and Wetherbe 1999). With such systems, firms can utilize profiles of individual visitors' consumption preferences in order to provide superior services. Yet such systems are inflexible; oblivious to the contextual nature of knowledge, they pose sets of queries to anybody in an attempt to accumulate information that fits patterns of information.

Third, tools such as e-mail, intranets, and programs for customizing information that is sent to individuals increase the efficiency of sharing and disseminating information. For example, software that helps write logical documents or groupware for collaborative prototyping allows numerous members in different locations to join in a common process through computer networks. Groupware, such as Lotus Notes, use available memory and facilitate the communication and sharing of information and knowledge. Interactive exchange of large amounts of data by means of rich, versatile tools, such as computer-mediated communication, roomware, and community-ware helps communicate information and knowledge by emulating face-to-face communication (Büchel and Raub, Ch. 23 in this volume; Ishida 1998; Ishii and Ullmer 1997; Small 1998). But these sophisticated tools still fail to adapt to changing contexts and relationships.

Fourth, there are tools promoting an increased use of information and knowledge. One of them is workflow-management software that supports decision-making processes in product development projects and concurrent engineering. Such tools as graphical user interfaces (GUI), browsers based on Hypertext

Markup Language (HTML), drawing-assistants, and navigators support the easy use of databases and help users efficiently utilize their organization's stored information for their own needs. However, the emphasis is more on access to information or existing knowledge (McKenna 1997) than on the creation of knowledge.

Fifth, increasing the possibilities to free access requires the protection of proprietary information and knowledge. Tools such as firewalls around intranets and encryption technology for interactive exchange, net-based communication, or electronic commerce (e-commerce) are needed in order to protect knowledge and information from unauthorized access. Creating barriers to the free flow of information and knowledge, these protective tools can become barriers to knowledge creation.

There are several problems with the current use of IT tools in the interest of knowledge management. Because the challenge for IT is to facilitate a dynamic process of knowledge creation, not a static process of information management, one of the problems is that concepts such as 'company as computer', 'information-age company', and 'intelligent' companies emphasize efficiency in processing existing information thereby fail to help people see a company as a knowledge-creating organization. Even in fairly recent research (Choo 1998; Fuld 1995) scholars still portray knowledge creation as a cycle of scanning, monitoring, and discovering information in the environment (sense-making), numerically capturing that information (measuring), acquiring further information from outside the organization (organizational learning), and applying and exploiting the gathered information (decision-making). The continuance of this viewpoint shows that the legacy of the deterministic model of decision-making processes and information flows (Simon 1976) is still prevalent in today's knowledge management literature.

Second, current IT-based knowledge management focuses only on explicit knowledge, which can be expressed in words and numbers and easily shared, and fails to deal with tacit knowledge. Tacit knowledge, such as intuitions, hunches, and gut feelings, is hard to verbalize or communicate because it cannot be articulated and because it is embedded in particular contexts and actions (Polanyi 1966). IT-based knowledge management began to address the issue of the contextuality of knowledge with such tools as video conferencing, which provides visual, real-time communication. Yet the contribution of IT to the sharing of tacit knowledge is still limited. Although dissipative structures, synergetics, and complexity theory (Haken 1977; Kauffmann 1995; Prigogine 1996) have offered nondeterministic, but statistical, models for integrating and supporting the contextuality of knowledge (Kelly and Allison 1999; Sherman and Schultz 1998), business applications of such models are still rare.

Third, most knowledge-management tools are designed to extract profits through knowledge economies of scale by combining or reusing existing explicit knowledge, not to create new knowledge. This emphasis on combining existing knowledge reflects a lack of commitment to innovation (Cohen 1998). Many knowledge-management projects and knowledge-based systems are initiated by consultants in order to connect knowledge, compensate for lack of staff, expertise, time, or quality; or achieve operational effectiveness (Berthoin Antal and Krebsbach-Gnath, Ch. 21 in this volume; Earl and Scott 1998; Gill 1995; Porter 1996). The time span of knowledge initiatives and projects is rather short and lacks the long-term view needed to foster the knowledge-based competence of a company (see Weber and Berthoin Antal, Ch. 15 in this volume). The diffusion of best practices in the use of IT is rapid, and knowledge management that relies only on such packaged tools cannot gain sustainable competitive advantage (Davenport 1998; Porter 1996). Instead, firms should develop new visions (Dierkes, Marz, and Teele, Ch. 12 in this volume) and the capability of creating new knowledge (Teece, Pisano, and Shuen 1997) in order to make these visions a reality. What firms need to manage is the continuous and dynamic *process* of knowledge

creation rather than some particular knowledge or information at one point in time. To
foster knowledge creation, IT is needed that
both facilitates an efficient and effective knowledge-conversion process and increases the
speed and ease of switching from one such process to another.

The Knowledge-creating Process and Information Technology

In order to develop the knowledge-creation
framework for IT, we first need to explain the
basic theory of knowledge itself. As stated
above, there are two types of knowledge: explicit knowledge and tacit knowledge. They are
mutually complementary, and they interact
and interchange with each other. There are
four modes of interactions, or conversions, between explicit and tacit knowledge: Socialization (from tacit to tacit), Externalization (from
tacit to explicit), Combination (from explicit to
explicit), and Internalization (from explicit to
tacit). These four modes of knowledge conversion form a continuous spiral process, the SECI
process, out of which new knowledge is created
(Nonaka and Konno 1998; Nonaka and Takeuchi
1995). The SECI model is the theoretical framework for our analysis of the present state of and
opportunities for using IT to increase the
productivity of knowledge-workers (Kunifuji
1999; Nonaka, Umemoto, and Senoo 1996).

As seen in the previous section, the use of IT
in knowledge management has mainly focused
on information or, at best, on explicit knowledge. Thus, IT currently covers only one mode
of knowledge conversion, that is, combination.
The emphasis on combination impedes organizational innovation because (a) insightful variation through human sense-making and
improvisation (Weick 1998) is excluded and (b)
IT relies only on algorithmically accumulated
data to select new explicit knowledge that fits
patterns. Thus, one can discover patterns with
IT but cannot explain the meaning of the new
patterns. However, the creation of knowledge
calls for all four modes of knowledge conver-

sion and a contingent balance between them
(Davenport, De Long, and Beers 1998; Nonaka
and Reinmöller 1998). It is a dynamic and continuous process that requires management
by means of IT. One has to facilitate all four
knowledge-conversion processes and should
promote a continuous movement along the
knowledge-creation spiral (see Fig. 37.1). For
such purposes, we propose that CSTools be
used to facilitate each mode of knowledge conversion and that ART systems be used to trigger
the spiral movement among the different
modes of knowledge conversion.

CSTools

CSTools regulate and facilitate each mode of
knowledge conversion by building and sustaining platforms of knowledge-work, which we
refer to as *ba* (roughly means 'place'). *Ba* is the
context in which knowledge is shared, created,
and utilized (Nonaka, Toyama, and Byosière,
Ch. 22 in this volume; Nonaka and Konno
1998). *Ba* is where meaning is created. The
power to create knowledge is seated not just in
an individual but also in *interactions* with other
individuals or with the environment as well as
within the context in which such interactions
take place, that is, *ba*. Unlike abstract space
(Boisot 1998), knowledge emerges only from a
physical context, for 'there is no creation without place' (Casey 1997: 16). Each mode of knowledge conversion is supported by a different
kind of *ba*.

Socialization

Socialization is the process of sharing tacit
knowledge through joint experiences, and it is
supported by personal and face-to-face interactions, which we call the originating *ba*. Originating *ba* provides tacit knowledge to individuals
and organizations and hence goes beyond imports, facilitating the endogenous creation of
knowledge (Nonaka and Reinmöller 1998).
Physical, face-to-face interaction is best suited
to transmitting tacit knowledge, for only these
interactions can bring to bear the full range
of the human being's physical senses and

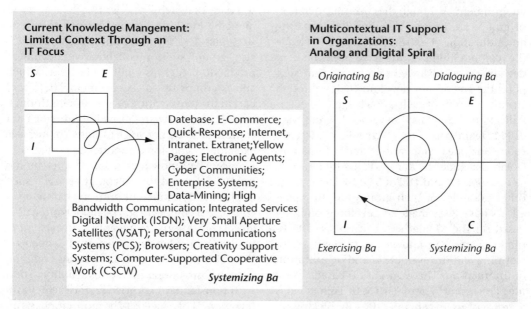

Fig. 37.1. The necessity of managing the knowledge-creation spiral—socialization, externalization, combination, and internalization (SECI)—through information technology (IT) and platforms of knowledge work (*ba*)

psychoemotional reactions, such as the sense of ease or discomfort. Hence, as implied by the notion of ontological interaction within a chaotic regime (Boisot 1998), the use of IT in socialization process is rather limited. However, interactive multimedia communication, such as video conferencing can create the impression of an encounter in virtual space, simulating the originating *ba* (Miyahara, Ino, Taniho, and Algazi 1998; Miyahara, Kotani, and Algazi 1998). Because the picture and sound quality of video conferences has improved a great deal, exchange is becoming possible within the tacit dimension of knowledge as well. Such technologies permit the attempt to convey part of the context, as happens during 'virtual conferences', in which participants share virtual, three-dimensional spaces or in which real persons become part of virtual environments (avatar). They also permit the attempt to increase opportunities to share tacit knowledge (Billinghurst, Weghorst, and Furness 1998; Churchill and Snowdon 1998). Furthermore, CSTools can facilitate socializa-

tion by allowing the organizational members to find out who has the knowledge they need. Sophisticated, IT-based yellow-page systems, such as the E. Prime at Hewlett-Packard or the system used at NTT Kanto, facilitate access to knowledge resources within a company (Carrozza 1998; Nonaka and Reinmöller 1999; Ushioda 1998).

Externalization

Externalization is the process of articulating tacit knowledge as explicit knowledge, such as concepts or diagrams, by means of dialogue, particularly dialogue in which metaphors or analogies are used frequently (Bohm 1980; Nichol 1996). This process is supported by what we call dialoguing *ba*, face-to-face interactions between people in a group. CSTools facilitate externalization by providing a virtual place for dialogues. Groupware, such as Lotus Notes, has been developed in order to support a group of users working on a common task and provide a virtual interface to a shared environment. Although the current generation of groupware focuses mainly on the sharing and utilization of existing explicit knowledge (i.e. combination), efforts have been made to develop more advanced groupware that supports the creation of new knowledge through the articulation of tacit knowledge (i.e. externalization). IBM has developed groupware called TeamFocus, an electronic conference room for idea generation and evaluation. Colab, developed by Xerox's Palo Alto Research Center (PARC) and DEFACTO, by Dentsu, are other examples of such groupware. In Japan, efforts have been made to develop groupware based on the KJ method, a card-based technique of creating knowledge through brainstorming and the evaluation and organization of information. The workstation-based Group Idea Processing System (GrIPS) by Fujitsu helps a group of users generate ideas by picking up virtual 'cards'. It uses electronic whiteboards and drawing diagrams with the help of software programs. This kind of IT exemplifies the attempt to support social cognition through network technology.

Combination

Combination is the process of connecting explicit knowledge from different sources into new or newly systemized knowledge, such as product specifications. This mode of knowledge conversion is supported by systemizing *ba*, or indirect interactions among people in a group. As noted above, the use of IT has mainly focused on facilitating this mode of knowledge conversion because IT is best suited to dealing with explicit knowledge and because it allows a large number of people to participate in the process. Combination requires ordered regimes (Boisot 1998). Tools such as data-mining and knowledge discovery in databases are algorithms that 'consist largely of some specific mix of three components', that is, the model, preference criteria, and the search algorithm (Fayyad, Piatetsky-Shapiro, and Smyth 1996: 31; Fayyad and Uthurusamy 1996).

An example of CSTools for combination is what is generally called an 'outline processor',

software that helps one write a logical document by breaking a topic down into several subtopics and then arranging them. There is also groupware for collaborative document production, such as Quilt by Bellcore, which allows groups up to sixteen members to take part in the joint writing of a document through e-mail. The software provides functions for comments in text or voice formats, for message exchanges, and for computer-supported conferences. Workflow-management software has been widely used for collaborative work, such as product development projects that involves concurrent engineering. The models often used are classifications, regressions, clusters, summaries, dependencies, links, and sequences. They therefore share the limitations common to such abstractions, including inability to deal with nonstandard knowledge or to achieve integration. 'There needs to be more emphasis on human–computer interaction and less emphasis on total automation' (Fayyad, Piatetsky-Shapiro, and Smyth 1996: 33).

Internalization

Internalization is the process of embodying explicit knowledge as tacit, operational knowledge through exercise, disciplined apprehension and energy-intensive processes, such as learning-by-doing and simulations. This mode of knowledge conversion is supported by personal and indirect interactions, which we call exercising *ba*. A person reading a manual in order to understand and assimilate the explicit knowledge written in it is a quintessential example of internalization. Information technology, including the Internet or intranets, provides 'open information spaces' and 'virtual universities' in the form of virtual exercising *ba* (Handa 1996; Hiltz and Wellman 1997).

Internalization is facilitated by CSTools such as expert systems, digitalized manuals, and networking technologies, which allow for asynchronous learning and remote communication, for which teachers and students do not have to be in the same place at the same time (Hiltz and Wellman 1997). Explicit knowledge to be internalized can be provided through on-line manuals, videos, Frequently Asked Questions (FAQ) lists, on-line narrative tools, on-line group discussions, computer-supported cooperative work, and three-dimensional avatars (Bers 1998; Orlikowski 1997; Turban, McLean, and Wetherbe 1999).

It is important to note that knowledge-conversion processes take place not only intraorganizationally but also interorganizationally. Interactions with customers or suppliers are important in the knowledge-creating process. We distinguish between four different levels of knowledge interactions with business partners, such as customers or suppliers (see Fig. 37.2). At level 1, only the explicit knowledge of customers or suppliers is gathered, combined, and utilized. At level 2, companies support customers or suppliers to externalize their own tacit knowledge. At this level of interaction, companies facilitate and stimulate externalization through customers and then capture the new explicit knowledge. At level 3, companies share tacit knowledge with a group of customers or partners and externalize it in order to improve their products or services for that group. At this level, companies engage in limited socialization. At level 4, knowledge is widely shared on the market so that companies can innovate. Interpretations of archetypes

and of key metaphorical visuals are a way to gain access to this universal, tacit knowledge (Zaltman and Coulter 1995). The externalization of tacit knowledge on this intertemporal, interregional, intercultural, iconological, and mythical level goes beyond segmentation and reflects the commitment of companies to universal values such as beauty and truth. CSTools must support interaction with business partners at all four levels.

ART systems in support of the Knowledge-creation Spiral

CSTools support each of the four previously explained knowledge-conversion processes. For knowledge to be created continuously and dynamically, these four modes must shift into each other, creating a spiral movement. We propose that the ART system serve as a conceptual model with which to account for information technology that triggers the spiral. CSTools and ART systems complement each other in terms of how they affect the conversion processes. As an integrated system, the two work together to help run an organizational engine for the knowledge-creating process. CSTools provide the systems with efficient conversion, that is, with fuel for the engine. At the

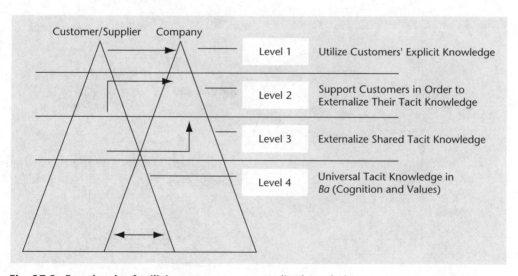

Fig. 37.2. Four levels of utilizing customer or supplier knowledge

same time, ART systems complement the engine with triggers for creative conversion, that is, with the ignition.

ART systems facilitate the process of shifting from one conversion mode to the next on the knowledge-creation spiral by sensing discrepancies between them and utilizing those discrepancies as triggers. Hence, ART systems trigger continual shifts from sharing (socialization), to articulating (externalization), to connecting (combination), to embodying (internalization), and on again to sharing along the knowledge-creation spiral, thereby advancing efficient knowledge-conversion processes (see Fig. 37.3). ART systems comprise affordances, novelties, and differences that lead to action and reflection. ART systems are used, for example, in pop-up interfaces that require the interactive input of data or in scheduled queries that remind users to act. Besides digital systems, the physical environment, too, can provide effective triggers.

ART systems trigger creative conversion by employing rhythms (i.e. recurring sequences), signals of urgency, or crisis that drive human beings to take action or to step back and reflect. ART systems trigger changes by stopping organizational members from doing the things they have been doing and forcing them to start new things. In contexts where multiple experiences lead to the accumulation of rich tacit knowledge, triggers are needed to stimulate people to consider sharing this tacit knowledge (socialization) or to articulating it as explicit knowledge (externalization). This reflection then triggers action to connect explicit knowledge (combination) or to embody explicit knowledge (internalization). Action then needs to be followed by reflection prompted by physical encounter and shared experience (socialization) so that movement continues along the knowledge spiral. The alteration between reflection and action is essential to knowledge creation.

ART systems link analog and digital systems in order to create effective support modes of knowledge creation. ART systems are not just IT but a complex gestalt of technology, human factors, and dialogue interactions between IT and human-based systems. Interactive ques-

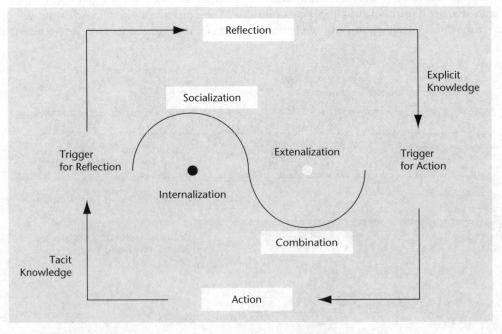

Fig. 37.3. Action–reflection-triggering systems for knowledge creation

tioning, GUI, and real or virtual encounters enable the shift to externalization from socialization. At the Fuji Xerox FX Palo Alto Laboratory, monthly reports on research results are posted on the intranet. Because these results have to be prepared by the individual researchers, these people are under pressure to create new ideas and knowledge. Weekly meetings for idea presentations constantly push organizational members to put their ideas into words that will be selected and included in databases. Placing limits on the quantity or quality of generated ideas and hypotheses triggers a shift from externalization to combination. Algorithms can help combine explicit knowledge into patterns. These patterns can be linked to the need for action and hence can initiate internalization. One can trigger a shift from combination to internalization by putting limits such as sales targets, on the number of experiments. If sales targets are met, the experiment is automatically justified and rolled out for internalization. Other triggers can be provided through training sessions, assignments, or regularly recurring periods of action (scheduling). Time limits on the number of successfully completed exercises can be used as triggers to end asynchronous learning and initiate new socialization.

As described above, ART systems trigger the dynamism of conversion. They utilize triggers for action that avoid excessive accumulation of data (paralysis by analysis) and triggers for reflection in order to avoid action without concepts. Integrated with CSTools, ART systems enhance the knowledge-creating process of a firm. In the following section, we look at one case study on each of two companies, Wal-Mart and Seven-Eleven Japan, to understand how they use CSTools and ART systems in their respective knowledge-creating processes.

Two Case Studies: Seven-Eleven Japan and Wal-Mart

We had a number of reasons for selecting Seven-Eleven Japan and Wal-Mart for study.

First, the industry in which they operate, retailing, has been adopting IT faster than other industries. Second, Seven-Eleven Japan and Wal-Mart outperform other retailers in terms of sales and profits. Third, both companies radically changed retailing through their use of IT. Fourth, at a time when increasing diffusion of standard IT systems has seriously threatened the corporate strategies of many companies, Wal-Mart and Seven-Eleven Japan have established unique prototypes of integrated systems for knowledge creation that support their strategies. Finally, Seven-Eleven Japan and Wal-Mart sell the knowledge that they create. Seven-Eleven Japan is a franchise company that sells knowledge to franchisees. Wal-Mart leads a large network of suppliers that purchase access to Wal-Mart's knowledge.

The configuration, integration, and utilization of IT in organizational knowledge-creating activities is more important to knowledge creation than hardware is. Wittgenstein (1984: 3.203) defined the meaning of tools as their use in practice. By the same token, we understand the meaning of information technology to be the function of its use in corporate practice.

The equifinality of both companies' use of IT creates more similarities than differences. This is a kind of family resemblance (Wittgenstein 1958). The identities of both companies, however, are distinct and strengthened because CSTools reinforce the underlying corporate values. Seven-Eleven Japan and Wal-Mart employ different IT systems and emphasize different functions. They strive, however, to achieve similar results—to create knowledge. This shared goal of using IT to create knowledge throughout the company is pursued differently (see Table 37.1). Seven-Eleven Japan and Wal-Mart differ in terms of perspective, complexity, and the ways in which their CSTools and ART systems are utilized. First, Wal-Mart emphasizes digital integration. Seven-Eleven Japan invests in both analog and digital systems. Second, Wal-Mart has a small number of large stores offering a large number of items with low margins of profit. Seven-Eleven Japan has a large number of small stores offering a small number of items with high margins of profit. Third,

Table 37.1. Resemblance and identity: Information technology at Seven-Eleven Japan and Wal-Mart

Family resemblance	Seven-Eleven Japan	Wal-Mart	Different identities
Complexity			
Large numbers of retail units and employees	Franchise system, small retailers, 7,000 shops and few employees	Ownership of large stores, 2,857 stores and 780,000 employees	Relative difference in size
Coverage of domestic markets	Large number of stores in densely populated areas	Stores located in rural, mid-town locations	Store location
Internationalization	Shops concentrated in Japan	Growth strategy; active globally	Importance of growth
Dominant strategy	Bottom-up; focus on coverage of local area	Top-down; integration of domestic network	Store-development process
Customers	7 million a day; young, male, frequent	90 million a day; families	Core customers
Chain stores	Few test shops managed directly	Chains of different format, direct management	Autonomy/control
Partners/vendors	Approx. 1,000	300–500	Network
Perspective			
Products and variety	Fresh meals, snacks, fresh bread, fast-food	Food, bulk goods, grocery	Freshness (needs), low price (supply)
Fast turnover	Multiple deliveries per day; 'public refrigerator'	'Just-in-time'	Purpose of speed (value or volume)
Importance of shop floor	Importance of place (bura-bura, i.e. walking around, employees, field counselors)	Importance of space (KDD[b], data-mining)	Place (genba), space (knowledge colonies)
Conversion-support tools and action–reflection-trigger systems			
Human-based information systems	Multiple systems to share local knowledge (triggers)	Building of regional expertise (by regional managers)	Level of knowledge
Data-mining	Purchase, POS[a], and 'raw' customer data	Purchase and POS data	Input (quality/quantity)
Information technology system	Below 3,500 items; POS; itemized analysis	Approx. 100,000 items; large-scale system (next to Pentagon)	Scale of IT systems
Integration of human-based and IT systems	Built-in triggers to shift from human-based to IT systems	Stress on efficiency of digital integration	Decentralization
Generation of hypotheses	All organizational members are stimulated to generate new ideas	Ideas are collected, concept discovery through IT, managers' ideas	Division of creative work
Testing	POS data, top management, shops	POS data	Type of experiments

[a] Point-of-sale.
[b] KDD = Knowledge discovery in database.

Wal-Mart aims to achieve a high degree of systemization of the knowledge processes and concept discovery by accumulating large pools of explicit data. Seven-Eleven Japan aims to maximize the tacit knowledge that is captured through direct encounters with customers in multiple places (*ba*). Seven-Eleven Japan's emphasis on customers' knowledge and local markets helps continuously develop new products with high value-added. Wal-Mart's focus on internal knowledge processes and its value chain provide the basis for its ability to offer low prices. What Wittgenstein (1958) called family resemblance can be observed in the two companies' prototypical approaches to using IT. This resemblance consists in the efforts of the two companies to create knowledge continuously. Fourth, Wal-Mart and Seven-Eleven Japan differ in the relative weight they give their ART systems. In their attempt to sustain organizational knowledge creation, the two companies integrate complementary human-based systems and technology-based systems with different emphasis.

Seven-Eleven Japan

Despite its image of inefficiency, the Japanese distribution and retailing sector has recently been said to be setting standards in efficiency worldwide (Drucker 1998*b*). Seven-Eleven Japan is the most profitable retailer in Japan in terms of both profits and sales–profit ratio. Seven-Eleven Japan is a franchiser of convenience stores that capitalizes on market knowledge by using ART systems (Nonaka, Reinmöller, and Senoo 1998). Seven-Eleven Japan emphasizes the embeddedness of technology within the contexts of purchasing and interaction.

In 1973 Ito-Yokado, a Japanese supermarket chain, and Southland Corporation, the operator and franchiser of 7-Eleven stores in the United States,[1] reached a licensing agreement on convenience store operation. Ito-Yokado established Seven-Eleven Japan and opened the

first Seven-Eleven store in 1978. In 1991 it acquired the Southland Corporation. Today, the number of stores in the chain of Japan Seven-Eleven stores has increased to over 7,000. Each store sells some 3,000 items, of which about 70 per cent are replaced every year. Every day seven million customers buy at stores of Seven-Eleven Japan. Their buying behavior is characterized by frequent, brief stops at the stores. Seventy per cent of the customers visit a store two times or more, and 55 per cent stay less than five minutes (Usui 1998).

In order to understand Seven-Eleven Japan, it is crucial to remember that the company is a franchiser that sells knowledge. The company charges its franchisees for services, receives royalties for trademarks, and collects leasing fees for equipment such as its information system, display racks, and refrigerated cases. To provide these services to the franchisees, Seven-Eleven Japan makes extensive use of quintessential explicit knowledge, such as manuals for store operation, employee training, and franchisee recruiting or training. This heavy reliance on explicit knowledge differentiates Seven-Eleven Japan from most other Japanese companies.

Yet the outstanding success of Seven-Eleven Japan is largely based on its capitalization on knowledge about its customers and its more than 1,000 business partners (Mitsugi, Takimoto, and Yamazaki 1998). Toshifumi Suzuki, the CEO of Seven-Eleven Japan, de-emphasizes growth as a key goal for future development. He has clearly stated that Seven-Eleven Japan will continue to achieve high margins by offering high value-added in innovative products rather than by offering high volumes with commodities at low margins (Suzuki 1998). Seven-Eleven Japan has pursued a multidynamic approach to knowledge management by striking a balance between supportive information technology and human insight (Usui 1998). In this approach, several *ba* are linked by means of CSTools, especially ART systems.

CSTools at Seven-Eleven Japan

Seven-Eleven Japan shuns the introduction of a computerized, automatic ordering-replenishing system and emphasizes the importance of

---

[1] The stores in the chain started in the United States belong to 7-Eleven Inc. The separate group of stores started up later in Japan are referred to everywhere as Seven-Eleven Japan.

systems that process information together with context. Suzuki explained that customers buy superior products, not IT. The key to understanding Seven-Eleven Japan is its successful use of IT together with human-based systems. For Seven-Eleven Japan, human insights are the most important resource for its operation, and IT is a tool that helps its human-based knowledge-creating system by providing speed and efficiency. Point-of-sale (POS) systems help in aggregating data and obtaining detailed information on the purchasing behaviors of customers. 'But this is only the data about the past. It does not make sense to extrapolate from the data to forecast the future' (Suzuki 1998: 44, our translation). Moreover, POS data 'do not explain why something did sell well' (Kunitomo 1998: 243).

At over 7,500 Seven-Eleven stores in Japan, store owners and part-time employees alike can place orders through easy-to-use, handheld computers called 'graphic-order terminals'. Owners and employees pay close attention to each item on the shelves and to customers' buying behaviors. When they place orders, they draw on their tacit knowledge in order to create their own hypotheses about what items will sell well, how much or how many will sell, and how they can be sold.

They gain tacit knowledge through experience-based intuitions that they accumulate through socialization with the customers. In this sense, each local store is an originating *ba*, where tacit knowledge is created and shared through face-to-face interactions with customers at levels 2 and 3 (see Fig. 37.2). It is therefore important for store owners and employees to take their human insights into consideration when placing the orders most suitable for their outlets. For example, through a leisurely conversation with a customer, a part-time employee might learn that there will be a festival at a local school the next day. The employee then uses his or her experience and insight when making an order for boxed lunches, generating a hypothesis about how many extra boxed lunches will be sold the next day. Hence, it is human insight, not IT, that makes the difference. CSTools, such as detailed POS

data, graphic-order terminals, and Seven-Eleven Japan's telecommunications network, help store owners and their employees efficiently and effectively externalize such tacit knowledge into hypotheses.

Each hypothesis is tested by an actual order, with confirmation or rejection being based on the POS data that are generated through the experimental order. Such data might show changes of sales or of profit-per-piece that are related to the order. Field counselors or owner consultants, who regularly visit local stores in order to listen to store owners and give advice, collect successful hypotheses. Selected hypotheses are presented at headquarters during a weekly conference attended by all field counselors, top management, and headquarters staff. Hence, the weekly conference works as a systemizing *ba*, where the combination of explicit knowledge takes place.

The field counselors then bring back the hypotheses to the Seven-Eleven Japan stores that they visit and encourage store owners and employees to test them in their stores as well. Thus, local employees' knowledge of and insight in customer needs are shared with other employees, combined, and made part of the organizational knowledge of Seven-Eleven Japan. Training for owners, including intensive periods of computer analysis, preparation, and simulations on how to run a Seven-Eleven store, support internalization. Store situations that engage both body and mind are enacted in order to familiarize new owners with explicit knowledge about the franchise system. On-the-job training is emphasized throughout one's career at Seven-Eleven Japan. New employees follow a career path that starts on the shop floor, as their first exercising *ba*, and leads up to the management positions. Although Seven-Eleven Japan runs only a few directly managed stores, these stores are important exercising *ba*, where young entrants internalize knowledge of the company, the business, and the market.

Seven-Eleven Japan has been investing heavily in state-of-the-art IT which is epitomized by the POS system. The data warehouse accumulates more than one year's worth of sales data per item and supports refined analysis in order to forecast sales (Okamoto 1998). The *tanpin kanri* (itemized inventory management) system accumulates 4.5 terabytes of data, that is, twenty-four million entries generated daily by seven million customers. The Integrated Services Digital Network (ISDN) and the fifth generation of Seven-Eleven Japan's information system were introduced in order to leverage high-speed on-line information exchange. Computers with substantial processing power were installed in all stores and integrated by satellite data transmission in order to increase productivity and reduce costs. Another tool is the graphic-order terminal, which is used in the stores in order to simplify and speed up the ordering process and delivery (Mitsugi, Takimoto, and Yamazaki 1998). Despite this considerable investment in technology, Seven-Eleven Japan emphasizes the importance of context for knowledge creation.

ART systems at Seven-Eleven Japan

ART systems manage the interface between the analog human factors and digital IT in order to trigger continual shifting along the knowledge spiral. Seven-Eleven Japan has established ART systems that generate routines to shift from one mode of knowledge conversion to another. This shifting comes about through (a) solicitation of action and reflection, (b) reinforcement of organizational culture, and (c) the scheduling of encounters for starting or terminating action and reflection.

First, soliciting hypotheses by using GUI helps employees of Seven-Eleven Japan absorb new information on sales performance and develop hypotheses easily. The employees using the graphic-order terminals stand before the racks as they input and transmit orders and are therefore able to respond directly to the current situation in the stores. ART systems fuse digital data and the insights of employees through terminals, providing for simple articulation of new ideas.

Second, changes from one mode of knowledge to another are also triggered by the organizational culture of Seven-Eleven Japan, which reinforces the attention paid to customers

and helps articulate differences. Seven-Eleven Japan has a business creed: Adapt to change and keep to basics. The four principles of the creed are freshness, the best assortment of goods, cleanliness, and friendliness to customers. These principles are continually disseminated throughout the company in order to reinforce the consistency of Seven-Eleven Japan's corporate culture and behavioral routines. They provide criteria for all operational procedures as well as guidelines for store owners, full-time employees, and part-timers. This organizational culture is reinforced by the IT system, for it imposes a rhythm on activities. For example, IT supports the task of ordering and the receipt of the several deliveries needed each day in order to maintain the high standards of freshness and quality of Seven-Eleven's food assortment. The daily order of merchandise and the multiple daily deliveries to Seven-Eleven Japan keep the chain's employees focused on constant changes in sales and customer behavior.

Third, regular encounters and meetings are frequently used for triggering action to produce ideas at various levels. On the shop floor, employees encounter customers every day and field counselors each week. Employees externalize their hypotheses in the act of ordering or in interaction with the field counselors. Field counselors meet their peers on a weekly basis in Tokyo and keep in contact with headquarters and their offices via e-mail and voice mail. At headquarters, the managers have a group meeting with their leader every Monday in order to discuss current problems. The participants of the meeting are well prepared with the statistical and digital data available at Seven-Eleven Japan and are ready to make presentations about their field of responsibility. Suzuki expects the managers who are facing problems to leave the meeting so that they can immediately solve these problems and then return to report on the actions taken as well as on the early results of these actions. Thus, Suzuki triggers immediate action by intensive face-to-face communication. The field counselors meet in Tokyo every Tuesday for a meeting and a speech by Suzuki. On these occasions, representatives from all areas of Japan attend (at a high cost to Seven-Eleven Japan) and engage in dialogue in a shared space. After the meeting they return to their stores and develop ideas locally or implement ideas externalized during the meeting.

In summary, Seven-Eleven Japan triggers action and reflection in four phases (see Fig. 37.4): (a) IT is used as a trigger for the conversion of frontline knowledge into ideas; (b) insights of employees trigger experimentation with the POS data; (c) verification of hypotheses in the database leads to experimentation in other regions; and (d) justified new knowledge (proven hypotheses) is disseminated among and utilized in all stores. Thus, Seven-Eleven Japan uses a series of triggers that alternate between action and reflection. The generation of ideas is continuously stimulated, and a rigid selection process allows for the instant verification of ideas ensuring that only valuable ideas are selected.

Wal-Mart

Sam Walton was convinced that consumers would appreciate a discount store with a wide assortment of merchandise and friendly service. He opened his first store in 1962, and a success story in the history of retailing began. In 1998 the Wal-Mart[2] group employed more than 780,000 people in the United States (with an additional 130,000 abroad) and served ninety million customers a week in its discount stores (Wal-Mart), grocery stores (supercenters), membership warehouse clubs (SAM's Clubs), and deep discount warehouse outlets (Bud's Discount City) (Wal-Mart 1998a).

Growth is of great importance to Wal-Mart. David G. Glass, the president, has asserted that he wants to 'meet aggressive growth targets that enhance shareholder value' 'through continued and steady expansion into new communities both inside and outside the United States' (Wal-Mart 1997a, b). As of November 1998, there were 2,857 Wal-Mart stores in the

---

[2] Data on Wal-Mart are courtesy of NCR 1998; Wal-Mart 1996, 1997b; Wal-Mart 1998a, b, d.

United States, supported by nine food centers and thirty-five merchandise centers. Wal-Mart plans to open forty new discount stores, approximately 150 new supercenters, and between ten and fifteen new SAM's Clubs in 1999. In total, Wal-Mart will expand store square-footage by 9 per cent. Internationally, Wal-Mart has expanded to Canada, South America, Asia, and Europe. Aggressive store growth is also planned for 1999, with Asia being 'an important part of [Wal-Mart's] long-term growth strategy' (Wal-Mart 1996, 1998d). Wal-Mart is also promoting Internet-based e-commerce. In 1997 Wal-Mart offered twenty-seven categories with more than 40,000 items and introduced a new payment card security mechanism (Secure Electronic Transaction) in promoting itself on-line.

Wal-Mart aspires to offer low prices and high levels of customer service everyday. Walton believed that each store should be managed individually in order to reflect the values and aspirations of its regional customer base. Bob L. Martin, president and CEO of Wal-Mart International, stated that the goal of enhancing and internationalizing the Wal-Mart shopping experience for customers shall be achieved by earning their trust in local markets. Thus, Wal-Mart engages in scanning the environment and in making sense of changes taking place at each location. Each store's hometown identity is a factor in its popularity with consumers.

CSTools at Wal-Mart

Wal-Mart's leaders are convinced that the degree of detail considered in analyses of purchase data plays a decisive role in the satisfaction of customers. Therefore, new information technologies are used to analyze single-item sales or purchase patterns. Wal-Mart has trademarked the term 'knowledge colony' as the proprietary label identifying and protecting the company's large investments in sophisticated IT systems. A knowledge colony, like a learning organization, includes methods such as best-practice circles; simulations; information coaching; recognition and reward systems for large-scale, fact-based empowerment; and decision and measurement systems. A know-

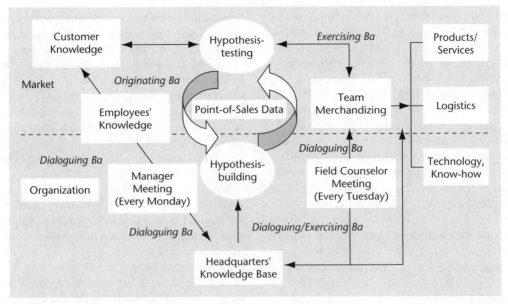

Fig. 37.4. Conversion-support tools, action–reflection-triggering systems, and platforms of knowledge-work (*ba*) at Seven-Eleven Japan

ledge colony refers to the collection of information that is used to make specific strategic decisions for regional approaches to inventory management. Wal-Mart aims to reinforce localization within a business system characterized by the centralized integration of explicit knowledge.

Since its early beginnings, Wal-Mart has aggressively invested in IT (Caldwell 1996) and has exchanged and compiled explicit knowledge with its business partners (level 1 of interaction). In 1997, Wal-Mart tripled the capacity of its data warehouse by installing new NCR Inc. equipment having up to 24 terabytes and investing in a satellite system for data transfer. At the Wal-Mart discount stores, the NCR Top End system offers a unified computing environment for centralized analysis of sales data so that headquarters can analyze and systemize explicit knowledge. In order to speed up data-processing, the stores are equipped with Telzon 960 wireless handheld terminals. These devices were introduced in 1995, and each store uses twenty to thirty terminals. Terminals and bar codes help Wal-Mart check both information

on the sales of each product in the previous year and detect problems. Today, Wal-Mart leads the retail industry in the use of highly integrated information systems that allow for superior asset management, quick response, e-commerce, and system-assisted replenishing of merchandise (Humphrey 1997; Turban, McLean, and Wetherbe 1999; Wal-Mart 1998c).

Wal-Mart attempts to integrate its digital systems in order to automate decision-making so that efficiency can be maximized. The fundamental achievements of Wal-Mart's IT systems are trend analysis, inventory management, and customer behavior analysis. The complexity arising from the increasing scale and scope of Wal-Mart's activities requires centralization of decision-making processes. IT is employed in order to facilitate the development of ideas at headquarters through discovery of meaningful patterns in large amounts of data. Sales of individual items at individual stores are analyzed in order to calculate seasonal profiles of each item (Turban, McLean, and Wetherbe 1999). Consumption patterns are detected and substantiated by means of integrated data about past purchases. The accumulated POS data can offer detailed information about when individual products were purchased, in which store, and what the remaining stock per item is. The data-mining software enables analysts to calculate the seasonal trends of store items, and build predictive models for system-assisted replenishment and tactical purchasing decisions. This system contributes to efficient management of Wal-Mart's 700 million unique store/item combinations and decreases the costs of delivery and inventory. Although Wal-Mart's sales in 1997 rose at a rate of 12 per cent these information systems helped reduce stock by 3 per cent and achieved inventory rates of 96 per cent (Wal-Mart 1997b, 1998a). At Wal-Mart this system for efficiently converting explicit knowledge is called 'just-in-time' replenishment.

IT is used not only for placing orders and internally sharing knowledge but also for facilitating the interactions between Wal-Mart and its suppliers and customers. For instance, customers can verify prices and check data on merchandise by reading the bar code. Another example of IT's utility is Collaborative Planning Forecasting and Replenishment, which aims to build an information system for interaction with Wal-Mart's vendors and other allies in order to automate interaction and the testing of new products. The system is a standardized tool that reduces costs and improves the integration of Wal-Mart and its partners.

The goals for IT at Wal-Mart are retail merchandising, the integration of store and product analysis, and supply-chain and profitability management. Through technology the time needed for the flow of information from stores to headquarters and suppliers has been reduced from seven days to two.

The backbone of Wal-Mart's supply-chain management is Retail Link. Retail Link enables on-line surfing and systematic searches for data and patterns. It is a systemizing *ba* that connects knowledge from buyers and vendors or partners in order to improve inventory and sales management. It solicits data, such as prices and specifications, and digitally conveys orders and requirements. The program allows buyers and vendors to monitor inventory and sales and to customize assortment and quantity at each store. Buyers and vendors account for 35,000 of the queries made to the data warehouse each week. For new partners, Wal-Mart offers training classes, videos, and help via telephone or e-mail. The company thereby creates access to the data and interests in hidden public knowledge shared by its partners, and it stimulates knowledge conversion beyond organizational boundaries.

Wal-Mart uses CSTools mostly to improve inventory rates, and little data are available on the context of each purchase. Wal-Mart emphasizes the accumulation of, combination of, and interaction with the explicit knowledge of customers (level 1). Now that large investments in IT have been made, top managers admit that they do not yet know what to do with the ocean of data at their disposal. Besides conventional schemes for proposals, there are a few CSTools that facilitate the articulation of new hypotheses (Levels 2 and 3).

ART systems at Wal-Mart

ART systems provide for the shifts between conversion modes through (a) solicitation of action and reflection, (b) reinforcement of organizational culture, and (c) the scheduling encounters for starting or terminating action and reflection. At Wal-Mart, however, ART systems mostly provide for elicitation of data input rather than for articulation of new hypotheses. Furthermore, not all employees are solicited to articulate new ideas. Regional managers and headquarters management are required to articulate new insights, but store employees are not. Automated replenishing and a high volume of interaction with partners decrease the importance of people in the task of ensuring the flow of merchandise. Thus, ART systems are de-emphasized, and machines divorce action from reflection by automating action patterns.

Because Wal-Mart's information system is highly centralized, the company needs to maintain a strong corporate culture and a solid base of shared values in order to balance centralization and focus on regional areas. The Wal-Mart cheer in each of the stores reinforces the organizational culture every day. Similarly, broadcasting strengthens organizational culture and identity even in the outlying stores by exposing all organizational members to electronically mediated corporate communication from headquarters.

Wal-Mart's evolving culture resonates in the use and meaning of IT in the company. Vice President Turner strongly emphasizes the efficiency of IT and recommends automating a process if it cannot be eliminated. The local focus evident in Sam Walton's motto of 'one store at a time', however, still expresses the vision of a retailer able to respond to local needs (Walton and Huey 1993). The concept of knowledge colonies reflects this vision yet also emphasizes the regional integration of explicit data.

Schedules help trigger action and reflection. The twenty-four regional managers at six locations visit their areas each week in order to engage in dialogue with local managers. The regional managers then gather at the corporate headquarters in Bentonville, Arkansas every Thursday in order to discuss what they have seen and heard during their days walking the shop floors and to articulate hypotheses on changing customer preferences. Furthermore, corporate broadcasting on Fridays puts pressure on the leaders to communicate Wal-Mart's essential values and new ideas about how to accommodate recent changes in customer behavior (see Fig. 37.5).

An important function of ART systems is to start and end combination precisely as scheduled. The high degree of automation of Wal-Mart's IT systems partly internalizes the start and end of combination. Data-mining with POS data is performed on a daily basis. The combination of explicit knowledge prompts the automatic replenishment systems to provide the stores with merchandise. In short, Wal-Mart relies on a loop of automated

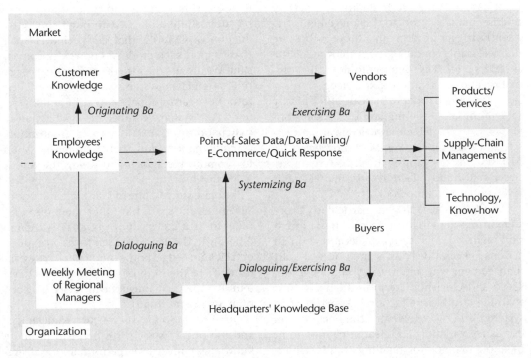

Fig. 37.5. Conversion-support tools, action–reflection-triggering systems, and platforms of knowledge work (*ba*) at Wal-Mart

systemization and utilization of data, human interference is minimized.

IT is used to trigger internalization according to a schedule and to discrepancies or patterns that are discovered. Such patterns can trigger the company's nationwide internalization, for they may be raised first in manager meetings and then in company-wide communications. Patterns in local knowledge, however, are difficult to detect, so they have no compelling effect on the behavior of organizational members. Indeed, Wal-Mart recently introduced different store formats, such as neighborhood markets, in order to improve the sensitivity of Wal-Mart's system.

In summary, Wal-Mart triggers action and reflection in three phases: (a) IT is used to search for patterns in databases of explicit knowledge. These patterns can trigger the combination of ideas. (b) Experimentation based on accumulated data is triggered by automatic pattern recognition. Global patterns extracted from databases are used for experiments in limited areas, a practice that increases the knowledge base of Wal-Mart. In addition, orders by middle managers or top management frequently trigger experiments, though they are not necessarily conducted by employees on the shop floor. (c) IT is used to promote the automation and acceleration of knowledge-conversion processes in order to increase efficiency by integrating sales, ordering, and logistics. Regional managers share tacit knowledge and articulate and collect ideas. Wal-Mart, however, uses ART systems that automatically alternate between action and reflection at the management level, not on the shop floor.

The CSTools at Wal-Mart, particularly those supporting combination, receive more attention than do ART systems. Because human actions are negatively associated by Wal-Mart management with redundancy and variation, speed and efficiency are more highly valued than the creative interaction between human systems and IT. However, the lack of redundancy, variation, and creative change result in lower margins for retailing standard merchandise and even higher pressure to be efficient.

Conclusion

The paradigm shift from information-processing to knowledge creation has promoted knowledge management in both theory and practice. These advances are valuable in specific areas of knowledge-creation management, such as combination, but they do not represent a balanced approach to implementing the theory of knowledge creation. In order to support theory development and practical application, the strong emphasis that current knowledge management places on information technology needs to be complemented with CSTools and ART systems.

We have extended knowledge-creation theory by introducing a framework of integrated IT for knowledge creation. The framework involves two complementary concepts, CSTools and ART systems. They construct technologically enhanced platforms for knowledge-conversion processes, or *ba*. The problem of current knowledge management, with its focus on combination and systemization, can be successfully addressed through the introduction of CSTools, that is, specific IT tools that support each mode of knowledge conversion. We discuss the idea of embedding the use of IT as efficient systems and creative triggers into the organizational context of human systems. ART systems compel an organization to switch from socialization, to externalization, to combination, and then to internalization to promote the movement along the knowledge spiral.

Two case studies, one of Wal-Mart and one of Seven-Eleven Japan, have illustrated opportunities to elicit knowledge through IT. Although differing in the degree of their focus on explicit or tacit knowledge, both companies have established IT in the form of CSTools and ART systems in order to manage the interface between humans and machines.

Opportunities for successful management and use of ART systems in order to promote knowledge conversions, performable by all employees—conversions such as socialization and externalization—have been illustrated through examples taken from the case of Seven-Eleven Japan. The importance of top-down leadership and corporate culture in seizing opportunities to increase efficiency through combination and internalization of knowledge has been shown through examples taken from the Wal-Mart case. The equifinality of the system at Wal-Mart and that at Seven-Eleven Japan highlights the importance of using IT to support sustained knowledge creation. Despite the family resemblance in the objectives behind the use of IT, the contingency of CSTools and ART systems implies that certain aspects of organizational knowledge creation in the one retail chain are distinctly identical with those in the other.

We recommend the use of CSTools and ART systems rather than of IT that is restricted solely to the function of combining existing explicit knowledge, as is the case in current knowledge management. CSTools support all knowledge conversions; they routinize conversion processes and build organizational discipline. ART systems alternately trigger action and reflection in order to promote the shifting from one mode of knowledge to another along the knowledge spiral.

The integration of CSTools and ART systems in the support of knowledge creation poses some interesting tasks for future research. First, for example CSTools and ART systems need to be studied in more depth than they have been in order to enrich multidynamic knowledge creation management efficiently and effectively. In this regard the quality of CSTools and ART systems is important. The tacit knowledge embodied in such tools and systems determines the sustainability of advantage gained by their use. However, the more the system configuration and implementation relies on tacit knowledge, the more difficult the system will be to transfer and the more uncertain and unsustainable the outcome will be. These contradictory effects call for additional research with an eye to the design of integrated systems for knowledge creation. Second, research is needed for development of technologies that can increase awareness of authenticity, originality, and usefulness in a chaotic environment, that is, technologies that can sharpen appreciation of meaningful, discrete occurrences. Tools and systems use existing relationships. CSTools, for instance, stimulate dialogue, and ART systems use schedules and discrepancies to evoke action and reflection. Synthesizing such CSTools and ART systems means providing a mechanism that supports self-organized conversion support and action-reflection units in order to capture the emergence of new meaning in changing contexts. Research is needed for development technologies that can increase awareness of authenticity, originality, and usefulness in a chaotic environment, that is, technologies that can sharpen appreciation of meaningful discrete knowledge-creation management. Third, the recognized importance of the link between technology and human values makes it seem promising to develop integrated information technology for relating knowledge creation to specific values. That kind of management calls for research on information technology and for philosophical inquiry into the essence of fundamental human values and knowledge.

References

Albert, S. and Bradley, K. (1997). *Managing Knowledge: Experts, Agencies and Organizations*. Cambridge: Cambridge University Press.

Bers, M. U. (1998). 'A Constructionist Approach to Values through On-line Narrative Tools'. *ICLS 1998 Proceedings*. Atlanta: Association for the Advancement of Computing in Education.

Billinghurst, M., Weghorst, S., and Furness, T. (1998). 'Shared Space: An Augmented Reality Approach for Computer Supported Collaborative Work'. *Virtual Reality*, 3/1: 25–36.

Bohm, D. (1980). *Wholeness and the Implicate Order*. London: Routledge.

——(1996). *On Dialogue* (L. Nichol, ed.). London: Routledge.

Boisot, M. H. (1998). *Knowledge Assets: Securing Competitive Advantage in the Information Economy.* New York: Oxford University Press.

Caldwell, B. D. (1996). 'Wal-Mart Ups the Pace'. *Information Week,* 9 December: 40–2.

Carrozza, T. (1998). *Connex: The HP Knowledge Network.* Working paper, Palo Alto, Calif.: Hewlett Packard Laboratory Library.

Casey, E. S. (1997). *The Fate of Place: A Philosophical History.* Berkeley: University of California Press.

Choo, C. W. (1998). *The Knowing Organization: How Organizations Use Information to Construct Meaning, Create Knowledge, and Make Decisions.* New York: Oxford University Press.

Churchill, E. F. and Snowdon, D. (1998). 'Collaborative Virtual Environments: An Introductory Review of Issues and Systems'. *Virtual Reality,* 3/1: 3–15.

Ciborra, C. U. (1993). *Teams, Markets and Systems: Business Innovation and Information Technology.* Cambridge: Cambridge University Press.

Clancey, W. J. (1997). *Situated Cognition: On Human Knowledge and Computer Representations.* Cambridge: Cambridge University Press.

Cohen, D. (1998). 'Toward a Knowledge Context: Report on the First Annual U. C. Berkeley Forum on Knowledge and the Firm'. *California Management Review,* 40/3 (Special issue on Knowledge and the Firm): 22–39.

Davenport, T. H. (1998). 'Putting the Enterprise into the Enterprise System'. *Harvard Business Review,* 76/4: 121–31.

——De Long, D. W., and Beers, M. C. (1998). 'Successful Knowledge Management Projects'. *Sloan Management Review,* 39/2: 43–57.

——and Pearlson, K. (1998). 'Two Cheers for the Virtual Office'. *Sloan Management Review,* 39/4: 51–65.

——and Prusak, L. (1998). *Working Knowledge: How Organizations Manage What They Know.* Boston: Harvard Business School Press.

Drucker, P. (1994). *Post Capitalist Society.* New York: Harper Business.

——(1998*a*). *Knowledge Work.* Video-tape speech presented at the 2nd Annual Knowledge Management Conference. University of California at Berkeley, Haas School of Business, 22–24 September.

——(1998*b*). 'In Defence of Japanese Bureaucrats'. *Foreign Affairs,* 77/5: 68–83.

Dyer, J. H. and Singh, H. (1998). 'The Relational View: Cooperative Strategy and Sources of Interorganizational Competitive Advantage'. *Academy of Management Review,* 23: 660–79.

Earl, M. J. (1996). *Information Management: The Organizational Dimension.* New York: Oxford University Press.

——and Scott, I. (1998). *What on Earth Is a CKO?* Working paper, London Business School.

Fayyad, U., Piatetsky-Shapiro, G., and Smyth, P. (1996). 'The KDD Process for Extracting Useful Knowledge from Volumes of Data'. *Communications of the ACM,* 39/11: 27–34.

——and Uthurusamy, R. (1996). 'Data Mining and Knowledge Discovery in Databases'. *Communications of the ACM,* 39/11: 24–6.

Fuld, L. M. (1995). *The New Competitor Intelligence: The Complete Resource for Finding, Analyzing, and Using Information about Your Competitors.* New York: John Wiley and Sons.

Gill, T. G. (1995). 'High-Tech Hidebound: Case Studies of Information Technologies that Inhibited Organizational Learning'. *Accounting, Management and Information Technologies,* 5/1: 33–5.

Granovetter, M. E. (1985). 'Economic Action and Social Structure: The Problem of Embeddedness'. *American Journal of Sociology,* 91: 481–510.

Haken, H. (1977). *Synergetics: Nonequilibrium Phase Transitions and Self-organization in Physics, Chemistry and Biology.* Berlin: Springer.

Handa, M. (1996). *Chino Kankyou Ron* (Intelligence Ambient). Tokyo: NTT Shuppan.

Hiltz, S. R. and Wellman, B. (1997). 'Asynchronous Learning Networks as a Virtual Classroom'. *Communications of the ACM,* 40/9: 44–9.

Holsapple, C. W., Johnson, L. E., and Waldron, V. R. (1996). 'A Formal Model for the Study of Communication Support Systems'. *Human-Communication Research,* 22: 422–47.

Humphrey, S. (1997). Wal-Mart Deploys NeoVista Decision Series Data Mining Software into its Production Decision Support Environment. Bentonville, Ark.: *Wal-Mart Communications*. Available: http://wal-mart.com

Ishida, T. (ed.) (1998). *Community Computing: Collaboration over Global Information Networks*. New York: John Wiley and Sons.

Ishii, H. and Ullmer, B. (1997). 'Tangible Bits: Towards Seamless Interfaces between People, Bits, and Atoms'. *Proceedings of CHIP 1997*. Atlanta: ACM, 234–41.

Kauffmann, S. (1995). *At Home in the Universe: Search for the Laws of Self-organization and Complexity*. New York: Oxford University Press.

Kelly, S. and Allison, M. A. (1999). *The Complexity Advantage: How the Science of Complexity Can Help Your Business Achieve Peak Performance*. New York: McGraw-Hill.

Koepp, S. (1987). 'Make that Sale, Mr. Sam'. *Time*, 18 May: 30–2.

Kunifuji, S. (1999). 'Ofisu ni okeru chiteki seisansei kojo no tame no chishiki sozo hohoron to chishiki sozo shuen tsuru' (Knowledge Creation Methodology and Supporting Knowledge Creation for Productivity Increase in the Office). *Jinko Chino gakkaishi*, 14/3: 50–7.

Kunitomo, R. (1998). *Seven-Eleven no Joho Shisutem* (The Information System of Seven-Eleven). Tokyo: Paru Shuppan.

Lave, J. and Wenger, E. (1991). *Situated Learning: Legitimate Peripheral Participation*. Cambridge: Cambridge University Press.

McKenna, R. (1997). *Real Time Marketing: Preparing for the Age of the Never Satisfied Customer*. Cambridge, Mass.: Harvard University Press.

Mitsugi, Y., Takimoto, T., and Yamazaki, M. (1998). 'Waga Kuni Kourigyo no Shinryutsu Senryaku to Johogijutsu' (New Retail Strategy and Information Technology in Our Country's Retail Business). *Chiteki Shisan Sozo*, 6/2: 18–29.

Miyahara, M., Ino, T., Taniho, S., and Algazi, R. (1998). 'Important Factors to Convey High Order Sensation'. *IEICE Trans. CQ*, E-81-113/11 November.

——Kotani, K., and Algazi, R. (1998). 'Objective Picture Quality Scale (PQS) for Image Coding'. *IEEE Trans. On Communications*, COM-46/9 September.

NCR (1998). Unpublished company information material.

Nonaka, I. (1990). *Chishiki Souzou Keiei* (Knowledge Creation Management). Tokyo: Touyoukeizai.

——(1994). 'A Dynamic Theory of Organizational Knowledge Creation'. *Organization Science*, 5: 14–37.

——and Konno, N. (1998). 'The Concept of "Ba": Building a Foundation for Knowledge Creation'. *California Management Review*, 40/3: 40–54.

——and Reinmöller, P. (1998). 'The Legacy of Learning: Towards Endogenous Knowledge Creation for Asian Economic Development', in H. Albach, M. Dierkes, A. Berthoin Antal, and K. Vaillant (eds.), *Organisationslernen—institutionelle und kulturelle Dimensionen*. *WZB Jahrbuch 1998*. Berlin: edition sigma, 401–32.

————and Senoo, D. (1998). 'The ART of Knowledge: Systems to Capitalize on Market Knowledge'. *European Management Journal*, 16: 673–84.

——and Takeuchi, H. (1995). *The Knowledge-creating Company: How Japanese Companies Create the Dynamics of Innovation*. New York: Oxford University Press.

——Umemoto, K., and Senoo, D. (1996). 'From Information Processing to Knowledge Creation: A Paradigm Shift in Business Management'. *Technology in Society*, 18: 203–18.

Okamoto, H. (1998). *Yokado Group: Koshueki he no Shisutemu Kakushin* (Yokado Group: The System Revolution toward High Profits). Tokyo: Paru Shuppan.

Orlikowski, W. J. (1997). 'Learning from Notes: Organizational Issues in Groupware Implementation'. *The Information Society*, 9: 237–50.

Papow, J. P. and Papow, D. M. (1998). *Enterprise.Com: Market Leadership in the Information Age*. New York: Perseus Books.

Polanyi, M. (1966). *The Tacit Dimension*. London: Routledge and Kegan Paul.

Porter, M. E. (1996). 'What Is Strategy?' *Harvard Business Review*, 74/6: 61–70.

Prigogine, I. (1996). *The End of Certainty*. New York: Free Press.

Quinn, J. B. (1992). *Intelligent Enterprise: A Knowledge and Service Based Paradigm for Industry.* New York: Free Press.

Ruggles, R. (1998). 'The State of the Notion: Knowledge Management in Practice'. *California Management Review,* 40/3 (Special issue): 80–9.

Schank, R. (1997). *Virtual Learning: A Revolutionary Approach to Building a Highly Skilled Workforce.* New York: McGraw-Hill.

Schendel, D. (1995). 'Introduction to "Technological Transformation and the New Competitive Landscape"'. *Strategic Management Journal,* 16 (Summer special issue): 1–6.

Sherman, H. and Schultz, R. (1998). *Open Boundaries: Creating Business Innovation through Complexity.* New York: Perseus Books.

Shout, P. (1999). 'Towards the Realization of One-to-One with 30 Million Profiles'. *Nikkei Multimedia,* 12/2: 104–5.

Simon, H. A. (1976). *Administrative Behavior: A Study of Decision-making Processes in Administrative Organization* (3rd edn). New York: Free Press.

Small, D. (1998). 'Graspable Interfaces: Experiments and Their Lessons' (Presentation material). *Semantics in Design,* Munich, 18 February.

Spender, J. C. and Grant, R. M. (1996). 'Knowledge and the Firm: Overview'. *Strategic Management Journal,* 17 (Winter special issue): 5–9.

Suzuki, K. (1998). 'Tsuyoi "Ishi" to "Tetteiryoku" koso ga subete' (Strong 'Intention' and 'Determination' Are Everything). *2020AIM,* 156/5: 40–5.

Teece, D. J., Pisano, G., and Shuen, A. (1997). 'Dynamic Capabilities and Strategic Management'. *Strategic Management Journal,* 18: 509–33.

Turban, E., McLean, E., and Wetherbe, J. (1999). *Information Technology for Management: Making Connections for Strategic Advantage.* New York: John Wiley and Sons.

Ushioda, K. (1998). *NTT ni okeru atarashii Choryu* (New Trends at NTT) (Presentation material). *NTT Kanto,* 19 December.

Usui, M. (1998). *Kigyo wo kaeru Web Kompyutingu—henka taiou to atarashii shisutemu moderu* (Web Computing Changes the Firm: Adaptation to Change and New System Models) (Presentation material). Seven-Eleven Japan, Information System Division.

Wal-Mart (1996). 'Wal-Mart and Sam's Club Journey into Cyberspace'. *Wal-Mart Communications.* Available: http://wal-mart.com/newsreleases

—— (1997a). 'Wal-Mart Announces Global Expansion Plans for 1998'. *Wal-Mart Communications.* Available: http://wal-mart.com/newsreleases

—— (1997b). 'Wal-Mart Deploys NeoVista Decision Series Data Mining Software into its Production Decision Support System'. *Wal-Mart Communications.* Available: http://wal-mart.com/newsreleases

—— (1998a). 'Wal-Mart Announces Expansion Plans'. *Wal-Mart Communications.* Available: http://wal-mart.com/newsreleases

—— (1998b). 'Wal-Mart International Announces German Acquisition'. *Wal-Mart Communications.* Available: http://wal-mart.com/newsreleases

—— (1998c). 'Wal-Mart Files Legal Action Against Amazon.com'. *Wal-Mart Communications.* Available: http://wal-mart.com/newsreleases

—— (1998d). 'Wal-Mart Names New Retailing Concept: The Wal-Mart Neighborhood Market'. *Wal-Mart Communications.* Available: http://wal-mart.com/newsreleases

Walton, S. and Huey, J. (1993). *Sam Walton: Made in America.* New York: Bantam Books.

Weick, K. E. (1998). 'Improvisation as a Mindset for Organizational Analysis'. *Organization Science,* 9: 543–55.

Wenger, E. (1998). *Communities of Practice: Learning, Meaning and Identity.* Cambridge: Cambridge University Press.

Wittgenstein, L. (1984). *Tractatus logico-philosophicus: Werkausgabe* (Vol. 1). Frankfurt am Main: Suhrkamp. (Original work published 1922).

—— (1958). *The Blue and Brown Books.* Oxford: Blackwell.

Zaltman, G. and Coulter, R. (1995). 'Seeing the Voice of the Customer: Metaphor-based Advertising Research'. *Journal of Advertising Research,* 35/4: 35–51.

38 Scenarios and Their Contribution to Organizational Learning: From Practice to Theory

Graham S. Galer and Kees van der Heijden

In this chapter an organizational learning perspective is adopted in an attempt to make sense of the experience gained through the use of scenarios as a vehicle for management thinking. Over many years of practice a typology of scenarios and their uses has emerged and we identify first two types that have proved the most important: framework and project scenarios. The significance of this typology's evolution is then considered in relation to an established theory of organizational learning. Because scenario planning is largely a practitioner's art, it can be interpreted most fruitfully as experiential learning that integrates crucial aspects such as reflection, theory building, and action, as modeled in the learning cycle described by Kolb (Kolb and Rubin 1991).

Applying the experiential learning cycle to organizations requires one to deal with the two domains in which the world codifies the managerial task, the world of business (strategizing, i.e. the external entrepreneurial aspects) and the world of management (organizing, i.e. the internal organizational aspects). Although Kolb's model (Kolb and Rubin 1991) suggests that all learning always straddles both domains of thinking, most of the organizational learning literature tends to stay within the world of management. The practical use of framework and project scenarios, however, permits the conclusion that, if properly executed, they offer management one of the few organizational learning tools that has the potential to integrate the thinking of both the world of business and the world of management within one process. This feature of the use of scenarios allows management to think about strategizing within the context of organizing and vice versa. Such potentially strong integration is a valuable facet of the methodology of scenario use, and it may well be an important reason for its practical success.

What is the relationship between the use of scenarios (for strategic planning and other purposes) and organizational learning? Organizational learning covers many different topics. One important topic, the study of which may lead to much further learning, is the future, or rather the many possible alternative futures, of the 'business environment', that is, the characteristics of the world in which the organization will develop and carry on its activities. The objective of studying the future is to develop with the organization a shared understanding of what is structurally determined in the surrounding environment and what is indeterminate—essential input for making decisions about an organization's future business. To use scenario planning is to acknowledge that many different futures are feasible and that sound management requires preparation for their possible occurrence.

A scenario has been defined as 'a coherent set (or sequence) of possibilities to the realization of which no fatal obstacle is perceived' (Loasby 1990: 52–3). In other words, a scenario can be thought of as a story about the future that is plausible and internally consistent. Based on the use of more than one scenario, scenario planning expresses the fact that much of the future is indeterminate, that more than one future exists.

Scenario planning is a way to learn about these futures through seeking, in an informed and disciplined way, to map the many different ways in which they could evolve. It develops and uses people's understanding of underlying structures and driving forces[1] in order to help identify possible future discontinuities and other significant changes in the business environment. If such change were to occur without warning, it would no doubt occasion useful learning, but only at great cost, including lost opportunities. Scenario planning provides a means of avoiding, or substantially reducing, such future costs. (This line of thinking is extensively developed in de Geus 1988.) It does so essentially by preparing the organization for change. An organization that has not undergone this type of preparation will take a long time to make sense of a new reality, and that time is lost for the process of reaction and adaptation.

In the 1950s and 1960s it seemed to most corporate and governmental decision-makers that economic and business growth could continue indefinitely at more or less constant rates. Consequently, there was little need to give serious thought to the future, beyond ensuring the continued availability of markets and supplies. By contrast, the 1970s were a period of uncertainty, limits to growth, the oil shocks of 1973 and 1979, and not coincidentally, the development of considerable interest in the use of scenarios. The reported use of scenarios declined somewhat during the 1980s, perhaps because the doomsday anticipated by some observers during the 1970s did not come about.

During the 1990s, scenarios made a powerful comeback, and their use is still growing rapidly (see, for instance, the many examples given in Ringland 1997). To our knowledge, the reasons for this renewed popularity of scenario use have not been the subject of disciplined research but we conjecture that managers find the scenario approach to thinking about the future to be a valuable learning device in times when major structural change has become a normal feature of business life.

Scenario planning has always been, and essentially remains, a craft with an articulated theoretical background that is only now slowly emerging. However, the methodology of scenario planning is sufficiently widespread and embedded in mainstream management to enable one to analyze categories of use and purpose and to relate them to effectiveness in terms of 'learning'. Our purpose in this chapter is to offer just such an analysis of the most frequently encountered categories in scenario planning.

Concepts and Purposes of Scenario Planning

Since the early 1980s, an extensive body of literature on the development and use of scenarios as an aid to management thinking has developed. In many of the publications, the scenario method has served as a framework for analysis and speculation. These publications include Central Planning Bureau of the Netherlands (1992), Fahey and Randall (1997), Galer and Kasper (1982), Gausemeier, Fink, and Schlake (1996), Kahane (1992), Kahn (1979), Kasper, Blandy, Freebairn, Hocking, and O'Neill (1980), Ringland (1997), Schwartz (1991), Tucker and Scott (1992), Yergin and Gustafson (1993).

The Royal Dutch/Shell Group (hereafter referred to as 'Shell') is widely recognized as a pioneering exponent of scenario planning, and methodology developed at Shell has been reported over the years in articles and presentations by various Shell authors, including

---

[1] A 'driving force' is a variable that analysis shows to have a relatively high level of explanatory power for the systemic structure underlying the situation under study. For example, the 'demand for mobility' is a major driving force for the oil industry.

Wack (1985*a*, 1985*b*), van der Heijden (1997, 1999), and Galer and van der Heijden (1992). Shell planners and managers have gone through experiential learning in scenario planning, a process that began in the late 1960s, when the first scenarios were developed and presented. (Our direct experience in working with Shell ended in 1990 (van der Heijden) and 1993 (Galer).)

Many aspects of the future are impossible to forecast accurately: Obvious examples include the prices of raw materials, developments in technology, regime changes, and rates of economic growth. Nevertheless, managers have to take decisions about the commitment of resources and, lacking reliable forecasts, need some other tool that will help them cope with the problems of risk, uncertainty, and lack of knowledge about aspects of the future business environment that are important to them. Such a tool is provided through the development and use of scenarios, which can be used in business or government (indeed, in any other field of endeavor as well) in order to explore poorly understood future environments. Scenarios can be used as the basis for developing new strategies or for testing existing ones, or they can contribute to building a shared language for the discussion of alternative future environments. In all these ways, scenarios facilitate shared learning on the part of managers in the organizations concerned. Although some aspects of the scenario approach may not be altogether intellectually rigorous, their use has proved to be of practical value.

Because many futures are possible, scenarios inevitably come in many forms. The methodology leads to the discovery of 'pre-determined elements', that is, factors that are considered predictable to an extent. These factors are reflected identically in all scenarios, but uncertainties will play out differently in the various scenario stories. In most management situations no more than four scenarios of alternative futures are developed. One reason for this limit is that increasing the number of scenarios proportionately increases the time and effort invested in the decision-making process yet reduces the proportionate contribution that

additional scenarios make to the insights on which the decision is based. At Shell, using more than four scenarios tended to lead to a feeling of diminishing returns. Second, introducing a greater number of scenarios leads to loss of overview in the decision-making discussion, increasing the difficulty of integrating the multiple scenario perspectives into one conclusion and decision. Third, the use of three scenarios can sometimes result in one of the three being seen as an average 'minimum-regret' or 'middle' way. This tendency is particularly evident if the scenario project focuses on one variable only. It leads to relative neglect of the other two, more extreme and perhaps more interesting, scenarios. Practitioners therefore often prefer to work with either two or four scenarios, depending on the circumstances of the situation under study.

Scenarios are usually derived from consideration of (a) the variables assumed to be most significant in the environment of a particular organization or business and (b) the multiple interrelationships of the driving forces affecting these variables. Scenarios tend to be built around a framework determined by the variables that combine 'importance' of the activities in question and 'uncertainty' about the ways in which these activities will develop. This method of looking for underlying structure, which characterizes the scenario approach, helps flush out and highlight the significance of importance–uncertainty variables.

In terms of content, it is possible to distinguish between two principal kinds of scenarios, each having its own place in the manager's toolbox: *Framework scenarios* cover a broad spectrum (the geopolitics and economics of the whole world, in some cases) and need to be narrowed down before they can be used for the development of strategy or the review of projects. By contrast, *project scenarios* cover a more precisely defined area of interest that is based on an expression of concern about a strategically important issue that needs to be better understood than it is.

Within each of these main categories, four types of scenarios can be identified:

1. *Focused* scenarios are prepared specifically for strategy development, for strategic decision-making, or for both purposes, normally against the background of a set of framework or project scenarios.

2. *Exploratory* scenarios are a means of testing the outcomes of 'what if' questions. They can be used in the early stages of a scenario project to explore, perhaps later mostly to reject, some of the wilder and more unlikely possibilities.

3. *First-generation* scenarios are a first attempt to think through the relationships over time of the variables being considered. Rather than producing the end product of the exercise, these scenarios help indicate areas where further analytical work is required for further learning about the basic driving forces of the situation under study. In *second-generation* scenarios, the responses of various actors (e.g. governments and consumers) identified in the first-generation scenarios are considered, and consequent adjustments are made to the scenario logic.

4. *Normative* scenarios (e.g. 'What would we like to have happen, and how can we bring it about?') combine environmental factors and elements of strategy. In most industrial enterprises the preference is to develop scenarios in the contextual environment, that is, in the part of the business environment that one believes cannot be influenced. However, some consultants use normative scenarios, which can be of value in bringing people's value and goal systems to the surface. Normative scenarios are often used in the public sector, where more of the environment may seem capable of being controlled or influenced than in the private sector. However, they are less suited to strategy-testing work, for they preempt managers' choice of strategic options.

Most of the early work in scenario planning (e.g. Kahn 1979) dealt only with the provision of information based on research and analysis. It was a content-based approach to learning through scenarios. As interesting and often challenging as this kind of information was, however, Shell discovered quite soon that managers frequently did not give it significant weight in their decision-making. In order to bring about change, in order to cause organizational learning to take place—it would have been necessary to give thought to the practical ways in which scenarios might be used in decision-making. Subsequently, it was found that some of the scenarios developed by groups of experts from inside and outside the company failed to attract significant senior management attention. In these cases, it was found that 'ownership' of scenarios could be secured by involving senior management in the development process and by arranging for staff to act as facilitators of the process rather than as experts on the content of scenarios. Thus, the ways in which scenarios were arrived at also came under review. Should they be developed by 'experts' or rather through a facilitated process involving managers themselves? These two different issues, practical relevance and ownership, made the resolution of questions about process central to Shell's productive use of scenarios (Kahane 1992; for further documentation of Shell's learning experience with the use of scenarios, see de Geus 1988, 1997; Galer and Kasper 1982; Galer and van der Heijden 1992; van der Heijden 1997, 1999; and Wack 1985a, b). It now has become widely accepted at Shell that the conduct of a successful exercise in scenario planning requires careful attention to both content and process.

Framework and Project Scenarios

What are the main aspects of the experience gained at Shell in the light of our subsequent sense-making? First, the use of scenarios over some twenty-five years by planners and managers at Shell had resulted, by the early 1990s, in the adoption of two somewhat different approaches to scenario work. The framework approach was part of a long-term process whose purpose was to provide a structured way to become aware of and learn more about the world in which the Shell Group as a whole had to operate and make strategy. Framework scenarios were the periodic output of a continuous program of work on issues of central importance to the oil, gas, and chemical industries and were carried out in Group Planning[2] in partnership with planning groups in operating companies and other business sectors in the Shell Group. Typically, the scenarios made reference to global issues in the economy, politics, technology, the energy business, and, on occasion, society in general. During the 1980s and early 1990s, framework scenarios were produced and promulgated in the Shell Group every two or three years.

Published, presented, and circulated, the framework scenarios provided a background (hence, 'framework') for strategic planning throughout Shell for the next two or three years. They would often be used as the basis for more detailed scenario thinking in operating companies or other business sectors of the group. An instructive account of the use of this approach in practice was given by Kahane (1992), who described the current scenarios for worldwide energy supply and demand.

The project approach was invoked as issues arose. This kind of exercise would begin with the expression of concern about an issue, such as, 'How might anticipated developments in the European Community affect our business?', or 'What is going on in China? How might things turn out there, and what threats and opportunities might these outcomes represent for us?'. The common characteristics of such issues were that they were normally of strategic importance and that both the current situation and the potential future outcomes were poorly understood. Framework scenarios might have raised these issues as something significant to the company but were too broad to provide a detailed analysis.

After some time, these feelings of uncertainty would become fairly widespread among actors whose business interests they might affect.

Support would develop for the view that resources should be committed to improving the understanding of the situation, and a director or other senior manager might commission a dedicated specialist group (Group Planning) to carry out a study. The expectation was that this study would result in project scenarios, backed up with expert research and analysis.

The first step to be taken by the study team would then be to interview appropriate Shell managers (i.e. managers directly involved in the situation or whose business might be affected by developments in it), who would help identify both the elements that they assumed might be of importance to the business and the areas of the environment about which they felt uncertain or ill-informed. Experts and other well-informed people outside the company, who might be able to shed light on the uncertainties that managers had identified, were also interviewed. More useful than acknowledged experts, often, were iconoclasts from inside or outside the company, that is, people with independent views who might ask challenging questions and challenge preconceptions. Such people became popularly known within Shell as 'remarkable persons', and relationships with them were carefully cultivated.

Having completed their interviews, members of the planning team would break the problematic situation down into a series of modules and organize—or locate and, if necessary, purchase—initial research into these aspects of the subject area. A workshop, or a series of workshops, would normally be held on each module, a practice that brought together some members of the planning team, one or more outside experts or remarkable persons, and, usually, some Shell managers. The purpose of these workshops was to test the preliminary conclusions of the scenario team and, by involving senior managers at this early stage, to develop a sense of ownership.

For example, a scenario project on aspects of the future of the European Community (EC) relevant to the oil industry was carried out at Shell in 1989–90, at which time one of the authors was responsible for a module on

[2] Group Planning was a division within Shell's central offices, which reported to the chairman of the managing directors. Most large operating companies and business divisions in the Shell Group also had planning departments, which, though responsible to local management, also worked in close cooperation with Group Planning.

decision-making in the European Commission. After preliminary interviews and research had been conducted, a one-day workshop was held at which the material that had accumulated was presented and discussed, particularly in order to identify the areas of greatest future uncertainty. The three groups mentioned were pre-presented by two members of the Group Planning team, the head of a policy studies institute based in Brussels (who had assisted with the research), and the general managers of four European Shell operating companies, each of whom, being based in an EC country, had a commercial interest in and first-hand knowledge of the topic.

By this stage in the work, the planning team would normally feel ready to draft preliminary (first-generation) scenarios and would run one or more additional workshop sessions for this purpose. Informal presentations would be made to appropriate managers and outsiders in order to test the logic of these scenarios. This exercise normally raised questions about aspects of the problem situation, indicating that the scenarios were not sufficiently understood and pointing out further areas of research that could deepen knowledge of the underlying systems. With the new understanding following from this supplementary research, the scenarios would be further developed and made more internally consistent. Another round of testing would follow. This process of testing, research, and scenario updating would continue until diminishing returns set in, after which the scenarios would be finalized and fully written up.

The scenarios would then be presented, usually on several occasions, to the original sponsors and other interested groups. This stage would normally lead to the definition of a number of strategic issues that had been raised by the scenarios, and working parties would often be set up both to develop the issues further in relation to the scenarios and to develop proposals.

The project approach, sketched above, used scenario methods as part of a process of managing strategic options. Scenarios helped in both identifying and evaluating options, and the particular value of the scenario approach was that it enabled its users, through an iterative process of raising research questions and considering related research, to identify both predictable structure and irreducible uncertainty within a situation. This information was then available as input for enhanced strategy design.

Whether scenarios were produced via the project-based route or the framework route, there were several managerial purposes of scenarios as used in the Shell Group:

1. To challenge 'mental maps'. Managers often have a set of beliefs and preconceptions about their business and the environment in which it operates. These beliefs and preconceptions have been built up over time and have served the managers well. If learning is to occur, these mental maps need to be tested from time to time and perhaps modified. The scenario method has proved to be a very effective means of triggering this process, for by presenting alternative futures, it provides a manager with possibilities that can be challenging without committing the manager to a particular, 'correct' line of action.

2. To identify trends. 'Scanning' and 'monitoring' are vital aspects of maintaining an understanding of the business environment. Scanning is the activity of disciplined exploration, of looking systematically at what is going on, searching for new developments, and trying to identify weak signals of change. Significant trends can be identified without recourse to scenarios but scenarios alert the organization to the fact that there are more futures possible than just the one, official prediction found in organizations that do not use scenarios. Scenarios draw attention to the need to look more openly at possible developments that would otherwise escape notice. In this way, scenario planning increases the range of vision of the organization.

3. To monitor important trends. Monitoring is the activity of keeping track of variables that out of the long list of items scanned, have proved to be significant. As in the process of trend identification, scenario thinking can

help in monitoring trends, in this case also by improving understanding of the driving forces that influence trends and by comparing the present status of those trends to the evolution anticipated for them in past scenarios.

4. To test existing strategies, or projects. By asking the question 'How would this strategy or project play out in scenario X?' and by posing the question for other scenarios as well, one can form a better idea of the risk involved and of the chances that the strategy or project will prove robust and profitable in the long run.

5. To develop new strategic thinking. Scenarios can be used to develop new strategic thinking by prompting one to ask questions such as 'What threats and opportunities does this scenario raise for our business?' and 'What options would these threats and opportunities create for the development of new strategies?' Developing a broad understanding of either threats or opportunities can lead within the organization to a shared awareness of an external imperative for change, which is one of the preconditions for intended strategic change (an important conclusion reached by Pettigrew and Whipp (1991) in their extensive research into change projects within organizations.

The aforementioned learning process undergone by Shell managers and planners as scenario planning developed in the organization is known as 'deutero-learning' (Argyris and Schön 1978: 26), in which the organization 'learned how to learn'. How could the business value of all this work be assessed? Although scenario planning had become part of the way of life at Shell during this period, and although many successes could be identified, there was no feasible way to construct an alternative history for the company that could indicate how the company might have behaved had it not adopted scenario planning methods.

In an internal review conducted in 1995, to which we authors were given access, surrogates for such an analysis were proposed. None of them need be associated solely with the use of scenarios, but, taken together, they give confidence that scenarios have indeed contributed significantly to learning at Shell. These surrogates are, among others (a) Shell's reputation in the world of international business for good planning, (b) Shell's growth in market capitalization in relation to significant competitors, (c) the significant influence that scenario analysis had on investment decisions associated with the threat of energy scarcity and security of supply, and (d) the contribution that scenario work made to the identification of many trends, such as the take-off and slow-down in Japan and the rest of the Pacific Basin, the conservation of energy, and the whitening of the oil barrel (i.e. a relative increase in demand for the lighter fractions—principally motor gasoline—in crude oil, a shift which had important consequences for investment in oil refining). It must be recognized that recent developments, including Shell's experience with the disposal of the Brent Spar North Sea platform and developments in Nigeria, may throw doubt on some of these propositions. It may take time for these events to be properly evaluated, a task that we must leave for future papers.

At Shell, though, scenarios increasingly came to be seen as part of the corporate culture, which encouraged a great deal of debate in the spirit of learning. An awareness had grown that the motivation to learn increases in situations of uncertainty and that scenarios were therefore needed as part of the learning process. In this way, the scenarios came to provide a vehicle both for structuring internal debate (which came to be termed 'strategic conversation') and for permitting the introduction of new and sometimes surprising information.

Scenario Planning Interpreted as a Cyclical Learning Process

All five aforementioned purposes for using scenarios—challenging mental maps, identifying trends, monitoring important trends, testing existing strategies or projects, and developing new strategic thinking—clearly represent opportunities for learning about the external environment of the organization and the options that it faces. How can this learning be modeled more explicitly?

As already noted, the scenario method is still essentially a craft, and learning is largely experiential. In order to map the activities of business planners, we have adopted the model of the experiential learning cycle presented in Kolb and Rubin (1991). This model has been found to provide a useful perspective on the ways in which scenario planning contributes to learning (Galer and van der Heijden 1992).

Kolb identified a cycle of experiential learning (Kolb and Rubin 1991), moving from 'experiencing' to 'reflecting' to 'conceptualizing' to 'planning new action' (see Fig. 38.1). In the experiencing phase the organization takes action and experiences both the consequences of actions that it has taken and the effects of actions taken by others. The organization then 'reflects' on these experiences (particularly those that deviate from expectations based on existing theories), internalizing them, relating them to other experiences, and assigning them a place in its 'memory'. The next step, 'conceptualizing', involves relating the organization's total memory of experiences to its working hypotheses about how the world functions. This step also entails explaining and understanding the most recent experiences and perhaps modifying to some degree the organization's store of theories about the world. Then the organization is ready to 'plan new action'—take strategic decisions—and begin the cycle again.

This simple model provides a means of addressing the question 'Is this organization capable of learning from its past experience?' If the organization can be shown to possess processes that perform the functions of registering experience, reflection, conceptualization, planning, and implementation, then, the organization can be said to be capable of 'learning' as long as these processes work effectively.

We believe that the significance of scenario planning as a management tool can best be appreciated in the context of a model of organizational learning and that Kolb (Kolb and Rubin 1991) provides an appropriate model. There is a complication, however. The Kolb model requires both thinking and action if learning is to take place, but in Kolb's original model (Kolb and Rubin 1991), thinking and action are seated in an individual learner. Extending the model to include organizations is not as straightforward as it may seem. An organization consists of a number of individual learners who each go through the Kolb cycle and who

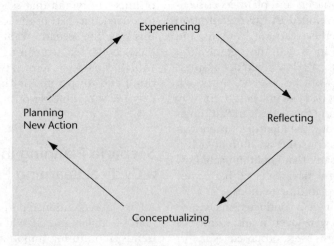

Fig. 38.1. Kolb's (1991) learning model

Arrows denote the relationship of the content of each element to the preceding element (A→B means A influences B)

therefore take individual action. Interpreting organizational action as simply the sum of the actions of its members leads to problems for such an equation would make an organization indistinguishable from a mob. What makes an organization different is that there is a degree of coherence in its action, a coherence based on alignment of thinking that issues from a shared theory of the world. That shared theory creates common expectations and overlapping experiences, reflection, and conceptualization. The notion of the organization as a unitary actor can be applied to points of the learning cycle at which the individual can assert that he or she is thinking on behalf of the collective—the steps of reflection and conceptualization. But the individual cannot assume to represent the totality of the organization's action and experience. That assumption requires consideration of the processes that translate individual action and experience into collective action and experience. In order to understand the full power of scenario planning as an organizational learning tool one therefore needs to consider how individual thinking and collective action relate to organizations.

Thinking and action can be related to the organizational executive's two 'worlds' of thinking: the rational world of business and the processual world of management (Normann and Ramirez 1994). Although few problems that managers encounter fall exclusively into just one of these areas of focus, the manner in which management thinking has developed has led to disciplinary thinking that tends to focus primarily on one of them or the other. This convention will be used as a convenient way to discuss these two crucial aspects of the scenario approach.

The World of Business

In the world of business, managers think about the organization as a unitary actor that interacts with other actors in its environment. In order for the organization to survive and flourish, the manager needs to understand the other actors with whom he or she is interacting, needs to map out their strengths and weaknesses relative to those of the organization so that it can develop a promising position in the world.

Outside observers of organizations tend to take this perspective. For example, one speaks of 'Shell developing a North Sea oil field', the 'European Union changing its trading regulations', and 'the Green Party adopting new policies'. One might even go as far as to consider the organization to be 'alive' (de Geus 1997). All such notions are metaphors that emerge from the activity of thinking in terms of unitary actors in the world of business.

The discipline conventionally called 'business policy' or 'strategic management' is essentially a set of activities that deal with thinking and acting in the world of business. In the process of strategic management, the potential of the organization is considered in relation to the environmental forces that have an impact on it. Fundamental to this rational thinking process is the notion of 'fit' between the organization and its environment. A good fit (a situation in which the organization has strengths that are scarce in the world) allows the organization to thrive and grow. A poor fit (the absence of such strengths) causes the organization to struggle and possibly even go under. A company without an articulated strategy defining the ways in which fit is to be achieved is often marked down by outside agencies, such as the stock markets.

Note that an assessment of fit requires an understanding of both the environment and the organization itself. Although scenarios are helpful in developing a better understanding of the environment, understanding the organization in terms of what might be called its 'formula for success' is also necessary for strategy development. Many organizational leaders do not have this formula at their fingertips. Abiding success seems to create mind-sets in which components of the success formula are taken for granted. Exposing this formula by articulating a company's 'business idea' is often surprisingly revealing to the managers of the organization (see van der Heijden 1997: 59–81).

The World of Management

Although world-of-business thinking needs to take place before a manager can reflect on experience and update the organization's model of its place in the world, the manager simultaneously needs to be able to shift his or her thinking inward at a moment's notice toward the world of management. Strategizing in the external world alone is not enough. As discussed above, the Kolb model of organizational learning (Kolb and Rubin 1991) suggests that no learning can take place without action. And action requires that the organization be seen not as one unitary actor but as a complex system with many subsystems and individual actors, each with their own objectives, perceptions, and learning processes, each following their own interests. In order to create conditions that cause strategy to be implemented, the manager needs to be skillful in intervening in this system. Without action in the world of management, no amount of strategic thinking in the world of business will lead to action or, therefore, to learning. The world of management is the world of creating action, of bringing in and motivating people, of organizing methods and work, of resolving conflict, and generally of dealing with issues of agency.

In the world of management the organization has become many people, who together need to make things happen. In this respect, there are many potential problems facing the manager. The organization may have become fragmented, and a 'house divided' has difficulty achieving objectives. There may be problems looming at the opposite end of communication as well, where Groupthink sets in and the organization lacks the requisite variety (Ashby 1983) for dealing successfully with the range of outside disturbances coming at it.

Whereas the discipline of 'strategic management' codifies thinking and acting in the world of business, thinking and acting in the world of management corresponds to the discipline referred to as 'organizational development' or 'change management' (Pettigrew and Whipp 1991). In change management the focus is on processual issues, and the activity is instrumental rather than content-driven, as in strategic management. The fundamental notion in change management is transition from the current situation toward a desired future, however that future is formulated. Whereas the strategist thinks about what an appropriate fit would look like (between the business and future environments), the change manager takes up the challenge of 'getting there', wherever 'there' may be.

In the world of the manager, a vision for the organization and the organization's business idea are crucially interwoven (see Dierkes, Marz, and Teele, Ch. 12 in this volume). An organization without ideas about how to attain a comfortable fit with the environment will not survive, for it will be unable to appropriate the economic rent required to generate surpluses for investment in its future. Effective strategizing is not enough, however. Fragmented companies that do not lack good ideas from their people but that simply lose the ability to implement these ideas will lose their ability to learn and hence their fit with the environment. These organizations will eventually disappear. For these reasons, managers need to be skillful in the world of business as well as in the world of management. Managers must be able to create organizations that not only strategize skillfully but also implement effectively and in this way learn from experience. Table 38.1 summarizes the principal characteristics of the two worlds just discussed.

Although the work of the manager takes place in both worlds, the available management tools as presented in textbooks on strategic management and on change management tend to be relevant in either one or the other domain. An exception is scenario planning. The scenario approach is a tool that requires work in both the world of business (experiencing, reflecting, conceptualizing, making decisions) and the world of management (aligning conceptualization, aligning planning, creating organizational action). The various stages of scenario work can therefore be mapped onto the complete Kolb cycle (as interpreted for organizations), so the approach can be under-

Table 38.1. Principal characteristics of the world of business and the world of management

The world of business	The world of management
The organization as a unitary actor	The organization as many individuals
One single learning loop	Multiple learning loops that need to be in alignment
Strategy	Change management
Rationalist logic	Processual logic
Focus: Fit between the business idea and the environment	Focus: Transition from current reality to vision
Success: Finding a good fit	Success: Making it happen
Question: Is the business idea sound?	Question: Does the organization have the ability to change?

stood to be a tool for integrated organizational learning.

This dual character—the fact of having both a content and a process aspect—may help account for the popularity of scenario work. It is a powerful analytical tool of considerable value for learning about the world of business. It is also a team activity that achieves powerful results in the world of management through the alignment and motivation of people for joint reflection, conceptualization, and action. In terms of the learning schema set out in the chapter by Pawlowsky, Forslin, and Reinhardt (Ch. 35 in this volume), the scenario approach can facilitate learning at all four system levels (individual, group, organizational, or network), mainly through learning types II and III in all three learning modes (cognitive, cultural, and actional), and in all four phases of the learning process (identification, diffusion, integration, and action).

Learning with Scenarios in the World of Business

In the world of business, scenarios are used as a reflective analytical tool. They help deal with the strategic question about the degree of fit between the business idea of the organization and the future environment, both of which need to be articulated and assessed. In this assessment the future environment is delineated in a series of scenarios that project some of the inherent uncertainties that the organization faces.

Clearly, thinking about future fit has value only if it can be agreed that there is *something* predictable in the business environment. As discussed earlier in this chapter, the scenario approach is an attempt to capture this 'something' through the concepts of causal structure and predetermined elements. A strategist who looks at a new situation for the first time may not be totally aware of the predetermined elements. Initially, everything may seem confused and ambiguous. Such a state of mind gives rise to exclamations such as, 'I wish the market would make up its mind' or 'This competitor behaves utterly irrationally'. What is needed is a way to quickly build understanding of what is structural and predetermined (within a relevant time frame) and of what is uncertain, not because it is not understood but because the elements are fundamentally indeterminate. This task is not a simple one. Why is it that scenarios can help here?

There is much turbulence in the world of events, and, without looking closer, one may gain the impression that very little is predictable. However, on closer inspection, patterns emerge in the events observed. The human mind is skillful at recognizing patterns (sometimes even seeing them where there are none). Some patterns present themselves as trends over time. One approach to analyzing a situation is to regard trends as indications of where the future is going. Extrapolating in this way produces the 'most likely' future, which, although couched in terms of the future, in fact describes a world based on relationships of the past. Although such extrapolation may give a sense of predictability and control, the future invariably catches up with those who limit themselves to fighting yesterday's battles.

However, more can be done with trends. Trends invite a causal explanation. Questions are asked, such as 'What is continuously driving up this element (e.g. a price or a business sector)?' By looking for, and finding, causal explanations, one can construct another layer of structure beneath the observed trends, an invisible world of interrelated driving forces that may be assumed to have caused these trends (Senge 1990). Scenario planners assume that causal structure is less volatile than events or trends, and the search for understanding begins to focus on systemic causal analysis. For example, the long-term outlook for the demand and supply of oil and other energy products is determined principally by geological factors and the state of technology for producing and using energy. This 'structure' changes more slowly than the flux of events in the political and economic marketplace.

Trying to define and compose internally consistent stories about the future forces the storyteller to become reasonably explicit about causal structure. The attempt helps create awareness of instances in which existing mental models of reality inadequately take account of causal structure and instances in which systemic analysis will be productive. Scenario planning in the world of business is a process in which intuition alternates with rigorous analysis to gradually sharpen understanding of the underlying causality in the business environment. It is an iterative process of scenario building and systemic analysis, a process in which scenario building indicates where systems research is required, which in turn produces new systemic understanding that indicates the direction in which the scenarios need to be adjusted. The process goes through a first, a second, and often a third generation until further effort shows diminishing returns (see the diversion of scenario taxonomy, above).

In the world of business, scenarios are important because of what they teach about the business environment. Projects for developing scenarios of this kind are not trivial; they often extend over many months and require significant resources to research the systemic questions that arise. An example was the 'Crossroads' study in Australia, which foreshadowed many of the liberalizing reforms undertaken by the Hawke government in the 1980s. In this study, which was sponsored by industry, a group of academics worked for almost a year to produce a report, cast in the form of scenarios, that explored different futures for Australia, each based principally on differing approaches to economic policy. It led to vigorous debate in the press and to the formation of several discussion groups and hence to learning on the part of industrialists and policy-makers (Kasper, Blandy, Freebairn, Hocking, and O'Neill 1980). If useful, productive scenarios are expected to result from a simple one-day workshop, disappointment is inevitable. But if investment is made in the full iterative process of a project, as happened at Shell, then understanding does develop and the scenario team gradually does grasp the reality that initially seemed so confusing and disturbing.

Learning with Scenarios in the World of Management

The message of the preceding sections is not that brief and limited scenario projects are always a waste of time. Any benefit derived from such projects is, however, strictly confined to the world of management. One reason for this limitation is that managers who believe that organizations need to change from time to time face a fundamental contradiction in the world of management. On the one hand, organizational change deriving from change in the business environment can obviously happen only if managers are clearly aware of such external change. In order to create a system that is capable of perceiving change in the outside world, managers need to develop requisite variety within the organization. People can perceive only what approximates the mental models that already exist in their minds. Therefore, the existence of a broad range of views among members of an organization helps broaden the range of perception of the organization at large. Differentiation is crucial for effective organizational learning.

On the other hand, learning cannot take place without action, which, in turn, can come about only if views are aligned closely enough to motivate members of the organization to participate in joint action. Without such alignment, there is no organizational action, only individual actions, and the organization might as well not exist. The economic logic of the organization requires it to be capable of integrating around a joint line of action so that it can have new experiences, learn, and move forward in the world. Managers therefore face the contradiction that both the integration and differentiation of views and mental models are desirable features of a sound organization. However, one cannot increase integration and differentiation at the same time. Increasing one will decrease the other, and a danger exists that an organization can move into either the extreme of differentiation (i.e. fragmentation) or the extreme of integration (i.e. Groupthink). Managers therefore need to carry out a careful balancing act, intervening whenever the system is moving too much toward one of the two extremes. Typical examples of such interventions are team-building activities (increasing integration), and 'bringing in new blood from the outside' (increasing differentiation).

Our experience at Shell showed that scenarios help overcome the contradiction between integration and differentiation. The most important characteristic of this methodology is its ability to introduce multiple perspectives into a strategic review. As stated above, scenarios start from the premise that there is more than one possible alternative future. They therefore provide more than one view of a situation, allowing for differentiation in perspective.

Many scenario projects are designed specifically to bring in new views and alternative voices. As noted above, one valuable resource is the remarkable person, who participates in a project as an insightful outsider, perhaps as an iconoclast, in order to throw new light on a situation and to help insiders transcend the limits of their normal thinking. Setting up an effective conversation with an insightful outsider is not a trivial matter if the necessary shared language is missing. The scenario methodology provides a structure that enhances the likelihood of an insightful conversation. Most of the successful projects that we have experienced have been undertaken in this way, the aim being to break out of conventional thinking and give the organization a new perspective on the world through a reframing process.

Scenarios are also developed as a disciplined group process. The most powerful barrier to group work in organizations is political posturing. Once two parties are locked in a power battle, the productive exchange of views ends. Many strategic debates in organizations deteriorate into a struggle to make one's view prevail. Such circumstances are not optimal for a mutual consideration of views and a gradual convergence until a conclusion is jointly agreed upon.

One way to overcome this problem is to move the strategic debate away from the normal decision-making process. For example, an 'away-day' from the office is often granted. By removing the threatening need to reach a decision, this device enables people to drop their defensive stance and open up to another line of argument. Because scenarios are not meant to figure out 'what will happen' but to address the question of 'what *could* happen', they have the same liberating effect. People who initially approach a situation from very different perspectives will see their own specific point of view reflected in at least one of the interpretative scenarios. In the knowledge that one's own view is clearly on the agenda, it becomes possible for one to listen to alternative points of view. A well-known example of this conversational and integrative use of scenarios is the Mont Fleur project in South Africa (Kahane 1995; for a somewhat similar report, see Tucker and Scott 1992), which has been hailed as one of the significant events that brought disparate parties closer together in the early 1990s. Similar, albeit less visible, projects are now becoming popular in the public sector in general, where they are used to create imaginative conversations around difficult societal issues. One example is a group of senior civil servants who gather regularly to consider the future of governance in an information society (Rosell 1995). Another example is the development of alternative scenarios for the provision of health services (e.g. the 'Hemingford scenarios' developed for the British National Health Service, described in Ringland 1997: 291).

In business this integrative approach is also being increasingly used in matters involving more than one organization, such as efforts to develop partnerships and to improve customer relations. The dearth of articles on this experience is perhaps a measure of its value, for corporate confidentiality may be entailed.

Scenario projects that enhance the process of organizational 'strategic conversation' can be short and limited in scope, and such projects can be useful in opening up channels of communication. But if the conversation is to lead to a significant integration of views, sufficient time is required for points of view to start shifting. Therefore, as in the world of business, only limited results can be expected unless significant investment is made (mainly of time).

Project Scenarios and Framework Scenarios in the World of Management and the World of Business

In the first pages of this chapter a distinction was made between project scenarios and framework scenarios. The use of these two approaches has different characteristics, depending on whether they are employed in the world of business or the world of management. In the former, project scenarios help most when there is a need to learn about some poorly understood situation, such as a potential new market or a new regulatory regime. Similarly, new business ventures or major projects can often benefit from the application of scenario thinking. Framework scenarios in the world of business are of a broader scope than framework scenarios in the world of management, and can be used as the background for rather general strategic thinking and for specific project scenarios.

In the world of management, project scenarios are effective at helping achieve the balance between integrative and differentiated thinking. Framework scenarios perform this function as well, and in so doing they may serve a useful purpose by providing a common language and a set of concepts through which the strategic conversation may be conducted and qualitatively upgraded. This common language and set of concepts can be thought of as a kind of corporate glue that fosters cohesion and consistency in management thinking within the organization. At the same time, multiple scenarios provide for a more differentiated view of the world than that communicated by one-line company forecast or the 'official future' that they replace. These ideas on the purposes of scenarios in the world of business and the world of management are summarized in Table 38.2.

Although we have treated the use of scenarios in the world of business (analysis) separately from their use in the world of management (organizational process), it must be remembered that organizational learning is an iterative process in which reflection, reconceptualization, action, and experience are equally important. Both uses are necessary in order to close the learning loop. It is only with the integration of reflection and theory-building (the world of business) and with the integration of theory-sharing and jointly created action (the world of management), that the cycle is

Table 38.2. The purposes of scenarios

	World of business	World of management
Project	To understand an unfamiliar environmental situation To assess prospects for a new business venture	To find the right balance of integration and differentiation in management views
Framework	To set out a broad background for strategic management, including the assessment of existing strategy and the development of new strategy	To provide 'corporate glue'

completed and learning actually occurs. The fact that scenario methodology plays such an important role in both worlds of thinking makes it one of the most powerful organizational learning tools available.

Summary

Applications of the scenario technique to organizational learning have been categorized according to various dimensions. In order to clarify the role of scenarios, we found it useful to consider organizational learning in the context of the two worlds of thinking in which managers operate, the world of business and the world of management. In the former, scenario projects are tools for reflective analysis, allowing strategists to look at a situation from different experiential perspectives, to generate relevant research questions, and thereby to develop deep structural and relevant understanding of a business environment (one that initially seemed foggy and confusing), which can then serve as a basis for skillful action.

But Kolb's (Kolb and Rubin 1991) model of experiential learning suggests that learning requires *action*. In the world of management, scenario projects help managers by providing space for their different views so that they can work together toward a common line of action. Differentiation through effective interaction with insightful outsiders allows individuals to reframe their views of the environment and thus helps them and the organization become more skillful observers of the outside world. Scenarios thereby overcome political barriers and create a powerful strategic debate, or 'conversation', within the organization, enabling forces to gather around agreed lines of implementation and action. An important motivational aspect in this context is the fact that the scenario process projects challenges outside the organization, encouraging people to align their ideas in order to face the 'common enemy' or gain 'the common prize'. Scenarios help people come to a shared concept of their 'business idea', which is the very basis of their company.

In each of these activities, progress requires significant investment, mainly of time. Organizational learning does not come for free. A significant scenario project must be measured in months rather than in days or weeks. In practice, the time required for an effective intervention is often underestimated, and projects are often underdesigned, a flaw that dulls the perception of results and generates disappointment.

Scenarios help in the process of experiencing, for they affect managers' perceptions of the world. They also help in the process of reflecting on experience, adapting mental models, and creating organizational action, the other three stages of the learning loop. In this way, they can contribute substantially to the overall process of organizational learning.

References

Ashby, W. R. (1983). 'Self-regulation and Requisite Variety', in F. E. Emery (ed.), *Systems Thinking*. Harmondsworth: Penguin, 105–24.

Central Planning Bureau of the Netherlands (1992). *Scanning the Future: A Long-term Scenario Study of the World Economy*. The Hague: Sdu Publishers.

de Geus, A. (1988). 'Planning as Learning'. *Harvard Business Review*, 66/2: 70–4.

——(1997). *The Living Company: Habits for Survival in a Turbulent Business Environment*. Boston: Harvard Business School Press.

Fahey, L. and Randall, R. (1997). *Future Mapping: The Art of Gaining Competitive Advantage through Scenario Planning*. Chichester: John Wiley and Sons.

Galer, G. and Kasper, W. (1982). 'Scenario Planning for Australia'. *Long Range Planning*, 15/4: 50–5.

——and van der Heijden, K. (1992). 'The Learning Organization: How Planners Create Organizational Learning'. *Marketing Intelligence and Planning*, 10/6: 5–12.

Gausemeier, J., Fink, A., and Schlake, O. (1996). *Szenario-Management: Planen und Führen mit Szenarien*. Munich: Carl Hanser.

Global Business Network (GBN). Emeryville, Calif. Available: Internet public home page: http:\\www.gbn.org

Kahane, A. (1992). 'Scenarios for Energy: Sustainable World versus Global Mercantilism'. *Long Range Planning*, 25/4: 38–46.

——(1995). 'Learning from Mont Fleur'. *Deeper News*, 7/1: 1–20.

Kahn, H. (1979). *World Economic Development: 1979 and Beyond*. Boulder, Colo.: Westview.

Kasper, W., Blandy, R., Freebairn, J., Hocking, D., and O'Neill, R. (1980). *Australia at the Crossroads: Our Choices to the Year 2000*. Sydney: Harcourt Brace Jovanovich.

Kolb, D. and Rubin, I. M. (1991). *Organizational Behavior: An Experiential Approach*. Englewood Cliffs, NJ: Prentice Hall.

Loasby, B. L. (1990). 'The Use of Scenarios in Business Planning', in S. F. Frowen (ed.), *Unknowledge and Choice in Economics: Proceedings of a Conference in Honor of G. L. S. Shackle*. Basingstoke: Macmillan, 52–3.

Normann, R. and Ramirez, R. (1994). *From Value Chain to Value Constellation: Designing Interactive Strategy*. Chichester: Wiley.

Pettigrew, A. M. and Whipp, R. (1991). *Managing Change for Competitive Success*. Oxford: Blackwell.

Ringland, G. (1997). *Scenario Planning: Managing for the Future*. Chichester: John Wiley and Sons.

Rosell, S. A. (1995). *Changing Maps: Governing in a World of Rapid Change*. Ottawa: Carleton University Press.

Schwartz, P. (1991). *The Art of the Long View*. New York: Doubleday Currency.

Senge, P. M. (1990). *The Fifth Discipline: The Art and Practice of the Learning Organization*. New York: Doubleday Currency.

Tucker, B. and Scott, B. (1992). *South Africa: Prospects for Successful Transition*. Cape Town: Juta.

van der Heijden, K. (1997). *Scenarios: The Art of Strategic Conversation*. Chichester: John Wiley and Sons.

——(1999). 'The Art of Maverick Thinking'. *Scenario and Strategic Planning*, 1/1: 19–24.

Wack, P. (1985a). 'Scenarios: Uncharted Waters Ahead'. *Harvard Business Review*, 63/5: 72–90.

——(1985b). 'Scenarios: Shooting the Rapids'. *Harvard Business Review*, 63/6: 139–50.

Yergin, D. and Gustafson, T. (1993). *Russia 2010*. New York: Random House.

39 Barriers to Organizational Learning

Ariane Berthoin Antal, Uwe Lenhardt, and Rolf Rosenbrock

The literature on organizational learning is dominated by contributions stressing the competitive advantages that organizations can reap from engaging in learning and the rewarding experience employees can expect to enjoy in learning organizations. The tenor of most publications is optimistic, suggesting that learning is a natural, ongoing process or at least that it will progress smoothly through the phases defined by the theories once a learning process has been initiated. In reality, however, organizational learning is neither an effortless nor an automatic process, for the media continues to report regularly on troubled and failing organizations. What, then, are the blockages to organizational learning?

Unfortunately, the literature provides no systematic analysis of barriers to organizational learning. Explicit references to impediments to learning are thinly dispersed in the publications of the last twenty-five years. Furthermore, most of these barriers have been theoretically derived, and they have not yet been empirically explored in organizations. The purpose of this chapter is, therefore, to provide an overview of the factors that can block organizational learning and to illustrate them with examples from four cases.

Barriers Explicitly Identified in the Literature

The barriers specifically maintained in the literature on organizational learning can be grouped into three categories: interrupted learning processes, psychological and cultural blockages to learning, and obstacles related to organizational structure and leadership.

Interrupted Learning Processes

The most systematic discussion of barriers to organizational learning was offered as early as 1975 by March and Olsen, and their list was later expanded by other authors, such as Hedberg (1981) and Kim (1993). Using a model of learning that highlighted the linkages between individual beliefs, individual action, organizational action, and environmental response, March and Olsen (1975) identified four types of interruption to the learning cycle (see Fig. 39.1). With regard to the first incomplete learning cycle, March and Olsen theorized that an interruption in the connection between individual beliefs and individual action would result if individuals were limited by their role in the organization and unable to act on their learning. They called this first barrier 'role-constrained learning' (p. 158). A second type of incomplete learning cycle, according to March and Olsen, is to be found when individuals change their own behavior but cannot persuade others to change the organizational rules for behavior. They termed this barrier 'audience learning' (p. 159) to highlight the idea that the link between individual action and organizational action is interrupted. The third incomplete learning cycle that March and Olsen described occurs when organizational members draw incorrect conclusions about the impact of organizational actions on the environment. They characterized such

The authors thank Ilse Stroo and Mieke Willems for their assistance in the literature search on barriers to organizational learning.

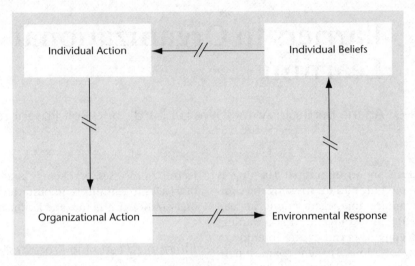

Fig. 39.1. Learning cycle and interruptions

Adapted from figs. 2–5 in March and Olsen 1975

conclusions as 'superstitious learning' (p. 158; see also Levitt and March 1988). The fourth incomplete learning process, which March and Olsen called 'learning under ambiguity' (p. 156), occurs when changes in the environment cannot be clearly identified.

Kim (1993) added three new types of interruptions to the model proposed by March and Olsen (1975), whereby only two of them are barriers.[1] When learning occurs, but is forgotten or not codified for later use, as frequently happens in crisis management, Kim called it 'situational learning' (p. 46). 'Fragmented learning', when one actor or unit learns but the whole does not, is typical in 'very decentralized organizations that do not have the networking capability to keep the parts connected' (Kim 1993: 46).

Hedberg (1981) also built on the learning cycle used by March and Olsen when he introduced

the concept of unlearning to the field of organization studies. He believed that 'slow unlearning is a crucial weakness of many organizations' (p. 3) and explained the need for unlearning as follows: 'Knowledge grows, and simultaneously it becomes obsolete as reality changes. Understanding involves both learning new knowledge and discarding obsolete and misleading knowledge. The discarding activity—unlearning—is as important a part of understanding as is adding new knowledge' (p. 3). The inability to stop certain skilled behaviors impedes the performance of new behaviors, and the inability to discard established mental models hinders the development and application of new ideas in an organization. Schein (1993) pointed out that it is more difficult to unlearn behaviors that have been learned from negative feedback than it is to unlearn behaviors that have been learned through rewards. Starbuck and Hedberg (Ch. 14 in this volume) show how organizational structures and politics militate against unlearning. Past learning becomes embedded in current structures, and key members of the organization have a stake in maintaining the structures and power relations that are advantageous to them (see also Coopey 1995).

---

[1] The third type of interrupted learning cycle identified by Kim (1993) is not a barrier to organizational learning but rather a strategy to bypass standard ways of doing things in an organization in order to achieve learning in one part of it. This happens when actors 'want to sever the link between shared mental models and organizational action in order to seize an opportunity that cannot wait for the whole organization to change (or it may not be desirable for the whole organization to change)' (Kim 1993: 46).

Psychological and Cultural Types of Barriers

Some writers have identified barriers to organizational learning by drawing on findings from psychology relating to individuals and groups—or even by analogy to research on animals (see Maier, Prange, and Rosenstiel, Ch. 1 in this volume). Argyris (1990, 1991, 1993; Argyris and Schön 1978, 1996) has worked extensively on the topic of defensive routines that individuals develop to protect themselves from threatening situations, such as 'critically examining their own role in the organization' (Argyris 1991: 101). The effect of these defensive routines is that they impede people's ability to discover 'how the very way they go about defining and solving problems can be a source of problems in its own right' (Argyris 1991: 100). In other words, they block the ability to learn to see or do things differently. Argyris has also explored how organizational cultures reinforce the defensive routines of their members and thereby build barriers to organizational learning (see also Friedman, Ch. 17 in this volume). Such defensive routines maintain themselves in organizational cultures that externalize blame and generate a sense of hopelessness and cynicism (Argyris 1990: 45).

Schein (1993), too, drew on psychology to illustrate the role of anxiety as an obstacle to organizational learning (see also Scherer and Tran, Ch. 16 in this volume). In his frequently cited article about the 'Green Room', he observed how dogs that have received electric shocks in experiments persist in their fear of entering the green room long after the electrical circuits there have been turned off. 'Once the pattern has been learned, the anxiety alone is enough to keep the behavior going, even if no shocks are ever again administered' (Schein 1993: 87). With this analogy, Schein surmised that organizations build and maintain similar anxiety-generating mechanisms that act as powerful hindrances to learning. In companies characterized for a long time by restrictive, controlling management styles and systems that have long dealt punitively with employees who deviated from the organizational norm or overstepped the boundaries of their jobs, it will be difficult to persuade employees that learning is safe. 'To the extent that our present managerial theories emphasize the stick over the carrot, we are building in strong resistances to new learning' (Schein 1993: 87).

Psychologists have long studied the role of success and failure in learning processes (for reviews in this volume, see Maier, Prange, and Rosenstiel, Ch. 1; Scherer and Tran, Ch. 16; and Starbuck and Hedberg, Ch. 14). There are contradictory views in the literature about how success and failure can block organizational learning. An international study of organizational learning in China, Germany, and Israel revealed that, in spite of the significant differences between the experiences in these three countries, long periods of success were believed to be a blockage to organizational learning (Berthoin Antal, Dierkes, and Marz 1999). Respondents in all three countries reported that crises were useful triggers for learning. Starbuck and Hedberg (Ch. 14 in this volume) explain that members of successful organizations become complacent and usually expect success to continue. Members tend to discard dissonant signals either as irrelevant or as irregularities that are outside their control. Sitkin (1992), too, found that success becomes a barrier because it leads to managerial overconfidence in the ability to foresee risks. In his view, crises are deemed necessary to shake an organization out of its complacency. Nevertheless, he added, learning is also seen to require positive feedback from successful experiences.

March (1991a) and the scholars with whom he has published (Levinthal and March 1993; Levitt and March 1988; March and Olsen 1995) have written about both success and failure as learning traps. As they portray it, success blocks learning when existing competences are exploited at the expense of exploring new ideas. Organizations can get caught in a failure trap when one idea after another is tried out and then abandoned before enough experience has been accumulated for it to be used successfully. 'Organizations are turned into frenzies of experimentation, change, and innovation by a dynamic of failure. Failure leads to search and change, which leads to failure, which leads to more search and so on' (Levinthal and March 1993: 105–6). The link between success and failure has been characterized by Sull (1999) as a trap of learning, a trap he refers to as 'active inertia' (p. 42). He observed that when long-successful companies start to experience failure, they tend to engage in 'flurries of activity' (p. 45) rather than question the assumptions underlying their organizational strategy, processes, and practices. These actions tend to aggravate the problem and multiply failures, because they are not based on a revised understanding of the market. According to Schein (1993), frequent failures can generate anxiety great enough to paralyze an organization so that it cannot learn. Sull (1999) pointed out that managers who engage in a flurry of activities do so precisely because they believe that paralysis is the greatest enemy (p. 43). The tension between the characterization of success as a barrier to learning and failure as a trigger of learning is heightened in the literature by the observation that organizations suffer from the tendency to 'oversample successes and undersample failures' (Levinthal and March 1993: 110). In other words, more attention is paid to successes than to failures, suggesting that the ability of the organization to learn is not just a matter of the number of successes or failures that have been experienced but also of the way in which they are perceived, interpreted, and remembered.

The idea that perceptions play a significant role in building barriers to learning is reflected in the two other barriers identified by Levinthal and March (1993). They draw an analogy to shortsightedness, theorizing that organizations suffer from spatial and temporal myopia. These impairments of sight inhibit the ability of organizations to learn by favoring effects that occur near the learner at the expense of the larger picture and by favoring the short run over the long run. Work by scholars such as Schein (1993) has revealed how perceptions become shared by a group and embedded into the culture of an organization. They have cautioned that 'the widely-shared, tacit assumptions which constitute an organization's

culture can preclude organizational learning' (Edmondson and Moingeon 1996: 23). The reasoning behind this warning is that the assumptions underpinning a culture act as a filter for perceiving and making sense of the information in and around an organization (Berthoin Antal, Dierkes, and Hähner 1997; Büchel and Raub, Ch. 23 in this volume). Perceptual filters enable some things to be seen more clearly by blending out others. 'Mental models not only help us make sense of the world we see, they can also restrict our understanding to that which makes sense within the mental model' (Kim 1993: 39; see also Sull 1999: 45).

Schein (1996) reminded readers that organizations are not monolithic cultures, that they are composed of subcultures often having different goals and using different languages (see Czarniawska, Ch. 5 in this volume). Such subcultures can develop in organizational units, occupational professions, and hierarchical levels. If the members of the subcultures do not understand each other's terminology, metaphors, or stories, organizational learning will be impeded.[2] Furthermore, culture-based barriers in communication can occur between actors inside and outside a given organization. Building on March (1991b), for example, Kieser (1998) showed how the diverse professional cultures of managers, consultants, and academics entail such different languages and goal systems that their ability to learn together is limited (see also Berthoin Antal and Krebsbach-Gnath, Ch. 21 in this volume).

Barriers Related to Organizational Structures and Leadership

Some writers have mentioned structures as barriers to organizational learning. For example, Fiol and Lyles (1985) suggested that centralized structures block learning because

---

[2] A certain amount of organizational learning can occur within subcultures. In fact the learning that takes place in subcultures can often serve as the motor for learning across the organization (Sackman 1992). However, when learning requires interactions with other parts of the system, communication problems will impede learning.

'a centralized, mechanistic structure tends to reinforce past behaviors, whereas an organic, more decentralized structure tends to allow shifts of beliefs and actions' (p. 805). Pawlowsky (1992: 223), too, cited hierarchy as a barrier to organizational learning. This viewpoint appears plausible (and attractive because it corresponds to currently popular ideas in favor of flatter organizations), but the dimensions of structure remains overly general and somewhat contradictory. Empirical research does not consistently support the hypothesis that a hierarchical structure is a barrier to organizational learning. The three-country study reported by Berthoin Antal, Dierkes, and Marz (1999) found evidence of effective and long-term learning in centralized and hierarchical structures as well as in decentralized structures. A more specific type of structural barrier is mentioned by Morgan (1986), who pointed out that departmental structures can inhibit organizational learning by focusing the attention of members on parochial rather than organization-wide problems. Structures can therefore lead to Kim's (1993) fragmented learning and, because they reflect and are shaped by an organization's cultural assumptions, can exacerbate the effects of the perceptual filter called spatial myopia by Levinthal and March (1993).

Probably the fuzziest notion of a barrier has to do with leadership. Authors such as Schein (1985: 317) have mentioned lack of good leadership as an impediment to organizational learning, but this formulation is very vague. Sadler's review of the literature on leadership (see Sadler, Ch. 18 in this volume) indicates that theories of leadership have long focused almost exclusively on top managers as heroic and all-knowing leaders (see also Child and Heavens, Ch. 13 in this volume). This picture suggests that lack of good leadership has a quantitative as well as a qualitative dimension. In other words, learning is impeded when there are not enough leaders and when the behavior of available leaders is not conducive to learning. As Sadler points out, leaders can block organizational learning when they behave as though knowing were a greater virtue than learning.

He also notes that leaders who relegate people to followership and limit the ability of others to participate in leadership curtail opportunities for learning. Models that enable leadership to be shared and distributed among many actors at different levels of the organization have been described in research in other areas, and they could be promising for organizational learning. For example, research on transformation processes in eastern and central Europe has documented the usefulness of the 'tandem' approach to sharing leadership as a way of developing synergies between local and market-oriented management (see Merkens, Geppert, and Antal, Ch. 10 in this volume). Studies on innovation processes have revealed how effectively new ideas can be introduced and implemented through combinations of actors holding status-based power and actors with expertise-based power, particularly when they build coalitions across organizational boundaries (Berthoin Antal 1992; Freeman 1982; Kanter 1988).

This overview of the barriers described in the literature on organizational learning indicates that the conceptualization is still quite thin and fragmented. Some ideas, such as the typologies of interruptions to learning processes, are intellectually appealing, but their usefulness in practice remains to be seen. The literature on the impact that success, and other factors have on organizational learning structures, contains contradictory findings. Far too little is known about how various leadership models can block or enable organizational learning. Possibly the most significant shortcoming of the literature is that each of these concepts has been treated separately. The interaction of different factors has not yet been considered. This gap is probably due to the fact that discussions about barriers have tended to emerge as byproducts of studies intended to portray ideal processes of organizational learning. Barriers have not often been treated as the focal point of research. A first step toward correcting some of these deficits can be taken by looking at a set of cases in which different degrees of organizational learning were achieved.

Barriers in Practice: Evidence from Four Cases

The introduction of a new program involves all the processes encompassed in phase models of organizational learning (see, for example, Huber 1991). Ideas need to be acquired, developed, and agreed upon by a large group of members of the organization, then must be implemented and embedded in the organization's structures and processes. Whether an idea for a new program originates from experience in another organization or from an internal source, its development within the organization is a creative process that involves the sharing of tacit and explicit knowledge (Czarniawska and Sevón 1996; Nonaka and Takeuchi 1995).

The field of preventive health care offers very instructive examples of how organizations need to learn and change their mental maps and administrative processes in order to introduce new programs effectively. There is much evidence that companies can benefit from improvements in protecting and promoting employees' health (e.g. reduction of sick-leaves and related costs, increase of work satisfaction, motivation, and quality). Nevertheless, in reality health at work is usually treated as a rather weak and marginal issue within the organization. Even when organizational structures and routines of preventive action have been established, they have often been far too insufficient to meet the demands of modern occupational health policy (Rosenbrock and Lenhardt 1999). This field represents a classic case of the need for what Argyris and Schön (1978) called second-order organizational learning. It is not sufficient to improve a few rules and regulations.

Instead, significant changes in mindsets and practices are needed in organizations in order to improve health promotion. First and foremost, a more comprehensive understanding of work-related health problems is required in organizations. Traditionally, occupational health and safety has focused on reducing risks and health-damaging events (mainly those of a physical and chemical nature) characterized by clear cause–effect relationships and amenable to quantitative measurement methods. Numerous health problems that do not fit into this pattern need to be attended to. For example, psychosocial stress related to organizational weaknesses, hierarchical conflicts, and inadequate work design remain invisible and untreated under the traditional approach to work-related health.

Second, if these problems are to be acted upon effectively in organizations, different strategies and methods are required than those currently pursued for managing occupational health and safety. Prevention is usually delegated to medical and technical experts, who tend to have only marginal status in organizations. Such experts lack the power necessary to achieve significant change. And they are not able to build a power base, for they usually act individualistically and selectively within their area of professional expertise. Effective prevention has to be planned and organized systematically and cooperatively. In other words, companies must find ways to integrate health issues into all levels of managerial decision-making. Continuous learning processes have to be established in order to facilitate regular evaluations of health and adjustment of preventive action. Employee participation in designing, implementing, and evaluating preventive health care has proven crucial in organizations. This approach, too, is something many organizations have yet to learn how to do.

A study on attempts to introduce preventive health programs in several German organizations (Lenhardt, Elkeles, and Rosenbrock 1997; Lenhardt and Rosenbrock 1998; Lenhardt, Rosenbrock, and Elkeles 1996) provides a rich range of experience for exploring barriers to organizational learning. The processes of changing mindsets and introducing new strategies in order to develop and implement more effective and far-reaching preventive health care approaches were examined in four organizations selected on the basis of information obtained from literature and experts. The sample was composed specifically with an eye to including organizations that represent varying ranges of activities undertaken and different stages of successful policy innovation. It was comprised in a community hospital, a large chemical company, a large manufacturer of automobile parts, and a medium-sized public transportation company. Data collection consisted of interviews in the companies with experts (e.g. physicians and physiotherapists) and decision-makers (e.g. personnel directors, plant directors, and members of the works council), interviews with managers at the health insurance funds providing coverage for the company's employees, and evaluation of internal documents. Some of the respondents turned out to be key actors in the innovation process, a fortunate, but not predictable, circumstance.

A comparison of the learning processes and outcomes in these four very different organizations sheds light on how organizational learning can be blocked by different factors at various points in the process.

Case A

In the community hospital presented as case A, the exploration of new possibilities in prevention focused on attempts to establish a program for training employees how to avoid back pain. The idea for a new preventive exercise course was introduced by the staff person responsible for training and development at the hospital. She had been recruited recently and was unaware of an earlier initiative. Her problem awareness and her solution stemmed from personal experience. Having originally been a nurse, she had experienced the demands of the job and the back strains it incurred. Furthermore, she had worked for a self-help organization before taking on the training and development position at the hospital, so she believed in preventive treatment. She asked for and obtained permission from the hospital management to offer relevant courses. However, the management did not become actively committed to the project and did not establish a budget to fund such courses. The very limited resources provided by the management and the sporadic availability of the external trainer

resulted in an irregular program (four or five courses were held) rather than in a preventive approach that became embedded in the organization.

It is striking how little was achieved in case A, particularly since a hospital—an organization dedicated to health care—appears to be an ideal environment in which to introduce preventive programs for employees. Attention to the health of the organization's employees could be expected to be a logical extension of (or even antecedent to) providing care to the organization's clients, its patients. However, adopting a preventive rather than a remedial approach to health care often involves changing the organizational mindset. Similarly, learning to focus on the needs of the staff often requires an organization to avoid seeing its employees simply as instruments for delivering services to patients. The interviews revealed barriers embedded in the culture of the hospital. The descriptions of the reasons for the back pains that many staff members suffered and the possible ways of dealing with the pains revealed very different perceptions of the problem. The findings show how difficult it is for an organization to learn a preventive approach under these conditions.

Case A also illustrates how lack of leadership can block a learning process early in its development. It is telling of the leadership situation that the medical director of the hospital felt that the issue of preventive health promotion for employees was not relevant enough for him to meet with the research team, so he passed the interview request on to the head of nursing services. The head of personnel believed that there was little the hospital could do to prevent back pains, which he saw as an unavoidable side effect of the work there. According to him, the difficulty faced by the hospital was to find other jobs for these employees, but since ever fewer alternatives could be found, the employees who could no longer fulfill their tasks had to be dismissed. Although he agreed to introduce the courses for back pains, he did not see them as a way of reducing the health problems. His skepticism about the courses as ways of preventing the problem at the hospital was also related to the fact that he believed that some people reported having back pains simply to avoid work. Furthermore, he felt that employees were not committed enough to caring for their backs, for too few of them were willing to register for classes outside of work time. The interview with him also showed that the hospital had introduced other types of preventive programs, but only in order to meet legislated requirements.

The two members of the works council supported the idea of introducing preventive courses against back pains, but they believed that the problem of employee health was much larger and that this initiative was of only marginal significance. They emphasized that the back pains were due not only to the tasks that involved lifting and carrying but also to the overall working conditions, which they described as very stressful. They had succeeded in launching various improvements over the years by bringing in external authorities to check on the hospital and to mandate ergonomically safe equipment. However, they noted that employees neither used the new equipment sufficiently nor followed the preventive procedures consistently, often because of time pressures on the job. The courses against back pains were not a central concern to the employee representatives, so they did not feel it was necessary to invest their political capital, although they had tried (unsuccessfully) to obtain permission from the hospital management to have the courses offered during work time.

The negative impact of management's disinterest in a preventive approach to employee health and the importance of external actors for triggering change in the organization was also highlighted by the physiotherapist who had run courses about preventing back pain a few years earlier. She had been with the hospital for some years as a physiotherapist for patients and had gradually become involved with employees' back pains when several colleagues asked her for advice and help. She had tried to get management support for courses for the employees but had been turned down until the company doctor proposed to the manage-

ment that such a course could be introduced and financed through the health insurance fund to which most of the employees belonged.[3] The physiotherapist found that her course was attended by many participants who already suffered from chronic back pain. She could not both help them and provide preventive care for other employees. In addition, she was concerned that her courses were not job-related enough and hence not as helpful as they could be for the employees. She appealed in vain for the management and the personnel representative to support an expansion of the program to increase its effectiveness. The employees' disinclination to take courses outside of work time was regarded by the physiotherapist as symptomatic of their low interest in preventive care. After two years, she discontinued the courses out of frustration with the lack of commitment to a preventive approach at the hospital.

The company physician who had spearheaded the introduction of this earlier program had only recently been succeeded by a new physician who believed that management's sincere commitment would be needed in order for the hospital to learn about preventing back pain. Although she thought that courses against back pain should be offered, they would not have more than a marginal impact on the problem until employees' tasks and working conditions were altered. She therefore recommended that management employ a staff person with expertise in preventive work practices, someone who could observe and advise employees at the workplace. The proposal was rejected on the grounds that it could not be financed. After this negative experience, the doctor decided to wait and work in the background with a variety of actors in the organiza-

[3] This arrangement was possible because the regulation of statutory health insurance funds underwent a major change in Germany in 1989. Article 20 of the Health Reform Act granted health insurance funds the right to establish health promotion services of their own. This change led to a significant expansion of preventive programs in the following years, mainly driven by intensified competition between the insurance funds. An interesting aspect of this development was that health insurance funds suddenly became actively involved particularly in health promotion activities at the workplace (Lenhardt 1999).

tion before making any new large-scale proposals.

The case provides an instructive example of an interrupted learning process. The previous courses about preventing back pain had been terminated and had left no visible traces in the memory of the organization. The interruption cannot be categorized easily into one of March and Olsen's (1975) four types, but it might be considered an example of Kim's (1993) situational learning. There is no evidence that success served as a barrier to learning in the case. Nor is there evidence that failure blocked organizational learning, although the failure of past initiatives or of proposals for new initiatives may have dissuaded their champions from making new attempts.

Among the most striking features of this case are the absence of a shared problem definition and the corresponding lack of agreement on the way to deal with it. Each of the interviewed actors held a view of the problem that corresponded to his or her professional role in the organization. There is no evidence that any of the respondents questioned their definitions of the problem or attempted to expand their views by learning from those of others. The greatest barrier appears to have been the culture of the hospital. The idea of preventive care for employees was foreign to the culture of the organization, and neither top management nor other actors exercised the leadership necessary to develop a different mindset. The new head of training and development was not powerful enough alone to suffice as a leader, and she did not get far in building a coalition with other leaders. She had not acquired sufficient information about past experience in the hospital before introducing her idea to management. There is no evidence that she had attempted to combine her views of the problem and her ideas for solutions with those of other key actors (other than her loose, informal contacts with the new company doctor, that is, another weak actor). An organization cannot learn how to do something new if there is no process by which the members generate a common view on what needs to be learned and why.

Case B

The chemical company in the sample had built up a certain amount of experience with preventive programs. Its employee social services and commitment to health and safety were part of a long-standing tradition typical of this industry in Germany (Dierkes, Hähner, and Berthoin Antal 1997). The company also had a sound relationship with the health insurance fund that provided coverage for the company's employees. In recent years, the health insurance had launched a number of innovative programs for preventive care that were open not only to the employees of the company but also to those of other companies. Such innovative behavior was largely driven by the Health Reform Act of 1989 (see note 3). A further incentive to introduce attractive preventive programs for employees was cost reduction. The director of the health insurance fund reported that studies documented how the increased participation of employees in health-promoting programs reduced medical costs and absenteeism, an argument he also used in persuading the management of the company to support new initiatives. The insurance fund played a central role in triggering learning initiatives in the area of prevention and health promotion. It offered preventive training courses and counseling for the company's employees, helped the company establish a work group for health matters, and contributed significantly to planning a company health report. Compared to the hospital in case A, the chemicals company had already developed a broader mindset to health issues, it had a strong external partner to design and deliver new initiatives, and it had launched a much broader range of health-promoting activities.

According to the director of the health insurance fund, the management of the chemicals company was generally quite receptive to innovations. However, the level of commitment to the different activities varied depending on the amount of organizational change and involvement the activity required from the company. For example, the management was willing to support the wide range of courses and advisory services provided by the health insurance fund, but the employees could not participate during their work time. This limitation signaled to the fund that the management was not yet taking preventive approaches seriously enough.

One might have expected the works council to take up the issue actively in the interests of employees. However, as the representative of the works council noted quite self-critically, the members of the council had traditionally focused on toxicological health issues and had responded to problems rather than promoting a preventive approach. It had not been in their mindset, he explained, to play a proactive role, and they had kept a distance from preventive activities run by the insurance fund or other medical services within the company.

The barriers to learning within the company become even more evident in the experience of the work group on health matters that was initiated by the health insurance fund and then handed over to the company. This group did not succeed in institutionalizing itself. It met irregularly, and its main project objective, the introduction of a company-wide health report, encountered resistance that the group was not able to overcome. The employee representatives first blocked the initiative for reasons of data protection. Once these concerns had been resolved, the works council favored the preparation of such a report because it hoped it would document that working conditions needed to be improved. By contrast, the management hoped that the report would show that absenteeism was not only a matter of working conditions but also of employees' attitudes and behaviors.

The interviews reveal that the participants themselves did not perceive their different views to be irreconcilable. In the process of discussing issues in the work group and in the data several respondents saw that the health report was expected to provide constructive opportunities to improve understanding and arrive at shared solutions for various health-related problems in the company. However, these opportunities for learning remained unused.

The barrier lay less in the existence of differing views than in the absence of leadership to ensure that the issues were actively tackled and decided. None of the internal actors regarded the topic of preventive health care in general, nor the company health report in particular, as central to his or her agenda.

Looking back at the experience with this work group, the director of the health insurance fund reflected that it had probably been a mistake to launch the group under the auspices of his organization. The leadership of the work group during its formative phase lay with the health fund, not with the company. When it was transferred to the company, the corporate officer who took over the responsibility did not have the necessary influence on health matters to push things through.

In the opinion of all the actors who were interviewed, progress on these initiatives had been impeded because they had been launched at a time when the company was undergoing significant restructuring. These actors pointed out that competing issues on the corporate agenda had distracted attention from preventive health care projects. For example, serious rationalization and a significant reduction in staff had become necessary for the company. Some members of the management believed that early retirement would not be sufficient, so they recommended dismissals, especially of workers who were often sick-listed. Such action was a taboo in the organization's culture and past practice, and the personnel director believed that breaking it would seriously threaten the company's harmonious labor relations, which were based on mutual trust and cooperation. In order to ward off dismissals, he considered two approaches essential. First, he thought more attention to the problem of absenteeism had to be demonstrated by a more systematic use of control methods. Second, at least a temporary tactical retreat from the 'health promotion arena' seemed necessary to avoid irritating hard-liners and raising unmeetable expectations among employees. The work of the health committee and discussions about new health promotion activities were therefore brought to a standstill.

Company B appears at first to have achieved more organizational learning than did the organization in case A, for the former undertook many more activities than the latter in order to promote preventive healthcare for employees. However, the amount of learning that actually took place in company B is questionable because there is no evidence that old ways of thinking or behaving were challenged and unlearned or that new procedures were institutionalized. The entire program of courses was designed and run for the employees by the insurance fund at its health center. The work group on health issues and the company-wide health report did not get off the ground. Even though the management of company B was perceived to be receptive to new initiatives and the culture of the organization supported ideas related to the health and safety of the employees, activities whose implementation would have required changes in mindsets, processes, or structures in the organization became stuck at the discussion stage. One barrier seems to be that the leadership for learning remained outside the organization. The health insurance fund's active process of developing and implementing new ideas suggests that this organization learned a great deal, but although it was able to trigger learning in the chemicals company, it could not be responsible for achieving that learning. The centrality of the health insurance fund in developing and running new programs meant that the company itself played too marginal a role (see Berthoin Antal and Krebsbach-Gnath, Ch. 21 in this volume). One organization cannot learn for another, and an imbalance in the relationship between learner and supporter can become a barrier for organizational learning.

There is somewhat more evidence in this case than in the previous one of discussions between various actors to find common ground in the definition of problems and of appropriate solutions. However, the differences between the management's view of the company-wide health report and the view held by the employee's representatives were not used as an opportunity for organizational learning. Instead of engaging the conflict, which could

have led to learning (see Rothman and Friedman, Ch. 26 in this volume), the actors allowed it to block further learning.

There is a hint in the interviews that a past failure might have contributed to blocking learning in this case. An attempt had been made a few years earlier to institute a 'health circle', a team in which the workers could analyze their work situation and propose how to improve it. But it had failed, and the manager involved in that activity reported having learned to be much more careful and skeptical about such initiatives. This experience was not mentioned by other respondents, so it may be more appropriate to interpret the earlier example as illustrating an interrupted learning cycle and lack of organizational memory than as evidence of the negative impact that past failure may have on future learning.

The high level of agreement among the respondents that the then-current pressures of restructuring were to blame for the lack of attention to health initiatives in the company is striking. Their reasoning may be a legitimate explanation or it might be symptomatic of the blaming and avoiding behavior characteristic of defensive routines (Argyris 1993). Whether or not it is fair to place the blame so squarely on another issue, the explanation of competing agenda items confirms the observation in case A that a main barrier to organizational learning is the lack of shared commitment to learning in a given area.

Case C

The order books of the automobile-parts manufacturer were so full that the high levels of absenteeism that had characterized the plant for some years became a serious problem. The company chose to introduce a participative approach to improving the health of employees at work in order to reduce absenteeism. After piloting ergonomics work groups formed by employees at the shop-floor level in three departments with particularly high incidences of absenteeism, the company extended the approach to twelve departments. It was considered successful by all involved.

The initiative for launching the project had been taken by the department responsible for work design and safety after senior management had signaled that the problem of high absenteeism had to be tackled in the company. The statistics on absenteeism had long been available, and the health insurance fund had pointed out some years earlier that the numbers in this company were above the average for comparable employees in the area. But no comprehensive approach to analyzing and dealing with the causes for the problem had been undertaken. The internal medical service was neither technically equipped for such data collection and analysis, nor trusted enough by employees for it to be able to lead such an initiative. The idea of introducing participative work groups came from discussions with corporate headquarters, after the managers there reported positive experiences with a similar approach in another plant.

It is at first surprising that the initiative for the project came from the work-design department; that unit is not usually influential in plants. However, the work designers had built up positive personal relations in the company over time and had expanded their scope of activity beyond what is traditionally seen to be their responsibility, so the department was well accepted as an innovator. The head of the department strategically chose a senior manager to support the project, a person he knew he could count on to be enthusiastic about an unusual approach and to give it the necessary political backing. The department quickly found other supporters for the idea of a 'participative ergonomic project' among middle management and brought in the works council from the very beginning in order to ensure its commitment as well. The close involvement of the works council helped create a sense of security and openness for the employees throughout the process, enabling them to express their concerns about a broad range of issues at work without fearing repercussions.

A project group with a mix of members from different functions and levels in the organization was formed to design the project. This group selected the pilot departments, informed the employees in these departments of the purpose and procedure of the project, conducted an unstructured written survey of all these employees about their work conditions, and requested their suggestions. The members of the project group believed that absenteeism was related to a mix of factors in which subjective perceptions play a significant role. The objective was not to generate a scientifically valid survey of health and safety factors designed to identify key factors responsible for absenteeism. The members of the project group wanted to create an opportunity for employees to report in their own words—unhampered by experts' categories and terminology—how they experienced their work. A number of work groups were created in each department to discuss the results of the survey, identify ideas generated by the survey, develop the ones that they considered worth pursuing, and establish priorities. A coordinating body then checked the proposals and decided which of them were to be implemented. The employees were continually informed about the suggestions and the progress of the work groups. Both the staff person who facilitated the work groups and the member of the works council who worked intensely on this project emphasized the importance of actively updating employees about actions taken and about the reasons for not following up on certain suggestions.

The smooth process and positive outcomes of the three pilot groups led to the expansion of this approach to further units in the company. The respondents mentioned three kinds of outcomes, although no formal evaluation of results was conducted. Many observable improvements were made in order to reduce or eliminate physical problems encountered by the employees at work. There was also a reduction in absenteeism, but the respondents generally did not particularly highlight this outcome. The most important result stressed in the interviews was the change in the relationship between management and employees. Some managers had been skeptical at the outset whether the investment in the work groups would actually generate a significant number of useful suggestions. However, they were soon impressed by the wealth of constructive ideas that were generated by the employees in the survey and then developed in the work groups. Managers learned that when they took employees seriously, employees were willing to understand business issues and pressures. Those employees who had been skeptical of management's willingness to listen and really follow up on ideas originating from the lower echelons of the organization were soon persuaded by management actions that it was worth making suggestions. According to the respondents, a cultural shift occurred in the plant. Old behaviors, mindsets, and structures were unlearned, and new understandings, processes, and structures were developed.

The respondents reported no serious barriers. They encountered some initial skepticism based on past experience and on a negative culture of interaction between management and employees, but these problems appear to have been overcome quickly. The most important factor in enabling members of the organization to learn how to resolve technical problems and how to interact at the workplace in a respectful and constructive way was the constellation of leadership for learning that was put into place from the outset. The two central actors from the work-design department and the works council did not hold hierarchically powerful positions, but they were well networked in the organization and well trusted. They had the strong backing of senior management at both a strategic level (headquarters had said it wanted something done about absenteeism) and a practical level (they secured the support of a production manager who was open to innovative approaches).

In case C success was an important motor for learning rather than a barrier. The overall business success of the plant, with its full order books, set the stage for the problem of absenteeism to be taken seriously by senior management. Several respondents also noted that it had enabled managers to feel they could invest the necessary funds to follow up on the useful suggestions generated by the work groups. The interviews show that the key actors had sought out managers in other departments who had experienced success with other innovations and who had therefore been willing to experiment again. Lastly, the successful implementation of suggestions from the work groups fueled the commitment to the project among employees and managers alike and expanded the effort from the one original department to twelve.

An intriguing facet of this case is that this company's work groups on health matters were no longer meeting at the time the interviews were conducted for this case study. A new team-based work organization had recently been introduced in the plant and the range of responsibility vested in the teams included (at least formally) the health and safety of its members. Managers and the staff person who facilitated the work groups believed that the success of those groups is what had enabled a smooth transition into a team-structured organization. They felt that the work groups had fulfilled their function well and that they were no longer needed. The works council, however, feared that one cost of this organizational transition might be a loss of attention devoted to preventive health care. Although the company's general learning about participative and cooperative work relations was maintained in the new structure, attention to health-related issues may have slipped from the agenda. This case can be seen either as an illustration of a completed learning cycle that had successfully embedded itself into a new organizational structure or as an interruption of learning despite significant initial achievements. Follow-up research would be needed to see whether the transition did indeed divert the learning away from health-related issues and whether the diversion has become a problem in the organization. If the transition has had effect, then diversion would represent a new type of interrupted learning cycle.

Case D

The privately owned public transportation company that was studied had rapidly expanded in the years prior to the interviews and had introduced new technologies and services to prepare itself to face increased competition in its region. The organization had suffered from very poor relations between managers and staff, a phenomenon that was accompanied by demotivation and absenteeism. A major difference between this case and cases A, B, and C is that the definition of the problem was very broad and that the approach taken to dealing with them was unusually open and flexible. Health-related concerns and preventive approaches had not been at the center of the initiative. Instead, they had emerged from the open-ended organizational development process. All the respondents agreed that the organization would be able to attend appropriately to specific issues such as health problems only if it unlearned negative behaviors and learned to change its culture.

The former head of the works council, who had previously worked as a bus driver for the company[4] started the ball rolling. Believing that improvements could be achieved only if the company's management style changed, he had joined forces with a staff person and two middle managers. Together they had persuaded top management to introduce a number of activities to promote a more cooperative management style with the help of an external consultant. New management principles had been developed, and managers had participated in training courses to develop a more participative leadership style.[5] A work group had then been established with members from different departments and different levels of the organization in order to identify the causes for the apparently deep-seated organizational problems and to develop and implement solutions to these problems. The changes had included investments in ergonomic equipment selected by employees, expanded training and development opportunities, a dramatic improvement in communication between management and employees, and organizational

innovations that gave the employees the power to determine their schedules.

All the respondents stressed two key factors responsible for the success of the learning process. First, there had been general agreement on the nature of the problem. Second, no predetermined focus or approach had been imposed from the outset. The consensus on the problem had been very broadly defined as 'management style—motivation—absenteeism'. Some subgroups in the organization had had different perceptions of the problem, but they had been variations in emphasis rather than significant conceptual disagreements. The autonomous nature of the process had meant that the initiators had been free to select the members of the work group and that the work group had then decided on how it wanted to work. The initiators had obtained an agreement from management that the group could make and implement decisions rather than having to seek management approval in order to act on proposals. Proposals entailing sizeable investment had been submitted to management, but they, too, had been handled flexibly.

In order to identify the problems in the organization from the perspective of employees, the work group had first conducted a survey of the bus drivers. Next, the group had worked through the resulting long list of very diverse problems and concerns and had developed suggestions for dealing with them. These suggestions had been posted for all to see. The very fact that the bus drivers had seen their concerns being taken seriously and that solutions were also being posted had significantly improved the work climate. While thinking about long-term problems, the group had taken measures to resolve the short-term problems immediately so that changes were visible. By building on these successes, the group had overcome any remnants of employee skepticism that change could be achieved in the organization. A great deal of attention had been paid to communicating with employees throughout the process, not only to inform them about changes that were being made but also to continue learning from their feedback and new ideas.

---

[4] At the time of the interviews he had been appointed head of social services.

[5] A manager who proved unable to adapt to the new style had to leave the company. This consequence was seen as proof of serious commitment to changing at the organization.

As in case C, the leadership for learning in this case was based on an effective constellation of internal actors. In company D leadership had started with the head of the works council who had built a coalition with a few middle managers. The leadership had then obtained top management support. With this backing, the initiators had approached the organization's rank-and-file and had engaged directly with the frontline employees. In other words, this case represents neither the traditional top-down, nor the currently popular bottom-up approach. Instead, it is an example of middle-top-bottom leadership for learning (Nonaka and Takeuchi 1995). Significantly, the selection of other key actors had entailed both positive and negative decisions. People had been chosen because the initiators believed they would work well in the group, and conscious choices had been made to include divergent views. Equally importantly, the respondents mentioned that they had decided not to bring in the people who are often automatically present in committees unless it was believed that these individuals could contribute productively. The learning and change process had been driven by internal actors, who had drawn on external expertise where they had felt it was useful (e.g. an external organizational development consultant and the health insurance fund). This example therefore illustrates an appropriate balance between centrality and marginality of internal and external actors in organizational learning (Berthoin Antal and Krebsbach-Gnath, Ch. 21 in this volume).

There is no clear beginning or end to this case, and no interruptions to the learning cycle emerge from the descriptions. Although segments of the process can be described as a progression from knowledge acquisition, diffusion and sense-making, implementation, and storage in memory, the overall process cannot be captured appropriately by a phase-type model of learning, even when one conceives of the phase model as functioning in iterative mode. An ongoing spiral of knowledge conversion and action is a more appropriate image to represent the experience reflected in the interviews.

Discussion

The four cases described in this chapter clearly document that learning cannot be assumed to be a natural, continuous process in organizations. It must be triggered in order to overcome a variety of barriers (see also Nonaka, Reinmöller, and Toyama, Ch. 37 in this volume). Our analysis also revealed that once learning processes are started, their momentum needs to be actively maintained because there is a high risk that they will be interrupted learning. The cases show that the culture of an organization can act as a powerful barrier to learning and that if this barrier is not grappled with explicitly, attempts to develop new ideas or behaviors will not take hold. Lack of leadership proved to be a serious problem with various forms: absence of support from top management; too strong a lead from outside the organization without a strong counterpart inside the organization; and individual, unconnected initiatives from lower levels in the hierarchy.

Not all the barriers identified in the literature could be explored in these case studies. Some may have been present but not visible through the methodology used in collecting the data, for the objective of the original research was not specifically to develop organizational learning theories. For example, it is likely that examples of defensive routines (Argyris 1990, 1991, 1993) could have been elicited if the researchers had been looking for them, particularly in cases A and B, and probably also in the other two. For the same methodological reasons, the cases unfortunately do not illustrate the processes involved in unlearning (Hedberg 1981), although it is probable that unlearning was a barrier that the actors in cases A and B did not overcome and that useful ideas could have been derived from cases C and D. Other potential barriers might have been neutralized in these cases because of the size of the organization or the nature of the policy issue, so these possibilities should be the subject of future empirical studies dedicated specifically to identifying barriers and their effects. For example, the concept of spatial myopia suggested by Levinthal and March (1993) is more likely to be relevant in organizations that are spread across multiple locations, such as multinational corporations, international joint ventures, or networks, than in organizations with only a single site.

The case studies shed fresh light on the barriers on which there is no consensus in the literature—success, failure, and centralized or hierarchical structures. The case studies show that organizational learning requires networking in every type of structure. The successful actors in cases C and D had developed a personal network that they could draw on across the organization, so the structure of the current organization was less important than the ability to build a network across it. The effect of failure as a barrier emerged weakly in the cases of interrupted learning. Actors who had experienced failures in attempts to launch initiatives in the past were not willing to take the risk again. It would probably be an exaggeration, however, to see in this behavior the 'Green Room effect' described by Schein (1993), for the consequences of earlier attempts were not severe and certainly not comparable to the pain of electric shocks. These case studies provide no documentation for success as a barrier to organizational learning; instead, success played a positive role in the learning process. The members of the leadership constellation in cases C and D actively sought examples of success to build on in order to help other members of the organization see that their ideas were being heard and were bearing fruit. Although none of the cases involved an outright crisis, case D did illustrate how problems embedded in a period of success can trigger learning. The level of absenteeism that had been problematic, but accepted, until the company became very successful suddenly became an intolerable problem that threatened the ability of the company to deliver all the orders it received. The company avoided a crisis by taking action and initiating a learning process. The fact that the launching of initiatives was preceded by a process of problem analysis that was specifically designed to give voice to different mindsets rather than limit itself to the dominant management view enabled the company to avoid the barrier of active inertia defined by Sull (1999).

In each of the cases, the representatives of different functions in the organization had function-specific mindsets. This diversity proved to be an insuperable barrier in case A and a significant barrier in case B, whereas in cases C and D the participants succeeded in developing a common platform on which their different priorities fitted together. In case A there was no evidence of attempts by the organization's members to generate a shared picture of the problem and of possible solutions to it. What the members of the organization did seem to share was a tendency to externalize blame and a sense that the problem lay beyond their control. These conditions fueled a sense of hopelessness and cynicism, as predicted by Argyris (1990). The few attempts by individual actors to initiate courses were met by the skepticism felt by members of other groups. Consequently, the experience with the courses served more to confirm existing views than to challenge and shift mindsets. The situation was better in case B, where more activities were undertaken. However, a close look revealed that these activities were led and implemented by an external organization and were not embedded in the company itself. They did not require the company to learn how to think or do anything differently. Those initiatives (particularly the company health report) that required the members of the organization to open themselves to new ways of thinking or acting and to come to a shared view of how things could be done differently became bogged down.

The concept of interrupted learning proved useful for observing the processes in three of the case studies, although the specific types of interruptions suggested by March and Olsen (1975) and Kim (1993) do not lend themselves easily to differentiating between the experiences. A course against back pain had been started and stopped a few years earlier in case A, and a quality circle had been launched unsuccessfully in the past in case B. It might be possible to categorize these two experiences as examples of audience learning because the individuals involved learned something. However, other members of the organization did not even remember the event in case A, so it was not an example of Kim's (1993) fragmented learning. Even if these examples could be correctly placed into one of the existing categories of interrupted learning processes, it is not clear what conclusions this categorization might help scholars or managers arrive at. The categories appear theoretically interesting but sterile when confronted with reality.

However, if the concept of interrupted learning cycles is linked to the phase model of organizational learning, the combination provides helpful insights into the dynamics of barriers in learning processes. In case A, there was some internal knowledge about how to take a preventive approach to back pains, but the lack of agreement on the nature of the problem and on the most appropriate approach made it impossible for this knowledge to be used. In case B the knowledge was acquired through an external organization, but the learning process was interrupted early because the knowledge did not become integrated into the company. In case C the new work structure meant that the work groups were no longer meeting, a fact that could represent a new kind of interruption: a diversion from the original learning process to a new one.

In all four organizations, the initial culture was not conducive to preventive care for employees. The relations between the various groupings in the organization were described as lacking understanding, respect, and trust. Management styles and procedures were controlling and employees demotivated, conditions that were reflected in problematic levels of absenteeism. These cultural barriers impeded learning in cases A and B, but in cases C and D the participants succeeded in changing the culture and improving preventive care. Two closely related strategic differences between the learning processes in the two sets of cases explain why the cultural barriers were not overcome in cases A and B. The first difference was the focus on the culture rather than on symptoms; the second, the presence or absence of a constellation of distributed leadership. The participants in cases A and B limited themselves to tackling back pains and absenteeism, but the attempts were blocked because these maladies were actually symptoms of the cultural problems in the organizations. By contrast, the participants in cases C and D explicitly labeled the culture as a source of the problems and emphasized that this deeper level had to be dealt with directly in order for changes to be achieved at other levels.

What enabled the change to occur in cases C and D was the emergence of a constellation of distributed leadership, whereas no such leadership grew in cases A and B. The individualistic approach taken in case A could not generate enough common ground to support learning initiatives. In case B the leadership was outside the company, and although the health fund director had good relations with various actors in the chemicals company, this constellation was not turned into an internal leadership coalition. The leadership constellation in cases C and D was entirely internal and included members from different departments and levels of the organization. Actors without significant status developed ideas and obtained backing for their initiatives from individuals higher up in the organization and from people in different departments at various other levels. In both cases the most important role of senior managers was to create legitimate space for learning to proceed, but their provision of the necessary resources to finance new ideas should not be overlooked.

Implications for a Coherent Approach to Barriers

Barriers to organizational learning need to be analyzed as interrelated factors rather than as distinct and independent elements. Strategies for overcoming barriers can then be developed in a coherent fashion. Some barriers may be more readily apparent than others but may not be the most serious obstacles to organizational learning. Successes, failures, and hierarchies, for example, may not deserve as much attention as they have received in the literature so far unless they are treated as symptoms of other, deeper barriers. Not until the underlying barriers relating to the structure, culture, and leadership of the organization have also been identified and grappled with can processes of organizational learning be actively engaged.

The structure, culture, and leadership of organizations are closely intertwined. For analytical purposes, it is possible to start with any one of the three and explore its connections to the other two. An organization's structure usually reflects the values and mental maps embedded in its culture, and the dominant leadership style tends to suit the given structure and the culturally shaped norms of the organization (see Berthoin Antal, Dierkes, and Marz 1999). Consequently, cultural barriers maintain and in turn, are maintained by, aspects of the organizational structure as well as by the behavior of leaders.

For practical purposes it makes no difference which of these three factors one starts with. The most effective approach is to focus first and foremost on ensuring that the organization does not suffer from a quantitative or qualitative lack of leadership. There are two reasons for beginning with leadership. First, it is the resource that can most readily be increased regardless of the organization's size, structure, or financial situation. Second, it is only through the exercise of leadership that barriers embedded in the culture and structure of an organization can be overcome.

If leadership responsibilities are taken at different levels of the organization by individuals who then build links to other members with related interests, then barriers in the structure or culture of the organization can be surmounted. The leadership potential within the organization is thereby augmented and distributed. The leadership constellation found in the cases where barriers to learning were overcome replicates the champion–sponsor network found in innovative organizations (Berthoin Antal 1992; Freeman 1982 reported similar re-

sults). Champions in the middle or lower ranks of the organization ensure support for their ideas by seeking a sponsor at the top of the organization to provide legitimacy. Initiatives that have a sponsor but no champion, or a champion but no sponsor, tend to founder quickly. An equally important dimension of the constellation is the network of relationships that the champions draw on in the organization (and, where appropriate, outside it). These people build up effective working relationships with others in different parts of the organization and are therefore trusted. For each issue they actively seek out other stakeholders and jointly develop a shared picture of the situation and what needs to be done (see also Kanter 1988). The actual job description of the champions is less significant than their personal characteristics, such as their intense commitment to an issue and their ability to link their perspectives on a problem to the strategic interests of other actors.

What are the implications for overcoming structural barriers? Leadership constellations that are effective for learning require networking across the organization in every type of structure. Distributed leadership can grow in different organizational structures. The strategies required in centralized organizations in order to develop a personal network that can be drawn on for specific initiatives differ somewhat from the strategies required for that purpose in decentralized organizations, but such development is not necessarily easier or more difficult to achieve in one type than in the other.

Learning leaders (see Sadler, Ch. 18 in this volume) at all levels have a responsibility for ensuring the cultural factors impeding organizational learning are brought to the surface so that the members of the organization do not become frustrated and cynical by fighting against mere symptoms. In order to stimulate organizational learning, leaders need to create space for processes in which the problems can be defined in ways that convey the reality experienced by members of the organization. It is essential that leaders enable people to avoid colluding with the dominant and culturally acceptable definition of the problem. The experiences in the four case studies presented in this chapter confirm the conclusion drawn by Berthoin Antal and Krebsbach Gnath (Ch. 21 in this volume) that problem definition needs to be added to current phase models. Learning does not begin with knowledge acquisition. If there is not sufficient agreement on problem definition at the outset, the learning process will be interrupted in one of the next phases. The responsibility of leadership goes beyond initiating learning processes. The likelihood that learning processes will be interrupted is particularly high when new items are placed on the agenda. To maintain the momentum for learning on other issues, leaders must foster the continuity of that learning. They need to ensure that the learning process is not interrupted before enough progress has been achieved to embed the new ways of thinking and behaving into the culture, structure, and processes of the organization. An interrupted learning process might be labeled and remembered as a failure, an outcome that could well impede future learning initiatives.

The practical implications for organizations have both a cautionary and an encouraging dimension. The confirmation that there are multiple barriers to organizational learning, even once a process appears to have been successfully initiated, should alert managers to be skeptical of articles or speeches that paint organizational learning in brilliant and happy colors. They need to be prepared to invest actively and consistently in the process if it is to start effectively and maintain the necessary momentum. The findings about the role of culture as an impediment to organizational learning should also serve as a warning to people at all levels of the organization that learning cannot start with a treatment of specific concerns that are actually symptoms of underlying cultural problems. The features of an organizational culture that block cooperation and understanding between the members must be grappled with in order for learning to take hold. Challenging elements of the organizational culture may appear to be an impossible task, but the insights from the preceding cases and from other studies (e.g. Friedman, Ch. 17 in this volume) show that the courage and energy to undertake such a challenge is available among the members of all organizations. It is neither a matter of waiting for the right hero to arrive, nor of recruiting a specialist for organizational learning. Employees in all functions and at all levels can seek out partners for distributed leadership on issues that they care deeply about and that they believe the organization should learn to deal with.

References

Argyris, C. (1990). *Overcoming Organizational Defenses: Facilitating Organizational Learning*. Boston: Allyn and Bacon.

——(1991). 'Teaching Smart People How to Learn'. *Harvard Business Review*, 69/3: 99–109.

——(1993). *Knowledge for Action: A Guide to Overcoming Barriers to Organizational Change*. San Francisco: Jossey-Bass.

——and Schön, D. A. (1978). *Organizational Learning: A Theory of Action Perspective*. Reading, Mass.: Addison-Wesley.

————(1996). *Organizational Learning*: Vol. 2. *Theory, Method, and Practice*. Reading, Mass.: Addison-Wesley.

Berthoin Antal, A. (1992). *Corporate Social Performance: Rediscovering Actors in Their Organizational Contexts*. Frankfurt am Main: Campus.

——Dierkes, M., and Hähner, K. (1997). 'Business Perception of Contextual Changes: Sources and Impediments to Organizational Learning'. *Business and Society*, 36: 387–407.

————and Marz, L. (1999). 'Organizational Learning in China, Germany and Israel'. *Journal of General Management*, 25/1: 63–88.

Coopey, J. (1995). 'The Learning Organization: Power, Politics and Ideology'. *Management Learning*, 26: 193–214.

Czarniawska, B. and Sevón, G. (1996). *Translating Organizational Change*. Berlin: de Gruyter.

Dierkes, M., Hähner, K., and Berthoin Antal, A. (1997). *Das Unternehmen und sein Umfeld: Wahrnehmungsprozesse und Unternehmenskultur am Beispiel eines Chemiekonzerns*. Frankfurt am Main: Campus.

Edmondson, A. and Moingeon, B. (1996). 'When to Learn How and When to Learn Why: Appropriate Organizational Learning Processes as a Source of Competitive Advantage', in B. Moingeon and A. Edmondson (eds.), *Organizational Learning and Competitive Advantage*. London: Sage, 17–37.

Fiol, C. M. and Lyles, M. A. (1985). 'Organizational Learning'. *Academy of Management Review*, 10: 803–13.

Freeman, C. (1982). *The Economics of Industrial Innovation*. Boston: MIT Press.

Hedberg, B. L. T. (1981). 'How Organizations Learn and Unlearn', in P. C. Nystrom and W. H. Starbuck (eds.), *Handbook of Organizational Design*: Vol. 1. *Adapting Organizations to Their Environments*. Oxford: Oxford University Press, 3–27.

Huber, G. P. (1991). 'Organizational Learning: The Contributing Processes and the Literatures'. *Organization Science*, 2: 88–115.

Kanter, R. M. (1988). 'When a Thousand Flowers Bloom: Structural, Collective, and Social Conditions for Innovation in Organization', in B. M. Staw and L. L. Cummings (eds.), *Research in Organizational Behavior: An Annual Series of Analytical Essays and Critical Reviews* (Vol. 10). Greenwich, Conn.: JAI Press, 169–211.

Kieser, A. (1998). *How Management Science, Consultancies and Business Companies (Do Not) Learn from Each Other: Applying Concepts of Learning to Different Types of Organizations and to Interorganizational Learning*. Discussion paper No. 98–20, University of Mannheim, Sonderforschungsbereich 504: Mannheim, Germany.

Kim, D. H. (1993). 'The Link between Individual and Organizational Learning'. *Sloan Management Review*, 35/1: 37–50.

Lenhardt, U. (1999). *Betriebliche Gesundheitsförderung durch Krankenkassen: Rahmenbedingungen—Angebotsstrategien—Umsetzung*. Berlin: edition sigma.

——Elkeles, T., and Rosenbrock, R. (1997). *Betriebsproblem Rückenschmerz: Eine gesundheitswissenschaftliche Bestandsaufnahme zu Verursachung, Verbreitung und Verhütung*. Weinheim: Juventa.

—— and Rosenbrock, R. (1998). 'Gesundheitsförderung als betriebliches Lernfeld', in H. Albach, M. Dierkes, A. Berthoin Antal, and K. Vaillant (eds.), *Organisationslernen—institutionelle und kulturelle Dimensionen*. *WZB Jahrbuch 1998*. Berlin: edition sigma, 135–60.

—— —— and Elkeles, T. (1996). *Bedingungs- und Akteurskonstellationen für Gesundheitsförderung im Betrieb: Ergebnisse aus vier Fallstudien*. WZB Discussion paper P96–201: Wissenschaftszentrum Berlin für Sozialforschung.

Levinthal, D. A. and March, J. G. (1993). 'The Myopia of Learning'. *Strategic Management Journal*, 14 (Winter special issue): 95–112.

Levitt, B. and March, J. G. (1988). 'Organizational Learning'. *Annual Review of Sociology*, 14: 319–40.

March, J. G. (1991a). 'Exploration and Exploitation in Organizational Learning'. *Organization Science*, 2: 71–87.

——(1991b). 'Organizational Consultants and Organizational Research'. *Journal of Applied Communications Research*, 19/1–2: 20–31.

—— and Olsen, J. P. (1975). 'The Uncertainty of the Past: Organizational Learning under Ambiguity'. *European Journal of Political Research*, 3: 147–71.

Morgan, G. (1986). *Images of Organization*. Beverly Hills, Calif.: Sage.

Nonaka, I. and Takeuchi, H. (1995). *The Knowledge-creating Company: How Japanese Companies Create the Dynamics of Innovation*. New York: Oxford University Press.

Pawlowsky, P. (1992). 'Betriebliche Qualifikationsstrategien und organisationales Lernen', in W. H. Staehle and P. Conrad (eds.), *Managementforschung* (Vol. 2). Berlin: de Gruyter, 177–237.

Rosenbrock, R. and Lenhardt, U. (1999). *Die Bedeutung von Betriebsärzten in einer modernen betrieblichen Gesundheitspolitik*. Gütersloh: Bertelsmann Stiftung.

Sackman, S. A. (1992). 'Culture and Subcultures: An Analysis of Organizational Knowledge'. *Administrative Science Quarterly*, 37: 140–61.

Schein, E. H. (1985). *Organizational Culture and Leadership: A Dynamic View*. San Francisco: Jossey-Bass.

——(1993). 'How Can Organizations Learn Faster? The Problem of Entering the Green Room'. *Sloan Management Review*, 34/2: 85–92.

——(1996). 'Three Cultures of Management: The Key to Organizational Learning'. *Sloan Management Review*, 38/1: 9–20.

Sitkin, S. B. (1992). 'Learning through Failure: The Strategy of Small Losses', in B. M. Staw and L. L. Cummings (eds.), *Research in Organizational Behavior: An Annual Series of Analytical Essays and Critical Reviews* (Vol. 14). Greenwich, Conn.: JAI Press, 231–66.

Sull, D. N. (1999). 'Why Good Companies Go Bad'. *Harvard Business Review*, 77/4: 42–52.

40 Applying Theory to Organizational Transformation

Camilla Krebsbach-Gnath

The theories and concepts of organizational learning, as they have been described and discussed in numerous articles in this handbook and other volumes (Albach, Dierkes, Antal, and Vaillant 1998; Argyris and Schön 1978; Garrat 1990; Krebsbach-Gnath 1996; Moingeon and Edmondson 1996; Pedler, Burgoyne, and Boydell 1991; Senge 1990), certainly sound convincing and promising. But they hardly provide a framework for action. As Garvin (1993) pointed out, 'the recommendations are far too abstract, and too many questions remain unanswered' (p. 78). Managers who want to prepare their companies for the future often ask questions such as 'How does it work? How do I make it happen? Do you know of any learning organizations that we can learn from?' How can the existing knowledge about organizational learning be applied to the real life of companies?

Drawing on a seven-year case study, I describe one company's transformation and explore the dimensions of organizational learning within that organization. The processes that took place and the methods that were used are examined and analyzed in terms of their 'theoretical architecture', their main stages; their contextual, psychological, and behavioral conditions; and the interdependence of driving forces. I then draw conclusions about key factors that promote success. The case provides a rich opportunity for exploring in a real-life setting many of the threads presented in other chapters of this handbook. It is a clear instance of 'double-loop learning' (Argyris and Schön 1978: 21), that is, the thorough examination of standards

and norms which build the frame of the interpretation scheme of reality. It demonstrates how tacit knowledge in a company is converted into explicit knowledge and then used to create both a new understanding of the environment and new strategic options.

This case study allows for the exploration of a variety of tools, concepts, processes, and agents and illustrates which of them did and did not work well. The successful organizational learning described in the study may serve as a benchmark for process-oriented learning.

At this point the difference between organizational learning and organizational change should be emphasized. Whereas the latter includes the result of the process of change, organizational learning concentrates on the process that brings such changes about (Krebsbach-Gnath 1996). The aims of organizational learning show how it differs from the classical concepts of organizational development. Not only is individual or team learning important, so is the transformation of the organization in terms of a change of paradigms, provided that the ability to learn in this way entails permanent capacity for change (Krebsbach-Gnath 1996). Understood in this sense, organizational learning approximates 'double-loop learning' more closely than it does 'single-loop learning' (Argyris and Schön 1978: 21), the identification and correction of deviations from existing norms, values, and aims. According to Kanter, Stein, and Jick (1992), organizational learning is a 'Change with a capital C', not incremental learning ('change with a small c') (p. 10). This interpretation of organizational learning means that organizational transformation is 'a second-order change, one that requires the learning of new viewpoints, new schemes of interpretation, and a new paradigm' (Staehle 1991: 836; my translation). Organizational transformation thus 'entails both an intellectual or cognitive reframing and a material structural change' (Child and Smith 1987: 582).

As important as these conceptual distinctions are for analytical purposes, they played no role in the actual thinking and behavior of the managers in this case study. The company at the center of the study, Adler Modemärkte GmbH, a well-known fashion discounter in Germany, had never heard of the concept of 'learning organization', let alone called or understood itself as such. During its organizational learning, the company therefore never consciously applied a theory of the process. Management simply had an urgent economic need to change in order to survive and once again be successful on the market. And they succeeded.

Structure and Process of Organizational Learning in Adler Fashion Markets, GmbH

The Point of Departure

Adler Modemärkte was founded in 1960 as a family business. It produced garments for women, men, and teenagers. The first Adler clothing store was opened in Aschaffenburg in 1971 and was followed by ten additional outlets throughout West Germany over the next nine years. In keeping with the company's philosophy—'bargain sales from the factory on up'— the volume of the assortment was large and the product variety limited. The shop floors were correspondingly Spartan. The company was extraordinarily successful in its early years, when its marketing consisted of offering lower- to middle-income consumers apparel of perfect quality at especially reasonable discount prices.

In 1982 Wolfgang Adler sold his company to Asko AG,[1] a group of major German department stores whose subsidiaries are quite independent, each having its own character. The Adler name was retained, however. In subsequent years several stores were opened annually. Today, there are approximately 100 Adler stores in Germany.

The company remained successful for years, with sales volume increasing by 10 per cent a year as a rule. But this success blinded the company's management team to changes in the environment that were relevant to the company. Problems with adaptation were obscured by steady growth, which served as the main index of success. Sales volume climbed from DM 510 million in 1983 to DM 910 million in 1987. These figures hid the fact that sales in existing outlets were declining because of a net loss of customers and the company's negative image as an utterly outdated purveyor of poor-quality brand merchandise.

The executive board of the parent company was not oblivious to these confusing figures, though. The board chairman at the parent company appointed a new managing director to Adler, the clear objective being to bring the company back onto a successful course. As Tainio, Lilja, and Santalainen (Ch. 19 in this volume) clearly show, intervention by the board is a strong indicator heralding a company's deterioration. Hence, the point of departure was a crisis. The need to change and learn was clearly being triggered by outside market forces, the 'world of business' (Galer and van der Heijden, Ch. 38 in this volume), where Adler's strategy no longer fitted and the company had to struggle for survival. The need to change also emanated from the 'world of management' (Galer and van der Heijden, Ch. 38 in this volume), where knowledge and action are created by individuals and groups, where methods of work are organized, where conflicts are resolved, and, generally, where issues of agency are dealt with.

---

[1] Asko AG merged with Metro AG, Düsseldorf, in 1996.

The Situation in 1987

The business was run by seven general managers, most of whom had been with the company since the 1970s. They did not get along with each other especially well, however. Board meetings were tedious and often unproductive. The organizational structure was highly complex. The managers of the shops reported through several levels of hierarchy to the individual members of the board, who still performed functional tasks at headquarters: purchasing, distribution and logistics, personnel administration, legal counsel, advertising, finances, and general administration.

Approximately 70 per cent of the employees were part-timers. The turnover rate and absenteeism were high, and motivation was low. Within the company, there was little or no feeling of partnership towards others. People were merely given information and instructions. There was no dialogue.

With the assistance of external consultants, Adler employees at all levels closely analyzed parts of the environment relevant to the company and carefully examined changes and trends within them (see Berthoin Antal and Krebsbach-Gnath, Ch. 21 in this volume). The results showed that—

(1) consumer behavior had shifted in several ways, some of which even indicated a societal change of values toward individuality and away from mass marketing;
(2) prosperity was increasing for broad sections of the population, intensifying consumer demand for improved goods and services;
(3) totally new types of marketing philosophy based heavily on pricing and ambience had been developed by Hennes and Mauritz, Benneton, and other competitors, whose pitch, though aimed at young shoppers, also had an impact on the expectations held by Adler's target groups; and
(4) the number and professionalism of competitors was increasing.

There was no marketing concept in Adler in the sense of running the business with the customer in mind. Instead, the clothing stores were perceived as places for selling off what the company produced. With its range of merchandise centered excessively on in-house production, and given the described changes in its business environment, Adler was no longer fit for the world in which it was operating. In addition, the company was experiencing especially great problems arising from headlong corporate growth, which was evident from the soaring number of clothing stores.

The mismatch between corporate performance and the company's business environment was expressed through a detailed inventory of Adler's weaknesses by 1987. Specialists, managers, and employees worked together to pinpoint the main internal shortcomings in corporate performance. They identified problems with—

(1) logistically coping with the increased volume of merchandise;
(2) controlling product range, pricing, advertising, and other aspects of sales policy, not to mention ensuring the ability of the stores to carry and sell certain items now that the company had grown into such a large group of outlets;
(3) dealing administratively and organizationally with the sudden increase in the volume of business;
(4) recruiting and ensuring the continued occupational development of managers and employees;
(5) managing distribution;
(6) working within obsolete organizational structures and outdated approaches to corporate management; and
(7) using irrational, uneconomical work procedures.

In addition, it was noted that—

(1) the product range, being hampered by the restrictions of in-house production, was not meeting market demands for modernity, fashion, and availability;
(2) an absence of appropriate employee information and systems for channeling it was hindering optimal distribution of the company's merchandise;

(3) Adler's historical development as a company that sold directly from the factory was preventing its merchandise from meeting market demands; and

(4) Adler, if present at all in the consumer's mind, was seen mainly as a mass-market store that offered reasonable prices but dubious quality and an unsatisfactory shopping experience.

Confronting the company with a different reality and defining the problems—this first step in the learning cycle (see Berthoin Antal and Krebsbach-Gnath, Ch. 21 in this volume)—thereby linked members of the company at all levels. It facilitated the identification of knowledge and its diffusion in the company (see Pawlowsky, Forslin, and Reinhardt, Ch. 35 in this volume). Tacit knowledge was converted into explicit knowledge.

The Change Process

Adler's new managing director introduced a process of change marked by a special basic concept and structural pattern (see Fig. 40.1). The overall concept had four distinct emphases:

(1) the focus of a vision in which the world of business and the world of management were oriented to the future (see Dierkes, Marz, and Teele, Ch. 12 in this volume);

(2) the active participation of specialists, managers, and a broad selection of employees throughout the company in identifying and diffusing knowledge and thereby in bringing the overall concept to a level where learning occurs;

(3) a broad investment in communication and training, in order to widen and deepen the diffusion of knowledge in the company;

(4) the role of leadership and cooperation in integrating and modifying the knowledge gained for the organization.

An important part of the fourth focal point was the introduction of evaluation workshops as 'checkpoints' throughout the process. They created further basic conditions for learning, such as tolerance for admitting error and

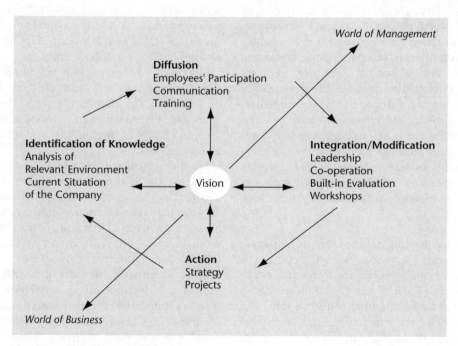

Fig. 40.1. The process of learning

doubt (see Friedman, Lipshitz, and Overmeer, Ch. 34 in this volume) and provision of room for reflection. As a whole, the overall concept expressed acknowledgment of important contextual and behavioral conditions for organizational learning, such as egalitarianism, inquiry, and transparency (see Friedman, Lipshitz, and Overmeer, Ch. 34 in this volume).

The overall approach was also reflected in individual processes, particularly those relating to changing the philosophy and activities of human resource development and of marketing. Analyses of changes in the relevant parts of the business environment and constant analyses of its current state served as starting points for developing ideas of conditions that should be aimed for. These ideas were then brought into projects and applied to the relevant area. The fundamental positions of the vision thereby served as orientations.

The change process began in May 1987. Of course, change processes often have no definite beginning or end. For programmatic purposes, a fixed starting point was chosen for this case study, the acknowledgment that the company was in a crisis and the hiring of a new managing director. First, the organizational framework for the overall process was created. New organizational charts were prepared, a new business responsibility plan was passed, new areas were created, and scopes of authority were redefined. 'Naturally, people also wrestled for power, but we did not battle over organizational territory and job descriptions. . . . The work on the vision and its implementation was much more arduous', a senior manager explained in an interview. In addition, weekly board meetings and informational meetings of the area and departmental managers took place.

In a closed meeting in June 1987, the managing board decided to proceed with the concept of integrated management and corporate development (see Galer and van der Heijden, Ch. 38 in this volume), simultaneously tackling the world of business (the strategy in the external world) and the world of management (the internal process for making this strategy happen).

In July 1987 the members attended a seminar entitled 'Loving Change' by the new managing director and run by consultants he had hired. In that gathering the reasoning and experience of the consultants in charge dispelled the board's skepticism about having all levels of the company actively participate in the change process. The board then decided to try out the concept with all senior employees, which meant having to have the desired culture developed in a series of workshops during the year. After massive pressure and persuasion by the managing director, the members of the managing board agreed to have the worker's council included in the processes from the outset.

Based on analyses of Adler's business environment, the changes made in it, and a detailed analysis of the company's state in 1987, the concept of change consisted in trying to develop a shared vision of what the Adler company should be in the future. This vision was to be adopted as the guiding image not only of the company but also of the change process itself. All other conceptual considerations and practical measures were developed accordingly. Ultimately, the vision created the framework for what was to be learned and set the contextual, psychological, and behavioral conditions for that learning (see Friedman, Lipshitz, and Overmeer, Ch. 34 in this volume).

The approach begins with the recognition that purely operational solutions to problems are not enough to change a company. The solutions must be embedded in a process of mental change, change in the thinking and actions of all participants.

For that reason, different viewpoints on the future of the company were collected and grouped in a series of workshops attended by all Adler managers and many of their subordinates. The participants first assessed the developmental trends in the relevant settings (such as ecological environment, demographic trends, household incomes, time budgets). After descriptions of the company's perceived strengths were compiled, the perceived weaknesses were identified and categorized. Then visions of a possible future were outlined: 'How do we have to be and how do we want to be in order to be successful in the future we have envisioned?'

The second step was to summarize the results of the workshop. From this summary, the consultants prepared the first draft of a vision, which was submitted for group discussion. The participants worked on proposed changes, producing a second draft of the vision. The management board passed the final version (for the process of developing a vision, see also Dierkes, Marz, and Teele, Ch. 12 in this volume).

What was new about this vision? What of the past was retained for the future? The corporate self-image as a 'discounter', the focus on the customer, and the orientation to qualified growth were traditional values and perspectives that 'we've always had and that we've been able to build on', as several managers stated in the interviews. Significantly, these values and perspectives were also the first three points in the vision, serving as the foundation upon which a new corporate identity could be built. A 'sense of safety' (Friedman, Lipshitz, and Overmeer, Ch. 34 in this volume), a central condition for learning, was thereby ensured.

What was new was the management philosophy (the importance of well-informed employees, joint efforts to make the company what it strived to be, the team idea), the sense of common purpose based on fairness and credibility, unusual market performance (moving away from the practice of selling directly from the factory toward the idea of making shopping an experience in itself), and long-term economic thinking. As one manager put it: 'Short-term thinking in terms of turnover used to dominate. That led to a lot of actionism.' Today, the idea of turnover is less important than calculations of returns are. The name of the vision ('Loving Change') was also indicative. It emphasized an ongoing process rather than a fixed point in the future.

The vision was elaborated on by employees and managers in the Adler group together with the managing board in numerous workshops. The result was not a glossy brochure, a piece of paper that was going to disappear into the desk drawers and waste baskets of the employees

and managers, but a map, a set of guiding rules for the future, that has remained the focus for all further effort.

The first step toward translating the Adler vision into reality was taken with the creation of project teams assigned to work out specific ideas for its implementation, an arrangement that facilitated experimentation with a new form of cooperation (quasi-autonomous project work) and started to change the company's traditional authoritarian culture of 'command and obey'. A total of twenty-one project teams were formed (with six to eight members each), with 150 managers and employees involved. Participation was voluntary, and 'they all went about it very enthusiastically', according to several managers and employees. The members of the vision groups worked on such topics as openness to families, ideas for making the shopping experience come alive, a tailoring shop, customer discounts, type and flow of employee information, customer management, a restaurant, parking service, quality fun, money-back guarantees, and natural environment (the managing board made the final decision about which were to be worked on).

Each project team had to choose a project director from among its members. The project teams acted autonomously. Only their planned and unplanned budgets required board approval. At first, each team was to develop a rough concept along with its necessary measures, budget plan, and schedule for presentation to the board. The subsequent, detailed concept was prepared in the same manner.

Most of the project teams worked for two years. In May 1990, the project directors gave the management board a comprehensive final report, in which the results were closely evaluated with an eye to their implementation. This 'issue orientation' (Friedman, Lipshitz, and Overmeer, Ch. 34 in this volume) clearly enhanced the learning process, and the success of the change project was related to the collective effort to make sense of the shared underlying vision.

In 1988, a year after Adler had developed and broadly communicated its vision, the strategy was formulated, again in cooperation with the managers and employees. The difference between the vision, as the desirable culture, and the strategy, as the formulation of the company's competitive scope and advantage, is laid out in an internal memo from the management board to managers and employees:

We stated our basic mission and our basic values in the vision. We stated that we want to be a discount clothing store for the whole family, that we are to strive for positive thinking and perfection in all we do, and so forth. . . . But that certainly did not formulate precisely how Adler intended to set itself apart on the market, which advantages the company is seen to have over competitors, why the customer should shop at Adler's rather than somewhere else. In short, it did not state what the very special, unique aspect of Adler is. Our vision does express that we want to offer unusual service, such as the tailoring shop, but that alone does not constitute the competitive advantage that draws masses of customers away from our competitors and into our stores.

What it is that sets Adler distinctly apart on the market should be spelled out in the strategy. The advantages and strengths that the company already has should be taken as the basis for formulating additional characteristics that will help to dominate the market. It should also be clearly stated what kind of impact this result will have on the design of the stores, on advertising, on product-line policy, and the like.

Five strategic components of success were defined by the management board after consultation with consultants, managers, and a variety of employees: (a) projection of creativity and the sense that one really cares; (b) unusual, engaging displays in the stores; (c) discount prices; (d) the company's own brands; and (e) unusual service. These five strategic components of success have led to general definitions that have, in turn, focused attention on operational business decisions related to advertising, demands on types of distribution and sites, the stores' interior design, policy on prices and product range, layout and the display of merchandise, store furnishings, and the development and introduction of unusual services (such as a tailoring shop). New fields of business have likewise been developed with this

strategy. The strategy concludes with an analysis of its implications for various functional areas—sales, purchasing, warehousing, procurement, personnel, controlling, finance and accounting, organization, data-processing, and logistics.

It is significant, and new in terms of the company's self-concept, that the separate functions were to be seen as service providers. They 'lose the justification for their existence as soon as certain services are no longer required or marketable at a reasonable price', as one of the senior managers clearly stated in an interview.

Essentially, then, the strategy constituted the practical formulation of the vision as well as the formulation and establishment of the operational essentials for entering the market. At Adler, knowledge of the market and the customers had already been updated by the analysis of the environment. Further specific analyses verified and refined those insights.

Market and Customer Orientation

Market and customer orientation was both the basis for and the result of brainstorming done in all twenty-one projects and the strategy development at Adler. It therefore constituted the real focus, not a fashionable management buzzword. In order to translate the results into daily action by the employees, a special internal paper was written for the special purpose of formulating the strategic components of success in simple, understandable language suited to the world of the frontline employees. Humorous illustrations enhanced the paper's attractiveness.

To the Adler company, market and customer orientation also means intensifying the tie to the customer and learning from the customer. For example, regular customers are offered special conditions (e.g. opening an hour earlier for them during the clearance sale, coupons). In direct-mail campaigns customers are asked to let the company know why they have not shopped in the stores since a certain date. As one of Adler's marketing managers reported, 'We get back a lot of letters from which we learn.' In some stores special tables have been set up for the store managers to meet and talk with regular customers.[2]

Leadership and Cooperation

In 1987 the atmosphere and cooperation within the managing board as well as the cooperation between the board and other managers and employees was marked by great 'frustration'. Members of the board were unable to talk to each other. There was no room for creativity, innovation, or dynamic interaction. The barrier between the board and the other managers and employees was as discernible as it was between the board members themselves. Wishing to risk nothing, the directors in particular stonewalled. All parties clung to what they considered to be right, allowing no new interpretations and thwarting every effort to deal with crises. Disputes continued into the early morning hours with little or nothing getting accomplished. Entrenched, ossified, command-oriented thinking prevailed, a mind-set that permitted no criticism from below and no ideas from the outside. Organizational power blocked necessary unlearning and learning.

At this juncture, the power of the newly appointed managing director helped to overcome the barriers. To break the gridlock it was first necessary to have the managers develop a philosophy of leadership that enabled people to direct and motivate themselves. This philosophy was understood as a logical result of the corporate vision, which emphasized team-thinking, joint effort to transform the company in the desired way, and the self-responsibility of the employees. Of course, not all managers could adopt this thinking, and many of those who could not accept it decided to leave the company.

In a number of workshops, several hundred Adler employees articulated the standards that they set for 'fair leadership' (leadership that was

'right' from their point of view). On this foundation, ten principles of management and cooperation ('Positive Leadership') were formulated in a committee in which all management groups were represented. The principles, which were subsequently printed and disseminated throughout the company, were understood as guidelines for action and as a yardstick for judgment by the employees. All managers had to attend a leadership seminar in which these principles and the management philosophy were discussed and practiced with examples based on everyday situations. Today, these leadership seminars are a basic part of the management development program in the Adler stores. The management principles also serve as guidelines for the assessment center, which has assisted in the selection of new employees since 1990.

This concept of leadership is similar to the concept of leaders as learners and teachers (Sadler, Ch. 18 in this volume): individuals who empower their employees, encourage their learning, teamwork, and participation. In that capacity, the manager serves as both a facilitator and a role model for learning.

Test: Built-in Evaluation

A key feature of the entire implementation process is that the people responsible for it have repeatedly organized workshops in which the participants analyze and evaluate what part of the vision has been achieved and which special objectives, such as fair leadership, have been experienced. Several questions have been typical: 'What have we been able to achieve of the vision?' 'What was translated well into action, and what is going smoothly?' 'Where are there problems with the implementation?' 'What can and must be adapted or improved?' There have always been specific suggestions to work on.

The way in which Adler developed its corporate strategy illustrates evaluation processes of this type. The company's strategy was made public to all employees in 1989. 'But it was already clear at that time that this version could

---

[2] The practice of managers talking with customers in order to learn about their demands and ideas as an essential tool of knowledge creation is also mentioned by Nonaka, Reinmöller, and Toyama (Ch. 37 in this volume) in case studies on Wal-Mart and Seven-Eleven Japan.

not be the final one. The strategy based on our vision has to be constantly adapted to market demands,' stated one marketing director in an interview. In order to do just that, a project group composed of representatives from every area of the organization from trainees to the board was formed in 1993. It reformulated the strategy, basing its work on the latest data pertaining to changes in the company's environment (its markets and customers)—and on numerous discussions with employees. The new brochure was immediately published and widely discussed.

Resistance

Resistance was encountered at all levels from managers who feared that they were not up to the new tasks or who could not or would not believe that the new concept would be implemented consistently. 'For a year, half of the managers did not believe in it,' according to one senior manager. As Adler's human resource manager explained, there was also resistance from young managers 'who still thought in the classical terms of moving up the ladder. We weren't able to offer as much in that respect anymore. Hierarchical opportunities for upward mobility were reduced by the reorganization.' Managers who were unable to identify with the new company proposed in the vision, with the strategy, and with the management principles also left the company. Massive resistance came from a group of senior managers who, on several occasions, urged the board of the parent company to terminate the entire process. In the end they either came to be convinced by the board or they left the company.

At the outset, the group of people with a wait-and-see attitude (Krebsbach-Gnath 1992) was 'considerable' (p. 39), according to Adler's human resource manager. Additional intense integration and a great deal of communication were necessary in order to persuade them to join in the process of change and learning. 'Our consistency and visible success helped a lot in that regard', he said.

The Process of Communication

The company's whole transformation process was accompanied by intense efforts to communicate. As one member of the managing board explained, 'If anyone does too little, the entire process will falter. The effort to facilitate communication cannot be overestimated. The messages must be repeated over and over. There was not enough communication at the beginning. We underestimated that.' This observation supports Kotter's (1995) analysis of efforts that more than 100 companies had made to initiate change. His results showed that the factor of communication was always underestimated 'by a factor of 10' (p. 63). To explain the strategy, the vision, and the individual projects and to evaluate the various workshops, a variety of channels were used, including brochures, numerous workshops and seminars, and many employee meetings. For example, from May 1989 through April 1994, all but three issues of the employee newspaper, *Der Adler*, carried detailed and prominently placed articles explaining topics pertaining to the vision, the strategy, and the management principles. The paper reported on projects and advances and published evaluation results (such as those of the employee questionnaire about management behavior and perceived strengths and weaknesses of the company). The achievements were described at length in its pages. This communication process ensured transparency, a central condition for organizational learning (see Friedman, Lipshitz, and Overmeer, Ch. 34 in this volume). But communication was by no means one-way. New forums, such as employee and departmental discussions, were introduced, with the regional sales directors being requested to check whether and how these gatherings were being held in the stores reporting to them.

In addition, the then newly appointed managing director modeled the open communication process called for in the corporate vision. In his initial appearances he spoke to managers and employees about numbers and plans, candor that, to one senior manager who was interviewed, came across as outright shocking because such information 'had never been the business of employees and managers before'. The managing director's successful approach left a deep impression on Adler managers. As a result, open and targeted information is now an organizational strength.

Key Learnings

Which Mistakes? What Kind of Learning?

The implementation process had had its share of mistakes, too. The first brochure presenting the vision had to be recalled. Written in a style that most of the employees did not understand, it had been roundly criticized at their meetings, in the seminars, and during the workshops. 'We learned—and that impressed people,' said a senior manager. Several interviewed employees agreed, stating: 'The board showed credibility.' A new version of the brochure is already in its fourth printing and contains a more understandable formulation of the vision.

Mistakes had also been made in organizing the production of ideas. Basically, it had not been possible to guide the twenty-one project groups properly. The members of these groups had been 'world champions in elaborating concepts', explained one manager. He added, however, that they were not professional project managers and that it had been difficult for the ideas interlinking the individual groups to be distilled for practical action. In his estimation, 'The project groups should have been supervised more closely so that the company could have benefited more efficiently from such brainstorming. The work of the project groups raised the expectations of the employees a good deal. We had to set time dimensions, had to establish the link between the creative production of ideas and reality.'

Results

From 1987 through 1994, Adler changed. First and foremost, it became a highly successful company again in economic terms—a very practical output indicator of learning.

1. Adler grew. In 1995 the company had more stores, greater sales volume, much better yields, and many more employees than it used to have.

2. Adler's range of merchandise is completely different from what it was earlier (almost none of its own brands, many branded goods).

3. Adler has a new advertising concept and a new commercial corporate identity (change of the company's logo, color, and advertising image).

At first glance, one could conclude that Adler today is more of the same, except that everything is a bit better-looking, cleverer, and more diversified than it used to be. Yet, those are not sufficient indicators of organizational learning, however (Krebsbach-Gnath 1996). The question of organizational learning goes much further: Has the company successfully abandoned its hitherto predominant organizational paradigm? Has it managed to develop a new structure and set the required frame in order to implement the new basis of knowledge, perspective, or schemes of interpretation in a practical way? Does the company understand learning and change to be continuous processes?

One therefore has to look at the company's current structural and cultural components that define its external and internal relations and influence practical thinking and action. External relations are created by the perception and interpretation of the relevant environment, the dimensions that Galer and van der Heijden (Ch. 38 in this volume) refer to as new relations to the world of business or that Pawlowsky, Forslin, and Reinhardt (Ch. 35 in this volume) describe as 'identification'. Internal relations are defined by 'rules' of leadership and cooperation; the process that takes place in the world of management, is described by Pawlowsky, Forslin, and Reinhardt (Ch. 35 in this volume) as the 'differentiation, motivation, and integration' of knowledge, and encompasses the contextual, psychological, and behavioral conditions for organizational learning (Friedman, Lipshitz, and Overmeer, Ch. 34 in this volume).

The change that Adler went through was more than just cosmetic. The company is not just more of the same. It *is* 'more' (stores, employees, range of merchandise, turnover, yields) but certainly *not* 'of the same'. A transformation occurred in the sense of a changed paradigm, and fundamental changes in the way the company sees itself are observable. It changed in terms of leadership and cooperation, employee motivation, and personnel management. New media were introduced to support the vision. At Adler today, learning has acquired new value, and there are new constellations of power. The perception and interpretation of the relevant environments, markets, and behavior also changed.

Adler went through a fundamental change in its corporate culture. Given the principles of management and cooperation embraced today, given the inclusion of the employees and the guidelines for personnel management, one sees that the paradigm for understanding how to work with each other and with the customers changed. Today's perception and interpretation of the relevant environments and markets reflect a profound change in external relations. The new value accorded to learning and the company's new self-concept also indicate that important values radically changed.

Adler now has new and different managers than those who were in place in 1987. Not only was the number of board members greatly reduced from eight to three, but two of the people on the now three-member board have come to the company from outside.

Actually, everything about the current management philosophy is new. As Adler's human resource manager explained, 'Learning by making mistakes is almost revolutionary. All we used to do was look for people who were at fault. We did not have a written management philosophy. But there was a philosophy: command and obey. Evaluation was strictly top down.'

Today Adler uses anonymous upward evaluation. To ensure that the management principles do not remain mere written intentions, the employees have thus far been surveyed three times about the managerial behavior of their superiors in an effort to determine where the company is on the learning curve. The results for the company as a whole have been published and commented on in *Der Adler*. For each store and each department at headquarters there has been a separate analysis that each supervisor must discuss with his or her employees in order to set new interim objectives.

New Ways of Working Together

The principles of management and cooperation are manifested in new ways of dealing with each other. At all levels, conflicts are resolved more quickly and objectively than they used to be. According to one senior manager, 'Today, it is easier for us to separate the issue from the person. After a conflict, we do not remain on bad terms with each other as long as we used to. Instead, we are now able to learn from conflicts.'

Discussion, too, is openly practiced and encouraged. Regularly held departmental discussions are sources of information for the employees and are meant 'to facilitate dialogue' as a means for mutual learning. They are planned a year in advance and usually take place each month at a set time on a specified day as a kind of 'sacred appointment' that all those concerned can and should note in their calendars. Another new idea in this regard is the introduction of employee discussions in which the participants systematically review their ways of working and their performance.

The frankness of this interpersonal communication appears not only in the departmental and employee discussions but also in the disclosure of corporate considerations and performance figures that never used to be shared outside the boardroom. Managers receive a 'manager's bulletin' containing extensive information (which, however, must be treated confidentially). 'Old rules like "Knowledge is power" and "We'll leave our employees in the dark" or "It's none of their business" belong to the past. We don't treat each other that way anymore,' said several of the senior managers interviewed. The contextual and behavioral conditions for learning described by Friedman, Lipshitz, and Overmeer (Ch. 34 in this volume), such as inquiry, egalitarianism, and transparency, are well illustrated by this attitude.

New Media and Instruments to Support the Vision

To support the learning process, Adler introduced new instruments and media and thoroughly revised existing ones that are used in operational planning, personnel management, and communication. The entire annual planning procedure was fundamentally changed, for example. Whereas Adler employees usually used to receive instructions from the top (centralized procedure), the planning process now flows upward, in a decentralized, participatory procedure. The employees in administration and stores submit their own plans, which they go over with their supervisors. These plans are then compiled and revised by headquarters and again talked over with the superiors. This planning procedure, which is closer to an agreement than to a pure dictate, increases the supervisors' commitment to achieving the objectives.

In 1993 an agreement between the employees and the management established a company suggestion box. The objectives were to streamline procedures and cut costs through the creative collaboration of all employees and to identify weak points in operations and find ways to remedy them. In the realm of personnel policy, regular workshops for employees have been organized in addition to the previously mentioned employee discussions. The workshops are conducted in either an intra- or interdepartmental context in order to reveal shortcomings and work on joint solutions to them.

In the sphere of communication, the employee newspaper (*Der Adler*) was completely reconceived in its layout, and a new edition now appears every two weeks rather than at irregular intervals. Discussion and communication of key points of the vision are always given prominent coverage, so that employees constantly experience the meaning of the vision through this channel as well.

All these media and instruments amplify the learning process enormously because they demonstrate selected principles of the company's vision and management practice ('achieve objectives', 'include others in decision-making', 'inform others', 'seek ideas for and commitment to constant innovation'), and thereby provide tangible models for emulation.

Personnel Management

Personnel management at Adler changed from pure administration to active human resource management. This shift is demonstrated by the previously mentioned introduction of employee discussions, team days, and workshops. An analysis of the company's training program revealed an increase in the number of seminars on leadership, communication, teamwork, and other nontechnical skills. According to Adler's human resource manager, human resource management is understood today as 'translation of the vision and management principles into action', as work in which 'we are constantly learning—with the outcome being open-ended'.

Basic and further training is accorded higher priority at Adler today than it was in the past. The value attached to it is shown not only in the expanded range of seminars being offered but also in the number of Adler's skilled personnel, which increased among specialized sales consultants, for example. The training, which is certified by the Chamber of Commerce, is offered to employees internally and free of charge.

Employee Motivation and Identification

The information gathered in this case study does not allow for valid statements about any change in motivation of the employees or their identification with the company. However, the change process has included the introduction of employee and departmental discussions as well as transfer seminars in which participants have worked out solutions for pending issues, which can limit motivation if left unresolved. From time to time, people have also been asked (albeit unsystematically) why they like working at Adler and what could be improved. The results of these surveys have been published from time to time in *Der Adler*, and the management has also responded briefly to each point of criticism, commenting on what is being done to eliminate the problem or explaining which problems cannot be eliminated immediately.

Evaluation of Learning

As clearly signaled by the name of the vision, 'Loving Change', learning has been given a completely different priority. This change is also evident from the principles of management and cooperation, in which it is explicitly stated that 'mistakes are learning opportunities'. The passage about this principle reads:

As understanding as we are in dealing with the mistakes of others, it is just as important to acknowledge our own mistakes and learn from them. The motto is to be imaginative and from now on only make new mistakes. Admitting your mistakes is what strengthens you personally and enhances your standing. As managers, we have no way of keeping mistakes a secret anyhow, so it is better to tackle them head-on.

The company has applied this principle many times in the course of the change process. Interim evaluations of the measures that were introduced have made it possible to correct mistakes straightforwardly and openly.

Learning also means constantly observing the environment, markets, and customers and drawing conclusions in order to respond accordingly. Since 1987, for example, personnel from the purchasing and sales departments have formed work groups in which they regularly discuss market and customer trends on the basis of results from customer surveys and observations about competitors passed on by store managers and regional sales managers. (For a description of similar procedures at Wal-Mart and Seven-Eleven Japan, see Nonaka, Reinmöller, and Toyama, Ch. 37 in this volume.)

New Constellations of Power

Adler's internal constellations of power changed as well. According to many Adler managers, it used to be said that general managers 'had all the say; no one could really challenge them'. Moreover, they used to have a highly operational style of leadership (micromanagement). Today, however, work groups, project groups, and specialists from various levels have considerable influence on decision-making. This arrangement has distinctly altered how the world is perceived and interpreted, what is considered important and unimportant, and how work is understood.

Conclusion

Adler has managed to change the structural and cultural components of the system fundamentally, for today's self-conception, future orientation, leadership, and cooperation differ markedly from the paradigms that existed in 1987. The basis of knowledge and the potential of control have been altered by and for the learning process. As a result, new ways of thinking have been introduced, and they perceptibly influence internal and external behavior.

However, these structures are also intended to allow for further changes. Power is not limited to the managing board but is also exercised by functional areas and project groups. At the same time the transparency of the system is increasing. Consequently, the power to define and interpret within Adler is less concentrated and less restricted than it used to be. The system is built on a structure that allows for learning.

These observations hint at plausible answers to the question posed at the outset of this chapter: How can existing knowledge about organizational learning be applied to the real life of companies? It is generally acknowledged that the results of a case study cannot be statistically generalized. The evidence underlying the results presented in case studies is not acquired through empirical material but rather through analytical generalization. When considering the results in light of existing theories and concepts of organizational learning, one develops a mental map of the central variables of organizational change, organizational transformation, and the underlying organizational learning process.

That process has two key determinants. One is the existence of open environmental monitoring, that is the perception of developments within the environment relevant to the organization. The company's open-mindedness, tolerance, and its awareness of the environment are crucial. The other key determinant is the relations within the organization, which are determined by conflict, communication, and learning.

In all probability, different views on developments within the organizational environment are produced if the organization's environmental monitoring is transparent. Therefore, conflicting assessments of changes and their consequences are inevitable. A culture that allows conflict and promotes communication in order to solve problems is crucial for the success of organizational learning processes. In this context learning as a determinant of change means that all levels of the company—employees as well as managers—are involved. This point leads to other determinants of learning:

1. The existence or development of a management with the ability to learn. In this context, skills or styles of leadership that managers should have in general, especially with regard to change, are of less interest than individual characteristics, such as the ability to communicate and argue, orientation to process rather than to structure, and curiosity and sensitivity backed up by strong self-confidence.

2. An orientation to the future, developed and formulated into a vision. This vision implies those goals and values that determine organizational decisions in the long run and the behavior of the organization's members.

3. Additional and precise structural guidelines. These guidelines issue from and aim at a binding vision and govern the development, implementation, and evaluation of the necessary steps.

The organization's learning process is initiated and supported by those determinants. The process has a number of central variables:

1. The active participation of all members as well as the consultation of internal and external experts. Only by opening up the 'prevailing corporate philosophy' in this way can the members of an organization challenge and, if necessary, alter its actual construction and definition of reality (Berger and Luckmann 1980) and its internal and external references. This variable expresses the elementary implementation of conflict, communication, and learning.

2. The successive implementation and rehearsal of new behavior patterns. These patterns are affected by formal instruments of planning and control and by systematic decisions.

3. Permanent and intensive training of employees and managers as part of the change process.

4. Integrative evaluation for measuring success and correcting divergences and mistakes.

It becomes clear that the process is permanent and cannot be terminated. It is initiated by establishing the determinants for organizational learning considering the demands of the process.

But in what way does practical application benefit from theoretical results? Organizational learning as a process is both unceasing and interminable—a fact of special importance in goal- and project-oriented processes. Moreover, organizational learning is incredibly complex, as conveyed by the interrelation of determinants and process variables described in this chapter. Lastly, concentration on a restricted number of central issues of this complex network, as would be necessary for practical application of this knowledge, would merely produce the illusion of speed and efficiency but 'never a satisfying result' (Kotter 1995: 59).

In discursive interaction with similar studies and practical experience, the results of this case study can provide a guideline for the learning organization. It is necessary to see these results not as the ingredients of a recipe but as parts of a checklist for the analysis and design of the actual learning process. This approach may increase the likelihood of success in an organization's learning process.

The large number of experiments and strategies in this area still blurs the picture that has been drawn by scientific research. It is therefore advisable to avoid copying manifestations of specific preconditions and process steps. More promising and more relevant to practice would be the implementation of the principles behind the manifestations. This suggestion implies:

(1) introducing continuous open environmental monitoring;

(2) shaping an organizational culture that allows for conflicts, communication, and learning;

(3) creating the possibility to acquire new competencies that allow one to test and rehearse new ideas;

(4) recruiting and training managers with the ability to learn.

It is equally important to develop a vision that can guide the process of change at all times. Each member of the company should be able to identify personally with the procedure. Integrative evaluation is also a key component of the process.

And even when these points are used as a check list for the learning process in an organization, the organization is never relieved of the hard work entailed by the process of development and learning.

References

Albach, H., Dierkes, M., Berthoin Antal, A., and Vaillant, K. (eds.) (1998). *Organisationslernen—institutionelle und kulturelle Dimensionen. WZB Jahrbuch 1998*. Berlin: edition sigma.

Argyris, C. and Schön, D. A. (1978). *Organizational Learning: A Theory of Action Perspective*. Reading, Mass.: Addison-Wesley.

Berger, P. L. and Luckmann, T. (1980). *Die gesellschaftliche Konstruktion der Wirklichkeit: Eine Theorie der Wissenssoziologie* (M. Plessner, trans.). Frankfurt am Main: Fischer. (Original work published 1966)

Child, J. and Smith, C. (1987). 'The Context and Process of Organizational Transformation: Cadbury Limited in Its Sector'. *Journal of Management Studies*, 24: 565–93.

Dierkes, M. (1994). *Definition von Organisationslernen*. Paper presented at the first Ladenburg Kolleg Meeting on Organizational Learning, Ladenburg, Germany, Gottlieb Daimler- and Karl Benz-Foundation, 12–13 October.

Duncan, R. and Weiss, A. (1979). 'Organizational Learning: Implications for Organizational Design', in B. M. Staw (ed.), *Research in Organizational Behavior: An Annual Series of Analytical Essays and Critical Reviews* (Vol. 1). Greenwich, Conn.: JAI, 75–123.

Garratt, B. (1990). *Creating a Learning Organisation: A Guide to Leadership, Learning and Development*. Cambridge: Director Books.

Garvin, D. A. (1993). 'Building a Learning Organization'. *Harvard Business Review*, 71/4: 78–91.

Kanter, R. M., Stein, B. A., and Jick, T. D. (1992). *The Challenge of Organizational Change*. New York: Free Press.

Kotter, J. P. (1995). 'Leading Change: Why Transformation Efforts Fail'. *Harvard Business Review*, 73/2: 59–67.

Krebsbach-Gnath, C. (ed.) (1992). *Den Wandel in Unternehmen steuern: Faktoren für ein erfolgreiches Change Management*. Frankfurt am Main: FAZ Verlag.

——(1996). *Organisationslernen, Theorie und Praxis der Veränderung*. Wiesbaden: Gabler, Deutscher Universitätsverlag.

Moingeon, B. and Edmondson, A. (eds.) (1996). *Organizational Learning and Competitive Advantage*. London: Sage.

Nonaka, I. and Reinmöller, P. (1998). 'The Legacy of Learning: Toward Endogenous Knowledge Creation for Asian Economic Development', in H. Albach, M. Dierkes, A. Berthoin Antal, and K. Vaillant (eds.), *Organizationslernen—institutionelle und kulturelle Dimensionen. WZB Jahrbuch 1998*. Berlin: edition sigma, 401–32.

Pedler, M., Burgoyne, J., and Boydell, T. (1991). *The Learning Company: A Strategy for Sustainable Development*. London: McGraw-Hill.

Senge, P. M. (1990). *The Fifth Discipline: The Art and Practice of the Learning Organization*. New York: Doubleday Currency.

Staehle, W. H. (1991). *Management: Eine verhaltenswissenschaftliche Perspektive* (6th edn). Munich: Franz Vahlen.

41 Multimodal Organizational Learning: From Misbehavior to Good Laboratory Practice in the Pharmaceutical Industry

Christoph de Haën, Lai Si Tsui-Auch, and Marcus Alexis

Theories of organizational learning could benefit from an increase in the number of large, detailed cases with which to assess their pertinence, explanatory power, and predictive ability. The emergence of governmental regulations on Good Laboratory Practice (GLP) and their implementation in the pharmaceutical industry offers precisely that kind of material. The processes of developing and implementing GLP regulations reveal multiple modalities of organizational learning, such as cognitive knowledge acquisition, organizational imitation, and behavioral and cultural change. These processes have involved a variety of actors, permitting an exploration of the dynamics of learning processes across different hierarchical levels of government and industry. To help put the chosen case into perspective, we begin by briefly introducing three theoretical frameworks for organizational learning and their relevant concepts. A detailed account of the GLP case follows, providing empirical data collected with aspects of organizational learning in mind. Theories are then applied to the case with the aim of assessing their epistemological merits. Finally, new insights are highlighted, and territories uncharted by present theories are identified.

The creation of a legislative framework and of GLP regulations in the United States involved parliament, government agencies, professional and trade associations, companies, international organizations, media agencies, public interest groups, and the public at large, including some outspoken activists. An account of the interaction between these agencies, groups, and individuals during the advent of GLP regulations (1963–1979) could alone have sufficed to illuminate interorganizational learning processes. However, our analysis benefited greatly from occasional comparisons with the preceding period (1950–1963), during which the 'current Good Manufacturing Practice' regulations were produced.

Both periods were followed by implementation phases within the governmental regulatory agency that was involved, namely, the U.S. Food and Drug Administration (FDA), as well as within companies, with the two efforts temporarily overlapping somewhat. For the purposes of this chapter, focus on the implementation phase of GLP regulations is confined to their application within companies. GLP implementation illustrates the conditions, agents, processes, and outcomes of learning mostly within organizations, that is, intraorganizational learning. Although inter- and intraorganizational learning are seldom mutually exclusive, we make the distinction because the two types of learning were found to characterize two consecutive phases, respectively. The following presentation is therefore chronological.

GLP regulations originated in the United States, as had the ones on current Good Manufacturing Practice. Similar regulations are in force in most of the world today. The European experience, at least, falls well in line with that in the United States, particularly with regard to GLP implementation. It was therefore appropriate to choose the United States as the focus for our sectorial case study of the rise and application of GLP regulations.

Our case research is based on several research methods: (a) documentation of related historical developments reflected in newspapers (*The New York Times*), and various types of publications from the government (e.g. United States Code Annotated and the *Federal Register*), trade associations, and academia (Shulman, Hewitt, and Manocchia 1995; Wardell and Lasagna 1975), with relevance to organizational learning as the key criterion; (b) personal, informal conversation and discussion with dozens of managers and researchers in organizations ranging from small venture capital companies to giant multinationals; (c) participation by one of the authors in the implementation of GLP as a manager in a European-based multinational company; (d) company visits; (e) observation of training courses; and (f) examination of research, inspection, and corrective action reports.

Theoretical Frameworks for Organizational Learning

Learning as a Cognitive-behavioral Process

The cognitive-behavioral models of organizational learning emphasize the analogical similarity between learning by organizations and learning by individuals (Maier, Prange, and von Rosenstiel, Ch. 1 in this volume). In these models organizational learning is conceived of as a relatively lasting change that a response to experience brings about in cognition, potential behavior, and/or actual behavior (for a summary, see Starbuck

and Hedberg, Ch. 14 in this volume; Tsang 1997). The organization is conceptualized as a system marked by a boundary and separated from the external, constantly changing environment (Lawrence and Lorsch 1967; Cyert and March 1963). In order to solve the problems stemming from a changing and uncertain environment, organizations presumably need to acquire information that enables them to develop new understanding and skills, to design appropriate strategies, rules, and actions or to do both.

As conceptualized in the cognitive-behavioral approach, learning is a linear sequence of information-processing, such as the acquisition, diffusion, interpretation, and storage of information and experience in organizational memory (for a summary, see Huber 1991), a view consistent with the image of the organization as an 'input–output system'. Most often, leaders and top management are considered the agents who manage and effect organizational learning and unlearning. Whereas behavioral theorists see organizational learning as an activity of adaptation to environmental changes of a contingent nature, cognitive theorists suggest that organizational learning can be planned and controlled. Behavioral theorists emphasize the maintenance of continuity; cognitive theorists focus on organizational change. Most authors see the importance of both control and contingency in maintaining the balance between organizational change and continuity (Cohen, March, and Olsen 1972; Hedberg 1981; March 1991). For example, Hedberg (1981) described unlearning as the intentional process of an organization to delete its cognitive maps, data, or standard operating procedures (SOP) in order to make way for new learning. However, he admitted that disregarding old habits and concepts is very difficult and suggested that this process is often triggered by crises rather than by rational planning. The paradoxes of continuity and change that result from organizational learning were viewed by Levinthal and March (1993) from the perspective of behavioral conditioning. According to them, on the one hand, failure may trigger excessive exploration of new solutions and may lead to a neglect of continuity, an outcome that would make the organization vulnerable in the long run (the 'exploration trap'). On the other hand, success may reinforce an overreliance on the existing routine, reducing the organization's future capability to cope with the changing environment (the 'exploitation trap').

Learning as a Cultural Process

In the cultural approach organizational learning is conceived of less as a change in cognition and behavior than as a change in collective identity. Organizations are conceptualized as cultures (Cook and Yanow 1993; Schein 1993). Cultures operate as a means of public persuasion, as ways of knowing, and as options for managing identities and political control. Organizations enact their own rules, structures, and environments through social interaction (Weick 1979). Meanings and actions are culturally and socially constructed and thus reflect the cultural and structural embeddedness of organizations (Child and Heavens, Ch. 13 in this volume). Cook and Yanow (1993) defined organizational learning as 'the acquiring, sustaining, or changing of inter-subjective meanings through the artifactual vehicles of their expression and transmission and the collective actions of the group' (p. 384). Authors taking this perspective, like those taking the cognitive-behavioral one, are concerned with change and the maintenance of continuity. They juxtapose the exploitation of an old identity and the exploration of new situations, illuminating the tension between the continuation of the old order and the adoption of a new one.

Learning as a Social Process

The 'learning organizing' approach (Czarniawska 1997), the 'learning-in-organizing' approach (Gherardi and Nicolini, Ch. 2 in this volume), and the 'knowledge-creation' theory (Nonaka, Toyama, and Byosière, Ch. 22 in this volume; Nonaka and Takeuchi 1995) have a central tenet in common—the pragmatic perspec-

tive on organizational learning, which creates no schism between cognition and interpretation or between knowledge and action. Although their proponents do not object to the idea that knowledge is stored in human minds, they conceive of organizational learning as inherently social. They therefore focus on the social, rather than the cognitive and behavioral, character of learning. They do not reduce knowledge to information that can be collected, programmed, and processed as it 'exists'. They conceive of knowledge as (a) relational, (b) in context, and (c) in action. Knowledge is developed, reproduced, and negotiated through the ongoing interaction and practices of actors who are bounded by material and social circumstances in a particular time and space. Knowledge can be formalized and made explicit in some ways, but for the most part it is tacitly rooted in individuals' (Polanyi 1966) experience and is spread through direct communication.

Although the learning organizing and learning-in-organizing approaches and the theory of organizational knowledge creation share the pragmatic perspective on learning, they have different focuses. Learning organizing and learning-in-organizing focus on the imitation process across boundaries of individual organizations over time and space. Proponents of these approaches suggest that organizational imitation involves a recontextualization of knowledge developed in the original context and that it is therefore a creative and transformative learning process. Learning changes individual action patterns, an effect that, if reinforced by interaction of individuals, leads to an expanding wave of change. Learning may bring about not only intended but also unintended consequences, and not only institutionalization (e.g. rule development) but also deinstitutionalization (e.g. rule violation).

The theory of organizational knowledge creation emphasizes knowledge creation and development within an organization. Proponents of this theory identify middle managers (e.g. knowledge engineers, line supervisors) as the key agents in bridging the ideals of top managers and the views of frontline workers. They advocate a 'middle-down-up' management model as the best strategy for knowledge creation. Nonaka and Konno (1998) have extended the knowledge-creation theory to include the concept of knowledge management, specifying the role of top management and leaders. What distinguishes their approach from the currently dominant models of information-processing and knowledge management is the tendency of the knowledge-creation theory to focus on the nurturing and cultivating of tacit knowledge and individual and collective experience more than on the processing of information through advanced technologies. The knowledge-creation theory largely reflects the organizational structure, corporate culture, and industrial relations of large Japanese companies; its applicability to other organizations and countries remains to be explored.

The Focus of the Inquiry

A number of questions are addressed in our GLP case analysis. How was organizational learning triggered? To which hierarchical levels within a system of organizations or within individual organizations do the initiators of learning belong? How did previous experience within the organizations referred to in the study and within unrelated organizations shape the learning processes? What circumstances favored interorganizational learning? Where was experience stored, and to whom was it readily available? Are there differences in the effectiveness of positive and negative experience? Which learning modalities were actually used, and why were they chosen? How were various learning modalities integrated? What kinds of impediments to learning were encountered? Which of the three discussed theoretical frameworks for organizational learning accounts best for various observed learning situations? Do any of the frameworks provide useful tools for future learning? What organizational learning needs are not adequately covered by theory?

Case Analysis: The Emergence of U.S. Government Regulations on GLP and their Implementation in the Pharmaceutical Industry

Interorganizational Learning: Learning to Regulate Laboratory Drug Safety Documentation

In the 1950s, the appearance of 'wonder drugs' (antibiotics, psychoactive drugs, steroids) on the market (Healy 1998) and the simultaneous rise of the consumer protection movement (Carson 1962; Chase and Schlink 1927; Lear 1959) led to unpredicted public interest in the pharmaceutical industry and its physician customers. Acrimonious congressional hearings that revealed corporate and professional misconduct entailing potential risks for the patient laid the inner workings of the pharmaceutical industry bare for the first time and shook the trust that the public had felt in both the industry and physicians (Harris 1964a, b, c). Pressure to take remedial action mounted. At first, massive opposition by trade and professional associations to increased government control was able to stalemate new legislation. However, shock over the tragic birth defects caused by thalidomide (Contergan®) led to amendment of existing U.S. legislation in 1962. Henceforth, the FDA, which since 1938 had operated under the legislative mandate to assure the safety of new drugs through regulation of safety-testing and marketing authorization, had the further responsibility of assuring, among other things, drug efficacy (benefit) and Good Manufacturing Practice.

In order to assess the risk–benefit relationships of drugs, the FDA obtained data on safety and efficacy from pharmaceutical companies. Whereas laboratory data, especially on safety, were generated either in house or at contract research organizations, clinical safety and efficacy information was produced at the request of the companies by potential prescribers who had performed clinical trials. The data were then evaluated by the FDA, often with the help of outside experts (peer review). This mechanism of risk–benefit assessment, which is based almost exclusively on the evaluation of data generated by the industry or under its supervision, is still considered satisfactory in principle. The tacit assumption then was that the data had been honestly produced and accurately and thoroughly reported to the FDA. However, there came a time in the 1960s when the risk–benefit assessment itself was seen to be at risk, for it was realized that the data required for such assessments could be flawed or could be selectively withheld from the FDA. Especially, transparency of laboratory data and accountability (or 'soundness', as it is called in banking) for their generation needed to be assured.

In 1963, with minimal involvement of the pharmaceutical industry, the FDA had produced the current Good Manufacturing Practice regulations. They represented the first effort to regulate not only the quality of the final drug product but also manufacturing processes and their documentation. They embodied an innovative regulatory concept aimed primarily at increasing both the transparency of procedures and accountability for actions taken. The concept was so convincing that the World Health Organization published its own, very similar Good Manufacturing Practice regulations in 1968. Moreover, what had been learned could be applied to the previously mentioned problem of transparency and accountability of documentation on drug safety. Consequently, the same approach was later adopted for GLP and Good Clinical Practice regulations. In particular, the Good Manufacturing Practice regulations set a learning precedent for the GLP regulations, on which our case study is chiefly focused.

After the introduction of Good Manufacturing Practice regulations, the FDA, some influential politicians, and some consumer-rights advocates (e.g. Mintz 1965) were not satisfied with the achieved improvement in drug safety. However, as revealed by the decline in the number of related articles in the *New York Times*, public interest waned for a while after the amendment of U.S. food and drug legislation in 1962. This waning interest, together with organizational struggles at the FDA and resistance by the pharmaceutical industry and trade associations, resulted in postponement of further legislative and regulatory action. Prompted partly by irregularities in reporting laboratory safety data on drugs (Flagyl®, Aldactone®) by G. D. Searle and Co. and the contract research organization it had used, and partly by Searle's resistance to FDA laboratory inspections, Senator Edward M. Kennedy conducted public hearings on compliance with drug-safety regulations in 1975. The proceedings involved a number of individuals who had played prominent roles in the hearings that had culminated in the 1962 legislation and current Good Manufacturing Practice regulations. These participants contributed their active memories of actors, processes, and both successful and failed strategies. Through practice they had developed skills that became the patrimony of their organizations, whether they had or had not changed from one to another. Most members of Congress and all top managers were novices in the field. Their lack of experience with the issue points to the important role of mid-level personnel in preserving the know-how of organizations over significant time spans.

The first category of problems aired at the hearings involved questionable scientific judgment in research design, data evaluation, and data presentation to the FDA. Clearly, these problems were caused by a combination of factors, such as employment of unqualified scientists and undue pressure by management to accelerate drug registration processes at the expense of safety. A second category of problems was the operational deficiencies of the studies (i.e. poor planning, inadequate adherence to protocols, incomplete data collection, lost data, failure to check for errors of transcription, and inadequate training of personnel). The poor laboratory practice led the FDA to impose a stay of effectiveness on G. D. Searle and Co.'s artificial sweetener, Aspartame®. This dramatic sanction could not be taken lightly by the company's top management.

In contrast to U.S. Congress and the FDA, some industries had evidently not learned in a timely manner to extrapolate from the bad experiences of the 1950s and from the Good Manufacturing Practice regulations of that time to other areas of drug validation. Good Manufacturing Practice was considered an issue of production management and thus a matter unworthy of particular attention from either top management or R&D management. Disciplinary compartmentalization might have caused the failure to detect the close similarities between the new situation and the history that led to current Good Manufacturing Practice regulations. In some industries this failure, in turn, generated shortsighted responses to criticism and inadequate corrective action.

At congressional hearings in 1976, the FDA commissioner called for a strengthening of the legislative mandate to regulate drug safety. In the same year, the U.S. Congress approved discretionary regulatory authority in the requested domains and a substantial budget for the creation of a Bioresearch Monitoring Program. The FDA decided to focus on improving transparency and accountability regarding the generation of laboratory data on drug safety. It adopted a command-and-control type of regulation that had considerable interpretative flexibility (Gifford 1989), an approach similar to the one already practiced in current Good Manufacturing Practice regulations. In 1976 the FDA presented the proposed GLP regulations for public scrutiny, as required by law. Representatives of industry immediately criticized the proposal for its bureaucratization of research through burdensome organizational requirements and for inappropriate intrusion into research by quality-assurance units. Actually, companies were mostly worried about additional costs.

Conducted concurrently with the regulatory effort, the FDA's field examination of 67 studies in 39 laboratories consolidated the view that poor laboratory practice was widespread. These findings convinced most companies and industrial associations of the justification of additional regulation. Meanwhile, the FDA's drastic punitive response to questionable la-

boratory documentation regarding the safety of Aspartame® triggered a revision of top management attitudes at G. D. Searle and Co. Instead of opposing all moves by the FDA, the company began voluntarily assisting the FDA in revising the proposed GLP regulations and hence became a partner in the change process. The Pharmaceutical Manufacturers Association did the same. The FDA welcomed this switch from regulatory policy-making based on adversarial representation of interests to policy-making based on the idea of negotiating regulations with the parties involved.

Regulation negotiation, a process given the name 'RegNeg', stemmed from a learning process in the 1970s (especially within the Federal Trade Commission) that had shown the adversarial approach to be ineffective and inefficient (Boyer 1989). Yet, the FDA had to guard against being perceived as a captive of the industry. It therefore moved quickly to assert its mandate, without waiting for a completion of consensus-building. On 22 December 1978, the FDA published the final version of the *Good Laboratory Practice for Nonclinical Laboratory Studies* (Food and Drug Administration 1978) and set 20 June 1979 as the date on which it was to go into effect. Preexisting regulations regarding Investigative New Drugs and New Drug Applications were amended to require a declaration of compliance for each study subject to GLP regulations, that is, any laboratory study whose purpose was to assess the safety of a drug. The regulations initially centered on selected professional specialties, above all toxicology, analytical testing of clinical specimens, the pharmaceutics of test and control articles, and quality control. Initially categorized outside the domain of GLP requirements, animal pharmacokinetics has meanwhile come to be considered part of safety studies, and laboratory information technology is in the process of becoming included as well. Studies exclusively addressing drug efficacy in laboratory animals were not placed under GLP regulations, for final assessment of efficacy by the FDA is ultimately based on human data. Obviously, research activities aimed at the discovery and understanding of drugs also remained unregulated. Almost identical GLP regulations were adopted by western European countries, Japan, and international organizations (e.g. the OECD). Moreover, GLP regulations were expanded to cover other areas, such as environmental studies in general and those involving herbicides and pesticides in particular. The progression of GLP applicability is thus clear to see.

Also, the implementation of the legislators, mandate to the FDA showed progression. At first, this primarily spelled out the safety principle and set a focus on the transparency and accountability of generating data on laboratory drug safety. Only in subsequent steps was specific guidance for various activities provided.

Despite extensive deregulation in the U.S. industrial sector in general, further regulatory efforts in the drug sector continued for a time after the enactment of the GLP regulations. Noting later the overall improvement in the submitted drug documents, however, the FDA was willing to renegotiate some details of existing regulations. Consequently, GLP regulations were amended in 1987 in order to reduce unnecessary regulatory burden and to increase the operational flexibility of laboratories while maintaining the basic objective of optimizing protection of the public. Similar regulatory relief in the area of current Good Manufacturing Practice and Good Clinical Practice regulations was announced at the end of 1997.

Intraorganizational Learning: Learning to Implement GLP Regulations in the Industry

The first individuals in a company to become familiar with GLP regulations were those from middle management. They typically were persons responsible for preclinical drug-safety assessment and regulatory compliance, and they usually followed new developments in the regulatory arena by reading the relevant literature and attending conventions. This group included toxicologists, safety pharmacologists, and specialists in pharmaceutics, quality control, and regulatory affairs. In fact, some of them had already helped formulate GLP regu-

lations as members of trade or professional associations, as partners in regulatory negotiation with the FDA, or in both capacities. After collecting all available documentation on the regulations, they began to introduce the principles and guidelines to their companies and to help implement the regulations. With middle management taken as the starting point, middle-down and middle-up learning processes were initiated. Through budget approvals and occasionally through written and verbal affirmation, the top management of most companies embraced the new regulations, although in several cases support for the implementation of GLP regulations was reluctant, even inadequate. Top management found it very difficult to accept that the costs of regulated activities increased between 15 and 30 per cent, depending on how far from compliance a given firm had been. A minority of companies simply decided to outsource all development work requiring GLP. They thereby demonstrated awareness that extensive in-house learning would have been required and reduced the organizational and economic burdens of in-house learning by sharing the labor with specialized service providers. They accepted a solution of minimized learning.

With the guidance of middle management, the corporate units in charge of in-house training organized courses and invited internal or external experts to impart the principles and guidelines to the employees. Alternatively, personnel was enrolled in courses organized by trade or professional organizations, private training companies, pharmaceutical company consortia, contract research organizations, or regulatory agencies. In these courses, however, the abstract, formalized principles were illustrated only through examples, if at all. Abstract, formalized knowledge transmission, though certainly essential, did not in itself prepare employees sufficiently for compliance with new regulations. The translation of principles and guidelines into action also required social interaction and practice. Because the knowhow behind the implementation of the regulations had the nature of a public good, competitive companies were happy to share training opportunities and discuss best practices, an attitude that added an interorganizational learning component to the otherwise primarily intraorganizational learning processes.

The task of adjusting to GLP regulations was often overwhelming, depending on the degree to which the actual situation diverged from the goals set by the regulations and from the deadline set for compliance. The most typical response of employees who were sent for GLP training was disbelief in the practicability of applying the abstract principles to their company's specific context. Compliance required the creation or remodeling of facilities and the reorganization of tasks and organization charts. Along with having to design or equip facilities such as GLP archives, animals' quarters, clean rooms, and dressing rooms, a company had to revise its SOP (Parks 1988), work organization, and job descriptions. Employees' participation in these activities was essential for translating the principles and written guidelines into operational know-how.

Some know-how of GLP regulations was also acquired when managers and other personnel paid visits to 'expert organizations', companies that had successfully implemented the new regulations. When the visitors encountered satisfaction with the new regulations and their effects on working conditions, they became motivated to achieve similar results in their own company. Finally, companies sometimes acquired advanced know-how by hiring expert personnel, an option used mostly by latecomers.

Know-how was consolidated through practice, especially through the feedback loops provided by frequent and obligatory study audits performed by the company's quality-assurance unit. In fact, compliance with GLP regulations required, among other things, a written response that addressed critique by the internal quality-assurance unit or the FDA inspectors. If the feedback loop had to be run through more than once, employees often got frustrated. Frustration, in turn, discouraged further rule violation. Frequently, corrective action required changes in SOP, the creation of new SOP, and/

or improvement of facilities. This formalized process was designed to optimize learning from errors by making personnel accountable for corrective action.

Compliance with GLP regulations necessitated the cooperation of many people. For instance, GLP required that research protocols be endorsed by several investigators, for example, a pharmacotoxicologist, veterinarian, statistician, manager, and a representative of a quality-assurance unit. Researchers with an individualist mentality lost their role in such a context. This change made some employees uncomfortable with GLP regulations and had the potential to retard learning or drive away valuable personnel.

All activities falling under GLP regulations within a company have involved one or more hierarchical systems of SOP. These SOP are characterized by their marked concreteness. They refer to specific people, positions, equipment, rooms, forms, and rhythms. Once institutionalized and strictly observed, they mirror how the company works. Procedural changes take place only if the relevant SOP are replaced. GLP requires all originals of SOP, including replaced ones, to remain archived for thirty years. Authorized copies of active SOP, which may not be copied further, are in the hands of named operators, and all copies of replaced SOP in the hands of operators must be retrieved and destroyed at the time of their replacement. Together, these requirements have made SOP the collective and depersonalized memory of a company's procedural knowledge. They fulfil this function especially for the successful implementation of GLP, including corrections after failures. SOP are meant to be regularly consulted, so they constituted active memory. Obviously, they need to be constantly updated, but experience has shown that frequent changes, especially those of only minor import or of a purely formal nature, create SOP fatigue and noncompliance. In any case, compliance with GLP has required a change of habits. This shift was uncomfortable for researchers, for it sometimes lacked scientific rationale. After all, many researchers had been used to carrying out experiments in university settings, which typically enjoy operational flexibility that fosters chance discovery. These conditions are alien to the standard set forth in GLP regulations. For these reasons discovery research, especially in chemistry, biochemistry, and general pharmacology, have continued to be managed outside the realm of GLP regulations, even within companies.

As time went on, companies became creative in fostering employees' compliance with GLP regulations by complementing cognitive with subliminal means of persuasion. For example, by encouraging many researchers to take part in writing SOP, managers showed that they treated subordinates as partners in processes of behavioral and cultural change. The creation of symbols and incentives was especially effective. In some instances, special job titles such as 'head of drug-testing facility', 'archivist', or 'quality controller of the drug-testing center' were created in order to meet the psychological need for peer recognition. Recognizing personnel as experts by granting them the authority to instruct novices or to sign off on documents also provided incentives. Peer pressure within teams provided an additional source of motivation. In other contexts, say, pharmaceutical development or animals' quarters, new special garments, badges, and access permits to off-limit areas were created, and these symbols provided emotional crutches for ceasing the old behavior and embracing the new. These subliminal incentives to behavioral change and compliance were, in some cases, complemented by material incentives, such as bonuses and festivities after a company's successful FDA inspection or speedy drug approvals. The majority of managers who were informally consulted on ways to make such transitions considered these approaches important for effecting cultural change.

Factors Inhibiting Learning Processes

The implementation of GLP regulations required additional personnel and enlarged facilities and therefore substantially increased the cost of the same amount of work. For top management understandably out of touch with the intricacies of the GLP implementation, the sudden change in efficiency and the demand for resources was hard to digest. In some cases denial of demands for increased resources led to failure of individual studies, necessitating costly repetitions. On rare occasions, it even caused delays in the approval of new drugs, although the FDA preferred to force progress through less dramatic, more gradual means. In any case, FDA inspections have shown that GLP violations still occur at a significant rate despite the fact that enough time to learn has passed (Food and Drug Administration 1998). Management's failure to provide enough resources of the right kind (insufficiently qualified research directors, inadequate facilities) has been a principal reason for lack of regulatory compliance with GLP, and it is an even greater problem in regulatory compliance with current Good Manufacturing Practice.

Thus, the middle-up learning processes encountered more difficulties than did the middle-down learning processes mentioned above. Top management tended to underestimate the scope of the regulatory change. The miscalculation of top management's role in meeting regulatory compliance was probably in part related to the inclusion of the word 'laboratory' in GLP regulations, vocabulary that allowed the issue of compliance to be relegated to a company's technical functions. Furthermore, top management was sometimes reluctant to learn from subordinates. Finally, there existed a deeply rooted aversion to government interference with the pharmaceutical industry.

In addition to the factors discussed thus far, the way firms dealt with the memory of criticism and failure was a factor that could impede learning. Companies at times responded to criticism with excessively limited interventions, for example, in selected facilities or SOP pertaining to a single product if that was where the deficiency lay. However, more systemic obstacles to general compliance could then be overlooked.

The exchange of criticisms and responses between operative units and the quality-assurance unit and between regulatory authorities and companies (e.g. audit reports, warning letters, injunctions, and registration denials) was always documented. However, distribution of the documents tended to be limited for fear that the information might prompt an FDA inspection or tarnish the company image. The active memory of deficiencies and failures and causes thereof was found to reside only in the minds of individuals. We found that archived documentation of failure was not used and that it constituted passive memory at most. This corporate amnesia was an obstacle to learning within a company and an even greater impediment to learning across companies.

Learning GLP: Results and Paradoxes

Today the pharmaceutical industry has completely embraced GLP regulations wherever they are applicable, and serious violations are rarely seen. This outcome is not surprising given the frequency of FDA inspections and the sanctions and other consequences of noncompliance. Considering the additional costs, the required facilities, and the general aversion to regulation, one could have expected industry to implement GLP only where strictly required. In many companies, however, the regulations have been followed even in studies to which they did not initially apply—animal pharmacokinetics and safety pharmacology, for instance. This response may have been due partly to the anticipation at that time that such studies, too, would soon be subject to the regulations. But such utilitarian motives do not explain why GLP-like working conditions were extended to even further activities. It seems instead that a new attitude toward quality assurance emerged, one imbued with the quest for transparency and accountability as important ingredients of total quality.

The rise of this new attitude has facilitated further learning, such as that started by the British Department of Health in 1989. Its objective is to ensure transparency and accountability in the acquisition and manipulation of computerized laboratory data. The FDA is still collaborating with international organizations on draft guidelines in this area. For the moment, it suffices to demonstrate during inspec-

tions that a sincere effort is being made to achieve transparency and accountability. In any case, much laboratory equipment for which no evidence of malfunction exists has to be replaced solely because there exists no economically reasonable way to validate the performance of its information-technology function. This new requirement, too, creates additional costs. However, a culture with a positive attitude toward GLP is now widespread, and this acceptance facilitates compliance. Thus, some instances in which the pharmaceutical industry extends GLP to unregulated activities testify to organizational learning as a cultural change.

The process of learning GLP has had both intended and unintended effects. GLP regulations were established in order to help elevate the quality of research (a process) and science (a body of knowledge). However, by no means can work performed under GLP regulations be equated with quality research and science. It is perfectly possible to perform scientifically nonsensical experiments in compliance with GLP regulations. Compliance with GLP only means maximum transparency and accountability for what has been planned, executed, observed, written down, archived, and communicated.

The introduction of GLP was accompanied by a bureaucratization of experimentation and a restriction on investigative flexibility for those investigators working under the regulations. Investigators who were compelled to operate under GLP regulations tended not to admit that they were being excessively restricted, but they represented a select group of individuals who felt comfortable in their situation. Unlearning both spontaneity and improvisation in experimentation—a necessary component of learning GLP—produced undesired side effects, namely, a quenching of highly creative research and a reduction in the number of surprise findings (serendipity). The time-consuming process of protocol approval and the need to convince others of an experiment's worthiness reduced the ludic acquisition of knowledge, in which intuition is followed, often prior to the formulation of testable hypotheses. Moreover, the more closely experiments followed rigid protocols under GLP regulations, the easier it was to delegate their execution to subordinates, who were generally less prepared to recognize the unusual and the surprising, which were unforeseen by the protocol. Restrictions on flexibility and the inducement to delegate conspired to reduce the number of occasions for discovery. Personnel working under the GLP regulations were removed even further from the possibilities of discovery than they normally were in their professional specialities. The situation appeared to be aggravated by the tendency of personnel, after habituation to GLP, to find working under the regulations more comforting than experimentation under individual responsibility. To the extent that discovery is part of the quality of research and science, GLP regulations paradoxically have the potential to adversely affect that desired quality.

The pharmaceutical industry has obviously had a need for both GLP-conditioned drug development and creative research for drug discovery, even in the professional specialties targeted by the regulations. Large corporations often opted to keep the two types of activity completely separate in terms of both personnel and physical spaces. That dichotomy, however, risked creating separate cultures and hence communication problems. The impracticality of completely separating the two activities in small and medium-sized companies has remained a concern. Balancing regulatory compliance with satisfactory discovery efforts required astute management of available human resources. Perceiving GLP regulations as a threat to creativity and a potential drain on economic resources, most universities ceased registration-related pharmacotoxicological drug-testing, leaving service gaps to be filled by the then newly emerging organizations in the business of contract research. Customers who relied entirely on this service for activities subject to GLP regulations allowed themselves to minimize their learning. Similarly, universities avoided learning. Thus, the regulations decreased rather than increased the number of organizations living up to the new standards of quality assurance.

Reflection on Theories

Interorganizational learning

Measured by any of the theoretical criteria briefly introduced above, the emergence of U.S. governmental regulations on GLP and their implementation in the pharmaceutical industry from 1963 to 1979 showed a good deal of organizational learning. Interorganizational learning was prominent in terms of concepts and procedures during the formative stage of legislation and regulations. The period clearly showed the benefits of organizational learning in the earlier, current Good Manufacturing Practice related period (1950–1963). Adoption of the RegNeg approach was the result of an interorganizational learning process among different government agencies. Evidently, learning occurred among organizations across time and space. The processes leading to GLP regulations consequently ran much more smoothly than the earlier ones leading to Good Manufacturing Practice. Legislation leading to Good Manufacturing Practice regulations in the 1960s needed the thalidomide birth defects tragedy to take the hurdle, just as the elixir of the sulfanilamide affair seemed to have been necessary to trigger safety legislation in 1938. In contrast, Congress passed legislation (1976) that prepared the way to GLP regulations without having to be prompted by such catastrophes. Unfortunately, a significant number of individuals who participated in the legislative process culminating in the congressional action in 1976 had already participated in the legislative process that brought about the 1963 legislation, but some individuals did so representing different organizations. Thus, it is impossible to determine whether the observed organizational learning had occurred in a depersonalized way or whether it had been intrinsically linked to individuals.

Problem analysis and the corresponding legislated processes of knowledge acquisition through public congressional hearings formally followed a cognitive paradigm of organizational learning, namely, one in which knowledge, like a substance, was 'acquired', 'received', 'diffused', 'stored', and 'retrieved'. This procedure was probably adopted because the outcome to be achieved, a statutory law, required learning processes of the same kind for its initial interpretation and implementation.

Study of the Congressional Record, legislative histories, and social science analyses (e.g. Harris 1964a, b, c; Peltzman 1973) of the earlier period pertaining to Good Manufacturing Practice (1950s) and similar documentation of other governmental regulatory efforts led to processes and solutions in the GLP era that bordered on imitation. In these instances, however, imitation efforts could not be clearly distinguished from cognitive learning.

In contrast to problem analysis, the creation of remedial legislation and regulation could not be satisfactorily understood in terms of the handling and exchange of knowledge as a good. The creation of remedial legislation and regulation involved processes of a pronounced social character: the negotiation of norms. Similarly, exegesis of the initial version of the GLP regulations required intensive interorganizational discussions and the sharing of concerns. The new regulations provided both general principles and particular guidelines that nonetheless maintained substantial interpretative flexibility. An understanding of them required discussion and interpretation among professionals and went beyond the grasp of any one individual. Such discussion; the way middle managers gathered information and lobbied through professional associations and various business networks; the way they assisted the FDA in revising proposed regulations and subsequent guidelines; and the manner in which they shared news about regulations, including information and their own interpretations, opinions, and anxieties about possible cost increases and restructuring of work processes—all these aspects are accommodated best by a perspective in which learning is seen as a social process.

Knowledge as a continuously negotiated state in constant flux is a useful concept for characterizing the negotiation phase of new legislation or regulation at the interorganiza-tional level. In addition, the observed gradual increase of regulatory stringency followed by relaxation indicates that the type of knowledge that is of interest in this context is not primarily delimited, unequivocally deducible from sources, but rather an entity that is relational (i.e. derived from negotiation of regulations and agreement on norms), in context (responsive to failure rate and achieved progress in the documentation of drug safety), and in action (expressed through inspection practices that help establish criteria) (Gherardi 1997; Nonaka and Takeuchi 1995). Again, the view of learning as a social process is the perspective most suited for describing these aspects.

If one considers the international acceptance of Good Manufacturing Practice and GLP regulations, the adaptations of them to fields outside the pharmaceutical industry, the readiness of the regulatory body to renegotiate regulations, and the subsequent voluntary introduction of very similar measures to improve safety and quality (ISO norms) in many commercial sectors, a change in culture becomes evident. What once gave rise to major contention between industry and government has now become widely accepted. Involved organizations have changed their self-understanding and public image in a manner best described in terms of learning as a cultural process.

It appears, however, that antecedent cognitive-behavioral learning was a condition for cultural change, and at several junctures social processes were crucial for passing from one cognitive-behavioral state to another. This impression suggests that the three theoretical approaches are not mutually independent frameworks but nested ways to illuminate the observations.

Intraorganizational learning

Implementation of GLP regulations within companies required intraorganizational learning above all, but it was accompanied by a degree of interorganizational learning. Organizational learning modalities analogous to principal modalities of individual learning theory were discerned: cognitive knowledge acquisition, reinforcement, conditioning, and imitation.

The initial phases of GLP implementation in companies were dominated by cognitive learning processes. Information about new legislation and GLP regulations was acquired by middle managers, who diffused it within their companies, and operational personnel regularly had to become acquainted with it. Learning often took place in group study and committee work. Given the written format of laws and regulations and of the documentation to be produced, the personnel had no choice but to begin learning in this way.

However, the cognitive learning processes were complemented by behavioral ones. Reinforcement by group-specific incentives was used in a planned manner by middle management in order to consolidate desired behavioral change. Apart from material incentives, a particular role was given to symbols, such as titles, access badges, and special garments.

Behavioral conditioning was the principal learning modality through which the quality-assurance units of a company or the FDA achieved their goal. The obligation to keep written documentation of remedial responses to critiques by these company or governmental sources, multiple rounds through corrective feedback loops, and finally, sanctions were all intended to discourage repeated rule violation. This approach was used not only for operative units within a company but also for the company as a whole, including its top management. Obviously, learning by conditioning is adaptive and is contingent on rule violation. It is effective when the required stringency of compliance is set at levels that lead to low, but nonzero, violation frequencies.

Certainly, the imitation recognizable in the results of visits to expert organizations was not merely a process of mechanistic reproduction. SOP from expert organizations served at best as general guidelines for the creation of a version fitted to one's own environment. A company needed to compare its own quantity and quality of resources (human, spatial, financial), drug development processes, and work cultures with those of other companies and to translate the observed corporate best practice into its own context. The translation process involved the reorganization of workspace, tasks, and charts; the rewriting of rules, including SOP; experimentation with the new procedures; the evaluation of the results; and further changes in procedures. Writing and rewriting SOP or study protocols again and again allowed knowledge to mature into skill or know-how, a form of knowledge that, like a reflex, allowed one to make shortcuts when transforming cognitive knowledge into action. It was a form of tacit knowledge that, unlike some other forms, could be verbalized at any moment.

Finally, when through emotional processes the know-how had impregnated the whole organizational culture and had in part become tacit, operators at all levels had learned how to be or behave (Badoux 1997): They had developed a new attitude (e.g. voluntary application of regulations and a low level of regulatory violations) and they had altered their culture. Visits to expert organizations also provided opportunity for tapping into this tacit knowledge of how to interpret and implement the regulations.

In many companies techniques aimed at stimulating cultural change were applied. As described in this sectorial case study, the transmission of abstract, formalized knowledge did not prepare employees sufficiently for compliance with the new regulations. Some employees in GLP training were reluctant to unlearn their habits and doubted that complete compliance was practicable. Recognizing the emotional and psychological sensibilities of the employees, companies created various symbols in order to render compliance with GLP regulations appealing.

Several managers in this case study considered symbolic and material incentives important for bringing about both behavioral and cultural changes that would gradually make GLP an industrial norm and encourage companies to explore a new corporate identity as more socially responsible organizations. Recognizing the importance of emotions in organizational change processes and using appropriate symbols helps ease resistance to change. The cultural perspective of organizational learning captures this angle of GLP's realization in the pharmaceutical industry best. Moreover, this theory leads one to expect that the described symbols that were successfully used in the processes of implementing GLP regulations constitute a tool kit that is applicable to similar situations. The theory allows prediction.

Although cognitive-behavioral approaches and the cultural perspective provided strong conceptual scaffolds for many observations, they were unable on their own to capture the full richness of observed organizational learning. The learning unit was always a group. We found not a single case of learning specifically aimed at the individual, for instance, 'computer-programmed self-learning'. This focus on groups signifies at least implicit acknowledgment of a social component in organizational learning needed for the implementation of GLP regulations. Moreover, the activities did not take place as discrete processes in a neat sequence described by the information-processing approach. The process of translating principles into practice involved discussion, interaction, visits of expert organizations, rule development, and consensus-building. By writing SOP, designing facilities in teams, and repeatedly going through the process of collective protocol-writing, participants delineated competence and negotiated the meanings of terms. These processes can be illuminated best if organizational learning is understood as social processes.

Not all organizational learning was driven by the necessity to adapt to pressures from outside the company. Frequently, a company's response to failure entailed a change in existing SOP or the creation of new ones, the improvement of facilities, or the hiring of new personnel who were not immediately necessary. In short, an active restructuring process was primed. Adaptive and active restructuring processes were not mutually exclusive. Instead, active restructuring was sometimes part of adaptation. They can take place simultaneously, depending on the corporate culture, personnel, firm size, and resources involved.

Once the FDA had followed up the initial GLP regulations with relatively specific guidances, the need to explore conceptually new solutions in order to respond to criticisms was alleviated. Hence, the clear definition of failure to learn regulations left no room for impulsive learning, the exploration trap, or the failure trap. By contrast, the clear definition of success was more likely to lead a company into a competence- or exploitation-driven learning trap. Positive feedback from the regulatory agency confirmed the usefulness of the existing rules. The institutionalization of the rules provided a sense of order and comfort for researchers and reduced the risks of experimenting in their own way. It facilitated management control over experimentation under the noble and fashionable banner of total quality. Once established, the exploitation of the GLP routines resulted in the bureaucratization of laboratory activities. Certain managers suspected an exploitation trap in some of their units, one resulting from the cognitive and behavioral homogeneity among researchers, scientists, and subordinate managers, which posed a restriction on highly innovative pursuits. However, the exploitation trap was a conjecture in some companies only. In others, the unintended impacts that GLP regulations were expected to have on creative research were overcome by proactive measures, such as complete separation of drug discovery and drug development or the practice of subcontracting one of them, discovery to venture capital companies or universities and development to contract research organizations.

Middle management was found to be the driving agent behind the learning of GLP regulations, whereas top management, at best, refrained from impeding the process. Being highly cost- and efficiency-conscious, top management perceived the learning of GLP only as a mundane, operational, technical 'laboratory'-type task imposed by an interventionist, big government. An aversion to learning from subordinates exacerbated the situation in some instances. By contrast, middle managers were agents of information acquisition, organizational imitation, enhancement of social interaction, restructuring of the work process, and change of habits and practices. Nevertheless, the U.S. pharmaceutical firms in this sectorial case study provided no evidence to support the middle-down-up strategy of knowledge creation strategy observed in Japanese corporations, where conflicts between hierarchical layers are downplayed. Instead, there seemed to be a dichotomous middle-down and middle-up process, with more obstacles being encountered in the latter than in the former.

Conclusions and Future Research Directions

The emergence of GLP regulations and their implementation in the pharmaceutical industry presented a favorable occasion to study organizational learning under simplified boundary conditions. First, Good Manufacturing Practice regulations had already been introduced through processes involving the same institutional actors, a step that had set both procedural and structural precedents. For our case study, it also provided an opportunity to examine the process of learning from experience. Second, numerous organizations of very similar nature faced identical substantive and temporal challenges, especially after GLP regulations had been created.

Interorganizational learning was particularly evident in congressional fact-finding efforts and in the creation of legislative frameworks and regulations for ensuring that pharmaceutical products were safe for the public. It was in this arena that the interests of associations, industry, and government clashed. Finding appropriate solutions required complex processes of interorganizational learning. By contrast, interorganizational learning became relatively straightforward when the knowledge to be elaborated had the nature of a public good, such as experience with regulatory negotiation or knowledge of regulations and their interpretation and implementation. The fact that power conflicts played a subordinate role goes a long way to explain this relationship between the facility with which organizations learn

from each other and the perceived character of the knowledge they exchange.

Intraorganizational learning in its various facets was evident particularly in the implementation of GLP within companies. As with interorganizational learning, the theoretical frameworks discussed in this chapter proved to be more useful as complementary conceptualizations of the observations than as independent and competing ones.

Beyond the interpretations presented within the theoretical frameworks we have applied, this case study contains a number of insights that merit attention. The first has to do with difficulties arising from the need for distinct middle-down and middle-up learning processes. For the middle-down direction, a large armory of learning tools was available, many of which proved efficacious. In contrast to the middle-down learning processes, the middle-up direction lacked suitable tools and posed significantly more obstacles. Similarly, the middle-up learning processes that have been brought to light in this study do not support the prevalent view that top management is always the key agent in organizational learning. The latter two issues of practical relevance constitute uncharted territory that deserves further exploration.

The second insight has to do with the nature and function of organizational memories of success and failure. In this study the roles of written and oral intermediaries are differentiated according to the nature and type of collective memory they carry. First, the evidence suggests that it is justified to distinguish static, or passive, purely archival memory from the dynamic, or active, collective memory of individuals in terms of each's availability as resource for organizational learning from experience. Second and more distinct, it shows that continually revised and distributed copies of SOP constitute a depersonalized active memory of success, whereas the active memory of failure is found only in individuals. This asymmetry in a company's memory of success and failure stems from the fragmentation of written sources, the desire to keep failure confidential, and the habit of 'forgetting' the archives.

Because learning from failure is at least as important as learning from success (Starbuck and Hedberg, Ch. 14 in this volume), individuals' memories and narratives are crucial for knowledge development. In both intra- and interorganizational learning, organizations with high personnel turnover are likely to be less capable of learning from past failures than organizations with low personnel turnover. In this industry-wide case study certain individuals actively remembered both successful and unsuccessful strategies during similar proceedings in which they earlier had played a part. This finding, too, points to the importance that personnel continuity has in stabilizing what is learned at the institutional level over prolonged periods. In contrast to politicians, who tend to remain in office for a long time, the top personnel of companies or government agencies too frequently leave their positions before they have occasion to use again within the same organization what they have learned.

In future research and theory development, researchers may consider addressing the following questions:

• What and who carries which types of memory?
• What are the differences between the memory of employees who remain with the company and employees who have retired or gone to another organization?
• What are the differences between the memory of individuals in one functional and hierarchical position and the memory of those in another?

The creation of GLP regulations and their implementation in the pharmaceutical industry involved multimodal organizational learning processes, which are best captured by a combination of various theoretical frameworks. Almost all companies that decided to implement GLP succeeded, so there does not seem to be any single 'right' way of going about the task. In order to reach a conclusion about which organizational learning strategy was optimal in the formulation and implementation of GLP regulations, one would have to quantify all costs, including opportunity costs, as a function of the mix of the types of learning processes. Such analyses are unlikely to be available in the foreseeable future. In fact, strategies and knowledge are often 'discovered' in interactive, informal processes and made sense of only retrospectively (Hedberg and Wolff, Ch. 24 in this volume). Hence, it is doubtful that the optimal strategy or 'best practices' to organizational learning can be identified. At best, organizational learning studies, including this chapter, can present organizational learning experiences in an organized fashion and thereby stimulate ideas about how to translate the collective experience into a specific context, how to create one's own proper mode of learning. Thus, managers must continue to rely mostly on their intuitive management skills, but it is to be hoped that they will also be inspired by studies like the present one.

References

Badoux, B. (1997). *Practising the Learning Organization: Course Manual*. Brussels: Management Center Europe.

Boyer, B. (1989). 'The Federal Trade Commission and Consumer Protection Policy: A Postmortem Examination', in K. Hawkins and J. M. Thomas (eds.), *Making Regulatory Policy*. Pittsburgh: University of Pittsburgh Press, 93–132.

Carson, R. (1962). *Silent Spring*. Boston: Houghton Mifflin.

Chase, S. and Schlink, F. J. (1927). *Your Money's Worth*. New York: Macmillan.

Cohen, M. D., March, J. G., and Olsen, J. P. (1972). 'A Garbage Can Model of Organizational Choice'. *Administrative Science Quarterly*, 17: 1–25.

Cook, S. D. N. and Yanow, D. (1993). 'Culture and Organizational Learning'. *Journal of Management Inquiry*, 2: 373–90.

Cyert, R. M. and March, J. G. (1963). *A Behavioral Theory of the Firm*. Englewood Cliffs, NJ: Prentice Hall.

Czarniawska, B. (1997). 'Learning Organizing in a Changing Institutional Order: Examples from City Management in Warsaw'. *Management Learning*, 28: 475–95.

Food and Drug Administration (FDA, United States of America). (1978). 'Good Laboratory Practice for Nonclinical Laboratory Studies'. *Federal Register*, 43/247 (22 December): 60013–20.

—— (1998). Center for Drug Evaluation and Research Office of Compliance, Bioresearch Monitoring Program 7348.808. Good Laboratory Practice, Quarterly Compliance Report. Inspection Update 31 March.

Gherardi, S. (1997). *Learning in the Face of Mystery*. Paper presented at the conference on 'Modes of Organizing, Power/Knowledge Shifts'. Warwick, U.K., 3–4 April.

Gifford, D. J. (1989). 'Discretionary Decision-Making in Regulatory Agencies: A Conceptual Framework', in K. Hawkins and J. M. Thomas (eds.), *Making Regulatory Policy*. Pittsburgh: University of Pittsburgh Press, 233–61.

Harris, R. (1964a). 'Annals of Legislation: The Real Voice I'. *The New Yorker*, 40/4: 48–106.

—— (1964b). 'Annals of Legislation: The Real Voice II'. *The New Yorker*, 40/5: 75–154.

—— (1964c). 'Annals of Legislation: The Real Voice III'. *The New Yorker*, 40/6: 46–135.

Healy, D. (1998). *The Antidepressant Era*. Cambridge, Mass.: Harvard University Press.

Hedberg, B. L. T. (1981). 'How Organizations Learn and Unlearn', in P. C. Nystrom and W. H. Starbuck (eds.), *Handbook of Organizational Design*: Vol. 1. *Adapting Organizations to Their Environments*. Oxford: Oxford University Press, 3–27.

Huber, G. P. (1991). 'Organizational Learning: The Contributing Processes and the Literatures'. *Organization Science*, 2: 88–115.

Lawrence, P. R. and Lorsch, J. W. (1967). *Organization and Environment: Managing Differentiation and Integration*. Boston: Harvard Business School Press.

Lear, J. (1959). 'Taking the Miracle out of the Miracle Drugs'. *Saturday Review*, 3 January: 35–41.

Levinthal, D. A. and March, J. G. (1993). 'The Myopia of Learning'. *Strategic Management Journal*, 14 (Winter special issue): 95–112.

March, J. G. (1991). 'Exploration and Exploitation in Organizational Learning'. *Organization Science*, 2: 71–87.

Mintz, M. (1965). *The Therapeutic Nightmare: A Report on the Roles of the United States Food and Drug Administration, the American Medical Association, Pharmaceutical Manufacturers, and Others in Connection with the Irrational and Massive Use of Prescription Drugs That May Be Worthless, Injurious, or Even Lethal*. Boston: Houghton Mifflin.

Nonaka, I. and Konno, N. (1998). 'The Concept of "Ba": Building a Foundation for Knowledge Creation'. *California Management Review*, 40/3: 40–54.

—— and Takeuchi, H. (1995). *The Knowledge-creating Company: How Japanese Companies Create the Dynamics of Innovation*. New York: Oxford University Press.

Parks, A. E. (1988). 'Standard Operating Procedures: One Element of a Program for Compliance with Good Laboratory Practice Regulations'. *American Chemical Society Symposium Series*, 369: 47–54.

Peltzman, S. (1973). 'An Evaluation of Consumer Protection Legislation: The 1962 Drug Amendments'. *Journal of Political Economy*, 81: 1049–91.

Polanyi, M. (1966). *The Tacit Dimension*. New York: Doubleday.

Schein, E. H. (1993). 'On Dialogue, Culture, and Organizational Learning'. *Organizational Dynamics*, 22/2: 40–51.

Shulman, S. R., Hewitt, P., and Manocchia, M. (1995). 'Studies and Inquiries into the FDA Regulatory Process: A Historical Review'. *Drug Information Journal*, 29: 385–413.

Tsang, E. W. K. (1997). 'Organizational Learning and the Learning Organization: A Dichotomy between Descriptive and Prescriptive Research'. *Human Relations*, 50: 73–89.

Wardell, W. M. and Lasagna, L. (1975). *Regulation and Drug Development*. Washington, DC: American Enterprise Institute for Public Policy Research.

Weick, K. E. (1979). *The Social Psychology of Organizing* (2nd edn). Reading, Mass.: Addison-Wesley.

PART IX

CONCLUSION

42 Organizational Learning and Knowledge: Reflections on the Dynamics of the Field and Challenges for the Future

Ariane Berthoin Antal, Meinolf Dierkes, John Child, and Ikujiro Nonaka

This handbook has been designed to cover a substantial range of approaches to organizational learning and knowledge. Such diversity is a natural part of the maturation process in a dynamic intellectual field. From the multiple narratives, however, we discern certain trends in the treatment of key themes over the past three decades and certain tendencies in the development of the language to describe and analyze organizational learning processes. This concluding chapter traces the developments we perceive as relating to language and themes in the field. It then outlines the ideas we feel are the most stimulating to pursue in the coming years.

Reflections on the Language of Organizational Learning

It is symptomatic of the dynamics of the development of the field that the one element on which there is no agreement is the definition of 'organizational learning' itself. The very definition of organizational learning is subject to controversy and flux. The discussion involved is no sterile academic debate but rather the

logical consequence of the active participation by scholars from an increasing number of disciplinary and cultural backgrounds, and it is a testimony to the deepening understanding about the complexity of the topic. The inability to come to a consensus may also be a result of a heightened sensitivity to the importance of language, particularly among scholars influenced by postmodernism (see, for example, Czarniawska, Ch. 5; Fear, Ch. 7; Gherardi and Nicolini, Ch. 2).

The definition of organizational learning provided in 1978 by Argyris and Schön provided a point of departure, and much debate continues to surround various dimensions of their definition. They used the term 'organizational learning' as a metaphor for processes in which 'members of the organization act as learning agents for the organization by detecting and correcting errors in organizational theory-in-use and embedding the results of their inquiry in private images and shared maps of the organization' (p. 29). This definition has inspired some authors in this handbook (e.g. Friedman, Ch. 17), and it has been sharply criticized by others (e.g. Nonaka, Reinmöller, and Toyama, Ch. 37; Nonaka, Toyama, and Byosière, Ch. 22) for its emphasis on problem detection and

The authors thank Jeff Fear, Victor Friedman, Silvia Gherardi, Camilla Krebsbach-Gnath, Klaus Scherer, and John Stopford for their insightful comments on an earlier version of this chapter.

correction. In an effort to overcome this limitation, the field has been expanded to include knowledge creation so as to ensure that processes leading to the generation of new ideas and behaviors are accorded appropriate attention as well.

Another source of controversy over the definition by Argyris and Schön (1978) is their positioning of the individual as the key agent of organizational learning. Their assumption is shared by numerous authors, but it is amended or challenged by others. The March school of research (e.g. March and Olsen 1976; see also Kieser, Beck, and Tainio, Ch. 27) does not deny the significance of individuals as the primary actors in the learning process but rather supplements this view by stressing the function of rules and standard operating procedures as vehicles of organizational learning. Scholars of this school highlight the significance of structures for organizational learning. Merkens, Geppert, and Antal (Ch. 10) choose a definition of organizational learning based on organizational culture in order to focus on the organization as the unit of learning. In this vein, Czarniawska (Ch. 5) draws on anthropology to point out that the focus on individuals is a peculiarity of certain cultures. She suggests it might be more appropriate to take the lead from those cultures in which relations, not individuals, are considered the key units of life.

There is growing recognition that the locus of organizational learning is not limited to traditional legal entities. Key terms encountered in this context are 'networks', 'communities of practice', and 'organizational culture'. These terms have been generated in other research fields and have been imported as central categories in organizational learning. Networks can be formal and informal, and their members can be individuals or larger entities, such as companies and their suppliers. Researchers are finding that the application of the concept of networks to organizations rather than just to individuals has extended the boundaries of the field. Community of practice—a closely related, but more specialized, concept—refers to groupings of individuals in which professional knowledge is shared and created through the experience of working together. Since communities of practice cut across boundaries both inside and between organizations, the term enables researchers to focus on units of analysis other than individuals and traditionally defined organizational structures (see Hedberg and Holmqvist, Ch. 33; Stopford, Ch. 11).[1] The concept of 'organizational culture' is central to research on organizational learning and knowledge creation because it highlights the context within which learning occurs, and it provides the framework for understanding how the outcomes of past learning become engrained in structures, norms, and routines in organizations. The culture of an organization shapes members' perceptions of past and current events and forms their 'mental models' or 'mental maps'. These shared conceptions of what needs to be learned how and why underlie the orientation of future learning in organizations. Authors in this handbook take the concept of mental maps further to explore how they develop not only within organizations but also within networks (Lane, Ch. 31) and across industries (Dierkes, Marz, and Teele, Ch. 12; de Haën, Tsui-Auch, and Alexis, Ch. 41).

The fact that past learning, embedded in organizational cultures and mental maps, is able not only to serve as a useful orientation but also to act as an impediment for learning gave rise to the term 'unlearning', which is closely associated with early work in the field by Hedberg (1981). It has since been used widely by other scholars as well (see, for example, Friedman, Lipshitz, and Overmeer, Ch. 34; Krebsbach-Gnath, Ch. 40; Weber and Berthoin Antal, Ch. 15) and has caught the imagination of managers. Unlearning is necessary because learning is not simply a cumulative process. It sometimes requires old ways of seeing and doing things to be questioned and cast aside in order for new behaviors and new mental maps to be developed. Organizations that do not recognize the need to unlearn run the risk of falling into 'competency traps' (Levitt and March 1988: 322) because they

---

[1] The Japanese term *'ba'* was introduced by Nonaka and Konno (1998) as a useful way of referring to the virtual and real spaces needed to nurture learning and knowledge creation.

continue to invest in perfecting current skills at the expense of developing radically new ones that would be more appropriate for conditions undergoing change (see Tainio, Lilja, and Santalainen, Ch. 19). March (1991) spoke of the need to balance the 'exploitation' of existing knowledge and competencies in an organization and of the 'exploration' of new ones.

Nevertheless, the value of past learning should not be underrated. As Fear points out in his analysis of the role of history (Ch. 7), past learning lays the groundwork for new knowledge to be perceived as relevant and useful. The concept of 'absorptive capacity' denotes the ability of an organization to harness its prior related knowledge, to recognize the value of new information, and then to assimilate and apply it. This capacity is rooted in past experience, but experience alone does not guarantee absorptive capacity. Several authors build on this concept in the handbook. They show how the development of an organization's absorptive capacity can both promote and hinder learning in multinational organizations (Lyles, Ch. 30; Macharzina, Oesterle, and Brodel, Ch. 28). On the one hand, previous experience in different settings lays the foundation for learning more about international affairs. On the other hand, the accumulation of insights and experiences within some units of an organization may hamper the ability to communicate ideas to other organizational units in which different cultures and different knowledge bases have been built up.

An issue that researchers continue to grapple with is the relationship between learning and 'change' in organizations. A commonality between psychological definitions of learning is that relatively permanent behavioral changes are considered essential indicators of learning (Maier, Prange, and Rosenstiel, Ch. 1), but not all authors agree that this assumption holds for organizational learning. For example, Child and Heavens (Ch. 13) note that change can occur in organizations without necessarily being the result of learning. Adaptation to changed environmental conditions may occur without inducing learning. Conversely, Berthoin Antal and Krebsbach-Gnath (Ch. 21)

point out that learning may in fact lead to the decision not to change. Rosenstiel and Koch (Ch. 8) illustrate the complex possible relationships between learning and change by considering value changes in society as triggers of organizational learning. The paradoxical relationship between continuity and change is highlighted by Fear (Ch. 7) in his longitudinal review of cases in Germany and Japan (see also Merkens, Geppert, and Antal, Ch. 10; and Tsui-Auch, Ch. 32).

A concept that has long been associated with learning is that of 'cycles'. Some behavioral and system models (building on the work by such scholars as March and Olsen 1976) speak of learning cycles in terms of feedback between the action of an organization and changes in the environment (e.g. Pawlowsky, Ch. 3; Starbuck and Hedberg, Ch. 14). Models linking cognitive and behavioral learning are based implicitly or explicitly on Kolb's (1984) learning cycles, which involve reflection and planning as well as action and experimentation (e.g. Friedman, Lipshitz, and Overmeer, Ch. 34; Galer and van der Heijden, Ch. 38; Pawlowsky, Forslin, and Reinhardt, Ch. 35). Blockages to organizational learning are often found when learning cycles are interrupted (Berthoin Antal, Lenhardt, and Rosenbrock, Ch. 39). The exploration of links between learning and timing (Weber and Berthoin Antal, Ch. 15) brings in different types of cycles. For example, Tainio, Lilja, and Santalainen (Ch. 19) explore stages of corporate life cycles for what they imply about the ability and willingness of companies to learn. Other authors map organizational learning onto the issue-attention cycle of organizations (Kädtler, Ch. 9; LaPalombara, Ch. 6).

An important, but possibly confusing, feature of the field is that numerous types of organizational learning have been differentiated over the years (for an overview, see Pawlowsky, Ch. 3). Probably the most commonly used distinction is based on Bateson's (1972) conceptualization of first-, second-, and third-order learning, which Argyris and Schön (1978) redefined as 'single-loop', 'double-loop', and 'deutero-learning'. Single-loop learning refers to incremental improvements in existing ways of

924   Berthoin Antal, Child, Dierkes, Nonaka

doing things, whereas double-loop learning involves reflexivity—the questioning of what is being done and leads to the learning of new behaviors rather than the refining of current skills. Deutero-learning is an even higher level of reflexivity that is said to occur when the learning process itself is examined and learned anew. However, very little research has been done on this concept (for an exception, see Dierkes, Marz, and Teele, Ch. 12). Double-loop learning has been considered particularly important during phases of major change and is associated with management concepts like renewal, transformation, and reengineering. There has been a tendency in past years to consider this kind of learning to be more significant and valuable than single-loop learning.

Another bias underlying the discussion of organizational learning has been that 'imitation learning' was long considered to be of less value than the ability and willingness to embark on radical change. Recent thinking has shifted away from this bias, and the amount of research on the nature and role of different forms of learning has increased. Imitation learning has become recognized as a creative learning process in its own right because the learner must actively work with the ideas or behaviors observed in another organization in order to fit them to the new situation (e.g. Czarniawska, Ch. 5; Tsui-Auch, Ch. 32). Another form of learning, 'learning-by-doing', although central to the psychology of individual learning, has essentially been taken for granted by most writers on organizational learning in recent years. It is now attracting renewed interest from several quarters, particularly because economists and economic historians are finding it an increasingly important topic (Boerner, Macher, and Teece, Ch. 4).

As the field of organizational learning has expanded to include knowledge creation, so has the degree to which knowledge-related vocabulary is shared. The differentiation between 'explicit' and 'tacit' (or 'implicit') knowledge, usually attributed to Polanyi (1966) is a crucial one that is now recognized and used by most authors in the field. Explicit knowledge is codified and can be transmitted in formal and systematic language, whereas tacit knowledge refers to what is known by individuals or groups and transmitted by action and observation. More attention has traditionally been paid to explicit knowledge in organizations than to tacit knowledge because the former is easier to formalize and quantify. However, the significance of tacit knowledge has become increasingly evident over the past years. Efforts are being undertaken to develop tools of 'knowledge management' that are capable of capturing and improving the use of both explicit and tacit knowledge (Büchel and Raub, Ch. 23; Nonaka, Reinmöller, and Toyama, Ch. 37). As a complement to assessments of other organizational resources, work is also being conducted to develop measurements of 'intellectual capital' that can do justice to all forms of 'knowledge assets' embedded in an organization (Reinhardt, Bornemann, Pawlowsky, and Schneider, Ch. 36).

Language is not static. The vocabulary continues to grow under the influence of different disciplines and as a result of detailed investigations into particular areas that require terminological differentiation. There are terms that may be about to enter the shared language of research on organizational learning if connections between that field and those of economics and political science become closer than they currently are. For example, concepts like the 'learning curve', 'learning trajectories', and 'transaction costs' that have been developed by economists promise to be useful in understanding processes and outcomes of organizational learning and knowledge creation (see Boerner, Macher, and Teece, Ch. 4; Macharzina, Oesterle, and Brodel, Ch. 28; and Reinhardt et al., Ch. 36). Increased research on dimensions of organizational learning that have received too little attention so far, such as power and conflict, emotions, and time, will bring additional concepts into the language used by members of the community of scholars and practitioners in this area. When well defined and precisely used, such terms from different disciplines will enrich the language and thereby support efforts to deepen understanding of the processes of learning and knowledge creation.

Making Sense of the Dynamics We Observe

Having worked in the field of organizational learning and knowledge creation for about a decade ourselves, and having engaged intensively with the authors of this handbook during the drafting and redrafting of the chapters, we editors have moved frequently back and forth between focusing on the forest and the trees. In so doing, we have developed a view of how research in this area has progressed and where some key challenges lie (see also Dierkes and Albach 1998; Berthoin Antal 1998; Dierkes *et al.* 1999). Although time periods can be categorized in different ways depending on one's perspective, we suggest considering the development of organizational learning in four periods: origins (1960s and 1970s), the early phase (1980s), the past decade (1990s), and the emerging challenges to be tackled in the coming years. The use of decades is practical but should not be interpreted too strictly, for the boundaries between thinking and publication at the beginning or end of decades are obviously fluid. We also identify eight dimensions in which the most significant changes in the field of organizational learning appear to have occurred. Table 42.1 presents an overview of the key trends that have struck us as significant. The divisions, however, should not be interpreted as hard and fast boundaries between periods.

The Cultural Contexts

One of the most striking achievements in the field of organizational learning is the shift from the purely Anglo-Saxon origins of the research to a much broader cultural range. The early writings stemmed from scholars in the United States, who assumed that their concepts were universally applicable. Not until the late 1980s and early 1990s did researchers from various western European countries and Japan join the field and explore organizational learning processes in organizations in their own cultures. During the 1990s, when the collapse of the East Bloc and the challenge of transformation placed organizational learning high on the agenda of organizations and researchers alike, research extended into eastern and central Europe (Lyles, Ch. 30; Merkens, Geppert, and Antal, Ch. 10). Research has also started to extend to organizational learning in several Asian economies (Nonaka, Toyama, and Byosière, Ch. 22; Tsui-Auch, Ch. 32). The challenge ahead lies in expanding the variety of countries in the research and in increasing the number of internationally comparative research projects. Such growth will not only allow scholars to test the reach and limits of concepts developed to date, it will also pave the way for the generation of new concepts that can provide fresh ways of looking at processes both in their countries of origin and in a global context (Berthoin Antal and Dierkes 1992).

The Intellectual Traditions

Another major step forward in the field can be seen in the intellectual traditions feeding into it. At the outset, publications came predominantly from management scientists with a grounding in psychology, political science, or economics. These scholars were dissatisfied with the models at that time, which were dominated by assumptions of hyperrationality. They therefore turned to concepts from psychology to describe processes of decision-making and learning. The field of organizational learning soon attracted scholars from other areas such as sociology and organization studies, leading to a large variety of models. They, too, often borrowed from psychology to describe organizational learning. Later, scholars used concepts from a relatively wide range of disciplines, including anthropology. During the late 1990s, interest in knowledge management emerged and came to expand the intellectual territory.

The process of including other disciplines continues. The interest in knowledge management has been closely linked to discussions about competitiveness, a factor that may be

Table 42.1. The development of organizational learning as a field of inquiry

Dimension	Origins (1960s–1970s)	Early phase (1980s)	Developments over the past decade (1990s)	Emerging challenges
Cultural contexts of research	From Anglo-Saxon perspectives claiming universality…		To the inclusion of Japanese and western European experiences…	Toward internationally comparative research and the inclusion of other regions
Intellectual contexts, traditions underpinning research	From management scholars dissatisfied with existing rational models building on concepts from psychology…	To development of a large variety of models still borrowing heavily from psychology…	To the inclusion of concepts from anthropology and an increased interest of other disciplines; emergence of knowledge in the management field…	Toward transdisciplinary building on a broadened base of disciplinary knowledge, including rediscovery of precursors
Relationship between theory and practice	From conceptual writing based on case study experience…	To a division between largely conceptual writing and attempts to satisfy demand for immediate practical advice; multitude of publications by practitioners, including 'recipes'…		Toward knowledge creation through closer cooperation between scholars and practitioners
Types of organizations studied	From a few examples from quite different traditional organizations (government agencies, educational institutions, and business)…	To narrowing of focus primarily to business…	To the gradual rediscovery of other entities such as public administrations and unions…	Toward networks of organizations; communities and environments of learning
Processes and models of organizational learning	From behavioral approaches, stimulus–response models with some cognitive elements and evolutionary concepts…		To recognition of interpretive dimensions; competing stage and spiral models…	Toward learning and knowledge creation as embedded processes
Agents of organizational learning	From the individual as agent, usually senior managers…	To teams, units, and subcultures as agents…		Toward actors at all levels and communities of practice crossing organizational boundaries

Tone/color of treatment of organizational learning in the literature	From a few early writings recognizing how politics distorts learning and the emotional barriers that can be encountered in learning processes . . .	To a predominance of publications that treated learning as a nonpolitical process leading automatically to a positive outcome . . .	Toward organizational learning and knowledge creation as political and emotional processes to which conflict is integral and whose outcome may not be seen to be positive
Trends in organizational learning practices	From learning as an 'intuitive' matter, or as training and development activity Some scenario planning . . .	To popularization of organizational learning as an element of change processes (e.g. turnaround, reengineering, restructuring) . . .	Toward learning as strategic intent; benchmarking; knowledge management; institutionalization of roles (e.g. Chief Learning Officer) and structures (e.g. corporate universities); experiments with loosely structured methods (e.g. dialogue, open-space technology).

Note: An earlier version of this table was developed in Berthoin Antal 1998: 47–8.

intensifying the role of economists in the community of scholars who are exploring organizational learning and knowledge creation. As Boerner, Macher, and Teece (Ch. 4) point out, economists have for many decades been treating phenomena related to learning and knowledge creation but have often done so implicitly, rarely engaging with scholars from other fields to ensure a cross-fertilization of ideas and theories. As economists enter the field of organizational learning, attention to the resource-based view of the firm and to the notion of competencies may well increase. The strong tradition of economists in research on innovation may also lead to the rediscovery of relevant findings that other disciplines contributed to this aspect of the subject in past decades (e.g. Burns and Stalker 1961; Schumpeter 1951). We hope too, that political scientists and historians will continue to enrich the field, building on the two chapters by LaPalombara (Chs. 6 and 25) and the one by Fear (Ch. 7). The participa-

tion of scholars from these two areas of research is likely to bring recognition of early thinking that, though not conducted under the banner of organizational learning, offers stimulating insights for the field. For example, the work by Mary Parker Follett (1942) may be seen as a precursor to the current attempts to see conflict as a dimension of organizational learning.

If the field of organizational learning is to build effectively on its multiple intellectual traditions, the challenge to be managed in the coming years is to develop transdisciplinary approaches based on a solid understanding of how each discipline can shed light on the processes of organizational learning and knowledge creation. By taking stock of present and past developments from the perspective of several disciplines, this handbook should provide the groundwork for such transdisciplinary integration. Furthermore, we believe that the insights gained through research on organizational learning and knowledge creation can flow back into the disciplines to stimulate fresh thinking there as well (see the suggestions in Czarniawska, Ch. 5; Fear, Ch. 7; and LaPalombara, Ch. 6) and reduce some of the barriers between them.

The Relationship between Theory and Practice

The relationship between theory and practice in the field of organizational learning and knowledge creation has shifted over the past decades. The early conceptual thinking was solidly rooted in case studies. Subsequently, however, a division emerged between largely conceptual writing and attempts to satisfy demand for immediate practical advice. Pressure to provide 'recipes' for success intensified in the late 1980s and during all of the 1990s. Practitioners became involved in the field. For example, managers opened their companies for case studies, and some tried to turn their companies into 'learning organizations', and this period was a heyday for consultants. Quite a few academics took on two hats and engaged in consulting. Ideally, such engagements should allow in-depth research because consultants gain extensive access to people and data in organizations during interventions, and they can be present at meetings to which external researchers are only rarely admitted. However, few theoretically meaningful studies have been published after consulting interventions (Argyris 1993 is one of the exceptions), possibly because time pressures cut projects short or because companies prefer to keep the research results for themselves.

A further factor impeding theory-building by the consultant-academic is that the freedom to research is difficult to combine with the politics and economics of consulting contracts (Berthoin Antal and Krebsbach-Gnath, Ch. 21). When research needs or findings conflict with the interests of the employer, they tend to be sacrificed. Not only has theory-building suffered, the expectations of managers have often remained unfulfilled. Hopes of rapid change and smooth, almost effortless transferability of best practices from other organizations have often proved illusory.

In future, project designs and forms of financing that permit relatively long-term studies of organizational learning and knowledge creation processes will be needed. One promising route in this direction is to conduct field experiments and action research in which academics and reflective practitioners collaborate on developing theory grounded in practice and applications grounded in theory.

The Types of Organizations Studied

The concept of organizational learning has been applied predominantly to companies in the private sector. This tendency has not always existed, however. The earliest writings by Cyert and March (1963) and their colleagues and by Argyris and Schön (1978) were based on experiences in governmental agencies and educational institutions as well as in companies. Strangely, this original work was essentially forgotten in the intervening period. Only in the past few years have practitioners taken an active interest in a wide range of organizations, such as unions (see, for example, Drinkuth, Riegler, and Wolff, Ch. 20 in this volume) schools, and the military (Friedman, Lipshitz, and Overmeer, Ch. 34). Researchers, too, have recently broadened the scope of their analyses and now also include nonprivate-sector organizations, such as public administrations and political organizations (see LaPalombara, Chs. 6 and 25), and increasingly fluid conceptions of organizations, such as social movements (e.g. Kädtler, Ch. 9), industry networks (Lane, Ch. 31), imaginary organizations (Hedberg and Holmqvist, Ch. 33), and *ba*, the space within which organizational learning and knowledge creation can flourish (Nonaka, Toyama, and Byosière, Ch. 22).

As the authors of these chapters argue, the inclusion of networks and nonprivate-sector organizations is not simply a quantitative change in the range of organizational types under study. It challenges some of the basic tenets of theory-building about processes of organizational learning and knowledge creation, for those fundamentals have been derived solely from experiences in individual companies. Such research is in its infancy, and much more of it will be needed in the coming years.

The Processes and Models of Organizational Learning

The way in which organizational learning has been conceptualized and modeled has undergone significant change over the past decades. Early conceptions of organizational learning were based on behavioral approaches, with cognitive processes and evolutionary concepts receiving a certain amount of recognition. Some of these models have been criticized for being too mechanistic or too passive (see, for example, Stopford, Ch. 11). Gradually, insights from cognitive learning theories and research on organizational culture enriched conceptualizations of organizational learning. Models came to include the role of interpretation and sense-making processes, leading recently to an awareness of political processes that are entailed in competing multiple interpretations and contested learning (Child and Heavens, Ch. 13). Research on perceptual filters revealed that they enable certain information to be seen at the expense of other signals. Starbuck and Hedberg (Ch. 14) analyze how perceptual filters also influence how information is interpreted (or misinterpreted) and can thereby influence the direction of learning in an organization. Kädtler's comparison (Ch. 9) of how companies have responded to challenges from social movements shows how perceptual filters are built up over time but also how they can be expanded to become more sensitive to emerging issues in order for the organization to learn early in the development of an issue-attention cycle. The scenario-planning techniques described by Galer and van der Heijden (Ch. 38) draw on organizational members' diverse perceptions as inputs into the process of learning in preparation for possible futures.

The key challenge to models of organizational learning is to recognize how its processes are embedded in social contexts. Originally, either organizational learning was treated as an outcome of behavior and engrained into organizational memory through rules, routines, and repertoires, or its relation to work processes was not made clear. However, several authors in this handbook argue for a revision that places learning more squarely in its contexts. They indicate how those contexts can be delineated in terms of the participating groups and their cultures as well as in terms of task systems, organizational structures, and environmental forces. Gherardi and Nicolini (Ch. 2) propose using the expression 'learning-in-organizing' to capture this significant shift in the way learning is conceptualized. Such a term recognizes that learning is not a separate activity but rather one that is embedded in processes of working and of organizing. This approach resonates with the findings in the chapter by Hedberg and Wolff (Ch. 24), who trace the similarities in the way conceptualizations of strategy, learning, and organizations have developed over the past few decades. They note that emphasis on process has increased in each of these areas, a shift that makes organizing a more useful concept than organization, and strategizing more appropriate than strategy.

This emphasis on process leads to a recognition that strategizing, learning, and organizing interact dynamically. The contribution by Merkens, Geppert, and Antal (Ch. 10) treats the complex interrelationship between processes of learning and organizing. Drawing on work by Weick and Westley (1996), they suggest that the two processes can be seen as antithetical because organization involves a reduction of variety, whereas learning necessarily entails at least some increase in variety. Merkens, Geppert, and Antal show that this antithesis is helpful in understanding why, particularly in phases requiring significant changes in mental maps, *dis*organizing, that is, the dismantling of existing structures, roles, and patterns of thinking, is required in order for learning to occur.

The nature of learning processes is probably the issue over which scholars still diverge most.

Some early models were based on feedback loops between the organization and its environment, whereas others portrayed learning in terms of steps or phases—usually starting at knowledge acquisition and continuing through diffusion and sense-making to action and then storage. Recently, a spiral model has emerged as a way of capturing the dynamic process of knowledge creation (Nonaka and Takeuchi 1995).

The current research landscape shows that all three types of models are worth developing further. The phase model underlies the chapters by Büchel and Raub (Ch. 23); Kieser, Beck, and Tainio (Ch. 27); and Lyles (Ch. 30). Child and Heavens (Ch. 13) implicitly apply the feedback-loop model, as do Starbuck and Hedberg (Ch. 14). Nonaka, ever since he started publishing in the field, has taken issue with both ways of depicting organizational learning processes. The two contributions he has written with his colleagues (see Chs. 22 and 37) represent further elaborations of the spiral model by illustrating how companies engage in the knowledge-creation process. The handbook contains evidence of attempts to resolve this controversy between competing frameworks. In the contribution by de Haën, Tsui-Auch, and Alexis (Ch. 41), the insights from the spiral model of knowledge creation are limited to the conception of organizational learning as a cultural process. The analysis of the four case studies by Berthoin Antal, Lenhardt, and Rosenbrock (Ch. 39) suggests that the phase model and the spiral model can complement each other in processes of inquiry into organizational learning.

The emerging challenge for research is to develop models that can treat learning and knowledge creation as embedded processes and can shed more light on how their cognitive and behavioral features are context-bound. This assertion raises a number of significant questions. In which ways and to what extent is organizational learning constrained by the context in which it takes place? If knowledge is to be transferred from one context to another, say, from one country or alliance partner to another, does it have to be reformulated to suit the new context (as suggested by Child,

Ch. 29)? What scope do agents of organizational learning have for pushing back contextual constraints on the learning process by offering new interpretations, identifying new solutions, and engendering enthusiasm among the people involved?

The Agents of Organizational Learning

Another change in the field of organizational learning since its beginnings surrounds the question of the agents of organizational learning. When the network of contributors to this handbook started meeting in the mid-1990s, a criticism leveled at the field was that it was focused too narrowly on an elitist view of organizations. Theories of organizational learning at that time reflected an exclusively top-down view of organizational processes. The work by Nonaka and Takeuchi (1995) in Japanese companies highlighted this bias in the Anglo-Saxon publications that dominated the field. Their research led them to point out an alternative pattern of organizational learning, one in which the agency of middle managers became more visible than it had been: the 'middle-up-down model'.

The chapters in this handbook show how much progress has been achieved on this topic. The overly narrow focus on top management is being replaced by an awareness of explorations by many more actors and of more complex constellations of leadership in learning processes. A far greater variety of types of actors has been studied in the past decade than in the early phase of research. These types include some agents that are not permanently based inside the organization: unions (Drinkuth, Riegler, and Wolff, Ch. 20), supervisory boards (Tainio, Lilja, and Santalainen, Ch. 19), and consulting services (Berthoin Antal and Krebsbach-Gnath, Ch. 21). The significance of actors who can serve as boundary-spanners—that is, individuals or groups who build links between the organization and its environment—is underscored by Rosenstiel and Koch (Ch. 8) in their analysis of value changes in society as triggers of organizational learning.

Several chapters document the effectiveness of leadership diffused among actors at various levels of the organization (Berthoin Antal, Lenhardt, and Rosenbrock, Ch. 39; Friedman, Ch. 17; Sadler, Ch. 18). These contributions help clarify the role that top management needs to play in learning processes, namely, that of articulating a clear vision that can orient the direction of learning and knowledge creation in an organization. This specification of the responsibility of top management does not, however, presage a return to the original simplistic elite view of organizational learning. Comparing public sector and private sector leadership, LaPalombara (Ch. 25) concludes that leaders in large organizations in both sectors have little direct control over resources. He notes that the ability to build relationships across the organization is becoming increasingly important to the achievement of goals. As the case study by Krebsbach-Gnath (Ch. 40) illustrates, the development of a vision by senior management is most effective when the process involves members of the organization at different levels. The recent multiplication of techniques for achieving these aims is striking. Pawlowsky, Forslin, and Reinhardt (Ch. 35) describe a range of innovative ways to involve large numbers of people quite intensely across the organization.

An additional advance in the literature is that all the chapters on the different kinds of agents emphasize how members of an organization, whether they are at the board level or low in the hierarchy, are capable not only of promoting but also of impeding organizational learning and knowledge creation. The emerging challenge to research in this area is to explore the range of agents of learning as they interact in different constellations of organization, including networks, communities of practice, and imaginary organizations.

The Tone or Color of the Discussion

There has been a notable shift in the tone, or color, of the discussion about organizational learning. The earliest works showed a keen awareness of the way politics distorts learning, and authors like Cyert and March (1963) have always expressed a certain skepticism about claims that learning is purely and simply good for all involved. However, most of the publications in the subsequent decades treated learning as a politically neutral process with a positive, rosy outcome for organizations and their members. Articles in the leading business journals have tended to enthusiastically encourage readers to develop and find learning organizations in which to work. Exceptions were Levitt and March (1988), who catalogued numerous learning problems that result in undesirable behavior or incorrect knowledge, and Argyris (1985) introduced the concept of defensive routines to recognize the role of fear and defensiveness that individuals may experience when having to challenge their mental models.

However, few scholars followed up on these ideas until the 1990s. Until then critical responses to organizational initiatives conducted under the banner of learning were treated as resistance that had to be overcome. Schein's (1993) treatment of the role of anxiety and fear in organizational learning helped put the subject on the agenda. Fortunately, in the past few years there has been growing recognition that emotions, power, and conflict could influence learning. Nevertheless, there has been almost no empirical research on this point, possibly because each of these factors were seen as antithetical to learning.

The challenges for the future will be to nurture the recent attempts to grapple with the role of emotions, power, and conflict in organizational learning. Several chapters in the handbook can serve as points of departure for such research. Improved understanding of the role of emotions in learning can be expected when today's generally accepted duality between rationality and emotions in organizational research is overcome. Taking a step in this direction, Scherer and Tran (Ch. 16) show the variety of ways in which emotions can either support or impede organizational learning. It is equally important that future research challenge the implicit assumption that conflict should be avoided or minimized in organizations. Rothman and Friedman (Ch. 26) lay the groundwork for such work by exploring different types of conflicts for which alternative responses are possible, and they indicate how under certain conditions, an active engagement of conflict can stimulate learning.

It is striking that the issue of power in organizational learning is only beginning to move out of silent shadows, although the concern about elitism and the topic of leadership have been on the research agenda for several years. The first article devoted specifically to this topic appeared in the mid-1990s (Coopey 1995). Two contributors to the handbook explicitly discuss theoretical dimensions of power in organizations by exploring what the disciplines of sociology (Ch. 2) and political science (Ch. 6) can offer. It may be symptomatic for the future development of the field that the richest insights about the impacts of power on learning and knowledge emerge from the chapters on interorganizational learning (see Part VI). The negative impact that asymmetric distribution of power has on the ability and willingness of different partners to share knowledge is brought out particularly well in each of the chapters on different kinds of networks. For example, Tsui-Auch's study (Ch. 32) shows how the control of resources by leaders in a field hampers the ability of latecomers to catch up. Macharzina, Oesterle, and Brodel (Ch. 28) suggest that the powerful position of headquarters in traditionally structured multinationals has impeded the flow of knowledge between subsidiaries and has blinded headquarters from perceiving the value of knowledge coming from subsidiaries. As Lane (Ch. 31) points out, such findings from research on interorganizational learning can lead to significant breakthroughs for theory-building by taking the research out of the trap of extrapolating from theories on individual learning. Far more research is needed to deepen understanding of organizational learning and knowledge creation as political and emotional processes, in which conflicts are a natural phenomenon.

The Trends in Organizational Learning Practices

Yet another dimension worth tracing over the past decades is the change in organizational learning practices. There used to be a sense among managers that learning simply happened intuitively: Organizations either succeeded and survived, or they failed. To the extent that learning was invested in directly by organizations, it took the form of training and development courses for individuals. The need to attend to how structures and processes could be improved to support organizational learning grew slowly. The organizational development activities launched primarily in the United States and the United Kingdom can now be seen to have been precursors of organizational learning. Initiatives like quality circles and quality-of-work programs of the mid- to late 1970s and the 1980s, which were introduced in Germany and Sweden, were not treated under the banner of organizational learning at the time, but with hindsight one can see how they laid the groundwork for later developments in this area.

Except for some advanced experiments with scenario-planning in the 1970s (Galer and van der Heijden, Ch. 38), conscious attempts to introduce organizational learning practices did not emerge in the United States or Europe until the late 1980s, when Japanese companies became the object of intense attention from managers as well as scholars. The popularization of organizational learning came on the back of attempts to introduce rapid and radical change programs, such as turnaround management, reengineering, and organizational restructuring. Learning as a strategic intent was put on the agenda in the 1990s, with various organizational and structural techniques being discussed. Benchmarking as a means of exploring different practices and learning from the experiences of others became a widespread practice.

The challenges for the future will lie in experimenting with additional new ideas and in monitoring the effects of these experiments. Among the recent introductions into corporate practices are dialogue and 'open-space-tech-nology' events (large-scale, relatively unstruc-tured meetings at which participants present their ideas and seek supporters to develop initiatives). With the advent of knowledge management have come recent attempts at in-stitutionalizing learning roles in the form of the Chief Learning Officer or Chief Knowledge Officer, and corporate universities have mush-roomed (see Pawlowsky, Forslin, and Rein-hardt, Ch. 35, for detailed descriptions of numerous practices). The speed at which new ideas are being introduced suggests a danger of faddishness and superficiality. The extent to which these practices actually help organiza-tions achieve learning goals will depend on how earnestly and critically their members en-gage in assessing their experiences. It will also depend on how well the roles and activities designed to assist learning are integrated into organizational processes. If they are marginal-ized or regarded as peripheral, the investment is likely to be wasted, as occurred when R&D ac-tivities were kept at a distance from the core activities of companies, such as the innova-tions that Xerox failed to adopt from its Palo Alto Research Center. This is one of the chal-lenges that corporate universities face.

Research That Matters

The contributions to this handbook contain numerous stimulating suggestions for further research within their particular focus area. In this concluding chapter we take a step further and propose a few overarching themes for fu-ture work that we believe would be useful for advancing the field as a whole. They grow out of our current map of the field's development and are influenced by our perceptions, our own research interests, and our experience. The themes on our agenda therefore reflect our sense of what is worthwhile to pursue in the coming years, and we hope that researchers and practitioners coming from varied cultural and professional backgrounds will be intrigued en-ough to join in pursuing some of these issues.

We emphasize this point because the spirit in which research is undertaken is a factor that is rarely addressed, an omission that often makes research agendas dry and ritualistic texts. In selecting overarching themes in this conclu-sion, we are driven by a sense that research on organizational learning and knowledge crea-tion is a deeply humanistic endeavor that should lead to insights that can benefit mem-bers at all levels of organizations. Equally im-portant, we believe that the actual research process should be designed to include diverse interests and perspectives. Learning and creat-ing knowledge entails moving into new terri-tories and taking risks, trying out different approaches, and engaging with people and ideas that seem contradictory and foreign. Scholars seeking to advance knowledge in this area and to generate research that matters in the future will do well to embed these consid-erations in the agendas they shape and the methodologies they select.

Moving Out of the Comfort Zone

Considering the range of cultures and the vari-ety of organizations in the world today, re-searchers have only begun to scratch the surface with the studies conducted so far. The validity of our theories will remain quite lim-ited until we significantly expand the types of conditions to which they have been exposed. Conducting research in different settings often means moving out of the comfort zone, intel-lectually and even physically. It is uncomfort-able not to understand what is going on in a different culture (e.g. national or organiza-tional), where the language and the behavioral norms are not those we are used to. It is not very comfortable to take the risk of disconfirm-ing ideas we have held to be true. Nor is travel-ing to distant places always glamorous and enjoyable. Nevertheless, it is essential to under-take such uncomfortable research in the com-ing years so that the map of places (countries as well as types of organizations) that have been studied does not remain one of predominantly virgin territory. For example, far too little is known about knowledge creation in the countries of the African continent and the Middle East. English-language publications contain next to nothing on experiences in South American organizations. Only a few of the former East-bloc countries have been included in research projects on organizational learning and knowledge creation. And most of the Asian nations, too, have received only scant attention.

In terms of organizations, a far greater diversity needs to be studied than has been the case thus far. Organizations in industries that are subject to very rapid change should be compared with organizations that epitomize consistency and stability. For example, the Internet and dot.com enterprises, independent film production teams, or the fashion industry could be compared with the Catholic Church or museums. Such comparisons would generate insights into the role of time and organizational life cycles in learning and into ways in which memory is built and accessed under different structural conditions. In other words, research on organizational learning and knowledge creation in highly varied settings will not only expand the database but also refine the understanding of already familiar organizations and thereby improve the quality of theory-building.

Grappling with the Politics of Organizational Learning and Knowledge Creation

If we want to generate knowledge that can serve humanitarian goals, we need to come to grips with the political dimensions of learning processes in and between organizations. Ideas are almost always associated with interests: the acquisition of new knowledge, the interpretation of past events, or the development of a concept are most likely to benefit some parties more than others. Studies of organizational learning have tended to be 'bloodless' in the sense that the political competition over ideas and knowledge between subgroups in organizations has been overlooked or masked by technocratic

rationalizations. A few exceptions to this tendency, such as those cited by Child and Heavens (Ch. 13), show how in practice such political competition tends to be inherent in the very process of developing the rationales for how new technologies are to be used. They point to the contested nature of much learning within organizations, an insight that deserves to be followed up in further work. This gap in the literature is all the more surprising because innovation research has shown that breakthrough ideas have often tended to come from the periphery rather than from representatives of the dominant mind-set.

Among the types of studies that we editors are curious to see in the coming years are those that look at the role that gender, the dynamics of the periphery, and ideologies play in organizational learning. Organizational learning has been studied as a gender-neutral process despite the fact that the role of gender has been shown to be significant in many other organizational processes. The cost of this oversight is probably twofold: Bodies of knowledge as well as learning strategies are remaining invisible and untapped. For example, many occupations and networks remain largely segregated by gender both within and between organizations, so it is likely that organizations dominated by women create and store bodies of knowledge different from those of organizations dominated by men.

The dynamics between the periphery and mainstream can be studied in terms of gender groups, but other constellations should be studied as well. For example, the power differences that exist between organizational departments, between headquarters and subsidiaries, or between organizational units in countries considered to be advanced and those labeled as less developed are likely to have significant impacts on the political career of ideas. Under which conditions do ideas generated at the periphery, that is, by units or groups that have lower status, have a chance of being heard and implemented?

The third type of research that we feel is particularly worth pursuing in the coming years is the role of ideologies. Work in this area should be focused on how ideologies are used to legitimate certain areas and actors for knowledge creation and how other topics and actors are repressed and silenced. Something that has rapidly gained currency across national boundaries over the past decade is the ideology of shareholder value, which clearly places the power in the hands of certain stakeholders at the expense of other constituencies. How and what do organizations learn under the pressures of this ideology? What is the impact of shareholder value on an organization's long-term capacity for knowledge creation? Furthermore, because part of the political game is to use labels in order to continue pursuing one's own ends, work in this area will also generate insights into continuity and change under different ideological labels.

Giving Luck a Chance

A third research area of a quite different nature that we are curious about is the role of luck, or chance, in organizational learning and knowledge creation. At a time when scholars and practitioners are proposing and introducing so many new strategies, roles, and instruments designed to increase the speed and efficiency with which organizations learn, it seems particularly important to explore the aspects of the process that are not directly subject to planning. Windows of opportunity, which may be unique constellations of ideas, people, and resources, appear to be significant, but they are little understood. Are they simply serendipitous moments or can they be created? What are the limits to planning, organizing, and analyzing organizational learning and knowledge creation? For example, firms invest enormous sums in acquisitions, often hoping to reap the benefits of expanded knowledge bases and competencies in their newly obtained units. Nevertheless, the resources often do not lead to the expected knowledge creation. Problems that arise are often attributed to bad luck, unfortunate circumstances, or bad timing. But is the decision to provide for a category labeled 'chance' simply a way of avoiding the matter, an easy way out of questions that cannot be easily resolved? By consciously examining the role of chance or luck, both good and bad, that is attributed by people to explain success and failure in organizational learning processes, researchers might discover new factors that have hitherto been masked, or the dynamics between known factors might become clearer. Such inquiry could draw on studies of creativity, the role of serendipity in research and development processes, and intuition in decision-making. These additions would once more expand the boundaries of the field of organizational learning.

Daring to be Persistent

It is likely to surprise most readers that we believe the role of experience in organizational learning to be a fourth overarching theme that should be studied in the coming years. Experience is at the heart of learning and has been the focus of most theories in the field, so one would not expect it to be high on the agenda at this point. However, the role of experience is still not well understood. There is a need for persistence in pursuing some of the most basic questions in the field. For example, under rapidly changing conditions, how can organizations improve their posthoc evaluation processes in order to channel experience directly into their repository of knowledge on what works well and what does not? It is a major challenge to classify, store, and disseminate knowledge in large complex organizations such as the modern multinational with its many far-flung units, in which people from diverse cultures need access to the lessons of experience. Given the unpredictability of future events and circumstances, it is very difficult to identify a priori which experience is actually relevant. Indeed, relevance may become apparent only as part of the learning process itself. Two of the traps that may be encountered in posthoc evaluations of experiences are rationalization and sanitization, both of which can be used by certain parties in an organization to place decisions in a more favorable light than they deserve. How can research help to identify and avoid these problems? By developing links with scholars who have built up experience in evaluation research, those who study organizational learning could strengthen the field. The connection between knowledge creation and experience needs further study. Are some of the organizational barriers that impede knowledge creation also those that stand in the way of access to experience? Do they in addition inhibit the ability of organizational members to reflect adequately on that experience? Lastly, there is a need to expand knowledge about which type and quality of experience can provide a significant input into the learning process. For example, we editors are perplexed to observe that companies with previous experience in strategic alliances often fail to apply the lessons from that experience when they engage in new alliances. They continue to set unrealistic expectations and make gross mistakes in the alliance relationship.

Methodological Implications

We believe that if research on organizational learning and knowledge creation is to make significant progress in the coming years, the community of scholars and practitioners will need to make good use of the diversity of lines of thinking at their disposal. Research methodologies that build on this diversity of perspectives are required. But it is not enough to call once more for a mix of methods, which all too often leads to the accumulation of research findings that are difficult to compare and integrate. We therefore recommend that more studies be conducted in mixed teams and that the research be designed in ways that enable multiple views of reality to be treated. In effect, researchers themselves need to learn how to learn better—in other words, they need to apply some of the lessons from the study of organizational learning to their own research process.

Mixed Teams

In order to overcome culturally shaped blind spots in conducting research in different settings, teams with members from different cultural and professional backgrounds need to be involved in each phase of the process (Berthoin Antal and Dierkes 1992: 605–6). Bringing different perspectives into the research team from the outset of a project design and retaining them through the field work and the analysis of the research results ensures that cultural biases are exposed and challenged. In our experience, the cooperation in each phase, including a mix of 'native' and 'naive' perspectives during the field work for data collection, significantly improves the quality of the research. The 'naive' outsiders to the culture pose questions about things 'natives' takes for granted, and the 'natives' can provide the contextual insights needed to avoid interpreting phenomena according to their cultural frames of reference. Building a mixed research team from the very start of a project maximizes the probability that the members will move out of their intellectual comfort zone, for each idea and concept is subject to scrutiny and challenge.

Multiple Perspectives

Research on organizational learning and knowledge creation could benefit from the multiple-perspective models used in political science by Allison (1971) and in organization studies by Morgan (1986). Both scholars showed how much value can be gained from looking at the same situation through different theoretical lenses or metaphors. Rather than seeking to tell a single story and find a single truth, we recommend (and will initiate) studies that explore competing views. For example, the entrance of a company into a new industry can be treated analytically as the story about how a visionary leader enabled his organization to enter into the new field. Alternatively, it can be studied as the story about how the company built up its absorptive capacity by making strategically sound acquisitions of new units in the relevant business area. Another possibility is that the company did nothing more than catch up with industry trends, imitating the leaders relatively late in the game. Yet another logical and fruitful angle to reconstruct is how the company started to learn to restructure itself once it had been pushed into the new field that entailed a completely different concept of knowledge management. Each of these stories throws light on different aspects, actors, and interests in the given situation.

By taking a multiple-story approach and rigorously pitting each story against the others, a mixed research team can explore the dynamics of how the outcome of organizational learning is shaped by different groupings in the organization. Such groups interpret information, build networks, and interact in promoting their agendas. They compete for resources to legitimate their intentions and achievements and to secure their vision for the future, and in so doing, they submerge alternative possibilities. A research team with members from varied disciplinary backgrounds could draw on views about power from sociology and political science; on innovation and resource based theories from economics; on creativity theories; on leadership concepts from management and political science; on theories of knowledge acquisition and knowledge creation; and on ideas relating to time, windows of opportunity, and, yes, possibly also luck.

Organizational Learning and Knowledge: Speculating about the Future

The study of organizations, especially in the field of management science, has seen many concepts come and go. For example, Taylorism, management by objectives, and diversification were propagated, followed by total quality management, reengineering, and business-process optimization, to name but a few. Each of these concepts was accompanied by frameworks within which to study organizations and by platforms from which to provide advice to leaders about how to manage change and achieve success. Core competencies, globalization, and shareholder value have appeared in the recent flurry of concepts that are strongly

promoted both as normative recommendations to organizations and as research foci. A final question to consider in this handbook, therefore, is whether organizational learning and the related concepts will soon fade from the scene and be relegated to the list of passing fads. Or will organizational learning and knowledge creation remain one of the paradigmatic bases to describe organizational life and development? As editors of this handbook, we cannot know the future any better than others, but we can offer some reflective speculations grounded in long-term observation and involvement in the study of organizations.

The case for the long-term significance of organizational learning and knowledge creation as a field of academic inquiry can be made on two levels: practical relevance and conceptual fruitfulness. The broad spectrum of literature on modernization and informed projections about the future fabric of our societies all suggest that learning and knowledge will become even more important in future than they are today. Learning as a competence and knowledge as a resource are key factors not only for economic competitiveness but also for access to participating in many dimensions of social, cultural, and political life. There is a broadly based consensus that change will remain a dominant feature of our societies in the foreseeable future, requiring both incremental adjustment and radical innovation. There is no indication in the literature or in informed discussions among scholars or practitioners that organizations are likely to decline as relevant societal or economic entities. Rather, the prediction is that new organizational forms will emerge to replace or complement existing organizations. We can therefore safely assume that the need of organizations to learn and to create and use new knowledge will continue to grow, although the label for the field may well change, particularly as a result of business schools' needs to generate new items for managers' learning agendas.

The conceptual rationale for the long-term life expectancy of organizational learning and knowledge creation as useful paradigmatic foundations for research is possibly even stronger than the argument of practical relevance. The chapters in the first section of this handbook document just how deeply rooted key concepts of organizational learning and knowledge creation are in numerous disciplinary traditions. This field of inquiry provides a focal platform for bringing together the interests of scholars from different disciplines who are seeking to understand the factors, conditions, and processes facilitating and inhibiting the acquisition, creation, and use of knowledge in societies. The intellectual innovativeness of

the field was fueled for many years largely by scholars who were attracted to the exploration of what often appeared to be peripheral, even unorthodox, questions in their disciplines. A challenge will now be to maintain that momentum while mining the core of the disciplines as well. The research agenda remains long and rich, as shown by each chapter in this volume. We therefore see this handbook as providing both a guide to existing knowledge in the field and a basis for future inquiry.

References

Allison, G. T. (1971). *Essence of Decision: Explaining the Cuban Missile Crisis*. Boston: Little, Brown.

Argyris, C. (1993). *Knowledge for Action: A Guide to Overcoming Barriers to Organizational Change*. San Francisco: Jossey-Bass.

——(1985). *Strategy, Change, and Defensive Routines*. Boston: Pitman.

—— and Schön, D. (1978). *Organizational Learning: A Theory of Action Perspective*. Reading, Mass.: Addison-Wesley.

Bateson G. (1972). *Steps to an Ecology of Mind: A Revolutionary Approach to Man's Understanding of Himself*. New York: Ballantine Books.

Berthoin Antal, A. (1998). 'Die Dynamik der Theoriebildungsprozesse zum Organisationslernen', in H. Albach, M. Dierkes, A. Berthoin Antal, and K. Vaillant (eds.), *Organisationslernen—institutionelle und kulturelle Dimensionen. WZB Jahrbuch 1998*. Berlin: edition sigma, 31–52.

—— and Dierkes, M. (1992). 'Internationally Comparative Research in Europe: The Underutilized Resource', in M. Dierkes and B. Biervert (eds.), *European Social Science in Transition: Assessment and Outlook*. Frankfurt am Main: Campus Verlag, 585–610.

Burns, T. and Stalker, G. (1961). *The Management of Innovation*. London: Tavistock.

Coopey, J. (1995). 'The Learning Organization: Power, Politics, and Ideology'. *Management Learning*, 26: 193–213.

Cyert, R. M. and March, J. (1963). *A Behavioral Theory of the Firm*. Englewood Cliffs, NJ: Prentice Hall.

Dierkes, M. and Albach, H. (1998). 'Lernen über Organisationslernen', in H. Albach, M. Dierkes, A. Berthoin Antal, and K. Vaillant (eds.), *Organisationslernen—institutionelle und kulturelle Dimensionen. WZB Jahrbuch 1998*. Berlin: edition sigma: 15–30.

——Alexis, M., Berthoin Antal, A., Hedberg, B. L. T., Pawlowksy, P., Stopford, J. M., and Tsui-Auch, L. S. (eds.) (1999). *The Annotated Bibliography of Organizational Learning*. Berlin: edition sigma. Also available: http://duplox.wz-berlin.de/oldb/bibliography.html

Follett, M. P. (1942). *Dynamic Administration: The Collected Papers of Mary Parker Follett* (H. C. Metcalf and L. Urwick, eds.). New York: Harper & Brothers.

Hedberg, B. L. T. (1981). 'How Organizations Learn and Unlearn', in P. C. Nystrom and W. Starbuck (eds.), *Handbook of Organizational Design*: Vol. 1. *Adapting Organizations to Their Environments*. Oxford: Oxford University Press, 3–27.

Kolb, D. (1984). *Experiential Learning: Experience as the Source of Learning and Development*. Englewood Cliffs, NJ: Prentice Hall.

Levitt, B. and March, J. (1988). 'Organizational Learning'. *Annual Review of Sociology*, 14: 319–40.

March, J. G. (1991). 'Exploration and Exploitation in Organizational Learning'. *Organization Science*, 2: 71–87.

——and Olsen J. P. (1976). *Ambiguity and Choice in Organizations*. Bergen: Universitetsforlaget.

Morgan, G. (1986). *Images of Organization*. Beverly Hills, Calif.: Sage.

Nonaka I. and Takeuchi, H. (1995). *The Knowledge-creating Company: How Japanese Companies Create the Dynamics of Innovation*. New York: Oxford University Press.

——and Konno, N. (1998). 'The Concept of "Ba": Building a Foundation for Knowledge Creation'. *California Management Review*, 40/3: 40–54.

Polanyi, M. (1966). *The Tacit Dimension*. Garden City, NY: Doubleday.

Schein, E. (1993). 'How Can Organizations Learn Faster? The Challenge of Entering the Green Room'. *Sloan Management Review*, 34/2: 85–92.

Schumpeter, J. A. (1951). *The Theory of Economic Development*. Cambridge, Mass.: Harvard University Press.

Weick, K. and Westley, F. (1996). 'Organizational Learning: Affirming an Oxymoron', in S. R. Clegg, C. Hardy, and W. R. Nord (eds.), *Handbook of Organization Studies*. London: Sage, 440–58.

NAME INDEX

Aadne, J. H. 685, 686, 687, 692, 696
Abbott, A. S. 26
Abell, D. F. 356, 436
Abelson, R. 19, 599
Abernathy, W. J. 64
Abrahamson, E. 462, 472, 476
Abrahamsson, B. 559
Abramson, L. Y. 381
Acker, J. 124
Acland, D. 803
Adidam, P. T. 214
Adizes, I. 357
Adler, N. 648
Adler, P. 98, 601, 602, 605, 619
Adler, Wolfgang 887
Aharoni, Y. 631, 638
Ahlstrand, B. 540
Akerlof, G. A. 93
Akers, John 379
Akert, R. M. 20
Alasoini, T. 449
Albach, H. 89, 94, 96, 97, 257, 359, 364,
    699, 886, 925
Albert, S. 827
Albracht, G. 227, 230
Albrow, M. 166, 369
Alchian, A. A. 91, 93, 98, 107
Aldag, R. 329
Aldrich, H. 62, 518, 606, 608
Alexander, R. C. 267
Alexandersson, O. 123
Alexeev, M. 683, 694
Alexis, Marcus 91, 92, 96, 505, 728,
    825–6, 902–17, 922, 925, 930
Algazi, R. 831
Allen, Bill 419
Allen, D. 146
Allen, L. 646, 647
Allen, N. 210, 211
Allison, G. 157, 616, 936
Allison, M. A. 828, 829
Allport, G. W. 199
Alter, C. 700
Altvater, E. 447
Alvesson, M. 36, 43–4
Alvestand, H. 292
Amatori, F. 169
Amburgey, T. L. 272, 333
Amsden, A. H. 172, 721, 722–3
Anand, V. 27
Ancona, D. G. 320
Andersen, O. 638

Anderson, B. 182
Anderson, C. A. 335, 345, 802
Anderson, J. C. 688
Anderson, J. R. 15, 19, 20, 21
Anderson, P. 104
Andersson, Å. E. 448
Andersson, L. M. 410
Andorka, R. 243, 244
Andréasen, L.-E. 448
Andrews, K. R. 433, 540
Angelmar, R. 381
Ansoff, H. I. 525, 540
Antal, David 37, 110, 196, 242–59, 457,
    670, 681–2, 689, 869, 886, 922–3, 925,
    929
Antal-Mokos, Z. 693
Antoni, C. 211, 212
Aoki, M. 708, 709
Apolte, T. 243
Appleby, J. 163, 167, 178, 182
Apter, D. E. 122–3
Arches, J. 604
Ardener, E. 129
Argote, L. 16, 26, 27, 98, 332
Argyris, Chris 3, 15, 17, 40, 63–6, 69–70,
    72–4, 76–7, 137, 150, 198, 209, 214,
    246, 272, 276, 283–4, 308, 357, 376,
    390, 399–400, 403, 405–7, 430, 438,
    442, 451, 465, 467, 472–3, 492, 535,
    537–8, 544, 563, 582, 587–90, 592–4,
    611, 637, 648, 660, 669, 702, 718,
    737, 757–8, 760–3, 766, 771, 855,
    867, 870, 875, 879–80, 886, 921–3,
    928, 931
Ariss, S. A. 357
Aristotle 127
Armour, H. O. 108
Arnold, O. 735
Aronson, E. 20
Arora, A. 103
Arrighetti, A. 706, 707, 710, 711
Arrow, K. J. 97, 98, 635
Arthur, J. B. 809, 811
Arthur, W. B. 95, 105, 110
Arujo, L. 39
Ashby, W. R. 68, 510, 858
Asher, H. 98
Ashforth, B. E. 369, 373, 599, 687
Astley, G. 44, 62, 734
Astrachan, J. H. 371
Asun, D. 372
Athenstaedt, U. 378
Audretsch, D. B. 643, 710

Aumann, R. 92, 96
Avolio, B. J. 418
Axelrod, R. 69, 156, 560, 589, 663
Aydin, C. 524
Azar, E. 590

Babai, D. 146
Bacdayan, P. 494
Bach, N. 207
Bach, V. 777
Bachmann, R. 705, 706, 707, 708, 709,
    710, 711
Bäckius, P. 736, 740
Backman, Stanley J. 811
Badaracco, J. L. 735
Baddely, A. D. 381
Baden-Fuller, C. W. F. 268, 269, 271, 273,
    404, 434
Badoux, B. 913
Bahnmüller, R. 449
Bailey, F. G. 573
Bailey, S. J. 142, 143
Bain, J. S. 634
Bair, J. 524
Baird, I. S. 684, 686
Baitsch, C. 70
Baker, W. E. 209, 214
Bala, V. 94
Baldridge, J. V. 587
Bales, R. F. 75
Baliga, B. R. 432
Ball, G. A. 378
Bammé, A. et al. 289
Bandura, A. 19, 23, 354, 363
Banerjee, A. V. 94
Banks, M. 591
Bantel, K. A. 25
Barkema, H. G. 254, 639, 669, 686
Barker, V. L. III, 337
Barley, S. 25, 42
Barnard, Chester I. 68, 106, 139, 140,
    535, 573, 602, 805
Barnes, B. 636
Barnett, C. K. 64
Barnett, W. P. 333
Barnevik, Percy 419, 421
Barney, J. B. 492, 704
Baron, R. A. 370
Barrett, N. I. 638
Barrios-Choplin, J. 520
Barteson, G. 39
Barth, M. 202, 210
Barthes, Roland 177

Bartholomew, S. 643
Bartlett, C. A. 274, 315, 447, 448, 631, 640, 642, 644, 645, 647, 648
Bartlett, F. C. 69
Bartoli, A. 449
Bass, B. M. 418, 420
Bassi, L. J. 801
Bateson, G. 69, 76, 77, 119, 121, 246, 276 n., 283, 284, 407, 492, 584, 649, 923
Batra, B. 332
Bauks, J. C. 685
Baum, J. A. C. 332, 333, 334, 717
Bauman, Z. 52
Baumard, P. 39, 336, 549, 552, 734, 738, 746
Bay, T. 736, 740
Baysinger, B. 428, 429
Bazeal, D. V. 404
Bazerman, M. H. 328, 717
Beamish, P. W. 685, 687, 688, 733
Bechert, H. 122
Beck, Nikolaus 39, 109, 382, 386, 435, 465, 476, 478, 489–90, 529, 594, 598–620, 633, 637, 647, 665, 737, 922, 930
Beck, U. 36, 52, 202
Becker, B. E. 809
Becker, G. S. 97, 98, 802
Beckérus, Å. 449
Beckhard, R. 675
Beckman, S. L. 27
Beer, M. 463 n., 477, 760, 762, 809
Beer, S. 68, 538
Beers, M. C. 827, 830
Behr, M. 448
Behrens, B. 478
Bell, C. H., Jr 63, 462
Bell, J. H. J. 254, 669
Bell, T. E. 341
Bello, W. 717, 726
Bellon, B. P. 175
Benassi, V. A. 328
Bender, C. 448
Benders, J. 472
Benedict, Ruth 121
Bengtsson, L. 657, 662, 663, 733, 735, 736, 749
Benkard, L. C. 98–9
Bennett, C. J. 572
Bennis, W. 274, 284, 420
Berger, P. L. 41, 64, 351, 457, 636, 689, 899
Berger, S. 726
Berggren, C. 449
Berghoff, H. 176
Bergin, R. S. 789
Bergmann, W. 352
Berle, A. A. 559
Berliner, D. C. 23
Berman, R. 809
Bernheim, B. D. 96
Bernstein, B. 40
Bernstein, J. R. 173

Berque, J. 123
Berridge, K. C. 371
Berry, A. J. 314 n.
Berry, M. A. 236
Bers, M. U. 833
Bertalanffy, L. V. 68
Berthoin Antal, Ariane 1–7, 38, 122, 200, 203, 205, 207–8, 210, 214–15, 221, 237–8, 245, 248, 255–7, 294, 306, 310, 316, 336, 351–65, 373, 397, 431, 435–6, 447, 462–80, 508, 519, 563, 660, 676, 687, 699, 824, 829, 865–83, 887, 890, 895, 921–38
Bertold, O. 291
Bettis, R. 269, 492
Bharadwaj, S. G. 214
Bierach, B. 463, 464, 470, 477, 478
Bieri, J. 71
Bieri, P. 351
Bierly, P. E. 537, 551
Biernacki, R. 181
Bies, R. J. 386
Biggart, N. W. 311
Bihl, G. 212
Bijker, W. 287
Bikhchandani, S. 94
Bilello, U. 247
Bilkey, W. J. 638
Billett, S. 51
Billinghurst, M. 831
Bilsky, W. 199, 204
Binney, G. 421, 422, 424, 426
Bion, W. 75, 591, 769
Birkinshaw, J. M. 641, 647
Björkman, T. 449
Blackler, F. 42, 49, 51
Blake, R. R. 63, 416, 421, 589
Blandy, R. 850, 860
Blau, Peter 36, 38, 140–1
Bleeke, J. 662, 663
Bleicher, K. 76, 352, 355
Bliemel, F. 810
Bloch, Marc 121, 127, 128, 164
Block, P. 419, 420, 423, 426, 463, 470, 479
Blomstrom, M. 721, 726
Blondel, J. 143
Blonski, M. 94
Bloomfield, B. 297
Bluedorn, A. C. 351, 352
Blumberg, H. H. 385
Blumer, H. 41
Boas, Franz 120, 121
Boerner, Christopher S. 12, 89–111, 924, 926
Böhling, K. 245, 257, 687
Bohm, D. 786, 831
Böhmann, T. 778
Boisot, M. 61, 523, 660, 814, 827, 830, 831, 832
Boje, D. M. 45, 636
Boland, R. 14, 42
Bollinger, H. 72

Bolman, L. 584, 586
Boltanski, L. 221
Bolton, M. K. 309
Bomke, P. 65
Bonifert, M. S. 689, 690
Bonini, C. P. 537
Bonjean, C. M. 604
Borg, M. R. 26
Bornemann, Manfred 62, 503, 632, 756, 794–814, 924
Bornstein, M. 244
Borucki, C. C. 272
Borys, B. 601, 602, 605, 619, 659, 687, 734
Bouchard, D. F. 181
Boudreau, J. W. 809
Bouffard-Bouchard, T. 23
Bougon, M. G. 69, 70, 74, 407, 519, 528, 771
Boulding, K. 70, 78, 591
Bourdieu, P. 49, 805
Bourgeois, L. J. III, 584, 588, 592, 593, 762
Bower, G. H. 381
Bower, J. L. 271, 277
Bowman, M. J. 802
Boydell, T. 65, 74, 417, 778, 788, 886
Boyer, B. 907
Bradach, J. L. 747
Bradley, K. 827
Bradner, S. 292
Brahm, R. A. 734
Brannen, M. Y. 633, 637
Bransford, J. D. 20
Branyiczki, I. 684
Brehmer, B. 757
Breslauer, G. W. 156
Bresnahan, T. 103
Brewer, G. 149
Brigham, E. F. 797
Brilman, J. 446
Broadbent, D. E. 345
Broadbent, J. 314 n.
Brock, G. W. 103
Brodbeck, F. C. 16, 25
Brödel, Dietmar 247, 275, 627, 631–50, 704, 716, 923, 924, 932
Brooking, A. 795
Brousseau, K. R. 739
Brown, A. L. 20
Brown, B. 588
Brown, D. R. 334
Brown, G. W. 96
Brown, John Seely 42, 47, 49, 51, 65, 267, 268, 273, 465, 492, 499, 690, 718, 735
Brown, R. 375
Brown, W. B. 635
Bruhn, M. 810
Brulin, G. 448, 450
Bruner, J. 44
Brunsson, N. 536, 553
Brusco, S. 449

Bruszt, L. 243, 251
Brutti, P. 449
Bryson, P. J. 244
Büchel, Bettina 14, 465, 471, 487–8,
    518–32, 640, 646, 672, 675, 739, 828,
    868, 924, 930
Buckley, P. J. 631, 635, 688
Buhr, R. 289, 290
Burchell, B. 710
Burgelmann, R. A. 89, 266, 274, 338,
    403
Burgmaier, S. 463
Burgoyne, J. 65, 74, 417, 778, 788, 886
Burkhard, B. 16, 18, 19
Burns, J. M. 573, 575
Burns, L. R. 332
Burns, T. 62, 317, 927
Burrell, G. 45, 47, 717
Burros, P. 722
Burt, R. S. 805, 806
Burton, J. 590
Busemeyer, J. R. 21
Bush, R. 590, 592
Bushe, G. 758
Butera, F. 39
Butler, H. 429
Butterfield, K. D. 378
Byosière, Philippe 72, 272, 319, 433,
    442, 487, 491–513, 528, 632, 648, 701,
    703–5, 709, 716, 733, 739, 743, 780,
    830, 904, 921, 925, 928, 930
Byrne, J. 464

Cabral, L. M. B. 99
Cacioppo, J. T. 373
Caldwell, B. D. 841
Caldwell, D. F. 320
Calhoun, C. 716
Calistri, F. 449
Callan, V. J. 371
Cameron, K. S. 63, 245, 308, 335, 357
Campbell, A. 541
Campbell, D. T. 126
Campbell, J. P. 16
Cangelosi, V. 15, 64
Canning, K. 180
Cantwell, J. A. 640, 643
Canzler, W. 284, 291
Carbonneau, T. 588
Carendi, Jan 743, 744
Carleton, W. 429
Carley, K. 27, 363, 463 n.
Carlin, W. 245, 250, 255, 256
Carlson, P. 528
Carlson, W. B. 174
Carlyle, T. 166
Carnevale, A. P. 802
Carnevale, P. J. D. 381
Carqueville, P. 468, 469, 470
Carr, D. K. 447
Carr, E. H. 167
Carrol, S. J. 687
Carroll, N. 183

Carrozza, T. 831
Carson, R. 905
Cartwright, D. 75
Cascio, W. 803
Casey, E. S. 830
Cassel, D. 243
Cassis, Y. 170
Casson, M. 631, 635, 688
Castrogiovanni, G. 432
Cattero, B. 449
Caves, R. E. 631, 634, 635
Cavusgil, S. T. 638
Cerf, V. 292
Cesarani, D. 183
Cesaria, R. 39
Chak, A. M. 37
Chakravarthy, B. S. 642
Champy, J. 547
Chandler, Alfred D., Jr 164, 169, 170
Chapin, A. 293, 296
Chase, S. 905
Chatman, J. A. 805
Chesbrough, H. W. 278, 320, 735
Chen, M.-J. 340
Chess, C. 548
Chew, D. H. 807 n.
Chi, M. T. H. 20
Child, John 1–7, 63, 123, 221, 242–3, 245,
    247, 256, 266, 305, 308–23, 352, 358,
    375, 422, 428–30, 433, 436, 498, 503,
    559, 593, 628, 636, 637, 657–77, 682,
    684, 688, 691, 699, 716, 735, 749, 828,
    869, 887, 904, 921–38
Chirac, Jacques 229
Chiu, S. 717
Choi, C. J. 657
Choo, C. W. 465, 491, 828, 829
Christensen, C. 25, 26, 28, 104
Christianson, S.-A. 381, 382
Christie, B. 520
Christienson, S. 432
Churchill, E. F. 828, 831
Churchland, P. M. 128
Ciborra, C. U. 49, 50, 310, 316, 649, 664,
    699, 705, 828
Clancey, W. J. 828
Clark, B. 336
Clark, E. 247, 255
Clark, K. 98, 103
Clark, K. B. 65, 110, 508
Clark, N. K. 26
Clark, P. 352, 353
Clegg, S. R. 36, 43, 46, 47, 563, 564, 566,
    568, 569, 571, 576, 704, 729
Coase, Ronald H. 106, 107, 111, 268, 549,
    634
Cockburn, I. 491
Cocking, R. R. 20
Cohen, A. 122, 124
Cohen, D. 76, 780, 827, 828, 829
Cohen, J. 351, 352
Cohen, M. 97, 494, 536, 537, 538, 548,
    560, 616, 618, 772, 903

Cohen, P. S. 126
Cohen, S. G. 29
Cohen, W. 24, 101, 103, 108, 320, 525,
    639, 645, 668, 681, 689, 691
Coldwell, J. B. 315
Coleman, D. C. 169
Coleman, J. S. 270, 805
Collin, S.-O. 734
Collins, A. 47, 49
Collins, G. 186
Collins, J. C. 275, 286, 294–5, 296, 417,
    419, 507
Collins, R. 35, 37, 38, 39, 40, 729
Comer, D. E. 292
Conger, J. A. 411
Conlisk, J. 92, 97
Conner, K. R. 633, 805
Conrad, P. 447
Consolini, P. M. 383
Conway, M. 335, 344
Cook, Captain James 132
Cook, S. D. N. 36, 38, 50, 72–3, 245, 358,
    398, 464, 904
Cooke, P. 706, 708, 709
Cool, K. 108, 110, 491
Cooley, C. H. 41
Cooper, C. 129
Cooper, J. 561, 562
Cooper, R. 45, 383
Coopey, J. 37, 318, 473, 563–6, 569, 573,
    577, 719, 729, 866, 932
Copeland, T. E. 457
Corazza, R. 356
Coriat, B. 448
Coser, L. A. 318, 585, 586
Cossentino, F. 449
Costigliola, F. 178
Coulter, R. 833
Cournot, A. 96
Courtney, J. F. 718
Crainer, S. 425
Crampton, T. 720
Crawford, R. G. 107
Crick, D. 638
Crosby, F. J. 239
Crossan, M. 14, 671, 673, 733
Crowder, R. G. 17
Crozier, M. 36, 604, 605
Cruikshank, J. 588
Crump, N. 51
Cunniff, M. K. 204
Currall, S. C. 687
Cusumano, M. A. 759, 760
Cyert, R. M. 3, 38, 63–6, 77, 142, 150,
    337–8, 437, 491–2, 536–7, 544,
    586–7, 599, 606, 609, 615, 618,
    638, 717, 733, 739, 746, 903, 928,
    931
Czaban, L. 255
Czarniawska, Barbara 12–13, 42, 93,
    118–33, 171, 439, 457, 475, 524, 528–9,
    632, 718–19, 868, 870, 904, 921–2,
    924, 928

Czarniawska-Joerges, Barbara 43, 45, 245, 247, 617
Czeglédy, A. P. 242, 243, 245, 254, 255, 256, 657, 682, 684, 687, 691
Czinkota, M. R. 638

Dacin, T. 333
Daft, R. L. 69, 70, 214, 269, 400, 465, 492, 519, 520, 521, 522, 525, 526, 527, 528, 532
Dahl, R. 562, 573, 585
Dahlgren, G. 536, 549, 734
Dahrendorf, R. 168
Daily, C. 429, 439
Dalton, M. 36, 118
Dankbaar, B. 448
Darly, J. M. 22
Darnton, R. 177
Darwin, C. 120
Davenport, T. H. 206, 508, 518, 827, 828, 829, 830
David, P. 95, 105, 110, 429, 668
Davidow, W. H. 536, 740
Davidson, W. H. 635, 639
Davies, G. 670, 802
Davies, J. 760
Davies, M. F. 385
Davis, G. 223, 332, 429, 528
Davis, J. H. 26
Davis, K. 463
Davis, Peter 464
Dayan, Moshe 764
De Dreu, C. 582
de Geus, A. 269, 424, 759, 850, 852, 857
de Goeje, J. 351
de Haën, Christoph 505, 728, 825–6, 902–17, 922, 930
De Long, D. W. 827, 830
De Rivera, J. 372
Deakin, S. 701, 706, 707, 710, 711
Deal, T. 584, 586
Dean, A. L. 141, 561
Dearborn, D. 584
Debreu, G. 62
Deering, C. J. 143, 150, 565
Deetz, S. 43–4, 45
Deiaco, E. 794
Delaney, J. T. 809
Delany, E. 462
Delios, A. 684
DeMarie, S. 297
Demb, A. 434
Denhardt, D. B. 351, 352
Denis, J. E. 639
Denison, D. R. 372
Dennis, A. 526
Denzin, N. K. 636
Depelteau, D. 639
Derrida, Jacques 43, 177
DeSanctis, G. 518
Descartes, René 49, 119 n.
Destler, I. M. 561
Deutsch, Karl 149, 157, 221, 576

Deutsch, M. 575, 589
Devadas, R. 332
Devanna, M. A. 416, 418, 419
Dewey, J. 41, 74, 399, 762
DiBella, A. J. 245, 252, 254, 354, 465, 704, 708, 709, 710, 758, 759, 760
Dickie, R. B. 207
Dickinson, J. 465
Dickson, W. J. 586
Diehl, M. 26
Dierickx, I. 108, 110, 491
Dierkes, Meinolf 1–7, 72, 105, 196–7, 200, 203, 205–6, 208, 210, 214, 237, 245, 256, 276, 282–93, 336, 352, 358, 386, 464, 476, 505, 563, 699, 804, 829, 858, 867–9, 873, 882, 886, 889, 891, 921–38
Dill, W. R. 15, 64
DiMaggio, P. J. 127, 148, 245, 310, 541, 561, 604, 613, 641, 702
Dimberg, U. 18
Disraeli, Benjamin 154
DiTomaso, N. 420
Dixon, N. 209, 778, 782
Djarrahzadeh, M. 199
Dobbing, J. 227
Dobbins, G. H. 420
Dobers, P. 544
Dodgson, M. 65, 308, 492, 645, 699, 701, 708, 717, 733, 758
Dolan, S. L. 371
Dollard, John 121, 245
Domjan, M. 16, 18, 19
Donahue, W. A. 371
Donaldson, L. 717
Donati, E. 39
Donnellon, A. 74, 519, 528, 690
Dopson, S. 505
Dörner, D. 69, 779
Dörr, G. 243, 248, 249, 251, 252, 253, 256, 257, 682, 687
Dosi, G. 100, 101, 102, 103, 104, 105, 107, 108, 109, 110, 164, 642
Dougherty, D. 338, 739
Dougherty, J. W. D. 121
Douglas, Mary 40, 125, 129
Down, Jim 475
Downey, H. K. 329
Downs, A. 153
Downs, L. L. 180
Doz, Y. L. 542, 642, 648, 665, 677
Dragonetti, N. 794, 795, 796, 797, 799, 812
Drexel, I. 448
Dreyfus, H. L. and S. E. 335
Drinkuth, Andreas 75, 154, 396–7, 423, 446–58, 928, 930
Driver, M. J. 69, 71, 331, 333, 374, 739
Drucker, P. 428, 491, 544, 794, 827, 837
Drüke, H. 448
Drummond, A., Jr 314, 672, 674, 675
Duguid, P. 42, 47, 49, 51, 65, 267, 268, 273, 465, 492, 499, 690, 718, 735

Duhaime, I. M. 337
Duke, V. 243
Dukerich, J. M. 328
Dunbar, R. L. M. 336
Duncan, R. 15, 29, 40, 64, 65, 70, 78, 492, 544, 649
Dunning, J. H. 634
Durkheim, Emile 11, 36, 39–41, 121, 129, 130, 138, 167, 168
Dussauge, P. 657
Dutton, J. 98
Dutton, J. E. 273, 617
Dutton, J. M. 336
Duverger, Maurice 144, 154
Dyer, J. H. 828
Dyerson, R. 319
Dyllick, T. 225, 226, 227, 229

Eagleton, T. 177
Eagly, A. H. 420
Earl, M. J. 828, 829
Easterby-Smith, M. 37, 198, 760
Easton, D. 558
Eatwell, J. 89
Ebbinghaus, H. 14
Eberl, P. 65, 68, 70, 72
Eccles, R. G. 518, 747
Eden, C. 779
Eden, D. 22
Edgerton, R. B. 121
Edison, S. W. 214
Edmondson, A. 64, 65, 464, 699, 702, 868, 886
Edström, A. 449, 648, 649
Edvinsson, Leif 491, 743, 794, 795, 796, 797, 799, 805, 812
Edwards, M. 786
Edwards, W. 328
Egelhoff, W. G. 640
Egri, C. P. 204, 213
Ehn, P. 48
Ehrlich, C. J. 809
Ehrlich, S. B. 328
Einhorn, H. J. 21, 22
Einsiedler, H. E. 199
Eisenhardt, K. E. 584, 588, 592, 593, 762
Eisenstat, R. 463 n., 477
Ekman, P. 371
Elias, N. 357, 803
Eliasson, G. 802
Elkeles, T. 870
Ellen, R. F. 129
Ellison, G. 92, 94
Ellstrand, A. 429, 439
Elster, J. 232
Elvander, N. 449
Emery, F. E. 68, 211, 591, 788
Engardio, P. 722
Engelhard, N. 245, 255
Engels, Friedrich 36
Engestrom, Y. 49
English, A. C. 543
English, H. B. 543

Ensign, P. C. 642
Epple, D. 27, 98, 332
Eran, M. 772
Erera, I. P. 371
Ericson, A. 539
Ericsson, K. A. 20
Eriksson, K. 639
Erlicher, L. 310, 316
Ernst, D. 662, 663
Ernst, M. 683, 694
Ertl, R. 207, 213
Esch, K. 341
Espejo, R. 247
Estes, W. K. 331
Estevers, F. 18
Estrada, C. A. 381
Etheridge, L. S. 137, 138, 140, 153, 558
Etzioni, A. 36, 210
Evans, P. 108, 110, 521
Evans, R. J. 163, 177, 178, 184
Evenson, R. E. 101
Eysenck, M. W. 19, 20

Fahey, L. 850
Fairholm, G. W. 150, 155, 572
Faulkner, D. 657, 664, 665, 673
Favereau, O. 222
Fay, B. 163, 177, 178
Fayerweather, J. 632
Fayol, H. 586
Fayyad, U. 832
Fazio, R. H. 22
Fear, Jeffrey R. 13, 95, 145, 147, 162–86,
    921, 923, 927, 928
Feather, N. T. 199
Featheringham, T. R. 473
Feher, J. 689, 690
Feinstein, C. H. 165
Feldman, D. C. 370
Feldman, J. 22
Feldman, M. P. 643
Feldman, M. S. 527
Fenno, R. 142
Ferner, A. 449
Ferrell, O. C. 214
Festinger, L. 344, 345
Fichman, M. 669
Fiedler, F. 421
Field, R. H. G. 415, 416
Fincham, R. 470, 472–3
Fineman, S. 369, 371, 375, 605
Fink, A. 850
Fiol, C. M. 17, 40, 64, 65, 70, 77, 358,
    398, 526, 582, 690, 717, 868–9
Firth, R. 119, 124, 125
Fisch, R. 335
Fischer, M. M. J. 131
Fisher, George 417, 418
Fisher, R. 588, 591
Fiske, S. T. 20
Fitz-Enz, J. 803, 809
Flam, H. 369
Flamholtz, E. G. 803, 804

Fleck, Ludwig 125
Fleischmann, P. 468, 469
Flores, F. 48, 509
Florida, R. 637
Floyd, S. W. 273
Flynn, P. 42, 51
Folger, J. 590, 592
Follett, Mary Parker 139, 140, 318, 584,
    588, 927
Ford, Henry 165
Ford, J. K. 23
Forrester, J. W. 68, 537
Forsgren, M. 647, 648
Forslin, Jan 11, 74, 76, 80, 207, 382, 755,
    775–91, 858, 889, 895, 923, 931, 933
Foster-Fishman, P. G. 26
Foucault, Michel 43, 44, 177, 178,
    180–1, 182, 183
Fox, F. V. 335
Fox, R. G. 119
Fox, S. 45
Francks, P. 172
Frank, R. H. 372
Franz, T. M. 26
Frazer, James George 120
Freebairn, J. 850, 860
Freeman, C. 642, 869, 882
Freeman, J. 62, 163, 164, 245, 247, 264,
    272, 274, 508
Frei, F. 448
Freimuth, J. 205, 206, 207
French, W. L. 63, 462
Frese, M. 16, 29, 370
Freud, S. 120
Fricke, W. 286, 447
Fried, Y. 599
Friedberg, E. 221, 600
Friedman, Victor J. 6, 12, 36, 156, 237,
    318, 384, 387, 395, 398–412, 425, 430,
    438, 440, 449, 456, 464, 472, 475,
    489, 562, 566, 582–94, 739, 755,
    757–72, 867, 875, 883, 890–1, 894–6,
    921, 923, 928, 931–2
Friedrich, H. F. 15
Friedrich, W. 204
Friesen, P. 357, 431, 434
Frijda, N. H. 370, 371, 376
Frohman, A. L. 400, 401, 404, 407, 410,
    411
Frost, A. G. 26
Frost, P. J. 72, 74, 353, 358
Fruin, W. Mark 169, 170, 172, 185, 633,
    637
Fry, Art 375
Fudenberg, D. 92, 94
Fujimoto, T. 110, 508
Fujimura, J. 51
Fujita, K. 717
Fulbrook, M. 183
Fuld, L. M. 829
Fulk, J. 518, 520, 521, 523, 524
Furness, T. 831
Fürstenberg, F. 210, 215

Furubo, J. E. 575
Futoran, G. C. 353, 355, 360

Gabriel, Y. 605
Gaciarz, B. 247, 248, 251, 254, 256
Gage, N. L. 23
Gagliardi, P. 50, 353
Galambos, L. 174
Galbraith, J. R. 519, 588, 648, 649
Galer, Graham 80, 207, 269, 364, 475,
    615, 759, 788, 824, 849–63, 887, 890,
    895, 923, 929, 932
Galgóczi, B. 253, 254, 255
Gallhofer, S. 181
Gallupe, R. 526
Galton, F. 120, 415
Gambardella, A. 103
Gamson, W. A. 587
Ganesh, U. 663, 665, 688, 729
Ganter, H.-D. 266, 309, 316
Gapenski, L. C. 797
Gardner, H. 274, 275
Gardner, W. 518
Garfinkel, H. 36, 41, 51
Gargiulo, M. 669
Garratt, B. 14, 65, 77, 440, 657, 757, 886
Garud, R. 336
Garvin, D. A. 14, 110, 216, 352, 398, 582,
    593, 758, 886
Gates, Bill 798
Gattiker, U. 468
Gausemeier, J. 850
Geen, R. G. 23
Geertz, Clifford 121, 122, 131, 132, 177
Gehlen, A. 284
Gensicke, T. 199, 202, 203, 204, 210
Gephart, R. P. 636
Geppert, Mike 37, 110, 196, 242–59, 457,
    670, 681, 682, 689, 869, 922, 923, 925,
    929
Gergen, Kenneth 44, 131
Gergs, H.-J. 255
Geringer, J. M. 662
Gerlach, F. 224 n., 450
Gerlach, M. L. 709
Geroski, P. 103
Gersick, C. J. G. 353, 355, 356, 357, 360
Geschka, H. 364
Geschlössl, A. 224 n.
Gherardi, Silvia 11, 35–54, 150, 167, 179,
    181, 185, 198, 221, 268, 308, 352–3,
    355, 357–8, 364, 384, 458, 465, 586,
    594, 610, 718, 729, 904, 913, 921, 929
Ghoshal, S. 264–6, 270, 274, 278, 315,
    447–8, 631, 640, 642, 644–5, 647–8,
    805–6
Gibbons, M. et al. 813–14
Giddens, A. 43, 52, 310, 321, 457, 458,
    600, 601, 637, 647, 649, 670, 737
Gierschner, H. C. 69
Gifford, D. J. 907
Gill, T. G. 829
Gilmore, T. 384, 473, 476, 478, 479

Ginsberg, A. 334, 462, 472, 476
Gioia, D. A. 19, 69, 70, 74
Gladstone, William Ewart 154
Glaser, R. 20
Glass, David G. 840
Glavin, T. L. 717
Gleick, J. 509
Glick, W. H. 27
Gloger, A. 472
Gluck, C. 165, 174
Glynn, M. A. 328, 329
Goffman, E. 40, 41
Goldberg, S. 588
Golden, M. 152, 155
Goldman, S. L. 735
Goldstein, J. 155
Gomez, P. 68, 807
Gomez, P.-Y. 222
Gomez-Meija, L. 429
Gonzalez, J. L. 372
Goodenough, W. H. 127
Gooding, R. Z. 328
Goody, J. 128, 129
Gorman, L. 640
Gortner, H. F. 141, 559, 560, 566
Goto, A. 103
Gould, J. M. 245, 252, 254, 354, 465,
    704, 708, 709, 710, 758, 759, 760
Gould, Stephen J. 121
Gouldner, A. W. 36, 118, 512, 602
Govindarajan, V. 631, 640, 643, 645,
    646, 647
Goyal, S. 94
Grabher, G. 243, 244, 699, 700, 701,
    703, 708
Grabner, L. 214
Gradous, D. B. 803
Grafton-Small, R. 45
Graham, P. 139, 318
Granel, M. 212
Granovetter, M. 271, 309, 828
Granovetter, M. S. 740, 805
Grant, R. M. 266, 491, 508, 619, 805, 814,
    827
Gray, B. 74, 207, 208, 215, 357, 519, 528,
    684, 686, 690
Green, D. F. 147
Green, E. 588
Greenberg, M. 548
Greening, D. W. 207, 208, 215
Greenwood, R. 247
Greiner, L. E. 63
Greitemeyer, T. 25
Grenier, R. 735, 736, 740
Grether, D. M. 97
Greve, A. 329, 339, 345, 431, 435, 616
Greyser, S. A. 379
Griffith, T. L. 520, 526, 527, 530
Griliches, Z. 103
Grime, V. 243
Grimes, M. D. 604
Grin, J. 282, 285
Grinyer, P. H. 311, 327, 338, 432

Gronhaug, K. 802
Gross, B. M. 573, 574
Grossman, S. R. 282
Gruber, H. 98
Grund, M. A. 810
Grundstein, M. 798 n.
Grundy, T. 72
Grunwald, A. 282, 285
Guatto, T. 14
Gul, F. A. 803
Gulati, R. 658, 661, 669, 747
Gulick, L. 153
Gulliver, F. R. 759
Gupta, A. K. 631, 640, 643, 645, 646, 647
Gurevitch, Z. D. 590
Gustafson, D. A. 204
Gustafson, T. 850
Gustavsen, B. 447, 448, 449, 458
Guzzo, R. A. 25

Haas, Ernst 145, 146, 151, 152
Haas, R. D. 757
Habermas, J. 52, 169
Habgood, A. J. 465
Hacker, W. 29
Hackman, J. R. 370
Hage, J. 700
Hagedoorn, J. 733
Hähner, K. 200, 203, 205, 206, 208, 210,
    214, 237, 336, 358, 464, 868, 873
Håkansson, H. 536
Haken, H. 829
Hale, R. 735
Hale, S. 374
Hall, E. T. 351
Hall, J. F. 16
Hall, P. 157
Hall, R. 802
Hall, R. A. 137
Hall, R. I. 70
Hamal, G. 72, 108, 110, 267, 275, 313
Hämäläinen, T. 537, 551
Hambrick, D. 431, 435
Hamel, G. 447, 491, 536, 540, 541, 640,
    662, 666, 667, 670, 672, 687, 733, 735,
    736, 739, 802
Hamilton, G. 717, 723, 725
Hammer, M. 547
Hammer, R. 364
Hampden-Turner, C. 421, 476, 540, 541
Handa, M. 832
Handy, Charles 80, 422, 566, 571, 573,
    576-7
Haney, D. S. 810
Hanf, K. 150
Hanna, C. 26
Hannan, M. 62, 163, 164, 245, 247, 264,
    272, 274, 508
Hannerz, U. 186
Hansen, M. H. 704
Hansen, M. T. 333
Hanson, J. 536, 549, 687, 734
Hard, K. J. 447

Hardy, C. 46, 47, 338, 563, 564, 566, 568,
    569, 571, 576, 704, 706, 729
Hare, A. P. 385
Hargie, O. 527
Harrell, A. M. 803
Harrigan, K. R. 735
Harris, R. 905, 913
Harrison, B. 278, 700
Harrison, J. 433
Harrison, R. 762
Hart, H. 447
Hartmann, H. 185
Hartwick, J. 26
Harvey Jones, John 419
Hasii, R. R. 246
Haslam, J. 181
Hassard, J. 351, 353, 357, 358
Hatch, N. W. 98
Hatfield, E. 373
Hattam, V. C. 147
Haunschild, P. 332, 333, 339, 340
Hauriou, M. 284
Hauser, A. 352
Havas, A. 252, 253, 254, 255, 257
Hawkins, P. 72
Hawlett, M. 572
Hayek, F. A. von 100, 106, 108, 111, 494,
    607
Hayes, P. 168
Hayes, R. H. 65
Healy, D. 905
Heap, S. H. 139
Heath, L. R. 352
Heath, P. S. 690, 693
Heavens, Sally J. 221, 256, 305, 308-23,
    375, 422, 428-30, 433, 436, 503, 559,
    593, 636-7, 661, 663, 669, 674, 677,
    828, 869, 904, 923, 929-30, 934
Heckhausen, H. 23
Heclo, H. 148, 565, 572
Hedberg, Bo L. T. 13, 15, 24, 37, 65, 77-8,
    157, 270, 272, 276, 305-6, 308, 313,
    319, 327-45, 351-4, 357-8, 380, 400,
    422, 431, 435-6, 439, 464, 466, 472,
    476, 488, 498, 509, 535-53, 576,
    615-17, 629-30, 637, 641, 649, 668,
    733-49, 757, 865-7, 879, 903, 917,
    922-3, 925, 928-9
Hedlin, P. 806, 807
Hedlund, G. 642, 644, 645, 675, 686,
    690, 738, 739, 746
Hedlund, J. 528
Heenan, D. A. 642
Heene, A. 733
Heidegger, M. 48, 49
Heidenreich, M. 243, 244, 256
Heider, F. 71, 328
Heifetz, Ronald A. 425, 769
Heijl, P. M. 68 n.
Heimann, S. E. 810
Heiner, R. A. 92
Hellman, S. 154
Hellriegel, D. 329, 691

Helluloid, D. 733
Helmers, S. 292, 293
Helper, S. 704, 706, 709, 710
Henderson, J. 717
Henderson, R. 103, 491
Hendricks, J. 803
Hendricks, R. 473, 475, 477
Hennart, J. 635, 684, 687
Henriksson, K. 657, 662, 663, 733, 749
Henry, G. 576
Henry, R. A. 26
Henzler, Herbert 477
Herbert, W. 199, 202, 203
Heriott, S. R. 318
Herkenhoff, R. 243, 252
Herkströter, C. 231
Herman, E. 429
Hermanson, R. H. 803
Herriott, S. R. 311, 561, 613
Herskovits, M. J. 120, 124, 125, 132
Hertle, H. H. 229
Hertog, J. F. den 446, 447, 448
Herzberger, S. D. 239
Heuer, F. 382
Hewitt, P. 903
Hewlett, Bill 419
Hewstone, M. 376
Hickson, D. J. 316
Hikino, T. 164, 169, 170
Hilgard, E. R. 331
Hilger, S. 170
Hill, F. E. 165
Hill, R. C. 691, 717
Hiltz, S. R. 832
Hinings, C. R. 247
Hinsz, V. B. 25, 26, 373
Hinterhuber, H. H. 185
Hippler, H. J. 199, 202
Hirsch, W. Z. 98
Hirsch-Kreinsen, H. 448, 706, 708, 710
Hirschhorn, L. 384, 409, 410, 448, 769
Hirschleifer, D. 94
Hirschman, A. 574
Hirst, P. 710
Hisrich, R. D. 684
Hitt, M. 247, 297, 492, 541
Hlawacek, S. 468, 469
Hobbes, Thomas 564, 585
Hobday, M. 717, 720, 721, 722–3
Hobsbawm, Eric 182
Hochschild, A. R. 369
Hocker, J. 585
Hocking, D. 850, 860
Hodgkinson, G. P. 330, 339
Hodgson, P. 425
Hoffman, L. 69
Hoffmann, U. 282, 285, 292, 293
Hoffmann, W. 468, 469
Hofmann, D. A. 28
Hofmann, J. 289, 292, 293, 296, 466 n.
Höfner, K. 807
Hofstede, G. H. 247, 420–1

Hogarth, R. M. 21, 22, 336
Holden, N. J. 129
Holland, D. 121, 127, 128
Holland, J. H. 21
Hollander, E. 449
Hollenbeck, J. 25, 528
Holmes, J. 700
Holmqvist, Mikael 313 n., 422, 498, 629–30, 733–49, 922, 928
Holmstrom, B. R. 633
Holsapple, C. W. 827
Holt, D. A. 204
Holt, J. 210
Holyoak, K. J. 21
Holzinger, I. W. 332, 339, 340
Homans, George C. 36, 38, 354
Homburg, C. 810
Homp, C. 207
Hooijberg, R. 420
Hooley, G. et al. 682, 683
Hopwood, A. 44, 181
Hörnell, E. 794
Hornsby, J. S. et al. 403
Horvath, J. A. 334
Hoskisson, R. 428, 429
Hotte, A. M. 200
Hough, J. B. 155, 570
House, R. 28, 282
Howard, R. 757
Howell, D. L. 174
Howells, J. 447
Howes, M. B. 19
Howitt, P. 801
Huber, G. P. 17, 65, 69, 78, 106, 157, 209, 212, 266, 308, 320, 382, 398, 464, 474, 518–20, 525–6, 528–9, 582, 619–20, 637, 646, 663, 703, 708, 717, 733, 870, 903
Huey, J. 843
Huff, A. 328
Hughes, T. 287
Huitema, C. 292
Huizenga, E. 446
Hull, C. 14
Hull, I. V. 178
Hult, G. T. M. 214
Humble, J. 315–16
Humphrey, R. H. 369, 373, 687
Humphrey, S. 841
Hunt, L. 163, 167, 178, 182
Hurley, R. F. 214
Huselid, M. A. 809
Husserl, Edmund 36
Hutchins, E. 49, 118, 121
Huysman, M. 53
Hyman, R. 449
Hymer, S. H. 631, 634

Iacocca, Lee 419
Ibielski, D. 462
Ichijo, K. 503, 510, 686
Ichiro, N. 725
Ijiri, Y. 806

Iles, P. 778
Ilgen, D. 528
Ilinitch, A. Y. 314
Ilkè, F. 156
Illich, I. 47
Imai, K. 65, 508, 709, 710
Imrie, R. 706, 709, 710
Inglehart, R. 199, 201, 202, 203, 204, 210
Inglis, S. 74
Ingram, P. 332, 333
Inkpen, A. C. 642, 657, 658, 663, 667, 668, 669, 671, 672, 673, 686, 687, 690, 733
Ino, T. 831
Inoue, R. 721
Insko, C. A. 27
Ireland, R. D. 247
Isaacs, W. 583
Isen, A. M. 370, 381
Ishida, T. 827, 828
Ishii, H. 828
Itami, H. 709, 710, 802
Itó Denschichi 171
Ittermann, P. 477
Izard, C. E. 376

Jackson, T. 463, 464, 478
Jacob, M. 163, 167, 178, 182
Jacobi, O. 450
Jaeger, H. 169
Jaffe, A. 103
Janis, I. L. 388, 439, 588
Jansanoff, S. 287
Jansen, J. 374
Jantsch, E. 492
Jaques, E. 118
Jarillo, J. C. 648
Jarvie, I. L. 130 n.
Jelinek, M. 72, 75, 539, 648
Jemison, D. B. 659, 687, 734
Jenkins, K. 178, 184
Jensen, M. 429, 432, 435, 439
Jensen, M. C. 62, 317, 508
Jervis, R. 156
Jewell, M. E. 143
Jick, T. D. 886
Jilge, S. 29
Jin, J. 89, 94, 96, 97
Job, Steve 267
Joerges, B. 118, 125, 287
Johansen, R. 536
Johanson, J. 631, 633, 638–9
Johns, G. 16
Johnson, B. M. 600
Johnson, B. T. 420
Johnson, Carver 479
Johnson, D. A. 226
Johnson, G. 310, 671
Johnson, H. T. 175, 181
Johnson, J. L. 429, 439
Johnson, J. P. 686
Johnson, L. E. 827

Johnson, R. 429
Johnson-Laird, P. N. 494
Johnstone, B. 722, 729 n.
Jones, Dan 424
Jones, G. 315–16
Jones, J. W. 521, 526
Jones, S. 779
Jones, T. C. 181
Jonsson, E. 430, 431, 432
Jönsson, S. 336, 338, 551, 552, 671
Jorgensen, J. 739
Joskow, P. L. 98, 107
Jürgens, U. 448, 706, 708, 709, 710, 711

Kabanoff, B. 210
Kachel, P. 251
Kädtler, Jürgen 149, 150, 195–6, 197,
    221–39, 923, 928, 929
Kahane, A. 850, 852, 853, 862
Kahn, H. 850, 852
Kahn, R. 68, 410
Kahneman, D. 22, 97
Kahwajy, J. L. 584, 588, 592, 593, 762
Kakabadse, A. 604
Kamehameha III, of Hawaii 132
Kamiyama, K. 648
Kanter, R. M. 763, 869, 882, 886
Kanungo, R. N. 411
Kao, J. 720, 723, 725
Kaplan, A. 149
Kaplan, R. S. 61, 175, 181, 808, 809
Kaplan, S. L. 177
Kapstein, E. B. 447
Karahanna, E. 520, 521
Karahannas, M. V. 675
Kaschube, J. 205, 209
Kasper, W. 850, 852, 860
Kast, F. E. 68
Kasvio, A. 449
Katz, A. N. 199
Katz, D. 68
Katz, R. 320
Katzenbach, J. R. 75
Kauffmann, S. 829
Kaufman, H. 561
Kaufmann, F. X. 370
Kay, J. 425
Keats, B. 297
Keesing, F. M. 120, 121
Keller, B. 450
Kelly, G. A. 407
Kelly, J. R. 353, 355, 360
Kelly, M. 700
Kelly, S. 828, 829
Kelly, W. H. 127, 130
Kelman, H. 591
Kennedy, Edward M. 906
Kenney, M. 637
Kent, M. V. 385
Keohane, R. O. 155
Kern, H. 710
Kerr, S. 345, 378
Kerramilli, M. K. 639

Kessel, T. 243, 248, 249, 251, 252, 253,
    256, 257, 682, 687
Kets de Vries, M. F. R. 649
Kettl, D. E. 573
Key, V. O. 143
Keynes, J. M. 94
Keys, C. B. 26
Khanna, T. 661
Kidder, D. L. 216
Kidder, J. T. 315
Kidwall, R. 432
Kieser, Alfred 39, 109, 266, 309, 316, 352,
    382, 386, 435, 465–6, 472–3, 476,
    478–9, 489–90, 529, 594, 598–620,
    633, 637, 647, 665, 737, 868, 922, 930
Kiesler, C. A. 328, 344
Kilduff, M. 636, 637, 648
Killing, P. 686, 688
Killingsworth, M. R. 98
Kilman, R. H. 72, 358
Kim, D. H. 308, 357, 400, 407, 465, 537,
    611, 701, 702, 717, 718, 865, 866, 868,
    869, 873, 880, 881
Kim, J.-Y. 332, 339, 340
Kim, K. I. 638
Kimberly, J. R. 357, 434
Kindleberger, C. P. 634
King, M. J. 282
Kirscheimer, O. 144
Kislev, Y. 101
Kitschelt, H. P. 223, 226
Kiyosawa, T. 504
Kjellberg, A. 448, 450
Klages, H. 199, 201, 202, 203, 210, 211,
    212
Klandermans, B. 222
Klein, B. 107
Klein, P. G. 107
Klein, W. 243
Kleiner, A. 68, 587
Klepper, S. 101
Klick, H. D. 803
Klimecki, R. 65, 68, 70, 72
Kline, S. J. 100, 102
Klink, M. 370
Kluckhohn, Clyde 121, 127, 130, 199
Kmieciak, P. 199
Knapp, A. 812
Knie, A. 284, 291
Knight, J. 96
Knorr Cetina, Karin 129
Kobrin, S. J. 647
Koch, Stefan 195, 198–216, 923, 930
Koch, U. 619
Kocka, Jürgen 168, 177
Koestler, A. 780
Kofman, F. 357
Kogut, B. 107, 110, 253, 267, 619, 632,
    636, 640, 642, 658, 685, 688, 689,
    692, 703, 705, 805, 814
Kogut, I. 710
Kohama, H. 721
Kojima, K. 721

Kolb, D. 74, 78, 357, 403, 660, 772, 787,
    788, 824, 849, 856, 858, 863
Kolb, S. 923
Kompa, A. 205
Konno, N. 72, 272, 493, 499, 500, 502,
    511, 719, 780, 781, 830, 905, 922, 930
Koput, K. W. 278, 320, 332, 657, 733
Korhonen, P. 617
Kornai, J. 243, 681, 690, 693
Kosaka, S. 511
Koselleck, R. 358
Kotani, K. 831
Kothari, R. 153
Kotler, P. 810
Kotter, J. B. 563, 566
Kotter, J. P. 312, 894, 899
Krackhart, D. 687
Krantz, J. 473, 476, 478, 479
Krcmar, H. 778, 812
Krebsbach-Gnath, Camilla 122, 397,
    462–80, 519, 825, 829, 868, 875, 879,
    883, 886–900, 922–3, 928, 930–1
Kreikebaum, H. 364
Kreitner, R. 18
Kreps, D. M. 90, 92, 95
Kreuter, A. 65
Kreuzig, H. W. 69
Kriesberg, L. 222, 574
Kristiansen, C. M. 200
Kroeber, Alfred 121
Krugman, P. 642, 643
Krull, D. S. 335, 345
Krupp, C. 284
Kubicek, H. 810
Kubik, J. 182, 183
Kubr, M. 463, 466, 467, 468, 479
Kuchhar, R. 429
Kuhn, T. S. 178
Kuisel, R. 179
Kulatilaka, N. 640
Kulik, J. 375
Kumar, K. 716
Kumar, R. 371, 381
Kumer, P. K. 491
Kunda, G. 42, 369
Kunifuji, S. 830
Kunitomo, R. 838
Kurbjuweit, D. 463, 464, 472, 477, 478
Kurke, L. 518
Küster, N. 462
Kuznets, S. 802
Kwolek-Folland, A. 180
Kyllönen, M. 449

LaCapra, Dominick 177
Ladd, D. 26
LaFarge, V. V. S. 371
Lainema, M. 433, 434, 437, 739
Lake, D. 310
Lall, S. 716, 721, 722–3
Lamoreaux, N. R. 170
Lampel, J. 540
Lancaster, K. L. 465

Landsman, W. R. 796
Lane, Christel 253, 424, 628–9, 657, 699–712, 716, 737, 741, 745, 922, 928, 932
Lane, P. J. 685, 692, 693
Lane, S. J. 683, 684, 686, 687, 688, 689, 690
Lange, A. 463
Langford, N. 379
Lant, T. K. 328, 329, 332, 335
Lanzara, G. F. 49, 50
LaPalombara, Joseph 12, 137–57, 322, 488–9, 557–78, 923, 927–8, 931
LaPorte, T. 149, 287, 383, 576
Larivée, S. 23
Larson, J. R., Jr 25, 26, 28
Larson, M. S. 310
Larsson, R. 657, 662, 663, 733, 734, 735, 736, 749
Larwood, L. 468
Lasagna, L. 903
Lash, S. 52
Lasswell, Harold D. 149, 558
Latham, G. P. 23, 335
Latour, Bruno 50, 51, 125–6, 128, 287
Latow, B. 719
Lau, C. M. 682
Laughlin, R. 45, 246, 247
Laurent, A. 632, 642, 648
Lauschke, K. 166, 171
Lave, J. 42, 49, 51, 264, 499, 828
Law, J. 49, 51, 287
Lawler, E. E. 803
Lawrence, P. R. 62, 317, 318, 319, 328, 588, 640, 645, 717, 809 n., 903
Lawrence, T. 706
Lazarus, R. S. 372
Leach, Edmund R. 129, 132, 345
Lear, J. 905
Leberl, D. 364
Lederach, J. P. 590
Lee, C. R. 465
Lee, D. H. K. 227
Lee, H. 638
Lee, K. M. 720, 722
Lee, S. 657, 718
Leeb, Axel 477
Leeuw, F. L. 559
Lehr, W. 292, 294
Lei, D. 398, 492, 582, 593, 760, 763
Leibenstein, H. 804
Lengel, R. H. 519, 520, 521, 522, 526, 527, 528, 532
Lenhardt, Uwe 38, 294, 316, 508, 676, 824, 865–83, 923, 930, 931
Lenin, V. I. 154
Leonard-Barton, D. 72, 267, 272, 309–10, 491, 507, 508
Leontyev, A. N. 49
Lerner, D. 149
Leroy, F. 328, 330, 344
Lester, S. 726
Leung, C. K. 725

Lev, B. 807, 811
Levi-Strauss, Claude 129
Levin, M. 141–2, 559, 562, 568, 575
Levine, J. M. 25, 26
Levinson, H. 475
Levinthal, D. A. 24, 39, 103, 108, 247, 274, 276, 311, 318, 320, 331, 337, 435, 492, 525, 561, 613, 615, 617–18, 639, 645, 668–9, 681, 689, 691, 718, 867–9, 880, 903
Levitas, E. 429
Levitt, B. 29, 38–9, 64, 67, 69, 106, 125, 266, 271, 308, 339, 354, 358, 363, 377, 379, 382, 398–9, 430, 435, 508, 548, 582, 599, 608, 613–14, 616, 699, 702–3, 718, 739, 757, 866, 867, 922, 931
Levitt, E. A. 332, 334
Levy, S. 155, 157, 267
Lewin, A. Y. 314
Lewin, Kurt 63, 71, 75, 199, 357, 410–11, 584, 591, 775
Lewontin, Richard 121
Li, J. 639
Liang, D. W. 26
Lieber, R. B. 475, 477, 478, 479
Liebeskind, J. P. 107, 267
Lievegoed, B. C. 63
Liker, J. K. 633, 637
Likert, J. 75, 589
Likert, R. 63, 75, 421, 589, 803, 809
Lilja, Kari 396, 398, 428–43, 474, 763, 887, 923, 930
Lillrank, P. 320, 661
Lim, J. S. 638
Limlingan, V. S. 723, 725
Lincoln, J. R. 709
Lindblom, C. E. 142, 565
Lindholm, N. 659
Lindzey, G. 199
Linenthal, E. T. 165
Linstead, S. 35, 45
Linton, R. 120, 125
Lippert, I. 448, 707, 708, 710
Lipshitz, Raanan 400, 404, 407, 410, 475, 566, 584, 739, 755, 757–72, 890–1, 894–6, 922–3, 928
Litterer, J. A. 75
Littlepage, G. E. 26
Ljungberg, F. 740
Llewellyn, S. 246
Loasby, B. L. 850
Lockart, C. 155
Locke, E. A. 23, 335
Löfgren, O. 131
Loftus, E. F. 328
Lombardi Bullen, M. 803, 804
Lorange, P. 430, 657, 665
Lord, R. G. 20
Lorsch, J. 62, 317–19, 328, 429–30, 432–4, 440–1, 588, 640, 645, 717, 903
Louis, M. R. 72, 353, 358
Lounamaa, P. H. 247, 613

Lovas, B. 264, 265, 266, 278
Loveridge, R. 318
Lowenberg, G. L. 143
Lowenthal, D. 182
Lowie, Robert 121
Lu, Y. 310, 677, 688
Lubatkin, M. 685
Luce, R. 38
Luckman, T. 41, 64, 351, 457, 636, 689, 899
Lüdtke, A. 177
Luhmann, N. 52, 68 n., 76, 602
Lui, James 726
Lui, T. L. 717
Luig, M. 448
Lullies, V. 72
Lundberg, C. C. 70, 72, 77, 78, 353, 358, 760
Lundin, R. 336, 551, 671
Lundvall, B.-A. 703, 704, 705
Lungwitz, R. 245, 255
Luria, A. R. 49
Luthans, F. 18
Luther, Martin 185
Lyles, Marjorie A. 17, 40, 64–5, 70, 77, 244–5, 358, 398, 582, 628, 648, 657, 664, 670, 681–94, 717, 868–9, 923, 925, 930
Lyman, S. F. 222
Lyotard, J. 43

McAdam, D. 222
McAllister, D. J. 371
McCallion, S. W. 172
McCarthy, J. H. 222
McColl-Kennedy, J. 810
McCormick, S. 640
McCraw, T. K. 169
McCulloch, W. 509
McDonald, S. 51
MacDonald, S. 525
MacDuffie, J. P. 809
McEvily, B. 688
McFertridge, D. 635
McGill, M. E. 398, 582, 593, 760, 763
McGrath, J. E. 17, 27, 351, 352, 353, 355, 360, 364
McGregor Burns, J. 418
McGregor, D. 421, 587, 809
McGuire, W. J. 76
Macharzina, Klaus 247, 275, 627, 631–50, 704, 716, 923, 924, 932
Macher, Jeffrey T. 12, 89–111, 924, 926
Machlup, F. 492, 802
McHugh, P. 447
MacIntosh, N. B. 519, 521
MacIver, E. 433, 434
McKelvey, B. 62, 606, 608
McKenna, R. 829
McKern, B. 648
McKersie, R. B. 589
McKiernan, P. 311, 432, 639
McKnight, William 419

McLean, E. 828, 833, 841
McLean, R. I. G. 807
McLean Parks, J. 216
McLeod, R. 526
McManus, J. 635
MacMillan, I. C. 273
MacMurrer, D. 801
McNutty, T. 429, 432, 433, 434, 438
Magee, S. P. 635
Maher, K. J. 20
Mahler, J. 141, 559, 560, 566
Mahnke, V. 71, 681
Mahnkopf, B. 447
Mahon, J. 207, 665
Mahon, R. 448
Maier, Günter W. 13, 14–29, 43, 352,
     372, 377–8, 380, 383–4, 464, 867, 903,
     923
Mair, L. 119
Majkgård, A. 639
Makhija, M. V. 663, 665, 688, 729
Makino, S. 682, 684
Malerba, F. 98, 101, 102, 104, 105
Malhotra, Y. 518
Malik, F. 68
Malinowski, B. 120, 284
Malmström, L. 342
Malone, Michael S. 491, 536, 740, 743,
     794, 795, 799, 805
Malsch, T. 255
Mambrey, P. 284, 285
Mandl, G. 810
Mandl, H. 15, 207
Mandler, G. 199, 201
Mann, F. C. 63
Mannheim, K. 36
Manocchia, M. 903
Mansfield, E. 100, 103
Manz, C. C. 27
Mao Zedong 570
Maravelias, C. 734, 736, 742, 747
March, James G. 3, 15, 29, 38–40, 63–7,
     69, 77, 97, 103, 106, 125, 140–2,
     149–50, 176, 247, 266, 271, 274–6,
     308, 311, 312, 318, 332–4, 337–9, 345,
     354, 358, 363, 375, 377, 379–80, 382,
     386, 398–400, 430, 434–5, 437, 442,
     466, 474, 492, 508, 529, 536–8, 544,
     548, 561–3, 582, 586–7, 599–602,
     605–6, 608–18, 638, 699, 702–3,
     717–18, 733, 739, 746, 757, 762,
     865–9, 873, 880, 903, 922–3, 928, 931
Marcus, G. 131
Marer, P. 681, 683, 684, 694
Markides, C. 273, 274
Markle, G. E. 287
Markóczy, L. 659, 682, 684, 687
Markus, M. L. 520, 521, 522, 523, 524,
     525
Marr, R. 803
Marriott, F. 464
Marshall, A. 89, 111
Martell, R. F. 26

Martin, Bob L. 840
Martin, J. 72, 353, 358, 528
Martin, T. 449
Martinez, J. 648
Marx, Karl 36, 166, 167
Marz, Lutz 105, 245, 256, 276, 282–93,
     358, 386, 423, 476, 505, 829, 858, 867,
     869, 882, 889, 891, 922, 924
Maslow, A. H. 202
Mason, L. 520
Masten, S. E. 107
Matsubara, T. 371
Matthies, H. 448
Mattimore, K. L. 809
Maturana, H. 68 n., 71
Mauss, Marcel 40, 121, 129, 130
Mavrinac, S. C. 807
May, E. R. 157
May, Karl 179
Maybey, C. 778
Mayes, D. G. 311, 432
Mayhew, D. 143, 562
Mayntz, Renate 148, 150, 287, 558
Mead, G. H. 36, 41, 246, 636, 649
Mead, Margaret 118, 121, 122
Means, B. 381
Means, G. C. 559
Meckling, W. H. 317
Meehan, J. 107
Mehra, A. 636
Meindl, J. R. 328
Mellar, T. 255
Menon, A. 214
Merck, George W. 419
Merkens, Hans 37, 110, 196, 242–59,
     457, 670, 681–2, 689, 869, 922–3, 925,
     929
Merli, G. 447
Mertlik, P. 249, 250, 252, 254, 257
Merton, R. 40, 512, 604, 805
Mesquita, B. 371
Metcalfe, S. 100, 101
Metes, G. 735, 736, 740
Meulemann, H. 203
Meyer, A. 207, 212, 213
Meyer, J. 210, 211, 345, 541, 604, 613
Meyer, M. W. 152, 271
Meyerson, D. E. 410
Mezias, J. 329, 690
Meznar, M. B. 43, 53
Michels, Robert 36, 139–40, 144
Mickler, O. 245, 255
Middleton, D. 49
Miglani, A. 223, 224
Mikula, B. 247
Mikula, G. 378
Miles, R. E. 355, 357, 699, 705, 735
Milgate, M. 89
Milgrom, P. 96
Milhofer, P. 224 n.
Miller, D. 223, 224, 273, 338, 340, 357,
     431, 434, 539
Miller, J. H. 127

Miller, N. E. 245
Miller, P. 181
Miller, R. B. 810
Milliken, F. J. 328, 329, 332, 334, 335,
     341, 528
Mills, A. J. 603
Mills, C. W. 168
Mills, D. Q. 809 n.
Milmer, K. 417
Milward, H. B. 559
Miner, A. S. 272, 274, 332, 333, 339, 340,
     690
Miner, J. B. 404
Mintinko, M. 518
Mintz, M. 906
Mintzberg, H. 63, 274, 308, 357, 518,
     540, 549, 550, 551, 604, 739
Mitchell, T. R. 336
Mitroff, I. 72, 223, 224, 473
Mittman, J. 212
Miyahara, M. 831
Mizruchi, M. 429
Mizuno, S. 371
Mjoen, H. 688, 690
Mladek, J. 244, 252
Mody, A. 661
Moe, T. 141
Moesel, D. 429
Mohrman, A. M., Jr and S. A. 29
Moingeon, B. 64, 65, 464, 699, 702, 868,
     886
Monks, R. 429
Montgomery, J. 518
Moon, J. 638
Moore, B. 168
Moore, Dave 760
Moore, L. F. 72, 353, 358
Moore, W. E. 352
Móra, M. 243
Morecroft, J. D. W. 68, 789
Moreland, R. L. 25, 26
Morgan, G. 47, 74, 179, 536, 552, 717,
     869, 936
Morgenthau, Hans 145, 585
Morgeson, F. P. 28
Morikawa, H. 169, 170
Morill, C. 592
Morishita, K. 722
Morling, B. 20
Morrill, C. 582
Morris, J. 370, 706, 709, 710
Morrison, A. J. 641, 647
Morrison, A. M. 420
Morrison, M. 464
Motowildo, S. J. 371
Moulin, H. 96
Mouritsen, J. 44
Mouton, J. S. 63, 416, 421, 589
Mowery, D. C. 98, 108, 110, 658, 690
Mückenberger, U. 448
Mueller, F. 319
Muldur, U. 447
Müller-Jentsch, W. 450

Mulrooney, C. 778, 788
Mumby, D. K. 369
Mumford, E. 473, 475, 477
Munro, R. 44
Murgatroyd, S. J. 603
Murray, A. 25
Murray, E. 665
Murray, E. A. 207
Murray, R. P. 411
Muskie, Edward 227
Myant, M. *et al.* 249, 250, 251, 252, 253, 254
Myatt, J. 492

Nadler, D. A. 70, 519
Nagel, R. N. 735
Nahapiet, J. 270, 805, 806
Naidu, G. M. 638
Nakagawa, K. 171–2
Nam, S. 336
Nanda, A. 711
Nandy, A. 124
Nanus, B. 284
Narus, J. A. 688
Narver, J. C. 212, 214
Nasierowski, W. 247
Nass, C. 520
Naugle, D. G. 802
Naylor, J. C. 21
Neale, M. A. 717
Neeman, Z. 94
Negandhi, A. R. 643
Neill, John 423–4
Neisser, U. 407
Nelson, J. 429
Nelson, R. 430
Nelson, R. R. 39, 62, 65, 90–1, 100–1,
   105, 108–9, 164, 173, 175, 264, 274,
   332, 491–2, 529, 601, 606, 642, 691,
   737
Nerdinger, F. W. 212
Nesse, R. M. 371
Neubauer, F. 434
Neuberger, O. 205
Neumann, P. 18
Neustadt, R. 157
Nevins, A. 165
Nevis, E. C. 245, 252, 254, 354, 465, 704,
   708, 709, 710, 758, 759, 760
Newell, A. 335
Newman, K. L. 637
Newman, P. 89
Newman, W. 313, 432
Newstrom, J. W. 463
Nichol, L. 831
Nicholson, J. B. 141, 559, 560, 566
Nicolini, Davide 11, 35–54, 150, 167,
   179, 181, 185, 198, 268, 308, 384, 458,
   465, 586, 594, 610, 729, 904, 921, 929
Nicoll, D. 419
Nicotera, A. M. 156
Nietzsche, Friedrich 181
Nilsson, K. 245, 247

Nisbett, R. 21, 272, 328
Nishida, Kitaro 499
Noda, T. 272, 277
Noe, R. A. 23
Noelle-Neumann, E. 199, 202
Nohria, N. 642, 644, 661, 699, 708
Nolan, M. 179
Nollen, S. D. 637
Nonaka, Ikujiro 1–7, 29, 39, 65, 70, 72,
   75, 78, 89, 106, 110, 162, 174, 179, 206,
   247, 267, 272, 283, 308, 316, 319,
   335–7, 351, 353, 375–6, 382, 384,
   398–400, 403, 407, 424, 430, 433,
   442, 449, 465, 487, 491–513, 519–20,
   528, 552, 557, 583, 589, 592, 601, 632,
   639–40, 642, 648, 670–1, 674–5, 686,
   691–2, 699, 701–5, 709, 716, 718–19,
   733, 738–9, 743, 746, 757, 780–1, 795,
   812, 823, 827–45, 870, 879, 898,
   904–5, 913, 921–38
Nood, M. L. 153
Noordewier, T. 209, 214
Norburn, D. 327, 338
Nordhaug, O. 802
Nordström, K. A. 639
Normann, R. 72, 329, 358, 548, 550, 857
North, K. 796, 812, 813
Northcraft, G. B. 520, 526, 527, 530
Norton, D. P. 61, 808, 809
Noss, C. 65, 465, 466, 467
Novick, P. 163, 167, 171
Nowotny, H. 351
Nutzinger, H. G. 447
Nystrom, P. C. 270, 272, 338, 345, 536,
   537, 543, 616

Obeysekere, G. 132
O'Brien, P. 177, 181
O'Connor, E. J. 356
O'Connor, K. M. 17, 27
Odagiri, H. 103
Odella, F. 37, 41
Oehlke, P. 449
Oehman, A. 18
Oesterle, Michael-Jörg 247, 275, 627,
   631–50, 704, 716, 923, 924, 932
Offe, C. 448
Ohmae, Kenichi 186, 642
Ohno, Taiichi 172–3
Okamoto, H. 839
O'Keefe, R. M. 718
O'Leary-Kelly, A. M. 16
Oliver, J. 803
Oliver, N. 709
Olsen, J. P. 38, 64, 67, 97, 140, 334, 345,
   379, 398–400, 536–8, 548, 562, 582,
   609–12, 618, 718, 757, 762, 865–7,
   873, 880, 903, 922, 923
Olson, M. 38
Olve, N.-G. 536, 549, 734
O'Neill, R. 850, 860
Opaschowski, H. W. 203, 213
Orléan, A. 221

Orlikowski, W. J. 833
Orosel, G. O. 94
Orr, J. 42, 718
Orsenigo, L. 100
Orton, J. D. 603
Oesterle, Michael-Jörg 777
Ostrogorski, Moisie 140, 144
Otley, D. 314 n.
Ouchi, W. 40, 740
Overmeer, Wim 475, 566, 739, 755,
   757–72, 890–1, 894–6, 922–3, 928
Owen, Harrison 781
Oxley, J. E. 110, 658, 690
Oz, S. 400, 410, 763, 768

Pablo, A. L. 548
Paez, D. 372
Palumbo, D. J. 138, 559
Panebianco, Angelo 144, 154, 559,
   561
Panków, W. 247, 248, 251, 254, 256
Papalekas, J. C. 284
Papanastassiou, M. 640
Papow, D. M. 827
Papow, J. P. 827
Parent, S. 23
Pareto, Vilfredo 138
Park, O. S. 371
Parkhe, A. 684
Parks, A. E. 909
Parks, D. 525
Parsons, Talcott 38, 40, 168, 169, 586
Pascale, R. 419, 472
Pasmore, W. A. 446
Patel, P. 100, 103
Patriotta, G. 310, 316
Patterson, S. C. 143
Pautzke, G. 65, 70, 72
Pavitt, K. 100, 103, 642
Pavlov, I. 14, 18, 377
Pawlowsky, Peter 11, 39, 61–81, 207, 283,
   382, 471, 503, 632, 660, 749, 755,
   775–91, 794–814, 858, 869, 889, 895,
   923–5, 931, 933
Payne, R. L. 329
Pearce, J., III 428, 429, 432, 434, 436,
   437
Pearce, J. L. 684
Pearce, R. D. 640
Pearlson, K. 828
Pearn, M. 778, 788
Pearson, R. D. 546
Peck, M. J. 103
Pederson, P. 465
Pedler, M. 65, 74, 417, 778, 788, 886
Peirce, C. 36, 41
Pekrun, R. 370
Pelled, L. H. 370
Pells, R. 179
Peltzman, S. 913
Peng, M. W. 681, 682, 690, 693
Penn, R. 474
Penrose, E. T. 108, 109, 638, 639

Pentland, B. 519, 600
Perich, R. 352, 353, 355, 356, 364
Perkins, D. N. T. 762
Perkoff, B. 811
Perlmutter, H. V. 632, 642, 644, 648
Perrone, V. 688
Perrow, C. 36, 383, 562, 563
Peter, E. 448
Peters, L. H. 356
Peters, T. 416, 505, 604
Petersen, J. C. 287
Peterson, Ford Motor Co.
    president 419
Petkoff, B. 778, 795
Petrella, R. 447
Petri, K. 781
Petterson, R. B. 688
Pettigrew, A. 123, 247, 311–12, 319, 429,
    432–4, 438, 587, 855, 858
Peukert, D. 177
Pfeffer, J. 62, 275, 313, 425, 429, 559, 563,
    566, 577, 587, 809
Phillips, N. 706
Phillips, W. A. 381
Phills, J. A. 472, 473
Piasecki, M. 71
Piatetsky-Shapiro, G. 832
Pickel, A. 244
Pickus, P. S. 809
Pinch, T. 287
Pinchot, C. 577
Pinchot, E. 577
Pinchot, G., III 205, 403, 504
Pintrich, P. R. 23
Piore, M. 164, 716
Pisano, G. 108, 109, 110, 491, 492, 827,
    829
Piscitello, D. 293, 296
Platz, S. T. 420
Plumpe, Werner 175
Pocztovski, A. 245
Pogash, R. 71
Pohl, A. 807
Pohlmann, M. 255
Polanyi, M. 48, 72, 100, 267, 336, 494,
    505, 660 n., 718, 829, 904, 924
Pomper, P. 163, 177, 178
Pondy, L. R. 74, 593
Pontusson, J. 152
Pooyan, A. 356
Popp, W. 185
Pöppel, E. 353
Popper, K. 96
Popper, M. 758, 761, 762, 763, 768
Porac, J. 70, 271, 336
Porras, J. I. 275, 286, 294–5, 296, 417,
    419, 507
Porter, M. E. 63
Porter, M. E. 540, 542, 547, 631, 640,
    641, 642, 643, 644, 709, 829
Posner, G. J. 16
Post, J. E. 207
Postman, L. 334

Powell, W. W. 127, 148, 245, 278, 310,
    320, 332, 541, 561, 604, 613, 641, 657,
    699–702, 733–5
Power, J. 520, 523, 524
Power, M. 45
Poynter, T. 642
Poznanska, J. K. 252, 254
Poznański, K. Z. 252, 254
Prahalad, C. K. 72, 108, 110, 267, 269,
    275, 313, 447, 491, 536, 540–2, 640,
    642, 648, 736, 802, 805
Prange, Christiane 13, 14–29, 43, 352,
    372, 377–8, 380, 383–4, 464, 672, 867,
    903, 923
Preiss, K. 735
Preissler, H. 207
Pressman, J. 149
Presthus, R. 36
Preston, L. E. 804
Prigogine, I. 509, 829
Probst, G. 14, 65, 68, 70, 72, 672, 778,
    779, 780, 782
Prokesh, S. 582, 593
Prusak, L. 206, 508, 518, 828
Prusko, G. F. 789
Pucik, V. 663, 672
Pulic, A. 798
Putnam, L. 369
Putnam, R. 449, 758, 763, 771, 805
Pyke, F. 449

Quick, J. C. 356
Quinn, J. B. 61, 274, 491, 505, 827
Quinn, N. 121, 127, 128
Quinn, R. E. 63, 137, 308, 357, 411

Raasch, S. 448
Rabin, M. 97
Rabinow, P. 181
Rabl, K. 810
Racht, D. 222, 223
Radcliffe-Brown, A. R. 120
Rafaeli, A. 369, 370
Raff, D. M. G. 170
Raghuram, S. 336
Rahim, M. A. 589
Raifa, H. 38, 588
Rainey, H. G. 559
Raisinghani, D. 550, 551
Rall, Wilhelm 471
Ralston, D. A. 204, 213
Ramanantsoa, B. 328, 330, 344
Ramesh, C. R. 371
Ramirez, R. 549, 550, 857
Ramistad, P. M. 809
Randall, R. 850
Ranger, T. 182
Ranke, Leopold von 163, 165, 166, 170,
    171, 174, 184
Rao, C. P. 639
Rao, T. R. 638
Rapaport, D. 382

Rappaport, A. 119 n., 121, 807
Rapping, L. 98
Rapson, R. L. 373
Raske, M. 206
Raub, Steffen 465, 471, 487–8, 518–32,
    640, 646, 675, 739, 778–80, 782, 828,
    868, 924, 930
Rayner, B. 759, 762
Reason, D. 129
Reason, P. 475
Reber, G. 17
Redding, S. G. 717, 724
Reddington, K. 26
Redfield, R. 119, 120, 125
Reed, M. 46, 50
Rehäuser, J. 812
Rehder, R. R. 637
Reichers, A. E. 372
Reichheld, F. F. 796, 810
Reid, S. D. 638
Rein, M. 584
Reinhardt, Rüdiger 11, 62, 65, 68–9, 71,
    76, 80, 207, 382, 503, 632, 755,
    775–91, 794–814, 858, 889, 895,
    923–4, 931, 933
Reinmöller, Patrick 206, 283, 424,
    519–20, 528, 699, 701, 709, 719, 739,
    823, 827–45, 879, 898, 921, 924
Reisberg, D. 382
Reischauer, C. 463
Reither, F. 69
Renaud, S. 371
Rennie, M. 798
Resnik, L. B. 49
Revans, R. W. 74, 418, 788
Rey, F. 804
Reynolds, M. 778
Rice, R. E. 520, 523, 524, 525
Richards, D. 257
Ridderstråle, J. 641, 647
Riegler, Claudius H. 75, 154, 396–7, 423,
    446–58, 928, 930
Rifkin, J. 351
Ring, P. S. 699, 704, 705
Ringland, G. 850, 862
Riordan, M. H. 99
Rist, R. C. 138, 157, 559
Ritzer, G. 604
Rivers, W. H. R. 120
Roberts, C. 68
Roberts, J. 96
Roberts, K. H. 383
Robinson, S. L. 16
Robinson, W. 26
Roche, E. M. 646
Roderick, C. 778, 788
Rodrigues, S. 321, 660, 661, 670
Roehl, H. 207
Roehl, T. 802
Roethlisberger, F. J. 586
Rogers, E. M. 72, 125, 721
Rogers, J. 447, 448, 449
Rogers, R. 284, 286

Rogoff, B. 49
Rogow, A. 149
Rogulic, B. 681
Rokeach, M. 199, 201
Rolander, D. 642, 644, 645
Romanelli, E. 313, 323, 339, 432, 463 n.
Romer, P. M. 103
Romero, A. A. 27
Romhardt, K. 778, 779, 780, 782, 783
Rondinelli, D. A. 236
Roos, G. 794, 795, 796, 797, 799, 812
Roos, J. 69, 71, 636, 641, 657, 665, 687,
    690, 691, 794, 795, 796, 797, 799, 812
Rosa, J. A. 336
Rosaldo, R. 131
Rose, N. L. 98
Rose, R. 157, 573, 576
Rosell, S. A. 862
Rosen, M. 127
Rosen, S. 97
Rosenberg, N. 100, 101, 102, 103, 108
Rosenbloom, R. S. 104
Rosenbrock, Rolf 38, 294, 316, 508, 676,
    824, 865–83, 923, 930, 931
Rosener, J. B. 420
Rosenfield, S. 717, 726
Rosenstiel, Lutz von 13, 14–29, 43, 195,
    198–216, 352, 372, 377–8, 380, 383–4,
    464, 867, 903, 923, 930
Rosenzweig, J. E. 68
Ross, A. 139
Ross, J. 335
Ross, K. 167
Ross, L. 272
Ross, M. 335, 344
Ross, R. 68, 778
Rost, D. 361
Rotchford, N. L. 351, 352, 364
Roth, George 784
Roth, K. 647
Rothman, Jay 12, 36, 156, 237, 318, 384,
    387, 409, 425, 430, 438, 440, 456,
    472, 489, 562, 582–94, 875, 932
Rothschild, M. 547
Rottenburg, R. 245
Rotter, J. B. 328
Rourke, F. E. 153
Rousseau, D. M. 28, 216, 604
Røvik, K.-A. 457
Rowan, B. 345, 541, 604, 613
Rowlinson, M. 123
Rubenstein, R. 149
Rubin, I. M. 849, 856, 858, 863
Rubin, J. 588
Rudy, I. A. 518 n., 524
Rueter, H. H. 600
Ruggles, R. 828
Rugman, A. M. 635, 640
Ruling, C.-C. 672
Rumelhart, D. E. 69
Rumelt, R. 109
Rupesinghe, K. 590
Ryan, P. 802

Sabel, C. 164, 716
Sackmann, S. A. 72, 73, 803, 804, 868 n.
Sadler, Philip 157, 205, 237, 252, 274,
    311–12, 395–6, 398, 415–26, 428,
    432, 476, 572, 674, 763, 869, 882,
    893, 931
Sadowski, D. 804
Sahlin-Andersson, K. 339, 537, 539
Sahlins, M. 118, 121, 123, 126, 132
Sakakibara, K. 103
Sako, M. 704, 706, 709, 710
Salancik, G. 70, 429, 577
Salk, J. E. 648, 684, 685, 686, 687, 688,
    689, 690, 691, 692, 693
Salzer, M. 337, 537
Sampler, J. 269
Sanchez, R. 733
Sandelands, L. E. 70, 273, 617
Sander, F. 588
Sandole, D. J. D. 574
Sanger, M. B. 141–2, 559, 562, 568, 575
Santalainen, Timo J. 396, 398, 428–43,
    617, 763, 887, 923, 930
Santangelo, G. D. 640
Sapir, Edward 121
Saro-Wiwas, Ken 231 n.
Sarvary, M. 464, 467
Sasajima, Y. 448
Saunders, C. 521, 526
Saussure, Ferdinand de 177
Savage, C. M. 736, 739
Saxenian, A. 278, 716
Saxton, M. J. 358
Sayer, A. 716
Sayles, L. 403, 419
Scarbrough, H. 318–19
Schacht, O. 659, 665, 666, 677
Schank, R. 19, 599, 827
Scharfstein, D. 94
Scharpf, Fritz 148, 150, 151, 558
Schein, E. H. 63, 72, 74, 177, 179, 209,
    247, 353–5, 357–8, 380, 410, 416,
    422–3, 467, 529, 583, 758, 760, 762,
    866–9, 880, 904, 931
Scheinman, L. 146
Schelsky, H. 284
Schendel, D. 542, 827
Scherer, Klaus R. 18, 73, 78, 249, 306,
    369–89, 410, 471, 493, 527, 529, 867,
    931
Scherer, U. 370
Scherler, Patrik 230
Schiller, F. 162
Schlake, O. 850
Schlink, F. J. 905
Schmidt, E. 448
Schmidt, G. W. 26
Schmidt, H. 803
Schmitz, J. 520, 521, 523, 524
Schmögnerova, B. 254
Schneider, B. 372
Schneider, L. S. 649
Schneider, S. 25, 70, 269, 381

Schneider, Ursula 62, 446, 503, 632,
    756, 794–814, 924
Schnierer, T. 202
Schoeller, W. F. 351
Scholl, W. 69
Schomer, C. 243, 252
Schön, D. A. 3, 15, 17, 40, 63–6, 69–70,
    74, 76–7, 137, 150, 198, 209, 214, 246,
    272, 276, 283–4, 308, 357, 376, 390,
    399–400, 403, 405–7, 410, 430, 438,
    442, 451, 465, 467, 492, 494, 511, 535,
    537, 544, 563, 582, 584, 587, 589–90,
    592, 594, 611, 649, 660, 669, 702, 718,
    737, 757–62, 766, 770–1, 855, 867,
    870, 886, 921–3, 928
Schoonhoven, C. B. 72
Schrader, S. 24
Schreyögg, G. 62, 65, 68, 447, 465, 466,
    467
Schroder, H. M. 69, 71, 331, 333, 374
Schuler, R. S. 809 n.
Schultz, R. 829
Schultz, T. W. 802
Schulz, M. 608, 619
Schumann, J. 62
Schumann, M. 224 n.
Schumann, W. 247
Schumpeter, Joseph A. 100, 109, 111,
    139, 185, 310, 927
Schunk, D. H. 23
Schutz, Alfred 36, 41
Schwan, E. S. 803
Schwaninger, M. 247
Schwartz, B. 17, 18
Schwartz, P. 543, 544, 850
Schwartz, S. H. 199, 204
Schwarz, M. 100
Schweiger, D. M. 647
Schwenk, C. R. 70, 328, 691
Schwerdtfeger, O. A. 227, 230
Scott, B. 850, 862
Scott, I. 829
Scott, J. W. 178
Scott, R. W. 561
Scott, W. A. 71
Scott, W. R. 62, 310, 541, 604
Searle, J. R. 407
Seemann, P. 207
Seidman, H. 567
Seifert, M. 76
Seim Elvander, A. 449
Selby, R. W. 759, 760
Seligman, C. 199
Selikoff, I. J. 227
Selvini Palazzoli, M. et al. 63
Selznick, P. 36, 138, 154, 155, 314, 457,
    512, 575, 586
Semlinger, K. 699, 700, 701, 705, 706,
    708, 716
Senge, P. M. 65, 68–70, 75, 76 n., 77, 89,
    276, 312, 382, 398, 400, 407–8, 419,
    423, 428, 475, 492, 535, 563, 583, 757,
    760, 781, 786–7, 789, 860, 886

Sengenberger, W. 449
Senoo, D. 830, 837
Serieyx, Hervé 422
Serpa, R. 358
Service, E. R. 118, 121
Sethi, S. P. 226, 227
Sevón, G. 126, 127, 131, 457, 718, 719, 870
Sewell, W. H. 177
Shamir, B. 282
Shan, W. 703, 705, 710
Shani, A. 758
Shapira, Z. 616
Shapiro, A. C. 796
Shapiro, E. 472, 477, 478
Shapiro, I. 147
Sharkey, T. W. 638
Sharma, D. D. 639
Sharp, W. 153
Shaw, R. B. 762
Shea, G. P. 25
Shelanski, H. A. 107
Shenkar, O. 254, 669, 688
Shepard, H. 589
Sheppard, B. H. 26
Sherman, H. 829
Shillingford, J. 297
Shimada, J. Y. 688
Shimizu, H. 499
Shleifer, A. 429
Shook, D. E. 523
Shore, B. 131
Short, J. 520
Shout, P. 828
Shrivastava, P. 25, 64, 65, 70, 77, 223, 224, 269, 398, 544, 548, 582, 649
Shuen, A. 108, 109, 491, 492, 827, 829
Shulman, L. E. 108, 110
Shulman, S. R. 903
Sidow, H. 810
Siegert, T. 807
Silbiger, H. 26
Silverman, B. S. 110, 658, 690
Simmel, G. 138, 687
Simmons, M. 420
Simon, Herbert A. 36, 38, 66, 91–2, 97, 103, 140–1, 149, 335, 398, 491, 504, 511, 529, 584, 586, 599, 602–3, 615, 638, 647, 733, 737, 739, 810, 829
Simon, L. 670
Simonin, B. L. 669, 733
Simons, R. 314–15
Sims, Arden C. 759–60
Sims, D. 44, 605, 779
Sims, H. P., Jr 69, 70, 371
Simson, A. J. 284
Singer, B. 328
Singh, H. 828
Singh, J. V. 333
Singh, S. 640
Sinkula, J. M. 209, 212, 213, 214
Sit, F. S. 720, 725
Sitkin, S. B. 24, 273, 337, 338, 354, 383, 520, 548, 867

Sitsugi, Y. 837, 839
Sitter, L. U. 448
Sixl, K. I. 812
Skinner, B. F. 14, 18, 345
Skocpol, T. T. 147
Skowronek, S. 147
Slater, S. F. 212, 214
Slavin, R. E. 23
Sloan, Alfred P. 275
Slocum, J. W. 329, 345, 398, 582, 593, 760, 763
Slocum, K. 69, 71, 690, 691
Small, D. 828
Smircich, L. 69, 74, 476, 603
Smith, Adam 97, 566
Smith, B. 180
Smith, B. J. 68
Smith, C. 123, 247, 311, 312, 358, 887
Smith, D. 590, 758, 763, 771
Smith, D. K. 75, 267
Smith, K. G. 687
Smith, Roger 275
Smith, S. S. 143, 150, 565
Smith, T. 174
Smith-Doerr, L. 278, 320, 332, 657, 733
Smithburg, D. W. 140
Smyth, P. 832
Snehota, I. 536
Snell, R. 37
Snow, C. C. 355, 699, 705, 735
Snowdon, D. 828, 831
Snyder, E. 107
Soete, L. 642
Solinas, G. 449
Sölvell, Ö. 641
Somogyi, P. 685
Sonnemans, J. 371
Sonnichsen, R. C. 559
Sormunen, J. 525
Soulsby, A. 247, 255
Sparks, J. 733, 749
Sparks-Graham, J. 657, 662, 663
Spector, B. 463 n. 477, 760, 762, 809 n.
Spencer, Herbert 120
Spencer, L. 803
Spencer, L. M. and S. M. 29
Spencer, M. 222
Spender, J. C. 39, 43, 267, 308, 332, 339, 491, 539, 551, 703, 814, 827
Sperling, H. -J. 448, 450, 477
Spiceland, D. J. 803
Spindler, G. and L. 119, 120
Spiro, H. J. 141
Spranger, E. 199
Spratt, M. F. 809
Spreitzer, G. M. 411
Sproull, L. S. 176, 344, 375, 380, 386, 614, 615
Squire, L. R. 21
Srubar, I. 243, 244
Stablein, R. E. 70
Staehle, W. H. 364, 463, 476, 887
Stajkovic, A. D. 18

Stalin, Josef 155, 570
Stalk, G. 108, 110
Stalker, G. 62, 317, 927
Stanfill, C. 335
Staniszkis, J. 243
Star, S. L. 51, 53
Starbuck, William H. 13–14, 24, 36, 40, 70, 77, 270, 272, 305–6, 327–45, 352–4, 358, 431, 435–6, 464, 466, 472, 528, 536–7, 543, 599, 615–16, 866–7, 903, 917, 923, 929–30
Stark, D. 243, 251
Starkey, K. 699
Starr, J. A. 273
Stasser, G. 26
Stata, R. 65, 308
Staüdel, T. 69
Staute, J. 463, 475, 477
Staw, B. M. 273, 335, 370, 617
Steensma, K. 657, 670, 688, 690, 693
Stegmüller, R. 65
Stein, B. A. 886
Stein, J. 94
Steiner, G. 121
Steiner, I. D. 26
Steinfield, C. 520, 523, 524
Steinmann, H. 68
Steinmueller, W. E. 103
Stengel, M. 211
Stengers, I. 509
Stephenson, G. M. 26
Sterman, J. D. 69
Stern, J. M. 807 n.
Sternberg, R. J. 24, 29, 810
Stevenson, M. K. 21
Steward, J. 429
Steward, S. 204, 213
Stewart, G. B. 807 n.
Stewart, R. 505
Stewart, T. A. 447, 794, 795, 798, 807 n.
Steyrer, J. 462
Stigler, G. J. 93, 94
Stinchcombe, A. L. 163, 173, 309
Stocking, G. W., Jr 120
Stopford, John M. 42, 196–7, 264–78, 404, 434, 465, 505, 632, 922, 925, 929
Storey, R. 329
Strasser, H. 468
Strassman, P. A. 811
Strathern, M. 130 n.
Strati, A. 42, 50, 52, 352, 353, 355, 357, 358, 364
Straub, D. 520, 521
Strauss, A. 264
Strauss, C. 127, 128
Strebel, P. 312
Streeck, W. 447, 448, 449
Streich, R. K. 199
Streufert, S. 69, 70, 71, 331, 333, 374
Streufert, S. C. 70, 71
Strickland, O. J. 26
Strike, K. A. 16
Stroebe, W. 26

Strongman, K. T. 373
Stubbart, C. 69, 74, 476
Stucky, S. 42
Sturgeon, T. J. 710
Suarez-Orozco, M. M. 119, 120
Suchman, L. 42, 51
Sull, Donald N. 272–3, 276, 298, 868, 880
Susskind, L. 588
Sutcliffe, K. 520
Sutton, R. I. 369, 370
Suzuki, Toshifumi 837, 838, 839
Sveiby, K. E. 61, 62, 491, 794, 795, 798, 799, 805, 812
Swanson, B. E. 522
Swanson, R. A. 803
Swezey, R. W. 69, 70
Swieringa, J. 266
Swigart, R. 536
Sydow, J. 76, 700, 701
Sylwan, P. 448
Szirmai, P. 684
Szulanski, G. 267, 685

Tainio, Risto 39, 109, 382, 386, 396, 398, 428–43, 465, 474, 476, 478, 489–90, 529, 594, 598–620, 633, 637, 647, 665, 737, 763, 887, 922–3, 930
Tajfel, H. 670
Takai, J. 371
Takeuchi, H. 39, 65, 70, 72, 75, 89, 106, 110, 162, 174, 179, 206, 267, 283, 316, 336–7, 351, 353, 375–6, 382, 384, 398–400, 403, 407, 430, 449, 465, 491, 493, 495, 498, 503, 505–6, 508, 510–12, 552, 557, 583, 589, 592, 601, 632, 670–1, 674–5, 691–2, 718, 780, 795, 812, 827, 830, 870, 879, 904, 913, 930
Takimoto, T. 837, 839
Tallman, S. 688, 690
Tam, S. 720, 723, 724
Tambiah, S. J. 122
Tamuz, M. 176, 375, 380, 386, 548, 614, 615
Tan, B. 526
Tan, J. J. 682
Tanoho, S. 831
Tarrow, S. 222, 223
Taylor, F. W. 216, 316, 491, 504, 586, 587
Taylor, L. A. 26
Teece, David J. 12, 89–111, 278, 320, 491–2, 635, 735, 812, 827, 829, 924, 926
Teele, Casey 276, 282–93, 386, 423, 476, 505, 829, 858, 889, 891, 922, 924
Temin, P. 165
Tenbrock, C. 797
Tenbrunsel, A. E. 717
Tenkasi, R. 14, 42
Tepper, A. 284, 285
Terpstra, R. H. 204, 213
Tesar, G. 638

Thagard, P. R. 21
Thanheiser, H. 542
Thatchenkery, T. J. 636
Théorèt, A. 550, 551
Thévenot, L. 221
Thieme, J. 244, 252, 253
Thom, N. 462
Thomas, H. 271
Thomas, J. 98
Thomas, K. 589
Thomas, W. 42, 129
Thomas-Hunt, M. 28
Thompson, E. P. 169, 177
Thompson, J. D. 62
Thompson, J. K. 637
Thompson, T. A. 223, 429
Thompson, V. 140
Thorelli, H. B. 700, 734
Thorlakson, A. J. H. 411
Thorndike, E. L. 14, 18
Thorsrud, E. 211, 591
Thulestedt, B. M. 74
Thyssen, August 174
Tichy, N. M. 312, 416, 418, 419
Tiedge, J. 362
Tindale, R. S. 25, 373
Tiratsoo, N. 170
Tirole, J. 633
Titus, W. 26
Tjosvold, D. 584, 586, 589, 593–4
Tobin, J. 796
Toffler, A. 491
Tolman, E. C. 14, 66
Tomassini, L. A. 803
Tomassini, M. 40
Tomasson, R. F. 239
Tomer, J. F. 804, 805
Tong, C. K. 720
Toniolo, G. 165
Töpfer, H. 810
Tosi, H. 329
Touama, Ryoko 823, 827–45
Touraine, A. 222, 223
Tourish, D. 527
Townley, B. 44
Toyama, Ryoko 72, 206, 283, 319, 424, 433, 442, 487, 491–513, 519–20, 528, 632, 648, 701, 703–5, 716, 719, 733, 739, 743, 780, 879, 893, 898, 904, 921, 924–5, 928, 930
Toyoda, Eiji 173
Toyoda, Kiichiro 172–3
Toyoda, Sakichi 172
Trahant, W. J. 447
Tran, Véronique 18, 73, 78, 249, 306, 369–89, 410, 471, 493, 527, 529, 867, 931
Traweek, S. 119
Trentin, B. 447
Trevino, L. K. 378, 519, 520, 521, 523, 526, 527, 528, 532
Tripp, T. M. 386
Tripsas, M. 339

Trist, E. L. 68
Trommsdorf, G. 199, 201, 204
Trompenaars, F. 421, 476
Trossmark, P. 123
Tsang, E. W. K. 46, 64, 266, 400, 447, 757, 903
Tsoukas, H. 39, 42, 512, 814
Tsui-Auch, Lai Si 313 n., 381, 505, 629, 701, 703, 716–29, 825–6, 902–17, 922–5, 930, 932
Tsurumi, E. P. 172
Tucker, B. 850, 862
Turban, E. 828, 833, 841
Turner, B. 50
Turner, J. R. 463
Turner, V. 127
Turnipseed, D. 314
Tushman, M. L. 70, 104, 313, 320, 321, 323, 339, 432, 463 n., 519
Tversky, A. 22, 97
Tyler, B. B. 541
Tyler, Edward Burnett 120
Tyre, M. J. 718

Uggla, H. 734, 736, 742
Ulich, E. 210
Ullmer, B. 828
Ulrich, D. 809
Ulrich, H. 779
Ulrich, P. 68
Ulrich, R. 248
Ulrich, U. 243
Umemoto, K. 830
Unger, R. 51
Ungson, G. R. 14, 24, 28, 29, 65, 358, 529, 717
Urata, S. 721
Urwich, L. 153
Ury, W. 588
Useem, M. 428
Ushioda, K. 831
Usui, M. 837
Uthurusamy, R. 832

Vahlne, J. -E. 631, 633, 638–9
Vaillant, K. 699, 886
Valpola, A. 434
van Bijsterveld, M. 472
van de Ven, A. H. 62, 699, 704, 705
Van de Vliert, E. 582
van den Berg, R. -J. 472
van der Heijden, Kees 80, 207, 269, 364, 475, 540, 541, 615, 759, 788, 824, 849–63, 887, 890, 895, 923, 929, 932
van der Merwe, H. 574
Van Goozen, S. 371
van Maanen, J. 25, 42, 119, 354, 369, 632, 642, 648
Van Reenen, J. 245, 250, 255, 256
Van Seters, D. A. 415, 416
Van Velsor, E. 420
Vanberg, V. 607
Vann, R. T. 163, 177, 178

Varela, F. J. 68 n., 71
Varillo, J. C. 735
Vattimo, G. 43, 51
Veranen, J. 429
Vermeulen, F. 254, 639, 669, 686
Vernon, P. E. 199
Vernon, R. 640, 641, 642
Vester, F. 68, 779
Vicari, S. 71, 632
Vickery, G. 794
Vico, Giambattista 119 n.
Victorin, A. 448
Villinger, R. 669
Virany, B. 339, 463 n.
Vishny, R. 429
Vitale, M. R. 807
Vogel, A. 475
Vogler, P. 777
Vollrath, D. A. 25, 373
von Alemann, H. 475
von Foerster, H. 68, 509
von Hippel, E. 48, 267, 718
von Krogh, G. 69, 71, 503, 510, 636,
    641, 657, 681, 685, 686, 687, 690,
    691, 692
von Oetinger, B. 465
Voss, M. 463, 464, 473
Vurdubakis, T. 297
Vygotsky, L. S. 49

Wack, Pierre 269, 851, 852
Wade, R. 720, 722
Wageman, R. 370
Wagner, J. A., III. 328
Wagner, R. K. 810
Wagner, S. 100
Wahren, H. K. 64
Waldo, D. 118
Waldron, V. R. 369, 371, 827
Walesa, Lech 255
Walker, B. 245, 255
Walker, G. 703, 705, 710
Wallace, William 146
Wallenberg, J. 449
Walls, G. 268
Walsh, J. P. 14, 24, 28, 29, 65, 358, 429,
    529, 717
Walton, R. E. 589, 809 n.
Walton, Sam 840, 843
Waltz, D. 335
Wardell, W. M. 903
Wargliem, M. 40
Warner, M. 89
Warwick, D. P. 147, 311
Waterman, R. H. 604
Waterman, R. W. 153, 561, 573, 575
Wathne, K. 687
Watson, R. 526
Watt, I. 129
Watzlawick, P. 335
Wayne, K. 64
Weakland, J. H. 335
Webb, C. 145

Webber, A. M. 384
Weber, B. 708
Weber, Christiana 238, 246, 248, 250,
    286, 306, 310, 351–65, 431, 435–6,
    660, 829, 922, 923
Weber, Max 36, 42, 120, 130, 138, 167–8,
    169, 181, 287, 369, 511, 561, 601, 602,
    603, 604
Webster, J. 523
Webster, L. 683
Weghorst, S. 831
Wegner, D. M. 26
Wehler, H.-U. 163, 168, 178
Wehrfritz, G. 726
Wei, K. 526
Weick, K. E. 37, 41, 43, 69–71, 75, 118,
    214, 245, 266, 268–70, 309, 331,
    336–7, 383, 400, 407, 457, 465, 492,
    511, 519, 525, 528, 536, 543–5, 547,
    550–1, 553, 603, 618, 727, 757, 771,
    830, 904, 929
Weiner, B. 22, 345
Weiner, E. S. C. 284
Weingart, P. 287, 293
Weinkamm, M. 211
Weir, M. 147
Weisbach, M. 429
Weisbord, M. E. 763
Weisbord, M. R. 788
Weiss, A. 15, 18, 29, 40, 64, 65, 70, 78,
    492, 544, 649
Weitz, B. 688
Weitzel, W. 430, 431, 432
Welch, I. 94
Welch, Jack 384, 419
Welch, John 312
Welge, M. K. 643
Wellhöner, V. 172
Wellman, B. 832
Welskopp, T. 166, 171
Weltz, F. 72
Wendorff, R. 351
Wenger, E. 42, 47, 51, 264, 499, 828
Wenzeler, G. 243, 244, 255
Wernerfelt, B. 108
Westenholz, A. 432
Westerman, Swedish economist 802
Westley, F. 37, 246, 308, 545, 728, 739,
    757, 929
Westney, D. E. 103, 165, 172, 644, 647,
    648
Westphal, J. D. 429, 440
Wetherbe, J. 828, 833, 841
Weyrather, I. 450
Wheeler, W. A., III. 447
Wheelwright, S. C. 65
Whetten, D. 432
Whipp, R. 855, 858
Whisler, E. W. 26
White, Hayden 177, 183
White, R. 420, 425, 642
Whitehead, A. N. 493
Whiteley, R. 810

Whitlam, P. 735
Whitley, R. 255
Whittington, R. 321
Wholey, D. R. 332
Whyte, G. 439
Whyte, W. 168
Wiegand, M. 64, 65, 76, 353, 354, 363,
    381
Wierdsma, A. 266
Wiersema, M. F. 25
Wiesenthal, H. 244, 255
Wikström, S. 72
Wildavsky, A. B. 149–50, 153, 157
Wilensky, H. L. 70, 150
Wilkins, A. 40
Wilkins, M. 492
Wilkinson, B. 709
Wilkinson, F. 701, 707, 710
Wilkinson, I. F. 638
Wilks, I. 122
Willard, R. 758
Williams, C. 421, 422, 424, 426
Williams, E. 520
Williams, J. R. 491, 736
Williams, M. P. 146
Williamson, Oliver E. 95 n., 92, 106,
    107, 111, 222, 549, 635, 700, 734, 740
Willke, H. 68, 448
Willms, B. 284
Wills, G. 179
Wilmot, W. 585
Wilson, C. 91
Wilson, D. A. 778
Wilson, J. Q. 576
Wilson, P. F. 546
Wilson, S. R. 156
Wilson, T. D. 20, 328
Wimmer, R. 477
Winiecki, J. 244, 252
Winograd, T. 48, 509
Winter, S. G. 62, 65, 90–2, 100–1, 105,
    108–9, 164, 173, 175, 264, 274, 332,
    491, 494, 529, 599, 601, 606, 642, 691,
    737
Wintermantel, R. E. 809
Wise, C. R. 574
Wiseman, R. 429
Witte, E. H. 202, 206
Wittgenstein, L. 50, 835, 837
Wixforth, H. 172
Wolf, E. R. 118, 121
Wolfe, T. 245, 250, 255, 256
Wolfers, Arnold 145
Wolff, Rolf 75, 154, 396–7, 423, 446–58,
    476, 488, 509, 535–53, 637, 641, 649,
    917, 928–30
Wong, S. L. 720, 723, 725
Wood, B. D. 153, 561, 573, 575
Wood, D. J. 207, 215
Wood, M. 447
Woodside, A. G. 685
Woodward, J. 62
Wooldridge, B. 273

Wright, T. P. 98
Wruck, K. H. 508
Wunderer, R. 212
Wurster, T. S. 521
Wyszomierski, T. 726

Yalman, N. 124 n.
Yamamura, K. 172
Yamazaki, M. 837, 839
Yan, A. 684, 686, 690
Yan, Y. 677, 688
Yanow, D. 50, 72–3, 245, 358, 398, 464,
    904
Yates, J. 175
Yergin, D. 850
Yeung, A. K. 809
Yeung, S. 541
Yip, G. 71, 636, 641

Yorges, S. L. 26
Young, M. J. 381
Yovetich, N. 27
Yu, K. 204, 213
Yutaka, N. 449

Zaheer, A. 688
Zahra, S. 428, 429, 432, 434, 436, 437
Zald, M. N. 222, 223
Zaleznik, A. 185
Zaltman, G. 833
Zand, D. E. 76, 747
Zander, A. 75
Zander, I. 641
Zander, U. 107, 110, 267, 619, 636, 640,
    685, 688, 689, 692, 805, 814
Zapf, D. 29
Zaunbrecher, H. C. 803

Zebrowitz, L. A. 334
Zeira, Y. 688
Zeitlin, J. 164, 710
Zeniuk, Nick 789
Zerubavel, E. 352
Zhou, X. 619
Zimmerman, F. O. 736–7
Zimmerman, L. J. 62
Zimmerman, M. B. 98
Zink, K. 805
Zmud, R. W. 521
Znaniecki, F. 129
Zoll, R. 448
Zuboff, S. 36
Zucchermaglio, C. 42, 49
Zucker, L. G. 310, 604, 705
Zuscovitch, E. 100

SUBJECT INDEX

ability to learn 465, 480, 518, 535
abnormal returns 542–3, 546, 685
absorptive capacity 24, 104, 525, 628,
  645, 659, 668, 676, 681, 685, 689, 692,
  694, 923
abstract knowledge 127, 660–1, 908, 914
acceleration-deceleration of
  learning 306
access 205–6, 522–4, 527, 531, 829
accountability 45, 51–2, 65, 440,
  559–60, 755, 760–2, 768–71, 906–9,
  911
accounting 44, 61, 175, 181–3, 700, 796,
  801, 804, 806–7, 811–12
accounts, intellectual capital 799–800
acculturation 120–1, 125–6, 131
Acer 722
achievement emotions 385–8
acquisition of knowledge 50, 78,
  126–7, 638–9, 758
  Chinese enterprise networks 717,
    722, 725, 727
  economic theory 89, 95, 99, 101,
    110–11
  emotions and 374, 381, 385–6
  future research 930, 935, 937–8
  joint ventures 628, 681–2, 684–94
  media and 519–20, 525–6, 530
  multimodal learning 902–3, 909,
    911–12, 914–15
  psychology 14–15, 17, 21, 25, 29
  strategic alliances 657–8, 663–4, 666,
    668–9, 676
  supplier networks 699–700, 702,
    704–5
action 814, 923–4, 930
  information technology 823, 829,
    833–5, 839–45
  scenario planning 824, 849, 856–9,
    861–3
  theory of 64, 399–400, 407, 457,
    537–8, 548, 551, 766
  theory and transformation 889, 892
  tools of learning 755, 775–7, 781–3,
    787–91
action-driven learning process 270–1
adaptation 15, 38–9, 163, 239, 491–2,
  572–3, 627, 659, 769, 775, 850, 887,
  923
  anthropology 121, 124
  Chinese enterprise networks 716–17,
    721, 727–8
  conflict and identity 587–8, 590

economic theory 106, 110–11
  emotions and 371, 382–4, 387
  joint ventures 687, 692, 694
  leadership 396, 415, 417, 419, 426
  management science 11, 62–4, 74–5
  market signals 266, 277
  multimodal learning 903, 915
  multinationals 631–2, 637, 642, 648,
    650
  political science 140, 142, 144, 150–5
  rules 603, 607, 609, 612–14
  social constitution of
    organization 308, 313–14
  socioeconomic values 196, 198–9,
    205, 214, 216
  strategizing 537, 544, 546, 553
  success and failure 327, 334–7
  supplier networks 702, 710–11
  technological vision 289, 295, 298
  time and 351, 356, 358
Adler Modemärkte 825, 887–99
administrative systems and market
  signals 265, 269, 271–4
adverse selection 93
aesthetic reflexivity 52
affluence 202, 204, 888
age 357–8, 477, 608–9, 619
agents:
  boards 428–43
  consultants 462–80
  economic 90–4, 97, 99, 106–7
  future research 921, 930
  individuals 64, 398–412
  leadership 415–26
  multimodal learning as social 904,
    915–16
  research future 926, 930–1
  retailing 825
  unions 446–58
aircraft industry 98–9, 102
alliances 567, 594, 642, 727, 733–6,
  747–8
  strategic 628, 657–77
alternative histories 185
altruism 614–15
ambiguity 24, 562, 590, 866
  management science 64, 67
  media choice 519–23, 525–6, 528, 531
  rules 600, 610–12, 614–15
  sociology 39, 52–3
  strategizing 538, 552
American Political Science Review 146–7
analog knowledge 494

analogy 495, 552, 831
anarchies, organizational 536, 543,
  548
anger 386, 388, 409–10, 478
Annales school 167, 177
anniversary history 169
antagonistic emotions 385–8
anthropology 12, 39–40, 89, 118–33,
  166–7, 169, 171, 177, 184, 528, 806,
  922, 925
anthropomorphism 400, 466
anxiety 247, 249, 380–6, 388, 867–8, 931
Apple 267, 276
appraisal and emotions 371–2, 377, 388
approach emotions 385–8
archives 166, 170–2, 174–8, 184, 528–31
arenas, multiple and imaginary
  organizations 745–7, 749
ARIS Toolset 778
arousal, emotional 370–1, 375–6
ART (action-reflection triggering) 823,
  827, 830, 833–5, 837, 839–40, 842–5
articulation and imaginary
  organizations 738–9, 742
artifacts 72, 201, 210, 287–8, 293, 296–7,
  541
asbestos crisis and Eternit 224, 228–30,
  233–5, 237–8
Asea Brown Boveri 337
aspirations 335, 404, 599, 604, 609,
  617–18
assets:
  dynamic knowledge 493, 501–3,
    507–8, 513
  economic theory 89, 107, 109–11
  intellectual capital 794–6, 798–9,
    804, 807–9, 811–13
  management science 61–2
  multinationals 631–2, 635–6, 640–1,
    643, 645–6, 649
associated learning 378–83
associations, professional 310
asymmetric learning 662–3
AT&T 664
attitudes to media 523–5
Audi 24, 253
audience learning 610–12, 865, 881
authority 155, 181–2, 439, 451, 511, 526,
  589, 617
  imaginary organizations 739, 743
  individual change agents 403, 411
  leadership 422, 425–6
  power and politics 558, 569–70, 573

social constitution of
    organization 308, 310, 312–17
automotive industry 24, 252–7, 289–92,
    294–6, 449, 706–8, 711
autonomy 39, 526, 616, 640, 674,
    769–70, 878
    dynamic knowledge 503–5, 508
    management science 68, 73
    power and politics 559–61, 571
    social constitution of
        organization 305, 312–17
    supplier networks 700–1, 705, 710
    time and 354, 364
autopoiesis theory 71
axiomatic knowledge 73

ba 487, 493, 498–501, 503, 505, 508, 513,
    520, 528, 719, 830, 837, 843–4, 928
balanced scorecard approach to
    intellectual capital 808–9
Banco Santander 664–5
bandwidth and media choice 521
bankruptcy 248–50, 343–4, 436, 720
bargaining 447, 450, 452, 586–9, 591–2,
    662, 665, 667, 688, 741–3, 746
barriers to learning 40, 81, 307, 361,
    456, 488, 706, 823, 824–5, 829,
    865–83, 893
    conflict and identity 489, 583
    consultants 470–80
    future research 922–3, 931, 936
    individual change agents 395,
        407–8, 410, 412
    joint ventures 687, 689
    multimodal learning 910–11, 916
    political science 139, 141, 149–50
    psychology 16, 22
    rules 598, 605, 609–10
    scenario planning 861, 863
    social constitution of
        organization 305, 308, 312, 318, 322
    strategic alliances 628, 659, 661,
        669–76
    success and failure 330, 334
    tools of learning 756, 776, 782–3, 785
    vision 287–96
base-rate information 22
Bayer AG 665
Bayesian updating 92, 96–7
BCG Matrix 332
behavior 306, 307, 397, 416, 487,
    489–90, 637–9, 702–3
    anthropology 125, 130
    barriers to learning 865–6, 868–9,
        873, 875, 877–9, 882
    boards 429–4, 437–8, 442
    Chinese enterprise networks 629,
        717–19, 727–9
    conditions for learning 755, 757–63,
        767, 770–1
    conflict and identity 582, 587, 590,
        594
    consultants 464–7, 471–2, 476–9

dynamic knowledge 487, 492–4,
    497, 501–3, 507
economic theory 90–6, 99, 107, 109
emotions and 369–72, 376–87
European transformation
    process 196, 242, 245–8, 251, 253–4,
        256, 258–9
future research 922–4, 929–30, 933
history and 166, 174, 176, 178–80,
    185–6
imaginary organizations 736, 739,
    747
individual change agents 395,
    398–400, 403–4, 406–9, 411–12
information technology 838–9, 844
intellectual capital 794, 796, 801–10
joint ventures 682, 686–7, 691, 694
management science 11, 62–4, 66–7,
    69, 72, 74–81
market signals 264–8, 270–6
media choice 518–19, 523–4, 526–9
multimodal learning 902–5, 908,
    910, 913–15
multinationals 627, 631–2, 647
organizational constitution 305,
    309, 314, 317–18, 320–3
organizational crisis 221, 225–6, 229,
    233, 236–7
political science 139–40, 143–4,
    146–8, 152, 156
power and politics 557–9, 561–2, 564,
    566–7, 571, 573–7
psychology 13, 15–19, 21–5, 28–9
scenario planning 849, 851, 857
sociology 35, 37–9, 41–3, 46, 49–51, 53
strategic alliances 663, 665, 667, 671,
    674
strategizing 488, 535–9, 543–6, 549,
    551–3
success and failure 305, 327–35,
    337–40, 342–5
theory and rules 598–620
theory and transformation 886–7,
    890, 895–6, 898–9
time and 352–5, 357, 360, 364–5
tools of learning 777–8, 782, 787–8
unions 397, 446–9, 456–7
value change 195, 198–200, 209–10,
    214, 216
vision 282–6, 289, 298
belief perseverance 97
belief-driven learning process 270–1,
    277
benefits of learning 661–2, 664, 666,
    669, 672, 805, 811, 863
Berlin-Chemie 251
best practice 62, 829, 909, 914, 917, 928
best-reply dynamics 96
bias, information 150
bidimensional value space 202
biotechnology 726
black-box model 802
BMW 24, 208, 212

boards 887–8, 890–1, 893, 896, 898, 930
    role of 428–43
bodies, public and political
    science 151–3
book value 795–8, 801, 807
bottom-up management 19, 169, 174,
    244, 277, 355, 375, 503–6, 540, 571,
    718, 801, 879
boundaries 103, 196, 206–7, 355, 602,
    627, 674–5, 769, 780, 842, 869
    boards 396, 429, 432–3, 441–2
    Chinese enterprise networks 717,
        723
    consultants 397, 465
    dynamic knowledge 492, 495,
        498–500, 506, 508–9, 513
    future research 922, 930, 935
    imaginary organizations 733, 735–6,
        747
    market signals 264, 267–70, 277–8
    multimodal learning 903–4, 916
    multinationals 631–41, 647, 649
    organizational constitution 305,
        308, 313, 315, 317–22
    power and politics 558, 573
    sociology 45, 47, 51, 53
    strategizing 541, 549
    supplier networks 700, 703, 705,
        708–10
    unions 446–7, 450, 453–7
    vision 284–5, 294–6, 298
brain workers and value change 205
braindrain 125
brainstorming 741, 895
brands 736
Brent Spar crisis 215, 230–2, 233, 236, 855
budgets 561–2, 564, 571
buffering 798
bureaucracy 36–7, 167–9, 359, 362,
    503–4, 511–13, 558, 561, 565, 572–3,
    576–7, 598, 602–4, 718
business history 169–70, 172–4, 178, 282
business theory 544–7

capabilities 15, 67, 169, 603, 704–6, 758,
    779, 829
    Chinese enterprise networks 722,
        725
    economic theory 101, 103, 105,
        107–11
    intellectual capital 801, 805–6
    joint ventures 681–2, 685–6, 689–91,
        694
    multimodal learning 904, 917
    multinationals 632–3, 642–3
    power and politics 567, 572
    scenario planning 856, 861
    strategic alliances 668–9, 672
    strategizing 542–3, 547
capacity for learning 12, 24, 89, 98, 140,
    142–5, 155, 157, 163, 666–7, 676
capital and unions 446, 450, 456
capitalism 709

caretaker boards 437–9
cascade, informational 94
catastrophe and learning 223–4, 315
catch-all parties 144
Caterpillar Inc. 583–4
causality 21–2, 25, 29
center/network oriented activities and
    multinationals 642–7
centralization 339, 568, 570–2, 681–2,
    841–3, 868–9, 897
Challenger disaster 340–2
champion-sponsor networks 882
change 397, 491–2, 510–11, 757, 825
    anthropology 12, 119–26
    barriers to learning 870–3, 875, 881
    boards 429–32, 434–5, 441
    Chinese enterprise networks 717–19,
        725–8
    conflict and identity 587, 590–1, 594
    consultants 397, 463–6, 472–3, 477
    economic theory 89–90, 93, 103–6,
        110
    emotions 306, 374, 376, 380, 384, 387
    European transformation
        process 246–8, 250, 256, 259
    future research 923, 928, 932, 934–5,
        937
    history and 163–70, 174, 180, 182–4,
        185
    imaginary organizations 737, 740–1
    individual agents 399, 404–6, 409–11
    information technology 840, 844
    joint ventures 628, 691
    leadership 396, 415–26
    management science 11, 61–3, 66–8,
        70–4, 80
    market signals 266, 270–2, 274–5
    multimodal learning 902–4, 909–10,
        915
    multinationals 627, 647
    organizational constitution 305,
        308–14, 322–3
    political science 139, 141, 144, 146–8,
        150–2, 154–7
    power and politics 561–2, 565, 567–8,
        571–2, 575–8
    psychology 14, 16–17, 24
    rules 489, 598, 600–1, 604–5, 607–20
    scenario planning 824, 850, 852, 858,
        860–1
    social movements 222–5, 233, 238
    socioeconomic values and 198–216
    sociology 40, 46, 52
    strategic alliances 665, 671
    strategizing 535, 537–9, 545–7, 551,
        553
    success and failure 306, 329, 331–6,
        338–9, 344–5
    supplier networks 701, 705, 710–11
    theory and transformation 886–900
    time and 351, 353–5, 357, 364
    unions 396, 446–9, 451–2, 455–7
    vision 283–7, 290, 294–5, 297–8

chaos 504, 508–9, 510, 672, 703, 711, 831
character of knowledge 812–13
charisma and leadership 419, 426
chief knowledge officers 508
child-rearing, parents and value
    change 201
China 204, 213, 658, 667, 676
    local enterprise networks 629,
        716–29
choice 142, 313, 488, 559, 637
    economic theory 90–1, 93, 107
    history and 162, 165, 180
    management science 62–3, 73
    market signals 265–6, 270–2, 274–7
    rules 599, 602, 605–6, 609, 618
    strategizing 488, 544
    success and failure 330, 332, 333–6,
        338
class, social 36–8, 176
classification 129–30, 132, 636, 659–60,
    777, 935
clients and consultants 462, 464,
    466–72, 474–80
climate, emotional 306–7, 371–3,
    376–7, 381–2, 384–8
coalitions 575, 577, 586–7, 869, 873
Coca-Cola 186
coercion 602, 604–5, 613
cognition 145–6, 195, 285, 529, 561,
    636–7, 705, 717–18, 805, 825, 832, 859
    consultants 464–5, 473
    dynamic knowledge 487, 494
    economic theory 91–4, 99, 103
    emotions and 371, 373–4, 381
    future research 923, 929–30
    individual change agents 399, 407–8
    management science 11, 63, 65–7,
        69–72, 74–6, 78–81
    market signals 266, 277
    multimodal learning 902–5, 912–15
    psychology 15, 20–2, 25
    rules 602–3, 616
    social constitution of
        organization 310, 314, 317, 321
    social movements 221, 234, 238
    sociology 45, 49, 51–3
    strategic alliances 660, 665, 672–3
    strategizing 539, 547
    success and failure 305, 327–8, 330,
        333–45
    tools of learning 775–7, 779–80,
        782–5, 787, 791
cognitive anthropology 119, 127–8
cognitive psychology 127, 536–7
cohesion and leadership 417, 423
collaboration 110, 227, 436, 479, 500,
    542, 605, 691, 897, 911
    conflict and identity 589–90, 592
    imaginary organizations 629, 733–4,
        737–40, 743–4
    information technology 828, 832
    market signals 275, 278
    multinationals 642, 644, 647, 649

political science 145–6, 155–6
power and politics 560, 566, 572, 574
social constitution of
    organization 318, 320
strategic alliances 628, 657, 659,
    661–7, 670–2, 674–5, 677
supplier networks 703, 708, 711
collectivity 155, 195, 421, 529, 666, 691,
    801, 857, 891
    anthropology 122, 129–30
    boards 429–30, 440
    Chinese enterprise networks 719,
        723, 729
    conditions for learning 757, 763, 771
    conflict and identity 583, 590
    emotions 306–7, 372–3, 377–8, 382
    history and 162–3, 166, 176, 180
    imaginary organizations 733, 735,
        739
    management science 67, 69, 71–4,
        76–80
    market signals 268, 270, 273, 276
    multimodal learning 904–5, 915–17
    multinationals 638, 646
    power and politics 566, 568, 572,
        575
    social constitution of
        organization 313, 315, 318
    social movements 221–5, 232–4
    sociology 41, 47, 51
    strategizing 544, 552–3
    supplier networks 704, 706, 709
    tools of learning 776–7, 779, 782, 786
    vision 284–5, 296, 298
colonialism 123–4
combination 353, 493, 495–8, 500, 503,
    511, 513, 738–9, 742, 823, 830–5,
    843–5
combines and European
    transformation process 245–6,
    250, 258–9
commitment 141, 403–4, 456, 529, 604,
    897
    barriers to learning 872–3, 875, 877
    conditions for learning 761–3,
        767–70
    dynamic knowledge 492–3, 500,
        505, 510–11
    information technology 828–9, 833
    joint ventures 685–6, 688, 690, 694
    multinationals 638–9, 647
    strategic alliances 669, 672–3, 676
    supplier networks 708, 710
communication 49, 80, 439–40, 490,
    589, 718, 807, 825–6, 923
    barriers to learning 868, 878
    conditions for learning 763, 770
    consultants 466, 471, 475–7
    dynamic knowledge 494, 501,
        505–6, 509
    economic theory 106, 109
    emotions and 372, 388
    history and 175, 178, 180, 183–4

imaginary organizations 742, 744–5, 748

individual change agents 399, 402–3, 406, 409

information technology 829, 831–2, 843–4

joint ventures 685–8, 690–2

media choice 487–8, 518–24, 526–8, 531

multimodal learning 904, 912

multinationals 636, 640, 645, 649, 650

political science 140, 156

power and politics 568, 570, 573

rules 600, 603, 605, 613

scenario planning 858, 862

social constitution of organization 312–15, 317, 319, 321–3

strategic alliances 666, 669, 674–6

strategizing 536, 542, 545, 549

success and failure 332, 335–6, 339–40

supplier networks 703, 705–6, 708–9

theory and transformation 889, 891, 894, 896–7, 899–900

time and 354, 360, 363

tools of learning 778, 783

unions 447, 456–7

value change 206–7, 212

vision 284, 292–3

communism 154–5

community 42, 46, 65, 167–8, 322, 354, 425, 471, 497, 552, 607, 646, 724, 759, 805

anthropology 122, 124–5, 126, 129

imaginary organizations 733, 736–7, 740

political science 152, 156

power and politics 559, 561, 563–4, 566

sociology 40–3, 49, 51–3

community of practice 42, 47, 51, 264, 268, 270, 272–5, 277–8, 465–6, 479, 499, 501, 735, 922, 931

comparative advantage 72, 666, 726, 794, 865, 892

economic theory 12, 89, 108

information technology 827, 829

multinationals 631–2, 640–3, 645

political science 145, 155

supplier networks 700, 703, 706–7

competences 122, 164, 196, 208, 257, 338–9, 630, 706, 824, 829, 867, 900

boards 430, 432, 435–7

Chinese enterprise networks 629, 718, 725, 727

conditions for learning 758, 762, 768, 772

consultants 467, 477

dynamic knowledge 491, 500–1, 507, 510

economic theory 91, 93, 97, 99, 101, 103, 105, 107–10

emotions and 371, 385–6

future research 922–4, 927, 935, 937

imaginary organizations 733, 735–7, 740, 744

individual change agents 395, 398, 403

intellectual capital 801–2, 811

joint ventures 628, 681–2, 686, 691–2

leadership 417, 426

management science 61, 71–2

market signals 273, 277

multimodal learning 903, 915

multinationals 642–3, 645–7, 649–50

organizational constitution 305, 309, 311, 315, 317–19, 322

power and politics 561, 565, 573, 575

psychology 14–16, 21

rules 601, 606–8, 616

social movements 221, 226–7, 232, 234, 237–9

sociology 39, 41, 48, 51, 53

strategic alliances 657, 662–3, 665, 667–74, 676

strategizing 536, 542–3, 547, 549–50

unions 397, 448, 450–1, 455–6

vision 286–7, 293

competency trap 608, 615–17, 619

competition 14, 145, 196–7, 288, 358, 425, 429, 627, 780–1, 810, 827, 888, 908

Central European transformation 248–50, 259

Chinese enterprise networks 629, 716, 718, 720, 722, 725–6

conflict and identity 587–9, 592

consultants 464, 474–5

dynamic knowledge 491–2, 501, 507, 510

economic theory 12, 108–11

future research 925, 934, 937

history and 164, 170, 183

imaginary organizations 736, 741

joint ventures 628, 681–3, 690

market signals 267–9, 275, 278

multinationals 632, 634–5, 641–4

power and politics 560, 563, 566, 568, 571–2, 575, 577

rules 613, 617

strategic alliances 628, 659, 661–70

strategizing 488, 540–2, 546–7, 549

success and failure 333, 338–9

supplier networks 700, 705, 707–12

unions 453, 457

value change 212, 214

complexity theory 71, 331

compromise 574, 577, 586, 593, 741, 743, 746

computers 49–50, 335–6, 518, 521, 524, 528, 537, 646, 700–1, 722, 728

conceptual knowledge 501–3, 701–3, 705–11, 825

conceptual model of strategizing 543–9

conceptualization 824, 856–9, 862

conditioning 17–19, 63, 151, 155, 377–80, 385, 903, 914

conditions for learning 305–7, 755, 757–72

conflict 25, 283–4, 425–6, 529, 729, 875, 916

boards 438–9, 442

conditions for learning 755, 757, 762–3

emotions and 370, 376, 387

future research 924, 927, 931–2

identity and 582–94

imaginary organizations 746, 749

individual change agents 408, 412

joint ventures 685, 688

knowledge creation 487, 489–90

multinationals 647, 649

political science 142, 144–5, 147, 150, 156

power and politics 489, 560, 562–4, 566–7, 573–5

rules 604, 614, 617

social constitution of organization 318–19, 322

social movements 226–7, 229, 232–3, 236–8

sociology 35–8, 44, 46

supplier networks 701–3, 711

theory and transformation 887, 896, 899–900

unions 451–2, 456, 458

connoisseurs knowledge 50

consensus 50, 64, 156, 355, 545, 707–8

media choice 526, 528, 530

multimodal learning as social 907, 915

power and politics 565, 568, 571, 574, 588

rules 602, 605, 611

conservatism 266, 309, 321, 435–6, 561

consortia 628, 657, 674

constellation of events 356, 361–3

constitution of organization, social 305, 307, 308–23

construction/discovery of strategy 535–53

construction industry in Sweden 342–4

constructionism 35, 42, 45–7, 52–3, 74, 407–11, 636

constructivism 124, 178, 183, 242, 247, 249–52, 254–9, 323

consultants 397, 450–3, 607, 829, 890–2, 895–6, 898–900, 928, 930

marginality 462–80

consumers and economic theory 90, 93, 102

contagion, emotional 373, 384

content/process consultants 467–9, 471

context 20–3, 126, 139, 374, 566, 703–4, 784, 824
  Chinese enterprise networks 718–19, 723–4, 729
  conditions for learning 760–2, 767, 772
  conflict and identity 584, 593
  dynamic knowledge 493–5, 499, 501
  economic theory 94, 97, 104, 106
  future research 922, 925, 929–30
  information technology 823, 828–31, 834, 838–9, 845
  joint ventures 684, 691
  media choice 488, 520, 523–6, 528–31
  multimodal learning as social 904, 910, 913–14, 917
  multinationals 631–3, 636, 640–50
  rules 490, 616, 619
  scenario planning 849, 852, 856
  sociology 35, 39–41, 45, 51, 53
  strategic alliances 664, 669, 671
  theory and transformation 886, 890, 895–6
contingency approaches 62–3, 416, 547, 589
continuity 12, 49, 144, 247, 283, 305, 337, 375, 466, 497–8, 745–7, 837, 850
  barriers to learning 870, 879, 883
  Chinese enterprise networks 718–19, 725–8
  future research 923, 935
  history and 169, 173
  multimodal learning 903–4, 917
  social constitution of organization 309, 311–12
  theory and transformation 895, 899
  time and 358, 364
contracts and strategic alliances 673, 677
contradiction and individual change agents 403–5, 408
control 20, 73, 305, 360–2, 384, 420, 644–6, 808–9, 898–9, 931
  boards 428–9, 432, 436, 439, 442
  conditions for learning 755, 757, 772
  conflict and identity 586–7, 589–90
  European transformation process 245–7, 249, 251, 257
  imaginary organizations 735, 739
  joint ventures 685–6, 688–90, 694
  multimodal learning 903–4, 915
  political science 140, 144, 153–4, 156
  power and politics 560, 563–4, 569–74, 576–7
  rules 604, 617
  social constitution of organization 312–17, 319, 323
  sociology 36, 39, 44–5, 53
  strategic alliances 674, 677
  success and failure 330, 340, 344–5
  supplier networks 702, 705
convection/conduction, social 125

conventional model of organizational learning 716–18
conversation 46–7, 53, 757, 770–1, 861–3, 896–7, 915
cooperation 627, 687, 721–2, 805–6, 909
  conflict and identity 587, 589–90, 592, 594
  imaginary organizations 629–30, 735
  power and politics 564, 575
  rules 605, 619
  strategic alliances 628, 657–9, 662–5, 667, 673, 676–7
  supplier networks 628–9, 700–1, 705, 707–8, 711–12
  theory and transformation 889, 891–3, 895–6, 898
coordination 26, 109–10, 356, 404–5, 627, 808
  imaginary organizations 738–9, 741, 743–4, 746, 749
  multinationals 641, 643, 645–8
  supplier networks 699, 701, 704–5, 711
  unions 448–50, 452, 454
  vision 284–6, 296
costs 521, 657, 707, 747, 850
  Chinese enterprise networks 720, 722, 725
  intellectual capital 794–5, 803–4, 811
  joint ventures 687, 693
  multimodal learning as social 908, 910–11, 917
  multinationals 634–5, 639
  strategizing 536, 549
  transaction 106–8, 684
cotton textile industry 171–2
coupling 629, 700, 703, 705–6, 709–11, 723, 727, 736, 740, 747
creation of economic theory 89, 99
creation of knowledge 37–8, 336, 487–90, 709–12, 904–5
  Chinese enterprise networks 718–19, 726, 728–9
  as dynamic process 491–513
  economic theory 95, 99, 105–11
  emotions and 375–6, 382
  future research 922, 927–8, 930–8
  history and 174–6, 178–80, 184
  identity and conflict 582–94
  imaginary organizations 630, 733–4, 736–43, 745–6
  individual change agents 399, 407
  information technology 823, 827–45
  intellectual capital 802, 814
  learning into practice 824, 826
  management science 65, 71–2, 75, 78–80
  media choice 518–32
  multinationals 632–3, 636, 640–50
  political science 146, 155
  power and politics 557–78
  rules 598–620

strategic alliances 659–61, 672–4, 676
strategizing 535–53
time and 351, 353
tools of learning 756, 776–7, 779–83, 786, 791
creative destruction concept 139
creativity 647, 674, 771, 809, 823, 870, 893
  Chinese enterprise networks 717, 719, 721, 727
  conflict and identity 583–4, 587–9, 592
  emotions and 381, 386
  future research 924, 937
  joint ventures 689, 693
  multimodal learning as social 904, 910–11
  rules 604–6, 609
  tools of learning 780, 782
credibility 237, 448, 477, 693
Creole in Sierra Leone 122–3
crisis, organizational 63, 454, 509, 587, 617, 672, 760, 903
  barriers to learning 866–7, 880
  boards 396, 429–32, 434, 439, 442
  Chinese enterprise networks 718, 724
  organizational constitution 311, 315
  social movements 221–37
  strategizing 546, 548, 551, 553
  success and failure 329, 343, 345
  theory and transformation 887, 890, 893
  triggers of organizational learning 195, 268, 283, 286
critical theory 36, 520, 524, 527
Crossroads, Australia 860
CSTools (conversion-support) 519–20, 823, 827, 830–3, 835, 837–45
cues, multiple and media 521, 525, 528–9
culture 197, 270, 398, 507–8, 627, 756, 825
  anthropology 12, 118–21, 124–9, 131–2
  barriers to learning 825, 867–9, 871, 873–5, 877, 881
  Chinese enterprise networks 717–19, 723, 726
  conditions for learning 755, 758, 760–4, 768, 772
  consultants 462–3, 470, 473, 477
  emotions and 372–3, 388
  European transformation process 247–9, 254, 256–8
  future research 922–3, 925–6, 929–30, 933, 935–6
  history and 163, 176–82, 185–6
  imaginary organizations 736, 737–9, 743–4
  information technology 839, 842–3, 845
  joint ventures 682, 684

leadership 320–3, 396, 415–16, 426
learning and practice 756, 823
management science 11, 66–7, 72–6,
    78–81
media choice 488, 529
multimodal learning 902, 904–5,
    910–15
multinationals 632, 634, 636–7, 639,
    646–50
political science 139, 143, 149, 153–4
power and politics 564, 566–7,
    570–2
psychology 25, 29
rules 605, 619
scenario planning 855, 859
social constitution of
    organization 310–13, 320
social movements 227, 231, 238
sociology 36, 38–9, 42, 45, 47
strategic alliances 659, 661, 664,
    667–8, 670–1, 675
strategizing 541, 543–4, 547–8
success and failure 329, 336–7
supplier networks 629, 699, 705–6,
    708, 710–11
time and 351, 355, 357–60, 362, 364
tools of learning 756, 775–7, 779–83,
    785, 787, 790–1
unions 449–51, 453, 456, 458
value change 198–9, 201–4, 208–10,
    212, 214
vision 285–6, 288–9, 292–7
customers 369–70, 498, 549–50, 571,
    657–8, 810, 862, 905
imaginary organizations 733, 736–7,
    742, 745, 747–8
information technology 828, 833,
    837–8, 840, 842–3
intellectual capital 795–6, 799
theory and transformation 887–9,
    891–4, 896, 898
value change 200, 205, 207, 210,
    212–15
cybernetics 40, 46
cycle, learning 38, 488, 537–9, 564, 582,
    639, 660, 788, 824, 829, 889, 923, 934
barriers to learning 825, 866, 877, 881
dynamic knowledge 503, 513
individual change agents 399, 403
management science 67, 74
scenario planning 849, 855–9
time and 354, 357–8, 360–1, 363–5
cycle, life 351, 357–62, 396, 433–7, 540,
    608–11, 617, 665–6
Czech Republic and transformation
    process 242–59

Daimler-Benz 24
data 49, 93, 521–2, 529–31, 646, 660,
    828–9, 841–4, 903, 905–8
data-mining 810, 832, 843
deadlines 355, 359–60
deadlock 547–8

decentralization 26, 143, 150, 601, 627,
    642, 644–5, 647, 709–10, 723, 739,
    866, 869, 882, 897
decision-making 36, 207, 249, 284–6,
    318, 411, 472, 504, 739, 898–9, 925,
    935
barriers to learning 870, 878
boards 396, 431–5, 437–8, 440
conditions for learning 768, 770
conflict and identity 588, 591
economic theory 90–4, 97, 101
emotions and 371, 374, 378, 382, 384,
    388
history and 170–1, 174–6, 179, 181,
    183
information technology 828–9, 841
intellectual capital 756, 803, 806–8
joint ventures 682, 684–6, 688–9, 691
leadership 415, 421, 423
management science 11, 62, 64,
    66–7, 69, 71, 80
market signals 272–3, 275–6
media choice 524, 528–9
multinationals 637–8, 641–7
political science 140, 142, 149, 150,
    154–6
power and politics 562, 564, 567–9,
    572, 574, 577
psychology 24–7, 29
rules 601–3, 614, 616
scenario planning 849–52, 858, 861
social movements 223, 238
strategizing 536, 541, 544, 547, 550
success and failure 330, 335, 337, 345
time and 355, 358, 360–2, 364–5
tools of learning 779, 790
unions 397, 446, 448, 450–3, 456
declarative/procedural knowledge 21
decline, organizational 430–1, 435, 439
deconstructionism 43, 45, 177–8, 181,
    183–4
decoupling 604
deductive reasoning 96
defensive/offensive organizational
    learning 234–6, 238
defensive routines 65, 72–3, 80, 376–7,
    407–9, 473, 637, 648, 867, 875, 879,
    931
definitions 15–17, 118, 921–3
democracy 143, 446, 448, 458, 559–60,
    566, 568–9, 571, 578, 591
dependency 107, 420
design archetypes and European
    transformation process 247, 249,
    255–6, 258–9
designer, leader as 423
determinism 62, 829
deterrence emotions 385–8
deutero-learning 246, 664, 855, 923–4
management science 74, 76–7, 79
tools of learning 775–6, 782–3, 785,
    788–9, 791
vision 197, 283, 288, 296–8

deviations 76, 78
devolution 571
dialogue 786–7, 790–1, 933
dialoguing ba 499–501, 528, 831, 841,
    843
diamond model concept 642–3
dictionary knowledge 73
differentiation 71, 316, 317–19, 640, 647,
    669–70, 861–3, 895
diffusion of knowledge 175, 540, 613,
    690, 743, 759, 825, 859, 889
anthropology 13, 119, 121, 125–6
Chinese enterprise networks 717–18,
    720–1, 724, 727–9
economic theory 89, 100, 102, 107–10
emotions and 373, 381, 383–4
future research 924, 930, 935
imaginary organizations 733, 739
information technology 823,
    827–30, 840–1
intellectual capital 811, 814
joint ventures 681–94
management science 65, 72, 75,
    78–80
media 518–20, 523–7, 530–1
multimodal learning 903, 913
multinationals 627, 631–3, 635–7,
    639–40, 644–6
political science 143, 146
sociology 37–9, 42, 46, 50, 52
strategic alliances 628, 659–61,
    663–4, 667, 670–2, 676
success and failure 336, 339
supplier networks 699, 701–6,
    708–10
tools of learning 755, 776–7, 781–6,
    788–91
digital knowledge 494
direction 314, 396, 419, 428–9, 440, 442,
    505
directive/nondirective
    consultants 467–9
directory knowledge 73
discipline and value change 200,
    202–3
disciplines:
    anthropology 118–33
    economic theory 89–111
    history 162–86
    management science 61, 81
    political science 137–57
    psychology 14–29
    sociology 35–54
disconfirmability 755, 761–2
discontinuity 164, 173–4, 195, 225, 268,
    297, 313, 315, 824
discourses 11, 43–7, 49, 53
discrimination skills 691
discursive/practical systems 649
disease 228–9, 233, 586
distributed leadership 396, 419
diversity 569–71, 627, 631–2, 647, 649,
    706–11, 717, 745, 748, 933–4, 936

double-loop learning 40, 214, 246, 272,
    336, 467, 492, 525, 649, 702, 870,
    886–7, 923–4
    boards 396, 430, 432–3, 435, 438,
        441–3
    conditions for learning 757–8, 772
    conflict and identity 582–3, 585,
        590–4
    emotions 306, 376–7
    individual change agents 406, 407
    management science 65, 74–7, 79
    political science 137–8, 146, 150,
        155–6
    power and politics 565, 574–6
    strategic alliances 660, 669
    strategizing 535, 537–8, 546, 548
    tools of learning 775–7, 779, 782–3,
        789, 791
    unions 451–3, 455
    vision 197, 283, 287–9, 295, 297–8
doubt 761–3, 768–9, 890
Douwe Egberts 273
Dow Chemical 798
driving forces 850–2, 855, 860, 886
Durkheimian approaches 11, 39–41,
    46
dynamic process, knowledge creation
    as 487, 491–513, 542, 829
Dyula in Sudan 122–3

eclecticism 65
ecology 39, 46, 163, 266, 268, 274, 276–8,
    318, 606, 613–15, 717
economic theory 12, 89–111
economics 62, 167, 242–50, 254–9,
    716–17, 719–20, 795, 924–5, 927, 937
education 23, 41, 122–3, 202, 242, 255,
    257–9, 702, 743, 802, 804, 928
EEC 145–6
effectiveness 65, 232–9, 363–4, 388, 547,
    588, 674–5, 777, 870
    conditions for learning 759–60,
        762–3
    consultants 465–6, 475, 477
    dynamic knowledge 508, 511–12
    information technology 827, 830,
        834, 838
    intellectual capital 803–4, 812
    joint ventures 685, 690
    media choice 518–19, 524–5, 527–9,
        532
    multinationals 627, 632–3, 636, 641,
        649–50
    political science 150, 152–3, 157
    power and politics 562, 572–4
    rules 605–6, 615
    scenario planning 850, 856, 858,
        862–3
    social constitution of
        organization 313–14, 318–19
    strategic alliances 663, 669
    success and failure 327, 329–30, 332,
        335

efficiency 16–17, 108, 143, 310, 503, 728,
    743, 910, 935
    emotions and 371, 374–6
    information technology 827–30,
        833–4, 837–8, 841–5
    intellectual capital 804, 812
    market signals 271–2, 274
    media choice 518, 524
    multinationals 632, 635, 641, 644
    power and politics 557–8, 562, 570–1
    rules 489, 603, 613, 616, 618
    strategizing 537, 545, 547–8
egalitarianism 38, 139, 761–3, 769–71,
    890, 897
elections, direct in US 154
electronic media 520–4, 526–7, 530,
    646, 675–6, 741, 810, 828
electronics 706, 726, 728
elitism 12, 122–4, 139, 144, 154, 476
embeddedness 268, 271, 466, 561, 593,
    823, 828–9, 890, 904
    barriers to learning 866, 868, 877, 882
    dynamic knowledge 491, 499, 502
    economic theory 104, 109
    European transformation
        process 247, 256, 258
    future research 921–2, 929–30
    social constitution of
        organization 305–6, 308–12, 318,
        320–2
    sociology 47, 51–2
    time and 353, 358
emergent strategies 540–1, 543
emotions 18, 39–40, 285, 317, 354,
    409–10, 480, 672–3, 687, 914
    conditions for learning 306–7, 772
    conflict and identity 589
    dynamic knowledge 493, 499
    future research 924, 931–2
    learning process and 369–89
    management science 73, 76, 78
    media choice 521, 527
employment 183
employees 18, 329, 360–2, 369–70, 541,
    686, 739
    barriers to learning 865, 867, 870–8,
        883
    Chinese enterprise networks 716,
        723–4
    conflict and identity 591, 594
    consultants 463, 479
    European transformation
        process 247–52, 255–6, 258
    individual change agents 403,
        410–11
    information technology 838–40,
        842–4
    intellectual capital 804–5, 810
    leadership 396, 416–18, 422, 426
    multimodal learning as social 905,
        908–10, 914, 917
    multinationals 646, 648–9
    rules 600, 604, 607

strategic alliances 668, 672, 674
theory and transformation 888–99
unions 446–8, 450–4, 456
value change 200, 205–6, 210–15
vision 289–90
employment and unions 451–2, 456
empowerment 411, 416, 419–20, 443,
    448, 546, 569, 571, 594, 604, 676, 729
enablement 602–3, 605, 645
enactment/selection/retention and
    market signals 268–71, 274, 276
encoding 19–20, 25
enculturation 126–8, 131
engagement 225, 229, 232, 234–6, 396,
    457, 561, 590–2
enhancement memory 382
enrichment 542
entrepreneurship 185, 403–4, 437,
    504–6, 541, 549, 562, 723–5, 729,
    735
environment 15, 195–7, 398, 447, 490,
    588, 627, 663–4, 809, 824
    anthropology 118, 125
    barriers to learning 865–6, 871
    boards 396, 429–30, 432–3, 442
    Chinese enterprise networks 717–18,
        722
    consultants 467, 476
    dynamic knowledge 491–2, 498–9,
        501, 503, 509–10, 513
    economic theory 90, 93–4, 96–9
    emotions 306, 371–2, 375, 380, 384–7
    European transformation
        process 242, 245–6, 248, 255–7
    future research 923, 929–30
    history and 180, 185
    imaginary organizations 733, 735,
        738, 740, 746
    information technology 830, 832,
        834, 840
    joint ventures 682–3, 691–4
    leadership 396, 417–20, 426
    management science 11, 74–5, 77, 80
    market signals 265–6, 268–72, 274–6
    media choice 519, 524–5, 527, 530
    multimodal learning 903–4, 916
    multinationals 631–2, 641–2, 644–5
    political science 139–40, 144–6, 150,
        153, 155
    power and politics 559, 561–2, 564–7,
        573, 577
    rules 490, 603, 605–6, 608–11, 613–19
    scenario planning 849–54, 856–61,
        863
    social constitution of
        organization 305, 308, 320
    social movements 222, 224–6, 231–2,
        234, 236, 239
    sociology 38, 40, 46, 48–50, 53
    strategizing 488, 536–40, 542–4, 547,
        553
    success and failure 327–38, 340, 345
    supplier networks 629, 699, 701, 708

theory and transformation 886–8,
    890, 894–6, 898–900
time and 351, 353–6, 361, 364
tools of learning 756, 780–1, 787, 790
value change 198, 200, 205–7, 214–16
vision 282–6, 288–90, 292–6, 298
epistemology 69, 71–4
equilibrium 62, 90–2, 95–6, 106, 565,
    567–8, 573–4, 586
error 80, 145, 311, 327–30, 363, 909
    conditions for learning 755, 757,
        760–2, 768, 770–1
    emotions and 380, 383, 386
    psychology 16, 24–5, 29
    theory and transformation 889,
        895–6, 898–9
espoused theory 209, 399, 405–6, 472
establishment chain 639
externalization, success and
    failure 336
Eternit and asbestos crisis 224, 228–30,
    233–5, 237–8
ethnocentrism 120, 647–8, 650
ethnomethodology 41–2, 51
EU 152
Europe, transformation process
    in 195–6, 242–59
European Patent Office 421–2
evaluation 71, 150, 157, 170, 893–4, 896,
    899–900, 936
events and emotions 306
evolution 11, 15, 62–3, 108–9, 111,
    119–21, 129, 132, 162, 164, 176, 264–6,
    272, 274–7, 332, 337–8, 340–2, 489,
    549–50, 553, 605–9, 633–9, 665–6,
    677, 929
executive power 559
exercising ba 499–501, 831–2, 838, 841,
    843
expatriates and joint ventures 685,
    687, 692
expectations 469–72, 602, 604
experience 127, 199, 426, 739, 810, 826
    barriers to learning 865, 867–8, 870,
        873, 877
    boards 433, 435, 440–2
    Chinese enterprise networks 717–19,
        721, 728–9
    conditions for learning 757, 759–60,
        764, 766, 770, 772
    conflict and identity 583, 587
    consultants 463, 465–7, 473–5,
        477–9
    dynamic knowledge 494–5, 499,
        501, 508
    economic theory 97–100, 103, 108
    emotions and 369, 372, 374–5, 382–3,
        385
    European transformation
        process 245–8, 252, 254–5, 257–9
    future research 922–3, 933, 935–6
    history and 162, 164, 167, 172–3
    individual change agents 399, 403

information technology 823, 830,
    834, 838
joint ventures 684, 687–8, 691, 693
management science 64, 66–7, 72,
    74, 77, 80
market signals 272, 275
media choice 520, 529
multimodal learning 903–7, 916–17
multinationals 635, 638–9
political science and 139, 142, 146
psychology 15–16, 19
rules 489, 600, 603, 605–7, 609,
    612–19
scenario planning 824, 849, 851–2,
    856–8, 861–3
social constitution of
    organization 308, 311–12, 321
sociology 35, 37–9, 41–2, 46
strategic alliances 658, 661, 664, 667,
    669, 676
strategizing 544, 548
success and failure 329, 335, 339
supplier networks 629, 703, 711
time and 352, 354, 358–9, 361–2, 364
tools of learning 777, 781–2, 785,
    787–8, 790
experimental psychology 121
experimentation 24–5, 71–2, 109, 354,
    661, 703, 724, 824, 891
    barriers to learning 867, 877
    boards 396, 430–1, 434–5, 439, 442
    conditions for learning 755, 762,
        769–70, 772
    consultants 474, 476
    future research 923
    individual change agents 402,
        405–6
    information technology 840, 844
    market signals 265, 270–1, 273,
        276–7
    multimodal learning 911–12, 915
    power and politics 569, 572
    rules 599, 607, 609, 616–18
    strategizing 488, 547–8, 551, 553
    success and failure 333, 337–8
expertise 99, 146, 335, 418, 494, 708,
    780, 794, 852–3, 899
    barriers to learning 870, 876, 879
    boards 434, 438–41
    consultants 463, 466–7, 470–1, 474
    European transformation
        process 251, 257
    imaginary organizations 740–2,
        744–5
    joint ventures 684, 690
    multimodal learning 908–9, 914–15
    multinationals 643–6, 649
    psychology 20, 24, 26
    social constitution of
        organization 317, 319–20, 322
    sociology 37, 41
    strategic alliances 657, 659
    unions 450, 452

explicit knowledge 29, 72, 335–6, 470,
    584, 601, 646, 718, 780, 795, 825, 860,
    870, 904, 924
    boards 430, 433, 439, 441–2
    dynamic 493–8, 500–3, 506, 511, 513
    imaginary organizations 737–9, 742,
        747
    individual change agents 399, 403
    information technology 823, 827,
        829–30, 832–5, 837, 841–5
    joint ventures 686–8, 690
    social constitution of
        organization 320, 322
    sociology 39, 49, 51
    strategic alliances 660–1, 667, 677
    strategizing 549, 552
    supplier networks 702–3, 709
    theory and transformation 886, 889
exploitation 396, 434, 439, 442, 503,
    627, 631–6, 640–1, 662, 673, 718, 728,
    915
exploration trap 904
exploratory scenario 852
externalization 353, 493, 495–8, 500,
    502–3, 511, 513, 584, 724, 823, 830–5,
    838, 840

face-to-face interaction 128–9, 354,
    521–9, 646, 707, 741, 744, 830–1,
    838–9
Facit 539
fad-setting 472–3
failure 61, 354, 404, 478, 635, 667, 826
    barriers to learning 867–8, 873, 875,
        880, 882–3
    boards 429–30, 432, 434, 439, 442
    Chinese enterprise networks 718,
        723, 727–8
    emotions and 383–4, 386
    future research 932, 935
    joint ventures 685, 691
    multimodal learning 903, 909–11,
        915–17
    power and politics 561, 574
    rules 606, 609, 614–18
    strategizing 535, 544, 547–8
    success and 305–7, 327–45
    trap 617–19, 867
faxes 522–4, 526
fear 410, 439, 617
features of media 520–2, 525, 531
federalism 488, 568–72, 574
feedback 152–3, 170, 353, 417, 440, 465,
    536, 591, 606, 632–3, 674, 727, 742–3,
    801
    barriers to learning 867, 878
    economic theory 90, 95, 97, 102
    future research 923, 930
    management science 63, 69, 77
    media choice 521–2, 525, 528–9
    multimodal learning 909, 915
    power and politics 565, 570
    psychology 21, 24

feedback (*cont.*)
  success and failure 305, 327, 330–2, 334, 338, 340
  tools of learning 776, 780
Fiat 253–4, 316, 449
fictitious-play logic 96
filtering information 375–7
finance 316, 441, 571, 693, 704, 720, 723, 796, 798, 801, 807–9, 811–12
finance/nonfinance measurement of intellectual capital 796–9, 804, 806, 808
Firestone 272
firm, theory of 12, 89, 105–11, 317, 536–7, 627, 633–4
first-generation scenarios 852, 854
fishnet organizations 536
fit 63, 540, 543, 857, 859, 887–8
flashbulb memory 375
flexibility 803, 828
  Chinese enterprise networks 716, 725, 728
  imaginary organizations 736, 739
  joint ventures 687, 689, 691
  multimodal learning 907–8, 911–13
  multinationals 627, 640, 645, 647
  rules 603, 605
fluctuation 504, 508–9, 537
focal/subsidiary awareness 48
focused scenario 852
Food and Drug Administration (US) 902, 905–8, 910–11, 913–15
forced learning 237–9, 246
Ford 411
formalization 543, 600–5
fragmented learning 143, 612, 866, 869, 881
framework:
  conflict and identity 582, 584–94
  information technology 823
  intellectual capital 812–14
  management science 75–80
  organizational learning 902–5
  rules 611–12, 619
  scenario 849, 851–5, 862–3
  SECI 830, 844
France 165, 229–30, 235
franchises 795, 835, 837–8
Frankfurt school 36
French Revolution 182
frequency/probability 22
functional approaches to intellectual capital 806–12
functional school 145
functional/dysfunctional rules 598–605
functionalism 36, 38, 40, 47, 120, 152, 210
functionality of emotions 385–8
fundamental attribution bias 328
future:
  scenario planning 849–51, 853–4, 858–61

theory and transformation 890, 899

game theory 92, 95–6, 99
Gamma; Interactive Modeling in Teams 779, 791
gatekeepers 206–7, 305, 319, 451–3, 455, 458
GD Searle and Co 906–7
GDR and *Treuhandanstalt* 352, 359–62
gender 124, 178, 180, 186, 420–2, 934
General Electric Co. 384, 782–3
General Motors 253, 275, 668
generative learning 276–7, 492
geocentric mind-set 648
German Democratic Republic 242–53, 255–9
Germany 172, 174–5, 179–80, 201–4, 222, 228–32, 234–6, 450–1, 453–6, 707–11, 825
Global Climate Coalition 231, 235
global positioning and mobility 291
globalization 14, 153, 186, 197, 278, 937
  Chinese networks 716–29
  conflict and identity 585, 591, 594
  consultants 462, 464, 474
  imaginary organizations 733–49
  joint ventures 681–94
  multinationals 631–50
  power and politics 561, 566–7, 570–2, 578
  strategic alliances 657–77
  supplier networks 699–712
  unions 447, 450, 455–8
Globe Metallurgical Inc. 759–60, 762
goals 122, 275, 356, 723, 852, 868, 909
  boards 430, 433, 438
  conditions for learning 757, 767
  conflict and identity 582–4, 586–90, 592
  consultants 463, 465
  dynamic knowledge 509–10, 512
  economic theory 91, 101, 106
  emotions and 369–70, 373–6, 386–7
  future research 931, 933, 934, 937
  individual change agents 405–6, 407–9, 411
  information technology 837, 845
  intellectual capital 756, 806, 809, 813–14
  joint ventures 685, 688–9, 691–2
  leadership 415, 417–20
  management science 63, 66–7
  multinationals 637, 647
  political science 138, 140, 142, 148, 150, 154–5, 157
  power and politics 558–63, 565, 568–9, 572, 574–6
  psychology 23, 25
  rules 601–2, 609, 615, 618–19
  social constitution of organization 310, 312, 315–17

social movements 224, 232, 234, 238–9
strategic alliances 661–2, 664, 666–7, 672, 674, 676
strategizing 536, 544, 549
success and failure 327, 329, 335
supplier networks 701–2, 705
theory and transformation 886, 891, 899
tools of learning 756, 787–8, 790
value change 211, 213
vision 282–6, 295, 297–8
Good Laboratory Practice and pharmaceutical industry 902–17
Good Manufacturing Practice 902, 905–6, 907–8, 912–13, 916
good practice and learning 825–6
good work concept 449–50
goodwill 794–5, 810
governance 107, 396, 428–9, 432, 438, 441, 591, 632, 634–5, 642, 720
government:
  multimodal learning 902, 905–13
  political science 12, 137, 141, 143–4, 146–7, 148–9, 151–3, 157
  power and politics 558–62, 565, 567, 569–70, 572–5, 577
grapeVINE 784, 791
graphic-order terminal 839
Green Room concept 867, 880
Greenpeace 215, 230, 233
groups 109–10, 156, 163–4, 251, 285–6, 395–7, 458, 632, 717–18, 741, 801
  anthropology 119, 121–3, 126
  barriers to learning 867–8, 874–8
  conditions for learning 757, 770, 772
  conflict and identity 489, 584–5, 587–8, 591–2, 594
  consultants 464–6, 476
  dynamic knowledge 501, 504–6, 508, 512–13
  emotions and 372–3, 377, 385–9
  future research 922, 924, 929–30, 937
  individual change agents 398–400, 409
  joint ventures 687, 690
  leadership 415, 417, 423–4, 426
  management science 71–3, 75–6, 79–80
  media choice 526, 529
  power and politics 559, 562–3, 565, 568–71, 573
  psychology 16, 20, 22, 25–9
  rules 601, 604, 607
  scenario planning 853–4, 859, 861
  social constitution of organization 305, 313, 317–19, 322–3
  sociology 35, 37–8, 40–1
  strategic alliances 670, 675
  strategizing 537, 546, 552
  success and failure 331–3, 336
  theory and transformation 886–7

time and 353, 355–6, 360, 365
tools of learning 775–9, 780–3, 785–7, 789
value change 198, 200–4, 207, 209, 211–12, 216
Groupthink 388, 439, 588, 858
groupware 828, 831–2
Grundfos 424
guidance 196, 286, 296, 298, 314
guilt 386, 388

habituation 374, 383, 608
harvesting concept 659
headquarters of unions 449–51, 455–6
health care, preventative and barriers to learning 870–81
hedonism 203–4, 213
herd behavior 94
heterarchical multinational 644–5
hidden-profile situations 26
hierarchy 28, 41, 79, 107, 120, 170, 344, 362, 375, 541, 888, 931
    barriers to learning 869, 879–80, 882
    Chinese enterprise networks 718, 723, 729
    dynamic knowledge 504, 509, 511, 513
    imaginary organizations 734, 747, 749
    media choice 526, 530
    multimodal learning 905, 909, 916
    multinationals 635, 643, 645, 648
    political science 139, 147, 150, 154, 156
    power and politics 488, 558, 565, 568–9, 571–3, 577
    rules 601, 603, 619
    strategic alliances 658, 675
    supplier networks 700, 703, 709–11
historical institutionalism 12, 147–8
historicism 120–1
history 12–13, 89, 120–1, 138–41
    economic theory 95–6, 99
    future research 923, 927
    management science 64, 67, 71
    organizational learning and 162–86
    rules 599, 605–6, 614–15, 618
    time and 354, 358–9, 361–2
Hitachi 722
Hoechst AG 665
Hoffmann-LaRoche 779–80
Hohner 176
home base advantage and multinationals 641–4, 649
home-pages 828
homo oeconomicus 131–2
Honda 507
Hong Kong and Chinese enterprises 716–29
hopelessness 867, 880
hot-spot locations 278
human capital 97–9, 100, 196, 275, 316, 463, 587, 646, 684, 795–8, 802–5

human embodied/nonembodied knowledge 802
human relations 586
human resources 44, 78, 563–4, 672, 704, 740, 756, 777, 782, 799, 803–4, 809, 811, 890, 896–7
humanities 287
Hungary 242–59, 671, 681–94
hyperformalism 153
hyperlinks 828
hyperrationality 91–2
hypertext organization 511–13
hypothesizing 22
hypothetical histories 614–15

IBM 379
identification 25, 78–80, 212, 755, 776–80, 784, 791, 814
identity 29, 131, 138, 256, 271, 305, 358, 601–3, 646, 703, 805
    conflict 489, 582–94
    history 13, 174, 176, 178, 180, 182, 186
    information technology 840, 843
    multimodal learning 904, 914
    social constitution of organization 317, 320–3
    sociology 37, 41–5
    strategic alliances 661, 665, 670–1, 674
    theory and transformation 891, 895, 897–8, 900
ideology 934–5
IG Metall 450, 453–6
IKEA 337, 537
illusion of validity 22–3
Ilongot people 131
imaginary organizations 536, 543, 549–50, 629–30, 658, 733–49, 928, 931
imitation 52, 276–7, 457, 575, 627, 641, 685, 924
    anthropology 127, 131
    Chinese enterprise networks 629, 717–19, 721–2, 725–8
    economic theory 93–4, 97, 100, 103, 109
    emotions and 380–1, 384–5
    European transformation process 196, 245, 247–8, 258
    multimodal learning 902, 904, 913–15
    rules 606–7, 613–14
    strategizing 537, 539, 542–4, 549, 551
    success and failure 332–3, 339, 344–5
    supplier networks 702–3, 706
implementation and multimodal learning 902–3, 908–11, 913, 916
improvisation 511, 830
incentives 80, 107, 212, 322, 363, 431, 646, 672–3, 705, 762, 826
    emotions 306, 370–1, 378–9
    individual change agents 403, 405
    intellectual capital 805, 810

leadership 418, 426
market signals 265, 271, 275, 278
multimodal learning 910, 914
power and politics 560, 564, 574
rules 602, 617
success and failure 330–1, 333, 340, 344
tools of learning 783, 786
incremental learning 146, 164, 273, 315, 330, 340, 638–9, 707–11
    boards 431, 434
    Chinese enterprise networks 629, 721
    economic theory 103–5, 111
    future research 923, 937
    rules 606, 618–19
    strategizing 539–40, 544–6, 548, 551, 553
    vision 295, 298
independence 404–5, 438, 440, 627
individuals 195, 232–3, 305, 429, 489, 801–5, 826
    agents of learning 395, 398–412
    anthropology 119, 124–5, 131
    barriers to learning 865, 867, 870, 879
    Chinese enterprise networks 717–19, 729
    conditions for learning 757–8, 768, 770–2
    conflict and identity 582, 585, 587–90, 592, 594
    consultants 464, 466, 479
    dynamic knowledge 487, 492–5, 497–500, 503–5, 509–10, 513
    economic theory 89, 91, 94–5, 97–9, 106–7, 109–10
    emotions 307, 369, 371–8, 381–7, 389
    European transformation process 251, 256
    future research 922, 924, 930
    history and 162–4, 180–1
    imaginary organizations 737–8, 746–7
    information technology 828, 830
    joint ventures 687, 690
    leadership 415–18, 421–3, 426
    management science 64–5, 67, 69, 71–9
    market signals 264–5, 268, 270, 272–3, 275
    media choice 520, 524, 528–31
    multimodal learning 903–5, 911–13, 915–17
    multinationals 632, 636–8, 646–9
    political science 139, 142, 147–8, 150–1, 155, 157
    power and politics 559, 566, 568, 571, 573
    psychology 12–13, 14–29
    rules 490, 598–604, 607–9, 611–13, 615, 618–19
scenario planning 856–7, 859, 861, 863

individuals (*cont.*)
  social constitution of
    organization 308, 317–18, 322
  sociology 35–6, 38–42, 44, 47, 49
  strategic alliances 671, 673
  strategizing 536–8, 544, 546, 552–3
  success and failure 331–2, 335–6, 338, 345
  supplier networks 628, 702–3, 706
  theory and transformation 886–7, 890
  time and 352–3, 356–7, 361, 363–5
  tools of learning 775–7, 780, 787–8, 790
  unions 448, 449, 458
  value change 199, 201–7, 210, 212–13, 215
  vision 285–6, 298
indoctrination 603
inductive learning 21
industrial action 448, 453
industrial crisis 223–4
industrial knowledge 802
industrial relations 447–51, 584, 588, 629, 728, 905
industrialization and value
    change 195–6, 198, 201–4, 215
inertia 125, 298, 358, 410, 453, 508, 561
  barriers to learning 868, 880
  European transformation
    process 247, 256
  history and 163–4, 173
  market signals 196, 264–6, 272, 275–8
  strategizing 488, 535, 539, 553
  success and failure 306, 338, 340, 342–4
infant formula crisis and Nestlé 224, 226–8, 230, 233, 235–8
influence:
  boards 428–9, 431, 434, 438, 440–1
  consultants 466, 470–3
  leadership 396, 415–16, 418–20, 426
  unions 446–7
information 47, 128–9, 291, 627, 895–6
  boards 429–30, 433, 437–9, 442
  Chinese enterprise networks 629, 717, 719, 725–7
  conditions for learning 307, 759, 762, 769, 771
  consultants 464–5, 467, 471–2, 474–6
  dynamic knowledge 487, 491–2, 504–5, 509–10
  economic theory 93–4, 96–7, 107
  emotions and 373–7, 380–2
  future research 929, 937
  history and 169, 175–6, 178, 181, 183–4
  imaginary organizations 740, 742, 745
  individual change agents 408, 410
  intellectual capital 756, 796, 801, 803–4, 806, 808, 810, 812
  joint ventures 687–8, 693

management science 61, 66, 69, 71, 78, 80–1
media choice 487, 518–32
multimodal learning 903–4, 911, 915
multinationals 631–2, 634, 637–9, 640, 643–7
political science 142–3, 152–4, 156–7
power and politics 565–6, 570, 572, 574, 576–7
processing and value change 205–6, 212–14
psychology 17, 19–21, 25–9
rules 600, 604–5, 618
social constitution of
    organization 308, 310, 313–14, 317, 319–23
strategic alliances 660–1, 674–6
strategizing 488, 536–7, 543–4, 550
success and failure 328–30, 338–9
supplier networks 700–1, 703–5, 708, 710
time 306, 354, 356
tools of learning 778–9, 782–4, 786
unions 450
information technology 455, 474, 500, 549, 571, 646–7, 674–5, 823
  Chinese enterprise networks 717, 727
  imaginary organizations 734–6, 738–40, 744–5
  intellectual capital 756, 794, 807, 811
  media choice 518–19, 521, 531
  multimodal learning 907, 911
  practice, learning into 827–45
  strategizing 536, 549
inheritance and history 163–4, 173
inhibition 374–5, 384, 388
Inköpscentralernas AB 451–3, 456
innovation 26, 164–5, 214, 374–5, 477, 627, 794, 824, 855–6, 893
  anthropology 122, 125
  barriers to learning 867, 869, 873, 876, 879
  Chinese enterprise networks 629, 716–20, 722–9
  conditions for learning 757, 763
  conflict and identity 583–4, 589
  dynamic knowledge 491–2, 508, 510, 513
  economic theory 12, 89, 92–3, 98–109, 111
  future research 922, 927, 934, 937–8
  imaginary organizations 630, 733, 741–3
  individual change agents 402, 405–6, 411
  information technology 829–30, 833, 837
  joint ventures 687, 689, 691, 693–4
  management science 61, 72, 78, 80
  market signals 265, 270, 278
  multinationals 638, 641–5, 648–50
  power and politics 561, 568

rules 604, 607, 614, 618
social constitution of
    organization 308–9, 311–12, 314–16, 318, 320
social movements 222, 230, 236, 238–9
sociology 40–1, 51
strategic alliances 668, 674, 676
strategizing 542, 546
success and failure 331, 334, 337–8, 344
supplier networks 703, 705, 709–11
tools of learning 756, 780–3
unions 448–50, 455
vision 283, 288–94, 296–8
inquiry 544, 786–7, 930
  conditions for learning 755, 757, 760–2, 767–8, 770–2
  conflict and identity 489, 582–3, 587, 590–4
  individual change agents 399–400, 403–4, 406, 407–10
  theory and transformation 890, 897
insight/action inertia 539
inspirational leadership 418–19
institution theory 284, 310, 641–2
institutions 561, 608, 693, 734, 806, 933
  anthropology 123–5, 130
  Chinese enterprise networks 718, 721–3, 726
  economic theory 90–2, 94–5, 107
  history and 168, 174–5, 181–2
  management science 63–4, 68
  multimodal learning 904, 915
  political science 138–9, 141–5, 148, 151–2, 157
  sociology 35, 37, 41, 50, 52–4
  supplier networks 699, 704–8, 710
  value change 200, 206–8
instrumental learning 17–19
integration 247, 287, 358, 476, 542, 685–6, 720, 759–60, 870, 905
  conflict and identity 588–9, 592–3
  economic theory 107–8, 110
  emotions and 371, 375
  information technology 832, 835, 837, 841, 843–5
  intellectual capital 756, 812–14, 890
  management science 61, 64–5, 71, 75, 78–80
  multinationals 627, 632, 640, 644–8
  rules 601, 603, 612, 619
  scenario planning 824, 849, 851, 859, 861–2
  social constitution of
    organization 315–19, 322
  strategic alliances 659–60, 662, 666, 675
  supplier networks 700, 709
  theory and transformation 889–90, 894
  tools of learning 755, 775, 777, 784–7, 790–1

Intel Corporation 338
intellectual capital 270, 403, 418, 422,
    426, 748–9, 756, 794–814, 924
intellectual potential 812
intellectual property 110
intellectual tradition 925–8
intelligent organization concept 577
intent 16, 23–5, 28, 265–6, 274–7, 282,
    285, 541, 666, 669, 672–4, 676, 689,
    762, 776, 932
interaction 199, 314, 395, 487, 591, 779,
    805, 823, 826, 877, 893, 937
    anthropology 125, 130
    boards 396, 432, 436, 438–40, 442
    Chinese enterprise networks 723,
        727
    conditions for learning 760, 768
    consultants 465–6, 469–71, 473,
        475–6, 480
    dynamic knowledge 487, 492–3, 495,
        497–501, 503–5, 508–10, 513
    economic theory 94–5, 99–100, 109
    emotions and 370, 372–3
    imaginary organizations 629, 733,
        735, 738, 741–2, 744–7
    information technology 823, 830–4,
        837, 841–2
    joint ventures 628, 684–5, 687–94
    leadership 415–16, 419–20, 423
    management science 71–2, 78
    market signals 266, 273, 277
    media choice 521, 524, 528–9, 531
    multimodal learning 902, 904, 908,
        915
    multinationals 631, 637, 642, 648–50
    political science 139–40, 142–3, 145,
        147, 151–2, 156
    power and politics 558, 568, 572–4,
        577–8
    rules 600, 603–5, 607, 612–13, 615
    scenario planning 857, 863
    sociology 35, 38, 42–3, 47–53
    strategic alliances 658–62, 665–9,
        673, 676
    strategizing 488, 535–9, 544, 549,
        552–3
    supplier networks 629, 700–2, 704–5,
        707, 710
    time and 351, 354, 356
    unions 397, 450, 455
interdependence 42, 103, 153, 641, 644,
    647, 650, 709, 723
interest as emotion 376–7, 381, 383–8
interest groups 36, 148–53, 195, 207,
    221–39, 560, 565, 578
interests 410, 530, 663
    conflict and identity 489, 582,
        584–90, 592–4
    consultants 463, 476
    power and politics 560, 565, 568,
        575
    supplier networks 702, 710–11
    unions 446–8, 454, 456, 458

interfaces between society and
    organizations 198–9, 204–9
Interflug 359–60
internalization 336, 353, 603, 628, 706,
    721–2, 758, 856
    dynamic knowledge 493, 495–8,
        500–1, 503, 511, 513
    imaginary organizations 738–9, 742
    information technology 823, 830–5,
        838, 843–5
    joint ventures 688, 692
    multinationals 635, 648
International Organization 146–7
internationalization 12, 144–7, 148,
    153, 155–7, 540, 542, 840, 911, 923
    Chinese enterprise networks 716–29
    imaginary organizations 733–49
    joint ventures 681–94
    multinationals 631–50
    strategic alliances 657–77
    supplier networks 699–712
Internet 154, 289, 292–4, 296, 832, 840
Internet Engineering Task Force
    293–4, 296
Internet Standards Organization 293,
    296
Interorganizational learning 52, 79,
    110–11, 313, 320, 332, 381, 833, 932
    imaginary organizations 733–4, 737,
        739, 742–5, 747
    multimodal 902, 905–9, 912–13,
        916–17
    multinationals 631–50
interpersonal context 41
interpretation of knowledge 25, 382,
    636–7
    Chinese enterprise networks 717–18,
        729
    future research 929, 937
    history and 177–8, 180
    management science 64, 67, 69–71,
        78
    media 519–20, 525–6, 528, 530–1
    multimodal learning 903–4, 914, 916
    sociology 39, 43
interpretive anthropology 119, 121
interrupted learning processes 869,
    873, 875, 877, 879, 880–1, 883, 923
intervention 397, 887, 910, 928
    boards 430–1, 439
    conflict and identity 582, 584–5, 587,
        589–90, 592
    consultants 466–7, 469–71, 473–4,
        476, 478, 480
    European transformation
        process 250–1, 255
    intellectual capital 796, 801
    management science 64, 68, 74, 76
    political science 147, 151–2
    power and politics 559, 565, 568–9
    scenario planning 858, 861, 863
    tools of learning 755, 776, 779, 783,
        788, 790

intranets 745, 810–11, 828–9, 832
intraorganizational 76, 103, 629, 902,
    908–11, 913–17
intraorganizational relations, social
    constitution of organization
    317–18
intrapreneurs, individual change
    agents 403–4
intrapreneurs and value change 205
investment:
    boards 428–9, 440–1
    foreign direct 242, 248, 251–5, 257–9,
        634–6, 638, 640, 642, 682–4
    intellectual capital 794, 797–8, 801,
        803–5, 807–9, 811–12
Iron Triangle concept 565, 567
Israeli Air Force Ordnance Corps 759,
    762–5, 767–9, 770, 772
issues management 207–8, 761–3,
    768–9, 771, 891, 923, 929

Japan 165, 171–2, 337, 668, 671–2, 675,
    685, 708–11, 718, 720–1, 723–5, 728,
    795, 832
Jenoptik 250–1, 256–7
joint ventures 110, 628, 681–94, 720–1,
    880
    European transformation
        process 243, 252, 257
    imaginary organizations 735, 748
    strategic alliances 628, 657–9, 662–4,
        667, 669, 671, 673–4, 676–7
just-in-time 172, 700, 707, 709, 711, 842

kaizen 535, 539, 548
Kao Corporation 507, 510
knowledge 128–30, 384, 628, 630, 756
    boards 396, 429, 433–5, 438, 441–2
    Chinese enterprise networks
        716–19, 721–2
    conditions for learning 757, 772
    consultants 397, 463–5, 467, 470–1,
        473–4, 478–80
    economic theory 97–9, 102–5, 108–9,
        111
    European transformation
        process 196, 255, 257
    future research 821–38, 923
    history and 162, 179, 181–4
    individual change agents 402–3,
        406, 410
    leadership 416, 418, 426
    management science 11, 61–2, 64–5,
        67–74, 76, 78, 81
    market signals 264–74, 276–8
    multimodal learning 911, 916–17
    multinationals 627, 631–9
    political science 150, 156
    psychology 14–17, 19, 21–3, 26–7, 29
    scenario planning 851, 854
    social constitution of
        organization 309–13, 315–23
    social movements 221, 234, 238

knowledge (*cont.*)
  sociology 35–9, 41–54
  strategic alliances 659, 663, 672–4,
    677
  success and failure 332, 334, 336, 339
  theory and transformation 887,
    898
  time and 352, 354, 356, 358, 361–3
  tools of learning 778–80, 782, 785–6
  unions 447, 449, 457–8
  value change 206–7, 209, 213–14, 216
  vision 283, 288
  see also acquisition of knowledge;
    creation of knowledge; diffusion
    of knowledge; explicit
    knowledge; interpretation of
    knowledge; shared knowledge;
    tacit knowledge
knowledge colony 840–1, 843
knowledge identity 889, 895
knowledge management 794–814, 827,
  829, 905, 924, 925
knowledge management 837, 842,
  844–5
Korea conglomerates 672
Krupp–Rheinhausen case 453–4

labor:
  division of 40, 44, 49–50, 61, 504,
    510–11, 543
  organized 396–7
laboratories good practice 789–91, 825
language 20, 71–2, 511, 538, 594, 744,
  770, 868
  anthropology 121, 129
  Chinese enterprise networks 719,
    726
  future research 921, 924, 933–4
  history and 177–81, 185
  media choice 521–2, 528–9
  multinationals 634, 636
  rules 600–1, 619
  scenario planning 851, 861–2
  sociology 43–5, 47, 50
  strategic alliances 661, 668–9
  unions 447, 458
latecomers, Chinese enterprises 719,
  721–2, 726, 729, 932
lateral centralization 643–4
law 141–2, 148
leadership 74, 124, 205, 255, 306, 489,
  586, 640, 756, 903
  agents of learning 395, 415–26
  barriers to learning 825, 868–9, 871,
    873–5, 877, 879–93
  boards 428, 432, 440
  Chinese enterprise networks 717–19,
    724, 729
  dynamic knowledge 487, 505,
    508–10
  emotions and 373, 380
  future research 930–2, 937
  history and 166, 185

imaginary organizations 734, 736–7,
  739–41, 743, 745
individual change agents 402,
  405–6
market signals 196–7, 265, 274–5,
  277
political science 139–40, 144–5, 147,
  149–50, 154–7
power and politics 560, 563, 566, 572,
  574–7
social constitution of
  organization 308, 311–17, 321–2
strategizing 537, 540, 542
success and failure 328, 337, 345
theory and transformation 889, 893,
  895–6, 898–9
tools of learning 756, 790
vision 282, 286, 294, 296
leaky knowledge 267–8, 270
lean management 462, 478–9, 637
lean production 172–3
learning:
  contracts 788, 791
  curves 16, 61, 64, 92, 97–9, 109, 332,
    365
  histories 784–5, 791
  life-long 396, 419, 423, 426
  mechanisms 826
  trap 728, 867–8
learning-by-doing 92, 97–9, 101, 104,
  172, 497, 638, 832, 924
learning-by-searching 101, 104
learning-by-using 101–2, 104
learning-in-action 766
learning-in-organizing 35, 47–53, 904,
  929
legends and history 183–4
legislative organizations 142–3
legislatures 151, 153, 558–9, 561, 565, 573
legitimacy 37, 256–9
  boards 437, 439
  history and 162, 178–9, 181–4
  imaginary organizations 740, 742
  power and politics 559, 562, 564, 569
  rules 489, 601, 604, 613
  social constitution of
    organization 310, 312, 315, 321–2
  social movements 195, 221, 223–4
  strategizing 543, 545–6, 553
  unions 447–9, 456, 458
Leitbilds 284
levels of learning 755, 760, 775–7, 791
leverage 151, 408–9, 465, 643, 647, 693
life-space of individual 410–11
limits of rules 615–18
lists 128–9
lobbying 151
localism 446, 448–51, 454–7, 572, 632,
  634, 643–5, 648–50, 658, 663, 682,
  684, 687–9, 840–1, 844
lock-in 95, 105, 107, 233, 238–9, 254,
  708–9
Lockheed 99

logic, dominant 269–70, 272, 274
luck 95, 379, 385, 935, 937

machine-tool industry 708
Maekawa Seisakusho 509
maladaptive learning 39
management 289–90, 756, 825, 826
  barriers to learning 867–74, 876–81
  boards 396, 428–43
  Chinese enterprise networks 717–21,
    724, 728–9
  conditions for learning 307, 758,
    762–3
  conflict and identity 586, 588–94
  consultants 463–4, 469–79
  dynamic knowledge 487, 491, 501,
    503–11, 513
  economic theory 91–2, 106, 108–10
  emotions and 369–71, 374–5
  European transformation
    process 246, 249–52, 254–7, 259
  future research 922, 924, 930–1, 933,
    937
  history and 169–71, 175, 181–3, 185
  imaginary organizations 734,
    739–40, 743–5, 745–9
  individual change agents 395, 400,
    402, 405–6, 408, 411
  information technology 823, 839,
    842–4
  joint ventures 682–4, 686–7, 690–4
  market signals 196–7, 264–9, 272–7
  media choice 518–24, 526–8, 531–2
  multimodal learning 903–5, 908–10,
    913, 915–17
  multinationals 632–3, 635–8, 641–6,
    648–50
  political science 139, 145–6, 148, 155
  power and politics 557, 559–69,
    571–3, 577
  psychology 14, 24–6
  research future 928, 932
  rules 599, 601, 614, 616–17, 619
  scenario planning 849–53, 857–8,
    860, 863
  social constitution of
    organization 309–17, 319–20,
    322–3
  social movements 227, 231, 234, 237
  sociology 37, 44
  strategic alliances 628, 657–60,
    664–5, 670–6
  strategizing 535–6, 538–42, 546–8,
    550, 553
  success and failure 305, 327–9, 332,
    334–9, 345
  supplier networks 629, 708, 711–12
  theory and transformation 887–8,
    890–900
  time and 351, 356, 363–5
  tools of learning 755–6, 776, 782, 785
  unions 447, 450–5, 457
  value change 205–7, 210–12, 214

management science 11, 61–81, 89, 282, 925, 937
management theory 125, 139
manipulation 270
maps 50, 70, 333–4, 407, 503, 594, 660, 903
  barriers to learning 870, 882
  Chinese enterprise networks 718, 729
  conditions for learning 760–3, 767, 771–2
  future research 922, 929
  scenario planning 850, 854–5
  strategizing 550, 552
  supplier networks 699, 702, 704, 706–8, 711
  tools of learning 779–80, 791
marginality 397, 462–80, 875, 879
market 39, 62, 195–6, 291–4, 328–9, 447, 462, 513, 700–1, 937
  Chinese enterprise networks 716, 720–4, 726–7
  economic theory 91, 93–4, 97, 100, 106–8
  European transformation process 242–52, 255–9
  history and 163–4, 167
  imaginary organizations 734, 736–7, 740, 743, 745, 748–9
  intellectual capital 806–7, 809, 811
  joint ventures 681–3, 693–4
  multinationals 627, 631–2, 634–5, 638–9, 641, 644
  political science 152–3, 156
  power and politics 557, 561, 566–7, 571, 577–8
  signals, guided responses to 195–6, 264–78
  strategic alliances 658, 664, 666
  strategizing 536, 540, 542, 549
  theory and transformation 888–9, 892–4, 896, 898
  time and 359, 362
  value 794–8, 801, 803–4
marketing 212–15, 684, 809–11, 905
  consultants 466, 474, 479
  European transformation process 245–7, 249–51, 257–8
  social movements 226–7, 233, 236
  theory and transformation 888, 890
Marxism 36, 47, 49, 129, 167, 177, 184
materialism 202–4
materiality of knowledge 49, 51
matrix structure 588
Matsushita Electrics Industry Co Ltd 645
maturation 16, 63, 76
meaning, making 72–4, 318–19, 527–8, 762, 805, 904
  agents and 400, 457
  history and 167, 176–80, 183, 185
  information technology 828, 830, 845

multinationals 636–7, 640, 647–9
  strategizing 550–1, 553
measurement 71, 829
  knowledge and intellectual capital 794–814
media 154, 560–1, 565, 897
  choice 487–8, 518–32
mediation and leadership 573–4
memory 128–30, 156, 358, 417, 674, 702, 717, 785–6, 826, 856
  barriers to learning 873, 875
  consultants 465, 471, 478–9
  emotions 306, 371, 373, 375, 381–2
  future research 929, 934
  history and 13, 162, 164, 175–6, 179, 181, 186
  imaginary organizations 737–8
  intellectual capital 805
  internationalization 627
  management science 66–7, 70, 74, 78, 80
  media choice 520, 522, 529–31
  multimodal learning 903, 909–11, 916–17
  psychology 14, 17, 19–20, 26–8
  rules 603, 606
  sociology 42, 44
  strategizing 537, 544, 548
  success and failure 328, 334
Menarini 251
mental models 64–5, 382, 423, 737
  barriers to learning 866, 868
  Chinese enterprise networks 717, 729
  conflict and identity 587, 590
  development of learning 931
  dynamic knowledge 494, 497, 499–500
  economics 90–1
  future research 922, 926, 929–30
  individual change agents 400, 406–7
  rules 611–12, 617
  scenario planning 860–1, 863
  supplier networks 629, 702, 704–6
  tools of learning 780, 785, 790
metal industry 24, 180
metalevel learning 537–8
metaphor 46–7, 125, 164, 178–80, 185, 495, 497, 552, 831, 857, 936
methodology research 936–7
Michelin 272
micro/macro problems 38
microeconomics 90, 801–6
microinteraction 11, 36, 41–3, 46
Microsoft Corporation 759, 828
microworlds 789–90
middle-up-down management 174, 503, 505–11, 513, 674, 879, 905, 908, 910, 916, 930
military 98–9, 102, 165, 928
mimesis 127, 613
mind organizations 544, 547, 549

mind, social theory of 41
minorities and leadership 574
Mishlav Jaffa Vocation High School 764–9, 771–2
Mitsubishi Heavy Industry Ltd 583–4
mnemonics 128–9
mobility 291–2, 296, 894
mobilization 37, 46, 222–3, 228, 230, 232–3, 236–7, 239, 542, 574–5, 725
modeling 19, 24, 147, 757, 771, 779, 801
modernism 43, 52, 123, 128–31, 163, 167–9, 178, 181, 185, 202
modernization 12, 36, 52, 121–4, 131, 167–8, 184, 215, 449, 684, 720–1, 937
modes of learning 11, 76, 78, 80–1, 755, 775–7, 782, 785, 787, 790–1
modification 79–80, 776, 785–7, 791, 814
Modjokuto and Tabanan in Indonesia 122–3
monitoring 51–2, 73, 387, 429–30, 432, 442, 808, 825, 854–6, 899
monocracy 488, 568–72
monopoly and European transformation process 248, 250
Mont Fleur project, South Africa 862
mood-dependent recall 381–2, 385
mortality, infant 226
motivation 38, 211–12, 305, 360–1, 395, 418–20, 473, 543, 575, 582, 686, 739, 783, 909–10
  dynamic knowledge 495, 508
  emotions and 370–2, 374, 376–7, 380, 384–7
  individual change agents 398–9, 404, 409–11
  intellectual capital 803, 809
  psychology 23, 25
  rules 602–3, 605, 608, 618
  scenario planning 855, 859, 861, 863
  social constitution of organization 314, 319
  strategic alliances 657, 664, 668, 673
  theory and transformation 888, 893, 895–8
  vision 284–6, 296
Motorola 417–18, 507
movement of individual life-space 411
movements, social 195, 221–39
multimodal organization learning 902–17
multinationals 152, 463, 567, 570–1, 594, 627, 631–50, 658, 663, 671, 681–2, 688, 720, 880, 923, 932, 935
multiple story approach to research 936–7
myopia 39, 868–9, 880
myths 126, 551–2

narratives 12, 44–6, 128–9, 171–2, 176, 177–9, 182–4
NASA 306, 340–2

nationalism 585, 627, 670
  Chinese enterprise networks 726,
    729
  history and 166–7, 182–3
  multinationals 631–4, 639, 640–3,
    647–8, 650
  supplier networks 629, 706, 708–11
  unions 446, 449, 455–6, 458
NEC 508
needs 469–72, 489, 576, 588, 590–3
negotiation and political science 156
neoclassicism 91, 93, 96–7, 99, 164, 634,
    804, 806
neoinstitutionalism 541, 604, 613, 719
Nestlé Coordination Center for
    Nutrition 227
Nestlé Infant Formula Audit
    Commission 227
Nestlé and infant formula crisis 224,
    226–8, 230, 233, 235–8
networks 106, 148, 278, 317, 381, 627,
    805, 859
  barriers to learning 880, 882
  future research 922, 928, 931–2, 937
  imaginary organizations 629, 734–6,
    740–1, 744, 746
  information technology 832, 835
  joint ventures 687, 693
  management science 68, 78
  multinationals 627, 631–2, 640–9
  power 567–8, 577
  strategic alliances 657, 663
  strategizing 542, 549
  technological vision 293
  tools of learning 783
NHS 527
Nigeria 233, 855
nonverbal language 127
normative organizations 264, 285, 310,
    613, 702, 757, 852
  multinationals 642, 648
  power 557–8, 560–2, 564, 566, 570
  socioeconomic values 198, 210, 216
  strategizing 535, 541–2, 546, 548–9
noticing 334

objective/experimental
    knowledge 639
objective/psychosocial media 520
objectivity:
  history and 163, 171, 174, 176–8, 182
  subjectivity 352–3, 355
observational learning 19, 24, 128, 201,
    354, 361, 384
Olivetti Corporation 664
Olympia Büromaschinenwerke 276,
    289–90, 294
ombudsman 143, 153, 227, 236
Open Space Technology 781–2, 790–1,
    933
open-systems approach 246
openness 312, 403, 405, 669–70, 675,
    701, 704, 706–7, 711, 739, 755, 760, 763

operational learning 611, 628, 702–3,
    707–9, 711, 832
operationalization 17
opportunity 157, 224–5, 268, 386–7, 456,
    490, 567–8, 724, 771, 845, 914
  barriers to learning 869, 874, 876
  boards 430, 438, 441–2
  conflict and identity 582, 590–1
  consultants 463, 470, 474
  economic theory 90, 104, 109–10
  imaginary organizations 733–4, 736,
    745–8
  joint ventures 628, 682, 687, 692
  media choice 525, 531
  multinationals 631, 633, 639–43,
    645
  rules 605–6, 612, 616
  scenario planning 850, 855–6
  social constitution of
    organization 313, 315–16
  strategic alliances 657, 661–4, 666–9,
    673, 676–7
  strategizing 488, 537, 542, 550, 553
  success and failure 328, 334, 338
  supplier networks 701, 705, 711
  vision 283, 287, 289, 298
optimization 26, 90–1, 93, 102, 107
oral media 129, 521, 826
organic/mechanistic systems 317
organizational capital 795–6, 804–5
organizational learning mechanisms
    755, 758–9, 763–4, 768
organizing 37, 47, 110, 129, 849,
    929, 935
orientation 284–6, 296, 354–5, 361–2
originating ba 499–500, 830–1, 838,
    841, 843
other, knowledge of 130–1
Oticon 278
outcomes 43, 184, 245, 309, 430, 464,
    488, 548, 674, 709, 790, 852–3
  conditions for learning 762, 770
  conflict and identity 585–90, 594
  economic theory 90–2, 94–5, 106
  emotions and 370, 380–1, 386
  individual change agents 398, 406,
    409
  leadership 415, 417
  management science 67, 79–80
  power 568, 577
  psychology 16, 28
  rules 599, 609, 613–14, 618
  success and failure 328, 330–1, 334,
    344
outsiders and scenario planning 861,
    863
overarching visions 196–7, 285–91,
    293–8
overload 150, 196, 214, 269, 331, 364,
    375, 510, 568, 768
ownership 428–9, 436, 661, 685, 688–9,
    692–3, 720, 723–5, 740, 769, 806,
    838, 839, 852–3

parliamentary systems 151
participation 686, 756, 763, 825, 832,
    909
  barriers to learning 870, 873–4
  boards 437–9, 441–2
  conflict and identity 589, 591
  consultants 467–9, 476–7
  dynamic knowledge 499, 501
  future research 929, 937
  imaginary organizations 738, 741,
    743
  management science 65, 74
  media choice 524, 526, 529
  political science 145, 156
  power and politics 568–9, 571, 577
  rules 600, 605
  sociology 35, 42, 45, 47–51, 53
  theory and transformation 889–90,
    893, 897, 899
parties, political 140, 143–4, 148, 151,
    153–5, 560–1, 575, 578
partnerships 837, 862
  imaginary organizations 733–49
passivity 429, 437–8, 487, 492, 736
past:
  economic theory and 95–6, 99
  future orientation 355, 358, 361–2,
    364
  history and 162–4, 173, 176, 177–9,
    182, 185
patents 635, 794–5
path dependency 92, 95, 103–5, 110,
    162–3, 173–4, 642
patterns:
  of behavior 373, 384–5
  and planning 859–60
payoffs and economic theory 96
pepsiCo Inc. 675–6
perceptions 488–90, 494, 544–6, 868,
    929
  conflict and identity 584, 590
  consultants 464, 470, 473
  emotions and 370, 373–4, 378, 380
  individual change agents 408–9, 411
  market signals 264–6, 268–70, 272–3,
    276–7
  media choice 523–31
  multinationals 636, 648
  rules 599, 612, 614
  strategic alliances 662, 670
  success and failure 327–30, 333–6,
    339–40, 345
  time and 354, 356, 358, 362, 365
  value change 195, 198, 205, 207–9,
    214
  vision 282, 284–7, 289–90, 294–8
performance 38, 150, 181, 228, 276,
    355–6, 396, 447, 720, 827
  boards 428–30, 432, 439–41
  conditions for learning 757, 759,
    763, 769
  conflict and identity 582, 584, 587,
    589–90, 592

consultants 467, 473
economic theory 97–8, 100, 102–4, 107–9, 111
emotions and 370, 378, 387–8
imaginary organizations 735, 737, 747–8
individual change agents 403, 405–7, 410
intellectual capital 756, 794, 801–5, 808, 810
joint ventures 685–94
leadership 417, 420
management science 61, 71, 77
media choice 487, 518, 521, 531–2
multinationals 637, 641–2, 644
paths 434–7, 443
power and politics 561, 574
psychology 13, 16–17, 23, 26–9
rules 609, 616–19
social constitution of organization 311, 318
socioeconomic values 200, 215
strategic alliances 662, 671
strategizing 540, 542–3, 545–8, 551
success and failure 327–8, 330–5, 337, 339, 342, 344
supplier networks 704, 709
theory and transformation 888, 891
periphery dynamics 934
personality 149, 415–16, 426
personnel 27–8, 67, 237, 335, 572, 613, 803, 826
dynamic knowledge 499, 510
economic theory 100, 103
good laboratory practice 908–9, 912, 915, 917
multinationals 635, 648–9
social constitution of organization 311, 314–15, 317, 319–20
supplier networks 701–2, 705, 708
value change 206–7, 210–13
perspective, time 354–5, 358–61, 365
pharmaceutical industry 825, 902–17
Pharmaceutical Manufacturers Association 907
phase models 11, 77–80, 357–8, 825, 870, 881, 883, 930
learning tools 775–91
phenomenology 41, 47–9, 51–2
Philips Electrics NV 645
philosophy 41, 43
planning 327, 364, 466, 488, 607–8, 663, 808, 903
central, and European transformation process 243, 245–7, 256
future research 923, 935
joint ventures 681, 691
power 571, 575
strategizing 539–40, 543, 547–8, 550–1
theory and transformation 897, 899

pluralism 137, 148, 151, 488, 568–72, 574
point-of-sales 838, 840, 842–3
Poland and transformation process 242–59
policy 162, 540
political science 12, 138, 141, 145–6, 147–54, 156
power and politics 558–62, 565–76, 578
unions 447–51, 456, 458
political science 12, 137–57, 184, 297, 557, 562–4, 566, 573, 577–8, 924, 925, 932, 937
politics 124, 168, 174, 931–2, 934–5
population analysis 68
positioning strategy 547
positive/negative emotions 369–70, 373, 378–84, 385–7
positivism 178
postmaterialism 202, 204, 210
postmodernism 11, 36, 43–6, 52, 126, 130, 163, 166, 176–8, 181, 184, 186, 195, 202, 204, 636, 921
poststructuralism 43
potential, behavioral 16
power 20, 338, 396, 449–51, 487–90, 499, 627, 634–5, 662–3, 692, 736, 830, 916, 931–2
barriers to learning 869, 870
boards 428–9, 431–2, 435–9, 441–3
Chinese enterprise networks 629, 719, 722, 729
conflict and identity 585–91
consultants 470–1, 480
emotions and 384, 388
future research 924, 934–5, 937
history and 162, 168, 178–80, 183–4
leadership 419–22, 426
political science 12, 149–51, 153, 155, 157
politics and 557–78
social constitution of organization 310, 313, 315–16, 319, 322–3
social movements 221, 225, 228, 232, 234, 238
sociology 11–12, 36–9, 41, 43–6, 52–3
strategizing 543, 545, 550
struggles 562–7, 569, 572, 575, 577, 604, 861
supplier networks 699, 701, 705–6, 711
technological vision 290–1, 294–5, 298
theory and transformation 890, 893, 896, 898
practice:
sociology 47–54
time and 353, 363
trends 927, 932–3
practice, learning:
conditions for learning 757–72
intellectual capital 794–814

learning as 718–19
tools of learning 775–91
practice, learning into:
barriers to learning 865–83
information technology 827–45
scenario planning 849–63
pressure:
groups 151
time 354–6, 359–62, 364–5
prior learning 19, 25, 28, 65, 103–5, 162, 164, 172–3, 374, 385
prisoners dilemma 663
private/public 488–9, 628, 681–4, 802, 928, 931
political science 137, 139–43, 146–50, 152–3, 155–7
strategic alliances 557–78
privatization 243–4, 248–56, 258–9, 359–61
proactive management 397, 404, 429, 432–4, 437–9, 441–2, 452, 456–7, 561
problem-solving 145, 283, 354, 491–2, 675, 702, 717–18, 771, 801, 839, 888–90
barriers to learning 867, 873–8, 880, 883
conflict and identity 583–4, 587–8, 590, 592
consultants 462–3, 467–9, 471–80
economic theory 91, 94, 96–7, 106, 109
future research 921, 931, 935
history and 170, 185
individual change agents 404, 407, 409, 411
joint ventures 687, 690
leadership 418, 422, 425
management science 61–3, 67–8, 72, 74, 76–8
media choice 518–19, 525–7, 529–31
multimodal learning 903, 906, 912–13, 916
multinationals 637–8, 646, 650
power and politics 568, 574
psychology 18, 25
rules 598, 600, 603–9, 611, 616, 619
scenario planning 854, 858, 861
sociology 11, 38, 46
strategizing 538–9, 547, 552–3
success and failure 334–40
tools of learning 777–9, 781, 783, 788
procedural knowledge 21, 50
process, learning 125, 145–6, 270–1, 283, 398, 416–18, 429–30, 740, 755–6, 824–6
anthropology 118, 125
barriers to learning 824–5, 865–6, 870–1, 875, 877, 879–80, 883
Chinese enterprise networks 629, 717–18, 720–7
conditions for learning 757–8, 763, 767–8, 770–2
consultants 462, 465, 471–2, 476, 480

process, learning (cont.)
economic theory 94–5, 98, 100–6, 108
emotions 369–89
future research 921–2, 924, 934–5
history and 163–5, 169–76
information technology 823, 829–35
intellectual capital 796–7, 812–13
joint ventures 681–2, 685, 689, 691
management science 11, 66–7,
    69–70, 72–4, 77–81
multimodal learning 902–5, 908,
    911–17, 913
multinationals 638–9, 646
psychology 14–16, 19, 23–4, 26–8
research future 925, 929–33
scenario planning 824, 855–9
social constitution of
    organization 309–13, 315, 317–20,
    322–3
social movements 225, 232, 234,
    237–9
socioeconomic values 198–9, 209–15
sociology 42–3, 52–4
strategic alliances 660, 665, 674, 677
strategizing 535–7, 540–1, 543, 550–2
success and failure 330, 340
supplier networks 699, 701–2, 704
theory and transformation 886–900
time and 351, 353–65
transformation of Central
    Europe 242–59
productivity 61, 801, 803–5, 811, 813,
    827, 830
profitability 327, 333
Project SAPPHO 315
project scenario 849, 851–5, 862–3
project teams 512–13, 891, 894–5, 898
property rights 635, 794–5
protection 107, 170, 827–9
protest movements 183
psychological anthropology 119–21
psychology 12–13, 14–29, 43, 69, 96, 130,
    167, 415, 464, 546, 591, 618, 639, 828,
    867–8, 924–5
conditions for learning 760–3, 767
emotions and 371, 373, 378, 383
individual change agents 407, 411
success and failure 328, 330, 332, 345
theory and transformation 886,
    890, 895
public relations 207–8, 223–4, 226,
    228–32, 234, 237–8
punishment 126, 306, 330–1, 333, 340,
    344, 370, 378–80, 383–4, 560, 617,
    762
purposes of intellectual capital 801–2

quality 93, 356, 363, 707, 723, 726, 909,
    911–12, 914–15, 932
Quick Market Intelligence 778–9

race 186
ratio Q 796–8

rational choice theory 37–8, 147, 151
rational-utilitarianism 11, 36–9, 46
rationality 75, 96, 182, 345, 586, 638,
    705, 725, 931
bounded 69, 91–2
conditions for learning 762, 771
dynamic knowledge 494, 500
emotions and 369, 378, 387
political science 142, 146, 155
power and politics 558–9, 564, 569
rules 489, 598–9, 602, 604, 606, 609,
    615, 618
sociology 36–9, 46
strategizing 536, 541, 543
rationalization 167–9, 643–4, 935
reach 522, 658
reactive management 429, 431–2, 442,
    446, 451–3, 456–7, 561
readiness to learn 373–5
reality 181, 203, 269, 336, 423–4, 439,
    457, 471, 520, 545, 590, 615, 636, 674,
    746, 762, 882
Central European
    transformation 247, 250
dynamic knowledge 494, 505, 507
individual change agents 404,
    407–11
management science 67, 69, 71–6
scenario planning 850, 860
social movements 236, 238
sociology 41–3, 47
theory and transformation 889, 891,
    899
time and 355, 359, 363
tools of learning 779, 786–7
receptivity 667–8, 670, 676, 681
recipes 73, 128, 539, 551
reciprocity and supplier
    networks 700, 703–4, 711
reconstruction 12, 174–5, 177, 185
Red Queen effect 333
redundancy 509–10, 552, 645, 675, 703,
    706–7, 709, 844
reengineering 410, 462, 465, 473, 475,
    478–9, 535, 547–8, 809, 924, 932
refinement 546–8
reflection 146, 185, 344, 397, 438, 457–8,
    494, 615, 636, 686, 747, 890
conditions for learning 755, 757,
    759–60, 766, 769, 770
conflict and identity 591, 594
dynamic knowledge 494, 500–1
future research 923–4, 936
individual change agents 404,
    409–10
information technology 833–5,
    839–45
management science 71, 74–7, 79
scenario planning 824, 849, 856–9
sociology 47, 49
tools of learning 775–6, 779–80, 782,
    785, 787–9
reflection-in-action 511

reflexivity and sociology 35, 41, 51–3
regionalism 446, 449, 453–6, 572,
    640–3, 647, 719–20, 726, 729
regulations and multimodal
    learning 902–17
reinforcement 18, 21, 95, 126, 331, 344,
    352–4, 374–5, 377–80, 383, 385, 417,
    914
relatedness, business and joint
    ventures 689–90
relational knowledge 131
relevance detectors 306, 371, 376, 527
renewal 110, 337, 724–5, 728, 924
reorientation and boards 432, 436
repetition 165, 273, 330–1, 337, 343,
    353–4, 357, 360, 365, 379, 616, 737
representation, unions 447–50, 452,
    454, 456, 458
representationism 69
repression of information 382
requirements for learning 666–7
requisite variety and dynamic
    knowledge 510
research 102–3, 105, 107–8, 201, 213, 321,
    643, 810, 812–13, 826, 845, 937
organizational learning and
    future 921–38
resistance 63, 210, 272, 329, 396, 561,
    617, 647, 810, 874, 894, 931
Central European
    transformation 247, 252, 256
consultants 470, 473, 475
individual change agents 404, 412
multimodal learning 906, 914
social constitution of
    organization 309, 311–12
social movements 221, 225–30, 234–6
strategic alliances 670, 673
resolution of conflict 583–4, 586–92,
    594
resource, knowledge as 37, 756, 794–5
resources 38, 61, 108–11, 475, 541–2, 831,
    931–2
boards 429–30, 432, 437
Chinese enterprise networks 725,
    729
conflict and identity 489, 582,
    584–90, 592–4
dynamic knowledge 499, 501, 512
future research 924, 927, 935, 937
imaginary organizations 735–6, 740,
    745, 748
intellectual capital 756, 802, 805–6,
    812
joint ventures 684, 688–90
market signals 269–70, 274, 278
multimodal learning 912, 914
multinationals 639, 643, 645, 647
power and politics 560, 563–4, 572
rules 601, 604, 615
scenario planning 851, 853, 860–1
social constitution of
    organization 312–15, 322

strategic alliances 661, 668, 670
success and failure 333, 337–8, 342
supplier networks 701, 704–5
time and 356, 364
respect 747–8
responsibility 42, 246–7, 276, 362, 396,
409–11, 425, 455–8, 477–9, 511, 591,
605, 703, 781, 809, 882–3, 893, 931
boards 428, 431–2
conditions for learning 762–3, 771
multinationals 643–5, 648
social movements 226, 235, 237
success and failure 313, 327, 329, 336
value change 195, 200, 203, 208, 211,
215
restructuring 148, 448, 450–3, 479, 564,
571, 577, 637, 660, 681, 683, 825, 915,
932
Retail Link 842
retailing 823, 825, 827, 835, 837, 842
retention 352
retrieval 20–1, 25–8
return-on-assets 807
return-on-investment 807
richness, media 488, 520–3, 525–31
rigidity 155, 374–5
risk 383–4, 638, 664, 781, 893
barriers to learning 824, 867
Central European
transformation 247, 249
Chinese enterprise networks 720,
722, 725, 727
individual change agents and 398,
410–12, 422, 434–5, 470–2
joint ventures 688, 690
market signals 269–70, 273
power 561, 567, 570, 574–5
rules 605, 614, 617, 619
scenario planning 851, 855
social movements 221, 223, 225, 234
success and failure 337, 341
supplier networks 704, 711–12
risk society 36
risk-benefit and multimodal
learning 905–6
ritual 40, 49, 127, 181, 210, 345
role:
of boards 428–43
of change agents 410–12
of conflict 582–4, 587, 589
of consultants 397, 462, 464, 466–75,
477–80
of individuals 395
of learning 609–10, 933
of organization 601–2
of power 562–3
of unions 446–7, 449–50, 452,
455–7
role-constrained learning 865
rotation of personnel 510, 645–6, 685,
686
routines 27, 399, 465, 529–31, 839, 870
boards 430, 435–6, 438, 442

Central European
transformation 246–9, 256, 258–9
Chinese enterprise networks 718,
727–8
dynamic knowledge 491, 501–3,
507–8, 511, 513
economic theory 100–1, 109–11
future research 922, 929
history and 162, 164, 170, 173, 175–6
imaginary organizations 737–9,
742–3, 746
management science 67, 69, 78, 80
market signals 265, 271–2, 274–6
multimodal learning 904, 915
multinationals 633, 637, 647
rules 599–603, 606–7, 611, 613, 616–19
social constitution of
organization 310, 315–16, 319
sociology 39, 50
strategic alliances 661, 665, 669
strategizing 543, 545–6
success and failure 330–2, 344
supplier networks 702, 705–10
time and 357–9, 361, 365
tools of learning 781, 783
Royal Bank of Scotland 664–5
Royal Dutch Shell Group 215, 230–3,
235–8, 269–70
rugged individualism concept 710
Ruhrort Shipyard case 454
rules 49–50, 67, 96, 344, 373–4, 529, 544,
627, 637
future research 922, 929
imaginary organizations 743, 746
knowledge creation 487, 489–90,
598–620
multimodal learning 904, 915
political science 142, 147
power 559, 564
psychology 21–2, 24–5

safety 228–30, 232, 755, 761–3, 768–9,
891, 905–8
sanitization 935
satisfaction 335, 370, 377, 385, 411–12,
418, 590, 604, 803, 840
satisficing 91–2
scale 633, 657, 666, 728, 811, 829, 841
Scandinavian Personal Computer
Systems 734, 740–3
scanning 38, 157, 364, 561–2, 573, 577,
629, 840, 854–5
scarcity of time 360–2, 364
scenario planning 207, 269, 364, 547,
550, 615, 759, 824, 849–63, 929, 932
schemata 19–20
scientific knowledge 101–2, 104, 106,
267
scientific management 153, 316, 587
scope 488, 522–3, 525–31, 633, 642, 666,
828, 841, 892, 910
Scottish knitwear industry and market
signals 270–1

scripts 19, 599–600
searching information 375–7
SECI knowledge conversion 72, 493–8,
500, 503, 508, 511, 513, 780, 830–1,
844
security 357, 706, 716, 723–5, 785
self 39, 68, 131, 397, 446–7, 509, 604, 825,
913
agents and 420, 462
conflict and identity 584, 587,
589–92, 594
emotions and 370, 374, 382
sociology 38, 40–2
theory and transformation 892, 896,
898
time and 352, 356
self-development 195, 202–3, 210–11,
215–16
self-efficacy 23, 25
self-fulfilling prophecy 22
semantic knowledge 20
semiotics 41
Semp 672
sense-making 627, 670, 770, 829–30,
868, 891, 929–30
agents and 407, 457, 465, 476
knowledge creation 519, 528, 548–53
market signals 264–6, 268–71
success and failure 306, 329–30,
334–6, 343
sequential learning 171, 174, 176, 487,
494–5, 638–9, 717, 727, 903
service 433–6, 442, 467, 475
Seven-Eleven Japan 823, 827, 835–40,
844–5
shadowing 788–9, 791
shared knowledge 51, 107, 162, 758,
783–4, 810, 913
agents and 399, 465
barriers to learning 868, 880
Chinese enterprise networks 717,
723, 729
dynamic 495, 497, 499, 501–3, 505,
507–10
emotions 372–4, 376–8, 388
future research 922, 932
imaginary organizations 630, 733,
738–9, 743, 747, 749
information technology 828–30,
832, 838, 842
joint ventures 682, 685–7, 692, 694
management science 64, 70–1,
74–5
media choice 519–20, 526–30
mental models 611–12
multinationals 640, 645, 648
psychology 25, 29
scenario planning 851, 857, 861–2
strategic alliances 659, 661–2, 674–5
supplier networks 704, 706, 711
shareholders 428–9, 439–41, 457, 559,
795, 804, 806–7, 935, 937
Sharp 507–8

Shell Group 215, 230–3, 235–8, 269–70, 424–5, 850–5, 860–1
shock 66, 244, 251
shuttles, space 340–2
significance 180–1, 373, 377–81
Silicon Valley 643
simulations 537, 771, 789, 832
simultaneity 354, 356, 359–60, 494, 521–2, 526, 631
Singapore and Chinese enterprises 716–29
single-loop learning 405, 430–1, 467, 702, 757, 886, 923
  conflict and identity 585, 587, 590, 592–3
  management science 69, 76–7, 79
  political science 137, 150, 155–6
  power 564, 574–6
  strategic alliances 659, 669
  strategizing 537–8, 544, 546–8
  tools of learning 776–7, 779, 791
  unions 451–3, 455
  vision 196, 283, 287–9, 294–8
situation theory 520
situational learning 42, 45, 47, 51, 53, 416, 545–7, 611, 866, 873
size:
  of organization 144, 357–8, 361–2, 374, 434, 436, 441, 666, 722, 724
  of supplier networks 701, 707
Skandia Assurance and Finance Services 734, 743–5, 749
Skandia Navigator 798–800
Skoda 252–3, 255–7
slack, organizational 68, 337
small and medium enterprises:
  in China 629, 716–17, 719–20, 726, 728
  Hungarian joint ventures 681–3, 693–4
social capital 270, 275, 805–6
social contract theory 285
social history 167–8
social influence theory 520, 523–5
social learning 18–19, 24, 28, 92, 94–5
social movements 148–9, 928–9
  interest groups and 221–39
social order 36, 39–41, 51–2
social presence theory 520
social psychology 49, 76
social sciences 96, 118, 121, 130, 140, 149, 156, 162–3, 169, 177–8, 195, 199, 287, 330, 352–3, 415, 420, 557, 582, 716, 728, 805
social systems 266, 268, 274–5, 277, 284, 309–11, 321, 607
socialism 242–4, 246–50, 255–8, 681–3
socialization 127, 336, 543, 584, 702, 724, 804
  dynamic knowledge 493, 495–500, 502–3, 511, 513
  imaginary organizations 738–9, 741, 746

information technology 823, 830–1, 833–5, 838, 844
  multinationals 640, 648
  rules 600, 612–13
  sociology 40–2, 46
  time and 353–4, 357, 362–3
sociocognition 25–9
sociocultural learning 647–9
sociology 11, 35–54, 64, 138, 144, 148, 167–8, 178, 184, 268, 308, 411, 586, 716–17, 729, 925, 932, 937
sociopsychology 67, 139–40, 149, 671, 783, 785
sociotechnical systems 591
software 828
Solidarity 183
SONY 383
sources of knowledge and economic theory 102–5, 111
space 395, 487, 499–501, 512, 519, 522, 526–7, 530, 572, 646, 718, 781, 783
specialization 26–7, 317–19, 322, 338–9, 435, 439, 509–10, 602–3, 619
specifity, firm 285, 631–2, 805
speed of learning 61, 306, 352–7, 359–65, 374, 435, 439, 521, 612–13, 616–17, 935
spillovers, learning 99, 103–4, 643
spiral, learning as 110, 465, 493, 497–9, 503, 505, 509, 511, 513, 830–1, 833–5, 839, 844–5, 879
spontaneous/planned order 609
stability 130, 608, 667, 934
  Chinese enterprise networks 717, 723, 728
  joint ventures 628, 686, 688
  multinationals 627, 647
  political science 142, 155
  strategizing 537, 545
  supplier networks 700–1, 705–9, 711–12
stagnation 288–90, 295, 298, 385, 387, 435
stagnovation, vision and learning 288–92
stakeholders 296, 429, 450, 542, 586, 604, 694, 778, 806–8, 882, 935
  leadership 417, 424–5
  power 559, 569
  socioeconomic values 207, 214–15
standard operating procedures 38, 109, 435, 529, 737, 785, 825–6, 922
  management science 66–7, 77, 80
  multimodal learning 903, 909–10, 914, 916
  rules 600, 603, 605, 611–12
  strategizing 537, 539, 545, 547
  success and failure 337, 345
  time and 358–9, 360–1, 365
standards 236–7, 292–3, 296, 546, 590, 592, 661, 812
state 372, 569, 628

Chinese enterprise networks 720, 722
  history and 166–7, 179, 182–4
  ownership and European transformation process 243–4, 249, 251–2, 255
  political science 145, 148, 153, 155–6
static culture 119–20
static organizations 487, 492
static/dynamic routines 109
statutory boards 437–40
steel industry in Germany 453–4
stereotypes 20, 675
stewardship, leadership as 419–20, 423, 426
sticky knowledge 267–8, 270, 812
stimulus/response 17–19, 43, 63, 66–7, 330–1, 492, 536–7, 539, 543–8, 599–601, 603, 616, 618, 718, 720, 746
stochastic process, learning as 99
stock of knowledge 47, 795–6, 801–2, 805, 813
storage of information 175, 675, 785–6, 811, 829
  Chinese enterprise networks 717–18, 727
  emotions and 373, 381–3
  future research 930, 935
  media 518–22, 525–6, 529, 531
  multimodal learning 903, 905, 913
  psychology 17, 20–1, 25–9
  rules 489, 606
  time and 353, 358, 361
strategic alliances 628, 657–77
strategic knowledge 659–61, 665–6, 668, 670, 677
strategic management simulations 71
strategizing 488, 535–53, 929
strategy 39, 198, 313, 355, 417–18, 489–90, 508, 525, 613–14, 706, 736, 805, 825, 929
  barriers to learning 870, 876, 881–2
  boards 396, 429, 432–8, 440–2
  Chinese enterprise networks 629, 717, 720–8
  conditions for learning 758–60, 763
  conflict and identity 587, 589–90, 592, 594
  consultants 462–4, 472, 479
  economic theory 95–6, 108, 110–11
  emotions and 370–1, 374, 384, 386
  European transformation process 254, 256
  history and 170, 174, 179, 182, 185
  individual change agents 399, 402–3, 406, 408–9
  information technology 827, 835, 841
  intellectual capital 756, 799, 801, 808–11
  joint ventures 681, 691–2
  management science 61–4, 67, 80

market signals 264, 266, 269–70, 273–4, 276–7
multimodal learning 903, 916–17
multinationals 627, 631, 640–1, 643–5, 647, 650
political science 142, 154
power 569, 571
psychology 15, 25
scenario planning 824, 849, 851–9, 861–3
social movements 195, 225–38
success and failure 327, 329, 332, 337–9, 342–4
theory and transformation 886–7, 890–4
tools of learning 778, 785
unions 446–50, 452, 454–6
vision 197, 282–3, 285–7, 289, 293–8
structural anthropology 119, 121
structural capital 795, 799, 805
structuralism 39–40, 120–1, 242, 245, 247–55, 257–9
structuration concept 321, 637, 647, 649
structure 124, 196, 214, 361, 375–7, 488, 610, 756, 824, 825, 904–5
barriers to learning 866, 868–70, 875, 877, 880–3
boards 429, 432, 440
Chinese enterprise networks 716–17, 720, 728
conditions for learning 307, 755, 758–60, 764, 768, 772
conflict and identity 594
consultants 462–3, 465–6, 477
dynamic knowledge 506, 511–13
economic theory 89, 96, 107
European transformation process 196, 243–59
future research 922, 929, 932, 934
history and 168–70, 175–6
imaginary organizations 736–7, 739, 745
individual change agents 398, 403
internationalization 627, 630
joint ventures 628, 681, 686, 693
leadership 396, 416, 422
management science 62–3, 68–9, 71
market signals 268, 272, 277
multinationals 640–2, 645, 649
political science 139–41, 143–4, 148–9, 151, 153–4, 156–7
power and politics 557, 563–4, 566–7, 570–1, 577
psychology 21–2, 24–5
scenario planning 850–1, 854, 859–61, 863
social constitution 305, 309–11, 317, 319, 321–3
social movements 226, 232
sociology 41, 50, 52–3
strategizing 535, 537, 539–41, 545
success and failure 329, 339
supplier networks 629, 704–9, 711

theory and transformation 888, 895, 898–9
tools of learning 756, 780, 782–3, 790
unions 397, 446–50, 452–3, 455–7
vision 283, 287–8, 295
style 396, 420–1, 426, 470, 699, 701, 705–6, 708–11
subcontracting 243, 250, 908
Chinese enterprise networks 719–21, 724–6, 728
supplier networks 700, 706, 710
subsidiaries 627, 631–2, 639–45, 647, 669, 682, 685–6, 688–9, 720–1, 744, 932
substitution values 202
subsystems and European transformation process 247, 249, 256, 259
success 157, 214, 396, 405–7, 456, 487, 749, 782, 826, 837
barriers to learning 867–9, 873, 877, 880, 882
boards 431–2, 434–5, 439
Chinese enterprise networks 629, 718, 723, 725, 727–8
economic theory 93, 100–1, 105, 109
emotions 370, 385–6
failure and 305–7, 327–45
future research 932, 935, 937
intellectual capital 799, 810
joint ventures 691–2, 694
leadership 417, 420
management science 61–2, 71
multimodal learning 904, 909, 915–17
multinationals 632, 638, 649
power and politics 563, 567
psychology 13, 23–4, 28
rules 606–7, 609, 611, 613, 615–18
scenario planning 855, 857
social constitution of organization 312, 316, 322
strategic alliances 657, 660, 667
strategizing 535, 538–40, 543, 547–8, 553
theory and transformation 886–7, 891–2, 894–5, 899–900
time 306, 354, 357, 360
vision 283, 286, 289–90, 294, 296–8
suffrage, universal 154
suggestion box 897
superstitious learning 276, 334, 363, 378–9, 538, 610–11, 614, 866
supervisory boards 429, 432, 440
supplier networks 628, 699–712, 719, 741, 833, 835
surveys, use of 201
survival 15, 62, 423, 432, 671, 747, 763, 857–8, 887
Chinese enterprise networks 723, 725–6
joint ventures 688, 690, 694

political science and 140, 144–5
power 560, 562, 566, 569
rules 604, 617
strategizing 536, 538, 544, 546
success and failure 330, 332, 336, 343–4
unions 448, 451–2, 455
vision 197, 283, 286, 289
suspension of rules 608–9
Suzuki 252–3, 257
Sweden 228, 450–1, 455
Swiss Banking Corporation 779
symbolic interactionism 636, 649
symbolism 41, 71, 124, 181–3, 185, 225, 229, 234–6, 520, 527, 530–1
symmetrical anthropology 126
synchronization 354, 356–7, 359, 707, 711, 832, 835
synergy 103, 387, 629, 631, 640, 647, 650, 662, 665, 670, 695, 869
system, organization as 62, 65–71, 118, 353, 717, 903
systemic knowledge 313, 501–3, 659–61, 664–6, 668, 670, 677, 757, 759–60, 860
systemizing *ba* 499–501, 831–2, 838, 841–3
systems:
level and knowledge tools 755
management science 11, 73, 75–6, 78, 90–1
oriented technology 196, 287–9, 292–3, 296–7
strategizing 536, 539–40, 549
theory 205, 423, 642, 779

tacit knowledge 29, 718–19, 771, 780–1, 825, 924
barriers to learning 868, 870
boards 430, 433, 441–2
consultants 470, 479
dynamic 491, 493–503, 506, 509–13
economic theory 12, 100–1, 108–9
imaginary organizations 737–8, 742, 747
individual change agents 399, 403
information technology 823, 827, 829–34, 837–8, 844
intellectual capital 795, 810–12
joint ventures 686–8, 690–2
knowledge creation 487, 490–1
management science 72, 76
market signals 267–8, 270, 278
multimodal learning 904–5, 914
multinationals 643, 646–7, 649
rules 601, 606
social constitution of organization 312, 319–20, 322
sociology 39, 48–9, 51, 53
strategic alliances 658, 660, 663, 667, 676–7
strategizing 549, 552–3
success and failure 332, 335–7

tacit knowledge (*cont.*)
  supplier networks 701–3, 705, 708–9,
    711
  theory and transformation 886,
    889
tactical emotions 369–72
Taiwan and Chinese enterprises
    716–29
tandem management 256–7, 869
task analysis 525–6, 530–1
task forces 511–12, 718, 826
teacher, leader as 422–6, 893
teaching organizations 121–3
teams 28, 378, 512–13, 583, 646, 709, 738,
    782–3, 859, 936
  management science 71, 75, 78, 80
  multimodal learning 910, 914–15
  social constitution 309, 313
  strategic alliances 659, 674–5
  theory and transformation 891, 893,
    897–8
  tools of learning 779, 791
technical knowledge 494, 497, 659,
    661, 663, 665–6, 668, 673, 676, 684,
    688, 692, 738, 783
technical/nontechnical problems and
    individuals 405–6, 407
techno-analytic style 710
technology 15, 269, 316–18, 464, 487,
    542, 588, 905, 934
  Chinese enterprise networks 629,
    717, 719–22, 725–9
  economic theory 89, 92, 95, 98–105,
    107, 110
  European transformation
    process 248, 250, 254–5, 257–9
  history and 163–4, 174–5
  imaginary organizations 629, 746
  information technology 837, 839,
    842
  intellectual capital 797, 799, 810–11
  joint ventures 684, 686–90, 693
  management science 62, 67
  media choice 518, 524
  multinationals 635, 637, 640, 642–3,
    646–7
  rules 613–14, 616, 618
  social movements 223, 229, 231
  sociology 39, 49–50
  strategic alliances 657, 659, 663, 666,
    668
  success and failure 339
  supplier networks 708
  vision and development 195–7,
    282–98
telecommunications 646–7
teleconferencing 521–5, 646
telephones 128, 521–6, 741
Tennessee Valley Authority 575, 586
tension:
  agents and 396, 436, 466, 476, 478
  conditions shaping learning 305,
    307

knowledge creation 509, 563, 569,
    589
  multinationals 647
  social constitution of
    organization 308, 312, 315, 320–1,
    323
territory 558, 569–71, 575, 588
theory of organizational change 62–3
theory of organizational learning 64,
    119, 138, 183, 543, 615, 701–4, 795,
    849, 902
  economic theory 108, 111
  future research 930, 932
  power 557, 562, 566
theory of organizations 519, 599, 717
  anthropology 118, 127, 130, 133
  conflict and identity 582, 586, 588
  history 163–9, 171–2, 174–5, 177, 180,
    183–5
  political science 137–8, 141–3, 146,
    148, 150, 156–7
  power 568, 575, 577
  strategizing 535–6, 541
theory and practice 926, 928, 934
theory and transformation 886–90
theory-in-use 65, 73, 80, 209, 399,
    405–6, 544, 582, 587, 757–8, 761, 921
Thiokol 340–2
Third Way 144
threat 157, 355, 405–8, 442, 855
  conditions for learning 760, 762,
    768–70
  emotions and 380, 386
  knowledge creation 525, 531, 545,
    561, 576, 587, 590–1
  success and failure 334, 338
3M Corporation 315, 337, 375, 419, 507
Thyssen 172–4, 455
Tikopia peoples 119, 124
time 15, 196, 248, 306–7, 468, 561, 668,
    781, 923
  boards 430–2, 435, 439
  Chinese enterprise networks 718
  dynamic knowledge 499–501, 512
  future research 924, 934, 937
  media choice 518–19, 521–2, 525–6,
    528, 531
  organizational learning 351–65
  scenario planning 850, 863
  social constitution of
    organization 310, 314
  social movements 225–6, 229, 232,
    235–8
  strategizing 488, 536, 539–40
tone and color of research 927, 931–2
tools of learning 755–6, 775–91, 825,
    828, 916
top-down management 19, 169, 174,
    312, 355, 407, 412, 503–6, 540, 718,
    801, 845, 879, 930
Toshiba Corporation 672, 674
total quality management 410, 462,
    535, 539, 545–6, 548, 567, 809

total quality training 805
Toyota Motor Corporation 172–5, 668,
    709
traditionalism 123
traffic information and mobility
    291
training 97–8, 100, 685–6, 692–3, 772,
    777, 825, 837–8, 889, 897, 899, 900,
    908–9
traits 415–16, 563–4
transactional leadership 416, 418
transdisciplinary research 927–8,
    937–8
transferability of knowledge 502
transformation 416, 418–23, 426, 432,
    904, 924, 925
  Central Europe 144, 242–59, 869
transitional economies and
    Hungarian joint ventures 681–5,
    690–1, 693–4
translation 126, 728
transnationals 118, 186
transparency 42, 182, 605, 646, 795
  conditions for learning 755, 761–3,
    767–8, 771
  imaginary organizations 630, 739,
    745, 747–9
  multimodal learning as social
    906–8, 911
  power 565–6, 577
  strategic alliances 663, 670
  theory and transformation 890,
    894, 897–8
trauma, corporate 383–4
trend identification 854–6, 859–60,
    890
Treuhandanstalt 306, 352, 359–64
trial-and-error learning 18, 92–3, 100,
    143, 170, 250–1, 354, 361, 363, 380,
    383, 474, 489, 548, 602
trigger of learning:
  market signals as 264–78
  organizational learning 195–7
  social movements as 221–39
  socioeconomic values as 198–216
  technological vision as 282–98
  transformation in Central Europe
    as 242–59
true-income approach of intellectual
    capital 806
trust 39, 273, 319, 339, 397, 402–3,
    418–19, 438, 495, 549, 612, 627, 760,
    783, 805, 840, 905
  Chinese enterprise networks 629,
    725
  consultants 476, 480
  dynamic knowledge 500–1, 510–11
  imaginary organizations 630, 736,
    739, 744–5, 747–9
  joint ventures 628, 685–8, 692–4
  management science 76, 78
  strategic alliances 658, 662, 666, 669,
    672–5, 677

supplier networks 629, 699, 701, 704–8, 710–12
unions 448, 457–8
turnarounds 338, 434–5, 539, 551, 618, 749, 932
types:
of boards 437–41
of consultancy clients 468–9
of consultants 467–8
of emotions 385–7
of learning 76–8, 80–1, 288
of learning and tools 775–7, 779–80, 784, 789, 791
of learning under transformation 245–8
of management science 11
of organization 926, 928–9

U model concept 638–9
UK 428, 433, 668, 672–3, 707–11
uncertainty 52, 67, 150, 238, 282, 334, 359, 511–12, 723, 736, 903
agents and 405, 407, 409, 415, 419–21, 425, 429, 431, 476–7
conditions for learning 762–3, 766–72
economic theory 92–4, 96, 99–100, 102, 107
joint ventures 628, 694
media choice 519–20, 522–3, 526, 531
multinationals 635, 638–9, 641
rules 602–3, 618
scenario planning 851, 853–5, 859
strategizing 535, 551
supplier networks 704, 711
understanding 74, 520–1, 525, 528, 530, 631, 637, 860, 862–3, 866, 868, 874, 877, 883, 903
unemployment 248–9, 254–5, 362, 447–8, 453–4, 683
unions 152, 154–5, 224, 234, 237, 244, 255–6, 804, 928, 930
as agents of learning 396, 446–58
Unipart 423–4
uniqueness 353, 361
unitary systems 568–72, 574
unlearning 15, 43–6, 196, 310, 380, 488, 509, 616, 668, 691, 726, 757, 826, 893
barriers to learning 866, 875, 878–9
European transformation process 246, 248–9, 251, 255–9
future research 922, 929
history and 162, 174
imaginary organizations 743, 749
market signals 272, 276
multimodal learning 903, 911, 914
strategizing 537, 539, 545–6, 553
success and failure 338–9, 343

time and 351, 357–8, 361, 365
US 154, 179, 671–3, 683, 708–11, 794, 827, 840
boards 428, 440
Chinese enterprise networks 718, 724
multinationals 638, 642–3
pharmaceutical industry 902–3, 905–12
power and politics 562, 567, 570
US Congress 142–3, 147
US Postal Service 311
utilitarianism 11, 36–9, 46, 210
utilization 37, 102, 758, 938
economic theory 89, 99, 110–11
information technology 827–9, 830, 832, 835, 840, 844
joint ventures 681–2, 685–6, 689, 691–4
media knowledge 518, 524, 526–7, 531
political science 142, 155
psychology 15, 25–7, 29

validity 71, 73, 96, 138, 661, 810, 933
value-added 61, 632, 640–1, 643–4, 648, 794, 798, 807, 837
value-oriented personnel policy 212–13
values 76, 693, 705, 717, 757–8, 852, 882
agents and 399, 404–7, 418–19, 423, 425, 438, 457, 466, 475–6
change and socioeconomic 195–6, 198–216
conflict and identity 582–5, 587–8, 590–3
dynamic knowledge 493, 501, 505–7
emotions and 372–4, 376
future research 923, 930, 935, 937
history and 173, 178–9, 183
imaginary organizations 735–6, 740–1, 744–5, 747
information technology 823, 833, 835, 837, 842, 845
intellectual capital 803–4, 807–9
political science 139, 145, 150
power and politics 557–8, 561, 566, 570, 577
social constitution of organization 311, 315, 317
social movements 224, 228
strategic alliances 657, 663, 666
strategizing 540, 549–50
theory and transformation 888, 891, 896, 899
vision 285–6, 295, 298
variation of rules 607–9
videoconferencing 831

virtual organizations 536, 543, 549, 734, 736, 806
visibility and time 355
vision 29, 276, 583, 617, 645, 674, 691, 723–4, 829, 925
agents and 416, 418–19, 423, 454
dynamic knowledge 506–9, 511–13
emotions and 374, 381
future research 931, 937
imaginary organizations 734, 736, 739–41, 743–4
intellectual capital 801, 809
scenario planning 854, 858
social constitution of organization 309, 312
strategizing 540–3, 549–50
technology and development 195–7, 282–98
theory and transformation 889–94, 896–9
voice mail 521–4, 646
voucher privatization 244, 252, 254–5
VW 214–15, 252–3

wages 248, 250, 254, 257, 358, 447–8
Wal-Mart Stores Inc. 509, 778, 823, 827, 835–7, 840–5
warning signals 207, 306, 330, 343–4, 430, 435, 439, 442
waste, industrial crisis and Shell Group 230, 233, 235–8
welfare 447, 457–8, 803, 805
white water leadership 425
willingness to learn 23, 465, 468, 471–2, 480, 706, 708, 923–4, 932
windows of opportunity 306, 354, 356–7, 359–62, 364, 436, 935, 937
withdrawal emotions 385–8
word-processing industry and vision 289–90, 294–5
work-flow management 828, 832
works councils 175, 397, 446–9, 451, 872, 874, 876, 890
workshops 207, 853–4, 860, 889, 890–1, 893–4, 897
world of business 824, 849, 857–60, 862–3, 887, 889–90, 895
World Health Organization 906
world of management 824, 849, 857, 858–63, 887, 889–90
written media 129, 520–3, 526–7, 530, 717, 727, 826

Xerox 267–8, 274–6

Yale learning theory 121
yellow pages 779–80, 791, 831